CENGAGE LEARNING'S

GLOBAL ECONOMIC WATCH

GLOBAL ECONOMIC CRISIS RESOURCE CENTER

The credit collapse. Tumbling markets. Bailouts and bankruptcies. Surging unemployment. Political debate. Today's financial turmoil transforms academic theory into breaking news that affects every family and business sector — from Wall Street to Shanghai.

Cengage Learning's Global Economic Watch brings these pivotal current events into the classroom. It helps you answer the key questions of the day, including: "How did we get here?" and "Where do we go from here?"

The Watch, a first of its kind resource, stimulates discussion and understanding of the global downturn with easy-to-integrate learning solutions:

- **A content-rich blog** of breaking news, expert analysis and commentary — updated multiple times daily — plus links to many other blogs

- **A powerful real-time database** of hundreds of relevant and vetted journal, newpaper and periodical articles, videos, and podcasts — updated four times every day

- **A thorough overview and timeline of events** leading up to the global economic crisis

- **Student forums** for sharing questions, ideas, and opinions

History is happening now. Experience it in the classroom.

For more information on the power of The Watch, please visit **www.cengage.com/thewatch**.

12e

MANAGEMENT

StuartDuncanSmith/iStockphoto.com

ROBERT KREITNER
Arizona State University

CARLENE M. CASSIDY
Anne Arundel Community College

Australia • Brazil • Japan • Korea • Mexico • Singapore • Spain • United Kingdom • United States

SOUTH-WESTERN
CENGAGE Learning™

Management, Twelfth Edition
Robert Kreitner
Carlene M. Cassidy

Vice President of Editorial, Business:
Jack Calhoun

Publisher: Erin Joyner

Acquisitions Editor: Scott Person

Development Editor: Jennifer King

Editorial Assistant: Ruth Belanger

Media Editor: Rob Ellington

Marketing Manager: Jonathan Monahan

Sr. Marketing Communications Manager:
Jim Overly

Marketing Coordinator: Julia Tucker

Content Project Manager: Darrell E. Frye

Sr. Art Director: Tippy McIntosh

Manufacturing Planner: Ron Montgomery

Rights Acquisitions Specialist: John Hill

Production Service: S4Carlisle Publishing
Services

Cover and Internal Design: Mike Stratton,
Stratton Design

Cover Image: ©StuartDuncanSmith, iStock

For product information and technology assistance, contact us at
Cengage Learning Customer & Sales Support, 1-800-354-9706
For permission to use material from this text or product,
submit all requests online at **www.cengage.com/permissions**
Further permissions questions can be emailed to
permissionrequest@cengage.com

Exam*View*® is a registered trademark of eInstruction Corp. Windows is a registered trademark of the Microsoft Corporation used herein under license. Macintosh and Power Macintosh are registered trademarks of Apple Computer, Inc. used herein under license.

© 2008 Cengage Learning. All Rights Reserved.

Cengage Learning WebTutor™ is a trademark of Cengage Learning.

Library of Congress Control Number: 2011939109

ISBN-13: 978-1-111-22136-2

ISBN-10: 1-111-221367

South-Western
5191 Natorp Boulevard
Mason, OH 45040
USA

Cengage Learning products are represented in Canada by Nelson Education, Ltd.

For your course and learning solutions, visit **www.cengage.com**

Purchase any of our products at your local college store or at our preferred online store **www.cengagebrain.com**

Printed in China by China Translation & Printing Services Limited.
1 2 3 4 5 6 7 15 14 13 12 11

BRIEF CONTENTS

PART ONE   **THE MANAGEMENT CHALLENGE**   **1**

CHAPTER 1   Managers and Entrepreneurs   2
CHAPTER 2   The Evolution of Management Thought   34
CHAPTER 3   The Changing Environment of Management: Diversity, Global Economy, and Technology   64
CHAPTER 4   International Management and Cross-Cultural Competence   92
CHAPTER 5   Management's Social and Ethical Responsibilities   124

PART TWO   **PLANNING AND DECISION MAKING**   **149**

CHAPTER 6   The Basics of Planning and Project Management   150
CHAPTER 7   Strategic Management: Planning for Long-Term Success   182
CHAPTER 8   Decision Making and Creative Problem Solving   208

PART THREE   **ORGANIZING, MANAGING HUMAN RESOURCES, AND COMMUNICATING**   **237**

CHAPTER 9   Organizations: Effectiveness, Design, and Cultures   238
CHAPTER 10   Human Resource Management   268
CHAPTER 11   Communicating in the Internet Age   294

PART FOUR   **MOTIVATING AND LEADING**   **325**

CHAPTER 12   Motivating Job Performance   326
CHAPTER 13   Group Dynamics and Teamwork   358
CHAPTER 14   Influence, Power, and Leadership   386
CHAPTER 15   Change, Conflict, and Negotiation   416

PART FIVE   **ORGANIZATIONAL CONTROL PROCESSES**   **445**

CHAPTER 16   Organizational Control and Quality Improvement   446

CONTENTS

Preface   xv

PART 1   THE MANAGEMENT CHALLENGE   1

1   Managers and Entrepreneurs   2

THE CHANGING WORKPLACE
What Is the Secret to Zappos.com's Success?   3

Management Defined   5
Working with and Through Others 5;
Achieving Organizational Objectives 6;
Balancing Effectiveness and Efficiency 6;
Making the Most of Limited Resources 7;
Coping with a Changing Environment 8

GREEN MANAGEMENT:
TOWARD SUSTAINABILITY
Greater Efficiency Gives the Union Pacific
Railroad a Green Edge over Truckers   8

ETHICS: CHARACTER, COURAGE,
AND VALUES
Who Says College Students Can't Make
a Difference?   13

What Do Managers Do?   15
Managerial Functions 15; Managerial
Skills 17; Some Managerial Facts of Life (with
No Sugar Coating) 18

Learning to Manage   19
How Do Managers Learn to Manage? 19; How
Can Future Managers Learn to Manage? 20

Small-Business Management   21
Exploding Myths About Small Business 21;
Career Opportunities in Small Business 23;
Entrepreneurship 23

WINDOW ON THE WORLD
Harvard Test Identifies Global Entrepreneurs
Among Loan Applicants   25

Summary   26
Terms to Understand   27

ACTION LEARNING EXERCISE
Do You Have the Right Stuff
to Be an Entrepreneur?   27

ETHICS EXERCISE: DO THE RIGHT THING
The Offshoring of Jobs Issue   29

MANAGERS-IN-ACTION VIDEO
CASE STUDY
Preserve® by Recycline   30

CLOSING CASE
Jennifer Reingold Samples a Day
in the Life of a Manager   31

2   The Evolution of Management Thought   34

THE CHANGING WORKPLACE
Craigie Zildjian Carries
on a 14-Generation Tradition   35

The Practice and Study of Management   37
Information Overload 38; An Interdisciplinary
Field 38; No Universally Accepted Theory
of Management 38

The Universal Process Approach   39
Henri Fayol's Universal Management Process 39;
Lessons from the Universal Process Approach 41

The Operational Approach   41
Frederick W. Taylor's Scientific Management 41;
Taylor's Followers 43; The Quality Advocates 44;
Lessons from the Operational Approach 45

WINDOW ON THE WORLD
Norwegian Paper Maker Benefits from
a Detailed Model of Its Global Operations   46

The Behavioral Approach   46
The Human Relations Movement 46

Contents **vii**

ETHICS: CHARACTER, COURAGE, AND VALUES
American Express Puts Its People First 48

Organizational Behavior 49; Lessons from the Behavioral Approach 49

The Systems Approach 50
Chester I. Barnard's Early Systems Perspective 50; General Systems Theory 51

GREEN MANAGEMENT: TOWARD SUSTAINABILITY
Open-System Thinking Is the Right Stuff for Annie Leonard 52

New Directions in Systems Thinking 52; Lessons from the Systems Approach 53

The Contingency Approach 54
Contingency Characteristics 54; Lessons from the Contingency Approach 55

The Era of Management by Best Seller: Proceed With Caution 55
What's Wrong with Management by Best Seller? 57; How to Avoid the Quick-Fix Mentality 57; Putting What You Have Learned to Work 58

Summary 59

Terms to Understand 60

ACTION LEARNING EXERCISE
Open-System Thinking and Recycling 60

ETHICS EXERCISE: DO THE RIGHT THING
Putting the Recent Recession into Historical Perspective 61

MANAGERS-IN-ACTION VIDEO CASE STUDY
Mitchell Gold + Bob Williams 62

CLOSING CASE
Six Generations Have Fine Tuned This Guitar Maker 62

3 The Changing Environment of Management: Diversity, Global Economy, and Technology 64

THE CHANGING WORKPLACE
Looking Forward to the 2020 Workplace 65

The Social Environment 66
Demographics of the New Workforce 66; Nagging Inequalities in the Workplace 70

VALUING DIVERSITY
Another Crack in the Glass Ceiling 72
Managing Diversity 72

The Political-Legal Environment 73
The Politicization of Management 74; Increased Personal Legal Accountability 76; Political-Legal Implications for Management 76

The Economic Environment 77
The Job Outlook in Today's Service Economy, Where Education Matters 77; Coping with Business Cycles 78

BEST PRACTICES
How Patricia Tate Took the Gamble out of Her Tribe's Casino Business 79
The Challenge of a Global Economy 80

The Technological Environment 81
The Innovation Process 82

GREEN MANAGEMENT: TOWARD SUSTAINABILITY
Here Comes Biodegradable Plastic 83

Promoting Innovation Through Intrapreneurship 84

Summary 86

Terms to Understand 86

ACTION LEARNING EXERCISE
Crystal Ball Gazing 87

ETHICS EXERCISE: DO THE RIGHT THING
Should an Employer Tell a Muslim Woman Not to Wear a Head Scarf? 88

MANAGERS-IN-ACTION VIDEO CASE STUDY
Evo (formerly known as evogear) 89

CLOSING CASE
How Wal-Mart Won Chicago 90

4 International Management and Cross-Cultural Competence 92

THE CHANGING WORKPLACE
China Myths, China Facts 93

Global Organizations for a Global Economy 95
The Internationalization Process 95; From Global Companies to Transnational Companies 97

GREEN MANAGEMENT:
TOWARD SUSTAINABILITY
*The Global Race for Leadership in Green
Technology*   98

Toward Greater Global Awareness
and Cross-Cultural Effectiveness   98
*Needed: Global Managers with Cultural
Intelligence and Cross-Cultural
Competencies 99; Contrasting Attitudes
Toward International Operations 99; The
Cultural Imperative 102*

Are U.S. Global Corporations Turning the World
into a Single "Americanized" Culture?   103
Understanding Cultural Diversity 103

WINDOW ON THE WORLD
Do You Speak Globish?   107

Comparative Management Insights   107
*Made-in-America Management Theories
Require Translation 108; Management Styles
Vary Across Countries and Cultures 108; Lessons
in Leadership from the GLOBE Project 109*

Staffing Foreign Positions   111
*Why Do U.S. Expatriates Fail? 111;
Cross-Cultural Training 112*

WINDOW ON THE WORLD
*The Legal/Ethical Side of Cross-Cultural
Training*   114

*What About North American Women on
Foreign Assignments? 115; Relying on Local
Managerial Talent 115*

Summary   116

Terms to Understand   117

ACTION LEARNING EXERCISE
Look into the Cultural Mirror   117

ETHICS EXERCISE: DO THE RIGHT THING
*Google's Fight Against Chinese
Censorship*   119

MANAGERS-IN-ACTION VIDEO
CASE STUDY
Numi Organic Tea   120

CLOSING CASE
Tell the Kids We're Moving to Kenya   121

5 **Management's Social and Ethical
   Responsibilities**   **124**

THE CHANGING WORKPLACE
The Two Faces of Pfizer   125

Social Responsibility: Definition
and Perspectives   126
*What Does Corporate Social Responsibility
(CSR) Involve? 126; What Is the Role of
Business in Society? 128*

ETHICS: CHARACTER, COURAGE,
AND VALUES
Cleaning Up in a Socially Responsible Way 129
*Arguments for and Against Corporate Social
Responsibility 130*

Toward Greater Social Responsibility   131
*Social Responsibility Strategies 131; Who
Benefits from Corporate Social Responsibility? 132*

The Ethical Dimension of Management   134

GREEN MANAGEMENT:
TOWARD SUSTAINABILITY
Beware the Greenwashers!   134

*Practical Lessons from Business Ethics
Research 135; Personal Values as Ethical
Anchors 137; General Ethical Principles 138*

Encouraging Ethical Conduct   139
*Ethics Training 139; Ethical
Advocates 140; Codes of Ethics 140;
Whistle-Blowing 141*

Summary   143

Terms to Understand   144

ACTION LEARNING EXERCISE
The Rokeach Value Survey   144

ETHICS EXERCISE: DO THE RIGHT THING
*Does Ethics Instruction in College
Do Any Good?*   145

MANAGERS-IN-ACTION VIDEO
CASE STUDY
Greensburg Kansas   146

CLOSING CASE
A Personal Crusade   147

PART 2 PLANNING AND DECISION MAKING   **149**

6 The Basics of Planning and Project Management   **150**

THE CHANGING WORKPLACE
Facebook: From Dorm Room to Global Dominance at Web Speed   151

Coping With Uncertainty   152
Three Types of Uncertainty 153; How Individuals Handle Uncertainty 153; Organizational Responses to Uncertainty 154; Balancing Planned Action and Spontaneity in the Twenty-First Century 156

BEST PRACTICES
Whole Foods Co-founder John Mackey Says Business Is Like White Water Kayaking   156

The Essentials of Planning   157
Organizational Mission 157; Types of Planning 158; Objectives 158; Priorities (Both Strategic and Personal) 160; The Planning/Control Cycle 161

Management by Objectives and Project Planning   162
Management by Objectives 162; Project Planning and Management 164

GREEN MANAGEMENT: TOWARD SUSTAINABILITY
Walmart's Bold Sustainability Project   165

Graphical Planning/Scheduling/ Control Tools   168
Sequencing with Flow Charts 168; Scheduling with Gantt Charts 170; PERT Networks 171

Break-Even Analysis   172
Fixed Versus Variable Costs 173; The Algebraic Method 173; The Graphical Method 174; Break-Even Analysis: Strengths and Limitations 175

Summary   176

Terms to Understand   177

ACTION LEARNING EXERCISE
How to Write Good Objectives and Plans (Plan = What + When + How)   177

ETHICS EXERCISE: DO THE RIGHT THING
Death by Project   178

MANAGERS-IN-ACTION VIDEO CASE STUDY
Flight 001   178

CLOSING CASE
Ford's Hybrid Suv Project Team Races to the Finish   179

7 Strategic Management: Planning for Long-Term Success   **182**

THE CHANGING WORKPLACE
Looking Backward Is a Losing Strategy in the Age of New Media   183

Strategic Management = Strategic Planning + Implementation + Control   186

Thinking and Acting Strategically (Including Internet and Social Media Strategies)   187
Synergy 187; Porter's Generic Competitive Strategies 189

ETHICS: CHARACTER, COURAGE, AND VALUES
Wal-Mart Takes the High Road on Renewable Energy   190
Business Ecosystems 191; Strategies for the Internet and Social Media 192

The Strategic Management Process   194
Formulation of a Grand Strategy 195; Formulation of Strategic Plans 197

Strategic Implementation and Control   197
Implementation of Strategic Plans 197; Strategic Control 198; Corrective Action Based on Evaluation and Feedback 199

Forecasting   199
Types of Forecasts 199

GREEN MANAGEMENT: TOWARD SUSTAINABILITY
Experts Say Sustainability Is Changing the Competitive Landscape   200
Forecasting Techniques 200

Summary   203

Terms to Understand   204

ACTION LEARNING EXERCISE
Thinking Strategically: A SWOT Analysis   204

ETHICS EXERCISE: DO THE RIGHT THING
*Where is the Fine Line Between Free
Internet Content and Pirating?*   205

*MANAGERS-IN-ACTION VIDEO
CASE STUDY*
Preserve® by Recycline   205

CLOSING CASE
*Howard Schultz Gets Starbucks
Perking Again*   206

**8   Decision Making and Creative
Problem Solving**   **208**

THE CHANGING WORKPLACE
Boeing's Costly Outsourcing Decision   209
Challenges for Decision Makers   210
*Dealing with Complex Streams of
Decisions 210; Coping with Uncertainty 212;
Information-Processing Styles 214;
Avoiding Perceptual and Behavioral
Decision Traps 215*

Making Decisions   217
*Making Programmed Decisions 217; Making
Nonprogrammed Decisions 218*

*ETHICS: CHARACTER, COURAGE,
AND VALUES*
*Starbucks CEO Decides to Put His
Employees Ahead of Wall Street*   218

*A General Decision-Making Model 219;
Knowledge Management: A Tool for Improving
the Quality of Decisions 219*

Group-Aided Decision Making:
A Contingency Perspective   221
*Collaborative Computing 221; Group
Involvement in Decisions 222; The Problem
of Dispersed Accountability 222; Advantages
and Disadvantages of Group-Aided Decision
Making 223; A Contingency Approach is
Necessary 223*

Managerial Creativity   224
*What is Creativity? 224; Workplace
Creativity: Myth and Modern Reality 225;
Learning to Be More Creative 225*

Creative Problem Solving   226
*Identifying the Problem 226; Generating
Alternative Solutions 228*

*GREEN MANAGEMENT:
TOWARD SUSTAINABILITY*
*Community Building Through
Environmental Problem Solving*   229

*Selecting a Solution 230; Implementing
and Evaluating the Solution 230*

Summary   231
Terms to Understand   232

ACTION LEARNING EXERCISE
How Creative are You?   232

ETHICS EXERCISE: DO THE RIGHT THING
*Is Overtime the Right Decision
in This Situation?*   233

*MANAGERS-IN-ACTION VIDEO
CASE STUDY*
Greensburg Kansas   233

CLOSING CASE
The Phantasmagoria Factory   234

**PART 3   ORGANIZING, MANAGING
HUMAN RESOURCES, AND
COMMUNICATING**   **237**

**9   Organizations: Effectiveness,
Design, and Cultures**   **238**

THE CHANGING WORKPLACE
*A Culture of Truth Helps Create
a Learning Organization*   239

Organizational Structure and
Effectiveness   240
*Characteristics Common to all Organizations
240; Organization Charts 241; Organizations
as Open Systems 242; Organizational
Learning 244; Organizational
Effectiveness 245*

*GREEN MANAGEMENT:
TOWARD SUSTAINABILITY*
*Ecomagination: General Electric's Big
Bet on Green Technology Is Paying Off*   246

Contingency Design   246
*The Burns and Stalker Model 247; Basic
Departmentalization Formats 249; Span
of Control 252; Centralization and
Decentralization 253*

Effective Delegation   254
The Advantages of Delegation 255; Barriers to Delegation 256

The Changing Shape of Organizations   256
Hourglass Organizations 257; Cluster Organizations 257; Virtual Organizations 258

Organizational Cultures   259

VALUING DIVERSITY
Military Veterans Energize Southern Company's Corporate Culture   260

Characteristics of Organizational Cultures 260; Forms and Consequences of Organizational Cultures 261; The Process of Organizational Socialization 261; Strengthening Organizational Cultures 262

Summary   263

Terms to Understand   264

ACTION LEARNING EXERCISE
An Organizational X-Ray: Capturing the "Feel" of an Organization's Culture   264

ETHICS EXERCISE: DO THE RIGHT THING
Is Xerox's Corporate Culture too Nice?   265

MANAGERS-IN-ACTION VIDEO CASE STUDY
Evo (Formerly Known as Evogear)   266

CLOSING CASE
Zappos.com's CEO Tony Hsieh Explains How to Build a Strong Corporate Culture   266

10   Human Resource Management   268

THE CHANGING WORKPLACE
Talent Analytics at Google   269

Human Resource Strategy:
A People-Centered Approach   271
The Age of Human Capital 271; People-Centered Organizations Enjoy a Competitive Advantage 272

GREEN MANAGEMENT: TOWARD SUSTAINABILITY
What About Sustainable Human Resources?   272

Recruitment and Selection   273
Recruiting for Diversity in the Internet Age 273; The Selection Process: An Overview 273; Equal Employment Opportunity 274

VALUING DIVERSITY
Sexual Orientation Is Part of the Diversity Mix at REI   276

Employment Selection Tests 277; Effective Interviewing 277

Performance Appraisal   280
Making Performance Appraisals Legally Defensible 280; Alternative Performance Appraisal Techniques 281

Training   283
Today's Training: Content and Delivery 283; The Ingredients of a Good Training Program 285; Skill Versus Factual Learning 285; Training Program Evaluation: The Kirkpatrick Model 285

Contemporary Human Resource Challenges and Problems   286
Discouraging Sexual Harassment 286; Controlling Alcohol and Drug Abuse 288

Summary   290

Terms to Understand   291

ACTION LEARNING EXERCISE
Writing Behavioral Interview Questions   291

ETHICS EXERCISE: DO THE RIGHT THING
Is My Privacy Up in The Cloud?   291

MANAGERS-IN-ACTION VIDEO CASE STUDY
Maine Media Workshops   292

CLOSING CASE
How UPS Delivers Objective Performance Appraisals   293

11   Communicating in the Internet Age   294

THE CHANGING WORKPLACE
Maureen Chiquet, Global CEO, Chanel: "The Best Advice I Ever Got"   295

The Communication Process   297
Encoding 297; Selecting a Medium 298

Media Selection in Cross-Cultural Settings   298
Decoding 299; Feedback 300; Noise 300

Dynamics of Organizational Communication   301
Communication Strategies 301; The Grapevine 302

GREEN MANAGEMENT:
TOWARD SUSTAINABILITY
How Tasty Catering's Communication
Strategy Spawned a Green Business   303

*Words of Caution about the E-Grapevine
303; The Grapevine has a Positive Side
Despite Its Bad Reputation 303; Nonverbal
Communication 305; Upward
Communication 307*

WINDOW ON THE WORLD
How About a Big Hug? Better Yet,
a Fist Bump Will Do.   308

Communicating in the Digital Workplace 310

*Dealing with Information Overload 311;
Developing a Workplace Policy for Social
Networking Sites 311; Getting a Handle on
E-mail 311; Hello! Can We Talk About Cell
Phone Etiquette? 313; Videoconferencing 313;
Teleworking 314*

Becoming a Better Communicator   315
*Effective Listening 315; Effective Writing 316;
Running a Meeting 317*

Summary   318

Terms to Understand   319

ACTION LEARNING EXERCISE
Oh, No! What Have I Done?   319

ETHICS EXERCISE: DO THE RIGHT THING
Is it Time to Hang Up on Unofficial Digital
Communication in the Workplace?   320

*MANAGERS-IN-ACTION VIDEO
CASE STUDY*
Greensburg, Kansas   321

CLOSING CASE
Found in Translation: How to Make
the Multicultural Workforce Work   322

PART 4   MOTIVATING AND LEADING   325

12   Motivating Job Performance   326

THE CHANGING WORKPLACE
Rackspace Needs Fully Engaged Employees 327

Motivation Theories   328
*Maslow's Hierarchy of Needs Theory 328;
Herzberg's Two-Factor Theory 331;*

*Expectancy Theory 332; Goal-Setting
Theory 333*

Motivation Through Job Design   335
*Strategy One: Fitting People to Jobs 335;
Strategy Two: Fitting Jobs to People 337*

Motivation Through Rewards   339
*Extrinsic Versus Intrinsic Rewards 339;
Employee Compensation 340; Improving
Performance with Extrinsic Rewards 340*

Motivation Through Employee
Participation and Engagement   343
*Employee Engagement and Retention
Programs 343*

*GREEN MANAGEMENT:
TOWARD SUSTAINABILITY*
Patagonia's Yvon Chouinard Wants
Everyone to Help Save the Planet   344

*Open-Book Management 345; Self-Managed
Teams 345; Keys to Successful Employee
Participation Programs 347*

Motivation Through Quality-of-Work-Life
Programs   348
*Flexible Work Schedules 348; Family Support
Services 349*

BEST PRACTICES
Hospital CEO Margaret Sabin Works Up
a Sweat over Wellness   350

Wellness Programs 351; Sabbaticals 351

Summary   352

Terms to Understand   353

ACTION LEARNING EXERCISE
Quality-of-Work-Life Survey   353

ETHICS EXERCISE: DO THE RIGHT THING
Is Corporate CEO Pay Out of Control?   354

*MANAGERS-IN-ACTION VIDEO
CASE STUDY*
Flight 001   355

CLOSING CASE
Best Buy Smashes the Time Clock   356

13   Group Dynamics and Teamwork   358

THE CHANGING WORKPLACE
Show Them Some Love   359

Fundamental Group Dynamics   360
What Is a Group? 360

ETHICS: CHARACTER, COURAGE,
AND VALUES
Building Stronger Neighborhoods Through
Social Capital   360

    Types of Groups 361; Attraction to Groups 363;
    Roles 364; Norms 364

Group Development   365
    Characteristics of a Mature Group 365; Six
    Stages of Group Development 366

Organizational Politics   368
    What Does Organizational Politics Involve?
    369; Research on Organizational Politics
    369; Political Tactics 370; Antidotes to
    Political Behavior 370

Conformity and Groupthink   371
    Research on Conformity 371; Groupthink 372

Teams, Teamwork, and Trust   374
    Cross-Functional Teams 374

GREEN MANAGEMENT:
TOWARD SUSTAINABILITY
A Virtual Environmental Team Makes
Real Money   375

    Virtual Teams 375; What Makes Workplace
    Teams Effective? 376; Trust: A Key to Team
    Effectiveness 378

Summary   380

Terms to Understand   381

ACTION LEARNING EXERCISE
Management Teamwork Survey   381

ETHICS EXERCISE: DO THE RIGHT THING
The Art of Friendship   382

MANAGERS-IN-ACTION VIDEO
CASE STUDY
Numi Organic Tea   383

CLOSING CASE
True Team Spirit at Chicago's Total Attorneys   383

14   **Influence, Power, and Leadership**   **386**

THE CHANGING WORKPLACE
Charting Your Pathway To Influence
and Power   387

Influence Tactics in the Workplace   388

Power   390
    What is Power? 391; The Five Bases
    of Power 391; Empowerment 393

GREEN MANAGEMENT:
TOWARD SUSTAINABILITY
Nike's Point Person for Sustainability   393

Leadership   393
    Leadership Defined 394; Formal and
    Informal Leaders 394; The Issue of Leaders
    Versus Managers: A Middle Ground 394;
    Trait Theory 396; Behavioral Styles Theory
    398; Situational Theory 399; Transformational
    Leadership Theory 401; Putting to Work What
    You've Learned Using "Practical Intelligence"
    and Becoming a "Servant Leader" 403

Mentoring   404

ETHICS: CHARACTER, COURAGE,
AND VALUES
Lola Gonzalez Laid Herself Off to Help
Her Employees Keep Their Jobs   404

    Learning from a Mentor 405; Dynamics
    of Mentoring 405; New Approaches to
    Mentoring 406

Behavior Modification   406
    What is Behavior Modification? 407;
    Managing Antecedents 407; Managing
    Consequences 408; Positively Reinforce
    What is Right About Job Performance (the Art
    of "Bucket Filling") 408; Schedule Positive
    Reinforcement Appropriately 410

Summary   411

Terms to Understand   412

ACTION LEARNING EXERCISE
What Is Your Emotional Intelligence (EQ)?   412

ETHICS EXERCISE: DO THE RIGHT THING
Some Truth About Lying   413

MANAGERS-IN-ACTION VIDEO
CASE STUDY
Greensburg, Kansas   413

CLOSING CASE
Leadership Development GE-Style   414

15   **Change, Conflict, and Negotiation**   **416**

THE CHANGING WORKPLACE
In Search of the Paperless Office—Part 1   417

Change: Organizational and Individual
Perspectives   418
    Types of Organizational Change 418;
    Individual Reactions to Change 420

Overcoming Resistance to Change   422
*Why Do Employees Resist Change? 423;
Strategies for Overcoming Resistance to
Change 424*

*GREEN MANAGEMENT:
TOWARD SUSTAINABILITY
AT&T's Alicia Abella Wants Better
and Greener Communication Technologies*   425

Making Change Happen   427·
*Planned Change Through Organization
Development (OD) 427; Unofficial and
Informal Grassroots Change 429*

Managing Conflict   431
*Dealing with the Two Faces of Conflict 431;
Conflict Triggers 433; Resolving Conflict 433*

*VALUING DIVERSITY
Needed: Innovators + Implementers*   434

Negotiating   435
*Elements of Effective Negotiation 436;
Added Value Negotiating 438*

Summary   439

Terms to Understand   439

*ACTION LEARNING EXERCISE
Putting Conflict on Ice*   440

*ETHICS EXERCISE: DO THE RIGHT THING
I'm Wrong!*   441

*MANAGERS-IN-ACTION VIDEO
CASE STUDY
Scholfield Honda*   442

*CLOSING CASE
In Search of the Paperless Office—Part 2*   443

**PART 5 ORGANIZATIONAL CONTROL
PROCESSES   445**

**16 Organizational Control and Quality
Improvement   446**

*THE CHANGING WORKPLACE
Apple Takes a Bite Out of Customer
Service Hassles*   447

Fundamentals of Organizational Control   448
Types of Control 449

*GREEN MANAGEMENT:
TOWARD SUSTAINABILITY
Tod Dykstra Wants Us to Stop Driving
in Circles*   450

*Components of Organizational Control
Systems 451; Strategic Control 453;
Identifying Control Problems 454*

Crisis Management   455
*Crisis Management Defined 455; Developing
a Crisis Management Program 456*

The Quality Challenge   458
*Defining Quality 458; Five Types
of Product Quality 458; Unique Challenges
for Service Providers 459; Defining Service
Quality 461*

An Introduction to Total Quality
Management (TQM)   461
*1. Do It Right the First Time 461; 2. Be
Customer-Centered 462; 3. Make
Continuous Improvement a Way of Life 463;
4. Build Teamwork and Empowerment 464;
The Seven Basic TQM Process Improvement
Tools 464*

Deming Management   466
Principles of Deming Management 466

*WINDOW ON THE WORLD
Chinese Appliance Maker Succeeds
with a Lesson from Peter Drucker*   467

Deming's 14 Points 468

Summary   470

Terms to Understand   470

*ACTION LEARNING EXERCISE
Measuring Service Quality*   471

*ETHICS EXERCISE: DO THE RIGHT THING
Who's Really No. 1?*   472

*MANAGERS-IN-ACTION VIDEO
CASE STUDY
Preserve® by Recycline*   472

*CLOSING CASE
The Cure*   473

Today's managers face a complex web of difficult and exciting challenges. A global economy in which world-class quality is essential, increased diversity in the workforce, new technologies, and demands for more ethical conduct promise to keep things interesting. As trustees of society's precious human, material, financial, and informational resources, today's and tomorrow's managers hold the key to a better world. A solid grounding in management is essential to successfully guiding large or small, profit or nonprofit organizations in the twenty-first century. *Management,* Twelfth Edition, represents an important step toward managerial and personal success in an era of rapid change. It is a comprehensive, up-to-date, and highly readable introduction to management theory, research, and practice. This twelfth edition is the culmination of Bob Kreitner's many years in management classrooms and management development seminars around the world and Carlene Cassidy's rich experience as an entrepreneur, executive, and teacher. Its style and content have been shaped by interaction with thousands of students along with many instructors, reviewers, editors, and managers. All have taught us valuable lessons about organizational life, management, and people in general. Organized along a time-tested functional/process framework, *Management,* Twelfth Edition, integrates classical and modern concepts with a rich array of contemporary real-world examples, cases, captioned photos, and unique Interactive Annotations.

SIGNIFICANT CHANGES, IMPROVEMENTS, AND NEW TOPICS

Many changes have been made in response to feedback from students, colleagues, and managers who read the previous edition and reflecting the latest trends in management thinking. Significant improvements in the twelfth edition of *Management* include:

- A **new co-author, Carlene Cassidy,** who brings diversity, a fresh perspective, and a wealth of real-world management experience to this edition.
- A **fresh interior design** makes this new edition very readable, accessible, and user-friendly.
- **New** integrated and comprehensive coverage of the **impacts of social media and social networking** in the workplace, beginning in Chapter 1 and continuing in Chapter 7 (strategy), Chapter 10 (recruiting and job hunting), Chapter 11 (communication), and Chapter 13 (group dynamics).

- More extensive **ethics** coverage includes **11 in-text boxed features** titled **Ethics: Character, Courage, and Values** (each box includes a **discussion question**). A **New Ethics Exercise following every chapter** (with provocative discussion starters) helps students tackle tough real-world ethical dilemmas).
- **Forty-four (90%)** of the 49 **boxed features** are **new** to this edition.
- Topical variety has been enhanced with **five types of boxed features:** Ethics: Character, Courage, and Values (11); Green Management: Toward Sustainability (16); Window on the World (10); Valuing Diversity (5); and Best Practices (7).
- **Every boxed feature** now ends with a **question** to stimulate analytical and reflective thinking and class discussion.
- **New** to this edition are 16 boxed features titled **Green Management: Toward Sustainability** to show the creative and inspiring ways organizations and managers are turning environmental concerns into action.
- **Fifteen** of the 16 **chapter-opening cases are new** to this edition (answers to all of the discussion questions are in the *Instructor's Resource Manual*).
- **Forty-six** of the 76 (60%) **Interactive Annotations** in the margins are **new** (responses to every one of them are in the *Instructor's Resource Manual*).
- Four of the five **Valuing Diversity** boxed features throughout the text are **new.**
- Eight of the 10 **Window on the World** boxed features throughout the text are **new.**
- All 7 of the **Best Practices** boxed features throughout the text are **new.**
- **End-of-chapter activities** for each chapter have been expanded and improved to include a classroom-tested **Action Learning Exercise,** an **Ethics Exercise** (all 16 are new), and a **Managers-In-Action Video Case Study.** Eight of the 16 **chapter-closing cases** are **new** (answers to all of the discussion questions are in the *Instructor's Resource Manual*).
- All 16 of the Managers-In-Action Video Case Studies are new. In this edition, there are video case studies at the end of every chapter rather than at the end of each section. Each video case study is introduced with a synopsis along with pre-viewing questions (a new and unique feature) and post-viewing questions that help students apply chapter concepts to these real-world examples. The instructors' manual provides additional activities and projects to extend student learning beyond the textbook and videos.
- All **vital statistics** have been **updated** (e.g., workforce demographics, global economy, job outlook, female executives, job engagement/satisfaction, employee trust, small businesses).
- **New topics** include onshoring, greenwashing, Internet and social media technologies, Tapscott's Net Generation, America's education and skills crisis, retirement redefined, 2010 U.S. Supreme Court decision allowing independently-funded political ads, three components of cultural intelligence, management practices across 17 countries, triple bottom line (people, planet, profits), BP Gulf oil spill (ethics), how individuals handle uncertainty, social media business models (user-generated content), learning organizations, recruiting and job hunting with social media (LinkedIn), training gaps caused by new technology, training in today's 4-generation workplaces, Kirkpatrick's 4-level training evaluation model, four types of exit interview questions, communicating in the digital workplace, workplace policies for using social networking sites, teleworking pros and cons, four ways to measure motivation, employee engagement and retention (3 steps), PTO banks (paid-time-off), chronotype work scheduling, issue of friendships in the workplace, social media guidelines, six mentoring trends, and checklists as a control tool.

COMPLETE HARMONY WITH AACSB INTERNATIONAL'S REVISED ACCREDITATION STANDARDS

AACSB International (The Association to Advance Collegiate Schools of Business), the leading accrediting organization for business, management, and accounting programs, revised its Standards for Business Accreditation in 2003. Rather than specifying what courses need to be taught, AACSB now emphasizes mastery of knowledge and skill areas. These "learning experiences" (cross-referenced to key chapters in *Management*, Twelfth Edition) include:

- Communication abilities (Chapters 11, 12, 13, 14, and 15)
- Ethical understanding and reasoning abilities (Chapters 1, 3, and 5, eleven Ethics: Character, Courage, and Values boxed features, and an Ethics Exercise following every chapter)
- Analytic skills (all chapters, especially Chapter 6 and Action Learning Exercises following every chapter)
- Use of information technology (Chapters 1, 7, and 11 plus comprehensive new coverage of social media and social networking)
- Multicultural and diversity understanding (Chapters 3, 4, and 10 plus five Valuing Diversity boxed features)
- Reflective thinking skills (all chapters, especially Chapter 8, plus eleven Ethics: Character, Courage, and Values boxed features and an Ethics Exercise following every chapter)

Learning objectives at the beginning of each chapter and answered in the chapter summary make this entire textbook **"outcome-focused."**

Moreover, topical coverage in *Management*, Twelfth Edition, aligns very closely with AACSB International's list of "management-specific knowledge and skills." Among them are: "Ethical and legal responsibilities in organizations and society; Creation of value through the integrated production and distribution of goods, services, and information; Group and individual dynamics in organizations; Information technologies as they influence the structure and processes of organizations and economies, and as they influence the roles and techniques of management; Domestic and global economic environments of organizations." (*Source*: Excerpted from www.aacsb.edu/accreditation/process/documents/AACSB_STANDARDS_Revised_Jan08.pdf, pp. 15–16.)

MAJOR THEMES

The study of management takes in a great deal of territory, both conceptually and geographically. Therefore, it is important for those being introduced to the field to have reliable guideposts to help them make sense of it all. Five major themes guiding our progress through the fascinating world of management are change, ethics, skill development, diversity, and green (sustainability) practices.

An Overriding Focus on Change

It may be a cliché to say "the only certainty today is change," but it is nonetheless true. The challenge for today's and especially tomorrow's managers is to be aware of *specific* changes, along with the factors contributing to them and their likely impact on the practice of management. Unintended consequences also need to be thoughtfully anticipated. Change has been woven into the fabric of this new edition in the following ways:

- Under the heading of "The Changing Workplace," each chapter-opening case introduces students to real-world managers and changes at large and small, domestic and foreign organizations (15 of the 16 opening cases are new to this edition).
- Chapter 1 profiles twenty-first-century managers and ten major changes in the practice of management. New Internet and social media technologies are defined and put into context.
- Chapter 2 introduces complex adaptive systems theory.
- Chapter 3 is devoted entirely to the changing social, political/legal, economic, and technological environments of management. Workplace demographics document the changing face of the workforce. Business cycles and the innovation process are explained.
- Chapter 4 discusses the growth of global and transnational corporations and how to adapt to cross-cultural situations.
- Chapter 6 covers project planning/management, underscoring the ad hoc nature of today's workplaces.
- Chapter 7 covers seven basic Internet business models and a new section titled "Emerging Business Models for Social Media."
- Chapter 8 discusses knowledge management as a strategic tool for better decision making.
- Chapter 9 describes the new virtual organizations.
- Chapter 10 covers the concept of "human capital" and features Pfeffer's seven people-centered practices.
- Chapter 11 covers blogs, social networking, e-mail, text messaging, cell phone etiquette, videoconferencing, and teleworking.
- Chapter 13 covers virtual teams and how to build them.
- Chapter 14 covers emotional intelligence, a vital trait for adaptable managers and leaders, and six trends in mentoring.
- Chapter 15 offers comprehensive treatment of change, resistance to change, and how to bring about unofficial grassroots change.
- Chapter 16 covers the timely topic of crisis management.
- The Managers-in-Action video clips for chapters 2, 3, 6, 8, 9, 13, 14, and 15 all provide real-world examples of change and innovation.

Emphasis on Ethics and Social Responsibility

Simply put, society wants managers to behave better. Ethical concerns are integrated throughout this edition, as well as featured in Chapter 5. Ethical coverage is evidenced by:

- Eleven (9 new) **Ethics: Character, Courage, and Values** boxes throughout the text (each box contains a **discussion question**)
- **New** to this edition, one at the end of every chapter, are **16 Ethical Exercises** with discussion prompts to give students hands-on experience with real-world ethical questions, choices, and dilemmas facing today's managers.
- Also new to this edition are several **Managers-in-Action video clips** that emphasize ethics and corporate social responsibility, a particularly strong theme in the clips for chapters 2, 4, 5, 7, and 15.

- Offshoring of jobs controversy (Chapter 1)
- Discussion of management's ethical reawakening (Chapter 1)
- Chapter 5 (in Part One for up-front emphasis), devoted entirely to management's social and ethical responsibilities, provides an ethical context for the entire book
- Carroll's global corporate social responsibility pyramid (Chapter 5)
- Research: how people rationalize unethical conduct (Chapter 5)
- Ten general ethical principles (Chapter 5)
- Value judgments in decision making (Chapter 8)
- Ethical implications of social networking in the workplace (Chapter 11)
- Ethical implications of being friends with coworkers, group norms, and avoiding groupthink (Chapter 13)
- Greenleaf's ethical "servant leader" (Chapter 14)
- Covey's ethical win-win negotiating style (Chapter 15)

Emphasis on Skill Development

Managers tell us they want job applicants who know more than just management theory. They value people who can communicate well, solve problems, see the big picture, and work cooperatively in teams. Consequently, this edition has a very strong skills orientation.

- *How-to-do-it instructions* are integrated into the text for the following skills and tasks: preparing employees for foreign assignments, examining the ethics of a business decision, writing good objectives, using management by objectives (MBO), constructing flow charts and Gantt charts, building a PERT network, performing a break-even analysis, writing planning scenarios, making decisions, avoiding decision-making traps, managing creative people, promoting organizational learning, delegating, following cell phone etiquette, interviewing, evaluating training programs, discouraging sexual harassment, developing a social networking policy, communicating via e-mail, participating in a videoconference, listening, writing effectively, running a meeting, using rewards, making employee participation programs work, curbing organizational politics, preventing groupthink, building trust, modifying behavior, managing change, overcoming resistance to change, managing conflict, negotiating, using Deming's Plan-Do-Check-Act cycle, and improving product and service quality.
- *Best Practices boxes* distributed throughout the text (**all 7 are new**) describe how real managers are dealing with real problems.
- *Managers-in-Action Videos,* following each chapter there is a video case study that features managers in a variety of settings from organizations including: Numi Organic Teas, Scholfield Honda, Preserve/Recycline, Greensburg KS, Flight 001, Maine Workshops, Evo, and Gold & Williams. Management best practices and contemporary management challenges included in this new edition are evident in the associated videos. Emphasis is placed on the development of essential management skills including: managing and motivating employees, leading teams, embracing creativity, supply chain management in a global economy, leveraging technology for improved customer service, employee communication, quality control, and operations management, and aligning corporate culture and values with the mission and vision of the organization. While viewing these videos, students will learn from the managers' challenges and their successes. The managers demonstrate their strategies for adapting to change and managing scarce resources.

Emphasis on Diversity

Labor forces and customers around the globe, particularly in the United States, are becoming more diverse in terms of national origin, race, religion, gender, predominant age categories, and personal lifestyle preferences. Managers are challenged to manage diversity effectively to tap the *full* potential of *every* individual's unique combination of abilities and traits. The following diversity coverage and themes can be found in this edition:

- Five boxed features (**4 new**) throughout the text, titled **Valuing Diversity**, focus needed attention on breaking the glass ceiling, biased decision making, military veterans as valuable employees, sexual orientation diversity, and job category diversity (innovators and implementers).
- Women play important managerial roles in 17 cases and boxed inserts.
- A diverse selection of individuals is featured in cases, boxes, in-text examples, photos, and video case studies.
- Chapters 1 and 4 discuss the demand for multilingual and multicultural managers.
- Chapter 3 includes a section on managing diversity.
- Chapter 4 discusses managing across cultures and emphasizes the importance of learning foreign languages. Chapter 4 also describes management practices and leadership styles in different cultures.
- Chapter 5 discusses different value systems.
- Chapter 8 describes different information-processing styles and how to manage creative individuals.
- Chapter 10 discusses moving from tolerance to appreciation when managing diversity. It also covers equal employment opportunity, affirmative action, the Americans with Disabilities Act (ADA), and how to develop policies for sexual harassment and substance abuse. Protection of military personnel and veterans under the Uniformed Services Employment and Reemployment Rights Act is discussed.
- Chapter 12 discusses how to motivate a diverse work force and provides coverage of the U.S. Family and Medical Leave Act (FMLA).
- Chapter 13 includes major coverage of teamwork.
- Chapter 14 discusses women and the use of power as well as different leadership styles.
- Chapter 15 discusses *cooperative* conflict and describes different conflict resolution styles.
- The Manager-in-Action Video for Chapter 2, featuring Gold + Williams, is particularly relevant to any discussion of diversity.

Emphasis on Green Management (Sustainability)

A clear "ethical green thread" runs throughout *Management*, Twelfth Edition.

- **Sustainability** is defined in chapter 1 as a context for examples and discussion in later chapters.
- Efficient use of resources, sustainability, alternative energy sources, and recycling are emphasized in many in-text examples of real-world green management practices.
- **New** to this edition are 16 boxed features titled **Green Management: Toward Sustainability** that describe the bold green management initiatives leading organizations such as Walmart, General Electric, and IBM are taking.
- Green management and sustainability are themes woven throughout several of the **Manager-in-Action Videos,** particularly in chapters 1, 4, 5, 7, 8, 14, 15, and 16.

AN INTERACTIVE TEXTBOOK

Active rather than passive learning is the preferred way to go these days. As well it should be, because active learning is interesting and fun. This textbook employs two interactive-learning strategies: Web-linked interactive annotations and action learning exercises.

Interactive Annotations

This feature, unique to *Management,* was introduced back in the seventh edition. The original idea was to link the textbook and the Internet to create a dynamic, instructive, and interesting learning tool. In short, we wanted to make the textbook come alive. This pedagogical experiment has been a great success. (In fact, many students say they read the annotations first when turning to a new page.) Consequently, there are **76 interactive annotations** in this twelfth edition (46 are new) that integrate timely facts, provocative ideas, discussion questions, and back-to-the-opening-case questions into the flow of the book.

Answers and interpretations for the annotations are provided in the *Instructor's Resource Manual* and on the Student and Instructor Web sites.

At the instructor's discretion, many of the annotations provide stimulating opportunities for cooperative learning. Valuable new insights are gained and interpersonal skills are developed when students work together in groups and teams.

Action Learning Exercises

There is one Action Learning Exercise at the end of each chapter. These exercises strive to heighten self-awareness and build essential managerial skills. They have all been successfully classroom tested. The exercises can be completed alone or in cooperative-learning teams. Each exercise is followed by a set of questions for personal consideration and/or class discussion. The 16 Action Learning Exercises include: an entrepreneur's quiz, open-system thinking and recycling, rating the probability of futuristic predictions, a cultural-awareness survey, a personal values survey, how to write good objectives and plans, doing a strategic SWOT analysis, a creativity test, an organizational culture assessment, a field study on organization structure and design, writing behavioral interview questions, communicating in an awkward situation, a quality-of-worklife survey, a management teamwork survey, an emotional intelligence (EQ) test, managing a conflict, and measuring service quality.

SUCCESSFUL PEDAGOGICAL STRUCTURE FOR STUDENTS

As with the previous edition, pedagogical features of the text, along with student ancillaries, make *Management,* Twelfth Edition, a complete and valuable learning tool—one that will satisfy the needs of both students and professors. This is demonstrated by the following:

- Chapter learning objectives at the beginning of each chapter focus the reader's attention on key concepts.
- Key terms are emphasized in bold where first defined, repeated at the bottom of the page, and listed at the close of each chapter (with page numbers) to reinforce important terminology and concepts.

- A stimulating photo/art program and an inviting, user-friendly layout make the material in this edition visually appealing, accessible, and interesting. Captioned color photographs of managers in action and organizational life enliven the text discussion.
- In-text examples and boxes with five different themes—ethics, global management, diversity, green management (sustainability), and best practices—provide students with extensive, interesting real-world illustrations to demonstrate the application and relevance of topics important to today's managers.
- Clear, comprehensive chapter summaries (organized by learning objectives) refresh the reader's memory of important material.
- Cases at the beginning and end of each chapter provide a real-world context for handling management problems. Twenty-three (72 percent) of the cases in this edition are new.
- An Action Learning Exercise follows each chapter to provide interactive and experiential learning.
- An Ethics Exercise following each chapter gives students the opportunity to wrestle with contemporary tough ethics choices.
- Managers-in-Action Videos following each chapter foster experiential learning by providing real-world exposure to key managerial skills. The use of pre-viewing questions along with post-viewing questions further engage students and encourage them to apply what they have learned in the chapter. 100% of the video case studies in this edition are new.

ACKNOWLEDGMENTS

Countless people, including colleagues, students, and relatives, have contributed in many ways to the many editions of this book. It is amazing where life's journey leads when you have a clear goal, the support of many good people, and a bone-deep belief in the concept of continuous improvement. Whether critical or reinforcing, everyone's suggestions and recommendations have been helpful and greatly appreciated.

Warmest thanks are extended to the following colleagues who have provided valuable input for this and prior editions by serving as content advisers or manuscript reviewers:

Teshome Abebe
University of Southern Colorado

Benjamin Abramowitz
University of Central Florida

Raymond E. Alie
Western Michigan University

Stephen L. Allen
Northwest Missouri State University

Douglas R. Anderson
Ashland University

Mark Anderson
Point Loma Nazarene College

Eva Beer Aronson
Interboro Institute

Debra A. Arvanites
Villanova University

Robert Ash
Rancho Santiago College

Seymour Barcun
St. Frances College

R. B. Barton Jr.
Murray State University

Andrew J. Batchelor
Ohio University–Chillicothe

Dorman C. Batson
Glenville State College

Dr. Loretta Beavers
Southwest Virginia Community College

Walter H. Beck Sr.
Kennesaw State University and Reinhardt College

Roger Best
Louisiana College

Gerald D. Biby
Sioux Falls College

Banu Goktan Bilhan
University of North Texas at Dallas

Glenn M. Blair
Baldwin-Wallace College

Bruce Bloom
DeVry University

Bob Bowles
Cecils College

Barbara Boyington
Brookdale Community College

Steve Bradley
Austin Community College

Margaret Britt
Mount Vernon Nazarene University

Dr. Jon Bryan
Bridgewater State College

Molly Burke
Rosary College

Marie Burkhead
University of Southwestern Louisiana

John Cantrell
Cleveland State Community College

Thomas Carey
Western Michigan University

Elaine Adams Casmus
Chowan College

Julia M. Chambers
Bloomfield College

David Chown
Minnesota State University, Mankato

Anthony A. Cioffi
Lorain County Community College

Richard Coe
Richard Stockton College of New Jersey

George M. Coggins
High Point College

Jeff Cohu
Rochester College

Craig Cowles
Bridgewater State College

Naomi Berger Davidson
*California State
University–Northridge*

Pamela Davis
*Eastern Kentucky
University*

Richard A. Davis
Rosary College

H. Kristl Davison
University of Mississippi

Thomas Daymont
*Temple University–
Philadelphia*

Christine Delatorre
*Collin County Community
College*

Adva Dinur
Long Island University

Mark Dobeck, Ph.D.
*Cleveland State
University*

Tim Donahue
Sioux Falls College

Thomas Duda
*S.U.N.Y. Canton Tech
College*

Ken Dunegan
Cleveland State University

Deborah J. Dwyer
University of Toledo

Sally Martin Egge
Cardinal Stritch University

Gary Ernst
North Central College

Dr. Yvette Essounga-Njan
Long Island University

Janice Feldbauer
*Macomb Community
College*

John Finley
*Columbus State
University*

Jacque Foust
*University of Wisconsin–
River Falls*

Ellen Frank
*Southern Connecticut
State University*

Edward Fritz
*Nassau Community
College*

Phyllis Goodman
College of DuPage

Sue Granger
*Jacksonville State
University*

Judith Grenkowicz
*Kirtland Community
College*

Dennis Gresdo
Park University

John Hall
University of Florida

Susan C. Hanlon
University of Akron

Kimberly Harris
*Durham Technical
Community College*

Nell Hartley
Robert Morris College

Lindle Hatton
*University of Wisconsin–
Oshkosh*

Samuel Hazen
Tarleton State University

Rick Hebert
*East Carolina
University*

Dorothy Hetmer-Hinds
*Trinity Valley Community
College*

Brian R. Hinrichs
*Illinois Wesleyan
University*

Larry W. Howard
*Middle Tennessee State
University*

Jerome Hufnagel
Horry Georgetown Tech

Cathy Jensen
*University of Nebraska–
Lincoln*

Kathleen Jones
*University of North
Dakota*

Dr. Norma Juma
Washburn University

Marvin Karlins
*University of South
Florida*

Velta Kelly
University of Cincinnati

Sylvia Keyes
Bridgewater State College

Mary Khalili
Oklahoma City University

John Lea
Arizona State University

Charles Lee
Baldwin-Wallace College

Roger D. Lee
*Salt Lake Community
College*

Dr. David O. Linthicum
Cecil College

James LoPresti
*University of Colorado,
Boulder*

Bob Lower
Minot State University

James L. Mann
Ashland Community College

Randall Martin
Florida International University

Irvin Mason
Herkimer County Community College

Fredric L. Mayerson
CUNY–Kingsboro Community College

Daniel McAlister
University of Nevada, Las Vegas

Ann McClure
Ft. Hays State University

Pam McElligott
St. Louis Community College

Barbara McIntosh
University of Vermont

Debra Miller
Ashland Community College

Mark S. Miller
Carthage College

Peggy M. Miller
Ohio University–Athens

Ray Moroye
University of Denver & Metropolitan State College

John Nagy
Cleary College

James Nead
Vincennes University

Joan Nichols
Emporia State University

Alice E. Nuttall
Kent State University

Darlene Orlov
New York University

Robert Ottemann
University of Nebraska–Omaha

Clyde A. Painter
Ohio Northern University

Herbert S. Parker
Kean College of New Jersey

Joe Pastorino
Gus Petrides
Borough of Manhattan Community College

J. Stephen Phillips
Ohio University–Chillicothe

Allen H. Pike
Ferrum College

Khush Pittenger
Ashland University

Tracy H. Porter, M.S.
*Cleveland State University
Southwestern Community College*

Jyoti N. Prasad
Eastern Illinois University

Abe Qastin
Lakeland College

Delores Reha
Fullerton College

Lynn J. Richardson
Fort Lewis College

Robert W. Risteen
Ohio University–Chillicothe

Ralph Roberts
University of West Florida

Jake Robertson
Oklahoma State University

Robert Rowe
New Mexico State University–Alamogordo and Park College, Holloman Air Force Base

Daniel James Rowley
University of Northern Colorado

Wendell J. Roye
Franklin Pierce College

Doug Rymph
Emporia State University

Nestor St. Charles
Dutchess County Community College

John Sagi
Anne Arundel Community College

John T. Samaras
Central State University

Roger C. Schoenfeldt
Murray State University

Gregory J. Schulz
Carroll College

Barbara Scott
San Francisco State University

C. L. Scott III
Indiana University NW– Gary

Kathryn Severance
Viterbo College

Jane Shuping
Western Piedmont Community College

Marc Siegall
California State University–Chico

Peter Sietins
Bridgewater State College

G. David Sivak
Westmoreland County Community College

Mick Stahler
Stautzenberger College

Jacqueline Stowe
McMurray University

Sharon Tarnutzer
Utah State University

Margo Underwood
Brunswick College

John Valentine
Kean College of New Jersey

Candace Vogelsong
Cecil College

Dr. Leatha Ware
Waubonsee Community College

Ty Westergaard
Lincoln University

Timothy Wiedman
Ohio University–Lancaster

Mary Williams
College of South Nevada

James Wittman
Rock Valley College

Joe F. Walenciak
John Brown University

Dorothy Wallace
Chowan College

Stanley Welaish
Kean College of New Jersey

Richard A. Wells
Aiken Technical College

Our partnership with South-Western Cengage Learning has been productive and enjoyable. Many Cengage Learning people have contributed enormously to this project. We would like to offer a hearty thank you to everyone by acknowledging the following key contributors: Erin Joyner, Publisher; Scott Person, Executive Editor; Jennifer King, Developmental Editor; Jonathan Monahan, Marketing Manager; Tippy McIntosh, Senior Art Director; Rob Ellington, Media Editor; and Ruth Belanger, Senior Editorial Assistant.

The discussion of mentoring in Chapter 14 is dedicated once again to Professor Fred Luthans, University of Nebraska–Lincoln, for getting Bob Kreitner into the textbook business. Fred's love for our field of study and incredible work ethic continue to inspire. To Margaret—Bob's wife, best friend, and hiking buddy—thanks for being his center of gravity and for keeping the spirit of the dancing bears alive. Our long marriage is a cherished treasure. Our cats Yahoo and Sweetie Pie did a great job of "managing" Bob's home office. To Carlene's family, friends and colleagues—thank you for your encouragement, support, and wisdom. Laura, your patience, guidance, and love are immeasurable. To Bob—my mentor and partner on this project—words cannot describe my respect, admiration and gratitude. You are an inspiration in all aspects of life! Thank you for making a difference!

Finally, we would like to thank the thousands of introductory management students we have had the pleasure of working with through the years for teaching us a great deal about tomorrow's managers. Best wishes for a rewarding career in management.

Bob Kreitner
Carlene Cassidy

ABOUT ROBERT KREITNER

Robert Kreitner, Ph.D., is a Professor Emeritus of Management at Arizona State University. After a 26-year career at ASU, Bob was named to the W. P. Carey School of Business Faculty Hall of Fame.

Bob was born in Buffalo, New York. After a four-year enlistment in the U.S. Coast Guard, including service in Antarctica aboard the icebreaker Eastwind, he attended the University of Nebraska-Omaha on a football scholarship. He was a co-captain his senior year and received the Alumni Association's Scholar-Athlete Award. Bob received bachelor's and master's degrees in business from UNO in 1970 and 1971 and a Ph.D. in business from the University of Nebraska-Lincoln in 1974. He has taught at UNO, UNL, Western Illinois University, Thunderbird, and ASU. Bob also has taught in Micronesia, Albania, and Switzerland.

Margaret A. Sova

He is the author or co-author of seven college textbooks that have been through a total of 31 editions since 1975. His management and organizational behavior books are leaders in their field and have been translated into Spanish, French, Italian, and Mandarin Chinese. Bob continues to pursue his passion for learning and teaching by working on new editions of his textbooks.

Among his consulting and management development clients have been American Express, Nazarene School of Large Church Management, Ford Motor Company, SABRE Computer Services, Honeywell, Motorola, Salt River Project, Amdahl, the Hopi Indian nation, State Farm Insurance, Goodyear Aerospace, Doubletree Hotels, Bank One-Arizona, Caterpillar, and U.S. Steel.

Bob and his wife Margaret, a Nebraska native who is a retired Intel manager, live in Phoenix with their two cats, Yahoo and Sweetie Pie, and enjoy hiking, world travel, funding tuition and textbook scholarships for UNO students, and fishing in Alaska. Bob's other leisure pursuits are exercising, attending sports events at ASU, tree planting and tending, and wood carving. He has been a Habitat for Humanity volunteer.

ABOUT CARLENE CASSIDY

Carlene M. Cassidy, founder of Anne Arundel Community College's Entrepreneurial Studies Institute, has over 20 years of experience in business, management, and information systems. She has worked in a variety of industries, including health care, retail, computer information systems, and education. Prior to becoming a Business Management professor at Anne Arundel Community College, she was a partner and Chief Operating Officer for a multi-million-dollar regional computer consulting firm. In addition, Cassidy has managed mergers and acquisitions, and she has launched several start-up initiatives from a health care staffing company to her own consulting firm providing information systems and management consulting services to health care organizations, educational institutions, and small service companies.

Ms. Cassidy is frequently invited to speak at corporate events, conferences, and other colleges and universities. In addition to her inspiring and motivational presentations, she has experience teaching a variety of business and technology subjects in both college and corporate environments. Her specialty areas include Entrepreneurship, Leadership, Management, Supervision, Strategic Planning, Business Communication, and Computer Information Systems.

Bob Kreitner

Ms. Cassidy received the 2009 Entrepreneurship Faculty of the Year Award from the National Association for Community College Entrepreneurship. She also received Anne Arundel Community College Student Association's highest honor, the Distinguished Service Award, and she was the 2008 Faculty Advisor of the Year. She is a YWCA Tribute to Women in Industry Honoree, and she has been included multiple times in the Who's Who Among American Teachers.

Ms. Cassidy is co-author of a new textbook: *Supervision: Setting People Up For Success, 1st Edition* (© 2010 South-Western Cengage Learning). In her spare time she volunteers her services to the community by serving on multiple non-profit boards of directors and committees. She has a Bachelor of Science Degree in Health Services Administration from Providence College and a Master of Science Degree in Information Systems and Telecommunications from Johns Hopkins University.

CHAPTER 1   Managers and Entrepreneurs

CHAPTER 2   The Evolution of Management
             Thought

CHAPTER 3   The Changing Environment
             of Management: Diversity,
             Global Economy,
             and Technology

CHAPTER 4   International Management
             and Cross-Cultural
             Competence

CHAPTER 5   Management's
             Social and Ethical
             Responsibilities

The Management Challenge

P1

1 Managers and Entrepreneurs

*"Management is a practice that has to combine a good deal of **craft**, namely experience, with a certain amount of **art**, as vision and insight, and some **science**, particularly in the form of analysis and technique."*[1]
—HENRY MINTZBERG

The Changing Workplace

WHAT IS THE SECRET TO ZAPPOS.COM'S SUCCESS?

Background: *Tony Hsieh (pronounced "shay"), CEO of online retailer and shoe specialist Zappos.com, helped guide the firm from struggling start-up to incredible success. In 2009, just ten years after Hsieh joined Zappos as an investor/adviser, the company was sold to Amazon.com for $1.2 billion. As detailed in this excerpt from his new book* Delivering Happiness: A Path to Profits, Passion, and Purpose, *Hsieh explains how Zappo's wildly customer-focused and fun-loving company culture came into being. FYI: Zappos.com ranked number 15 on* Fortune *magazine's 2010 list of the "100 Best Companies to Work For." After the Amazon deal was complete, Hsieh assembled all 1,300 employees to assure them their cherished culture was safe and gave each one a Kindle and a retention bonus equaling 40 percent of their annual pay, in two annual installments.*[2]

Someone from our legal department suggested that we come up with a list of core values as a guide for managers to make hiring decisions. . . .

Over the course of a year, I e-mailed the entire company several times and got a lot of suggestions and feedback on which core values were the most important to our employees.

I was surprised the process took so long, but we wanted to make sure not to rush through the process because whatever core values we eventually came up with, we wanted to be ones that we could truly embrace. . . .

We wanted a list of committable core values that we were willing to hire and fire on. If we weren't willing to do that, then they weren't really "values."

We eventually came up with our final list of ten core values [from an initial list of 37], which we still use today:

1. Deliver WOW Through Service
2. Embrace and Drive Change
3. Create Fun and a Little Weirdness
4. Be Adventurous, Creative, and Open-Minded
5. Pursue Growth and Learning
6. Build Open and Honest Relationships with Communication
7. Build a Positive Team and Family Spirit
8. Do More with Less
9. Be Passionate and Determined
10. Be Humble

OBJECTIVES

- **Define** the term *management,* and **explain** the managerial significance of the terms *effectiveness* and *efficiency.*
- **Identify** and **summarize** five major sources of change for today's managers.
- **Distinguish** between managerial functions and skills, and **identify** the eight basic managerial functions.
- **Demonstrate** your knowledge of Wilson's three managerial skill categories, and **explain** the practical significance of his research findings.
- **Explain** how managers learn to manage.
- **Challenge** two myths about small businesses, and **describe** entrepreneurs.

. . . *Be Humble* is probably the core value that ends up affecting our hiring decisions the most. There are a lot of experienced, smart and talented people we interview that we know can make an immediate impact on our top or bottom line. But a lot of them are also really egotistical, so we end up not hiring them. At most companies, the hiring manager would probably argue that we should hire such a candidate because he or she will add a lot of value to the company, which is probably why most large corporations don't have great cultures.

Our philosophy at Zappos is that we're willing to make short-term sacrifices (including lost revenue or profits) if we believe that the long-term benefits are worth it. Protecting the company culture and sticking to core values is a long-term benefit.

Source: Excerpted from Tony Hsieh, *Delivering Happiness: A Path to Profits, Passion, and Purpose* (New York: Business Plus, 2010), pp. 155–158.

The Zappos.com story is inspiring for those striving to be successful managers and leaders someday. Tony Hsieh and other modern managers need vision, authenticity, and persistence to handle these four key realities:

1. The only certainty today is *change*. Challenging *goals* motivate people to strive for improvement and overcome obstacles and resistance to change.
2. *Speed, teamwork,* and *flexibility* are the orders of the day, from both strategic and operational standpoints.
3. Managers at all levels need to stay close to the *customer*. Product/service *quality* is the driving force in the battle to stay competitive.
4. Without *continuous improvement* and *lifelong learning*, there can be no true economic progress for individuals and organizations alike.

Try to keep these managerial realities in mind as you explore the world of management in this book.

Every one of us—whether as an employee, a customer, a stockholder, or a member of the surrounding community—has a direct stake in the quality of management. Joan Magretta, a management consultant who went on to become an editor at *Harvard Business Review*, offers this perspective:

> *Management's business is building organizations that work. Underneath all the theory and the tools, underneath all the specialized knowledge, lies a commitment to performance that has powerfully altered our economy and our lives. That, ultimately, is why management is everyone's business.*[3]

Accordingly, bad management is a serious threat to our quality of life. Terry Bragg, president of a management training company in Utah, put it this way: "For most employees, the immediate boss is the prime representative of the organization. . . . If they don't like their immediate boss, they don't like the company."[4] A recent survey put a sharper point on the issue when it found 28 percent of the 1,047 workers polled would lay off their boss if they could.[5]

Effective management is the key to a better world, but mismanagement squanders our resources and jeopardizes our well-being. Every manager, regardless of level or scope of responsibility, is either part of the solution or part of the problem. Management or mismanagement—the choice is yours. A basic knowledge of management theory, research, and practice will help prepare you for productive and gainful employment in a highly organized world in which virtually everything is managed.

MANAGEMENT DEFINED

We now need to define management, in order to highlight the importance, relevance, and necessity of studying it. Management is the process of working with and through others to achieve organizational objectives in a changing environment. Central to this process is the effective and efficient use of limited resources. (*Note:* The term *management*, when used to describe workers with supervisory duties, is a legal designation in the United States wrapped in controversy over issues such as who can join a union and who qualifies for overtime pay.)[6]

Five components of this definition require closer examination: (1) working with and through others, (2) achieving organizational objectives, (3) balancing effectiveness and efficiency, (4) making the most of limited resources, and (5) coping with a changing environment (see Figure 1.1).

Working with and Through Others

Management is, above all else, a social process. Many collective purposes bring individuals together—building cars, providing emergency health care, publishing books, and on and on. But in all cases, managers are responsible for getting things done by working with and through others.

Aspiring managers who do not interact well with others hamper their careers. This was the conclusion two experts reached following interviews with 62 executives from the United States, the

Figure 1.1 Key Aspects of the Management Process

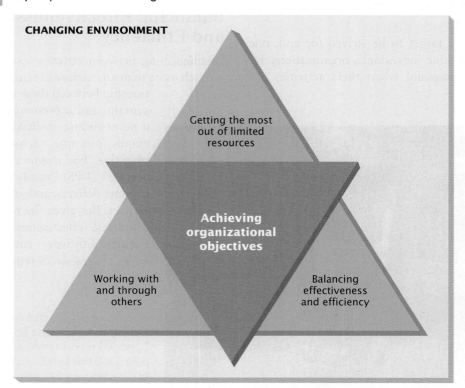

CHANGING ENVIRONMENT

Getting the most out of limited resources

Achieving organizational objectives

Working with and through others

Balancing effectiveness and efficiency

management the process of working with and through others to achieve organizational objectives in a changing environment

United Kingdom, Belgium, Spain, France, Germany, and Italy. Each of the executives was asked to describe two managers whose careers had been *derailed*. Derailed managers were those who had not lived up to their peers' and superiors' high expectations. The derailed managers reportedly had these shortcomings:

- Problems with interpersonal relationships
- Failure to meet business objectives
- Failure to build and lead a team
- Inability to change and adapt during a transition[7]

Significantly, the first and third shortcomings involve failure to work effectively with and through others. Derailed managers experienced a number of interpersonal problems; among other things, they were perceived as manipulative, abusive, untrustworthy, demeaning, overly critical, not team players, and poor communicators. The former CEO of PeopleSoft tripped over this particular hurdle when he was fired by the board of directors in 2004 for a number of reasons, including "managing abrasively."[8]

Achieving Organizational Objectives

An objective is a target to be strived for and, one hopes, attained. Like individuals, organizations are usually more successful when their activities are guided by challenging, yet achievable, objectives. From an individual perspective, scheduling a course load becomes more systematic and efficient when a student sets an objective, such as graduating with a specific degree by a given date.

Although personal objectives are typically within the reach of individual effort, organizational objectives or goals always require collective action. A good case in point involves PepsiCo's new strategic emphasis on healthier snacks—basically meaning less sugar, fat, and salt. "The company describes its current portfolio of 'healthy' fare as a $10 billion business—a figure CEO Indra Nooyi says she wants to see jump to $30 billion over the next decade."[9] This objective means the $43 billion-a-year soft drink and snack giant will have to mobilize its 203,000 employees to significantly revamp its product development and marketing programs.[10] This will be a huge collective effort requiring lots of skillful management.

Organizational objectives also serve later as measuring sticks for performance. Without organizational objectives, the management process, like a trip without a specific destination, would be aimless and wasteful.

Balancing Effectiveness and Efficiency

Distinguishing between effectiveness and efficiency is much more than an exercise in semantics. The relationship between these two terms is important, and it presents managers with a never-ending challenge. **Effectiveness** entails promptly achieving a stated objective. For instance, United Parcel Service (UPS) needs to meet its on-time-delivery and sales growth objectives. But given the reality of limited resources, effectiveness alone is not enough. **Efficiency** enters the picture when the resources required to achieve

PepsiCo employees, like these workers at the corporation's largest bottling plant in Domodedovo outside Moscow, Russia, are pulling together to help implement the snack and beverage giant's new strategies for growth.

AP Photo/Ivan Sekretarev

effectiveness a central element in the process of management that entails achieving a stated organizational objective | *efficiency a central element in the process of management that balances the amount of resources used to achieve an objective against what was actually accomplished*

an objective are weighed against what was actually accomplished. The more favorable the ratio of benefits to costs, the greater the efficiency. For giant companies such as UPS, seemingly small efficiencies can yield huge payoffs:

> UPS uses a sophisticated mapping-software system that directs its drivers not to make left turns unless absolutely necessary. The trucks actually drive a bit farther each day than if they took those left turns, but spend less time idling wastefully and burning fuel while waiting to turn.[11]

Managers are responsible for balancing effectiveness and efficiency (see Figure 1.2). Too much emphasis in either direction leads to mismanagement. On one hand, managers must be effective by getting the job done. On the other hand, managers need to be efficient by reducing costs and not wasting resources. Of course, managers who are too stingy with resources may fail to get the job done.

At the heart of the quest for both *productivity improvement* (a favorable ratio between inputs and output) and *sustainability* is the constant struggle to balance effectiveness and efficiency.[12] (See Green Management: Toward Sustainability.)

Making the Most of Limited Resources

We live in a world of scarcity. Even something as seemingly abundant as water is scarce when it comes to being drinking-quality water: "more than 800 million people worldwide lack clean water."[13] Those who are concerned with such matters worry not only about running out of renewable and nonrenewable natural resources but also about the lopsided use of those resources. The United States, for example, with under 5 percent of the world's population, is currently consuming roughly 25 percent of the world's annual oil production (60 percent of it imported) and generating 25 percent of the world's CO_2, a greenhouse gas linked to global warming.[14] Meanwhile, it takes a lot of water to support a modern lifestyle, as highlighted recently in *Fortune* magazine: "consider that the food you'll consume today required more

than 500 gallons to produce. The T-shirt you're wearing took 713 gallons. And each single sheet of paper in your 80-page presentation required about 2.5 gallons."[15]

Although experts and nonexperts alike may quibble over exactly how long it will take to exhaust our natural resources or come up with exotic new technological alternatives,[16] one bold fact remains: our planet is becoming increasingly crowded. Demographers who collect and study population statistics tell us that Earth's human population is growing each year by 57 million. Today's global population of nearly 6.9 billion is expected to grow to 8.9 billion by 2050.[17] Meanwhile, our planet's carrying capacity

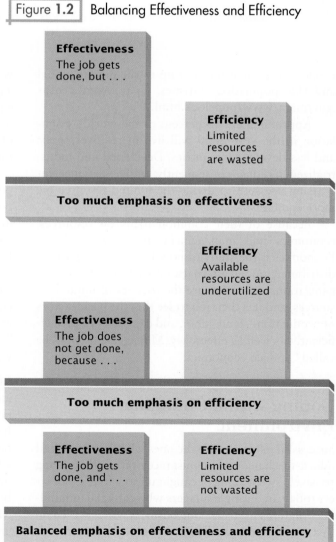

Figure **1.2** Balancing Effectiveness and Efficiency

Effectiveness
The job gets done, but . . .

Efficiency
Limited resources are wasted

Too much emphasis on effectiveness

Efficiency
Available resources are underutilized

Effectiveness
The job does not get done, because . . .

Too much emphasis on efficiency

Effectiveness
The job gets done, and . . .

Efficiency
Limited resources are not wasted

Balanced emphasis on effectiveness and efficiency

Green Management: Toward Sustainability

Greater Efficiency Gives the Union Pacific Railroad a Green Edge over Truckers

Trains are longer—on average . . . more than a mile long—and instead of just pulling the freight cars, locomotives are distributed throughout the trains so that they push as well. Information technology helps too: Locomotives with GPS track the fuel efficiency of every engineer, and those who use the least fuel get a share of the savings, between $200 and $400 a month.

That has enabled the Union Pacific, with the rest of the railroad industry, to tell a nice-sounding environmental story: The rail industry as a whole carries about 43% of all freight (as measured in ton-miles), but trains consume just 7% of the energy used to move freight. Trucks, by contrast, move 31% of the tonnage but use 66% of the energy. UPS, a big customer of Union Pacific, uses trains rather than trucks to move ground packages that travel 750 miles or more.

For Discussion: How do increased efficiency and productivity improvement help businesses protect the natural environment? What eco-friendly efficiencies can you achieve in your daily life?

Source: Excerpted from Marc Gunther, "Union Pacific: 'Building America,'" *Fortune* (July 5, 2010): 122, 124.

---

is open to speculation. (For up-to-the-minute global and U.S. population statistics, go to: **www.census.gov/main/www/popclock.html**.)

Approximately 83 percent of the world's population in the year 2020 will live in relatively poor and less-developed countries. Developed and industrialized nations, consequently, will experience increasing pressure to divide the limited resource pie more equitably.[18]

Because of their common focus on resources, economics and management are closely related. Economics is the study of how limited resources are distributed among alternative uses. In productive organizations, managers are the trustees of limited resources, and it is their job to see that the basic factors of production—land, labor, and capital—are used efficiently as well as effectively. Management could be called "applied economics."

Coping with a Changing Environment

Successful managers are the ones who anticipate and adjust to changing circumstances rather than being passively swept along or caught unprepared. Employers today are hiring managers who can take unfamiliar situations in stride. One business writer served up this amusing but challenging profile of tomorrow's managers: "The next generation of corporate leaders will need the charm of a debutante, the flexibility of a gymnast, and the quickness of a panther. A few foreign languages and a keen understanding of technology won't hurt either."[19] Also in the mix are a sense of humor, passion, and the ability to make decisions rapidly.

Chapter 3 provides detailed coverage of important changes and trends in management's social, political-legal, economic, and technological environments. At this point, it is instructive to preview major changes for managers doing business in the twenty-first century[20] (see Table 1.1). This particular collection of changes is the product of five overarching sources of change: globalization, the evolution of product quality, environmentalism/sustainability, an ethical reawakening, and the Internet and social media revolution. Together, these factors are significantly reshaping the work-a-day world and the practice of management.

GLOBALIZATION. The global economy cranks out an incredible $58 trillion worth of goods and services annually (equivalent to about 32 California economies).[21] It is a huge and dynamic force affecting virtually every one of us on a daily basis. What sort of work we do, whom we work for, how much we are paid, and how much things cost are all impacted at least indirectly by economic globalization and international trade.[22] Major shifts and changes are under way, led by fast-growing China. A few decades ago, China was a "backward" country of minor economic significance.

| Table **1.1** | The Twenty-First-Century Manager: Ten Major Changes |

	MOVING AWAY FROM	**MOVING TOWARD**
Administrative role	Boss/superior/leader	Team member/facilitator/teacher/sponsor/advocate/coach
Cultural orientation	Monocultural/monolingual	Multicultural/multilingual
Quality/ethics/environmental impacts	Afterthought (or no thought)	Forethought (unifying themes)
Power bases	Formal authority; rewards and punishments	Knowledge; relationships; rewards
Primary organizational unit	Individual	Team
Interpersonal dealings	Competition; win-lose	Cooperation; win-win
Learning	Periodic (preparatory; curriculum-driven)	Continuous (lifelong; learner-driven)
Problems	Threats to be avoided	Opportunities for learning and continuous improvement
Change and conflict	Resist/react/avoid	Anticipate/seek/channel
Information	Restrict access/hoard	Increase access/share

Now it has passed Japan to become the world's second-largest economy ($5 trillion), behind the United States ($14 trillion). "China's growth rate means it could surpass the U.S. as the world's largest economy as early as 2030."[23] By 2014, China is expected to consume more energy than the United States.[24] The shifting global economy is loaded with opportunities and pitfalls.

Companies have had to become global players just to survive, let alone prosper. Here are a couple of illustrative snapshots. McDonald's may be headquartered in Oak Brook, Illinois, but it is a global business "with more than 32,000 local restaurants serving more than 60 million people in 117 countries each day."[25] Germany's Siemens, an electronics and

DNY59/Shutterstock.com

industrial equipment maker, has 405,000 employees at 1,640 facilities in 190 countries around the world.[26] Does venturing abroad pay off? Yes, according to a recent study by Goldman Sachs. In 2009 American multinationals that made a significant portion of their revenue abroad returned nearly double the gains of the overall market.[27]

A controversial aspect of globalization is the practice of **offshoring**, the outsourcing of jobs from developed countries to lower-wage countries.[28] (See the Ethics Exercise at the end of this chapter.) This is a long-standing practice that has been going on for decades. Hundreds of thousands of jobs in the textile, steel, auto, and consumer electronics industries are long gone from the United States. Americans are stuck

offshoring controversial practice of sending jobs to low-wage countries on the horns of a dilemma: lost jobs versus abundant low-priced goods from mass importers such as Walmart. Thanks to the broadband Internet, offshoring has moved beyond manufacturing into the service sector. Skilled jobs in areas such as hardware and software engineering, architecture, tax return preparation, and medical diagnosis are being outsourced to well-educated workers in India, China, the Philippines, Eastern Europe, and Russia.[29] Andy Grove, the widely respected former CEO of computer chip maker Intel, is very concerned about the erosion of America's manufacturing foundation. In a recent *Bloomberg Businessweek* article, he framed the problem this way:

> *Some 250,000 Foxconn employees in southern China produce Apple's products. Apple, meanwhile, has about 25,000 employees in the U.S. That means for every Apple worker in the U.S. there are 10 people in China working on iMacs, iPods, and iPhones. The same roughly 10-to-1 relationship holds for Dell, disk drive maker Seagate Technology, and other U.S. tech companies.*
>
> *You could say, as many do, that shipping jobs overseas is no big deal because the high-value work—and much of the profits—remain in the U.S. That may well be so. But what kind of a society are we going to have if it consists of highly paid people doing high-value-added work—and masses of unemployed?*[30]

Balancing the global jobs equation a bit are these two factors: (1) 5.1 million employees in the United States are employed by foreign-owned companies, such as Japan's Toyota;[31] and (2) "onshoring," in which industrial giants such as General Electric, NCR, and Caterpillar are reversing the offshoring process by bringing production jobs back to the United States:

> *There are myriad reasons for the shifts. . . . Chinese wages and shipping costs have risen sharply in the past few years while U.S. salaries have stayed flat, or in some cases, fallen in the recession. Meanwhile,*

1a
It's a Small World

For more than a week after Iceland's Eyjafjallajökull volcano erupted in April of 2010, volcanic ash brought air traffic throughout Europe to a standstill, resulting in widespread repercussions on businesses around the world. Nissan Motors had to shut down three auto assembly lines in Japan because the plane carrying Nissan's next shipment of tire-pressure sensors was grounded, and BMW's auto plant in South Carolina had to slow production until more transmissions could be flown in from Germany.

QUESTION: How does this situation illustrate the pros and cons of economic globalization?

For further information about the interactive annotations in this chapter, visit our student Web site (see back cover for URL).

Sources: "Volcanic Ash Grounds Air Traffic Across Europe," April 15, 2010, http://www.msnbc.msn.com/id/36543312/ns/travel-news/; "Iceland Volcano Eruption of 2010," April 20, 2010, http://topics.nytimes.com/top/news/international/countriesandterritories/iceland/eyjafjallajokull/index.html; Carol Matlack, "The Growing Peril of a Connected World," *Bloomberg Businessweek* (December 6–12, 2010): 63.

U.S. manufacturers have been frustrated by the sometimes poor quality of goods made by foreign contractors, theft of their intellectual property and long product-delivery cycles.[32]

Time will tell if this is a durable trend and the United States emerges as a net winner or loser in the global merry-go-round of jobs. Meanwhile, the push for a well-educated and globally competitive American workforce needs to continue.

Today's model manager is one who is comfortable transacting business in multiple languages and cultures. There is a rapidly growing army of global managers from all corners of the world, and you can become a member of it through diligent effort and a clear sense of purpose. Chapter 4 is devoted to the topic of international management. The international cases and examples, and the Window on the World features throughout the text, are intended to broaden your awareness of international management.

AP Photo/CHINATOPIX

Hewlett-Packard (HP) may be based in California's Silicon Valley, but it has a worldwide round-the-clock workforce. These call center employees work at HP's facility in Dalian, China.

THE EVOLUTION OF PRODUCT QUALITY. Managers have been interested in the quality of their products, at least as an afterthought, since the Industrial Revolution. But thanks to U.S. and Japanese quality gurus such as W. Edwards Deming and Kaoru Ishikawa[33] (more about them in Chapter 2), product/service quality has become both a forethought and a driving force in effective organizations of all kinds. Today's hospitals, hotels, universities, and government agencies are as interested in improving product/service quality as are factories, mines, airlines, and railroads.

In its most basic terms, the emphasis on quality has evolved through four distinct stages since World War II—from "fix it in" to "inspect it in" to "build it in" to "design it in." Progressive managers are moving away from the first two approaches and toward the build-it-in and design-it-in approaches. Here are the key differences:

- The fix-it-in approach to quality

  Rework any defective products identified by quality inspectors at the end of the production process.

- The inspect-it-in approach to quality

  Have quality inspectors sample work in process and prescribe machine adjustments to avoid substandard output.
- The build-it-in approach to quality

  Make *everyone* who touches the product responsible for spotting and correcting defects. The emphasis is on identifying and eliminating *causes* of quality problems.
- The design-it-in approach to quality

  Intense customer and employee involvement drives the entire design-production cycle. The emphasis is on *continuous improvement* of personnel, processes, and product.

Notice how each stage of this evolution has broadened the responsibility for quality, turning quality improvement into a true team effort. Also, the focus has shifted from reactively fixing product defects to proactively working to prevent them and to satisfy the customer completely. Today's quality leaders strive to *exceed*, not just meet, the customer's expectations.

A common label for the build-it-in and design-it-in approaches to quality is *total quality management* (TQM).[34] TQM is discussed in detail in Chapter 16.

ENVIRONMENTALISM AND SUSTAINABILITY. Green issues have gone mainstream.[35] We read and hear concerns daily about deforestation; global warming; depletion of the ozone layer; toxic waste; food safety; rapid urbanization; and pollution of land, air, and water. Fundamentally, each of us has a big stake in the environment because we all want to breathe safe air and we all need drinkable water. Colleges and universities are competing to see who is greener in terms of solar and wind power, recycling, certified green architecture,[36] and environmental initiatives.[37] So are businesses (Hewlett-Packard ranked number 1 in a recent *Newsweek* poll).[38] Still, there is lively debate over global warming, control of carbon emissions, and jobs versus the environment. Unfortunately, there is no clear roadmap detailing how to proceed. Top climate scientist Bill Collins at California's Lawrence Berkeley National Laboratory summed it up this way: "We're running an uncontrolled experiment on the only home we have."[39]

In business circles, the old argument over jobs versus the environment has become obsolete. We need both good-paying jobs *and* a healthy environment for our families, not one or the other. The catalyst is the idea of *sustainability*. Linda Fisher, Chief Sustainability Officer at DuPont, defines "sustainability as meeting the needs of today without sacrificing future generations' ability to meet their needs."[40] In his landmark book, *The Ecology of Commerce: A Declaration of Sustainability,* entrepreneur Paul Hawken offered this instructive perspective of sustainability: "It can also be expressed in the simple terms of an economic golden rule for the restorative economy: Leave the world better than you found it, take no more than you need, try not to harm life or the environment, make amends if you do."[41] Corporate leaders are seeing opportunities in sustainability and environmental clean-up that will translate to jobs and profits:

> *A recent IBM survey found that two-thirds of executives see sustainability as a revenue driver, and half of them expect green initiatives to confer competitive advantage. This dramatic shift in corporate mind-set and practices over the past decade reflects a growing awareness that*

environmental responsibility can be a platform for both growth and differentiation.[42]

A great deal of work needs to be done to fulfill the promise of sustainable business practices. A recent series of surveys and interviews by the United Nations with nearly 1,000 CEOs detected an *implementation gap.* Specifically, sustainability needs to be embedded deep and wide into product design, supply chain management, training, and production and transportation processes.[43] Otherwise, slogans and hype will prevail and justly prompt claims of "greenwashing" (when advocates and advertisers make exaggerated or misleading environmental claims).[44] Green Management features in each chapter demonstrate practical real-world applications of the sustainability philosophy by individuals and organizations alike.

Encouragingly, researchers found 80 percent higher stock market valuations for multinational corporations adhering to strict environmental standards, compared with those taking advantage of the lax environmental standards often found in less-developed countries.[45] In short, investors tend to reward "clean" companies and to punish "dirty" ones.

AN ETHICAL REAWAKENING. Managers are under strong pressure from the public, elected officials, and respected managers to behave better. This pressure has resulted from years of headlines about discrimination, illegal campaign contributions, accounting fraud, price fixing, insider trading, the selling of unsafe products, investment scams, and other unethical practices. Here is a sampling from just two weeks of business news in 2010: Wall Street banker Goldman Sachs paid a $550 million fine to settle a fraud complaint by the U.S. Securities and Exchange Commission (SEC), General Electric paid the SEC a $23.4 million fine to settle charges of paying kickbacks to officials in Saddam Hussein's Iraqi government in 2000–2003, and Citigroup paid the SEC $75 million to settle charges of misleading investors about the money it lost on subprime mortgages.[46] It was a big month for government watchdogs and a big embarrassment for American business ethics.

Traditional values such as honesty are being reemphasized in managerial decision making and conduct. A case in point: "When the *Economist* magazine published a Top 10 list of leadership qualities…, a sound ethical compass was No. 1."[47] Ethics and honesty are everyone's concern: *yours, mine,* and

---

sustainability meeting today's needs without sacrificing future generations' needs

ETHICS: Character, Courage, and Values

Who Says College Students Can't Make a Difference?

Julie Markham is the kind of person who refuses to give up on a dream—even if some people think it's an impossible dream. And that has made a world of difference to the University of Denver student, who graduated [in 2010]. . . .

It has taken her to Cambodia, India, Bangladesh, the Middle East and, most recently, Kenya, where she is consulting with a local bank that is developing an eco-friendly village designed to move slum-dwellers into sustainable, affordable housing.

Markham, a real estate and finance major, has ignored naysayers who say microfinancing—sometimes called "barefoot banking"—won't lead to long-term social good. Or who think a college student could never play a role in transforming the lives of people across the globe.

For Discussion: What "big" idea or personal dream could you act on to make the world a better place? Why is it so hard to swim against the current of popular opinion when pursuing your dream?

Source: Excerpted from Mary Beth Marklein, "Students Defy Expectations," *USA Today* (June 9, 2010): 1D.

ours. Every day we have countless opportunities to be honest or dishonest. One survey of more than 4,000 employees uncovered the following ethical problems in the workplace (the percentage of employees observing the problem during the past year appears in parentheses).

- Lying to supervisors (56 percent)
- Lying on reports or falsifying records (41 percent)
- Stealing and theft (35 percent)
- Sexual harassment (35 percent)
- Abusing drugs or alcohol (31 percent)
- Conflict of interest (31 percent)[48]

Because of closer public scrutiny, ethical questions can no longer be shoved aside as irrelevant. The topic of managerial ethics is covered in depth in Chapter 5 and is explored in the Ethics: Character, Courage, and Values features throughout the text. Additionally, at the end of every chapter is an Ethics Exercise that will give you hands-on experience with tough ethical issues relevant to today's workplaces.

THE INTERNET AND SOCIAL MEDIA REVOLUTION. In concept, the Internet began as a U.S. Department of Defense (DOD) research project during the Cold War era of the 1960s. The plan was to give university scientists a quick and inexpensive way to share their DOD research data. Huge technical problems, such as getting incompatible computers to communicate in a fail-safe network, were solved in 1969 at UCLA when researchers succeeded in getting two linked computers to exchange data. The Internet was born. Other universities were added to the Internet during the 1970s, and applications such as e-mail gradually emerged. By 1983, technology made it possible to share complex documents and graphics on the Internet, and the World Wide Web came into existence.[49] Time passed and improvements were made. During the early 1990s, individuals and businesses began to log on to the "Web" to communicate via e-mail and to buy, sell, and trade things.

Growth of the **Internet**—the worldwide network of computers, routers and switches, servers, and wire and wireless transmission systems—has been explosive. No one owns the Internet in its entirety, and anyone with a computer modem can be part of it (see Table 1.2). Within its digital recesses are both trash and treasure. According to industry data, the number of Internet users worldwide was almost 2 billion in mid-2010. Asia, with 825 million people on the Internet (vs. 266 million in North America), but only a 22 percent market penetration (vs. 77 percent in North America), will be a big Internet growth driver going forward.[50]

A second generation of Internet use is evolving. Some call it Web 2.0; others simply use the term *social networking*. The content is user-generated. Think of Facebook, YouTube, and Twitter. **Social media** are defined by Harvard's Amy Campbell as platforms that give anyone the means to create and publish content online. The content on these mini-websites or web pages is created for the masses by

---

Internet *global network of servers and personal and organizational computers* | **social media** *Collaborative Internet tools such as Facebook, YouTube, and Twitter featuring end-user Web content*

Table 1.2   Sorting Out Internet Technologies and Tools

	DESCRIPTION	SELECTED APPLICATIONS/ SERVICES/EXAMPLES	UNIQUE FEATURES/COMMENTS
Internet	Global network of computers, servers, routers, and wire and wireless transmission technologies maintained by Internet service providers (ISPs) who, for a fee, provide access to anyone with a dial-up, cable, DSL broadband, or wireless modem.	Web access E-mail Instant messaging (not to be confused with text messaging on a cell phone) VoIP (voice over Internet) Data storage space	The Internet, in its entirety, belongs to no single person, organization, or government. A recent global survey of 28,000 people "found 87 percent of those who use the Net believe it should be a 'fundamental right.'" *
World Wide Web (WWW)	System for delivering content via the Internet using standardized http (hyper-text transfer protocol) language for Web sites and pages. Hypertext (html) coding links one Web site to another.	Web search engines such as Google, Yahoo, Bing Web domain registration Web hosting services Webinars (Web seminar or conference) Online meetings and video conferencing (e.g., WebEx) Web directories	The Web is not the same as the Internet, although the terms are commonly used interchangeably.
Social media (via the Internet)	Second-generation Web tools featuring highly interactive user-generated content.	Blogs (personal diaries and opinions) Social networking sites (e.g., Facebook, LinkedIn) Microblogging sites (e.g., Twitter users send 140-character or less text messages termed "tweets" to as many followers as they like) Photo and video sharing (e.g., YouTube, Flickr)	Bottom-up rather than top-down creation and delivery of content. Highly customized and collaborative content. "Every minute of the day, people post 24 hours' worth of videos to YouTube." **

Sources: Adapted in part from Amy Campbell, "Social Media—A Definition," January 21, 2010, http://blogs.law.harvard.edu/amy/2010/01/21/social-media-%E2%80%94-a-definition/; www.techterms.com, accessed August 19, 2010; and http://tweeternet.com, accessed August 19, 2010.

* Julia Baird, "The Front Line Is Online," *Newsweek* (June 14, 2010): 17.

** David Leiberman, "Google Wins Legal Dispute with Viacom," *USA Today* (June 24, 2010): 1B.

other members of the masses, rather than by media experts. Notes Campbell, "We become active participants in creating, commenting, rating and recommending content rather than passive consumers of it."[51] Social networking via Internet-based social media is personal, engaging, and addictive. In fact, a Nielsen media researcher recently reported that Americans spend nearly half their online time doing three activities: social networking, playing games, and e-mailing.[52]

While the technical aspects of the Internet are relevant and interesting, present and future managers and marketers need to appreciate how the Internet revolution has profoundly shaped those who grew up with it. They are today's younger employees and tomorrow's new hires. Don Tapscott calls the huge

81-million-member generation of Americans born between January 1977 and December 1997 the *Net Generation*. His research has identified the norms they (and those born since) embrace as a result of having 24/7 Internet access and Web content shape their lives:

> They value freedom—freedom to be who they are, freedom of choice. They want to customize everything, even their jobs. They learn to be skeptical, to scrutinize what they see and read in the media, including the Internet. They value integrity—being honest, considerate, transparent, and abiding by their commitments. They're great collaborators, with friends online and at work. They thrive on speed. They love to innovate.[53]

Vibrant Image Studio/Shutterstock

How well does this describe you? How do you differ in significant ways? How will it affect your workplace behavior?

Implications of this nearly instantaneous global interconnectedness for all of us (especially managers) are profound and truly revolutionary. Legal, ethical, security, and privacy issues, however, remain largely unresolved.[54] Dynamics of the Internet and social media revolution are explored throughout this book, with detailed coverage of Internet strategy in Chapter 7.

Considering the variety of these five overarching sources of change in the general environment, managers are challenged to keep abreast of them and adjust and adapt as necessary.

WHAT DO MANAGERS DO?

Although nearly all aspects of modern life are touched at least indirectly by the work of managers, many people do not really understand what the management process involves. Management is much more, for example, than the familiar activity of telling employees what to do. Management is a complex and dynamic mixture of systematic techniques and common sense. As with any complex process, the key to learning about management lies in dividing it into readily understood pieces. There are two different ways in which we can analyze the management process for study and discussion. One approach, dating back to the early twentieth century, is to identify managerial functions. A second, more recent approach focuses more precisely on managerial skills.

Managerial functions are general administrative duties that need to be carried out in virtually all productive organizations. Managerial skills, on the other hand, are specific observable behaviors that effective managers exhibit.[55] When we shift the focus from functions to skills, we are moving from general to specific. To put it another way, functions tell us *what* managers generally do, whereas skills tell us more precisely *how* they carry out those functions. We shall examine both perspectives more closely and then have a frank discussion of some managerial facts of life.

Managerial Functions

For nearly a century, the most popular approach to describing what managers do has been the functional view. It has been popular because it characterizes the management process as a sequence of rational and logical steps. Henri Fayol, a French industrialist-turned-writer, became the father of the functional approach in 1916 when he identified five managerial functions: planning, organizing, command, coordination, and control.[56] Fayol claimed that these five functions were the common denominators of all managerial jobs, whatever the purpose of the organization. Over the years, Fayol's original list of managerial functions has been updated and expanded by management scholars. This book, even though it is based on more than just Fayol's approach, is organized around eight different managerial functions: planning, decision making, organizing, staffing, communicating, motivating, leading, and controlling (see Figure 1.3). A brief overview of these eight managerial functions will describe what managers do and will preview what lies ahead in this text.

PLANNING. Commonly referred to as the primary management function, planning is the formulation of future courses of action. Plans and the objectives on which they are based give purpose and direction to the organization, its subunits, and contributing individuals.

DECISION MAKING. Managers choose among alternative courses of action when they make decisions.

Making intelligent and ethical decisions in today's complex world is a major management challenge.

ORGANIZING. Structural considerations such as the chain of command, division of labor, and assignment of responsibility are part of the organizing function. Careful organizing helps ensure the efficient use of human resources.

STAFFING. Organizations are only as good as the people in them. Staffing consists of recruiting, training, and developing people who can contribute to the organized effort.

COMMUNICATING. Today's managers are responsible for communicating to their employees the technical knowledge, instructions, rules, and information required to get the job done. Recognizing that communication is a two-way process, managers should be responsive to feedback and upward communications.

MOTIVATING. An important aspect of management today is motivating individuals to pursue collective objectives by satisfying needs and meeting expectations with meaningful work and valued rewards. Flexible work schedules can be motivational for today's busy employees.

LEADING. Managers become inspiring leaders by serving as role models and adapting their management style to the demands of the situation. The idea of visionary leadership is popular today.

CONTROLLING. When managers compare desired results with actual results and take the necessary corrective action, they are keeping things on track through the control function. Deviations from past plans should be considered when formulating new plans. BP's 2010 oil spill in the Gulf of Mexico is an instructive case study of how persistently weak organizational control can have disastrous and even deadly consequences. *Fortune* magazine's Geoff Colvin reported that after three consecutive accidents at a BP refinery in Texas City, Texas—one of which killed 15 people and injured 170 others—BP assembled an independent panel to investigate safety issues. During the investigation, in March 2006, another accident occurred in which a pipeline in Alaska leaked more than 200,000 gallons of crude oil. In January 2007, the panel published its report,

Figure **1.3** | Identifiable Functions
in the Management Process

repeatedly stating that, "BP has the right standards and programs but *cannot make them work*."[57]

Organizational control is covered in detail in Chapter 16.

Managerial Skills

Thanks to Clark L. Wilson's 30 years of research involving tens of thousands of managers, we have a very clear picture of what it takes to be an effective manager. It takes three skill categories—technical, teambuilding, and drive—that branch into the 12 specific managerial skills listed in Figure 1.4. Unfortunately, according to Wilson's research, about one-third of managers at all levels will not achieve an appropriate *balance* of managerial skills because they're unable to provide the technical and teambuilding skills needed when trying to exercise control. Wilson felt that unless managers learned to exercise their "up-front responsibilities" to communicate goals and coordinate teams, they would never successfully exercise control.[58]

This conjures up the image of effective managers as jugglers struggling to keep three balls in the air at once. Those balls are labeled technical skills, teambuilding skills, and drive skills. Not an easy chore, but today's and tomorrow's managers are challenged to get the job done amid constant change.

| Figure 1.4 | Wilson's Managerial Skills |

SKILL CATEGORY	SKILLS	DESCRIPTION
TECHNICAL Applying your education, training, and experience to effectively organize a task, job, or project	1. Technical expertise	Skills you have acquired by education and experience; to understand and communicate key technical details
	2. Clarification of goals and objectives	Your ability to organize and schedule the work of your unit so it is achieved when expected, and meets established standards
	3. Problem solving	Your ability to resolve issues you confront in the day's work; to develop team collaboration in facing problems
	4. Imagination and creativity	You demonstrate an ability to originate ideas, to correct and develop ways to improve productivity
TEAMBUILDING Listening carefully and communicating clearly to develop and coordinate an effective group or team	5. Listening for insights	Keeping aware of activities of your team and units close to you; underpinning your ability to continue being a manager
	6. Directing and coaching	Meeting your goals and standards; keeping your team's skills up to target levels
	7. Solving problems as teams	An important role is helping your team contribute ideas to improve their performance
	8. Coordinating and cooperating	Demonstrating a willingness to work with others: your group, individuals, and units close to you
DRIVE Setting goals, maintaining standards, and evaluating performance to achieve effective outcomes involving costs, output, product quality, and customer service	9. Standards of performance	Your effort to keep your part of the organization moving, your willingness to be busy and keep aimed toward new accomplishments
	10. Control of details	Overseeing the performance of work at a close level, to meet performance goals and standards
	11. Energy	Demonstrating to your team and colleagues a readiness and willingness to work and that you expect their cooperation
	12. Exerting pressure	Urging others to perform, by shaping your activity to be perceived as teamwork, not domination

Source: Quoted and adapted from Clark L. Wilson, *How and Why Effective Managers Balance Their Skills: Technical, Teambuilding, Drive* (Columbia, Md.: Rockatech Multimedia Publishing, 2003), pp. 13, 18–20. Used by permission of the author.

Some Managerial Facts of Life (with No Sugar Coating)

Managing is a tough and demanding job today. The hours are long and, at first anyway, the pay may not be generous. Worse yet, managers are visible authority figures who get more than their fair share of criticism and ridicule from politicians and Scott Adams's Dilbert cartoons.[59] Nevertheless, managing can be a very rewarding occupation for those who develop their skills and persist, as evidenced by American Management Association (AMA) research findings:

- Forty-six percent of U.S. managers say they feel more overwhelmed at work today than two years ago, and 22 percent more say they're "somewhat" more overwhelmed.
- Half of U.S. managers say they experience stress every day, but an even greater share—63 percent—say they feel enthusiasm for their jobs.[60]

A HECTIC PACE. According to Henry Mintzberg's classic observational studies of actual managers, the average manager is not the reflective planner and precise "orchestra leader" that the functional approach suggests.[61] Mintzberg characterizes the typical manager as follows: "The manager is overburdened with obligations; yet he cannot easily delegate his tasks. As a result, he is driven to overwork and is forced to do many tasks superficially. Brevity, fragmentation, and verbal communication characterize his work."[62]

1b
Back to the Opening Case

What evidence of the managerial functions (see Figure 1.3) and skills (see Figure 1.4) can you detect in the Zappos.com case?

In addition, according to Mintzberg's research, constant interruptions are the order of the day. A more recent study supported Mintzberg's view and provided a somewhat surprising insight into the reality of nonstop interruptions. Stephanie Winston interviewed 48 top U.S. executives, including the late Katharine Graham, former chief executive of the *Washington Post,* and discovered that constant interruptions are not a threat to successful top executives. Indeed, interruptions are what the work of top managers is all about and actually constitute a valuable resource. Winston concluded, "They use a fluid time style to make abundant connections and draw in streams of information. . . . The torrent of questions, comments, updates, requests, and expectations is a rich resource to be mined."[63]

Thus, the typical manager's day involves a hectic schedule, with lots of brief interactions. Interruptions and fragmentation are the norm. Extended quiet periods for reflection and contemplation are rare. An even quicker pace is in store for future managers. However, in line with Wilson's advice to balance one's managerial skills, Mintzberg urges managers to balance reflective thought and action:

> All effective managing has to be sandwiched between acting on the ground and reflecting in the

To be effective in today's business environment, managers need to learn to cope with a fast-paced, hectic schedule that often involves a lot of interruptions and brief exchanges with coworkers and colleagues.

Yuri Arcurs/Shutterstock.com

abstract. Acting alone is thoughtless—we have seen enough of the consequences of that—just as reflecting alone is passive. Both are critical. But today, one—reflection—gets lost.[64]

MANAGERS LOSE THEIR RIGHT TO DO MANY THINGS. Mention the word *manager,* and the average person will probably respond with terms such as *power, privilege, authority, good pay,* and so on. Although many managers eventually do enjoy some or all of these rewards, they pay a significant price for stepping to the front of the administrative parade. According to one management expert, when you accept a supervisory or managerial position, you give up your right to do any of the following:

- Lose your temper
- Be one of the gang
- Bring your personal problems to work
- Vent your frustrations and express your opinion at work
- Resist change
- Pass the buck on tough assignments
- Get even with your adversaries
- Play favorites
- Put your self-interests first
- Ask others to do what you wouldn't do
- Expect to be immediately recognized and rewarded for doing a good job[65]

We tell you this not to scare you away from what could be a financially and emotionally rewarding career, but rather to present a realistic picture so you can choose intelligently. Management is not for everyone—it is not for the timid, the egomaniacal, or the lazy. Management requires clear-headed individuals who can envision something better and turn it into reality by working with and through others.

LEARNING TO MANAGE

Students of management are left with one overriding question: "How do I acquire the ability to manage?" This question has stimulated a good deal of debate among those interested in management education. What is the key, theory or practice? Some contend that future managers need a solid background in management theory acquired through formal education. Others argue that managing, like riding a bicycle, can be learned only by actually doing it.[66] We

can leapfrog this debate by looking at how managers learn to manage, understanding how students learn about management, and considering how you can blend the two processes to your best advantage.

How Do Managers Learn to Manage?

We have an answer to this simple but intriguing question, thanks to the Honeywell study, which was conducted by a team of management development specialists employed by Honeywell.[67] In a survey, they asked 3,600 Honeywell managers, "How did you learn to manage?" Ten percent of the respondents were then interviewed for additional insights. Successful Honeywell managers reportedly acquired 50 percent of their management knowledge from job assignments (see Figure 1.5). The remaining 50 percent of what they knew about management reportedly came from relationships with bosses, mentors, and coworkers (30 percent) and from formal training and education (20 percent).

Fully half of what the Honeywell managers knew about managing came from the so-called school of hard knocks. To that extent, at least, learning to manage is indeed like learning to ride a bike. You get on, you fall off and skin your knee, you get

Figure 1.5 The Honeywell Study: How Managers Learn to Manage

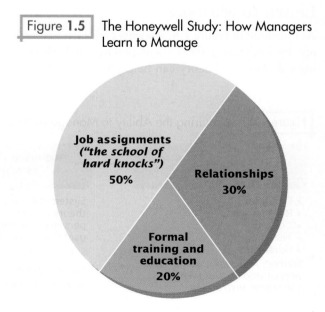

Source: Data from Ron Zemke, "The Honeywell Studies: How Managers Learn to Manage," *Training,* 22 (August 1985): 46–51.

back on a bit smarter, and so on, until you're able to wobble down the road. But in the minds of aspiring managers, this scenario raises the question of what classes are held in the school of hard knocks. A second study, this one of British managers, provided an answer. It turns out that the following are considered *hard knocks* by managers:

- Making a big mistake
- Being overstretched by a difficult assignment
- Feeling threatened
- Being stuck in an impasse or dilemma
- Suffering an injustice at work
- Losing out to someone else
- Being personally attacked[68]

As someone once said, "If you're not making mistakes, then you're not learning." Nike, for example, is a successful athletic apparel company because its managers learn from their mistakes and hard knocks. Some of its ad campaigns have bombed with viewers, and several of its products have failed miserably. The company's first golf shoes, for instance, were so uncomfortable that Nike insiders referred to them as "air-blisters." Yet Scott Bedbury, Nike's former advertising VP, credits the company's success to its willingness to embrace "a culture of screw-ups."[69]

How Can Future Managers Learn to Manage?

As indicated in Figure 1.6, students can learn to manage by integrating theory and practice and observing role models. Theory can help you systematically

1c
Learning Under Fire

As a Marine in Iraq, Brian Iglesias dodged bullets, ducked hand grenades, saw others lose limbs and wondered each morning if it would be his last.

Someone who lived through such horror might not want to remember those days—much less reflect upon them for inspiration. But Igelesis says the survival skills he learned as a soldier have helped him become a successful entrepreneur.

"Every day is a struggle," both in battle and in running a small business, he says.

QUESTIONS: Why is military combat experience a fertile training ground for managers and entrepreneurs? What can military veterans teach all of us about managing and life in general?

Source: Laura Petrecca, "Wounded Vets Trade Boots for Business Suits," *USA Today* (November 11, 2010): 1B.

analyze, interpret, and internalize the managerial significance of practical experience and observations. Although formal training and education contributed only 20 percent to the Honeywell managers' knowledge, they nonetheless can provide needed conceptual foundations. Returning to our bicycle example, a cross-country trip on a high-tech bike requires

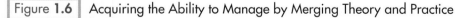

Figure **1.6**   Acquiring the Ability to Manage by Merging Theory and Practice

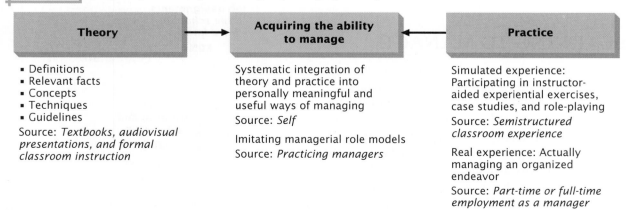

Theory	Acquiring the ability to manage	Practice
▪ Definitions ▪ Relevant facts ▪ Concepts ▪ Techniques ▪ Guidelines Source: *Textbooks, audiovisual presentations, and formal classroom instruction*	Systematic integration of theory and practice into personally meaningful and useful ways of managing Source: *Self* Imitating managerial role models Source: *Practicing managers*	Simulated experience: Participating in instructor-aided experiential exercises, case studies, and role-playing Source: *Semistructured classroom experience* Real experience: Actually managing an organized endeavor Source: *Part-time or full-time employment as a manager*

more than the mere ability to ride a bike. It requires a sound foundation of knowledge about bicycle maintenance and repair, weather and road conditions, and road safety. So, too, new managers who have a good idea of what lies ahead can go farther and faster with fewer foolish mistakes. Learning valuable lessons in the school of hard knocks is inevitable. But you can foresee and avoid at least some of the knocks.

Ideally, an individual acquires theoretical knowledge and practical experience at the same time, perhaps through work-study programs or internships. Usually, though, full-time students get a lot of theory and little practice. This is when simulated experience and real experience become important. If you are a serious management student, you will put your newly acquired theories into practice wherever and whenever possible (for example, in organized sports; positions of leadership in fraternities, sororities, or clubs; part-time and summer jobs; and internships). What really matters is your personal integration of theory and practice.[70]

Small-Business Management

Small businesses have been called the "engine" of the U.S. economy. Consider the stunning example of Walmart. It began in 1945 as a single discount store in Arkansas run by Sam and Helen Walton.[71] Walmart is now the largest company in the world, with annual revenues exceeding $408 *billion* and over 2.1 *million* employees.[72] Small businesses often are too small to attract much media attention, but collectively they (and their counterparts in other countries) are a huge and vibrant part of the global economy. As evidence, consider these facts about the millions of small businesses in the United States.

- Businesses with less than 500 employees make up 99.7 percent of all businesses and employ 50 percent of the civilian workforce.[73]
- According to the most recent U.S. Small Business Administration (SBA) data, "74 percent of the net new jobs [in 2007] were in small firms with fewer than 500 employees and 22 percent were in firms with fewer than 20 employees."[74]
- Also according to the SBA, 97.3 percent of U.S. exporting companies have fewer than 500 employees. Their annual exports total $263 billion.[75]

Interestingly, around 60 percent of them are "microbusinesses" with fewer than five employees, typically operating out of the owner's home (about 1 out of every 10 non-agricultural workers in the United States is self-employed, with about 40 percent of them incorporated).[76] Free-enterprise capitalism is a rough-and-tumble arena where anyone can play, but only the very best survive. The only guaranteed result for those starting their own business is that they will be tested to their limit.

Few would dispute the facts and claims cited above, but agreement on the definition of a small business is not so easily reached. The many yardsticks used to distinguish small from large businesses include number of employees, level of annual sales, amount of owner's equity, and total assets. For our present purposes, a small business is defined as an independently owned and managed profit-seeking enterprise employing fewer than 100 people. (If the small business is incorporated, the owner/manager owns a significant proportion of the firm's stock.)

The health of every nation's economy depends on how well its small businesses are managed. To get a better grasp of the realm of small-business management, we will clear up two common misconceptions, explore small-business career options, and discuss entrepreneurship.

Exploding Myths About Small Business

Mistaken notions can become accepted facts if they are repeated often enough. Such is the case with failure rates and job creation for small businesses. Fortunately, recent research sets the record straight.

THE 80-PERCENT-FAILURE-RATE MYTH. An often-repeated statistic says that four out of five small businesses will fail within five years.[77] This 80 percent casualty rate is a frightening prospect for anyone thinking about starting a business. But a study by Bruce A. Kirchhoff of the New Jersey

Netfalls/Shutterstock.com

small business an independently owned and managed profit-seeking enterprise with fewer than 100 employees

Institute of Technology found the failure rate for small businesses to be *only 18 percent during their first eight years.*[78] Why the huge disparity? It turns out that studies by the U.S. government and others defined business failures much too broadly. Any closing of a business, even if it occurred because someone died, sold the business, or retired, was recorded as a business failure. In fact, only 18 percent of the 814,000 small businesses tracked by Kirchhoff for eight years went out of business with unpaid bills. This should be a comfort to would-be entrepreneurs.

THE LOW-WAGE-JOBS MYTH. When it came to creating jobs in recent decades, America's big businesses were put to shame by their small and midsize counterparts. As documented above, most of the new job growth was generated by the smaller companies; massive layoffs were the norm at big companies. Critics, meanwhile, claimed that most of the new jobs in the small-business sector went to low-paid clerks and hamburger flippers. Such was not the case, according to a Cambridge, Massachusetts, study by researcher David Birch.

After analyzing new jobs created in the United States over a five-year period, Birch found that businesses with fewer than 100 employees had indeed created most new jobs. Surprisingly, however,

1d

Got a Good Business Idea? You've Got 45 Seconds

According to new-venture expert Elton B. Sherwin Jr., entrepreneurs who are trying to raise venture capital should be able to answer these "Seven Sacred Questions" in 45 seconds:

1. What is your product?
2. Who is the customer?
3. Who will sell it?
4. How many people will buy it?
5. How much will it cost to design and build?
6. What is the sales price?
7. When will you break even?

QUESTION: Can you pass this 45-second test with your idea for a new business? Give details.

Source: Marc Ballon, "Hot Tips," *Inc.,* 21 (April 1999): 104.

only 4 percent of those small firms produced 70 percent of that job growth.[79] Birch calls these rapidly growing small companies "gazelles," as opposed to the "mice" businesses that tend to remain very small. For the period studied, the gazelles added more high-paying jobs than big companies eliminated. Gazelles are not mom-and-pop operations. They tend to be computer software, telecommunications, and specialized engineering or manufacturing firms.[80] Thus, although small businesses on average pay less than big companies do and are about half as likely to offer health insurance benefits, they are *not* low-wage havens.[81]

The Internet has created numerous opportunities for entrepreneurs like Blake Ross, creator of the web browser Firefox, to create and build highly successful businesses.

Again, as in the case of failure rates, the truth about the prospects of starting or working for a small company is different—and brighter—than traditional fallacies suggest.

Career Opportunities in Small Business

Among the five small-business career options listed in Table 1.3, only franchises require definition. The other four are self-defining. A franchise is a license to sell another company's products and/or to use another company's name in business. Familiar franchise operations include McDonald's, the National Basketball Association, and Holiday Inn.[82] Notice how each of the career options in Table 1.3 has positive and negative aspects. There is no one best option. Success in the small-business sector depends on the right combination of ideas, money, talent, hard work, luck, and opportunity. If you've got a great business idea, a good starting point is being able to answer the "seven sacred questions" listed in the Interactive Annotation 1d. To be able to do so in 45 seconds tells potential partners, investors, venture capitalists, loan officers, and customers that you as an entrepreneur

- are future focused and optimistic,
- have a positive can-do attitude,
- have a good idea,

- have a solid plan for turning that idea into a marketable good or service,
- have the means to carry out your plan,
- and are dealing with real numbers, not fantasy.

Entrepreneurship

According to experts on the subject, "entrepreneurship is the process by which individuals—either on their own or inside organizations—pursue opportunities without regard to the resources they currently control."[84] In effect, entrepreneurs look beyond current resource constraints when they envision new possibilities. Entrepreneurs are preoccupied with "how to" rather than "why not." Entrepreneurs, as we discuss next, are risk takers—and all they want is a chance. If and when that chance pays off, the rewards can be psychological as well as monetary. Lee Goldberg had the following experience when his Orlando Poppa D's Nuts partnership finally had a winning streak:

> *A few weeks ago, Goldberg was in his local 7-Eleven and got an emotional—and financial— reward: He noticed a customer buying Poppa D's Nuts.*
>
> *"The satisfaction of watching someone pick the bag off the rack and buy it was like watching my child be born," he says. "Watching my child be born was one of the best experiences of my life—and this was close."*[85]

| Table **1.3** | Career Opportunities in Small Business

SMALL-BUSINESS CAREER OPTIONS	CAPITAL REQUIREMENTS	LIKELIHOOD OF STEADY PAYCHECK	DEGREE OF PERSONAL CONTROL	ULTIMATE FINANCIAL RETURN
1. Become an independent contractor/consultant	Low to moderate	None to low	Very high	Negative to high
2. Take a job with a small business	None	Moderate to high	Low to moderate	Low to moderate
3. Join or buy a small business owned by your family	Low to high	Low to high	Low to high	Moderate to high
4. Purchase a franchise	Moderate to high	None to moderate	Moderate to high	Negative to high
5. Start your own small business	Moderate to high	None to moderate	High to very high	Negative to very high

entrepreneurship process of pursuing opportunities without regard to resources currently under one's control

Table 1.4 | Contrasting Trait Profiles for Entrepreneurs and Administrators

ENTREPRENEURS TEND TO	ADMINISTRATORS TEND TO
Focus on envisioned futures	Focus on the established present
Emphasize external/market dimensions	Emphasize internal/cost dimensions
Display a medium to high tolerance for ambiguity	Display a low to medium tolerance for ambiguity
Exhibit moderate to high risk-taking behavior	Exhibit low to moderate risk-taking behavior
Obtain motivation from a need to achieve	Obtain motivation from a need to lead others (i.e., social power)
Possess technical knowledge and experience in the innovative arena	Possess managerial knowledge and experience

Source: Philip D. Olson, "Choices for Innovation-Minded Corporations," *The Journal of Business Strategy*, 11 (January–February 1990): Exhibit 1, p. 44. Reprinted from *Journal of Business Strategy* (New York: Warren, Gorham & Lamont). © 1990 Warren, Gorham & Lamont Inc. Used with permission.

A TRAIT PROFILE FOR ENTREPRENEURS. Exactly how do entrepreneurs differ from general managers or administrators? According to the trait profiles in Table 1.4, entrepreneurs tend to be high achievers who focus more on future possibilities, external factors, and technical details. Also, compared with general administrators, entrepreneurs are more comfortable with ambiguity and risk taking. It is important to note that entrepreneurs are not necessarily better or worse than other managers—they are just different. Jeff Bezos, the founder and CEO of Amazon.com, had this to say in an interview with *Inc.* magazine:

Entrepreneurship is really more about a state of mind than it is about working for yourself. It's about being resourceful, it's about problem solving. If you meet people who seem like really good problem solvers, step back, and you'll see that they are self-reliant. I spent summers on my grandfather's ranch, in a small town in Texas; from age four to 16 I probably missed only two summers. One of the things that you learn in a rural area like that is self-reliance. People do everything themselves. . . . If something is broken, let's fix it.[86]

Bezos instructively calls himself a "realistic optimist." He explains:

I believe that optimism is an essential quality for doing anything hard—entrepreneurial endeavors or anything else. That doesn't mean that you're blind or unrealistic, it means that you keep focused on eliminating your risks, modifying your strategy, until it is a strategy about which you can be genuinely optimistic.[87]

Guy Kawasaki, a California venture capitalist and author of the book *The Art of the Start,* offers a slightly different portrait of the entrepreneur: "It's confidence; it's also a little bit of denial. Part of being an entrepreneur is ignoring things too, because if you listen to all the naysayers, no one would ever start a company."[88] (See Window on the World.)

ENTREPRENEURSHIP HAS ITS LIMITS. Many successful entrepreneurs have tripped over a common stumbling block. Their organizations outgrow the entrepreneur's ability to manage them. In fact, according to "a poll by PricewaterhouseCoopers, about 40% of CEOs at the fastest-growing companies said that their own ability to manage or reorganize their business could be an impediment to

WINDOW ON THE WORLD

Harvard Test Identifies Global Entrepreneurs Among Loan Applicants

Do you like taking things apart to see how they work? . . . Do you enjoy going to parties? . . .

If your answers to these and about 150 other questions add up, you could run a small business in Nairobi. Or Lima. Or Bogotá. All because a new test [developed at Harvard] identifies the traits that make for successful entrepreneurs in developing economies. . . .

The 40-minute computer-based test assesses traits like honesty, ethics, intelligence, and motivation. . . . [Trial assessments] in South Africa, Kenya, Rwanda, Colombia,

and Peru have shown that the test achieves the same—or better—results than traditional ways of assessing a borrower's future success and ability to repay a loan. . . .

The resulting evaluation can be customized to reflect an applicant's business, company size, and country, though the core questions remain the same.

For Discussion: In your view, what are the two or three essential traits for a successful entrepreneur, regardless of country or culture?

Source: Excerpted from Caroline Winter, "Pass the Test, Get a Loan, Start a Company," *Bloomberg Businessweek* (July 19–25, 2010): 20.

growth."[89] Some refer to this problem as "founder's disease." Moreover, entrepreneurs generally feel stifled by cumbersome and slow-paced bureaucracies. One management consultant praised Microsoft's Bill Gates for knowing his limits in this regard:

In January [2000], Gates went from being CEO of the multibillion-dollar business he cofounded to naming himself "chief software architect" and handing over executive responsibility for his company to Steve Ballmer. . . . few people recognized it for what I think it was: a courageous leap into a self-esteem-threatening black hole.[90]

The trick, according to a recent study of great entrepreneurs such as Herb Kelleher of Southwest Airlines, is for company founders to keep some psychological distance between themselves and their companies:

. . . it's all in their heads. It's their ability to avoid thinking of themselves as one with their companies. "The most successful entrepreneurs think of their companies as a separate entity from themselves," says Nancy Koehn, a historian of entrepreneurship who is a professor at Harvard Business School. "It's incongruous, but they have a sense that if they have done their work well, the proof will be in their companies outgrowing, outpacing—and even outliving—them."[91]

Entrepreneurs who launch successful and growing companies face a tough dilemma: either grow with the company or have the courage to step aside and turn the reins over to professional managers who possess the administrative traits needed, such as those listed in Table 1.4.

SUMMARY

1. Formally defined, *management* is the process of working with and through others to achieve organizational objectives in a changing environment. Central to this process is the effective and efficient use of limited resources. An inability to work with people, not a lack of technical skills, is the main reason why some managers fail to reach their full potential. A manager is *effective* if he or she reaches a stated objective and *efficient* if limited resources are not wasted in the process.

2. Five overarching sources of change affecting the way management is practiced today are *globalization* (increased global commerce; controversy over offshoring of jobs to low-wage countries; greater need for global managers who can work effectively across cultures), *the evolution of product quality* (moving away from fix-it-in and inspect-it-in approaches; moving toward build-it-in and design-it-in approaches; emphasis on continuous improvement), *environmentalism* and sustainability (greater emphasis on making money without destroying the natural environment; leaving the planet better than we found it), *an ethical reawakening* (the public's low opinion of managers' ethical conduct is spurring renewed emphasis on honesty and ethical behavior), and *the Internet and social media revolution* (the Net Generation of 81 million young Americans will reshape the workplace with their creativity and collaboration).

3. Two ways to answer the question "What do managers do?" are the functional approach and the skills approach. *Managerial functions* generally describe *what* managers do, whereas *managerial skills* state in specific behavioral terms *how* they carry out those functions. This text is organized around eight managerial functions: planning, decision making, organizing, staffing, communicating, motivating, leading, and controlling.

4. Clark Wilson's three managerial skill categories are technical, teambuilding, and drive. His 30 years of research have uncovered an imbalance in managerial skills. About one-third of managers at all levels attempt to exercise control without first applying their technical and teambuilding skills. Thus, managers need to strive for an effective balance of skills.

5. Honeywell researchers found that managers learned 50 percent of what they know about managing from job assignments ("the school of hard knocks"). The remaining 50 percent of their management knowledge came from relationships (30 percent) and formal training and education (20 percent). A good foundation in management theory can give management students a running start and help them avoid foolish mistakes.

6. *Small businesses* (independently owned and managed profit-seeking companies with fewer than 100 employees) are central to job creation and a healthy economy. Contrary to conventional wisdom, 80 percent of new businesses do not fail within five years. In fact, one large study found only an 18 percent failure rate during the first eight years. The belief that small businesses create only low-wage jobs also has been shown to be a myth. Five career opportunities in the small-business sector are (1) becoming an independent contractor/consultant, (2) going to work for a small business, (3) joining or buying your family's business, (4) buying a franchise, and (5) starting your own business. Compared with general administrators, entrepreneurs tend to be high achievers who are more future-oriented, externally focused, ready to take risks, and comfortable with ambiguity.

TERMS TO UNDERSTAND

Management, p. 5
Effectiveness, p. 6
Efficiency, p. 6
Offshoring, p. 9

Sustainability, p. 12
Internet, p. 13
Social media, p. 13
Managerial functions, p. 15

Managerial skills, p. 15
Small business, p. 21
Entrepreneurship, p. 23

ACTION LEARNING EXERCISE

DO YOU HAVE THE RIGHT STUFF TO BE AN ENTREPRENEUR?

Instructions: Entrepreneurship isn't just about a good business idea. It's a matter of temperament. Some have it, some don't. Do you? Test yourself. And be honest; there are no "right" answers.

1. Where do you think you'll be in 10 years' time?

   a. I don't think that far ahead; my short-term goals are clear, though.

   b. I have a career path in mind, and I'm going to stick to it.

   c. I live and work from day to day.

   d. I know where I want to be and have ideas on how to get there, but if a better idea comes along, I'll take it.

2. How would you describe your attitude toward competition?

   a. I relish it. Winning isn't everything, it's the only thing.

   b. I avoid it. Competition brings out the worst in people.

   c. I compete hard when I have to, but have been known to bluff my rivals.

   d. I compete hard, but my eye is always on the payoff.

3. Your boss says, "That's the way we do things here." How do you react?

   a. I respect established procedures, but I know when to ignore them.

   b. I begin to think I should be working somewhere else.

   c. I accept it and proceed accordingly. After all, I want to keep my job.

   d. I may try to change his mind, but if I don't succeed quickly, I'll go along.

4. Which statement comes closest to describing your personal finances?

   a. My checkbook is always balanced, and I pay my bills when they come in.

   b. I have an interest-bearing bank account, and I wait until the end of the statement period to pay my bills. That way the bank doesn't get the interest.

   c. I have multiple credit cards, and every one of them is about maxed out.

   d. I separate my business and personal expenses by using different credit cards.

5. What gives you the greatest personal satisfaction at work?

   a. Having an idea and being allowed to run with it.

   b. Receiving praise for a job well done.

   c. Coming out ahead of an office rival.

   d. Knowing my office status is secure.

6. How do you handle criticism at work?

   a. It throws me off track and makes my next task more difficult.

   b. Other perspectives are often helpful, so I listen carefully and adjust if the criticism makes sense to me.

   c. While maintaining my dignity, I try to shift at least some of the blame to others.

   d. I don't like it, but what can I do? I absorb the criticism and move on.

7. What's best about your current job?

   a. My salary and perks. I do OK compared with people like me.

   b. The fine reputation of my company.

   c. I enjoy a certain amount of freedom to start my own projects.

   d. I get regular promotions, and there's a clear career path to the top.

8. Which statement best describes your attitude toward your projects at work?

   a. I like to start projects, but I tend to lose interest and delegate things to other people.

   b. I find myself moving on to new projects before I finish the current one.

   c. I always finish what I start. Personally.

   d. I've been known to put a project on hold if I run into difficulties.

9. How much time do you typically invest in your projects at work?

   a. I take pride in being on schedule, so I put in however many hours it takes. Then I take a breather.

   b. I work hard, but sometimes I'll take a day or two off in mid-project.

   c. I'm pretty much a 9-to-5er.

   d. My work is my life.

10. If you had what you thought was a good idea for a start-up, how would you finance it?

   a. A loan. That's why banks exist.

   b. To hold down my exposure, I'd hit up friends and family.

   c. I'd take out a second mortgage on my house.

   d. I'd *sell* my house if it came to that.

Scoring: Add up your score, using the following key.

1. a-2	b-3	c-1	d-4
2. a-3	b-1	c-2	d-4
3. a-3	b-4	c-1	d-2
4. a-1	b-3	c-4	d-2
5. a-4	b-2	c-3	d-1
6. a-1	b-4	c-3	d-2
7. a-2	b-1	c-4	d-3
8. a-2	b-3	c-4	d-1
9. a-4	b-2	c-1	d-3
10. a-1	b-2	c-3	d-4

RESULTS

10 TO 19 POINTS

You are probably a responsible employee, but not a self-starter. You wait to be assigned tasks. Security is important to you. Your tolerance of risk is relatively low. You may derive too much of your sense of self-worth from factors outside yourself, such as the prestige of the company you work for. Stay put.

20 TO 29 POINTS

You are capable of initiative, even if it doesn't seem that way. You try to advance your career, but are careful not to offend people along the way. You understand office politics, but are reluctant to make bold moves. If you aren't already in middle management, you may be a good candidate.

30 TO 35 POINTS

Lack of ambition is not one of your shortcomings. Neither is a willingness to work hard, and outside normal office hours. You may, however, be somewhat impatient, and reluctant to seek advice from others. These are not good qualities in an entrepreneur. Go for top management instead.

36 TO 40 POINTS

You have the makings of an excellent entrepreneur. You have a high tolerance for risk—an essential ingredient. You are passionate about your ideas. Equally important, you are able to balance your own ambition with interest in others' thoughts and regard for their feelings. Go for it.

Source: From *Newsweek*, © 2000, Newsweek, Inc. May 29, 2000. All rights reserved. Used by permission and protected by the Copyright laws of the United States. The printing, copying, redistribution, or retransmission of the Material without express written permission is prohibited.

FOR CONSIDERATION/DISCUSSION

1. Well, do you have the right stuff to be an entrepreneur? Is this a valid assessment tool? Why or why not?
2. Do you know someone who is a successful entrepreneur? If so, how well does the interpretation for an individual scoring 36 to 40 points characterize that person?
3. What would happen if everyone in the business world scored high on this quiz?
4. Is it an insult to score low on this quiz? Explain.

ETHICS EXERCISE

DO THE RIGHT THING

THE OFFSHORING OF JOBS ISSUE

An American Perspective:

Mount Airy, North Carolina, is a small town of less than 10,000 residents. At one point, the town's mainstay was textile manufacturing, but the town has lost more than 3,000 jobs since 1999—jobs that once provided people who have relatively little skills and education a chance to earn enough income to lead a middle-class lifestyle.

This small textile town is representative of other towns like it across the United States. In the last 10 years, the nation has lost more than 700,000 textile and apparel jobs, in part due to a 2005 trade pact that phased out quotas on textile imports.

"I understand that free trade opens the door for some American businesses," says former textile plant manager and college graduate Neil Hagwood. . . . "But that's hard to explain to a 50-year-old employee who's been running a loom or sewing blankets for 32 years."

An Indian Perspective:

The major Western consulting companies are adding to the turnover at their Indian competitors, as IBM, Capgemini, and Accenture all plan to strengthen their operations in India. Accenture [an Irish corporation headquartered in Chicago], for instance, is expected to have 50,000 employees in the country by the end of 2010. For someone looking to advance in the industry, says Vijay Gautam, an analyst in Mumbai with Jaypee Capital Services, "having a Western company on your résumé definitely helps."

The problem with high turnover is not just the higher costs that come with big pay raises. The average pay for an IT [information technology] worker in India is still $20,000, compared with as much as $85,000 for his or her counterpart in the West.

The real challenge is maintaining the quality of the workforce, as companies lose veteran workers in droves while at the same time hiring tens of thousands of new employees.

Sources: Adapted from Paul Wiseman, "When the Textile Mill Goes, So Does a Way of Life," *USA Today* (March 10, 2010): 1A–2A. Excerpted from Bruce Einhorn and Ketaki Gokhale, "Bangalore's Paying Again to Keep the Talent," *Bloomberg Businessweek* (May 24–30, 2010): 16.

What are the ethical implications of the following interpretations?

1. Corporations have an obligation to their customers and shareholders to hire the best talent anywhere in the world at the lowest cost.

2. Sending jobs to foreign countries is unpatriotic and unethical because it leads to unemployment and lower wages at home.

3. Employees in low-wage countries deserve the opportunity to work hard and get ahead in life by working for foreign-owned companies.

4. Your own ethical interpretation?

Managers-In-Action Video Case Study

 PRESERVE® BY RECYCLINE

Founder and company president Eric Hudson describes how he built this small, environmentally friendly company around solid business systems without the more traditional, stiff corporate culture. Several employees discuss various positive aspects of their work environment. The entrepreneurial spirit is apparent as they share how this small company develops green products and competes with big corporations like Gillette and Procter & Gamble.

For more information about Preserve, visit its Web site: www.preserveproducts.com.

Video Learning Objective

Learn how an entrepreneur created an environmentally friendly company where the people, their values, and the corporate culture significantly impacted a small company's success.

Before watching the video, answer the following questions:

1. From a management perspective, how would you describe efficiency and effectiveness?
2. What overarching societal changes are impacting managers and organizations today?
3. How do entrepreneurs and administrators differ?

After watching the video, answer the following questions:

4. As a small business, how does Preserve achieve both efficiency and effectiveness?
5. Of the five overarching changes mentioned in this chapter, choose one and discuss how Preserve is adapting to this change to gain a competitive advantage.
6. What unique aspects of Preserve's work environment and employee values allow its workers to collaborate, innovate, and make decisions quickly?
7. What do Zappos and Preserve have in common?
8. Why do you think company values are important, and how do they impact companies like Zappos and Preserve?

CLOSING CASE

JENNIFER REINGOLD SAMPLES A DAY IN THE LIFE OF A MANAGER

The lightning bolt wasn't a great sign. My first day on the job, and I was already losing control: A string of emails demanded split-second decisions for problems I had only just heard about; I needed to pull together a business-plan presentation for a product I had never laid eyes on; a rabid reporter lurked outside my door. Then, the single, jagged flash shot across my window. I gulped my Diet Dr Pepper. Maybe I wasn't meant to be an executive after all.

Not that I ever really thought I was. Sure, I've been covering management and leadership for 10 years, lambasting and lionizing executives, dismissing their best-laid plans with a few cutting words and anointing their successors with a few sparkling ones. But my actual experience with leading and managing has remained largely theoretical. Ironic? Sure, but I liked that.

Still, we all have to grow up sometime. So when Richard Wellins, an SVP at human-resources consulting firm Development Dimensions International (DDI), invited me to its intensive one-day "operational executive platform"—a simulation used to screen potential job candidates or identify and develop stars already in-house—I jumped at the chance. Over the course of one full day, I'd make strategic decisions, launch a new product, and deal with the challenges a boss typically faces. I'd be thrown curveballs by company brass, employees, customers, and media alike (all role-played by trained assessors). And then I'd receive an unvarnished evaluation of my work, a kind of psychographic leadership report card.

In the days running up to my visit, I logged on to DDI's Assessing Talent portal, which gave me financial and historical information about my fictitious company, Global Solutions, a robotics shop facing tough times in the year 2025. I also took a series of preliminary psych tests, or "leadership inventories," that would be analyzed in conjunction with my performance. Then I received my pseudo identity: Kelly Myers, a new VP whose predecessor at Global had just been canned.

Kelly and I, it turned out, had our work cut out for us: Margins were falling, inventories were rising, and the Jeeves—a robotic valet—had started doing odd things, such as cooking a client's favorite shoes and breaking into hotel rooms in the middle of the night.

The morning of the big day found me chugging coffee in my hotel room and trying to look the part, when the front desk called up to say my car had arrived. "But they're early!" I spat. "I'll be down when I can!" After I hung up on the poor woman, it occurred to me that I might have already blown my first test. Leadership? Yeah. In boot camp, maybe.

In the glass-skinned Pittsburgh headquarters of DDI, I was shown to my new "office." Ah! The faux-wood desk, the paper clips in the drawer, a suspicious box of tissues (would I be needing those?). A pleasant picture of boats distracted me from the view of the parking lot—and from the video camera recording my every move. I was disappointed to note that the workplace of 2025 was as drab as ever.

My email revealed a host of headaches, including a note about the Jeeves from a furious hotel manager and another from my boss: One of my direct reports was resisting the centralization of the sales and marketing functions. "It is imperative that you gain Marty's buy-in," he wrote.

Kelly and I dove in. First up was Marty, whom I motivated, I felt sure, with a deft application of both carrot and stick. Next came the hostile hotelier: I pulled out all the stops trying to placate her, offering a quick (and possibly nonexistent) fix that included temporarily substituting an earlier-generation robot. "This relationship is critical to our company, and we want to make you happy," I purred,

adding an eye roll that was promptly captured by the now-forgotten camera.

I suddenly realized I hadn't gotten a single email in hours. "Oh, dear," said the coordinator. It seems there had been a computer glitch, not part of the simulation. When I rebooted, a good dozen emails lay festering in my inbox: Design an agenda for our off-site! Decide whether to move a guy from Asia to the inventory-reduction task force—today! Determine why all of our new-hire MBAs are quitting! Write a business plan by 4 P.M.! And, oh, by the way, you have a TV interview to address concerns that one of our security robots caused a teenager's death.

It was at about this time that the lightning bolt struck. "Not fair," I whined to myself, pining for my messy desk, my writer's block. No time for that now, though—I had a dead teenager on my hands. At least the interview would be a breeze, I figured, given my day job in real life. But when I tried to stay cool, explaining our position on the "unfortunate event," the jerk kept putting words in my mouth.

The rest of the day was a blur. More vile emails. An inspirational voice mail I had to record to introduce Kelly to the staff (in a brilliant, if unauthorized, initiative, I announced $1,000-to-$25,000 bonuses to anyone with "ideas that help the company"). I swore a lot under my breath. And then it was time for the business-plan presentation. Without a clue about how to crunch the production numbers, I had opted to concentrate on the marketing side of the Jeeves product launch—and to talk so much that my boss wouldn't miss the margin calculations or the ad budget. Amazingly, he actually seemed to buy it.

I left feeling like the white-collar equivalent of Lucille Ball in the chocolate factory. I didn't think I had been a complete loser, but that just raised the question: If this ink-stained—and untrained—wretch could pass for management material, wasn't this whole exercise suspect? Could it really be worth the $4,000 to $12,000 that more than 1,000 companies have ponied up for DDI's full- or half-day assessments?

Kelly and I cuddled up together in the hotel for a brain-dead evening of reality TV, then returned to DDI the next morning for our results. . . .

To my delight and horror, the tests nailed me cold. My passion for new and different challenges, my hardworking, ambitious side, my love of socializing and interacting with others—all there. But so, too, were my tendency to get snappish at stressful moments and my "low interpersonal sensitivity" (i.e., extreme bluntness). DDI doesn't make yes-or-no job recommendations for candidates. Yet I came away with the strange—and somehow disturbing—conclusion that, warts and all, I could, with a lot of practice and probably a lot of therapy, be Kelly Myers. I didn't have much time to think about that, though. Thankfully, I had a story to write.

For Discussion:

1. How would you rate the effectiveness and efficiency of Jennifer Reingold (aka Kelly Myers)? Explain.

2. Which of the eight managerial functions are evident in this case? Explain.

3. In what respects is this a manager's typical day?

4. Based on the trait profiles in Table 1.4, did Jennifer Reingold act more like an administrator or an entrepreneur? Explain.

Source: Excerpted from Jennifer Reingold, "My (Long) Day at the Top," *Fast Company,* 106 (June 2006): 64–66. Copyright © 2006 by Mansueto Ventures LLC. Reproduced with permission of Mansueto Ventures LLC in the format Textbook via Copyright Clearance Center.

2

The Evolution
of Management Thought

"In the renewing society the historian consults the past
in the service of the present and the future."[1]
—JOHN W. GARDNER

The Changing Workplace

CRAIGIE ZILDJIAN CARRIES ON A 14-GENERATION TRADITION

The Zildjian Company, based in Norwell, Massachusetts, is the largest cymbal maker in the world and the oldest continuously family-run business in the United States. Founded in Turkey in 1623 by Armenian alchemist Avedis Zildjian, the company, with 2006 revenues of $52 million, is now run by 14th-generation descendent Craigie Zildjian, who took the reins from her father in 1999, becoming the first woman to head up the business. We spoke with Zildjian about the challenges of leading her nearly four-century-old company into the future. The following are edited excerpts from that interview.

What's the secret to keeping a centuries-old business on the cutting edge? Many of the things we do are what any good company should do, whether it's thinking one year out or 100. We're guided by our core values—a focus on continuous quality improvement, innovation, craftsmanship, customer collaboration, empowering employees, avoiding complacency, and reinvesting in the company. We don't have a secret formula for our strategy. It's just good management practice. That said, there's no question that our legacy keeps us all focused on preserving the business for the long haul. As my niece Cady, part of the 15th generation, said, "We'd never want to be the ones who have to sell the company."

How do you balance the fear of being "the Zildjian who sold the business" with the need to take risks? A sure way to damage the business would be to stop innovating and risk taking. We have an estimated 65% of the world cymbal market, but that market share isn't a given. We have fierce competitors. So, on the one hand, we preserve the family jewels—the secret formulas we use that go back centuries—but we're always working on product innovations and other improvements. For instance, we introduced the first titanium-coated cymbal as a limited edition line, which was a risky R&D [research and development] project but paid off. And we're in the middle of a major plant expansion that will give us more capacity than we currently need. We're betting on the future.

Does this long-range focus affect how you relate to your customers?

We've always collaborated with customers on products—something a lot of companies are just catching on to now. My grandfather Avedis, who set up the U.S. company in 1929, became good friends with Gene Krupa, Chick Webb, and Papa Jo Jones, and he worked closely with them to develop the modern drum kit. . . . My father was a natural at this type of collaboration. Today, we continue the tradition of bringing artists into the plant so our R&D manager and marketing people can meet directly with them. We also take employees into stores so they can see customers buying Zildjians—and the competition. Careful listening is part of our corporate strategy.

Source: Excerpted from Gardiner Morse, "A Formula for the Future," *Harvard Business Review*, 86 (July–August 2007): 23. Reprinted by permission of HBS Publishing.

Craigie Zildjian did not start with a blank slate at the company bearing her name. Her family tradition, corporate culture, and way of doing business continue to affect what she can and cannot do to keep Zildjian on the right course. In short, history matters at Zildjian Company. In a parallel sense, that is what this chapter is all about. Management historians believe that a better knowledge of the past will lead to a more productive future. They contend that students of management who fail to understand the evolution of management thought are destined to repeat past mistakes.[2] Moreover, historians and managers alike believe that one needs to know where management has been if one is to understand where it is going. While participating in a Harvard Business School roundtable discussion on the value of management history, a top-level executive put it this way:

It is always hard to communicate any sort of abstract idea to someone else, let alone get any acceptance of it. But when there is some agreement on the factual or historical background of that idea, the possibilities for general agreement expand enormously.[3]

Historians draw a distinction between history and historical perspective. According to one management scholar,

Historical perspective is the study of a subject in light of its earliest phases and subsequent evolution. Historical perspective differs from history in that the object of historical perspective is to sharpen one's vision of the present, not the past.[4]

This chapter qualifies as a historical perspective because it is part historical fact and part modern-day interpretation. Various approaches in the evolution of management thought are discussed relative to the lessons each can teach today's managers. The term *evolution* is appropriate here because management theory has developed in bits and pieces through the years. Moreover, pioneering contributors to management theory and practice have come from around the globe[5] (see Figure 2.1). A historical perspective puts these pieces together.

| Figure **2.1** | Management Is a Global Affair: Selected Contributors to Management Theory |

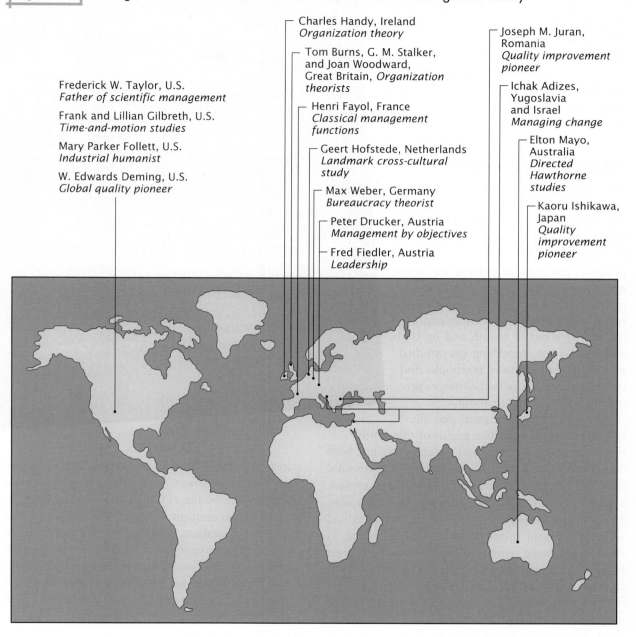

Frederick W. Taylor, U.S.
Father of scientific management

Frank and Lillian Gilbreth, U.S.
Time-and-motion studies

Mary Parker Follett, U.S.
Industrial humanist

W. Edwards Deming, U.S.
Global quality pioneer

Charles Handy, Ireland
Organization theory

Tom Burns, G. M. Stalker,
and Joan Woodward,
Great Britain, *Organization theorists*

Henri Fayol, France
Classical management functions

Geert Hofstede, Netherlands
Landmark cross-cultural study

Max Weber, Germany
Bureaucracy theorist

Peter Drucker, Austria
Management by objectives

Fred Fiedler, Austria
Leadership

Joseph M. Juran,
Romania
Quality improvement pioneer

Ichak Adizes,
Yugoslavia
and Israel
Managing change

Elton Mayo,
Australia
Directed Hawthorne studies

Kaoru Ishikawa,
Japan
Quality improvement pioneer

THE PRACTICE AND STUDY OF MANAGEMENT

The systemic study of management is relatively new. As an area of academic study, management is essentially a product of the twentieth century. Only three universities—Pennsylvania, Chicago, and California—offered business management courses before 1900.[6]

But the actual practice of management has been around for thousands of years. The pyramids of Egypt, for example, stand as tangible evidence of the ancient world's ability to manage. It reportedly took more than 100,000 individuals 20 years to construct the great pyramid honoring the Egyptian king Cheops nearly 5,000 years ago. This remarkable achievement was the result of systematically managed effort. Although the Egyptians' management techniques were crude by modern standards, many problems they faced are still around today. They, like today's managers, had to make plans, obtain and mobilize human and material resources, coordinate interdependent jobs, keep records, report their progress, and take corrective action as needed.

Information Overload

Since the building of the pyramids, entire civilizations have come and gone. In one form or another, management was practiced in each. Sadly, during those thousands of years of management experience, one modern element was missing: a systematically recorded body of management knowledge.[7] In early cultures, management was something one learned by word of mouth and by trial and error—not something one studied in school, read about in textbooks and on the Internet, theorized about, experimented with, or wrote about.

Thanks to modern print and electronic media, the collective genius of thousands of management theorists and practitioners has been compressed into a veritable mountain of textbooks, journals, research monographs, microfilms, movies, audio- and videotapes, computer files, and Web sites. Never before have present and future managers had so much relevant information at their fingertips, as close as a Google search on the Web or the nearest library. As an indication of what is available, a 1990 study identified 54 journals dealing with just the behavioral side of management.[8] There are many others, including *Bloomberg Businessweek, Fortune,* and *Fast Company* magazines. In fact, so much information on management theory and practice exists today that it is difficult, if not impossible, to keep abreast of all of it.[9]

An Interdisciplinary Field

A principal cause of the information explosion in management theory is its interdisciplinary nature. Scholars from many fields—including psychology, sociology, cultural anthropology, mathematics, philosophy,

2a
What About Factual Accuracy?

Apple Cofounder Steve Wozniak:

I think it's time to set the record straight. So much of the information out there about me is wrong. I've come to hate books about Apple and its history so much because of that. For instance, there are stories that I dropped out of college (I didn't) or that I was thrown out of the University of Colorado (I wasn't), that Steve [Jobs, Apple's cofounder and CEO,] and I were high school classmates (we were several years apart in school) and that Steve and I engineered those first computers together (I did them alone).

QUESTIONS: In general, how much do you trust the factual accuracy of historical accounts? What is the best way to get the *real* story?

For further information about the interactive annotations in this chapter, visit our student Web site.

Source: As quoted in a book review by Russ Juskalian, "Wozniak Sets Record Straight with Awkward, Charming Style," *USA Today* (October 9, 2006): 5B.

statistics, political science, economics, logistics, computer science, ergonomics, history, and various fields of engineering—have, at one time or another, been interested in management. In addition, administrators in business, government, religious organizations, health care, and education all have drawn from and contributed to the study of management. Each group of scholars and practitioners has interpreted and reformulated management according to its own perspective. With each new perspective have come new questions and assumptions, new research techniques, different technical jargon, and new conceptual frameworks.[10]

No Universally Accepted Theory of Management

We can safely state that no single theory of management is universally accepted today.[11] To provide a useful historical perspective that will guide our study of modern management, we shall discuss five different approaches to management: (1) the universal process approach, (2) the operational approach, (3) the behavioral approach, (4) the systems approach, and (5) the contingency approach. Understanding these general approaches to the theory and practice of management can help you appreciate how management has evolved, where it is today, and where it appears to be headed. Each of the five approaches to management represents a different conceptual framework for better understanding the practice of management. Cornell University professor Craig C. Lundberg explains the practical (and scientific) importance of conceptual frameworks:

> *When we have a known set of ideas, and the relationships among them are spelled out, we have a conceptual framework, or model. . . . In addition to helping us notice and comprehend something of interest as a frame of reference does, models also enable us to anticipate and discover relevant facts and to better understand how things really work. Over time, with continuing experiences and/or confirmation from research, models are modified by being fine-tuned to better and better represent the phenomena of interest, or they are discarded and replaced.[12]*

This chapter concludes with some cautionary words about slavishly following sure-fire success formulas in best-selling management books.

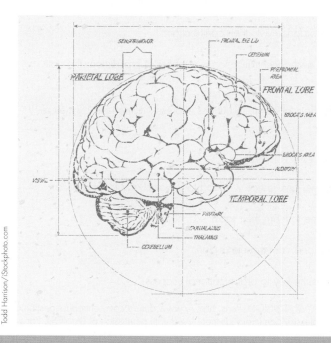

Todd Harrison/iStockphoto.com

THE UNIVERSAL PROCESS APPROACH

The universal process approach is the oldest and one of the most popular approaches to management thought. It is also known as the universalist or functional approach. According to the **universal process approach**, the administration of all organizations, public or private and large or small, requires the same rational process. The universalist approach is based on two main assumptions. First, although the purpose of organizations may vary (for example, business, government, education, or religion), a core management process remains the same across all organizations. Successful managers, therefore, are assumed to be interchangeable among organizations of differing purpose. A prime example is David Brandon, who left his job as CEO of Domino's Pizza (with an annual compensation of $2.6 million) to sign on as athletic director for his alma mater, the University of Michigan (annual salary? $825,000!).[13]

The second assumption is that the universal management process can be reduced to a set of separate functions and related principles. Early universal process writers emphasized the specialization of labor (who does what), the chain of command (who reports to whom), and authority (who is ultimately responsible for getting things done).

Henri Fayol's Universal Management Process

In 1916, at the age of 75, Henri Fayol published his now-classic book *Administration Industrielle et Générale*, although it was not widely known in Britain and the United States until an English translation became available in 1949.[14] Despite its belated appearance in the English-speaking world and despite its having to compete with enthusiastic scientific management and human relations movements in the United States, Fayol's work left a permanent mark on twentieth-century management thinking.

Fayol was first an engineer and later a successful administrator in a large French mining and metallurgical concern, which is perhaps why he did not resort to theory in his pioneering management book. Rather, Fayol was a manager who attempted to translate his broad administrative experience into

universal process approach assumes all organizations require the same rational management process

practical guidelines for the successful management of all types of organizations.

As we mentioned in Chapter 1, Fayol believed that the manager's job could be divided into five functions, or areas, of managerial responsibility—planning, organizing, command, coordination, and control—that are essential to managerial success. (Some educators refer to them as the POC[3] functions.) His 14 universal principles of management, listed in Table 2.1, were intended to show managers how to carry out their functional duties. Fayol's functions and principles have withstood the test of time because of their widespread applicability. In spite of years of reformulation, rewording, expansion, and revision, Fayol's original management functions still can be found in nearly all management textbooks because they have proven to be so useful. In fact, after an extensive review of studies of managerial work, a pair of management scholars concluded that "The classical functions provide clear and discrete methods of classifying the thousands of different activities that managers carry out and the techniques they use in terms of the functions they perform for the achievement of organizational goals."[15]

Table **2.1**	Fayol's 14 Universal Principles of Management

1. **Division of work.** Specialization of labor is necessary for organizational success.

2. **Authority.** The right to give orders must accompany responsibility.

3 **Discipline.** Obedience and respect help an organization run smoothly.

4. **Unity of command.** Each employee should receive orders from only one superior.

5. **Unity of direction.** The efforts of everyone in the organization should be coordinated and focused in the same direction.

6. **Subordination of individual interests to the general interest.** Resolving the tug of war between personal and organizational interests in favor of the organization is one of management's greatest difficulties.

7. **Remuneration.** Employees should be paid fairly in accordance with their contribution.

8. **Centralization.** The relationship between centralization and decentralization is a matter of proportion; the optimum balance must be found for each organization.

9. **Scalar chain.** Subordinates should observe the formal chain of command unless expressly authorized by their respective superiors to communicate with each other.

10. **Order.** Both material things and people should be in their proper places.

11. **Equity.** Fairness that results from a combination of kindliness and justice will lead to devoted and loyal service.

12. **Stability and tenure of personnel.** People need time to learn their jobs.

13. **Initiative.** One of the greatest satisfactions is formulating and carrying out a plan.

14. **Esprit de corps.** Harmonious effort among individuals is the key to organizational success.

Source: Excerpted from *Administration industrielle et générale*, by Henri FAYOL, DUNOD, Paris. http://www.dunod.com/entreprise-gestion/entreprise-et-management/strategie-et-politique-de-lentreprise/ouvrages-professio/administration-indu. Used with permission of DUNOD, Paris.

Lessons from the Universal Process Approach

Fayol's main contribution to management thought was to show how the complex management process can be separated into interdependent areas of responsibility, or functions. Fayol's contention that management is a continuous process beginning with planning and ending with controlling also remains popular today. Contemporary adaptations of Fayol's functions offer students of management a useful framework for analyzing the management process. But as we noted in Chapter 1, this sort of rigid functional approach has been criticized for creating the impression that the management process is more rational and orderly than it really is. Fayol's functions, therefore, form a skeleton that needs to be fleshed out with concepts, techniques, and situational refinements from more modern approaches. The functional approach is useful because it specifies generally what managers *should* do, but the other approaches help explain *why* and *how*.

THE OPERATIONAL APPROACH

The term operational approach is a convenient description of the production-oriented area of management dedicated to improving efficiency, cutting waste, and improving quality. Since the turn of the twentieth century, it has had a number of labels, including scientific management, management science, operations research, production management, and operations management. Underlying this somewhat confusing evolution of terms has been a consistent purpose: to make person-machine systems work as efficiently as possible. Throughout its historical development, the operational approach has been technically and quantitatively oriented.

Frederick W. Taylor's Scientific Management

The son of a Philadelphia lawyer born in 1856, Frederick Winslow Taylor was the epitome of the self-made man. Because a temporary problem with his eyes kept him from attending Harvard University, Taylor went to work as a common laborer in a small Philadelphia machine shop. In just four years he picked up the trades of pattern maker and machinist.[16]

Later, Taylor went to work at Midvale Steel Works in Philadelphia, where he quickly moved up through the ranks while studying at night for a mechanical engineering degree. As a manager at Midvale, Taylor was appalled at industry's unsystematic practices. He observed little, if any, cooperation between the managers and the laborers. Inefficiency and waste were rampant. Output restriction among groups of workers, which Taylor called "systematic soldiering," was widespread. Ill-equipped and inadequately trained workers were typically left on their own to determine how to do their jobs. Hence, the father of scientific management committed himself to the relentless pursuit of "finding a better way."[17] Taylor sought nothing less than what he termed a "mental revolution" in the practice of industrial management.[18]

According to an early definition, scientific management is "that kind of management which *conducts* a business or affairs by *standards* established by facts or truths gained through *systematic* observation, experiment, or reasoning."[19] The word *experiment* deserves special emphasis because it was Taylor's trademark. While working at Midvale and later at Bethlehem Steel, Taylor started the scientific management movement in industry in four areas: standardization, time and task study, systematic selection and training, and pay incentives.[20]

STANDARDIZATION. By closely studying metal-cutting operations, Taylor collected extensive data on the optimum cutting-tool speeds and the rates at which stock should be fed into the machines for each job. The resulting standards were then posted for quick reference by the machine operators. He also systematically catalogued and stored the expensive cutting tools that usually were carelessly thrown aside when a job was completed. Operators could go to the carefully arranged

Frederick W. Taylor, 1856–1915

Bettmann/CORBIS

tool room, check out the right tool for the job at hand, and check it back in when finished. Taylor's approach caused productivity to jump and costs to fall.

TIME AND TASK STUDY. According to the traditional rule-of-thumb approach, there was no "science of shoveling." But after thousands of observations and stopwatch recordings, Taylor detected a serious flaw in the way various materials were being shoveled: each laborer brought his own shovel to work. Taylor knew the company was losing, not saving, money when a laborer used the same shovel for both heavy and light materials. A shovel load of iron ore weighed about 30 pounds, according to Taylor's calculations, whereas a shovel load of rice coal weighed only 4 pounds. Systematic experimentation revealed that a shovel load of 21 pounds was optimum (permitted the greatest movement of material in a day). Taylor significantly increased productivity by having workers use specially sized and shaped shovels provided by the company—large shovels for the lighter materials and smaller ones for heavier work.

SYSTEMATIC SELECTION AND TRAINING. Although primitive by modern standards, Taylor's experiments with pig iron handling clearly reveal the intent of this phase of scientific management. The task was to lift a 92-pound block of iron (in the steel trade, a "pig"), carry it up an incline (a distance of about 36 feet), and drop it into an open railroad car. Taylor observed that on the average, a pig iron handler moved about 12 1/2 tons in a ten-hour day of constant effort. After careful study, Taylor found that if he selected the strongest men and instructed them in the proper techniques of lifting and carrying the pigs of iron, he could get each man to load 47 tons in a ten-hour day. Surprisingly, this nearly fourfold increase in output was achieved by having the pig iron handlers spend only 43 percent of their time actually hauling iron. The other 57 percent was spent either walking back empty-handed or sitting down. Taylor reported that the laborers liked the new arrangement because they were less fatigued and took home 60 percent more pay.

Management historians recently have disputed Taylor's pig iron findings, suggesting his conclusions were unfounded and/or exaggerated.[21] As mentioned earlier, our present historical perspective is an evolving blend of fact and interpretation.

2b

Piece-Rate Puzzle

Suppose you are a college student about to take a part-time job in the school library. The job involves taking books and bound periodicals from the sorting room and returning them on a hand cart to their proper shelves throughout the library. Library officials have observed that an average of 30 items can be reshelved during one hour of steady effort. You have the option of being paid $9 an hour or 30 cents per item reshelved. The quality of your work will be randomly checked, and 30 cents will be deducted from your pay for each item found to be improperly shelved.

QUESTIONS: How do you want to be paid? Why? Which pay plan is probably better for the library? Why?

PAY INCENTIVES. According to Taylor, "What the workmen want from their employers beyond anything else is high wages."[22] This "economic man" assumption led Taylor to believe that piece rates were important to improved productivity. Under traditional piece-rate plans, an individual received a fixed amount of money for each unit of output. Thus, the greater the output, the greater the pay. In his determination to find a better way, Taylor attempted to improve the traditional piece-rate scheme with his differential piece-rate plan.

Figure 2.2 illustrates the added incentive effect of Taylor's differential plan. (The amounts are typical rates of pay in Taylor's time.) Under the traditional plan, a worker would receive a fixed amount (for example, 5 cents) for each unit produced. Seventy-five cents would be received for producing 15 units and $1.00 for 20 units. In contrast, Taylor's plan required that a time study be carried out to determine the company's idea of a fair day's work. Two piece rates were then put into effect. A low rate would be paid if the worker finished the day below the company's standard, a high rate if the day's output met or exceeded the standard. As the lines in Figure 2.2

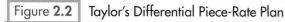

Figure **2.2**   Taylor's Differential Piece-Rate Plan

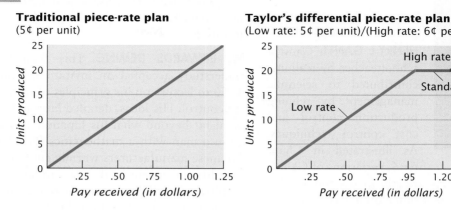

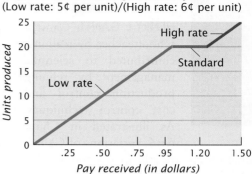

indicate, a hard worker who produced 25 units would earn $1.25 under the traditional plan and $1.50 under Taylor's plan.

Taylor's Followers

Among the many who followed in Taylor's footsteps, Frank and Lillian Gilbreth and Henry L. Gantt stand out.

FRANK AND LILLIAN GILBRETH. Inspired by Taylor's time studies and motivated by a desire to expand human potential, the Gilbreths turned motion study into an exact science. In so doing, they pioneered the use of motion pictures for studying and streamlining work motions. They paved the way for modern work simplification by cataloguing 17 different hand motions, such as "grasp" and "hold." These they called "therbligs" (the name *Gilbreth* spelled backwards with the *t* and *h* reversed). Their success stories include the following:

> In laying brick, the motions used in laying a single brick were reduced from eighteen to five—with an increase in output, from one hundred and twenty bricks an hour to three hundred and fifty an hour, and with a reduction in the resulting fatigue. In folding cotton cloth, twenty to thirty motions were reduced to ten or twelve, with the result that instead of one hundred and fifty dozen pieces of cloth, four hundred dozen were folded, with no added fatigue.[23]

Frank and Lillian Gilbreth were so dedicated to the idea of finding the one best way to do every job that 2 of their 12 children wrote *Cheaper by the Dozen*, a humorous recollection of scientific management and motion study applied to the Gilbreth household.[24]

Lillian M. Gilbreth, 1878–1972, at right, and Frank B. Gilbreth, 1868–1924, at left, with 11 of their dozen children.

Bettmann/CORBIS

Henry L. Gantt, 1861–1919

HENRY L. GANTT. Gantt, a schoolteacher by training, contributed to scientific management by refining production control and cost control techniques. As illustrated in Chapter 6, variations of Gantt's work-scheduling charts are still in use today.[25] He also humanized Taylor's differential piece-rate system by combining a guaranteed day rate (minimum wage) with an above-standard bonus. Gantt was ahead of his time in emphasizing the importance of the human factor and in urging management to concentrate on service rather than profits.[26]

The Quality Advocates

Today's managers readily attach strategic importance to quality improvement. The road to this enlightened view, particularly for U.S. managers, was a long and winding one. It started in factories and eventually made its way through service businesses, not-for-profit organizations, and government agencies. An international cast of quality advocates took much of the twentieth century to pave the road to quality. Not until 1980, when NBC ran a television documentary titled *If Japan Can . . . Why Can't We?* did Americans begin to realize fully that *quality* was a key to Japan's growing dominance in world markets. Advice from the following quality advocates finally began to sink in during the 1980s.[27]

WALTER A. SHEWHART. A statistician for Bell Laboratories, Shewhart introduced the concept of statistical quality control in his 1931 landmark text *Economic Control of Quality of Manufactured Product.*

KAORU ISHIKAWA. The University of Tokyo professor advocated quality before World War II and founded the Union of Japanese Scientists and Engineers (JUSE), which became the driving force behind Japan's quality revolution. Ishikawa proposed a preventive approach to quality. His expanded idea of the customer included both *internal and external customers.* Ishikawa's fishbone diagrams, discussed in Chapter 8, remain a popular problem-solving tool to this day.

W. EDWARDS DEMING. This Walter Shewhart understudy accepted an invitation from JUSE in 1950 to lecture on his principles of statistical quality control. His ideas, detailed later in Chapter 16, went far beyond what his Japanese hosts expected from a man with a mathematics Ph.D. from Yale. Japanese manufacturers warmly embraced Deming and his unconventional ideas about encouraging employee participation and striving for continuous improvement. His 1986 book *Out of the Crisis* is "a guide to the 'transformation of the style of American management,' which became a bible for Deming disciples."[28] Deming believed *every* employee, regardless of title or rank, is responsible for improving quality.

W. Edwards Deming, 1900–1993

JOSEPH M. JURAN. Juran's career bore a striking similarity to Deming's. Both were Americans (Juran was a naturalized U.S. citizen born in Romania) schooled in statistics, both strongly influenced Japanese managers via JUSE, and both continued to lecture on quality into their nineties. Thanks to extensive training by the Juran Institute, the concept of internal customers is well established today.[29] Teamwork, partnerships with suppliers, problem solving, and brainstorming are all Juran trademarks. Juran is also known for having developed the *Pareto analysis*, a technique used to separate major problems from minor ones. A Pareto analysis can be used to determine the 20 percent of possible causes leading to 80 percent of all problems. [30] (The 80/20 rule is discussed in Chapter 6 under the heading "Priorities.")

ARMAND V. FEIGENBAUM. While working on his doctorate at MIT, Feigenbaum developed the concept of *total quality control*. He expanded on his idea of an organizationwide program of quality improvement in his 1951 book *Total Quality Control*. He envisioned all functions of the business cycle—from purchasing and engineering, to manufacturing and finance, to marketing and service—as necessarily involved in the quest for quality. The *customer*, according to Feigenbaum, is the one who ultimately determines quality.[31]

PHILIP B. CROSBY. The author of the 1979 best seller *Quality Is Free*, Crosby learned about quality improvement during his up-from-the-trenches career at ITT (a giant global corporation in many lines of business). His work struck a chord with top managers because he documented the huge cost of having to rework or scrap poor-quality products. He promoted the idea of *zero defects,* or doing it right the first time.[32]

Lessons from the Operational Approach

Scientific management often appears rather unscientific to those who live in a world of genetic engineering, piloted space flight, industrial robots, the Internet, and laser technology. *Systematic management* might be a more accurate label. Within the context of haphazard, turn-of-the-twentieth-century industrial practices, however, scientific management was indeed revolutionary. Heading the list of its lasting contributions is a much-needed emphasis on promoting production efficiency and combating waste. Today, dedication to finding a better way is more important than ever in view of uneven productivity growth and diminishing resources.

Nevertheless, Taylor and the early proponents of scientific management have been roundly criticized for viewing workers as unidimensional economic beings interested only in more money. These critics fear that scientific management techniques have dehumanized people by making them act like mindless machines. Not all would agree. According to one respected management scholar who feels that Taylor's work is widely misunderstood and unfairly criticized, Taylor actually improved working conditions by reducing fatigue and redesigning machines to fit people. A systematic analysis of Taylor's contributions led this same management scholar to conclude that Taylor's insights are as valid today as they were in the context of his day.[33]

Contributions by the quality advocates are subject to less debate today. The only question is, Why didn't we listen to them earlier? (See Chapter 16.)

An important post–World War II outgrowth of the operational approach is operations management. Operations management, like scientific management, aims at promoting efficiency through systematic observation and experimentation. However, operations management (sometimes called operations research or production management) tends to be broader in scope and application than scientific management was. Whereas scientific management was limited largely to hand labor and machine shops, operations management specialists apply their expertise to all types of production and service operations, such as the purchase and storage of materials, energy use, product and service design, work flow, safety, quality control, and data processing. Thus, **operations management** is defined as developing tools and procedures to efficiently transform raw materials, technology, and human talent into useful goods and services.[34] As demonstrated at Norway's Norske Skog, one of the world's largest paper makers, operations managers are key players in the never-ending quest for productivity growth (see Window on the World).

WINDOW ON THE WORLD

Norwegian Paper Maker Benefits from a Detailed Model of Its Global Operations

Relying on two math whizzes in the New Zealand branch, it built a model of its global operations . . . [in 2008] that included everything from changing costs on freight to currency fluctuations.

This enabled managers to study the business with a new level of detail. They picked out money-losing operations in plants that appeared to be well-run. A manufacturing line in Korea, for example, was selling expensive recycled stock from the U.S. at a loss.

Norske Skog managers ran simulations of different scenarios, from soaring oil to cratering economies, for board members and union representatives. This helped make the case for where to cut capacity and 300 jobs. The union hired numbers experts of its own and, says employee representative [Kåre] Leira, "found nothing to complain about."

For Discussion: Why is this analytical approach superior to the usual us-versus-them approach to union-management relations?

Source: Excerpted from Stephen Baker, "A New Math for Cutting Costs," *Business Week* (May 11, 2009): 57.

THE BEHAVIORAL APPROACH

Like the other approaches to management, the behavioral approach has evolved gradually over many years. Advocates of the behavioral approach to management point out that people deserve to be the central focus of organized activity. They believe that successful management depends largely on a manager's ability to understand and work with people who have a variety of backgrounds, needs, perceptions, and aspirations. The progress of this humanistic approach from the human relations movement to modern organizational behavior has greatly influenced management theory and practice.

The Human Relations Movement

The human relations movement was a concerted effort among theorists and practitioners to make managers more sensitive to employee needs. It came into being as a result of special circumstances that occurred during the first half of the twentieth century. As illustrated in Figure 2.3, the human relations movement may be compared to the top of a pyramid.

Just as the top of a pyramid must be supported, the human relations movement was supported by three very different historical influences: (1) the threat of unionization, (2) the Hawthorne studies, and (3) the philosophy of industrial humanism.

THREAT OF UNIONIZATION. To understand why the human relations movement evolved, one needs first to appreciate its sociopolitical background. From the late 1800s to the 1920s, American industry grew by leaps and bounds as it attempted to satisfy the many demands of a rapidly growing population. Cheap immigrant labor was readily available, and there was a seller's market for finished goods. Then came the Great Depression in the 1930s, and millions stood in bread lines instead of pay lines. Many held business somehow responsible for the depression, and public sympathy swung from management to labor. Congress consequently began to pass pro-labor legislation. When the Wagner Act of 1935 legalized union-management collective bargaining, management began searching for ways to stem the tide of all-out unionization. Early human relations theory proposed an enticing answer: satisfied employees would be less inclined to join unions. Business managers subsequently began adopting morale-boosting

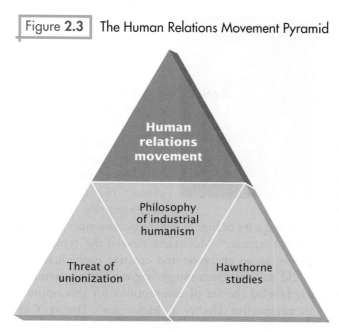

one way or another. After extensive interviewing of the subjects, it became clear to researchers that productivity was much less affected by changes in work conditions than by the attitudes of the workers themselves. Specifically, relationships between members of a work group and between workers and their supervisors were found to be more significant. Even though the experiments and the theories that evolved from them are criticized today for flawed methodology and statistical inaccuracies, the Hawthorne studies can be credited with turning management theorists away from the simplistic "economic person" model to a more humanistic and realistic view, the "social person" model.[35]

THE PHILOSOPHY OF INDUSTRIAL HUMANISM.

Although unionization prompted a search for new management techniques and the Hawthorne studies demonstrated that people were important to productivity, a philosophy of human relations was needed to provide a convincing rationale for treating employees better. Elton Mayo, Mary Parker Follett, and Douglas McGregor, although from very different backgrounds, offered just such a philosophy.

Born in Australia, Elton Mayo was a Harvard professor specializing in psychology and sociology when he took over the Hawthorne studies. His 1933 book *The Human Problems of an Industrial Civilization*, inspired by what he had learned at Hawthorne, cautioned managers that emotional factors were a more important determinant of productive efficiency than physical and logical factors. Claiming that employees create their own unofficial yet powerful workplace culture complete with norms and sanctions, Mayo urged managers to provide work that fostered personal and subjective satisfaction. He called for a new social order designed to stimulate individual cooperation.[36]

human relations techniques in an effort to discourage unionization.

THE HAWTHORNE STUDIES.

As the sociopolitical climate changed, a second development in industry took place. Behavioral scientists from prestigious universities began to conduct on-the-job behavior studies. Instead of studying tools and techniques in the scientific management tradition, they focused on people. Practical behavioral research such as the famous Hawthorne studies stirred management's interest in the psychological and sociological dynamics of the workplace.

The Hawthorne studies began in 1924 in a Western Electric plant near Chicago as a small-scale scientific management study of the relationship between light intensity and productivity. Curiously, the performance of a select group of employees tended to improve no matter how the physical surroundings were manipulated. Even when the lights were dimmed to mere moonlight intensity, productivity continued to climb! Scientific management doctrine could not account for what was taking place, and so a team of behavioral science researchers, headed by Elton Mayo, was brought in from Harvard to conduct a more rigorous study.

By 1932, when the Hawthorne studies ended, more than 20,000 employees had participated in

Elton Mayo, 1880–1949

Mary Parker Follett,
1868–1933

Mary Parker Follett's experience as a management consultant and her background in law, political science, and philosophy shaped her strong conviction that managers should be aware that each employee is a complex collection of emotions, beliefs, attitudes, and habits. She believed that managers had to recognize the individual's motivating desires to get employees to work harder. Accordingly, Follett urged managers to motivate performance rather than simply demanding it. Cooperation, a spirit of unity, and self-control were seen as the keys to both productivity and a democratic way of life.[37] (See Ethics: Character, Courage, and Values for a modern application of Follett's management philosophy.) Historians credit Follett, who died in 1933, with being decades ahead of her time in terms of behavioral and systems management theory.[38] Her influence as a management consultant in a male-dominated industrial sector was remarkable as well.

Douglas McGregor,
1906–1964

A third philosophical rallying point for industrial humanism was provided by an American scholar named Douglas McGregor. In his 1960 classic *The Human Side of Enterprise*, McGregor outlined a set of highly optimistic assumptions about human nature.[39] McGregor viewed the typical employee as an energetic and creative individual who could achieve great things if given the opportunity. He labeled the set of assumptions for this optimistic perspective Theory Y. McGregor's Theory Y assumptions are listed in Table 2.2, along with what he called the traditional Theory X assumptions. These two sets of assumptions about human nature enabled McGregor to contrast the modern, or enlightened, view he recommended (Theory Y) with the prevailing traditional view (Theory X), which he criticized for being pessimistic, stifling, and outdated. Because of its relative recency (compared with Mayo's and Follett's work), its catchy labels, and its intuitive appeal, McGregor's description of Theory X and Theory Y

ETHICS: Character, Courage, and Values

American Express Puts Its People First

. . . when it gave its global customer service division a makeover, it decided to focus on making life better for its 26,000 call-center employees. The theory: Happier employees mean happier customers. "We've learned the importance of the attitude of the employee," says Jim Bush, EVP [executive vice president] of world service. AmEx started by asking customer service employees what they wanted to see—and then delivered better pay, flexible schedules, and more career development. It also switched from a directive to keep calls short and transaction-oriented to engaging customers in longer conversations. Collectively, the moves have boosted service margins by 10%. "Great service starts with the people who deliver it," says [CEO Ken] Chenault. "We want American Express to be the company people recommend to their friends."

For Discussion: Why is this employee-centered management style both good business and a key workplace ethics issue?

Source: Excerpted from Christopher Tkaczyk, "American Express," *Fortune* (August 16, 2010): 14.

Theory Y McGregor's optimistic assumptions about working people

| Table **2.2** | McGregor's Theories X and Y |

THEORY X: SOME TRADITIONAL ASSUMPTIONS ABOUT PEOPLE	THEORY Y: SOME MODERN ASSUMPTIONS ABOUT PEOPLE
1. Most people dislike work, and they will avoid it when they can.	1. Work is a natural activity, like play or rest.
2. Most people must be coerced and threatened with punishment before they will work. They require close direction.	2. People are capable of self-direction and self-control if they are committed to objectives.
3. Most people prefer to be directed. They avoid responsibility and have little ambition. They are interested only in security.	3. People will become committed to organizational objectives if they are rewarded for doing so.
	4. The average person can learn to both accept and seek responsibility.
	5. Many people in the general population have imagination, ingenuity, and creativity.

has left an indelible mark on modern management thinking.[40] Some historians have credited McGregor with launching the field of organizational behavior.

Organizational Behavior

Organizational behavior is a modern approach to management that attempts to determine the causes of human work behavior and to translate the results into effective management techniques. Accordingly, it has a strong research orientation and a robust collection of theories. In fact, one review uncovered "73 established organizational behavior theories."[41] Organizational behaviorists have borrowed an assortment of theories and research techniques from all the behavioral sciences and have applied them to people at work in modern organizations. The result is an interdisciplinary field in which psychology predominates.[42] In spite of its relatively new and developing state, organizational behavior has had a significant impact on modern management thought by helping to explain why employees behave as they do. Because human relations has evolved into a practical, how-to-do-it discipline for supervisors, organizational behavior amounts to a scientific extension of human relations. Many organizational behavior findings will be examined in Part 4 of this text.

Lessons from the Behavioral Approach

Above all else, the behavioral approach makes it clear to present and future managers that *people* are the key to productivity.[43] According to advocates of the behavioral approach, technology, work rules, and standards do not guarantee good job performance. Instead, success depends on motivated and skilled individuals who are committed to organizational objectives.[44] Only a manager's sensitivity to individual concerns can foster the cooperation necessary for high productivity.

2c

Back to the Opening Case

Does Craigie Zildjian appear to be a Theory X or a Theory Y manager? Explain.

organizational behavior a modern approach seeking to discover the causes of work behavior and to develop better management techniques

On the negative side, traditional human relations doctrine has been criticized as vague and simplistic. According to these critics, relatively primitive on-the-job behavioral research does not justify such broad conclusions. For instance, critics do not believe that supportive supervision and good human relations will lead automatically to higher morale and hence to better job performance. Also, analyses of the Hawthorne studies, using modern statistical techniques, have generated debate about the validity of the original conclusions.[45]

Fortunately, organizational behavior, as a scientific extension of human relations, promises to fill in some of the gaps left by human relationists, while at the same time retaining an emphasis on people. Today, organizational behaviorists are trying to piece together the multiple determinants of effective job performance in various work situations and across cultures.

THE SYSTEMS APPROACH

A system is a collection of parts operating interdependently to achieve a common purpose. Working from this definition, the systems approach represents a marked departure from the past; in fact, it requires a completely different style of thinking.

Universal process, scientific management, and human relations theorists studied management by taking things apart. They assumed that the whole is equal to the sum of its parts and can be explained in terms of its parts. Systems theorists, in contrast, study management by putting things together and assume that the whole is greater than the sum of its parts. The difference is analytic versus synthetic thinking. According to one management systems expert, "Analytic thinking is, so to speak, outside-in thinking; synthetic thinking is inside-out." He adds that the two work in tandem, giving us a deeper understanding, especially of collective phenomena, than we could gain with either one individually.[46]

Systems theorists recommend synthetic thinking because management is not practiced in a vacuum. Managers affect, and are in turn affected by, many organizational and environmental variables. Systems thinking has presented the field of management with an enormous challenge: to identify all relevant parts of organized activity and to discover how they interact. Two management writers even predicted that systems thinking might one day produce a revolution in our understanding of organizations and their problems that would equal the impact of Taylor's theory of scientific management.[47]

Chester I. Barnard's Early Systems Perspective

In one sense, Chester I. Barnard followed in the footsteps of Henri Fayol. Like Fayol, Barnard established a new approach to management on the basis of his experience as a top-level manager. But the approach of the former president of New Jersey Bell Telephone differed from Fayol's. Rather than isolating specific management functions and principles, Barnard devised a more abstract systems approach. In his landmark 1938 book *The Functions of the Executive*, Barnard characterized all organizations as cooperative systems: "A cooperative system is a complex of physical, biological, personal, and social components which are in a specific systematic relationship by reason of the cooperation of two or more persons for at least one definite end."[48]

According to Barnard, willingness to serve, common purpose, and communication are the principal elements in an organization (or cooperative system).[49] He felt that an organization did not exist if these three elements were not present and working interdependently. As illustrated in Figure 2.4, Barnard viewed communication as an energizing force that bridges the natural gap between the individual's willingness to serve and the organization's common purpose.

Figure 2.4 Barnard's Cooperative System

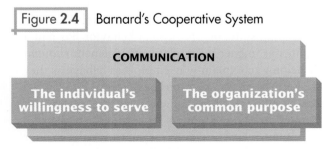

Barnard's systems perspective has encouraged management and organization theorists to study organizations as complex and dynamic wholes instead of piece by piece. Significantly, he was also a strong advocate of business ethics in his speeches and writings.[50] Barnard opened some important doors in the evolution of management thought.

General Systems Theory

General systems theory is an interdisciplinary area of study based on the assumption that everything is part of a larger, interdependent arrangement. According to Ludwig von Bertalanffy, a biologist and the founder of general systems theory, "In order to understand an organized whole we must know the parts and the relations between them."[51] This interdisciplinary perspective was eagerly adopted by Barnard's followers because it categorized levels of systems and distinguished between closed and open systems.

LEVELS OF SYSTEMS. Envisioning the world as a collection of systems was only the first step for general systems theorists. One of the more important recent steps has been the identification of hierarchies of systems, ranging from very specific systems to general ones. Identifying systems at various levels has helped translate abstract general systems theory into more concrete terms.[52] A hierarchy of systems relevant to management is the seven-level scheme of living systems shown in Figure 2.5. Note that each system is a subsystem of the one above it.

CLOSED VERSUS OPEN SYSTEMS. In addition to identifying hierarchies of systems, general systems theorists have distinguished between closed and open systems. A **closed system** is a self-sufficient entity, whereas an **open system** depends on the surrounding environment for survival. In reality, these two kinds of systems cannot be completely separated. The key to classifying a system as relatively closed or relatively open is to determine the amount of interaction between the system and its environment. A battery-powered digital watch, for example, is a relatively closed system; after the battery is in place, the watch operates without help from the outside environment. In contrast, a solar-powered clock is a relatively open system; it cannot operate without a continuous supply of outside energy. The human body is a highly open system because life depends on the body's ability to import oxygen and energy and to export waste. In other words, the human body is highly dependent on the environment for survival.[53]

Along the same lines, general systems theorists say that all organizations are open systems because organizational survival depends on interaction with the surrounding environment. Just as no person is an island, no organization or organizational subsystem is an island, according to this approach (see Green Management: Toward Sustainability).

| Figure **2.5** | Levels of Living Systems |

System level		Practical examples
Supranational	*General*	United Nations
National		Canada
Organizational		Walmart
Group		Family, work group
Organismic		Human being
Organic		Heart
Cellular	*Specific*	Blood cell

2d

Back to the Opening Case

Is Zildjian Company a closed or an open system? How can you tell?

general systems theory an area of study based on the assumption that everything is part of a larger, interdependent arrangement | closed system a self-sufficient entity | open system something that depends on its surrounding environment for survival

Green Management: Toward Sustainability

Open-System Thinking Is the Right Stuff for Annie Leonard

Where does all our stuff come from and where does it go when we throw it away? Annie Leonard spent 10 years researching this simple question and put her findings into The Story of Stuff, a provocative 20-minute film posted online in 2007 that illustrates how complicit we all are in our planet's destruction. With stick-figure-style animation and gee-whiz narration by the 45-year-old activist, the film has received more than 10 million hits from 238 countries, been incorporated into environmental studies in classrooms, and turned into a book.

For more, view Leonard's video at **www.storyofstuff.com/**.

For Discussion: How can this sort of open-system thinking help managers create more sustainable practices and products? What about all your "stuff"?

Source: Excerpted from Emilia Benton et al., "The 100 Most Creative People in Business 2010," *Fast Company*, 146 (June 2010): 118.

New Directions in Systems Thinking

Two very different streams of thought are taking systems thinking in interesting new directions today. No one knows for sure where these streams will lead, but they promise to stimulate creative ideas about modern organizations.

ORGANIZATIONAL LEARNING AND KNOWLEDGE MANAGEMENT.

An organizational learning perspective portrays the organization as a living and *thinking* open system. Like the human mind, organizations rely on feedback to adjust to changing environmental conditions. In short, organizations are said to learn from experience, just as humans and higher animals do. Organizations thus engage in complex mental processes such as anticipating, perceiving, envisioning, problem solving, and remembering. According to two organization theorists,

> Some forms of organizational learning occur regularly in many organizations. Human resource development activities, strategic and other planning activities, and the introduction and mastering of new technologies for doing work are three common learning processes. They often do not fulfill their potential for true organizational learning, however.
>
> Organizational learning is more than the sum of the learning of its parts—more than cumulative individual learning. The training and development of individuals with new skills, knowledge bases, theories, and frameworks does not constitute organizational learning unless such individual learning is translated into altered organizational practices, policies, or design features. Individual learning is necessary but not sufficient for organizational learning.[54]

When organizational learning becomes a strategic initiative to identify and fully exploit valuable ideas from both inside and outside the organization, a *knowledge management* program exists.[55] You will find more about knowledge management and how it relates to decision making in Chapter 8.

CHAOS THEORY AND COMPLEX ADAPTIVE SYSTEMS.

Chaos theory has one idea in common with organizational learning: systems are influenced by feedback. Work in the 1960s and 1970s by mathematicians Edward Lorenz and James Yorke formed the basis of modern chaos theory. So-called chaologists are trying to find order among the seemingly random behavior patterns of everything from weather systems to organizations to stock markets.[56] Behind all this is the intriguing notion that every complex system has a life of its own, with its own rule book. The challenge for those in the emerging field known as *complex adaptive systems theory* is to discover "the rules" in seemingly chaotic systems.

As indicated in Table 2.3, complex adaptive systems theory casts management in a very different light than do traditional models. Managers are challenged to be more flexible and adaptive than in the past.[57] They need to acknowledge the limits

| Table 2.3 | Complex Adaptive Systems Thinking Helps Managers Make Sense Out of Chaos |

COMPLEX ADAPTIVE SYSTEMS THEORY	CLASSICAL MANAGEMENT THEORY
Change and transformation are inherent qualities of dynamic systems. The goal of management is to increase learning and self-organizing in continuously changing contexts.	Organizations exist in equilibrium; therefore change is a nonnormal process. The goal of management is to increase stability through planning, organizing, and controlling behavior.
Organizational behavior is inherently nonlinear, and results may be nonproportional to corresponding actions. New models and methods are needed to understand change.	Organizational behavior is essentially linear and predictable, and results are proportional to causes. Thus linear regression models explain most of the variance of organizational change.
Inputs do not cause outputs. The elements of a system are interdependent and mutually causal.	System components are independent and can be analyzed by separating them from the rest of the system, as well as from their outcomes.
An organization is defined, first of all, according to its underlying order and principles. These give rise to surface-level organizing structures, including design, strategy, leadership, controls, and culture.	An organization can be completely defined in terms of its design, strategy, leadership, controls, and culture.
Change should be encouraged through embracing tension, increasing information flow, and pushing authority downward.	Change should be controlled by minimizing uncertainty and tension, limiting information, and centralizing decision making.
Long-term organizational success is based on optimizing resource flow and continuous learning. A manager's emphasis is on supporting structures that accomplish these goals.	Organizational success is based on maximizing resource utilization, to maximize profit and increase shareholder wealth. A manager's emphasis is on efficiency and effectiveness, and on avoiding both transformation and chaos.

Source: *Academy of Management Executive: The Thinking Manager's Source* by Benjamin Bregmann Lichtenstein. Copyright © 2000 by Academy of Management (NY). Reproduced with permission of Academy of Management (NY) in the format Textbook via Copyright Clearance Center.

of traditional command-and-control management because complex systems have *self-organizing* tendencies. (For example, labor unions have historically thrived in eras when management was oppressive.) The twenty-first-century manager, profiled in the previous chapter (Table 1.1), is up to the challenge. Significantly, chaos theory and complex adaptive systems theory are launching pads for new and better management models, not final answers. Stay tuned.

Lessons from the Systems Approach

Because of the influence of the systems approach, managers now have a greater appreciation for the importance of seeing the whole picture. Open-system thinking does not permit the manager to become preoccupied with one aspect of organizational management while ignoring other internal and external realities. The manager of a business, for instance, must consider resource availability, technological developments, and market trends when producing and selling a product or service. Another positive aspect of the systems approach is how it tries to integrate various management theories. Although quite different in emphasis, both operations management and organizational behavior have been strongly influenced by systems thinking.

There are critics of the systems approach, of course. Some management scholars see systems thinking as long on intellectual appeal and catchy terminology and short on verifiable facts and practical advice.

THE CONTINGENCY APPROACH

A comparatively new line of thinking among management theorists has been labeled the contingency approach. Advocates of contingency management are attempting to take a step away from universally applicable principles of management and toward situational appropriateness. In the words of Fred Luthans, a noted contingency management writer, "The traditional approaches to management were not necessarily wrong, but today they are no longer adequate. The needed breakthrough for management theory and practice can be found in a contingency approach."[58] Formally defined, the **contingency approach** is an effort to determine through research which managerial practices and techniques are appropriate in specific situations. Imagine using Taylor's approach with a college-educated computer engineer! According to the contingency approach, different situations require different managerial responses.

Generally, the term *contingency* refers to the choice of an alternative course of action. For example, roommates may have a contingency plan to move their party indoors if it rains. Their subsequent actions are said to be contingent (or dependent) on the weather. In a management context, contingency management has become synonymous with situational management. As one contingency theorist put it, the effectiveness of a management pattern depends on a variety of interrelated factors within a particular situation.[59] This means that the application of various management tools and techniques must be appropriate to the particular situation, because each situation presents unique problems. A contingency approach is especially applicable in intercultural dealings, where customs and habits cannot be taken for granted.

In real-life management, the success of any given technique is dictated by the situation. For example, researchers have found that rigidly structured organizations with many layers of

2e

Back to the Opening Case

What, if any, evidence of the contingency approach can you detect in this case? Explain.

management function best when environmental conditions are relatively stable. Unstable surroundings dictate a more flexible and streamlined organization that can adapt quickly to change. Consequently, traditional principles of management that call for rigidly structured organizations, no matter what the situation, have come into question.

Contingency Characteristics

Some management scholars are attracted to contingency thinking because it is a workable compromise between the systems approach and what can be called a purely situational perspective. Figure 2.6 illustrates this relationship. The systems approach is often criticized for being too general and abstract, while the purely situational view, which assumes that every real-life situation requires a distinctly different approach, has been called hopelessly specific. Contingency advocates have tried to take advantage of common denominators without lapsing into simplistic generalization. Three characteristics

Figure 2.6   The Contingency View: A Compromise

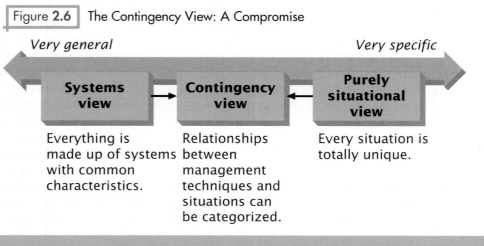

Very general   *Very specific*

Systems view	Contingency view	Purely situational view
Everything is made up of systems with common characteristics.	Relationships between management techniques and situations can be categorized.	Every situation is totally unique.

contingency approach research effort to determine which managerial practices and techniques are appropriate in specific situations

of the contingency approach are (1) an open-system perspective, (2) a practical research orientation, and (3) a multivariate approach.

AN OPEN-SYSTEM PERSPECTIVE. Open-system thinking is fundamental to the contingency view. Contingency theorists are not satisfied with focusing on just the internal workings of organizations. They see the need to understand how organizational subsystems combine to interact with outside social, cultural, political, and economic systems.

A PRACTICAL RESEARCH ORIENTATION. Practical research is that which ultimately leads to more effective on-the-job management. Contingency researchers attempt to translate their findings into tools and situational refinements for more effective management.

A MULTIVARIATE APPROACH. Traditional closed-system thinking prompted a search for simple one-to-one causal relationships. This approach is called bivariate analysis. For example, the traditional human relations assumption that higher morale leads automatically to higher productivity was the result of bivariate analysis. One variable, morale, was seen as the sole direct cause of changes in a second variable, productivity. Subsequent multivariate analysis has shown that many variables, including the employee's personality, the nature of the task, rewards, and job and life satisfaction, collectively account for variations in productivity. Multivariate analysis is a research technique used to determine how numerous variables interact to cause a particular outcome. For example, if an employee has a conscientious personality, the task is highly challenging, and the individual is highly satisfied with his or her life and job, then analysis might show that productivity could be expected to be high. Contingency management theorists strive to carry out practical and relevant multivariate analyses.

Lessons from the Contingency Approach

Although still not fully developed, the contingency approach is a helpful addition to management thought because it emphasizes situational appropriateness. People, organizations, and problems are too complex to justify rigid adherence to universal principles of management.[60] In addition, contingency thinking is a *practical* extension of the systems approach.

Assuming that systems thinking is a unifying synthetic force in management thought, the contingency approach promises to add practical direction.

The contingency approach, like each of the other approaches, has its share of critics. One has criticized contingency theory for creating the impression that the organization is a captive of its environment.[61] If such were strictly the case, attempts to manage the organization would be in vain. In actual fact, organizations are subject to various combinations of environmental forces and management practices.

Whether the contingency management theorists have bitten off more than they can chew remains to be seen. At present they appear to be headed in a constructive direction. But it is good to keep in mind that the contingency approach is a promising step rather than the end of the evolution of conventional management thought.[62]

THE ERA OF MANAGEMENT BY BEST SELLER: PROCEED WITH CAUTION

An interesting thing happened to the field of management over the last 25 years or so. It went mainstream. A fledgling field that had been pretty much limited to college classrooms and management development seminars began having a broader appeal. Peter F. Drucker, an Austrian-born management consultant, writer, and teacher living in the United States, deserves to be considered the father of this trend.[63] His now-classic books, such as *The Concept of the Corporation* (1946), *The Practice of Management* (1954), and *The Effective Executive* (1967), along with his influential articles in *Harvard Business Review* and elsewhere, appealed to academics and practicing managers alike. Drucker became the first management guru whose sage advice was sought by executives trying to figure out how to manage in increasingly turbulent times. Others, such as quality advocates Juran and Deming, followed.

The popularization of management shifted into high gear in 1982 with the publication of Peters and Waterman's *In Search of Excellence*. This book topped the nonfiction best-seller lists for months, was translated into several foreign languages, and soon appeared in paperback. Just five years later, an

---

multivariate analysis research technique used to determine how numerous variables combine to cause a particular outcome

astounding 5 million copies had been sold world-wide.[64] Other business management best sellers followed (see Table 2.4), and the popular appeal of management grew. The rest, as they say, is history. By 2004, best-selling authors such as Michael Hammer were collecting $82,000 per speaking engagement, worldwide sales of *The One Minute Manager* had reached 7 million copies,[65] and businessman Donald Trump was saying "You're fired!" on his reality TV hit *The Apprentice*.[66] Certain academics, meanwhile, worried about the instant gurus and their best sellers encouraging shoddy research and simplistic thinking, to say nothing of pandering to busy managers' desire for quick fixes.[67] Still, the era of management by best seller deserves serious discussion in any historical perspective on management thought, if for no other reason than the widespread acceptance among practicing managers of the books listed in Table 2.4.

Table 2.4   A Sampling of Business Management Best Sellers

NAME OF BOOK, AUTHOR(S), AND YEAR PUBLISHED	MAIN THEME/LESSONS
Theory Z: How American Business Can Meet the Japanese Challenge, William Ouchi, 1981	UCLA professor finds successful "Theory Z" U.S. firms such as IBM exhibit a blend of American and Japanese traits (e.g., participative decision making; teamwork + individual responsibility).
In Search of Excellence: Lessons from America's Best-Run Companies, Thomas J. Peters and Robert H. Waterman Jr., 1982	Consultants' analysis of 36 companies, including Johnson & Johnson and McDonald's, finds eight "attributes of excellence." Excellent companies reportedly focus on action, customers, entrepreneurship, people, values, the core business, simplicity, and balanced control and decentralization.
The One Minute Manager, Kenneth Blanchard and Spencer Johnson, 1982	Short parable of a young man who learns from experienced managers about the power of on-the-spot goals, praise, and reprimands.
High Output Management, Andrew S. Grove, 1983	Respected CEO of Intel Corp. urges managers to be output-oriented, teambuilders, and motivators of individual peak performance.
Iacocca: An Autobiography, Lee Iacocca (with William Novak), 1984	Legendary president of Ford and CEO of Chrysler details how being a master salesman helped him save Chrysler Corp.
The 7 Habits of Highly Effective People: Powerful Lessons in Personal Change, Stephen R. Covey, 1989	Professor/consultant charts pathway to personal growth in terms of good habits formed by balancing one's knowledge, skills, and desires.
Reengineering the Corporation: A Manifesto for Business Revolution, Michael Hammer and James Champy, 1993	Consultants recommend using information technology to radically redesign basic business practices to achieve lower costs, higher quality, and speed.
Built to Last: Successful Habits of Visionary Companies, James C. Collins and Jerry I. Porras, 1994	After studying 18 "visionary" companies, including American Express and Marriott, these professors/consultants urge managers to "preserve the core" (with strong cultures and internal promotions) and "stimulate progress" (with difficult goals and a hunger for continuous change).
The Death of Competition: Leadership & Strategy in the Age of Business Ecosystems, James F. Moore, 1996	Consultant advises firms to be as good at cooperating as they are at competing, especially with others in their ecosystem (e.g., Microsoft and Intel).

NAME OF BOOK, AUTHOR(S), AND YEAR PUBLISHED	MAIN THEME/LESSONS
Who Moved My Cheese? Spencer Johnson, 1998	Coauthor of *The One Minute Manager* spins a short fable about two mice who learn to adapt to change by facing their fears and enjoying the trip.
Fish! Stephen C. Lundin, Harry Paul, and John Christensen, 2000	Short story of a manager who turns her department around by applying four lessons learned at Seattle's Pike Place fish market.
Good to Great: Why Some Companies Make the Leap . . . and Others Don't, Jim Collins, 2001	Coauthor of *Built to Last* returns with list of 11 companies, including Gillette and Walgreens, that jumped from good to great by hiring great people, confronting reality, and becoming the world's best.
Jack: Straight from the Gut, Jack Welch (with John A. Byrne), 2001	Legendary CEO of General Electric explains his concept of the "boundaryless" organization dedicated to sharing ideas, building people into winners, and fighting bureaucracy.
Execution: The Discipline of Getting Things Done, Larry Bossidy and Ram Charan (with Charles Burck), 2002	Retired CEO of Honeywell and professor/consultant tell how to get results by hiring good people who are taught to link strategy with operations.
Outliers, The Story of Success, Malcolm Gladwell, 2008	Personal success is complex and requires much more than intelligence and ambition. Being in the right place at the right time, hard work, and diligent practice are key.

What's Wrong with Management by Best Seller?

Craig M. McAllaster, the Business School Dean at Florida's Rollins College, describes how easily a manager can get caught up in the potential for the latest business best seller's ability to solve all of the firm's problems with ease:

> *Fired up and sure of the prognosis and treatment, the executive returns to the organization . . . and calls a management meeting to announce the change. No diagnosis or assessment takes place to determine the real organizational problems.*[68]

The inevitable disappointment is not the fault of popular management books, which typically do contain some really good ideas; rather, the hurried and haphazard application of those generic, one-size-fits-all ideas is at fault. Our challenge, then, is to avoid the quick-fix mentality that makes management by best seller so tempting.

How to Avoid the Quick-Fix Mentality

In a follow-up study of Peters and Waterman's *In Search of Excellence*, Michael Hitt and Duane Ireland conducted a *comparative* analysis of "excellent" companies and industry norms. Companies that satisfied all of Peters and Waterman's excellence criteria turned out to be no more effective than a random sample of *Fortune* 1000 companies.[69] Similar disappointing results were uncovered in Bruce G. Resnick and Timothy L. Smunt's follow-up study of Jim Collins's still popular 2001 best seller *Good to Great*, in which the 11 "great" companies in the book did not continue to perform in a superior fashion, at least not when measured according to modern portfolio metrics.[70]

Hitt and Ireland's findings prompted them to offer five tips for avoiding what they termed "the quick-fix mentality" (see Table 2.5).

Alex Mares-Manton/Asia Images/Corbis

The business section of your local bookstore contains a mountain of information—both trash and treasure. Be wary of quick fixes based on shoddy research while gathering those pearls of wisdom.

2f
Practical Take-Aways

Jeffrey Pfeffer, Stanford University management professor:

If companies act on the basis of simplistic and inaccurate theories of human behavior and organizational performance, their decisions will not be good ones and the results will be poor.

QUESTION: What specific take-away lessons have you learned from studying this chapter that can help you avoid common "rookie" mistakes as a manager?

Source: Jeffrey Pfeffer, *What Were They Thinking? Unconventional Wisdom About Management* (Boston: Harvard Business School Press, 2007), pp. 7–8.

Putting What You Have Learned to Work

We need to put the foregoing historical overview into proper perspective. The topical tidiness of this chapter, while providing useful conceptual frameworks for students of management, generally does not carry over to the practice of management. Managers are, first and foremost, pragmatists. They use whatever works. Instead of faithfully adhering to a given school of management thought, successful managers tend to use a "mixed-bag" approach. This chapter is a good starting point for you to begin building your own personally relevant and useful approach to management by blending theory, the experience and advice of others, and your own experience. A healthy dose of common sense would help as well.

Table **2.5**	How to Avoid the Quick-Fix Mentality in Management

Our research suggests that practicing managers should embrace appealing ideas when appropriate but anticipate that solutions typically are far more complex than the type suggested by Peters and Waterman's search for excellence. To avoid the quick-fix mentality, managers should:

1. Remain current with literature in the field, particularly with journals that translate research into practice.

2. Ensure that concepts applied are based on science or, at least, on some form of rigorous documentation, rather than purely on advocacy.

3. Be willing to examine and implement new concepts, but first do so using pilot tests with small units.

4. Be skeptical when simple solutions are offered; analyze them thoroughly.

5. Constantly anticipate the effects of current actions and events on future results.

Source: *Michael A. Hitt and R. Duane Ireland, "Peters and Waterman Revisited: The Unended Quest for Excellence,"* Academy of Management Executive, *Vol. 2, no. 2 (May 1987): p. 96. Reprinted by permission.*

SUMMARY

1. Management is an interdisciplinary and international field that has evolved in bits and pieces over the years. Five approaches to management theory are (1) the universal process approach, (2) the operational approach, (3) the behavioral approach, (4) the systems approach, and (5) the contingency approach. Useful lessons have been learned from each.

   Henri Fayol's universal process approach assumes that all organizations, regardless of purpose or size, require the same management process. Furthermore, it assumes that this rational process can be reduced to separate functions and principles of management. The universal approach, the oldest of the various approaches, is still popular today.

2. Dedicated to promoting production efficiency and reducing waste, the operational approach has evolved from scientific management to operations management. Frederick W. Taylor, the father of scientific management, and his followers revolutionized industrial management through the use of standardization, time-and-motion study, selection and training, and pay incentives.

3. The quality advocates taught managers about the strategic importance of high-quality goods and services. Shewhart pioneered the use of *statistics* for quality control. Japan's Ishikawa emphasized *prevention* of defects in quality and drew management's attention to *internal* as well as external *customers*. Deming sparked the Japanese quality revolution with calls for *continuous improvement* of the entire production process. Juran trained many U.S. managers to improve quality through *teamwork, partnerships with suppliers*, and *Pareto analysis* (the 80/20 rule). Feigenbaum developed the concept of *total quality control*, thus involving all business functions in the quest for quality. He believed that the *customer* determined quality. Crosby, a champion of *zero defects*, emphasized how costly poor-quality products could be.

4. Management has turned to the human factor in the human relations movement and organizational behavior approach. Emerging from such influences as unionization, the Hawthorne studies, and the philosophy of industrial humanism, the human relations movement began as a concerted effort to make employees' needs a high management priority. Today, organizational behavior theorists try to identify the multiple determinants of job performance.

5. Advocates of the systems approach recommend that modern organizations be viewed as open systems. Open systems depend on the outside environment for survival, whereas closed systems do not. Chester I. Barnard stirred early interest in systems thinking in 1938 by suggesting that organizations are cooperative systems energized by communication. General systems theory, an interdisciplinary field based on the assumption that everything is systematically related, has identified a hierarchy of systems and has differentiated between closed and open systems. New directions in systems thinking are organizational learning and chaos theory.

6. A comparatively new approach to management thought is the contingency approach, which stresses situational appropriateness rather than universal principles. The contingency approach is characterized by an open-system perspective, a practical research orientation, and a multivariate approach to research. Contingency thinking is a practical extension of more abstract systems thinking.

7. "Management by best seller" occurs when managers read a popular book by a management guru and hastily try to implement its ideas and one-size-fits-all recommendations without proper regard for their organization's unique problems and needs. The quick-fix mentality that fosters this problem can be avoided by staying current with high-quality management literature, requiring rigorous support for claims, engaging in critical thinking, and running pilot studies.

TERMS TO UNDERSTAND

Universal process approach, p. 39   Theory Y, p. 48   Closed system, p. 51
Operational approach, p. 41   Organizational behavior, p. 49   Open system, p. 51
Scientific management, p. 41   System, p. 50   Contingency approach, p. 54
Operations management, p. 46   General systems theory, p. 51   Multivariate analysis, p. 55
Human relations movement, p. 46

ACTION LEARNING EXERCISE

OPEN-SYSTEM THINKING AND RECYCLING

Instructions: Open-system thinking involves trying to better understand (and manage) complicated situations. It requires one to connect the dots, so to speak, and see the big picture. The idea is to comprehend the interconnectedness of things and to anticipate (and ideally avoid) possible unintended consequences. Corrective actions can then be taken on the basis of your new, broader understanding. This exercise challenges you to tackle the twin problems of too much solid waste and too little recycling. For a 24-hour period, keep a log of all the tangible items you buy or consume (such as a meal, some clothing, cell phone, gum or candy bar, book or magazine, bottle of water, can of soda, and the like) and jot down what you did with any resulting packaging, material waste, or leftovers. Was the waste recycled, thrown away (where?), or poured down the drain? Be prepared to discuss your log in class, if requested by the instructor.

Consider this:

When done right, recycling saves energy, preserves natural resources, reduces green-house-gas emissions, and keeps toxins from leaking out of landfills.

So why doesn't everyone do it? Because it's often cheaper to throw things away. The economics of recycling depends on landfill fees, the price of oil and other commodities, and the demand for recycled goods. Paper, for example, works well: About 52% of paper consumed in the U.S. is recovered for recycling, and 36% of the fiber that goes into new paper comes from recycled sources. By contrast, less than 25% of plastic bottles are recycled, and we use five billion (!) a year.

Americans generated an average of 4.5 pounds of garbage per person per day in 2005, the EPA reports. About 1.5 pounds were recycled. That's a national recycling rate for municipal solid waste of just 32%.[71]

. . . and this:

That plastic water bottle you absent-mindedly toss out the car window could end up traveling through a storm drain or waterway to an ocean, where it can float around for decades or longer.

In just one day [in 2009] . . . , thousands of volunteers collected 7.4 million pounds of litter such as cigarettes, plastic bags and food wrappers from coastlines and inland waterways in 108 countries and locations worldwide, a report from the Ocean Conservancy says. . . .

The USA yielded far more debris than any other country: 4,253,650 pounds. The report says 60% to 80% of marine debris starts out on land and can travel thousands of miles. Some of it outlives us, such as tin cans that can take up to 50 years to decompose and baby diapers that don't break down for up to 450 years.[72]

. . . and this:

. . . 8% of global oil production is siphoned off to make plastic each year. Recycled plastic, however, requires 80% less energy to produce. Recycled aluminum burns

up 95% less energy. Recycled iron and steel use 74% less, while paper requires 64% less.[73]

FOR CONSIDERATION/DISCUSSION

1. Viewing yourself as part of a natural open system, how wasteful are you? What are the broader environmental implications of your consumption habits?

2. Did this exercise spur you to do a better job of recycling?

3. Should recycling be a high priority for business? Explain.

4. On local, national, and global scales, what needs to be done to significantly reduce the solid waste stream?

5. Why is open-system thinking useful for issues as complex as solid waste reduction?

6. What other tough societal problems could managers and government leaders better understand and manage through open-system thinking? Discuss.

ETHICS EXERCISE

 DO THE RIGHT THING

Putting the Recent Recession into Historical Perspective

John Gerzema, consumer-behavior researcher: When you consider layoffs, downsizing, delayed raises, and reduced hours, more than half of all American workers have suffered losses. This very real pain has driven us to reconsider our definition of the good life. People are finding happiness in old-fashioned virtues—thrift, do-it-yourself projects, self-improvement, faith, and community—and in activities and relationships outside the consumer realm. Our data show large numbers saying money is no longer as important to them. Seventy-six percent say the number of possessions they own doesn't affect how happy they are.

. . . we are moving from mindless to mindful consumption. That's a fact of life when housing values will no longer provide an ATM to fund our spending and people are working longer to repair lost wealth. From now on, we will spend money that is ours, not the bank's. Therefore, our purchases will become more considered.

What are the ethical implications of the following interpretations?

1. Yes, the so-called Great Recession has created what some economists call the "new normal," where Americans will live simpler lives for the foreseeable future. How will this new reality impact the workplace in terms of employee loyalty and motivation to work hard? What about the American Dream?

2. This is just an historical blip. When the economy eventually turns around, Americans will return to their traditional habit of spending like there's no tomorrow. Does this mean that each generation keeps making the same old mistakes and that we don't learn from the past?

3. Younger people entering the workforce today truly "get it." Family and friends come first—career success, wealth, and material possessions are not the keys to happiness. Balance is important. How should managers motivate and lead these less materialistic employees?

4. Your own ethical interpretation?

Sources: Excerpted from John Gerzema, as quoted in an interview by Leigh Buchanan, "Decoding the New Consumer," *Inc.*, 32 (September 2010): 159.

MANAGERS-IN-ACTION VIDEO CASE STUDY

MITCHELL GOLD + BOB WILLIAMS

Company founders Mitchell Gold and Bob Williams discuss their unique approach in the furniture industry when they started their company. They clearly demonstrate how successful companies can produce quality products while also providing a great place to work. Employees share their perspective, which makes it easy to understand why Mitchell Gold + Bob Williams has grown from 23 employees to more than 700.

For more information about Mitchell Gold + Bob Williams, visit its Web site: www .mgbwhome.com/.

Before watching the video, answer the following questions:

1. Describe quality management ideas and practices suggested by quality advocates Deming, Ishikawa, Juran, and Feigenbaum (discussed in this chapter in the Quality Advocates section).

2. What responsibility should a company have to its employees' quality of life and working conditions? Provide specific examples to support your answer.

3. How can business owners and managers get employees to produce their best work?

After watching the video, answer the following questions:

4. For each of the quality advocates referenced in question 1, identify a quality idea/ perspective and discuss a corresponding practice in place today at Gold + Williams.

5. How does the work environment at Gold + Williams impact quality and success?

6. From an employee recruitment and retention perspective, what benefits, policies, and management practices provide Gold + Williams with a competitive advantage? Explain why.

7. One of the five overarching changes mentioned in Chapter 1 was environmentalism and sustainability. Discuss how Gold + Williams is responding to this change and adapting its manufacturing practices.

CLOSING CASE

SIX GENERATIONS HAVE FINE TUNED THIS GUITAR MAKER

Chris Martin, CEO, C.F. Martin & Company, founded in 1833: "Our business in America started in Manhattan. The family moved to Nazareth [Pennsylvania] in 1839. They had come from a small town in southern Germany, and they didn't feel comfortable in a big metropolitan area. My great-great-great-grandfather was able to more consistently make perfect guitars than anyone from that era. People still say C.F. Martin set the standard for quality for American guitars.

"I was going to become a marine biologist and worked here summers. People were saying, 'Aren't you going to join the family business?' I remember I went to a trade show with my father when I was

14 or 15. My dad said that someone from CBS wanted to talk to us about selling the business and asked me what I thought. I said, 'I would like to think about joining the business—I can't guarantee that I will.' And we went over and met this gentleman at the show, sitting at a big desk, and my dad said, 'This is my son, and he may want to join the business someday, so we're not for sale.' I have a 3-year-old daughter named Claire Frances, so if she ever wants to be C.F. Martin, she can. She comes to work with me every once in a while, and we go out to the plant—right now we're watching a ukulele being made.

"When I took over, in 1986, the business was barely breaking even. We'd ridden the folk boom and then the folk-rock boom through the '60s and early '70s, and then business started to trail off with disco. Production peaked in the late '70s at around 20,000 units; by 1983, we were down to making and selling 3,000 guitars a year.

"The guitar started regaining popularity thanks to things like MTV Unplugged. We've got about 600 employees here in Nazareth and about 250 in Mexico, where we make our strings, our backpacker guitar, and our Little Martin travel guitar. Last year, we made 85,000 guitars.

"My father made a bunch of acquisitions. Aside from buying a string company, which was an astute move, none of these panned out. And when they didn't work out, he would take the people who were really smart here and send them to try to fix the acquisitions. As a result, the core business suffered. The people making the guitars were like, 'Hey, what about us?' And they'd hear, 'Oh, we've got to go fix the drum company! We've got to fix the banjo company!' It was really a distraction.

"I also found a very hierarchical situation: top-down, traditional, the boss tells the worker and the worker does it and goes home. As much as I knew there was a better way, forever and ever the old way was what everyone knew. I went on an Outward Bound course for a week, and I really learned the value of teamwork. I came back, and I was all fired up: If the Martin Company was going to move ahead, we needed to involve the workers more. We went through a lot of formal training, all the way down to the hourly level, about employee involvement. And since I came in, we've given out about $15 million to the employees in profit sharing.

"We hired a gentleman from Bethlehem Steel to formalize our quality assurance program a couple of years ago. One day he came in and said, 'Chris, people work really hard here, and I keep telling them, "Hey, we're not trying to make the perfect guitar!" ' And I said, ' Vince, we are trying to make the perfect guitar.' "

For Discussion:

1. Which of Fayol's 14 universal principles of management in Table 2.1 are evident in the C.F. Martin case? Explain your reasoning for each principle selected.

2. What would Mary Parker Follett probably say about Chris Martin's management style? Explain.

3. Is Chris Martin a Theory X or a Theory Y manager? Explain.

4. Is C.F. Martin a closed or an open system? Explain.

5. If you were responsible for designing and conducting a management training program for C.F. Martin's managers, which of the management best sellers listed in Table 2.4 would you have them read? Why?

Source: Adam Bluestein, "The Success Gene," *Inc.*, 30 (April 2008): 86.

3 The Changing Environment of Management

Diversity, Global Economy, and Technology

Greg Vote/Corbis

"*The best way to predict the future is to create it.*"[1]

—ALAN KAYE

The Changing Workplace

LOOKING FORWARD TO THE 2020 WORKPLACE

Employees in the 2020 workplace will communicate, connect, and collaborate with one another around the globe using the latest forms of social media. As they work in virtual teams with colleagues and collaborate with their peers to solve problems and propose new ideas for business, they will need to develop a new mind-set to thrive. This 2020 mind-set will incorporate abilities in:

Social participation: A belief that your network is the first place you go to ask questions, seek out advice, and disseminate your expertise.

Thinking globally: A capacity to think globally, have a deep understanding of how world events can impact your organization, and make decisions in ways that factor in cultural differences.

Ubiquitous learning: A commitment to learning new skills and, in the process, leveraging the latest technologies that are now a pervasive part of our lives, such as mobile devices; an openness to looking for new ideas in your area of expertise; and an ability to apply new knowledge to a fast-changing set of business conditions.

Thinking big, acting fast, and constantly improving: A desire to see opportunities as once-in-a-lifetime moments that must be acted upon with speed and clarity while believing in the power of continually improving beta [or temporary] solutions.

Cross-cultural power: A conviction that embracing a diverse community of employees, customers, and consumers representing many different backgrounds, skills, countries of origin, and ideas will result in superior business outcomes.

Source: Excerpted from Jeanne C. Meister and Karie Willyerd, *The 2020 Workplace: How Innovative Companies Attract, Develop, and Keep Tomorrow's Employees Today* (New York: Harper Business, 2010), pp. 222–223.

OBJECTIVES

- **Summarize** the demographics of the new American workforce.
- **Explain** why America's education and workplace readiness situation is a crisis.
- **Define** the term *managing diversity*, and **explain** why it is particularly important today.
- **Discuss** how the changing political-legal environment is affecting the practice of management.
- **Discuss** why business cycles and the global economy are vital economic considerations for modern managers.
- **Describe** the three-step innovation process, and **define** the term *intrapreneur*.

If you are to be successful in the 2020 workplace and beyond, you need to be aware of *how* things are changing in the world around you. Employees and managers need to do more than merely cope with change; they must learn to thrive on it.[2]

Ignoring the impact of general environmental factors on management makes about as much sense as ignoring the effects of weather and road conditions on high-speed driving. The general environment of management includes social, political-legal, economic, and technological dimensions. Changes in each area present managers with unique opportunities and obstacles that will shape not only the organization's strategic direction but also the course of daily operations. This challenge requires forward-thinking managers who can handle change and accurately see the greater scheme of things.

The purpose of this chapter, then, is to prepare you for constant change and help you see the *big picture* by identifying key themes in the changing environment of management.[3] It builds on our discussion in Chapter 1 of the five overarching sources of change for today's managers: globalization, the evolution of product quality, environmentalism and sustainability, an ethical reawakening, and the Internet and social media revolution.

THE SOCIAL ENVIRONMENT

According to sociologists, society is the product of a constant struggle between the forces of stability and change. Cooperation promotes stability, whereas conflict and competition upset the status quo. The net result is an ever-changing society. Keeping this perspective in mind, we shall discuss three important dimensions of the social environment: demographics, inequalities, and managing diversity. Each presents managers with unique and difficult challenges.

Demographics of the New Workforce

Demographics—statistical profiles of population characteristics—are a valuable planning tool for managers. Managers with foresight who study demographics can make appropriate adjustments in their strategic, human resource, and marketing plans. Selected demographic shifts reshaping the U.S. workforce are presented in Figure 3.1. (Other countries have their own demographic trends.) The projections in Figure 3.1 are not totally "blue-sky" numbers. They are based on people already born, most of whom are presently working. In short, the U.S. workforce demonstrates the following trends:

- *It is getting larger.* The U.S. labor force will continue to grow more rapidly than the national population. As the recession eases and employment improves, selective labor shortages will be a magnet for continued legal and illegal immigration.

- *It is becoming increasingly female.* Although women will still constitute slightly less than half of the U.S. civilian labor force, their share will grow faster than men's.

- *It is becoming more racially and ethnically diverse.* The white, non-Hispanic segment of the U.S. workforce will continue to be a shrinking majority, and Hispanics/Latinos have replaced African Americans as the second-largest segment. These figures simply mirror trends in the overall U.S. population: non-Hispanic whites down to a 60 percent majority by 2020 and Latinos becoming the majority by the end of the century.[4]

- *It is becoming older.* The median age of U.S. employees will continue to increase, with most vigorous growth for the 55-and-older group. Driving this shift is the aging post–World War II baby-boom generation: "In 2011, the bubble of 77 million baby boomers will begin turning 65. By 2050, the 65-and-over population will grow from 12% to 21% of the population, the U.S. Census Bureau predicts."[5] (Japan and Italy hit

demographics statistical profiles of human populations

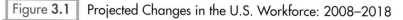

Figure **3.1**   Projected Changes in the U.S. Workforce: 2008–2018

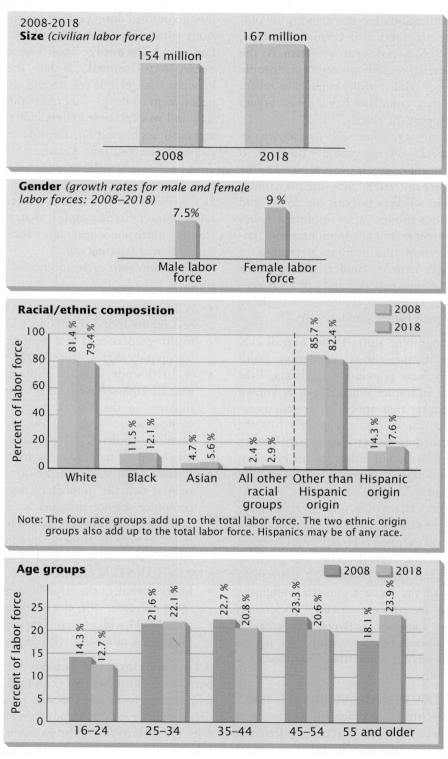

Note: The four race groups add up to the total labor force. The two ethnic origin groups also add up to the total labor force. Hispanics may be of any race.

Source: Data from U.S. Department of Labor, Bureau of Labor Statistics, "Overview of the 2008–18 Projections," *Occupational Outlook Handbook*, 2010–11 edition, **www.bls.gov/oco/oco2003.htm**.

the 20 percent threshold for citizens 65 and older back in 2008!)[6] This trend has major (some say troubling) implications for the viability of old-age assistance programs in developed countries, including the U.S. Social Security System. As the *Wall Street Journal* recently pointed out, "people are living longer while fertility rates have fallen. This means that countries have fewer young workers to support the elderly."[7]

- *It has growing age diversity.* As shown in Figure 3.1, the 25–34 age group is on track to become the second-largest age group in the U.S. labor force by 2018. This unique combination of more workers in both the 25–34 and 55-and-older age groups raises important issues regarding intergenerational communication, motivation, leadership, and training. According to human resource experts, "understanding of the needs, expectations, and demands of each generation will be crucial to creating a workforce development plan for the coming years."[8]

Parallel demographic shifts in the overall U.S. population have manufacturers redesigning products and targeting new population segments. Take Apple's iPad, for example: While Apple is known for creating products that appeal to younger generations, evidence shows that the elderly like the iPad as well. According to her blog, Marti Weston gave one to her 87-year-old father for his birthday. He soon declared it had become his "news and entertainment source."[9]

Similarly, products, services, and advertising are being tailored to the rapidly growing Hispanic/Latino population. A good example is Honey Nut Cheerios, America's best-selling cereal. The fast-growing Hispanic market has made Honey Nut Cheerios a success because of the cereal's cholesterol-fighting benefits and its sweetness—a Latino preference, according to the Latinum Network of Bethesda, Maryland.[10] Businesses cannot afford to ignore the $1 trillion in buying power the 50 million U.S. Hispanics/Latinos have.[11]

AMERICA'S EDUCATION AND WORKPLACE SKILLS CRISIS. Drew Greenblatt, president of Marlin Steel Wire in Baltimore, Maryland, recently purchased $700,000 worth of wire-bending robots to meet strong demand for his firm's custom stainless steel products. Unfortunately, says Greenblatt, the robots aren't in use because he doesn't have enough "smart people" to set them up.[12] So how can good-paying jobs go unfilled during one of America's worst recessions with millions of unemployed people eager to find work? The answer, according to manufacturing expert Jerry Jasinowski, is that "there's a mismatch between what people can do and what the economy needs them to do."[13] This raises the issue of education and workplace readiness in an era of increased technical sophistication. *Fortune* magazine's Geoff Colvin has noted that America's rising living standard has brought political and social stability. However, in order to maintain that high living standard, U.S. workers must be able to compete in the global labor market. To accomplish that, they need a constantly improving, world-class education, but American kids aren't getting one.[14]

Problems start early and persist in the education process:

- A 2009 National Assessment of Education Progress report found that "only about one-third of fourth-graders read at a 'proficient' level or better, up only slightly from 1992."[15]
- A 2010 study found slightly less than 69 percent of high school students earned a standard diploma in the normal four-year cycle. Those without a four-year diploma include 46 percent of black students, 44 percent of Latinos, and 49 percent of native Americans.[16]
- In the United States, the National Science Board reports that the number of degrees awarded in computer science declined by 27 percent from 2004 to 2007. Universities and high schools have failed to prepare students in science, technology, engineering, and math, leading to what some call America's STEM crisis.[17]
- Internationally, the United States ranks 12th (40.4 percent) for the "percentage of adults ages 25–34 with an associate degree or higher."[18] (Canada is number 1 with 55.8 percent.)

All this adds up to big problems for America's competitiveness in the global economy. Comprehensive education reform continues to muddle along with disappointing results. Meanwhile, employers are left with the task of filling the gaps with remedial education in basic reading, writing, and math; English language instruction; and general technical skills training. When done haphazardly, these costly and time-consuming programs distract managers from promptly getting products and services to market. Unfortunately, a survey of 217 employers led to this conclusion: New hires require readiness training, yet most companies rate their training programs as only moderately or somewhat successful.[19] The challenges for society and business are clear and urgent. Following are a couple of inspiring cases-in-point to demonstrate what can be done about this work-readiness crisis to improve education and job performance.

Computer-chip maker Intel's education initiatives show what can be done by progressive businesses to help improve education. One Intel program has sponsored technology training for more than 7 million teachers worldwide. Another involves donating $200 million in cash and equipment over ten years to upgrade science and math teaching. Yet another Intel program aims to train 100,000-plus elementary and secondary school science and math teachers in the United States over a three-year period.[20] (Visit www.intel.com/inside for details of these and other Intel education initiatives.) By enriching the talent pool of future employees, Intel is helping both itself and society in general.

Grand Rapids, Michigan-based Cascade Engineering Inc. had a hard time finding and hanging on to appropriately skilled workers. The maker of automotive parts and green products such as wind turbines had an employee turnover rate of 42 percent in 2000. After three tries with various welfare-to-work programs, Cascade found a winning formula for getting 40 of its 440 full-time employees off welfare rolls and onto the payroll. Its "Welfare-to-Career" program has yielded these lessons:

- *Provide a caseworker on-site by partnering with a state agency.*
- *Identify and remove barriers to employment, such as lack of transportation or child care.*
- *Deliver early training—onboarding—that includes information about the hidden behavioral rules of each socioeconomic class.*
- *Provide a career track that motivates entry-level employees to develop skills.*
- *Create a culture that respects the dignity of every employee.*[21]

Importantly, these comprehensive newcomer-friendly rules helped the *entire* company improve. By 2009, Cascade's turnover rate had plummeted to below 2 percent (for a savings of more than $3 million between 2000 and 2008).

MYTHS ABOUT OLDER WORKERS. As we have noted, the U.S. workforce is getting older. Those 55 and older are projected to be the largest age group in the U.S. workforce by 2018. Bolstering this trend is the ongoing redefinition of the concept of retirement, resulting from cultural shifts and a changing economic reality stemming from the recent recession. Because of their need for income—as well as a desire to stay busy and intellectually engaged—Baby Boomers at all economic levels now expect to continue working into their 70s.[22]

Older workers, defined by the U.S. Department of Labor as those aged 55 and up, tend to be burdened by negative stereotypes in America's youth-oriented popular culture. Researchers have identified and disproved five stubborn myths about older workers.

Myth. Older workers are less productive than the average worker.

Fact. Research shows that productivity does not decline with a worker's age. A recent report from AARP (formerly the American Association of Retired Persons) reported that older employees perform as well as younger workers in most jobs. This is confirmed by a recent survey conducted by the Center for Retirement Research, in which 56 percent of employers surveyed stated they believed that workers age 55+ are actually more productive than younger workers.

Myth. The costs of employee benefits for older workers outweigh any possible gain from hiring them.

Fact. According to AARP, the costs of health insurance do indeed increase with age, but health insurance is just one of a host of company-paid benefits that do not increase in price with the worker's age because the benefits are tied to length of service and level of salary. Gary M. Stern, writing in the Small Business Review, further counters this argument with reports that older workers tend to be more experienced, stable, reliable, and committed to the long term, all of which reduces a firm's employment expenses.

Myth. Older workers are more prone to illness and injury than younger workers.

Fact. Recent data from the CDC (Centers for Disease Control and Prevention) reveals that older workers have similar or lower rates for all injuries and illnesses combined compared with younger workers. AARP adds that older workers account for only 9.7 percent of all workplace injuries, while they make up a much larger percentage of the workforce.

Myth. Older workers are inflexible about the hours they will work.

Fact. A study conducted by the Boston College Center on Aging and Work found that 50 to 66 percent of older workers want "bridge jobs," meaning part-time work or short-term assignments, and the Bureau of Labor Statistics reports that a higher percentage of older workers are willing to work alternative work schedules than their younger counterparts.[23]

Like all employees, older workers need to be managed according to their individual abilities, not as members of a demographic group. Proactive steps need to be taken during diversity training to address any resentment younger employees might have as they compete with older workers for pay and promotions in leaner organizations. For their part, older employees need to become comfortable working with technically savvy teammates and younger bosses. Consider this recent advice to older workers: Even if younger colleagues are better at technology, and you think the old ways were better, hold those thoughts. Don't project them in "the way you talk, dress, or do business."[24] Older workers who integrate texting, Facebook, and tweets, for instance, into their work style demonstrate their commitment to lifelong learning.

Nagging Inequalities in the Workplace

Can the United States achieve full and lasting international competitiveness if a large proportion of its workforce suffers nagging inequalities?[25] Probably not. Unfortunately, women, minorities, and part-timers often encounter barriers in the workplace. Let's open our discussion by focusing on women, because all minorities share their plight to some degree.

UNDER THE GLASS CEILING. As a large and influential minority, women are demanding—and getting—a greater share of w orkplace opportunities. Women occupy 51 percent of the managerial

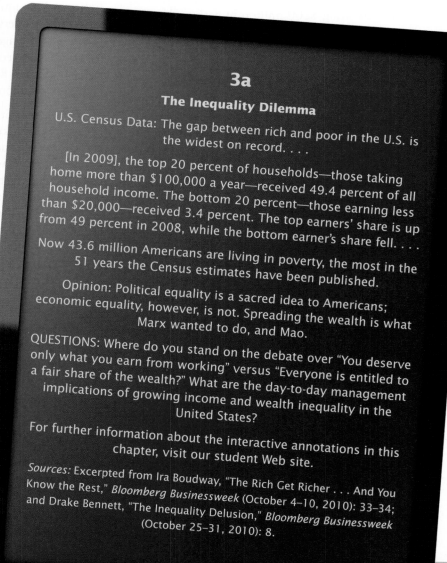

3a

The Inequality Dilemma

U.S. Census Data: The gap between rich and poor in the U.S. is the widest on record. . . .

[In 2009], the top 20 percent of households—those taking home more than $100,000 a year—received 49.4 percent of all household income. The bottom 20 percent—those earning less than $20,000—received 3.4 percent. The top earners' share is up from 49 percent in 2008, while the bottom earner's share fell. . . .

Now 43.6 million Americans are living in poverty, the most in the 51 years the Census estimates have been published.

Opinion: Political equality is a sacred idea to Americans; economic equality, however, is not. Spreading the wealth is what Marx wanted to do, and Mao.

QUESTIONS: Where do you stand on the debate over "You deserve only what you earn from working" versus "Everyone is entitled to a fair share of the wealth?" What are the day-to-day management implications of growing income and wealth inequality in the United States?

For further information about the interactive annotations in this chapter, visit our student Web site.

Sources: Excerpted from Ira Boudway, "The Rich Get Richer . . . And You Know the Rest," *Bloomberg Businessweek* (October 4–10, 2010): 33–34; and Drake Bennett, "The Inequality Delusion," *Bloomberg Businessweek* (October 25–31, 2010): 8.

Some Baby Boomers are working later in life to earn income, but others choose to continue working as a way to meet their fitness, social, and intellectual needs.

and professional positions in the U.S. workforce. Still, a large inequity remains. *Newsweek* recently summed up the situation: Data show that women with higher college GPAs earn 80 percent of what men do, and even women with MBAs earn less in their first job out of graduate school than their male counterparts. Motherhood has traditionally been the explanation for this pay gap, yet experienced, professional women without children also earn significantly less—on average, just 77 cents compared to one male dollar.[26]

In addition to suffering a wage gap, women (and other minorities) bump up against the so-called glass ceiling when climbing the managerial ladder.[27] "The glass ceiling is a concept popularized in the 1980s to describe a barrier so subtle that it is transparent, yet so strong that it prevents women and minorities from moving up in the management hierarchy."[28] It is not unique to the United States. Consider the situation in 2010: In the United States, *Fortune* 500 companies had 15 percent of their board seats filled by women, and 3 percent had female CEOS, while in Canada, *Financial Post* 500 companies had 14 percent of their board seats filled by women, and 4 percent had female CEOs. Of the 100 biggest companies on The London Stock Exchange, four had female CEOs.[29]

Why is there a glass ceiling? According to *Working Woman* magazine, women are being held back by a number of factors, including "the lingering perception of women as outsiders, exclusion from informal networks, male stereotyping and lack of experience."[30] Other research suggests women are too often placed in precarious leadership positions, where *anyone* would have a higher probability of failure.[31] (See Valuing Diversity for an inspiring program.)

Another force is also at work here, siphoning off some of the best female executive talent partway up the corporate ladder. Many women are leaving the corporate ranks to start their own businesses. According to the U.S. Small Business Administration, women-owned businesses total 9.1 million, employ 27.5 million people, and add $3.6 trillion dollars to the American economy.[32]

CONTINUING PRESSURE FOR EQUAL OPPORTUNITY. Persistent racial inequality is underscored by the fact that the unemployment rate for African Americans generally is about twice as high as that for whites during both good and bad economic times.[33] Women, African Americans, Hispanics/Latinos, Native Americans, the physically challenged, and other minorities who are overrepresented in either low-level, low-paying jobs or the unemployment line can be expected to press harder to become full partners in the world of work. Equal employment opportunity (EEO) and affirmative action are discussed in Chapter 10.

PART-TIMER PROMISES AND PROBLEMS. An increasing percentage of the U.S. labor force (about 17 percent) is now made up of contingent workers.[34] This "just-in-time" or "flexible" workforce includes a diverse array of part-timers, temporary workers, interns, on-call employees, and independent contractors. Some are part-timers because they want to be, while others work part time because they can't find a full-time job. Employers are relying more on part-timers for two basic reasons. First, because they are paid at lower rates and often do not receive the full range of employer-paid benefits, part-timers are

VALUING DIVERSITY

Another Crack in the Glass Ceiling

When [former Google executive] Sep Kamvar showed his newest batch of students how to color the text on their Web pages purple, they jumped up and squealed. . . . His students are 10- and 11-year-olds at Girls Prep Middle School, a New York City charter school that serves mostly low-income families.

Kamvar and his wife, Angie Schiavoni, recently launched CodeEd, a pilot program to introduce fifth-grade girls to computer science. Funded with $20,000 donated by the couple, it's the only such program in the U.S. geared to underprivileged preteen girls. "We're doing this because we saw a gender gap and a socioeconomic gap in computing," explains Kamvar. . . . Only 1 percent of girls who took the SAT in 2009 said they planned to major in the subject. This puts girls at a disadvantage in the global workplace, says Schiavoni, because "many of the new jobs being created are in the technology sector."

For Discussion From both practical business and ethical standpoints, why is it important to get more women working in computer science?

Source: Excerpted from Caroline Winter, "Innovators: Sep Kamvar, Angie Schiavoni," *Bloomberg Businessweek* (June 7–13, 2010): 39.

much less costly to employ than full-time employees. Second, as a flexible workforce, they can be let go when times are bad, without the usual repercussions of a publicized layoff. Starbucks and Costco are notable exceptions to this state of affairs.

On the downside, a comprehensive analysis of 38 studies involving 51,231 employees found lower "job involvement" among part-timers, compared with their full-time coworkers. (There were no significant differences in job satisfaction and organizational commitment, however.)[35] Also, critics warn of the risk of creating a permanent underclass of "disposable workers" burdened by low pay, inadequate health and retirement benefits, and low status.[36] Although some highly skilled professionals do enjoy good pay and greater freedom by working part time, most part-timers do not. The plight of the growing legion of part-timers could become a major social and political issue worldwide in the years to come.

Managing Diversity

The United States, a nation of immigrants, is becoming even more racially, ethnically, and culturally diverse. The evidence is compelling and controversial:

- Population figures from 2008 show that 12.5 percent were born outside the United States, close to the all-time high rate of 15 percent born outside the United States in the 1800s.[37]
- Babies born to illegal immigrants rose to 4 million in 2009, a roughly 50 percent increase from the 2.7 million born in 2003. These children, who are automatically given U.S. citizenship, total 5.4 percent of children under 18.[38]
- Whites represent less than 50 percent of the population in 303 counties in the United States, and 205 counties primarily in the South and West are nearing this mark.[39]
- America is gradually becoming a country of minorities. By 2050, whites are projected to represent 53 percent of the population, blacks 13.2 percent, Asians 8.9 percent, and Hispanics 24.3 percent.[40]
- With a population growth rate seven times greater than that of any other group, Hispanics/Latinos passed African Americans in 2003 to become the country's largest minority.[41]
- An estimated 12 million undocumented people are living in the United States illegally, with half from Mexico.[42]

Accordingly, the U.S. workforce is becoming more culturally diverse. For example, the employees at some Marriott Hotels speak 30 different languages.[43] Some Americans decry what they consider to be an invasion of their national, organizational, and cultural "territories." But many others realize that America's immigrants and minorities have always been a vitalizing, creative, and hardworking force. Progressive organizations are taking steps to better accommodate and more fully utilize America's more diverse workforce. **Managing diversity** is the process of creating an organizational culture that enables *all* employees, including women and minorities, to realize their full potential.[44]

MORE THAN EEO. Managing diversity builds on equal employment opportunity (EEO) and affirmative action programs (discussed in Chapter 10). EEO and affirmative action are necessary to get more women and minorities into the workplace. But getting them in is not enough. Comprehensive diversity programs are needed to create more *flexible* organizations where *everyone* has a fair chance to thrive and succeed. These programs need to include white males who have sometimes felt slighted or ignored by EEO and affirmative action; they, too, have individual differences (opinions, lifestyles, age, and schedules) that deserve fair accommodation. Managing diversity requires many of us to adjust our thinking. According to sociologist Jack McDevitt, "We don't want to have as a goal just tolerating people. We have to *value* them."[45] In addition to being the ethical course of action, managing diversity is a necessity; a nation cannot waste human potential and remain globally competitive.

PROMISING BEGINNINGS. Among the diversity programs in use today are the following:

- Teaching English as a second language
- Creating mentor programs (an experienced employee coaches and sponsors a newcomer)
- Providing immigration assistance
- Fostering the development of support groups for minorities
- Training minorities for managerial positions
- Training managers to value and skillfully manage diversity
- Encouraging employees to contribute to and attend cultural celebrations and events in the community
- Creating, publicizing, and enforcing discrimination and harassment policies
- Actively recruiting minorities[46]

Through mentoring programs, new employees learn the company's culture, and all employees learn to appreciate their diverse backgrounds and life situations more.

The scope of managing diversity is limited only by management's depth of commitment and imagination. For example, a supervisor learns sign language to communicate with a hearing-impaired employee. Or a married male manager attends a diversity workshop and becomes aware of the difficulties of being a single working mother. Perhaps a younger manager's age bias is blunted after reading a research report documenting that older employees tend to be absent less often and to have lower accident rates than younger ones.[47]

THE POLITICAL-LEGAL ENVIRONMENT

In its broadest terms, *politics* is the art (or science) of public influence and control. Laws are an outcome of the political process that differentiates good and bad conduct. An orderly political process is necessary because modern society is the product

managing diversity the process of helping all employees, including women and minorities, reach their full potential

of an evolving consensus among diverse individuals and groups, often with conflicting interests and objectives. Although the list of special-interest groups is long and is still growing, not everyone can have his or her own way. The political system tries to balance competing interests in a generally acceptable manner.

Ideally, elected officials pass laws that, when enforced, control individual and collective conduct for the general good. As we all know, however, variables such as hollow campaign promises, illegal campaign financing, and voter apathy throw sand into a democracy's political gears. Uninformed voters hamper the democratic process as well. In a recent survey of 1,000 American adults, 65 percent were unable to name a single U.S. Supreme Court justice—nine key people appointed by the president and approved by the U.S. Senate for life.[48] Managers, as both citizens and caretakers of socially, politically, and economically powerful organizations, have a large stake in the political-legal environment. Two key pressure points for managers in this area are the politicization of management and increased personal legal accountability.

DNY59/iStockphoto.com

The Politicization of Management

Prepared or not and willing or not, today's managers often find themselves embroiled in issues with clearly political overtones. Google is a good case in point. The comparatively young high-tech firm has had to quickly develop some political savvy in the face of calls for Web censorship around the world. Thus, Google asked U.S. trade officials to consider Internet restrictions as trade barriers, similar to tariffs. The move came in response to the increase in Net censorship in Asia and the Middle East, which hampers Google's business model that relies heavily on advertising revenues.[49] This sort of political climate has spurred the growth of a practice called *issues management*.

ISSUES MANAGEMENT. Issues management (IM) is the ongoing process of identifying, evaluating, and responding to relevant and important social, political, and reputation issues potentially impacting the organization's success.[50] According to a pair of experts on the subject, IM's purpose is mainly to reduce the unexpected effects of social and political change by alerting companies to possible threats and opportunities. It also triggers effective responses to issues through coordination and integration within the corporation.[51]

IM is not an exact science. It has been carried out in various ways in the name of strategic planning, public relations, community affairs, and corporate communications, among others. IM's main contribution to good management is its emphasis on systematic preparedness for social and political action. IM is more important than ever in the social media age where mischief and malicious news spread fast. Take this bizarre case, for example: A weak password ("happiness") allowed a hacker to enter Twitter's systems. The hacker then leaked the passwords used by Fox News and other high-profile users, such as President Obama. Some of these users' Twitter feeds were later filled with pornographic links and obscenities.[52] Reputation-destroying misinformation that goes viral requires a fast and precise IM response. (*Side lesson:* Avoid using common dictionary words for Web passwords.)

With this background in mind, let us turn our attention to three general political responses and four specific political strategies.

GENERAL POLITICAL RESPONSES. The three general political responses available to management can be plotted on a continuum, as illustrated in Figure 3.2. Managers who are politically inactive occupy the neutral zone in the middle and have a "wait and see" attitude. But few managers today can afford the luxury of a neutral political stance. Those on the extreme left of the continuum are politically active in defending the status quo and/or fighting government intervention. In contrast, politically

issues management ongoing process of identifying, evaluating, and responding to important social and political issues

Figure **3.2** Management's Political Response Continuum

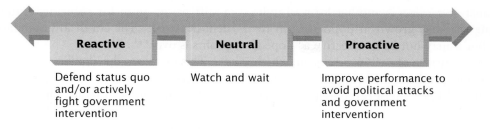

Reactive	**Neutral**	**Proactive**
Defend status quo and/or actively fight government intervention	Watch and wait	Improve performance to avoid political attacks and government intervention

active managers on the right end of the continuum try to identify and respond constructively to emerging political/legal issues. In recent years, more and more business managers have swung away from being reactive and have become proactive. Why? In short, they view prompt action as a way to avoid additional governmental regulation.

SPECIFIC POLITICAL STRATEGIES. Whether acting reactively or proactively, managers can employ four major strategies:[53]

1. *Campaign financing.* Although federal law has long prohibited U.S. corporations and labor unions from directly backing a specific candidate or party with the organization's name, funds, or free labor, legal loopholes are available for political spending. One way, broadened by a controversial 2010 U.S. Supreme Court decision, allows companies and unions to provide unlimited funding for campaign advertising in favor of or in opposition to federal candidates, provided the ads are independent of a candidate's political campaign.[54] It is too early to tell how the Court's decision, based on the principle of free speech, will play out, but critics worry about a political spending free-for-all by unions and cash-rich corporations.[55] Stay tuned.

Another established alternative involves forming political action committees (PACs) to solicit volunteer contributions from employees biannually for the support of preferred candidates and parties. Significantly, PACs are registered with the Federal Election Commission and are required to keep detailed and accurate records of receipts and expenditures. Some criticize corporate PACs for having too great an influence over federal politics. But an MIT study found no positive correlation between corporate political giving and subsequent profitability. The researchers

concluded that companies should spend their money in more productive ways.[56]

2. *Lobbying.* Historically, lobbying has been management's most popular and successful political strategy. Secret and informal meetings between hired representatives and key legislators in smoke-filled rooms have largely been replaced by a more forthright approach. Today, formal presentations by well-prepared company representatives are the preferred approach to lobbying for political support. For example, in a single day in Washington, DC, eBay's then-CEO Meg Whitman, accompanied by 51 eBay customers, conducted 36 political meetings in an attempt to get government understanding and support for their goal: keeping Internet sales free from taxation.[57] Despite reform legislation from the U.S. Congress intended to correct abuses, loopholes, and weak penalties for inappropriate gifts, corporate lobbyists remain a potent political force.[58]

3. *Coalition building.* In a political environment of countless special-interest groups, managers are finding that coalitions built around common rallying points are often necessary for political impact.

4. *Indirect lobbying.* Having learned a lesson from unions, business managers now appreciate the value of grassroots lobbying. Members of legislative bodies tend to be more responsive to the desires of their constituents than to those of individuals who vote in other districts. Employee and consumer letter-writing, telephone, and e-mail and social media campaigns are common. So, too, are television and print ads appealing to voters to contact their elected officials. For example, during the 2009 health care reform debate in Congress, pharmaceutical industry groups and companies spent $130 million in television ads to build public support for their positions.[59]

Advocacy advertising, the controversial practice of promoting a cause or point of view along with a product or service, is another form of indirect lobbying that has grown in popularity in recent years. But it may not be as effective as hoped, judging from a survey of 1,066 adults in which cause-supporting products with higher price tags appealed to only 14 percent of respondents.[60] What about you?

Increased Personal Legal Accountability

Recent changes in the political and legal climate have made it increasingly difficult for managers to take refuge in the bureaucratic shadows when a law has been broken. Managers in the United States who decide to take illegal courses of action stand a good chance of being held personally accountable in a court of law.

Things got even tougher in July 2002, when President George W. Bush signed the Sarbanes-Oxley Act into law. This sweeping corporate fraud bill, called SarbOx by many, garnered an unusually high degree of bipartisan support. The lawmakers were prodded into decisive action by public disgust over the fraud-tainted failures of corporate giants, including Enron, former "Big 5" accounting firm Arthur Andersen, WorldCom, and Adelphia. In addition to creating a federal board to oversee the accounting industry, the law increases penalties for accounting fraud and establishes a new felony with a stiff prison term for securities fraud. The president declared, "The era of low standards and false profits is over."[61]

This increases the likelihood of managers being held personally responsible for the illegal actions of their companies. Anyone who is skeptical about rich and powerful executives being held accountable for their misdeeds should consider this roster of prison inmates: Jeffrey Skilling, former Enron CEO (serving 24 years); Bernard Ebbers, former CEO of WorldCom (25 years); Dennis Kozlowski, former CEO of Tyco (up to 25 years); Sanjay Kumar, former CEO of Computer Associates (12 years); and champion Ponzi schemer Bernard Madoff (150 years).[62] Personal legal accountability for managerial misdeeds is evident in other countries as well. In China, the former head of an airport management company was recently executed for taking bribes.[63] And U.S. managers complain that SarbOx is too tough!

Political-Legal Implications for Management

Managers will continue to be forced into becoming more politically astute, whether they like it or not. Support appears to be growing for the idea that managers can and should try to shape the political climate in which they operate. But the vigilant media and a wary public can be expected to keep a close eye on the form and substance of managerial politics to ensure that the public interest is served. Managers who abuse their political power and/or engage in criminal conduct while at work will increasingly be held accountable.

Tougher standards and higher expectations in the United States are pushing law enforcement officials to hold business executives like now imprisoned Wall Street financier Bernard Madoff accountable for their actions like never before.

AP Photo/Louis Lanzano

advocacy advertising promoting a point of view along with a product or service

On the legal side, managers are attempting to curb the skyrocketing costs of litigation. Suing large companies with so-called deep pockets is a common practice in the United States, a country with more than 1 million lawyers. In a survey of large-company CEOs, 24 percent said litigation costs were their primary economic concern.[64] Indicative of the current legal climate is this recent news item: While following online directions on her mobile device, a pedestrian was hit by a car. She later filed a $100,000+ lawsuit against Google for providing a dangerous walking route.[65]

Okaaay, next case!

Not surprisingly, U.S. business leaders are pushing hard for tort (noncriminal) reform in which some sort of legislated cap is put on jury awards and damage claims.[66] Trial lawyers are pushing equally hard to squelch any such limitations, citing the need to protect the public. In the meantime, managers can better prepare their companies and, it is hoped, avoid costly legal problems by performing legal audits A legal audit looks at company operations in their entirety to find potential liabilities and legal problems.[67] For example, a company's job application forms and policy guidelines need to be carefully screened by human resource experts or lawyers to eliminate any questions that could trigger a discriminatory-hiring lawsuit. Another approach, called alternative dispute resolution (ADR), strives to curb courtroom costs by settling disagreements out of court through techniques such as arbitration and mediation. These traditional methods, plus newer methods involving mini-trial, summary jury trial, private judging, and regulatory negotiation, are used today. ADR also may involve variants and combinations of these methods.[68] As a technical point, a third-party arbitrator makes a binding decision, whereas a mediator helps the parties reach their own agreement.

THE ECONOMIC ENVIRONMENT

As we noted in Chapter 1, there is a close relationship between economics and management. Economics is the study of how scarce resources are used to create wealth and how that wealth is distributed. Managers, as trustees of our resource-consuming productive organizations, perform an essentially economic function. Sadly, economics is not a strong subject for the average American. In a nationwide survey by the University of Buffalo School of Management, "12th-graders answered only 52.3 percent of questions about personal finance and economics correctly."[69] A slight improvement over the 2002 results (50.2 percent of questions correctly answered) led the researcher to characterize U.S. high schoolers' knowledge of economics and finance as "dismal but improving."

Three aspects of the economic environment of management that deserve special consideration are jobs, business cycles, and the global economy.

The Job Outlook in Today's Service Economy, Where Education Matters

As in other important aspects of life, you have no guarantee of landing your dream job. However, as you move through college and into the labor force, one assumption is safe: you will most likely end up with a job in the service sector. Why? According to the U.S. Bureau of Labor Statistics (BLS), a continuation of the economic shift from producing goods to providing services is expected. In fact, service providers are expected to generate 14.5 million jobs between 2008 and 2018.[70] Also from the same BLS report is this employment projection relevant to the subject matter of this book:

> *Workers in management, business, and financial occupations plan and direct the activities of business, government, and other organizations. Their employment is expected to increase by 11 percent by 2018. These workers will be needed to help organizations navigate the increasingly complex and competitive business environment. A large portion of these jobs will arise in the management, scientific, and technical consulting industry sector. A substantial number, in addition, are expected in several other large or rapidly growing industries, including government, healthcare and social assistance, finance and insurance, and construction.*[71]

The traditional notion of the service sector as a low-wage haven of nothing but hamburger flippers

---

legal audit review of all operations to pinpoint possible legal liabilities or problems | alternative dispute resolution avoiding courtroom battles by settling disputes with less costly methods, including arbitration and mediation

and janitors is no longer valid. Well-paid doctors and dentists, lawyers, airline pilots, engineers, scientists, consultants, architects, and other professionals are all service-sector employees enjoying the fruits of a good education. BLS economists predict that the fastest growing occupations require a bachelor's degree. Likewise, the 20 occupations with the highest salaries require a bachelor's. Education is thus a key ingredient for a high-paying job.[72] Of course, you don't want to forget good-old networking when it comes to landing that dream job, as was the case with Minnie Ingersoll, a product manager at Google: Her mom saw a Google ad saying, "You're brilliant, we're hiring," and called Minnie, a Stanford graduate, who then decided to network with former classmates already employed at Google.[73] A solid educational foundation and networking skills are especially important in tough economic times.[74]

Coping with Business Cycles

The business cycle is the up-and-down movement of an economy's ability to generate wealth; it has a predictable structure but variable timing. Historical economic data from industrialized economies show a clear pattern of alternating expansions and recessions. In between have been peaks and troughs of varying magnitude and duration. According to Nobel Prize–winning economist Paul Samuelson, the four phases are like the changing seasons: "Each phase passes into the next. Each is characterized by different economic conditions. For example, during expansion we find that employment, production, prices, money, wages, interest rates, and profits are usually rising, with the reverse true in recession."[75]

Economic cycles are far more than fodder for academic discussions; they affect all of us one way or another. This has been especially true as the painful 2008–2010 "Great Recession" caused virtually everyone to revisit their priorities. For example, when *Money* magazine's Dan Kadlec recently asked his 20-year-old, a college student, what lessons the Great Recession had taught her, he expected her to shrug off the question. However, she explained that faculty cutbacks had forced the cancellation of a required class. Seeing how directly she was affected by this economic downturn made her realize she needed to learn to readily adapt to a shifting economic climate.

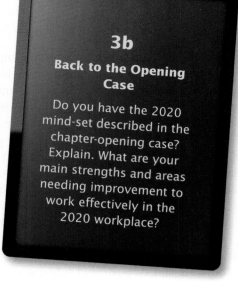

3b

Back to the Opening Case

Do you have the 2020 mind-set described in the chapter-opening case? Explain. What are your main strengths and areas needing improvement to work effectively in the 2020 workplace?

It showed her "the value of performing at work and of building a résumé," Kadlec added.[76] Managers need to adapt to the ups and downs of the economy as well.

CYCLE-SENSITIVE DECISIONS. Important decisions depend on the ebb and flow of the business cycle (see Figure 3.3). These decisions include ordering inventory, borrowing funds, increasing staff, and spending capital for land, equipment, and energy.

Timing is everything when it comes to making good cycle-sensitive decisions. Just as a baseball batter needs to start swinging before the ball reaches home plate, managers need to make appropriate cutbacks prior to the onset of a recession. Failure to do so, in the face of decreasing sales, leads to bloated inventories and idle productive resources—both costly situations. On the other hand, managers cannot afford to get caught short during a period of rapid expansion. Prices and wages rise sharply when everyone is purchasing inventories and hiring at the same time, and thus fueling inflation.

The trick is to stay slightly ahead of the pack. This is particularly true during recessions, when corporate strategy is tested to the fullest. Importantly, studies conclude that after a recession only 9 percent of firms are more effective and efficient.[77]

According to a leading management consultant those who are successful in a recession make systematic moves, not lucky gambles, to enhance their market positions and change the odds in favor of management.[78] (See, for example, Best Practices.)

business cycle the up-and-down movement of an economy's ability to generate wealth

Figure **3.3**   Business Cycles Affect Managerial Decisions

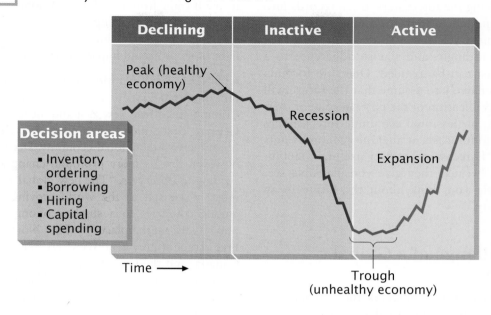

How Patricia Tate Took the Gamble out of Her Tribe's Casino Business

**BEST
PRACTICES**

Tate, 39, is vice president and chief financial officer at Casino Arizona and the recently-opened Talking Stick Resort [near Scottsdale].

There she has guided the businesses' finances through the modern-gaming industry's worst slump and oversaw the casino's $440 million investment in its new Talking Stick Resort, which opened in April [2010].

The casinos are operated by the Salt River Pima-Maricopa Indian Community, of which Tate is one of about 9,100 members.

"It's an honor to work for the tribe and give back to the community," she says.

She has been able to preserve jobs, despite falling revenue, through careful cash management and operating efficiencies. . . .

She also notes that the tribe was able to get the best prices on construction materials and the best-quality labor because it built the resort at a time when there were few other major construction projects.

For Discussion: Why is it so hard for most managers to make decisions out of sync with the general business cycle?

Source: Excerpted from Max Jarman, "Casino Finances Challenging for VP," *Arizona Republic* (June 4, 2010): D1, D4.

As mentioned repeatedly in this text, successful managers are *foresighted* rather than hindsighted. Accurate economic forecasts can be very helpful in this regard.

BENEFITING FROM ECONOMIC FORECASTS. Thanks to some widely publicized bad calls, economic forecasting has come under fire in recent years. A case in point: A survey conducted by the Federal Reserve Bank of Philadelphia predicted a 3.3 percent growth rate for 2001, but the economy shrank by 0.6 percent. This same group of survey respondents also predicted 0.1 percent growth in 2002, but growth reached a surprising 5 percent.[79] One wit chided economic forecasters by claiming they have predicted eight out of the last four recessions! How can managers get some value from the hundreds of economic forecasts they encounter each year?

A pair of respected forecasting experts recommends a *consensus approach*.[80] These experts urge managers to survey a wide variety of economic forecasts, taking the forecasters' track records into consideration, and to look for a consensus or average opinion. Cycle-sensitive decisions can then be made accordingly, and slavish adherence to a single forecast can be avoided. One sure formula for failure is naively to assume that the future will simply be a replication of the past. In spite of their imperfection, professional economic forecasts are better than no forecasts at all. One economist puts it this way: "Forecasters are very useful, in fact indispensable, because they give you plausible scenarios to help you think about the future in an organized way."[81]

The Challenge of a Global Economy

Nintendo's Wii game symbolizes the dynamic nature of today's truly globalized economy. *Fortune* magazine had an electronics expert disassemble a Wiimote, the system's remote-control device, and this is what he found: parts for the Japanese company's product were designed in Japan, the United States, Italy, and the Philippines; manufactured in the United States, Italy, Japan, Thailand, India, and Taiwan; and

assembled in China.[82] So where *did* the product come from? It came from the global economy.

Each of us is challenged to better understand the workings and implications of the global economy in light of its profound impact on our lives and work.

A SINGLE GLOBAL MARKETPLACE. Money spent on imported Japanese cars, French perfumes, Colombian coffee, New Zealand meat and produce, German beers, and Italian shoes may be evidence of an increasingly global economy. Deeper analysis, however, reveals more profound changes. First, according to observers, "The new global economy . . . must be viewed as the world moving from trade among countries to a single economy. One economy. One marketplace."[83] The North American Free Trade Agreement (NAFTA) among Mexico, Canada, and the United States, the 27-nation European Union, and the 153-nation World Trade Organization (WTO) represent steps toward that single global marketplace. Second, the size of the global economy has expanded dramatically, especially as billions of people from the former Soviet empire, China, India, Brazil, and elsewhere have begun to participate in the global marketplace. *Fortune* has called this "the most dramatic change in the geography of capitalism in history."[84]

This supersized container ship entering the Panama Canal from the Atlantic side is just a tiny cog in today's huge and growing global economy.

Margaret A. Sova

GLOBALIZATION IS PERSONAL. Economic globalization is a huge concept, stretching the limits of the imagination. For instance, try to grasp what it means that more than $1.5 trillion moves through the global banking network in a single day![85] Ironically, globalization is also a very personal matter affecting where we work, how much we're paid, what we buy, and how much things cost. Let us explore two personal aspects of the global economy.

1. *Working for a foreign-owned company.* One of the most visible and controversial signs of a global economy is the worldwide trend toward foreign ownership. Consider the case of Toyota Motor, for example. According to *Fortune* magazine's Global 500 list, it is the fifth-biggest company in the world, with over $204 billion in global sales and 320,590 employees.[86] Toyota's presence in the United States is huge: 28,783 direct employees; 163,880 indirect (dealer and supplier) employees; annual vehicle production of 870,570 units; $22.2 billion in purchases; and $18.3 billion invested in plants and equipment.[87] This sort of cross-border ownership raises fundamental questions. For instance, has the increase in foreign-owned companies in the United States been a positive or a negative? Economists have found evidence on the positive side. Gary Hufbauer, senior economist with the Institute for International Economics, reports that global companies are typically the most productive, hire the best workers in the countries they enter, and willingly pay a premium for those workers, often about 10 percent more than what local competitors are paying.[88]

A rigorous new study of differing management practices in 17 countries puts a sharper point on the matter. The researchers concluded that "foreign multinationals are better managed than domestic firms."[89] (More about this in Chapter 4.)

2. *Meeting world standards.* One does not have to work for a foreign-owned company to be personally affected by the global economy. Many people today complain of having to work harder for the same (or perhaps less) money. Whether they realize it or not, they are being squeezed by two global economic trends: higher quality and lower wages. The "offshoring" of jobs discussed in Chapter 1 is a major driver of these trends. Only companies striking the right balance between quality and costs can be globally competitive.

THE TECHNOLOGICAL ENVIRONMENT

Technology is a term that ignites passionate debates in many circles these days. Some blame technology for environmental destruction and cultural fragmentation. Others view technology as the key to economic and social progress. No doubt there are important messages in both perspectives. See Table 3.1 for technologies likely to have significant effects on our lives in the future.

3c
A Global Brand Quiz

Name the home country for each of these well-known brands.

Brand	Home country*
Nokia	_____
Lego	_____
Samsung	_____
Ericsson	_____
Adidas	_____

*See Chapter 3 endnote 103 for the correct answers and the results of a 1,000-student survey.[103]

QUESTIONS: When you buy something, is a product's country of origin more or less important than price and value? What implications does your answer have for the global economy and for the U.S. economy?

Source: Elizabeth Woyke, "Flunking Brand Geography" *Business Week* (June 18, 2007): 14.

| Table **3.1** | Science Fiction Is Becoming Reality with These Seven New Technologies |

- **Clean water** ("At least a billion people have access only to water contaminated by pathogens or pollution.") Stanford University researchers are developing an inexpensive filter that won't clog up. "The device, which uses a piece of cotton treated with nanomaterial inks, kills bacteria with electrical fields but uses just 20 percent of the power required by pressure-driven filters."
- **Plastic solar cells** "The new photovoltaics use tiny solar cells embedded in thin sheets of plastic to create an energy-producing material that is cheap, efficient, and versatile."
- **Printable mechatronics** Researchers are "developing processes that adapt ink-jet printing technology to build ready-to-use products, complete with working circuitry, switches, and movable parts."
- **Memory drugs** These drugs aim to help people with Alzheimer's and boost healthy people's memories by enhancing the brain's neural connections and functions.
- **Microfluidic testing** "Microfluidics is the science of moving fluids through tiny channels the thickness of a human hair. In microfluidic tests, blood, saliva, or urine samples are analyzed after coming into contact with tiny amounts of a chemical reagent."
- **Micro-opticals** Combining the functions of several present-day chips on one integrated optical chip will make telecommunication faster and less expensive.
- **Software radio** The goal of this new software is to create wireless communication devices that will work on all mobile networks—anywhere, anytime.

Sources: First item adapted and quoted from Katherine Bourzac, "Clean Water for the Developing World," *MIT Technology Review* (September 8, 2010), **www.technologyreview.com/computing/26232/?a=f**. Remaining items adapted and quoted from G. Pascal Zachary, Om Malik, David Pescovitz, and Matthew Maier, "Seven New Technologies That Change Everything," *Business 2.0,* 5 (September 2004): 82–90.

For our purposes, **technology** is defined as all the tools and ideas available for extending the natural physical and mental reach of humankind. A central theme in technology is the practical application of new ideas, a theme that is clarified by the following distinction between science and technology: "Science is the quest for more or less abstract knowledge, whereas technology is the application of organized knowledge to help solve problems in our society."[90] We're seeing that technology is facilitating the evolution of the industrial age into the information age, just as it once enabled the agricultural age to evolve into the industrial age. Development of infrastructure technologies led to a change from an agricultural to a manufacturing economy. Now the seismic shift is from an electromechanical to a computational infrastructure, according to Cornell's Stephen Barley.[91] Consequently, *information* has become a valuable strategic resource. Organizations that use appropriate information technologies to get the right information to the right people at the right time will enjoy a competitive advantage (Internet and social media strategies are discussed in Chapter 7).

Two aspects of technology with important implications for managers are the innovation process and *intra*preneurship.

The Innovation Process

New technology comes into being through the **innovation process**, the systematic development and practical application of a new idea.[92] According to *Bloomberg Businessweek*'s 2010 list of the "50 Most Innovative Companies," Apple and Google were numbers 1 and 2 for the second straight year. Consistency was the primary reason for Apple's number 1 ranking, and the consistency of these products has dramatically altered demand for digital technology. For example, the iPad has shifted the market away from the netbook and the laptop.[93]

A great deal of time-consuming work is necessary to develop a new idea into a marketable product or service. And many otherwise good ideas do not become technologically feasible, let alone marketable and profitable. According to one innovation expert, it takes 20 to 25 ideas to result in one

technology all the tools and ideas available for extending the natural physical and mental reach of humankind |
innovation process the systematic development and practical application of a new idea

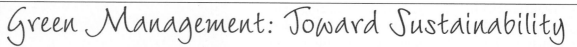

Green Management: Toward Sustainability

Here Comes Biodegradable Plastic

Only 7% of the plastic Americans consume gets recycled. The bulk is thrown into landfills or, worse, into our rivers, lakes, and oceans, where fish consume toxins that attach to the plastic. Then we consume the fish. . . .

[Metabolix CEO] Richard Eno . . . thinks he can help fix the problem. His solution? Making plastic out of plants. Plastic products made partly or wholly of plant matter already exist. But until now no one has been able to make a 100% bioplastic that is durable, stands up to extreme heat—and is biodegradable.

[The Cambridge, Mass., company] . . . has genetically engineered a microbe that eats sugar from corn and generates a plastic-like molecule called PHA. The plastic will after a few months decompose in water or soil and is so pure that you can throw containers into your backyard compost heap, where it will degrade into mulch for your vegetable garden.

For Discussion: Relative to the three-step innovation process in Figure 3.4, what challenges lie ahead for Metabolix? Are you willing to pay more for a plastic product that is biodegradable? How much more? 5 percent? 10 percent? Even more? Why?

Source: Excerpted from Brian Dumaine, "Feel-Good Plastic," *Fortune* (May 3, 2010): 36.

successful product, and only one out of every 10 to 15 new products becomes a top seller.[94] Nowhere is this uphill battle more apparent than in pharmaceutical research and development: Scientists screen countless chemicals against disease targets, and typically find that most compounds are unsatisfactory. Pfizer spends $152 million a week funding discovery projects that almost always fail.[95]

A better understanding of the innovation process can help improve management's chances of turning new ideas into profitable goods and services (see Green Management: Toward Sustainability).

A THREE-STEP PROCESS. The innovation process has three steps (see Figure 3.4). First is the conceptualization step, when a new idea occurs to someone. Development of a working prototype is the second step, called **product technology**. This involves actually creating a product that will work as intended.

The third and final step is developing a production process to create a profitable relationship among quantity, quality, and price. This third step is labeled **production technology**. Successful innovation depends on the right combination of new ideas, product technology, and production technology. A missing or deficient step can ruin the innovation process.

INNOVATION LAG. The time it takes for a new idea to be translated into satisfied demand is called **innovation lag**. The longer the innovation lag, the longer society must wait to benefit from a new idea. For example, fax machines came into wide use in the early 1990s. But the fax concept was patented by a Scottish clockmaker named Alexander Bain in 1843—an innovation lag of nearly a century and a half.[96] Over the years, the trend has been toward shorter innovation lags. Consider CEO Steve Jobs's story about the birth of the Apple iPhone: He wanted to develop a phone that everyone loved. As Jobs explained, the goal was to create a new phone that would be so indispensable that "you couldn't imagine going anywhere without it." After a three-year innovation lag, from concept to marketplace, Apple had a hit on its hands.[97]

| Figure **3.4** | The Three-Step Innovation Process |

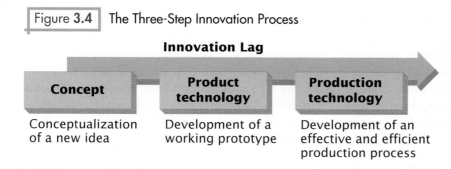

Innovation Lag

Concept	Product technology	Production technology
Conceptualization of a new idea	Development of a working prototype	Development of an effective and efficient production process

product technology second stage of the innovation process, involving the creation of a working prototype | production technology third stage of the innovation process, involving the development of a profitable production process | innovation lag time it takes for a new idea to be translated into satisfied demand

SHORTENING INNOVATION LAG. Reducing innovation lags should be a high priority for modern managers. Innovative companies generally rely on two sound management practices: *goal setting* and *empowerment*. These practices create the sense of urgency necessary for speedier innovation. Medtronic, the Minnesota-based leader in manufacturing heart pacemakers, uses goal setting skillfully. A powerful message is sent to its 25,000-plus employees worldwide about promptly getting new ideas to market when top management restates that the firm's objective is to have new products generate 70 percent of sales.[98] That is indeed a bold commitment.

Empowerment, discussed in Chapter 14, involves pushing decision-making authority down to levels where people with the appropriate skills can do the most good. Software giant Microsoft is strong in this regard, as illustrated by the following story told by the firm's now-retired chief operating officer.

> I was in a meeting where Bill Gates was quizzing a young manager—dressed in cutoffs, sandals, and a well-worn Microsoft T-shirt—about a new product proposal. After the meeting, I asked Bill, for whom this had been the first significant briefing on the product, what the next step would be. Would the manager prepare a memo summarizing the arguments, something top management could review before suggesting modifications to his proposal and granting final approval? Bill looked at me and smiled. "No, that's it. The key decisions got made," he said. "Now his group better hustle to implement things—or else."[99]

Another step in the right direction is a practice called *concurrent engineering*. Also referred to as parallel design or cross-functional teamwork, **concurrent engineering** is a team approach to product design. Such an approach lets research, design, production, finance, and marketing specialists have a direct say in the product design process from the very beginning. This contrasts with the traditional, and much slower, practice of having a product move step-by-step from research to design, from design to manufacturing, and so on down the line toward the marketplace. The time to hear about possible

marketing problems is while a product is still in the conceptualization stage, not after it has become a warehouse full of unsold goods.

Promoting Innovation Through Intrapreneurship

When we hear someone called an entrepreneur, we generally think of a creative individual who has risked everything while starting his or her own business. Indeed, as we saw in Chapter 1, entrepreneurs are a vital innovative force in the economy. A lesser-known but no less important type of entrepreneur is the so-called intrapreneur.

Gifford Pinchot, author of the book *Intrapreneuring*, defines an **intrapreneur** as an employee who takes personal "hands-on responsibility" for pushing any type of innovative idea, product, or process through a large organization. Pinchot calls intrapreneurs "dreamers who do." But unlike traditional entrepreneurs, who tend to leave the organizational

---

3d
Advice for Future Intrapreneurs

Among Gifford Pinchot's ten commandments for intrapreneurs are the following:

- "Come to work each day willing to be fired."
- "Do any job needed to make your project work, regardless of your job description."
- "Remember it is easier to ask for forgiveness than for permission."

QUESTIONS: How can these ideas enhance innovation in large organizations? Is this advice a formula for career success or sudden unemployment?

Source: Excerpted from Gifford Pinchot III, *Intrapreneuring: Why You Don't Have to Leave the Corporation to Become an Entrepreneur* (New York: Harper & Row, 1985), p. 2.

---

concurrent engineering team approach to product design involving specialists from all functional areas, including research, production, and marketing | intrapreneur an employee who takes personal responsibility for pushing an innovative idea through a large organization

Fionline digitale Bildagentur GmbH/Alamy

Apple—consistently considered one of the most forward-thinking technology companies—claims it sold more than 3 million of its innovative iPad devices in the first 80 days on the market.

confines to pursue their dreams, intrapreneurs strive for innovation *within* existing organizations. Intrapreneurs tend to have a higher need for security than entrepreneurs, who strike out on their own. They pay a price for being employees rather than owners. Pinchot explains:

> Corporate entrepreneurs [or intrapreneurs], despite prior successes, have no capital of their own to start other ventures. Officially, they must begin from zero by persuading management that their new ideas are promising. Unlike successful independent entrepreneurs, they are not free to guide their next ventures by their own intuitive judgments; they still have to justify every move.[100]

Kathleen Synnott, a division marketing manager for Pitney Bowes Inc., is the classic intrapreneur. After

seeing the potential of the versatile new Mail Center 2000, a computerized mail-handling and mail-stamping machine, Synnott became its enthusiastic champion. Just two things stood in her way: change-resistant managers and skeptical customers. "There were naysayers who didn't think we were ready," says Synnott, but the executives quickly changed their tune when she conducted more than 20 technical simulations to ensure that customers liked the new product.[101]

If today's large companies are to achieve a competitive edge through innovation, they need to foster a supportive climate for intrapreneurs like Synnott. According to experts on the subject, an organization can foster intrapreneurship if it does four things:

- Focuses on results and teamwork
- Rewards innovation and risk taking
- Tolerates and learns from mistakes
- Remains flexible and change-oriented[102]

Our discussions of creativity, participative management, and organizational cultures in later chapters contain ideas about how to encourage intrapreneurship of all types.

SUMMARY

1. Demographically, the U.S. workforce is becoming larger, older, more culturally diverse, and increasingly female. Remedial education programs are needed to improve the quality of the U.S. workforce. Researchers have disproved persistent myths that older workers are less productive and more accident-prone than younger coworkers.

2. America's education system has major problems at all levels. Many students simply do not have the basic reading, writing, math, and technical skills needed in today's technically sophisticated workplaces. This puts the United States at a competitive disadvantage in the global economy. When managers must devote time and money to remedial education and training for general work skills new hires should already possess, it takes longer to get marketable goods and services out the door. Educators and companies urgently need to enrich the U.S. labor pool.

3. The persistence of opportunity and income inequalities (and the so-called glass ceiling) among women and minorities is a strong stimulus for change. With part-timers playing a greater role in the U.S. workforce, there is genuine concern about creating a disadvantaged underclass of employees. Managing-diversity programs attempt to go a step beyond equal employment opportunity. The new goal is to tap *every* employee's *full* potential in today's diverse workforce.

4. Because of government regulations and sociopolitical demands from a growing list of special-interest groups, managers are becoming increasingly politicized. More and more believe that if they are going to be affected by political forces, they should be more active politically. Some organizations rely on issues management to systematically identify, evaluate, and respond to important social and political issues. Managers can respond politically in one of three ways: by being reactive, neutral, or proactive. Four political strategies that managers have found useful for pursuing active or reactive political goals are campaign financing, lobbying, coalition building, and indirect lobbying. There is a strong trend toward managers being held personally accountable for the misdeeds of their organizations. Alternative dispute resolution tactics such as arbitration and mediation can help trim management's huge litigation bill.

5. Managers can make timely decisions about inventory, borrowing, hiring, and capital spending during somewhat unpredictable business cycles by taking a consensus approach to economic forecasts. Business is urged to compete actively and creatively in the emerging global economy. By influencing jobs, prices, quality standards, and wages, the global economy affects virtually *everyone*. Multinational companies have been found to be better managed than domestic firms, thus they are more profitable and can pay more.

6. Consisting of conceptualization, product technology, and production technology, a healthy innovation process is vital to technological development. Innovation lags must be shortened. An organizational climate that fosters intrapreneurship can help. An intrapreneur is an employee who champions an idea or innovation by pushing it through the organization.

TERMS TO UNDERSTAND

Demographics, p. 66
Glass ceiling, p. 71
Contingent workers, p. 71
Managing diversity, p. 73
Issues management, p. 74
Advocacy advertising, p. 76

Legal audit, p. 77
Alternative dispute resolution, p. 77
Business cycle, p. 78
Technology, p. 82
Innovation process, p. 82

Product technology, p. 83
Production technology, p. 83
Innovation lag, p. 83
Concurrent engineering, p. 84
Intrapreneur, p. 84

ACTION LEARNING EXERCISE

CRYSTAL BALL GAZING

Instructions: Read these predictions from *The Futurist* magazine and rate how probable each is, according to the scale below. (*Note:* Use the year 2020 if a specific time frame is not mentioned.)

No chance									Virtually guaranteed	
0%	10%	20%	30%	40%	50%	60%	70%	80%	90%	100%

Prediction   **Probability of occurrence**

1. **Globalization could make foods less safe to eat.** As more   _____
   food is imported from far-flung local producers, national
   food-safety standards will become harder to enforce.
   Growing demand for fresh foods year-round makes
   refrigeration and other safe-transport issues more
   of a concern.

2. **Falling language barriers could spur more travel.** Automated   _____
   translation systems could enable most of the world's people
   to communicate directly with one another—each speaking
   and hearing in his or her own language—by about 2020.

3. **No more textbooks?** Printed and bound textbooks may   _____
   disappear as more interactive coursework goes online.

4. **"Internet universities" could lead to the demise of   _____
   traditional institutions.** Web-linked education services that
   offer franchised software and "college-in-a-box" courses
   from superstar teachers could lead to educational monopolies.
   Such "virtual" universities would have rigidly standardized
   curricula that undersell traditional courses in brick-and-mortar
   institutions.

5. **The era of cheap oil is NOT over.** Not only is the world   _____
   not running out of oil, but prices are likely to fall again
   and remain around $20 per barrel for the next decade.
   Reason: The current high prices make intensive exploration
   and development of new oil sources more attractive, thus
   ultimately increasing supply and lowering prices.

6. **Water shortages will become more frequent and severe.**   _____
   Most of the major cities in the developing world will
   face severe water shortages in the next two decades, as
   will one-third of the population of Africa. By 2040, at
   least 3.5 billion people will run short of water—almost
   10 times as many as in 1995—and by 2050, two-thirds
   of the world's population could be living in regions
   with chronic, widespread shortages of water.

7. **Tissue engineers may one day grow a "heart in a bottle."**   _____
   Using a fibrous "scaffold" that is seeded with stem cells,
   researchers could coax the cells to grow into the needed
   organ. Skin and cartilage have already been grown this

way. In the future, organ generation could help the tens of thousands of patients in need of organ transplants, predicts Vladimir Mironov, chief scientific officer with Cardiovascular Tissues Technology, Inc.

8. **Nanomachines will enhance our brains.** Nanocomputers may soon be placed inside human brains to enhance memory, thinking ability, visualization, and other tasks, according to futurist consultant Michael Zey, author of *The Future Factor*. Technologies will also be developed that allow us to connect our brains to a computer and either download or upload data.

9. **Touch-sensitive robots may make virtual reality more realistic.** The ability to collect and transmit tactile data—such as the way it feels to kick a soccer ball—could add to humans' ability to experience events.

10. **Hardware will soften up.** Instead of pounding on hard, plastic keyboards to do your computing, you'll soon be able to gently caress soft electronic fabrics. Among potential applications for smart textiles: tablecloths with piano keyboards and furniture slipcovers with TV remote controls.

Source: Originally published in the November–December 2001 issue of *The Futurist*. Used with permission from the World Future Society, 7910 Woodmont Avenue, Suite 450, Bethesda, Maryland 20814. Telephone: 301-656-8274; Fax: 301-951-0394; **www.wfs.org**

FOR CONSIDERATION/DISCUSSION

1. When you compare your ratings with those of others, do you envision things changing more rapidly or more slowly than they do? What does this imply about the way you, as a manager, would tend to deal with organizational and external changes?

2. What, if any, potentially profitable business ideas do you see in any of these predictions? Explain.

3. What are two or three of your own ten-year predictions for our sociocultural, political-legal, economic, or technological future?

4. What needs to be done to prepare for two or three selected predictions from *The Futurist*'s list (or from your own predictions)?

ETHICS EXERCISE

 DO THE RIGHT THING

SHOULD AN EMPLOYER TELL A MUSLIM WOMAN NOT TO WEAR A HEAD SCARF?

College sophomore Hani Khan had worked for three months as a stockroom clerk at a Hollister Co. clothing store in San Francisco when she was told the head scarf she wears in observance of Islam violated the company's "look policy."

The policy instructs employees on clothing, hair-styles, makeup and accessories they may wear to work. When supervisors told Khan she had to remove the scarf, known as a hijab, to work at the store, she refused on religious grounds. A week later, she says, she was fired.

. . . Khan filed a federal job discrimination complaint against Hollister and its parent company, Abercrombie & Fitch. She is among a growing number of Muslim women who are filing complaints of discrimination at work, in businesses or in airports.

Sources: Excerpted from Marisol Bello, "Controversy Shrouds Scarves," *USA Today* (April 15, 2010): 3A.

What are the ethical implications of the following interpretations?

1. Appearances are important in face-to-face interactions with customers, so employers need to specify and enforce dress and behavior codes. Any exceptions?

2. This is a grave religious insult, akin to making a devout Christian employee remove a necklace or pin with a cross symbol or telling a devout Jewish employee to remove a necklace with a Star of David or yarmulke (a skullcap worn by Orthodox Jewish men).

3. Reasonable dress codes can be enforced that permit religiously significant clothing and symbols. Specifics?

4. Your own ethical interpretation?

MANAGERS-IN-ACTION VIDEO CASE STUDY

EVO (FORMERLY KNOWN AS EVOGEAR)
A Borderless Marketplace

"evo explores the collaboration between culture and sport by seamlessly joining art, music, streetwear, skateboarding, snowboarding, skiing and wakeboarding." This quote from the evo Web site describes this Seattle, Washington-based business perfectly. The only element it leaves out is the growing company's international component. In this video, Bryce Phillips discusses his strategies to compete in what he describes as a global environment and borderless marketplace. He shares his plans for growth, expansion, and diversification, all in the context of the global marketplace. Phillips also mentions some of the challenges evo faces operating in the global economy. There are financial, political, and technological challenges that create another layer of complexity. The video begins with Phillips describing a ski trip to Japan where he had a chance encounter with evo customers from around the world.

For more information about evo, visit its Web site: www.evo.com/.

Before watching the video, answer the following questions:

1. Why is it important for managers to understand business cycles and the global economy?

2. What impact does the global economy have on companies and their labor force?

3. How does a borderless marketplace (economic globalization) affect you personally?

After watching the video, answer the following questions:

4. Although only about 5 percent of evo's sales are shipped outside the United States, the international component of its business impacts its management team. If you were the manager of evo's customer service team, what factors would you consider in setting your employees up for success?

5. How has technology helped evo grow, and what challenges has it created?

6. What do you think Bryce Phillips meant when he said, "Everything we are doing is connected globally"?

7. Is the statement above true for all U.S.-based companies, or just companies like evo? Explain why or why not.

CLOSING CASE

HOW WAL-MART WON CHICAGO

In a retail desert on the South Side of Chicago, amid vacant lots and signs promoting "affordable bankruptcy," sits a highly contested 200-acre plot that's the future of Wal-Mart. The company famous for low prices and high growth is nearly tapped out in the sticks and suburbs. Today, just 47 of its 4,300 Wal-Mart and Sam's Club stores are in big cities, and most of those are in Dallas and Houston. Urban America is the company's last frontier.

Since 2006 a single Wal-Mart has been homesteading in Austin, a mostly African American Chicago community with an unemployment rate of 40 percent, its alderman says. Now the company wants to put two dozen more stores in the city, including a 145,000-square-foot Supercenter on that 200-acre plot. In an area ravaged by poverty and desperate for the 400 jobs the Supercenter would provide, you'd think this would have been a slam dunk. It was not.

After the first Chicago Wal-Mart opened, unions and community organizations successfully lobbied the city council to pass an ordinance requiring Wal-Mart and other big box retailers to pay at least $10 an hour, with benefits. The legislation infuriated Wal-Mart and its chief advocate, Mayor Richard M. Daley. In response, Daley, the country's longest-tenured big-city mayor, exercised his first and only veto, then watched labor spend $3 million to elect a cadre of pro-union aldermen to the city council.

The mayor looked outside the city limits and saw that unions hadn't tried to stop Wal-Mart from operating in the suburbs. "Why didn't the unions object in the 'burbs? Suburbs are flooded with those stores," the mayor says. As for the argument that small businesses in the city would be imperiled, "go to New York and see all the small stores which have closed up. It's not because of Wal-Mart. It's because people are not spending." Daley also says Wal-Mart's management "got caught up in a national thing" by being too sensitive to attacks from unions.

The open warfare between labor and Wal-Mart showed no signs of ending until the recession forced both sides to reconsider. Chicago's political leaders realized the city couldn't continue to lose sales tax dollars to big boxes in the suburbs while failing to embrace the jobs offered by the Wal-Marts of the world. Wal-Mart had to feed the growth monster to keep shareholders happy. So on May 3 [2010] an unprecedented informal negotiation between company executives and labor leaders was held near O'Hare International Airport, according to three people who attended. The executives joked that Sam Walton would be turning in his grave if he knew about it, though the meeting itself hardly bridged the trust gap between the sides; the unionists, according to attendees, were required to sign confidentiality agreements, which they did.

With the door to rapprochement open a crack, Wal-Mart executives met Daley at a U.S. Conference of Mayors gathering last month [June 2010] in Oklahoma City to tell him about a "transformational" strategy. To win over Chicago, the company would build stores of various sizes, double its community spending to $20 million over five years, and ensure union construction of stores in the Chicago metropolitan area.

Starting wages were the final sticking point. First Wal-Mart signaled it would pay $8.75, or 50 cents more than the new Illinois minimum wage. When warned on the eve of a critical June 24 [2010] council vote that Wal-Mart was going to lose the Supercenter, negotiators agreed to a minimum 40 cents hourly hike after an employee's first year of service. Wal-Mart won't confirm any such deal, but according to union leaders, aldermen, and the mayor, the 45-0 council vote in favor was premised on those points. "I'm nervous about the camel's nose inside the tent," says Joe Moore, an alderman and Wal-Mart critic. "It's not a vote that was taken without mixed feelings. But the compromise on wages changed my vote."

Ultimately, Wal-Mart cracked Chicago by presenting a smart package of incentives and highlighting the lack of retail in the poorest communities, notably the absence of Chicago's two unionized supermarket chains, Jewel and Dominick's. The company may have blinked on wages—but so did labor, accepting an hourly figure it would have scoffed at a year ago. Everybody wins.

Except, not really. While unions were reflexively arguing that big box retailers are exploitative, Wal-Mart didn't endure much suffering. The unemployed did. So did shoppers on a budget. On a Monday trek to Chicago's current Wal-Mart, the parking lot in front of the store was packed by 10:30 a.m. Van Gooden, 56, a community representative for a nonprofit group, happily showed off his purchase: a white, button-down polo shirt slashed to $3.29 from an initial $12. Asked about Wal-Mart's impact on the impoverished ward, he said: "It's all about jobs and price."

For Discussion:

1. What role did demographics play in this case? Explain.

2. What specific mix of political and economic factors made Wal-Mart's job especially difficult in this case?

3. Could Wal-Mart have handled the situation better? Explain how.

4. Generally speaking, do you consider Wal-Mart to be a corporate "good guy," "bad guy," or some combination of the two? Explain your position.

Source: James Warren, "How Wal-Mart Won Chicago," *Bloomberg Businessweek* (July 19–25, 2010): 37.

4

International Management and Cross-Cultural Competence

"I've always thought of travel as a university without walls"[1]
—ANITA RODDICK, FOUNDER OF THE BODY SHOP

The Changing Workplace

CHINA MYTHS, CHINA FACTS

Chinese business culture is unique, but not in all the ways outsiders tend to assume. To identify the most common myths, we interviewed dozens of North American and European expats ["expatriots" who work in a foreign country] as well as some Chinese managers now working in the West, all of whom have spent at least three years doing business in China. Our research uncovered three principal myths, perpetuated informally through stereotypes and formally through management-training programs.

Anyone working with the Chinese will find a multifaceted, fast-changing culture. As one respondent notes, managers can tap Eastern and Western strengths alike by learning the nuances of both business cultures and developing the flexibility to work in either one. "The Chinese will often pop in to see you with no appointment," says one executive. "I've learned I can do this, too. If I have 30 minutes to spare, I just make a quick call from a taxi and visit someone working in the area."

MYTH 1: COLLECTIVISM

REALITY: INDIVIDUALISM

Wei Chen, a Chinese manager in Paris's luxury goods sector, attributes the rise in individualism to citizens' suppression for many generations: "As a child I was punished for stepping out of the box and told to 'be average.' But we have left this mentality with a passion. In China, we are so eager to move ahead. Westerners often feel our style is pushy and aggressive." An executive at a Canadian pharmaceutical company points out, "There is an intense self-interest [in China]—more important than company, community, or nation. It is like nothing I have experienced in the West. The U.S. is generally considered the most individualistic part of the world, but it has nothing on China." Interview subjects cited the Cultural Revolution, the one-child policy, and mass migration to big cities as factors in the unraveling collective spirit.

The part of the myth that's true: Decisions are often made in groups, and the Chinese are highly skilled at working in teams.

MYTH 2: LONG-TERM DELIBERATION

REALITY: REAL-TIME REACTION

Managers unanimously indicated that the speed of decision making and execution in China is extraordinary compared with the West, where "we spend time trying to predict the future and getting it wrong," says Frédéric Maury, a French executive in technical services. "In China no one thinks about the future." That's hyperbole, perhaps, but a manager who has worked for the World Bank in China for a decade agrees with the sentiment, saying that ad hoc logistics are quite common but amazingly well executed. "I've attended dozens if not hundreds of workshops in China, and not one has gone according to plan. Things change the night before: speakers, topics, even venues. But it all always ends up working out fine."

The part of the myth that's true: Business relationships and government policies are both built for the long term.

MYTH 3: RISK AVERSION

REALITY: RISK TOLERANCE

"In the West we like to debate something, print it out, debate it again, do some analysis," says British logistics executive Michael Drake. "But in China it's, 'Right, we've decided, boom, off we go!'" Many participants believe the appetite for risk is tied to growth. Edith Coron, a French intercultural consultant and coach, says, "In an environment where GDP is growing at over 10% a year, it's understandable that the level of entrepreneurship and risk taking should be so high." Chinese manager Wei Chen confirms, "We don't want to lose a single minute. We have a lot of confidence, and we are very comfortable with risk."

The part of the myth that's true: Chinese workers often hesitate to give individual opinions or brainstorm openly when more-senior people are present.

Source: Erin Meyer and Elisabeth Yi Shen, "China Myths, China Facts," *Harvard Business Review*, 88 (January–February 2010): 24.

Learning more about China is to know more about 20 percent of the world's population and a fast-growing economy responsible for 10 percent of the world's exports.[2] As documented in Chapters 1 and 3, striking evidence of the modern global marketplace is everywhere today, especially in the form of goods made in China. Take a trip to your local supermarket and you likely will find grapes from Chile, oranges from Australia, meat from Argentina, wines from France and South Africa, cheese from Italy, and cereals and cooking oil from Canada. Red Lobster, owned by Darden Restaurants, purchases fish in 30 countries.[3] A look at the labels on your clothes is yet another geography lesson, with countries of origin such as Mexico, Vietnam, Bangladesh, India, and China. World trade in goods and services totaled an incredible $15.5 trillion in 2009.[4] But, as the headlines tell us, this growth in global economic interconnectedness has come with tough problems. Among them: record trade deficits for the United States, foreign labor abuses and sweatshops, offshoring of jobs, infringement of intellectual property rights, and unsafe and unhealthy imported goods and foods.[5] Meanwhile, the challenge to be competitive on the global stage looms large for today's business managers. The U.S. Trade Representative's office shows that 95 percent of the world's consumers live outside the United States.[6]

Like any other productive venture, an international corporation must be effectively and efficiently managed. Consequently, *international management*, the pursuit of organizational objectives in international and intercultural settings, has

become an important discipline. Nancy Adler, a leading international management scholar at Canada's McGill University, sees it this way: "Managing the global enterprise and modern business management have become synonymous."[7] The purpose of this chapter is to define and discuss multinational and global corporations, stimulate global and cultural awareness, explore comparative management insights, and discuss the need for cross-cultural training.

GLOBAL ORGANIZATIONS FOR A GLOBAL ECONOMY

Many labels have been attached to international business ventures over the years. They have been called international companies, multinational companies, global companies, and transnational companies.[8] This section clarifies the confusion about terminology by reviewing the six-stage internationalization process as a foundation for contrasting global and transnational companies.

The Internationalization Process

There are many ways to do business across borders.[9] At one extreme, a company may merely buy goods from a foreign source, or, at the other, it may actually buy the foreign company itself. In between is an internationalization process with identifiable stages.[10] Companies may skip steps when pursuing foreign markets, so the following sequence should *not* be viewed as a lock-step sequence.

STAGE 1: LICENSING. Companies in foreign countries are authorized to produce and/or market a given product within a specified territory in return for a fee.[11] For example, under the terms of a ten-year licensing agreement, South Korea's Samsung Electronics got to use Texas Instruments' patented semiconductor technology for royalty payments exceeding $1 billion.[12]

Margaret A. Sova

Today's globalized, Internet-linked economy is a boon to developing countries. This busy ship container port in Manzanillo, the largest on Mexico's Pacific Coast, has thrived since the North American Free Trade Agreement (NAFTA) went into effect.

international management pursuing organizational objectives in international and cross-cultural settings

STAGE 2: EXPORTING.

Goods produced in one country are sold to customers in foreign countries. Exports amount to a large and growing slice of the U.S. economy.

STAGE 3: LOCAL WAREHOUSING AND SELLING.

Goods produced in one country are shipped to the parent company's storage and marketing facilities located in one or more foreign countries.

STAGE 4: LOCAL ASSEMBLY AND PACKAGING.

Components, rather than finished products, are shipped to company-owned assembly facilities in one or more foreign countries for final assembly and sales.

STAGE 5: JOINT VENTURES.

A company in one country pools resources with one or more companies in a foreign country to design, produce, store, transport, and market products, with resulting profits/losses shared appropriately. Joint ventures, also known as *strategic alliances* or *strategic partnerships,* have become very popular in recent years.[13] For example, consider the unique three-way alliance formed in 2010 between France's Renault, Japan's Nissan, and Germany's Daimler, which is designed to increase production of small, fuel-efficient cars and to bring electric and alternative-power cars to market.[14] All three companies hope to reduce costs by sharing know-how, parts, and technology, otherwise wastefully duplicated if each proceeded alone.

International joint ventures/strategic alliances have proven to be very difficult. Recent research by the management consulting firm McKinsey & Company concluded that only 50 percent of joint ventures show returns that exceed the cost of capital.[15] That's a dismal 50 percent failure rate, leaving lots of room for improvement.

Experts offer the following recommendations for successful international joint ventures/strategic alliances. First, exercise *patience* when selecting and building trust with a partner that has compatible (but not directly competitive) products and markets. Second, *learn* as fast and as much as possible without giving away core technologies and secrets. Third, establish firm *ground rules* about rights and responsibilities at the outset.[16]

4a
Is It Time to Go to Vietnam?

Explosive wage growth and labor strife in China and India, favored destinations for foreign investment in Asia, have multinationals taking a serious look at Vietnam as a low-cost alternative for new factories and call centers. "We're cheaper—much cheaper," says Nguyen Than Nam, chief executive officer of FPT, a Hanoi-based IT outsourcer and distributor of cell phones with $1 billion in revenue last year. Vietnam is ready to compete head-on for foreign investment, says Nam. "We are trying to be the 'one.'"

QUESTION: Is it time to do business in Vietnam, or would it be an insult to the aging American veterans of the Vietnam War? Explain your reasoning.

For further information about the interactive annotations in this chapter, visit our student Web site.

Source: Bruce Einhorn, "Vietnam: An Asian-Tiger Wannabe (Again)," *Bloomberg Businessweek* (June 21–27, 2010): 12.

STAGE 6: DIRECT FOREIGN INVESTMENTS.

Typically a company in one country produces and markets products through wholly owned subsidiaries in foreign countries. Global corporations are expressions of this last stage of internationalization.

Cross-border mergers are an increasingly popular form of direct foreign investment.[17] A cross-border merger occurs when a company in one country buys an entire company in another country. For instance, Intel recently spent $1.4 billion for Infineon Technologies AG's communications unit in Germany. Infineon possesses chips and licenses for many Internet devices, and Intel will be able to make use of Infineon's long-range wireless networks for consumers.[18] Unfortunately, as with joint ventures, cross-border mergers are not a quick and easy way to go global. Problems occur in all mergers, but special challenges arise in cross-border mergers due to cultural, distance, and language barriers. McKinsey & Company's research shows that nearly 40 percent of cross-border mergers end in failure.[19]

From Global Companies to Transnational Companies

The difference between these two types of international ventures is the difference between actual and theoretical. That is to say, transnational companies are evolving and represent a futuristic concept. Meanwhile, global companies, such as the giants in Table 4.1, do business in many countries simultaneously. They have global strategies for product design, financing, purchasing, manufacturing, and marketing. By definition, a **global company** is a multinational venture centrally managed from a specific country. For example, even though Colgate-Palmolive makes 75 percent of its sales and has 29,500 (85 percent) of its employees outside the United States, it is viewed as a U.S. company because it is run from a powerful headquarters in New York City.[20] The same goes for McDonald's, Coca-Cola, Ford, IBM, and Walmart, with their respective U.S. headquarters.

A **transnational company**, in contrast, is a global network of productive units with a decentralized authority structure and no distinct national identity.[21] Transnationals rely on a blend of global and local strategies, as circumstances dictate. Local values and practices are adopted whenever possible, because in the end, all *customer contacts* are local. Ideally, managers of transnational organizations "think globally, but act locally." Managers of foreign operations are encouraged to interact freely with their colleagues from around the world. Once again, this type of international business venture exists mostly in theory, although some global companies are moving toward transnationalism. For example, L.M. Ericsson, the Swedish telecommunications

| Table **4.1** | Corporate Giants Worldwide |

COMPANY	HOME COUNTRY	INDUSTRY	2009 SALES (U.S. $, BILLIONS)
Petrobrás	Brazil	Petroleum products	92
BP	Britain	Petroleum products	246
Nokia	Finland	Electronics	57
AXA	France	Insurance	175
Siemens	Germany	Electronics and industrial equipment	104
ENI	Italy	Petroleum products	117
Toyota Motor	Japan	Motor vehicles	204
Pemex	Mexico	Petroleum products	81
ING Group	Netherlands	Insurance	163
Samsung Electronics	South Korea	Electronics	109
Nestlé	Switzerland	Nutrition and food products	99
Walmart	United States	General retail and groceries	408

Source: Adapted from data in "Global 500: The World's Largest Corporations," *Fortune* (July 26, 2010): F-1–F-7.

global company a multinational venture centrally managed from a specific country | transnational company a futuristic model of a global, decentralized network with no distinct national identity

Green Management: Toward Sustainability

The Global Race for Leadership in Green Technology

Quick: which nation builds the most wind turbines? If you guessed America, with its blustery Great Plains dotted with whirring GE blades, you'd be wrong. In 2009, China became the planet's largest producer.

What's going on here? While America was digging itself out of its financial crisis, China quietly positioned itself to become a leader in what promises to be the largest emerging industry of the 21st century: green tech.

A new report...argues that China, along with Japan and Korea, will dominate the clean-energy race by out-investing America.

Asia's clean-tech tigers are already launching massive government investment programs to dominate this industry and, according to the report, have surpassed the U.S. in virtually all clean-energy areas, including wind, solar, and electric-car batteries.

For Discussion: Is this a major concern, or not? Explain. What should government and business managers do to tip the balance back into America's favor? What, if any, implications does the above trend have for your own life and career?

Source: Excerpted from Brian Dumaine, "Will China Win the Green-Tech War?" *Fortune* (February 8, 2010): 22.

equipment manufacturer, shifted its European headquarters to London to avoid Sweden's high tax burden and to get closer to investors and customers.[22] Ericsson's decision to relocate its headquarters was not constrained by national identity but, rather, guided by business and financial considerations.

Significantly, many experts are alarmed at the prospect of immense "stateless" transnational companies because of unresolved political, economic, and tax implications. If transnational companies become more powerful than the governments of countries in which they do business, who will hold them accountable in cases of fraud, human rights violations, and environmental degradation?[23] (See Green Management: Toward Sustainability.)

TOWARD GREATER GLOBAL AWARENESS AND CROSS-CULTURAL EFFECTIVENESS

Americans in general and American business students and managers in particular are often considered too narrowly focused for the global stage. Upon taking over as dean of Northwestern University's Kellogg School of Management in 2010, Sally

Blount stated that people must learn to have a global perspective and to span boundaries across geographies, ethnicities, and disciplines.[24] This state of affairs is slowly changing amid growth of international business and economic globalization. To compete successfully in a dynamic global economy, present and future managers need to develop their international and cross-cultural awareness. In this section, we discuss the need for global managers with cultural intelligence and specific cross-cultural competencies, examine attitudes toward international operations, and explore key sources of cultural diversity.

Shamleen/Shutterstock.com

Needed: Global Managers with Cultural Intelligence and Cross-Cultural Competencies

Successful global managers possess a characteristic called cultural intelligence (CQ), the ability of an outsider to read individual behavior, group dynamics, and situations in a foreign culture as well as the locals do.[25] (The initials CQ are a variation of the familiar label IQ, for intelligence quotient.) Just as a chameleon changes colors to blend in with its surroundings, a person with high CQ quickly analyzes an unfamiliar cultural situation and then acts appropriately and confidently. David C. Thomas and Kerr Inkson, in their helpful book *Cultural Intelligence: Living and Working Globally*, break down cultural intelligence into the following three components:

- *First, the culturally intelligent person requires **knowledge** of culture and of the fundamental principles of cross-cultural interactions. This means knowing what culture is, how cultures vary, and how culture affects behavior.*
- *Second, the culturally intelligent person needs to practice **mindfulness**, the ability to pay attention in a reflective and creative way to cues in the cross-cultural situations encountered and to one's own knowledge and feelings.*
- *Third, based on knowledge and mindfulness, the culturally intelligent person develops cross-cultural **skills** and becomes competent across a wide range of situations. These skills involve choosing the appropriate behavior from a well-developed repertoire of behaviors that are correct for different intercultural situations.*[26]

In short, CQ involves seeing the world as someone else sees it and adapting appropriately thanks to the right knowledge, mindfulness, and skills. CQ combines two topics we cover later—*impression management* (Chapter 13) and *emotional intelligence* (Chapter 14)—and puts them into a cross-cultural context. While noting that only 5 percent of managers studied possess high CQ, a pair of researchers shared this cautionary tale of

a manager with *low* CQ: When a French manager in the United States met his new female secretary, he kissed her on both cheeks, according to European custom. Outraged, the secretary filed a harassment complaint.[27] You can boost your cultural intelligence by mastering the nine cross-cultural competencies listed in Table 4.2 and understanding the concepts in this chapter.

Contrasting Attitudes Toward International Operations

Can a firm's degree of internationalization be measured? Some observers believe it can, and they claim a true global company must have subsidiaries in at least six nations. Others say that to qualify as a multinational or global company, a firm must have a certain percentage of its capital or operations in foreign countries. However, Howard Perlmutter insists that these measurable guidelines tell only part of the story and believes it is management's *attitude*

4b
In Search of Cultural Intelligence

A profile of Stephen A. Miles, a successful executive coach:

Born in Nairobi [Kenya] to a schoolteacher mother and an agro-economist father, Miles lived in South Africa, Iraq, and Argentina by the time he turned eight, then in Canada—New Brunswick, Ontario, and British Columbia—honing his adaptability and talent for observation all along the way. "You have to read people quickly to fit into the social network," says Miles, 43. "My whole world is about trying to read people, to find that one ticket in, and get them to do something differently."

Source: Diane Brady, "The Unknown Guru," *Bloomberg Businessweek* (November 29–December 5, 2010): 84.

QUESTIONS: Is the concept of cultural intelligence evident in this sketch? Explain. How would you rate your own cultural intelligence? Explain.

---

cultural intelligence (CQ) ability to interpret and act in appropriate ways in unfamiliar cultural surroundings

Table 4.2   Competencies Needed to Work Effectively Across Cultures

CROSS-CULTURAL COMPETENCY CLUSTER	KNOWLEDGE OR SKILL REQUIRED
1. Building relationships	Ability to gain access to and maintain relationships with members of host culture
2. Valuing people of different cultures	Empathy for difference; sensitivity to diversity
3. Listening and observation	Knows cultural history and reasons for certain cultural actions and customs
4. Coping with ambiguity	Recognizes and interprets implicit behavior, especially nonverbal cues
5. Translating complex information	Knowledge of local language, symbols, or other forms of verbal language and written language
6. Taking action and initiative	Understands intended and potential unintended consequences of actions
7. Managing others	Ability to manage details of a job, including maintaining cohesion in a group
8. Adaptability and flexibility	Views change from multiple perspectives
9. Managing stress	Understands own and others' mood, emotions, and personality

Source: *Academy of Management Learning & Education* by Yoshitaka Yamazaki and D. Christopher Kayes. Copyright © 2004 by Academy of Management (NY). Reproduced with permission of Academy of Management (NY) in the format Textbook via Copyright Clearance Center.

toward its foreign operations that really counts. He maintains that it is also necessary to consider how executives do business around the world. The orientation in host and home environments toward "foreign people, ideas, and resources" is paramount in gauging a firm's multinationality.[28]

Perlmutter identified three managerial attitudes toward international operations, which he labeled ethnocentric, polycentric, and geocentric.[29] Each attitude is presented here in its pure form, but all three are likely to be found in a single multinational or global corporation (see Table 4.3). The key question is "Which attitude predominates?"

ETHNOCENTRIC ATTITUDE. Managers with an ethnocentric attitude are home-country-oriented. Home-country personnel, ideas, and practices are viewed as inherently superior to those from abroad.

Foreign nationals are not trusted with key decisions or technology. Home-country procedures and evaluation criteria are applied worldwide without variation. Oklahoma-based Dominion Farms' 17,000-acre American-style agribusiness in Kenya is a clear case in point. Dominion's president Calvin Burgess is intent on proving that large-scale farming is superior to the African nation's tradition of small family farms, which he describes as "unproductive gardens." Burgess claims that he is unconcerned with preserving the local culture because "If you preserve it, people will starve."[30] Not surprisingly, Dominion Farms faces plenty of local opposition in Kenya.

Proponents of ethnocentrism say that it makes for a simpler and more tightly controlled organization. Critics believe this attitude makes for poor planning and ineffective operations because of inadequate feedback, high turnover of subsidiary

ethnocentric attitude view that the home country's personnel and ways of doing things are best

| Table **4.3** | Three Different Attitudes Toward International Operations |

ORGANIZATION DESIGN	ETHNOCENTRIC	POLYCENTRIC	GEOCENTRIC
Identification	Nationality of owner	Nationality of host country	Truly international company but identifying with national interests
Authority; decision making	High in headquarters	Relatively low in headquarters	Aim for a collaborative approach between headquarters and subsidiaries
Evaluation and control	Home standards applied for person and performance	Determined locally	Find standards that are universal and local
Communication; information flow	High volume to subsidiaries; orders, commands, advice	Little to and from headquarters; little between subsidiaries	Both ways and between subsidiaries; heads of subsidiaries part of management team
Perpetuation (recruiting, staffing, development)	Recruit and develop people of home country for key positions everywhere in the world	Develop people of local nationality for key positions in their own country	Develop best people everywhere in the world for key positions everywhere in the world

Source: Excerpted from Howard V. Perlmutter, "The Tortuous Evolution of the Multinational Corporation," *Columbia Journal of World Business,* 4 (January–February 1969): 12. Used with permission.

managers, reduced innovation, inflexibility, and social and political backlash.

In U.S.-Japanese business relations, ethnocentrism cuts both ways. Procter & Gamble failed to do its cultural homework when it ran a series of advertisements for Pampers in Japan. Japanese customers were bewildered by the ads, in which a stork carried a baby, because storks have no cultural connection to birth in Japan.[31] Similarly, Japanese companies operating in the United States seem to be out of touch with the expectations of American managers. In a survey of American managers employed by 31 such companies, the common complaint was too few promotions and too little responsibility.[32]

Ethnocentric attitudes can also cause problems in ethnically diverse countries. For example, in the United States, Spanish or Spanish Creole is spoken in more than 34 million homes, and Hispanics/Latinos are projected to make up nearly one-quarter of the population by 2050.[33] Marketers attempt to cater to this significant segment of the population, but many of their efforts have fallen flat when they have failed to account for differences among the 22 nationalities that make up this overall segment. To offer a case in point, Tropicana orange juice was advertised as "jugo de china" in Miami. While "china" means orange to Puerto Ricans, Miami's extensive Cuban population thought it was juice from China. Regarding a Jack in the Box commercial that featured a Mexican mariachi band playing while a Spanish flamenco dancer performed, marketing professor Bert Valencia quipped, "That's like having Willie Nelson sing while Michael Jackson does the moonwalk."[34]

POLYCENTRIC ATTITUDE. This host-country orientation is based on the assumption that because cultures are so different, local managers know what is best for their operations. A polycentric attitude leads to a loose confederation of comparatively independent subsidiaries rather than to a highly integrated structure. Because foreign operations are measured in terms of results (instead of culture), methods, incentives, and training procedures vary widely from location to location.

polycentric attitude view that local managers in host countries know best how to run their own operations

On the negative side, wasteful duplication of effort occurs at the various units within the confederation precisely because they are independent. Such duplication can erode the efficiency of polycentric organizations. Moreover, global objectives can be undermined by excessive concern for local traditions and success. But there is a positive side: "The main advantages are an intensive exploitation of local markets, better sales since local management is often better informed, more local initiative for new products, more host-government support, and good local managers with high morale."[35]

GEOCENTRIC ATTITUDE. Managers with a geocentric attitude are world-oriented. For example, it is easy to detect a geocentric attitude in this Q&A with David Rothkopf, a former high-ranking U.S. Commerce Department official: To be competitive, Rothkopf explained, "My approach would be not to look at geography as a limitation." He feels that all businesses—even start-ups—can find great people, valuable resources, and profitable markets anywhere in the world.[36] Skill, not nationality, determines who gets promoted or transferred to key positions around the globe in geocentric companies. Local and worldwide objectives are balanced in all aspects of operation. Collaboration between headquarters and subsidiaries is high, but an effort is made to maintain a balance between global standards and local discretion. Thus, a geocentric attitude is essential in global companies such as IBM.

Notice the geocentric attitude in this story: John Tolva, IBM's director of technology, can pinpoint the moment he realized the significance of a global perspective. He was on assignment in Ghana, and wound up playing Scrabble with his co-workers, who came from India, Germany, Brazil, and other countries. It was a challenge to find a common language, so they had to look for other points of connection. Tolva recognized that what linked the team members was "the values that IBM has instilled in us—a professional code."[37]

Of these three contrasting attitudes, only a geocentric attitude can help management take a long step toward success in today's vigorously competitive global marketplace.

The Cultural Imperative

Culture has a powerful impact on people's behavior. For example, consider the routine act of negotiating a business contract. Americans view a signed contract as binding. However, the Japanese consider renegotiation an option whenever a shift in the company's circumstances occurs, such as an unforeseen change in governmental tax policy, and the Chinese view a signed contract as only the start of negotiations.[38] Cross-cultural business negotiators who ignore or defy cultural traditions do so at their own risk. That means the risk of not making the sale or of losing a contract or failing to negotiate a favorable deal. Therefore, sensitivity to cross-cultural differences is imperative for people who do business in other countries or work with people from other cultures.

In this section, we define the term *culture* and address the fear of an "Americanized" world culture. Then, drawing primarily from the work of pioneering cultural anthropologist Edward T. Hall, we explore key sources of cross-cultural differences.

CULTURE DEFINED. Culture is the pattern of taken-for-granted assumptions about how a given collection of people should think, act, and feel as they go about their daily affairs.[39] Regarding the central aspect of this definition, *taken-for-granted assumptions*, Hall noted that culture is internalized. People from different cultures, whether they're American or Japanese or Arab, are not even aware that their deeply held beliefs stem from their culture, not from human nature.[40]

Ton Koene/Picture Contact BV/Alamy

Think globally, act locally. This McDonald's in Moscow, Russia, is successful because the food and service standards have been adapted to local tastes and expectations.

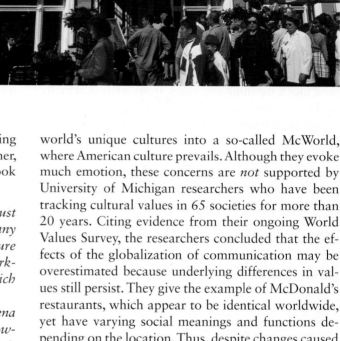

Timothy O'Keefe/Photolibrary

In Chapter 9, *organizational culture* is called the social glue binding members of an organization together. Similarly, at a broader level, *societal culture* acts as a social glue. That glue is made up of norms, values, attitudes, role expectations, taboos, symbols, heroes, beliefs, morals, customs, and rituals. Cultural lessons are imparted from birth to death via role models, formal education, religious teachings, and peer pressure.

Cultural undercurrents make international dealings immensely challenging. According to Fons Trompenaars and Charles Hampden-Turner, the Dutch and English authors of the landmark book *Riding the Waves of Culture,*

> *International managers have it tough. They must operate on a number of different premises at any one time. These premises arise from their culture of origin, the culture in which they are working, and the culture of the organization which employs them.*
>
> *In every culture in the world such phenomena as authority, bureaucracy, creativity, good fellowship, verification, and accountability are experienced in different ways. That we use the same words to describe them tends to make us unaware that our cultural biases and our accustomed conduct may not be appropriate, or shared.*[41]

world's unique cultures into a so-called McWorld, where American culture prevails. Although they evoke much emotion, these concerns are *not* supported by University of Michigan researchers who have been tracking cultural values in 65 societies for more than 20 years. Citing evidence from their ongoing World Values Survey, the researchers concluded that the effects of the globalization of communication may be overestimated because underlying differences in values still persist. They give the example of McDonald's restaurants, which appear to be identical worldwide, yet have varying social meanings and functions depending on the location. Thus, despite changes caused by global development, there will never be a uniform, "McWorld" global culture.[43] Cultural roots run deep, have profound effects on behavior, and are not readily altered.

ARE U.S. GLOBAL CORPORATIONS TURNING THE WORLD INTO A SINGLE "AMERICANIZED" CULTURE?

Protesters at World Trade Organization and global economic summit meetings in recent years have decried the growing global reach of McDonald's (in 117 countries)[42] and other American corporate giants. They worry about a homogenizing of the

Understanding Cultural Diversity

Dealing effectively with both coworkers and customers in today's diverse workplaces requires a good deal of cultural intelligence. For instance, the standard all-too-revealing hospital gown caused a unique cross-cultural problem for the Maine Medical Center in Portland, Maine. When the hospital's staff realized that Muslim women were canceling appointments to avoid the shame of being inadequately clothed, they created gowns for modest patients who desire coverage of their legs and backside.[44] Making this sort of cultural accommodation is a little easier when you know about the following important sources of cultural diversity.

HIGH-CONTEXT AND LOW-CONTEXT CULTURES.
People from European-based cultures typically assess people from Asian cultures such as China and Japan as quiet and hard to figure out. Conversely, Asians tend to view Westerners as aggressive, insensitive, and even rude. True, language differences are a significant barrier to mutual understanding. But something more fundamental is involved, something cultural. Anthropologist Edward T. Hall prompted better understanding of cross-cultural communication by distinguishing between high-context and low-context cultures.[45] The difference centers on how much meaning one takes from what is actually said or written versus who the other person is.

In high-context cultures, people rely heavily on nonverbal and subtle situational messages when communicating with others. The other person's official status, place in society, and reputation say a great deal about the person's rights, obligations, and trustworthiness. In high-context cultures, people do not expect to talk about such "obvious" things. Conversation simply provides general background information about the other person. Thus, in high-context Japan, the ritual of exchanging business cards is a social necessity, and failing to read a card you have been given is a grave insult. The other person's company and position determine what is said and how. Arab, Chinese, and Korean cultures also are high-context cultures.

People from low-context cultures convey essential messages and meaning primarily with words. Low-context cultures in Germany, Switzerland, Scandinavia, North America, and Great Britain expect people to communicate their precise intended meaning. Low-context people do read so-called body language, but its messages are secondary to spoken and written words. Legal contracts with precisely worded expectations are important in low-context countries such as the United States. However, according to international communications experts, strong business relationships are equally or more important than a written document in high-context cultures.[46] This helps explain why Americans tend to be frustrated with the apparently slow pace of

business dealings in Japan. For the Japanese, the many rounds of meetings and social gatherings are necessary to collect valuable contextual information as a basis for judging the other party's character. For the schedule-driven American, anything short of actually signing the contract is considered largely a waste of time. *Patience* is a prime virtue for low-context managers doing business in high-context cultures.

NINE DIMENSIONS OF CULTURE FROM THE GLOBE PROJECT.
The GLOBE (Global Leadership and Organizational Behavior Effectiveness) project was conceived by Robert J. House, a University of Pennsylvania researcher. Beginning with a 1994 meeting in Calgary, Canada, the GLOBE project has grown to encompass an impressive network of over 150 researchers from 62 countries. It is a massive ongoing effort in which researchers assess organizations in their own cultures and languages with standardized instruments to collect data from around the world, building a comprehensive model. If things go as intended, the resulting database will yield important new insights about both similarities and differences across the world's cultures.[47] More important, it promises to provide practical guidelines for international managers. Thanks to the first two phases of the GLOBE project, we have a research-based list of key cultural dimensions (see Table 4.4).

Interestingly, according to one GLOBE research report, mid-level managers in the United States scored high on assertiveness and performance orientation and moderately on uncertainty avoidance and institutional collectivism.[48]

OTHER SOURCES OF CULTURAL DIVERSITY.
Managers headed for a foreign country need to do their homework on the following cultural variables to avoid awkwardness and problems.[49] There are no rights or wrongs here, only cross-cultural differences.

Individualism Versus Collectivism. This distinction between "me" and "we" cultures deserves closer attention, because it encompasses two of the nine GLOBE cultural dimensions in Table 4.4. People in individualistic cultures focus primarily on individual rights, roles, and achievements. The United States and Canada are highly individualistic cultures.

Table **4.4**   Nine Cultural Dimensions from the GLOBE Project

DIMENSION	DESCRIPTION	COUNTRIES SCORING HIGHEST	COUNTRIES SCORING LOWEST
Power distance	Should leaders have high or low power over others?	Morocco, Argentina, Thailand	Denmark, Netherlands, South Africa (black sample)
Uncertainty avoidance	How much should social norms and rules be used to reduce future uncertainties?	Switzerland, Sweden, Germany (former West)	Russia, Hungary, Bolivia
Institutional collectivism	To what extent should society and institutions reward loyalty?	Sweden, South Korea, Japan	Greece, Hungary, Germany (former East)
In-group collectivism	To what extent do individuals value loyalty to their family or organization?	Iran, India, Morocco	Denmark, Sweden, New Zealand
Assertiveness	How aggressive and confrontational should one be with others?	Germany (former East), Austria, Greece	Sweden, New Zealand, Switzerland
Gender equality	How nearly equal are men and women?	Hungary, Poland, Slovenia	South Korea, Egypt, Morocco
Future orientation	How much should one work and save for the future, rather than just live for the present?	Singapore, Switzerland, Netherlands	Russia, Argentina, Poland
Performance orientation	How much should people be rewarded for excellence and improvement?	Singapore, Hong Kong, New Zealand	Russia, Argentina, Greece
Humane orientation	How much should people be encouraged to be generous, kind, and fair to others?	Philippines, Ireland, Malaysia	Germany (former West), Spain, France

Sources: Adapted from discussions in Mansour Javidan and Robert J. House, "Cultural Acumen for the Global Manager: Lessons from Project GLOBE," *Organizational Dynamics*, 29 (Spring 2001): 289–305; Robert House, Mansour Javidan, Paul Hanges, and Peter Dorfman, "Understanding Cultures and Implicit Leadership Theories Across the Globe: An Introduction to Project GLOBE," *Journal of World Business*, 37 (Spring 2002): 3–10; and Mansour Javidan, Robert J. House, and Peter W. Dorfman, "A Nontechnical Summary of GLOBE Findings," in Robert J. House, Paul J. Hanges, Mansour Javidan, Peter W. Dorfman, and Vipin Gupta, eds., *Culture, Leadership, and Organizations: The GLOBE Study of 62 Societies* (Thousand Oaks, Calif.: Sage, 2004), pp. 29–48.

People in collectivist cultures—such as Egypt, Mexico, India, and Japan—rank duty and loyalty to family, friends, organization, and country above self-interests. Group goals and shared achievements are paramount to collectivists; personal goals and desires are suppressed. It is important to remember that individualism and collectivism are extreme ends of a continuum along which people and cultures are variously distributed and mixed. For example, in the United States, one can find pockets of collectivism among Native Americans and recent immigrants from Latin America and Asia. This helps explain why a top-notch engineer born in Japan might be reluctant to attend an American-style recognition

collectivist cultures cultures that emphasize duty and loyalty to collective goals and achievements

dinner where individual award recipients are asked to stand up for a round of applause.[50]

Time. Hall referred to time as a silent language of culture. He distinguished between monochronic and polychronic time.[51] **Monochronic time** is based on the perception that time is a unidimensional straight line divided into standard units, such as seconds, minutes, hours, and days. In monochronic cultures, including North America and Northern Europe, everyone is assumed to be on the same clock, and time is treated as money. In the United States, it is common to hear people talk about "saving," "spending," or "wasting" time, as if it were money. The general rule is to use time efficiently, to be on time, and (above all) not to waste time. Google has made a science out of saving time. In 2010, Google vice president Marissa Mayer introduced Google Instant, a faster version of the firm's search engine that will help users shave two to five seconds off each 15-second query.[52]

In contrast, **polychronic time** involves the perception of time as flexible, elastic, and multidimensional. Latin American, Mediterranean, and Arab cultures are polychronic. Managers in polychronic cultures tend to view schedules and deadlines in relative rather than absolute terms. Different perceptions of time have caused many cultural collisions. For example, Grahame Maher, head of Vodafone in the Persian Gulf gas-rich emirate of Qatar, had to adjust to participating in the age-old custom called the "majlis," in which men gather to drink tea, smoke tobacco, and discuss world issues each evening. Says Maher: "I learned a way to do business that we have forgotten in the West because it takes too much time."[53] As Maher discovered, it is important to reset your mental clocks (and expectations) when living and working in a culture with a different time orientation or when working globally on a virtual team. (Virtual teams are discussed in Chapter 13.)[54]

Interpersonal Space. People in a number of cultures prefer to stand close when conversing. Many Arabs, Asians, and Pacific Islanders fall into this group. An interpersonal distance of only six inches is very disturbing to a Northern European or an American who is accustomed to conversing at arm's length. Cross-cultural gatherings in the Middle East often involve an awkward dance as Arab hosts strive to

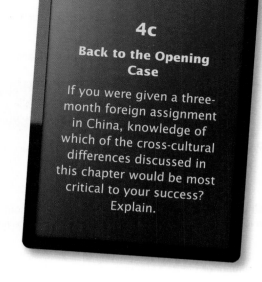

4c
Back to the Opening Case

If you were given a three-month foreign assignment in China, knowledge of which of the cross-cultural differences discussed in this chapter would be most critical to your success? Explain.

get closer while their American and European guests shuffle backward around the room to maintain what they consider a proper social distance.

Language. Foreign-language skills are the gateway to true cross-cultural understanding. Translations are not an accurate substitute for conversational ability in the local language. Consider, for example, the complexity of the Japanese language, which changes depending on the relationship between speaker and listener as well as the context of the conversation. The language shifts according to social conventions that are totally unfamiliar to Americans, making it easy for those with only a minimal understanding of the language to blunder.[55]

Language instructors who prepare Americans for foreign assignments say it takes from 150 to 350 hours of classroom work, depending on the difficulty of the language, to reach minimum proficiency (e.g., exchanging greetings, shopping and ordering meals, and asking for directions). The American Society for Testing and Materials has ranked the difficulty of learning foreign languages for native English speakers as follows. Romance and Germanic languages, such as Spanish or German, are the least difficult to master. Next come African and Eastern European languages, followed by Middle Eastern and Asian languages.[56] Historically, foreign languages have not been a strong suit for Americans. Indeed, almost 81 percent speak only English, and although 200 million Chinese are studying English, a paltry 24,000 American children are trying to master Chinese.[57] (See Window on the World.)

---

monochronic time a perception of time as a straight line broken into standard units | polychronic time a perception of time as flexible, elastic, and multidimensional

WINDOW ON THE WORLD

Do You Speak *Globish*?

The alumni of the vast people's University of China are typical of the post–Mao Zedong generation. Every Friday evening several hundred gather informally under the pine trees of a little square in Beijing's Haidian district, in the so-called English Corner, to hold "English conversation." Chatting together in groups, they discuss football, movies, and celebrities like Victoria Beckham and Paris Hilton in awkward but enthusiastic English. . . .

English is now used, in some form, by approximately 4 billion people on earth—perhaps two thirds of the planet—including 400 million native English speakers.

As a mother tongue, only Chinese is more prevalent, with 1.8 billion native speakers—350 million of whom also speak some kind of English. . . .

Having neatly made the transition from the Queen's English to the more democratic American version, it is now becoming a worldwide power, a populist tool increasingly known as Globish. . . .

For Discussion: Does this mean that foreign language skills are no longer important for native English speakers when doing business around the world? Explain.

Source: Excerpted from Robert McCrum, *www.newsweek.com/2010/06/12/globish.html,* accessed June 12, 2010.

Religion. Awareness of a business colleague's religious traditions is essential for building a lasting relationship.[58] Those traditions may dictate dietary restrictions, religious holidays, and Sabbath schedules, which are important to the devout and represent cultural minefields for the uninformed. For instance, the official work week in Saudi Arabia is Saturday through Wednesday, Saturday through Thursday in Iran, and Sunday through Thursday in Egypt. In Israel, where the official day off is Saturday, Burger King observes Jewish dietary law, which prohibits mixing milk and meat products. Unlike McDonald's, Burger King does not serve cheeseburgers.[59]

Of course, it is important to be aware of and follow applicable laws regarding religion in the workplace.

AP Photo/Gustavo Ferrari

COMPARATIVE MANAGEMENT INSIGHTS

Comparative management is the study of how organizational behavior and management practices differ across cultures. In this relatively new field of inquiry, as in other fields, there is

Expatriates working in countries such as Kuwait, where women have only recently been elected to the country's Parliament, need to be fully aware of cross-cultural and religious differences if they are to get the job done.

comparative management study of how organizational behavior and management practices differ across cultures

disagreement about theoretical frameworks and research methodologies.[60] Nevertheless, some useful lessons have been learned. This research-based foundation of understanding can come in handy for managers such as Nancy McKinstry, who lives and works across cultures. McKinstry, an American, is the CEO of Wolters Kluwer, a $4.3-billion-a-year Dutch publishing company based in Amsterdam with operations in 25 countries. In her experience, it has been relatively easy for her to adjust to working with her Dutch colleagues because the two cultures are fairly similar. It would be more challenging, she says, if the company was based in southern Europe, where long-term business relationships require more effort and decision making is more collaborative.[61]

In this section, we focus on (1) the applicability of American management theories in other cultures, (2) management styles across cultures, and (3) a GLOBE matrix of leadership styles.

Made-in-America Management Theories Require Translation

In the 1970s, Geert Hofstede, a Dutch organizational behavior researcher, surveyed 116,000 IBM employees from 40 different countries.[62] He classified each of his 40 national samples according to four different cultural dimensions. Hofstede found a great deal of cultural diversity among the countries he studied. For example, employee needs were ranked differently from country to country. The need for self-actualization was tops in the United States, Great Britain, and members of the former British Empire (Canada, Hong Kong, India, Australia, New Zealand, and South Africa). Social needs ranked the highest in Singapore, the Netherlands, and the Scandinavian countries. Countries ranking security needs the highest included Switzerland, Germany, Italy, Mexico, Japan, and Argentina.

The marked cultural differences among the 40 countries led Hofstede to recommend that American management theories be adapted to local cultures rather than imposed on them.[63] As we saw in Chapter 2, many popular management theories were developed within the U.S. cultural context. Hofstede believes that it is naive to expect those theories to apply automatically in significantly different cultures. For example, American-made management theories that reflect Americans' preoccupation with individualism

are out of place in countries such as Mexico, Brazil, and Japan, where individualism is discouraged.

Hofstede's research does not attempt to tell international managers *how* to apply various management techniques in different cultures. However, it does provide a useful cultural typology and presents a convincing case for the cultural adaptation of American management theory and practice.[64] In turn, Americans would do well to culturally adapt any management theories and practices acquired from other cultures.

Management Styles Vary Across Countries and Cultures

An extensive new study of how management is actually practiced in 17 countries adds weight to Hofstede's argument against a one-size-fits-all approach to international management. Factory managers at nearly 6,000 medium-sized companies (100 to 5,000 employees) were interviewed and rated from 1 = low to 5 = high on a list of 18 standard management practices. According to the lead researchers:

> This evaluation tool was developed by an international consulting firm, and it can be broadly interpreted as attempting to measure management practices in three broad areas: 1) **monitoring**— how well do companies monitor what goes on inside their firms and use this for continuous improvement? 2) **targets**—do companies set the right targets, track the right outcomes, and take appropriate actions if the two are inconsistent? 3) **incentives**—are companies promoting and rewarding employees based on performance, and trying to hire and keep their best employees?[65]

The researchers grouped the ratings of the managers they interviewed by country to look for national management styles. Table 4.5 lists the five countries ranked highest in "overall management," along with their scores for "monitoring," "targets," and "incentives" management. (*Note*: This is an abbreviated list for illustrative purposes, not a comprehensive list of all 17 countries studied.) It turns out that countries with strong overall management practices are *not* all alike. Countries have their own characteristic ways of implementing good management practices, according to this study. In the United States and Canada, greater emphasis is placed on

| Table **4.5** | Countries Place Differing Emphasis on Standard Management Practices |

	INTERNATIONAL RANKINGS (AMONG 17 COUNTRIES STUDIED)			
	OVERALL MANAGEMENT	MONITORING MANAGEMENT	TARGETS MANAGEMENT	INCENTIVES MANAGEMENT
United States	1	2	3	**1**
Germany	2 (tie)	3	**2**	3
Sweden	2 (tie)	**1**	4	5
Japan	3	7	**1**	4
Canada	4	4	5	**2**

Source: Adapted from data in Table 2 in Nicholas Bloom and John Van Reenen, "Why Do Management Practices Differ Across Firms and Countries?" *Journal of Economic Perspectives*, 24 (Winter 2010): 203–224.

attracting and motivating employees with incentives. Meanwhile, targets and goal setting receive comparatively greater emphasis in Germany and Japan. In Sweden, which tied Germany for second in good overall management, monitoring is emphasized.

What is the practical significance of these findings? In short, managers working internationally need to use their cultural intelligence to detect local management preferences. The management techniques may be familiar, but the emphasis may vary (e.g., "pulling" employees with incentives versus "pushing" them with targets and monitoring). These subtle but important differences in how otherwise standard management practices are emphasized can mean the difference between success and failure on a foreign assignment.

Lessons in Leadership from the GLOBE Project

The huge 62-society database compiled by the GLOBE researchers provides valuable insights into the applicability of leadership styles around the world. As listed along the top of the matrix in Figure 4.1, the GLOBE researchers focused on the following five different leadership styles:

- *Charismatic/value-based:* a visionary person who inspires high performance by exhibiting integrity and decisiveness

- *Team-oriented:* an administratively competent person and teambuilder who diplomatically emphasizes common purposes and goals
- *Participative:* a person who actively involves others in both making and carrying out decisions
- *Humane-oriented:* a compassionate, generous, considerate, and supportive person
- *Self-protective:* a self-centered and status-conscious person who tends to save face and stir conflict[66]

The matrix in Figure 4.1 rates these five leadership styles as most acceptable, moderately acceptable, or least acceptable for ten cultural clusters.

According to the matrix, the charismatic/value-based and team-oriented leadership styles have the greatest cross-cultural applicability. The self-protective leadership style definitely is *not* acceptable, regardless of the cultural setting. Humane-oriented leadership is perceived around the world as being only moderately acceptable, except within the southern Asian cultural cluster. This is probably because humane-oriented leaders are perceived in most cultures as not pushing hard enough to achieve goals and solid results. The picture for participative leadership is mixed, despite its general popularity in North and South America and in Germanic, Latin, and Nordic Europe.

A completely different study of employees in Russia's largest textile factory confirms the limited

Figure **4.1**   GLOBE Leadership Matrix

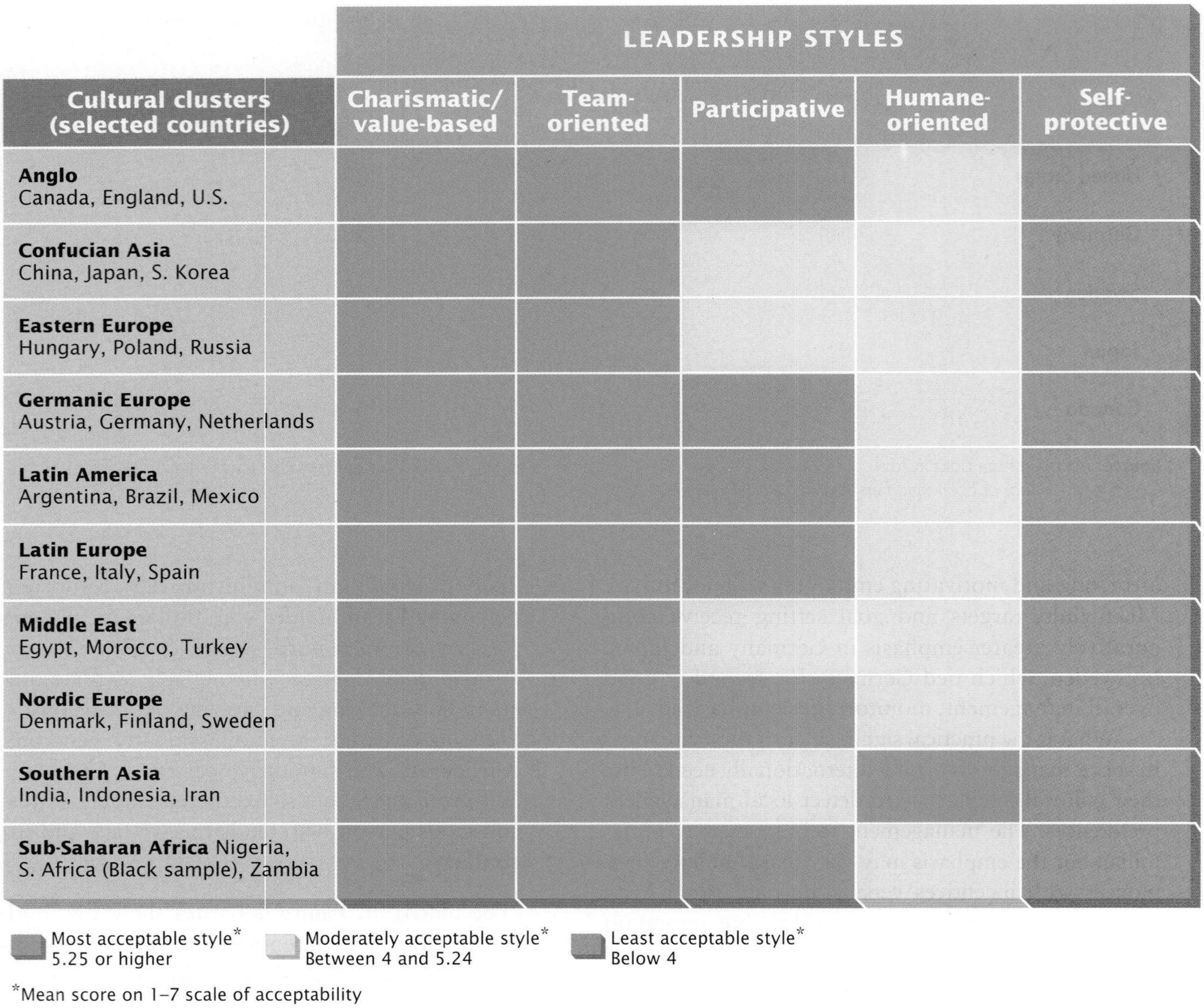

Cultural clusters (selected countries)	LEADERSHIP STYLES				
	Charismatic/ value-based	Team-oriented	Participative	Humane-oriented	Self-protective
Anglo Canada, England, U.S.					
Confucian Asia China, Japan, S. Korea					
Eastern Europe Hungary, Poland, Russia					
Germanic Europe Austria, Germany, Netherlands					
Latin America Argentina, Brazil, Mexico					
Latin Europe France, Italy, Spain					
Middle East Egypt, Morocco, Turkey					
Nordic Europe Denmark, Finland, Sweden					
Southern Asia India, Indonesia, Iran					
Sub-Saharan Africa Nigeria, S. Africa (Black sample), Zambia					

Most acceptable style* 5.25 or higher   Moderately acceptable style* Between 4 and 5.24   Least acceptable style* Below 4

*Mean score on 1–7 scale of acceptability

Sources: Adapted from data in Peter W. Dorfman, Paul J. Hanges, and Felix C Brodbeck, "Leadership and Cultural Variation: The Identification of Culturally Endorsed Leadership Profiles," in Robert J. House, Paul J. Hanges, Mansour Javidan, Peter W. Dorfman, and Vipin Gupta, eds., *Culture, Leadership, and Organizations: The GLOBE Study of 62 Societies* (Thousand Oaks, Calif.: Sage, 2004), pp. 669–719; and Vipin Gupta and Paul J. Hanges, "Regional and Climate Clustering of Societal Cultures," in *ibid.*, pp. 178–218.

applicability of participative leadership in Eastern Europe. That study documented how participative leadership triggered a *decrease* in output. Why? The researchers felt the Russians were influenced by their lack of faith in participative schemes that had proved untrustworthy during the communist era.[67]

It takes time for people in new democracies to get used to participative management. For example, American entrepreneur Michael Smolens took one step at a time at Danube Knitware Ltd., the textile mill he cofounded in Hungary. It was a learning experience for all involved at the 950-employee company, which later opened a sewing factory in neighboring Romania. Hungarian workers had to learn how to meet Western production standards and accept company priorities, while Smolens had to learn how to motivate his employees with better wages and other incentives, including an open, communicative work environment. At first, the workers did not trust the process, but they're starting to change. "We do see progress," Smolens adds. "They're starting to realize that what they say is being taken seriously."[68] Like Smolens, international managers need a full repertoire of leadership styles that they can use flexibly in a culturally diverse world.

STAFFING FOREIGN POSITIONS

In our global economy, successful foreign experience is becoming a required stepping stone to top management. For example, PricewaterhouseCoopers offers employees with more than three years of experience an opportunity for an international assignment, which the company views as an important ingredient in building a good résumé.[69]

Unfortunately, American expatriates reportedly have a higher-than-average failure rate. Failure in this context means foreign-posted employees perform so poorly that they are sent home early or voluntarily go home early. Estimates vary widely, from a modest 3.2 percent failure rate to an alarming 25 percent.[70] Whatever the failure rate, *any* turnover among employees on foreign assignments is expensive, considering that it costs an average of $1 to $2 million to send someone on a three- to four-year foreign assignment.[71] Predeparture training for the employee and education allowances for

children can drive the bill much higher. Managers are challenged not to waste this sort of investment. They need to do a better job of preparing employees for foreign assignments. Toward that end, let us examine why employees fail abroad and what can be done about it.

Why Do U.S. Expatriates Fail?

Although it has historically been a term for banishment or exile from one's native country, *expatriate* today refers to those who live and work in a foreign country. Living outside the comfort zone of one's native culture and surroundings can be immensely challenging—even overwhelming. Expatriates typically experience some degree of culture shock—feelings of anxiety, self-doubt, and isolation brought about by a mismatch between one's expectations and reality. Psychologist Elisabeth Marx offered these insights: "On average, managers in my study experienced culture shock symptoms for about seven weeks: 70 percent of managers reported these lasting up to five weeks and 30 percent had symptoms for up to ten weeks."[72]

Those who view culture shock as a natural part of living and working in a foreign country are better equipped to deal with it. More precise knowledge of why U.S. expatriates fail also is helpful. Thanks to a survey of 74 large U.S. companies, encompassing a total of 3.6 million employees and 12,500 expatriates, we have a clearer picture[73] (see Table 4.6). Job performance—either so poor that it prompted recall (48.4 percent) or so good that it attracted outside job offers (43.7 percent)—was the leading reason U.S. expatriates went home early. Also high on the list were factors related to culture shock (36.6 percent) and

Say *Ni hao* (Hello) to the first Apple store in Shanghai, China. Lots of cultural adaptation and training will be needed if Apple's made-in-America business model is to thrive in Shanghai.

Xinhua/Photoshot

culture shock negative feelings triggered by a mismatch between expectations and reality

Table 4.6 Research Findings on Why U.S. Expatriates Go Home Early

REASON	PERCENTAGE IN AGREEMENT
Not performing job effectively	48.4
Received other, more rewarding offers from other companies	43.7
Expatriate or family not adjusting to culture	36.6
Expatriate or family missing contact with family and friends at home	31.0
Received other, more rewarding offers from our company	12.2
Unable to adjust to deprived living standards in country of assignment	10.3
Concerned with problems of safety and/or health care in foreign location	10.3
Believed children's education was suffering	7.1
Feared that assignment would slow career advancement	7.1
Spouse wanted career	6.1
Compensation package was inadequate	0.0

Source: Reprinted from Gary S. Insch and John D. Daniels, "Causes and Consequences of Declining Early Departures from Foreign Assignments," *Business Horizons*, 45 (November–December 2002): Table 2, p. 41. Copyright © 2002 with permission from Elsevier.

homesickness (31 percent). Other factors trailed in relative importance. It behooves candidates for foreign assignments to prepare themselves not just to avoid failure as an expatriate but to be stimulated and productive in a foreign assignment.

Cross-Cultural Training

As we have defined it, culture is the unique system of values, beliefs, and symbols that fosters patterned behavior in a given population. It is difficult to distinguish the individual from his or her cultural context. Consequently, people tend to be very protective of their cultural identity. Careless defiance or ignorance of cultural norms or traditions by outsiders can result in grave personal insult and put important business dealings at risk. Fortunately, cultural sensitivity can be learned through appropriate cross-cultural training. Cross-cultural training is any form of guided experience aimed at helping people live and work successfully in another culture. Experts say successful cross-cultural adaptation requires practice and mastery of the nine competencies listed in Table 4.2, in our earlier discussion of cultural intelligence.

SPECIFIC TECHNIQUES. The nine cross-cultural competencies involve the *what* of cross-cultural training. Let us now consider *how* those competencies can be taught. Following is a list of five basic cross-cultural training techniques, ranked in order of increasing complexity and cost.[74]

Documentary Programs. Trainees read about a foreign country's history, culture, institutions, geography, and economics. Videotaped and Web-based presentations are often used. For example, Ambergris Solutions makes sure its 1,400 call center employees in the Philippines can comfortably converse with American clients of Texas-based companies by asking them to read *USA Today* and the Texas travel guide and to watch news shows from Texas. Being able to chat about Texas sports and weather may not seem terribly important, but operations manager Katherine Ann Fernando explains, "We can't afford to sound like we don't know anything about Texas."[75]

Culture Assimilator. Cultural familiarity is achieved through exposure to a series of simulated intercultural incidents, or typical problem situations. This technique has been used to quickly train those who are given short notice of a foreign assignment.[76]

Language Instruction. Conversational language skills are taught through a variety of methods. Months, sometimes years, of diligent study are required to master difficult languages. But as a cross-cultural communications professor noted, "To speak more than one language is no longer a luxury, it is a necessity."[77] A good role model is Tupperware's top management team made up of nine executives (all with foreign experience) who speak from two to four languages each.[78] Given the rapid decline of foreign language instruction in U.S. high schools and colleges,[79] access to translators may be a necessary fall-back option. For example, Eric Zuziak hired two people who spoke Mandarin when he recently was in Nanjing, China, designing a residential community.[80]

4d
Foreign Language Skills

Fact: Native English speakers are projected to be only 5 percent of the world's population by 2050, down from 9 percent in 1995.

Fact: Senior executives in the Netherlands speak an average of 3.9 languages. Their counterparts in both the United Kingdom and the United States speak an average of 1.5 languages.

Learning a foreign language is easier for some than for others. International business experts say it is worth the time and effort in order to

- Enhance the traveler's sense of mastery, self-confidence, and safety
- Show respect for foreign business hosts or guests
- Help build rapport and trust with foreign hosts or guests
- Improve the odds of a successful foreign business venture
- Build a base of confidence for learning other languages
- Promote a deeper understanding of other cultures
- Help travelers obtain the best possible medical care during emergencies
- Minimize culture shock and the frustrations of being an outsider

QUESTIONS: Could you conduct a business meeting in one or more foreign languages? What has been your experience with trying to learn foreign languages? How strong is your desire to speak a foreign language? Which language(s)? Why? Would a strong second language help you get a better job? Explain.

Sources: Data from "English Declining as World Language," *USA Today* (February 27, 2004): 7A; and "Bilingual Business," *USA Today* (April 11, 2000): 1B. Adapted from Gary P. Ferraro, "The Need for Linguistic Proficiency in Global Business," *Business Horizons*, 39 (May–June 1996): 39–46.

WINDOW ON THE WORLD

The Legal/Ethical Side of Cross-Cultural Training

U.S. prosecutors, empowered by the Foreign Corrupt Practices Act of 1977 (FCPA) to investigate allegations of bribery anywhere in the world, have been stepping up their activities in China, where a tradition of gift-giving in business often degenerates into serious graft. The FCPA bans U.S. companies from bribing foreign officials. It also applies to foreign companies like [Germany's] Siemens that list their securities on U.S. exchanges. Companies that violate the FCPA face millions in fines, and executives can go to prison. U.S. authorities have upped the number of bribery cases they

pursued to a resolution around the world, from 11 in 2005 to 34 . . . [in 2009].

The temptation to offer a bribe in China is strong because the practice is so common. The risks of getting caught, however, are increasing rapidly.

For Discussion: After selecting a specific foreign country (other than China) and doing some Internet research, what are the gift-giving traditions in that country, and how great an FCPA risk do those traditions likely pose for a visiting U.S. businessperson?

Source: Excerpted from Dexter Roberts and Justin Blum, "Bribery Is Losing Its Charm in China," *Bloomberg Businessweek* (July 12–18, 2010): 11–12.

Sensitivity Training. Experiential exercises teach awareness of the impact of one's actions on others in cross-cultural situations.[81]

Field Experience. Extensive firsthand exposure to ethnic subcultures in one's own country or to foreign cultures can build cultural intelligence.[82] PricewaterhouseCoopers, the major accounting and consulting company mentioned earlier, has developed an inspiring leadership development program involving cross-cultural field experience. The Ulysses Program sends mid-career employees to developing countries for eight-week community service projects, where they often have to break down barriers to communication. Tahir Ayub, for example, arrived in Namibia expecting to help village leaders deal with the growing AIDS epidemic. But almost immediately, he had to abandon his PowerPoint presentations in favor of low-tech, face-to-face conversations. In the end, Ayub says, he was thankful for the change in plans because he gained a new perspective while he was giving out information.[83]

PricewaterhouseCoopers considers the $15,000 per-person cost of the Ulysses Program to be a sound investment in human and social capital.

IS ONE TECHNIQUE BETTER THAN ANOTHER? A study of 80 (63 male, 17 female) managers from a U.S. electronics company attempted to assess the relative effectiveness of two different training techniques.[84] A documentary approach was compared with an interpersonal approach. The latter combined sensitivity training and local ethnic field experience. These techniques were judged equally effective at promoting cultural adjustment, as measured during the managers' three-month stay in South Korea. The researchers recommended a *combination* of documentary and interpersonal training. The importance of language training was diminished in this study because the managers dealt primarily with English-speaking Koreans.

Considering that far too many U.S. companies have no formal expatriate training programs, the key issue is not which type of training is better, but whether companies offer any systematic cross-cultural training at all. (See Window on the World.)

AN INTEGRATED EXPATRIATE STAFFING SYSTEM Cross-cultural training, in whatever form, should not be an isolated experience. Rather, it should be part of an integrated, selection-orientation-repatriation process focused on a distinct career path.[85] The ultimate goal should be a positive and productive experience for the employee and his or her family and a smooth professional and cultural re-entry back home.

During the selection phase, the usual interview should be supplemented with an orientation session for the candidate's family. This session gives everyone an opportunity to "select themselves out" before a great deal of time and money has been invested. Experience has shown that upon the expatriate's arrival at the foreign assignment, family sponsors or assigned mentors are effective at reducing culture shock.[86] Sponsors and mentors ease the expatriate family through the critical first six months by answering naive but important questions and by serving as cultural translators.[87]

Finally, repatriation should be "a forethought" rather than an afterthought.[88] Candidates for foreign assignments deserve a firm commitment from their organization that a successful tour of duty will lead to a step up the career ladder upon their return. Expatriates who spend their time worrying about being leapfrogged while they are absent from headquarters are less likely to succeed.

What About North American Women on Foreign Assignments?

Historically, companies in Canada and the United States have sent very few women on foreign assignments. Between the early 1980s and the late 1990s, the representation of women among North American expatriates grew from 3 percent to a still small 14 percent.[89] Conventional wisdom—that women could not be effective because of foreign prejudice—has turned out to be a myth.[90] Recent research and practical experience have given us these insights:

- North American women have enjoyed above-average success on foreign assignments.
- The greatest barriers to foreign assignments for North American women have been self-disqualification and prejudice among *home-country* managers. A recent survey concluded that American women can be as successful as men in management in foreign countries *if* they can convince their employers to give them assignments.[91]
- Culture is a bigger hurdle than gender. In other words, North American women on foreign assignments are seen as North Americans first and as women second.[92]

Testimonial evidence suggests that these last two factors are also true for African Americans, many of whom report smoother relations abroad than at home.[93] Thus, the best career advice for *anyone* seeking a foreign assignment is this: carefully prepare yourself, *go for it*, and don't take "no" for an answer![94]

Relying on Local Managerial Talent

In recent years, the expensive problem of expatriate failure and general trends toward geocentrism and globalism have resulted in a greater reliance on managers from host countries. Foreign nationals already know the language and culture and do not require huge relocation expenditures.[95] In addition, host-country governments tend to look favorably on a greater degree of local control. On the negative side, local managers may not have adequate knowledge of home-office goals and procedures. The staffing of foreign positions is necessarily a case-by-case proposition.

SUMMARY

1. The study of international management is more important than ever as the huge global economy continues to grow. Doing business internationally typically involves much more than importing and/or exporting goods. The six stages of the internationalization process are licensing, exporting, local warehousing and selling, local assembly and packaging, joint ventures, and direct foreign investments. There are three main guidelines for success in international joint ventures: (a) Be patient while building trust with a carefully selected partner; (b) learn as much information as fast as possible without giving away key secrets; and (c) establish clear ground rules for rights and responsibilities. Global companies are a present-day reality, whereas transnational companies are a futuristic vision. A global company does business simultaneously in many countries but pursues global strategies administered from a strong home-country headquarters. In contrast, a transnational company is envisioned as a decentralized global network of productive units with no distinct national identity. There is growing concern about the economic and political power that such stateless enterprises may acquire as they eclipse the power and scope of their host nations.

2. Cultural intelligence (CQ) is defined as the ability of an outsider to "read" individual behavior, group dynamics, and situations in a foreign culture as well as the locals do. Those with high CQ are cross-cultural chameleons who blend in with the local cultural situation. Global managers with high cultural intelligence possess these nine cross-cultural competencies: (1) building relationships; (2) valuing people of different cultures; (3) listening and observation; (4) coping with ambiguity; (5) translating complex information; (6) taking action and initiative; (7) managing others; (8) adaptability and flexibility; and (9) managing stress. According to Howard Perlmutter, management tends to exhibit one of three general attitudes about international operations: an ethnocentric attitude (home-country-oriented), a polycentric attitude (host-country-oriented), or a geocentric attitude (world-oriented). Perlmutter claims that a geocentric attitude will lead to better product quality, improved use of resources, better local management, and more profit than the other attitudes.

3. In high-context cultures such as Japan, communication is based more on nonverbal and situational messages than it is in low-context cultures such as the United States. The nine cultural dimensions identified by the GLOBE project are power distance, uncertainty avoidance, institutional collectivism, in-group collectivism, assertiveness, gender equality, future orientation, performance orientation, and humane orientation.

4. Comparative management is a new field of study concerned with how organizational behavior and management practices differ across cultures. A unique study by Geert Hofstede of 116,000 IBM employees in 40 nations classified each country by its prevailing attitude toward four cultural variables. In view of significant international differences on these cultural dimensions, Hofstede suggests that American management theory and practice be adapted to local cultures rather than imposed on them. According to a study of nearly 6,000 companies in 17 nations, countries have their own characteristic style of using standard management practices. Incentives are relatively more important in the United States and Canada, while targets and goal setting get emphasized in Germany and Japan. Swedish managers place emphasis on monitoring. Thus, international managers need to tailor their style to the local culture.

5. Across 62 societies in the GLOBE study, the charismatic/value-based (goal-directed visionary) and team-oriented (competent team-builder) leadership styles were found to be widely applicable. The self-protective (self-centered) leadership style was not acceptable in any culture. The participative leadership style (involving others in making and implementing decisions) had mixed applicability across cultures, as did the humane-oriented (supportive

and nurturing) style. Global managers need to use a contingency approach to leadership, adapting their styles to the local culture.

6. Culture shock is a normal part of expatriate life. Job performance issues, family and/or individual culture shock, and homesickness are the leading reasons why U.S. expatriates go home early (a costly problem). Systematic cross-cultural training—ideally including development of interpersonal, observational, language, and stress management competencies—is needed. Expatriates also must be flexible and able to handle ambiguity. Specific cross-cultural training techniques include documentary programs, training via a culture assimilator, language instruction, sensitivity training, and field experience.

7. North American women fill a growing but still small share of foreign positions. The long-standing assumption that women will fail on foreign assignments because of foreigners' prejudice has turned out to be false. Women from the United States and Canada have been successful on foreign assignments but face two major hurdles at *home:* self-disqualification and prejudicial managers. Culture, not gender, is the primary challenge for women on foreign assignments. The situation for African Americans parallels that for women.

TERMS TO UNDERSTAND

- **International management,** p. 95
- **Global company,** p. 97
- **Transnational company,** p. 97
- **Cultural intelligence (CQ),** p. 97

- **Ethnocentric attitude,** p. 100
- **Polycentric attitude,** p. 101
- **Geocentric attitude,** p. 102
- **Culture,** p. 102
- **High-context cultures,** p. 104
- **Low-context cultures,** p. 104
- **Individualistic cultures,** p. 105

- **Collectivist cultures,** p. 105
- **Monochronic time,** p. 106
- **Polychronic time,** p. 106
- **Comparative management,** p. 107
- **Culture shock,** p. 111
- **Cross-cultural training,** p. 112

ACTION LEARNING EXERCISE

LOOK INTO THE CULTURAL MIRROR

Instructions: Culture, as defined in this chapter, involves *taken-for-granted* assumptions about how we should think, act, and feel (relative to both ourselves and the world in general). Here is an opportunity to bring those assumptions to the surface. Remember, there are no right or wrong answers. Moreover, because this exercise has no proven scientific validity, it is intended for instructional purposes only. The idea is to see where you stand in the world's rich mosaic of cultural diversity by rating yourself on the cultural variables discussed in this chapter.

Low-context
("Put it in writing.")

1 _____ 2 _____ 3 _____ 4 _____ 5

High-context
("The situation is more important than words.")

Individualistic
("Me first.")

1 _____ 2 _____ 3 _____ 4 _____ 5

Collectivist
("It's all about us.")

Monochronic
("Do one thing at a time and be on time.")

1 _____ 2 _____ 3 _____ 4 _____ 5

Polychronic
("There's a time to go fast and a time to go slow. Do more than one thing at a time.")

Power Distance

Low   **High**
("Leaders are no better   ("Authority and power of leaders
than anyone else.")   should be respected.")
1 _____ 2 _____ 3 _____ 4 _____ 5

Uncertainty Avoidance

Low   **High**
("Take chances, bend the rules.")   ("Take no chances, follow the rules.")
1 _____ 2 _____ 3 _____ 4 _____ 5

Future Orientation

Low   **High**
("Live for today; instant gratification.")   ("Think long term; save for the future.")
1 _____ 2 _____ 3 _____ 4 _____ 5

Performance Orientation

Low   **High**
("Loyalty and belonging are what   ("Take the initiative; have a sense of urgency
really count.")   about getting results.")
1 _____ 2 _____ 3 _____ 4 _____ 5

Humane Orientation

Low   **High**
("Look out for yourself.")   ("Help others, especially the weak and vulnerable.")
1 _____ 2 _____ 3 _____ 4 _____ 5

Masculinity   **Femininity**
("Winning and material wealth   ("Relationships and quality of life
are what count.")   are what really matter.")
1 _____ 2 _____ 3 _____ 4 _____ 5

FOR CONSIDERATION/DISCUSSION

1. Did this exercise help you better understand any of the cultural variables discussed in this chapter? Explain.

2. Does your cultural profile help you better understand some of your family's traditions, values, rituals, or customs?

3. How does your cultural profile compare with that of others (spouse, friends, classmates)? Could the seeds of conflict and misunderstanding grow from any cultural differences with them?

4. Which of your positive cultural traits could become a negative if taken to extremes?

ETHICS EXERCISE

 DO THE RIGHT THING

GOOGLE'S FIGHT AGAINST CHINESE CENSORSHIP

Background: Google's...pull out of China has brought into sharp relief China's longstanding clampdown on personal freedom and foreign companies' access to its vast consumer market. It has continued these practices even as it revs up the capitalist-style advance of the world's fastest-growing economy.

In China, domestic "stability" is paramount. That means zero tolerance for political dissent at a time when Chinese consumers are being encouraged to embrace technologies that let them communicate and socialize much like their Western counterparts. Similarly, China has invited major tech players, such as Google, Microsoft and Yahoo, to help nurture its economic growth. Yet it imposes censorship and other restrictions and has paid little heed to intellectual-property rights....

Will Western values factor in or will China's tactics prevail? "The 21st century is about whether and where a converging balance will be found," says [an international law expert].

Google's executive chairman Eric Schmidt: When we filed for our IPO [initial public offering of stock], we attached to the document a statement about how we wanted to run our business. We said we were going to be different. We said that we were going to be motivated by concerns that were not always or strictly business ones. This is an extension of that view. This was not a business decision—the business decision would obviously have been to continue to participate in the Chinese market. It was a decision based on values. We tried to ask what would be best from a global standpoint.

The negotiated compromise: In order to comply with Chinese law without violating its own commitment not to censor search results, Google created a landing page [in July 2010] that appears after users in China enter a search term. When users click on a link on the new page, they get redirected to a search engine located in Hong Kong. (Chinese censorship rules don't apply in the former British colony because of Beijing's "one country, two systems" policy.) The extra steps are an inconvenience to users that will drive more people to [Chinese competitor] Baidu, analysts predict. And where users go, advertisers will follow.

Sources: Excerpted from Byron Acohido, Calum MacLeod, and Kathy Chu, "Google Clash Highlights How China Does Business," *USA Today* (January 25, 2010): 1B–2B. As quoted in an interview by Fareed Zakaria, "A Conversation with Google's Chairman and CEO," *Newsweek* (January 25, 2010): 36. Excerpted from Bruce Einhorn, Mark Lee, and Brian Womack, "Google Stays in China. And Baidu Keeps on Winning," *Bloomberg Businessweek* (July 19–25, 2010): 39–40.

What are the ethical implications of the following interpretations?

1. Despite its admirable business philosophy, Google is a profit-making corporation that is cheating its stockholders by fighting censorship in China, the world's most populous country with huge market potential.
2. Foreign-owned companies are guests in host countries and have no right to impose their cultural values. They are obligated to "play by the rules" by following local laws and customs. Any exceptions?
3. Google, as an Internet mainstay, has a moral obligation to promote free speech worldwide. Did the negotiated solution betray that moral obligation?
4. Your own ethical interpretation?

MANAGERS-IN-ACTION VIDEO CASE STUDY

 ## NUMI ORGANIC TEA
The Cultural Imperative and a Sustainable Supply Chain

Numi Organic Tea was started in 1999 in Oakland, California. Numi imports tea from Asia and exports it to more than 20 countries around the world. Brian Durkee, Director of Operations, and Ahmed Rahim, co-founder and CEO, discuss in this video how and why they source tea from growers in China. They share their approach in creating mutually beneficial partnerships that are respectful of cultural differences. They also describe how they have implemented a sustainable supply chain and leveraged technology to grow. This video provides a sample of Numi Organic Tea's secrets to success, as Numi achieves its commitment to people, planet, and profit.

For more information about Numi, visit its Web site: www.numitea.com/.

Before watching the video, answer the following questions:

1. How would you describe culture and cultural differences?

2. Why is it important for managers to compare and study how organizational behavior and management practices differ across cultures?

3. What competencies and skills does a manager need to have to work effectively across cultures?

After watching the video, answer the following questions:

4. In *The Changing Workplace* chapter opener, we describe myths and realities about China. Choose one of these and discuss how you think it is relevant to the management team at Numi Tea.

5. What steps has Numi Tea taken to fulfill its commitment to the planet?

6. How does Numi Tea maintain its commitment to profit and people while respecting cultural differences?

7. How has technology had a positive impact on Numi Tea's management practices?

CLOSING CASE

TELL THE KIDS WE'RE MOVING TO KENYA

Dale Pilger, General Motors Corp.'s new managing director for Kenya, wonders if he can keep his Kenyan employees from interrupting his paperwork by raising his index finger.

"The finger itself will offend," warns Noah Midamba, a Kenyan. He urges that Mr. Pilger instead greet a worker with an effusive welcome, offer a chair and request that he wait. It can be even trickier to fire a Kenyan, Mr. Midamba says. The government asked one German auto executive to leave Kenya after he dismissed a man—whose brother was the East African country's vice president.

Mr. Pilger, his adventurous wife and their two teenagers, miserable about moving, have come to...[Boulder, Colorado,] for three days of cross-cultural training. The Cortland, Ohio, family learns to cope with being strangers in a strange land as consultants Moran, Stahl & Boyer International give them a crash immersion in African political history, business practices, social customs and nonverbal gestures. The training enables managers to grasp cultural differences and handle culture-shock symptoms such as self-pity.

Cross-cultural training is on the rise everywhere because more global-minded corporations moving fast-track executives overseas want to curb the cost of failed expatriate stints. . . .

But as cross-cultural training gains popularity, it attracts growing criticism. A lot of the training is garbage, argues Robert Bontempo, assistant professor of international business at Columbia University. Even customized family training offered by companies like Prudential Insurance Co. of America's Moran Stahl—which typically costs $6,000 for

three days—hasn't been scientifically tested. "They charge a huge amount of money, and there's no evidence that these firms do any good" in lowering foreign-transfer flops, Prof. Bontempo contends.

"You don't need research," to prove that cross-cultural training works because so much money has been wasted on failed overseas assignments, counters Gary Wederspahn, director of design and development at Moran Stahl.

General Motors agrees. Despite massive cost cutting lately, the auto giant still spends nearly $500,000 a year on cross-cultural training for about 150 Americans and their families headed abroad. "We think this substantially contributes to the low [premature] return rate" of less than 1 percent among GM expatriates, says Richard Rachner, GM general director of international personnel. . . .

The Pilgers' experience reveals the benefits and drawbacks of such training. Mr. Pilger, a 38-year-old engineer employed by GM for 20 years, sought an overseas post but never lived abroad before. He finds the sessions "worthwhile" in readying him to run a vehicle-assembly plant that is 51 percent owned by Kenya's government. But he finds the training "horribly empty . . . in helping us prepare for the personal side of the move."

Dale and Nancy Pilger have just spent a week in Nairobi. But the executive's scant knowledge of Africa becomes clear when trainer Jackson Wolfe, a former Peace Corps official, mentions Nigeria. "Is that where Idi Amin was from?" Mr. Pilger asks. The dictator ruled Uganda. With a sheepish smile, Mr. Pilger admits, "We don't know a lot about the world."

The couple's instructors don't always know everything about preparing expatriates for Kenyan culture, either. Mr. Midamba, an adjunct international-relations professor at Kent State University and son of a Kenyan political leader, concedes that he neglected to caution Mr. Pilger's predecessor against holding business dinners at Nairobi restaurants.

As a result, the American manager "got his key people to the restaurant and expected their wives to be there," Mr. Midamba recalls. But "the wives didn't show up." Married women in Kenya view restaurants "as places where you find prostitutes and loose morals," notes Mungai Kimani, another Kenyan trainer.

The blunder partly explains why Mr. Midamba goes to great lengths to teach the Pilgers the art of entertaining at home. Among his tips: Don't be surprised if guests arrive an hour early, an hour late, or announce their departure four times.

The Moran Stahl program also zeros in on the family's adjustment (though not to Mr. Pilger's satisfaction). A family's poor adjustment causes more foreign-transfer failures than a manager's work performance. That is the Pilgers' greatest fear because 14-year-old Christy and 16-year-old Eric bitterly oppose the move. The lanky, boyish-looking Mr. Pilger remembers Eric's tearful reaction as: "You'll have to arrest me if you think you're going to take me to Africa."

While distressed by his children's hostility, Mr. Pilger still believes living abroad will be a great growth experience for them. But he says he promised Eric that if "he's miserable" in Kenya, he can return to Ohio for his last year of high school next year.

To ease their adjustment, Christy and Eric receive separate training from their parents. The teens' activities include sampling Indian food (popular in Kenya) as well as learning how to ride Nairobi public buses, speak a little Swahili and juggle, of all things.

By the training's last day, both youngsters grudgingly accept being uprooted from friends, her swim team and his brand-new car. Going to Kenya "no longer seems like a death sentence," Christy says. Eric mumbles that he may volunteer at a wild-game reserve.

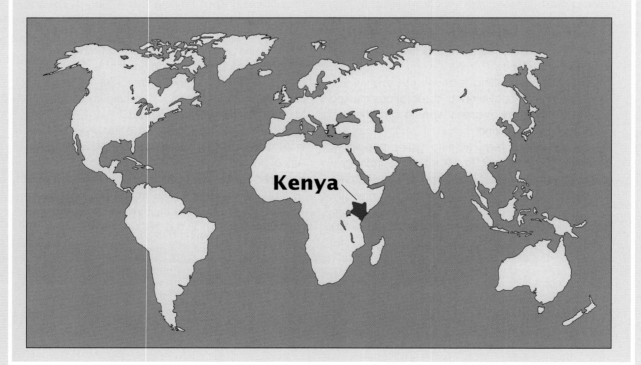

But their usually upbeat mother has become increasingly upset as she hears more about a country troubled by drought, poverty, and political unrest— where foreigners live behind walled fortresses. Now, at an international parenting session, she clashes with youth trainer Amy Kaplan over whether her offspring can safely ride Nairobi's public buses, even with Mrs. Pilger initially accompanying them.

"All the advice we've gotten is that it's deadly" to ride buses there, Mrs. Pilger frets. Ms. Kaplan retorts, "It's going to be hard" to let teenagers do their own thing in Kenya, but then they'll be less likely to rebel. The remark fails to quell Mrs. Pilger's fears that she can't handle life abroad. "I'm going to let a lot of people down if I blow this," she adds, her voice quavering with emotion.

For Discussion:

1. Does the Pilgers' son Eric seem to have an ethnocentric, polycentric, or geocentric attitude? Explain.

2. Would you label Kenya a monochronic or a polychronic culture, based on the evidence in this case? Explain.

3. Using Figure 4.1 as a guide, indicate which of the GLOBE leadership styles Pilger should use (and which he should avoid) in Kenya. Explain.

4. What were the positive and negative aspects of the Pilgers' predeparture training?

5. Do you think the Pilger family will end up having a productive and satisfying foreign assignment? Explain.

5

Management's Social and Ethical Responsibilities

"Would you want your actions posted as a clip on YouTube?"[1]

—*BRUCE WEINSTEIN*

BRENDAN MCDERMID/Reuters/Landov

The Changing Workplace

THE TWO FACES OF PFIZER

News item: In the largest health care fraud settlement in history, pharmaceutical giant Pfizer must pay $2.3 billion to resolve criminal and civil allegations that the company illegally promoted uses of four of its drugs, including the painkiller Bextra, the U.S. Department of Justice announced. . . .

As part of the settlement, Pfizer will pay a criminal fine of $1.195 billion, the largest criminal fine ever imposed in the USA for any matter, according to the Justice Department. . . .

Pfizer also has agreed to pay $1 billion in civil damages and penalties to compensate federal health care programs for false claims.

The investigation resulted from whistle-blower lawsuits, the first of which was filed by former Pfizer sales representative John Kopchinski, 45. . . .

Of the $102 million that will be divided among six whistle-blowers, Kopchinski [who was fired by Pfizer] will receive $51.5 million.

News item: During a spring management meeting at Pfizer, one executive floated a seductive idea: With millions of Americans struggling to make ends meet, maybe Pfizer should give away drugs to people who have lost their jobs. The 160-year-old company, which has long offered financial assistance to low-income patients, has never handed out freebies in response to a recession. But Pfizer CEO Jeffrey Kindler seized on the idea as a way both to support customers and to burnish Pfizer's reputation. "Five weeks after it was suggested, we just did it," he says.

Pfizer's free-drug program, called Maintain, is the latest effort by the pharmaceutical industry to repair its damaged public image and position itself as a standard bearer for social responsibility. For years, drug companies have been blasted for charging outlandish prices, holding generic drugs off the market, and paying doctors to help market their products.

Sources: Excerpted from Rita Rubin, "Pfizer Fined $2.3B for Illegal Marketing," *USA Today* (September 3, 2009): 1B; and Arlene Weintraub, "Will Pfizer's Giveaway Drugs Polish Its Public Image?" *Business Week* (August 3, 2009): 13.

OBJECTIVES

- **Define** the term *corporate social responsibility* (CSR), and **specify** the four levels in Carroll's global CSR pyramid.
- **Contrast** the classical economic and socioeconomic models of business, and **summarize** the arguments for and against CSR.
- **Identify** and **describe** the four social responsibility strategies, and **explain** the concept of enlightened self-interest.
- **Summarize** the four practical lessons from business ethics research.
- **Distinguish** between instrumental and terminal values, and **explain** their relationship to business ethics.
- **Identify** and **describe** at least four of the ten general ethical principles.
- **Discuss** what management can do to improve business ethics.

In terms of corporate social responsibility and business ethics, is Pfizer a corporate bad guy or good guy? When is it appropriate to blow the whistle on one's employer—an act of extreme organizational disloyalty in the eyes of some? Was Kopchinski's whistle-blower reward fair and appropriate? This chapter will help you tackle tough, ethically loaded questions such as these.

As the social, political, economic, and technological environments of management have changed, the practice of management itself has changed. This is especially true for managers in the private business sector. Today, in the wake of the recent economic meltdown and corporate bailouts, it is far less acceptable for someone in business to stand before the public and declare that his or her sole job is to make as much profit as possible.[2] The public is wary of the abuse of power and the betrayal of trust, and business managers—indeed, managers of all types of organizations—are expected to make a wide variety of economic and social contributions. Demands on business that would have been considered patently unreasonable 30 or 40 years ago have become the norm today. Stuart Graham, the American CEO of Skanska, a giant Swedish construction company with 12,000 projects worldwide, has even gone so far as to say that management has no choice but to improve in the future in order to meet these twin demands: shareholders demanding excellent financial performance and the public demanding social responsibility.[3] The purpose of this chapter is to examine management's broader social and ethical responsibilities.

SOCIAL RESPONSIBILITY: DEFINITION AND PERSPECTIVES

When John D. Rockefeller was at the zenith of his power as the founder of Standard Oil Company, he handed out dimes to rows of eager children who lined the street. Rockefeller did this on the advice of a public relations expert

Vova Shevchuk/Shutterstock.com

who believed the dime campaign would counteract his widespread reputation as a monopolist who had ruthlessly eliminated his competitors in the oil industry. The dime campaign was not a complete success, however, because Standard Oil was broken up under the Sherman Antitrust Act of 1890.[4] Conceivably, Rockefeller believed he was fulfilling some sort of social responsibility by passing out dimes to hungry children. Since Rockefeller's time, the concept of social responsibility has grown and matured to the point where many of today's companies are intimately involved in social programs that have no direct connection with the bottom line. These programs include everything from support of the arts and urban renewal to education reform and environmental protection. But like all aspects of management, social responsibility needs to be carried out in an effective and efficient manner.

What Does Corporate Social Responsibility (CSR) Involve?

Social responsibility, as defined in this section, is a relatively new concern of the business community. Like a child maturing through adolescence on the way to adulthood, the idea of corporate social responsibility is evolving. One expert defined corporate social responsibility (CSR) as "the notion that corporations have an obligation to constituent groups in society other than stockholders and beyond that prescribed by law or union contract."[5] As might be expected for any emerging area, disagreement remains over the exact nature and scope of management's *social* responsibilities.[6]

Nancy Lockwood, a researcher for the Society for Human Resource Management, characterizes CSR as financial, environmental, and social actions that allow a company to gain a competitive edge, make a profit, and enhance its reputation, all while serving others. She then expands the domain of CSR by adding that it is not limited to corporations; all types of organizations from labor

corporate social responsibility (CSR) the idea that business has social obligations above and beyond making a profit

| Figure **5.1** | Carroll's Global Corporate Social Responsibility Pyramid |

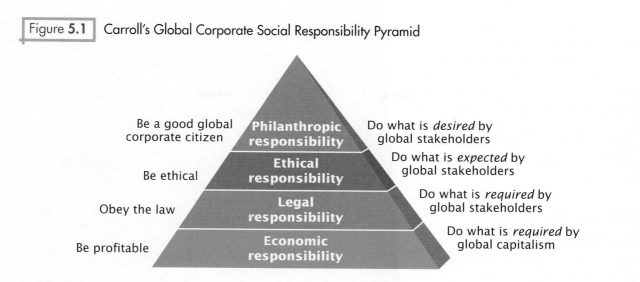

Source: *Academy of Management Executive: The Thinking Manager's Source* by Archie B. Carroll. Copyright 2004 by Academy of Management (NY). Reproduced with permission of Academy of Management (NY) in the format Textbook via Copyright Clearance Center.

unions to governmental agencies can and should employ these positive business strategies.[7] Some CSR advocates prefer the big-picture term *triple bottom line*—meaning "People, Planet, Profit."[8] The global economy is expanding the scope of CSR even more.

CSR FOR GLOBAL AND TRANSNATIONAL CORPORATIONS. Business ethics scholar Archie B. Carroll believes the burgeoning global economy requires a more encompassing perspective on CSR. According to his model, shown in Figure 5.1, today's global and transnational companies have four main areas of responsibility: economic, legal, ethical, and philanthropic. Working from bottom to top, this means the global corporation should:

- *Make a profit* consistent with expectations for international businesses
- *Obey the law* of host countries as well as international law
- *Be ethical in its practices*, taking host-country and global standards into consideration
- *Be a good corporate citizen*, especially as defined by the host country's expectations[9]

Carroll emphasizes that this is not a pick-and-choose approach to CSR. All four responsibilities are intertwined and need to be fulfilled if a global corporation—or *any* company in any situation, for that matter—is to be called socially responsible.

However, over the long term, a company must consistently satisfy the bottom three levels before exercising philanthropic responsibility. Carroll describes *philanthropic responsibilities* as activities not decreed by law or not considered a regular part of business in an ethical sense.[10] Tachi Kiuchi, managing director of Japan's Mitsubishi Electric Corp., offers his own all-encompassing perspective on CSR when he states that, in his opinion, serving the public—not just making a profit—is the real reason businesses exist: "People talk about businesses needing to be responsible as if it's something new we need to do on top of everything else. But the whole essence of business should be responsibility."[11]

CSR REQUIRES VOLUNTARY ACTION. An implicit feature of the above definition and perspective is that an action must be *voluntary* to qualify as socially responsible. For example, consider the actions of Paul Dolan at California's Fetzer Vineyards. Not only has he converted his 2,000-acre vineyard to an all-organic and "zero waste" operation, he requires his outside grape growers to be organic as well. His critics have claimed that "going organic, using alternative power sources, providing living wages for workers, and eliminating waste . . . are nice, fuzzy goals that don't make financial sense," yet Dolan attributes his success in this highly competitive industry to these very actions.[12]

Fetzer Vineyards is socially responsible because Dolan has *voluntarily* taken a creative and inspiring leadership role in the wine-making business to strike a workable balance between profit and the greater good. His actions did not involve reluctant compliance with new laws or court orders, nor are his actions a cynical public relations ploy to keep regulators at bay.

What Is the Role of Business in Society?

Much of the disagreement over what social responsibility involves can be traced to a fundamental debate about the exact purpose of a business. Is a business an economic entity responsible only for making a profit for its stockholders? Or is it a socioeconomic entity obligated to make both economic and social contributions to society?[13] Depending on one's perspective, social responsibility can be interpreted either way.

THE CLASSICAL ECONOMIC MODEL.

The classical economic model can be traced to the eighteenth century, when businesses were owned largely by entrepreneurs or owner-managers. Competition was vigorous among small

5a
Personal Social Responsibility

Survey: 1,018 employees were asked if the money for their year-end holiday party should go instead to charity: 51% said cancel the party; 49% said have the party.

Tips for giving: On Facebook you can use the Causes application to create a page for a charity you want to support. Then invite friends to join the cause and give money through the site. . . .

Don't underestimate the value of what you can provide [as a volunteer]. A typical volunteer hour at, say, a soup kitchen or in your parks department is worth $20.85 to the organization, according to Independent Sector, a group that tracks nonprofits.

QUESTIONS: Would you vote to cancel the party for charity? Explain. Why do people who unselfishly donate their time and money find it so personally rewarding? What is your experience (and future plan) as a donor or volunteer?

For further information about the interactive annotations in this chapter, visit our student Web site.

Sources: Survey data from Anne R. Carey and Paul Trap, "Give to Charity in Lieu of Office Holiday Party?" *USA Today* (December 17, 2010): 1A; and excerpted from Dan Kadlec, "How to Give Like a Billionaire," *Money,* 39 (December 2010): 121, 123.

operations, and short-run profits were the sole concern of these early entrepreneurs. Of course, the key to attaining short-run profits was to provide society with needed goods and services. According to Adam Smith, father of the classical economic model, an "invisible hand" promoted the public welfare. Smith believed the efforts of competing entrepreneurs had a natural tendency to promote the public interest when each tried to maximize short-run

Janine Wiedel Photolibrary/Alamy

The green movement is testing the limits of corporate social responsibility. Here, 50,000 people marched through the streets of London, demanding clean energy sources that are affordable *and* protect the environment.

E T H I C S : Character, Courage, and Values

Cleaning Up in a Socially Responsible Way

Dallas-based Soap Hope, [launched in 2009 by entrepreneur Salah Boukadoum,] . . . sells all-natural body-care products online (soaphope.com).

Soap Hope is a decidedly for-profit venture, but with a philanthropic twist. At the end of the year the company invests all its profits in nonprofits with an antipoverty mission, such as Chiapas International and the Plan Fund. Yet its investment is just a loan: The nonprofit recipient must pay back all the funds within 12 months. "All we're doing is delaying our [profits] by one year," says Boukadoum. Since any new loans are made with the next year's profits, he says, "there's actually a rolling investment."

Boukadoum dubbed his idea Good Returns and hopes it will morph into its own nonprofit, providing a "Good Housekeeping"-type certification for participating companies and offering insurance to guarantee the loans.

For Discussion: Why is this unique business strategy an example of the socioeconomic model? What are the pros and cons of this particular strategy?

Source: Excerpted from Abby Ellin, "From Tech Bubbles to Soap Bubbles," *Fortune* (July 5, 2010): 38.

profits. In other words, Smith believed the public interest was served by individuals pursuing their own economic self-interests.[14]

This model has survived into modern times. For example, *Business Week* quoted Robert J. Eaton, former chairman of Chrysler Corporation prior to the creation of DaimlerChrysler, as describing CSR as ridiculous, adding, "You'll simply burden industry to a point where it's no longer competitive."[15] Thus, according to the classical economic model of business, profitability and social responsibility are the same thing.

THE SOCIOECONOMIC MODEL. Reflecting society's broader expectations for business (for example, safe and meaningful jobs, clean air and water, charitable donations, safe products), many think the time has come to revamp the classical economic model, which they believe to be obsolete. Enron, the company that took a spectacular tumble from number 7 on the 2001 *Fortune* 500[16] list to a scandalous bankruptcy in 2002, has been cited as a prime case in point. Economist Robert Kuttner explained that Enron claimed to exemplify the philosophy that free markets cleanse themselves. But in fact, Enron's cronyism and disregard for the rules eroded the transparency that should be the foundation of an efficient free market system.[17]

Enron's 21,000 former employees—most of whom lost their life's savings along with their jobs—would probably agree. According to the socioeconomic model, proposed as an alternative to the classical economic model, business is just one subsystem among many in a highly interdependent society (see Ethics: Character, Courage, and Values).

Advocates of the socioeconomic model point out that many groups in society besides stockholders have a stake in corporate affairs. Creditors, current and retired employees, customers, suppliers, competitors, all levels of government, the community, and society in general have expectations, often conflicting, for management. Some companies go so far as to conduct a stakeholder audit.[18] This growing practice involves systematically identifying all parties that might possibly be affected by the company's performance (for an example,[19] see Figure 5.2). According to the socioeconomic view, business has an obligation to respond to the needs of all stakeholders while pursuing a profit.[20] Delivery giant UPS, for instance, responded quickly and effectively to the Haiti earthquake disaster in 2010 because it had a running start, thanks to its commitment to being a good corporate citizen. UPS has long believed that logistics is critical in a crisis, which is why the company—an acknowledged champion at logistics—encourages employees to volunteer during disasters and has a

stakeholder audit identification of all parties that might be affected by the organization

Figure 5.2 A Sample Stakeholder Audit for Walmart, the World's Largest Retailer

20-member logistics team in Asia, Europe, and the Americas trained to provide humanitarian aid when needed.[21]

Arguments for and Against Corporate Social Responsibility

As one might suspect, the debate about the role of business has spawned many specific arguments both for and against corporate social responsibility.[22] A sample of four major arguments on each side will reveal the principal issues.

ARGUMENTS FOR. Convinced that a business should be more than simply a profit machine, proponents of social responsibility have offered the following arguments:

1. *Business is unavoidably involved in social issues.* As social activists like to say, business is either part of the solution or part of the problem. There is no denying that private business shares responsibility for such societal problems as unemployment,

inflation, and pollution. Like everyone else, corporate citizens must balance their rights and responsibilities.

2. *Business has the resources to tackle today's complex societal problems.* With its rich stock of technical, financial, and managerial resources, the private business sector can play a decisive role in solving society's more troublesome problems. After all, without society's support, business could not have built its resource base in the first place.

3. *A better society means a better environment for doing business.* Business can enhance its long-run profitability by making an investment in society today. Today's problems can turn into tomorrow's profits.

4. *Corporate social action will prevent government intervention.* As evidenced by waves of antitrust, equal employment opportunity, and pollution-control legislation, government will force business to do what it fails to do voluntarily.

Arguments like these four give business a broad socioeconomic agenda.

ARGUMENTS AGAINST. Remaining faithful to the classical economic model, opponents of corporate social responsibility rely on the first two arguments below. The third and fourth arguments have been voiced by those who think business is already too big and powerful.

1. *Profit maximization ensures the efficient use of society's resources.* By buying goods and services, consumers collectively dictate where assets should be deployed. Social expenditures amount to theft of stockholders' equity.

2. *As an economic institution, business lacks the ability to pursue social goals.* Gross inefficiencies can be expected if managers are forced to divert their attention from their pursuit of economic goals.

3. *Business already has enough power.* Considering that business exercises powerful influence over where and how we work and live, what we buy, and what we value, more concentration of social power in the hands of business is undesirable.

4. *Because managers are not elected, they are not directly accountable to the people.* Corporate social programs can easily become misguided. The market system effectively controls business's economic performance but is a poor mechanism for controlling business's social performance.

These arguments are based on the assumption that business should stick to what it does best—pursuing profit by producing marketable goods and services. Social goals should be handled by individuals and other institutions, such as the family, schools, religious organizations, or government.

TOWARD GREATER SOCIAL RESPONSIBILITY

Is it inevitable that management will assume greater social responsibility? Some scholars believe so. It has been said that business is bound by an iron law of responsibility, which states that "in the long run, those who do not use power in a way that society considers responsible will tend to lose it."[23] This is an important concept, considering that cynicism about business runs deep today, despite a more pro-business political climate worldwide. In response to his company's 2010 22-nation trust and credibility survey, Richard Edelman, CEO of the public relations firm bearing his name, reported that while trust in business is growing, it still has a long way to go. Firms will have to prove to people that they can have both profit and purpose.[24] The call for business to act more responsibly is clear. If this challenge is not met voluntarily, government reform legislation is likely to force business to meet it. In this section, we look at four alternative social responsibility strategies and some contrasting expressions of corporate social responsibility.

Social Responsibility Strategies

Similar to management's political response continuum, discussed in Chapter 3, is its social responsibility continuum (see Figure 5.3), which is marked by four strategies: reaction, defense, accommodation, and proaction.[25] Each involves a distinctly different approach to demands for greater social responsibility.

REACTION. A business that follows a reactive social responsibility strategy will deny responsibility while striving to maintain the status quo. This strategy has been a favorite one for the tobacco industry, intent on preventing any legal liability linkage between smoking and cancer. So, for example, when European countries showed signs of adopting U.S.-style bans on secondhand smoke, Philip Morris reacted by initiating a campaign claiming that breathing secondhand smoke was less dangerous than drinking milk. France responded by banning the campaign, and Philip Morris soon faced a couple of lawsuits.[26]

DEFENSE. A defensive social responsibility strategy uses legal maneuvering and/or a public relations campaign to avoid assuming additional responsibilities. Toyota's foot dragging on vehicle recalls in recent years is a clear case in point. A study of lawsuits against the car manufacturer reveals that Toyota has often said that it lacked the required information to turn over or claimed that it couldn't retrieve the information from headquarters in Japan. Toyota has also been known to withhold test results and electronically stored vehicle data that could be

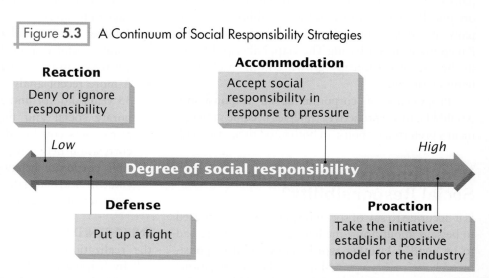

| Figure **5.3** | A Continuum of Social Responsibility Strategies

Reaction
Deny or ignore responsibility

Accommodation
Accept social responsibility in response to pressure

Low   **Degree of social responsibility**   *High*

Defense
Put up a fight

Proaction
Take the initiative; establish a positive model for the industry

iron law of responsibility those who do not use power in a socially responsible way will eventually lose it | *reactive social responsibility strategy* denying responsibility and resisting change | *defensive social responsibility strategy* resisting additional responsibilities with legal and public relations tactics

potentially damaging, and to ignore court orders to submit documents.[27] Consequently, Toyota's once sterling reputation for product quality and its corporate reputation have taken major hits that will require many years to rehabilitate.

ACCOMMODATION. The organization must be pressured into assuming additional responsibilities when it follows an **accommodative social responsibility strategy**. Some outside stimulus, such as pressure from a special-interest group or threatened government action, is usually required to trigger an accommodative strategy. For example, Apple had to be nudged into greater environmental transparency and actions, but the company's Web site now confirms that Apple has reduced its level of carbon emissions and has eliminated polyvinyl chlorides (PVCs) and bromide flame retardants (BFRs) in its products. CEO Steve Jobs acknowledges that Greenpeace motivated Apple to stop polluting the environment and to avoid working with suppliers that use toxic substances, but he objected strongly to the tactics Greenpeace used.[28]

PROACTION. A **proactive social responsibility strategy** involves taking the initiative with a progressive program that serves as an inspiring role model for the industry. Sportswear maker Patagonia is a prime example. Founder Yvon Chouinard describes one recent initiative in which Patagonia analyzed the fibers used in its clothing and found that industrially grown cotton, heavily loaded with pesticides, was the most damaging. Chouinard explains the company's response by saying, "What the switchover to organically grown cotton did was mobilize the company in a direction, and it's been more profitable." Patagonia is now advising The Gap, Nike, and Levi's in the use of organically grown cotton in clothing manufacturing.[29]

Proponents of corporate social responsibility would like to see proactive strategies become management's preferred response in both good times and bad.

Who Benefits from Corporate Social Responsibility?

Is it accurate to say of social responsibility what used to be said about home medicine, "It has to taste bad to be good"? In other words, does social responsibility have to be a hardship for the organization?

5b
Back to the Opening Case
Where would you plot Pfizer on the social responsibility continuum in Figure 5.3? Explain.

Those who answer *yes* believe that social responsibility should be motivated by **altruism**, an unselfish devotion to the interests of others.[30] This implies that businesses that are not socially responsible are motivated strictly by self-interest. In short-run economic terms, the tobacco industry's foot dragging has saved it billions of dollars. In contrast, 3M's decision to pull its popular Scotchgard fabric protector spray cans from the marketplace as soon as the company became aware of a possible health hazard cost the company an estimated $500 million in annual sales.[31] On the basis of this evidence alone, one would be hard pressed to say that social responsibility pays. Research paints a mixed but somewhat brighter picture:

- A study of 243 companies for two years found a positive correlation between industry leadership in environmental protection/pollution control and profitability. The researchers concluded, "It pays to be green."[32]
- Another study found a good reputation for corporate social responsibility to be a competitive advantage in recruiting talented people.[33]
- A more recent analysis of 167 studies spanning 35 years did *not* find a strong link between corporate social and financial performance. The researchers concluded that there is only a small correlation between profits and socially responsible corporate behavior. However, shareholder value is clearly negatively impacted when a company acts in a socially irresponsible manner.[34]

ENLIGHTENED SELF-INTEREST. Enlightened self-interest, the realization that business ultimately helps itself by helping to solve societal problems, involves balancing short-run costs and long-run benefits. For example, consider the beverage industry: Coke and United Resource Recovery started a facility to recycle polyethyleneterephthalate (PET) into new bottles, and Nestlé is working with Waste Management to recycle plastics to use as packaging for its Perrier, Poland Spring, and other food brands. Why go green? Public image plays a part in the decision, but recycled packaging also costs less than new PET, a petroleum-based product.[35] Is the elusive "triple bottom line" evident in this situation, or is it just a cost-saving tactic cloaked as corporate social responsibility? You be the judge.

Advocates of enlightened self-interest contend that social responsibility expenditures are motivated by profit. Research into **corporate philanthropy**, the charitable donation of company resources, supports this contention. (*Note*: 68 large U.S. companies responding to a *USA Today* survey donated $3.9 billion in cash to charities in 2009.)[36]

After analyzing Internal Revenue Service statistics for firms in 36 industries, researchers concluded that corporate giving is a form of *profit-motivated advertising*. They went on to observe that philanthropy is not a reliable gauge of a corporation's true spirit of giving.[37] This theory of profit-motivated advertising was further supported by a study of 130 large manufacturing firms in the United States. Companies that had committed significant crimes but donated a good deal of money had better responsibility ratings than companies that had committed no crimes but donated very little money.[38]

AN ARRAY OF BENEFITS FOR THE ORGANIZATION. In addition to the advertising effect, other possible long-run benefits for socially responsible organizations include the following:

- Tax-free incentives to employees (such as buying orchestra tickets and giving them to deserving employees).
- Retention of talented employees by satisfying their altruistic motives.
- Help in recruiting talented and socially conscious personnel.
- Swaying public opinion against government intervention.
- Improved community living standards for employees.
- Attracting socially conscious investors.
- A nontaxable benefit for employees in which company funds are donated to their favorite causes. Many companies match employees' contributions to their college alma maters, for example. (*Tip*: Be sure to ask about this during job interviews.)

John Sommers/Reuters/Corbis

As part of a win-win partnership between Major League Baseball and the Susan G. Komen for the Cure foundation, this Hillerich & Bradsby employee puts the finishing touches on pink versions of the firm's iconic baseball bats for a "Bats Against Breast Cancer" fundraiser.

corporate philanthropy charitable donation of company resources

Social responsibility can be a win-win proposition; both society and the socially responsible organization can benefit in the long run.[39] Meanwhile, in today's age of increased corporate accountability, efforts are under way to assess the benefits of philanthropy. According to one consultant, just as businesses invest in marketing or development, so should they view giving as a strategic investment.[40]

THE ETHICAL DIMENSION OF MANAGEMENT

There is widespread cynicism about business ethics these days. A Pew Research Center poll showed that 69 percent of those surveyed hold a negative opinion about banks and finance corporations, and 64 percent hold a negative view of any large firm.[41] This is not surprising, considering recent headlines. Bernie Madoff was sentenced to 150 years in prison in 2009 for a colossal investment scam.[42] Since then, blue-chip American companies Citigroup, General Electric, Goldman Sachs, and Hewlett-Packard collectively paid over $700 million in fines to the U.S. government for various misdeeds, including fraud and kickbacks.[43] More than ever,

the subject of ethics deserves serious attention in management circles.[44] (See Green Management: Toward Sustainability.)

Ethics is the study of moral obligation involving the distinction between right and wrong. *Business ethics*, sometimes referred to as management ethics or organizational ethics, narrows the frame of reference to productive organizations.[45] However, as a pair of ethics experts noted, business ethics is not a simple matter:

> *Just being a good person and, in your own way, having sound personal ethics may not be sufficient to handle the ethical issues that arise in a business organization. Many people who have limited business experience suddenly find themselves making decisions about product quality, advertising, pricing, hiring practices, and pollution control. The values they learned from family, church, and school may not provide specific guidelines for these complex business decisions. For example, is a particular advertisement deceptive? Should a gift to a customer be considered a bribe, or is it a special promotional incentive? . . . Many business ethics decisions are close calls. Years of experience in a particular industry may be required to know what is acceptable.[46]*

Green Management: Toward Sustainability

Beware the Greenwashers!

More than half of consumers say they would pay more for a product if they knew it was better for the environment, according to a [new] national poll. . . .

Yet, some of the spending is misplaced: Overhyped and overpriced enviro-friendly imposters share shelves with the truly planet- and human-friendly products. Misleading claims are so rampant, there is actually a term for it: greenwashing.

. . . "The concept of green is still evolving," and there are no easy answers for consumers, says Ed Stafford, a Utah State University professor who specializes in green marketing. "Even environmentalists conflict with one another about what is truly a green product."

No wonder more than 40% of consumers say they don't know how to verify whether a company really is green, according to [another recent study].

For Discussion: What evidence of greenwashing have you detected recently? How did you uncover it? How does greenwashing impact the drive for sustainability and the public's trust in business?

Source: Excerpted from Laura Petrecca and Christine Dugas, "Going Truly Green Might Require Detective Work," *USA Today* (April 22, 2010): 1B–2B.

ethics study of moral obligation involving right versus wrong

With this reality check in mind, we turn to a discussion of business ethics research, personal values, ethical principles, and steps that management can take to foster ethical business behavior.

Practical Lessons from Business Ethics Research

Empirical research is always welcome in a socially relevant and important area such as business ethics.[47] It permits us to go beyond mere intuition and speculation to determine more precisely who, what, and why. On-the-job research of business ethics among managers has yielded practical insights in four areas: (1) ethical hot spots, (2) pressure from above, (3) discomfort with ambiguity, and (4) the rationalization of unethical conduct.

ETHICAL HOT SPOTS. In a survey of 1,324 U.S. employees from all levels across several industries, 48 percent admitted to having performed (during the prior year) at least one illegal or unethical act from a list of 25 questionable practices. The list included everything from calling in sick when feeling well through cheating on expense accounts, forging signatures, and giving or accepting kickbacks, to ignoring violations of environmental laws. Also uncovered in the study were the top ten workplace hot spots responsible for triggering unethical and illegal conduct:

- Balancing work and family
- Poor internal communications
- Poor leadership
- Work hours, workload
- Lack of management support
- Need to meet sales, budget, or profit goals
- Little or no recognition of achievements
- Company politics
- Personal financial worries
- Insufficient resources[48]

PRESSURE FROM ABOVE. Numerous studies have uncovered the problem of perceived pressure to achieve results. As discussed in Chapter 13, pressure from superiors can lead to unhealthful conformity. How widespread is the problem? Very widespread, according to the ethical hot spots survey just discussed:

- Most workers feel some pressure to act unethically or illegally on the job (56 percent), but far

fewer (17 percent) feel a high level of pressure to do so. . . .
- Mid-level managers most often reported a high level of pressure to act unethically or illegally (20 percent). Employees of large companies cited such pressure more than those at small businesses (21 percent versus 14 percent).
- High levels of pressure were reported more often by those with a high school diploma or less (21 percent) versus college graduates (13 percent).[49]

By being aware of this problem of pressure from above, managers can (1) consciously avoid putting undue pressure on others and (2) prepare to deal with excessive organizational pressure.

An instructive case in point is Walt Pavlo, a former MCI collection manager who spent 18 months in prison for his part in a fraudulent scheme. Pavlo found out that MCI managers, who had purchased stock options, wanted to prevent the price per share from dropping. Wanting to be perceived as a team player, Pavlo felt that he should "fudge the numbers." He later explained his illegal actions by saying he believed there was a powerful, yet unspoken directive to avoid giving the managers any bad financial news.[50] Excessive pressure to achieve results is a serious problem because it can cause otherwise good and decent people to take ethical shortcuts just to keep their jobs. The challenge for managers is to know where to draw the line between motivating employees to excel and exerting too much pressure. Particularly troublesome are overly aggressive goal-setting schemes that create a pressure-cooker environment."[51]

AMBIGUOUS SITUATIONS. In a survey of 111 executives (27 percent female) from a diverse array of large companies, 78 percent said the existence of "ambiguous rules" was a common rationale for "bending the rules."[52] Surveys of purchasing managers and field sales personnel showed that respondents were uncomfortable with ambiguous situations in which there were no clear-cut ethical guidelines. As one research team noted, the survey showed just how much purchasing managers want a written policy.[53] In other words, those who often face ethically ambiguous situations want formal guidelines to help sort things out. Ethical codes, discussed later, can satisfy this need for guidelines.

RATIONALIZATION: HOW GOOD PEOPLE END UP DOING BAD THINGS. Rationalization is a fundamental part of everyday life. "They say dark chocolate is good for you. I think I'll have another big piece of that delicious chocolate cake." "Of course I cheat a little on my expense report, doesn't everybody? Besides, the company owes me." Such rationalizations involve perceiving an objectively questionable action

Chepe Nicoli/Shutterstock.com

as normal and acceptable. Rationalization may occur before and/or after the fact. A team of management researchers reviewed the behavioral science literature and came up with a list of six rationalization strategies that employees commonly use to justify misdeeds in the workplace (see Table 5.1). Those misdeeds can range from slightly wrong (e.g., exaggerating your knowledge of a software program to your coworkers) to absolutely

Table 5.1   How Employees Tend to Rationalize Unethical Conduct

STRATEGY	DESCRIPTION	EXAMPLES
Denial of responsibility	The actors engaged in corrupt behaviors perceive that they have no other choice than to participate in such activities.	"What can I do? My arm is being twisted." "It is none of my business what the corporation does in overseas bribery."
Denial of injury	The actors are convinced that no one is harmed by their actions; hence the actions are not really corrupt.	"No one was really harmed." "It could have been worse."
Denial of victim	The actors counter any blame for their actions by arguing that the violated party deserved whatever happened.	"They deserved it." "They chose to participate."
Social weighting	The actors assume two practices that moderate the salience of corrupt behaviors: 1. Condemn the condemner, 2. Selective social comparison.	"You have no right to criticize us." "Others are worse than we are."
Appeal to higher loyalties	The actors argue that their violation of norms is due to their attempt to realize a higher-order value.	"We answered to a more important cause." "I would not report it because of my loyalty to my boss."
Metaphor of the ledger	The actors rationalize that they are entitled to indulge in deviant behaviors because of their accrued credits (time and effort) in their jobs.	"We've earned the right." "It's all right for me to use the Internet for personal reasons at work. After all, I do work overtime."

Source: *Academy of Management Executive: The Thinking Manager's Source* by Vikas Anand, Blake Ashforth, and Mahendra Jo. Copyright 2004 by Academy of Management (NY). Reproduced with permission of Academy of Management (NY) in the format Textbook via Copyright Clearance Center.

criminal (e.g., accepting a bribe from a vendor). Both managers and nonmanagers need to be aware of these common rationalizations and resist the temptation to invoke them too often. New employees are particularly vulnerable to socialization tactics and influences infected with unhealthful rationalizations. The researchers concluded that there are strong pressures to continue questionable behavior and plenty of opportunities to rationalize transgressions because there is ambiguity in many current business environments. Employee education and the designation of an "ethics ombudsperson" can help protect against these rationalization tactics.[54]

A BOLD CALL TO ACTION. Corporate misconduct and the associated research findings underscore the importance of the following call to action. It comes from Bill George, Harvard professor and former CEO of Medtronic, a manufacturer of heart pacemakers and other medical devices: Ethical boundaries are determined by each individual, and an employee should stand up for his or her ethical principles if given a direct order that violates those principles, even if it means resigning from the job.[55] George's call is *personal*. It requires *courage*. His words suggest that each of us can begin the process of improving business ethics by looking in a mirror.

Personal Values as Ethical Anchors

Values are too often ignored in discussions of management.[56] This oversight is serious because personal values can play a pivotal role in managerial decision making and ethics. For example, Peter Löscher, CEO of German industrial giant Siemens (who was hired to clean up the company's international kickback scandal that resulted in $1.34 billion in fines[57]), recently offered the following advice to corporate leaders: "Stick to your principles. Have a clear ethical north. Be trusted and be the role model of your company." He added that leaders should have a set of core values they live by through life's ups and downs, and that winning can be accomplished through leadership and innovation.[58]

Contemporary social observers complain that many managers lack character and have turned their backs on ethical values such as honesty, and MIT management scholar Michael Schrage agrees that employees are increasingly willing to blame their betrayal of personal values on corporate imperatives. While talent and intelligence abound, Schrage says, "character may be the scarcer and more valuable commodity."[59]

Defined broadly, values are abstract ideals that shape an individual's thinking and behavior.[60] Let's explore two different types of values that act as anchors for our ethical beliefs and conduct.

INSTRUMENTAL AND TERMINAL VALUES. Each manager, indeed each person, values various means and ends in life. Recognizing this means-ends distinction, behavioral scientists have identified two basic types of values. An instrumental value is an enduring belief that a certain way of behaving is appropriate in all situations. For example, the time-honored saying

5c
Survey Says . . .

[The Josephson Institute of Ethics] surveyed 43,321 teens ages 15 to 18 from 78 public and 22 private schools. . . .

- 60% of the students said they had "cheated on a test," and 34% did so twice or more. Students at non-religious private schools cited the lowest percentage (33%), while 56% at religious schools said they cheated.

- 27% of the students said they "stole something from a store."

QUESTIONS: Has America, as some contend, become a "cheating culture" in which cheating is expected and tolerated? Can values and ethics be turned on and off to fit the situation (e.g., cheat in school but be an honest businessperson later in life)?

Source: Excerpted from Sharon Jayson, "Teens Say Bullying Is Widespread," *USA Today* (October 26, 2010): 1A.

values abstract ideals that shape one's thinking and behavior | instrumental value enduring belief in a certain way of behaving

"Honesty is the best policy" represents an instrumental value. A person who truly values honesty will probably behave in an honest manner under all circumstances. A terminal value, in contrast, is an enduring belief that a certain end-state of existence is worth striving for and attaining.[61] Whereas one person may strive for eternal salvation, another may strive for social recognition and admiration. Instrumental values (modes of behavior) help people achieve terminal values (desired end-states).

Because a person can hold a number of different instrumental and terminal values in various combinations, individual value systems are somewhat like fingerprints: each of us has a unique set. No wonder managers who face the same ethical dilemma often differ in their interpretations and responses.

IDENTIFYING AND ACTING UPON YOUR OWN VALUES. To help you discover your own set of values, refer to the Rokeach value survey in the Action Learning Exercise at the end of this chapter. Take a few moments now to complete this survey. (As a reality check on the "fit" between your intentions and your actual behavior, have a close friend, relative, or spouse evaluate you later with the Rokeach survey.)

If your results surprise you, it is probably because we tend to take our basic values for granted. We seldom stop to arrange them consciously according to priority. For the sake of comparison, compare your top five instrumental and terminal values with the value profiles uncovered in a

survey of 220 eastern U.S. managers. On average, those managers ranked their instrumental values as follows: (1) honest, (2) responsible, (3) capable, (4) ambitious, and (5) independent. The most common terminal value rankings were (1) self-respect, (2) family security, (3) freedom, (4) a sense of accomplishment, and (5) happiness.[62] These managerial value profiles are offered for purposes of comparison only; they are not necessarily an index of desirable or undesirable priorities. When addressing specific ethical issues, managers need to consider each individual's personal values.

Another reality check involves how faithful we are to our key values. For instance, it is reasonable to assume most people would say they value being "honest." However, in a recent survey of 1,000 employees representative of the general population, behavioral intentions were almost equally split between honest and dishonest actions. Fifty-two percent said they would *not* feel comfortable taking things such as office supplies, electronic files, and information about customers when leaving a job. Forty-eight percent said "Yes"—they would feel comfortable with such behaviors.[63] How about you? Are you faithful to your cherished values or are your value → behavior connections elastic and situational?

General Ethical Principles

Like your highly personalized value system, your ethical beliefs have been shaped by many factors, including family and friends, the media, culture, schooling, religious instruction, and general life experiences.[64] This section brings taken-for-granted ethical beliefs, generally unstated, out into the open for discussion and greater understanding. It does so by exploring ten general ethical principles. Even though we may not necessarily know how ethics scholars label them, we use ethical principles both consciously and

In recent years, ethics has become an increasingly important part of the curriculum in undergraduate management and MBA courses, which is intended to later ensure ethical conduct in the workplace.

Stock Connection Blue/Alamy

terminal value enduring belief in the attainment of a certain end-state

unconsciously when dealing with ethical dilemmas.[65] Each of the ten ethical principles is followed by a brief behavioral guideline.

1. *Self-interests.* "Never take any action that is not in the *long-term* self-interests of yourself and/or of the organization to which you belong."
2. *Personal virtues.* "Never take any action that is not honest, open, and truthful and that you would not be proud to see reported widely in national newspapers and on television."
3. *Religious injunctions.* "Never take any action that is not kind and that does not build a sense of community, a sense of all of us working together for a commonly accepted goal."
4. *Government requirements.* "Never take any action that violates the law, for the law represents the minimal moral standards of our society."
5. *Utilitarian benefits.* "Never take any action that does not result in greater good than harm for the society of which you are a part."
6. *Universal rules.* "Never take any action that you would not be willing to see others, faced with the same or a closely similar situation, also be free to take."
7. *Individual rights.* "Never take any action that abridges the agreed-upon and accepted rights of others."
8. *Economic efficiency.* "Always act to maximize profits subject to legal and market constraints, for maximum profits are the sign of the most efficient production."
9. *Distributive justice.* "Never take any action in which the least [fortunate people] among us are harmed in some way."
10. *Contributive liberty.* "Never take any action that will interfere with the right of all of us [to] self-development and self-fulfillment."[66]

Source: Excerpted from Hosmer, *Moral Leadership in Business*, pp. 39–41, © 1994, McGraw-Hill. Reproduced with permission of The McGraw-Hill Companies.

Which of these ethical principles appeals most to you in terms of serving as a guide for making important decisions? Why? The best way to test your ethical standards and principles is to consider a *specific* ethical question and see which of these ten principles is most likely to guide your *behavior.* Sometimes, in complex situations, a combination of principles would be applicable. For example, which ethical principle(s) would you apply to judge the rightness versus wrongness in this curious situation? A banker who illegally obtained account information from Swiss banks will receive $3.5 million from German authorities who wish to prosecute any tax evaders who might be among the account holders. Who says crime doesn't pay?[67] And do two wrongs make a right in this situation?

ENCOURAGING ETHICAL CONDUCT

Simply telling managers and other employees to be good will not work. Both research evidence and practical experience tell us that words must be supported by action. Four specific ways to encourage ethical conduct within the organization are ethics training, ethical advocates, codes of ethics, and whistle-blowing. Each can make an important contribution to an integrated ethics program.

Ethics Training

Managers lacking ethical awareness have been labeled *amoral* by CSR and ethics researcher Archie B. Carroll. **Amoral managers** are neither moral nor immoral but indifferent to the ethical implications of their actions. Carroll contends that managers in this category far outnumber moral or immoral managers.[68] If his contention is correct, there is a great need for ethics training and education, a need that too often is not adequately met. Consider these research findings:

- According to a survey of human resource executives, only 27 percent of large U.S. companies provide ethics training for corporate directors.[69]
- Only 28 percent of a sample of 1,001 U.S. employees had received any ethics training during the prior year.[70]
- An analysis of the core curricula at 50 leading U.S. business schools "found only 40% require an ethics or social responsibility course."[71]

These are surprising and disappointing statistics, in view of the wave of corporate misconduct in recent years.

Some say ethics training is a waste of time because ethical lessons are easily shoved aside in the heat of competition. For example, Dow Corning's

amoral managers managers who are neither moral nor immoral, but ethically lazy

model ethics program included ethics training but did not keep the company from getting embroiled in costly charges of selling leaky breast implants.[72] Ethics training is often halfhearted and intended only as window dressing. Hard evidence that ethics training actually improves behavior is lacking.[73] Nonetheless, carefully designed and administered ethics training courses can make a positive contribution. Key features of effective ethics training programs include

- Top-management support
- Open discussion of realistic ethics cases or scenarios
- A clear focus on ethical issues specific to the organization
- Integration of ethics themes into all training
- A mechanism for anonymously reporting ethical violations (Companies have had good luck with e-mail and telephone hot lines.)
- An organizational climate that rewards ethical conduct[74]

Ethical Advocates

An **ethical advocate** is a business ethics specialist who is a full-fledged member of the board of directors and acts as the board's social conscience.[75] This person may also be asked to sit in on top-management decision deliberations. The idea is to assign someone the specific role of critical questioner (see Table 5.2 for recommended questions). Problems with groupthink and blind conformity, discussed in Chapter 13, are less likely to arise when an ethical advocate tests management's thinking about ethical implications during the decision-making process.[76]

Codes of Ethics

An organizational code of ethics is a published statement of moral expectations for employee conduct. Some codes specify penalties for offenders. As in the case of ethics training, growth in the adoption of company codes of ethics has stalled in recent years.

Recent experience has shown codes of ethics to be a step in the right direction, but not a cure-all.[77] A glaring case in point is the disconnect between BP's ethical code and its disastrous 2010 oil spill in the Gulf of Mexico. Even though BP's written code opened with former CEO Tony Hayward stating that employees had "a responsibility to speak up" about their concerns and should not fear retribution,[78] these turned out to be empty words in practice. Eleven lives were lost in a preventable accident

| Table 5.2 | Twelve Questions for Examining the Ethics of a Business Decision |

1. Have you defined the problem accurately?
2. How would you define the problem if you stood on the other side of the fence?
3. How did this situation occur in the first place?
4. To whom and to what do you give your loyalty as a person and as a member of the corporation?
5. What is your intention in making this decision?
6. How does this intention compare with the probable results?
7. Whom could your decision or action injure?
8. Can you discuss the problem with the affected parties before you make your decision?
9. Are you confident that your position will be as valid over a long period of time as it seems now?
10. Could you disclose without qualm your decision or action to your boss, your CEO, the board of directors, your family, society as a whole?
11. What is the symbolic potential of your action if understood? If misunderstood?
12. Under what conditions would you allow exceptions to your stand?

Source: Exhibit from "Ethics Without the Sermon," by Laura L. Nash (November–December 1981). Reprinted by permission of HBS Publishing.

ethical advocate ethics specialist who plays a role in top-management decision making

on the Deepwater Horizon rig where long-standing safety violations were ignored in the face of a looming production deadline.[79]

To encourage ethical conduct, formal codes of ethics for organization members must satisfy two requirements. First, they should refer to specific practices, such as kickbacks, payoffs, receiving gifts, record falsification, safety violations, and misleading claims about products. For example, Xerox Corporation's 15-page ethics code says, "We're honest with our customers. No deals, no bribes, no secrets, no fooling around with prices. A kickback in any form kicks anybody out. Anybody."[80] General platitudes about good business practice or professional conduct are ineffective—they do not provide specific guidance, and they offer too many tempting loopholes.

The second requirement for an organizational code of ethics is that it be firmly supported by top management and equitably enforced through the reward-and-punishment system. Selective or uneven enforcement is the quickest way to undermine the effectiveness of an ethics code, as in the BP oil spill. The effective development of ethics codes and monitoring of compliance are more important than ever in today's complex legal environment.[81]

Whistle-Blowing

Detailed ethics codes help managers deal swiftly and effectively with employee misconduct. But what should a manager do when a superior or an entire organization is engaged in misconduct? Yielding to the realities of organizational politics, many managers simply turn their backs or claim they were "just following orders." (Nazi war criminals who based their defense at the Nuremberg trials on the argument that they were following orders ended up with a rope around their neck.) Managers with leadership and/or political skills may attempt to work within the organizational system for positive change. Still others will take the boldest step of all, whistle-blowing. Whistle-blowing is the practice of reporting perceived unethical practices to outsiders such as the news media, government agencies, or public-interest groups. Several whistle-blowers made headlines in recent years. Sherron Smith Watkins foresaw Enron's financial collapse, and FBI agent Coleen Rowley went public with allegations of a mishandled terrorist lead. Noreen Harrington blew the whistle on illegal trading at Canary Capital Partners, resulting in a scandal that rocked the entire mutual fund industry.

Jay Mallin/Bloomberg/Getty Images

Former Brown & Williamson executive Jeffrey Wigand went to the CBS news program *60 Minutes* to blow the whistle on his company's practice of intentionally manipulating the effect of nicotine in cigarettes.

whistle-blowing reporting perceived unethical organizational practices to outside authorities

Military policeman Joseph Darby blew the whistle on the abuse of Iraqi prisoners by his fellow U.S. soldiers.[82]

Not surprisingly, whistle-blowing is a highly controversial topic among managers, many of whom believe that whistle-blowing erodes their authority and decision-making prerogatives. Because loyalty to the organization is still a cherished value in some quarters, whistle-blowing is criticized as the epitome of disloyalty. Consumer advocate Ralph Nader disagrees: "The willingness and ability of insiders to blow the whistle is the last line of defense ordinary citizens have against the denial of their rights and the destruction of their interests by secretive and powerful institutions."[83] Still, critics worry that whistle-blowers may be motivated by revenge.

Whistle-blowing generally means putting one's job and/or career on the line, even though the federal government and many states have passed whistle-blower protection acts.[84] A few whistle-blowers strike gold, such as the former Warner-Lambert employee who was awarded $26.6 million,[85] but most do not. After reviewing a wide variety of whistle-blower cases, *USA Today* reached the following conclusion: Whistler-blowers are heroes to those fed up with corporate greed, yet many end up broke with their lives in ruins. Still, say the whistle-blowers, their drive to expose scandals and protect consumers pushes them to endure whatever personal hardships their actions may cause.[86]

The challenge for today's management is to create an organizational climate in which the need to blow the whistle is reduced or, ideally, eliminated. Constructive steps include the following:

- Encourage the free expression of controversial and dissenting viewpoints.
- Streamline the organization's grievance procedure so that those who point out problems receive a prompt and fair hearing.

5d
A Strong Ethical Culture Pays

Companies with weak ethical cultures experience 10 times more misconduct than companies with strong ethical cultures, according to a survey of about 500,000 employees in more than 85 countries conducted by The Corporate Executive Board in Arlington, Va.

In strong ethical cultures, employees are comfortable speaking up about their concerns without fear of retaliation. . . .

Companies whose leaders strongly encourage open communication deliver shareholder returns that average 5 percent higher than their competitors' returns, researchers found.

QUESTIONS: What workplace lessons have you learned from working in either strong or weak ethical cultures? In the role of a management consultant, what advice would you give present and future managers about building a strong ethical culture?

Source: Excerpted from Dori Meinert, "Strong Ethical Culture Helps Bottom Line," *HR Magazine*, 55 (December 2010): 21.

- Find out what employees think about the organization's social responsibility policies, and make appropriate changes.
- Let employees know that management respects and is sensitive to their individual consciences.
- Recognize that the harsh treatment of a whistle-blower will probably lead to adverse public opinion.[87]

In the final analysis, individual behavior makes organizations ethical or unethical. Organizational forces can help bring out the best in people by clearly identifying and rewarding ethical conduct.[88]

SUMMARY

1. Corporate social responsibility is the idea that management has broader responsibilities than just making a profit. A strict interpretation holds that an action must be voluntary to qualify as socially responsible. Accordingly, reluctant submission to court orders or government coercion is not an example of social responsibility. Carroll's global corporate social responsibility pyramid encompasses, from bottom to top, four responsibilities: economic, legal, ethical, and philanthropic.

2. The debate over the basic purpose of the corporation is long-standing. Those who embrace the classical economic model contend that business's social responsibility is to maximize profits for stockholders. Proponents of the socioeconomic model disagree, saying that business has a responsibility, above and beyond making a profit, to improve the general quality of life. The arguments *for* corporate responsibility say businesses are members of society with the resources and motivation to improve society and avoid government regulation. Those arguing *against* corporate responsibility call for profit maximization because businesses are primarily economic institutions run by unelected officials who have enough power already.

3. Management scholars who advocate greater corporate social responsibility cite the iron law of responsibility. This law states that if business does not use its socioeconomic power responsibly, society will take away that power. A continuum of social responsibility includes four strategies: reaction, defense, accommodation, and proaction. The reaction strategy involves *denying* social responsibility, whereas the defense strategy involves actively *fighting* additional responsibility with political and public relations tactics. Accommodation occurs when a company must be *pressured into* assuming additional social responsibilities. Proaction occurs when a business *takes the initiative* and becomes a positive model for its industry. In the short run, proactive social responsibility usually costs the firm money. But according to the notion of enlightened self-interest, both society and the company will gain in the long run. Research indicates that corporate philanthropy actually is a profit-motivated form of advertising.

4. Business ethics research has taught these four practical lessons: (1) 48 percent of surveyed workers reported engaging in illegal or unethical practices; (2) perceived pressure from above can erode ethics; (3) employees desire clear ethical standards in ambiguous situations; and (4) rationalization sometimes enables good people to do bad things. The call for better business ethics is clearly a *personal* challenge.

5. Managers cannot afford to overlook each employee's personal value system; values serve as anchors for one's beliefs and conduct. Instrumental values are related to desired behavior, whereas terminal values involve desired end-states. Values provide an anchor for one's ethical beliefs and conduct.

6. The ten general ethical principles that consciously and unconsciously guide behavior when ethical questions arise are self-interests, personal virtues, religious injunctions, government requirements, utilitarian benefits, universal rules, individual rights, economic efficiency, distributive justice, and contributive liberty.

7. The typical manager is said to be *amoral*—neither moral nor immoral—just ethically lazy or indifferent. Management can encourage ethical behavior in the following four ways: conduct ethics training; use ethical advocates in high-level decision making; formulate, disseminate, and consistently enforce specific codes of ethics; and create an open climate for dissent in which whistle-blowing becomes unnecessary.

TERMS TO UNDERSTAND

Corporate social responsibility
(CSR), p. 126
Stakeholder audit, p. 129
Iron law of responsibility, p. 131
Reactive social responsibility
strategy, p. 131
Defensive social responsibility
strategy, p. 131

Accommodative social responsibility
strategy, p. 132
Proactive social responsibility
strategy, p. 132
Altruism, p. 132
Enlightened self-interest, p. 132
Corporate philanthropy, p. 133
Ethics, p. 134

Values, p. 137
Instrumental value, p. 137
Terminal value, p. 138
Amoral managers, p. 139
Ethical advocate, p. 140
Whistle-blowing, p. 141

ACTION LEARNING EXERCISE

THE ROKEACH VALUE SURVEY

Instructions: Study the following two lists of values, then rank the instrumental values in order of importance to you (1 = most important, 18 = least important). Do the same with the list of terminal values.

Instrumental values		Terminal values	
Rank		**Rank**	
_____	Ambitious (hardworking, aspiring)	_____	A comfortable life (a prosperous life)
_____	Broadminded (open-minded)	_____	An exciting life (a stimulating, active life)
_____	Capable (competent, effective)	_____	A sense of accomplishment (lasting contribution)
_____	Cheerful (lighthearted, joyful)	_____	A world at peace (free of war and conflict)
_____	Clean (neat, tidy)	_____	A world of beauty (beauty of nature and the arts)
_____	Courageous (standing up for your beliefs)	_____	Equality (brotherhood, equal opportunity for all)
_____	Forgiving (willing to pardon others)	_____	Family security (taking care of loved ones)
_____	Helpful (working for the welfare of others)	_____	Freedom (independence, free choice)
_____	Honest (sincere, truthful)	_____	Happiness (contentedness)
_____	Imaginative (daring, creative)	_____	Inner harmony (freedom from inner conflict)
_____	Independent (self-sufficient)	_____	Mature love (sexual and spiritual intimacy)
_____	Intellectual (intelligent, reflective)	_____	National security (protection from attack)
_____	Logical (consistent, rational)	_____	Pleasure (an enjoyable, leisurely life)
_____	Loving (affectionate, tender)	_____	Salvation (saved, eternal life)
_____	Obedient (dutiful, respectful)	_____	Self-respect (self-esteem)
_____	Polite (courteous, well-mannered)	_____	Social recognition (respect, admiration)

_____ Responsible (dependable, reliable)   _____ True friendship (close companionship)

_____ Self-controlled (restrained, self-disciplined)   _____ Wisdom (a mature understanding of life)

Source: Copyright 1967, by Milton Rokeach, and reproduced by permission of Halgren Tests, 873 Persimmon Avenue, Sunnyvale, CA. 94087.

FOR CONSIDERATION/DISCUSSION

1. How does this value survey help you better understand yourself? Or others?

2. Do you believe that values drive behavior (including ethical and unethical behavior)? Explain.

3. Value *conflict* can make life troublesome in three ways. First, there can be incompatibility among one's highly ranked instrumental values (e.g., honest vs. polite; courageous vs. obedient). Second, it may be difficult to achieve one's top terminal values via one's highly ranked instrumental values (e.g., ambitious and responsible vs. happiness and an exciting life). Third, your important instrumental and terminal values may clash with those of significant others—such as friends, spouse, coworkers, or an organization. What sorts of potential or actual value conflict do you detect in your survey responses? Explain. What can you do to minimize these conflicts?

ETHICS EXERCISE

 DO THE RIGHT THING

DOES ETHICS INSTRUCTION IN COLLEGE DO ANY GOOD?

Nitin Nohria, new dean of the Harvard Business School: Business itself is at an inflection point. Society's trust in business has certainly been shaken. As a result, some of society's trust in business education has been shaken as well. My hope at Harvard Business School is to restore that trust in business and business education. What we have to ask ourselves as business leaders and as a school is what can we do to restore this trust that has been lost so widely. I believe this trust can be repaired. . . .

Not all of this is about ethics. It's a broader thing. There's something about the way that we began to run business that made the pursuit of short-term profit maximization more important than creating long-term sustainable businesses.

Source: Excerpted from an interview by John Lauerman, "Speed Dial: Nitin Nohria," *Bloomberg Businessweek* (May 10–16, 2010): 22.

What are the ethical implications of the following interpretations?

1. Ethics instruction in college is probably a waste of time because students' value systems solidify earlier in life. What percent of students do you think are fundamentally honest, trustworthy, and ethical, and what percent are fundamentally dishonest, untrustworthy, and unethical?

2. There should be coverage of ethics because at least some students will be positively influenced. How should ethics instruction be handled for college students?

3. Ethics should be emphasized in virtually every college course to increase the likelihood of better conduct later in life. Will corrupting influences and pressure for results in the workplace tend to cancel out ethics lessons learned in college?

4. Your own ethical interpretation?

MANAGERS-IN-ACTION VIDEO CASE STUDY

GREENSBURG KANSAS

Social Responsibility: A Kansas Town Goes Green

The town of Greensburg, Kansas, was wiped out by a tornado. Rather than letting this tragedy devastate the community, residents and business leaders bonded as they launched a green rebuilding initiative. In this video, city leaders, business owners, and students share how the rebuilding of Greensburg has impacted them, their city, and local businesses. Social responsibility is evident throughout the town. A John Deere dealership owner is paving the way for the next generation of green dealers. The newly formed Greensburg GreenTown nonprofit organization is providing resources and information for residents, business owners, and others who are interested in resource conservation and the green initiative. This is an inspiring story about how one town of approximately five hundred residents turned a disaster into something great through social responsibility and a commitment to sustainability.

For more information about Greensburg and the green initiative, visit the Greensburg GreenTown Web site: www.greensburggreentown.org.

Before watching the video, answer the following questions:

1. How would you describe corporate social responsibility (CSR)?
2. Do you think a company can be socially responsible and still be profitable? Explain why or why not.
3. Choose a company that you are familiar with that demonstrates social responsibility. Describe the company's corporate policies and practices that illustrate its commitment to CSR.

After watching the video, answer the following questions:

4. How have the citizens of Greensburg and the Greensburg GreenTown organization demonstrated social responsibility?
5. Who was the champion for change and the green initiative? How were advocates successful in getting buy-in and support from residents, business owners, and government officials?
6. What legacy programs have been created, as a result of this initial green movement in Greensburg, that will provide sustainability for the future?
7. As a manager, how can you incorporate the lessons learned from the town of Greensburg to implement more corporate social responsibility at your place of work?

CLOSING CASE

A PERSONAL CRUSADE

The senior leaders of DM Bicycle Company filed into the conference room, their hands full of coffee containers, BlackBerrys, and the agenda for that morning's meeting. With the end of the fiscal year in sight, the CEO, Gino Duncan, wanted to discuss sales projections for FY11.

"Good morning, everyone," he said. "Thanks for coming in early. I know y'all can't wait to break down the budget, but before we get started, do you notice anything unusual outside?" He gestured at the window behind him.

Carolyn Bridges, DMBC's HR [human resource] director, peered down on what looked from the 10th floor like a procession of shiny beetles scuttling down the Bicentennial Greenway. They were actually bikers wearing helmets that reflected the bright North Carolina sunlight. "Lots of cyclists out this morning," she said. Carolyn had ridden the Greenway many times since she joined the company, but she couldn't remember ever seeing so much traffic.

"Bingo!" Gino said. "More and more people are biking to work, and that's good news for us."

Gino had created DMBC, now a public company, out of his passion for the outdoors and his eye for unique bicycle designs. The company's 1,500 employees all worked at its headquarters and factory in Greensboro. The bikes were called "Greenies," as a tribute to their hometown.

Everyone in the room knew that orders were coming in at a record rate. Carolyn relished the thought of finally being able to staff up for increased production. She hoped that the strong sales growth meant the company could reinstate the bonus pool that had been discontinued when the financial crisis struck. But her excitement was short-lived.

Gino's face grew serious. "As most of you know," he said, his emotion nearly overcoming him, "about eight months ago my nine-year-old daughter, Nicole, was diagnosed with Batten disease."

His listeners nodded sympathetically. Most of them could remember Nicole and her brothers riding their bikes around the office on training wheels. Gino had taken Nicole's diagnosis very hard and had spent several months working from Rochester, New York, while she was undergoing experimental treatment.

"It's an inherited neurological disorder that affects two to four out of every 100,000 born in the U.S. each year," Gino continued. "They start exhibiting symptoms between the ages of five and 10, and don't make it past their early twenties. They go blind, become mentally impaired, and are afflicted with seizures . . ." His voice began to crack. After a moment, he said, "As you can see from our projections, we're about to have the best year in our 23-year history. I'd like to divide the windfall between a new CSR program focused on Batten disease and employee bonuses."

The room was silent. Then one of the executives asked the question that was on everyone's mind. "Just for clarification—by 'divide between' do you mean split equally?"

Gino's eyes flicked toward the speaker. "To be blunt, which do you think is more important? Finding a cure for a devastating disease, or putting a little extra padding in someone's wallet?"

Carolyn was shocked. The company had not given raises in three years and in some cases had been forced to cut salaries, yet Gino seemed to want to direct the bulk of the expected profits toward fighting for his daughter's life. She respected his fatherly feelings, but was this really a corporate responsibility?

For Discussion:

1. Is diverting a portion of corporate profits to fighting a childhood disease a legitimate CSR activity for DMBC? What percent of profits would be appropriate? Explain.

2. Where on Carroll's global CSR pyramid (Figure 5.1) would you put Gino Duncan's idea? Explain.

3. Which, if any, of the ten general ethical principles presented in this chapter seem to drive

Gino Duncan's profit-sharing decision? Which ethical principle should drive any decision about corporate profit sharing? Explain.

4. If you were a member of DMBC's corporate board of directors, what would you advise Gino Duncan to do? Explain your ethical reasoning.

Source: Excerpted from Randle D. Raggio, "When the CEO's Personal Crusade Drives Decisions," *Harvard Business Review*, 88 (June 2010): 118, 120.

CHAPTER 6   The Basics of Planning and Project Management

CHAPTER 7   Strategic Management: Planning for Long-Term Success

CHAPTER 8   Decision Making and Creative Problem Solving

Planning and Decision Making

P2

6

The Basics of Planning and Project Management

"Management is a balancing act between the short term and the long term, between different objectives at different times."[1]
—PETER F. DRUCKER

The Changing Workplace

FACEBOOK: FROM DORM ROOM TO GLOBAL DOMINANCE AT WEB SPEED

Sophomore Mark Zuckerberg arrived at his dorm room in Harvard's Kirkland House in September 2003 dragging an eight-foot-long whiteboard, the geek's consummate brainstorming tool. It was big and unwieldy, like some of the ideas he would diagram there. There was only one wall of the four-person suite long enough to hold it—the one in the hallway on the way to the bedrooms. Zuckerberg, a computer science major, began scribbling away.

The wall became a tangle of formulas and symbols sprouting multicolored lines that wove this way and that. Zuckerberg would stand in the hall staring at it all, marker in hand, squeezing against the wall if someone needed to get by. Sometimes he would back into a bedroom doorway to get a better look. "He really loved that whiteboard," recalls Dustin Moskovitz, one of Zuckerberg's three suite-mates. "He always wanted to draw out his ideas, even when that didn't necessarily make them clearer." Lots of his ideas were for new services on the Internet. He spent endless hours writing software code, regardless of how much noncomputing classwork he might have. Sleep was never a priority. If he wasn't at the whiteboard he was hunched over the PC at his desk in the common room, hypnotized by the screen. Beside it was a jumble of bottles and wadded-up food wrappers he hadn't bothered to toss.

Right away that first week, Zuckerberg cobbled together Internet software he called Course Match, an innocent enough project. He did is just for fun. The idea was to help students pick classes based on who else was taking them. You could click on a course to see who was signed up, or click on a person to see the courses he or she was taking. If a cute girl sat next to you in Topology, you could look up next semester's Differential Geometry course to see if she had enrolled in that as well, or you could just look under her name for the courses she had enrolled in. As Zuckerberg said later, with a bit of pride at his own prescience, "you could link to people through things." Hundreds of students immediately began using Course Match. The status-conscious students at Harvard felt very differently about a class depending on who was in it. Zuckerberg had written a program they wanted to use.

Source: Excerpted from David Kirkpatrick, *The Facebook Effect: The Inside Story of the Company That Is Connecting the World* (New York: Simon & Schuster, 2010), pp. 19–20.

OBJECTIVES

- **Distinguish** among state, effect, and response uncertainty.
- **Identify** and **define** the three types of planning.
- **Write** good objectives, and **discuss** the role of objectives in planning.
- **Describe** the four-step management by objectives (MBO) process, and **explain** how it can foster individual commitment and motivation.
- **Discuss** project planning within the context of the project life cycle, and **list** six roles played by project managers.
- **Compare** and **contrast** flow charts and Gantt charts, and **discuss** the value of PERT networks.
- **Explain** how break-even points can be calculated.

There is an old saying in management circles about the need to plan: "Organizations that fail to plan, plan to fail." Facebook has evolved from a college project into what co-founder Mark Zuckerberg envisions as a profitable global social networking giant with more than a billion members.[2] He and his growing organization are formulating detailed plans and carrying them out with creative diligence to realize his vision. But even Facebook can't eliminate uncertainty in the global marketplace, as evidenced by growing concerns about privacy, cyber bullying, over-commercialization, and potential government regulation.[3] Yes, amid all the uncertainty, even *success* can be a problem for today's planners.

Planning is the process of coping with uncertainty by formulating future courses of action to achieve specified results. Planning enables humans to achieve great things by envisioning a pathway from concept to reality. The greater the mission, the longer and more challenging the pathway. For example, imagine the challenges awaiting Pollo Campero ("country chicken"), a fast-food chain based in Guatemala. It plans to have 1,750 stores worldwide by 2020. That's a big step up from 325 locations in 13 countries in 2010.[4] Planning is a never-ending

process because of constant change, uncertainty, new competition, unexpected problems, and emerging opportunities.[5]

Because planning affects all downstream management functions (see Figure 6.1), it has been called the primary management function. With this model in mind, we shall discuss uncertainty, highlight five essential aspects of the planning function, and take a close look at management by objectives and project planning. We shall also introduce four practical tools (flow charts, Gantt charts, PERT networks, and break-even analysis).

COPING WITH UNCERTAINTY

Ben Franklin said the only sure things in life are death and taxes. Although this is a gloomy prospect, it does capture a key theme of modern life. We are faced with a great deal of uncertainty. Organizations, like individuals, are continually challenged to accomplish something in spite of general uncertainty.[6] Organizations meet this challenge largely through

| Figure **6.1** | Planning: The Primary Management Function |

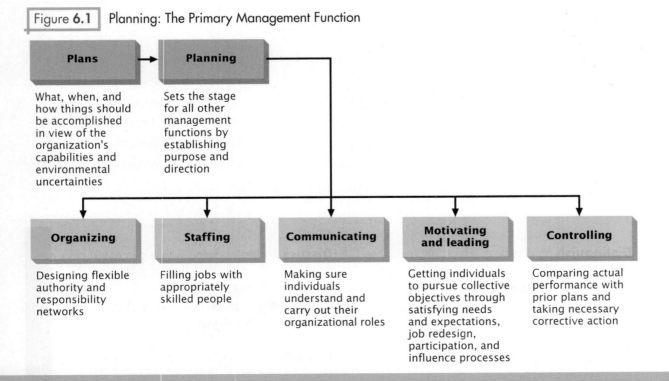

planning coping with uncertainty by formulating courses of action to achieve specified results

planning and then making appropriate adjustments as uncertainties evolve. For instance, the delivery date for 863 of Boeing's innovative new 787 Dreamliners slipped by a frustrating three years, mostly due to problems with international suppliers that were scheduled to provide components for assembly at the Washington plant.[7]

As a context for our discussion of planning in this and the following chapter, let us explore general uncertainty from three perspectives: (1) types of uncertainty; (2) how individuals deal with uncertainty; and (3) organizational responses to environmental uncertainty.

Three Types of Uncertainty

Through the years, *environmental uncertainty* has been a catch-all term among managers and researchers. However, research indicates that people actually perceive three types of environmental uncertainty: state uncertainty, effect uncertainty, and response uncertainty. **State uncertainty** occurs when the environment, or a portion of the environment, is considered unpredictable. A manager's attempt to predict the *effects* of specific environmental changes or events on his or her organization involves **effect uncertainty**. **Response uncertainty** is inability to predict the *consequences* of a particular decision or organizational response.[8]

A simple analogy can help us conceptually sort out these three types of uncertainty. Suppose you are a golfer, and on your way to the course you wonder whether it is going to rain; this is *state uncertainty*. Next, you experience *effect uncertainty* because you are not sure whether it will rain hard enough, if it does rain, to make you quit before finishing nine holes. Soon you begin weighing your chances of making par if you have to adjust your choice of golf clubs to poor playing conditions; now you are experiencing *response uncertainty*. Each of the three types of perceived uncertainty could affect

your golfing attitude and performance. Similarly, managers are affected by their different perceptions of environmental factors. Their degree of uncertainty may vary from one type of uncertainty to another. A manager may, for example, be unsure about whether a key employee is about to quit (considerable state uncertainty) but very sure that productivity would suffer without that individual (little effect uncertainty).

How Individuals Handle Uncertainty

Individual managers and employees perceive and deal with uncertainty in different ways. This becomes an important dimension of human diversity when individuals gather in organizations to make

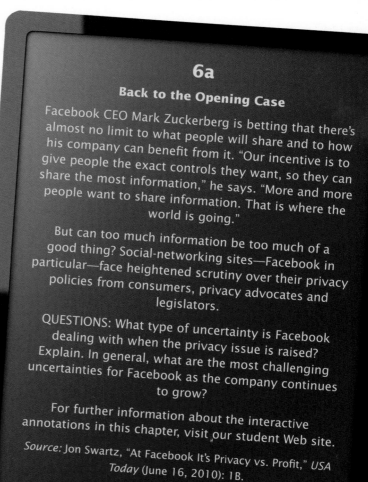

6a
Back to the Opening Case

Facebook CEO Mark Zuckerberg is betting that there's almost no limit to what people will share and to how his company can benefit from it. "Our incentive is to give people the exact controls they want, so they can share the most information," he says. "More and more people want to share information. That is where the world is going."

But can too much information be too much of a good thing? Social-networking sites—Facebook in particular—face heightened scrutiny over their privacy policies from consumers, privacy advocates and legislators.

QUESTIONS: What type of uncertainty is Facebook dealing with when the privacy issue is raised? Explain. In general, what are the most challenging uncertainties for Facebook as the company continues to grow?

For further information about the interactive annotations in this chapter, visit our student Web site.

Source: Jon Swartz, "At Facebook It's Privacy vs. Profit," *USA Today* (June 16, 2010): 1B.

state uncertainty environment is unpredictable | *effect uncertainty* impacts of environmental changes are unpredictable. | *response uncertainty* consequences of decisions are unpredictable

plans and accomplish something together. Kerry Sulkowicz, M.D., a psychoanalyst who consults with CEOs about psychological issues in the workplace, suggests that dealing with uncertainty can be particularly challenging for those who require order, are concrete thinkers, or who lack self-confidence.[9] Although people can learn to improve their tolerance for uncertainty, it's probably best for teams and work groups to be made up of individuals with varying comfort levels.

Organizational Responses to Uncertainty

Some organizations do a better job than others of planning amid various uncertainties. This is due in part to differing patterns of response to environmental factors beyond the organization's immediate control. As outlined in Table 6.1, organizations cope with environmental uncertainty by adopting one of four positions vis-à-vis the environment in which they operate. These are the positions taken by defenders, prospectors, analyzers, and reactors,[10] and each position has its own characteristic impact on planning.

DEFENDERS. A defender can be successful as long as its primary technology and narrow product line remain competitive. But defenders can become stranded on a dead-end road if their primary market seriously weakens. A prime example of a defender is Harley-Davidson, which sold its recreational vehicle division and other nonmotorcycle businesses to get back to basics. Harley-Davidson enjoys such fierce brand loyalty among Hog riders that many sport a tattoo of the company's logo. Can you imagine a Coca-Cola or Exxon tattoo? But Harley-Davidson

Table 6.1	Different Organizational Responses to an Uncertain Environment
TYPE OF ORGANIZATIONAL RESPONSE	**CHARACTERISTICS OF RESPONSE**
1. Defenders	Highly expert at producing and marketing a few products in a narrowly defined market Opportunities beyond present market not sought Few adjustments in technology, organization structure, and methods of operation because of narrow focus Primary attention devoted to efficiency of current operations
2. Prospectors	Primary attention devoted to searching for new market opportunities Frequent development and testing of new products and services Source of change and uncertainty for competitors Loss of efficiency because of continual product and market innovation Simultaneous operations in stable and changing product/market domains
3. Analyzers	In relatively stable product/market domain, emphasis on formalized structures and processes to achieve routine and efficient operation In changing product/market domain, emphasis on detecting and copying competitors' most promising ideas
4. Reactors	Frequently unable to respond quickly to perceived changes in environment Make adjustments only when finally forced to do so by environmental pressures

Source: Adapted from *Organizational Strategy, Structure, and Process,* by Raymond E. Miles and Charles C. Snow. Copyright © 1978, McGraw-Hill Book Company, p. 29. Used with permission of McGraw-Hill Book Company.

runs the risk of having its narrow focus miss the mark in an aging America. Specifically, the median age of Harley buyers rose from 35 in 1987 to 46 in 2002. Harley-Davidson is therefore seeking to lure younger riders who prefer sleek bikes away from Honda and other Japanese rivals.[11]

PROSPECTORS. Prospector organizations are easy to spot because they have a reputation for aggressively making things happen rather than waiting for them to happen. Take Amazon.com, Inc., for example. Founder Jeffrey P. Bezos first shifted Amazon beyond book sales to media, electronics, and other products. His latest idea is to sell extra computing capacity and storage space in Amazon's distribution centers to other companies. Bezos says the company's continual evolution reflects its "never ending need to search for the next source of tech growth."[12]

Prospectors (or pioneers) traditionally have been admired for their ability to gain what strategists call a *first-mover advantage*. In other words, the first one to market wins. Following the Internet crash, when many dot-com pioneers were the first to go bankrupt, the first-mover advantage was given a second look.

Two researchers, one from the United States and the other from France, discovered that with both industrial and consumer goods companies, later entrants were typically more profitable because early movers usually struggled with persistently high costs that diminished any sales gains.[13] Prospectors need to pick their opportunities very carefully, selecting those with the best combination of feasibility and profit potential. This is especially true for entrepreneurs starting small businesses.

ANALYZERS. A comparatively conservative strategy of following the leader marks an organization as an analyzer. It is a "me too" response to environmental and market uncertainty. Analyzers let market leaders take expensive research and development (R&D) risks and then imitate or build upon what works. Importantly, as detailed recently by an Ohio State University researcher, successful analyzers are active (not passive) imitators. They search worldwide for ideas to imitate, and learn to cut costs and make improvements along the way. The researcher showed that imitators aim to create "an offering based on the market reaction to [the original]."[14]

This patient, more studied approach can pay off when the economy turns down and prospectors stumble. Generic drug maker Teva Pharmaceutical Industries is a classic example of a very successful analyzer. This Israel-based company is the number one maker of generic pharmaceuticals and fills 22 percent of all generic prescriptions in the United States. Thanks to its past success and future potential, Teva's market capitalization has outpaced many of the biggest names in "big pharma."[15]

Although analyzers such as generic drug companies may not get a lot of respect, they perform the important economic function of breaking up overly concentrated industries. Customers appreciate the resulting lower prices, too.

Lightning strikes such as this one during a severe storm in Clifton Park, New York, are a major source of both "state" and "effect" uncertainty for everyone, including business owners, airlines, and electric utilities.

AP Photo/Mike Groll

REACTORS. The reactor is the exact opposite of the prospector. Reactors wait for adversity, such as declining sales, before taking corrective steps. They are slow to develop new products to supplement their tried-and-true ones. Their strategic responses to changes in the environment are often late. An instructive example is Kodak's situation. The company was very slow to embrace digital technology when it first emerged on the scene, choosing instead to stick with its historic strength—film. In recent years, however, Kodak has tried to transition into digital photography, but best-selling management author Michael Raynor likens the move to "leaping on a train when it's going 70 miles per hour."[16]

Not surprisingly, Kodak's global workforce was cut by one-third (about 31,000 employees) over a ten-year period.[17] According to one field study, reactors tended to be less profitable than defenders, prospectors, and analyzers.[18]

Balancing Planned Action and Spontaneity in the Twenty-First Century

In the obsolete command-and-control management model, plans were considered destiny. Top management formulated exacting plans for every aspect of operations and then kept everything under tight control to "meet the plan." All too often, however, plans were derailed by unanticipated events, and success was dampened by organizational inflexibility. Today's progressive managers see plans as general

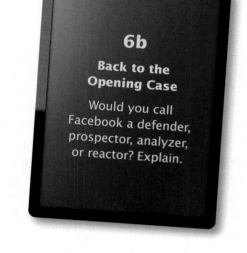

6b

Back to the Opening Case

Would you call Facebook a defender, prospector, analyzer, or reactor? Explain.

guidelines for action, based on imperfect and incomplete information. Planning is no longer the exclusive domain of top management; it now typically involves those who carry out the plans because they are closer to the customer. Planning experts, who use terms such as *strategic agility* and *ambidextrous strategy*,[19] say managers need to balance planned action with the flexibility to take advantage of surprise events and unexpected opportunities (see Best Practices). Another good analogy is to an improvisational comedy act.[20] The stand-up comic has a plan for the introduction, structure of the act, some tried-and-true jokes, and closing remarks. Within this planned framework, the comic will play off the audience's input and improvise as necessary. Accordingly, Twitter had a plan for encouraging innovation that allowed it to quickly respond to users' desire to stream photos, video clips, and maps along with standard 140-character tweets.[21] Planning should be a springboard to success, not a barrier to creativity.

BEST PRACTICES

Whole Foods Co-founder John Mackey Says Business Is Like White Water Kayaking

Q: Describe Whole Foods 30 years from now.

A: I don't like to play that game. The world changes too quickly. That makes anyone in the prediction business look like a fool. It's challenging enough to try to look three years out.

The trick is to be in the flow of the world. Like a kayaker in white water, you need to be in the flow and navigate and contribute your own creativity and good intentions to the overall flow. Whole Foods will continue to be in the flow and evolve.

For Discussion: How can managers make a go-with-the-flow strategy work in the long run? What are the major obstacles to this planning style?

Source: Excerpted from an interview by Bruce Horovitz, "Whole Foods CEO Goes with the Flow of the World," *USA Today* (August 31, 2010): 2B.

THE ESSENTIALS OF PLANNING

Planning is an ever-present feature of modern life, although there is no universal approach. Virtually everyone is a planner, at least in the informal sense. We plan leisure activities after school or work and we make career plans. Personal or informal plans give purpose and direction to our lives. In a similar fashion, more formalized plans enable managers to mobilize their intentions to accomplish organizational purposes. A **plan** is a specific, documented intention consisting of an objective and an action statement. The objective portion is the end, and the action statement represents the means to that end. Stated another way, objectives give management targets to shoot at,

Boston's annual marathon attracts more than 20,000 participants. Event planners from the Boston Athletic Association have much to consider in terms of planning for traffic, security, promotions, and caring for and accommodating the athletes.

whereas action statements provide the arrows for hitting the targets. Properly conceived plans tell *what*, *when*, and *how* something is to be done.

In spite of the wide variety of formal planning systems that managers encounter on the job, we can identify some essentials of sound planning. Among these common denominators are organizational mission, types of planning, objectives, priorities, and the planning/control cycle.

Organizational Mission

To some, defining an organization's mission might seem to be an exercise in the obvious. But exactly the opposite is true. Some organizations drift along without a clear mission. Others lose sight of their original mission. Sometimes an organization, such as the U.S. Army Corps of Engineers, finds its original mission no longer acceptable to key stakeholders. In fact, the Corps is stepping back from its tradition of building dams and levees, in favor of more environmentally sensitive projects. It has tackled "a 30-year, $7.8 billion restoration of the Florida Everglades"[22] that will involve tearing down levees to restore the natural flow of the Kissimmee River. Periodically redefining an organization's mission is both common and necessary in an era of rapid change.

A clear, formally written, and publicized statement of an organization's mission is the cornerstone of any planning system that will effectively guide the organization through uncertain times. The satirical definition by Scott Adams, the Dilbert cartoonist, tells us how *not* to write an organizational mission statement: "A Mission Statement is defined as a long, awkward sentence that demonstrates management's inability to think clearly."[23] This sad state of affairs, too often true, can be avoided by a well-written mission statement that does the following things:

1. *Defines* your organization for key stakeholders
2. Creates an *inspiring vision* of what the organization can be and can do
3. Outlines *how* the vision is to be accomplished
4. Establishes key *priorities*
5. States a *common goal* and fosters a sense of togetherness
6. Creates a *philosophical anchor* for all organizational activities
7. Generates *enthusiasm* and a "can-do" attitude

plan an objective plus an action statement

8. *Empowers* present and future organization members to believe that *every* individual is the key to success[24]

A good mission statement provides a North Star for the entire planning process. Google's mission statement is to "organize the world's information and make it universally accessible and useful."[25] In your view, how many of the eight criteria of a well-written mission statement does it satisfy? Where does it fall short?

Types of Planning

Ideally, planning begins at the top of the organizational pyramid and filters down. The rationale for beginning at the top is the need for coordination. It is top management's job to state the organization's mission, establish strategic priorities, and draw up major policies. After these statements are in place, successive rounds of strategic, intermediate, and operational planning can occur. Figure 6.2 presents an idealized picture of the three types of planning, as carried out by different levels of management.

STRATEGIC, INTERMEDIATE, AND OPERATIONAL PLANNING. Strategic planning is the process of determining how to pursue the organization's long-term goals with the resources expected to be available.[26] A well-conceived strategic plan communicates much more than general intentions about profit and growth. It specifies *how* the organization will achieve a competitive advantage, with profit and growth as necessary by-products. Intermediate planning is the process of determining the contributions that subunits can make with allocated resources. Finally, operational planning is the process of determining how specific tasks can best be accomplished on time with available resources. Each level of planning is vital to an organization's success and cannot effectively stand alone without the support of the other two levels.

PLANNING HORIZONS. As Figure 6.2 illustrates, planning horizons vary for the three types of planning. The term planning horizon refers to the time that elapses between the formulation and the execution of a planned activity. As the planning process evolves from strategic to operational, planning horizons shorten and plans become increasingly specific. Naturally, management can be more confident—and hence more specific—about the near future than about the distant future.

Note, however, that the three planning horizons overlap, their boundaries being elastic rather than rigid. The trend today is toward involving employees from all levels in the strategic planning process. Also, it is not uncommon for top and lower managers to have a hand in formulating intermediate plans. Middle managers often help lower managers draw up operational plans as well. Hence Figure 6.2 is an ideal instructional model with countless variations in the workplace.

Figure **6.2** Types of Planning

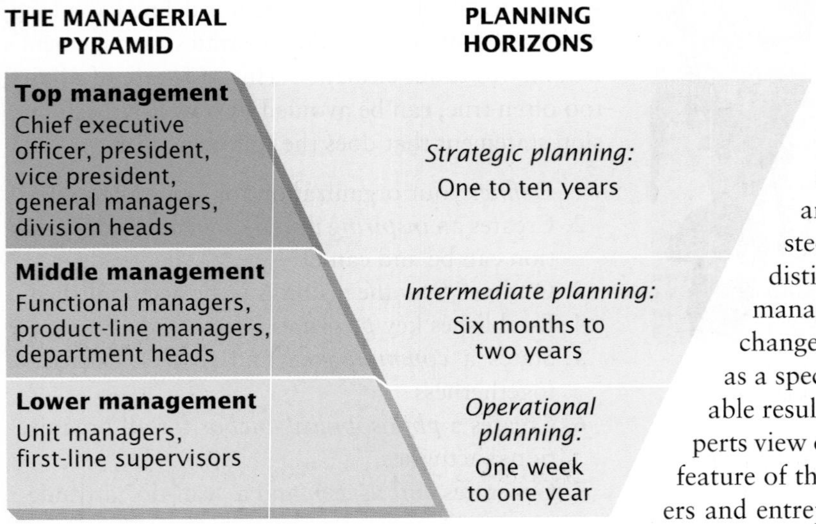

THE MANAGERIAL PYRAMID / **PLANNING HORIZONS**

Top management
Chief executive officer, president, vice president, general managers, division heads

Strategic planning: One to ten years

Middle management
Functional managers, product-line managers, department heads

Intermediate planning: Six months to two years

Lower management
Unit managers, first-line supervisors

Operational planning: One week to one year

Objectives

Just as a distant port is the target or goal for a ship's crew, objectives are targets that organization members steer toward. Although some theorists distinguish between goals and objectives, managers typically use the terms interchangeably. A goal or an objective is defined as a specific commitment to achieve a measurable result within a given time frame. Many experts view objectives as the single most important feature of the planning process. They help managers and entrepreneurs build a bridge between their dreams, aspirations, and visions and an achievable *reality*. Dan Sullivan, a consultant for entrepreneurs, explains that goals and objectives, by definition, should be real and measurable. Sullivan says, "I'm constantly amazed at how many people—and entrepreneurs in particular—confuse their goals with their ideals."[27]

It is important for present and future managers to be able to write good objectives, to be aware of their importance, and to understand how objectives combine to form a means-ends chain.

WRITING GOOD OBJECTIVES. An authority on objectives recommends that "as far as possible, objectives [should be] expressed in quantitative, measurable, concrete terms, in the form of a written statement of desired results to be achieved within a given time period."[28] In other words, objectives represent a firm commitment to accomplish something specific. A well-written objective should state what is to be accomplished and when it is to be accomplished. In the following sample objectives, note that the desired results are expressed *quantitatively*, in units of output, dollars, or percentage of change:

- To increase subcompact car production by 240,000 units during the next production year
- To reduce bad-debt loss by $50,000 during the next six months

- To achieve an 18 percent increase in Brand X sales by December 31 of the current year

For actual practice in writing good objectives and plans, see the Action Learning exercise at the end of this chapter.

THE IMPORTANCE OF OBJECTIVES. From the standpoint of planning, carefully prepared objectives benefit managers by serving as targets and measuring sticks, fostering commitment, and enhancing motivation:[29]

- *Targets.* As mentioned earlier, objectives provide managers with specific targets. Without objectives, managers at all levels would find it difficult to make coordinated decisions. People quite naturally tend to pursue their own ends in the absence of formal organizational objectives.
- *Measuring sticks.* An easily overlooked, after-the-fact feature of objectives is that they are useful for measuring how well an organizational subunit or individual has performed. When appraising performance, managers need an established standard against which they can measure performance. Concrete objectives enable managers to weigh performance objectively on the basis of accomplishment, rather than subjectively on the basis of personality or prejudice.
- *Commitment.* The very process of getting an employee to agree to pursue a given objective gives that individual a personal stake in the success of the enterprise. Thus objectives can be helpful in encouraging personal commitment to collective ends. Without individual commitment, even well-intentioned and carefully conceived strategies are doomed to failure.
- *Motivation.* Good objectives represent a challenge—something to reach for. Accordingly, they have a motivational aspect. People usually feel good about themselves and what they do when they successfully achieve a challenging objective. Moreover, objectives give managers a rational basis for rewarding performance. Employees who believe they will be equitably rewarded for achieving a given objective will be motivated to perform well.

John Evans/Shutterstock.Com

objective commitment to achieve a measurable result within a specified period

THE MEANS-ENDS CHAIN OF OBJECTIVES. Like the overall planning process, objective setting is a top-to-bottom proposition. Top managers set broader objectives with longer time horizons than do successively lower levels of managers. In effect, this downward flow of objectives creates a means-ends chain. Working from bottom to top in Figure 6.3, supervisory-level objectives provide the means for achieving middle-level objectives (ends) that, in turn, provide the means for achieving top-level objectives (ends).

The organizational hierarchy in Figure 6.3 has, of course, been telescoped and narrowed at the middle and lower levels for illustrative purposes. Usually, two or three layers of management would separate the president and the product-line managers.

Another layer or two would separate product-line managers from area sales managers. But the telescoping helps show that lower-level objectives provide the means for accomplishing higher-level ends or objectives.

6c

Clear Priorities

Chew Choon Seng, CEO of widely admired Singapore Airlines:

Even as we scaled back supply to match the impact of the global financial crisis on demand, we made it a point not to touch spending on safety and security, nor on staff training and skills development.

QUESTIONS: Why are firmly established and clearly communicated strategic priorities crucial for organizational success today? What are your personal priorities, and will they help get you where you want to go?

Source: As quoted in Anna Bernasek, "Who Does Business Trust?" *Fortune* (March 22, 2010): 126.

Priorities (Both Strategic and Personal)

Defined as a ranking of goals, objectives, or activities in order of importance, **priorities** play a special role in planning. By listing long-range organizational objectives in order of their priority, top management prepares to make later decisions regarding the allocation of resources. Limited time, talent, and financial and material resources need to be channeled into more important endeavors and away from other areas in proportion to the relative priority of the areas. Establishment of priorities is a key factor in managerial and organizational effectiveness. Strategic priorities give both insiders and outsiders answers to the questions "Why does the organization exist?" and "How should it act and react during a crisis?" An inspiring illustration of the latter occurred for American Express after the September 11, 2001, terrorist attacks. Newly appointed CEO Kenneth Chenault immediately waived delinquent fees, increased credit limits, and helped more than half a million stranded, cash-starved cardholders reach home, even going so far as to provide airplanes and buses to transport them. American Express's primary concerns were to keep their employees safe and to serve their customers.[30]

Figure 6.3 A Typical Means-Ends Chain of Objectives

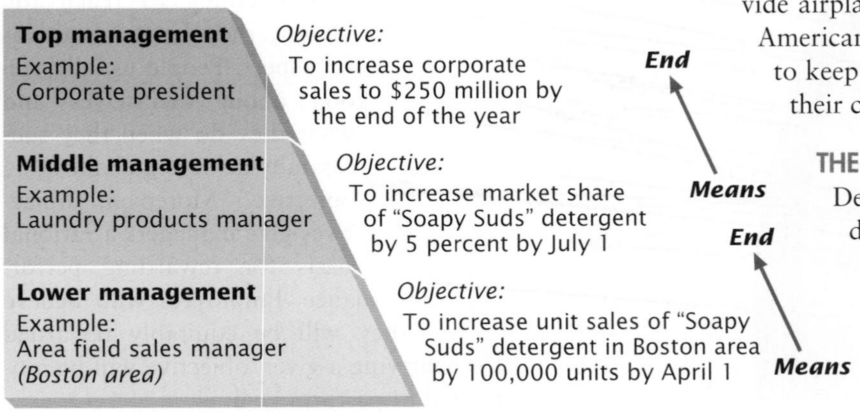
Top management
Example:
Corporate president
Objective:
To increase corporate sales to $250 million by the end of the year
End
Middle management
Example:
Laundry products manager
Objective:
To increase market share of "Soapy Suds" detergent by 5 percent by July 1
Means
End
Lower management
Example:
Area field sales manager
(Boston area)
Objective:
To increase unit sales of "Soapy Suds" detergent in Boston area by 100,000 units by April 1
Means

THE A-B-C PRIORITY SYSTEM. Despite time-management seminars, day planners, and computerized "personal digital assistants," establishing priorities remains a subjective process affected by organizational politics and value conflicts.[31] Although

priorities goals, objectives, or activities ranked in order of importance

there is no universally acceptable formula for carrying out this important function, the following A-B-C priority system is helpful:

A. "Must do" objectives *critical* to successful performance. They may be the result of special demands from higher levels of management or other external sources.
B. "Should do" objectives *necessary* for improved performance. They are generally vital, but their achievement can be postponed if necessary.
C. "Nice to do" objectives *desirable* for improved performance, but not critical to survival or improved performance. They can be eliminated or postponed to achieve objectives of higher priority.[32]

Home Depot uses an interesting and effective color-coded variation of this approach: ". . . when a to-do list for managers arrives electronically, it is marked in green. If it isn't done by the set date, it changes to red—and district managers can pounce."[33]

THE 80/20 PRINCIPLE. Another proven priority-setting tool is the 80/20 principle (or Pareto analysis, as mentioned in Chapter 2). "The 80/20 principle asserts that a minority of causes, inputs, or effort usually leads to a majority of the results, outputs, or rewards."[34] Care needs to be taken not to interpret the 80/20 formula too literally—it is approximate. Managers can leverage their time by focusing on the *few* people, problems, or opportunities with the *greatest* impact. Consider this situation that occurred when Apple partnered with AT&T to roll out the iPhone in 2007. AT&T's network was nearly crippled when just 3 percent of the new smart phone customers began using 40 percent of AT&T's bandwidth. The long-term result of this partnership that was meant to bolster both companies' business? Apple's stock has since risen by 110 percent, but AT&T is down 38 percent.[35]

For profit-minded banks and other businesses, all customers are not alike. Indeed, ING Bank, the U.S. subsidiary of the Dutch insurance giant ING, stops doing business with those customers who absorb too much time, thus saving the company more than $1 million a year."[36] How would business purists who say "The customer is always right" feel about this practice?

AVOIDING THE "BUSYNESS" TRAP. These two simple yet effective tools for establishing priorities can help managers avoid the so-called *busyness trap*.[37] In these fast-paced times, managers should not confuse being busy with being effective and efficient. *Results* are what really count. Activities and speed, without results, are an energy-sapping waste of time. By slowing down a bit, having clear priorities, and taking a strategic view of daily problems, busy managers can be successful *and* "get a life."[38]

Finally, managers striving to establish priorities amid lots of competing demands would do well to heed Peter Drucker's advice—that the most important skill for setting priorities and managing time is simply learning to say "no."

The Planning/Control Cycle

To put the planning process in perspective, it is important to show how it is connected with the control function. Figure 6.4 illustrates the cyclical relationship between planning and control. Planning gets things headed in the right direction, and control keeps them headed in the right direction. Because of the importance of the control function, it is covered in detail in Chapter 16. Basically, each of the three levels of planning is a two-step sequence followed by a two-step control sequence.

The initial planning/control cycle begins when top management establishes strategic plans. When those strategic plans are carried out, intermediate and operational plans are formulated, thus setting in motion two more planning/control cycles. As strategic, intermediate, and operational plans are carried out, the control function begins. Corrective action is necessary when either the preliminary or the final results deviate from plans. For planned activities still in progress, the corrective action can get things back on track before it is too late. Deviations between final results and plans, on the other hand, are instructive feedback for the improvement of future plans. The broken lines in Figure 6.4 represent the important sort of feedback that makes the planning/control cycle a dynamic and evolving process. Our attention now turns to some practical planning tools.

80/20 principle a minority of causes, inputs, or effort that tends to produce a majority of results, outputs, or rewards

| Figure 6.4 | The Basic Planning/Control Cycle

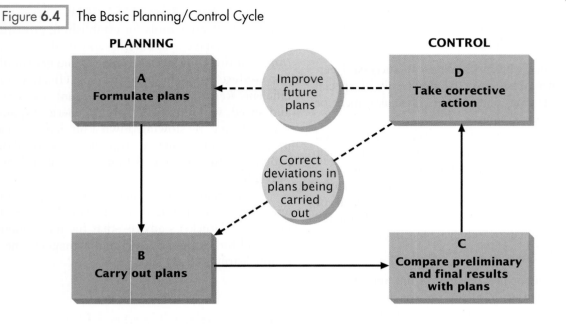

MANAGEMENT BY OBJECTIVES AND PROJECT PLANNING

In this section we examine a traditional planning technique and a modern planning challenge. Valuable lessons about planning can be learned from each.

Management by Objectives

Management by objectives (MBO) is a comprehensive management system based on measurable and participatively set objectives. MBO has come a long way since it was first suggested by Peter Drucker in 1954 as a means of promoting managerial self-control.[39] MBO theory[40] and practice subsequently mushroomed and spread around the world. In one form or another, and under various labels, MBO has been adopted by most public and private organizations of any significant size. For example, at Cypress Semiconductor Corporation, the San Jose, California, electronics firm, computerization paved the way for high-tech MBO. T. J. Rodgers, the company's founder and chief executive officer, explains that Cypress employees use a computer database to set and monitor goals on a weekly basis, a system Rodgers designed based on MBO techniques he learned in the 1970s. Rodgers attributes a great part of the

company's success to its goal setting system, adding, "It is a detailed guide to the future."[41]

The common denominator that has made MBO programs so popular in management theory and practice is the emphasis on objectives that are both *measurable* and *participatively set*.

THE MBO CYCLE. Because MBO combines planning and control, the four-stage MBO cycle corresponds to the planning/control cycle outlined in Figure 6.4. Steps 1 and 2 make up the planning phase of MBO, and steps 3 and 4 are the control phase.

1. *Step 1: Setting objectives.* A hierarchy of challenging, fair, and internally consistent objectives is the necessary starting point for the MBO cycle and serves as the foundation for all that follows. All objectives, according to MBO theory, should be reduced to writing and put away for later reference during steps 3 and 4. Consistent with what was said earlier about objectives, objective setting in MBO begins at the top of the managerial pyramid and filters down, one layer at a time.

    MBO's main contribution to the objective-setting process is its emphasis on the participation and involvement of people at lower levels. There is no place in MBO for the domineering manager ("Here are the objectives I've written for you") or for the passive manager ("I'll go along with

management by objectives (MBO) comprehensive management system based on measurable and participatively set objectives

whatever objectives you set"). MBO calls for a give-and-take negotiation of objectives between the manager and those who report directly to him or her.

2. *Step 2: Developing action plans.* With the addition of action statements to the participatively set objectives, the planning phase of MBO is complete. Managers at each level develop plans that incorporate objectives established in step 1. Higher managers are responsible for ensuring that their direct assistants' plans complement one another and do not work at cross-purposes.

3. *Step 3: Periodic review.* As plans turn into action, attention turns to step 3, monitoring performance. Advocates of MBO usually recommend face-to-face meetings between a manager and his or her people at three-, six-, and nine-month intervals. (Some organizations, such as Cypress, rely on shorter cycles.) These periodic checkups permit those who are responsible for a particular set of objectives to reconsider them, checking their validity in view of unexpected events—added duties or the loss of a key assistant—that could make them obsolete. If an objective is no longer valid, it is amended accordingly. Otherwise, progress toward valid objectives is assessed. Periodic checkups also afford managers an excellent opportunity to give their people needed and appreciated feedback.

4. *Step 4: Performance appraisal.* At the end of one complete cycle of MBO, typically one year after the original goals were set, final performance is compared with the previously agreed-upon objectives. The pairs of superior and subordinate managers who mutually set the objectives one year earlier meet face to face once again to discuss how things have turned out. MBO emphasizes results, not personalities or excuses. The control phase of the MBO cycle is completed when success is rewarded with promotion, merit pay, or other suitable benefits and when failure is noted for future corrective action.

After one round of MBO, the cycle repeats itself, with each cycle contributing to the learning process. A common practice in introducing MBO is to start at the top and to pull a new layer of management into the MBO process each year. Experience has shown that plunging several layers of management into MBO all at once often causes confusion, dissatisfaction, and failure. In fact, even a moderate-sized organization usually takes five or more years to evolve a full-blown MBO system that ties together such areas as planning, control, performance appraisal, and the reward system. MBO programs can be facilitated by using off-the-shelf software programs. Such programs offer helpful spreadsheet formats for goal setting, timelines, at-a-glance status boards, and performance reports. MBO proponents believe that effective leadership and greater motivation—through the use of realistic objectives, more effective control, and self-control—are the natural by-products of a proper MBO system.[42]

STRENGTHS AND LIMITATIONS OF MBO. Any widely used management technique is bound to generate debate about its relative strengths and weaknesses, and MBO is no exception.[43] Present and future managers will have more realistic expectations for MBO if they are familiar with both sides of this debate. The four primary strengths of MBO and four common complaints about it are compared in Figure 6.5.

This debate will probably not be resolved in the near future. Critics of MBO, such as the late quality expert W. Edwards Deming, point to both theoretical and methodological flaws.[44] Meanwhile, MBO advocates insist that it is the misapplication of MBO, not the MBO concept itself, that leads to problems. In the final analysis, MBO will probably work when organizational conditions are favorable and will probably fail when those conditions are unfavorable. A favorable climate for MBO includes top-management commitment, openness to change, Theory Y management, and employees who are willing and able to shoulder greater responsibility.[45]

Figure 6.5   MBO's Strengths and Limitations

Strengths

- MBO blends planning and control into a rational system of management.
- MBO forces an organization to develop a top-to-bottom hierarchy of objectives.
- MBO emphasizes end results rather than good intentions or personalities.
- MBO encourages self-management and personal commitment through employee participation in setting objectives.

Limitations

- MBO is too often sold as a cure-all.
- MBO is easily stalled by authoritarian (Theory X) managers and inflexible bureaucratic policies and rules.
- MBO takes too much time and effort and generates too much paperwork.
- MBO's emphasis on measurable objectives can be used as a threat by overzealous managers.

Research justifies putting *top-management commitment* at the top of the list. In a review of 70 MBO studies, researchers found that "when top-management commitment was high, the average gain in productivity was 56 percent. When such commitment was low, the average gain in productivity was only 6 percent."[46] A strong positive relationship was also found between top-management commitment to MBO program success and employee job satisfaction.[47] The greater management's commitment, the greater the satisfaction.

Project Planning and Management

Project-based organizations are becoming the norm today. Why? Concept-to-market times are being honed to the minimum in today's technology-driven world, where a great deal of work is outsourced to specialty contractors.[48] The more than 500,000-member Project Management Institute (**www.pmi.org**) defines a project as follows: It is **temporary,** with a specific start and finish date and a defined scope and set of resources. It is **unique** because it is a set of tasks that meet a specific goal.[49]

Typically, teams of people with different technical skills are brought together on a temporary basis to complete a specific project by an assigned deadline. Project teams are often virtual, meaning most if not all of their interaction is electronic rather than face-to-face. Members often come from different time zones and countries.

Projects, like all other activities within the management domain, need to be systematically planned and managed. What sets project planning/management apart is the *temporary* nature of projects, as contrasted to the typical ongoing or continuous activities in organizations. Projects may be pursued within the organization or performed for outside clients. When the job is done, project members disband and move on to other projects or return to their usual work routines. Time is usually of the essence for project managers because of tight schedules and deadlines. For example, put yourself in the shoes of the executive project manager at book publisher Scholastic, who was faced with the challenge of printing

The longest suspension bridge in the world, Japan's Akashi-Kaikyo Suspension Bridge crosses one of the world's busiest sea lanes and must be able to withstand winds in excess of 180 mph. Imagine what the project managers had to consider when constructing this technological marvel.

project a temporary endeavor undertaken to achieve a particular aim

and delivering 12 million copies of a new Harry Potter book to thousands of retailers around the United States simultaneously so that no one could spoil the ending for the rest of the series' fans. Scholastic began its strategic planning even before the author finished writing the book.[50]

On a much grander scale, imagine yourself in charge of the $5.25 billion Panama Canal project in which a third lane is being added. This mega-project, scheduled for completion in 2014, will double the Canal's capacity and accommodate the world's largest cargo ships.[51] Project management is the usual thing on Hollywood movie sets and at construction companies building homes, roads, and skyscrapers. But it is newer to manufacturers, banks, insurance companies, hospitals, and government agencies. Unfortunately, much of this Internet-age project management leaves a lot to be desired. In fact, the track record for a typical information technology (IT) project, which usually involves converting an old computer system to new hardware, software, and work methods, is fairly dismal. Ohio-based benchmarking firm Hackett Group completed a study that showed that firms finish only 37 percent of IT projects on time and only 42 percent within budget.[52] Clearly, a broader and deeper understanding of project management is in order.

Project managers face many difficult challenges. First and foremost, they work outside the normal organizational hierarchy or chain of command because projects are ad hoc and temporary. Consequently, they must rely on excellent "people management skills" instead of on giving orders.[53] Those skills include, but are not limited to, communication, motivation, leadership, teambuilding, conflict resolution, and negotiation (see Chapters 11–15).

Project *planning* deserves special attention in this chapter because project managers have the difficult job of being both intermediate/tactical and operational planners. They are responsible for both the big picture and the little details of their project. A project that is not well planned is a project doomed to failure (see Green Management: Toward Sustainability). So let us take a look at the project life cycle, project management software, the six roles project managers play, and guidelines for project managers.

THE PROJECT LIFE CYCLE. Every project, from developing a new breakfast cereal to staging a benefit rock concert, has a predictable four-stage life cycle. As shown in Figure 6.6, the four stages are conceptualization, planning, execution, and termination. Although they are shown equally spaced in Figure 6.6, the four

---

Green Management: Toward Sustainability

Walmart's Bold Sustainability Project

Activity and skepticism have been the first by-products of Walmart's audacious plan to create a label that would tell a shopper the environmental toll of every product it sells, from the greenhouse-gas emissions of an Xbox to the water used to produce your Sunday bacon. . . .

Even though Walmart execs have said that its index won't be ready before 2013, the early discussions reveal just how roiling this initiative will be.

Although Walmart is framing its Sustainability Index as something positive for both consumers and companies, Matt Kistler, senior vice president of sustainability, acknowledges that "it is creating a new level of competition in ways that, historically, manufacturers have not competed."

. . . analysts estimate that just 10% of Walmart suppliers are prepared to measure and report their sustainability [as of early 2010].

For Discussion: What are the keys to making this sustainability project a reality? What roadblocks will need to be overcome? How big an impact will this project likely have? Explain.

Source: Excerpted from Kate Rockwood, "Attention, Walmart Shoppers: Clean-up in Aisle Nine," *Fast Company*, 142 (February 2010): 30.

Figure **6.6**   The Project Life Cycle and Project Planning Activities

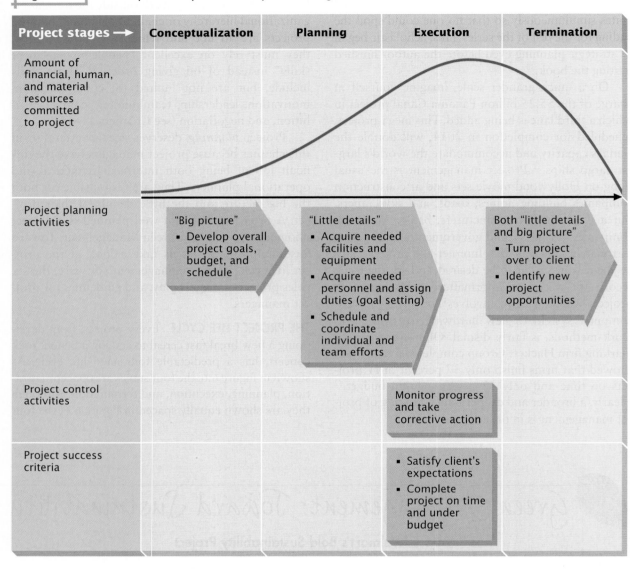

stages typically involve varying periods of time. Sometimes the borders between stages blur. For example, project goal setting actually begins in the conceptualization stage and often carries over to the planning stage. During this stage, project managers turn their attention to facilities and equipment, personnel and task assignments, and scheduling. Work on the project begins in the execution stage, and additional resources are acquired as needed. Budget demands are highest during the execution stage because everything

is in motion. To some, the label "termination" in stage 4 might suggest a sudden end to the project. But more typically, the completed project is turned over to an end user (for example, a new breakfast cereal is turned over to manufacturing) and project resources are phased out.[54]

PROJECT MANAGEMENT SOFTWARE. Recall from our earlier discussion of the basic planning/control cycle (Figure 6.4) how planning and control are intertwined. One cannot occur without the other. The same is true for project planning. Making sure planned activities occur when and where appropriate and taking corrective action when necessary can be an overwhelming job for the manager of a complex project. Fortunately, a host of computer software programs can make the task manageable. But which one of the many available programs—such as Microsoft Project for Windows—should a project manager use? Thanks to project management experts, we have a handy list of screening criteria for selecting the right tool. Judging from the list that follows, the overriding attributes of good project management software packages are *flexibility* and *transparency* (meaning quick and up-to-date status reports on all important aspects of the project).[55]

- Identify and ultimately schedule need-to-do activities
- Ability to dynamically shift priorities and schedules, and view resulting impact
- Provide critical path analysis
- Provide flexibility for plan modifications
- Ability to set priority levels
- Flexibility to manage all resources: people, hardware, environments, cash
- Ability to merge plans
- Management alerts for project slippage
- Automatic time recording to map against project
- Identification of time spent on activities[56]

SIX ROLES PLAYED BY PROJECT MANAGERS. In a research report, interviews with 40 project managers (and their clients) revealed what it takes to be effective.[57] The managers studied were working with outside clients on IT projects involving software development, systems integration, and technical support. In addition to the key role of "implementer," effective project managers played the roles of entrepreneur, politician, friend, marketer, and coach (see Table 6.2). Each role has its own set of challenges and appropriate strategies for meeting those challenges. It takes a highly skilled and motivated person to play all of these roles successfully in today's business environment. As one project management educator put it, every cent invested must be accounted for and must yield visible results. The value of any

project management initiative is always the first thing executives ask about.[58]

PROJECT MANAGEMENT GUIDELINES. Project managers need a working knowledge of basic planning concepts and tools, as presented in this chapter. Beyond that, they need to be aware of the following special planning demands of projects:

- *Projects are schedule-driven and results-oriented.* By definition, projects are created to accomplish something specific by a certain time. Project managers require a positive attitude about making lots of quick decisions and doing things in a hurry. They tend to value results more than process.
- *The big picture and the little details are of equal importance.* Project managers need to keep the overall project goal and deadline in mind when attending to day-to-day problems and personnel issues. This is difficult because distractions are constant.
- *Project planning is a necessity, not a luxury.* Novice project managers tend to get swept away by the pressure for results and fail to devote adequate time and resources to project planning.
- *Project managers know the motivational power of a deadline.* A challenging (but not impossible) project deadline is the project manager's most powerful motivational tool. The final deadline serves as a focal point for all team and individual goal setting.[59]

6d
Oh, My Aching Deadlines!

QUESTIONS: How do you respond to deadlines? Which types of deadlines motivate you and which kind do not? Why are deadlines such a powerful motivational tool?

Table 6.2   Roles, Challenges, and Strategies for Effective Project Managers

PROJECT MANAGER ROLE	CHALLENGES	STRATEGIES
Implementer	—Effectively plan, organize, and accomplish the project goals. —Navigate unfamiliar surroundings. —Survive in a "sink or swim" environment.	—Extend this role to include the newly identified roles described. —Build relationships with a number of different stakeholders.
Entrepreneur	—Manage the unexpected.	—Use persuasion to influence others. —Be charismatic in the presentation of new approaches.
Politician	—Understand two diverse corporate cultures (parent and client organizations). —Operate within the political system of the client organization.	—Align with the powerful individuals. —Obtain a senior/politically savvy client sponsor to promote and support the project.
Friend	—Determine the important relationships to build and sustain outside the team itself. —Be a friend to the client.	—Build friendships with key project managers and functional managers. —Identify common interests and experiences to bridge a friendship with the client.
Marketer	—Access client corporate strategic information. —Understand the strategic objectives of the client organization. —Determine future business opportunities.	—Develop a strong relationship with the primary client contact and with top management in the client organization. —Align new ideas/proposals with the strategic objectives of the client organization.
Coach	—Blend team members from multiple organizations. —Motivate team members without formal authority. —Reward and recognize team accomplishments with limited resources.	—Identify mutually rewarding common objectives. —Provide challenging tasks to build the skills of the team members. —Promote the team and its members to key decision makers.

Source: *Academy of Management Executive: The Thinking Manager's Source* by Sheila Simsarian Webber and Maria Torti. Copyright 2004 by Academy of Management (NY). Reproduced with permission of Academy of Management (NY) in the format Textbook via Copyright Clearance Center.

GRAPHICAL PLANNING/ SCHEDULING/CONTROL TOOLS

Management science specialists have introduced needed precision into the planning/control cycle through graphical analysis. Three graphical tools for planning, scheduling, and controlling operations are flow charts, Gantt charts, and PERT networks. They can be found in project management software programs.

Sequencing with Flow Charts

Flow charts have been used extensively by computer programmers for identifying task components and by TQM (total quality management) teams for *work simplification* (eliminating wasted steps and activities).

Beyond that, flow charts are a useful sequencing tool with broad application.[60] Sequencing is simply arranging events in the order of their actual or desired occurrence. For instance, this book had to be purchased before it could be read. Thus the event "purchase book" would come before the event "read book" in a flow chart for completing assignments in this course.

A sample flow chart is given in Figure 6.7. Note that the chart consists of boxes and diamonds in addition to the start and stop ovals. Each box contains a major event, and each diamond contains a yes-or-no decision.

Managers at all levels and in all specialized areas can identify and properly sequence important events

Figure **6.7**   A Sample Flow Chart

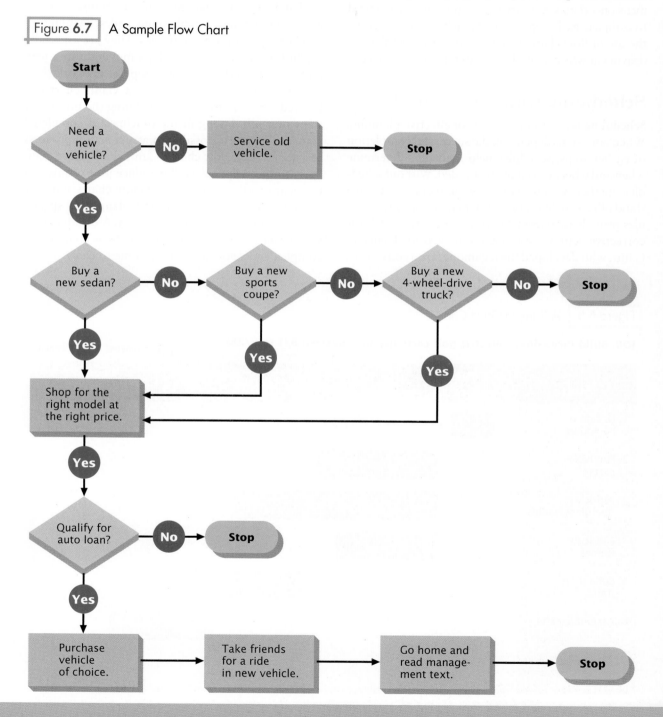

and decisions with flow charts of this kind. User-friendly computer programs make flow-charting fun and easy today. Flow charts force people to consider all relevant links in a particular endeavor, as well as their proper sequence. This is an advantage because it encourages analytical thinking. But flow charts have two disadvantages. First, they do not indicate the time dimension—that is, the varying amounts of time required to complete each step and make each decision. Second, the use of flow charts is not practical for complex endeavors in which several activities take place at once.

Scheduling with Gantt Charts

Scheduling is an important part of effective planning. When later steps depend on the successful completion of earlier steps, schedules help managers determine when and where resources are needed. Without schedules, inefficiency creeps in as equipment and people stand idle. Also, like any type of plan or budget, schedules provide management with a measuring stick for corrective action. Gantt charts, named for Henry L. Gantt, who developed the technique, are a convenient

scheduling tool for managers.[61] Gantt worked with Frederick W. Taylor at Midvale Steel beginning in 1887 and, as discussed in Chapter 2, helped refine the practice of scientific management. A *Gantt chart* is a graphical scheduling technique historically used in production operations. Things have changed since Gantt's time, and so have Gantt chart applications. Updated versions like the one in Figure 6.8 are widely used today for planning and scheduling all sorts of organizational activities. They are especially useful for large projects such as moving into a new building or installing a new computer network.[62]

Figure 6.8 also shows how a Gantt chart can be used for more than just scheduling the important steps of a job. Filling in the timelines of completed activities makes it possible to assess *actual* progress at a glance. Like flow charts, Gantt charts force managers to be analytical as they reduce jobs or projects to separate steps. Moreover, Gantt charts improve on flow charts by allowing the planner to specify the time to be spent on each activity. A disadvantage Gantt charts share with flow charts is that overly complex endeavors are cumbersome to chart.

Figure **6.8**   A Sample Gantt Chart

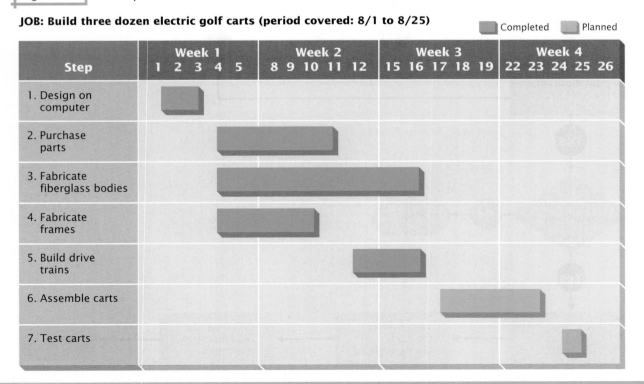

JOB: Build three dozen electric golf carts (period covered: 8/1 to 8/25)

Gantt chart graphical scheduling technique

PERT Networks

The more complex the project, the greater the need for reliable sequencing and scheduling of key activities. Simultaneous sequencing and scheduling amounts to programming. One of the most widely recognized programming tools used by managers is a technique referred to simply as PERT. An acronym for Program Evaluation and Review Technique, PERT is a graphical sequencing and scheduling tool for large, complex, and nonroutine projects.

HISTORY OF PERT. PERT was developed in 1958 by a team of management consultants for the U.S. Navy Special Projects Office. At the time, the navy was faced with the seemingly insurmountable task of building a weapon system that could fire a missile from the deck of a submerged submarine. PERT not only contributed to the development of the Polaris submarine project but also was credited with helping to bring the system to combat readiness nearly two years ahead of schedule. News of this dramatic administrative feat caught the attention of managers around the world. But, as one user of PERT reflected, "No management technique has ever caused so much enthusiasm, controversy, and disappointment as PERT."[63] Realizing that PERT is not a panacea, but rather a specialized planning and control tool that can be appropriately or inappropriately applied, helps managers accept it at face value.[64]

PERT TERMINOLOGY. Because PERT has its own special language, four key terms must be understood:

- *Event.* A PERT event is a performance milestone representing the start or finish of some activity. Handing in a difficult management exam is an event.
- *Activity.* A PERT activity represents work in process. Activities are time-consuming jobs that begin and end with an event. Studying for a management exam and taking the exam are activities.
- *Time.* PERT times are estimated times for the completion of PERT activities. PERT times are weighted averages of three separate time estimates: (1) *optimistic time* (T_o)—the time an activity should take under the best of conditions; (2)

most likely time (T_m)—the time an activity should take under normal conditions; and (3) *pessimistic time* (T_p)—the time an activity should take under the worst possible conditions. The formula for calculating estimated PERT time (T_e) is

$$T_e = \frac{T_o + 4T_m + T_p}{6}$$

- *Critical path.* The critical path is the most time-consuming chain of activities and events in a PERT network. In other words, the longest path through a PERT network is critical because if any of the activities along it are delayed, the entire project will be delayed accordingly.[65]

PERT IN ACTION. A PERT network is shown in Figure 6.9. The task in this example, the design and construction of three dozen customized golf carts for use by physically challenged adults, is relatively simple for instructional purposes. PERT networks are usually reserved for more complex projects with hundreds or even thousands of activities. PERT events are coded by circled letters, and PERT activities, shown by the arrows connecting the PERT events, are coded by number. A PERT time (T_e) has been calculated and recorded for each PERT activity.

Before reading on, see if you can pick out the critical path in the PERT network in Figure 6.9. By calculating which path will take the most time from beginning to end, you will see that the critical path turns out to be A-B-C-F-G-H-I. This particular chain of activities and events will require an estimated 21.75 workdays to complete. The overall duration of the project is dictated by the critical path, and a delay in any of the activities along this critical path will delay the entire project.

POSITIVE AND NEGATIVE ASPECTS OF PERT. During the 50 years that PERT has been used in a wide variety of settings, both its positive and its negative aspects have become apparent.

On the plus side, PERT is an excellent scheduling tool for large, nonroutine projects, ranging from

---

Program Evaluation and Review Technique (PERT) graphical sequencing and scheduling tool for complex projects | PERT event performance milestone; start or finish of an activity | PERT activity work in process | PERT times weighted time estimates for completion of PERT activities | critical path most time-consuming route through a PERT network

Figure **6.9** | A Sample PERT Network

TASK: Build three dozen customized golf carts for use by physically challenged adults

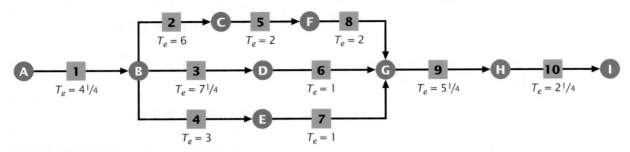

PERT events
A. Receive contract
B. Begin construction
C. Receive parts
D. Bodies ready for testing
E. Frames ready for testing
F. Drive trains ready for testing
G. Components ready for assembly
H. Carts assembled
I. Carts ready for shipment

PERT activities and times				
Activities	T_o	T_m	T_p	T_e*
1. Prepare final design	3	4	6	4¼
2. Purchase parts	4	5	12	6
3. Fabricate bodies	5	7½	9	7¼
4. Fabricate frames	2½	3	4	3
5. Build drive trains	1½	2	3	2
6. Test bodies	½	1	1½	1
7. Test frames	½	1	1½	1
8. Test drive trains	1	1½	5	2
9. Assemble carts	3	5	9	5¼
10. Test carts	1	2	5	2¼

*Rounded to nearest ¼ workday

constructing an electricity generation station to launching a space vehicle. PERT is a helpful planning aid because it forces managers to envision projects in their entirety. It also gives them a tool for predicting resource needs, potential problem areas, and the impact of delays on project completion. If an activity runs over or under its estimated time, the ripple effect of lost or gained time on downstream activities can be calculated. PERT also gives managers an opportunity, through the calculation of optimistic and pessimistic times, to factor in realistic uncertainties about planning horizons.

On the minus side, PERT is an inappropriate tool for repetitive assembly-line operations in which scheduling is dictated by the pace of machines. PERT also shares with other planning and decision-making aids the disadvantage of being only as good as its underlying assumptions. False assumptions about activities and events and miscalculations of PERT times

can render PERT ineffective. Despite the objective impression of numerical calculations, PERT times are derived rather subjectively. Moreover, PERT's critics say it is too time-consuming: A complex PERT network prepared by hand may be obsolete by the time it is completed, and frequent updates can tie PERT in knots. Project management software with computerized PERT routines is essential for complex projects because it can greatly speed the graphical plotting process and updating of time estimates.

BREAK-EVEN ANALYSIS

In well-managed businesses, profit is a forethought rather than an afterthought. A widely used tool for projecting profits relative to costs and sales volume is break-even analysis. In fact, break-even analysis is often referred to as cost-volume-profit analysis. By using either the algebraic method or the graphical method, planners can calculate the break-even point, the level of sales at which the firm neither suffers a loss nor realizes a profit. In effect, the break-even point is the profit-making threshold. If sales are below that point, the organization loses money. If sales go beyond the break-even point, it makes a profit. Break-even points, as discussed later, are often expressed in units. An example is Europe's Airbus Industrie's huge 555-passenger commercial airliner that went into service in 2007. The break-even point for the $300 million double-deck A380 reportedly is about 250 units.[66]

From a procedural standpoint, a critical part of break-even analysis is separating fixed costs from variable costs.

Fixed Versus Variable Costs

Some expenses, called fixed costs, must be paid even if a firm fails to sell a single unit. Other expenses, termed variable costs, are incurred only as units are produced and sold. Fixed costs are contractual costs that must be paid regardless of the level of output or sales. Typical examples include rent, utilities, insurance premiums, managerial and professional staff salaries, property taxes, and licenses. Variable costs are costs that vary directly with the firm's production and sales. Common variable costs include costs of production (such as labor, materials, and supplies), sales commissions, and product delivery expenses. As output and sales increase, fixed costs remain the same but variable costs accumulate. Looking at it

another way, fixed costs are a function of *time* and variable costs are a function of *volume*. You can now calculate the break-even point.

The Algebraic Method

Where the following abbreviations are used,

FC = total fixed costs
P = price (per unit)
VC = variable costs (per unit)
BEP = break-even point

the formula for calculating break-even point (in units) is

$$BEP(\text{in units}) = \frac{FC}{P-VC}$$

The difference between the selling price P and per-unit variable costs VC is referred to as the contribution margin. In other words, the contribution margin is the portion of the unit selling price that falls above and beyond the variable costs and that can be applied to fixed costs. Above the break-even point, the contribution margin contributes to profits.

Variable costs are normally expressed as a percentage of the unit selling price. As a working example of how the break-even point (in units) can be calculated, assume that a firm has total fixed costs of $30,000, a unit selling price of $7, and variable costs of 57 percent (or $4 in round numbers).

$$BEP(\text{in units}) = \frac{30,000}{7-4} = 10,000$$

This calculation shows that 10,000 units must be produced and sold at $7 each if the firm is to break even on this particular product.

PRICE PLANNING. Break-even analysis is an excellent "what-if" tool for planners who want to know what impact

Dairy farming is an endless struggle with break-even analysis. Like most American dairy farmers, Lisa Kaiman, seen here with some heifers on her 33-acre farm in Chester, Vermont, is being squeezed by higher costs and lower milk prices.

Spencer Platt/Getty Images

break-even point level of sales at which there is no loss or profit | fixed costs contractual costs that must be paid regardless of output or sales. | variable costs costs that vary directly with production and sales | contribution margin selling price per unit minus variable costs per unit

price changes will have on profit. For instance, what would the break-even point be if the unit selling price were lowered to match a competitor's price of $6?

$$BEP(\text{in units}) = \frac{30,000}{6-4} = 15,000$$

In this case, the $1 drop in price to $6 means that 15,000 units must be sold before a profit can be realized.

PROFIT PLANNING. Planners often set profit objectives and then work backwards to determine the required level of output. Break-even analysis greatly assists such planners. The modified break-even formula for profit planning is

$$BEP(\text{in units}) = \frac{FC = \text{desired profit}}{P - VC}$$

Assuming that top management has set a profit objective for the year at $30,000 and that the original figures above apply, the following calculation results:

$$BEP(\text{in units}) = \frac{30,000 + 30,000}{7-4} = 20,000$$

To meet the profit objective of $30,000, the company would need to sell 20,000 units at $7 each.

The Graphical Method

If you place the dollar value of costs and revenues on a vertical axis and unit sales on a horizontal axis, you can calculate the break-even point by plotting fixed costs, total costs (fixed + variable costs), and total revenue. As illustrated in Figure 6.10, the break-even point is where the total costs line and the total sales revenue line intersect.

Although the algebraic method does the same job, some planners prefer the graphical method because it presents the various cost-volume-profit relationships at a glance, in a convenient visual format.

Figure **6.10**   Graphical Break-Even Analysis

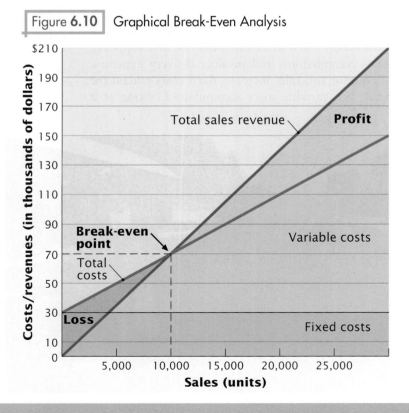

Break-Even Analysis: Strengths and Limitations

Like the other planning tools discussed in this chapter, break-even analysis is not a cure-all. It has both strengths and limitations.

On the positive side, break-even analysis forces planners to acknowledge and deal realistically with the interrelatedness of cost, volume, and profit. All three variables are connected such that a change in one sends ripples of change through the other two. As mentioned earlier, break-even analysis allows planners to ask what-if questions concerning the impact of price changes and varying profit objectives.

The primary problem with break-even analysis is that neatly separating fixed and variable costs can be very difficult. General managers should enlist the help of accountants to isolate relevant fixed and variable costs. Moreover, because of complex factors in supply and demand, break-even analysis is not a good tool for setting prices. It serves better as a general planning and decision-making aid.

SUMMARY

1. Planning has been labeled the primary management function because it sets the stage for all other aspects of management. Along with many other practical reasons for planning, managers need to plan in order to cope with an uncertain environment. Three types of uncertainty are state uncertainty ("What will happen?"), effect uncertainty ("What will happen to our organization?"), and response uncertainty ("What will be the outcome of our decisions?"). Individual differences in tolerance to uncertainty need to be considered when staffing teams and work groups. To cope with environmental uncertainty, organizations can respond as defenders, prospectors, analyzers, or reactors.

2. A properly written plan tells what, when, and how something is to be accomplished. A clearly written organizational mission statement tends to serve as a useful focus for the planning process. Strategic, intermediate, and operational plans are formulated by top, middle, and lower management, respectively.

3. Objectives have been called the single most important feature of the planning process. Well-written objectives spell out, in measurable terms, what should be accomplished and when it is to be accomplished. Good objectives help managers by serving as targets, acting as measuring sticks, encouraging commitment, and strengthening motivation. Objective setting begins at the top of the organization and filters down, thus forming a means-ends chain. Priorities affect resource allocation by assigning relative importance to objectives. Plans are formulated and executed as part of a more encompassing planning/control cycle.

4. Management by objectives (MBO), an approach to planning and controlling, is based on measurable and participatively set objectives. MBO basically consists of four steps: (1) setting objectives participatively, (2) developing action plans, (3) periodically reevaluating objectives and plans and monitoring performance, and (4) conducting annual performance appraisals. Objective setting in MBO flows from top to bottom.

MBO has both strengths and limitations and requires a supportive climate favorable to change, participation, and the sharing of authority.

5. Project planning occurs throughout the project life cycle's four stages: conceptualization, planning, execution, and termination. "Big-picture" tactical planning—project goal, budget, and schedule—occurs during stage 1 and into stage 2. During stage 2 and into the execution phase in stage 3, project planning deals with the "little details" of facilities and equipment, personnel and job assignments, and scheduling. Starting near the end of stage 3 and carrying into the termination stage, both little-details and big-picture planning are required to pass the project along and identify new project opportunities. Planning is central to project success because projects are schedule-driven and results-oriented. Project planners need to keep constantly abreast of both the big picture and the little details. Novice project managers too often shortchange planning. Challenging but realistic project deadlines are project managers' most powerful motivational tool. Six roles performed by effective project managers are implementer, entrepreneur, politician, friend, marketer, and coach.

6. Flow charts, Gantt charts, and PERT networks, found in project management software packages, are three graphical tools for more effectively planning, scheduling, and controlling operations. Flow charts visually sequence important events and yes-or-no decisions. Gantt charts, named for Frederick W. Taylor's disciple Henry L. Gantt, are a graphical scheduling technique used in a wide variety of situations. Both flow charts and Gantt charts have the advantage of forcing managers to be analytical. But Gantt charts realistically portray the time dimension, whereas flow charts do not. PERT, which stands for Program Evaluation and Review Technique, is a sequencing and scheduling tool appropriate for large, complex, and nonroutine projects. Weighted PERT times enable managers to factor in their uncertainties about time estimates.

7. Break-even analysis, or cost-volume-profit analysis, can be carried out algebraically or graphically. Either way, it helps planners gauge the potential impact of price changes and profit objectives on sales volume. A major limitation of break-even analysis is that specialized accounting knowledge is required to identify relevant fixed and variable costs.

TERMS TO UNDERSTAND

Planning, p. 152
State uncertainty, p. 153
Effect uncertainty, p. 153
Response uncertainty, p. 153
Plan, p. 157
Strategic planning, p. 158
Intermediate planning, p. 158
Operational planning, p. 158
Planning horizon, p. 158

Objective, p. 158
Priorities, p. 160
80/20 principle, p. 161
Management by objectives
(MBO), p. 162
Project, p. 164
Gantt chart, p. 170
Program Evaluation and Review
Technique (PERT), p. 171

PERT event, p. 171
PERT activity, p. 171
PERT times, p. 171
Critical path, p. 171
Break-even point, p. 175
Fixed costs, p. 175
Variable costs, p. 175
Contribution margin, p. 175

ACTION LEARNING EXERCISE

 HOW TO WRITE GOOD OBJECTIVES AND PLANS (PLAN = WHAT + WHEN + HOW)

Instructions: Well-written objectives are the heart of effective planning. An objective should state *what* is to be accomplished (in measurable terms) and *when* it will be accomplished. An objective becomes a plan when the *how* is added. Here is an everyday example of a well-written plan: "I will ("what?") lose 5 pounds ("when?") in 30 days ("how?") by not eating desserts and walking a mile four days a week."

Remember the following handy three-way test to assess how well your plans are written:

- Test 1: Does this plan specify *what* the intended result is, and is it stated in *measurable* terms?
- Test 2: Does this plan specify *when* the intended result is to be accomplished?
- Test 3: Does this plan specify *how* the intended result is to be accomplished?

Write a plan that passes all three tests for each of the following areas of your life.

Self-improvement plan: What? _____
                        When? _____
                        How? _____

Work-related plan: What? _____
                    When? _____
                    How? _____

Community-service plan: What? _____
                         When? _____
                         How? _____

FOR CONSIDERATION/DISCUSSION

1. In terms of the above three-way test, which of your plans is the best? Why? Which is the worst? Why?

2. What is the hardest part of writing good plans? Explain.

3. From a managerial standpoint, why is it important to have plans written in measurable terms?

4. What is the managerial value of formally written plans, as opposed to verbal commitments?

5. Why would some employees resist writing plans according to the specifications in this exercise? Explain.

ETHICS EXERCISE

 DO THE RIGHT THING

DEATH BY PROJECT

Firing someone is legally risky and requires lots of paperwork. One way to get rid of an employee easily is to assign him projects that he can't possibly complete successfully. . . .

For example, if you know Bob is not a detail person and not neat and precise in recordkeeping, what do you do to get rid of him? Assign Bob to be the recordkeeper for a tediously detailed project.

Source: Excerpted from Casey Hawley, *100+ Tactics for Office Politics*, 2nd ed. (Hauppauge, N.Y.: Barron's, 2008), p. 108.

What are the ethical implications of the following interpretations?

1. This dirty trick is clearly unethical, regardless of the people or circumstances involved. It should be avoided. Explain.

2. This could be a challenging make-or-break opportunity for someone who has been performing below his or her potential. Poor performers sometimes need a wake-up call. Explain your measured use of this tactic.

3. This is a good idea for that rare occasion when time is short and one individual is keeping a project from being successful. Explain.

4. Your own ethical interpretation?

MANAGERS-IN-ACTION VIDEO CASE STUDY

FLIGHT 001

Planning for Growth

Flight 001 co-founders Brad John and John Sencion share their plans for growth, expansion, and recognition as the travel authority throughout the world. They discuss the impact the economic downturn has had on their strategic plan and the adjustments they have made. Crew development manager Emily Griffin provides an overview of her role in helping the organization achieve its goals. She offers insights and shares how she learned to plan. Learn from this video how a relatively young, ambitious company is using strategic planning and goal setting to grow and achieve success.

For more information about Flight 001, visit its Web site: http://www.flight001.com.

Before watching the video, answer the following questions:

1. Describe what you think are the essential roles for project managers to play in an organization.
2. Why is it important for managers to spend time planning?
3. What are three types of planning used in most companies?

After watching the video, answer the following questions:

4. How has Flight 001 demonstrated the concept that strategic plans are not just written every five years and left on a shelf; rather, they are living documents that require monitoring and adjustments?
5. How did the crew development manager, Emily Griffin, learn to plan? What lessons can you learn from her approach to help you be a more efficient and effective manager and planner?
6. What are the keys to success for Flight 001 in implementing its strategic plan (flight plan)?
7. What will it take for Flight 001 to achieve its goals for growth, expansion, and recognition as the travel authority throughout the world?

CLOSING CASE

FORD'S HYBRID SUV PROJECT TEAM RACES TO THE FINISH

In the spring of 2003, Phil Martens saw trouble down the road. As head of product development for Ford, he was supervising the creation of what could be one of the most important vehicles in company history. While the car wasn't due to come out until the fall of 2004, the team needed to be in launch mode right then to stay on schedule.

It wasn't. It was still pulling marathon hours just trying to get the thing running properly.

The vehicle was the much-anticipated gas-electric hybrid that CEO Bill Ford Jr. had been touting for a couple of years as emblematic of the new, environmentally friendly Ford. The Ford Escape Hybrid would be the first hybrid SUV; it would handle like a muscular V-6, yet sip gas—36 miles per gallon, about 50% better than a standard Escape; its emissions would be minuscule. It was the most technically advanced product the automaker had ever attempted to put into mass production.

The hybrid team was packed with PhDs, but for all of their technical prowess, the brainiacs had one weakness: little launch experience. Martens needed someone to crack the whip without destroying morale, someone to persuade the scientists to stop perfecting and start finishing the vehicle. That someone was Mary Ann Wright—part spark plug, part disciplinarian, and all Ford.

A self-described "car nut," Wright, 42, has launched Sables, Tauruses, and Lincolns. Her discipline is legendary. Twelve-plus-hour days. Five hours of sleep. Four A.M. workouts. She has blond bangs, blue eyes, a firm handshake, and the confidence of someone who doesn't miss deadlines. "My launches are really, really good," she says. Somehow this doesn't come across as a boast.

Even with Wright on board, staying on schedule wasn't a sure thing. Introducing one major technology is a challenge. The Escape Hybrid contains nine such technologies. By the time Ford sends it to dealers in September, this SUV will have been in the works for a little more than five years. In addition to overcoming herculean technical hurdles, Ford collaborated with suppliers around the globe. "This is an unusually complex team with little or no experience with hybrid technology," says Martens, "and they're introducing this unusually complex technology into a mainstream manufacturing system without any flaws." . . .

Creating a dramatically different product is a staggering challenge for any organization, but for the oldest and second-largest American automaker, it's a higher, steeper mountain to scale. Ford Motor Co. has been making cars for 101 years—cars with one motor. Open the hood of a hybrid, and you'll find two: one gas, the other electric.

As a "full" hybrid, the Escape can run on either motor. Its network monitors an array of computers to determine which motor can drive the wheels most efficiently. In an instant, the vehicle balances the dueling demands for power and acceleration and for high mileage and low emissions. For team member Tom Gee, Ford's announcement of a mass-produced hybrid was "the equivalent of Kennedy saying, 'We're going to the moon by the end of the decade.'" At Ford, vehicle programs are typically ranked 1 to 10, according to the complexity of the power train. "This was a 20," says longtime researcher Mike Tamor.

The stakes are particularly high because Honda and Toyota introduced their hybrids in the United States first—in 1999 and 2000, respectively. Although they lacked the power and roominess of conventional cars, the first gas-electric models found a niche audience. Last year, Toyota released a zippier Prius, but Ford insists that its Escape is going where no hybrid has gone before: into the mainstream. The pitch? No compromises on acceleration, towing capacity, cargo space, fuel economy, or emissions. Not only is it the first hybrid manufactured by an American automaker, but it's also the first hybrid SUV. Ford has plenty of competition in the rearview mirror, though; over the next three years, the major automakers plan to release 20 new hybrids, many of them SUVs and trucks. . . .

Ford's Escape Hybrid program got its start in a Toyota Prius, of all places. After being tapped to head the team in late 1998, Prabhaker Patil went for a test drive with then-chairman Alex Trotman. As the two had suspected, the soon-to-be-released Prius sacrificed too much performance. Trotman insisted that Ford's hybrid do better.

To develop its unconventional vehicle, Ford created an unconventional team. Typically, researchers and product engineers don't work closely together. At Ford, in fact, they work in different buildings. Researchers act as consultants; they share their expertise while commuting from the Ford Scientific Research Laboratory. But Ford's team would itself be a hybrid: scientists and product engineers inventing and building software and hardware together, then shepherding their creation through production. "The people story is as interesting as the technology story," says Wright.

Patil, 54, was a hybrid himself, a PhD scientist who worked in Ford's lab for more than 15 years and then in product development for the past four. He sought team members he knew would be open to collaboration. They included Anand Sankaran, 39, who holds a doctorate in electrical engineering and is a nine-year veteran of the research lab. "It has always been my wish to take something into product production," he says. Still, Sankaran was curious about the fit. "There was a little bit of concern, because I come from a background where I deal more with solving problems technically but it's not fine-tuned to be put easily into production."

The creative tension often centered on deadlines. "On one side, you have people with program discipline who said, 'This has to happen at this point and at this point,'" Patil says, "and the other side would say, 'Oh you want to time an invention?'" . . .

Internally, the hybrid team is simply Team U293. It occupies a long stretch of gray cubicles a one-minute walk from the tinted glass door of one of Bill Ford's offices. The bulletin board celebrates new babies and new patents ("Method for controlling an internal combustion engine during engine shutdown to reduce evaporative emissions"). Schedules wallpaper the conference room, along with a banner that says, "By When?"

The office feels ordinary, but for Ford it is revolutionary. Engineers and scientists work in adjacent cubicles. "Before, it might have been a half a mile apart, but even one building away is a barrier compared with what we have now," says Gee. "It makes a huge difference." Group lunches in the nearby cafeteria evolve into meetings. Hallway chats lead to impromptu problem solving. Once, a couple of engineers at the soda machine discovered a discrepancy in a power-train specification and corrected the issue before the code was written. With thousands of tasks on the to-do list, preventing a problem is as sweet as solving one.

The hybrid group has become the envy of other Ford engineers. "I have engineers who say, 'I wish I could be on that team,'" says Craig Rigby, a technical support supervisor. "Then I tell them the hours." As a way of motivating his weary team, Patil would remind them how fortunate they were. "This was a product that if you did it right, it was going to do a great deal for customers and the company and the country and the environment," he says. "You rarely get a chance to go after something like this in your career. It's what I call the nobility of the cause." . . .

After putting his foot down in the spring of 2003 about the Escape Hybrid's launch, Martens gave the team a rare gift: no outside interruptions. From May through December, it wouldn't have to do management reviews and other presentations. Martens would check in periodically and test-drive the latest prototype so he could keep his bosses informed. "I was getting questions from above," he says. "Weekly." A grin. "Daily."

During this "dark period," Martens says, "I allowed them to be entrepreneurial, and they doubled their productivity." Issues that had been stalled for months got resolved: reaching the fuel economy goal and building the first preproduction model. "The same people who had been coming into my office saying, 'I don't know how we're going to get there,' were saying within weeks and months, 'My God, we can get there,'" Wright recalls. . . .

Wright put the pedal to the metal. "Every day is a lost day," she would tell the team. She quickly established a launch plan and a "meeting cadence": daily get-togethers at 8 A.M. for two hours, with suppliers in Germany and Japan participating by video. There were also weekly meetings with chief engineers and technical forums to tackle specific issues. Wright devoured the details. "Most chiefs won't do that. I find it helps motivate people and helps educate me."

Launch mode meant acting as an even more integrated team. During the design phase, small groups had focused on each system to master its separate technology. Now the challenge was orchestrating the interaction between systems. "I told them, 'If one person is struggling, we're all struggling,'" says Wright. She could be tough, but Martens believed she was what the team needed, just as Patil and his more collegial style had been effective in development. She was the hybrid team's second motor; if Patil's job was to inspire invention, hers was to wrap it up.

Letting go didn't come naturally to scientists like Sankaran. One of his goals was eliminating extraneous engine noise. Like a conductor with extraordinary hearing, he could detect an occasional, almost imperceptible high-pitched tone even though the transmission met the noise requirements. Technically—officially—it was good to go. But, Sankaran says, "as an engineer I wanted to say, 'What are the physics behind this sound? I can do better.'" Ultimately, though, he was persuaded to let it go by taking consolation in another of Wright's reminders: "This isn't the only one we'll do." There will be more hybrids down the road.

For Discussion

1. Which stages of the project life cycle in Figure 6.6 are evident in this case? Explain.

2. Was it a good idea for Phil Martens, head of product development, to have two project managers—first Prabhaker Patil and then Mary Ann Wright—to head the Escape Hybrid project? Explain.

3. From a project manager's standpoint, what are the toughest challenges with this sort of high-visibility, high-risk project? Explain.

4. Which of the project manager roles in Table 6.2 did Mary Ann Wright play in this case? Explain.

5. Would you like to have been a member of this team? Why or why not?

Source: Excerpted from Chuck Salter, "Ford's Escape Route," *Fast Company*, 87 (October 2004): 106–110. Reprinted by permission.

7

Strategic Management: Planning for Long-Term Success

"The minute you've developed a new business model, it's extinct, because somebody is going to copy it."

—INDRA NOOYI, CEO, PEPSICO

The Changing Workplace

LOOKING BACKWARD IS A LOSING STRATEGY IN THE AGE OF NEW MEDIA

The audience that had once belonged to broadcast television moved to cable, to video on demand, to DVDs, to YouTube and Facebook and Guitar Hero. TiVo and DVRs allowed viewers to become their own programmers. This was great for viewers but not so great for the television business.

. . . the three television networks were slow to recognize the seismic shift that cable heralded, missing their chance to own rather than compete with cable networks. They were not alone in disdaining the new. When Robert Pittman cofounded MTV in 1981, Coca-Cola and McDonald's refused to buy advertising on a television network that did not reach at least 55 percent of the nation. Pittman did persuade Pepsi to place some ads, and for the next several years Pepsi had a de facto exclusive advertising platform that greatly boosted its market share. It took Coca-Cola and McDonald's four or five years, Pittman recalled, to change their minds. Likewise, most traditional media companies in the Google era concentrated more on defending their turf rather than extending it. Belatedly, most have begun to dip their toes, and in some cases entire feet, into new media efforts, hoping technology [can save the day]. . . .

Yahoo! and Microsoft were tossed in the digital storm. With better search and advertising technology, Google's search widened its lead. With the promise of cloud computing and free software applications, Google menaced Microsoft's packaged software business. Everywhere they turned, new technologies were disrupting businesses faster than they could respond.

Source: Excerpted from Ken Auletta, *Googled: The End of the World As We Know It* (New York: Penguin Press, 2009), pp. 238–239.

OBJECTIVES

- **Define** the term *strategic management,* and **explain** its relationship to strategic planning, implementation, and control.
- **Explain** the concept of synergy, and **identify** four kinds of synergy.
- **Describe** Porter's model of generic competitive strategies.
- **Identify** and **explain** the major contribution the business ecosystems model makes to strategic thinking.
- **Identify** seven basic Internet business models and **discuss** the strategic significance of social media.
- **Identify** and **describe** the four steps in the strategic management process.
- **Explain** the nature and purpose of a SWOT analysis.
- **Describe** the three types of forecasts.

This chapter is about strategic farsightedness, something missing on the part of many players in the opening case. Strategic management drives the effort to succeed long-term amid constant change, uncertainty, and obstacles. In fact, a statistical analysis of 26 published studies documented the positive impact of strategic planning on business performance.[2]

Executives responding to a Gallup Poll said they spend the largest proportion of their time (39 percent) on "strategic thinking/planning."[3] For instance, Amazon.com's founder Jeff Bezos credited long-term thinking for his company's strength during the recent Great Recession, emphasizing that the company's focus remained on their core competencies: providing a broad selection at low prices with reliable service. Regarding their ongoing success, Bezos says, "It's the cumulative effect of having this approach for 14 years."[4]

Many people assume that strategy is the exclusive domain of top-level management. But that simply is not true.[5] Its relevance for those lower in the organization may not be as apparent, but it is relevant for *everyone* in the organization. A management student who is 10 to 20 years away from a top-level executive position might reasonably ask, "If top managers formulate strategies and I'm headed for a supervisory or staff position, why should I care about strategic management?" There are three good reasons why staff specialists and managers at all levels need a general understanding of strategic management.

First, in view of widespread criticism that American managers tend to be shortsighted,[6] a strategic orientation encourages farsightedness (see Table 7.1). Second, employees who think in strategic terms tend to understand better how top managers think and why they make the decisions they do. In other words, the rationale behind executive policies and decisions is more apparent when things are viewed from a strategic perspective. Unfortunately, as a survey of 143 strategic management professionals revealed, things seem to be headed in the wrong direction: Only 5 percent of the companies represented in the survey share their strategy with their employees.[7]

A third reason for promoting a broader understanding of strategic management is related to a recent planning trend. Specifically, greater teamwork and cooperation throughout the planning/control cycle are eroding the traditional distinction between those who plan and those who implement plans. In terms of the five strategy-making modes shown in Table 7.2, there is a clear trend *away from* the command, symbolic, and rational modes and *toward* the transactive and generative modes.[8] In other words, the traditional idea of top-management strategists as commanders, coaches, or bosses is giving way to a view of them more as participative facilitators and sponsors. In each of the traditional modes, people below the top level must

7a
Back to the Opening Case

Being king of the web is a short-lived gig. Only several years ago the web was navigated by search and Google was the clear king of innovation. Now, as the web takes on an increasingly social structure we seem to be heading into the Age of Facebook.

By some measures, it will be an age where Google isn't welcome. The company has long been seen as a one-trick pony, gifted at search and little else. It's stumbled again and again in social media with Orkut, Buzz and Wave—efforts that were at best mixed successes.

QUESTION: In terms of Table 7.1, what sort of strategic farsightedness can keep Google from being pushed aside by Facebook?

For further information about the interactive annotations in this chapter, visit our student Web site.

Source: Kevin Kelleher, "How Google Can Thrive in the Age of Facebook," *Fortune* (December 6, 2010), http://tech.fortune.cnn.com/2010/12/06/how-google-can-thrive-in-the-age-of-facebook/.

Table 7.1	Key Dimensions of Strategic Farsightedness

	SHORTSIGHTED	FARSIGHTED
1. Organizational strategy	No formally documented strategies.	A formally written and communicated statement of long-term organizational mission.
2. Competitive advantage	"Follow the leader." No attention devoted to long-term competitive edge.	"Be the leader." Emphasis on gaining and holding a strategic competitive edge.
3. Organizational structure	Rigid structure emphasizing status quo, downward communication, and predictability.	Flexible structure encouraging change, upward and lateral communication, adaptability, and speed.
4. Research and development	Emphasis on applying competitors' good ideas.	Heavy emphasis on developing new products and services and on innovations in production, marketing, and human resource management.
5. Return	Emphasis on short-term profits.	Emphasis on increased market share, growth, and future profit potential.
6. Human resources	Emphasis on stopgap hiring and training. Labor viewed as a commodity. Layoffs common.	Emphasis on long-term development of employees. Labor viewed as a valuable human resource. Layoffs seen as a last resort.
7. Problem solving	Emphasis on chasing symptoms and blaming scapegoats.	Emphasis on finding solutions to emerging problems.
8. Management style	Emphasis on day-to-day firefighting, owing to short-term orientation.	Multilevel strategic thinking that encourages managers to consider long-term implications of their actions and decisions.

be obedient, passive, and reactive. In the *transactive* strategy-making mode, continuous improvement is the order of the day, as middle- and lower-level managers and staff specialists actively participate in the process. They go a step further, becoming risk-taking entrepreneurs, in the *generative* mode. Here is a case in point: The J. M. Smucker Co. asked 140 employees to devote half of their work time over a six-month period to gathering information from all 2,000 employees and to generating new ideas. The result? The team developed more than 10 initiatives that could potentially double the company's revenues in five years. Co-CEO Richard K. Smucker says the participative team approach

". . . brought to the surface a lot of people with special talents."[9]

This strategic exercise certainly paid off because some key purchases, including Crisco oil and Jif peanut butter from Procter & Gamble, helped boost Smucker's annual sales to over $2 billion eight years later.[10]

Thus you, today's management student, are not as far away from the strategic domain as you may think. The time to start thinking strategically is *now*. This chapter defines strategic management, looks at ways to think and act strategically (including Internet and social media strategies), explores the strategic management process, and discusses forecasting.

| Table **7.2** | Five Different Strategy-Making Modes |

	TRADITIONAL MODES		MODERN MODES		
	COMMAND	**SYMBOLIC**	**RATIONAL**	**TRANSACTIVE**	**GENERATIVE**
Style	*Imperial* Strategy driven by leader or small top team	*Cultural* Strategy driven by mission and a vision of the future	*Analytical* Strategy driven by formal structure and planning systems	*Procedural* Strategy driven by internal process and mutual adjustment	*Organic* Strategy driven by organizational actors' initiative
Role of Top Management	*Commander* Provide direction	*Coach* Motivate and inspire	*Boss* Evaluate and control	*Facilitator* Empower and enable	*Sponsor* Endorse and support
Role of Organizational Members	*Soldier* Obey orders	*Player* Respond to challenge	*Subordinate* Follow the system	*Participant* Learn and improve	*Entrepreneur* Experiment and take risks

Source: Adapted from Stuart L. Hart, "An Integrative Framework for Strategy-Making Processes," *Academy of Management Review,* 17 (April 1992): 334. Reprinted by permission.

STRATEGIC MANAGEMENT = STRATEGIC PLANNING + IMPLEMENTATION + CONTROL

Strategic management is the ongoing process of ensuring a competitively superior fit between an organization and its changing environment.[11] In a manner of speaking, strategic management is management on a grand scale, management of the "big picture." Accordingly, **strategy** has been defined as an integrated and externally oriented perception of how the organization will achieve its mission.[12] The strategic management perspective is the product of a historical evolution and is now understood to include budget control, long-range planning, and strategic planning.[13]

Significantly, strategic management does not do away with earlier, more restricted approaches. Instead, it synthesizes and coordinates them all in a more systematic fashion. For example, consider the relationship between strategic planning, as defined in Chapter 6, and strategic management. Recall that *strategic planning* is the process of determining how to pursue the organization's long-term goals with the resources expected to be available. Note that

nothing is said in this definition about adjustment or control. But just as astronauts and space scientists need to make mid-flight corrections to ensure that space shuttles reach their distant destinations, strategic adjustment and control are necessary. The more encompassing strategic management concept is useful today because it effectively merges strategic planning, implementation, and control.

Managers who adopt a strategic management perspective appreciate that strategic plans are living documents. They require updating and fine-tuning as conditions change. They also need to draw on all available talent in the organization. Stephen Haines, CEO of an international strategic management consulting firm, recently observed that strategic thinking requires a holistic view from a longer-term perspective, yet it is also personal and immediate. He notes, "Strategic thinking is a broad and innovative way of thinking on a daily basis about the overall goals of your job, team, and organization."[14]

It is longer-term-oriented with a more systemic and holistic view of your department/unit in its environment.

The strategic management process is discussed in greater detail later in this chapter. But first we need to consider alternative ways to encourage strategic thinking.

THINKING AND ACTING STRATEGICALLY (INCLUDING INTERNET AND SOCIAL MEDIA STRATEGIES)

Effective strategic management involves more than just following a few easy steps. It requires *every* employee, on a daily basis, to consider the "big picture" and think strategically about gaining and keeping a competitive edge. ABB Power Technologies, based in Alamo, Tennessee, uses a teambuilding business simulation to get its employees to think strategically. Working in teams of four, participants in ABB's day-long, decision-making workshop run a company together, which gives them a chance to see how all employees' choices—not just the managers' decisions—directly impact the organization. Says Eduardo Miller, ABB manager and workshop co-instructor, "If all of us are not learning to make the right decisions, we can burn the business."[15]

This section presents four alternative perspectives for thinking innovatively about strategy in today's fast-paced global economy: synergies, Porter's generic strategies, business ecosystems, and Internet and social media strategies.

Glasshouse Images/SuperStock

Synergy

Although not necessarily a familiar term, *synergy* is a well-established and valuable concept for business strategists. **Synergy** occurs when two or more variables (for example, chemicals, drugs, people, and organizations) interact to produce an effect greater than the sum of the effects of all of the variables acting independently. Some call this the $1 + 1 = 3$ effect; others say Reese's Peanut Butter Cups are a tasty synergy of peanut butter and chocolate. Either way, the whole is greater than the sum of its parts. The key is to focus on the bonus effect in synergistic relationships. In strategic management, managers are urged to achieve as much *market, cost, technology*, and *management synergy* as possible when making strategic decisions. Those decisions may involve mergers,[16] acquisitions, new products, new technology or production processes, or executive replacement. When Procter & Gamble bought pet-food maker Iams, executives trumpeted the potential synergies, which turned out to be real. P&G's scientists upgraded the pet food to address pet owners' concerns about health, and the firm's extensive retail network was able to dramatically increase distribution. Over the next five years, Iams' sales doubled and its profits tripled, making it the top-selling pet food brand on the market."[17]

MARKET SYNERGY. When one product or service fortifies the sales of one or more other products or services, market synergy has been achieved. Examples of market synergy are common in the business world. For instance, it has proved profitable for Costco to build 268 gas stations alongside its retail warehouses. The cash-only stations are unbranded and self-service, making them more cost efficient. The gas business now earns more than $3 billion in revenue, or about 5 percent of Costco's annual total.[18]

COST SYNERGY. This second type of synergy can occur in almost every dimension of organized activity. When two or more products can be designed by the same engineers, produced in the same facilities, distributed through the same channels, or sold by the same salespeople, overall costs will be lower than they would be if each product received separate treatment. In an interesting example of cost synergy, major hotels are trying to squeeze more value from their costly real estate. At the airport in Miami, Marriott offers three hotels at three levels of hotel service—full, midprice, and economy—on the same plot of land.[19] Cost synergy also can be achieved by recycling by-products and hazardous wastes that would normally be thrown away.[20] Human imagination is the only limit

---

synergy the concept that the whole is greater than the sum of its parts

to creating cost synergies through recycling. Cost synergy through waste reduction and recycling is good business ethics, too.

TECHNOLOGICAL SYNERGY. The third variety of synergy involves transferring technology from one application to another, thus opening up new markets. For example, consider this marriage of technologies from two very different industries: ConocoPhillips and Tyson Foods are collaborating on producing lower carbon-emission diesel fuel out of fat from Tyson's beef, pork, and poultry products. The partnership combines Tyson's scientific knowledge with Conoco's marketing and processing skills.[21] Thanks to this sort of technological synergy, profitable new markets can be tapped with existing equipment and technical know-how.

MANAGEMENT SYNERGY. This fourth type of synergy occurs when a management team is more productive because its members have complementary rather than identical skills. For example, the top two corporate officers of global mining giant Freeport-McMoRan Copper & Gold, chairman James R. Moffett and CEO Richard C. Adkerson, are a strong team. Says Adkerson, "We complement each other's skills. . . . He knows geology and I know finance."[22] Management synergy also is achieved when an individual with multiple skills or talents is hired for an administrative position.

You may find it difficult, if not impossible, to take advantage of all four types of synergy when developing new strategies. Nonetheless, your strategies are more likely to be realistic and effective if you give due consideration to all four types of synergy as early as possible and try to mix and match synergies. For example, Coca-Cola achieved the following mix of market and cost synergies with its aluminum contour bottle: The new bottle is more modern and user-friendly, yet less costly to manufacture. As for sustainability, the bottle is not only made from recycled aluminum, it is also recyclable.[23]

Johnson Controls recently showed off a bit of technological synergy at the Detroit Auto Show with its Home Recharging Station. As consumers buy more plug-in electric vehicles, they'll need recharging stations like this one.

Porter's Generic Competitive Strategies

In 1980 Michael Porter, a Harvard University economist, developed a model of competitive strategies. During a decade of research, Porter's model evolved to encompass these four generic strategies: (1) cost leadership, (2) differentiation, (3) cost focus, and (4) focused differentiation.[24] As shown in Figure 7.1, Porter's model combined two variables, *competitive advantage* and *competitive scope*.

On the horizontal axis is competitive advantage, which can be achieved via low costs or differentiation. A competitive advantage based on low costs, which means lower prices, is self-explanatory. Differentiation, according to Porter, "is the ability to provide unique and superior value to the buyer in terms of product quality, special features, or after-sale service."[25] Differentiation helps explain why consumers willingly pay more for branded products such as Sunkist oranges, Apple iPhones, and Lexus motor vehicles.[26] On the vertical axis is competitive scope. Is the firm's target market broad or narrow? Dell, which sells many types of computers all around the world, serves a very broad market. A neighborhood pizza parlor offering one type of food in a small geographic area has a narrow target market.

Like the concept of synergy, Porter's model helps managers think strategically: it enables them to see the big picture as it affects the organization and its changing environment. Each of Porter's four generic strategies deserves a closer look.

COST LEADERSHIP STRATEGY. Managers pursuing this strategy have an overriding concern for keeping costs, and therefore prices, lower than those of competitors. Normally, this means extensive production or service facilities with efficient economies of scale (low unit costs of making products or delivering services). Productivity improvement is a high priority for managers following the cost leadership strategy. A prime example of the cost leadership strategy, Walmart's marketing concept is to sell quality products in a clean, family-friendly atmosphere. But rather than appeal to customers with endless discounts and sales, the retailer is grounded in "everyday low prices."[27] Walmart's computerized warehousing network gives it an additional cost advantage over its less efficient competitors. (See Ethics: Character, Courage, and Values.)

In manufacturing firms, the preoccupation with minimizing costs flows beyond production into virtually all areas: purchasing, wages, overhead, research and development (R&D), advertising, and selling. A relatively large market share is required to accommodate this high-volume, low-profit-margin strategy.

DIFFERENTIATION STRATEGY. For this strategy to succeed, a company's product or service must be considered unique by most of the customers in its industry. Advertising and promotion help the product to stand out from the crowd. Specialized design (BMW automobiles), a widely recognized brand (Crest toothpaste), leading-edge technology (Intel), or reliable service (Caterpillar) also may serve to differentiate a product in the industry. Because customers with brand loyalty will usually spend more for what they perceive to be a superior product, the differentiation strategy can yield larger profit margins than the low-cost strategy. But if a brand's image is not carefully nurtured and protected, brand loyalty and customers' willingness to pay a premium price can erode. For businesses sticking to a differentiation strategy, it is important to note that cost reduction is not ignored; it simply is not the highest priority.

| Figure 7.1 | Porter's Generic Competitive Strategies |

differentiation buyer perceives unique and superior value in a product

ETHICS: Character, Courage, and Values

Wal-Mart Takes the High Road on Renewable Energy

In 2005, Wal-Mart set the goal of being 100% reliant on renewable energy. It didn't give a time frame and hasn't said how far it's come. But given Wal-Mart's 8,400 locations worldwide, it's barely made a dent in the goal. Nonetheless, the world's biggest retailer is running real-world tests on green-energy technologies [including solar and wind power]. Because of its heft, it could quickly deploy winning technologies and propel them into the mass market while proving to other companies that the economics work, renewable-energy experts say.

"'If these technologies can pass the Wal-Mart hurdle,' other people will say, 'We ought to look into it. It's not just a novelty,'" says Gwen Ruta, vice president of the Environmental Defense Fund.

Wal-Mart—one of the USA's largest private users of electricity—isn't pursuing renewables just for good PR. It'll turn to green energy, but only if it costs the same as or less than traditional power.

For Discussion: As a Wal-Mart executive, how would you justify your company's renewable-energy strategy to a skeptical Wal-Mart stockholder on *both* cost leadership and ethical grounds?

Source: Excerpted from Julie Schmit, "Wal-Mart Raises Bar on Going Green," *USA Today* (September 20, 2010): 4B.

COST FOCUS STRATEGY. Organizations with a cost focus strategy attempt to gain a competitive edge in a narrow (or regional) market by exerting strict cost control. For instance, Singapore Airlines manages to win rave reviews from business travelers and lots of awards for its high-quality service while at the same time minimizing costs. Compared to American and European airlines' costs, which range anywhere from 7 to 16 cents per available seat kilometer (ASK), Singapore Airlines' cost is just 4.58 cents per ASK. In fact, Singapore Airlines keeps its costs lower than most budget airlines.[28]

FOCUSED DIFFERENTIATION STRATEGY. This generic strategy involves achieving a competitive edge by delivering a superior product and/or service to a limited audience. The Mayo Clinic's world-class health care facilities—in Rochester, Minnesota; Jacksonville, Florida; and Scottsdale, Arizona—are an expression of this strategy.[29] Companies pursuing a focused differentiation strategy typically charge premium prices for their goods and services.

A contingency management approach is necessary for determining which of Porter's generic strategies is appropriate. Research on Porter's model indicates a positive relationship between long-term earnings growth and a good fit between strategy and environment.[30]

Charles Pertwee/Bloomberg/Getty Images

Businesses can choose any number of strategies to help differentiate themselves from their competitors. For example, award-winning Singapore Airlines is known for the quality of its service and its ability to minimize costs.

Business Ecosystems

Researchers recently have given new meaning to the saying "It's a jungle out there." They have extended the concept of ecosystems from nature to business. In his bestseller *The Death of Competition: Leadership and Strategy in the Age of Business Ecosystems*, James F. Moore writes, "It is my view that executives need to think of themselves as part of organisms participating in an ecosystem in much the same way that biological organisms participate in a biological ecosystem."[31] A business ecosystem is an economic community of organizations and all of their stakeholders, including suppliers and customers.[32] This evolving model makes one very important contribution to modern strategic thinking: *organizations need to be as good at cooperating as they are at competing if they are to succeed.*

A BUSINESS ECOSYSTEM IN ACTION. Within a business ecosystem, key organizations selectively cooperate and compete to achieve both their individual and collective goals. A prime example is the relationships among major computer and networking companies. In public, the executives of all the major tech players appear to cooperate and get along, and in a very real sense, the companies must learn to make their products work well together in order to satisfy their communal customers. But don't be mislead by the outward appearance of collaboration. *Fortune* magazine recently observed that these tech giants are becoming more and more competitive in the race to win the trillion dollars in sales that will be made each year, and the magazine warns ". . . it's going to get bloody."[33]

The tension of alternating between cooperation and competition extends to talent as well. When Mark Hurd resigned under pressure from his CEO post at Hewlett-Packard in 2010, he promptly was hired as Oracle's new president.[34]

Another robust business ecosystem to watch is Apple's computer/telephone/entertainment combination and its hugely successful "apps" business.[35] In the meantime, things won't be dull in the business jungle.

NEEDED: MORE STRATEGIC COOPERATION. Through the years, the terms *strategy* and *competition* have become synonymous. Business ecologists now call for greater cooperation, even among the toughest of competitors. In fact, James F. Moore has even observed that it is the inability to prompt cooperation among diverse communities that has posed the

7b
Runway Fashion on a Budget

Jenn Hyman and Jenny Fleiss, Cofounders of RentTheRunway, New York City designer dress rental company:

Hyman: "Women feel this constant pressure to wear something new, especially now that pictures are posted on sites like Facebook. We want to enable women to have a new dress for every occasion."

Fleiss: "Pick a dress you love, and we'll send it in two sizes to ensure the perfect fit. When you're finished, pop it in the mailbox, and we'll take care of the dry cleaning. Renting costs $50 to $300, just 10% of the retail value. Women today have a cost-per-wear mentality, and it's stylish to be thrifty. We have more than 750,000 members, and we're adding 20,000 every week."

Hyman: "We've developed personal relationships with more than 100 brands to make sure we get the most current inventory."

QUESTIONS: Which of Porter's four generic competitive strategies is being followed here? Explain your choice. How would you tweak RentTheRunway's strategy to ensure continued success?

Source: "Fast Talk: Jenny Fleiss and Jenn Hyman," *Fast Company*, 151 (December 2010–January 2011): 80. For more see: www.renttherunway.com/about.

business ecosystem economic community of organizations and all their stakeholders

biggest stumbling block to innovation, not a lack of good ideas, technology, or capital.[36] In ecosystem terms, companies need to "coevolve" with key strategic partners (and sometimes even with their competitors) if they are to thrive today. For example, Apple allowed developers of iPhone and iPad apps to write programs both for Apple and Android, produced by Google, because the company recognized the mutual benefits of that cooperative action.[37]

Strategies for the Internet and Social Media

The Internet is not a fixed thing. It is a complex bundle of emerging technologies at various stages of development. The original Internet has evolved into such things as the mobile Internet, smart phones, cloud computing, social media, and augmented reality.[38] Corporate strategists and entrepreneurs are challenged to build business models based on *where they expect these technologies to be* X years down the road. This exercise is akin to hitting a moving target from a moving platform—very difficult, at best. But L. L. Bean, the nearly 100-year-old outdoor gear retailer, proved it is possible to keep pace in the Internet age. Thanks to online features like customer reviews, lower return shipping charges, simple package tracking, and instant access to live customer service representatives, the company now sells more merchandise through e-tailing than through its traditional catalogs. "Wherever they want to shop, we have to be there," says Terry Sutton, vice-president for customer satisfaction.[39] E-business experts predict major changes ahead for several industries, including software development and distribution, real estate, telecommunications, bill payment, jewelry, and advertising.

The purpose of this section is to build a framework of understanding for squeezing maximum value from the Internet and social media.

BASIC INTERNET BUSINESS MODELS. Relative to buying, selling, and trading things on the Internet,

Arthur Kwiatkowski/arsenik/ iStockphoto.com

it is possible to fashion a strategy around one or a combination of seven basic business models (see Table 7.3).[40] eBay, for example, has been hugely successful with the commission-based model. Google, on the other hand, makes its money via an advertising-based model. As indicated in Table 7.3, each of the Internet business models has its own unique set of opportunities for strategic competitive advantage. Our challenge is to take what we have learned about synergy, Porter's competitive strategies, and business ecosystems and develop a winning strategy.

THERE IS NO ONE-SIZE-FITS-ALL INTERNET STRATEGY. Harvard's Michael Porter, whose generic competitive strategies we just covered, cautions us to avoid putting Internet strategies into one basket. Instead, he sees two major categories:

At this critical juncture in the evolution of Internet technology, dot-coms and established companies face different strategic imperatives. Dot-coms must develop real strategies that create economic value. They must recognize that current ways of competing are destructive and futile and benefit neither themselves nor, in the end, customers. Established companies, in turn, must stop deploying the Internet on a stand-alone basis and instead use it to enhance the distinctiveness of their strategies.[41]

These two types of businesses have been called dot-coms and dot-corps. Porter urges established "bricks-and-mortar" businesses to weave the Internet into the very fabric of their operations—in short, to become true e-businesses.

CUSTOMER LOYALTY IS BUILT WITH RELIABLE BRAND NAMES AND "STICKY" WEB SITES. Web surfers have proved to have very short attention spans. Seemingly attractive Web sites can have many visitors ("hits"), but few or no sales. When doing business at Internet speed, Web sites need to satisfy four criteria: (1) high-quality layout and graphics; (2) fast, responsive service; (3) complete and up-to-date information; and (4) high ranking on search engines such as Google.[42] A trusted brand name can further

| Table **7.3** | Seven Basic Internet Business Models |

TYPE	FEATURES AND CONTENT	SOURCES OF COMPETITIVE ADVANTAGE
Commission-based	Commissions charged for brokerage or intermediary services. Adds value by providing expertise and/or access to a wide network of alternatives.	Search Evaluation Problem solving Transaction
Advertising-based	Web content paid for by advertisers. Adds value by providing free or low-cost content—including customer feedback, expertise, and entertainment programming—to audiences that range from very broad (general content) to highly targeted (specialized content).	Search Evaluation
Markup-based	Reselling marked-up merchandise. Adds value through selection, distribution efficiencies, and the leveraging of brand image and reputation. May use entertainment programming to enhance sales.	Search Transaction
Production-based	Selling manufactured goods and custom services. Adds value by increasing production efficiencies, capturing customer preferences, and improving customer service.	Search Problem solving
Referral-based	Fees charged for referring customers. Adds value by enhancing a company's product or service offering, tracking referrals electronically, and generating demographic data. Expertise and customer feedback are often included with referral information.	Search Problem solving Transaction
Subscription-based	Fees charged for unlimited use of service or content. Adds value by leveraging strong brand name, providing high-quality information to specialized markets or access to essential services. May consist entirely of entertainment programming.	Evaluation Problem solving
Fee-for-service-based	Fees charged for metered services. Adds value by providing service efficiencies, expertise, and practical outsourcing solutions.	Problem solving Transaction

Source: Reprinted from *Organizational Dynamics*, 33, no. 2, G. T. Lumpkin and Gregory G. Dess, "E-Business Strategies and the Internet Business Models: How the Internet Adds Value," p. 169, Copyright 2004, with permission from Elsevier.

enhance what e-businesspeople call the *stickiness* of a Web site—that is, the ability to draw the same customer back again and again. A great deal of work is needed in this area, considering the results of one study: two-thirds of the visitors to online stores did not return within a year.[43] Even though e-retailing might appear to be a quick-and-easy and impersonal process, loyal customers still expect a personal touch

and some "hand holding" when they have questions, problems, or suggestions.

EMERGING BUSINESS MODELS FOR SOCIAL MEDIA. As indicated back in Chapter 1 (Table 1.2), social media are second-generation Web tools. They include but are not limited to Internet blogs, social networking sites such as Facebook and LinkedIn, microblogging sites such as Twitter, and photo and video sharing sites such as Flickr and YouTube. What distinguishes social media from first-generation Internet offerings is the advent of *user-generated content*. Social media empower us to create our own Internet content and distribute it as narrowly or broadly as we choose. When businesses hear that hundreds of millions of people around the world are exchanging treasure troves of information on Facebook, YouTube, and Twitter, they envision immense profit opportunities.[44] However, the major challenge (and potential landmine) for companies and advertisers is to join the social media conversation without over-commercializing something users view as inherently free, relatively unmanaged, and personal in nature.

Marketers are advised to aim for the following sort of "soft-sell" interaction: Followers on Twitter will read your company blog, which encourages them to link to your Facebook Fan page, which publicizes your YouTube videos.[45] Of course, the last crucial step is for social media users to then pay a fee or buy something based on this Internet version of heard-it-from-a-friend advertising. Consider Ford's approach to introducing the 2011 Explorer: As a new marketing approach, Ford is bypassing auto shows and instead using social networking, launching its Explorer on Facebook, which has nearly 500 million members. Scott Monty says, "Customers may . . . be found hanging out online."[46]

Social media strategies clearly are a work in progress as new technologies are unfolding. Importantly, this is *not* a green light for companies to ignore social media. Why? Company reputations and brand names can be seriously damaged by both valid and invalid criticism (for example, see the Starbucks case at the end of this chapter). Rumors and negative images that "go viral," meaning they spread quickly from one person to many others like a cold virus, need to be nipped in the bud. Thus, *at the very minimum*, both large and small companies need to monitor social media and respond promptly and constructively to postings that put reputations and brand names at risk. According to *Inc.* magazine, a number of online services, such as Google Alerts, Social Mention, and HootSuite, can be used to track online mentions of any product or service, enabling

7c
A CEO Gets Comfortable with Social Media
Brian Dunn, CEO Best Buy:

In my office, I now have a large monitor of all the activity where we're mentioned. I want to know what's out there. I don't have to respond to all of it, but I write everything on my Twitter and Facebook accounts myself—and I'm the one who's posting. I'm responsible for what I say online, and I expect the same of my employees. The only guideline is that they act within our values. You can engage with social media and get comfortable with the messiness of it. We're past the tipping point. You have to be where the people are.

QUESTIONS: What are the pros and cons of Dunn's heavy involvement with social media? Is it wise to rely on the company's values for controlling employee abuse of social media?

Source: As quoted in Diane Brady, "Hard Choices: Brian Dunn," *Bloomberg Businessweek* (December 6–12, 2010): 104.

the organizations behind them to respond immediately. Says social media expert Nate Bagley, "It's a good way to gather business intelligence."[47] The need for companies to have social media policies in place for their employees is discussed in Chapter 11.

THE STRATEGIC MANAGEMENT PROCESS

Strategic plans are formulated during an evolutionary process with identifiable steps. In line with the three-level planning pyramid covered in Chapter 6, the strategic management process is broader and more general at the top and filters down to narrower and more specific terms. Figure 7.2 outlines the four major steps of the strategic management process: (1) formulation of a grand strategy, (2) formulation of strategic plans, (3) implementation of strategic plans, and (4) strategic control. Corrective action based on evaluation and feedback takes place

Figure **7.2**   The Strategic Management Process

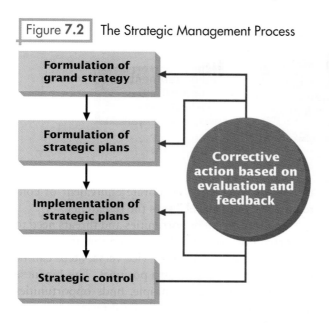

- Formulation of grand strategy
- Formulation of strategic plans
- Implementation of strategic plans
- Strategic control

Corrective action based on evaluation and feedback

throughout the entire strategic management process to keep things headed in the right direction.[48]

It is important to note that this model represents an ideal approach for instructional purposes. Because of organizational politics, as discussed in Chapter 13, and different planning orientations among managers, a somewhat less systematic process typically results.

Nevertheless, it is helpful to study the strategic management process as a systematic and rational sequence in order to better understand what it involves. Although he noted that rational strategic planning models should not be taken literally, Henry Mintzberg acknowledged their profound instructional value. They teach necessary vocabulary and implant the notion "that strategy represents a fundamental congruence between external opportunity and internal capability."[49]

Formulation of a Grand Strategy

As pointed out in Chapter 6, a clear statement of organizational mission serves as a focal point for the entire planning process. Key stakeholders inside and outside the organization are given a general idea of why the organization exists and where it is headed. Working from the mission statement, top management formulates the organization's **grand strategy**, a general explanation of *how* the organization's mission is to be accomplished. Grand strategies are not drawn out of thin air. They are derived from a careful *situational analysis* of the organization and its environment. A clear vision of where the organization *is* headed and of where it *should be* headed is the gateway to competitive advantage.[50] As a bold example, Volkswagen's CEO Martin Winterkorn has proclaimed to all that the German automaker intends to pass Toyota by 2018.[51]

SITUATIONAL ANALYSIS. A **situational analysis** is a technique for matching organizational strengths and weaknesses with environmental opportunities and threats to determine the right niche for the organization (see Figure 7.3). Many strategists refer to this process as a SWOT analysis. SWOT stands for strengths, weaknesses, opportunities, and threats. (You can perform an actual SWOT analysis in the Action Learning

KAREN BLEIER/AFP/Getty Images

Promotional tie-ins between different types of businesses and different types of products—like this one between McDonald's and the Star Wars movies—have become a popular way for corporations to strategically cross-promote their products to common markets.

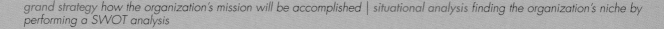

grand strategy how the organization's mission will be accomplished | *situational analysis* finding the organization's niche by performing a SWOT analysis

Figure 7.3 | Determining Strategic Direction Through Situational (SWOT) Analysis

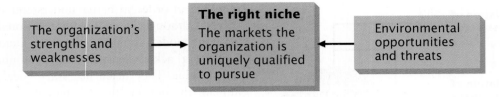

Exercise at the end of this chapter.) Every organization should be able to identify the purpose for which it is best suited. But this matching process is more difficult than it may first appear. Strategists are faced not with snapshots of the environment and the organization but with a video of rapidly changing events. As one researcher said, "The task is to find a match between opportunities that are still unfolding and resources that are still being acquired."[52] For example, Google's executive chairman Eric Schmidt explains how his company tackles this task:

There's tremendous opportunity before us, so we're organized around taking advantage of . . . technology discontinuities as they occur. And therefore we spend a lot of time trying to make sure that we're busy seeing them. And that's our competitive advantage. You have to be set up to shift your focus quickly so that you spend most of your energies inventing the new business instead of blindly optimizing the old one.[53]

Forecasting techniques, such as those reviewed later in this chapter, help managers cope with uncertainty about the future while conducting situational analyses.

Strategic planners, whether top managers, key operating managers, or staff planning specialists, have many ways to scan the environment for opportunities and threats. They can study telltale shifts in the economy, recent technological innovations, growth and movement among competitors, market trends, labor availability, and demographic patterns.

Unfortunately, according to a survey of executives at 100 U.S. corporations, not enough time is spent looking outside the organization: Less than half of the respondents' planning time involved evaluating competition and markets (external factors) compared with 48 percent spent on internal factors—budget, organizational factors, and human resources. "That's the corporate equivalent of contemplating one's navel," says the researcher.[54]

Environmental opportunities and threats need to be sorted out carefully. A perceived threat may turn out to be an opportunity, or vice versa. Steps can be taken to turn negatives into positives. The Japanese company Omron, for example, finds opportunities by researching customers' unsolved problems.[55]

CAPABILITY PROFILE. After scanning the external environment for opportunities and threats, management's attention turns inward to identifying the organization's strengths and weaknesses.[56] This subprocess is called a capability profile. The following are key capabilities for today's companies:

- Quick response to market trends
- Rapid product development
- Rapid production and delivery
- Continuous cost reduction
- Continuous improvement of processes, human resources, and products
- Greater flexibility of operations[57]

Diversity initiatives are an important way to achieve continuous improvement of human resources.[58] Also note the clear emphasis on *speed* in this list of key organizational capabilities.

THE STRATEGIC NEED FOR SPEED. Speed has become an important competitive advantage. Warren Holtsberg, a Motorola corporate vice president, notes that due to customer demand, the company has gone from rolling out a new cellular telephone every two years to rolling one out every four to six months, a change of pace that he describes as refreshing and invigorating.[59]

I find the impatience of the new economy refreshing. The concept that fast is better than perfect bodes well, particularly for the technology industry. At Motorola, we used to be able to introduce a cellular telephone, and it would have a life expectancy in the marketplace of about two years. Now we face cycle times of four to six months. People continue to demand new things. They demand change. They're impatient. Bringing that into a big corporation is invigorating.

Accordingly, the new strategic emphasis on speed involves more than just doing the same old things faster. It calls for rethinking and radically redesigning the entire business cycle, a process called **reengineering**.[60] The idea is to have cross-functional teams develop a whole new—and better—production process, one that does not let time-wasting mistakes occur in the first place. (The related topic of horizontal organizations is covered in Chapter 9.)

Formulation of Strategic Plans

In the second major step in the strategic management process, general intentions are translated into more concrete and measurable strategic plans, policies, and budget allocations.[61] This translation is the responsibility of top management, although staff planning specialists and middle managers often provide input. From our discussion in the last chapter, recall that a well-written plan consists of both an objective and an action statement. Plans at all levels need to specify by whom, what, when, and how things are to be accomplished and for how much. Many managers prefer to call these specific plans "action plans" to emphasize the need to turn good intentions into action. Even though strategic plans may have a time horizon of one or more years, they must meet the same criteria that shorter-run intermediate and operational plans meet. They should do the following:

1. Develop clear, results-oriented objectives in measurable terms.
2. Identify the particular activities required to accomplish the objectives.
3. Assign specific responsibility and authority to the appropriate personnel.
4. Estimate times to accomplish activities and their appropriate sequencing.

5. Determine resources required to accomplish the activities.
6. Communicate and coordinate the above elements and complete the action plan.[62]

All of this does not happen in a single quick-and-easy session. Specific strategic plans usually evolve over a period of months as top management consults with key managers in all areas of the organization to gather their ideas and recommendations and, one hopes, to win their commitment.

STRATEGIC IMPLEMENTATION AND CONTROL

As illustrated earlier in Figure 7.2, the third and fourth stages of the strategic management cycle involve implementation and control. The entire process is only as strong as these two traditionally underemphasized areas.

Implementation of Strategic Plans

Because strategic plans are too often shelved without adequate attention to implementation, top managers need to do a better job of facilitating the implementation process and building middle-manager commitment.[63]

A SYSTEMATIC FILTERING-DOWN PROCESS. Strategic plans require further translation into successively lower-level plans. Top-management strategists can do some groundwork to ensure that the filtering-down process occurs smoothly and efficiently. Planners need answers to four questions, each tied to a different critical organizational factor:

1. *Organizational structure.* Is the organizational structure compatible with the planning process, with new managerial approaches, and with the strategy itself?

maxstockphoto/Shutterstock.Com

---

reengineering radically redesigning the entire business cycle for greater strategic speed

2. *People.* Are people with the right skills and abilities available for key assignments, or must attention be given to recruiting, training, management development, and similar programs?

3. *Culture.* Is the collective viewpoint on "the right way to do things" compatible with strategy, must it be modified to reflect a new perspective, or must top management learn to manage around it?

4. *Control systems.* Is the necessary apparatus in place to support the implementation of strategy and to permit top management to assess performance in meeting strategic objectives?[64]

Strategic plans that successfully address these four questions have a much greater chance of helping the organization achieve its intended purpose than those that do not. In addition, field research

These Yellowstone National Park bison occasionally wander into neighboring grazing lands, carrying diseases harmful to cattle. A comprehensive strategic control program attempts to maintain a healthy herd within the park and minimize damage elsewhere, yet none of the stakeholders—including ranchers, hunters, and environmentalists—are entirely happy with the program.

AP Photo/Laura Rauch, File

indicates the need to *sell* strategies to all affected parties. New strategies represent change, and people tend to resist change for a variety of reasons, which means that the strategist must also convince key stakeholders of a strategy's merit.[65] FedEx founder and CEO Fred Smith explains how strategy is "sold" throughout his company: Once the senior management team has hammered out its strategic plans at its annual meeting, it communicates the strategy to employees through its mission statement, its employee handbooks, its written business plans, its incentive plans, and even through its own industrial TV network.[66] This brings us to the challenge of obtaining commitment among middle managers.

BUILDING MIDDLE-MANAGER COMMITMENT. Resistance among middle managers can kill an otherwise excellent strategic management program. A study of 90 middle managers who wrote 330 reports about instances in which they had resisted strategic decisions documented the scope of this problem. It turned out that to protect their own self-interests, the managers in the study frequently derailed strategies. This finding prompted the researchers to conclude that without buy-in from middle managers, top management's decisions will yield less efficient results and may not get implemented at all. Researchers added that, "in dynamic competitive environments, securing commitment is crucial because rapid implementation is so important."[67]

Participative management (see Chapter 12) and effective leadership (see Chapter 14) can foster middle-management commitment. Ford Motor Company's CEO Alan Mulally makes sure all key players are committed to achieving strategic objectives by communicating directly with his leadership team. He says, "Everyone has to know the plan, its status, and areas that need special attention." To ensure this, Mulally holds a Business Plan Review, which is a weekly meeting with all 12 of his direct reports that takes place every Thursday morning.[68]

Strategic Control

Strategic plans, like our more informal daily plans, can go astray, so a formal control system is needed to keep strategic plans on track.[69] Software programs that synchronize and track all contributors' goals in real time are indispensable today. And strategic control systems need to be carefully designed ahead of time, not merely tacked on as an afterthought.[70] Before strategies are translated downward, planners should set up and test channels for information on progress, problems, and strategic assumptions about the environment or organization that have proved to be invalid. If a new strategy varies significantly from past ones, then new production, financial, or marketing reports will probably have to be drafted and introduced.

The ultimate goal of a strategic control system is to detect and correct downstream problems in order to keep strategies updated and on target, without stifling creativity and innovation in the process. A survey of 207 planning executives found that in high-performing companies there was no tradeoff between strategic control and creativity. Rather, the two were delicately balanced.[71]

Corrective Action Based on Evaluation and Feedback

As illustrated in Figure 7.2, corrective action makes the strategic management process a dynamic cycle. A rule of thumb is that negative feedback should prompt corrective action at the step immediately before.[72] Should the problem turn out to be more deeply rooted, then the next earlier step also may require corrective action. The key is to detect problems and initiate corrective action, such as updating strategic assumptions, reformulating plans, rewriting policies, making personnel changes, or modifying budget allocations, as soon as possible. In the absence of prompt corrective action, problems can rapidly worsen.

Let us now turn to forecasting. Without the ability to obtain or develop reliable environmental forecasts, managerial strategists have little chance of successfully navigating their way through the strategic management process.

FORECASTING

An important aspect of strategic management is anticipating what will happen in the years ahead. Forecasts may be defined as predictions, projections, or estimates of future events or conditions in the environment in which the organization operates. The idea is to sketch a rough outline of the future to enable better strategic decision making *today*[73] (see Green

Management: Toward Sustainability). Forecasts may be little more than educated guesses, or they may be the result of highly sophisticated statistical analyses. They vary in reliability, as we all know from off-the-mark weather forecasts.[74] They may be relatively short run—a few hours to a year—or long run—five or more years. A combination of factors determines a forecast's relative sophistication, time horizon, and reliability. These factors include the type of forecast required, management's knowledge of forecasting techniques, and how much money management is willing to invest.[75] Poor forecasting can be very costly. For example, after Toyota's U.S. sales of full-size pickup trucks fell way below expectations, evidence showed the firm's sales forecasts were based on faulty assumptions and research. Research revealed that Toyota's Tundra appealed to a much smaller pool of people than the traditional customer base for big pick-ups made by Ford, GM, and Chrysler.[76]

Types of Forecasts

There are three types of forecasts: (1) event outcome forecasts, (2) event timing forecasts, and (3) time series forecasts.[77] Each type answers a different general

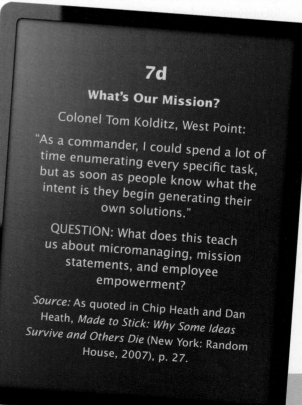

7d
What's Our Mission?
Colonel Tom Kolditz, West Point:

"As a commander, I could spend a lot of time enumerating every specific task, but as soon as people know what the intent is they begin generating their own solutions."

QUESTION: What does this teach us about micromanaging, mission statements, and employee empowerment?

Source: As quoted in Chip Heath and Dan Heath, *Made to Stick: Why Some Ideas Survive and Others Die* (New York: Random House, 2007), p. 27.

forecasts predictions, projections, or estimates of future situations

Green Management: Toward Sustainability

Experts Say Sustainability Is Changing the Competitive Landscape

Business history is marked by periods of relative stability punctuated by fundamental shifts in the competitive landscape that create inescapable threats and game-changing opportunities. Sustainability is an emerging business megatrend, like electrification and mass production, that will profoundly affect companies' competitiveness and even their survival.

. . . fueling this megatrend, thousands of companies are placing strategic bets on innovation in energy efficiency, renewable power, resource productivity, and pollution control. . . . What this all adds up to is that managers can no longer afford to ignore sustainability as a central factor in their companies' long-term competitiveness.

For Discussion: What hard evidence of this sustainability megatrend have you observed in how businesses are being run today? Is the sustainability movement likely to be just a fad? Explain.

Source: Excerpted from David A. Lubin and Daniel C. Esty, "The Sustainability Imperative," *Harvard Business Review,* 88 (May 2010): 44–45.

question (see Table 7.4). Event outcome forecasts are used when strategists want to predict the outcome of highly probable future events. For example: "How will an impending strike affect output?"

Event timing forecasts predict when, if ever, given events will occur. Strategic questions in this area might include "When will the prime interest rate begin to rise?" or "When will our primary competitor introduce a certain product?" Timing questions such as these typically can be answered by identifying leading indicators that historically have preceded the events in question. For instance, a rising inflation rate often prompts major banks to raise their prime interest rate, or a competitor may flag the introduction of a new product by conducting market tests or ordering large quantities of a new raw material.

Time series forecasts seek to estimate future values in a sequence of periodically recorded statistics. A common example is the sales forecast for a business. Sales forecasts need to be as accurate as possible because they affect decisions all along the organization's supply chain as well as inventory levels.[78]

Forecasting Techniques

Modern managers may use one or a combination of four techniques to forecast future outcomes, timing, and values. These techniques are informed judgment, scenario analysis, surveys, and trend analysis.

INFORMED JUDGMENT. Limited time and money often force strategists to rely on their own intuitive judgment when forecasting. Judgmental forecasts

| Table **7.4** | Types of Forecasts |

TYPE OF FORECAST	GENERAL QUESTION	EXAMPLE
1. **Event outcome forecast**	"What will happen when a given event occurs?"	"Who will win the next Super Bowl?"
2. **Event timing forecast**	"When will a given event occur?"	"When will a human set foot on Mars?"
3. **Time series forecast**	"What value will a series of periodic data have at a given point in time?"	"What will the Dow Jones Industrial Average stock index close at on January 5, 2015?"

event outcome forecasts predictions of the outcome of highly probable future events | event timing forecasts predictions of when a given event will occur | time series forecasts estimates of future values in a statistical sequence

are both fast and inexpensive, but their accuracy depends on how well informed the strategist is. Frequent visits with employees—in sales, purchasing, and public relations, for example—who regularly tap outside sources of information are a good way of staying informed. A broad reading program to stay in touch with current events and industry trends, and refresher training through management development programs, are also helpful. Additionally, customized news clipping services (delivered by e-mail), spreadsheet forecasting software, and a competitive intelligence-gathering operation can help keep strategic decision makers up to date. The trick is to separate key bits of information from extraneous background noise. For example, The announcement of Hitachi's ultra-thin hard drive sparked an accurate prediction that Apple would soon start producing the iPod mini.[79]

Of course, informed judgment is no panacea. It generally needs to be balanced with data from other forecasting techniques and formal market research.[80]

SCENARIO ANALYSIS. This technique also relies on informed judgment, but it is more systematic and disciplined than the approach just discussed. Scenario analysis (also called scenario planning) is the preparation and study of written descriptions of *alternative* but *equally likely* future conditions.[81] Scenarios are visions of what "could be." The late futurist Herman Kahn is said to have first used the term *scenario* in conjunction with forecasting during the 1950s. The two types of scenarios are longitudinal and cross-sectional.

Longitudinal scenarios describe how the present is expected to evolve into the future. Cross-sectional scenarios, the most common type, simply describe possible future situations at a given time.

While noting that *multiple forecasts* are the cornerstone of scenario analysis, one researcher offered the following perspective: As a qualitative process, scenario writing stems from hunches as much as quantitative models. The assumption is that the future does not replicate the past. It is a combination of many forces that can be predicted, but it is best understood by the human mind, not merely mathematical computations.[82]

The same researcher recommends developing two to four scenarios (three being optimal) for narrowly defined topics. Likely candidates for scenario

analysis are specific products, industries, markets, or catastrophic events.[83] For example, a grain-exporting company's strategists might look five years into the future by writing scenarios for three different likely situations: (1) above-average grain harvests, (2) average harvests, and (3) below-average harvests. These scenarios could serve as focal points for strategic plans concerning construction of facilities, staffing and training, and so on. As the future unfolds, the strategies written to accompany the more realistic scenario would be followed.

This approach has been called "no-surprise" strategic planning. The results of a poll uncovered a crying need for such an approach when more than 95 of the 140 respondents admitted that they had failed to predict and strategize for numerous significant events that had impacted their organizations over the last five years.[84] In another study, an amazing 97 percent of the respondents admitted their companies had no means of detecting potentially problematic events before they happened.[85] The case for scenario planning has been framed this way:

> *If you envision multiple versions of the future and think through their implications, you will be better prepared for whatever ends up happening. In effect, you won't be seeing the future for the first time. You'll be remembering it. The alternative won't cut it: Those who cannot remember the future are condemned to be taken by surprise.*[86]

The key to good scenario writing is to focus on the few readily identifiable but unpredictable factors that will have the greatest impact on the topic in question. Because scenarios look far into the future, typically five or more years, they need to be written in general and rather imprecise terms.

SURVEYS. Surveys are a forecasting technique involving face-to-face or telephone interviews and mailed, e-mail, or Web panel questionnaires.[87] They can be used to pool expert opinion or to fathom consumer tastes, attitudes, and opinions. When carefully constructed and properly administered to representative samples, surveys can give management comprehensive and fresh information. They suffer the disadvantages, however, of being somewhat difficult to construct, time-consuming to administer and interpret, and expensive. Although costs can be trimmed by purchasing an off-the-shelf or "canned"

---

scenario analysis preparing written descriptions of equally likely future situations | longitudinal scenarios describing how the future will evolve from the present | cross-sectional scenarios describing future situations at a given point in time

survey, standardized instruments too often either fail to ask precisely the right questions or ask unnecessary questions.

TREND ANALYSIS. Essentially, a trend analysis is the hypothetical extension of a past pattern of events or time series into the future. An underlying assumption of trend analysis is that past and present tendencies will continue into the future.[88] Of course, surprise events such as the September 11, 2001, terrorist attacks can destroy that assumption. Trend analysis can be fickle and cruel to reactive companies. If sufficient valid historical data are readily available, then barring disruptive surprise events, trend analysis can be a reasonably accurate, fast, and inexpensive strategic forecasting tool. An unreliable or atypical database, however, can produce misleading trend projections.

Each of these forecasting techniques has inherent limitations. Consequently, strategists are advised to cross-check each source of forecast information with one or more additional sources.

7e
Calling All Oddball Curiosities and Failures

More often than not, indicators look like mere oddball curiosities or, worse, failures, and just as we dislike uncertainty, we shy away from failures and anomalies. But if you want to look for the thing that's going to come whistling in out of nowhere in the next years and change your business, look for interesting failures—smart ideas that seem to have gone nowhere.

QUESTION: Among the failed businesses and product flops you have observed recently, which ones are "interesting failures" that, given the right conditions, could be profitable ideas? Explain.

Source: Paul Saffo, "Six Rules for Effective Forecasting," *Harvard Business Review*, 85 (July–August 2007): 128.

"We're looking for a more comprehensive research strategy than simply 'Google it.' "

trend analysis hypothetical extension of a past series of events into the future

SUMMARY

1. Strategic management sets the stage for virtually all managerial activity. Managers at all levels need to think strategically and to be familiar with the strategic management process for three reasons: farsightedness is encouraged, the rationale behind top-level decisions becomes more apparent, and strategy formulation and implementation are more decentralized today. Strategic management is defined as the ongoing process of ensuring a competitively superior fit between the organization and its ever-changing environment. Strategic management effectively merges strategic planning, implementation, and control.

2. Strategic thinking, the ability to look ahead and spot key organization-environment interdependencies, is necessary for successful strategic management and planning. Four perspectives that can help managers think strategically are synergy, Porter's model of competitive strategies, the concept of business ecosystems, and e-business models and lessons. Synergy has been called the $1 + 1 = 3$ effect because it focuses on situations where the whole is greater than the sum of its parts. Managers are challenged to achieve four types of synergy: market synergy, cost synergy, technological synergy, and management synergy.

3. According to Porter's generic competitive strategies model, four strategies are (1) cost leadership, (2) differentiation, (3) cost focus, and (4) focused differentiation. Porter's model helps managers create a profitable "fit" between the organization and its environment.

4. Contrary to the traditional assumption that strategy automatically equates to competition, the business ecosystems model emphasizes that organizations need to be as good at *cooperating* as they are at competing. By balancing competition and cooperation, competitors can *coevolve* into a dominant economic community (or business ecosystem).

5. Seven basic Internet business models are the commission-based, advertising-based, markup-based, production-based, referral-based, subscription-based, and fee-for-service-based models. Each model affords its own opportunities for competitive advantage. Two Internet strategy lessons learned in recent years are: (1) there is no one-size-fits-all strategy, and (2) reliable brand names and "sticky" Web sites are needed to build customer loyalty. Businesses and advertisers are excited about the potential of social media such as Facebook, Twitter, and YouTube. But a "soft sell" is needed to avoid the perception of over-commercializing media where personal user-generated content prevails. At a minimum, businesses of all sizes need to regularly monitor social media and respond quickly and constructively to postings that threaten the company's reputation and/or brands.

6. The strategic management process consists of four major steps: (1) formulation of a grand strategy, (2) formulation of strategic plans, (3) implementation of strategic plans, and (4) strategic control. Corrective action based on evaluation of progress and feedback helps keep the strategic management process on track. Results-oriented strategic plans that specify what, when, and how are then formulated and translated downward into more specific and shorter-term intermediate and operational plans. Participative management can build needed middle-manager commitment during implementation. Problems encountered along the way should be detected by the strategic control mechanism or by ongoing evaluation and subjected to corrective action.

7. Strategists formulate the organization's grand strategy after conducting a SWOT analysis. The organization's key capabilities and appropriate niche in the marketplace become apparent when the organization's strengths (S) and weaknesses (W) are cross-referenced with environmental opportunities (O) and threats (T). Strategic speed has become an important capability today, sometimes necessitating radical reengineering of the entire business cycle.

8. Event outcome, event timing, and time series forecasts help strategic planners anticipate and prepare for future environmental circumstances. Popular forecasting techniques among today's managers include informed judgment, scenario analysis, surveys, and trend analysis. Each technique has its own limitations, so forecasts need to be cross-checked against one another.

TERMS TO UNDERSTAND

Strategic management, p. 186
Strategy, p. 186
Synergy, p. 187
Differentiation, p. 191
Business ecosystem, p. 191
Grand strategy, p. 195

Situational analysis, p. 195
Capability profile, p. 296
Reengineering, p. 297
Forecasts, p. 299
Event outcome forecasts, p. 200
Event timing forecasts, p. 200

Time series forecasts, p. 200
Scenario analysis, p. 201
Longitudinal scenarios, p. 201
Cross-sectional scenarios, p. 201
Trend analysis, p. 202

ACTION LEARNING EXERCISE

THINKING STRATEGICALLY: A SWOT ANALYSIS

Instructions: This exercise is suitable for either an individual or a team. First, pick an organization as the focal point of the exercise. It can be a large company, a unit of a large company, a small business, or a nonprofit organization such as a college, government agency, or religious organization. Next, look inward and list the organization's strengths and weaknesses. Turning the analysis outward, list opportunities and threats in the organization's environment. Finally, envision workable strategies for the organization by cross-referencing the two sets of factors. Be sure to emphasize organizational strengths that can exploit environmental opportunities and neutralize or overcome outside threats. Also think about what needs to be done to correct organizational weaknesses. The general idea is to create the best possible fit between the organization and its environment (the "right niche").

Note: A SWOT analysis also can be a powerful career guidance tool. Simply make *yourself* the focus of the exercise and go from there.

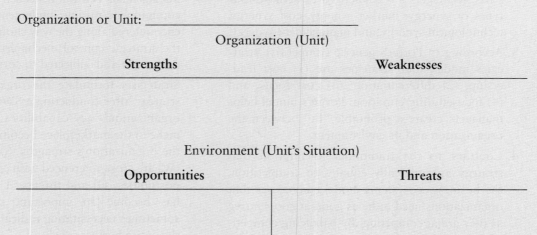

Organization or Unit: _____

Organization (Unit)

Strengths	Weaknesses

Environment (Unit's Situation)

Opportunities	Threats

FOR CONSIDERATION/DISCUSSION

1. Which of the four elements—strengths, weaknesses, opportunities, threats—turned out to be the most difficult to develop? Why? Which was the easiest? Why?

2. What valuable insights about your focal organization did you gain during your SWOT analysis?

3. Why should every manager know how to do a SWOT analysis?

4. What "right niche" did your SWOT analysis yield?

5. How can a personal SWOT analysis improve your career prospects?

ETHICS EXERCISE

 ## DO THE RIGHT THING

WHERE IS THE FINE LINE BETWEEN FREE INTERNET CONTENT AND PIRATING?

I am willing to pay for a newspaper, yet I expect an article downloaded from the Internet to be free. Researchers say "44 percent say they have taken songs . . . and 'remixed' them."

Sources: Adapted from Andrew Zolli, "The Future Won't Be Free," *Newsweek* (March 8, 2010): 10. Excerpted from Del Jones, "Authorship Gets Lost on Web," *USA Today* (August 1, 2006): 3B.

What are the ethical implications of the following interpretations?

1. Any information you can access for free on the Internet is fair game. That's what the Web is all about, greater and greater access to information for more and more people around the world. In your circle of acquaintances, how common is pirating music and plagiarizing?

2. Those who create original intellectual property (e.g., music, visual art, or literary works) deserve to be fairly compensated for their creativity and effort and not have it stolen via the Internet. What are the practical business implications for entrepreneurs and companies attempting to make money with an Internet strategy?

3. The Internet is an evolving technology still in its infancy, and the dividing line between free and paid content needs to be sorted out by lawmakers and the competitive marketplace. Any suggestions?

4. Your own ethical interpretation?

MANAGERS-IN-ACTION VIDEO CASE STUDY

PRESERVE® BY RECYCLINE

Strategic Partnerships

Recycline company executives Eric Hudson, C. A. Webb, and Ben Anderson discuss how strategic partnerships impact their Preserve® brand's marketing and product development. Hudson, president of Recycline, considers partnerships with companies like Stoneyfield Farm to be a core advantage, as the company is able to provide service beyond its size. From college campuses to yogurt manufacturers, learn how strategic partnerships are giving Preserve® a competitive advantage.

For more information about Preserve®, visit its Web site: www.preserveproducts.com.

Before watching the video, answer the following questions:

1. What is meant by the concept "strategic thinking"?

2. Describe what is involved in a SWOT analysis.

3. When and why should a company conduct a SWOT analysis?

After watching the video, answer the following questions:

4. Explain the process and approach the executives at Preserve® follow to determine whom they will partner with.

5. Describe the impact partnerships have on synergy and a sustainable supply chain.

6. What are potential risks and rewards of using partners as part of the Preserve® brand's overall strategy?

7. Based on what you learned from the video and from visiting the Preserve® Web site, complete a SWOT analysis.

CLOSING CASE

HOWARD SCHULTZ GETS STARBUCKS PERKING AGAIN

Background: By the time Howard Schultz stepped down as chief executive of Starbucks, in 2000, the coffee chain was one of the world's most recognizable brands—and on a steady trajectory of growth. Eight years later Starbucks was suffering from a rough economy and its own strategic missteps, and Schultz felt compelled to return to the CEO seat. His previous tenure had seen promising growth, but now he faced a challenging mission: to lead a turnaround of the company he had built. [Here are excerpts from Schultz's interview with *Harvard Business Review*:]

HBR: We thought we knew the Howard Schultz story. You had a vision, built a successful company, and moved on. But then Starbucks ran into trouble, and two years ago you had to return as CEO. How hard has it been to get things right?

Schultz: The past two years have been transformational for the company and, candidly, for me personally. When I returned, in January 2008, things were actually worse than I'd thought. The decisions we had to make were very difficult, but first there had to be a time when we stood up in front of the entire company as leaders and made almost a confession—that the leadership had failed the 180,000 Starbucks people and their families. And even though I wasn't the CEO, I had been around as chairman; I should have known more. I am responsible. We had to admit to ourselves and to the people of this company that we owned the mistakes that were made. Once we did, it was a powerful turning point. It's like when you have a secret and get it out: The burden is off your shoulders. . . .

Also, you were suddenly facing serious competition.

We had never had much competition. Everything we did more or less worked. And that produced a level of hubris that caused us to overlook what was coming. Big-time people began to notice that this coffee business is a good business and highly profitable. McDonald's and Dunkin' Donuts were on the very low end. Let's characterize them as willing to do anything to capture or intercept customers—free coffee, coupons, say anything, do anything. We respect them as companies, but we didn't respect their practices. At the higher end were the independents who went to school on Starbucks. And there was this feeling of "Let's support the local companies." So Starbucks was being squeezed to the middle, and that is an undesirable place for us to be.

And by this time, bloggers were making life tough for you.

Social media suddenly started defining Starbucks. We were an easy target. Bloggers were putting holes in the equity of the brand, and it was affecting consumer confidence, our people, everything. I woke up one day and went to my desk, and I had 75 to 100 e-mails and phone calls about an issue I had never heard of. There was a sensational story in the *Sun*, in London, that Starbucks was wasting water through something called the "dipper well." My phone rang, and it was a reporter asking me to comment on the dipper well. "I have no idea what you're talking about," I said. The reporter said, "Mr. Schultz, I suggest you Google Starbucks real fast." The *Sun* claimed that we were pouring "millions of litres of precious water down the drain" as a result of the method we used to sanitize equipment. The report was wildly exaggerated, and we had been working for several years to find a better solution, but we suddenly became the target of conservation groups. We had a real problem. The lesson was that the world had changed. Something that had happened in London had created a worldwide story that positioned Starbucks with venom and disrespect. And we didn't know how to respond. The issues of social media, digital media, and getting smart about the rules of engagement emerged as a tremendous weakness for the company. Ultimately our reputation didn't suffer, but we spend countless hours defending ourselves when in fact we have a very strong track record in environmental stewardship.

What was the low point after your return?

The challenge was how to preserve and enhance the integrity of the only assets we have as a company: our values, our culture and guiding principles, and the reservoir of trust with our people. There was unbelievable pressure from multiple constituents. I've saved every analyst's report and major story, and what was said about us and about me. My favorite was "Never give an 800-pound gorilla caffeine." There was a death march of comments like "Starbucks's days are numbered," "It's no longer relevant," "McDonald's will definitely kill Starbucks," and "How could the board bring back Schultz, who is responsible for all this?"

How had things gone so wrong?

There was a different team here—very good people, who deserve respect and not the burden of responsibility, because I was chairman of the company, and I am culpable. Success is not sustainable if it is defined by how big you become or by growth for growth's sake. Success is very shallow if it doesn't have emotional meaning. I think there was a herd mentality—a reason for being that somehow became linked to PE [the price/earnings ratio of the common stock], the stock price, and a group of people who felt they were invincible. Starbucks isn't the first company that has happened to, and thankfully we caught it in time.

Do you feel there's a clash between trying to be a premium destination with a premium-priced product and being a public company?

I don't think so. Hundreds of public companies have a premium position in their categories. I think the tension is about can you be big and stay "small"? Can you maintain intimacy with your customers and your people? We understand our business very well, and we understand our customers. And to a person, we understand that we are only as good as yesterday and we have to come to work every day and try to exceed the expectations of our people and customers.

Yet every company that begins small and "authentic" eventually finds it hard to retain that image as it expands. How can you combat that?

You have to have a 100% belief in your core reason for being. There was tremendous pressure in the first three or four months after my return to dramatically change the strategy and the business model of the company. The marketplace was saying, "Starbucks needs to undo all these company owned stores and franchise the system." That would have given us a war chest of cash and significantly increased return on capital. It's a good argument economically. It's a good argument for shareholder value. But it would have fractured the culture of the company. You can't get out of this by trying to navigate with a different road map, one that isn't true to yourself. You have to be authentic, you have to be true, and you have to believe in your heart that this is going to work. Someone said to me, "You are roasting 400 million pounds of coffee a year. If you reduce the quality 5%, no one would know. That's a few hundred million dollars!" We would never do that.

For Discussion

1. Which strategy-making mode in Table 7.2 does Howard Schultz appear to follow? What are the pros and cons of this approach?

2. Which of Porter's generic competitive strategies in Figure 7.1 is apparent in this case? What are the pros and cons of this strategy? Explain.

3. Using your imagination and any additional research, if needed, who is included in Starbucks's business ecosystem? What does Starbucks need to do to maintain a healthy business ecosystem?

4. How does this case illustrate the dynamic strategic management process in Figure 7.2?

5. Using your imagination and making reasonable assumptions, how would a SWOT analysis for Starbucks look? (Tip: Use the Action Learning Exercise at the end of this chapter as a guide.)

6. What valuable lesson(s) did Howard Shultz learn about the strategic importance of social media?

Source: Excerpted from Adi Ignatius, "We Had to Own the Mistakes," *Harvard Business Review*, 88 (July–August 2010): 109–111.

8 Decision Making and Creative Problem Solving

"Every now and then, I'm reminded that the difference between success and failure in business is often one decision. You make the right one, and you survive. You make the wrong one, and you don't."[1]

—*NORM BRODSKY, ENTREPRENEUR*

The Changing Workplace

BOEING'S COSTLY OUTSOURCING DECISION

Boeing, the world's largest airplane manufacturer, has long used outside suppliers. Traditionally, Boeing engineers designed a plane and sent the detailed blueprints to suppliers, a system they called "build-to-print." This process allowed Boeing to control key design and engineering functions while lowering overall costs. But for its newest plane, the 787 Dreamliner, Boeing opted to have the suppliers both design and build the airplane sections, leaving only the final assembly to its own mechanics. The company hoped to pare two years from its historical go-to-market time and envisioned assembling a 787 in just three days, one-tenth the normal time for a plane that size.

The program was a disaster. Despite being a best-seller with almost nine hundred orders, the plane saw its launch repeatedly delayed as the program slipped well over a year behind schedule. The problem was that the suppliers were unable to deliver fully functional sections of the plane for Boeing's final assembly. While Boeing designed the production system to integrate twelve hundred components, the first plane came in thirty thousand pieces, costing the company substantial time and money as it had to pull design work back in house. . . .

[The decision error was] embracing a strategy without fully understanding the conditions under which it succeeds or fails. Outsourcing is not universally good. For example, outsourcing does not make sense for products that require the complex integration of disparate subcomponents. The reason is that coordination costs are high, so just getting the product to work is a challenge.

Source: Excerpted from Michael J. Mauboussin, *Think Twice: Harnessing the Power of Counterintuition* (Boston: Harvard Business Press, 2009), p. 90.

OBJECTIVES

- **Specify** at least five sources of decision complexity for modern managers.
- **Explain** what a *condition of risk* is and what managers can do to cope with it.
- **Define** and **discuss** the three decision traps: framing, escalation of commitment, and overconfidence.
- **Discuss** why programmed and nonprogrammed decisions require different decision-making procedures, and **distinguish** between the two types of knowledge in knowledge management.
- **Explain** the need for a contingency approach to group-aided decision making.
- **Identify** and briefly **describe** five of the ten "mental locks" that can inhibit creativity.
- **List** and **explain** the four basic steps in the creative problem-solving process.
- **Describe** how causes of problems can be tracked down with fishbone diagrams.

Decision making is the process of identifying and choosing among alternative courses of action in a manner appropriate to the demands of the situation.[2] The act of choosing implies that alternative courses of action must be identified, weighed, and weeded out. Decisions typically are made amid lots of change and uncertainty, including incomplete information about competitors, the economy, and future customers. As underscored by the Boeing 787 fiasco, good judgment and common sense are fundamental to effective decision making. Boeing's strategists made invalid assumptions about key situational factors. Today's organizational decision making requires courage, steady nerves, and the ability to handle complexity, as in the case of Nike's CEO Mark Parker. After taking the helm, he reorganized the company into units that focused on individual sports, put a higher emphasis on Asian markets, and managed to bring Nike through the recent recession with strong revenues and increasing earnings.[3] This chapter highlights major challenges for decision makers, introduces a general decision-making model, discusses group-aided decision making, and examines creativity and problem solving.

CHALLENGES FOR DECISION MAKERS

Decision making has never been easy, but it is especially challenging for today's managers. In an era of accelerating change, the complexity of decision making has accelerated. Recent interviews with 1,541 CEOs and executives in 60 countries revealed that more than half had high levels of complexity and even more expected very high complexity in the future, but less than half of them felt prepared to handle the future.[4] A host of tough challenges accounts for increased decision complexity. Those that we will discuss here are (1) complex streams of decisions, (2) uncertainty, (3) information-processing styles, and (4) perceptual and behavioral decision traps.

Dealing with Complex Streams of Decisions

Above all else, today's decision-making contexts are not neat and tidy. A pair of experts lent realism to the subject by using this analogy: Making a

decision is like floating in a stream, with countless bits of information flowing in random order around you. The stream of information doesn't stop and it doesn't deliver neat solutions, so decision makers must learn to find anchors by taking action.[5] Yet, it is important to note that this analogy is a recognition of complexity, *not* an admission of hopelessness. A working knowledge of eight intertwined factors contributing to decision complexity can help decision makers successfully navigate the stream (see Figure 8.1).

1. *Multiple criteria.* Typically, a decision today must satisfy a number of often-conflicting criteria representing the interests of different groups, so decision makers must balance the needs of all stakeholders. For example, the Denver International Airport was designed and built with much more than airplanes in mind. Because airports are typically quite challenging for people with disabilities to navigate, the city of Denver invited a number of disabled people to participate in the building's design to ensure that it was completely accessible for all travelers."[6]

2. *Intangibles.* Factors such as customer goodwill, employee morale, increased bureaucracy, and aesthetic appeal (for example, negative reaction to a

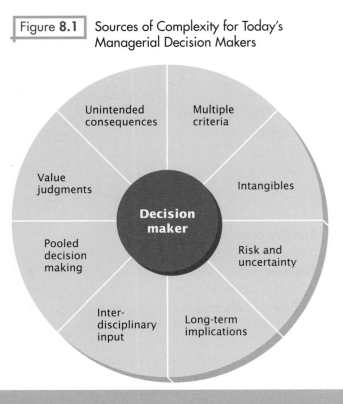

Figure **8.1**   Sources of Complexity for Today's Managerial Decision Makers

billboard on a scenic highway), although difficult to measure, often determine decision alternatives.

3. *Risk and uncertainty.* Along with every decision alternative comes the chance that it will fail in some way. Poor choices can prove costly. Yet the right decision can open up whole new worlds of opportunity, as illustrated in this legendary example: After drilling seven dry holes in 1967 in Alaska, Atlantic Richfield's CEO decided to try one more. The result was Prudhoe Bay, the greatest petroleum find in North America.[7] Because of the importance of this particular aspect of decision complexity, we shall devote special attention to it in the next section.

4. *Long-term implications.* Decisions that sound good in the near-term can turn out to be unworkable as circumstances unfold. Overlooked situational factors and/or faulty assumptions can derail decisions, as in the case of this recent example from the United Kingdom: At Boots, a national chain of drugstores, CEO Steve Russell thought he could differentiate the stores by adding health-care and dental services, but the strategy flopped because store managers weren't equipped with the right skills and many markets yielded little profit. The failed plan cost Russell his job.[8]

5. *Interdisciplinary input.* Decision complexity is greatly increased when technical specialists such as lawyers, consumer advocates, tax advisers, accountants, engineers, and production and marketing experts are consulted before making a decision.

This process can become even more complex and time-consuming in traditional societies such as China, where it is common practice to consult *feng shui* experts about superstitious beliefs. Literally, *feng* (meaning wind) and *shui* (meaning water) refer to the creation of harmony between people and their environment.[9] The principles of *feng shui* are used, for example, to guide the position and orientation of a building and the colors chosen for the decor. Foreigners who ignore what they deem to be superstitious nonsense do so at the peril of their business dealings with their Chinese partners.

6. *Pooled decision making.* Rarely is a single manager totally responsible for the entire decision process. For example, consider the approach of Brian Ruder, the successful president of Heinz's U.S. unit: He formed a board of directors from mentors, advisors, and his father to get their opinions when facing a difficult decision. Ruder says, "I rely on them for total frankness and objectivity."[10] After pooled input, complex decisions wind their way through the organization, with individuals and groups interpreting, modifying, and sometimes resisting. Minor decisions set the stage for major decisions, which in turn are translated back into local decisions. Typically many people's fingerprints are on final decisions in the organizational world.

7. *Value judgments.* As long as decisions are made by people with differing backgrounds,

Local small businesses in Kentucky fear being driven out of business by look-alike, big-box stores. Thus, their advertising message challenges consumers—not to mention the managers of those superstores—to consider the long-term implications of their decisions.

AP Photo/Brian Bohannon

perceptions, aspirations, and values, the decision-making process will be marked by disagreement over what is right or wrong, good or bad, and ethical or unethical.[11] For example, following the Virginia Tech massacre in 2007, Facebook made a value judgment to reverse its policy of removing the pages of deceased users out of respect. As reported by *USA Today* at the time, online protests and a letter-writing campaign inspired Facebook to keep these pages available as a place where friends and family can memorialize their lost loved ones.[12]

8. *Unintended consequences.* The law of unintended consequences, according to an expert on the subject, "states that you cannot always predict the results of purposeful action."[13] In other words, there can be a disconnect between intentions and actual results. Although unintended consequences can be positive, negative ones are most troublesome and have been called the Frankenstein monster effect.[14] For example, consider this looming environmental disaster: Asian carp—originally introduced into ponds in the South to clean up algae—are making their way north to the Great Lakes, where they could starve out native fish and threaten the region's fishing industry.[15] And therein lies the crux of the problem of unintended consequences. Namely, *hurried and/or narrowly focused decision makers typically give little or no consideration to the full range of*

8a
Back to the Opening Case

Based on the facts of this case and any reasonable assumptions, how many of the eight sources of decision complexity are evident in the Boeing case? Explain.

For further information about the interactive annotations in this chapter, visit our student Web site.

likely consequences of their decisions. Unintended consequences cannot be altogether eliminated in today's complex world.[16] Still, they can be moderated to some extent by giving them creative and honest consideration when making important decisions.

Coping with Uncertainty

Among the valuable contributions of decision theorists are classification schemes for types and degrees of uncertainty. (Recall our discussion in Chapter 6 about state, effect, and response uncertainty.)

Bad weather is a major source of uncertainty for supply chain managers. Heavy snowfalls often strand truckers and motorists on Interstate 5, a primary link between Los Angeles, Sacramento, and northern California.

law of unintended consequences results of purposeful actions are often difficult to predict

Unfortunately, life is filled with varying degrees of these types of uncertainties. Managers are continually asked to make the best decisions they can, despite uncertainties about present and future sources of risk. Identifying and dealing effectively with risks is at the heart of successful entrepreneurship. If every risk and uncertainty were considered, products might never be launched. Still, entrepreneurs must make an effort to spot risks and resolve them quickly and cheaply. A great example is Reed Hastings, the founder of Netflix, who simply mailed himself a CD to confirm that one could be sent through the postal system without damage. This simple test conducted before he went into business eliminated one of the operational risks he had considered.[17]

Managers who are able to assess the degrees of certainty in a situation—whether conditions are certain, risky, or uncertain—are able to make more effective decisions. As illustrated in Figure 8.2, there is a negative correlation between uncertainty and the decision maker's confidence in a decision. In other words, the more uncertain a manager is about the principal factors in a decision, the less confident she or he will be about the successful outcome of that decision. The key, of course, lies not in eliminating all sources of uncertainty, which is impossible, but rather in learning to work within an acceptable range of uncertainty.

CERTAINTY. A condition of certainty exists when there is no doubt about the factual basis of a particular decision, and its outcome can be predicted accurately. Much like the economic concept of pure competition, the concept of certainty is useful mainly as a theoretical anchor point for a continuum. In a world filled with uncertainties, certainty is relative rather than absolute. For example, the decision to order more rivets for a manufacturing firm's fabrication department is based on the relative certainty that the current rate of use will exhaust the rivet inventory on a specific date. But even in this case, uncertainties about the possible misuse or theft of rivets creep in to reduce confidence. Because nothing is truly certain, conditions of risk and uncertainty are the general rule for managers, not the exception.

RISK. A condition of risk is said to exist when a decision must be made on the basis of incomplete but reliable factual information. Reliable information, though incomplete, is still useful to managers coping with risk because they can use it to calculate the probability that a given event will occur and then to select a decision alternative with favorable odds.

The two basic types of probabilities are objective and subjective probabilities.[18] Objective probabilities are derived mathematically from reliable historical data, whereas subjective probabilities are estimated on the basis of one's past experience or judgment. Decision making based on probabilities is common in all areas of management today. For instance, laundry product manufacturers would not think of launching a new detergent without determining the probability of its acceptance via consumer panels and test marketing. A number of inferential statistical techniques can help managers objectively assess risks.[19]

Figure **8.2**   The Relationship Between Uncertainty and Confidence

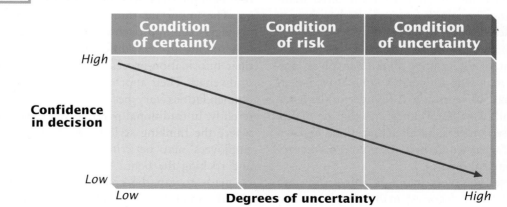

UNCERTAINTY. A condition of uncertainty exists when little or no reliable factual information is available. Still, judgmental or subjective probabilities can be estimated. Decision making under conditions of uncertainty can be both rewarding and nerve-racking for managers. Just ask executives in the biotechnology industry: It takes up to 15 years and tens of millions of dollars to create and test a drug, yet many drugs never make it past the clinical trials.[20] Decision confidence is lowest when a condition of uncertainty prevails because decisions are then based on educated guesses rather than on hard factual data.

Information-Processing Styles

Thinking is one of those activities we engage in constantly yet seldom pause to examine systematically. But within the context of managerial decision making and problem solving, it is important that one's thinking not get into an unproductive rut. The quality of our decisions is a direct reflection of how we process information.[21]

Researchers have identified two general information-processing styles: the thinking style and the intuitive style.[22] One is not superior to the other. Both are needed during organizational problem solving. Managers who rely predominantly on the *thinking* style tend to be logical, precise, and objective. They prefer routine assignments requiring attention to detail and systematic implementation. Conversely, managers who are predominantly *intuitive* find comfort in rapidly changing situations in which they can be creative and follow their hunches and visions. Intuitive managers see things in complex patterns rather than as logically ordered bits and pieces. They typically rely on their own mental shortcuts and detours.[23] An interesting example of intuitive thinking involves Jann Wenner, the man who founded *Rolling Stone* magazine more than 40 years ago. A founder of the Rock and Roll Hall of Fame, Wenner says that he makes decisions based on personal preferences and his own ideas about "what would be fun," not on market research or financial reports.[24]

Of course, not every manager falls neatly into one of these two categories; many people process

8b
How Intuitive Are You?

Rate yourself on each item with the following 1-to-5 scale. The higher your total score, the more intuitive you are.

Not at all like me 1-2-3-4-5 Very much like me

1. You can identify something you haven't seen clearly.
2. You look at a cloud and many images come to mind.
3. You always know when it's the ideal time to strike.
4. You're good at hunches.
5. You're good at detective work; you know what elements fit together.

Total score: ____

QUESTIONS: How intuitive are you? Would your close friends and relatives agree with your score? How do others tend to react to your level of intuition? How can your intuition (or lack of it) help or hinder you as a manager?

Source: Questionnaire items excerpted from Daniel Cappon, "The Anatomy of Intuition," *Psychology Today,* 26 (May–June 1993): 42–43.

information through a combination of the two styles. For example, Bonnie Reitz, a senior vice president for sales at Continental Airlines, told *Fast Company* magazine, "I believe in unshakable facts." She believes that coupling facts with intuition generally results in the right decisions.[25] (See Table 8.1.)

The important thing to recognize here is that managers can approach decision making and problem solving in very different ways, depending on their information-processing styles.[26] It is a matter of diversity. Their approaches, perceptions, and recommendations vary because their minds work differently. In traditional pyramid work organizations, where the thinking style tends to prevail, intuitive employees may be criticized for being imprecise and rocking the boat. A concerted effort needs to be made to tap the creative skills of "intuitives" and the implementation abilities of "thinkers." An

condition of uncertainty no reliable factual information available

| Table 8.1 | How to Sharpen Your Intuition |

RECOMMENDATION	DESCRIPTION
1. **Open up the closet**	To what extent do you: experience intuition; trust your feelings; count on intuitive judgments; suppress hunches; covertly rely upon gut feel?
2. **Don't mix up your I's**	Instinct, insight, and intuition are not synonymous; practice distinguishing between your instincts, your insights, and your intuitions.
3. **Elicit good feedback**	Seek feedback on your intuitive judgments; build confidence in your gut feel; create a learning environment in which you can develop better intuitive awareness.
4. **Get a feel for your batting average**	Benchmark your intuitions; get a sense for how reliable your hunches are; ask yourself how your intuitive judgment might be improved.
5. **Use imagery**	Use imagery rather than words; literally visualize potential future scenarios that take your gut feelings into account.
6. **Play devil's advocate**	Test out intuitive judgments; raise objections to them; generate counter-arguments; probe how robust gut feel is when challenged.
7. **Capture and validate your intuitions**	Create the inner state to give your intuitive mind the freedom to roam; capture your creative intuitions; log them before they are censored by rational analysis.

Source: *Academy of Management Executive: The Thinking Manager's Source* by Eugene Sadler-Smith and Erella Shefy. Copyright 2004 by Academy of Management (NY). Reproduced with permission of Academy of Management (NY) in the format Textbook via Copyright Clearance Center.

appreciation for alternative information-processing styles needs to be cultivated because they complement one another.

Avoiding Perceptual and Behavioral Decision Traps

Behavioral scientists have identified some common human tendencies that are capable of eroding the quality of decision making. Three well-documented ones are framing, escalation, and overconfidence. Awareness and conscious avoidance of these traps can give decision makers a competitive edge.

FRAMING ERROR. One's judgment can be altered and shaped by how information is presented or labeled. In other words, labels create frames of reference with the power to bias our interpretations.

Framing error is the tendency to evaluate positively presented information favorably and negatively presented information unfavorably.[27] Those evaluations, in turn, influence one's behavior. A study with 80 male and 80 female University of Iowa students documented the framing-interpretation-behavior linkage. Half of each gender group was told about a cancer treatment with a 50 percent success rate. The other two groups heard about the same cancer treatment but were told it had a 50 percent failure rate. The researchers discovered that re-framing the "failure rate" in terms of a "success rate" made the students perceive the treatment as more effective and made them more inclined to recommend it to others.[28] Framing thus influenced both interpretations and intended behavior. Given the importance of the information in this study (cancer treatment), ethical questions arise about the potential abuse of framing error.

framing error how information is presented influences one's interpretation of it

In organizations, framing error can be used constructively or destructively. Advertisers, for instance, take full advantage of this perceptional tendency when attempting to sway consumers' purchasing decisions. A leading brand of cat litter boasts of being 99 percent dust-free. Meanwhile, a shampoo claims to be fortified with 1 percent natural protein. Thanks to framing error, we tend to perceive very little dust in the cat litter and a lot of protein in the shampoo. Managers who couch their proposals in favorable terms hope to benefit from framing error. And who can blame them? On the negative side, prejudice and bigotry thrive on framing error.[29] A male manager who believes women can't manage might frame an interview report so that Max looks good and Maxine looks bad.

ESCALATION OF COMMITMENT. Why are people slow to write off bad investments? Why do people stay in bad relationships? Why do companies stick to unprofitable strategies? And why are government officials reluctant to scrap over-budget and behind-schedule programs? Escalation of commitment is a possible explanation for these diverse situations.[30] Escalation of commitment is the tendency of individuals and organizations to get locked into losing courses of action because *quitting is personally and socially difficult.* This decision-making trap has been called the "throwing good money after bad" dilemma. Those victimized by escalation of commitment are often heard talking about "sunk costs" and "too much time and money invested to quit now." Within the context of management, psychological, social, and organizational factors conspire to encourage escalation of commitment[31] (see Figure 8.3).

Jack and Suzy Welch claim that large, diversified companies too often fail to unload broken businesses for any number of reasons, including sentimentality, false hope, and inertia. They say, "Companies should only keep trying to fix businesses as long as they serve a strategic purpose. And they should face reality and give up hope . . . as soon as they don't."[32] Reality checks, in the form of comparing actual progress with goals and timetables, can help keep escalation in check.[33]

OVERCONFIDENCE. The term *overconfidence* is commonplace and requires no formal definition. We need to comprehend the psychology of overconfidence because it can expose managers to

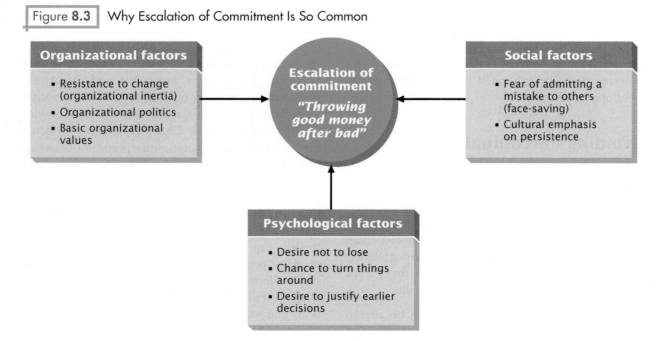

Figure **8.3** | Why Escalation of Commitment Is So Common

Source: Adapted from discussion in Barry M. Staw and Jerry Ross, "Understanding Behavior in Escalation Situations," *Science*, 246 (October 13, 1989): 216–220.

escalation of commitment people get locked into losing courses of action to avoid the embarrassment of quitting or admitting error

unreasonable risks. For example, in his book *Why Smart Executives Fail—and What You Can Learn from Their Mistakes,* Sydney Finkelstein offers this helpful caution:

> *Movies, television shows, and journalists all offer us instantly recognizable vignettes of the dynamic executive making a dozen decisions a minute, snapping out orders that will redirect huge enterprises, dealing with numerous crises at once, and taking only seconds to size up situations that have obviously stumped everyone else for days. . . .*
>
> *The problem with this picture of executive competence is that it is really a fraud. In a world where business conditions are constantly changing and innovations often seem to be the only constant, no one can "have all the answers" for long. Leaders who are invariably crisp and decisive tend to settle issues so quickly that they have no opportunity to grasp the ramifications. Worse, because these leaders need to feel that they already have all the answers, they have no way to learn new answers. Their instinct, whenever something truly important is at stake, is to push for rapid closure, allowing no periods of uncertainty, even when uncertainty is appropriate.*[34]

Ironically, researchers have found a positive relationship between overconfidence and task difficulty. In other words, the more difficult the task, the greater the tendency for people to be overconfident.[35] Easier and more predictable situations foster confidence, but generally not unrealistic overconfidence. People may be overconfident about one or more of the following: accuracy of input data; individual, team, or organizational ability; and the probability of success. There are various theoretical explanations for overconfidence. For example, overconfidence may often be necessary to generate the courage needed to tackle difficult situations.

As with the other decision traps, managerial awareness of this problem is the important first step toward avoiding it. Careful analysis of situational factors, critical thinking about decision alternatives, and honest input from stakeholders can help managers avoid overconfidence. Yet another remedy is to make what management consultants call "deliberate mistakes" that allow experienced managers to shake up the status quo and test the boundaries of their knowledge.[36]

MAKING DECISIONS

It stands to reason that if the degree of uncertainty varies from situation to situation, there can be no single way to make decisions.[37] Managers do indeed make decisions in every conceivable way. One of the oddest examples is how the stacked potato chips we know as Pringles got their name. It seems that employees at Procter & Gamble pulled it out of a phone book.[38] Even doing nothing can qualify as decision making. Behavioral economists explain that while delays and procrastination may appear to be easy choices, they are "as consequential as any other choice."[39] How often a particular decision is made is another important consideration. Some decisions are made frequently, perhaps several times a day. Others are made infrequently or just once. Consequently, decision theorists have distinguished between programmed and nonprogrammed decisions.[40] Each of these types of decisions requires a different procedure.

Making Programmed Decisions

Programmed decisions are those that are repetitive and routine. Examples include hiring decisions, billing decisions in a hospital, supply reorder decisions in a purchasing department, consumer loan decisions in a bank, and pricing decisions in a university bookstore. Managers tend to devise fixed procedures for handling these everyday decisions. Most decisions made by the typical manager on a daily basis are of the programmed variety.

angelo.samacchiaro/Shutterstock.Com

programmed decisions repetitive and routine decisions

At the heart of the programmed decision procedure are decision rules. A **decision rule** is a statement that identifies the situation in which a decision is required and specifies how the decision will be made. Behind decision rules is the idea that standard, recurring problems need to be solved only once. Decision rules enable busy managers to make routine decisions quickly without having to go through comprehensive problem solving over and over again.[41] Generally, decision rules should be stated in "if-then" terms. A decision rule for a consumer loan officer in a bank, for example, might be: *If* the applicant is employed, has no record of loan default, and can put up 20 percent collateral, *then* a loan not to exceed $50,000 can be authorized. Carefully conceived decision rules can streamline the decision-making process by allowing lower-level managers to shoulder the responsibility for programmed decisions and freeing higher-level managers for relatively more important, nonprogrammed decisions. Checklists with if-then reminders can be helpful with programmed decisions.[42]

Making Nonprogrammed Decisions

Nonprogrammed decisions are those made in complex, important, and nonroutine situations, often under new and largely unfamiliar circumstances. This kind of decision is made much less frequently than programmed decisions. Examples of nonprogrammed decisions include deciding whether to merge with another company, how to replace an executive who died unexpectedly, whether a foreign branch should be opened, and how to market an entirely new kind of product or service. The following six questions need to be asked prior to making a nonprogrammed decision:

1. What decision needs to be made?
2. When does it have to be made?
3. Who will decide?
4. Who will need to be consulted prior to the making of the decision?
5. Who will ratify or veto the decision?
6. Who will need to be informed of the decision?[43]

The decision-making process becomes more sharply focused when managers take the time to answer these questions.

One respected decision theorist has described nonprogrammed decisions as situations in which there is no hard and fast rule for resolving the issue because it is either without precedent, very complex, or so critical that it requires a customized response.[44]

Nonprogrammed decision making calls for creative problem solving (see Ethics: Character, Courage, and Values). The four-step problem-solving process introduced later in this chapter helps managers make effective and efficient nonprogrammed decisions.

ETHICS: Character, Courage, and Values

Starbucks CEO Decides to Put His Employees Ahead of Wall Street

Howard Schultz: Our health care costs over the past 12 months were approximately $300 million. [Starbucks offers health care benefits to any eligible employee who works at least 20 hours a week.] . . . Within this past year I got a call from one of our institutional shareholders. He said, "You've never had more cover to cut health care than you do now. No one will criticize you." And I just said, "I could cut $300 million out of a lot of things, but do you want to kill the company, and kill the trust in what this company stands for? There is no way I will do it, and if that is what you want us to do, you should sell our stock." What I stand for is not just to make money; it's to preserve the integrity of what we have built for 39 years. . . .

For Discussion: Are decisions with major ethical implications more likely to be programmed or nonprogrammed decisions? Explain.

Source: Excerpted from an interview by Adi Ignatius, "We Had to Own the Mistakes," *Harvard Business Review,* 88 (July–August 2010): 112.

---

decision rule tells when and how programmed decisions should be made | *nonprogrammed decisions decisions made in complex and nonroutine situations*

A General Decision-Making Model

Although different decision procedures are required for different situations, it is possible to construct a general decision-making model. Figure 8.4 shows an idealized, logical, and rational model of organizational decision making. Significantly, it describes how decisions can be made, but it does not portray how managers actually make decisions.[45] In fact, on-the-job research found that managers did not follow a rational and logical series of steps when making decisions.[46] Why, then, should we even consider a rational, logical model? Once again, as in the case of the strategic management process in Chapter 7, a rational descriptive model has instructional value because it identifies key components of a complex process. It also suggests a better way of doing things.

The first step, a scan of the situation, is important, although it is often underemphasized or ignored altogether in discussions of managerial decision making. Scanning answers the question "How do I know a decision should be made?" Many years ago, Chester I. Barnard gave one of the best answers to this question, stating that "the occasions for decision originate in three distinct fields: (a) from authoritative communications from superiors; (b) from cases referred for decision by subordinates; (c) from cases originating in the initiative of the [manager] concerned."[47] In addition to signaling when a decision is required, scanning reveals the degree of uncertainty and provides necessary information for pending decisions.

When the need for a decision has been established, the manager should determine whether the situation is routine. If it is routine and there is an appropriate decision rule, the rule is applied. But if it turns out to be a new situation demanding a nonprogrammed decision, comprehensive problem solving begins. In either case, the results of the final decision need to be monitored to see whether any follow-up action is necessary.

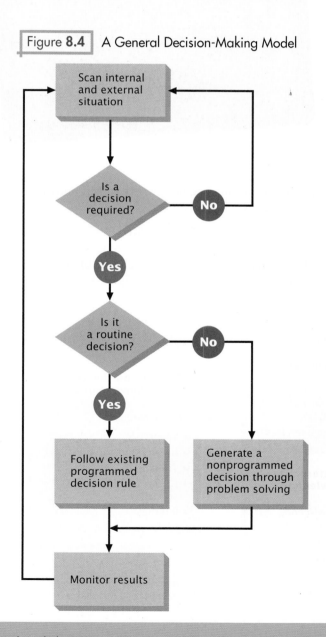

Figure 8.4   A General Decision-Making Model

Knowledge Management: A Tool for Improving the Quality of Decisions

Armies of academics, consultants, and managers have rallied around the concept of knowledge management during the last dozen years. Although some may dismiss it as a passing fad, knowledge management is a powerful and robust concept that deserves a permanent place in management theory and practice.[48] Authorities on the subject define **knowledge management** (KM) as "the development of tools, processes, systems, structures, and cultures explicitly to improve the creation, sharing, and use of knowledge critical for decision making."[49] KM is at the heart of what organizational theorists call *learning organizations,* a topic we cover in the next chapter.[50] Our purpose here is to explore the basics of KM, with an eye toward better organizational decisions.

knowledge management developing a system to improve the creation and sharing of knowledge critical for decision making

After all, decisions are only as good as the information on which they are based.

TWO TYPES OF KNOWLEDGE. KM specialists draw a fundamental distinction between two types of knowledge: tacit knowledge and explicit knowledge (see Figure 8.5). Tacit knowledge is personal, intuitive, and undocumented information about how to skillfully perform tasks, solve problems, and make decisions. People who are masters of their craft have tacit knowledge (or "deep smarts") accumulated through years of experience. Their deep wells of knowledge allow them to see patterns and resolve problems effortlessly, yet the process is often so quick and reflexive that they often can't explain how they arrived at the answer. Dorothy Leonard and Walter Swap write that experienced managers ". . . chalk up to gut *feel* what is really a form of gut *knowledge*."[51]

Experts with deep smarts simply "do" the task; they have a "feel" for the job; they know when they are "in the zone." For example, ask really good golfers or tennis players how they know their stroke is just right.[52]

Meanwhile, explicit knowledge is readily sharable information because it is in verbal, textual, visual, or numerical form. It can be found in presentations and lectures, books and magazines (both hard copy and online), policy manuals, technical specifications, training programs, databases, and software programs. In short, explicit knowledge is

public (to varying degrees), whereas tacit knowledge is private.

IMPROVING THE FLOW OF KNOWLEDGE. As indicated in Figure 8.5, knowledge resides in different places and needs to be shared. Each type of knowledge is important in its own way. Each needs to be carefully

---

8c
A Recipe for Good Decisions

"Good decisions are forward-looking, take available information into account, consider all available options, and do not create conflicts of interest."

QUESTIONS: How does a specific decision recently made by either you or a manager measure up to each of these four criteria? How did the quality of the decision-making process affect the outcome?

Source: Dan Ariely, "Good Decisions. Bad Outcomes." *Harvard Business Review,* 88 (December 2010): 40.

| Figure **8.5** | Key Dimensions of Knowledge Management |

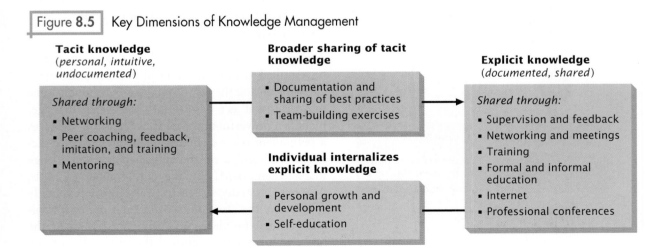

Sources: Adapted from discussion in Kiujiro Nonaka, "The Knowledge-Creating Company," *Harvard Business Review on Knowledge Management* (Boston: Harvard Business School Publishing, 1998), pp. 21–45; and Roy Lubit, "Tacit Knowledge and Knowledge Management: The Key to Sustainable Competitive Advantage," *Organizational Dynamics,* 29 (Winter 2001): 164–178.

---

tacit knowledge personal, intuitive, and undocumented information | explicit knowledge documented and sharable information cultivated. The sharing of constructive tacit knowledge between coworkers is a top priority, as indicated in Figure 8.5. Organizational support is needed to help individuals feel comfortable about giving and receiving useful task-related knowledge on demand.[53]

Sophisticated new KM software is proving very useful and cost-effective in large organizations for sharing both tacit and explicit knowledge.[54] For example, consider the experience of Werner Hinz, a lead engineer at defense contractor Northrop Grumman: When preparing a bid for the design of an unmanned aircraft for the Pentagon, Hinz needed high-level expertise on hypersonics. He used ActiveNet, a KM software application, to identify two colleagues who possessed the necessary expertise within minutes.

In a sense, KM software is sort of like an Internet dating service, but for informational rather than romantic purposes. Intra-company social networking applications represent the newest step in that direction.[56] According to KM advocates, it is important to know what you know, to know what you don't know, and to know how to find what you need to know. The result: better and more timely decisions.

You will encounter many topics in this book to improve the various knowledge flows in Figure 8.5. Among them are organizational cultures, training,

communication, empowerment, participative management, virtual teams, transformational leadership, and mentoring.

GROUP-AIDED DECISION MAKING: A CONTINGENCY PERSPECTIVE

Decision making, like any other organizational activity, does not take place in a vacuum. Typically, decision making is a highly social activity with committees, study groups, review panels, or project teams contributing in a variety of ways.

Collaborative Computing

Computer networks, the Internet, and the advent of collaborative computing guarantee even broader participation in the decision-making process. Collaborative computing software—also known as "groupware"—allows people to work together across time and space, sharing information, collaborating, and networking as needed. Other features of collaborative computing software include video

Some creative group-aided decision making between the Little Traverse Bay Bands of Odawa Indians and Harbor Springs Public Schools led to an interesting nonprogrammed decision. Harbor Springs is the only public school system in Michigan to offer a for-credit course in a Native American language.

collaborative computing teaming up to make decisions via a computer network programmed with groupware conferencing, calendar management, e-mail messaging, and integrated team support.[57]

Unfortunately, according to research, groupware is typically plagued by low-quality implementation. Sixty-five percent of the survey respondents used it simply as a communication tool, to send and receive e-mail, which is analogous to using a personal computer for word processing only. Groupware users need to be taught how to *collaborate* via computer (for instance, jointly identifying and solving problems). If users are given the proper training, groupware can have a tremendous positive impact on both job performance and customer satisfaction.[58]

Group Involvement in Decisions

Whether the situation is a traditional face-to-face committee meeting or a global e-meeting, at least five aspects of the decision-making process can be assigned to groups:

1. Analyzing the problem
2. Identifying components of the decision situation
3. Estimating components of the decision situation (for example, determining probabilities, feasibilities, time estimates, and payoffs)
4. Designing alternatives
5. Choosing an alternative[59]

Assuming that two (or more) heads may be better than one and that managers can make better use of their time by delegating various decision-making chores, there is a strong case for turning to groups when making decisions. But before bringing others into the decision process, managers need to be aware of the problem of dispersed accountability and consider the trade-off between the advantages and disadvantages of group-aided decision making. In view of these problems and of research evidence comparing individual and group performance, a contingency approach is recommended.

The Problem of Dispersed Accountability

There is a critical difference between group-aided decision making and group decision making. In the first instance, the group does everything except make the final decision. In the second instance, the group actually makes the final decision. Managers

8d
Collective Wisdom

James Surowiecki, author of the book *The Wisdom of Crowds*:

. . . under the right circumstances, groups are remarkably intelligent, and are often smarter than the smartest people in them. . . .The best collective decisions are the product of disagreement and contest, not consensus or compromise.

QUESTION: Do you agree or disagree? Explain.

Source: As quoted in Brad Wieners, "Why It Pays to Heed the Herd," *Business 2.0,* 5 (May 2004): 32.

who choose the second route face a dilemma. Although a decision made by a group will probably reflect the collective experience and wisdom of all those involved, personal accountability is lost. Blame for a joint decision that fails is too easily passed on to others. For example, when Robert Palmer was hired to turn Digital Equipment around, he discovered that no one person or team was responsible for actually running the company. Everything was done by committee and consensus, which meant that no one was ever held accountable for problems.[60] This legacy of dispersed accountability proved too much for Palmer, and Digital was sold to Compaq Computer, which eventually became part of Hewlett-Packard.

The traditional formula for resolving this problem is to make sure that a given manager is personally accountable for a decision when the responsibility for it has to be traced. According to this line of reasoning, even when a group is asked to recommend a decision, the responsibility for the final outcome remains with the manager in charge. For managers who want to maintain the integrity of personal accountability, there is no such thing as group decision making; there is only group-*aided* decision making. There are three situations in which individual accountability for a decision is necessary:

- The decision will have significant impact on the success or failure of the unit or organization.
- The decision has legal ramifications (such as possible prosecution for price-fixing, antitrust, or product safety violations).
- A competitive reward is tied to a successful decision. (For example, only one person can get a promotion.)

In less critical areas, the group itself may be responsible for making decisions.

Advantages and Disadvantages of Group-Aided Decision Making

Various combinations of positive and negative factors are encountered when a manager brings others into the decision-making process. The advantages and disadvantages are listed in Table 8.2. If there is a conscious effort to avoid or at least minimize the disadvantages, managers can gain a great deal by sharing the decision-making process with diverse peers, outside consultants, and team members.[61] However, some important contingency factors need to be taken into consideration.

A Contingency Approach Is Necessary

Are two or more heads actually better than one? The answer depends on the nature of the task, the ability of the contributors, and the form of interaction (see Table 8.3). An analysis of dozens of individual-versus-group performance studies conducted over a 61-year period led one researcher to the following conclusions: (1) groups tend to do quantitatively and qualitatively better than the *average* individual; and (2) *exceptional* individuals tend to outperform the group, particularly when the task is complex and the group is made up of relatively low-ability people.[62]

Table 8.2 Advantages and Disadvantages of Group-Aided Decision Making and Problem Solving

ADVANTAGES	DISADVANTAGES
1. **Greater pool of knowledge.** A group can bring much more information and experience to bear on a decision or problem than can an individual acting alone.	1. **Social pressure.** Unwillingness to "rock the boat" and pressure to conform may combine to stifle the creativity of individual contributors.
2. **Different perspectives.** Individuals with varied experience and interests help the group see decision situations and problems from different angles.	2. **Domination by a vocal few.** Sometimes the quality of group action is reduced when the group gives in to those who talk the loudest and longest.
3. **Greater comprehension.** Those who personally experience the give-and-take of group discussion about alternative courses of action tend to understand the rationale behind the final decision.	3. **Logrolling.** Political wheeling and dealing can displace sound thinking when an individual's pet project or vested interest is at stake.
4. **Increased acceptance.** Those who play an active role in group decision making and problem solving tend to view the outcome as "ours" rather than "theirs."	4. **Goal displacement.** Sometimes secondary considerations such as winning an argument, making a point, or getting back at a rival displace the primary task of making a sound decision or solving a problem.
5. **Training ground.** Less experienced participants in group action learn how to cope with group dynamics by actually being involved.	5. **"Groupthink."** Sometimes cohesive "in groups" let the desire for unanimity override sound judgment when generating and evaluating alternative courses of action. (Groupthink is discussed in Chapter 13.)

| Table **8.3** | Individual Versus Group Performance: Contingency Management Insights from 61 Years of Research |

NATURE OF TASK	INSIGHTS FROM RESEARCH
Problem-solving task	Individuals are faster, but groups tend to produce better results
Complex task	Best results achieved by polling the contributions of individuals working alone
Brainstorming task	Same as for complex task
Learning task	Groups consistently outperform individuals
Concept mastery/creative task	Contributions from average-ability group members tend to improve when they are teamed with high-ability group members

Source: Based in part on research conclusions found in Gayle W. Hill, "Group Versus Individual Performance: Are N + 1 Heads Better Than One?" *Psychological Bulletin*, 91 (May 1982): 517–539.

Consequently, busy managers need to delegate aspects of the decision-making process (specified earlier) according to the contingencies in Table 8.3. More is said about delegation in the next chapter.

MANAGERIAL CREATIVITY

Demands for creativity and innovation make the practice of management endlessly exciting (and often extremely difficult).[63] Nearly all managerial problem solving requires a healthy measure of creativity as managers mentally take things apart, rearrange the pieces in new and potentially productive configurations, and look beyond normal frameworks for new solutions. This process is like turning the kaleidoscope of one's mind. Thomas Edison used to retire to an old couch in his laboratory to do his creative thinking. Henry Ford reportedly sought creative insights by staring at a blank wall in his shop. Although the average manager's attempts at creativity may not be as dramatically fruitful as Edison's or Ford's, workplace creativity needs to be understood and nurtured. As a steppingstone to the next section on creative problem solving, this section defines creativity, discusses the management of creative people, and identifies barriers to creativity.

What Is Creativity?

Creativity is a rather mysterious process known chiefly by its results and is therefore difficult to define. About as close as we can come is to say that creativity is the reorganization of experience into new configurations.[64] According to a management consultant specializing in creativity, it requires actively trying to connect bits of information into new patterns, and then evaluating and developing these small ideas into real possibilities.[65] Donna Kacmar, an architect in Houston, Texas, exemplifies our definition of creativity: She says, "My creativity lies in trying to explore new possibilities for what might be considered a dumb or mundane problem." She encourages others to develop their creative abilities by challenging assumptions, looking for new relationships, and viewing a familiar situation from a different vantage point.[66] Creativity is often subtle and may not be readily apparent to the untrained eye. But the combination and extension of seemingly insignificant day-to-day breakthroughs lead to organizational progress.

Identifying general types of creativity is easier than explaining the basic process. One pioneering writer on the subject isolated three overlapping domains of creativity: art, discovery, and humor.[67] These have been called the "ah!" reaction, the "aha!" reaction, and the "haha!" reaction, respectively.[68]

The discovery ("aha!") variation is the most relevant to management. Entirely new businesses can spring from creative discovery. Here is a prime example: When Gary Goldberg learned how hard it was to fight allergen-related illnesses, he developed mattresses and pillow covers that prevent sleepers from breathing in allergens that typically reside in bedding, like dust mites.[69]

Workplace Creativity: Myth and Modern Reality

Research has shattered a long-standing myth about creative employees. According to the myth, creative people are typically nonconformists. But Alan Robinson's field research, like many other studies on creativity, paints a very different picture: In a survey of 600 innovative people, only three could accurately be described as nonconformists. The others were careful and patient individuals who had to build support among team members for their ideas.[70]

Thus, creative self-expression through unconventional dress and strange behavior does not necessarily translate into creative work.

Today's managers are challenged to create an organizational culture and climate capable of evoking the often hidden creative talents of *every* employee.[71] Consider, for instance, the birth of Frappuccino at Starbucks, as related by founder and CEO Howard Schultz: A West L.A. store manager started blending beverages and sampling them to customers. People were fascinated, and the Frappuccino was born. Schultz says, "Frappuccino today is a multi-hundred-million-dollar business in our stores."[72]

Learning to Be More Creative

Some people naturally seem to be more creative than others. But that does not mean that those who feel the need cannot develop their creative capacity. It does seem clear that creative ability can be learned, in the sense that our creative energies can be released from the bonds of convention, lack of self-confidence, and narrow thinking. We all have the potential to be more creative.

The best place to begin is by trying consciously to overcome what creativity specialist Roger von Oech calls *mental locks*. The following mental locks are attitudes that get us through our daily activities but tend to stifle our creativity:*

1. *Looking for the "right" answer.* A given problem may have several right answers, depending on one's perspective.
2. *Always trying to be logical.* Logic does not always prevail, given human emotions and organizational inconsistencies, ambiguity, and contradictions.
3. *Strictly following the rules.* If things are to be improved, arbitrary limits on thinking and behavior need to be questioned.[73]
4. *Insisting on being practical.* Impractical answers to "what-if" questions can become steppingstones to creative insights.
5. *Avoiding ambiguity.* Creativity can be stunted by too much objectivity and specificity.
6. *Fearing and avoiding failure.* Fear of failure can paralyze us into not acting on our good ideas. This is unfortunate because we learn many valuable and lasting lessons from our mistakes.
7. *Forgetting how to play.* The playful experimentation of childhood too often disappears by adulthood.
8. *Becoming too specialized.* Cross-fertilization of specialized areas helps in defining problems and generating solutions.

8e
Quick Test of Your Creativity

You have a candle, some matches, and a box of tacks. How can you affix the burning candle to the wall without dripping any wax on the wall or the floor?

QUESTIONS: How quickly did you solve this puzzle? What was right or wrong about your approach? What does it say about your creativity? (See Ch. 8 endnote 92 for the answer.)

Source: Puzzle adapted from and answer quoted from Janet Paskin, "Happily Ever After," *Money,* 35 (June 2006): 28.

creativity *the reorganization of experience into new configurations*

From left to right, Samantha Richey of DeSoto, Texas; Sarah Fakhraldeen of Kuwait; and Sajid Mehmood of Somerset, New Jersey, use vital cross-cultural communication skills to tackle a creative problem-solving exercise at the Seeds of Peace summer camp in Otisfield, Maine.

AP Photo/Robert F. Bukaty

9. **Not wanting to look foolish.** Humor can release tensions and unlock creative energies. Seemingly foolish questions can enhance understanding.
10. **Saying "I'm not creative."** By nurturing small and apparently insignificant ideas, we can convince ourselves that we are indeed creative.[74]

Source: List adapted from *A Whack on the Side of the Head* by Roger von Oech, Warner Books, 1983. Reprinted by permission.

(Try the creativity exercise in the Action Learning Exercise at the end of this chapter.) If these mental locks are conquered, the creative problem-solving process discussed in the next section can be used to its full potential.

CREATIVE PROBLEM SOLVING

We are all problem solvers. But this does not mean that all of us are good problem solvers or even, for that matter, that we know how to solve problems systematically. Most daily problem solving is done on a haphazard, intuitive basis. A difficulty arises, so we look around for an answer, jump at the first workable solution to come along, and move on to other things. In a primitive sense, this sequence of events qualifies as a problem-solving process, and it works quite well for informal daily activities. But in the world of management, a more systematic

problem-solving process is required for tackling difficult and unfamiliar non-programmed decisions. In the context of management, problem solving is the conscious process of bringing the actual situation closer to the desired situation.[75] Managerial problem solving consists of a four-step sequence: (1) identifying the problem, (2) generating alternative solutions, (3) selecting a solution, and (4) implementing and evaluating the solution (see Figure 8.6).

Identifying the Problem

As strange as it may seem, the most common problem-solving difficulty lies in the identification of problems. Busy managers have a tendency to rush into generating and selecting alternative solutions before they have actually isolated and understood the real problem. According to Peter Drucker, the respected management scholar, "The greatest source of mistakes in top management is to ask the same questions most people ask. They all assume that there are the same 'right answers' for everyone. But one does not begin with answers. One begins by asking, 'What are our questions?'"[76] When problem finding, managers should probe with the right questions.[77] Only then can the right answers be found. Problem finding can be a great career booster, too, as Michael Iem discovered. It all started with his love of tough challenges:

This bricklayer's son has no formal job title and no office, but his career at Tandem Computers [now part of Hewlett-Packard] is on a tear. He personifies the advice that executive recruiter Robert Horton offers all who want to advance: "Find the biggest business problem your employer faces for which you and your skills are the solution." ... [Iem's problem-solving ability] made him known throughout Tandem, bringing promotions and a doubling of his $32,000

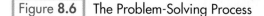

Figure **8.6**   The Problem-Solving Process

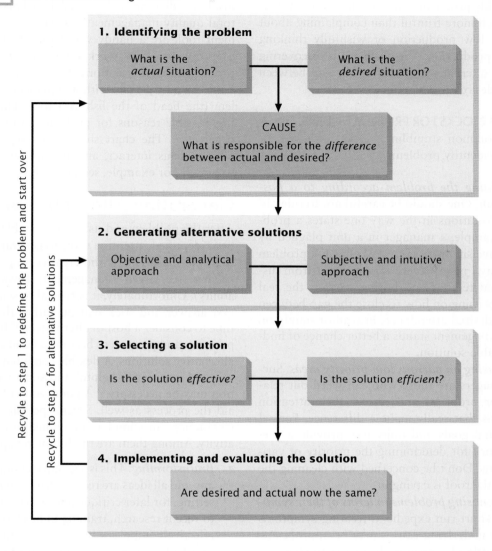

starting salary. . . . The company lets him decide what projects to take on, making him the youngest of perhaps a dozen employees with the broad mandate.[78]

WHAT IS A PROBLEM? Ask half a dozen people how they identify problems, and you are likely to get as many answers. Consistent with the definition given earlier for problem solving, a **problem** is defined as the difference between an actual state of affairs and a desired state of affairs. In other words, a problem is the gap between where one is and where one wants to be. Problem solving is meant to close this gap. For

example, a person in New York who has to make a presentation in San Francisco in 24 hours has a problem. The problem is not being in New York (the actual state of affairs), nor is it presenting in San Francisco in 24 hours (the desired state of affairs). Instead, the problem is the distance between New York and San Francisco. Flying would be an obvious solution. But thanks to modern communications technology such as videoconferencing, there are ways to overcome the 2,934-mile gap without having to travel.[79]

Managers need to define problems according to the gaps between the actual and the desired situations. A production manager, for example, would be wise to concentrate on the gap between the present level of weekly production and the desired level. This focus is much more fruitful than complaining about the current low production or wishfully thinking about high production. The challenge is discovering a workable alternative for closing the gap between actual and desired production.

STUMBLING BLOCKS FOR PROBLEM FINDERS. There are three common stumbling blocks for those attempting to identify problems:

1. *Defining the problem according to a possible solution.* One should be careful not to rule out alternative solutions in the way one states a problem. For example, a manager in a unit plagued by high absenteeism who says, "We have a problem with low pay," may prevent management from discovering that tedious and boring work is the real cause. By focusing on how to close the gap between actual and desired attendance, instead of simply on low pay, management stands a better chance of finding a workable solution.

2. *Focusing on narrow, low-priority areas.* Successful managers are those who can weed out relatively minor problems and reserve their attention for problems that really make a difference. Formal organizational goals and objectives provide a useful framework for determining the priority of various problems. Don't be concerned with cleaning the floor when the roof is caving in.

3. *Diagnosing problems in terms of their symptoms.* As a short-run expedient, treating symptoms rather than underlying causes may be appropriate. Buying a bottle of aspirin is cheaper than trying to find a less stressful job, for example. In the longer run, however, symptoms tend to reappear and problems tend to get worse. There is a two-way test for discovering whether one has found the cause of a problem: "If I *introduce* this variable, will the problem (the gap) disappear?" or "If I *remove* this variable, will the problem (the gap) disappear?" **Causes** are variables that, because of their presence in or absence from the situation, are primarily responsible for the difference between the actual and the desired conditions. For example, the *absence* of a key can cause a problem with a locked door, and the *presence* of a nail can cause a problem with an inflated tire.[80]

PINPOINTING CAUSES WITH FISHBONE DIAGRAMS. Fishbone diagrams, discussed in Chapter 16 as a total quality management (TQM) process improvement tool, are a handy way to track down causes of problems. They work especially well in group problem-solving situations. Construction of a fishbone diagram begins with a statement of the problem (the head of the fish skeleton). The bones list the possible reasons for problems in order of their occurrence. The chart shows how separate causes for problems interact, and this assists in problem solving.[81] For example, see Figure 8.7.

Generating Alternative Solutions

After the problem and its most probable cause have been identified, attention turns to generating alternative solutions. This is the creative step in problem solving (see Green Management: Toward Sustainability). Unfortunately, it is typical to seize upon the first answer and stick with it, rather than take the time to consider a host of alternatives.[82] It takes time, patience, and practice to become a good generator of alternative solutions. A flexible combination of analysis and intuition is helpful and some experimentation may be necessary.[83] A good sense of humor can aid the process as well. Several popular and useful techniques can stimulate individual and group creativity. Among them are the following approaches:

- *Brainstorming.* This is a group technique in which any and all ideas are recorded, in a *nonjudgmental* setting, for later critique and selection. According to recent research, training in how to brainstorm effectively improves both the quantity and quality of ideas generated.[84] Brainstorming with the use of computer network systems is proving worthwhile now that sophisticated groupware is available.[85] IBM's CEO Samuel J. Palmisano believes in the creative potential of brainstorming and does it on a truly grand scale. In a project called Innovation Jam, he hosts online townhall meetings to harness the power of 100,000 creative minds and discover new innovations that will transform industries, change human behavior, and open new businesses.[86]

- *Free association.* Analogies and symbols are used to foster unconventional thinking. For example, think of your studies as a mountain requiring special climbing gear and skills.

causes factors, because of their presence or absence in a situation, that are primarily responsible for a problem

Figure **8.7** | Sample Fishbone Diagram

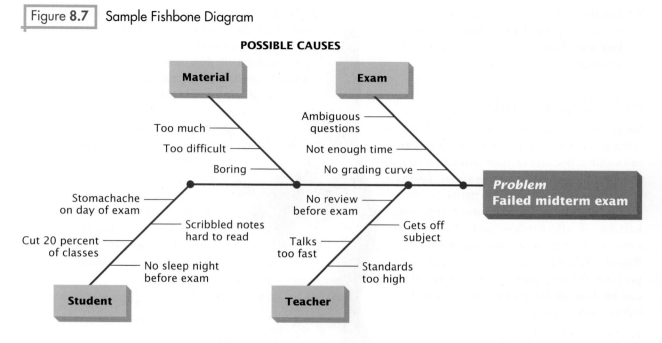

POSSIBLE CAUSES

- *Edisonian method.* Named for Thomas Edison's tedious and persistent search for a durable lightbulb filament, this technique involves trial-and-error experimentation: Back in 1897, after 18 months, 1,200 failures, and $40,000 in expenses, Edison and his team finally created a lightbulb that worked.[87] The rest, as they say, is history.

- *Attribute listing.* Ideal characteristics of a given object are collected and then screened for useful insights.
- *Scientific method.* Systematic hypothesis testing, manipulation of variables, situational controls, and careful measurement are the essence of this rigorous approach.

Green Management: Toward Sustainability

Community Building Through Environmental Problem Solving

"There are South Bronxes all over the country," says Majora Carter, 43, seated in her down-to-earth South Bronx offices, adjacent to the highway and above an auto-glass repair shop. She rattles off a few: New Orleans, northeastern North Carolina, Detroit. That realization prompted her in 2008 to make the leap from not-for-profit to for-profit entrepreneur. . . .

Through TED [Technology, Entertainment, Design conference] presentations, numerous speeches, and appearances on the Sundance Channel series *The Green*, Carter has galvanized people around a provocative vision: Clean up environmental problems in a blighted community and you start a positive chain of events. Improve water and air quality, and you'll lower residents' health-care costs. Train them for new jobs restoring critical wetlands, or installing solar panels on roofs, and you'll lift families out of poverty. Those changes, in turn, create and attract businesses, and a community that was once a burden on local government becomes a resource.

For Discussion: How can the problem-solving process in Figure 8.6 help keep this sort of complex community-building program focused and productive?

Source: Excerpted from Chuck Salter, "Majora Carter: Founder, Majora Carter Group," *Fast Company*, 146 (June 2010): 101.

satisfice to settle for a solution that is good enough

- *Creative leap.* This technique involves thinking up idealistic solutions to a problem and then working back to a feasible solution.

Selecting a Solution

Simply stating that the best solution should be selected in step 3 (refer to Figure 8.6) can be misleading. Because of time and financial constraints and political considerations, *best* is a relative term. Generally, alternative solutions should be screened for the most appealing balance of effectiveness and efficiency in view of relevant constraints and intangibles. Russell Ackoff, a specialist in managerial problem solving, contends that three things can be done about problems: they can be re-solved, solved, or dissolved.[88]

RESOLVING THE PROBLEM. When a problem is resolved, a course of action that is good enough to meet the minimum constraints is selected. The term satisfice has been applied to the practice of settling for solutions that are good enough rather than the best possible.[89] A badly worn spare tire may satisfice as a replacement for a flat tire for the balance of the trip, although getting the flat repaired is the best possible solution. According to Ackoff, most managers rely on problem resolving. This nonquantitative, subjective approach is popular because managers claim they do not have the information or time necessary for the other approaches. Satisficing, however, has been criticized as a short-sighted and passive technique emphasizing expedient survival instead of improvement and growth.

SOLVING THE PROBLEM. A problem is solved when the best possible solution is selected. Managers are said to optimize when, through scientific observation and quantitative measurement, they systematically research alternative solutions and select the one with the best combination of benefits.

DISSOLVING THE PROBLEM. A problem is dissolved when the situation in which it occurs is changed so that the problem no longer exists. Problem dissolvers

Aaron Amat/Shutterstock.Com

are said to idealize because they actually change the nature of the system in which a problem resides. Managers who dissolve problems rely on whatever combination of nonquantitative and quantitative tools is needed to get the job done. The replacement of automobile assembly-line welders with robots, for instance, has dissolved the problem of costly absenteeism among people in that job category.

Whatever approach a manager chooses, the following advice from Ackoff should be kept in mind: "Few if any problems . . . are ever permanently resolved, solved, or dissolved; every treatment of a problem generates new problems."[90]

Implementing and Evaluating the Solution

Time is the true test of any solution. Until a particular solution has had time to prove its worth, the manager can rely only on his or her judgment concerning its effectiveness and efficiency. Ideally, the solution selected will completely eliminate the difference between the actual and the desired in an efficient and timely manner. Should the gap fail to disappear, two options are open. If the manager remains convinced that the problem has been correctly identified, he or she can recycle to step 2 to try another solution that was identified earlier. This recycling can continue until all feasible solutions have been given a fair chance or until the nature of the problem changes to the extent that the existing solutions are obsolete. If the gap between actual and desired persists in spite of repeated attempts to find a solution, then it is advisable to recycle to step 1 to redefine the problem and engage in a new round of problem solving.

In any case, timely response is vital in today's problem-filled world. Doug McMillon, CEO of Walmart International, the giant retailer's fastest-growing division, tells us: "Act with a sense of urgency. Problems don't age well."[91]

---

optimize to systematically identify the solution with the best combination of benefits | *idealize to change the nature of the situation in which a problem has arisen*

SUMMARY

1. Decision making is a fundamental part of management because it requires choosing among alternative courses of action. In addition to having to cope with an era of accelerating change, today's decision makers face the challenges of dealing with complexity, uncertainty, the need for flexible thinking, and decision traps. Eight factors that contribute to decision complexity are multiple criteria, intangibles, risk and uncertainty, long-term implications, interdisciplinary input, pooled decision making, value judgments, and unintended consequences.

2. Managers must learn to assess the degree of certainty in a situation—whether conditions are certain, risky, or uncertain. Confidence in one's decisions decreases as uncertainty increases. Managers can respond to a condition of risk—incomplete but reliable factual information—by calculating objective or subjective probabilities. Today's managers need to tap the creative potential of intuitive employees and the implementation skills of those who process information as thinkers.

3. Researchers have identified three perceptual and behavioral decision traps that can undermine the quality of decisions. Framing error occurs when people let labels and frames of reference sway their interpretations. People fall victim to escalation of commitment when they get locked into losing propositions for fear of quitting and looking bad. Oddly, researchers find that overconfidence tends to grow with the difficulty of the task.

4. Decisions, generally, are either programmed or nonprogrammed. Because programmed decisions are relatively clear-cut and routinely encountered, fixed decision rules can be formulated for them. In contrast, nonprogrammed decisions require creative problem solving because they are novel and unfamiliar. Decision making can be improved with a knowledge management (KM) program. KM is a systematic approach to creating and sharing critical information throughout the organization. Two types of knowledge are *tacit* (personal, intuitive, and undocumented) and *explicit* (documented and sharable) knowledge.

5. Managers may choose to bring other people into virtually every aspect of the decision-making process. However, when a group rather than an individual is responsible for making the decision, personal accountability is lost. Dispersed accountability is undesirable in some key decision situations. Group-aided decision making has both advantages and disadvantages. Because group performance does not always exceed individual performance, a contingency approach to group-aided decision making is advisable.

6. Creativity requires the proper combination of knowledge, imagination, and evaluation to reorganize experience into new configurations. The domains of creativity may be divided into art, discovery (the most relevant to management), and humor. Contrary to myth, researchers have found only a weak link between creativity and nonconformity. A fun and energizing workplace climate can tap *every* employee's creativity. By consciously overcoming ten mental locks, we can become more creative.

7. The creative problem-solving process consists of four steps: (1) identifying the problem, (2) generating alternative solutions, (3) selecting a solution, and (4) implementing and evaluating the solution. Inadequate problem finding is common among busy managers. By seeing problems as gaps between an actual situation and a desired situation, managers are in a better position to create more effective and efficient solutions. Depending on the situation, problems can be resolved, solved, or dissolved. It is important to remember that today's solutions often become tomorrow's problems.

8. A clear and concise statement of the problem forms the "head" of the fishbone skeleton. Each of the "bones" extending out from the backbone of the fishbone diagram represents a possible cause of the problem. More likely causes are located closer to the head of the diagram. Possible explanations for each cause are attached to each particular "bone."

TERMS TO UNDERSTAND

Decision making, p. 210

Law of unintended consequences, p. 212

Condition of certainty, p. 213

Condition of risk, p. 213

Objective probabilities, p. 213

Subjective probabilities, p. 213

Condition of uncertainty, p. 214

Framing error, p. 215

Escalation of commitment, p. 216

Programmed decisions, p. 217

Decision rule, p. 218

Nonprogrammed decisions, p. 218

Knowledge management, p. 219

Tacit knowledge, p. 220

Explicit knowledge, p. 220

Collaborative computing, p. 221

Creativity, p. 225

Problem solving, p. 227

Problem, p. 227

Causes, p. 228

Satisfice, p. 229

Optimize, p. 230

Idealize, p. 230

ACTION LEARNING EXERCISE

HOW CREATIVE ARE YOU?

Instructions: This exercise is for both individuals and teams. Assume that a steel pipe is embedded in the concrete floor of a bare room as shown below. The inside diameter is .06 inch larger than the diameter of a ping-pong ball (1.50 inches) that is resting gently at the bottom of the pipe. You are one of a group of six people in the room, along with the following objects:

- 100 feet of clothesline
- Carpenter's hammer
- Chisel
- Box of Wheaties
- File
- Wire coat hanger
- Monkey wrench
- Light bulb

List as many ways you can think of (in five minutes) to get the ball out of the pipe without damaging the ball, tube, or floor.

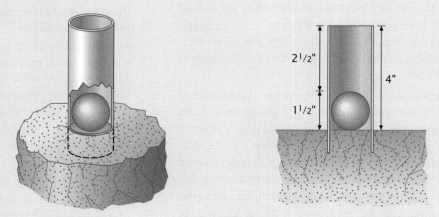

Source: From *Conceptual Blockbusting* by James L. Adams. Reprinted by permission of Da Capo Press, a member of Perseus Books Group.

FOR CONSIDERATION/DISCUSSION

1. In terms of the definition in this chapter, what is the "problem" here?

2. What assumptions did you make about any of the objects?

3. How would you rate your creativity on this exercise on a scale of 1 = low to 10 = high?

4. How many of the eight resource objects did you manage to employ? Which was the most useful? Why?

5. How many solutions did you develop? Which one is the "best"? Why?

ETHICS EXERCISE

 DO THE RIGHT THING

IS OVERTIME THE RIGHT DECISION IN THIS SITUATION?

Quality Float Works of Schaumburg, Ill., laid off three employees in 2009 and put its remaining 18 on a four-day workweek.

Now [mid 2010], sales are surging for the company, which makes metal balls that businesses use to signal when water levels get too high or low in tanks and troughs. Customers depleted their inventories in the slowdown and are panicked, says company President Sandra Westlund-Deenihan.

She's giving workers up to nine hours of overtime weekly. Although she hired two staffers recently, she's holding off on further additions. Existing employees "went through the hard times, and I felt I owed it to them first," she says.

Some workers are going straight from part time to overtime duty.

Source: Excerpted from Paul Davidson, "Employees Work More to Meet Demand," *USA Today* (June 21, 2010): 3B.

What are the ethical implications of the following interpretations?

1. This is a very fair arrangement—a classic case of "share the pain, share the gain." Besides, it gives Westlund-Deenihan some room to maneuver in case the economy softens again.

2. Bringing back all the laid-off employees (those who desired to return) for at least part-time work, before granting overtime to existing employees, would have better served the greater good. After all, the laid-off employees suffered the most.

3. In the spirit of employee empowerment and participative management, Westlund-Deenihan should have polled the employees to see if a majority wanted to go the overtime route or first bring back all laid-off employees, and acted accordingly.

4. Your own ethical interpretation?

MANAGERS-IN-ACTION VIDEO CASE STUDY

 ### GREENSBURG KANSAS

Decision Making: The 100-Year Decision

Following the tornado that devastated the town of Greensburg, Kansas, leaders and residents were faced with a major decision—what to do next. The residents could move, or stay and be part of the rebuilding. Prior to the tornado, residents were looking for ways to create a better town by increasing efficiency and effectiveness and decreasing waste. As a result, they saw this storm as an opportunity to rebuild the town with a new direction. In this video, the city administrator shares his approach to what he describes as the 100-year decision. Current and former residents provide their perspectives and offer both positive and negative commentary on the decision-making process. Through this video you will gain greater insight into the complex challenges managers face in the decision-making process.

For more information about Greensburg and the 100-year decision to go green, visit the Greensburg GreenTown Web site: www.greensburggreentown.org.

Before watching the video, answer the following questions:

1. Describe the decision-making process.
2. What factors may complicate the decision-making process?
3. What are some of the keys to success for managers faced with a difficult decision that impacts their entire team?

After watching the video, answer the following questions

4. What did city leaders do to gain buy-in and support for their decision to go green in the rebuilding process?
5. Critique the town of Greensburg's approach to the 100-year decision.
6. Compare and contrast the decision from the perspective of current and former residents, evaluating the positive and negatives presented.
7. Would you do anything different if you were the city administrator? If yes, explain what and why. If no, explain why not.

CLOSING CASE

THE PHANTASMAGORIA FACTORY

To understand what a Cirque du Soleil circus is like, you first have to forget every childhood memory of ringmasters, clown cars, and lion tamers. Get ready instead for a dancing headless man carrying an umbrella and a bowler hat (in *Quidam*, one of Cirque's five touring shows). Or a clown acting a pantomime of lost love, then disappearing in an elaborately staged blizzard (in *Alegria*, another touring show). Or trapeze artists dropping into a huge indoor lake that then "evaporates" before the audience's eyes (in *O*, Cirque's resident show at the Bellagio in Las Vegas).

Cirque du Soleil (French for "circus of the sun") is one of the rare companies that utterly redefine

their industries. It takes the circus's raw materials—trapeze artists, contortionists, strong men, clowns—combines them with surreal costumes, nonstop New Age music, and dazzling stagecraft, and then ties it all together with a vaguely profound theme, like "a tribute to the nomadic soul" *(Varekai)* or "a phantasmagoria of urban life" *(Saltimbanco)*. The result is a spectacle that leaves audiences cheering—and flailing for metaphors. "It's like a tour of Dante's Inferno designed and cast by Federico Fellini," reads one review of *O*.

Though considerably less surreal than its shows, Cirque's business model is another crowd pleaser. Bobby Baldwin, CEO of Mirage Resorts, whose Treasure Island casino in Las Vegas hosts Cirque's *Mystère*, calls Cirque "the most successful entertainment company in the world." He isn't referring strictly to profits: The private, Montreal-based company nets more than $100 million a year on $500 million in revenue; that's not peanuts, but it's no more than Disney's live entertainment division.

Instead, Baldwin is talking about the power of the brand. In two decades and 15 separate productions, Cirque du Soleil has never had a flop. By comparison, 9 out of 10 shows on Broadway—productions aimed at the same sophisticated, big-ticket audience as Cirque—fail to earn back the money invested in them. Cirque's reputation for never missing is so strong that, in exchange for half the profits, four Las Vegas resorts, as well as Disney World, each agreed to spend tens of millions of dollars to build a custom theater to house a Cirque show and foot half the show's production costs, which can hit $25 million. No traditional circus has ever inspired such an outpouring of capital from business partners. And who can blame them? According to a recent survey, some 5 percent of all Las Vegas tourists—1.8 million a year—cite Cirque's shows as their main reason for visiting.

Much of the credit goes, appropriately, to the company's performers and artists—especially Franco Dragone, the Belgian director who headed the creative team for six of Cirque's nine current productions. Cirque's president for shows and new ventures, Daniel Lamarre, is only too happy to agree. A 50-year-old former television executive who seems slightly amused to find himself in the constant company of world-class acrobats, contortionists, designers, and musicians, Lamarre says he knows exactly why his business works: "We let the creative people run it.". . .

Cirque du Soleil was hatched in 1984 by two high school dropouts—Guy Laliberté, a 23-year-old Montreal fire breather, and Daniel Gauthier, 24, a youth hostel manager. In what had to be one of the entertainment industry's most audacious acts of persuasion, they talked the Quebec government into granting them just over $1 million to develop a show around local street performers as part of a festival celebrating the 450th anniversary

of Montreal's founding. The pair hired Dragone in 1985, and what he calls the "transdisciplinary experience" of circus blended with stagecraft, live music, and song became Cirque's trademark and a hit across Canada.

The moment of truth arrived in 1987 when Laliberté and Gauthier took their act to the LA Arts Festival. The pair knew that if the show flopped, they couldn't afford to fly the cast and equipment home. They needn't have worried, however: The standing ovation went on for five minutes, and by the time the box office opened the next morning, 500 people were standing in line. Cirque du Soleil was no longer a nonprofit organization.

The new business was less than four years old when the founders made perhaps their most crucial decision. As word had spread of Cirque's blockbuster success, offers flooded in from other production companies eager to license touring versions of the show. No doubt the road shows could have made money. Ringling Bros. and Barnum & Bailey Circus, for example, has built its business on touring shows that have been offering up basically the same trained-lions-and-traditional-trapeze fare for generations. And for a Broadway musical, tours can be the main source of profit. But Gauthier and Laliberté refused. World-class circus performers are simply too scarce a resource, they reasoned, and a wave of road shows could only dilute the genius of the original. Rather than compromise on quality, they decided that every show bearing the Cirque name would be created in-house and be unlike any show that went before. "We said, 'Each show is a new member of the family, and we never want twins,'" Gauthier says. (Gauthier left Cirque in 2001, but Laliberté, now CEO and sole proprietor of Cirque, has never budged from that resolution.)

Lamarre freely admits that the decision has restricted the company's growth. "People tell me we're leaving a lot of money on the table by not duplicating our shows," he says. "And you know what? They're right." But he says he has no regrets, adding that Cirque's success is the best proof that the founders were right to choose quality over quick profits. The same holds for the company's deliberate pace of production. Cirque will release just one new show a year through 2007. Since the company builds each show from scratch—a three-year process—a faster schedule would spread creative resources too thin, as the company learned in 1998 when it produced both *La Nouba* and *O*.

At the moment, five Cirque shows tour the world, each a one-of-a-kind production accompanied by its own 2,500-seat tent. Another four play in permanent venues built exclusively for Cirque in Las Vegas and Orlando. Such arrangements are not cheap. To launch *Zumanity,* for example, New York-New York owner MGM Mirage put up $51 million, including the cost of building the theater, while Cirque kicked in $7.5 million.

So far, though, Cirque has repaid its partners' investments—and then some. The brand draws a decidedly upscale college-educated audience, skewing toward women. Such patrons appreciate Cirque's ambitious themes and, just as important, don't blink at ticket prices that range from $45 to $150. The company sells 97 percent of available seats. . . .

True to Lamarre's assertion that the creative minds lead the company, he and his business staff never get involved with a show's three-year-long creative gestation. At conception, Lamarre meets with the team of director, circus director, choreographer, composer, and set and lighting designers and agrees on a production budget and an opening date. After that, the director can spend the budget—typically on the order of $10 million to $25 million—as he or she sees fit. "Cirque allows you to approach shows with the artistic priority first," Dragone confirms. "I never had to worry about the money or the business and instead could focus on the show." While it seems hard to believe, Lamarre says no director has ever come begging for more money.

That doesn't mean, of course, that the business office is irrelevant. Indeed, one key to each new show's electrifying originality is Lamarre's massive investment in research and development. While he won't be specific, Lamarre hints at an annual outlay of some $40 million. The payback:

astonishing effects like a swirling snowstorm in *Alegria*. Perhaps the most amazing invention is *O*'s indoor lake, which can shrink from a 25-foot-deep pool to a puddle in a matter of seconds, thanks to a hydraulically powered floor that rises through the water. The specially equipped theater cost $70 million alone, paid for entirely by MGM Mirage, which also shouldered nearly half the $22 million in production costs.

Ideas on the drawing board include a nightclub called Club Cirque and a Cirque Resort in Vegas that would feature New Age music, brightly colored furniture, and theatrical lighting throughout the building. Cirque's entertainers would also have roles; Lamarre says he envisions jugglers as room service waiters. "We want to challenge our creative people to work in new mediums," he says.

For Discussion

1. Which of the eight sources of complexity for today's decision makers (Figure 8.1) are evident in this case? Explain your choices.

2. Is most of the decision making discussed in this case programmed or nonprogrammed? Explain.

3. What was "the key decision" in this case? Could it have any unintended consequences? Explain.

4. What does Cirque du Soleil do to foster a healthy climate for creativity? What else could it do?

5. How does Cirque du Soleil create a profitable balance between artistic creativity and business discipline?

6. What is the secret of Cirque du Soleil's success?

Source: From Geoff Keighley, "The Phantasmagoria Factory," *Business 2.0* (January–February 2004): 103–107. © 2004 Time Inc. All rights reserved.

CHAPTER 9   Organizations: Effectiveness, Design, and Cultures

CHAPTER 10   Human Resource Management

CHAPTER 11   Communicating in the Internet Age

Organizing, Managing Human Resources, and Communicating

P3

9 Organizations: Effectiveness, Design, and Cultures

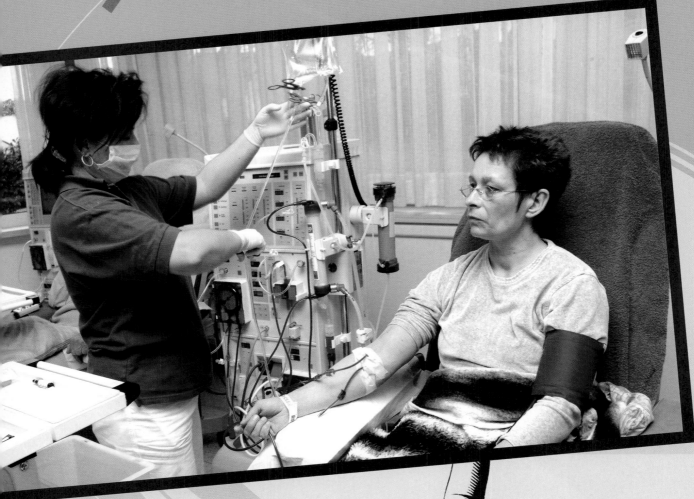

Klaus Rose/Photolibrary

"You have to think small to grow big."[1]
—*SAM WALTON, FOUNDER OF WALMART*

The Changing Workplace

A CULTURE OF TRUTH HELPS CREATE A LEARNING ORGANIZATION

Creating a culture where people feel free to admit they need help, where they have an attitude of wisdom—knowing what they know and knowing what they don't know—also requires CEOs and other senior leaders to stop bluffing their way through situations. Instead of making stuff up, admit what you don't know when asked a question, and promise to find out. That's precisely the approach that Kent Thiry, CEO of kidney dialysis company DaVita does. At every employee gathering he or other leaders attend, it is a requirement that there be a "town meeting" where employees are free to ask any questions they want. . . . His response, even in front of 440 front-line employees, is "I don't know. I'll have to get back to you on that." And he makes it his business to find out the answer and respond. This creates an environment in which people can admit their own uncertainties and what they don't know. And this is the first step toward learning.

. . . good management requires telling the truth, asking for help, and learning. Building a culture where people are rewarded for identifying problems and telling the truth—and even better, for suggesting solutions—isn't easy, as it goes against the natural human tendencies to like those who agree with us and to prefer happy talk, even if it isn't true. But truth telling and admissions of ignorance are crucial requirements for long-term business success.[2]

Source: Excerpted from Jeffrey Pfeffer, *What Were They Thinking? Unconventional Wisdom About Management* (Boston: Harvard Business School Press, 2007), pp. 125–126.

OBJECTIVES

- **Identify** and **describe** four characteristics common to all organizations, and **distinguish** between line and staff positions.
- **Describe** a business organization in terms of the open-system model, and **explain** the term *learning organization*.
- **Describe** the time dimension of organizational effectiveness.
- **Explain** the concept of contingency organization design, and **distinguish** between mechanistic and organic organizations.
- **Identify** and briefly **describe** the five basic departmentalization formats.
- **Describe** how a highly centralized organization differs from a highly decentralized one.
- **Define** the term *delegation*, and **list** at least five common barriers to delegation.
- **Explain** how the traditional pyramid organization is being reshaped.
- **Describe** at least three characteristics of organizational cultures, and **explain** the cultural significance of stories.

Organizations are an ever-present feature of modern society. We look to organizations for food, clothing, education, employment, entertainment, health care, transportation, and protection of our basic rights. DaVita, for its part, is a thriving business meeting patients' chronic health care needs. For better or for worse, virtually every aspect of modern life is influenced in one way or another by organizations. Douglas Smith, a management consultant/author who is concerned about ethics and values in our era of giant global corporations, has suggested that organizations are communities where people work together to make a difference for themselves and others, as well as the planet as a whole. Thus, there is a need for increased corporate transparency and accountability to make sure the greater good is served. Smith adds, "Organizations are not just places where people have jobs."[3]

In Chapter 1 we said the purpose of the management process is to achieve *organizational* objectives in an effective and efficient manner. Organizations are social entities that enable people to work together to achieve objectives they normally could not achieve alone. This chapter explores the organizational context in which managers and all other employees operate. It examines the structure, effectiveness, and design of organizations. The importance of delegation and the changing shape of organizations are discussed. The chapter concludes with the interesting topic of organizational cultures.

ORGANIZATIONAL STRUCTURE AND EFFECTIVENESS

An **organization** is defined as a cooperative social system involving the coordinated efforts of two or more people pursuing a shared purpose.[4] In other words, when people gather and formally agree to combine their efforts for a common purpose, an organization is the result.

There are exceptions, of course, such as when two strangers agree to push a car out of a ditch. This task is a one-time effort based on temporary expediency. But if the same two people decided to pool their resources to create a towing service, an organization would be created. The "coordinated efforts" portion of our definition, which implies a degree of formal planning and division of labor, is present in the second instance but not in the first.

Characteristics Common to All Organizations

According to Edgar Schein, an organizational psychologist, all organizations share four characteristics: (1) coordination of effort, (2) common goal or purpose, (3) division of labor, and (4) hierarchy of authority.[5]

COORDINATION OF EFFORT. As we noted in the last chapter, two heads are sometimes better than one. Individuals who join together and coordinate their mental and/or physical efforts can accomplish great and exciting things. Building the great pyramids, conquering polio, sending astronauts to the moon—all these achievements far exceeded the talents and abilities of any single individual. Coordination of effort multiplies individual contributions.

COMMON GOAL OR PURPOSE. Coordination of effort cannot take place unless those who have joined together agree to strive for something of mutual interest. A common goal or purpose gives the organization focus and its members a rallying point. Constantly reminding employees of that common purpose and getting them to rally around it is a key managerial challenge. For instance, DaVita, featured in the opening case for this chapter, strives to feel and act like a "village." CEO Kent Thiry recently told *Training* magazine in an interview that DaVita puts its employees first because the company has found that creating a positive workplace ultimately leads to better care for the patients. Says Thiry, "Early on, we adopted a strategy of training and caring for our teammates as a way to truly live our mission and values."[6]

DIVISION OF LABOR. By systematically dividing complex tasks into specialized jobs, an organization can use its human resources efficiently. Division of labor permits each organization member to become more proficient by repeatedly doing

James Hoenstine/Shutterstock.com

the same specialized task. (But, as is discussed in Chapter 12, overspecialized jobs can breed boredom and alienation.)

The advantages of dividing labor have been known for a long time. One of its early proponents was the pioneering economist Adam Smith. While touring an eighteenth-century pin-manufacturing plant, Smith observed that a group of specialized laborers could produce 48,000 pins a day. This was an astounding figure, considering that each laborer could produce only 20 pins a day when working alone.[7]

HIERARCHY OF AUTHORITY. According to traditional organization theory, if anything is to be accomplished through formal collective effort, someone should be given the authority to see that the intended goals are carried out effectively and efficiently. Organization theorists have defined authority as the right to direct the actions of others. Without a clear hierarchy of authority, coordination of effort is difficult, if not impossible, to achieve.[8] Accountability is also enhanced by having people serve in what is often called, in military language, the *chain of command*. For instance, a grocery store manager has authority over the assistant manager, who has authority over the produce department head, who in turn has authority over the employees in the produce department. Without such a chain of command, the store manager would have the impossible task of directly overseeing the work of every employee in the store.

The idea of hierarchy has many critics, particularly among those who advocate flatter organizations with fewer levels of management.[9] Yet, one organization theorist answers those critics by noting that his research has demonstrated some advantages to managerial hierarchy, such as providing a productive structure, encouraging creative energy, and improving morale.[10]

The construction of these ancient ruins atop the Acropolis in Athens, Greece, remind us that the four characteristics common to all organizations are timeless: coordination of effort, a common goal, division of labor, and a hierarchy of authority.

PUTTING ALL THE PIECES TOGETHER. All four of the foregoing characteristics are necessary before an organization can be said to exist. Many well-intentioned attempts to create organizations have failed because something was missing. In 1896, for example, Frederick Strauss, a boyhood friend of Henry Ford, helped Ford set up a machine shop, supposedly to produce gasoline-powered engines. But while Strauss was busy carrying out his end of the bargain by machining needed parts, Ford was secretly building a horseless carriage in a workshop behind his house.[11] Although Henry Ford eventually went on to become an automobile-industry giant, his first attempt at organization failed because not all of the pieces of an organization were in place. Ford's and his partner's efforts were not coordinated, they worked at cross-purposes, their labor was vaguely divided, and they had no hierarchy of authority. In short, they had organizational intentions, but no organization.

Organization Charts

An **organization chart**, such as the one in Figure 9.1, is a diagram of an organization's official positions and formal lines of authority. In effect, an organization chart is a visual display of an organization's structural skeleton. With their familiar pattern of boxes and connecting lines, these charts (some call

Courtesy of Robert Kreitner

---

authority right to direct the actions of others | *organization chart visual display of an organization's positions and lines of authority*

Figure **9.1**   A Simplified Sample Organization Chart

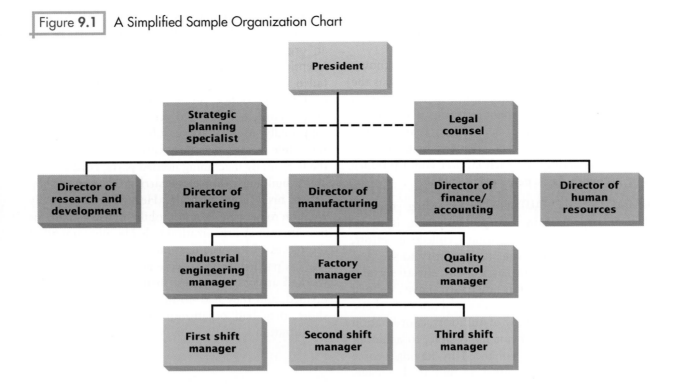

them tables) are a useful management tool because they offer an organizational blueprint for deploying human resources.[12] Organization charts are common in both profit and nonprofit organizations.

VERTICAL AND HORIZONTAL DIMENSIONS. Every organization chart has two dimensions, one representing *vertical hierarchy* and one representing *horizontal specialization*. Vertical hierarchy establishes the chain of command, or who reports to whom. The five directors in Figure 9.1 report directly to the president. Also note the unmistakable chain of command from the president, down through the director of manufacturing and factory manager, to the shift managers who oversee the factory workers. Horizontal specialization establishes the division of labor. For example, the directors of marketing and finance/accounting in Figure 9.1 have very different specialized skill sets.

LINE VERSUS STAFF POSITIONS. Technically, Figure 9.1 is a line and staff organization. In a **line and staff organization**, a distinction is made between line positions, those in the formal chain of command (connected by solid lines), and staff positions, those

serving in an advisory capacity outside the formal chain of command (indicated by broken lines). Line managers have the authority to make decisions and give orders to those lower in the chain of command. In contrast, those who occupy staff positions merely advise and support line managers. Staff authority is normally restricted to immediate assistants (for example, Figure 9.1 shows that the legal counsel directs his or her staff).[13]

Organizations as Open Systems

Open-system thinking puts the concepts we have been discussing in motion by considering the dynamic interaction between an organization and its environment.[14] (Recall our discussion of general systems theory in Chapter 2.) An open-system model encourages managers to think about the organization's life-support system (see Figure 9.2). A business must acquire various *inputs*: capital, either through selling stock or borrowing; labor, through hiring people; raw materials, through purchases; and market information, through research. On the *output* side of the model, goods and services are marketed,

| Figure **9.2** | Open-System Model of a Business |

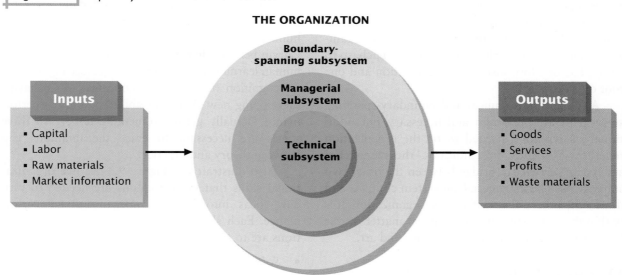

profits (or losses) are realized, and waste materials are discarded (if not recycled).[15] There are other inputs and outputs as well. This open-system model, although descriptive of a business organization, readily generalizes to all types of organizations.

By using the open-system premise that systems are made up of interacting subsystems, we can identify three prominent organizational subsystems: technical, boundary-spanning, and managerial. Sometimes called the production function, the technical subsystem physically transforms raw materials into finished goods and services. But the ability to turn out a product does not in itself guarantee organizational survival. Other supporting subsystems working in concert are also needed.

Whereas technical subsystems may be viewed as being at an organization's very core, boundary-spanning subsystems are directed outward toward the general environment. Most boundary-spanning jobs, or interface functions, as they are sometimes called, are easily identified by their titles. Purchasing and supply-chain specialists are responsible for making sure the organization has a steady and reliable flow of raw materials and subcomponents.[16] Public relations staff are in charge of developing and maintaining a favorable public image of the organization. Strategic planners have the responsibility of surveying the general environment for actual or potential opportunities and threats. Sales personnel probe the

One major takeaway from viewing organizations and the world as open systems is that we're all in this together. When an International Red Cross disaster assistance team is called to a site, it deploys technical, boundary-spanning, and managerial subsystems to help those in need.

environment for buyers for the organization's goods or services. Purchasing agents, public relations staff, strategic planners, and sales personnel have one common characteristic: they all facilitate the organization's interaction with its environment. Each, so to speak, has one foot inside the organization and one foot outside.[17]

Although the technical and boundary-spanning subsystems are important and necessary, one additional subsystem is needed to tie the organization together. As Figure 9.2 indicates, the managerial subsystem serves as a bridge between the other two subsystems. The managerial subsystem controls and directs the other subsystems in the organization. It is within this subsystem that the subject matter of this book is practiced as a blend of science and art.

Organizational Learning

The idea of organizational learning, and its companion topic of knowledge management discussed in Chapter 8, dates back to the 1980s.[18] It took Peter Senge's 1990 best-seller, *The Fifth Discipline*, to popularize this extension of open-system thinking.[19] Many management writers and consultants then jumped on the bandwagon and confusion prevailed.

Fortunately, Harvard's David A. Garvin did a good job of sorting things out and clarifying the concept. According to Garvin, a learning organization is one that can create, acquire, and transfer knowledge, and can then adapt its behavior accordingly.[20] One could view Garvin and others as having extended the open-system model of organizations by putting a human head on the biological (open-system) model. Garvin believes that organizational learning, just like human learning, involves three stages (see Figure 9.3): (1) cognition (learning new concepts), (2) behavior (developing new skills and abilities), and (3) performance (actually getting something done). All three stages are necessary to erase the infamous gap between theory and practice.

Also illustrated in Figure 9.3 are five organizational skills that Garvin claims are needed to turn new ideas into improved organizational performance. Each skill is important if today's organizations are to *thrive*, not just survive.

- *Solving problems.* Problems, as discussed in Chapter 8, are the gap between actual and desired situations. Everyone in the organization needs to be skilled at identifying problems and helping to creatively solve them.
- *Experimenting.* W. Edwards Deming's plan-do-check-act (PDCA) cycle, covered in Chapter 16, is an excellent tool for learning through systematic experimentation.
- *Learning from organizational experience and history.* Role models and oft-told stories of success and failure embedded in the organization's culture teach vital lessons. However, there are times when an organization has to

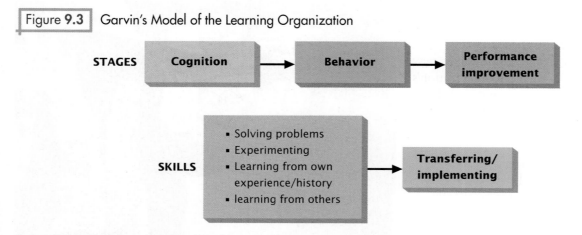

Figure **9.3**   Garvin's Model of the Learning Organization

Source: Adapted from discussion in David A. Garvin, "Building a Learning Organization," *Harvard Business Review,* 71 (July–August 1993): 78–91; and David A. Garvin, Amy C. Edmondson, and Francesca Gino, "Is Yours a Learning Organization?" *Harvard Business Review,* 86 (March 2008): 109–116.

learning organization an organization skilled at creating, acquiring, and transferring knowledge to improve performance "unlearn" some of its practices in order to become innovative and build new competencies.[21]

- *Learning from others*. Two prime sources of valuable knowledge in this regard are benchmarking (learning best practices from market leaders), also discussed in Chapter 16, and customer input and feedback.
- *Transferring and implementing*. All the other skills are for naught if actions are not taken to make the organization perform better. Training (Chapter 10) and effective communication (Chapter 11) are key bridges spanning the gap between ideas and skills and superior organizational performance.

The concept of learning organizations is a valuable addition to managers' toolkits because it helps them deal more effectively with today's only certainty—*change*.[22]

Organizational Effectiveness

The practice of management, as defined in Chapter 1, challenges managers to use organizational resources effectively and efficiently. Effectiveness is a measure of whether organizational objectives are accomplished. In contrast, efficiency is the relationship between outputs and inputs. In an era of diminishing resources and increasing concern about civil rights, society is reluctant to label "effective" any organization that wastes scarce resources or tramples on civil rights. Management's definition of organizational effectiveness therefore needs to be refined.

NO SILVER BULLET. According to one management scholar, there is not a single approach to evaluating effectiveness that works in all situations.[23] More and more, the effectiveness criteria for modern organizations are being prescribed by society in the form of explicit expectations, regulations, and laws. In the private sector, profitability is no longer the sole criterion of effectiveness.[24] Winslow Buxton, CEO of Pentair, Inc., a Minnesota manufacturing company with $2 billion in annual revenue and 10,000 employees, has noted that nearly everyone defines success in terms of growth. But that "growth" means different things to different stakeholders, including employees, managers, customers, investors, and financial analysts.[25]

Moreover, today's managers are caught up in an enormous web of laws and regulations covering employment practices, working conditions, job safety, pensions, product safety, pollution, and competitive practices. To be truly effective, today's productive organizations need to strike a generally acceptable balance between organizational and societal goals. Direct conflicts, such as higher wages for employees versus lower prices for customers, are inevitable. Therefore, the process of determining the proper weighting of organizational effectiveness criteria is an endless one that requires frequent review and updating.[26] (See Green Management.)

A TIME DIMENSION. To build a workable definition of organizational effectiveness, we shall introduce a time dimension. As indicated in Figure 9.4, the organization needs to be effective in the near, intermediate, and distant future. Consequently, organizational effectiveness can be defined as meeting organizational objectives and prevailing societal expectations in the near future, adapting and developing in the intermediate future, and surviving into the distant future.[27]

Most people think only of the near future. It is in the near future that the organization has to produce goods or render services, use resources efficiently, and satisfy both insiders and outsiders with its activity. But this is just the beginning, not the end. To grow and be effective (and ultimately survive), an organization must adapt to new environmental demands and must mature and learn in the intermediate future (two to four years).

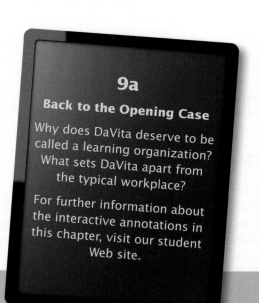

9a
Back to the Opening Case

Why does DaVita deserve to be called a learning organization? What sets DaVita apart from the typical workplace?

For further information about the interactive annotations in this chapter, visit our student Web site.

organizational effectiveness being effective, efficient, and satisfying today; adapting and developing in the intermediate future; and surviving in the long term

Green Management: Toward Sustainability

Ecomagination: General Electric's Big Bet on Green Technology Is Paying Off

GE . . . is pumping $10 billion into the project's R&D [research and development] over the next 5 years—effectively doubling its investment from the past 5 years. The reason is simple: ecomagination is a cash cow, generating $70 billion in revenue since its inception in 2005.

The ecomagination technologies span multiple sectors . . . and have a pervasive theme of increased efficiency, the surest way to find cost-effective sustainable energy solutions.

So far, ecomagination has spawned everything from low-energy digital mammography machines and aircraft engines to gas turbines and nuclear plants. There's plenty more on the way, including a massive battery plant in New York, a $2 billion wind project in Oregon, and a series of high-end energy-efficient front-load washers and dryers set to be manufactured in Kentucky. And we can't forget GE's ambitious plan to integrate appliances (i.e., hot water heaters, microwaves, and oven ranges) with smart grid technology.

For Discussion: Which of the organizational effectiveness criteria in Figure 9.4 are evident in this situation? Explain.

Source: Excerpted from Ariel Schwartz, "GE Boosts Ecomagination Initiative with an Extra $10 Billion," FastCompany.com, June 25, 2010, *www.fastcompany.com/1664033/ge-boosts-ecomagination-initiative-with-an-extra-10-billion*. Accessed June 27, 2010.

| Figure **9.4** | The Time Dimension of Organizational Effectiveness |

Source: Adapted from James L. Gibson, John M. Ivancevich, and James H. Donnelly Jr., *Organizations: Behavior, Structure, Processes,* 5th ed. (Homewood, Ill.: Richard D. Irwin, Inc.), p. 37. © 1991.

CONTINGENCY DESIGN

Recall from our discussion in Chapter 2 that contingency thinking amounts to situational thinking. Specifically, the contingency approach to organizing involves taking special steps to make sure the organization fits the demands of the situation. In direct contrast to traditional thinking, contingency design is based on the assumption that there is no single best way to structure an organization. **Contingency design** is the process of determining the degree of environmental uncertainty and adapting the organization and its subunits to the situation. This does not mean that all contingency organizations necessarily differ

contingency design fitting the organization to its environment

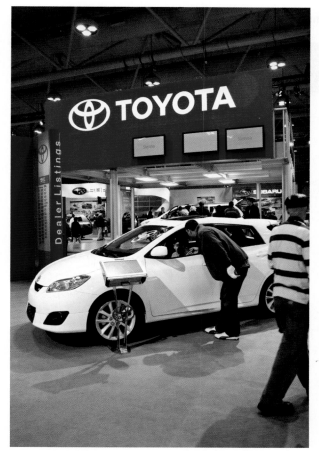

Toyota's organizational effectiveness, which had always been highly respected, was widely criticized when the company issued three back-to-back recalls in 2009 affecting millions of vehicles. The car manufacturer lost more than sales in the aftermath—it had to repair its credibility.

from each other. Instead, it means that managers who take a contingency approach select from a number of standard design alternatives to create the most situationally effective organization possible. Contingency managers typically start with the same basic collection of design alternatives but end up with unique combinations of them as dictated by the demands of their situations.

The contingency approach to designing organizations boils down to two questions: (1) How much environmental uncertainty is there? (See Table 9.1 for a handy way to answer this question.) (2) What combination of structural characteristics is most appropriate? Let us set the stage by examining a landmark contingency model to establish the validity of the contingency approach.

The Burns and Stalker Model

Tom Burns and G. M. Stalker, both British behavioral scientists, proposed a useful typology for categorizing organizations by structural design.[28] They distinguished between mechanistic and organic organizations. **Mechanistic organizations** tend to be rigid in design and have strong bureaucratic qualities. In contrast, **organic organizations** tend to be quite flexible in structure and adaptive to change. Actually, these two organizational types are the extreme ends of a single continuum. Pure types are difficult to find, but it is fairly easy to check off the characteristics listed in Table 9.2 to determine whether a particular

| Table 9.1 | Determining Degree of Environmental Uncertainty |

	LOW	MODERATE	HIGH
1. How strong are social, political, and economic pressures on the organization?	Minimal	Moderate	Intense
2. How frequent are technological breakthroughs in the industry?	Infrequent	Occasional	Frequent
3. How reliable are resources and supplies?	Reliable	Occasional, predictable shortages	Unreliable
4. How stable is the demand for the organization's product or service?	Highly stable	Moderately stable	Unstable

mechanistic organizations rigid bureaucracies | *organic organizations:* flexible, adaptive organization structures

| Table 9.2 | Mechanistic Versus Organic Organizations |

CHARACTERISTIC	MECHANISTIC ORGANIZATIONS	ORGANIC ORGANIZATIONS
1. Task definition for individual contributors	Narrow and precise	Broad and general
2. Relationship between individual contribution and organization purpose	Vague	Clear
3. Task flexibility	Low	High
4. Definition of rights, obligations, and techniques	Clear	Vague
5. Reliance on hierarchical control	High	Low (reliance on self-control)
6. Primary direction of communication	Vertical (top to bottom)	Lateral (between peers)
7. Reliance on instructions and decisions from superior	High	Low (superior offers information and advice)
8. Emphasis on loyalty and obedience	High	Low
9. Type of knowledge required	Narrow, technical, and task-specific	Broad and professional

Source: Adapted from Tom Burns and G. M. Stalker, *The Management of Innovation* (London: Tavistock, 1961), pp. 119–125. Reprinted by permission.

organization (or subunit) is relatively mechanistic or relatively organic. It is notable that a field study found distinctly different communication patterns in mechanistic and organic organizations. Communication tended to be the formal command-and-control type in the mechanistic factory and to be participative in the organic factory.[29]

TELLING THE DIFFERENCE. Here is a quick test of how well you understand the distinction between mechanistic and organic organizations. Read the following description of how an Emeryville, California, company maximizes the security of its clients' Web site data, and then attach a mechanistic or organic label. Before landing a position as a customer support specialist at the SiteROCK command center, employees must master the standard operating procedures found in several three-inch-thick binders. Then,

when each employee starts the workday, he or she must sort through an hour and a half of paperwork in order to stay on top of the latest developments.[30]

If you said mechanistic, you're right. Using Table 9.2 as a guide, we see evidence of precise task definition, low task flexibility, clear definition of techniques, and high emphasis on obedience. Indeed, SiteROCK is staffed mostly by former military personnel and is run with military precision.

An organic organization would have basically the opposite characteristics. An extreme example is The Sky Factory, a Fairfield, Iowa, maker of backlit sea and sky displays used to decorate hotels and restaurants. According to founder Bill Witherspoon, the Sky Factory has no managers. Every week a different person facilitates the general meeting, and anyone can assume the leadership position in any given situation. As Witherspoon explains, "People who see a job do the job because they don't feel constrained."[31] There are not even any "employees" at The Sky Factory, so to speak, because everyone is an owner.

SITUATIONAL APPROPRIATENESS. Burns and Stalker's research uncovered distinct organization-environment patterns indicating the relative appropriateness of both mechanistic and organic organizations. It revealed that *successful organizations in relatively stable and certain environments tended to be mechanistic.* Conversely, Burns and Stalker also discovered that *relatively organic organizations tended to be the successful ones when the environment was unstable and uncertain.*

For practical application, this means that mechanistic design is appropriate for environmental stability, and organic design is appropriate for high environmental uncertainty. Today, the trend necessarily is toward more organic organizations because uncertainty is the rule. *Management Review* summed up the situation this way: Because of shorter life cycles, reorganizations, initiatives, and even product launches occur in months, not years. Both globalization and technology have increased the complexities of change, forcing companies to be more flexible and adaptive.[32] This is not to say that organic is good and mechanistic is bad. Mechanistic organizations have their place. SiteROCK's mechanistic structure, for example, makes it highly resistant to human error, technical failures, and attacks by hackers and terrorists.

Basic Departmentalization Formats

Aside from the hierarchical chain of command, one of the most common ways to coordinate an organization is departmentalization. It is through **departmentalization** that related jobs, activities, or processes are grouped into major organizational subunits. For example, all jobs involving staffing activities such as recruitment, hiring, and training are often grouped into a human resources department. Grouping jobs through the formation of departments, according to management author James D. Thompson, is a cost-effective way to handle coordination.[33] A degree of coordination is achieved through departmentalization because members of the department work on interrelated tasks, are guided by the same departmental rules, and report to the same department head. It is important to note that although the term *departmentalization* is used here, it does not always literally apply; managers commonly use labels such as *division*, *group*, or *unit* in large organizations.

Five basic types of departmentalization are functional departments, product-service departments, geographic location departments, customer classification departments, and work flow process departments.[34]

FUNCTIONAL DEPARTMENTS. Functional departments categorize jobs according to the activity performed. Among profit-making businesses, variations of the functional production-finance-marketing arrangement in Figure 9.5A are the most common forms of departmentalization. Functional departmentalization is popular because it permits those with similar technical expertise to work in a coordinated subunit. Of course, functional departmentalization is not restricted to profit-making businesses. Functional departments in a nonprofit hospital might be administration, nursing, housekeeping, food service, laboratory and x-ray, admission and records, and accounting and billing.

Restaurants tend to be mechanistic organizations because they have to meet strict cleanliness and public health standards.

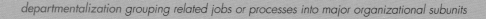

departmentalization grouping related jobs or processes into major organizational subunits

A negative aspect of functional departmentalization is that it creates "technical ghettos," in which local departmental concerns and loyalties tend to override strategic organizational concerns. For example, when Bruce L. Claflin was named head of IBM's newly formed mobile computing division, he recalls that "gridlock" among the marketing, design, and manufacturing departments brought the development of the Think-Pad 700C to a standstill.[35] Situations like this prompted a major reorganization at IBM and the eventual sale of its PC unit to a Chinese company.[36]

PRODUCT-SERVICE DEPARTMENTS. Because functional departmentalization has been criticized for encouraging specialization at the expense of coordination, a somewhat more organic alternative has evolved. It is called product-service departmentalization because a product (or service), rather than a functional category of work, is the unifying theme. As diagrammed in Figure 9.5B, the product-service approach permits each of, say, two products to be managed as semiautonomous businesses. Organizations rendering a service instead of turning out a tangible product might find it advantageous to organize around service categories. In reality, however, many of today's companies turn out *bundles* of products and services for customers. General Electric, for example, reorganized around these major product/service categories: energy (power

generation equipment), transportation (aircraft engines and rail locomotives), NBC-Universal (television and films), health care (diagnostic equipment), and consumer and industrial products and services.[37] Ideally, those working in this sort of product-service structure have a broad "business" orientation rather than a narrow functional perspective. As Figure 9.5B shows, it is the general manager's job to ensure that these mini-businesses work in a complementary fashion, rather than competing with one another.[38]

GEOGRAPHIC LOCATION DEPARTMENTS. Sometimes, as in the case of organizations with nationwide or worldwide markets, geography dictates structural format (see Figure 9.5C). Geographic dispersion of resources (for example, mining companies), facilities (for example, railroads), or customers (for example, chain supermarkets) may encourage the use of a geographic format to put administrators "closer to the action." One can imagine that drilling engineers in a Houston-based petroleum firm would be better able to get a job done in Alaska if they actually went there. Similarly, a department-store marketing manager would be in a better position to judge consumer tastes in Florida if working out of a regional office in Orlando rather than out of a home office in Salt Lake City or Toronto.

Long lines of communication among organizational units have traditionally been a limiting factor with geographically dispersed operations. But Internet-age telecommunications technology has created some interesting regional advantages. A case in point is Omaha, Nebraska. Its central location, along with the absence of a distinct regional accent among Nebraskans, has made Omaha the 1–800 capital of the country. Every major hotel chain and most of the big telemarketers have telephone service centers in Omaha.[39]

Global competition is pressuring managers to organize along geographic lines. This structure allows multinational companies to serve local markets better.

Figure 9.5 Alternative Departmentalization Formats

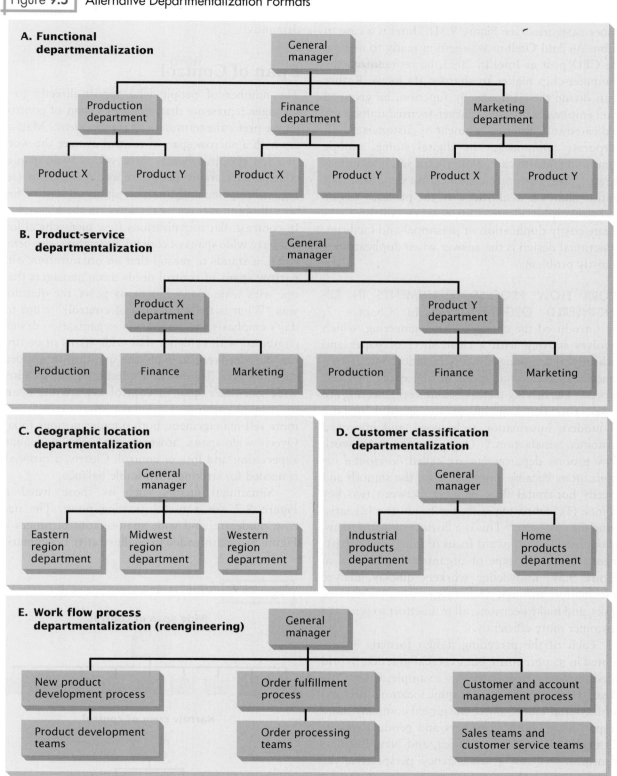

CUSTOMER CLASSIFICATION DEPARTMENTS. A fourth structural format centers on various customer categories (see Figure 9.5D). Intel is a case in point. As Paul Otellini was getting ready to assume the CEO post at Intel in 2005, he reorganized the computer-chip maker to sharpen its focus. Rather than divide the company by function, he grouped Intel employees into five market-focused units, each dedicated to a different segment of customer needs: corporate computing, the digital home, mobile computing, health care, and PCs for small manufacturers.[40] Yet, customer classification departmentalization shares a weakness with the product-service and geographic location approaches: all three can create costly duplication of personnel and facilities. Functional design is the answer when duplication is a costly problem.

WORK FLOW PROCESS DEPARTMENTS IN REENGINEERED ORGANIZATIONS. In Chapter 7, we introduced the concept of reengineering, which involves starting with a clean sheet of paper and radically redesigning the organization into cross-functional teams that speed up the entire business process. The driving factors behind reengineering are lower costs, better quality, greater speed, better use of modern information technology, and improved customer satisfaction.[41] Organizations with work flow process departments are called *horizontal organizations* because emphasis is on the smooth and speedy horizontal flow of work between two key points: (1) identifying customer needs and (2) satisfying the customer.[42] This is a distinct *outward* focus, as opposed to the inward focus of functional departments. Inside the type of organization depicted in Figure 9.5E, knowledge workers quickly analyze information through technology, combine related tasks, and make decisions, all in an effort to serve the customer more efficiently.[43]

Each of the preceding design formats is presented in its pure form, but in actual practice, hybrid versions occur frequently. For example, Coca-Cola created a mix of three geographic location units and a functional unit to make the global company more responsive to both customers and product trends: "Americas, Asia, Europe/Africa, and New Business Ventures."[44] From a contingency perspective, the five departmentalization formats are useful starting points rather than final blueprints for organizers.

Numerous structural variations show how the basic formats can be adapted to meet situational demands.

Span of Control

The number of people who report directly to a manager represents that manager's span of control. (Some prefer the term *span of management*.) Managers with a narrow span of control oversee the work of a few people, whereas those with a wide span of control have many people reporting to them (see Figure 9.6). Generally, narrow spans of control foster tall organizations (many levels in the hierarchy). In contrast, flat organizations (few hierarchical levels) have wide spans of control. Everything else being equal, it stands to reason that an organization with narrow spans of control needs more managers than one with wide spans. For many years, the question was "What is the ideal span of control?"[45] But today's emphasis on contingency organization design, combined with evidence that wide spans of control can be effective, has made the question of an ideal span obsolete. The relevant question today is "How wide *can* one's span of control be?" Wider spans of control mean less administrative expense and more self-management, both popular notions today. Overly wide spans, however, can mean inadequate supervision and loss of control. Clearly, a rationale is needed for striking a workable balance.

Situational factors such as those listed in Figure 9.7 are a useful starting point. The narrow, moderate, and wide span-of-control ranges in Figure 9.7 are intended to be illustrative benchmarks

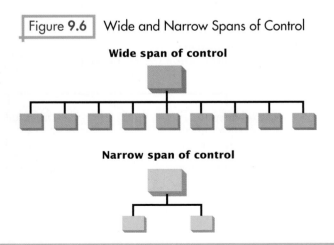

Figure 9.6 Wide and Narrow Spans of Control

span of control: number of people who report directly to a given manager

| Figure **9.7** | Situational Determinants of Span of Control |

	Wide span of control appropriate (10 or more)	Moderate span of control appropriate (5 to 9)	Narrow span of control appropriate (2 to 4)
1. Similarity of work performed by subordinates	Identical		Distinctly different
2. Dispersion of subordinates	Same work area		Geographically dispersed
3. Complexity of work performed by subordinates	Simple and repetitive		Highly complex and varied
4. Direction and control required by subordinates	Little and/or infrequent		Intensive and/or constant
5. Time spent coordinating with other managers	Little		A great deal
6. Time required for planning	Little		A great deal

rather than rigid limits. Each organization must do its own on-the-job experimentation. At Federal Express, for example, the span of control varies with different areas of the company. Departments that employ many people doing the same job or very similar jobs—such as customer service agents, handlers/sorters, and couriers—usually have a span of control of 15 to 20 employees per manager. Groups performing multiple tasks, or tasks that require only a few people, are more likely to have spans of control of five or fewer.[46] No ideal span of control exists for all kinds of work.

Centralization and Decentralization

Where are the important decisions made in an organization? Are they made strictly by top management or by middle- and lower-level managers? These questions are at the heart of the decentralization design alternative. Centralization is at one end of a continuum, and at the other end is decentralization.

9b
Wider Is Better, for the Head of Cisco Systems

Says John Chambers, CEO of Cisco Systems Inc.: "I learned a long time ago that a team will always defeat an individual. And if you have a team of superstars, then you have a chance to create a dynasty." That's one reason why Chambers has two to three times as many people reporting to him as does the average executive in his company: It forces him to empower those directly under him with greater autonomy, because he can't possibly keep up with every detail of their work.

QUESTION: What are the keys to making Chambers's wide span of control work?

Source: John Byrne, "The Global Corporation Becomes the Leaderless Corporation," *Business Week* (August 30, 1999): 90.

| Figure 9.8 | Factors in Relative Centralization/Decentralization |

	Highly centralized organization	Highly decentralized organization
How many decisions are made at lower levels in the hierarchy?	Very few, if any	Many or most
How important are the decisions that are made at lower levels (i.e., do they impact organizational success or dollar values)?	Not very important	Very important
How many different functions (e.g., production, marketing, finance, human resources) rely on lower-level decision making?	Very few, if any	All or most
How much does top management monitor or check up on lower-level decision making?	A great deal	Very little or not at all

Centralization is defined as the relative retention of decision-making authority by top management. Nearly all decision-making authority is retained by top management in highly centralized organizations. In contrast, decentralization is the granting of decision-making authority by management to lower-level employees. Decentralization increases as the degree, importance, and range of lower-level decision making *increase* and the amount of checking up by top management *decreases* (see Figure 9.8).

When we speak of centralization or decentralization, we are describing a comparative degree, not an absolute. The challenge for managers, as one management consultant observed, is to strike a workable balance between two extremes—centralization, which offers cost-saving shared resources, and decentralization, which offers improved market responsiveness. Successful managers will evaluate and choose the optimal organizational solution on a case-by-case basis, even if it creates a somewhat "messy mixture of decentralized units sharing cost-effective centralized resources."[47]

Support for greater decentralization in the corporate world has come and gone over the years in faddish waves. Today, the call is for the type of balance just discussed. The case against extreme decentralization can be summed up in three words: *lack of control*. Consider the case of health care giant Johnson & Johnson (J&J) with over 250 operating units, each acting as a stand-alone profit center.[48] Recent costly and embarrassing product recalls stemming from quality problems suggest J&J has become too decentralized and out of control.[49] Centralization of certain strategically vital functions may be appropriate, as in the case of product research and development at Apple. CEO Steve Jobs reviews all new product ideas and suggestions for new features on existing products, and he's quick to turn down most of them.[50] Again, the contingency approach dictates which end of the centralization-decentralization continuum needs to be emphasized throughout the organization.[51]

EFFECTIVE DELEGATION

Delegation is an important common denominator that runs through virtually all relatively organic design alternatives. It is vital to successful decentralization. Formally defined, delegation is the process of assigning various degrees of decision-making

centralization the retention of decision-making authority by top management | decentralization management's sharing of decision-making authority with lower-level employees | delegation assigning various degrees of decision-making authority to lower-level employees

Figure 9.9 The Delegation Continuum

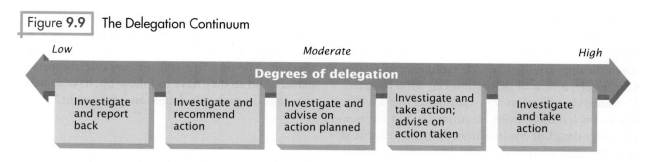

Low   Moderate   High

Degrees of delegation

| Investigate and report back | Investigate and recommend action | Investigate and advise on action planned | Investigate and take action; advise on action taken | Investigate and take action |

authority to lower-level employees.[52] As this definition implies, delegation is not an all-or-nothing proposition. There are at least five different degrees of delegation[53] (see Figure 9.9).

A word of caution about delegation is necessary, because there is one thing it does *not* include. Former President Harry Truman is said to have had a little sign on his White House desk that read, "The Buck Stops Here!"[54] Managers who delegate should keep this idea in mind because, although authority may be passed along to people at lower levels, ultimate responsibility cannot be passed along. Thus delegation is the sharing of authority, not the abdication of responsibility. Chrysler's former CEO Lee Iacocca admittedly fell victim to this particular lapse by turning his attention to finance, marketing, and sales issues, while ignoring the planning of new models. He says, "If I made one mistake, it was delegating all the product development and not going to one single meeting."[55] Iacocca corrected this mistake prior to his retirement, and customers liked Chrysler's bold new designs.

The Advantages of Delegation

Managers stand to gain a great deal by adopting the habit of delegating. By passing along well-defined tasks to lower-level people, managers can free more of their time for important chores such as planning and motivating. Regarding the question of exactly *what* should be delegated, Intel's former chairman, Andy Grove, suggests

delegating the activities you know best—and thus can easily monitor from a distance—and keeping the rest for yourself so you can remain heavily involved.[56] But Grove cautions that delegators who follow his advice will experience some psychological discomfort because they will quite naturally want to continue doing what they know best.

In addition to freeing valuable managerial time,[57] delegation is also a helpful management

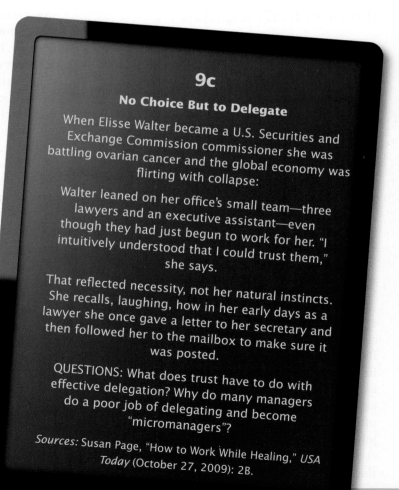

9c
No Choice But to Delegate

When Elisse Walter became a U.S. Securities and Exchange Commission commissioner she was battling ovarian cancer and the global economy was flirting with collapse:

Walter leaned on her office's small team—three lawyers and an executive assistant—even though they had just begun to work for her. "I intuitively understood that I could trust them," she says.

That reflected necessity, not her natural instincts. She recalls, laughing, how in her early days as a lawyer she once gave a letter to her secretary and then followed her to the mailbox to make sure it was posted.

QUESTIONS: What does trust have to do with effective delegation? Why do many managers do a poor job of delegating and become "micromanagers"?

Sources: Susan Page, "How to Work While Healing," *USA Today* (October 27, 2009): 2B.

training and development tool. Moreover, lower-level managers who desire more challenge generally become more committed and satisfied when they are given the opportunity to tackle significant problems. Conversely, a lack of delegation can stifle initiative. Consider the situation of a California builder who insists on handling every negotiation and overseeing every detail of construction. A former executive with the man's firm points out that turnover is high because bright and talented employees felt disempowered and useless.[58]

Perfectionist managers who avoid delegation can become overwhelmed by minute details. Omar Hamoui, who founded and then sold the mobile ad network company AdMob to Google for $750 million, learned this lesson from the school of hard knocks. Now he wishes he had learned to stop micromanaging and start trusting his employees sooner.[59]

Barriers to Delegation

There are several reasons why managers generally do not delegate as much as they should:

- Belief in the fallacy expressed in the advice "If you want it done right, do it yourself"
- Lack of confidence and trust in lower-level employees
- Low self-confidence
- Fear of being called lazy
- Vague job definition
- Fear of competition from those below
- Reluctance to take the risks involved in depending on others
- Lack of controls that provide early warning of problems with delegated duties
- Poor example set by bosses who do not delegate[60]

Managers can go a long way toward effective delegation by recognizing and correcting these tendencies both in themselves and in their fellow managers. Because successful delegation is habit-forming, the first step usually is the hardest. Properly trained and motivated people who know how to take initiative in challenging situations often reward a delegator's trust with a job well done.[61]

Once managers have developed the habit of delegating, they need to remember this wise advice from Peter Drucker: "Delegation . . . requires that delegators follow up. They rarely do—they think they have delegated, and that's it. But they are still accountable for performance. And so they have to follow up, have to make sure that the task gets done—and done right."[62]

THE CHANGING SHAPE OF ORGANIZATIONS

Management scholars have been predicting the death of traditional pyramid-shaped bureaucracies for over 40 years.[63] Initial changes were slow in coming and barely noticeable. Observers tended to dismiss the predictions as naïve and exaggerated. However, the pace and degree of change have picked up dramatically since the 1980s. All of the social, political-legal, economic, and technological changes discussed in Chapter 3 threaten to make traditional organizations obsolete. Why? Because they are too slow, unresponsive, uncreative, costly, and hard to manage. It is clear today that no less than a reorganization revolution is under way. Traditional pyramid organizations, though still very much in evidence, are being questioned as never before. General Electric's legendary CEO Jack Welch notes that some degree of control is still needed, but that today's organizations need more freedom than ever.[64]

Consequently, to be prepared for tomorrow's workplace, we need to take a look at how organizations are evolving.[65] Figure 9.10 illustrates three different ways in which the traditional pyramid organization is being reshaped. They are the hourglass organization, the cluster organization, and the virtual organization. To varying extents, these new

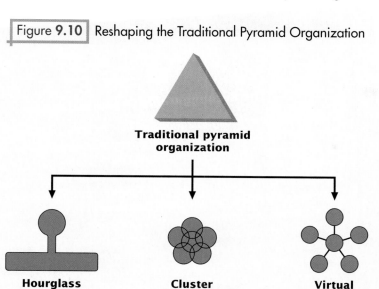

| Figure **9.10** | Reshaping the Traditional Pyramid Organization

Traditional pyramid organization

Hourglass organization

Cluster organization

Virtual organization

Hourglass Organizations

The hourglass organization consists of three layers, with the middle layer distinctly pinched. A strategic elite is responsible for formulating a vision for the organization and making sure it becomes reality. A significantly shrunken middle-management layer carries out a coordinating function for diverse lower-level activities. Thanks to computer networks that flash information directly from the factory floor or retail outlet to the executive suite and back again, fewer middle managers are needed to simply serve as conduits for warmed-over information. Also unlike traditional middle managers, hourglass middle managers are generalists rather than narrow specialists. They are comfortable dealing with complex cross-functional problems. A given middle manager might deal with an accounting problem one day, a product design issue the next, and a marketing dilemma the next—all within cross-functional team settings.

At the bottom of the hourglass is a broad layer of technical specialists who act as their own supervisors much of the time. Consequently, the distinction between supervisors and rank-and-file personnel is blurred. Employees at this operating level complain about a very real lack of promotion opportunities. Management tries to keep them motivated with challenging work assignments, lateral transfers, skill-training opportunities, and pay-for-performance schemes. Union organizers attempt to exploit complaints about employees "having to act like managers, but not being paid like managers."

Cluster Organizations

Another new configuration shown in Figure 9.10 is the cluster organization. This label is appropriate because teams are the primary structural unit.[69] At Oticon Inc., for example, self-directed work teams form to work on a project and then disband when the project is completed. The company's 1,500 employees, located in Denmark and the United States, are usually organized into about 100 different project teams, and most employees are working on more than one project team at a time.[70]

configurations embody three current organizational trends:

- *Fewer layers.* A recent study of the U.S. military found that there were about 30 layers of hierarchy between Robert Gates, former Secretary of Defense under Barack Obama, and the average line officer. Gates described the system as having "the fine motor skills of a dinosaur."[66]

  In the corporate world, meanwhile, CEO Andrea Jung streamlined Avon's hierarchy by 7 layers—from 15 layers down to 8—to enable the beauty products firm to respond faster to quickly changing consumer tastes.[67]
- *Greater emphasis on teams.*
- *Smallness within bigness.* When *Fortune* magazine asked Google's co-founder Larry Page how Google could retain its culture as it grows, Page explained the importance of working in groups of two hundred or less. Page describes these groups as "a natural size for human organizations."[68]

The new configurations may overlap, as when an hourglass organization relies extensively on teams. The new structures have important implications for both the practice of management and the quality of work life. Let us examine them and take an imaginary peek into the not-too-distant future of work organizations.

Imagining ourselves working in a cluster organization, we see multiskilled people moving from team to team as projects dictate. Pay for knowledge is a common practice. Motivation seems to be high, but some complain about a lack of job security because things are constantly changing. Stress levels rise when the pace of change quickens. Special training efforts, involving teambuilding exercises, are aimed at enhancing everyone's communication and group involvement skills.[71]

Virtual Organizations

From the time of the Industrial Revolution until the Internet age, the norm was to build an organization capable of designing, producing, and marketing products. Bigger was assumed to be better. And this approach worked as long as large batches of look-alike products were acceptable to consumers. But then along came the Internet, e-business, and mass customization. *Speed*—in the form of faster market research, faster product development, faster production, and faster delivery— became more important than organizational size. Meanwhile, global competition kept a lid on prices. Suddenly, consumers realized they could get exactly what they wanted, at a good price, and fast. Many lumbering organizational giants of the past were not up to the task.

Enter virtual organizations, flexible networks of value-adding subcontractors, linked by the Internet and modern telecommunications technology.[72] Probably the most extreme example of a virtual organization that we can find today is Linux. What started in 1991 as Linus Torvalds's student project at Finland's University of Helsinki has evolved into a huge global enterprise with a product competing head-to-head with Microsoft's Windows operating system: It is a cooperative venture with no headquarters or CEO. Workers—some employed at any of two dozen companies and others employed as

9d
The Reconfigurable Organization

The reconfigurable organization consists of both stable portions and dynamic portions, and it configures and reconfigures itself around opportunities. There are two main stable parts of the organization. The first stable part is the basic structure, and the second stable part is the set of common business practices. As people move from one team assignment to another, the processes are common and stay the same. The financial systems, the new product development process, the customer relationship process, the performance management process, and so on are the same everywhere. Certainly, there are process "owners" who constantly try to improve them, but business processes are stable and common throughout the organization.

The variable parts of the organization are the teams that form and reform, and the management decision-making groups that allocate resources and determine priorities. Teams are formed by gathering people from functional areas across the company.

QUESTIONS: Does this describe a relatively mechanistic or organic organization? Explain. Why is this type of organization necessary in today's faster-paced world? What type of employees will thrive in reconfigurable organizations?

Source: Jay R. Galbraith, "The Multi-Dimensional and Reconfigurable Organization," *Organizational Dynamics*, 39 (April–June 2010): 119–120.

individual contractors or volunteers—collaborate to improve Linux software. The tech companies pay programmers and generate revenue through sales and service.[73] Torvalds studiously monitors the quality of changes to his open-source software from his home in Oregon via the Internet. Aside from the Torvalds legacy, what holds this far-ranging virtual organization together is a common passion for creating world-class software.

Other virtual organizations are taking shape as large companies strive to cut costs by outsourcing functions ranging from manufacturing and shipping to payroll and accounting.

virtual organizations Internet-linked networks of value-adding subcontractors

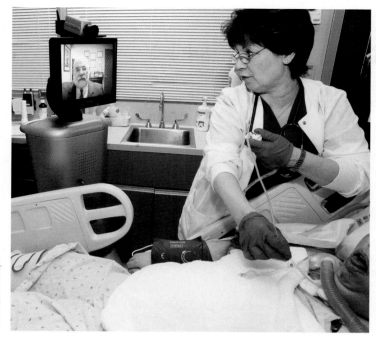

Sometimes it's useful to have an expert peering over your shoulder while you work. Thanks to modern technology, nurse Kathy Trimble attends to an intensive care patient at the Detroit Medical Center with the "virtual" guidance of Harper University Hospital's Dr. Joseph Bander via an RP-6 robot.

From a personal perspective, life in virtual organizations is *hectic*. Everything moves at Internet speed. Change and learning are constant. Cross-functional teams are the norm, and job reassignments are frequent. Project specialists rarely see a single project to completion because they are whisked off to other projects. Unavoidable by-products of constant change are stress and burnout. Unexpectedly, the need for face-to-face contact increases as geographically dispersed team members communicate via e-mail, instant messaging, groupware, and voice mail.[74] Only face-to-face interaction, both on and off the job, can build the rapport and trust necessary to get something done quickly with people you rarely see. The growing gap between information haves and have-nots produces resentment and alienation among low-paid workers employed by factory, data-processing, and shipping subcontractors.

ORGANIZATIONAL CULTURES

The notion of organizational culture is rooted in cultural anthropology.[75] Organizational culture is the collection of shared (stated or implied) beliefs, values, rituals, stories, myths, and specialized language that fosters a feeling of community among

organization members.[76] (See Valuing Diversity.) Culture, although based largely on taken-for-granted or "invisible" factors, exerts a potent influence on behavior. For example, a six-year study of more than 900 newly hired college graduates found significantly lower turnover among those who joined public accounting firms with cultures emphasizing respect for people and teamwork. New hires working for accounting firms whose cultures emphasized detail, stability, and innovation tended to quit 14 months sooner than their counterparts in the more people-friendly organizations. According to the researcher's estimate, the companies with people-friendly cultures saved $6 million in human resource expenses because of lower turnover rates.[77]

Unfortunately, there is a dark side to organizational cultures as well. Dysfunctional cultures anchored to irresponsible values and supportive of (or blind to) unethical conduct have been blamed for the collapse of Enron, Arthur Andersen, and WorldCom and for the crash of NASA's space shuttle *Columbia* that took the lives of its seven crew members.[78] The problem of "groupthink," discussed in Chapter 13, is associated with cultural misdirection. Today's managers need to understand the subtle yet powerful influence of organizational culture and appropriately manage it. For example, Alan R. Mulally faced this difficult situation when he was brought in from Boeing to be Ford's CEO. He immediately recognized that saving Ford would require more than just cutting expenses and developing new products; he needed to address "the most fundamental problem of all: Ford's dysfunctional, often defeatist culture."[79]

Some call organizational (or corporate) culture the "social glue" that binds an organization's members together. Accordingly, this final section binds together all we have said about organizations in this chapter. Without an appreciation for the cultural aspect, an organization is just a meaningless collection of charts, people, and job assignments. An

organizational culture shared values, beliefs, and language that create a common identity and sense of community

VALUING DIVERSITY

Military Veterans Energize Southern Company's Corporate Culture

Atlanta-based utility Southern Company has seen an increase in the hiring of military veterans over the past few years. In 2009, 24% of the external new hires were military veterans. "We are reaping the benefits of recent initiatives," says Martha Johnson, senior vice president of human resources and chief diversity officer, noting that the 26,000-employee company has initiated a new military recruiting and branding campaign, added a dedicated military recruiter, created a web site dedicated to military recruiting, and continues to offer benefits for reservists and their families when employees are called to active duty.

Southern Company finds that its corporate culture is a particularly good fit for those exiting the military. Brian Reed, a 42-year-old who spent 21 and a half years in the Navy, found echoes of its core values of "Honor, Courage, Commitment" in Southern Company's principles—"Unquestioned Trust, Superior Performance, and Total Commitment."

For Discussion: What characteristics and skills would you generally expect military veterans to bring to the job? Any potential negatives?

Source: Excerpted from Lynn Asinof, "On the Hiring Line," Special advertising section, *Fortune* (July 5, 2010): S4.

anthropologist-turned-manager cautions that corporate culture cannot be forced upon employees by top management or consultants. It is a reality of human social organization that must be taken into account during planning.[80]

Characteristics of Organizational Cultures

Given the number of variables involved, organizational cultures can vary widely from one organization to the next. Even so, authorities on the subject have identified six characteristics that most organizational cultures exhibit.[81] Let us briefly examine these common characteristics to gain a fuller understanding of organizational cultures.

1. *Collective.* Organizational cultures are *social* entities. An individual may exert a cultural influence, but it takes collective agreement and action for an organization's culture to assume a life of its own. Organizational cultures are truly synergistic (1 + 1 = 3). Jeffrey R. Immelt, soon after becoming the new head of General Electric, commented that even in a multibusiness company like his, culture is greater than the sum of its parts.[82]

2. *Emotionally charged.* People tend to find their organization's culture a comforting security blanket that enables them to deal with (or sometimes mask) their insecurities and uncertainties. Not surprisingly, people can develop a strong emotional attachment to their cultural security blanket. They will fight to protect it, often refusing to question its basic values. Corporate mergers often get bogged down in culture conflicts.[83]

3. *Historically based.* Shared experiences, over extended periods of time, bind groups of people together. We tend to identify with those who have had similar life experiences. Trust and loyalty, two key components of culture, are earned by consistently demonstrating predictable patterns of words and actions.[84] Traditions are important at companies with strong cultures. A fun example is the tradition of M&M Wednesdays at SAS. The privately held software company near Raleigh, North Carolina, ranked number 1 in *Fortune* magazine's 2010 list of The 100 Best Companies to Work For, goes through more than 22 tons of the little candies each year.[85] Fortunately, SAS headquarters also features an "on-site 66,000-square-foot recreation and fitness center" where employees can work off the M&Ms.[86]

4. *Inherently symbolic.* Actions often speak louder than words. Memorable symbolic actions are the lifeblood of organizational culture.[87] For instance, when Alan G. Lafley took the helm as CEO of personal care products giant Procter & Gamble,

Disney has been so successful at creating a productive and fun organizational culture at its Magic Kingdom theme parks that it conducts training sessions for other companies. Rob Morton (center), a Disney Institute business consultant, instructs a pair of Miami Airport employees at Florida's Walt Disney World.

he moved the top executives out of the Cincinnati headquarters' top floor and began converting that space into a training center for the firm's international cadre of employees.[88] The changes at P&G symbolically told top executives to focus less on power and privilege and more on employee development and open communication.

5. *Dynamic.* In the long term, organizational cultures promote predictability, conformity, and stability. Just beneath this apparently stable surface, however, change boils as people struggle to communicate and comprehend subtle cultural clues.[89] A management trainee who calls the president by her first name after being invited to do so may be embarrassed to learn later that "no one actually calls the president by her first name, even if she asks you to."

6. *Inherently fuzzy.* Ambiguity, contradictions, hidden agendas, and multiple meanings are fundamental to organizational cultures. Just as a photographer cannot capture your typical busy day in a single snapshot, it takes intense and prolonged observation to capture the essence of an organization's culture.

Forms and Consequences of Organizational Cultures

Figure 9.11 lists major forms and consequences of organizational cultures. To the extent that people in an organization share symbols, a common language, stories, and practices, they will tend to experience the four consequences. The degree of sharing and the intensity of the consequences determine whether the organization's culture is strong or weak.

Shared values are a pivotal factor. Unlike instrumental and terminal values, discussed in Chapter 5 as *personal* beliefs, organizational values are *shared* beliefs about what the organization stands for. Shared values, when deeply embedded in the organization's culture, become the equivalent of its DNA. Just as DNA in the cells of our bodies determines who we are, shared values define an organization. For example, Houston-based Bridgeway Funds stood out as a positive role model in the recent mutual fund trading scandal. Founder and president John Montgomery explained why: A solid culture of integrity acts as a safeguard. Montgomery adds that another guideline is answering the question, "What's in the long-term interest of current shareholders?"[90] Not surprisingly, Bridgeway does not own any tobacco stocks, and half the firm's profits are donated to charity.

The Process of Organizational Socialization

Organizational socialization is the process through which outsiders are transformed into accepted insiders.[91] Typically, each time a newcomer "violates" one of the organization's taken-for-granted assumptions, the veteran employees will respond with stories, advice, jokes, or lectures that serve to educate the newcomer about the firm's culture.[92] In effect, the socialization process helps newcomers make sense of their new situation and integrate into the organization's culture.

ORIENTATIONS. *Orientation programs*—in which newly hired employees learn about their organization's history, culture, competitive realities, and compensation and benefits—are an important first step in the socialization process. Too often today,

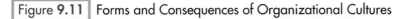

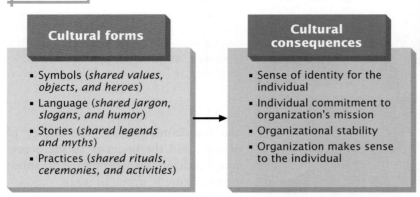

Figure 9.11   Forms and Consequences of Organizational Cultures

Cultural forms

- Symbols (*shared values, objects, and heroes*)
- Language (*shared jargon, slogans, and humor*)
- Stories (*shared legends and myths*)
- Practices (*shared rituals, ceremonies, and activities*)

Cultural consequences

- Sense of identity for the individual
- Individual commitment to organization's mission
- Organizational stability
- Organization makes sense to the individual

9e

Back to the Opening Case

How can the key aspects of DaVita's learning organization be integrated into another organization's culture and be successfully replicated?

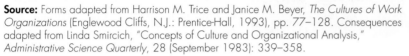

Source: Forms adapted from Harrison M. Trice and Janice M. Beyer, *The Cultures of Work Organizations* (Englewood Cliffs, N.J.: Prentice-Hall, 1993), pp. 77–128. Consequences adapted from Linda Smircich, "Concepts of Culture and Organizational Analysis," *Administrative Science Quarterly*, 28 (September 1983): 339–358.

however, orientations are hurried or nonexistent, and new employees are left to "sink or swim." This is a big mistake, according to workplace research. A study conducted at Corning Glass Works showed that employees who participated in a structured orientation program were far more likely to stay with the company long term than employees with no orientation program.[93] Furthermore, research at Texas Instruments revealed that an orientation enabled new employees to reach full productivity sooner.[94]

STORYTELLING. *Stories* deserve special attention here because, as indicated in Figure 9.11, they are a central feature of organizational socialization and culture. Company stories about heroic or inspiring deeds let newcomers know what "really counts."[95] For example, 3M's eleventh commandment—"Thou shalt not kill a new product idea"—has been ingrained in new employees through one inspiring story about the employee who accidentally discovered transparent cellophane tape. To convince the company's leaders of the product's value, he surprised the board members by using it during a board meeting. Once they saw the product in use, they gave it a try, and 3M's tape went on to become a resounding success.[96] Upon hearing this story, a 3M newcomer has believable, concrete evidence that innovation and persistence pay off. It has been said that stories are "social roadmaps" for employees, telling them where to go and where not to go and what will happen when they get there.

Moreover, stories are remembered longer than abstract facts or rules and regulations. How many times have you recalled a professor's colorful story but forgotten the rest of the lecture?

Strengthening Organizational Cultures

Given the inherent fuzziness of organizational cultures, how can managers identify cultural weak spots that need improvement? Symptoms of a weak organizational culture include the following:

- *Inward focus.* Has internal politics become more important than real-world problems and the marketplace?
- *Morale problems.* Are there chronic unhappiness and high turnover?
- *Fragmentation/inconsistency.* Is there a lack of "fit" in the way people behave, communicate, and perceive problems and opportunities?
- *Ingrown subcultures.* Is there a lack of communication among subunits?
- *Warfare among subcultures.* Has constructive competition given way to destructive conflict?
- *Subculture elitism.* Have organizational units become exclusive "clubs" with restricted entry?

Have subcultural values become more important than the organization's values?[97] Evidence of these symptoms may encourage a potential recruit to look elsewhere. Each of these symptoms of a weak organizational culture can be a formidable barrier to organizational effectiveness. Organizations with strong cultures do a good job of avoiding these symptoms.[98]

SUMMARY

1. Organizations need to be understood and intelligently managed because they are an ever-present feature of modern life. Whatever their purpose, all organizations exhibit four characteristics: (1) coordination of effort, (2) common goal or purpose, (3) division of labor, and (4) hierarchy of authority. If even one of these characteristics is absent, an organization does not exist. Line managers are in the formal chain of command and have decision-making authority, whereas staff personnel provide advice and support.

2. In open-system terms, business organizations are made up of interdependent technical, boundary-spanning, and managerial subsystems. As an open system, a business is dependent on its environment and has inputs and outputs. Harvard's David A. Garvin characterizes learning organizations as those capable of turning new ideas into improved performance. Five skills required to do this are (1) solving problems, (2) experimenting, (3) learning from organizational experience and history, (4) learning from others, and (5) transferring and implementing knowledge for improved performance.

3. Because there is no single criterion for organizational effectiveness, for-profit as well as non-profit organizations need to satisfy different effectiveness criteria in the near, intermediate, and distant future. In the near term, effective organizations accomplish their purposes, are efficient, and are a source of satisfaction to all stakeholders. They are adaptive and developing in the intermediate term. Ultimately, in the long term, effective organizations survive.

4. The idea behind contingency design is structuring the organization to fit situational demands. Consequently, contingency advocates contend that there is no one best organizational setup for all situations. Diagnosing the degree of environmental uncertainty is an important first step in contingency design. Field studies have confirmed the validity of the assumption that organization structure should vary according to the situation. Burns and Stalker discovered that mechanistic (rigid) organizations are effective when the environment is relatively stable and that organic (flexible) organizations are best when unstable conditions prevail.

5. There are five basic departmentalization formats, each with its own combination of advantages and disadvantages. Functional departmentalization is the most common approach. The others are product-service, geographic location, customer classification, and work flow process departmentalization. In actual practice, these pure types of departmentalization are usually combined in various ways.

6. As we have come to realize that situational factors dictate how many people a manager can directly supervise, the notion of an ideal span of control has become obsolete. In a centralized organization, top management retains all major decision-making authority and does a lot of checking up on subordinates. Decentralization, the delegation of decision authority to lower-level managers, has been praised as being democratic and has been criticized for reducing top management's control.

7. Delegation of authority, although generally resisted for a variety of reasons, is crucial to decentralization. Effective delegation permits managers to tackle higher-priority duties while helping train and develop lower-level managers. Although delegation varies in degree, it never means abdicating primary responsibility. Successful delegation requires that lower-level managers display plenty of initiative. Among the barriers to delegation are doing everything yourself, lack of confidence and trust in others, low self-confidence, fear of competition, reluctance to risk depending on others, and poor role models who do not delegate.

8. Many factors, with global competition leading the way, are forcing management to reshape the traditional pyramid bureaucracy. These new organizations are characterized by fewer layers, extensive use of teams, and manageably small subunits. Three emerging organizational configurations are the hourglass organization, the cluster organization, and the virtual organization. Each has its own advantages and pitfalls.

9. Organizational culture is the "social glue" binding people together through shared symbols, language, stories, and practices. Organizational cultures can commonly be characterized as collective, emotionally charged, historically based, inherently symbolic, dynamic, and inherently fuzzy (or ambiguous). Diverse outsiders are transformed into accepted insiders through the process of organizational socialization. Orientations and stories are powerful and lasting socialization techniques. Systematic observation can reveal symptoms of a weak organizational culture.

TERMS TO UNDERSTAND

Organization, p. 240
Authority, p. 241
Organization chart, p. 241
Line and staff organization, p. 242
Learning organization, p. 244
Organizational effectiveness, p. 245
Contingency design, p. 246

Mechanistic organizations, p. 247
Organic organizations, p. 247
Departmentalization, p. 249
Span of control, p. 252
Centralization, p. 254
Decentralization, p. 254
Delegation, p. 254

Hourglass organization, p. 257
Cluster organization, p. 257
Virtual organizations, p. 258
Organizational culture, p. 259
Organizational values, p. 261
Organizational socialization, p. 261

ACTION LEARNING EXERCISE

AN ORGANIZATIONAL X-RAY: CAPTURING THE "FEEL" OF AN ORGANIZATION'S CULTURE

Instructions: Working either alone or as part of a team, select an organization you are personally familiar with (such as your college or university or a place of present or past employment). Alternatively, you may choose to interview someone about an organization of their choice. The key is to capture a knowledgeable "insider's" perspective. Complete Parts A and B of this exercise with your target organization in mind. (*Notes:* This instrument is for instructional purposes only, because it has not been scientifically validated. Also, you may want to disguise the organization in any class discussion if your cultural profile could offend someone or is strongly negative.)

PART A

For each of the following adjective pairs, circle the number that best describes the "feel" of the organization, and then calculate a sum total.

Rejecting	1	2	3	4	5	6	7	8	9	10	Accepting
Destructive	1	2	3	4	5	6	7	8	9	10	Constructive
Uncomfortable	1	2	3	4	5	6	7	8	9	10	Comfortable
Unfair	1	2	3	4	5	6	7	8	9	10	Fair
Unsupportive	1	2	3	4	5	6	7	8	9	10	Supportive
Demeaning	1	2	3	4	5	6	7	8	9	10	Empowering
Dishonest	1	2	3	4	5	6	7	8	9	10	Honest
Dull, boring	1	2	3	4	5	6	7	8	9	10	Challenging
Declining	1	2	3	4	5	6	7	8	9	10	Improving
Untrustworthy	1	2	3	4	5	6	7	8	9	10	Trustworthy

Total score = _____

Interpretive scale

1. 10–39 = Run for your life!

2. 40–69 = Needs a culture transplant.

3. 70–100 = Warm and fuzzy!

PART B

Write a brief statement for each of the following:

1. What are the organization's key values (as enacted, not simply as written or stated)?

2. What story (or stories) best convey(s) what the organization is "really" like?

3. Does the organization have legends or heroes that strongly influence how things are done? Describe.

4. What traditions, practices, or symbols make the organization's culture stronger?

5. Does the organization have a larger-than-life reputation or mythology? Explain.

For Consideration/Discussion

1. Is the organization's culture strong or weak? How can you tell?

2. Is the organization's culture people-friendly? Explain.

3. Does the strength (or weakness) of the culture help explain why the organization is thriving (or suffering)? Explain.

4. Will the organization's culture attract or repel high-quality job applicants? Explain.

5. What can or should be done to improve the organization's culture?

ETHICS EXERCISE

 DO THE RIGHT THING

Xerox CEO Ursula Burns Worries About Her Corporate Culture Being Too Nice

[*Geoff Colvin,* Fortune *magazine*]: Xerox has a famously strong culture, but you've said it could use a little adjusting. What did you mean?

[Burns]: Let me note the strong points. We are nice. And I mean that in a very good way. If you get sick, we'll take care of you. We're not one of these mechanical cultures. We are real people working with real people. It's phenomenal.

We are a team-based company. Diversity is important. Everybody thinks racial and gender diversity is important for sure, but differences in how you work, what your points of view are, are things that we love.

Some of those things can become a hindrance, especially when you need to move quickly, which is just about every day. This niceness sometimes leads to lack of motion, lack of decision.

Source: Excerpted from Geoff Colvin, "Ursula Burns," *Fortune* (May 3, 2010): 101

What are the ethical implications of the following interpretations?

1. Xerox is a great American company with an admirable culture that took generations of hard work and trust-building to create. Don't mess with the organization's culture. Strategic and procedural changes are fine, but don't fiddle with what makes Xerox unique. Explain.

2. Xerox is an old company suffering from a case of bureaucratic hardening of the arteries. Xerox's employees have become too comfortable to be really creative and have a sense of urgency about being competitive. It's time for Burns to really shake things up. How?

3. Yes, a cultural change is in order. But in a company that truly values teamwork, the change should be driven by employee problem-solving teams at all levels and consensus building, not by orders from the top. Suggestions?

4. Your own ethical interpretation?

MANAGERS-IN-ACTION VIDEO CASE STUDY

EVO (FORMERLY KNOWN AS EVOGEAR)

Leading Teams: Storms and Norms

evo owner Bryce Phillips shares his perspective on leadership and forming successful teams. Several evo employees discuss the process they went through in forming a new creative team. They share challenges they faced as they tried to develop better team synergy and eliminate the "middle school mentality." Learn how team leaders address conflict and work toward group cohesion in an effort to increase creative output. Roles, responsibilities, communication, constructive feedback, and strategies for effective team formation are just a few of the many topics included in this video.

For more information about evo, visit its Web site: *www.evo.com/.*

Before watching the video, answer the following questions:

1. Do you believe teams improve creativity, innovation, and efficiency, or do you think they add complications and waste time? Explain.

2. Are you a team player? What personality traits do you possess that make you a good (or bad) team player?

3. What do you think is the best approach to team formation?

After watching the video, answer the following questions:

4. What company values and elements of corporate culture impact evo's approach to teamwork and team formation?

5. How are feedback and communication used to improve team performance?

6. How was conflict handled among team members?

7. What is the next stage of growth for the creative team at evo?

CLOSING CASE

ZAPPOS.COM'S CEO TONY HSIEH EXPLAINS HOW TO BUILD A STRONG CORPORATE CULTURE

Note: Read the Chapter 1 opening case for background on Tony Hsieh and Zappos.com and a list of the company's ten core values.

What's the best way to build a brand for the long term?

In a word: culture.

At Zappos, our belief is that if you get the culture right, most of the other stuff—like great customer service, or building a great long-term brand, or passionate employees and customers—will happen naturally on its own.

We believe that your company's culture and your company's brand are really just two sides of the same coin. The brand may lag the culture at first, but eventually it will catch up.

Your culture is your brand.

So how do you build and maintain the culture that you want?

It starts with the hiring process. At Zappos, we actually do two different sets of interviews. The hiring manager and his/her team will do the standard set of interviews looking for relevant experience, technical ability, fit within the team, etc. But then our HR [human resources] department does a separate set of interviews, looking purely for culture fit. Candidates have to pass both sets of interviews in order to be hired.

We've actually said no to a lot of very talented people that we know can make an immediate impact on our top or bottom line. But because we felt they weren't culture fits, we were willing to sacrifice the short-term benefits in order to protect our culture (and therefore the brand) for the long term.

After hiring, the next step to building the culture is training. Everyone that is hired into our headquarters goes through the same training that our Customer Loyalty Team (call center) reps go through, regardless of department of title. You might be an accountant, or a lawyer, or a software developer—you go through the exact same training program.

It's a 4-week training program, in which we go over company history, the importance of customer service, the long-term vision of the company, our philosophy about company culture—and then you're actually on the phone for 2 weeks, taking calls from customers. Again, this goes back to our belief that customer service shouldn't just be a department, it should be the entire company.

At the end of the first week of training, we make an offer to the entire class. We offer everyone $2,000 to quit (in addition to paying them for the time they've already worked), and it's a standing

offer until the end of the fourth week of training. We want to make sure that employees are here for more than just a paycheck. We want employees that believe in our long-term vision and want to be part of our culture. As it turns out, on average, less than 1% of people end up taking the offer.

One of the great advantages of focusing on culture is when reporters come and visit our offices. Unlike most companies, we don't give reporters a small list of people they're allowed to talk to. Instead, we encourage them to wander around and talk to whoever they want. It's our way of being as transparent as possible, which is part of our culture. . . .

Many companies have core values, but they don't really commit to them. They usually sound more like something you'd read in a press release. Maybe you learn about them on day 1 of orientation, but after that it's just a meaningless plaque on the wall of the lobby.

We believe that it's really important to come up with core values that you can commit to. And by commit, we mean that you're willing to hire and fire based on them. If you're willing to do that, then you're well on your way to building a company culture that is in line with the brand you want to build. You can let all of your employees be your brand ambassadors.

For Discussion

1. Is Zappos an open system? Explain.

2. Why is Zappos probably an effective "learning organization," as described in this chapter?

3. Would you call Zappos a mechanistic or organic organization? Explain.

4. Would managers who want to delegate likely succeed at Zappos? Explain.

5. What are the three or four most important things Zappos does to create and maintain a strong corporate culture? Explain in terms of Figure 9.11.

Source: Excerpted from Tony Hsieh, *Delivering Happiness: A Path to Profits, Passion, and Purpose* (New York: Business Plus, 2010), pp. 152–154.

10 Human Resource Management

PETER DASILVA/The New York Times/Redux

"Business is a game, and as with all games, the team that puts the best people on the field and gets them playing together wins. It's that simple."[1]

—JACK AND SUZY WELCH

The Changing Workplace

TALENT ANALYTICS AT GOOGLE

The company's goal is to identify leading people-management practices and confirm them with data and analysis. To achieve it, Google created a people analytics function with its own director and staff of 30 researchers, analysts, and consultants who study employee-related decisions and issues. The People and Innovation Lab (PiLab) conducts focused investigations for internal clients.

Google has analyzed a variety of HR [human resource] topics and has often moved in new directions as a result. It has determined what backgrounds and capabilities are associated with high performance and what factors are likely to lead to attrition—such as an employee's feeling underused at the company. It has set the ideal number of recruiting interviews at five, down from a previous average of ten.

Google's Project Oxygen—so named because good management keeps the company alive—was established to determine the attributes of successful managers. The PiLab team analyzed annual employee surveys, performance management scores, and other data to divide managers into four groups according to their quality. It then interviewed high- and low-scoring managers (interviews were double blind—neither interviewers nor managers knew which category the managers were in) to determine their managerial practices. Google was eventually able to identify eight behaviors that characterized good managers and five behaviors that all managers should avoid.

Google's vice president of people operations, Laszlo Bock, says, "It's not the company-provided lunch that keeps people here. Googlers tell us that there are three reasons they stay: the mission, the quality of the people, and the chance to build the skill set of a better leader or entrepreneur. And all our analytics are built around these reasons."

Source: Thomas H. Davenport, Jeanne Harris, and Jeremy Shapiro, "Competing on Talent Analytics," *Harvard Business Review*, 88 (October 2010): 56–57.

OBJECTIVES

- **Explain** what human resource management involves.
- **Define** the term *human capital*, and **identify** at least four of Pfeffer's people-centered practices.
- **Identify** and briefly **explain** the seven steps in the PROCEED model of employee selection.
- **Distinguish** among equal employment opportunity, affirmative action, and managing diversity.
- **Explain** how managers can be more effective interviewers.
- **Discuss** how performance appraisals can be made legally defensible.
- **Contrast** the ingredients of good training programs for both skill and factual learning and **explain** training program evaluation.
- **Specify** the essential components of an organization's policies for dealing with sexual harassment and alcohol and drug abuse.

Staffing has long been an integral part of the management process. Like other traditional management functions, such as planning and organizing, the domain of staffing has become more sophisticated through the years. This evolution reflects increasing environmental complexity and greater organizational sophistication, as in the case of Google.[2] Early definitions of staffing focused narrowly on hiring people for vacant positions. Today, the traditional staffing function is just one part of the more encompassing human resource management process. **Human resource management** involves the acquisition, evaluation, retention, and development of human resources necessary for organizational success. This broader definition underscores the point that people are valuable *resources* requiring careful nurturing. In fact, what were once called personnel departments are now called human resource departments. This people-centered human resource approach emphasizes the serious moral and legal issues involved in viewing labor simply as a commodity to be bought, exploited to exhaustion, and discarded when convenient. Moreover, global opportunities and competitive pressures have made the skillful management of human resources more important than ever.[3]

Progressive and successful organizations treat all employees as valuable human resources. They go out of their way to accommodate their employees' full range of needs. A prime example is Analytical Graphics Inc. in Exton, Pennsylvania. The engineering company whose clients include NASA offers a host of free services for employees and their families, including free meals and snacks, laundry facilities, and a gym. Employees report that these perks increase productivity and help them keep their home and work lives in balance.[4]

Field research indicates that employees tend to return the favor when they are treated with dignity and respect. For instance, one study compared steel mills with either "control" or "commitment" human resource systems. Emphasis at the control-oriented steel mills was on cost cutting, rule compliance, and efficiency. Meanwhile, the other steel mills encouraged psychological commitment to the company with a climate of trust and participation. "The mills with commitment systems had higher productivity, lower scrap rates, and lower employee turnover than those with control systems."[5]

Figure 10.1 presents a model for the balance of this chapter; it reflects this strategic orientation. Note that a logical sequence of human resource management activities—human resource strategy, recruiting, selection, performance appraisal, and training—all derive from organizational strategy and structure. Without a strategic orientation, the management of people becomes haphazardly inefficient and ineffective. Also, as indicated in

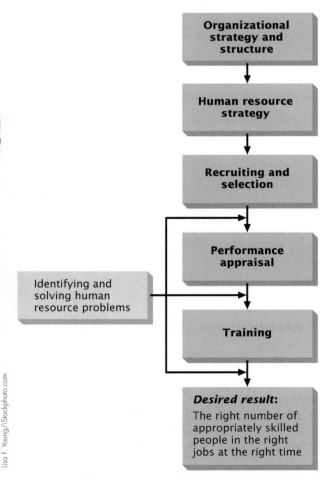

Figure **10.1** A General Model for Human Resource Management

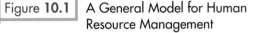

human resource management acquisition, evaluation, retention, and development of human resources

Figure 10.1, an ongoing process following the hiring decision involves identifying and solving human resource problems. Two contemporary human resource problems, explored in the last section of this chapter, are discouraging sexual harassment and controlling alcohol and drug abuse.

HUMAN RESOURCE STRATEGY: A PEOPLE-CENTERED APPROACH

Conventional wisdom about how employees should be perceived and managed has evolved greatly over the last 60 years. The pendulum has swung from reactive to proactive. Following World War II, personnel departments filled hiring requisitions and handled disciplinary problems submitted by managers. During the 1970s and 1980s, human resource (HR) departments became the norm, and a more encompassing approach evolved. HR departments attempted to forecast labor supply and demand, recruit and hire, manage payrolls, and conduct training and development programs. Too often, however, HR was treated as a support-staff function with only an indirect link to corporate strategy. Today, in well-managed companies, HR is being embedded in organizational strategy.[6] Other major HR trends: traditional HR functions are being decentralized throughout the enterprise and, in a more controversial move, being outsourced;[7] and HR is adapting to globalization.[8] But these transitions are far from complete, which has prompted some pundits to describe HR as a teenager: starting to mature but uncertain as to where it's going.[9] This section outlines a strategic agenda for human resource management.

The Age of Human Capital

This perspective requires open-system thinking, as discussed in Chapters 2 and 9. It is a "big picture" approach to managing people and staying competitive. According to the authors of *The HR Scorecard: Linking People, Strategy, and Performance*, a new era has arrived, which is characterized by speed, quality, and customer satisfaction. These shifts have brought the value of intangible assets such as knowledge, brand recognition, innovation, and human capital to light.[10]

The term **human capital** encompasses all present and future workforce participants and emphasizes the need to develop their fullest potential for the benefit of everyone. Central to this perspective is the assumption that every employee is a valuable asset, not merely an expense item. This broad concern

Andy Nelson/The Christian Science Monitor/Getty Images

Employers are more proactive than ever before in finding ways to seek out the best and brightest people who will help the employers reach their strategic goals. Job fairs, like this one in Houston, are just one method of recruiting new talent.

human capital the need to develop all present and future employees to their fullest potential

for possible *future* employees is a marked departure from traditional "employees-only" perspectives.

Intel, the Santa Clara, California–based maker of computer microprocessors, is committed to developing human capital. The company "adopts" primary and secondary schools—providing computers, teaching talent, and money—and encourages its employees to help. Intel donates $200 for every 20 hours of time that an employee volunteers at a local school.[11] As might be expected from a high-tech company, the emphasis is on math and science. Additionally, Intel matches employees' donations to their college alma maters up to $10,000 a year and awards $1,250,000 in school grants and scholarships each year to winners in a national science competition for high school seniors. Most of those who benefit from these initiatives will *not* end up working for Intel. That's what developing the *world's* human capital is all about—thinking big! (See Green Management: Toward Sustainability.)

People-Centered Organizations Enjoy a Competitive Advantage

In an era of nonstop layoffs, the oft-heard slogan "Employees are our most valuable asset" rings hollow. In fact, Dilbert cartoonist Scott Adams calls that statement "The First Great Lie of Management."[12] But such cynicism can be countered by looking at how leading companies build a bridge from progressive human resource practices to market success. Take, for instance, Southwest Airlines. Co-founder and former CEO Herb Kelleher told

---

10a

Back to the Opening Case

2010 Survey of 449 human resource professionals: *Nearly half the respondents (47 percent) said that obtaining human capital and optimizing human capital investments was the top investment challenge for businesses over the coming decade.*

QUESTION: Is Google's quantitative approach to managing human capital the right approach, or should experienced managers be trusted to rely on their judgment and "gut feelings" for hiring and promotion decisions?

For further information about the interactive annotations in this chapter, visit our student Web site.

Source: "Poll Identifies Top Challenges for HR During Next 10 Years," *HR Magazine*, 55 (November 2010): 80.

Green Management: Toward Sustainability

What About Sustainable Human Resources?

Even as businesses have appointed "eco-managers" to oversee company efforts to become more energy efficient and environmentally conscious, and even as companies track and publicly report carbon emissions from their activities, one would be hard-pressed to find similar efforts focused on employees. Just as there is a concern for protecting natural resources, there could be a similar level of concern for protecting human resources. For example, there has been no groundswell of reporting on employee physical and mental health and wellness, even though that might be an interesting and informative indicator of what companies are doing about the sustainability of their people. This lack of concern is puzzling given that health-care costs, which . . . are related in part to what companies do in the workplace, are an enormous problem in the United States and throughout the industrialized world.

For Discussion: Is it a good idea to extend the concept of sustainability to people and the organizations in which they work? Explain. What could be done to make employees and organizations more sustainable?

Source: Excerpted from Jeffrey Pfeffer, "Building Sustainable Organizations: The Human Factor," *Academy of Management Perspectives*, 24 (February 2010): 36.

Fortune magazine, "My mother taught me that your employees come first." When employees receive fair treatment, they treat the customers so well that they come back, which in turn pleases the shareholders.[13] Well, Herb's mom was right! Solid research support for this approach comes from Stanford's Jeffrey Pfeffer, who reported a strong connection between *people-centered practices* and higher profits and lower employee turnover. Pfeffer identified the following seven people-centered practices:

- Protection of job security (including a no-layoff policy)
- Rigorous hiring process
- Employee empowerment through decentralization and self-managed teams
- Compensation linked to performance
- Comprehensive training
- Reduction of status differences
- Sharing of key information

Pfeffer sees these practices as an integrated package and cautions against implementing them piecemeal. Unfortunately, according to Pfeffer's calculations, only about 12 percent of today's organizations qualify as being systematically people-centered.[14] Thus, we have a clear developmental agenda for human resource management. Ideas about how to enact people-centered practices can be found throughout the balance of this book.

RECRUITMENT AND SELECTION

Jim Collins, in his best-seller *Good to Great: Why Some Companies Make the Leap . . . and Others Don't*, uses the metaphor of a bus when referring to the organization and its employees.[15] He believes a busload of great people can go just about anywhere it wants. But a bus filled with confused and unruly passengers is destined for the ditch. A survey of CEOs reinforces the importance of getting the right people on the bus and keeping them there. When the CEOs were asked what they probably will look back on five years from now as the key to their success, the number one response was "Getting and retaining talent."[16] This section deals with that important challenge.

Recruiting for Diversity in the Internet Age

The ultimate goal of recruiting is to generate a pool of qualified applicants for new and existing jobs. Everyday recruiting tactics include internal job postings, referrals by present and past employees, campus recruiters, newspaper ads, Web sites and social media, public and private employment agencies, so-called headhunters, job fairs, temporary-help agencies, and union halls. Meanwhile, an underlying reality makes today's recruiting extremely challenging. Specifically, applicant pools need to be demographically representative of the population at large if diversity is to be achieved. One *Fortune* 500 company CEO stated that diversity is not a choice; it's a requirement for long-term success. She explains, "It has to be built into the fabric of the business."[17]

Social networking via the Web is rapidly becoming the tool of choice for both recruiters and job seekers. *Fortune* magazine recently reported that John Campagnino of Accenture plans to hire 40 percent of new employees through social media, especially the Web site LinkedIn. He explains, "This is the future of recruiting for our company."[18]

As many job seekers have learned the hard way, thorough Internet searches by recruiters have become commonplace. A Microsoft study showed that a significant majority of recruiters reviewed applications online and eliminated candidates based on their findings.[19] So here is a very important lesson for job seekers: *don't post anything to the Web that you wouldn't want your parents or a prospective employer to see.*

Caution also needs to be shown by recruiters when tapping social media for background information on job seekers. According to researchers, it is tempting to review an applicant's Facebook page, but caution should prevail. If a page contains false or prejudicial information or applicants are not on Facebook, selection could be biased.[20]

The Selection Process: An Overview

HR experts commonly compare the screening and selection process to a hurdle race. Equal employment opportunity (EEO) legislation in the United States and elsewhere attempts to ensure a fair and unprejudiced race for all job applicants.[21] The first two hurdles are résumé screening and reference checking. Both are very important because of discouraging evidence such as this: ADP Screening and Selection Services performed 2.6 million background checks and found that more than 41 percent of applicants lied about their work histories and education.[22]

Background checks for criminal records and citizenship/immigration status are more crucial than ever amid concerns about workplace violence and international terrorism. Consider this: "Between January 1998 and October 2000, American Background Information Services Inc. (ABI), based in Winchester, Va., found undisclosed criminal backgrounds on 12.6 percent of the people it screened."[23] Walmart now performs criminal background checks on all of its job applicants.[24]

Other hurdles may include psychological tests, physical examinations, interviews, work-sampling tests, and drug tests. The whole selection process can become quite complex and drawn out at companies such as Google, where rapid growth and the constant need for innovation means the steady hiring of the best and the brightest. Google's recruiters sift through more than 3,000 online job applications each day, selecting applicants for interviews. In addition to a rigorous round of interviews, those applicants are often asked to take on-the-spot tests to demonstrate their skills.[25]

Del J. Still, a respected author and trainer, summarizes the overall employee selection process with the acronym PROCEED, where each letter represents one of the seven steps involved (see Table 10.1). This model encourages managers to take a systems perspective, all the way from preparation to the final hiring decision. Before examining key elements of the PROCEED model in depth, we need to clarify what is involved in the first three action items for step 1. This is where job analysis and job descriptions come into play. **Job analysis** is the process of identifying basic task and skill requirements for specific jobs by studying superior performers. A **job description** is a concise document outlining the role expectations and skill requirements for a specific job. Some say they have become obsolete in today's fast-paced world, but up-to-date job descriptions foster discipline in selection and performance appraisal by offering a formal measuring stick.[26]

Table 10.1	The Employee Selection Process: Still's PROCEED Model

Step 1: PREPARE
- Identify existing superior performers.
- Create a job description for the position.
- Identify the competencies or skills needed to do the job.
- Draft interview questions.

Step 2: REVIEW
- Review questions for legality and fairness.

Step 3: ORGANIZE
- Select your interview team and your method of interviewing.
- Assign roles to your team and divide the questions.

Step 4: CONDUCT
- Gather data from the job candidate.

Step 5: EVALUATE
- Determine the match between the candidate and the job.

Step 6: EXCHANGE
- Share data in a discussion meeting.

Step 7: DECIDE
- Make the final decision.

Source: Del J. Still, *High Impact Hiring: How to Interview and Select Outstanding Employees*, 2nd ed., revised (Dana Point, CA.: Management Development Systems, 2001), pp. 43–44. Reprinted by permission.

Equal Employment Opportunity

Although earlier legislation selectively applies, the landmark EEO law in the United States is Title VII of the Civil Rights Act of 1964. Subsequent amendments, presidential executive orders, and related laws have expanded EEO's coverage. EEO law now provides a broad umbrella of employment protection for certain categories of disadvantaged individuals, making it virtually impossible for hiring organizations to discriminate on the basis of race, color, sex, religion, national origin, disabilities, or military service.[27] What all this means is that managers cannot refuse to hire, promote, train, or transfer employees

---

job analysis identifying task and skill requirements for specific jobs by studying superior performers | *job description document outlining role expectations and skill requirements for a specific job*

simply on the basis of these characteristics, nor can they lay off or discharge employees on these grounds. Returning U.S. military service members are protected against workplace discrimination under the 1994 Uniformed Services Employment and Reemployment Rights Act.[28] Sexual preference and gender identity have been added to the list in some local and state jurisdictions.[29] Selection and all other personnel decisions must be made solely on the basis of objective criteria, such as ability to perform or seniority.

Lawsuits and fines by agencies such as the U.S. Equal Employment Opportunity Commission (EEOC) are a powerful incentive to comply with EEO laws. In fact, racial discrimination settlements cost Texaco $176 million in 1996 and Coca-Cola $192.5 million in 2000.[30] In 2004, Boeing agreed to pay $72.5 million to settle a class-action lawsuit covering 29,000 women who claimed the aircraft maker discriminated against them when making pay and promotion decisions.[31]

AFFIRMATIVE ACTION. A more rigorous refinement of EEO legislation is affirmative action. An affirmative action program (AAP) is a plan for actively seeking out, employing, and developing the talents of those groups historically discriminated against in employment.[32] Affirmative action amounts to a concerted effort to make up for *past* discrimination. EEO, in contrast, is aimed at preventing *future* discrimination. Typical AAPs attack employment discrimination with the following four methods: (1) *active* recruitment of women and minorities, (2) elimination of prejudicial questions on employment application forms, (3) establishment of specific goals and timetables for minority hiring, and (4) statistical validation of employment testing procedures.

Like any public policy with legal ramifications, the EEO/AAP area is fraught with complexity.[33] Varying political and legal interpretations and inconsistent court decisions have sometimes frustrated and confused managers.[34] Researchers have uncovered both negative and positive findings about affirmative action. On the negative side, those hired through affirmative action are often deemed incompetent, even if they have superb qualifications.[35] On the positive side, a study based on nationwide U.S. Census Bureau data found that affirmative action had enhanced the promotion opportunities of black workers in both government and business

organizations. In fact, according to the researcher, women and blacks had better chances for promotion than white males, except in the public sector.[36] These findings disturb some white males, who claim to be the victims of "reverse discrimination."[37] At the same time, some minority employees complain of swapping one injustice for another when they take advantage of affirmative action. Legislated social change, however necessary or laudable, is not without pain. Much remains to be accomplished to eliminate the legacy of unfair discrimination in the workplace.

FROM AFFIRMATIVE ACTION TO MANAGING DIVERSITY. As discussed in Chapter 3, the "managing-diversity" movement promises to raise the discussion of equal employment opportunity and affirmative action to a higher plane. One authority on the subject, R. Roosevelt Thomas Jr., reminds us that diversity issues include age, education, background, and personality differences that should be of concern to all people. Notes Thomas, "The objective [of affirmative action and equal employment opportunity] is not to assimilate minorities and women into a dominant white male culture but to create a dominant heterogeneous culture."[38] In short, diversity advocates want to replace all forms of bigotry, prejudice, and intolerance with tolerance and, ideally, appreciation of interpersonal differences.[39] (See Valuing Diversity.) They also want to broaden the message of inclusion to make it globally applicable in multinational organizations.

ACCOMMODATING THE NEEDS OF PEOPLE WITH DISABILITIES. From the perspective of someone in a wheelchair, the world can be a very unfriendly place. Curbs, stairways, and inward-swinging doors in small public toilet stalls all implicitly say, "You're not welcome here; you don't fit in." Prejudice and discrimination worsen the situation. Cheri Blauwet, a world-class wheelchair racer from Larchwood, Iowa, who was paralyzed below the waist in a farm accident at 15 months of age, has commented that she feels that when people see her, they just see her wheelchair, not a Stanford medical school student who is strong and capable.[40]

Human disabilities vary widely, but historically, disabled people have had one thing in common—unemployment. Consider these telling statistics: About 20 percent of the population is disabled. One out of five disabled adults is a high school dropout,

affirmative action program (AAP) making up for past discrimination by actively seeking and employing minorities

VALUING DIVERSITY

Sexual Orientation Is Part of the Diversity Mix at REI

Recreational Equipment Inc. (REI) may be well known for its commitment to green issues, but the retailer is also focused on the rainbow: It is a truly welcoming place for lesbian, gay, bisexual, and transgender people.

Inclusion is the name of the game at REI, where LGBT employees can be found on the board of directors as well as in its 112 retail stores. Since 1992 the cooperative has had an anti-discrimination policy that includes sexual orientation.

Same-sex partners receive full health-care coverage, adoption assistance, and FMLA [U.S. Family and Medical Leave Act] and bereavement leave. Also included: medical leave, follow-up treatments, and hormone therapy after gender-reassignment surgery.

"The obvious answer is it's the right thing to do," says CEO Sally Jewell.

For Discussion: What is the business argument for including sexual orientation in the organization's diversity plan?

Source: Excerpted from Christopher Tkaczyk, "100 Best Companies to Work For: No. 14; REI," *Fortune* (June 14, 2010): 52.

and more than 70 percent of the disabled aged 18 to 55 are unemployed.[41]

Reducing the unemployment rate for people with disabilities is not just about jobs and money. It is about self-sufficiency, hopes, and dreams. With enactment of the Americans with Disabilities Act of 1990 (ADA), disabled Americans hoped to get a real chance to take their rightful place in the workforce.[42] But according to research, this hope remains largely unfulfilled. In a 2010 survey, 61 percent of disabled

adults said the ADA had made no difference in their lives; 23 percent said it had made their lives better.[43]

The ADA, enforced by the EEOC, requires employers to make *reasonable* accommodations to meet the needs of present and future employees with physical and mental disabilities. As the ADA was being phased in to cover nearly all employers, many feared their businesses would be saddled with burdensome expenses and many lawsuits. But a 1998 White House–sponsored survey "determined that the mean

The world changed for Carmen Jones when a car accident during her junior year at Virginia's Hampton University left her in a wheelchair for life. But she's gone on to earn a marketing degree and found Solutions Marketing Group in Arlington, Virginia, which helps businesses reach and better serve disabled people.

Ron Ceasar

cost of helping disabled workers to overcome their impairments was a mere $935 per person."[44]

New technology is also making accommodation easier.[45] Large-print computer screens for the partially blind, Braille keyboards and talking computers for the blind, and telephones with visual readouts for the deaf are among today's helpful technologies. Here are some general policy guidelines for employers:

- Audit all facilities, policies, work rules, hiring procedures, and labor union contracts to eliminate barriers and bias.
- Train all managers in ADA compliance and all employees in how to be sensitive to coworkers and customers with disabilities.
- Do not hire anyone who cannot safely perform the basic duties of a particular job with reasonable accommodation.

With lots of low-tech ingenuity, a touch of high tech, and support from coworkers, millions of disabled people can help their employers win the battle of global competition.

Employment Selection Tests

EEO guidelines in the United States have broadened the definition of an employment selection test to include any procedure used as a basis for an employment decision. This means that in addition to traditional pencil-and-paper tests, numerous other procedures qualify as tests, such as unscored application forms; informal and formal interviews; performance tests; and physical, educational, or experience requirements.[46] This definition of an employment test takes on added significance when you realize that in the United States, the federal government requires all employment tests to be statistically valid and reliable predictors of job success.[47] Historically, women and minorities have been victimized by invalid, unreliable, and prejudicial employment selection procedures. Similar complaints have been voiced about the use of personality tests, polygraphs, drug tests, and AIDS and DNA screening during the hiring process[48] (see Table 10.2). Despite questions about the practice, and despite its potential drawbacks, the Association of Test Publishers noted that over the last several years, employment testing, including personality tests, has been increasing at about 10 to 15 percent each year.[49]

Effective Interviewing

Interviewing warrants special attention here because it is the most common employee selection tool.[50] Line managers at all levels are often asked to interview candidates for job openings and promotions and should be aware of the weaknesses of the traditional unstructured interview. The traditional unstructured or informal interview, which has no fixed question format or systematic scoring procedure, has been criticized on grounds such as the following:

- It is highly susceptible to distortion and bias.
- It is highly susceptible to legal attack.
- It is usually indefensible if legally contested.
- It may have apparent validity, but no real validity.
- It is rarely totally job-related and may incorporate personal items that infringe on privacy.
- It is the most flexible selection technique, thereby being highly inconsistent.
- There is a tendency for the interviewer to look for qualities he or she prefers, and then to justify the hiring decision based on these qualities.
- Often the interviewer does not hear about the selection mistakes.
- There is an unsubstantiated confidence in the traditional interview.[51]

THE PROBLEM OF CULTURAL BIAS. Traditional unstructured interviews are notorious for being culturally insensitive. Evidence of this problem surfaced in a study of the interviewing practices of 38 general managers employed by nine different fast-food chains. According to the researcher, looking someone in the eye and offering a firm handshake are very important in the hiring process. In fact, 9 percent of applicants are turned down purely for inappropriate or insufficient eye contact.[52]

Managers can be taught, however, to be aware of and to overcome cultural biases when interviewing. This is particularly important in today's era of managing diversity and promoting greater sensitivity to disabled people.

STRUCTURED INTERVIEWS. Structured interviews are the recommended alternative to traditional unstructured or informal interviews.[53] A **structured interview** is a set of job-related questions with standardized answers applied consistently across all interviews for a specific job.[54] Structured interviews are constructed, conducted, and scored by a committee of three to six members to try to eliminate individual bias. The systematic format and scoring of structured interviews eliminate the weaknesses inherent in unstructured interviews. Four types of questions typically characterize structured interviews: (1) situational, (2) job knowledge, (3) job sample simulation, and (4) worker requirements (see Table 10.3).

Table 10.2   Employment Testing Techniques: An Overview

TYPE OF TEST	PURPOSE	COMMENTS
Pencil-and-paper psychological and personality tests	Measure attitudes and personality characteristics such as emotional stability, intelligence, and ability to deal with stress.	Renewed interest based on claims of improved validity. Can be expensive when scoring and interpretations are done by professionals. Validity varies widely from test to test.
Pencil-and-paper honesty tests (integrity testing)	Assess the degree of risk of a candidate's engaging in dishonest behavior.	Inexpensive to administer. Promising evidence of validity. Growing in popularity since recent curtailment of polygraph testing. Women tend to do better than men.
Job skills tests (clerical and manual dexterity tests, math and language tests, assessment centers, and simulations)	Assess competence in actual "hands-on" situations.	Generally good validity if carefully designed and administered. Assessment centers and simulations can be very expensive.
Polygraph (lie detector) tests	Measure physical signs of stress, such as rapid pulse and perspiration.	Growing use in recent years severely restricted by federal (Employee Polygraph Protection Act of 1988), state, and local laws. Questionable validity.
Drug tests	Check for controlled substances through urine, blood, or hair samples submitted to chemical analysis.	Rapidly growing in use despite strong employee resistance and potentially inaccurate procedures.
Handwriting analysis (graphoanalysis)	Infer personality characteristics and styles from samples of handwriting.	Popular in Europe and growing in popularity in the United States. Sweeping claims by proponents leave validity in doubt.
AIDS/HIV antibody tests	Find evidence of AIDS virus through blood samples.	An emerging area with undetermined legal and ethical boundaries. Major confidentiality issue.
Genetic/DNA screening	Use tissue or blood samples and family history data to identify those at risk of costly diseases.	Limited but growing use strongly opposed on legal and moral grounds. Major confidentiality issue.

| Table **10.3** | Types of Structured Interview Questions |

TYPE OF QUESTION	METHOD	INFORMATION SOUGHT	SAMPLE QUESTION
Situational	Oral	Can the applicant handle difficult situations likely to be encountered on the job?	"What would you do if you saw two of your people arguing loudly in the work area?"
Job knowledge	Oral or written	Does the applicant possess the knowledge required for successful job performance?	"Do you know how to do an Internet search?"
Job sample simulation	Observation of actual or simulated performance	Can the applicant actually do essential aspects of the job?	"Can you show us how to compose and send an e-mail message?"
Worker requirements	Oral	Is the applicant willing to cope with job demands such as travel, relocation, or hard physical labor?	"Are you willing to spend 25 percent of your time on the road?"

Source: Updated from "Structured Interviewing: Avoiding Selection Problems," by Elliott D. Pursell, Michael A. Campion, and Sarah R. Gaylord, copyright November 1980. Reprinted with permission of *Personnel Journal*, Costa Mesa, California; all rights reserved.

BEHAVIORAL INTERVIEWING. Behavioral scientists tell us that past behavior is the best predictor of future behavior. We are, after all, creatures of habit. Situational-type interview questions can be greatly strengthened by anchoring them to actual past behavior (as opposed to hypothetical situations).[55] Structured, job-related, behaviorally specific interview questions keep managers from running afoul of the problems associated with unstructured interviews, as listed earlier.

In a *behavior-based interview*, candidates are asked to recall and describe specific actions taken in job-related circumstances. Candidates should include verifiable details about names, dates, and locations, and they should use "I" statements (rather than "we") to communicate their personal roles in the situations.[56] If the questions are worded appropriately, the net result should be a good grasp of the individual's relevant skills, initiative, problem-solving ability, and ability to recover from setbacks and learn from mistakes. (For practice, see the Action Learning Exercise at the end of this chapter.)

10b
What's Your Story?

Stories can also aid hiring, says John Berisford, head of human resources at Pepsi Beverages. "I often ask one question, whether I'm interviewing a senior-level executive or a campus person: Tell me your story," said Berisford, who learned storytelling from his grandmother in West Virginia. "It's the best way to get to know the entire human being."

QUESTIONS: How can this approach be worked into behavior-based interviewing? How can you tell your story to make you an attractive job candidate?

Source: Vickie Elmer, "How Storytelling Spurs Success," *Fortune* (December 6, 2010): 76.

behavior-based interview detailed questions about specific behavior in past job-related situations

PERFORMANCE APPRAISAL

Annual performance appraisals are such a common part of modern organizational life that they qualify as a ritual. As with many rituals, the participants repeat the historical pattern without really asking the important questions: "Why?" and "Is there a better way?" Both appraisers and appraisees tend to express general dissatisfaction with performance appraisals. Stanford's Jeffrey Pfeffer observed that managers don't like giving appraisals any more than employees like getting them.[57] This is a major threat to productivity because, according to a survey, more than 70 percent of managers agree that it is challenging to be tough on a poorly performing employee.[58] UCLA management professor and consultant Samuel A. Culbert has even gone so far as to describe a boss-administered review as a "dysfunctional pretense" that poses a barrier to communication and teamwork and generates low morale.[59] Considering that experts estimate the average cost of a *single* performance appraisal to be $1,500, the waste associated with poorly administered appraisals is mind-boggling.[60]

Performance appraisal can be effective and satisfying if systematically developed and implemented techniques replace haphazard methods. For our purposes, **performance appraisal** is the process of evaluating individual job performance as a basis for making objective personnel decisions.[61] This definition intentionally excludes occasional coaching, in which a supervisor simply checks an employee's work and gives immediate feedback. Although personal coaching is fundamental to good management, formally documented appraisals are needed both to ensure equitable distribution of opportunities and rewards and to avoid prejudicial treatment of protected minorities.

In this section, we will examine two important aspects of performance appraisal: (1) legal defensibility and (2) alternative techniques.

Making Performance Appraisals Legally Defensible

Lawsuits challenging the legality of specific performance appraisal systems and resulting personnel actions have left scores of human resource managers asking themselves, "Will my organization's performance appraisal system stand up in court?" From the standpoint of limiting legal exposure, it is better to ask this question in the course of developing a formal appraisal system than after it has been implemented. Managers need specific criteria for legally defensible performance appraisal systems. Fortunately, researchers have discerned some instructive patterns in court decisions.

After studying the verdicts in 66 employment discrimination cases in the United States, one pair of researchers found that employers could successfully defend their appraisal systems if these systems satisfied four criteria:

1. A *job analysis* was used to develop the performance appraisal system.
2. The appraisal system was *behavior-oriented*, not trait-oriented.
3. Performance evaluators followed *specific written instructions* when conducting appraisals.
4. Evaluators *reviewed the results* of the appraisals with the ratees.[62]

Each of these conditions has a clear legal rationale. Job analysis, discussed

Blend Images/Photolibrary

Performance evaluations can take many different forms, but they almost always involve the manager observing the employee, recording these observations and perhaps other relevant data, and then sharing this feedback with the employee.

---

performance appraisal evaluating job performance as a basis for personnel decisions

earlier relative to employee selection, anchors the appraisal process to specific job duties, not to personalities. Behavior-oriented appraisals properly focus management's attention on *how* the individual actually performed his or her job. Performance appraisers who follow specific written instructions are less likely to be plagued by vague performance standards and/or personal bias. Finally, by reviewing performance appraisal results with those who have been evaluated, managers provide the feedback necessary for learning and improvement. Managers who keep these criteria for legal defensibility and the elements in Table 10.4 in mind are better equipped to select a sound appraisal system from alternative approaches and techniques.

Alternative Performance Appraisal Techniques

The list of alternative performance appraisal techniques is long and growing. Appraisal software programs also are proliferating. Unfortunately, many are simplistic, invalid, and unreliable. In general terms,

Table **10.4**	Elements of a Good Performance Appraisal

Appraisals can be used to justify merit increases, document performance problems or simply "touch base" with employees. Experts say HR first must decide what it wants the appraisal to accomplish [and] then customize the form and the process to meet that goal.

Elements to consider:

1. Objectives set by the employee and manager at the last appraisal.
2. List of specific competencies or skills being measured, with examples of successful behaviors.
3. Ratings scale appropriate to the organization.
4. Space for employee's self-appraisal.
5. Space for supervisor's appraisal.
6. Space for specific comments from the supervisor about the employee's performance.
7. Suggestions for employee development.
8. Objectives to meet by the next appraisal date.

Source: *HR Magazine* by Carla Johnson. Copyright 2001 by Society for Human Resource Management (SHRM). Reproduced with permission of Society for Human Resource Management (SHRM) in the format Textbook via Copyright Clearance Center.

an *invalid* appraisal instrument does not accurately measure what it is supposed to measure. *Unreliable* instruments do not measure criteria in a consistent manner. Many other performance appraisal techniques are so complex that they are impractical and burdensome to use. But armed with a working knowledge of the most popular appraisal techniques, a good manager can distinguish the strong from the weak. Once again, the strength of an appraisal technique is gauged by its conformity to the criteria for legal defensibility discussed previously. The following are some of the techniques used through the years:

- *Goal setting.* Within a management by objectives (MBO) framework, performance is typically evaluated in terms of formal objectives set at an earlier date. This is a comparatively strong technique if desired outcomes are clearly linked to specific behavior. For example, a product design engineer's "output" could be measured in terms of the number of product specifications submitted per month.
- *Written essays.* Managers describe the performance of employees in narrative form, sometimes in response to predetermined questions. Evaluators often criticize this technique for consuming too much time. This method is also limited by the fact that some managers have difficulty expressing themselves in writing.[63]
- *Critical incidents.* Specific instances of inferior and superior performance are documented by the supervisor when they occur. Accumulated incidents then provide an objective basis for evaluations at appraisal time. The strength of critical incidents is enhanced when evaluators document specific behavior in specific situations and ignore personality traits.[64]
- *Graphic rating scales.* Various traits or behavior are rated on incremental scales. For example, "initiative" could be rated on a 1(= low)—2—3—4—5(= high) scale. This technique is among the weakest when personality traits are employed. However, **behaviorally anchored rating scales (BARS)**, defined as performance rating scales divided into increments of observable job behavior determined through job analysis, are considered one of the strongest performance appraisal techniques. For example, managers at credit card issuer Capital One use performance rating scales

with behavioral anchors such as "Do you get things done well through other people? Do you play well as a team member?"[65]

- **Weighted checklists.** Evaluators check appropriate adjectives or behavioral descriptions that have predetermined weights. The weights, which gauge the relative importance of the randomly mixed items on the checklist, are usually unknown to the evaluator. Following the evaluation, the weights of the checked items are added or averaged to permit interpersonal comparisons. As with the other techniques, the degree of behavioral specificity largely determines the strength of weighted checklists.

- **Rankings/comparisons.** Coworkers in a subunit are ranked or compared in head-to-head fashion according to specified accomplishments or job behavior. A major shortcoming of this technique is that the absolute distance between ratees is unknown. For example, the employee ranked number one may be five times as effective as number two, who in turn is only slightly more effective than number three. Rankings/comparisons are also criticized for causing resentment among lower-ranked, but adequately performing, coworkers. *Fortune* magazine recently reported that this controversial practice resulted in employees filing class action lawsuits against some of the biggest corporations around, such as Microsoft, Ford, and Conoco.[66] Ford and Microsoft have since dropped their forced ranking systems.[67] This technique can be strengthened by combining it with a more behavioral technique, such as critical incidents or BARS.

- **Multirater appraisals.** This is a general label for a diverse array of nontraditional appraisal techniques involving more than one rater for the focal person's performance. The rationale for multirater appraisals is that "two or more heads are less biased than one." One approach

Ayoaz Rattansi/iStockphoto.com

that enjoyed faddish popularity in recent years involves 360-degree feedback. In a **360-degree review**, a manager is evaluated by his or her boss, peers, and subordinates. The results may or may not be statistically pooled and are generally fed back anonymously.[68] The use of 360-degree reviews as a performance appraisal tool has produced mixed results.[69]

A recent cross-cultural study found 360-degree feedback to be more effective in individualistic ("me") cultures than in collectivist ("we") cultures.[70] Researchers also found that 360-degree *feedback* is an effective management development technique, especially when paired with coaching.[71] Consider, for example, how 360-degree feedback is used at Procter & Gamble to evaluate its general managers. Once every six months, each manager's boss, peer managers, and direct reports use a two-page form called the GM Performance Scorecard to assess the manager's performance, leadership skills, and team-building abilities.[72]

360-degree review pooled, anonymous evaluation by one's boss, peers, and subordinates

TRAINING

No matter how carefully job applicants are screened and selected, typically a gap remains between what employees *do* know and what they *should* know. Present employees also develop knowledge and skill gaps in the face of progress and new technologies. Researchers say that knowledge in general is doubling every three years, and in some arenas, such as the medical field, knowledge can double every eighteen months.[73] Training is needed to help fill these knowledge and skill gaps. In 2009, U.S. companies with more than 100 employees spent $52.2 billion on training.[74] Huge as this number sounds, it was the smallest amount (in constant 2008 dollars) going back as far as 1986. The general trend in training budgets, worsened by the recent deep recession, has been going down since 1996.[75] This is bad news in terms of developing the human capital needed to keep the United States globally competitive. General Electric wisely sees the money it spends on training as an investment, not a cost, willingly devoting $1 billion a year to training and weeks or months to evaluating talent. Professor Brooks C. Holtom of Georgetown University notes, "Their investment is formidable," which perhaps explains why GE is known for its deep pool of talent.[76]

Formally defined, training is the process of changing employee behavior and/or attitudes through some type of guided experience. In this section, we explore the nature of today's training, list the ingredients of a good training program, examine two types of learning, and discuss training program evaluation.

Today's Training: Content and Delivery

Training magazine's annual survey of companies with at least 100 employees gives us a revealing snapshot of current training practices. The top portion of Figure 10.2 lists the nine most common types of training. How that training was delivered is displayed in the bottom portion of the figure. Surprisingly, despite all we read and hear about computer-based training and e-learning via the Internet, the majority of today's training is remarkably low-tech. We anticipate growth in e-learning and other nontraditional methods as the technology becomes more user-friendly, more conveniently mobile, and more affordable.[77] Consider, for example, this breakthrough application: Intuition, an Irish technology company, has developed "the world's first fully trackable mobile e-learning course" for PDAs such as BlackBerry. The course will make training easier and more convenient for both users and their employers.[78]

Meanwhile, the old standbys—classroom PowerPoint presentations, workbooks/manuals, DVDs, and seminars—are still the norm. For better or for worse, the typical college classroom is still a realistic preview of what awaits you in the world of workplace training.

Which instructional method is best? There are probably as many answers to this question as there are trainers. Given variables such as interpersonal differences, budget limitations, and instructor capabilities, it is safe to say that there is no one best

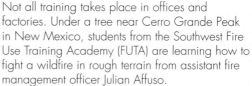

Not all training takes place in offices and factories. Under a tree near Cerro Grande Peak in New Mexico, students from the Southwest Fire Use Training Academy (FUTA) are learning how to fight a wildfire in rough terrain from assistant fire management officer Julian Affuso.

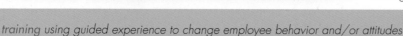

training using guided experience to change employee behavior and/or attitudes

Figure 10.2 | The Content and Delivery of Today's Training

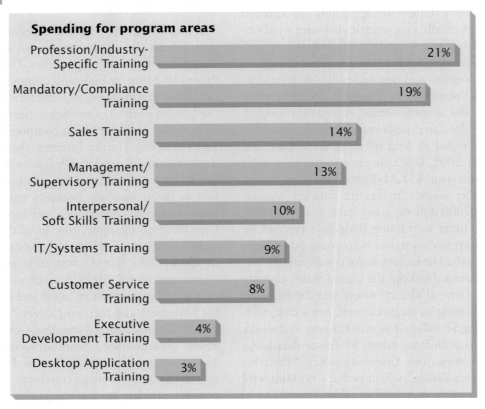

Spending for program areas

Program area	Percent
Profession/Industry-Specific Training	21%
Mandatory/Compliance Training	19%
Sales Training	14%
Management/Supervisory Training	13%
Interpersonal/Soft Skills Training	10%
IT/Systems Training	9%
Customer Service Training	8%
Executive Development Training	4%
Desktop Application Training	3%

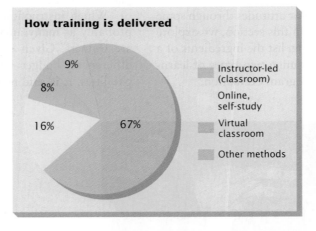

How training is delivered

- 67% Instructor-led (classroom)
- 16% Online, self-study
- 8% Virtual classroom
- 9% Other methods

Source: Data from "2008 Industry Report: Gauges and Drivers," *Training*, 45 (November–December 2008): 16–34.

training technique. This is especially true in today's four-generation workplaces. For example, inVentiv Health's chief learning officer Peter Marchesini says his firm is very aware of the diversity among its 7,000 employees worldwide. Thus, inVentiv delivers its training on a variety of platforms, from classroom to digital offerings, which allows employees to choose which teaching format best suits their learning styles and technical abilities.[79] Looking down the road, training content and delivery will be like a neat business outfit that is tailored to fit the individual—no longer a one-size-fits-everybody situation.[79]

The Ingredients of a Good Training Program

Although training needs and approaches vary, managers can get the most out of their training budgets by following a few guidelines. According to two training specialists, every training program should be designed along the following lines to maximize retention and transfer learning to the job:

1. Maximize the similarity between the training situation and the job situation.
2. Provide as much experience as possible with the task being taught.
3. Provide for a variety of examples when teaching concepts or skills.
4. Label or identify important features of a task.
5. Make sure that general principles are understood before expecting much transfer.
6. Make sure that the trained behaviors and ideas are rewarded in the job situation.
7. Design the training content so that the trainees can see its applicability.
8. Use adjunct questions to guide the trainee's attention.[80]

Skill Versus Factual Learning

The ingredients of a good training program vary according to whether skill learning or factual learning is involved, but should always include goal setting, modeling, practice, and feedback. This entails telling someone what to do, showing how to do it, letting someone try it, and giving corrective feedback.[81]

When factual learning is involved, the same sequence is used, except that in step 2, "meaningful presentation of the materials" is substituted for modeling. Keep in mind that the object of training is *learning*. Learning requires thoughtful preparation, carefully guided exposure to new ideas or behavior, and motivational support.

Training Program Evaluation: The Kirkpatrick Model

Virtually all teachers and trainers, at one time or another, have been haunted by the question, "Did anyone really learn anything today?" The answer lies in effective program evaluation. According to Donald L. Kirkpatrick's time-honored model, there are four ways to evaluate training program effectiveness. They evolve from most superficial and easy to most rigorous and difficult. The four levels of program evaluation in the Kirkpatrick model are:

- *Reaction*—Did the trainee enjoy the program and find it useful and relevant?
- *Learning*—Did the trainee acquire the knowledge and/or skills intended?
- *Behavior*—Did the trainee perform the newly acquired behavior(s) on the job (e.g., more effective conflict resolution, greater teamwork, increased compliance with regulations)?
- *Results*—Were the trainee's newly acquired behavior(s) responsible for measurable improvement in key outcomes (e.g., higher productivity, better quality, lower costs)?[82]

10d
Is Experience the Best Teacher?

Folk wisdom both trumpets the significance of experience and warns of its inadequacies. On the one hand, experience is described as the best teacher. On the other hand, experience is described as the teacher of fools, of those unable or unwilling to learn from accumulated knowledge or the teaching of experts.

QUESTIONS: Who can likely teach you the most, someone who has done the same job for 20 years or someone who has 20 years of varied experience? Explain. How can you effectively blend valuable lessons from both your own experience and the wisdom of others?

Source: James G. March, *The Ambiguities of Experience* (Ithaca, N.Y.: Cornell University Press, 2010), p. 1.

Post-training surveys are typically used to assess *re-action*, and quizzes or hands-on demonstrations are used to assess *learning*. *Behavior* and *results* fall into the category of what trainers call "transfer of training," involving the crucial jump from concept to application. Generally, training program evaluations are long on assessing reactions and short on documenting actual learning, behavior change, and on-the-job results. More rigorous measurement at the behavior and results levels is needed if training budgets are to be justified to top-management strategists.

Let us turn our attention to modern human resource management problems that have serious implications for the well-being of today's organizations and employees.

CONTEMPORARY HUMAN RESOURCE CHALLENGES AND PROBLEMS

Modern organizations are a direct reflection of society in general. People take societal influences to work (such as attitudes toward gender differences). Along with these predispositions, they take their social, emotional, behavioral, and health-related problems to work. Like it or not and prepared or not, managers face potential problems such as sexual harassment and alcohol and drug abuse. Today's challenge to deal effectively with human resource problems of this nature cannot be ignored because organizational competitiveness is at stake.

Discouraging Sexual Harassment

A great deal of misunderstanding surrounds the topic of sexual harassment because of sexist attitudes, vague definitions, differing perceptions,[83] and inconsistent court findings. Sexual harassment, defined generally as unwanted sexual attention or conduct, has both behavioral and legal dimensions (see Table 10.5). Important among these are the following:

- Although it is typically female employees who are the victims of sexual harassment, both women and men (in the United States) are protected under Title VII of the Civil Rights Act of 1964. For example, consider this recent case in Peoria, Arizona: Managers at Arrowhead Honda knew that one of

the general sales managers had been accused of inappropriately touching other employees and did nothing, according to a lawsuit filed with the Equal Employment Opportunity Commission. The two salesmen who claimed to have been harassed eventually resigned from their jobs.[84]

- Sexual harassment includes, but is not limited to, unwanted physical contact. Gestures, displays, joking, and language also may create a sexually offensive or hostile work environment. In fact, according to the courts, any behavior that diminishes an employee's work performance or psychological well-being contributes to a hostile work environment.[85]

- It is the manager's job to be aware of and correct cases of sexual harassment. Ignorance of such activity is not a valid legal defense. This was the case with Amanda West, a former Tyson Foods, Inc., employee in Kentucky, who recently was awarded $1.2 million in a sexual harassment claim. West informed her trainer and her supervisor that she was being sexually harassed, but they told her to ignore the behavior and asked her not to report it to the human resources department. Several weeks later, after she had resigned from

Table **10.5**   Behavioral and Legal Dimensions of Sexual Harassment

What exactly is sexual harassment? The Equal Employment Opportunity Commission (EEOC) says that unwelcome sexual advances, requests for sexual favors, and other verbal or physical conduct of a sexual nature constitute sexual harassment when submission to such conduct is made a condition of employment; when submission to or rejection of sexual advances is used as a basis for employment decisions; or when such conduct creates an intimidating, hostile, or offensive work environment. These EEOC guidelines interpreting Title VII of the Civil Rights Act of 1964 further state that employers are responsible for the actions of their supervisors and agents and that employers are responsible for the actions of other employees if the employer knows or should have known about the sexual harassment.

Source: "Sexual Harassment, 1: Discouraging It in the Work Place," by B. Terry Thornton. Reprinted by permission of the publisher, from *Personnel*, April 1986, © 1986. American Management Association, New York, N.Y. All rights reserved.

sexual harassment unwanted sexual attention that creates an offensive or intimidating work environment

As at any co-ed college or university, sexual harassment is a potential problem at the U.S. Naval Academy in Annapolis, Maryland. In response, the academy asked midshipmen Josh Foxton and Joy Dewey to jointly conduct a peer education session about sexual harassment.

the job, she reported the harassment to the HR manager, who also did not investigate her claim.[86]

Research evidence indicates that sexual harassment is commonplace. In one survey, 35 percent of women and 17 percent of men reported having been sexually harassed at work.[87] Employees who use e-mail systems must also contend with problems of sexual harassment in the form of rape threats and obscene words and graphics. Importantly, "if an employee uses company e-mail or a company business cell phone to harass another employee or if an employee is using personal e-mail or a personal cell phone during work hours to harass another employee, these situations could lead to employer liability if not addressed."[88] Harassment begins early—according to a new survey of 43,321 public and private school students ages 15 to 18: "50% said they had 'bullied, teased or taunted someone at least once' and 47% had been 'bullied, teased or taunted in a way that seriously upset me at least once.'"[89] According to research, people generally agree that unwanted sexual propositions, promises, or threats tied to sexual favors, lewd comments/gestures/jokes, and touching/grabbing/brushing qualify as sexual harassment. Beyond that, opinions differ.[90] Personal tastes and sensibilities vary widely

from individual to individual. In view of the foregoing evidence, preventive and corrective actions need to be taken both by the victims of sexual harassment and by management.

WHAT CAN THE VICTIM DO? Employees who believe they are victims of sexual harassment can try to live with it, fight back, complain to higher-ups, find another job, or sue their employer. Those who choose to file a lawsuit need to know how to arrange the odds in their favor. An analysis of sexual harassment cases revealed that the following five factors are likely to lead to success. Victims of sexual harassment tended to win their lawsuits when

- the harassment was severe.
- there were witnesses.
- management had been notified.
- there was supporting documentation.
- management had failed to take action.[91]

The more of these factors that apply, the greater the chances that a sexual harassment lawsuit will be successful. Courtrooms are the last line of defense for victims of sexual harassment. Preventive and remedial actions are also needed. Harassers need to be told by their victims, coworkers, and supervisors that their actions are illegal, unethical, and against company policy. As more organizations develop and enforce sexual harassment policies, the problem can be greatly reduced without costly court battles and the loss of valued employees.

WHAT CAN THE ORGANIZATION DO? Starting with top management, an organizationwide commitment to eliminating sexual harassment should be established. A clear policy statement, with behavioral definitions of sexual harassment and associated penalties, is essential. Like all policies, sexual harassment policies need to be disseminated and uniformly enforced if they are to have the desired impact. Appropriate training, particularly for new employees, can alert people to the problem and consequences of sexual harassment.[92] Finally, in accordance with EEOC guidelines, management can remain adequately informed of any sexual harassment in the organization by establishing a grievance procedure. Harassed employees should be able to get a fair hearing of their case without fear of retaliation.

Controlling Alcohol and Drug Abuse

Statistics tell a grim story about the number-one drug problem—alcohol. Research done by the National Institute on Alcohol Abuse and Alcoholism shows that more than 30 percent of American adults abuse alcohol or are alcoholics. Those who receive treatment usually don't get help until an average of eight years after they develop a dependency on drinking, and nearly one-fourth of alcoholics never receive treatment at all.[93]

Once believed to be a character disorder, alcoholism is now considered a disease in which an individual's normal social and economic roles are disrupted by the consumption of alcohol. Very few alcoholics are actually down-and-out folks on skid row; most are average citizens with jobs and families. Alcoholism cuts across all age, gender, racial, and ethnic categories. Experts say a glance in the mirror shows what the average alcoholic looks like.

Close on the heels of employee alcoholism as a growing problem is workplace drug abuse. As a general point of reference, a survey of people 12 and older by the U.S. Department of Health and Human Services found that 46 percent had used illicit drugs during their lifetime. The government defines illicit

drugs as "marijuana, hashish, cocaine, crack, heroin, hallucinogens, inhalants, or any prescription-type psychotherapeutic (non-medical usage)".[94] As with harassment, the problem starts early, with abuse of prescription drugs and marijuana among school-age youth.[95]

Because drug fads come and go, the drug problem is a moving target. A drug use study by the U.S. Department of Health and Human Services found that "10.5 percent of full-time employed adults and 11.9 percent of part-time employed adults were classified with dependence or abuse."[96] Compared with nonabusers, alcoholic employees and drug abusers are one-third less productive, ten times more likely to be absent, three times more likely to be involved in an accident, and responsible for 300 percent higher health care costs.[97]

One way employers are attempting to curb this costly erosion of human resources is with the controversial practice of drug testing for job applicants and employees. But does this tactic work? At least in part, the answer is "yes," according to Quest Diagnostics, which performs 7.3 million drug tests annually. Between 1988 and 2006, the rate for "positives" dropped from 13.6 percent to 3.8 percent (a 72 percent decline). Marijuana remained by far the most common cause for a positive test result.[98] Because drug testing is not necessarily a cure, however, the issue of employee drug abuse remains. Additional tactics are needed.

Unfortunately, it will be an uphill battle in view of this recent assessment that drug use is rampant in the United States and that related violence is even more fierce and widespread than ever before. About 460 tons of illegal drugs are sold in the United States each year, most of it brought in from other countries. The Office of National Drug Control Policy reports that the $320 billion annual global drug industry now accounts for 1 percent of all commerce on the planet.[99]

THE LEGAL SIDE OF WORKPLACE SUBSTANCE ABUSE. Businesses doing contract work for the U.S. government are squeezed on two sides by the law. On the one side, alcoholics and drug addicts are protected from employment discrimination by the Vocational Rehabilitation Act of 1973. They are presumed to have the same employment rights as any disabled person.[100] On the other side, employers with federal contracts exceeding $25,000 are subject to the Federal

alcoholism a disease in which alcohol abuse disrupts one's normal life

Drug-Free Workplace Act of 1988. These employers "must certify that they will maintain a drug-free workplace."[101] The idea is to rid federal contractors' workplaces of the production, distribution, and possession of controlled substances. Alcohol is not considered a controlled substance by the 1988 act. Companies found to be in violation of the act may lose their right to do business with the U.S. government.

Do these two legal thrusts work in opposite directions? Actually, the two laws work in combination because they make *rehabilitation* the best option.

REFERRAL AND REHABILITATION. Alcoholism and drug abuse typically reveal themselves to the manager in the form of increased absenteeism, tardiness, sloppy work, and complaints from coworkers. As soon as a steady decline in performance is observed, the manager should confront the individual with his or her poor performance record. Experts advise supervisors *not* to make accusations about alcohol or drug abuse. It is the employee's challenge to admit having such a problem. Management's job is to refer troubled employees to appropriate sources of help. Managers are cautioned against "playing doctor" when trying to help the alcohol- or drug-abusing employee. If the organization has an *employee assistance program* (EAP), counselors, or a company doctor, an in-house referral can be made.[102] One study tracked 25,000 employees for four years and found that for every dollar the company spent on its EAP, it saved four dollars in health claims and missed work days.[103]

Managers in small organizations without sophisticated employee services can refer the alcoholic employee to community resources such as Alcoholics Anonymous. Similar referral agencies for drug abusers exist in most communities. The overriding objective for the manager is to put troubled employees in touch with trained rehabilitation specialists as soon as possible.

10e
Medical Marijuana and the Workplace

Recent U.S. government survey: *Daily marijuana use has increased significantly among eighth-, 10th- and 12th-graders. . . .The survey found that for the second year in a row, more 12th-graders said they used marijuana than smoked cigarettes in the previous month.*

Case study: *Gary Ross had worked about three days as a systems administrator at a California telecommunications firm when the company withdrew its job offer—not because of Ross' poor performance, but because he had tested positive for marijuana in a drug screen conducted before he was hired. Ross, an Air Force veteran, used marijuana with a doctor's permission for an otherwise untreatable pain in his back. . . .*

[The California Supreme Court backed his employer.] Laws allowing medical marijuana use don't undercut an employer's right to dictate drug use standards for their workforces.

Firing medical marijuana users because they have it in their bodies amounts to disability discrimination and a form of wrongful discharge, "compassionate use" advocates claim.

So far, the courts aren't buying their claims. But workplace testing issues continue to smolder.

QUESTIONS: Should it be "zero tolerance" in the workplace with pre-employment and random drug testing? Or is it time for a different approach, given the growing number of states legalizing medical marijuana?

Sources: Rita Rubin, "Daily Marijuana Use Increases in Students," *USA Today* (December 15, 2010): 3A; and Diane Cadrain, "Medical Marijuana Testing Issues Smolder," *Society for Human Resource Management* (September 14, 2010), http://www.shrm.org/Publications/HRNews/Pages/MarijuanaTesting.aspx.

SUMMARY

1. Human resource management involves human resource acquisition, retention, and development. Four key human resource management activities necessarily linked to organizational strategy and structure are (1) human resource strategy, (2) recruitment and selection, (3) performance appraisal, and (4) training. After an employee has joined the organization, part of the human resource management process involves dealing with human resource problems such as sexual harassment and alcohol and drug abuse.

2. A systems approach to human resource strategy views both present and future employees as human capital that needs to be developed to its fullest potential. Pfeffer's seven people-centered practices can serve as a strategic agenda for human resource management. The seven practices are provision of job security, rigorous hiring practices, employee empowerment, performance-based compensation, comprehensive training, reduction of status differences, and sharing of key information.

3. Managers need to recruit for diversity to increase their appeal to job applicants and customers alike. The hurdle-like selection process can be summed up in the seven-step PROCEED model. The seven steps are (1) prepare (job analysis, job descriptions, and interview questions), (2) review (ensure the legality and fairness of the questions), (3) organize (assign the questions to an interview team), (4) conduct (collect information from the candidate), (5) evaluate (judge the candidate's qualifications), (6) exchange (meet and discuss information about the candidate), and (7) decide (extend a job offer or not).

4. Federal equal employment opportunity laws require managers to make hiring and other personnel decisions on the basis of ability to perform rather than personal prejudice. Affirmative action (making up for past discrimination) is evolving into managing diversity. Appreciation of interpersonal differences within a heterogeneous organizational culture is the goal of managing-diversity programs. The Americans with Disabilities Act of 1990 (ADA) requires employers to make reasonable accommodations so that disabled people can enter the workforce.

5. All employment tests must be valid predictors of job performance. Because interviews are the most popular employee screening device, experts recommend structured rather than traditional, informal interviews.

6. Legally defensible performance appraisals enable managers to make objective personnel decisions. Four key legal criteria are job analysis, behavior-oriented appraisals, specific written instructions, and discussion of results with ratees. Seven common performance appraisal techniques are goal setting, written essays, critical incidents, graphic rating scales, weighted checklists, rankings/comparisons, and 360-degree reviews.

7. Today, training is a huge business in itself. Unfortunately, America's global competitiveness is threatened by a steady decline in training budgets. Managers can ensure that their training investment pays off by using techniques appropriate to the situation. Training programs should be designed with an eye toward maximizing the retention of learning and its transfer to the job. Successful skill learning and factual learning both depend on goal setting, practice, and feedback. But skills should be modeled, whereas factual information should be presented in a logical and meaningful manner. According to the Kirkpatrick model, training program evaluation can occur at four increasingly rigorous levels: reaction, learning, behavior, and results. More emphasis is needed on the behavior and results levels to ensure transfer of training to the job.

8. Sexual harassment and alcohol and drug abuse are contemporary human resource problems that require top-management attention and strong policies. A sexual harassment policy needs to define the problem behaviorally, specify penalties, and be disseminated and enforced. Useful ways to fight substance abuse in the workplace include drug testing for job applicants and employees and referral to professional help and rehabilitation.

TERMS TO UNDERSTAND

Human resource management, p. 270
Human capital, p. 271
Job analysis, p. 274
Job description, p. 274
Affirmative action program
(AAP), p. 275

Employment selection test, p. 277
Structured interview, p. 277
Behavior-based interview, p. 279
Performance appraisal, p. 280
Behaviorally anchored rating scales
(BARS), p. 281

360-degree review, p. 282
Training, p. 283
Sexual harassment, p. 286
Alcoholism, p. 288

ACTION LEARNING EXERCISE

WRITING BEHAVIORAL INTERVIEW QUESTIONS

Instructions: Working either alone or as a member of a team, select a specific job and write *two* behavioral interview questions for at least *five* of these categories:

Being a self-starter and demonstrating initiative

Being a leader

Being an effective communicator

Being ethical

Being able to make a hard decision

Being a team player

Being able to handle conflict

Being able to handle a setback, disappointment, or failure

Tips: If you pick a higher-level job, this exercise will be easier because people at higher levels have more responsibility and engage in a broader range of behavior. Be sure to prepare by rereading the Behavioral Interviewing section in this chapter.

FOR CONSIDERATION/DISCUSSION

1. How well will each of your questions uncover *actual past job-related behavior?*

2. Would any of your questions put the candidate at a disadvantage because of his or her gender, race, ethnicity, religion, disability, marital status, or sexual preference?

3. When others hear your questions, are they judged to be *fair* questions?

4. Which question is your absolute best? Why? Which is your weakest? Why?

5. What (if anything) do you like about behavioral interviews? What (if anything) do you dislike about them?

ETHICS EXERCISE

 DO THE RIGHT THING

IS MY PRIVACY UP IN THE CLOUD?

It sounds like a privacy breach waiting to happen: Take some of your company's most classified information—employee records containing Social Security numbers, salaries— and put it on a bunch of remote servers that let you access the data via the public Internet.

Yet Workday, a private, venture-backed company, is successfully getting companies such as Sony Pictures and Flextronics to move their human resources software to an Internet-based system.

Workday . . . contends it can securely lower customers' tech costs (fewer servers to purchase and maintain) and improve efficiency (software upgrades take days, not months) by delivering complex applications and information over the Net, also known as the "cloud."

"It cost me less than half of what I would have paid to do it in-house," says Andy Schlei, vice president of information technology for Sony Pictures, which switched to Workday's offering last year.

Source: Excerpted from Jon Fortt, "A New Way to Cut Your Payroll Costs," *Fortune* (April 12, 2010): 26.

What are the ethical implications of the following interpretations?

1. This is a good way for companies to be more efficient and cut information technology costs. The privacy issue here is no greater than with all our other sensitive personal information such as Social Security and bank account numbers already stored on Internet servers around the world.

2. This cost-cutting move is acceptable if management makes sure all sensitive employee information and data are password protected on high-security networks. Is any Internet-linked database security system ever really fail-safe?

3. This is a bad idea because just one hacking incident could destroy employees' trust in management and have costly legal consequences. Protecting the confidentiality of an employer's human resource and pay records is a sacred trust that should not be outsourced.

4. Your own ethical interpretation?

MANAGERS-IN-ACTION VIDEO CASE STUDY

MAINE MEDIA WORKSHOPS

Human Resources Management: Building a Contingent Workforce

This media workshop organization offers weeklong courses in filmmaking and photography at its scenic Rockport, Maine, location. Mimi Edmunds, Director of Film Programs, and Elizabeth Greenberg, Director of Education, share their approach to attracting and retaining contingent faculty to instruct the workshops. They face many challenges, including rapid growth and working with industry professionals who may have last-minute scheduling conflicts and other, more lucrative commitments. Learn how this organization manages last-minute cancellations and leverages its vast network to recruit and retain top talent.

For more information about Maine Media Workshops, visit its Web site: www.mainemedia.edu/.

Before watching the video, answer the following questions:

1. What are the most effective recruiting methods to attract top talent for an organization?
2. What is a contingent workforce?
3. What industries are more likely to hire contingent workers?

After watching the video, answer the following questions:

4. What challenges does Maine Media Workshops face in hiring contingent faculty instructors?
5. What are its strategies to recruit the best talent and keep those individuals coming back to teach year after year?
6. How does Main Media Workshops ensure consistency and quality from one week to the next with new instructors coming in all the time?
7. What would you do the same and what would you do differently to recruit and train contingent faculty for Maine Media Workshops?

CLOSING CASE

HOW UPS DELIVERS OBJECTIVE PERFORMANCE APPRAISALS

Determining whether a supervisor is using enough objectivity during the employee review is one of the most difficult aspects of any company's employee evaluation process.

With this in mind, the United Parcel Service (UPS), based in Washington D.C., is deploying personal digital assistants (PDAs) to its supervisors to use in on-road driver evaluations. The PDAs are equipped with proprietary software that standardizes the evaluation process, helping to ensure that each driver review is as objective as possible.

"Our supervisors do ride-alongs to see if the driver is following procedures and adhering to our health and safety policies," says Cathy Callagee, vice president of applications development for UPS's operations portfolio. "But this is problematic because supervisors have to write notes on paper, then bring their notes back to the office and type them into reports."

Paper is eliminated with the help of PDAs, which display a series of checklists for the supervisor to use during the evaluation. The checklists guide the supervisors through a list of duties the driver should be performing. The supervisor simply checks off each duty as the driver completes it. Additionally, the checklists are uniform across the UPS network, so each driver receives the same evaluation, regardless of who is conducting the review.

The new PDAs also are helpful for supervisors because they serve as a remote office, allowing supervisors to receive e-mail and check the status of other activities while they are on the road with drivers. Currently, UPS has 1,400 PDAs in the field, with plans to deploy an additional 600 this year.

"Supervisors can now electronically write how their drivers are doing and if they are following procedures," Callagee says. "If not, the supervisor can bring the applied methods right up on the PDA and walk the driver through it."

Before PDAs, drivers and supervisors were forced to memorize these instructions or put notes in their back pocket, but since the data is transmitted electronically, they can simply plug the PDA into their PC and it automatically uploads the information to the PC.

"The use of PDAs eliminates paperwork, makes the rides more consistent and complete, improves the accountability of UPS supervisors and also increases the professionalism for the group," Callagee says. "This is going to become a way of life for UPS supervisors."

The PDAs also identify training needs, which will be particularly helpful to new drivers who might need additional safety training. "Our objective is to have drivers follow procedures that will help make their job safer, [make them] more efficient and provide better service for customers," Callagee says. "From a workforce perspective, the use of PDAs will make training easier so we can accomplish these goals."

For Discussion

1. Would Jeffrey Pfeffer be likely to call UPS a people-centered company? Why or why not?

2. Which one (or what combination) of the performance appraisal techniques discussed in this chapter is UPS using? Explain.

3. How would you rate the legal defensibility of UPS's driver evaluation program? Explain.

4. From an ethical standpoint, there is a thin line between supervision and "snoopervision." In your opinion, has UPS crossed that line? Explain.

5. How could UPS improve its driver evaluation program?

Source: From Gail Johnson, "Online Objectivity," *Training*, 41 (July 2004): 18. © VNU Business Media, Inc. Reprinted with permission.

11 Communicating
in the Internet Age

"It is a luxury to be understood."[1]
—RALPH WALDO EMERSON

The Changing Workplace

MAUREEN CHIQUET, GLOBAL CEO, CHANEL: "THE BEST ADVICE I EVER GOT"

Early in my career, I worked at the Gap as a merchant in women's denim. I worked with designers to choose styles for the stores, with planners to determine how much inventory to buy, and with a sourcing team to manage production. A year into this job, I came up with what I thought was a terrific style: a stovepipe jean, with a wider leg, in a great new wash. Both research and instinct told me the product could be huge. So when our CEO—Mickey Drexler, who now runs J. Crew—called one day from a conference room and asked if I could come present to him and the head of marketing, I felt ready and pretty proud.

The marketing chief loved the samples and immediately started talking excitedly about an approach to advertising. But Mickey was not so sure. "Why wouldn't we use that same wash," he asked, "with Classic Fit jeans instead?"

Now, I was a very confident young merchant: I knew what was happening, what was cool, and what should and shouldn't be in the store. And instead of acquiescing, I began to argue my agenda, offering all kinds of reasons why that wash and style belonged together. Mickey kept asking questions, getting louder and progressively angrier. Finally I shut up and slunk back to my office, depressed, wondering if I'd lost my job for talking back to one of the most prominent retail executives in the country. A few minutes afterward, however, he called. "Maureen!" he bellowed, "I'm going to give you some important advice. You're a terrific merchant. But you've gotta learn to *listen!*"

Of course, Mickey was right about using the wash with the Classic Fit style, and we successfully launched those jeans. And 20 years later, his words continue to have a profound effect on how I think about my company's products and interact with its employees, customers, and other stakeholders. In retail—as well as in other industries—you've got to have a strong point of view and present it effectively. But to lead effectively and achieve real

OBJECTIVES

- **Identify** each major link in the communication process.
- **Explain** the concept of media richness and the Lengel-Daft contingency model of media selection.
- **Identify** the five communication strategies, and **specify** guidelines for using them.
- **Discuss** why it is important for managers to know about grapevine and nonverbal communication.
- **Explain** at least four ways managers can encourage upward communication.
- **Explain** how to deal with information overload, and **outline** a workplace policy for social networking sites.
- **List** two practical tips for each of the three modern communication technologies (e-mail, cell phones, and videoconferences), and **summarize** the pros and cons of telecommuting.
- **Specify** at least three practical tips for improving each of the following communication skills: listening, writing, and running a meeting.

business results as the head of any enterprise, you have to listen. You've got to constantly ask questions and seek out diverse opinions, and remain humble enough to change your mind—whether about a product or a person.

Whenever I'm in a Chanel boutique, I ask the store employees what's selling, how consumers are responding, and what we should be doing differently. Their frontline observations help me refine my own thoughts about the business—and sometimes change my mind outright about a piece of merchandise or even a big strategy. Back in the office, I spend about 75% of my time listening to my direct reports' insights, and I make regular dates with our partners around the world to hear their perspectives, too. I'm always seeking information from as many varied sources as possible: I'll check YouTube, for example, just to see what people are watching. I keep my ears open and my eyes peeled for new trends in culture, the arts, film, theater, and the like.

Listening has its drawbacks because sometimes you realize that people are just telling you what they want you to hear. Yet, ultimately, what's good for this business—surrounding myself with talented teams and relying on their expertise—is good for me personally, too. If I hadn't taken Mickey's advice, put a piece of tape over my mouth, and really listened to people when I got to Chanel, I wouldn't have been successful for very long.

Source: As quoted in Daisy Wademan Dowling, "The Best Advice I Ever Got," *Harvard Business Review*, 86 (November 2008): 30.

One of the most difficult challenges for management is getting individuals to understand and voluntarily pursue organizational objectives. Effective communication, as used by Maureen Chiquet to get everyone at Chanel on the same page, is vital in meeting this challenge—a challenge that has grown in the digital age. During a recent guest lecture at the University of Pennsylvania, she made a telling observation about communicating today: There is a powerful disconnect between the traditional Chanel model of one-way communications and the new two-way digital world of communications. Every rule set in stone about high-end branding is overturned in the age of the Internet.[2] Good thing Chiquet is a careful listener.

Organizational communication takes in a great deal of territory. Virtually every management function and interaction with internal and external stakeholders (advertising and media relations included) requires effective communication. Planning and controlling require a good deal of communicating, as do organizational design and development, decision making and problem solving, leadership, and staffing. Organizational cultures would not exist without communication. Studies have shown that both organizational and individual performance improve when managerial communication is effective. An international study of 264 companies concluded that there is a strong correlation between effective communication and high levels of employee engagement.[3] Given today's team-oriented organizations, where things need to be accomplished with and through people over whom managers often have no direct authority, communication skills are more important than ever. In fact, a survey of 133 executives revealed that good communication is the most highly-valued management skill, followed by vision, honesty, decision-making ability, and relationship building.[4]

Thanks to modern technology, we can communicate more broadly and quickly and less expensively than ever before. Ironically, many believe the *quality* of workplace communication has gotten worse. In a 2010 survey of 2,115 managers, over 51 percent rated their employees' communication skills as "only average."[5] Turning the tables, a survey of 493 employees found only 37 percent saying they are getting more frequent corporate updates than the year before.[6] The challenge to improve this situation is both immense and immediate. But before managers, or anyone else for that matter, can become more effective communicators, they need to appreciate that communication is a complex process subject to a great deal of perceptual distortion and many problems. This is especially true for the apparently simple activity of communicating face to face.

THE COMMUNICATION PROCESS

Management scholar Keith Davis defined communication as "the transfer of information and understanding from one person to another person."[7] Communication is inherently a social process. Whether one communicates face to face with a single person or with a group of people via a video feed or Twitter, it is still a social activity involving two or more people. By analyzing the communication process, one discovers that it is a chain made up of identifiable links (see Figure 11.1). Links in this process include sender, encoding, medium, decoding, receiver, and feedback.[8] The essential purpose of this chain-like process is to send an idea from one person to another in a way that will be understood by the receiver. Like any other chain, the communication chain is only as strong as its weakest link. For example, a recent survey uncovered this weak link: the majority of respondents stated they did not receive enough positive feedback or constructive criticism from their supervisors.[9] Sound familiar?

Encoding

Thinking takes place within the privacy of your brain and is greatly affected by how you perceive your environment. But when you want to pass along a thought to someone else, an entirely different process begins. This second process, communication, requires that you, the sender, package the idea for understandable transmission. Encoding starts at this point. The purpose of encoding is to translate internal thought patterns into a language or code that the intended receiver of the message will probably understand.

Managers usually rely on words, gestures, or other symbols for encoding. Their choice of symbols depends on several factors, one of which is the nature of the message itself. Is it technical or nontechnical, emotional or factual? Perhaps it could be expressed better with colorful PowerPoint slides than with words, as in the case of a budget report. To express skepticism, merely a shrug might be enough. More fundamentally, will the encoding help get the attention of busy and distracted people?

Greater cultural diversity in today's global workplace also necessitates careful message encoding.[10] E-mail translation programs promise to make the encoding process a bit easier when communicating across cultures.

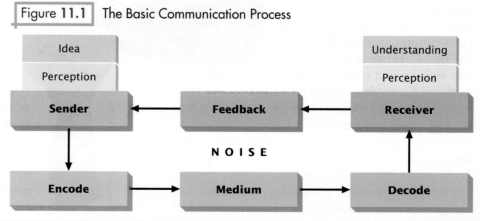

Figure 11.1   The Basic Communication Process

Idea
Perception
Sender

Feedback

Understanding
Perception
Receiver

N O I S E

Encode → **Medium** → **Decode**

communication interpersonal transfer of information and understanding

In organizational life, effective communicators, such as this manager, get the desired response by skillfully using each link in the basic communication process. Sometimes a little appropriate humor can help, too.

Selecting a Medium

Managers can choose among a number of media: face-to-face conversations, phone calls, e-mails, memos, letters, computer reports and networks, photographs, bulletin boards, meetings, organizational publications, and others. Communicating with those outside the organization opens up further possibilities, such as news releases, press conferences, and advertising on television and radio or in magazines and newspapers, billboards, or on the Internet.

MEDIA SELECTION IN CROSS-CULTURAL SETTINGS

The importance of selecting an appropriate medium is magnified when one moves from internal to cross-cultural dealings. Recall the distinction between low-context and high-context cultures that we made in Chapter 4; managers moving from low-context cultures to high-context cultures need to select communication media with care: In low-context cultures like North America and Europe, the message's content is more important than the delivery method, so business communication formats like videoconferencing and e-mail are acceptable. But in high-context cultures, such as Asia and the Middle

East, the setting or context conveys as much or even more meaning than the words, so face-to-face interaction is essential.[11]

A CONTINGENCY APPROACH. A contingency model for media selection was developed by Robert Lengel and Richard Daft.[12] It pivots on the concept of media richness. Media richness describes the capacity of a given medium to convey information and promote learning. As illustrated in the top portion of Figure 11.2, media vary in richness from high (or rich) to low (or lean). Face-to-face conversation is a rich medium because it (1) simultaneously provides *multiple information cues*, such as message content, tone of voice, facial expressions, and so on; (2) facilitates immediate *feedback*; and (3) is *personal* in focus. In contrast, bulletins and general computer reports are lean media; that is, they convey limited information and foster limited learning. Lean media, such as general e-mail announcements, provide a single cue, do not facilitate immediate feedback, and are impersonal.

Management's challenge, indicated in the bottom portion of Figure 11.2, is to match media richness with the situation. Nonroutine problems are best handled with rich media such as face-to-face, telephone, or video interactions. John Chambers, the highly respected CEO of Cisco Systems, explained why he prefers richer media when he said, "I'm a voice person. I communicate with emotion." Chambers leaves as many as 50 voice mails a day and routinely uses video on demand so employees and customers can watch his videotaped messages

media richness a medium's capacity to convey information and promote learning

Figure **11.2** The Lengel-Daft Contingency Model of Media Selection

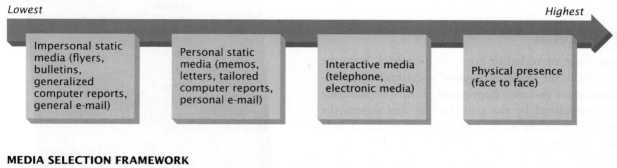

MEDIA RICHNESS HIERARCHY

Lowest   *Highest*

Impersonal static media (flyers, bulletins, generalized computer reports, general e-mail)

Personal static media (memos, letters, tailored computer reports, personal e-mail)

Interactive media (telephone, electronic media)

Physical presence (face to face)

MEDIA SELECTION FRAMEWORK

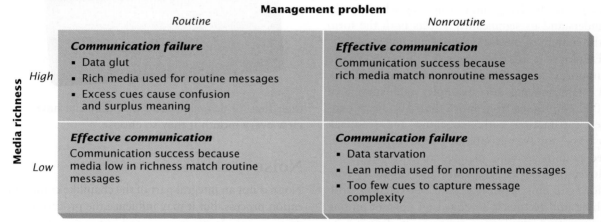

Management problem

Routine   *Nonroutine*

Communication failure
- Data glut
- Rich media used for routine messages
- Excess cues cause confusion and surplus meaning

Effective communication
Communication success because rich media match nonroutine messages

Effective communication
Communication success because media low in richness match routine messages

Communication failure
- Data starvation
- Lean media used for nonroutine messages
- Too few cues to capture message complexity

Media richness — High / Low

Source: Updated from Robert H. Lengel and Richard L. Daft, "The Selection of Communication Media as an Executive Skill," *Academy of Management Executive*, 2 (August 1988): 226, 227, exhibits 1 and 2. Reprinted by permission.

at their convenience.[13] Lean media, on the other hand, are more appropriate for routine problems.

Examples of mismatched media include reading a corporate annual report at a stockholders' meeting (data glut) or announcing a layoff with an impersonal e-mail (data starvation). Examples of mismatches abound: 400 workers at Radio Shack's Texas headquarters received e-mails terminating their employment, and a London-based business fired an employee via a text message.[14] Imagine being on the receiving end of these poor media-selection decisions.

Decoding

Even the most expertly fashioned message will not accomplish its purpose unless it is understood. After physically receiving the message, the receiver needs to comprehend it. If the message has been properly encoded, decoding is supposed to take place rather routinely. But perfect decoding is nearly impossible in our world of many languages and cultures. Case in point: language problems have been cited as a major reason why workplace deaths among Hispanic workers jumped 76 percent between 1992 and 2007, according to the most recent U.S. Bureau of Labor Statistics data.[15]

Successful decoding also is more likely if the receiver knows the jargon and terminology used in the message. American sports jargon is particularly troublesome in cross-cultural business dealings. Imagine how confusing it must be if you're a businessperson in Brazil or India, and your American colleague is telling you to "make a pitch" about a "home-run product."[16] These baseball references would mean nothing to you (and if they don't to you right now, ask a baseball-loving classmate). It helps, too, if the receiver understands the sender's purpose and background situation. Effective listening is given special attention later in this chapter.

Feedback

Some sort of verbal or nonverbal feedback from the receiver to the sender is required to complete the communication process. Appropriate forms of feedback are determined by the same factors that govern the sender's encoding decision. Without feedback, senders have no way of knowing whether their ideas have been accurately understood. Communicating without feedback amounts to flying blind. Knowing whether others understand us significantly affects both the form and the content of our follow-up communication.

Employee surveys consistently underscore the importance of timely and personal feedback from management. For example, one survey of 500,000 employees from more than 300 firms contrasted satisfaction with "coaching and feedback from boss" for two groups of employees: (1) committed employees who planned to stay with their employer for at least five years and (2) those who intended to quit within a year. Satisfaction with coaching and feedback averaged 64 percent among the committed employees, whereas it dropped to 34 percent among those ready to quit.[17] At accounting firm PricewaterhouseCoopers, new employees decide when to hold their first performance review with their boss. It just needs to happen sometime in

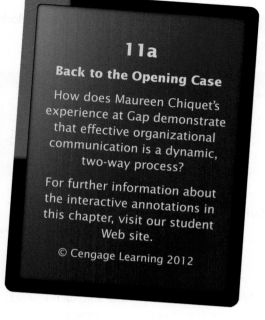

11a

Back to the Opening Case

How does Maureen Chiquet's experience at Gap demonstrate that effective organizational communication is a dynamic, two-way process?

For further information about the interactive annotations in this chapter, visit our student Web site.

© Cengage Learning 2012

their first 90 days, but after that they can have a review every month if they so choose.[18]

Noise

Noise is not an integral part of the chainlike communication process, but it may influence the process at any or all points. As the term is used here, noise is any interference with the normal flow of understanding from one person to another. This is a very broad definition. Thus, a speech impairment, garbled technical transmission, a negative attitude, lies, misperception, illegible print or pictures, cell phone static, partial loss of hearing, and poor eyesight all qualify as noise. Understanding tends to diminish as noise increases. In general, the effectiveness of organizational communication can be improved in two ways. Steps can be taken to make verbal and written messages more understandable. And at the same time, noise can be minimized by foreseeing and neutralizing sources of interference.

It's a noisy world, and sometimes we have to compete with distractions when we're communicating. We need to take all possible sources of noise into consideration, tailoring our messages and selecting our media accordingly.

Miles Schuster/SuperStock

noise any interference with the normal flow of communication

DYNAMICS OF ORGANIZATIONAL COMMUNICATION

As a writer on the subject pointed out, human co-operation is the foundation of civilization, and communication is the key to cooperation.[19] Accordingly, effective communication is also essential for cooperation within productive organizations. At least four dynamics of organizational communication—communication strategies, the grapevine, nonverbal communication, and upward communication—largely determine the difference between effectiveness and ineffectiveness in this important area.

Communication Strategies

A good deal of effort goes into plotting product development, information technology, financial, and marketing strategies these days. Much less attention, if any, is devoted to organizational communication strategies.[20] Hence, organizational communication tends to be haphazard and often ineffective. A more systematic approach is needed. This section introduces five basic communication strategies, with an eye toward improving the overall quality of communication.

A COMMUNICATION CONTINUUM WITH FIVE STRATEGIES.
A team of authors led by communication expert Phillip G. Clampitt created the useful communication strategy continuum shown in Figure 11.3. Communication effectiveness is the vertical dimension of the model, ranging from low to high. A message communicated via any of the media discussed earlier is effective if one's intended meaning is conveyed fully and accurately to the receiver. The horizontal dimension of Clampitt's model is the amount of information transmitted, which may range from great to little. Plotted on this quadrant are five common communication strategies. Let us examine each one more closely.

- *Spray & Pray.* This is the organizational equivalent of a large lecture section where passive receivers are showered with information in the hope that some of it will stick. Managers employing the Spray & Pray strategy assume "more is better." Unfortunately, as employees who are swamped by corporate e-mail directives and

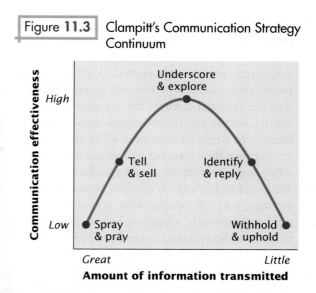

Figure 11.3   Clampitt's Communication Strategy Continuum

announcements will attest, more is *not* necessarily better. This strategy suffers from being one-way, impersonal, and unhelpful because it leaves receivers to sort out what is actually important or relevant.

- *Tell & Sell.* This strategy involves communicating a more restricted set of messages and taking time to explain their importance and relevance. Top executives often rely on Tell & Sell when introducing new strategies, merger plans, and reorganizations. A potentially fatal flaw arises when more time is spent polishing the presentation than assessing the receivers' actual needs.

- *Underscore & Explore.* Key information and issues closely tied to organizational success are communicated with this give-and-take strategy. Priorities are included and justifications are offered. Unlike the first two strategies, this one is two-way. Receivers are treated as active rather than passive participants in the process. Giving employees the creative freedom to explore their ideas in a disciplined manner generates feedback.[21] Listening, resolving misunderstandings, building consensus and commitment, and addressing actual or potential obstacles are fundamental to success with the Underscore & Explore strategy.

- *Identify & Reply.* This is a reactive and sometimes defensive strategy. Employee concerns about prior communications are the central focus here. Employees are not only viewed as active participants; they essentially drive the process because they are assumed to know the key issues. According to Clampitt and his colleagues, those using the Identify & Reply strategy need to be good listeners because they respond to rumors and gossip while employees set the actual agenda.[22]

- *Withhold & Uphold.* With this communication strategy, you tell people what you think they need to know only when you believe they need to know it. Secrecy and control are paramount. Because information is viewed as power, it is rationed and restricted. Those in charge cling to their rigid and narrow view of things when challenged or questioned. If you think this sounds like the old Theory X command-and-control style of management, you're right. The Withhold & Uphold communication strategy virtually guarantees rumors and resentment.

In organizational life, one can find hybrid combinations of these five strategies. But usually there is a dominant underlying strategy that may or may not be effective.

SEEKING A MIDDLE GROUND. Both ends of the continuum in Figure 11.3 are problematic: On one end workers receive copious information while at the other end they receive next to none. For both extremes, workers cannot frame or make sense out of organizational events, and they wind up developing their own personal interpretations of the information rather than receiving a consistent, cohesive message.[23]

Accordingly, managers need to follow this set of guidelines when selecting a communication strategy appropriate to the situation: (1) avoid Spray & Pray and Withhold & Uphold; (2) use Tell & Sell and Identify & Reply sparingly; and (3) use Underscore & Explore as much as possible (see Green Management: Toward Sustainability).

MERGING COMMUNICATION STRATEGIES AND MEDIA RICHNESS. Present and future managers who effectively blend lessons from Figure 11.2 (media selection) and Figure 11.3 (communication strategies) are on the path toward improved organizational communication. The trick is to select the

richest medium possible (given resource constraints) when employing the Tell & Sell, Identify & Reply, and Underscore & Explore strategies. Face-to-Face communication is generally best when the development of an interpersonal relationship is at stake, such as when giving instruction, coaching, counseling, or delivering urgent or bad news.[24]

The Grapevine

In every organization, large or small, there are actually two communication systems, one formal and the other informal. Sometimes these systems complement and reinforce each other; at other times they come into direct conflict. Although theorists have found it convenient to separate the two, distinguishing one from the other in real life can be difficult. Information required to accomplish official objectives is channeled

---

11b
Quick Quiz

Pontish Yeramyan, management consultant:

Assume that by virtue of your being a boss, people are already guarded and worried about what you think of them. Ease that tension by sharing things about yourself. That means speaking from the "I" perspective—how it is for you. One CEO we work with is loved and respected. When he talks about growth, he explains what he's working on for his own development—that he needs to be more expressive and demanding—rather than talking in a sterile and objective way. It lets his employees see him as human and think, "I can be real because he's being real."

QUESTIONS: This describes which one of Clampitt's five communication strategies? What are the strengths and limitations of this strategy?

Source: As quoted in Beth Kowitt, "Building the (Workplace) Ties That Bind," *Fortune* (December 6, 2010): 78.

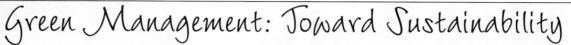

Green Management: Toward Sustainability

How Tasty Catering's Communication Strategy Spawned a Green Business

Tasty Catering's [54] employees participate in virtually all important decisions, including those involving company structure and health care policy. The [Elk Grove Village, Ill.] company encourages an entrepreneurial spirit among employees: Anyone with an idea for a new business can pitch it to management, and if the idea flies, the company provides various forms of support. Recently, an employee wanted to create an environmentally friendly gift-basket company. Tasty Catering helped with the business plan and provided the funding. It now runs out of Tasty Catering's facilities as a sister business.

For Discussion: Why is this just plain good management, from so many different angles? Why are upward communication and participative decision making so motivating and empowering for today's employees?

Source: Excerpted from "First, People: Tasty Catering," *Inc.*, 32 (June 2010): 67.

---

throughout the organization via the formal system. By definition, official or formal communication flows in accordance with established lines of authority and structural boundaries. Media for official communication include all those channels discussed earlier. But intertwined with this formal network is the grapevine, the unofficial and informal communication system. The term *grapevine* can be traced back to Civil War days, when vine-like telegraph wires were strung from tree to tree across battlefields.[25] *Inc.* magazine offered this observation about the grapevine: People gossip, and bad or embarrassing news travels at lightening speed.[26] Indeed, according to one survey, most employees spend about 65 hours of office time gossiping each year.[27] All the more reason to learn more about the grapevine and how to deal with it.

WORDS OF CAUTION ABOUT THE E-GRAPEVINE

The Internet has been a boon to the grapevine, vastly and instantly extending its reach via e-mail and other Web tools such as Twitter. But this new communication landscape holds some nasty surprises for the unwary. Lacking the nonverbal cues and interactivity of face-to-face interaction, e-mail makes it difficult for employees to interpret the messages they receive. Thus, smart employees do not engage in e-gossip.[28]

Another reason savvy employees avoid e-gossip is that it leaves an electronic trail that could be read by anyone. The same goes for blogs and online social networking sites such as Facebook and Twitter. The e-grapevine is one more area where lawmakers, ethics specialists, and company policy makers are racing to catch up with new technology. According to legal experts, policies to get workplace blogging (and social networking) under control should:

- Define the appropriate level of social networking at work.
- Specify that a blog offers an employee's opinion, not the company's opinion.
- Assure employees that their information is confidential.[29]

THE GRAPEVINE HAS A POSITIVE SIDE DESPITE ITS BAD REPUTATION

One survey of 341 participants in a management development seminar uncovered predominantly negative feelings among managers toward the grapevine. Moreover, first-line supervisors perceived the grapevine to be more influential than did middle managers. This second finding led the researchers to conclude that at the lower levels of the managerial hierarchy, the grapevine is more prevalent and impactful.[30] Finally, the survey found that employees of relatively small organizations (fewer than 50 people) viewed the grapevine as less influential than did those from larger organizations (more than 100 people).

---

grapevine unofficial and informal communication system

Ryan Howe/istockphoto.com

The Internet and the availability of mobile devices make it easier than ever for workers to communicate through the grapevine, except now it's an e-grapevine. This "global e-grapevine" is both good and bad news for organizations and managers.

A logical explanation for this last finding is that smaller organizations are usually more informal.

In spite of the negative attitude that many managers harbor toward it, the grapevine does have a markedly positive side. In fact, experts estimate grapevine communication to be about 75 percent accurate.[31] Even though the grapevine has a reputation among managers as a bothersome source of inaccurate information and vicious gossip, it helps satisfy a natural desire to know what is really going on and gives employees a sense of belonging. A recent study of social interactions in the workplace revealed that positive gossip is actually more common than negative gossip, and it confirmed that gossip helps staff members reach a better understanding of the social environment, which may enable them to have greater influence.[32] Moreover, grapevine communication can carry useful information through the organization

11c
Should I Tell Him?

Letter to an advice column:

I spotted a memo from the CEO on my boss's desk—and proceeded to find out who will be the targets of downsizing. I don't need a lecture about wandering eyes, but I wonder if I should tell my co-worker that he's on the list.

QUESTIONS: What is the ethical thing to do here? What would you do? Explain your rationale.

Source: As quoted in Evelyn Nussenbaum, "I Know Something I Shouldn't Know," *Business 2.0,* 5 (January–February 2004): 115.

with amazing speed and help management learn how employees truly feel about policies and programs.

COPING WITH THE GRAPEVINE. Considering how the grapevine can be an influential and sometimes negative force, what can management do about it? First and foremost, the grapevine *cannot be extinguished.* In fact, attempts to crush the grapevine and stop the rumor mill may serve instead to stimulate it. Staying attuned, subtly monitoring the grapevine, and officially correcting or countering any potentially damaging misinformation is about all any management team can do. This has been especially true during the recent waves of layoffs and downsizings. Former governor and presidential candidate Mitt Romney, who specializes in corporate turnarounds, has noted that rumors and fears are often much worse than the reality of a situation.[33] Rumor-control hot lines and in-house Web sites with answers to frequently asked questions (FAQs) have proved useful for neutralizing disruptive and inaccurate rumors and grapevine communication.

For your part, you would do well to follow this time-honored advice from *Training* magazine's editor-in-chief:

Whether it's something you're hearing or some-thing you're telling, ask yourself: Is it the truth? Is it fair to all concerned? Will it build goodwill and better friend-ships? And finally, will it be beneficial to all concerned? If you answer "no" to even one of those questions, don't open your mouth. If you're on the receiving end, you are equally responsible. You should decline to participate in the conversa-tion, and the onus is also on you to try to cut it off at the source.[34]

Michoela Stejskalova/Shutterstock.Com

New Image, to give her a new, more professional look and wardrobe that would help her project enough author-ity to win a major promotion. "Like it or not," she ex-plains, "we're a society that's built on first impressions."[37]

In the same vein, the defini-tion of "office casual" is causing some conflict in workplaces to-day. Just how casual is too casual? Clinton Kelly, co-host of The Learning Channel's *What Not to Wear*, believes that Americans dress very casually because of a lack of fashion role models. He notes that out-rageous people get the most attention, but that doesn't mean it's okay to dress like Lady Gaga at the office.[38] Managers need to communicate, demonstrate, and consistently enforce reasonable appearance standards in the workplace.[39] Broad ac-ceptance over time will embed those expectations into the organization's culture.

Nonverbal Communication

In today's hurried world, our words are often taken to have meanings that were not intended. Facial ex-pressions and body movements that accompany our words can either enhance communication or worsen matters. This nonverbal communication, sometimes referred to as body language, is an important part of the communication process. In fact, one expert contends that only 7 percent of the impact of our face-to-face communication comes from the words we utter; the other 93 percent comes from our vocal intonations, facial expressions, posture, and appear-ance.[35] Even periods of silence can carry meaning. Consider this advice: A manager has to learn to hear what people are leaving out of a conversation, so if someone is silent during an interview or meeting, avoid interrupting unless the person clearly needs your intervention.[36] Silence may indicate doubt, lack of understanding, or polite disagreement (often the case in high-context cultures).

Even the whole idea of "dressing for success" is an attempt to send a desired nonverbal message about oneself. Image consultants have developed a thriving business helping aspiring executives look the part. For example, youthful and petite Vanda Sachs (a pseudonym) hired Emily Cho, founder of

TYPES OF BODY LANGUAGE. There are three kinds of body language: facial, gestural, and postural.[40] Without the speaker or listener consciously think-ing about it, seemingly insignificant changes in fa-cial expressions, gestures, and posture send various messages. A speaker can tell whether a listener is interested by monitoring a combination of nonverbal cues, including an attentive gaze, an upright posture, and confirming or agreeing gestures. Unfortunately many people in positions of authority—parents, teachers, and managers—ignore or misread nonver-bal feedback. When this happens, they become inef-fective communicators.

RECEIVING NONVERBAL COMMUNICATION. Like any other interpersonal skill, sensitivity to nonverbal cues can be learned (see Table 11.1).

Listeners need to be especially aware of subtle-ties, such as the fine distinctions between an attentive gaze and a glaring stare and between an upright pos-ture and a stiff one. Knowing how to interpret a nod, a grimace, or a grin can be invaluable to managers. If at any time the response seems inappropriate to what one is saying, it is time to back off and reassess one's approach. It may be necessary to explain things

body language nonverbal communication based on facial expressions, posture, and appearance

| Table 11.1 | Reading Body Language |

UNSPOKEN MESSAGE	BEHAVIOR
"I want to be helpful."	Uncrossing legs Unbuttoning coat or jacket Unclasping hands Moving closer to other person Smiling face Removing hands from pockets Unfolding arms from across chest
"I'm confident."	Avoiding hand-to-face gestures and head scratching Maintaining an erect stance Keeping steady eye contact Steepling fingertips below chin
"I'm nervous."	Clearing throat Expelling air (such as "Whew!") Placing hand over mouth while speaking Hurried cigarette smoking
"I'm superior to you."	Peering over tops of eyeglasses Pointing a finger Standing behind a desk and leaning palms down on it Holding jacket lapels while speaking

Source: Adapted from William Friend, "Reading Between the Lines," *Association Management*, 36 (June 1984): 94–100. Reprinted by permission of the publisher.

more clearly, adopt a more patient manner, or make other adjustments.

Nonverbal behavior can also give managers a window on deep-seated emotions. For example, consider the situation Michael C. Ruettgers encountered shortly after joining EMC Corp., a leading manufacturer of computer data storage: Every piece of equipment they'd recently sold was failing because EMC engineers had not detected an entire batch of faulty disk drives. Ruettgers met face-to-face with as many customers as he could, sometimes even finding them in tears because their computer operations had been destroyed. "Nothing can really prepare you for that," Ruettgers later recalled.[41] After his promotion to CEO, Ruettgers helped make EMC a leader in product quality. No doubt his face-to-face interaction with frustrated customers, who conveyed powerful nonverbal emotional messages, drove home the need for improvement.

GIVING NONVERBAL FEEDBACK. What about the nonverbal feedback that managers give rather than receive? A research study carried out in Great Britain suggests that nonverbal feedback from authority figures significantly affects employee behavior. Among the people who were interviewed, those who received nonverbal approval from the interviewers in the form of smiles, positive head nods, and eye contact behaved quite differently from those who received nonverbal disapproval through frowns, head shaking, and avoidance of eye contact. Those receiving positive nonverbal feedback were judged

These Habitat for Humanity volunteers in Port Huron, Michigan, know the importance of nonverbal communication when getting instructions from the team leader. Ear plugs, sawing and hammering, and roaring machinery all conspire to make verbal communication difficult.

Dennis MacDonald/PhotoEdit

by neutral observers to be significantly more relaxed, more friendly, more talkative, and more successful in creating a good impression.[42]

Positive nonverbal feedback to and from managers is a basic building block of good interpersonal relations. A smile or nod of the head in the appropriate situation tells the individual that he or she is on the right track and to keep up the good work. Such feedback is especially important for managers, who must avoid participating in the subtle but powerful nonverbal discrimination experienced by women in leadership positions.[43] When samples of men and women leaders in one study offered the same arguments and suggestions in a controlled setting, the women leaders received more negative and less positive nonverbal feedback than the men.[44] Managing-diversity workshops target this sort of "invisible barrier" to women and minorities. Similarly, cross-cultural training alerts employees bound for foreign assignments to monitor their nonverbal gestures carefully (see Window on the World). For example, the familiar thumbs-up sign tells American employees to keep up the good work. Much to the embarrassment of poorly informed expatriates, that particular nonverbal message does not travel

well. The same gesture would be a vulgar sign in Australia, would say "I'm winning" in Saudi Arabia, and would signify the number one in Germany and the number five in Japan. Malaysians use the thumb, instead of their forefinger, for pointing.[45]

Two other trends in nonverbal communication are offering etiquette classes for students and management trainees[46] and teaching sign language to coworkers of deaf employees.

Upward Communication

As used here, the term upward communication refers to a process of systematically encouraging employees to share their feelings and ideas with management. Although upward communication is more important than ever, a recent survey of 439 full-time employees found a great deal of *self-censorship* (keeping quiet) that seriously restricted the upward flow of good ideas. This was true regardless of gender, amount of education, or income level. Leading reasons for the self-censorship were not wanting to waste one's time and fear of negative consequences. According to the researchers, silent employees and uninvolved managers gloss over constructive criticism and important truths.

upward communication encouraging employees to share their feelings and ideas with management

WINDOW ON THE WORLD

How About a Big Hug? Better Yet, a Fist Bump Will Do.

John Sexton, the president of New York University, typically greets students, faculty, and even strangers with a bear hug, and word has spread. When he taught a class in Abu Dhabi, where NYU is about to open a campus, three male students from the United Arab Emirates opened their arms to him. Knowing that Middle East convention barred him from touching female students, Sexton decided he needed a technique to cover both genders. So the 67-year-old, white-bearded president gave each student a fist bump.

"I told them I will not give them a hug until they have an NYU degree," Sexton says. "I just didn't want to be too violative of social norms."

For Discussion: Do you have favorite nonverbal gestures that are second nature in your own culture but could cause problems when doing business with foreigners? Explain.

Source: Excerpted from John Hechinger, "Abu Dhabi's Man in New York," *Bloomberg Businessweek* (May 31–June 6, 2010): 73.

Most importantly, good ideas for the organization never surface.[47] A refreshing exception is IBM's CEO, Sam Palmisano. Even though he leads a workforce of 400,000, Palmisano reads every single e-mail he receives from IBM employees. He even telephones mid-level managers to ask for their opinions.[48]

At least seven different options are open to managers who want to improve upward communication.

FORMAL GRIEVANCE PROCEDURES. When unions represent rank-and-file employees, provisions for upward communication are usually spelled out in the collective bargaining agreement. Typically, unionized employees utilize a formal grievance procedure for contesting managerial actions and oversights. Grievance procedures usually consist of a series of progressively more rigorous steps.[49] For example, union members who have been fired may talk with their supervisor in the presence of the union steward. If the issue is not resolved at that level, the next step may be a meeting with the department head. Sometimes the formal grievance process includes as many as five or six steps, with a third-party arbitrator as the last resort. Formal grievance procedures are also found in nonunion situations.

EMPLOYEE ATTITUDE AND OPINION SURVEYS. Both in-house and commercially prepared surveys can bring employee attitudes and feelings to the surface. Thanks to commercial software packages, time-saving and paperless electronic surveys are popular in today's workplaces.[50] Employees will usually complete surveys if they are convinced that meaningful changes will result. For example, Business Research Lab of Houston, a service that conducts about 70 employee surveys each year, describes one client that used a survey to pinpoint the cause of its retention problem. Not only did the firm reduce its turnover rate from 55 percent to 14 percent, it saved $2 million annually in HR costs. The lab's director of client relations, Gregg Campa, notes, "Taking time to implement action plans based on survey results translates into big bucks."[51] Similarly, a researcher found that unionized companies conducting regular attitude surveys were less likely to experience a labor strike than companies that failed to survey their employees.[52] On the other hand, surveys with no feedback or follow-up action tend to alienate employees, who feel the surveys are just wasting their time.

SUGGESTION SYSTEMS. Who knows more about a job than someone who performs that job day in and day out? This rhetorical question is the primary argument for suggestion systems, which can be a wellspring of good ideas. At Ernst & Young, the New York–based accounting firm, an employee suggested creating a confidential ethics hotline.[53]

AP Photo/Ted S. Warren

Customer feedback is a vital part of the upward communication process. At an annual meeting, Starbucks employees read customer comments that have been posted on the mystarbucksidea.com Web site.

Fairness and prompt feedback are keys to successful suggestion systems. Managers at Dixon Schwabl, a Victor, New York, advertising firm guarantee a 48-hour reply to any employee suggestions.[54] Monetary incentives can help, too. For example, at Winnebago Industries, the recreational vehicle maker in Forest City, Iowa, employees have submitted more than 10,000 reasonable suggestions since the company started its program in 1991, and a third of these ideas have been implemented. Employees get 10 percent of whatever the company saves in the first year of implementation, and so far they've earned more than $500,000 in incentives. Better yet, their ideas have saved Winnebago nearly $6 million.[55] Nice return on investment! (The 10 percent rule is also used at Chicago's famous chewing gum and candy company, Wm. Wrigley Jr.)[56] Also, a study of U.S. government employees found a positive correlation between suggestions and productivity.[57]

OPEN-DOOR POLICY. The open-door approach to upward communication has been both praised and criticized. Proponents say problems can be nipped in the bud when managers keep their doors open and employees feel free to walk in at any time and talk with them. But critics contend that an open-door policy encourages employees to leapfrog the formal chain of command (something that happens a lot these days because of e-mail and social media). They argue further that it is an open invitation to annoying interruptions when managers can least afford them. A limited open-door policy—afternoons only, for example—can effectively remedy this particular problem.

Another problem that needs to be overcome is the tendency for hard-charging managers and entrepreneurs to be too defensive. *Inc.* magazine cautions that feedback should always be viewed as professional, even when it feels personal. Christine White, an Internet entrepreneur, asks for negative feedback through her "open door" policy, but she admits that she sometimes gets defensive and has to remind herself that it's just part of doing business.[58]

INFORMAL MEETINGS. Employees may feel free to air their opinions and suggestions if they are confident that management will not criticize or penalize them for being frank. But they need to be given the right opportunity. At the Lodge at Vail in Colorado, for example, HR director Mandy Wulfe invites small groups of employees to have lunch with the hotel manager, Wolfgang Triebnig, at the hotel's five-star restaurant. The program is called "Wolfgang's Lunch Gang," and every employee gets a chance to participate. By demonstrating how much they value their employees and their ideas, these managers hope the employees will in turn demonstrate how much the hotel values its customers.[59]

SOCIAL MEDIA. As emphasized in Chapter 7, companies cannot afford to ignore what is being said about them on social media. By subscribing to services that scan blogs, Facebook, LinkedIn, Twitter, and other relevant social networking sites, management can try to keep potentially damaging information from going viral. Malicious gossip and unfounded rumors need to be promptly challenged and corrected. At the same time, valuable upward communication can be collected for analysis. All this requires courage and thick skin. For example, Nokia has taken a proactive approach to upward communication by creating Blog-Hub, an intranet for its employees worldwide. Using nicknames, workers can post brutally candid opinions about Nokia and other related topics, and managers welcome both their opinions and their complaints.[60]

EXIT INTERVIEWS. Employees leaving the organization, for whatever reason, no longer fear possible recrimination from superiors. Consequently, they can offer unusually frank and honest feedback, obtained in a brief, structured exit interview. For example, Bill Klingelsmith, an executive at the Quad/Graphics printing plant in Martinsburg, Virginia, was tasked with helping to reduce turnover. Klingelsmith called former employees to learn why they had left, and discovered that a lack of training had been a major source of frustration. Quad then increased its training programs, and Klingelsmith hasn't heard that complaint since the change.[61]

On the other hand, exit interviews have been criticized for eliciting artificially negative feedback because the employee may have a sour-grapes attitude toward the organization. Research finds the use of exit interviews to be spotty and haphazard, although many employers claim to use them. Managers agree that exit interviews can uncover problems and point out trends.[62] Exit interviewers are advised to probe the following four categories:

Management. Unsatisfactory management or supervisory interactions with staff.
Competitive practices. Less-than-favorable working conditions, pay, benefits or recognition incentives when compared with competitors.
Career potential. Lack of career path, job growth, or development plans.
Work/life balance. Lifestyle issues, hours of work, and family commitments.[63]

Systematic use of exit interviews is recommended, not only for feedback purposes, but also for "harvesting" valuable knowledge from retiring experts. This needs to be done within the context of a comprehensive *knowledge management* (KM) program as discussed in Chapter 8. For example, Halliburton, the oil-services contractor, collects and shares vital knowledge from exit interviews, particularly with managers who have not been mentoring or training any obvious successors. Halliburton's managers then turn this knowledge into graphics-rich flowcharts available for online training.[64] This use of exit interviews for KM is especially important in view of the coming wave of post–World War II baby boom retirees.

In general, attempts to promote upward communication will be successful only if employees truly believe that their contributions will have a favorable impact on their employment. Halfhearted or insincere attempts to get employees to open up and become involved will do more harm than good.

COMMUNICATING IN THE DIGITAL WORKPLACE

Digital technology has permanently altered how, where, and how fast we communicate. Computers and other digital devices speak a language of 1s and 0s used to code software and applications. Today, every imaginable sort of information—including text, numbers, still and moving pictures, and sound—is available in digital format. Digital technology has been revolutionary for the computer, telecommunications, consumer electronics, publishing, defense, and entertainment industries. Organizational communication, already significantly reshaped by computerization, is undergoing its own digital revolution. As a sign of things to come, consider the use of "virtual desktop infrastructure" at CB Richard Ellis (CBRE), a global real estate firm based in Los Angeles. In a pilot program with 2,000 of its employees, the company is using virtualization technology from VMware to give these employees access to all of the firm's e-mail, databases,

exit interview brief, structured interview with a departing employee

and business applications through any PC available, including smartphones and tablets.[65] Having such a flexible business communication tool that works on *any* device *anywhere* promises to be a liberating and empowering experience for CBRE's employees.

This section does *not* attempt to explain the fine points of emerging communication technologies, ranging from speech recognition software through wireless broadband Internet to virtual reality and cloud computing. Rather, it explores some practical workplace implications of digital-age communication. Our objective is to more effectively use the digital communication technologies we have and to prepare for those to come.

Dealing with Information Overload

Anyone who has stayed at a party too long knows what it means to have too much of a good thing. So it is with information today. According to data analytics specialist SAS, a company in the right business to know, "digital data in the world is quadrupling *daily*."[66] The central challenge for managers is to avoid drowning in information overload. A good place to begin is with the foundation management concepts of objectives and priorities, as covered in detail in Chapter 6. *Clear objectives* and *priorities* sharpen one's focus and foster selective perception amid all the noise and clutter. The off buttons on our 24/7 digital devices could use a little exercise, too. Microsoft vice president Linda Stone describes the common practice of people repeatedly checking and using their handheld devices during meetings as "continuous partial attention."[67]

Are you paying attention? In his best-seller *The Shallows: What the Internet Is Doing to Our Brains*, Nicholas Carr worries that digital-age multitasking, with its constant interruptions, is rewiring our brains in harmful ways. He writes that current research has proven that "frequent interruptions scatter our thoughts, weaken our memory, and make us tense and anxious."[68] Knowing how much distractions

can impair a person's train of thought, Marvin R. Ellison, executive vice president of U.S. stores at Home Depot, implemented new policies to address the problem of information overload: He drastically cut the number of reports and messages from the corporate office so that managers who once received 200 e-mails a day now get one. Everything else is online.[69] Now check your e-mail and tweets!

Developing a Workplace Policy for Social Networking Sites

Recent employee surveys have provided these important insights:

- Forty-five percent said they visit social networking sites such as LinkedIn, Facebook, Twitter, and YouTube at least four times a week.[70]
- Twenty-four percent reported visiting social networking sites while using corporate computers.[71]
- Just over half said that an employer should not be concerned about the contents of employees' social networking pages.[72]
- In a survey of 7,200 managers, 64 percent answered "No" to the question, Does your company monitor posts on social-networking sites?[73]

In short, online social networking by employees is commonplace, controversial, and poorly controlled.[74] Therefore, an organizational policy framework like the one in Table 11.2 is recommended for blogs and other social media.

Getting a Handle on E-mail

E-mail is a two-headed beast: easy and efficient, while at the same time grossly abused and mismanaged.[75] There are even moral implications. For instance, a recent experiment demonstrated that individuals are more inclined to lie more frequently via e-mail than in a written letter or memo.[76] By managing e-mail effectively, the organization can take a big step toward properly using online communication.

Radu Razvan/Shutterstock.com

Table 11.2	Policy Guidelines for Using Social Networking Sites at Work

- Company approval is required for authors who use electronic resources of the company to send "tweets" or other public messages.
- Any identification of the author, including usernames, pictures or logos, or "profile" web pages should not use logos, trademarks or other intellectual property of the company without approval from the company.
- If he or she is not providing an official message from the company, an employee who comments on any aspect of the business must include a disclaimer in his or her "profile" or "bio" that the views are his or her own and not those of the company.
- A message should not disclose any confidential or proprietary information of the company.

Source: Rex Stephens, "In a Dither over Twitter? Get a Policy," *HR Magazine*, 54 (June 2009): 30.

Table 11.3	How to Compose a CLEAR E-Mail Message

Concise. A brief message in simple conversational language is faster for you to write and more pleasant for your readers to read.

Logical. A message in logical steps, remembering to include any context your readers need, will be more easily understood.

Empathetic. When you identify with your readers, your message will be written in the right tone and in words they will readily understand.

Action-oriented. When you remember to explain to your readers what you want them to do next, they are more likely to do it.

Right. A complete message, with no important facts missing, with all the facts right, and with correct spelling, will save your readers having to return to you to clarify details.

Source: Joan Tunstall, *Better, Faster Email: Getting the Most Out of Email* (St. Leonards, Australia: Allen & Unwin, 1999), p. 37. Reprinted by permission.

An organizational e-mail policy, embracing the following recommendations from experts, can help.

- The e-mail system belongs to the company, which has the legal right to monitor its use. Research by the American Management Association found that two-thirds of employers surveyed monitor their employees' Internet and e-mail use, and half of employers track computer content and time at the keyboard.[77] *Conclusion*: **never** assume privacy with company information technology or e-mail accounts. Of course, this raises major privacy and ethical issues largely unresolved in both the courts and public opinion.[78]
- Workplace e-mail is for business purposes only.
- Harassing and offensive e-mail will not be tolerated.
- E-mail messages should be concise (see Table 11.3). As in all correspondence, grammar and spelling count because they reflect on your diligence and credibility. Typing in all capital letters makes the message hard to read and amounts to SHOUTING in cyberspace. (All capital letters can be appropriate, for contrast purposes, when adding comments to an existing document.)
- Lists of bullet items (similar to the format you are reading now) are acceptable because they tend to be more concise than paragraphs.

- Long attachments defeat the quick-and-easy nature of e-mail.
- Recipients should be told when a reply is *unnecessary*.
- An organization-specific priority system should be used for sending and receiving all e-mail.
- "Spam" (unsolicited and unwanted e-mail) that gets past filters should be deleted without being read. Despite passage of a federal anti-spam law in the United States, spam still constitutes about 60 to 70 percent of all e-mail.[79] So-called spy-ware and adware should be blocked and should be uninstalled when a system has been infected.
- To avoid file clutter, messages unlikely to be referred to again should not be saved.[80]

Once again, clear objectives and priorities can help busy managers cut through e-mail clutter. Mark Hurst, author of Bit Literacy, recommends fighting e-mail overload by immediately moving any e-mails that require action—such as a meeting request or decision to be made—to a separate place, like a calendar or to-do list.[81]

Hello! Can We Talk About Cell Phone Etiquette?

According to industry data, there were over 293 million wireless subscribers (with over 61 million smart phone subscribers) in the United States in mid 2010.[82] The market penetration rate for cell phones in the United States is 93 percent. As a sign of the times, an entire 8,000-person engineering group at Ford Motor Company traded in their desktop phones for cell phones.[83] Like e-mail, cell phones have proved to be both a blessing and a curse. Offsetting the mobility and convenience are concerns about drivers being distracted while talking and texting on handheld wireless devices, loud and obnoxious cell phone conversations in public places, electronic eavesdropping, and health issues from overuse.[84] Managers need to be particularly sensitive to the risk of inadvertently broadcasting proprietary company information, names, and numbers. Competitors or identity theft criminals could be standing in the same airport line or sitting in the next restaurant booth. Table 11.4 offers some practical tips to help make the use of cell phones more effective, secure, and courteous.

Camera phones also require restrictions in the workplace because of concerns about privacy and information security.

Videoconferencing

A videoconference is a live television or broadband Internet video exchange between people in different locations. The decreasing cost of steadily improving videoconferencing technologies and the desire to reduce travel time and expense have fostered wider use of this approach to organizational communication. Options range from Web services such as low-cost Skype and more sophisticated VidyoOne, to hotel videoconference facilities rented by the hour, to expensive TelePresence gear from Cisco Systems. Cisco saved half a million dollars in travel expenses the first year it switched to videoconferencing, and TNT, a courier company in Europe, saved $1.6 million over three years through online video exchange.[85]

videoconference live television or broadband Internet video exchange between people in different locations

Table 11.4	Five Commandments of Cell Phone Etiquette

1. *Thou shalt not subject defenseless others to cell phone conversations.* Cell phone etiquette, like all forms of etiquette, centers on having respect for others.
2. *Thou shalt not set thy ringer to play La Cucaracha every time thy phone rings.* It's a phone, not a public address system.
3. *Thou shalt turn thy cell phone off during public performances.* Set your phone on vibrate when in meetings or in the company of others and, if necessary, take or return the call at a polite distance.
4. *Thou shalt not dial while driving.* If you must engage in cell phone conversations while driving, use a hands-off device.
5. *Thou shalt not speak louder on thy cell phone than thou would on any other phone.* It's called "cell yell" and it's very annoying to others.

Source: Five basic commandments in italics excerpted from Dan Briody, "The Ten Commandments of Cell Phone Etiquette," *InfoWorld*, February 5, 2005, **www.infoworld.com.**

11d
Are You a Supertasker? Don't Bet Your Life on It

Recent University of Utah study:

Talking on a cellphone while driving is distracting and potentially dangerous unless you are a "supertasker." This group—just 2.5% of the population—can do two things at once without noticeable impairment. . . .

In the study, 200 participants completed a task (simulated freeway driving) and then repeated it while adding a hands-free cellphone conversation that included memorizing words and doing math. While multitasking, 97.5% of participants' performance declined. But "supertaskers" displayed no changes in braking or following distance and their math ability was fine. Their memory even improved 3%.

QUESTION: If you habitually multitask while driving, are you willing to bet your life that you are among the rare "supertaskers"?

Source: Excerpted from Sharon Jayson, "Just 2½% of Us Can Do 2 Things at Once," *USA Today* (March 30, 2010): 7D. Reprinted with Permission.

Communication pointers for videoconference participants include the following:

- Test the system before the meeting convenes.
- Dress for the occasion. The video image is distorted by movement of wild patterns and flashy jewelry. Solid white clothing tends to "glow" on camera.
- Make sure everyone is introduced.
- Check to make sure everyone can see and hear the content of the meeting.
- Do not feel compelled to direct your entire presentation to the camera or monitor. Directly address those in the same room.
- Speak loudly and clearly. Avoid slang and jargon in cross-cultural meetings where translations are occurring.
- Avoid exaggerated physical movements that tend to blur on camera.
- Adjust your delivery to any transmission delay, pausing longer than usual when waiting for replies.
- Avoid side conversations, which are disruptive.
- Do not nervously tap the table or microphone or shuffle papers.

Teleworking

Telecommuting has evolved into **teleworking** because working from home, in lieu of commuting, is being supplanted by working from *anywhere*, thanks to mobile Internet technology. The long-standing dream of working from the beach or ski slope has arrived! (Perhaps that's why some prefer the term *virtual working*.) A survey of 812 white-collar employees found 51 percent supporting the idea of teleworking for anyone capable, 40 percent supporting it but worrying it could be abused, and 3 percent saying it hurts productivity.[86] Research by the Society for Human Resource Management reveals that the ranks of telecommuters/teleworkers is modest and growing slowly. Although most companies have some telecommuters, few have more than 10 percent of their employees doing so.[87] A recent Brigham Young University study of 24,436 people employed by IBM in 75 countries found that a personalized combination of working from home and flexible work hours at the office minimized work/life conflict.[88] Despite being a popular concept, teleworking is not for everyone. Barriers to success can involve location-specific work (e.g., assembly-line worker or bank teller), one's temperament (highly social), or circumstances (family conflict). (See Table 11.5.) Consider this turn of events: Tony Bacigalupo was glad to work from home when his employer first went virtual, but a year later, Tony felt isolated, missed his office friends, and thought he might go stir-crazy.[89]

Table 11.5   Telecommuting/Teleworking: Promises and Problems

PROMISES	POTENTIAL PROBLEMS
1. Significantly boosts individual productivity.	1. Can cause fear of stagnating at home.
2. Saves commuting time and travel expenses (lessens traffic congestion).	2. Can foster sense of isolation due to lack of social contact with coworkers.
3. Taps broader labor pool (such as mothers with young children, disabled and retired persons, and prison inmates).	3. Can result in competition or interference with family duties, thus causing family conflict.
4. Eliminates office distractions and politics.	4. Can disrupt traditional manager–employee relationship.
5. Reduces employer's cost of office space.	5. Can cause fear of being "out of sight, out of mind" at promotion time.

teleworking working from home or anywhere else thanks to the mobile Internet

Jochen Tack/Glow Images

Virtual teams and telecommuting are a common part of today's global workplace. Fortunately, there are many tools available for effective communication, regardless of how far apart the workers may be.

BECOMING A BETTER COMMUNICATOR

Three communication skills as important as ever in today's rapidly changing world are listening, writing, and running meetings. Managers who master these skills generally have fewer interpersonal relations problems. Moreover, effective communicators tend to move up the hierarchy faster than poor ones do. *Training* magazine summed up the importance of communication this way: A manager's greatest challenge is communication, an important dimension of leadership. Good communication leads to strong employee commitment. Without it, employees fail to achieve business goals or develop teamwork skills.[90]

Effective Listening

Nearly all training in oral communication in high school, college, and management development programs is in effective speaking. But what about listening, the other half of the communication equation? Listening is the forgotten factor in communication skills training. This is unfortunate in view of recent research involving 4,000 managers in various industries in the United States that uncovered a *listening gap*. In short, managers tended to rate themselves as much better listeners than their coworkers did, and the disconnect was the greatest when dealing with difficult issues.[91] Quite simply, managers often subtly communicate that they don't want to hear bad news, and their subordinates respond by keeping the news to themselves.[92]

Listening takes place at two steps in the verbal communication process. First, the receiver must listen in order to decode and understand the original message. Then the sender becomes a listener when attempting to decode and understand subsequent feedback. Identical listening skills come into play at both ends. Former CEO Anne Mulcahy, who brought Xerox back from the brink before recently retiring, describes listening as easier said than done. "I'm talking about listening in a way that actually treasures and absorbs criticism and makes a point of getting honest feedback," she notes.[93]

We can hear and process information much more quickly than the normal speaker can talk. According to researchers, our average rate of speaking is about 125 words per minute, whereas we are able to listen to about 400 to 600 words a minute.[94] Thus, listeners have up to 75 percent slack time during which they can daydream or, alternatively, analyze the information and plan a response. Effective listeners know how to put that slack time to good use. Here are some practical tips for more effective listening:

- Tolerate silence. Listeners who rush to fill momentary silences cease being listeners.
- Ask stimulating, open-ended questions that require more than merely a yes-or-no answer.
- Encourage the speaker with attentive eye contact, alert posture, and verbal encouragers such as "umhum," "yes," and "I see." Occasionally repeating the speaker's last few words also helps.
- Paraphrase. Periodically restate in your own words what you have just heard.
- Show emotion to demonstrate that you are a sympathetic listener.
- Know your biases and prejudices and attempt to correct for them.

SAUL LOEB/AFP/Getty Images

How would you handle this tough communication situation? Imagine being the BP Oil representative sent out to address these U.S. citizens protesting the oil spill in the Gulf of Mexico.

English teacher in Alexandria, Virginia, recently observed that high-tech devices designed to facilitate communication are actually helping to destroy it. Texting is a language unto itself, unrelated to the common standards of good writing, and most students do not proofread or rewrite their work.[98] Moreover, spelling and grammar checkers used by those who compose at the computer keyboard are not cure-alls. (There really is no adequate substitute for careful proofreading.) As a learned skill, effective writing is the product of regular practice. Students who do not get the necessary writing practice in school are at a disadvantage when they enter the job market.

Good writing is a key form of encoding in the basic communication process. If it is done skillfully, potential barriers can be surmounted. Caterpillar's publications editor offered four helpful reminders:

- Avoid premature judgments about what is being said.
- Summarize. Briefly highlight what the speaker has just finished saying to bring out possible misunderstandings.[95]

For their part, speakers need to randomly insert comprehension checks, or what John Baldoni, a Michigan communication consultant, calls the "briefback." He recommends asking your listeners to tell you what you have just told them so you can both confirm a clear understanding of the discussion.[96]

Effective Writing

Managers often complain about poor writing skills. For example, Larry Kensington, president of a firm in Michigan, scanned dozens of resumes and job applications for three job openings he had, but had a hard time finding candidates who could write adequately and spell correctly, which were requirements for the jobs.[97]

Writing difficulties stem from an educational system that requires students to do less and less writing. Essay tests have given way in many classes to the multiple-choice variety and term papers are being pushed aside by team activities and projects. Quick-and-dirty e-mails and instant messages, tweets, and cell phone text messaging at home, school, and the workplace also have contributed to the erosion of writing quality in recent years. Patrick Welsh, a high school

1. *Keep words simple.* Simplifying the words you use will help reduce your thoughts to essentials; keep your readers from being "turned off" by the complexity of your letter, memo, or report; and make it more understandable.
2. *Don't sacrifice communication to rules of composition.* Most of us who were sensitized to the rules of grammar and composition in school never quite recovered from the process. As proof, we keep trying to make our writing conform to rigid rules and customs without regard to style or the ultimate purpose of the communication. (Of course, employees need to be sensitive to the stylistic preferences of their bosses.)
3. *Write concisely.* This means expressing your thoughts, opinions, and ideas in the least number of words consistent with effective composition and smoothness. But don't confuse conciseness with mere brevity; otherwise, you may write briefly without being clear or complete.
4. *Be specific.* Vagueness is one of the most serious flaws in written communication because it

destroys accuracy and clarity, leaving the reader to wonder about your meaning or intent.[99]

Also, avoid irritating your readers with useless phrases such as "to be perfectly honest," "needless to say," "as you know," and "please be advised that."

Running a Meeting

Meetings are an ever-present feature of modern organizational life. Whether they are convened to find facts, solve problems, or pass along information, meetings typically occupy a good deal of a manager's time. Sadly, much of that time is wasted. Management consultant Stuart R. Levine summed up what he learned from a study of mid- and upper-level managers' experiences with meetings: Although they spent 70 percent of their time at meetings, those meetings had clear objectives only 40 percent of the time and the objectives were reached only 28 percent of the time.[100] No surprise that in a 2010 survey of 1,043 people, 49 percent said "Yes" and 51 percent said "No" to the question: "Are most company meetings a waste of time?"[101] A good first step toward better meetings, according to author Patrick M. Lencioni, is to categorize meetings for a sharper focus. Four general categories that he recommends using are:

Daily check-in. A five-minute morning huddle to report on activities that day.
Weekly tactical. A 45- to 90-minute meeting to review the firm's critical metrics (revenue, expenses, etc.) and solve problems.
Monthly strategic. Executives wrestle with, debate, analyze, and decide the big critical issues that will affect the bottom line.
Quarterly off-site review. These reviews focus on four areas—strategy, team, personnel, and competitors—to help avoid turning into the "touchy-feely boondoggle" that such meetings can become.[102]

Whatever the reason for a meeting, managers who convene meetings owe it to themselves and their organization to use everyone's time and talent efficiently. Here are ten pointers for conducting successful meetings:

- Meet for a specific purpose, not simply as a ritual.
- Create an agenda and distribute it at least one day in advance.
- Communicate expectations for attendees to help them come prepared with proper data and documentation.
- Limit attendance to essential personnel.
- Open the meeting with a brief overview of what has been accomplished and what lies ahead.
- Deal with the most difficult/challenging agenda items quite early in the meeting while the energy level is still high.
- Encourage broad participation, while sticking to the agenda.
- Selectively use stimulating visual aids to make key points and, according to one expert, do not use more than three PowerPoint slides for every ten minutes of presentation.[103]
- Make sure everyone understands what action items they are responsible for after the meeting.
- Begin and end the meeting on time, and follow up as necessary.[104]

With practice, these guidelines will become second nature. Running a meeting brings into focus all the components of the communication process, including coping with noise and barriers. Effective meetings are important to organizational communication and, ultimately, to organizational success in today's team-oriented workplaces.

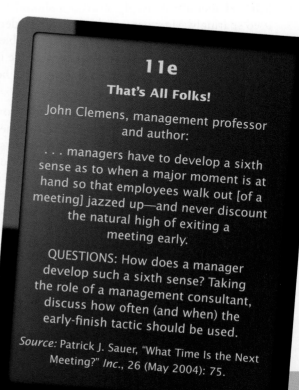

11e
That's All Folks!
John Clemens, management professor and author:

. . . managers have to develop a sixth sense as to when a major moment is at hand so that employees walk out [of a meeting] jazzed up—and never discount the natural high of exiting a meeting early.

QUESTIONS: How does a manager develop such a sixth sense? Taking the role of a management consultant, discuss how often (and when) the early-finish tactic should be used.

Source: Patrick J. Sauer, "What Time Is the Next Meeting?" *Inc.,* 26 (May 2004): 75.

SUMMARY

1. Modern technology has made communicating easier and less costly but has had the unintended side effect of information overload. Managers are challenged to improve the *quality* of their communication because it is a core process for everything they do. Communication is a social process involving the transfer of information and understanding. Links in the communication process include sender, encoding, medium, decoding, receiver, and feedback. Noise is any source of interference.

2. According to the Lengel-Daft contingency model, media richness is determined by the amount of information conveyed and the amount of learning promoted. Rich media such as face-to-face communication are best for nonroutine problems. Lean media such as impersonal bulletins are suitable for routine problems.

3. Organizational communication is typically too haphazard. Clampitt's communication continuum indicates that the five basic strategies are not equally effective. The Spray & Pray and Withhold & Uphold strategies are generally ineffective and should be avoided. The Tell & Sell and Identify & Reply strategies should be used sparingly. Managers need to use the Underscore & Explore strategy as much as possible. Media richness needs to be as high as possible if the preferred communication strategies are to be effective.

4. The unofficial and informal communication system that sometimes complements and sometimes disrupts the formal communication system has been labeled the grapevine. A sample of managers surveyed had predominantly negative feelings toward it. Recognizing that the grapevine cannot be suppressed, managers are advised to monitor it constructively. Nonverbal communication (including facial, gestural, and postural body language) accounts for most of the impact of face-to-face communication. Managers can become more effective communicators by doing a better job of receiving and giving nonverbal communications.

5. Upward communication can be stimulated by using formal grievance procedures, employee attitude and opinion surveys, suggestion systems, an open-door policy, informal meetings, social media, and exit interviews.

6. Information overload is a by-product of the digital communication age. Clear objectives and priorities are fundamental to cutting through the clutter and noise. A workplace policy for using social networking sites needs to satisfy these four criteria: approval for authoring public messages with company resources; no unauthorized use of company logos, trademarks, or intellectual property; personal opinions should be labeled as such; and no disclosure of confidential or proprietary company information.

7. E-mail, supposedly a real time saver, has quickly become a major time waster. Organizations need to create and enforce a clear e-mail policy to improve message quality and curb abuses. Cell phone users need to be discreet and courteous to avoid broadcasting privileged information and/or offending others. Videoconferencing restricts how people communicate because televised contacts are more mechanical than face-to-face meetings. Although telecommuting/teleworking can reduce travel time and expense and can offer employment to nontraditional employees, it restricts normal social contact and face-to-face communication in the workplace.

8. Listening does not get sufficient attention in communications training. Active, cooperative listening is to be encouraged. Writing skills are no less important in the computer age. Written messages need to be specific, simply worded, and concise. Meetings, an ever-present feature of organizational life, need to be focused and agenda-driven if time is to be used wisely.

TERMS TO UNDERSTAND

Communication, p. 297
Media richness, p. 298
Noise, p. 304

Grapevine, p. 303
Body language, p. 305
Upward communication, p. 307

Exit interview, p. 310
Videoconference, p. 313
Teleworking, p. 314

ACTION LEARNING EXERCISE

OH, NO! WHAT HAVE I DONE?

Situation: It's almost 6 P.M. and you're back at your office putting the finishing touches on next week's annual presentation to top management. Your stomach is churning, partly from hunger and partly from the stress of having missed another one of your twins' soccer matches. As the corporate director of product design at a large multinational company, you don't need to be reminded about the importance of next week's presentation. Between 3 P.M. and a few minutes ago, you had hidden out in a remote conference room fine-tuning it. Your cell phone was with you but had a dead battery, as you just noticed.

Back at your desk, having just replaced your cell phone battery, you are staring in disbelief at a text message on your phone. The three-word message "WHERE WERE YOU!" burns into your mind. This particular text is from your firm's director of marketing. She called and then texted you an hour ago from her home after a late-afternoon meeting with two executives from a company that has been a customer for over ten years. During a quick chat in the hallway yesterday, you had promised the marketing director you'd attend today's meeting to provide technical support. This customer is one of your smaller accounts, but there is potential for a big jump in business this year. The marketing director's idea was to have a brief "let's explore possibilities" meeting.

The plain truth is you simply forgot about the meeting. You've been on major overload. You never bothered to put it on your electronic calendar because the commitment was made just yesterday and you thought you'd surely remember it. Well, you didn't!

Your mind races, weighing the situation and what to do about it. Losing this customer would be very bad for your career because your CEO is a table-pounder about customer service. Whom should you contact first—the marketing director, your boss, the customer, your family? And how should you communicate with them? It's dinnertime now. What about calling later tonight? Can everything but your family wait until tomorrow? Should you leave a voice mail or text message? What about e-mails? You know both your boss and the marketing director check their BlackBerry e-mails later each evening at home. Should you stop by anybody's home tonight to deliver a personal apology and explanation? What should you do? What should you say? How should you say it? Your stomach tightens a couple more notches.

Instructions: Working either alone or as a member of a team, quickly develop a communication plan for this awkward situation. Your plan should involve (1) specifying your assumptions and objectives, (2) choosing an appropriate medium for each message (face to face, cell phone, telephone/voice mail, or e-mail), and (3) composing messages to the relevant parties.

FOR CONSIDERATION/DISCUSSION

1. What assumptions did you make in this case? How did they influence your response?

2. What were your priorities in this situation? How did they influence your actions?

3. Whom did you contact first? How and why?

4. How did you communicate with each party? Why did you choose that way?

5. What practical lessons about communication did you learn from this exercise? Explain.

ETHICS EXERCISE

DO THE RIGHT THING

IS IT TIME TO HANG UP ON UNOFFICIAL DIGITAL COMMUNICATION IN THE WORKPLACE?

High-tech small company employee: I'm 46, the second-oldest person in my company. I know my twenty-something colleagues do even more stuff online and with tech toys than I do. So if I need to, of course I handle personal stuff at work. I surf for news on the web. I check in on friends and family on Facebook. I read tweets. I've even posted to my personal blog, which is about politics and midlife concerns. And, yeah, while I've got the kids trained not to call or text me or their mom at the office, I've arranged a lot of stuff by phone, text or chat for their soccer leagues. It can get crazy during the soccer season.

In our office, people Twitter just to get random thoughts off their minds. But our firm also taps social media to get its message out to the public.

Credit union vice president: . . . as I stroll our operations, everyone has a [company] phone on their desk or nearby.

So why does everyone also need a personal cell phone at work? Why shouldn't we ban them on the job?

We're seriously considering it. We just barred access on our computers to social media sites like Facebook and Twitter. We don't give smart phones and PDAs access to our network, either. But people can use their cell phones to get on social media sites on the job—and to me, that makes cell phones a workplace issue.

We've already got some rules and we talk a lot about common sense practices with cell phones and other personal electronic devices. We want to trust our people. . . .

But that approach isn't working.

. . . here's what's most critical for us: We handle something dear to our customers—their money. We can't make mistakes.

Don Tapscott, author of the best-seller Grown Up Digital: How the Net Generation is Changing Your World: Net Geners [born between 1978 and 1997] use the Internet at work to do their jobs and to recharge or eliminate boredom. Most visit social networking sites, catch up on news headlines, Google, IM with friends or watch videos on YouTube several times a day. Many perceive that taking a "virtual coffee break" for 10 minutes allows them to return to their work even more focused. They don't view such activities as abusing the system.

Far too many executives make no effort to learn from young employees. Too often, young people go to work and hit a wall of corporate procedure and a deeply entrenched hierarchy.

The widespread banning of Facebook at work is a classic example of misguided supervision. The Net Generation wants to take a digital break; Boomer employers shut them down. Get ready for the generational clash at work as a generational firewall builds up frustration.

Sources: As quoted in Craig Matsuda, "Yes, I Blog at the Office," *Entrepreneur,* 38 (March 2010): 72. As quoted in Craig Matsuda, "Hello? You've Got a Job to Do," *Entrepreneur,* 38 (March 2010): 73. As quoted in an interview by Aliah D. Wright, "Millennials: 'Bathed in Bits,'" *HR Magazine,* 55 (July 2010): 40.

What are the ethical implications of the following interpretations?

1. Let's face it, communication technologies are clearly out of control in the workplace today. Strict policies need to be in place to ban nonwork-related cell phone and digital communication during working hours. Any job-specific exceptions?

2. Wake up, it's the twenty-first century so electronic communication and social media are essential to modern life and should be unrestricted in the workplace. Any job-specific exceptions?

3. Communication training is needed to let employees know what is fair and reasonable when using personal cell phones and wireless devices and company communication technology for personal business. If you can't trust your employees, why did you hire them?

4. Your own ethical interpretation?

MANAGERS-IN-ACTION VIDEO CASE STUDY

GREENSBURG, KANSAS

Managing Communication—Lessons from a Crisis

For Darin Headrick, Superintendent of Schools in Greensburg, Kansas, communication was one of the biggest challenges following the tornado. His school system lost everything from buildings to books and buses. With the front seat of his pick-up truck serving as his office, he leveraged available technology to communicate as efficiently as possible with his staff, parents, and board members. During this video, he shares how he relied on technology but continued to conduct staff meetings. Learn from Headrick's perspective how he balanced the use of technology with face-to-face communication.

For more information about Greensburg, visit the Greensburg GreenTown Web site: www.greensburggreentown.org. For more information about the school system, visit the Kiowa County USD 422 school district Web site: www.usd422.org.

Before watching the video, answer the following questions:

1. What are three examples of modern communications technology?

2. What are the pros and cons of each of these technologies when used for the purpose of business communication?

3. In comparison, what are the pros and cons of face-to-face group communication?

4. When would a face-to-face group meeting be a more effective medium for communicating with employees?

After watching the video, answer the following questions:

5. As a manager, what lessons can you learn from this video about preparing a contingency plan to manage communication following a crisis?

6. While text messaging proved to be very useful following the tornado, do you think it is an appropriate tool for business communication? Explain.

7. Provide an example from the video of when school superintendent Darin Headrick used the Underscore & Explore strategy for communication.

CLOSING CASE

FOUND IN TRANSLATION: HOW TO MAKE THE MULTICULTURAL WORKFORCE WORK

At City Fresh Foods, CEO Glynn Lloyd likes to hire from the neighborhood. And because the 12-year-old food-service company is headquartered in Boston's polyglot Dorchester neighborhood, Lloyd's payroll resembles a mini–United Nations. Some 70 percent of his 65 employees are immigrants, from places like Trinidad, Brazil, Nigeria, the Dominican Republic, and Cape Verde, off the West Coast of Africa. They speak half a dozen languages, not to mention the myriad cultural differences. "Visitors can see that we're a community of people from all over. They pick up on it right away," says Lloyd, 38. "You walk in, and you can feel the vibe of all those places."

Immigrants will account for nearly two-thirds of the country's population growth between now and 2050, according to the U.S. Department of Labor. Minority groups will constitute almost half of the population by then, meaning that successful managers will have to understand how to develop and retain employees who come from more cultures than any CEO could master. Indeed, while policymakers struggle to find an acceptable posture on border security, Lloyd has been working hard to figure out his own urgent question: How can managers best ensure that employees from so many different cultures work side by side productively?

He's come up with an ad hoc series of practices and processes that are achieving that aim. The highest hurdle, of course, has been communication. Lloyd tried overcoming it by providing about 40 hours of ESL [English as a second language] classes to his workers so that all 65 of them would use English. But that bar seemed too high, so Lloyd has lowered it. Instead, he requires his employees to learn the more limited language of City Fresh Foods—terms like "delivery ticket," "checkout sheet,"

and "ice packs." "I spend a little extra time trying to help them read what they need to know," says Kurt Stegenga, the company's logistics manager, who grew up in Mexico. "It takes a bit of clarification so that they can reach into the refrigerator and know what it is they are grabbing—say, cream cheese and not cheese sticks." But once they know those terms, productivity begins humming, Lloyd says.

At monthly companywide meetings, meanwhile, multilingual employees volunteer to serve as translators. Rosemary De la Cruz, a 26-year-old administrator from the Dominican Republic, sits next to employees who need the Spanish version and translates. Delivery manager Jose Tavares makes notes about his department meetings; his assistant translates them into Portuguese and Spanish for the company's 26 drivers. He's also ready to jump on the phone and solve any problems that might occur when an immigrant driver cannot answer a customer's question. Cotumanama "Toby" Peña—many employees adopt nicknames to further the cause of simplification—learned English words such as "safe" and "out" by watching baseball in his native Dominican Republic and picked up the alphabet from *Sesame Street*. "The English I speak is broken," says Peña, a cook. "For me, it's sometimes better to write things down." (Nonetheless, he often finds himself translating for one of his fellow cooks who is among the 40 percent of employees who don't speak English.)

When it comes to company material that is typically communicated with words—training manuals, say—Lloyd sticks mainly to visual tools, an outgrowth of the knack he had to develop for using gestures to make himself understood. To learn how to stack a cooler, for instance, employees study photos of how the contents can be arranged so that drivers don't have to reach deep inside to grab any drinks. How does City Fresh pack bread? Employees take turns using a machine that pumps air into a bag, slipping a loaf inside the bag, and then using another machine to tape it up. "A demonstration is better than words," says Lloyd.

City Fresh also counts on numbers to serve as a universal language. For instance, Lloyd worked with his managers to design a checklist that employees use to keep track of how many meals still need to be produced—the company ships out 4,000 daily, mostly to institutional customers ranging from charter schools to nursing homes—and for which accounts. The bulk packers can tell how many pounds of green beans they'll need. The expediters who match the beverages and desserts to each meal know what time it has to leave and who will be delivering it. Everybody can use the document, no matter what language they speak, says Lloyd.

But anybody with designs on rising into a management position has to master English. City Fresh will contribute up to $1,000 per person a year to help; it allocates $12,000 a year for education. These days, one assistant manager is getting 90 minutes of private tutoring a week. Rather than hauling everyone into a classroom, "we're going to start using this kind of learning more strategically," Lloyd says. "It will be a reward for the people who we think will get the most value from it." Otherwise, he says, ESL classes come and go without much to show for them. Nobody gets sufficiently immersed in English at work because "they don't need to know it," he says. "They can talk to each other in whatever language they want."

Lloyd goes to such lengths not just to ease communication but also because it's good for his customers. Many, especially the elderly, are from ethnic communities themselves and have "a taste for the authentic," as he puts it. Chefs from the Caribbean know how to whip up such specialties as mondongo (cow intestine), stewed goat, and salted codfish. And if employees sometimes run into problems with customers because they do not speak English, they've also been known to save the day when an English-speaking staffer encounters a customer from another country.

For Discussion

1. What role does the basic communication process in Figure 11.1 play in this case? Explain.

2. Which of the five communication strategies in Figure 11.3 does CEO Glynn Lloyd rely on the most at City Fresh Foods? Explain.

3. How should Glynn Lloyd stimulate upward communication at City Fresh Foods? Explain.

4. How would you rate Glynn Lloyd as a listener? Explain.

5. How comfortable would you be managing this type of multicultural organization? Explain.

Source: Excerpted from Joshua Hyatt, "Found in Translation: How to Make the Multicultural Workforce Work," *Inc.*, 28 (October 2006): 41–42. Copyright 2006 by Mansueto Ventures LLC. Reproduced with permission of Mansueto Ventures LLC in the format Textbook via Copyright Clearance Center.

Motivating and Leading

P4

CHAPTER 12 Motivating Job Performance

CHAPTER 13 Group Dynamics and Teamwork

CHAPTER 14 Influence, Power, and Leadership

CHAPTER 15 Change, Conflict, and Negotiation

12 Motivating Job Performance

Helen King/Comet/Corbis

"We need to use 100% of an employee—not just their backs and minds, but their innovation, enthusiasm, energy, and fresh perspective."[1]

—MARK MEUSSNER

The Changing Workplace

RACKSPACE NEEDS FULLY ENGAGED EMPLOYEES

San Antonio-based Rackspace provides web-hosting and information technology solutions to its clients, but that role is secondary, says Wayne Roberts, vice president of human resources. "Our mission statement is to be among the world's greatest service companies."

Engagement drivers at Rackspace relate to improving customer service and increasing customer loyalty, thereby affecting the bottom line. It starts with recruiting and being honest about Rackspace's culture, Roberts says. "We do strengths assessments on each recruit or employee and assign them the right job for them in the company. It's not uncommon for candidates to come to us for one job, and we hire them because their values align with ours, but we place them in a different role."

Giving people the opportunity to do what they do best fosters engagement at the company. Good job fit has translated into lower-than-industry-average turnover and a connection with customers. Quarterly performance reviews stress employees' contributions to business strategy. "Discretionary effort comes from an employee understanding the connection between the 'fanatical' customer service she provides and the overall health of the organization" and how that ties to her future, Roberts says.

Rackspace employees also want transparency, so senior leaders hold monthly open-book financial sessions, Roberts says.

He adds that Rackspace doesn't tie managers' bonuses or salary increases to engagement scores; the scores are looked at only for promotions. "I will not use our engagement surveys as weapons," Roberts says. "We want candid, open and unfiltered feedback. Engagement is a team sport, and the scores are reflective of the team, not just the manager."

Source: Excerpted from Adrienne Fox, "Raising Engagement," *HR Magazine*, 55 (May 2010): 39.

OBJECTIVES

- **Explain** the motivational lessons taught by Maslow's theory, Herzberg's theory, and expectancy theory.
- **Describe** how goal setting motivates performance.
- **Discuss** how managers can improve the motivation of personnel who perform routine tasks.
- **Explain** how job enrichment can be used to enhance the motivating potential of jobs.
- **Distinguish** extrinsic rewards from intrinsic rewards, and list four rules for administering extrinsic rewards effectively.
- **Explain** how employee engagement and retention programs, open-book management, and self-managed teams promote employee participation.
- **Explain** how companies are striving to motivate today's diverse workforce with quality-of-work-life programs.

The factors motivating how hard and effectively we work are as varied as our personalities, occupations, and opportunities. Innovative initiatives such as the employee engagement program at Rackspace are needed to provide a spark. As used here, the term *motivation* refers to a psychological process that gives behavior purpose and direction. Researchers measure employee motivation in four ways: "engagement, satisfaction, commitment, and intention to quit."[2] Managers attempt to "motivate" individuals to pursue organizational objectives willingly and persistently and be loyal to the organization. They generally do so through administering rewards fairly, building trust and teamwork, and creating a stimulating work environment. Motivation theories are generalizations about the "why" and "how" of purposeful behavior.

Figure 12.1 is an overview model for this chapter. The final element in this model, job performance, is the product of a combination of an individual's motivation and ability. Both are necessary. All the motivation in the world, for example, will not enable a computer-illiterate person to sit down and create a computer spreadsheet. Ability and skills, acquired through training and/or on-the-job experience, are also required. The individual's motivational factors—needs, satisfaction, expectations, and goals—are affected by challenging work, rewards, and participation.[3] We need to take a closer look at each key element in this model. A review of four basic motivation theories is a good starting point.

MOTIVATION THEORIES

Although there are dozens of different theories of work motivation, four have emerged as the most influential: Maslow's theory of the hierarchy of needs, Herzberg's two-factor theory, expectancy theory, and goal-setting theory. Each approaches the motivation process from a different angle, each has supporters and detractors, and each teaches important lessons about motivation to work.

Maslow's Hierarchy of Needs Theory

In 1943 psychologist Abraham Maslow proposed that people are motivated by a predictable five-step hierarchy of needs.[4] Little did he realize at the time that his tentative proposal, based on an extremely limited clinical study of neurotic patients, would become one of the most influential concepts in the field of management. Perhaps because it is so straightforward and intuitively appealing, Maslow's theory has strongly influenced those interested in work behavior. Maslow's message was simply this: people always have needs, and when one need is relatively fulfilled, others emerge in a predictable sequence to take its place. From bottom to top, Maslow's needs hierarchy includes physiological, safety, love, esteem, and self-actualization needs (see Figure 12.2). According to Maslow, most individuals are not consciously aware of these needs, yet we all supposedly proceed up the hierarchy of needs, one level at a time.

 Figure **12.1**   Individual Motivation and Job Performance

motivation psychological process giving behavior purpose and direction

PHYSIOLOGICAL NEEDS. At the bottom of the hierarchy are needs based on physical drives, including the need for food, water, sleep, and sex. Fulfillment of these lowest-level needs enables the individual to survive, and nothing else is important when these bodily needs have not been satisfied. As Maslow observed, "It is quite true that man lives by bread alone—when there is no bread."[5] But today the average employee experiences little difficulty in satisfying physiological needs. Figuratively speaking, the prospect of eating more bread is not motivating when one has plenty of bread to eat.

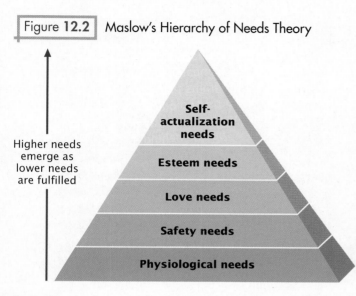

| Figure **12.2** | Maslow's Hierarchy of Needs Theory

Higher needs emerge as lower needs are fulfilled

Self-actualization needs
Esteem needs
Love needs
Safety needs
Physiological needs

Source: Data for diagram are from A. H. Maslow, "A Theory of Human Motivation," *Psychological Review*, 50 (July 1943): 370–396.

SAFETY NEEDS. After our basic physiological needs have been relatively well satisfied, we next become concerned about our safety from the elements, enemies, and other threats. For reasons that are not entirely clear (terrorism? workplace violence?), researchers have documented a recent jump in the need for feeling safe and secure in the work environment.[6] Yet most of us, by virtue of earning a living, achieve a reasonable degree of fulfillment in this area. Unemployment assistance is a safety net for those between jobs. Insurance also helps fulfill safety needs, a point not lost on Coca-Cola Femsa, Mexico's primary bottler of Coke, which used group health insurance as an incentive to encourage shopkeepers to sell more Coke. (The incentive was so powerful that the program resulted in a 13 percent boost in the cola's sales!)[7]

Now here's someone who can tell school children a thing or two about self-actualization needs. Grammy Award–winning singer and songwriter Alicia Keys fires up a classroom of eighth graders at the Betty Shabazz International Charter School in Chicago.

AP Photo/Nam Y. Huh

LOVE NEEDS. A physiologically satisfied and secure person focuses next on satisfying needs for love and affection. This category is a powerful motivator of human behavior. People typically strive hard to achieve a sense of belonging with others. For instance, consider this situation reported by author and consultant Patrick Lencioni: A woman he met could not pinpoint why she felt unfulfilled in her job until she returned from maternity leave. Her supervisor never once expressed any interest in her personal life, not even in the birth of her child.[8] As with the first two levels of needs, relative satisfaction of love needs paves the way for the emergence of needs at the next higher level.

ESTEEM NEEDS. People who perceive themselves as worthwhile are said to possess high self-esteem.[9] Self-respect is the key to esteem needs. Much of our self-respect, and therefore our esteem, comes from being accepted and respected by others. It is important for those who are expected to help achieve organizational objectives to have their esteem needs relatively well fulfilled. But esteem needs cannot emerge if lower-level needs go unattended.

SELF-ACTUALIZATION NEEDS. At the very top of Maslow's hierarchy is the open-ended category *self-actualization needs*. It is open-ended because, as Maslow pointed out, it reflects the need to reach one's potential.[10] One may satisfy this need by striving to become a better homemaker, plumber, rock singer, or manager. As an inspiring example, Microsoft co-founder Bill Gates has taken his career to a new level by devoting his time to persuading heads of state and other influential people to increase their humanitarian aid for underdeveloped countries. Friend Warren Buffett observes that Gates is translating his past accomplishments into changing the quality of life for all people.[11]

According to one management writer, the self-actualizing manager has the following characteristics:

1. Has warmth, closeness, and sympathy.
2. Recognizes and shares negative information and feelings.
3. Exhibits trust, openness, and candor.
4. Does not achieve goals by power, deception, or manipulation.
5. Does not project own feelings, motivations, or blame onto others.
6. Does not limit horizons; uses and develops body, mind, and senses.
7. Is not rationalistic; can think in unconventional ways.
8. Is not conforming; regulates behavior from within.[12]

Granted, this is a rather tall order to fill. It has been pointed out that it is uncommon to find a completely self-actualized person in any organization.[13] Whether productive organizations need more self-actualized individuals is subject to debate. On the positive side, self-actualized employees might help break down barriers to creativity and steer the organization in new directions. On the negative side, too

12a
Quick Quiz

Howard Schultz, chairman of Starbucks, explains his company's formula for "exceeding employee expectations" so that they, in turn, will do the same for customers:

We provided comprehensive health care as well as equity in the form of stock options to all employees. For the first time in America's history, not only did part-time workers have a stake in the financial outcome of the company, but they had the kind of health-care programs that gave them the sense of security and a psychological contract with the company that the company was not going to leave people behind.

QUESTIONS: Starbucks is trying to satisfy which particular needs in Maslow's hierarchy? Explain. Is this an effective approach to motivating today's employees?

For further information about the interactive annotations in this chapter, visit our student Web site.

Source: As quoted in Jeremy B. Dann, "How to Find a Hit as Big as Starbucks," *Business 2.0*, 5 (May 2004): 66.

many unconventional nonconformists could wreak havoc with the typical administrative setup dedicated to predictability.

RELEVANCE OF MASLOW'S THEORY FOR MANAGERS. Behavioral scientists who have attempted to test Maslow's theory in real life claim it has some deficiencies.[14] Even Maslow's hierarchical arrangement has been questioned. Practical evidence points toward a two-level rather than a five-level hierarchy. In this competing view, physiological and safety needs are arranged in hierarchical fashion, as Maslow contends. But beyond that point, any one of a number of needs may emerge as the single most important need, depending on the individual. Edward Lawler, a leading motivation researcher, has observed that most people pursue a variety of same-level needs all at the same time.[15]

Although Maslow's theory has not stood up well under actual testing, it teaches managers one important lesson: a *fulfilled* need does not motivate an individual. For example, the promise of unemployment benefits may partially fulfill an employee's need for economic security (the safety need). But the added security of additional unemployment benefits will probably not motivate fully employed individuals to work any harder. Effective managers anticipate each employee's personal need profile and provide opportunities to fulfill *emerging* needs. Because challenging and worthwhile jobs and meaningful recognition tend to enhance self-esteem, the esteem level presents managers with the greatest opportunity to motivate better performance.

Herzberg's Two-Factor Theory

During the 1950s, Frederick Herzberg proposed a theory of employee motivation based on satisfaction.[16] His theory is especially relevant today because, according to a 2009 Conference Board survey, "only 45 percent of workers claimed to be satisfied with their jobs—a significant decrease from 61 percent in 1987."[17] Worse yet, another recent survey documented growing job *dissatisfaction* among younger workers.[18] Herzberg believed that a satisfied employee is motivated from within to work harder and that a dissatisfied employee is not self-motivated and has to be pushed. Herzberg's research uncovered two classes of factors associated with employee

Table 12.1 Herzberg's Two-Factor Theory of Motivation

DISSATISFIERS: FACTORS MENTIONED MOST OFTEN BY DISSATISFIED EMPLOYEES	SATISFIERS: FACTORS MENTIONED MOST BY SATISFIED EMPLOYEES
1. Company policy and administration	1. Achievement
2. Supervision	2. Recognition
3. Relationship with supervisor	3. Work itself
4. Work conditions	4. Responsibility
5. Salary	5. Advancement
6. Relationship with peers	6. Growth
7. Personal life	
8. Relationship with subordinates	
9. Status	
10. Security	

Source: Adapted from an exhibit from "One More Time: How Do You Motivate Employees?" by Frederick Herzberg (January–February 1968). Copyright © 1968 by the President and Fellows of Harvard College; all rights reserved. Reprinted by permission of HBS Publishing.

satisfaction and dissatisfaction (see Table 12.1). As a result, his concept has come to be called Herzberg's two-factor theory.

DISSATISFIERS AND SATISFIERS. Herzberg compiled his list of dissatisfiers by asking a sample of about 200 accountants and engineers to describe job situations in which they felt exceptionally bad about their jobs. An analysis of their responses revealed a consistent pattern. Dissatisfaction tended to be associated with complaints about the job context or factors in the immediate work environment.

Herzberg then drew up his list of satisfiers, factors responsible for self-motivation, by asking the same accountants and engineers to describe job situations in which they had felt exceptionally good about their jobs. Again, a patterned response emerged, but this time different factors were described: the opportunity to experience achievement, receive recognition, work on an interesting job, take responsibility, and experience advancement and growth. Herzberg observed that these satisfiers centered on the nature of the task itself. Employees appeared to be motivated by *job content*—that is, by what they actually did all day long. Consequently, Herzberg concluded that enriched jobs were the key to self-motivation. The work itself—not pay, supervision, or some other environmental factor—was the key to satisfaction and motivation.

IMPLICATIONS OF HERZBERG'S THEORY.

By insisting that satisfaction is not the opposite of dissatisfaction, Herzberg encouraged managers to think carefully about what actually motivates employees. According to Herzberg, "the opposite of job satisfaction is not job dissatisfaction, but rather *no* job satisfaction; and similarly, the opposite of job dissatisfaction is not job satisfaction, but *no* dissatisfaction."[19] Rather, the dissatisfaction–satisfaction continuum contains a zero midpoint at which both dissatisfaction and satisfaction are absent. An employee stuck on this midpoint, although not dissatisfied with pay and working conditions, is not particularly motivated to work hard because the job itself lacks challenge. Herzberg believes that the most managers can hope for when attempting to motivate employees with pay, status, working conditions, and other contextual factors is to reach the zero midpoint. But the elimination of dissatisfaction is not the same as truly motivating an employee. To satisfy and motivate employees, an additional element is required: meaningful, interesting, and challenging work. Herzberg believed that money is a weak motivational tool because, at best, it can only eliminate dissatisfaction.

Like Maslow, Herzberg triggered lively debate among motivation theorists. His assumption that job performance improves as satisfaction increases has been criticized for having a weak empirical basis. But a recent analysis of studies encompassing a total of 7,939 business units at 36 companies lends weight to Herzberg's model. The researchers concluded that changes in management practices that increase job satisfaction are likely to increase productivity and profits, while decreasing turnover and accidents.[20]

On the negative side, other researchers found that one person's dissatisfier may be another's satisfier (for example, money).[21] Nonetheless, Herzberg made a major contribution to motivation theory by emphasizing the motivating potential of enriched work. (Job enrichment is discussed in detail in the next section.)

Expectancy Theory

Both Maslow's and Herzberg's theories have been criticized for making unsubstantiated generalizations about what motivates people. Practical experience shows that people are motivated by lots of different things. Fortunately, expectancy theory, based largely on Victor H. Vroom's 1964 classic *Work and Motivation*, effectively deals with the highly personalized rational choices individuals make when faced with the prospect of having to work to achieve rewards. Individual perception, though secondary in the Maslow and Herzberg models, is central to expectancy theory. Accordingly, expectancy theory is a motivation model based on the assumption that motivational strength is determined by perceived probabilities of success. The term expectancy refers to the subjective probability (or expectation) that one thing will lead to another. Work-related expectations, like all other expectations, are shaped by ongoing personal experience. For instance, an employee's expectation of a raise, diminished after a request for a raise has been turned down, later rebounds when the supervisor indicates a willingness to reconsider the matter.

A BASIC EXPECTANCY MODEL.

Although Vroom and other expectancy theorists developed their models in somewhat complex mathematical terms, the descriptive model in Figure 12.3 is helpful for basic understanding. In this model, one's motivational strength increases as one's perceived effort–performance and performance–reward probabilities increase. All this is not as complicated as it sounds. For example, estimate your motivation to study if you expect to do poorly on a quiz no matter how hard you study (low effort–performance probability) and you know the quiz will not be graded (low performance–reward probability). Now contrast that estimate with your motivation to study if you believe that you can do well on the quiz with minimal study (high

---

expectancy theory model that assumes that motivational strength is determined by perceived probabilities of success |
expectancy the belief or expectation that one thing will lead to another

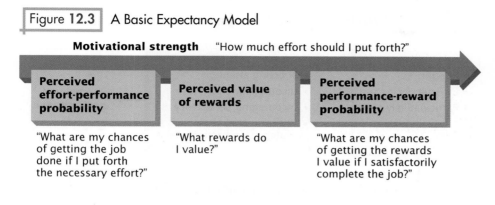

Figure **12.3** A Basic Expectancy Model

Motivational strength   "How much effort should I put forth?"

Perceived effort-performance probability	Perceived value of rewards	Perceived performance-reward probability
"What are my chances of getting the job done if I put forth the necessary effort?"	"What rewards do I value?"	"What are my chances of getting the rewards I value if I satisfactorily complete the job?"

effort–performance probability) and that doing well on the quiz will significantly improve your grade in the course (high performance–reward probability). Like students, employees are motivated to expend effort when they believe it will ultimately lead to rewards they themselves value. This expectancy approach not only appeals strongly to common sense; it also has received encouraging empirical support from researchers.[22]

RELEVANCE OF EXPECTANCY THEORY FOR MANAGERS. According to expectancy theory, effort → performance → reward expectations determine whether motivation will be high or low. Although these expectations are in the mind of the employee, they can be influenced by managerial action and organizational experience. Training, combined with challenging but realistic objectives, gives people reason to believe that they can get the job done if they put forth the necessary effort. But perceived effort–performance probabilities are only half the battle. Listening skills enable managers to discover each individual's perceived performance–reward probabilities. Employees tend to work harder when they believe they have *a good chance* of getting *personally meaningful* rewards. Both sets of expectations require managerial attention. Each is a potential barrier to work motivation.

Goal-Setting Theory

Think of the three or four most successful people you know personally. Their success may have come via business or professional achievement,

Our expectations affect our motivation to engage in all sorts of work and nonwork behavior. Although jockey Tony McCoy once suffered a fractured vertebrae in a riding accident, he returned to professional racing, placing second aboard Kruguyrova in this major Irish steeplechase race.

politics, athletics, or community service. Chances are they got where they are today by being goal-oriented. In other words, they committed themselves to (and achieved) progressively more challenging goals in their professional and personal affairs. A prime example is Martina Navratilova, Hall of Fame tennis star and champion of 18 Grand

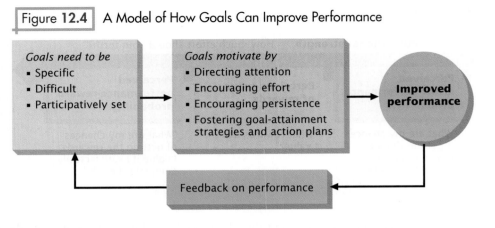

Figure 12.4   A Model of How Goals Can Improve Performance

Goals need to be
- Specific
- Difficult
- Participatively set

Goals motivate by
- Directing attention
- Encouraging effort
- Encouraging persistence
- Fostering goal-attainment strategies and action plans

Improved performance

Feedback on performance

Slam singles tournaments. She says, "You set your goals and then break it down and try to figure out how to get there." In other words, successful people use their goals to help them strategize solutions that become part of their daily routines.[23] Biographies and autobiographies of successful people in all walks of life generally attest to the virtues of goal setting. Accordingly, goal setting is acknowledged today as a respected and useful motivation theory.

Within an organizational context, goal setting is the process of improving individual or group job performance with formally stated objectives, deadlines, or quality standards. Management by objectives (MBO), discussed in Chapter 6, is a specific application of goal setting that advocates participative and measurable objectives. Also, recall from Chapter 6 that managers tend to use the terms *goal* and *objective* interchangeably.

A GENERAL GOAL-SETTING MODEL. Thanks to motivation researchers such as Edwin A. Locke and Gary P. Latham, there is a comprehensive body of knowledge about goal setting.[24] Goal setting has been researched more rigorously than the three motivation theories just discussed.[25] Locke and Latham pinpointed the power of goals in their summary of goal-setting research evidence: A goal creates "constructive discontent" with your current performance and leads you to set a new desired level of performance proficiency.[26]

Important lessons from goal-setting theory and research are incorporated in the general model in Figure 12.4. This model shows how properly conceived goals trigger a motivational process that improves performance. Let us explore the key

components of this goal-setting model, while keeping in mind that a Franklin Covey survey of workers in the United States found that only 19 percent had well-defined work goals.[27]

PERSONAL OWNERSHIP OF CHALLENGING GOALS. In Chapter 6, the discussion of MBO and writing good objectives stressed how goal effectiveness is enhanced by *specificity, difficulty,* and *participation.* Measurable and challenging goals encourage an individual or group to stretch while trying to attain progressively more difficult levels of achievement. For instance, parents who are paying a college student's tuition and expenses are advised to specify a challenging grade point goal rather than simply to tell their daughter or son, "Just do your best." Otherwise, the student could show up at the end of the semester with two Cs and three Ds, saying, "Well, I did my best!" John Krafcik, CEO of Hyundai USA, explains that his company promotes those who see the wisdom of the company's philosophy: Never set a target you know how to hit. Put another way, Hyundai rewards people who reach for higher levels of performance within themselves and within their work environments.[28] It is important to note that goals need to be difficult enough to be challenging, but they should not be impossible. Impossible goals hamper performance; they are a handy excuse for not even trying.[29]

Participation in the goal-setting process gives the individual *personal ownership.* From the employee's viewpoint, it is "something I helped develop, not just my boss's wild idea." Feedback on performance operates in concert with well-conceived goals. Feedback lets the person or group know if things are on track or if corrective action is required to reach the goal.

goal setting process of improving performance with objectives, deadlines, or quality standards

An otherwise excellent goal-setting program can be compromised by lack of timely and relevant feedback from managers. Researchers have documented the motivational value of matching *specific goals* with *equally specific feedback*.[30] Sam Walton, the founder of Walmart, was a master of blending goals and feedback. Take, for example, this exchange between Sam Walton and an employee during one of his regular store visits: When a top-selling employee said that her pet department accounted for 3.1 percent of sales and that she was aiming to increase to 3.3 percent, Walton complimented her and said that the average pet department does only 2.4 percent.[31]

HOW DO GOALS ACTUALLY MOTIVATE? Goal-setting researchers say goals perform a motivational function by doing the four things listed in the center of Figure 12.4. First, a goal is an exercise in selective perception because it directs one's *attention* to a specific target. Second, a goal encourages one to exert *effort* toward achieving something specific. Third, because a challenging goal requires sustained or repeated effort, it encourages *persistence*. Fourth, because a goal creates the problem of bridging the gap between actual and desired, it fosters the creation of *strategies and action plans* (prompted by the "constructive discontent" Locke and Latham mentioned earlier). When Marriott hotels implemented a 15-minute delivery guarantee on breakfast room service orders, for example, employees came up with ideas for meeting the goal, including using walkie-talkies for faster communication.[32] In effect, the service-guarantee program told Marriott employees that prompt room service was important, and they rose to the challenge with persistent and creative effort. Clear, reasonable, and challenging goals, reinforced by specific feedback and meaningful rewards, are indeed a powerful motivational tool.[33]

PRACTICAL IMPLICATIONS OF GOAL-SETTING THEORY. Because the model in Figure 12.4 is a generic one, the performance environment may range from athletics to academics to the workplace. The motivational mechanics of goal setting are the same, regardless of the targeted performance. If you learn to be an

effective goal setter in school, that ability will serve you faithfully throughout life.

Anyone tempted to go through life without goals should remember the smiling Cheshire Cat's good advice to Alice when she asked him to help her find her way through Wonderland: When Alice asked which way to walk, the Cheshire Cat replied, "That depends a good deal on where you want to get to."[34]

MOTIVATION THROUGH JOB DESIGN

A job serves two separate but intertwined functions. It generates value for the organization and income for the individual. Thus job design, the delineation of task responsibilities as dictated by organizational strategy, technology, and structure, is a key determinant of individual motivation and ultimately of organizational success. Considering that the average adult spends about half of his or her waking life at work, jobs are a central feature of modern existence. A challenging and interesting job can add zest and meaning to one's life. Boring and tedious jobs, on the other hand, can become a serious threat to one's motivation to work hard, not to mention their negative effect on one's physical and mental health. Concern about uneven productivity growth, product quality, and declining employee satisfaction has persuaded managers to consider two job design strategies.[35]

Strategy One: Fitting People to Jobs

For technological or economic reasons, work sometimes must be divided into routine and repetitive tasks. At Chung's Gourmet Foods in Houston, Texas, Paula Villalta and her co-workers spend eight hours a day doing nothing but filling and wrapping egg rolls. Yet Villalta routinely completes 6,000 egg rolls per shift, as compared to her colleagues' average of 4,000, because of her intense focus.[36]

BW Folsom/Shutterstock.Com

job design creating task responsibilities based on strategy, technology, and structure

In routine tasks, steps can be taken to avoid chronic dissatisfaction and bolster motivation. Three proven alternatives are realistic job previews, job rotation, and limited exposure. Each involves adjusting the person rather than the job in the person–job equation. Hence, each entails creating a more compatible fit between an individual and a routine or fragmented job. (In line with this approach is the employment of mentally disadvantaged workers, often in sheltered workshops.)

REALISTIC JOB PREVIEWS. Unrealized expectations are a major cause of job dissatisfaction, low motivation, and turnover. Managers commonly create unrealistically high expectations in job applicants to entice them to accept a position. This has proved particularly troublesome with regard to routine tasks. Dissatisfaction too often sets in when lofty expectations are brought down to earth by dull or tedious work. **Realistic job previews** (RJPs), honest explanations of what a job actually entails, have been successful in helping to avoid employee dissatisfaction resulting from unrealized expectations. On-the-job and laboratory research have demonstrated the practical value of giving a realistic preview of both positive and negative aspects to applicants for highly specialized and/or difficult jobs.

A statistical analysis of 40 different RJP studies revealed these patterns: fewer dropouts during the recruiting process, lower initial expectations, and lower turnover and higher performance once on the job. The researcher recommended a contingency approach to the form and timing of RJPs. *Written* RJPs are better for reducing the dropout rate during the recruiting process, whereas *verbal* RJPs more effectively reduce post-hiring turnover (quitting). Similarly, RJPs provided before hiring help prevent high turnover, while RJPs provided after hiring can help improve employee performance.[37]

JOB ROTATION. As the term is used here, **job rotation** involves periodically moving people from one specialized job to another. Such movement prevents stagnation. Other reasons for rotating personnel include compensating for a labor shortage, enhancing safety, training, and preventing fatigue.[38] *Carpal tunnel syndrome* and other painful and disabling injuries stemming from repetitive-motion tasks can be reduced significantly through job rotation. For example, at Nissan's U.S. vehicle assembly plants, workers are given four separate tasks in an eight-hour period to help reduce repetitive-motion injuries. This strategy has led to a 60 percent decline in injury rates in two years.[39] Meanwhile, the FBI rotates its agents off the drug squad periodically to

Fans of the Discovery Channel's *Dirty Jobs* love the wild and crazy situations host Mike Rowe gets himself into, yet the show helps us to empathize with the folks who perform the dirty work that makes modern life possible.

Elfi Kluck/Index Stock Imagery/Photolibrary

realistic job previews honest explanations of what a job actually entails | job rotation moving people from one specialized job to another

discourage corruption.[40] If highly repetitive and routine jobs are unavoidable, job rotation, by introducing a modest degree of novelty, can help prevent boredom and resulting alienation.

Of course, a balance needs to be achieved—people should be rotated often enough to fight boredom and injury and acquire valuable cross-training, but not so often that they feel unfairly manipulated or disoriented.

LIMITED EXPOSURE. Another way of coping with the need to staff a highly fragmented and tedious job is to limit the individual's exposure to it. A number of organizations have achieved high productivity among personnel doing routine tasks by allowing them to earn an early quitting time.[41] This technique, called contingent time off (CTO) or earned time off, involves establishing a challenging yet fair daily performance standard, or quota, and letting employees go home when it is reached. At a large manufacturing plant, for example, workers were promised a shorter work day if they could produce more units with fewer rejects. Within a week, the employees had increased production, significantly decreased rejections, and shortened their work days by more than an hour.[42] Some employees find the opportunity to earn eight hours of pay for fewer hours of steady effort extremely motivating.

Companies using contingent time off report successful results. Impressive evidence comes from a large-scale survey of 1,598 U.S. companies employing about 10 percent of the civilian workforce. Among nine nontraditional reward systems, "earned time off" ranked only eighth in terms of use (5 percent of the companies). But among those using it, earned time off ranked *second* in terms of positive impact on job performance—an 85 percent approval rating.[43] Thus, the use of contingent time off has not yet reached its excellent potential as a motivational tool.

Strategy Two: Fitting Jobs to People

The second job-design strategy calls for managers to consider changing the job instead of the person. Two job-design experts have proposed that managers address the question: "How can we get a person-job fit that leads to both high productivity and job satisfaction?[44] Two techniques for moving in this direction are job enlargement and job enrichment.

JOB ENLARGEMENT. As used here, job enlargement is the process of combining two or more specialized tasks in a work flow sequence into a single job. Aetna Life & Casualty, for example, gave some of its office employees a measure of relief from staring at a video display terminal (VDT) all day by reorganizing tasks among 10 data-entry clerks and 10 others whose jobs involved mainly paperwork and telephoning. Now nobody stares at a VDT screen more than 70 percent of the day, and both productivity and morale have increased for those 20 workers.[45] Although a moderate degree of complexity and novelty can be introduced in this manner, critics claim that two or more potentially boring tasks do not necessarily make one challenging job. Furthermore, organized labor has criticized job enlargement as a devious ploy for getting more work for the same amount of money. But if pay and performance are kept in balance, boredom and alienation can be kept somewhat at bay by job enlargement.

JOB ENRICHMENT. In general terms, job enrichment is redesigning a job to increase its motivating potential.[46] Job enrichment increases the challenge of one's work by reversing the trend toward greater specialization. Unlike job enlargement, which merely combines equally simple tasks, job enrichment builds more complexity and depth into jobs by introducing planning and decision-making responsibility normally carried out at higher levels. Thus, enriched jobs are said to be *vertically loaded*, whereas enlarged jobs are *horizontally loaded*. Managing an entire project can be immensely challenging and motivating thanks to vertical job loading. Scott Nichols, a home construction foreman, describes the process of transforming a vacant lot into a home as rewarding. Nichols says, "A lot of times you'll build a house for a family . . . that's pretty gratifying."[47]

Jobs can be enriched by upgrading five core dimensions of work: (1) skill variety, (2) task identity, (3) task significance, (4) autonomy, and (5) job feedback. Each of these core dimensions deserves a closer look.

- *Skill variety.* The degree to which the job requires a variety of different activities in carrying out the work, involving the use of a number of different skills and talents of the person

- *Task identity.* The degree to which the job requires completion of a "whole" and identifiable piece of work; that is, doing a job from beginning to end with a visible outcome
- *Task significance.* The degree to which the job has a substantial impact on the lives of other people, whether those people are in the immediate organization or in the world at large
- *Autonomy.* The degree to which the job provides substantial freedom, independence, and discretion to the individual in scheduling the work and in determining the procedures to be used in carrying it out
- *Job feedback.* The degree to which carrying out the work activities required by the job provides the individual with direct and clear information about the effectiveness of his or her performance[48]

Figure 12.5 shows the theoretical connection between enriched core job characteristics and high motivation and satisfaction. At the heart of this job-enrichment model are three psychological states that highly specialized jobs usually do not satisfy: meaningfulness, responsibility, and knowledge of results.

12b
Back to the Opening Case

Which of the five core dimensions of work can you detect in the Rackspace case? Explain. What is the motivational potential of the core dimensions you identified?

It is important to note that not all employees respond favorably to enriched jobs. Personal traits and motives influence the connection between core job characteristics and desired outcomes. Only those with the necessary knowledge and skills plus a desire for personal growth will be motivated by enriched work. Furthermore, in keeping with Herzberg's two-factor theory, dissatisfaction with factors such as pay, physical working conditions, or supervision can neutralize

| Figure 12.5 | How Job Enrichment Works |

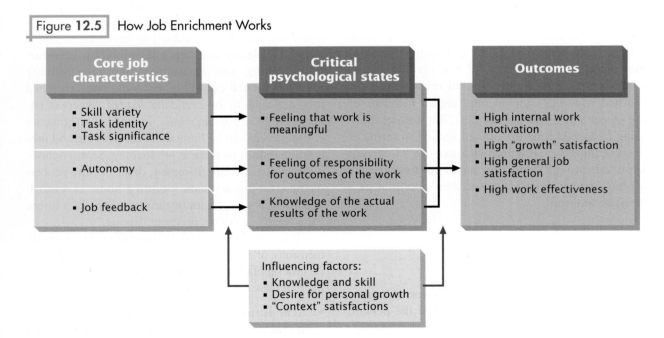

Source: J. Hackman/G. Oldham, *Work Redesign* (Figure 4.6). © 1980. Reprinted by permission of Pearson Education, Inc., Upper Saddle River, New Jersey.

enrichment efforts. Researchers have reported that fear of failure, lack of confidence, and lack of trust in management's intentions can stand in the way of effective job enrichment. But job enrichment can and does work when it is carefully thought out, when management is committed to its long-term success, and when employees desire additional challenge.[49]

MOTIVATION THROUGH REWARDS

All workers, including volunteers who donate their time to worthy causes, expect to be rewarded in some way for their contributions. Rewards can be defined broadly as the material and psychological payoffs for performing tasks in the workplace. Managers have found that job performance and satisfaction may be improved by properly administered rewards. Today, rewards vary greatly in both type and scope, depending on one's employer and geographic location. One indicator of the vastness of this topic is the book *The 1001 Rewards & Recognition Fieldbook.*[50]

In this section, we distinguish between extrinsic and intrinsic rewards, review alternative employee compensation plans, and discuss the effective management of extrinsic rewards.

Extrinsic Versus Intrinsic Rewards

There are two different categories of rewards. Extrinsic rewards are payoffs granted to the individual by other people. Examples include money, employee benefits, promotions, recognition, status symbols, and praise. The second category consists of intrinsic rewards, which are self-granted and internally experienced payoffs. Among intrinsic rewards are a sense of accomplishment, self-esteem, and self-actualization. For example, Audrey Tsao, a surgeon in Arizona who specializes in hip and knee replacements, says, "My patients keep me going." People often arrive in Tsao's office immobile and in pain, and after surgery, they can walk again and enjoy life, which Tsao finds very rewarding.[51]

Usually, on-the-job extrinsic and intrinsic rewards are intermingled. For instance, employees often experience a psychological boost, in addition to reaping material benefits, when they are empowered and enjoy their work experience. Such is the case at Trader Joe's, the popular chain of trendy grocery stores. Admittedly, workers there are motivated by the better-than-average salaries and benefits, but they also enjoy the fun-loving and empowering work environment where the "uniform" is a loud Hawaiian shirt and khakis.[52]

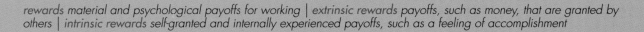

Aboard Cunard's luxury ocean liner *Queen Mary 2,* pay and recognition are welcome extrinsic rewards for the pastry chefs. They also get powerful intrinsic rewards when their efforts result in perfection.

Courtesy of Robert Kreitner

rewards material and psychological payoffs for working | **extrinsic rewards** payoffs, such as money, that are granted by others | **intrinsic rewards** self-granted and internally experienced payoffs, such as a feeling of accomplishment

Employee Compensation

Compensation deserves special attention at this point because money is the universal extrinsic reward. Managers need to be effective and efficient in this area because, when nonwage benefits are added in, labor costs typically make up about two-thirds of total costs.[53] Employee compensation is a complex area fraught with legal, ethical, and tax implications. Although an exhaustive treatment of employee compensation plans is beyond our present purpose, we can identify major types. Table 12.2 lists and briefly describes ten different pay plans. Two are nonincentive plans, seven qualify as incentive plans, and one plan is in a category of its own. Each type of pay plan has advantages and disadvantages. Therefore, there is no single best plan suitable for all employees. Indeed, two experts at the U.S. Bureau of Labor Statistics say the key words in compensation for the next 25 years will be *flexible* and *varied*. A diverse workforce will demand an equally diverse array of compensation plans.[54]

Mike Foley/Therapist Studios

Improving Performance with Extrinsic Rewards

Extrinsic rewards, if they are to motivate job performance effectively, need to be administered in ways that (1) satisfy operative needs, (2) foster positive expectations, (3) ensure equitable distribution, and (4) reward results. Let us see how these four criteria can be met relative to the ten different pay plans in Table 12.2.

REWARDS MUST SATISFY INDIVIDUAL NEEDS. Whether it is a pay raise or a pat on the back, a reward has no motivational impact unless it satisfies an operative need. Not all people need the same things, and one person may need different things at different times. Money is a powerful motivator for those who seek security through material wealth. But the promise of more money may mean little to a financially secure person who seeks ego gratification from challenging work. People's needs concerning when and how they want to be paid also vary.

Because cafeteria compensation is unique and particularly promising, we shall examine it more closely. Cafeteria compensation (also called life-cycle benefits) is a plan that allows each employee to determine the makeup of his or her benefit package.[55] In addition to receiving a core set of insurance benefits, vacation pay, and retirement funding, employees can choose optional benefits that best fit their needs and salaries. For example, an older worker might choose higher retirement fund contributions, while a young parent might choose additional insurance coverage for the kids.[56] Because today's nonwage benefits are a significant portion of total compensation, the motivating potential of such a privilege can be sizable.

Although some organizations have balked at installing cafeteria compensation because of added administrative expense, the number of programs in effect in the United States has grown steadily. Cafeteria compensation enhances employee satisfaction, according to at least one study,[57] and represents a revolutionary step toward fitting rewards to people, rather than vice versa.

EMPLOYEES MUST BELIEVE EFFORT WILL LEAD TO REWARD. According to expectancy theory, an employee will not strive for an attractive reward unless it is perceived as being attainable. For example, the promise of an expenses-paid trip to Hawaii for the leading salesperson will prompt additional efforts at sales only among those who feel they have a decent chance of winning. Those who believe they have little chance of winning will not be motivated to try any harder than usual. Incentive pay plans, especially merit pay, profit sharing, gain sharing, and stock options, need to be designed and communicated in a way that will foster believable effort–reward linkages.[58]

cafeteria compensation plan that allows employees to select their own mix of benefits

| Table 12.2 | Guide to Employee Compensation Plans |

PAY PLAN	DESCRIPTION/CALCULATION	MAIN ADVANTAGE	MAIN DISADVANTAGE
Nonincentive			
Hourly wage	Fixed amount per hour worked	Time is easier to measure than performance	Little or no incentive to work hard
Annual salary	Contractual amount per year	Easy to administer	Little or no incentive to work hard
Incentive			
Piece rate	Fixed amount per unit of output	Pay tied directly to personal output	Negative association with sweatshops and rate-cutting abuses
Sales commission	Fixed percentage of sales revenue	Pay tied directly to personal volume of business	Morale problem when sales personnel earn more than other employees
Merit pay	Bonus granted for outstanding performance	Gives salaried employees incentive to work harder	Fairness issue raised when tied to subjective appraisals
Profit sharing	Distribution of specified percentage of bottom-line profits	Individual has a personal stake in firm's profitability	Profits affected by more than just performance (for example, by prices and competition)
Gain sharing	Distribution of specified percentage of productivity gains and/or cost savings	Encourages employees to work harder and smarter	Calculations can get cumbersome
Pay-for-knowledge	Salary or wage rates tied to degrees earned or skills mastered	Encourages lifelong learning	Tends to inflate training and labor costs
Stock options	Selected employees earn right to acquire firm's stock free or at a discount	Gives individual a personal stake in firm's financial performance	Can be resented by ineligible personnel; morale tied to stock price
Other			
Cafeteria compensation (life-cycle benefits)	Employee selects personal mix of benefits from an array of options	Tailored benefits package fits individual needs	Can be costly to administer

REWARDS MUST BE EQUITABLE. Something is equitable if people perceive it to be fair and just. Each of us, figuratively speaking, carries in our head a pair of scales upon which we weigh equity. Figure 12.6 shows one scale for *personal equity* and another for *social equity*. The personal equity scale tests the relationship between effort expended and rewards received. The social equity scale, in contrast, compares our own effort–reward ratio with that of someone else in the same situation. We are motivated to seek personal and social equity and to avoid inequity.[59] An interesting aspect of research on this

Figure **12.6** Personal and Social Equity

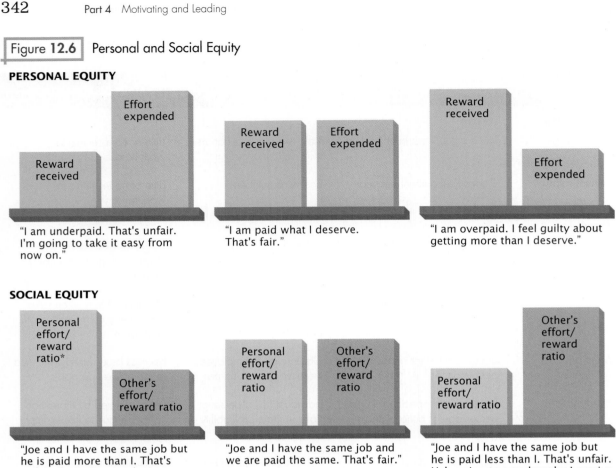

PERSONAL EQUITY

Reward received | Effort expended
"I am underpaid. That's unfair. I'm going to take it easy from now on."

Reward received | Effort expended
"I am paid what I deserve. That's fair."

Reward received | Effort expended
"I am overpaid. I feel guilty about getting more than I deserve."

SOCIAL EQUITY

Personal effort/reward ratio* | Other's effort/reward ratio
"Joe and I have the same job but he is paid more than I. That's unfair. I'm going to take it easy. Is Joe special?"

Personal effort/reward ratio | Other's effort/reward ratio
"Joe and I have the same job and we are paid the same. That's fair."

Personal effort/reward ratio | Other's effort/reward ratio
"Joe and I have the same job but he is paid less than I. That's unfair. He's going to wonder why I receive special treatment."

* The lower the effort/reward ratio, the greater the motivation.

topic is its demonstration that inequity is perceived by those who are *overpaid* as well as by those who are underpaid.[60] In a recent survey of 557 employees, 51 percent said they were underpaid, 46 percent felt they were paid the right amount, and 3 percent believed they were overpaid.[61] Because perceived inequity is associated with feelings of dissatisfaction and anger, jealousy, or guilt, inequitable reward schemes tend to be counterproductive and are ethically questionable. Record-setting executive pay in recent years of painful downsizings, massive layoffs, and stock market underperformance has been roundly criticized as inequitable and unfair. Take Terry Semel, for instance. The former CEO of Yahoo took home $71.7 million in 2006, a year when Yahoo's stock took a 38 percent dive.[62] In fact, when 400 college-educated people were asked, "What has undermined your trust in companies?" 60 percent said exceedingly

high pay for top management.[63] One notable exception to this trend occurred at Continental Airlines after a money-losing 2009 when CEO Jeff Smisek refused to accept a paycheck until the airline returned to profitability.[64]

REWARDS MUST BE LINKED TO PERFORMANCE. Ideally, there should be an if-then relationship between task performance and extrinsic rewards. Traditional hourly wage and annual salary pay plans are weak in this regard. They do little more than reward the person for showing up at work. Managers can strengthen motivation to work by making sure that those who give a little extra get a little extra. In addition to piece-rate and sales-commission plans, merit pay, profit sharing, gain sharing, and stock option plans are popular ways of linking pay and performance. Cash bonuses, when paid promptly to maximize the *positive reinforcement* effect, can boost motivation. At Salary.com, where on-the-spot bonuses run anywhere from $50 to $500, senior vice president of compensation Bill Coleman feels they are more effective at highlighting the value of exceptional behavior than annual bonuses, which are appreciated but not necessarily associated with specific behaviors.[65] Positive reinforcement is discussed in Chapter 14, in the context of behavior modification.

The concept of team-based incentive pay as a way of rewarding teamwork and cooperation has been slow to take hold in the United States for two reasons: (1) it goes against the grain of an individualistic culture, and (2) poorly conceived and administered plans have given team-based pay a bad reputation.[66]

All incentive pay plans should be carefully conceived because undesirable behavior may inadvertently be encouraged. Consider, for example, this story told by the head of Nucor Corporation, a successful mini-mill steel company, that withholds an employee's daily bonus if they are out sick or arrive even five minutes late to work.

> *One of the workers came in one day and said that Phil [another worker] had been in an automobile accident and was sitting beside his car off of Route 52, holding his head. So the foreman asked, "Why didn't you stop and help him?" And the guy said, "And lose my bonus?"*[67]

Like goals, incentive plans foster selective perception.[68] Consequently, managers need to make sure goals and incentives point people in ethical directions.

MOTIVATION THROUGH EMPLOYEE PARTICIPATION AND ENGAGEMENT

While noting that the term *participation* has become a "stewpot" into which every conceivable kind of management fad has been tossed, one management scholar helpfully identified four key areas of participative management. Employees may participate in (1) setting goals, (2) making decisions, (3) solving problems, and (4) designing and implementing organizational

changes.[69] Thus, **participative management** is defined as the process of empowering employees to assume greater control of the workplace.[70] When personally and meaningfully involved, above and beyond just doing assigned tasks, employees are said to be more engaged, motivated, and productive. In fact, a study of 164 New Zealand companies with at least 100 employees found lower employee turnover and higher organizational productivity among firms using participative management practices.[71]

This section focuses on three approaches to participation. They are employee engagement and retention programs, open-book management, and self-managed teams. After taking a closer look at each, we consider four keys to successful employee participation programs.

Employee Engagement and Retention Programs

Managers are responsible for building the organization's talent pool through careful hiring, needed training, and rigorous performance appraisal. But

12c
Does Money Buy Happiness?

Gallup poll: Even if they won a $10 million lottery jackpot, 55 percent of working Americans would continue to work.

George Lucas, director of Star Wars movies: Money can buy pleasure, but pleasure isn't happiness. Happiness is a feeling that goes beyond pleasure.

QUESTIONS: Some management theorists say money isn't a motivator. Do you agree or disagree? Why? When it comes to motivating you to do your best, what role does money play?

Sources: Data from "The Stat," *Business Week* (October 4, 2004): 16; and Lucas as quoted in Craig Wilson, "How Much Would Make You Smile?" *USA Today* (December 27, 2004): 2B.

participative management empowering employees to assume greater control of the workplace

are they doing a good job of tapping each employee's full potential and keeping key players from leaving? Evidently not, judging from this evidence: A 2009 Gallup poll of 42,000 workers showed that 33 percent of them are engaged, meaning they work with passion, drive innovation, and move the organization forward. Another 49 percent say they're simply putting in their time, and 18 percent admit they're actively acting out against their employers. These disengaged workers cost American businesses an estimated $350 billion a year.[72]

Buried in that astounding figure is the expense of paid unplanned absences. For all job categories, employees average 5.4 days of unplanned absences annually.[73] Also factored in is the cost of replacing potentially excellent people who quit out of frustration.[74]

A FEELING OF PROGRESS IS KEY. If you are presently employed, what is your engagement category, absenteeism record, and desire to quit? More to the point, what would it take for you to be fully engaged? (See Green Management: Toward Sustainability.) Researchers have discovered a perception gap on this matter. Employees do not hunger for what their bosses think they want most. Specifically, employers think their people want to be recognized for their good work, above all else. Meanwhile, workers say they want *a sense of progress* more than anything else—recognition is well down their list of desires.

12d

Back to the Opening Case

In terms of what you have learned in this chapter about employee motivation, does Rackspace have a good employee engagement program? What is the single most important component of the program? Explain.

The researcher, Harvard University's Teresa M. Amabile, explains that when workers believe they're making progress and receiving support, they feel positive and motivated to succeed. But when they face roadblocks to accomplishment, motivation wanes.[75] Consequently, managers are challenged to implement comprehensive engagement and retention programs that fit their employees' needs. Here is a basic three-step approach.

A SURVEY-DRIVEN PROCESS. Step 1 is to develop an employee engagement survey for the organization, with input from inside and outside human resource and survey research experts. Short, convenient, and

Green Management: Toward Sustainability

Patagonia's Yvon Chouinard Wants Everyone to Help Save the Planet

Chouinard is owner and founder of the clothing company Patagonia. . . . The $314.5 million company, based in Ventura, California, is legendary for its environmental focus and beloved by employees, who enjoy an almost unparalleled degree of autonomy and flexibility. . . .

Chouinard: For every opening at Patagonia, we have an average of 900 applicants. I think that's because people know we're in business to try to save this planet and influence other companies that green business is good business. Our people are young and idealistic. They want to do more than just get a paycheck. . . .

We give employees two weeks' paid time to volunteer at the environmental organization of their choice. . . .

Openness creates trust. . . . They know what we give to environmental causes. It's part of an overall message where there is no hierarchy and everything is very honest.

For Discussion: What roles do intrinsic and extrinsic rewards and participation and engagement play in Patagonia's green management style?

Source: Excerpted from an interview by Leigh Buchanan, "A Little Enlightened Self-Interest," *Inc.*, 32 (June 2010): 56–60.

anonymous surveys with questions such as "Do you have the necessary tools to do a good job?" and "Is the company's mission clear to you?" should be administered at least annually. Zappos.com's online engagement survey is monthly.[76] Engagement surveys are more behaviorally specific than traditional attitude surveys. For instance, it is better to ask "How often does your manager provide helpful coaching and tips?" instead of "Do you like your manager?" Step 2 involves analyzing the survey data department by department, looking for patterns of problems. Step 3 is the remedial phase when problems are addressed head on. While one size does not fit all, employee engagement and retention programs need to satisfy these basic criteria:

- Be forthcoming about trends in your company and industry.
- Keep everyone abreast of both good and bad news.
- Trust employees' experience and ideas.
- Ask for employees' suggestions and comments, then take action.
- Remain optimistic.
- Foster innovation.
- Don't waste employees' time.[77]

A concerted effort to enhance engagement and retention by United Health Group's 6,000 managers produced measurable results within two years: engagement up 6 percent; total employee turnover down 9 percent; turnover of key personnel down 6 percent; turnover of new employees within their first year down 10 percent; and internal promotions up 13 percent.[78]

Open-Book Management

Open-book management (OBM) involves giving employees access to financial records, as well as explaining what the numbers mean and how their work contributes to the financial success of the company.[79] Clearly, this is a bold break from traditional management practice. Many companies claim to practice OBM, but few actually do.[80] Why? OBM asks managers to correct three typical shortcomings by (1) displaying a high degree of trust in employees, (2) having a deep and unwavering commitment to employee training, and (3) being patient when waiting for results.[81] Once again, as we saw earlier with his masterful blending of goals and feedback, Walmart's founder Sam Walton was a pioneer in

open-book management and employee participation. Former Walmart CEO David Glass recalls that Walton treated everyone as a partner and shared information because he believed it encouraged every employee to take ownership and contribute to the company's success.[82]

A four-step approach to OBM is displayed in Figure 12.7. The S.T.E.P. acronym stands for *share, teach, empower,* and *pay.* Skipping or inadequately performing a step virtually guarantees failure. A systematic process is needed. Experts tell us it takes at least two complete budget cycles (typically two years) to see positive results. In step 1, employees are exposed to eye-catching public displays of key financial data. Sales, expense, and profit data for both the organization and relevant business units are shared in hallways, in cafeterias, and on password-protected Web sites. Of course, without step 2, step 1 would be meaningless. Comprehensive, ongoing training gives *all* employees a working knowledge of the firm's business model. At Jelly Belly University, all Jelly Belly Candy Co. employees learn how to make the candy, review results, oversee product evaluations, handle scheduling, and control inventory.[83] Thus, Jelly Belly's employees not only learn how to make great jelly beans, they learn what it takes to make a profit in the process.

In OBM companies, finance specialists teach other employees how to read and interpret basic financial documents such as profit-loss statements. Entertaining and instructive business board games and computer simulations have proved effective. Remedial education is provided when needed.

Armed with knowledge about the company's workings and financial health, employees are ready for step 3. Managers find it easier to trust empowered employees to make important decisions when the employees are adequately prepared (more on empowerment in Chapter 14). In step 4, employees enjoy the fruits of their efforts by sharing profits and/or receiving bonuses and incentive compensation. There is no magic to OBM. It simply involves doing *important* things in the *right* way.

Self-Managed Teams

According to the logic of this comprehensive approach to participation, self-management is the best management because it taps people's full potential.

open-book management sharing key financial data and profits with employees who are trained and empowered

Figure **12.7**   The Four S.T.E.P. Approach to Open-Book Management

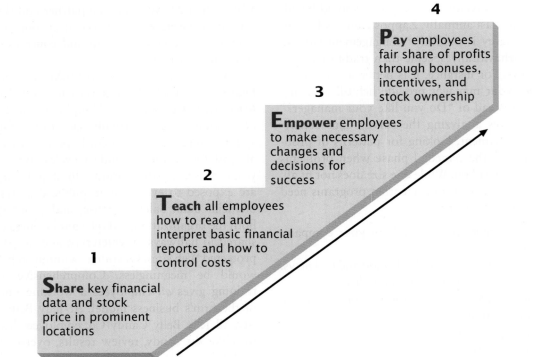

4

Pay employees fair share of profits through bonuses, incentives, and stock ownership

3

Empower employees to make necessary changes and decisions for success

2

Teach all employees how to read and interpret basic financial reports and how to control costs

1

Share key financial data and stock price in prominent locations

Source: Based in part on Raj Aggarwal and Betty J. Simkins, "Open Book Management—Optimizing Human Capital," *Business Horizons*, 44 (September–October 2001): 5–13.

Advocates say self-management fosters creativity, motivation, and productivity. **Self-managed teams**, also known as autonomous work groups or high-performance work teams, take on traditional managerial tasks as part of their normal work routine.[84] They can have anywhere from 5 to more than 30 members, depending on the job. Cross-trained team members typically rotate jobs as they turn out a complete product or service. Any supervision tends to be minimal, with managers acting more as *facilitators* than as order givers.

VERTICALLY LOADED JOBS. In the language of job enrichment, team members' jobs are vertically loaded. This means non-managerial team members assume duties traditionally performed by managers. But specifically which duties? A survey of industry practices at 1,456 U.S. companies by *Training* magazine gave us some answers. Over 60 percent of the companies using self-managed teams let team members determine work schedules, deal directly with

customers, and conduct training. Between 30 and 40 percent of the teams were allowed to manage budgets, conduct performance appraisals, and hire people. Only 15 percent of the teams were permitted to fire coworkers. The researchers concluded that *true* self-managed teams are still in the early growth stage.[85] Google's engineers, for example, are divided into self-managing teams of three, and each team is empowered to solve problems without consulting anyone. It took them some time to get used to the new system, but it worked. "There's faith here in the ability of smart, well-motivated people to do the right thing," says chief engineer Wayne Rosing.[86]

MANAGERIAL RESISTANCE. Not surprisingly, managerial resistance is the number one barrier to self-managed teams. More than anything else, self-managed teams represent *change*, and lots of it. Using teams requires the removal of layers of management and bureaucratic barriers. However, companies gain

self-managed teams high-performance teams that assume traditional managerial duties such as staffing and planning

wavebreakmedia ltd/Shutterstock.Com

Proponents of self-managed work teams say they foster creativity, motivation, and productivity. Team members often take turns performing particular job duties and tasks, including leading the team.

the commitment and knowledge of workers, and see increases in productivity, sometimes as much as 30 percent.[87] Yet, traditional authoritarian supervisors view autonomous teams as a threat to their authority and job security. For this reason, *new* facilities built around the concept of self-managed teams, so-called greenfield sites, tend to fare better than reworked existing operations.

Managers who take the long view and switch to self-managed teams are finding it well worth the investment of time and money. Self-managed teams even show early promise of boosting productivity in the huge service sector. (Teamwork is discussed in the next chapter.)

Keys to Successful Employee Participation Programs

According to researchers, four factors build the *employee* support necessary for any sort of participation program to work:

1. A profit-sharing or gain-sharing plan
2. A long-term employment relationship with good job security

3. A concerted effort to build and maintain group cohesiveness
4. Protection of the individual employee's rights[88]

Working in combination, these factors can help employee participation programs involving engagement and retention, open-book management, or self-managed teams succeed.

It should be clear by now that participative management involves more than simply announcing a new program, such as open-book management. To make sure a supportive climate exists, a good deal of background work often needs to be done. This is particularly important in view of the conclusion drawn by researchers who analyzed 41 participative management studies: Participation positively influences both satisfaction and productivity. However, organizational factors strengthen or weaken the effect of participation. For example, workers typically find more satisfaction in a generally participative climate than in actually participating in decisions.[89] In the end, effective participative management is as much a managerial attitude about sharing power as it is a specific set of practices. In some European countries, such as Germany, the supportive climate is reinforced by government-mandated participative management.

MOTIVATION THROUGH QUALITY-OF-WORK-LIFE PROGRAMS

Workforce diversity has made *flexibility* and *accommodation* top priorities for managers today. This chapter concludes with a look at ways of accommodating emerging employee needs. For example, a big concern these days involves striking a proper balance between work and life beyond the workplace. The dilemmas facing Dan Rosensweig, Yahoo!'s chief operating officer, and teacher Carmen Alvarez are typical today:

> *Rosensweig: The biggest challenge is, when you're given an opportunity like this, how do you give it everything you have because it deserves it, and also recognize and appreciate that the most important things in your life are your wife and daughters. I'm envious of people who have been able to find better balance.*[90]
>
> *Alvarez: Each day after teaching fourth graders, Carmen Alvarez, 35, cooks for her three daughters, helps them with their homework and finds time to attend at least one of their games. "I feel responsible for everything." Alvarez, who is separated from the girls' father, finished Ph.D. coursework at Boston College. Now she's trying to complete her dissertation. "How do you find time to put yourself first?"*[91]

Ironically, more time at home for telecommuters and entrepreneurs often fails to translate into better work/life balance. "The technology that allows parents to spend more time at home—laptops and cell-phones and mobile e-mail—is blurring the lines between work and personal life and distracting them from the 'family time' they crave."[92] For many, modern technology has not been as liberating as promised.

Harvard's Rosabeth Moss Kanter believes employers need to be part of the solution. Our society will not be able to reap the rewards of employing so many talented people if they're not given opportunities to strike a healthy work/life balance. Kanter notes that there are several good role models out there, but that companies could be doing more.[93] By meeting these needs in creative ways, such as flexible work schedules, family support services, wellness programs, and sabbaticals, managers hope to enhance motivation and job performance.

Flexible Work Schedules

The standard 8 A.M. to 5 P.M., 40-hour workweek has come under fire as dual-income families, single parents, and others attempt to juggle hectic schedules. One alternative is flextime, a work-scheduling plan that allows employees to determine their own arrival and departure times within specific limits.[94] All employees must be present during a fixed core time (see the center portion of Figure 12.8). If an eight-hour day is required, as in Figure 12.8, an early bird can put in the required eight hours by arriving at 7:00 A.M., taking half an hour for lunch, and departing at 3:30 P.M. Alternatively, a late starter can come in at 9:00 A.M. and leave at 5:30 P.M.

When given the choice between "flexible work hours" and an "opportunity to advance" in a survey, 58 percent of the women opted for flexible hours. Forty-three percent of the men chose that option.[95] This comes as no surprise given an aging population in need of caregivers for ailing relatives. About one-third of American adults are caregivers, and of these, about two-thirds are full-time working women.[96] Some progressive organizations, such as Mitre, in McLean, Virginia, take flextime to an extreme by

Figure 12.8	Flextime in Action

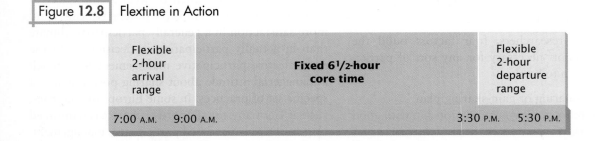

flextime allows employees to choose their own arrival and departure times within specified limits

Comstock/Jupiterimages

Today's employees are striving for a better work–life balance, and they're looking for employers that can help them achieve it. To that end, some larger corporations, like Cisco Systems, provide on-site daycare for their employees with small children.

Family Support Services

Family-friendly companies recognize that employees have lives and priorities outside the workplace and make appropriate accommodations. They strive to help their employees achieve a productive and satisfying balance between work and life with supportive policies, programs, and culture. This last factor—culture—is particularly important because it is driven by the organization's core values. A company that claims to

allowing employees to set their own schedules entirely as long as they put in 40 hours of work in every seven-day period.[97]

Another increasingly popular flexible scheduling option is paid-time-off (PTO) banks, also called leave banks. With a **PTO bank**, normal paid-time-off days—vacation allotment, sick days, personal days—are lumped together into a time bank that employees can draw from in hourly increments whenever they need to and for whatever reason. Will this mean the end of lame excuses such as "My grandmother died" (for the fourth time)? Generally, paid federal holidays are not included and limits are placed on how many hours can be carried over from one year to the next. About one-third of companies in the United States currently have PTO banks. At Pinnacol Assurance, a Denver insurance firm, human resources director Cecelia Muir has used employee surveys to trace the firm's high levels of engagement and satisfaction and low turnover (about 6 or 7 percent) back to the PTO bank.[98]

Other work-scheduling variations include *compressed workweeks* (40 or more hours in fewer than five days), *permanent part-time* (workweeks with fewer than 40 hours), *job sharing* (complementary scheduling that allows two or more part-timers to share a single full-time job), and *chronotype scheduling* (scheduling "morning people" and "night people" according to their internal clocks).[99]

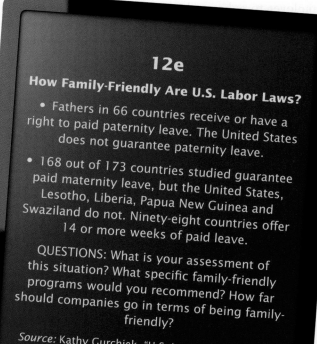

12e
How Family-Friendly Are U.S. Labor Laws?

- Fathers in 66 countries receive or have a right to paid paternity leave. The United States does not guarantee paternity leave.

- 168 out of 173 countries studied guarantee paid maternity leave, but the United States, Lesotho, Liberia, Papua New Guinea and Swaziland do not. Ninety-eight countries offer 14 or more weeks of paid leave.

QUESTIONS: What is your assessment of this situation? What specific family-friendly programs would you recommend? How far should companies go in terms of being family-friendly?

Source: Kathy Gurchiek, "U.S. Lags in Policies That Are Worker-Friendly," *HR Magazine,* 52 (April 2007): 29, 32.

PTO bank vacation, sick, and personal leave time is pooled into a single account and drawn upon at will | family-friendly companies companies that recognize and accommodate employees' nonwork lives and priorities

be family-friendly, yet promotes only those who log 60-hour weeks, values total dedication more than work/life balance. A study by the Society for Human Resource Management identified "the top five family-friendly benefits":

1. Dependent care flexible spending accounts (71 percent)
2. Flextime (55 percent)
3. Family leave above required leave of the federal Family and Medical Leave Act (39 percent)
4. Telecommuting on a part-time basis (34 percent)
5. Compressed workweeks (31 percent)[100]

It is important to note that the U.S. Family and Medical Leave Act (FMLA), which took effect in 1993, has significant holes and limitations. First, only companies with 50 or more employees are required to comply with the law mandating up to 12 weeks of *unpaid* leave per year for family events such as births, adoptions, and sickness. Because the vast majority of U.S. businesses (95 percent) employ fewer than 50 people, millions of working Americans (43 percent) are left unprotected by FMLA. Second, employees can be required by their employer to exhaust their sick leave and vacation allotments before taking FMLA leave. Fortunately, individual states and businesses have plugged some of the holes in FMLA.[101]

True family-friendly companies go way beyond the legal minimum, as these recent inspiring examples show:

- *Nugget Market, Woodland, California.* Because of the recession, the supermarket chain gives employees discount cards for groceries every month.
- *Cisco Systems, San Jose.* It offers on-site child care for 800 children, making it one of the largest providers of this service, and parents at HQ can use their computers to check on their children.
- *Nustar Energy, San Antonio.* The company provides no-cost health insurance for employees and their families.
- *Johnson Financial Group, Racine, Wisconsin.* Employees receive their salaries even when they miss work due to an emergency.
- *Southern Ohio Medical Center, Portsmouth, Ohio.* Adoption benefits up to $3,500 are provided, and after 20 years of employment, workers get an extra week of vacation.[102]

As more and more companies offer family-friendly benefits, cost-conscious managers properly ask, "What is the return on our investment?" Recent studies of companies with family-friendly practices have documented financial payoffs from easier recruitment, lower absenteeism and turnover, and greater productivity.[103]

BEST PRACTICES

Hospital CEO Margaret Sabin Works Up a Sweat over Wellness

Striding the halls of Penrose Hospital [in Colorado Springs], one of four hospitals she runs, Margaret Sabin looks every bit the president and CEO she is—perfectly tailored suit, stylish coif, purposeful air.

Twenty minutes later, not so much. The confidence and determination remain, but now she's in workout garb, sweating, laughing, shouting as she leads 30 or so folks in a kick-butt exercise class in the hospital fitness room.

Twice a week, no matter what thorny issues she's wrangling with, Sabin, 53, does her quick-change routine into workout instructor (she has been certified since 2001).

"You guys are animals today," she bellows happily to the class, which includes the hospital CFO [chief financial officer] and the manager of the GI lab, and is often attended by the now-trim head of the oncology unit (who has lost 40-plus pounds)....

"We are a health care system," she points out. "We should be role models."

For Discussion: Generally speaking, what are the keys to making a workplace wellness program successful? What does (or should) your own personal wellness program involve?

Source: Excerpted from Sharon L. Peters, "Hospital Chief Leads by Example," *USA Today* (September 20, 2010): 5D.

Employees at the European Commission's headquarters in Brussels, Belgium, have free access to a fleet of 200 bicycles for short work-related trips, thus combining eco-friendly transportation and employee fitness.

Wellness Programs

Stress and burnout are all too common consequences of modern work life. Stress is tough on employees, productivity, and relationships. Family-versus-work conflict, long hours, overload, hectic schedules, deadlines, frequent business travel, and accumulated workplace irritations are taking their toll. Progressive companies are coming to the rescue with *wellness programs* featuring a wide range of offerings. Among them are stress reduction, healthy eating and living clinics, quit-smoking and weight-loss programs, exercise facilities, massage breaks, behavioral health counseling, and health screenings. The ultimate objective is to help employees develop healthy habits in their personal and work lives, with win-win benefits all around[104] (see Best Practices). A good example is Fieldale Farms, a chicken processor in Baldwin, Georgia, where the $50,000 tab each time an employee had a heart attack was making health insurance unaffordable. Its solution was to provide gym memberships, health screenings, nutritional counseling, and sessions about heart disease, diabetes, and other conditions as part of a new wellness program. The company thinks the $200,000 annual tab is worth it, given that the company spends about half what other companies spend on health insurance plans.[105]

Sabbaticals

Some progressive companies in the United States (about 2 percent) give selected employees paid sabbaticals after a certain number of years of service. Computer chip-maker Intel is the gold standard when it comes to corporate sabbaticals: In 2009, 6,000 employees took a sabbatical of eight paid weeks after putting in seven years of service.[106] An extended period of paid time off gives the employee time for family, recreation, service, or travel. The idea is to refresh dedicated employees and, it is hoped, bolster their motivation and loyalty in the process.

SUMMARY

1. Maslow's five-level hierarchy of needs, though criticized on the basis of empirical evidence of deficiencies, makes it clear to managers that people are motivated by emerging rather than fulfilled needs. Assuming that job satisfaction and performance are positively related, Herzberg believed that the most that wages and working conditions can do is eliminate sources of dissatisfaction. According to Herzberg, the key to true satisfaction, and hence motivation, is an enriched job that provides an opportunity for achievement, responsibility, and personal growth. Expectancy theory is based on the idea that the strength of one's motivation to work is the product of perceived probabilities of acquiring personally valued rewards. Both effort–performance and performance–reward probabilities are important in expectancy theory.

2. Goals can be an effective motivational tool when they are specific, difficult, participatively set, and accompanied by feedback on performance. Goals motivate performance by directing attention, encouraging effort and persistence, and prompting goal-attainment strategies and action plans.

3. Managers can counteract the boredom associated with routine-task jobs through realistic job previews, job rotation, and limited exposure. This third alternative involves letting employees earn an early departure time.

4. Job enrichment vertically loads jobs to meet individual needs for meaningfulness, responsibility, and knowledge of results. Personal desire for growth and a supportive climate must exist for job enrichment to be successful.

5. Both extrinsic (externally granted) and intrinsic (self-granted) rewards, when properly administered, can have a positive impact on performance and satisfaction. There is no single best employee compensation plan. A flexible and varied approach to compensation will be necessary in the coming years because of workforce diversity. The following rules can help managers maximize the motivational impact of extrinsic rewards: (1) rewards must satisfy individual needs, (2) one must believe that one's effort will lead to reward, (3) rewards must be equitable, and (4) rewards must be linked to performance. Gain-sharing plans have great motivational potential because they emphasize participation and link pay to actual productivity.

6. Participative management programs foster direct employee involvement in one or more of the following areas: goal setting, decision making, problem solving, and change implementation. Recent research discovered that employees want to feel a sense of progress more than anything else. Employee engagement and retention programs involve three steps: anonymous employee surveys with behaviorally specific questions about their workplace, department-by-department analysis of results to spot problems, and remedial action with emphasis on transparency and trust. The S.T.E.P. model of open-book management encourages employee participation when managers (1) *share* key financial data with all employees, (2) *teach* employees how to interpret financial statements and control costs, (3) *empower* employees to make improvements and decisions, and (4) *pay* a fair share of profits to employees. Employees assigned to self-managed teams participate by taking on tasks that have traditionally been performed by management. Profit sharing or gain sharing, job security, cohesiveness, and protection of employee rights are keys to building crucial employee support for participation programs.

7. Quality-of-work-life programs are being used to accommodate and motivate today's diverse workforce. Flextime, a flexible work-scheduling scheme that allows employees to choose their own arrival and departure times, has been effective in improving employee–supervisor relations while reducing absenteeism. Employers are increasingly providing family-friendly services such as child care, elder care, parental leaves, and adoption benefits. Employee wellness programs and sabbaticals are offered by some companies to reduce health insurance costs, build loyalty, and boost motivation.

TERMS TO UNDERSTAND

Motivation, p. 328
Expectancy theory, p. 332
Expectancy, p. 332
Goal setting, p. 334
Job design, p. 335
Realistic job previews, p. 336
Job rotation, p. 336

Contingent time off, p. 337
Job enlargement, p. 337
Job enrichment, p. 337
Rewards, p. 339
Extrinsic rewards, p. 339
Intrinsic rewards, p. 339
Cafeteria compensation, p. 340

Participative management, p. 343
Open-book management, p. 345
Self-managed teams, p. 346
Flextime, p. 348
PTO bank, p. 349
Family-friendly companies, p. 349

ACTION LEARNING EXERCISE

QUALITY-OF-WORK-LIFE SURVEY

Instructions: Think of your present job, or one you had in the past, and circle one number for each of the following items. Add the circled numbers to get a total quality-of-work-life score. Alternatively, you can use this survey to interview another jobholder to determine his or her quality of work life. (*Note:* This survey is for instructional purposes only because it has not been scientifically validated.)

General Job Satisfaction

Most of the time, my job satisfaction is

Very low   **Very high**
1   2   3   4   5   6   7

Quality of Supervision

The person I report to respects me, listens to me, and supports me.

Never   **Always**
1   2   3   4   5   6   7

Quality of Communication

The organization keeps me well informed about its mission and pending changes.

Never   **Always**
1   2   3   4   5   6   7

Organizational Climate

My workplace generally feels like

A cold, rainy day   **A warm, sunny day**
1   2   3   4   5   6   7

Job Design

The work I do is

Routine and boring   **Varied and challenging**
1   2   3   4   5   6   7

Unimportant   **Important**
1   2   3   4   5   6   7

Feedback and Compensation

I am given timely and constructive feedback.

False   **True**
1   2   3   4   5   6   7

I am paid fairly for what I do.

False   **True**
1	2	3	4	5	6	7

Coworkers

My coworkers are

Negative and unfriendly   **Positive and friendly**
1	2	3	4	5	6	7

Work Hours and Schedules

My work hours and schedules are flexible and accommodate my lifestyle.

Never   **Always**
1	2	3	4	5	6	7

Organizational Identification

I have a strong sense of commitment and loyalty to my work organization.

False   **True**
1	2	3	4	5	6	7

Stress

The degree of unhealthy stress in my workplace is

Very high   **Very low**
1	2	3	4	5	6	7

Total quality-of-work-life score = _____

Scale

12–35 = Warning—this job could be hazardous to your health
36–60 = Why spend half your waking life settling for average?
61–84 = T.G.I.M. (Thank goodness it's *Monday!*)

FOR CONSIDERATION/DISCUSSION

1. Which of these various quality-of-work-life factors is of overriding importance to you? Why? Which are least important? Why?

2. How strongly does your quality-of-work-life score correlate with the amount of effort you put into your job? Explain the connection.

3. How helpful would this survey be in your search for a better job? Explain.

4. How much does your total score reflect your attitude about life in general?

5. What should your managers do to improve the quality-of-work-life scores for you and your coworkers?

6. How important is quality of work life to your overall lifestyle and happiness? Explain.

ETHICS EXERCISE

 DO THE RIGHT THING

IS CORPORATE CEO PAY OUT OF CONTROL?

Graef Crystal, a pioneer in compensation consulting, analyzed the 2009 pay of 271 chief executive officers. His findings? "Simply put," Crystal says, "companies don't pay for performance."

Although there is no standard method for analyzing compensation, Crystal, 76, developed the formulas he uses over the course of 30 years advising companies such as CBS, Coca-Cola, and American Express on their pay practices. In an ideal world, Crystal and many investors agree, stock performance and CEO pay would be closely aligned. But no matter how he parsed the numbers, Crystal discovered no relationship between shareholder returns and CEO compensation. . . .

Crystal recommends awarding stock options with a strike price that's the average of the last 90 days and can't be exercised for five years to avoid "opportunistic" pricing. He also suggests reducing bonuses if incentive targets aren't met.

[According to Crystal, average CEO pay in 2009 was $9.95 million, ranging from $128,751 to $43.2 million.]

Dan Ariely, Duke University behavioral economist: CEOs care about stock value because that's how we measure them. If we want to change what they care about, we should change what we measure.

Human beings adjust behavior based on the metrics they're held against. Anything you measure will impel a person to optimize his score on that metric. What you measure is what you'll get. Period. . . .

To change CEO's behavior, we need to change the numbers we measure. . . .

What are those numbers? Ideally, they'd vary by industry, situation, and mission, but here are a few obvious choices: How many new jobs have been created at your firm? How strong is your pipeline of new patents? How satisfied are your customers? Your employees? What's the level of trust in your company and brand? How much carbon dioxide do you emit?

Sources: Excerpted and data drawn from Jessica Silver-Greenberg and Alexis Leondis, "How Much Is a CEO Worth?" *Bloomberg Businessweek* (May 10–16, 2010): 70. Excerpted from Dan Ariely, "You Are What You Measure," *Harvard Business Review* 88 (June 2010): 38.

What are the ethical implications of the following interpretations?

1. CEO pay should be determined by the marketplace, like it is with top professional athletes, musicians, and movie stars, and not subject to arbitrary limits by the government or stockholders. Top talent requires top money.

2. CEO pay is definitely out of control. Corporate executives need to exercise some self-restraint when it comes to their compensation packages to avoid alienating their employees and customers.

3. CEO and executive pay should be tied to measurable performance. What dimensions of performance?

4. Your own ethical interpretation?

MANAGERS-IN-ACTION VIDEO CASE STUDY

FLIGHT 001

Motivating Employees

Crew development manager Emily Griffin discusses the personal connection employees have to Flight 001 and how this affects recruitment, retention, and performance. Retail store leaders share their perspective and what motivates them—and it is not just money! Learn from this video how the owners' values and attitudes impact employees and what motivates their employees to do their best.

For more information about Flight 001, visit its Web site: www.flight001.com

Before watching the video, answer the following questions:

1. What motivates you to do your best?

2. What are a few examples of intrinsic motivators?

3. What do you think are the top three extrinsic motivators?

After watching the video, answer the following questions:

4. Motivation is often a challenge in retail stores. What has Flight 001 done to ensure a happy and motivated workforce?

5. How do the values, attitudes, and actions of the Flight 001 owners impact employee behavior?

6. In this chapter you learned about motivation through employee participation. Provide a few examples of how Flight 001 demonstrates a participative management approach.

7. In this chapter you also learned about employee engagement. What are the benefits to Flight 001 as a result of its employee engagement efforts?

CLOSING CASE

BEST BUY SMASHES THE TIME CLOCK

Jason Dehne's brother called him one day in March and asked if he might like to have lunch and then visit the annual auto show in downtown Minneapolis. Without even checking his schedule, Dehne—a human resource manager of retirement and wealth strategies at Best Buy—agreed to the plan. The brothers spent a blissful Tuesday afternoon walking through showrooms full of the latest vehicles.

The story might not seem unusual if it were not for the fact that Dehne did not need to inform his boss of his whereabouts—he knew his boss could not care less. Nor did he feel guilty about it, since his job allows him to work wherever and whenever he wants as long as he completes projects on a timely basis.

Dehne participates in the consumer electronics retailer's novel Results-Only Work Environment (ROWE) program, which allows almost all of its 4,000 corporate employees to have the same freedom.

"Three years ago, if I was going to go to the car show I would have felt so guilty about it, I would have probably first worked the entire day and then left after 6 p.m. to get to the show [for] an hour or two" before closing time, Dehne says. Now, he continues, "people I work with don't know where I am all the time, but they know how to reach me—I have e-mail; I have a cell phone; I have voice mail. I don't report all of my activities, and I don't feel guilty about it anymore."

Begun four years ago at Best Buy's suburban Minneapolis campus, ROWE has been so successful that the company created a division, CultureRx, to promote it to other companies. Meanwhile, Best Buy has started rolling out ROWE to the 100,000 employees in its retail stores. Figuring out just how that will work remains to be seen, however, since retail requires time clocks—anathema to the program's operating philosophy. . . .

ROWE was created by Jody Thompson and Cali Ressler when they were Best Buy employees; both now serve as principals of CultureRx. They share a passion for shaking up the American workplace and replacing the 9-to-5 paradigm with one that emphasizes freedom for employees and results for employers.

In a time when many white-collar Americans complain of being chained to desks for 50 to 70 hours a week and of having too little time for families and hobbies, CultureRx offers a remedy for the prevailing zeitgeist—a prescription that has attracted the attention of national media such as "60 Minutes," National Public Radio, the *New York Times* and *Business Week*.

ROWE [offers] Best Buy employees whose departments participate in it the opportunity to do their work wherever and whenever they wish. They might play tennis in the morning, go windsurfing on a lake one afternoon, take a two-hour lunch or run a couple of days a week, as Dehne does.

Best Buy supervisors have been retrained to think less about line-of-sight management (Jim is at his desk, so he must be working) and more about the results of employees' work. Some employees work outside the office just one day a week, while others spend the majority of their time at home or other locations.

Thompson likens ROWE to the college lifestyle, in which studying and writing papers can be done anytime and anywhere—the library, the dorm room or a coffeehouse. "Going from college to the workforce is like going back to elementary school—you have no control," she says. "The conundrum is that managers are always trying to manage people—instead of results. Think about it. People come into the workforce as adults, and they're treated like children."...

Results from and reactions to ROWE have been encouraging. Productivity has increased an average of 35 percent within six to nine months in Best Buy units implementing ROWE, a figure based on metrics reported or estimated by managers using the new system. Voluntary turnover has dropped between 52 percent and 90 percent in three Best Buy divisions that CultureRx has studied. The three divisions were chosen because they were otherwise unaffected by company reorganizations or other initiatives.

Ressler cites this voluntary turnover figure as an indication that employees who once would have left Best Buy decided to stay put after ROWE was implemented. Thompson says one procurement division, an early adopter, saw voluntary turnover drop from 36.6 percent a year to less than 6 percent annually.

A CultureRx study of attitudes of ROWE participants found that feelings of pressure and a sense of working too hard have changed. "They feel happier about work. They feel more ownership of their work. They feel more clear about what they're doing for the company, and they see it [ROWE] as a benefit that's almost more important than any other," says Thompson. "They talk about it as if to say, 'Someone else could offer me more money, but I wouldn't go because I now have control over my time.'"

Phyllis Moen, sociology professor at the University of Minnesota, is studying ROWE and has looked at other work arrangements around the country. She finds the favorable results no surprise. Her own studies, and a large body of related workplace research, show "schedule control" leads to lower turnover, increased productivity and employee wellness. Having control over work schedules enhances "health, life quality and productiveness," she wrote in an e-mail interview. . . .

Managers "are scared to death" when the training process begins, Thompson says, but they soon come to realize freedom is rewarded with exceptional work. "Everyone wants the benefit, everyone is jazzed up about it, and no one wants to screw it up," she says. "Managers get better work and more work out of people because they've allowed employees their freedom. Managers find out pretty quickly they can trust people."

For Discussion

1. How important is goal setting to the success of Best Buy's ROWE program? Explain the motivational mechanism.

2. Should ROWE be widely adopted as an employee engagement and retention tool? Explain. What sorts of jobs or industries would not be appropriate settings for ROWE? Explain.

3. Why is (or isn't) this a case of participative management at its best? What are the biggest threats to the success of ROWE-type programs? Explain.

4. How well do you think open-book management would work at Best Buy? Why?

5. Which of the keys to successful employee participation programs are evident in this case? Explain.

6. Would you like to work at a company with a ROWE program? Why or why not?

Source: Excerpted from Frank Jossi, "Clocking Out," *HR Magazine*, 52 (June 2007): 46–50. Copyright 2007 by Society for Human Resource Management (SHRM). Reproduced with permission of Society for Human Resource Management (SHRM) in the format Textbook via Copyright Clearance Center.

13

Group Dynamics
and Teamwork

Bloomberg/Getty Images

*"When I'm working with a group now, I can honestly say that
I think about the team first. The 'I first' approach has been drilled
out of me."*[1]

—*JIM VESTERMAN, U.S. MARINE COMBAT VETERAN
AND MBA STUDENT*

The Changing Workplace

SHOW THEM SOME LOVE

Stanford University Professor Robert I. Sutton: Joel Podolny is the boss who taught me the power of showing a little love. Joel is a former dean of the Yale School of Management and currently an Apple vice president and dean of their internal "University." I knew Joel as an associate dean at the Stanford Business School, where he did a masterful job. Joel is the only academic dean I've ever met who wandered the halls several times a week, talking to faculty about what they were doing and the challenges they faced. Joel had thousands of things to do, but he always took time to listen to and show appreciation to the faculty he served. Joel was well loved. . . .

I was especially impressed with Joel's approach when a faculty member asked for a raise and threatened to move to another university—a routine part of any dean's job. Joel told me something like "I always get to the money eventually, but when a faculty member is talking about leaving they often aren't feeling sufficiently appreciated, so I start out by telling them how much I love and appreciate them and all the ways that their colleagues do, too. After we work through that, I turn to the money. It nearly always turns out that the love and appreciation issue is bigger than the money." Bosses in hundreds of occupations can learn from Joel—spend less time on those endless routine chores . . . and spend more time showing a little love.

Source: Robert I. Sutton, *Good Boss, Bad Boss: How to Be the Best . . . and Learn from the Worst* (New York: Business Plus, 2010), pp. 114–115.

OBJECTIVES

- **Define** the term *group*.
- **Explain** the significance of cohesiveness, roles, norms, and ostracism in regard to the behavior of group members.
- **Identify** and briefly **describe** the six stages of group development.
- **Define** *organizational politics*, and **summarize** relevant research insights.
- **Explain** how groupthink can lead to blind conformity.
- **Define** and **discuss** the management of virtual teams.
- **Discuss** the criteria and determinants of team effectiveness.
- **Explain** why trust is a key ingredient of teamwork, and discuss what management can do to build trust.

As the Joel Podolny story shows, relationships rule in modern organizations. The more managers know about building and sustaining good working relationships, the better. In fact, in a study involving 1,040 managers and 208 focus groups, the two leading causes of managerial failure were ineffective communication skills/practices (81 percent) and poor work relationships/interpersonal skills (78 percent).[2] Andrea Wong, CEO of Lifetime Networks, recently commented that many people assume that hard work is all it takes to earn rewards, but she believes that building relationships within your immediate organization and beyond is the key to success.[3]

What is involved here is the concept of **social capital**: strong relationships, goodwill, and trust resulting in opportunities for productivity.[4] In line with our discussion of human capital in Chapter 10, managers need to build social capital by working on strong, constructive, and mutually beneficial relationships (see Ethics: Character, Courage, and Values). This can involve lots of delicate balancing acts—from trying not to play favorites to deciding if it is a good idea to mix business and pleasure with coworkers on a social networking site.[5] The purpose of this chapter is to build a foundation of understanding about how groups and teams function in today's organizations.

FUNDAMENTAL GROUP DYNAMICS

According to one organization theorist, "All groups may be collections of individuals, but all collections of individuals are not groups."[6] This observation is more than a play on words; mere togetherness does not automatically create a group. Consider, for example, this situation. Half a dozen people who worked for different companies in the same building often shared the same elevator in the morning. As time passed, they introduced themselves and exchanged pleasantries. Eventually, four of the elevator riders discovered that they all lived in the same suburb. Arrangements for a car pool were made, and they began to take turns picking up and delivering one another. A group technically came into existence only when the car pool was formed. To understand why this is so, we need to examine the definition of the term *group*.

What Is a Group?

From a sociological perspective, a **group** can be defined as two or more freely interacting individuals who share a common identity and purpose.[7] Careful analysis of this definition reveals four important dimensions (see Figure 13.1). First, a group must be

---

ETHICS: Character, Courage, and Values

Building Stronger Neighborhoods Through Social Capital

A decade ago, Archie Williams, the founder of a small printer-toner distribution company in the impoverished Boston neighborhood of Roxbury, happened to play a round of golf with Tom Stemberg, the founder and then-chief executive of office supply mega-retailer Staples. Through 18 holes, the pair pitched, putted, and chatted—and became fast friends. Soon, Stemberg started buying printer cartridges from Williams' company, Roxbury Technology.

The deal turned out to be a win for both Staples and Roxbury—the company and the neighborhood. The office supply giant found a reliable supplier for an important product and Roxbury got a partner that could distribute its goods nationally. Stemberg soon became a mentor to Williams' company, helping with strategic planning, finance, and legal advice. Roxbury Technology is now a preferred supplier to Staples . . . , [with nearly $17 million in annual sales, and] almost all of Roxbury's 65 employees live in the neighborhood or nearby.

For Discussion: Why is this a prime example of an informal group evolving into a formal group? Do you believe large company executives have a moral obligation to help build the communities in which they do business? Explain.

Source: Excerpted and adapted from Michael Porter, "How Big Business Can Help Itself by Helping Its Neighbors," *Bloomberg BusinessWeek* (May 31–June 6, 2010): 56.

---

social capital productive potential of strong relationships, goodwill, trust, and cooperation | group two or more freely interacting individuals with a common identity and purpose

Figure **13.1** What Does It Take to Make a Group?

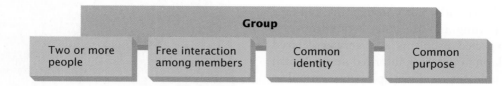

Group

| Two or more people | Free interaction among members | Common identity | Common purpose |

made up of two or more people if it is to be considered a social unit. Second, the individuals must freely interact in some manner. An organization may qualify as a sociological group if it is small and personal enough to permit all of its members to interact regularly with each other. Generally, however, larger organizations with bureaucratic tendencies are made up of many overlapping groups. Third, the interacting individuals must share a common identity. Each must recognize himself or herself as a member of the group. Fourth, these interacting individuals who have a common identity must also have a common purpose. That is, there must be at least a rough consensus on why the group exists.

Types of Groups

Human beings belong to groups for many different reasons. Some people join a group as an end in itself. For example, an accountant may enjoy the socializing that is part of belonging to a group at a local health club. That same accountant's membership in a work group is a means to a professional end. Both the exercise group and the work group satisfy the sociological definition of a group, but they fulfill very different needs. The former is an informal group, and the latter is a formal group.

INFORMAL GROUPS. As Abraham Maslow pointed out, a feeling of belonging is a powerful motivator. People generally have a great need to fit in, to be liked, to be one of the gang. Whether a group meets at work or during leisure time, it is still an informal group if the principal reason for belonging is friendship.[8] Informal groups usually evolve spontaneously. They serve to satisfy esteem needs because one develops a better self-image when one is accepted, recognized, and liked by others. Sometimes, as in the case of a group of friends forming an investment club, an informal group may evolve into a formal group.

Managers cannot afford to ignore informal groups, because grassroots social networks can either

Purdue University's Professor Dan Raftery (second from right) and a team of students use a mass spectrometer to search for biomarkers for early-stage cancer. If the students socialize apart from their schoolwork, this formal group would also qualify as an informal group.

AP Photo/Journal & Courier, John Terhune

informal group collection of people seeking friendship

advance or threaten the organization's mission.[9] As experts on the subject have explained, highly adaptive informal networks cut through the red-tape of formal reporting and are often very effective in solving unexpected problems and getting delayed projects back on target. Still, informal networks can block communication and stir up opposition unless managers learn to work with and direct them.[10]

FORMAL GROUPS. A formal group is a group created for the purpose of doing productive work. It may be called a team, a committee, or simply a work group. Whatever its name, a formal group is usually formed for the purpose of contributing to the success of a larger organization. Formal groups tend to be more rationally structured and less fluid than informal groups. Rather than joining formal task groups, people are assigned to them according to their talents and the organization's needs. One person normally is granted formal leadership responsibility to ensure that the members carry out their assigned duties. Informal friendship groups, in contrast, generally do not have officially appointed leaders, although informal leaders often emerge by popular demand. For the individual, the formal group and an informal group at the place of employment may or may not overlap. In other words, one may or may not be friends with one's coworkers. This raises some important issues that we need to discuss.

WHAT ABOUT FRIENDSHIPS IN THE WORKPLACE?
The overlapping of formal and informal groups at work has both positive and negative implications. Two important ones are bosses being friends with those who report to them and putting limits on social media interaction. Traditional cautions about making friends at work have pretty much gone by the wayside. Only 37 percent of 1,017 workers 18 and older in a recent survey answered "Yes" to the question: "Is it smart to keep personal and professional lives separate?"[11] Another recent survey asked 1,050 women about the coworkers they had invited to their wedding. Only 23 percent did *not* invite *any* coworkers.[12] However, as uncovered in the first survey, there are pros and cons to workplace friendships. The positive side of workplace friendships: 70 percent said they create a more supportive workplace and 69 percent said they increase teamwork. On negative side, 44 percent said they feed gossip and 37 percent said they encourage favoritism.[13]

13a
Survey Says . . .

In a survey of 905 employees, 57% said "Yes" and 37% said "No" when asked "Do you consider what your boss would think when you post comments, photos, etc. on social-network websites?"

QUESTION: What is your answer to this question, and what are the broader implications of your actions? Is it ethical for employers to monitor the leisure-time social media postings of their employees? Explain.

For further information about the interactive annotations in this chapter, visit our student Web site.

Source: Jae Yang and Julie Snider, "Social-Networking and the Boss," *USA Today* (June 24, 2009): 1B.

Should managers be friends with their direct reports? Management experts Jack and Suzy Welch offer this helpful advice: "Boss-subordinate friendships live or die because of one thing: complete, unrelenting candor." While frankness is important in any relationship, it is imperative when there is a social component involved in a work relationship. If that kind of honesty can be there, then friendships between managers and their subordinates will probably make the work environment more fun for everyone.[14] The same professional working relationship is recommended when hiring and working with family members.[15]

As we discussed in Chapters 7 and 11, clear policies are needed for using social media and social networking sites on the job and discussing company business. Otherwise, employees have an open invitation to cyberbullying, sexual harassment, and leaking privileged or damaging information. A good social media policy should help employees appropriately handle these types of issues. Workplace etiquette consultant Barbara Pachter recommends using Facebook for family and friends and LinkedIn for work. This makes it easier to decide what is appropriate to share and in what context.[16]

formal group collection of people created to do something productive

Attraction to Groups

What attracts a person to one group but not to another? And why do some groups' members stay whereas members of other groups leave? Managers who can answer these questions can take steps to motivate people to join and remain members of a formal work group. Individual commitment to either an informal or a formal group hinges on two factors. The first is *attractiveness*, the outside-looking-in view.[17] A nonmember will want to join a group that is attractive and will shy away from a group that is unattractive. The second factor is cohesiveness, the tendency of group members to follow the group and resist outside influences. This is the inside-looking-out view. In a highly cohesive group, individual members tend to see themselves as "we" rather than "I." Cohesive group members stick together.[18]

Factors that either enhance or destroy group attractiveness and cohesiveness are listed in Table 13.1. It is important to note that each factor is a matter of degree. For example, a group may offer the individual little, moderate, or great opportunity for prestige and status. Similarly, group demands on the individual may range from somewhat disagreeable to highly disagreeable. What all this means is that both the decision to join a group and the decision to continue being a member depend on a net balance of the factors in Table 13.1. Naturally, the resulting balance is colored by one's perception and frame of reference, as it was in the case of Richard Dale, a former manager of distribution at Commodore International, during his first meeting with the company's founder,

| Table 13.1 | Factors that Enhance or Detract from Group Attractiveness and Cohesiveness |

FACTORS THAT ENHANCE	FACTORS THAT DETRACT
1. Prestige and status	1. Unreasonable or disagreeable demands on the individual
2. Cooperative relationship	2. Disagreement over procedures, activities, rules, and the like
3. High degree of interaction	3. Unpleasant experience with the group
4. Relatively small size	4. Competition between the group's demands and preferred outside activities
5. Similarity of members	5. Unfavorable public image of the group
6. Superior public image of the group	6. Competition for membership by other groups
7. A common threat in the environment	

Source: Table adapted from *Group Dynamics: Research and Theory*, 2nd ed., by Dorwin Cartwright and Alvin Zander. New York: HarperCollins Publishers, Inc.

Dog lovers will be attracted to this fundraising group at Pierce College in southern California. The annual Nuts for Mutts dog show benefits New Leash on Life Animal Rescue, a nonprofit animal rescue and placement organization.

cohesiveness *tendency of a group to stick together*

Jack Tramiel. Tramiel grilled Dale for over an hour, pronounced his philosophy of business "all wrong," and then openly expressed his anger when he found boxes of computers sitting in the warehouse, waiting to be shipped.[19]

Dale's departure within a few months of this episode is not surprising in view of the fact that Tramiel's conduct utterly destroyed work group attractiveness and cohesiveness.

Roles

According to Shakespeare, "All the world's a stage, and all the men and women merely players." In fact, Shakespeare's analogy between life and play-acting can be carried a step further—to organizations and their component formal work groups. Although employees do not have scripts, they do have formal positions in the organizational hierarchy, and they are expected to adhere to company policies and rules. Furthermore, job descriptions and procedure manuals spell out how jobs are to be done. In short, every employee has one or more organizational roles to play. An organization that is appropriately structured, in which everyone plays his or her role(s) effectively and efficiently, will have a greater chance for organizational success.

A social psychologist has described the concept of *role* as follows: A role is a set of expectations about an individual's behavior in a specific job, and an individual's actual workplace behavior. It is assumed that any person in the position would behave similarly to any other person in that position.[20]

A role, then, is a socially determined prescription for behavior in a *specific* position. Roles evolve out of the tendency for social units to perpetuate themselves, and roles are socially enforced. Role models are a powerful influence. They are indispensable to those trying to resolve the inherent conflicts between work and family roles, for example.[21]

Norms

Norms define "degrees of acceptability and unacceptability."[22] More precisely, norms are general standards of conduct that help individuals judge what is right or wrong or good or bad in a given social setting (such as work, home, play, or religious organization). Because norms are culturally derived, they vary from one culture to another. For example, public disagreement and debate, which are normal in Western societies, are often considered rude in Eastern countries such as Japan.

Norms have a broader influence than roles, which focus on a specific position. Although usually unwritten, norms influence behavior enormously.[23]

Every mature group, whether informal or formal, generates its own pattern of norms that constrains and directs the behavior of its members. Norms are enforced for at least four different reasons:

1. To facilitate survival of the group
2. To simplify or clarify role expectations
3. To help group members avoid embarrassing situations (protect self-images)
4. To express key group values and enhance the group's unique identity[24]

As illustrated in Figure 13.2, norms tend to go above and beyond formal rules and written policies. Compliance is shaped with social reinforcement in the form of attention, recognition, and acceptance. Those who fail to comply with the norm may be criticized or ridiculed. For example, consider the pressure Gwendolyn Kelly experienced in medical school: The clear message from both instructors and peers was that those who go into family practice or pediatrics are considered less academic and less intelligent than those who specialize in surgery or tertiary medicine, which involve complex diagnostic procedures.[25] Thus, reformers of the U.S. health care system, who want to increase the number of primary-care (family-practice) doctors, need to begin by altering medical school norms.

Worse than ridicule is the threat of being ostracized. Ostracism, or rejection from the group, is figuratively the capital punishment of group dynamics. Informal groups derive much of their power over individuals through the ever-present threat of ostracism. Thus, informal norms play a pivotal role in on-the-job ethics.[26] Police officers, for example, who honor the traditional "code of silence" norm—which demands *total* loyalty to one's fellow officers—face a tough moral dilemma when they encounter a "bad cop."

---

role socially determined way of behaving in a specific position | *norms general standards of conduct for various social settings* | *ostracism rejection from a group*

Figure **13.2**   Norms Are Enforced for Different Reasons

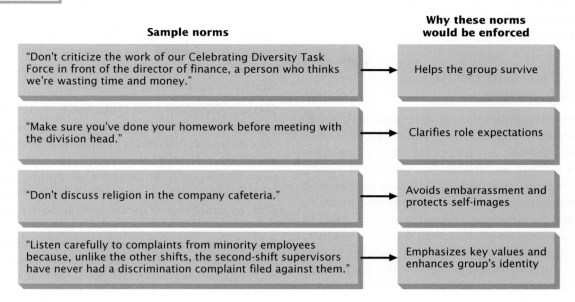

Sample norms

"Don't criticize the work of our Celebrating Diversity Task Force in front of the director of finance, a person who thinks we're wasting time and money."

"Make sure you've done your homework before meeting with the division head."

"Don't discuss religion in the company cafeteria."

"Listen carefully to complaints from minority employees because, unlike the other shifts, the second-shift supervisors have never had a discrimination complaint filed against them."

Why these norms would be enforced

Helps the group survive

Clarifies role expectations

Avoids embarrassment and protects self-images

Emphasizes key values and enhances group's identity

GROUP DEVELOPMENT

Like inept youngsters who mature into talented adults, groups undergo a maturation process before becoming effective. We have all experienced the uneasiness associated with the first meeting of a new group, be it a class, club, or committee. Initially, there is little mutual understanding, trust, or commitment among the new group members, and their uncertainty about objectives, roles, and leadership doesn't help. The prospect of cooperative action seems unlikely in view of defensive behavior and differences of opinion about who should do what. Someone steps forward to assume a leadership role, and the group is off and running toward eventual maturity (or perhaps premature demise). A working knowledge of the characteristics of a mature group can help managers envision a goal for the group development process.

Characteristics of a Mature Group

If and when a group takes on the following characteristics, it can be called a mature group:

1. Members are aware of their own and each other's assets and liabilities vis-à-vis the group's task.
2. These individual differences are accepted without being labeled as good or bad.

3. The group has developed authority and interpersonal relationships that are recognized and accepted by the members.
4. Group decisions are made through rational discussion. Minority opinions and dissension are recognized and encouraged. Attempts are not made to force decisions or a false unanimity.
5. Conflict is over substantive group issues such as group goals and the effectiveness and efficiency of various means for achieving those goals. Conflict over emotional issues regarding group structure, processes, or interpersonal relationships is at a minimum.
6. Members are aware of the group's processes and their own roles in them.[27]

Effectiveness and productivity should increase as the group matures. Research with groups of school teachers found positive evidence in this regard. The researchers concluded, faculty members who function at higher developmental levels produce students who score higher on standard achievement tests.[28] This finding could be fruitful for those seeking to reform and improve the American education system.

A hidden but nonetheless significant benefit of group maturity is that individuality is strengthened, not extinguished.[29] Protecting the individual's right to dissent is particularly important in regard to the problem of blind obedience, which we shall consider later in this chapter. Also, as indicated in the fifth item on the list, members of mature groups tend to be emotionally mature.[30] This paves the way for building much-needed social capital.

Six Stages of Group Development

Experts have identified six distinct stages in the group development process[31] (see Figure 13.3). During stages 1 through 3, attempts are made to overcome the obstacle of uncertainty over power and authority. Once this first obstacle has been surmounted, addressing uncertainty over interpersonal relations becomes the challenge. This second obstacle must be cleared during stages 4 through 6 if the group is to achieve maturity. Each stage confronts the group's leader and contributing members with a unique combination of problems and opportunities.

STAGE 1: ORIENTATION. Attempts are made to "break the ice." Uncertainty about goals, power,

and interpersonal relationships is high. Members generally want and accept any leadership at this point. Emergent leaders often misinterpret this "honeymoon period" as a mandate for permanent control. According to a recent survey of 900 executives, 42 percent of team members said "their team rarely, if ever, gets off to the right start."[32]

STAGE 2: CONFLICT AND CHALLENGE. As the emergent leader's philosophy, objectives, and policies become apparent, individuals or subgroups advocating alternative courses of action struggle for control. This second stage may be prolonged while members strive to clarify and reconcile their roles as part of a complete redistribution of power and authority. Many groups never continue past stage 2 because they get bogged down as a consequence of emotionalism and political infighting. Organizational committees often bear the brunt of jokes (we've all heard that a camel is a horse designed by a committee) because their frequent failure to mature beyond stage 2 prevents them from accomplishing their goals.[33]

| **Figure 13.3** | Group Development from Formation to Maturity |

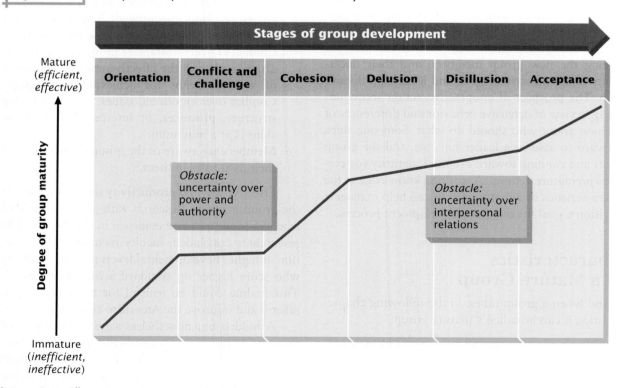

Source: *Group Effectiveness in Organizations,* by Linda N. Jewell and H. Joseph Reitz, p. 20. Used with permission of the authors.

Diversity is both an advantage and a challenge to group development. People from different backgrounds—like these strategists in Nike's Ethnic Diversity Council—bring different perspectives, values, and issues to the table.

Mark Richards/PhotoEdit

STAGE 3: COHESION. The shifts in power started in stage 2 are completed, under a new leader or the original leader, with a new consensus on authority, structure, and procedures. A "we" feeling emerges as everyone becomes truly involved. Any lingering differences over power and authority are resolved quickly. Stage 3 is usually of relatively short duration. If not, the group is likely to stall.

STAGE 4: DELUSION. A feeling of "having been through the worst of it" prevails after the rather rapid transition through stage 3. Issues and problems that threaten to break this spell of relief are dismissed or treated lightly. Members seem committed to fostering harmony at all costs. Participation and camaraderie run high because members believe that all the difficult emotional problems have been solved.

STAGE 5: DISILLUSION. Subgroups tend to form as the illusion of unlimited goodwill wears off, and there is a growing disenchantment with how things are turning out. Those with

13b
The Business of Golf

Ask people why they golf with business associates, and the answer is always the same: It's a great way to build relationships. They say this far more about golf than about going to dinner or attending a baseball game, and for good reason. Indeed, this may be the central fact about corporate golf, though it's rarely said: When people golf together, they see one another humiliated. At least 95% of all golfers are terrible, which means that in 18 holes everyone in the foursome will hit a tree, take three strokes in one bunker, or four-putt, with everyone else watching. Bonding is simply a matter of people jointly going through adversity, and a round of golf will furnish plenty of it.

QUESTIONS: Why does shared adversity foster strong relationships and bonding? How can managers get task group members who do not play golf to bond like this?

Source: Geoffrey Colvin, "Why Execs Love Golf," *Fortune* (April 30, 2001): 46.

unrealized expectations challenge the group to perform better and are prepared to reveal their personal strengths and weaknesses if necessary. Others hold back. Tardiness and absenteeism are symptomatic of diminishing cohesiveness and commitment.[34]

STAGE 6: ACCEPTANCE. It usually takes a trusted and influential group member who is concerned about the group to step forward and help the group move from conflict to cohesion. This individual, acting as the group catalyst, is usually someone other than the leader. Members are encouraged to test their self-perceptions against the reality of how others perceive them. Greater personal and mutual understanding helps members adapt to situations without causing problems. Members' expectations are more realistic than ever before. Because the authority structure is generally accepted, subgroups can pursue different matters without threatening group cohesiveness. Consequently, stage 6 groups tend to be highly effective and efficient.[35]

Time-wasting problems and inefficiencies can be minimized if group members are consciously aware of this developmental process. Just as it is impossible for a child to skip being a teenager on the way to adulthood, committees and other work groups will find there are no shortcuts to group maturity. Some emotional stresses and strains are inevitable along the way.

ORGANIZATIONAL POLITICS

Only in recent years has the topic of organizational politics (also known as impression management) begun to receive serious attention from management theorists and researchers.[36] But as we all know from practical experience (and the back-stabbing on Donald Trump's television show *The Apprentice*),[37] organizational life is often highly charged with political wheeling-and-dealing. For example, consider this complaint from a first-year marketing manager: I offer strategies at meetings, but then others change them slightly and take credit for them. Company bonuses are based on how many of each person's ideas are used, so it's a serious problem.[38]

Workplace surveys reveal that organizational politics can hinder effectiveness and be an irritant to employees. A three-year study of 46 companies attempting to establish themselves on the Internet discovered that the top two barriers to change are poor communication and political infighting.[39] Meanwhile, 44 percent of full-time employees and 60 percent of independent contractors listed "freedom from office politics" as extremely important to their job satisfaction.[40]

Productive political maneuvering will be required at Procter & Gamble's headquarters as Edgar Sandoval (right) attempts to integrate the Puerto Rico-based Hispanic marketing unit into the North American multicultural team in Cincinnati, Ohio.

AP Photo/Al Behrman

Whether they themselves are politically motivated or not, managers need to be knowledgeable about organizational politics because their careers will be affected by it. A recent survey of 522 employees asked how they dealt with office politics. Sixteen percent said they actively participate, 29 percent avoid it, and 54 percent know what is happening but do not participate.[41] New managers, particularly, should be aware of the political climate in their organization and develop important networking skills without becoming shameless politicians.[42] As "new kids on the job," they might be more easily taken advantage of than other, more experienced managers. Certain political maneuvers also have significant ethical implications.

What Does Organizational Politics Involve?

As the term implies, self-interest is central to organizational politics. In fact, organizational politics has been defined as "the pursuit of self-interest at work in the face of real or imagined opposition."[43] Political maneuvering is said to encompass all self-serving behavior above and beyond competence, hard work, and luck.[44] For example, in a recent article in the *Wall Street Journal*, a veteran Wall Street analyst described how she would set easily achievable annual goals so she could claim to have excelled in her performance. She went on to explain how she would collect any written praise to use in her annual review, and how she would point out her colleagues' "wasteful" spending habits to her supervisor, but never in writing so the information couldn't be traced back to her.[45]

Although self-serving people such as this have given the term *organizational politics* a negative connotation, researchers have identified both positive and negative aspects: Legitimate political behaviors include exchanging favors and information, creating coalitions, and building relationships with upper-level sponsors. Questionable behaviors include whistle-blowing, revolutionary coalitions, threats, and sabotage.[46] Recall our discussion of whistle-blowing in Chapter 5.

Employees resort to political behavior when they are unwilling to trust their career solely to competence, hard work, and luck. One might say that organizational politicians help luck along by relying

on political tactics. Whether employees will fall back on political tactics has a lot to do with an organization's climate or culture. A culture that presents employees with unreasonable barriers to individual and group success tends to foster political maneuvering. Consider this situation, for example: Corvette lovers within General Motors "lied, cheated, and stole" to keep the sports car from being removed from production during the firm's tumultuous period of the late 1980s and early 1990s.[47] The redesigned Corvette finally made it to market in 1997, thanks in part to the Corvette team giving high-level GM executives thrilling unauthorized test rides in the hot new model.

Research on Organizational Politics

Researchers in a landmark study of organizational politics conducted structured interviews with 87 managers employed by 30 electronics firms in southern California. Included in the sample were 30 chief executive officers, 28 middle managers, and 29 supervisors. Significant results included the following:

- The higher the level of management, the greater the perceived amount of political activity.
- The larger the organization, the greater the perceived amount of political activity.
- Personnel in staff positions were viewed as more political than those in line positions.
- People in marketing were the most political; those in production were the least political.
- "Reorganization changes" reportedly prompted more political activity than any other type of change.
- A majority (61 percent) of those interviewed believed that organizational politics helps advance one's career.
- Forty-five percent believed that organizational politics distracts from organizational goals.[48]

Regarding the last two findings, it was clear that political activities were seen as helpful to the individual. On the other hand, the interviewed managers were split on the question of the value of politics to the organization. Managers who believed political behavior had a positive impact on the organization felt that it could get new ideas off the ground,

organizational politics the pursuit of self-interest in response to real or imagined opposition

enhance communication, and help bond teams and groups together.[49] The most-often-cited negative effect of politics in the study was its distraction of managers from organizational goals. Misuse of resources and conflict were also mentioned as typical problems.

Political Tactics

As defined earlier, organizational politics takes in a lot of behavioral territory. The following six political tactics are common expressions of politics in the workplace:

- *Posturing.* Those who use this tactic look for situations in which they can make a good impression. "One-upmanship" and taking credit for other people's work are included in this category.
- *Empire building.* Gaining and keeping control over human and material resources is the principal motivation behind this tactic. Those with large budgets usually feel more safely entrenched in their positions and believe they have more influence over peers and superiors.
- *Making the supervisor look good.* Traditionally referred to as "apple polishing," this political strategy is prompted by a desire to favorably influence those who control one's career ascent. Anyone with an oversized ego is an easy target for this tactic.
- *Collecting and using social IOUs.* Reciprocal exchange of political favors can be done in two ways: (1) helping someone look good or (2) preventing someone from looking bad by ignoring or covering up a mistake. Those who rely on this tactic feel that all favors are coins of exchange rather than expressions of altruism or unselfishness.
- *Creating power and loyalty cliques.* Because there is power in numbers, the idea here is to face superiors and competitors as a cohesive group rather than alone.
- *Engaging in destructive competition.* As a last-ditch effort, some people will resort to character assassination through suggestive remarks, vindictive gossip, or outright lies. This tactic also includes sabotaging the work of a competitor.[50]

Obvious illegalities notwithstanding, one's own values and ethics, as well as organizational sanctions, are the final arbiters of whether these tactics

are acceptable. (See Table 13.2 for a practicing manager's advice on how to win at office politics.)

Antidotes to Political Behavior

The foregoing political tactics vary in degree. The average person will probably acknowledge using at least one of these strategies. But excessive political maneuvering can become a serious threat to productivity when self-interests clearly override the interests of the group or organization. Organizational politics can be kept within reasonable bounds by applying the following five tips:

- Strive for a climate of openness and trust.
- Measure performance results rather than dwelling on personalities.
- Encourage top management to refrain from exhibiting political behavior that will be imitated by employees.
- Strive to integrate individual and organizational goals through meaningful work and career planning.
- Practice job rotation to encourage broader perspectives and understanding of the problems of others.[51]

13c
Time to Crush the Boss?

Letter to *Fortune* magazine:

I am a 31-year-old executive at a company headed by a friendly but fiercely competitive CEO. We get along fine, but here's the thing: We both play racquet-ball, and he's mentioned repeatedly that we should play sometime. I keep putting off setting a date for a game because I'm an excellent player and I'm pretty sure I would crush him, which I'm afraid would be career suicide. Should I agree to play? If so, should I play to win?—Killer Backhand

QUESTIONS: What advice would you give to Killer Backhand? How "political" is your answer?

Source: Anne Fisher, "Will I Lose if I Beat the Boss at Racquetball?" *Fortune* (January 24, 2005): 36.

Table **13.2**	One Manager's Rules for Winning at Office Politics

1. Find out what the boss expects.

2. Build an information network. Knowledge is power. Identify the people who have power and the extent and direction of it. Title doesn't necessarily reflect actual influence. Find out how the grapevine works. Develop good internal public relations for yourself.

3. Find a mentor. This is a trusted counselor who can be honest with you and help train and guide you to improve your ability and effectiveness as a manager.

4. Don't make enemies without a very good reason.

5. Avoid cliques. Keep circulating in the office.

6. If you must fight, fight over something that is really worth it. Don't lose ground over minor matters or petty differences.

7. Gain power through allies. Build ties that bind. Create IOUs, obligations, and loyalties. Do not be afraid to enlist help from above.

8. Maintain control. Don't misuse your cohorts. Maintain the status and integrity of your allies.

9. Mobilize your forces when necessary. Don't commit your friends without their approval. Be a gracious winner when you do win.

10. Never hire a family member or a close friend.

Source: Adapted from David E. Hall, "Winning at Office Politics," *Credit & Financial Management*, 86 (April 1984): 23. Reprinted with permission from Credit & Financial Management. Copyright April 1984, published by the National Association of Credit Management, 475 Park Avenue South, New York, NY 10016.

CONFORMITY AND GROUPTHINK

Conformity means complying with the role expectations and norms perceived by the majority to be appropriate in a particular situation. Conformity enhances predictability, which is generally thought to be good for rational planning and productive enterprise. How can anything be accomplished if people cannot be counted on to perform their assigned duties? On the other hand, why do so many employees actively participate in or passively condone illegal and unethical organizational practices involving discrimination, environmental degradation, accounting fraud, and unfair competition?[52] The answers to these questions lie along a continuum with anarchy at one end and blind conformity at the other. Socially responsible management is anchored to a point somewhere between them.[53]

Research on Conformity

Social psychologists have discovered much about human behavior by studying individuals and groups in controlled laboratory settings. One classic laboratory study conducted by Solomon Asch was designed to answer the following question: How often will an individual take a stand against a unanimous majority that is obviously wrong?[54] Asch's results were both intriguing and unsettling.

THE HOT SEAT. Asch began his study by assembling groups of seven to nine college students, supposedly to work on a perceptual problem. Actually, though, Asch was studying conformity. All but one member of each group were Asch's confederates, and Asch told them exactly how to behave and what to say. The experiment was really concerned with the reactions of the remaining student—called the naïve subject—who didn't know what was going on.

All the students in each group were shown cards with lines similar to those in Figure 13.4. They were instructed to match the line on the left with the one on the right that was closest to it in length. The differences in length among the lines on the right were obvious. Each group went through 12 rounds of the matching process, with a different set of lines for every round. The researcher asked one group member at a time to announce his or her choice to the group.

Figure **13.4**	The Asch Line Experiment

Standard line   Comparison lines

1   2   3

conformity complying with prevailing role expectations and norms

Thanks to general conformity and stifled dissent at a Communist Party Congress at Beijing's Great Hall of the People, Chinese President Hu Jintao can consistently maintain his power base.

AP Photo/Greg Baker

Things proceeded normally for the first two rounds as each group member voiced an opinion. Agreement was unanimous. Suddenly, on the third round only one individual, the naïve subject, chose the correct pair of lines. All of the other group members chose a different (and obviously wrong) pair. During the rounds in which there was disagreement, all of Asch's confederates conspired to select an incorrect pair of lines. It was the individual versus the rest of the group.

FOLLOWING THE IMMORAL MAJORITY. Each of the naïve subjects was faced with a personal dilemma. Should he or she fight the group or give in to the obviously incorrect choice of the overwhelming majority? Among 31 naïve subjects who made a total of 217 judgments, two-thirds of the judgments were correct. The other one-third were incorrect; that is, they were consistent with the majority opinion. Individual differences were great, with some subjects yielding to the incorrect majority opinion more readily than others. *Only 20 percent of the naïve subjects remained entirely independent in their judgments*. All of the rest turned their backs on their own perceptions and went along with the group at least once. In other words, 80 percent of Asch's subjects knuckled under the pressure of group opinion at least once, even though they knew the majority was dead wrong.

Replications of Asch's study in the Middle East (Kuwait) and in Japan have demonstrated that this tendency toward conformity is not unique to American culture.[55] Indeed, a statistical analysis of 133 Asch conformity studies across 17 countries concluded that blind conformity is a greater problem in collectivist ("we") cultures than in individualist ("me") cultures. Japan is strongly collectivist, whereas the United States and Canada are highly individualistic cultures.[56] (You may find it instructive to ponder how you would act in such a situation.)[57]

Because Asch's study was a contrived laboratory experiment, it failed to probe the relationship between cohesiveness and conformity. Asch's naïve subjects were outsiders. But more recent research on "groupthink" has shown that a cohesive group of insiders can fall victim to blind conformity.

Groupthink

After studying the records of several successful and several unsuccessful American foreign policy decisions, psychologist Irving Janis uncovered an undesirable by-product of group cohesiveness. He labeled this problem **groupthink** and defined it as a way of thinking that occurs in a cohesive group, when the desire for consensus outweighs the desire to examine

groupthink Janis's term for blind conformity in cohesive in-groups

"Damn it, Hopkins, didn't you get yesterday's memo?"

Source: © The New Yorker Collection 1998 Jack Ziegler from cartoonbank.com. All Rights Reserved.

alternative options realistically.[58] Groupthink helps explain how intelligent policy makers, in both government and business, can sometimes make incredibly unwise decisions.

One dramatic result of groupthink in action was the Vietnam War. Strategic advisers in three successive administrations rubber-stamped battle plans laced with false assumptions. Critical thinking, reality testing, and moral judgment were temporarily shelved as decisions to escalate the war were enthusiastically railroaded through. Although Janis acknowledges that cohesive groups are not inevitably victimized by groupthink, he warns group decision makers to be alert for the signs of groupthink—the risk is always there.

SYMPTOMS OF GROUPTHINK. According to Janis, the onset of groupthink is foreshadowed by a definite pattern of symptoms. Among these are excessive optimism, an assumption of inherent morality, suppression of dissent, and an almost desperate quest for unanimity.[59] Given such a decision-making climate, the probability of a poor decision is high. Managers face a curious dilemma here. While a group is still in stage 1 or stage 2 of development, its cohesiveness is too low for it to get much accomplished in the face of emotional and time-consuming power struggles. But by the time, in stage 3, that the group achieves enough cohesiveness to make decisions promptly, the

risk of groupthink is high. The trick is to achieve needed cohesiveness without going to the extreme of groupthink.

PREVENTING GROUPTHINK. According to Janis, one of the group members should periodically ask, "Are we allowing ourselves to become victims of groupthink?"[60] More fundamental preventive measures include:

- Avoiding the use of groups to rubber-stamp decisions that have already been made by higher management.
- Urging each group member to be a critical evaluator.
- Bringing in outside experts for fresh perspectives.
- Assigning someone the role of devil's advocate to challenge assumptions and alternatives.[61]
- Taking time to consider possible side effects and the consequences of alternative courses of action.[62]

Ideally, decision quality improves when these steps become second nature in cohesive groups. But groupthink remains a constant threat in management circles.

13d
It's My Way or the Highway

I'm a lawyer, and I have just joined my first corporate board. The chairman, a client of mine, runs meetings as if only his ideas matter; he seems more interested in impressing us than in using our counsel.

QUESTIONS: What is the risk of groupthink in this type of situation? Explain. How would you handle the situation if you were the lawyer? What are the ethical implications of your answer?

Source: Kerry J. Sulkowicz, "The Corporate Shrink," *Fast Company*, 82 (May 2004): 54.

One major area ripe for abuse is corporate governance. Corporate boards of directors are supposed to represent the interests of stockholders and to hold top executives accountable for results. Too often, however, domineering CEOs and pliable boards create the perfect environment for groupthink.[63] For example, consider Al Dunlap, as profiled in the book *Bad Leadership*, by Harvard's Barbara Kellerman. Dunlap, nicknamed "chainsaw Al" and "Rambo in pinstripes" by the business press, was hired as CEO of Sunbeam Corporation in 1996 to turn the company around. Less than two years later, after Dunlap had slashed 40 percent of Sunbeam's payroll while richly rewarding himself, the company was deeply in debt and on the verge of bankruptcy. Dunlap was fired amid claims of financial trickery. Kellerman explains that Dunlap fostered a climate conducive to groupthink by rapidly replacing the existing board members with people who supported him and didn't question his managerial decisions.[64] Disturbing? Yes. Unusual? Not really, especially when groupthink prevails.

Managers who cannot imagine themselves being victimized by blind conformity are prime candidates for groupthink.[65] Dean Tjosvold at Lingnan University in Hong Kong recommends "cooperative conflict," by encouraging dissent and free discussion of key issues. As a practical example, one Google insider says that co-founders Larry Page and Sergey Brin routinely use cooperative conflict during product strategy meetings. Page will present one side of the debate and Brin the other, and then let everyone else contribute to the conversation. Not only does it help Page and Brin arrive at a clear answer, it lets them know who's truly engaged and passionate about the issue at hand.[66] Groupthink is unlikely to occur in dynamic situations such as this. The constructive use of conflict is discussed further in Chapter 15.

TEAMS, TEAMWORK, AND TRUST

Teams are the organizational unit of choice today, especially teams that mix and match people with different skills and perspectives. Teams and teamwork are vital group dynamics in the modern workplace. For instance, consider what is happening in today's hospitals, which are borrowing teamwork techniques from the aviation industry. By training hospital staff to work in teams more effectively, such as by holding pre- and post-operation briefings, hospitals have reduced the number of deaths due to surgery by 18 percent.[67]

Unfortunately, team skills in today's typical organization tend to lag far behind technical skills.[68] It is one thing to be a creative software engineer, for example. It is quite another for that software specialist to be able to team up with other specialists in accounting, finance, and marketing to beat the competition to market with a profitable new product.[69] In this final section, we explore teams and teamwork by discussing cross-functional teams, virtual teams (see Green Management: Toward Sustainability), a model of team effectiveness, and the importance of trust.

Cross-Functional Teams

A cross-functional team is a task group staffed with a mix of specialists focused on a common objective. This structural innovation deserves special attention here because cross-functional teams are becoming commonplace (particularly for projects). They may or may not be self-managed, although self-managed teams (as discussed in Chapter 12) generally are cross-functional. Cross-functional teams stand in sharp contrast to the tradition of lumping specialists into functional departments, thereby creating the problem of integrating and coordinating those departments. Rather, cross-functional teams have exciting potential to overcome obstacles, especially if they are made up of adaptable self-starters. For

Mike Flippo/Shutterstock.Com

cross-functional team task group staffed with a mix of specialists pursuing a common objective

Green Management: Toward Sustainability

A Virtual Environmental Team Makes Real Money

Amy Gonzales, a geologist and wetlands scientist, played mentor to Kelly Caldwell, a biologist, at their former employer, for which they did environmental-impact studies of proposed gas pipelines and other energy projects. When Gonzales grew frustrated with her bosses, Caldwell, who was 17 years her junior, suggested they start their own company. The result is AK Environmental, which performs environmental surveys and manages construction projects nationwide. [AK's sales were $17.5 million in 2009.] The women run their company virtually—Gonzales lives in New Jersey; Caldwell, in North Carolina.

[According to Amy,] "Kelly makes a real effort to visit the staff out in the field, so she sees more of them than I do. We have done work in 20 states, so we have staff all over the place. We encourage everyone to call and talk to us. We also try to do marketing things together so that our clients can see the face of AK."

For Discussion: As Amy and Kelly's 40-person virtual team continues to grow and prosper, what will be their greatest challenges and how should they be handled?

Source: Excerpted from an interview by Darren Dahl, "How We Make This Work," *Inc.,* 32 (September 2010): 128.

example, a cross-functional team at Ford designed and produced an all-new diesel engine in just 36 months—12 months faster than the usual design timeframe—because team members from a range of departments were able to break out of their usual structure and work cooperatively. Team member Pat Morgan commented, "We saved months by knowing hourly what the other guys were thinking and what their problems were."[70]

Virtual Teams

Along with the move toward virtual organizations, discussed in Chapter 9, have come virtual teams. A **virtual team** is a physically dispersed task group linked electronically. A researcher elaborates that virtual team members interact electronically across time, space, culture, and organizational boundaries to reach a common goal.[71] Face-to-face contact among team members is usually minimal or nonexistent. E-mail, voice mail, videoconferencing, social media, Web-based project or collaboration software, and other forms of electronic interchange allow members of virtual teams from anywhere on the planet to accomplish a common goal.[72] It is commonplace today for virtual teams to have members from different organizations, different time zones, and different cultures.[73]

Speed is a primary selling point for virtual teams. For example, Claire Bonilla, senior director of disaster management at Microsoft, explains that her team

uses Bing and other software to assess damage, communicate with government officials, and stage simulations to determine the best course of action whenever a disaster occurs. In recent crisis areas such as Haiti and Chile, her team was able to complete in five days what might have taken an entire year in the past.[74]

Because virtual organizations and teams are so new, paced as they are by emerging technologies, managers are having to learn from the school of hard knocks. Old habits and assumptions need to be reality tested. As a case in point, here is a *quick quiz*: Who do you think would do better working remotely as a member of a virtual team, an introvert or an extrovert? In a recent study at Cisco Systems, researchers hypothesized that introverted, reclusive types would favor virtual work situations, but results showed that it was the extroverts who loved working virtually. These individuals stay connected to their clients and colleagues no matter where they are or what means of communication are used.[75]

Just as we noted (in Chapter 9) about virtual organizations, one reality of managing virtual teams is clear. *Periodic face-to-face interaction, trust building, and teambuilding are more important than ever when team members are widely dispersed in time and space.* Although faceless interaction may work in Internet chat rooms, it can doom a virtual team with a crucial task and a pressing deadline. Additionally, special steps need to be taken to clearly communicate role expectations, performance norms, goals,

virtual team task group members from dispersed locations who are electronically linked

Table 13.3	The Basics of Managing a Virtual Team

Forming the Team
- Develop a team mission statement along with teamwork expectations and norms, project goals, and deadlines.
- Recruit team members with complementary skills and diverse backgrounds who have the ability and willingness to contribute.
- Get a high-level sponsor to champion the project.
- Post a skill, biographical sketch, contact information, and "local time" matrix to familiarize members with each other and their geographic dispersion.

Preparing the Team
- Make sure everyone has a broadband connection and is comfortable with virtual teamwork technologies (e.g., e-mail, instant messaging, conference calls, online meeting and collaboration programs such as WebEx, and videoconferencing).
- Establish hardware and software compatibility.
- Make sure everyone is comfortable with *synchronous* (interacting at the same time) and *asynchronous* (interacting at different times) teamwork.
- Get individuals to buy-in on team goals, deadlines, and individual tasks.

Building Teamwork and Trust
- Make sure everyone is involved (during meetings and overall).
- Arrange periodic face-to-face work meetings, teambuilding exercises, and leisure activities.
- Encourage collaboration between and among team members on sub-tasks.
- Establish an early-warning system for conflicts (e.g., gripe sessions).

Motivating and Leading the Team
- Post a scoreboard to mark team progress toward goals.
- Celebrate team accomplishments both virtually and face-to-face.
- Begin each virtual meeting with praise and recognition for outstanding individual contributions.
- Keep team members' line managers informed of their accomplishments and progress.

Sources: Based on discussions in Jack Gordon, "Do Your Virtual Teams Deliver Only Virtual Performance?" *Training*, 42 (June 2005): 20–26; Deborah L. Duarte and Nancy Tennant Snyder, *Mastering Virtual Teams*, 3rd ed. (San Francisco: Jossey-Bass, 2006); Arvind Malhotra, Ann Majchrzak, and Benson Rosen, "Leading Virtual Teams," *Academy of Management Perspectives*, 21 (February 2007): 60–70; and Jack Welch and Suzy Welch, "The Connected Leader," *Business Week* (June 23, 2008): 86.

and deadlines (see Table 13.3). Virtual teamwork may be faster than the traditional face-to-face kind, but it is by no means easier.[76]

What Makes Workplace Teams Effective?

Widespread use of team formats—including project teams, self-managed teams, cross-functional teams, and virtual teams—necessitates greater knowledge of team effectiveness.[77] A model of team effectiveness criteria and determinants is presented in Figure 13.5. This model is the product of two field studies involving 360 new-product-development managers employed by 52 high-tech companies.[78] It is a generic model that applies equally well to all workplace teams.[79]

The five criteria for effective team performance in Figure 13.5 parallel the criteria for organizational effectiveness discussed in Chapter 9. Thus, team effectiveness feeds organizational effectiveness.

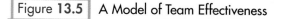

Figure **13.5**   A Model of Team Effectiveness

DETERMINANTS OF TEAM EFFECTIVENESS

People-related factors
- Personal work satisfaction
- Mutual trust and team spirit
- Good communications
- Low unresolved conflict and power struggle
- Low threat, fail-safe, good job security

Organization-related factors
- Organizational stability and job security
- Involved, interested, supportive management
- Proper rewards and recognition of accomplishments
- Stable goals and priorities

Task-related factors
- Clear objectives, directions, and project plans
- Proper technical direction and leadership
- Autonomy and professionally challenging work
- Experienced and qualified project/team personnel
- Team involvement and project visibility

Effective team performance
- Innovative ideas
- Goal(s) accomplished
- Adaptable to change
- High personal/team commitment
- Rated highly by upper management

Source: Reprinted from *Journal of Product Innovation Management*, 7, Hans J. Thamhain, "Managing Technologically Innovative Team Efforts Toward New Product Success," pp. 5–18. Copyright 1990, with permission from Elsevier Science.

Determinants of team effectiveness, shown in Figure 13.5, are grouped into people-, organization-, and task-related factors. Considered separately, these factors involve rather routine aspects of good management. But the collective picture reveals each factor to be part of a complex and interdependent whole. Managers cannot maximize just a few of them, ignore the rest, and hope to have an effective team. In the spirit of the Japanese concept of *kaizen*, managers and team leaders need to strive for "continuous improvement" on all fronts. Because gains on one front will inevitably be offset by losses in another, the pursuit of team effectiveness and teamwork is an endless battle with no guarantees of success.[80]

Let's focus on trust, one of the people-related factors in Figure 13.5 that can make or break work teams.

13e
Trust Me!

Trust is essential to building enduring connections with employees, suppliers, customers, and the communities in which we do business. . . . What most managers don't get, though, is that the best way to build trust is to extend it to others.

QUESTIONS: How do you build trust with others, both on and off the job? What causes you to mistrust someone? How should you deal with a coworker who mistakenly mistrusts you?

Source: Dov Seidman, "Building Trust by Trusting," *Business Week* (September 7, 2009): 76.

Robert LeSieur/Reuters/Corbis Wire/Corbis

That's trust and teamwork! Everyone on NASCAR driver Kyle Busch's cross-functional team consisting of driver, pit crew, support personnel, owner, and sponsors is focused on a single goal—a safe trip to the checkered flag.

Trust: A Key to Team Effectiveness

Trust, a belief in the integrity, character, or ability of others, is essential if people are to achieve anything together in the long run.[81] Participative management programs are very dependent on trust. According to Stanford's Jeffrey Pfeffer, employee retention and motivation hinge upon trust in management.[82] Sadly, trust is not one of the hallmarks of the current U.S. business and government scene:

- A 2009 Rasmussen survey showed that trust was lowest in CEOs, lower than all other professions. For example, only 25 percent of adults respected CEOs, whereas 30 percent of adults respected members of Congress.[83]
- A 2010 Pew Research Center survey showed that 22 percent of Americans trust the government in Washington most of the time. This is among the lowest ratings in 50 years.[84]

To a greater extent than they may initially suspect, managers determine the level of trust in the organization and its component work groups and teams.

Experts in the area of social capital tell us that no one can force trust. However, leaders can give people reasons to trust by exhibiting trustworthy behavior and not rewarding behavior built on distrust.[85]

ZAND'S MODEL OF TRUST. Trust is not a free-floating variable. It affects, and in turn is affected by, other group processes. Dale E. Zand's model of work group interaction puts trust into proper perspective (see Figure 13.6). Zand believes that trust is the key to establishing productive interpersonal relationships.[86]

Primary responsibility for creating a climate of trust falls on the manager. Team members usually look to the manager, who enjoys hierarchical advantage and greater access to key information, to set the tone for interpersonal dealings. Threatening or intimidating actions by the manager will probably encourage the group to bind together in cohesive resistance. Therefore, trust needs to be developed right from the beginning, when team members are still receptive to positive managerial influence.

Trust is initially encouraged by a manager's openness and honesty. Trusting managers talk *with*

trust belief in the integrity, character, or ability of others

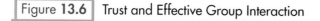

Figure **13.6** Trust and Effective Group Interaction

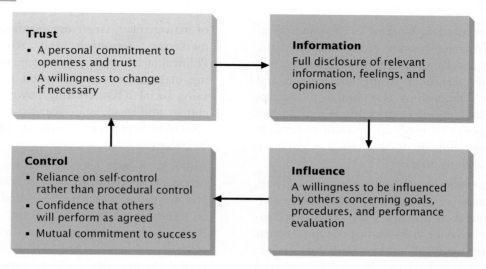

Source: Reprinted from "Trust and Managerial Problem Solving," by Dale E. Zand and published in *Administrative Science Quarterly*, 17, no. 2 (June 1972), by permission of Administrative Science Quarterly. © 1972 by Cornell University.

their people rather than *at* them. A trusting manager, according to Zand's model, demonstrates a willingness to be influenced by others and to change if the facts indicate a change is appropriate. Mutual trust between a manager and team members encourages *self-control,* as opposed to control through direct supervision.

Paradoxically, managerial control actually expands when committed group or team members enjoy greater freedom in pursuing consensual goals. Those who trust each other generally avoid taking advantage of others' weaknesses or shortcomings.[87]

SIX WAYS TO BUILD TRUST. Trust is a fragile thing. As most of us know from personal experience, trust grows at a painfully slow pace yet can be destroyed in an instant with a thoughtless remark. Mistrust can erode the long-term effectiveness of work teams and organizations. According to management professor and consultant Fernando Bartolomé, managers need to concentrate on six areas: communication, support, respect, fairness, predictability, and competence.

- *Communication.* Keep your people informed by providing accurate and timely feedback and explaining policies and decisions. Be open and honest about your own problems. Do not hoard information or use it as a political device or reward.
- *Support.* Be an approachable person who is available to help, encourage, and coach your people. Show an active interest in their lives and be willing to come to their defense.
- *Respect.* Delegating important duties is the sincerest form of respect, followed closely by being a good listener.
- *Fairness.* Evaluate your people fairly and objectively and be liberal in giving credit and praise.
- *Predictability.* Be dependable and consistent in your behavior and keep all of your promises.
- *Competence.* Be a good role model by exercising good business judgment and being technically and professionally competent.[88]

Managers find that trust begets trust. In other words, those who feel they are trusted tend to trust others in return.

SUMMARY

1. Managers need a working understanding of group dynamics because groups are the basic building blocks of organizations. Generating social capital through strong, constructive, and win-win relationships is essential to success today. Both informal (friendship) and formal (work) groups are made up of two or more freely interacting individuals who have a common identity and purpose.

2. After someone has been attracted to a group, cohesiveness—a "we" feeling—encourages continued membership. Roles are social expectations for behavior in a specific position, whereas norms are more general standards for conduct in a given social setting. Norms are enforced because they help the group survive, clarify role expectations, protect self-images, and enhance the group's identity by emphasizing key values. Compliance with role expectations and norms is rewarded with social reinforcement; noncompliance is punished by criticism, ridicule, and ostracism.

3. Mature groups are characterized by mutual acceptance, encouragement of minority opinion, and minimal emotional conflict. They are the product of a developmental process with identifiable stages. During the first three stages—orientation, conflict and challenge, and cohesion—power and authority problems are resolved. Groups are faced with the obstacle of uncertainty over interpersonal relations during the last three stages—delusion, disillusion, and acceptance. Committees have a widespread reputation for inefficiency and ineffectiveness because they tend to get stalled in an early stage of group development.

4. Organizational politics centers on the pursuit of self-interest. Research shows greater political activity to be associated with higher levels of management, larger organizations, staff and marketing personnel, and reorganizations. Political tactics such as posturing, empire building, making the boss look good, collecting and using social IOUs, creating power and loyalty cliques, and engaging in destructive competition need to be kept in check if the organization is to be effective.

5. Although a fairly high degree of conformity is necessary if organizations and society in general are to function properly, blind conformity is ultimately dehumanizing and destructive. Research shows that individuals have a strong tendency to bend to the will of the majority, even if the majority is clearly wrong. Cohesive decision-making groups can be victimized by groupthink when unanimity becomes more important than critical evaluation of alternative courses of action.

6. Teams are becoming the structural format of choice. Today's employees generally have better technical skills than team skills. Cross-functional teams are particularly promising because they facilitate greater strategic speed. Although members of virtual teams by definition collaborate via electronic media, there is still a need for periodic face-to-face interaction and teambuilding. Three sets of factors—relating to people, organization, and task—combine to determine the effectiveness of a work team.

7. Trust, a key ingredient of effective teamwork, is disturbingly low in the American workplace today. When work group members trust one another, there will be a more active exchange of information, more interpersonal influence, and hence greater self-control. Managers can build trust through communication, support, respect (primarily in the form of delegation), fairness, predictability, and competence.

TERMS TO UNDERSTAND

Social capital, p. 360
Group, p. 360
Informal group, p. 361
Formal group, p. 362
Cohesiveness, p. 363

Role, p. 364
Norms, p. 364
Ostracism, p. 364
Organizational politics, p. 369
Conformity, p. 371

Groupthink, p. 372
Cross-functional team, p. 374
Virtual team, p. 375
Trust, p. 378

ACTION LEARNING EXERCISE

MANAGEMENT TEAMWORK SURVEY

Instructions: Think of your present job (or a past one) and check one box for each of the following ten questions. Alternatively, you can ask a manager to complete this survey. The idea is to assess the organization's commitment to building cooperation and teamwork among managers. This instrument also pinpoints weak spots needing attention.

TO WHAT EXTENT DO …	Never	To a Limited Extent	To a Great Extent	Always
1. Our managers pursue common goals that focus on our customers and profitability?	☐	☐	☐	☐
2. We have team-based performance measurements and feedback devices?	☐	☐	☐	☐
3. Our top managers demonstrate and foster cooperation in their approach to leadership?	☐	☐	☐	☐
4. We provide incentives and rewards that encourage management cooperation?	☐	☐	☐	☐
5. We engage in ongoing teambuilding activities and skill development among our managers?	☐	☐	☐	☐
6. We identify and resolve problems/conflicts among managers in a timely fashion?	☐	☐	☐	☐
7. We create management team ownership of decision processes and outcomes?	☐	☐	☐	☐
8. We clarify each manager's roles and goals to each other?	☐	☐	☐	☐
9. We integrate planning, problem-solving, and communication activities among managers?	☐	☐	☐	☐
10. We build consensus and understanding around work processes and systems?	☐	☐	☐	☐

Interpretation: Scores in Columns 1 and 2 represent areas that damage management cooperation and teamwork; these areas should be systematically addressed to enhance organizational performance. Scores in Columns 3 and 4 represent practices that can and should be continued and improved to increase management cooperation and teamwork.

Source: Clinton O. Longenecker and Mitchell Neubert, "Barriers and Gateways to Management Cooperation and Teamwork." Reprinted with permission from *Business Horizons*, 43 (September–October 2000). Copyright 2000 by the Trustees at Indiana University, Kelley School of Business.

FOR CONSIDERATION/DISCUSSION

1. Why are cooperation and teamwork among managers so important today?
2. Overall, how does this organization measure up in terms of fostering managerial cooperation and teamwork?
3. Which areas are strongest? How can they be made even stronger?
4. Which areas are weakest and what needs to be done?
5. Which factors in this survey are most critical to organizational success today? Explain.

ETHICS EXERCISE

DO THE RIGHT THING

THE ART OF FRIENDSHIP

Peter Bregman, management consultant: To be a good friend, you have to give of yourself, but not so much that you lose yourself. You need to know what you want and pursue it, while helping others achieve what they want. You need to have personality while making room for, and supporting, other people's personalities. You need to care about, and even love, people you might disagree with. . . . You need to be willing to give at least as much, if not more, than you take.

Source: Excerpted from Peter Bregman, "Why Friends Matter at Work and in Life," *Harvard Business Review* (July 1, 2010). http://blogs.hbr.org/bregman/2010/07/why-friends-matter-at-work-and.html, accessed July 2, 2010.

What are the ethical implications of the following interpretations?

1. Friends come and go, but one's performance record at work is permanent. Friendships often get in the way of getting the job done quickly. It is best to keep your professional and personal lives separate.
2. True friendship is a treasure and the key to successful teamwork on the job. What are the pros and cons of working with your best friends?
3. Workplace friendships can be either productive or counterproductive, depending on the situation and personalities involved. Any recommendations or advice for new hires?
4. Your own ethical interpretation?

MANAGERS-IN-ACTION VIDEO CASE STUDY

NUMI ORGANIC TEA

Group Dynamics and Teamwork

Ahmed Rahim, co-founder and CEO of Numi Organic Tea, shares his secrets to success in fostering a work environment where employee passion inspires a work ethic where people go above and beyond what is expected to help the group achieve its goals. Having the right group dynamics—or, as Rahim describes it, *the right people and the right formula*—is integral to the company's growth. In this video, managers from Numi Tea share their insights about team development, corporate culture, and how values impact team cohesion and performance.

For more information about Numi Tea, visit its Web site: http://www.numitea.com/

Before watching the video, answer the following questions:

1. What are the keys to team effectiveness?
2. Why is there so much emphasis on group dynamics and teamwork in the workplace?
3. Trust has often been considered an essential ingredient for high-functioning teams. As a team leader, how can you build trust with your team members?

After watching the video, answer the following questions:

4. Several of the Numi Tea employees in this video mentioned passion as one of the essential characteristics for success. How would you describe passion in the workplace?
5. Do you agree that passion is important? Explain.
6. How does Numi Tea develop group cohesion to achieve its organizational goals?
7. What did you learn from Dannielle Oviedo, the distribution center manager, about leading teams?

CLOSING CASE

TRUE TEAM SPIRIT AT CHICAGO'S TOTAL ATTORNEYS

The first thing you notice when you walk into the Chicago offices of Total Attorneys, which provides software and services to small law firms, is the number of people on their feet. Every morning, the company's 180 employees gather around the office in groups of five to 10. Close your eyes, take in the often raucous banter and laughter, and it's easy to mistake Total Attorneys's headquarters for a college cafeteria. But these meetings, which last for about 15 minutes, are more than mere employee chitchat.

They are intended to create what CEO Ed Scanlan calls controlled chaos.

The inspiration for the gatherings comes from a process for designing software called agile development, which aims to promote flexibility, speed, and teamwork. But rather than limit participation to software engineers, Scanlan has deployed agile development concepts companywide, in a drive to make the seven-year-old business act more like the start-up it once was.

Scanlan became interested in agile development about a year ago. He had grown increasingly frustrated with his company's software-development process. When he founded Total Attorneys in 2002 to make customer-relationship-management software for law firms, he and a handful of employees would write code on the fly. Projects were completed quickly, and employees often worked late nights and weekends to launch new features and fix bugs. But as revenue grew to $24 million, the company abandoned the fly-by-the-seat-of-your-pants approach in favor of a more formal system. Sometimes referred to as the waterfall model, this system divides a software project into sequential stages, in which the work is handed off from designers to coders to quality-assurance testers.

But Scanlan found that the waterfall model made Total Attorneys move a lot more slowly—so slowly, in fact, that in some cases clients' needs had changed by the time a piece of software was complete. "We had more than a hundred employees, but we were getting a lot less done than when it was just me and three other people," Scanlan says. "Morale was suffering as well." Employees felt disconnected not only from the projects, Scanlan says, but also from their colleagues. Designers rarely interacted with developers, let alone anyone from the accounting department or the management team.

Scanlan's search for a solution led him to *Getting Real*, a book about agile development published by the software company 37signals. "I learned about cutting the 'big picture' into small pieces," Scanlan says. "You have to be able to change course as often as your customers' needs or market conditions dictate."

One way to accomplish this is by breaking down large departmental silos and creating small, cross-functional teams instead. A typical team might be made up of one project leader, one designer, one coder, and one quality-assurance tester. Large projects get carved into lots of mini projects, often with deadlines as short as a couple of weeks. Each team focuses on one mini project at a time and is given the freedom to make decisions. The teams hold daily meetings—or "scrums"—to discuss each member's progress and daily objectives.

Scanlan adopted the strategy and found that the software team's productivity improved. What's more, employees seemed happier. That got Scanlan thinking: Could he use agile development to change how the rest of his company operated as well? He decided to find out.

He grouped all employees into about 35 small teams. The 85 call center employees, for example, were divided into about 15 groups, which review calls and analyze performance metrics every morning. "We teach all of our customer reps to be open to change and to be ready for one day to be different than the rest," says Scott Hogan, the company's call center trainer. "We give our reps talking points instead of scripts so that they can adjust on the fly to help the customer. Whenever someone finds an effective way to connect, we share that with everyone else." Although call center reps aren't often on teams with software developers, Scanlan moved the departments to the same floor to bolster communication. "Now, rather than waiting to see how effective the latest changes to the call center software are, developers need only stand up to see how the reps are reacting to it," says Scanlan.

Another key to the agile approach is shorter deadlines. In software, that means building smaller pieces over shorter periods and evaluating them rapidly rather than waiting months to see if they hit the mark. In Total Attorneys's sales department, it means setting three-week sales goals instead of annual targets. That way, the sales team can more easily adjust its strategy and forecasts if the company introduces a new service or experiences fluctuations in demand. At the beginning of each three-week period, the company's sales managers, each of whom is responsible for a five-person team, set goals for their squads, such as landing a certain number of clients in a new sales territory. At the end of the period, the teams evaluate their results and devise new goals for the next three weeks. Because commissions are based on meeting targets set just three weeks prior, salespeople can strive for realistic objectives, which has boosted morale. "Sales jobs can get stale fairly quickly," says Brian Pistorius, the company's 2008 salesperson of the year. "But we are constantly changing and doing things differently to hit our goals. It makes a real difference to get a sense of achievement and recognition every three weeks rather than waiting until the end of the year."

Another strategy Scanlan has borrowed from agile development involves inviting a few customers to test and provide feedback on a product as it is being developed. Last fall, for example, Scanlan decided to launch a new service, legal process outsourcing. The service is aimed at clients like bankruptcy lawyers, who often must complete dozens of forms for each of their clients. Launching the service required hiring a team of paralegals and transcribers as well as building new software. "In the past, we might have developed a fancy system and just announced it to our customers," Scanlan says. "This time, we used agile development to put together a pilot program in less than three months."

For the pilot program, Total Attorneys created teams made up of operations employees and call center reps. The teams collected feedback from five firms that agreed to participate in the pilot. "We learned that not all our customers work the same way," says Scanlan. "Today, we have about 50 customers who love our product because we built it, step by step, using their input." One of those customers, Rustin Polk, a bankruptcy attorney in Dallas, can't wait to see what Total Attorneys comes up with next. "A lot of companies try to forecast or guess what their customers want," he says. "Ed Scanlan just listens to what his customers are telling him."

One downside to changing things on the fly, says Scanlan, is that it has become increasingly difficult to make accurate financial projections. That's why the accountants now like to sit in on daily scrums to keep better tabs on where the company is headed. "We are moving so fast in so many directions," Scanlan says. "But if we focus on communication and transparency, we can control the chaos, even when it seems like everyone is running in different directions."

For Discussion

1. What are the pros and cons of such extensive use of cross-functional teams?

2. What norms need to be embedded in the corporate culture to make cross-functional teams work effectively at Total Attorneys?

3. What can management do to help the firm's cross-functional teams reach the acceptance (maturity) stage of the group development process in Figure 13.3?

4. Are organizational politics and groupthink likely to be major problems in Total Attorneys's team-based organization? Explain.

5. How can team leaders build the trust necessary for effective cross-functional teamwork?

Source: Darren Dahl, "Fast, Flexible, and Full of Team Spirit: How to Work More Like a Start-Up," *Inc.*, 31 (May 2009): 95–97.

MARIO ANZUONI/Reuters/Landov

"Leaders need to exude positive energy. Define vision. Build great teams. Care. Reward. Teach. Decide. Innovate. Execute."[1]
—JACK AND SUZY WELCH

The Changing Workplace

CHARTING YOUR PATHWAY TO INFLUENCE AND POWER

Ron Meyer, the president and chief operating officer of Universal Studios since 1995, is the longest serving head of a major motion picture company. A powerful figure in the film industry, Meyer also provides an example of a life transformed. Ron Meyer dropped out of high school when he was 15 and a couple of years later he joined the U.S. Marines. After leaving the Marines he got a job at a talent agency as a chauffer, a position that permitted him to learn a lot about the entertainment business as he listened to the conversations of clients. After working as an agent for the William Morris Agency, Meyer and some friends founded the Creative Artists Agency, a position that helped establish him as a power broker in Hollywood.

Meyer, like many successful people, profoundly changed over the course of his life. He developed qualities that permitted him to obtain and hold on to influence. If you are going to do likewise, you need to successfully surmount three obstacles. First, you must come to believe that personal change is possible; otherwise, you won't even try to develop the attributes that bring power—you will just accept that you are who you are rather than embarking on a sometimes difficult path of personal growth and development. Second, you need to see yourself and your strengths and weaknesses as objectively as possible. This is difficult because in our desire to self-enhance—to think good things about ourselves—we avoid negative information and overemphasize any positive feedback we receive. And third, you need to understand the most important qualities for building a power base so you can focus your inevitably limited time and attention on developing those....

The two fundamental dimensions that distinguish people who rise to great heights and accomplish amazing things are *will*, the drive to take on big challenges, and *skill*, the

- **Identify** and **describe** eight generic influence tactics used in modern organizations.
- **Identify** the five bases of power, and **explain** what it takes to make empowerment work.
- **Explain** the concept of emotional intelligence in terms of Goleman's four leadership traits.
- **Summarize** what the Ohio State model has taught managers about leadership.
- **Describe** the path-goal theory of leadership, and **explain** how the assumption on which it

is based differs from the assumption on which Fiedler's contingency theory is based.
- **Describe** a transformational leader, and **explain** Greenleaf's philosophy of the servant leader.
- **Identify** the two key functions that mentors perform, and **explain** how a mentor can develop a junior manager's leadership skills.
- **Explain** the management of antecedents and consequences in behavior modification.

OBJECTIVES

capabilities required to turn ambition into accomplishment. The three personal qualities embodied in will are ambition, energy, and focus. The four skills useful in acquiring power are self-knowledge and a reflective mind-set, confidence and the ability to project self-assurance, the ability to read others and empathize with their point of view, and a capacity to tolerate conflict.

Source: Excerpted from Jeffrey Pfeffer, *Power: Why Some People Have It—and Others Don't* (New York: HarperCollins, 2010), pp. 36–37, 43.

What do the following situations have in common?

- A magazine editor praises her supervisor's new outfit shortly before asking for the afternoon off.
- A milling-machine operator tells a friend that he will return the favor if his friend will watch out for the supervisor while he takes an unauthorized cigarette break.
- An office manager attempts to head off opposition to a new Internet-use policy by carefully explaining how it will be fair and will increase productivity.

Aside from the fact that all of these situations take place on the job, the common denominator is "influence." In each case, someone is trying to get his or her own way by influencing someone else's behavior. The pathway to influence and power in the opening case, developed by Stanford University's Jeffrey Pfeffer, and the concepts in this chapter will guide you toward the skillful and responsible use of influence, power, and leadership.

Influence is any attempt by a person to change the behavior of superiors, peers, or lower-level employees. Influence is not inherently good or bad. As the foregoing situations illustrate, influence can be used for purely selfish reasons, to subvert organizational objectives, or to enhance organizational effectiveness. Managerial success is firmly linked to the ability to exercise the right sort of influence at the right time. A good example is Andrea Jung, CEO of Avon, as she was working her way up the executive ladder. While Jung lacked experience abroad, she was a daughter of Chinese immigrants and showed cultural sensitivity. On a trip to Mexico, for instance, she won the hearts of the local staff by using a few Spanish phrases in her presentation.[2] Jung's influence skills eventually paid off when she was named the first woman CEO of Avon in its 118-year history.

The purpose of this chapter is to examine different approaches to influencing others. We focus specifically on influence tactics, power, leadership, mentoring, and behavior modification.

INFLUENCE TACTICS IN THE WORKPLACE

A replication and refinement of an earlier groundbreaking study provides useful insights about on-the-job influence.[3] Both studies asked employees basically the same question: "How do you get your boss, coworker, or subordinate to do something you want?" The following eight generic influence tactics emerged:

1. *Consultation.* Seeking someone's participation in a decision or change
2. *Rational persuasion.* Trying to convince someone by relying on a detailed plan, supporting information, reasoning, or logic
3. *Inspirational appeals.* Appealing to someone's emotions, values, or ideals to generate enthusiasm and confidence

AP Photo/Will Kincaid

More than 100 Basin Electric Power Cooperative employees in Bismarck, North Dakota, were influenced to shave their heads as part of a fundraising event. The worthy cause was children's cancer research.

4. *Ingratiating tactics.* Making someone feel important or good before making a request; acting humble or friendly before making a request

5. *Coalition tactics.* Seeking the aid of others to persuade someone to agree

6. *Pressure tactics.* Relying on intimidation, demands, or threats to gain compliance or support

7. *Upward appeals.* Obtaining formal or informal support of higher management

8. *Exchange tactics.* Offering an exchange of favors; reminding someone of a past favor; offering to make a personal sacrifice[4]

These influence tactics are *generic* because they are used by various organizational members to influence lower-level employees (downward influence), peers (lateral influence), or superiors (upward influence). Table 14.1 indicates what the researchers found out about patterns of use for the three different directions of influence. Note that consultation, rational persuasion, and inspirational appeals were the three most popular tactics, regardless

14a

Quick Quiz

As chief executive [of Kraft Foods, Irene Rosenfeld] . . . has won most employees' cooperation for a wrenching reorganization. "When she is trying to persuade you of something, she will be relentless in coming back with facts and showing you she has the support of other people," says John Bowlin, who ran Kraft North America in the mid-1990s.

QUESTIONS: Which of the eight generic influence tactics are evident in Rosenfeld's approach? Would a different approach be more effective? Explain.

For further information about the interactive annotations in this chapter, visit our student Web site.

Source: Susan Berfield and Michael Arndt, "Kraft's Sugar Rush," *Bloomberg Businessweek* (January 25, 2010): 37.

Table 14.1	Use of Generic Organizational Influence Tactics

TACTIC	RANK ORDER (BY DIRECTION OF INFLUENCE)		
	DOWNWARD	LATERAL	UPWARD
Consultation	1	1	2
Rational persuasion	2	2	1
Inspirational appeals	3	3	3
Ingratiating tactics	4	4	5
Coalition tactics	5	5	4
Pressure tactics	6	7	7
Upward appeals	7	6	6
Exchange tactics	8	8	8

Source: Adapted from discussion in Gary Yukl and Cecilia M. Falbe, "Influence Tactics and Objectives in Upward, Downward, and Lateral Influence Attempts," *Journal of Applied Psychology*, 75 (April 1990): 132–140.

of the direction of influence.[5] Meanwhile, pressure tactics, upward appeals, and exchange tactics consistently were the least-used influence tactics. Ingratiating and coalition tactics fell in the midrange of use.[6] This is an encouraging pattern from the standpoint of getting things done through collaborative problem solving rather than through intimidation and conflict in today's team-oriented workplaces.

Frank Squillante, one of IBM's vice presidents, is a great example. He is tasked with developing the company's intranet strategies and applications, which are used by 325,000 employees and an additional 100,000 business partners. With only four direct reports working for him, Squillante says he has no real influence over many of his colleagues, so he uses cajoling and collaboration to convince them to help him reach his objectives. He notes, "If I tried to pull one of these 'I'm in charge so you have to do this' maneuvers, the whole thing would break down."[7]

Do women and men tend to rely on different influence tactics? Available research evidence reveals no systematic gender-based differences relative to

influencing others.[8] In contrast, the tactics used by employees to influence their bosses were found to vary with different leadership styles. Employees influencing authoritarian managers tended to rely on ingratiating tactics and upward appeals. Rational persuasion was used most often to influence participative managers.[9]

POWER

Power is inevitable in modern organizations. According to one advocate of the positive and constructive use of power, managers need power to influence those they rely upon, and it is essential in developing managers' self-confidence. From this vantage point, power is a natural part of any organization. Power does not need to be feared or avoided because it is powerlessness, not power, that has the real potential to damage an organization.[10] As a manager, if you understand power, its bases, and empowerment, you will have an advantage when it comes to getting things accomplished with and through others.[11]

What Is Power?

Power is the ability to accomplish something by organizing human, informational, and material resources.[12] Powerful people get their own way, despite obstacles and opposition.[13] Power affects organizational members in the following three areas:

1. *Decisions.* A packaging engineer decides to take on a difficult new assignment after hearing her boss's recommendations.
2. *Behavior.* A hospital lab technician achieves a month of perfect attendance after receiving a written warning about absenteeism from his supervisor.
3. *Situations.* The productivity of a product design group increases dramatically following the purchase of project management software.[14]

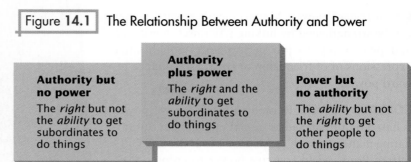

| Figure **14.1** | The Relationship Between Authority and Power |

Authority plus power
The *right* and the *ability* to get subordinates to do things

Authority but no power
The *right* but not the *ability* to get subordinates to do things

Power but no authority
The *ability* but not the *right* to get other people to do things

Religion exercises a powerful influence over the lives of many people around the world. This mosque minaret towering high above Dubai Creek calls the Islamic faithful to prayer five times a day. Business is not conducted on Fridays, the Islamic holy day, in Dubai, United Arab Emirates.

Another instructive way of looking at power is to distinguish among "power over" (ability to dominate), "power to" (ability to act freely), and "power from" (ability to resist the demands of others).[15]

By emphasizing the word *ability* in our definition and discussion of power, we can contrast power with authority. As defined in Chapter 9, authority is the "right" to direct the activities of others.[16] Authority is an officially sanctioned privilege that that may or may not get results. In contrast, power is the demonstrated *ability* to get results. As illustrated in Figure 14.1, one may possess authority but have no power, possess no authority yet have power, or possess both authority and power. The first situation, authority but no power, was experienced by some Albanian police in 1997, when Europe's poorest nation fell into anarchy over dissatisfaction with a corrupt government. According to *Newsweek* an unruly mob encircled the police, stripped off their uniforms, and set fire to their gear.[17] At the other end of the model in Figure 14.1, it is possible for an individual to have power but no authority. For example, employees may respond to the wishes of the supervisor's spouse.[18] Finally, a manager who gets employees to work hard on an important project has both authority and power.

The Five Bases of Power

Essential to the successful use of power in organizations is an understanding of the various bases of power. One widely cited classification of power bases identifies five types of power: reward, coercive, legitimate, referent, and expert.[19]

REWARD POWER. One's ability to grant rewards to those who comply with a command or request is the

power ability to marshal resources to get something done

key to reward power. Management's reward power can be strengthened by linking pay raises, merit pay, and promotions to job performance. Sought-after expressions of of friendship or trust also enhance reward power.

COERCIVE POWER. Rooted in fear, coercive power is based on threatened or actual punishment. Intimidating managers such as Amazon's founder and CEO Jeffrey Bezos wield coercive power to enforce their high standards. One former Amazon employee, in describing how Bezos makes people uncomfortable with his blunt and difficult questions, said, "That bellowing laugh? He would look at your spreadsheet and laugh you out of the room."[20]

LEGITIMATE POWER. Legitimate power is achieved when a person's superior position alone prompts another person to act in a desired manner. This type of power closely parallels formal authority, as discussed earlier. Parents, teachers, religious leaders, and managers who expect or demand obedience by virtue of their superior social position will find it simply won't work for two reasons. One, these leaders will sometimes find themselves dealing with people over whom they have no real authority, and two, in modern society, most people refuse to blindly obey orders, even when those orders come from a supervisor.[21]

One might reasonably conclude that legitimate power has been eroded by its frequent abuse (or overuse) through the years.[22] Moreover, legitimate power may exact a price that fewer are willing to pay these days. According to a recent survey, 60 percent of respondents said they had no interest in becoming a CEO, which is twice the number of respondents who said they'd decline the top job in 2001.[23]

REFERENT POWER. An individual has referent power over those who identify with him or her if they comply on that basis alone. Personal attraction is an elusive thing to define, let alone consciously cultivate. *Charisma* is a term often used in conjunction with referent power. Although leaders with the personal magnetism of Abraham

Jochen Tack/imagebroker/Age Fotostock

Lincoln, John Kennedy, or Martin Luther King Jr. are always in short supply, charisma in the workplace can be problematic. *Fortune* magazine noted that charismatic visionaries have the potential to lead individuals forward, but sometimes they can lead people astray when the leader's mission becomes an obsession. John Thompson, a leadership consultant says, "Leaders can cut corners on values and become self-driven."[24] Still, as we will see in our discussion of transformational leadership later in this chapter, charisma does have its positive side.

EXPERT POWER. Those who possess and can dispense valued information generally exercise expert power over those in need of such information. Information technology experts, for instance, are in a position today to wield a great deal of expert power.

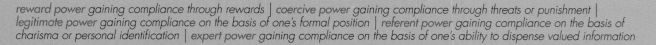

Anyone who has ever been taken advantage of by an unscrupulous computer technician knows what expert power in the wrong hands can mean.

Empowerment

Empowerment occurs when employees are adequately trained, provided with all relevant information and the best possible tools, fully involved in key decisions, and fairly rewarded for results.[25] Those who endorse this key building block of progressive management view power as an unlimited resource. Frances Hesselbein, the widely respected former head of the Girl Scouts of the USA, offered this perspective: "The more power you give away, the more you have."[26] This can be a difficult concept to grasp for traditional authoritarian managers who see empowerment as a threat to their authority and illusion of being in total control. Today, the issue is not empowerment versus no empowerment. Rather, the issue is how empowerment should take place (see Green Management: Toward Sustainability). At Homewood Suites where dissatisfied guests are assured a money-back guarantee, for example, every employee from housekeeper to manager is empowered to resolve a guest's problem without seeking approval. Here, empowerment has resulted in a 20-to-1 return on every dollar refunded.[27] Because of complex individual, group, and organizational factors, employee empowerment is like a puzzle with many vital pieces that cannot be ignored.

Much of the burden for successful empowerment falls on the *individual*. No amount of empowerment and supportive management can overcome dishonesty, untrustworthiness, selfishness, and inadequate skills.[28] Moreover, as we learned in the case of Enron, empowerment without proper oversight can lead to very bad consequences. There, inexperienced people were given authority to make $5 million decisions without approval, and intense pressure for results opened the door to abuses. A former Enron manager said, "Nobody at corporate was asking the right questions. It was completely hands-off management."[29] Enron ended up being one of the biggest bankruptcies in U.S. history. Once again, rigorous employee selection and training and ethics training, as discussed in Chapters 5 and 10, come to the forefront.

LEADERSHIP

Leadership has fascinated people since the dawn of recorded history. The search for good leaders has been a common thread running through human civilization.[30] In view of research evidence that effective leadership is associated with both better performance and more ethical performance, the search for ways to identify (or develop) good leaders needs

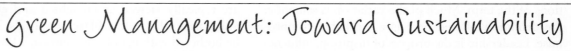

Green Management: Toward Sustainability

Nike's Point Person for Sustainability

Hannah Jones, vice president of sustainable business and innovation: A philosophy major who did a stint on pirate radio, she says she joined Nike's sustainability team to test whether it was "more effective to shout from the outside or work from the inside." Her conclusion: The creative combination of both is the most potent. She has paired Nike with NASA and venture capitalists to address water shortages; with Creative Commons to launch GreenXchange, a platform for companies to share green intellectual property; and with PopTech to create an Open Collaboration Lab for scientists and engineers. "We need to get to a place," Jones says, "where businesses leverage renewable energy, do not produce waste, and have clean water coming in and clean water coming out."

For Discussion: Which influence tactics and power bases would likely serve Jones the best when getting people inside and outside Nike to collaborate on sustainability initiatives?

Source: Excerpted from Danielle Sacks, "Hannah Jones, VP of Sustainable Business and Innovation: Nike," *Fast Company*, 146 (June 2010): 75.

empowerment making employees full partners in the decision-making process and giving them the necessary tools and rewards to continue.[31] Indeed, when 800 training and development managers were surveyed recently, 63 percent ranked "Developing potential leaders" as the number one management challenge.[32] As Peter Drucker pointed out, leadership is a difficult topic because great leaders come in all sizes, shapes, and temperaments. The legendary management scholar helpfully offered the following leader *effectiveness* criteria, which are common to all leaders, regardless of personality, values, or strengths:

What made them all effective is that they followed the same eight practices:

- *They asked, "What needs to be done?"*
- *They asked, "What is right for the enterprise?"*
- *They developed action plans.*
- *They took responsibility for decisions.*
- *They took responsibility for communicating.*
- *They were focused on opportunities rather than problems.*
- *They ran productive meetings.*
- *They thought and said "we" rather than "I."*[33]

Let us keep these effectiveness criteria in mind as we explore the topic of leadership, while resisting the temptation to embrace a one-size-fits-all leadership model.

Leadership Defined

Research on leadership has produced many definitions of the term. Much of the variation is semantic; the definition offered here is a workable compromise. Leadership is the process of inspiring, influencing, and guiding others to participate in a common effort.[34] In today's highly interconnected world, leadership extends beyond the office door or factory gate. Leaders emerge in nearly every facet of any organization, as well as among the organization's suppliers, customers, investors, shareholders, and beyond. The thing that unites these leaders is a common vision that helps them guide others toward reaching the organization's overarching goals.[35]

To encourage such broad participation, leaders supplement any authority and power they possess with their personal attributes, imagination, and social skills. Colin Powell, a leader admired in both

military and civilian circles, offers his own definition: "Leadership is the art of accomplishing more than the science of management says is possible."[36]

Formal and Informal Leaders

Experts on leadership distinguish between formal and informal leadership. Formal leadership is the process of influencing relevant others to pursue official organizational objectives. Informal leadership, in contrast, is the process of influencing others to pursue unofficial objectives that may or may not serve the organization's interests. Formal leaders generally have a measure of legitimate power because of their formal authority, whereas informal leaders typically lack formal authority.[37] Beyond that, both types rely on expedient combinations of reward, coercive, referent, and expert power. Informal leaders who identify with the job to be done are a valuable asset to an organization. Conversely, an organization can be brought to its knees by informal leaders who turn cohesive work groups against the organization.

The Issue of Leaders Versus Managers: A Middle Ground

A long-standing debate about the differences between leaders and managers sprang from Abraham Zaleznik's 1977 article in *Harvard Business Review* titled "Managers and Leaders: Are They Different?" Over the years, stereotypes developed characterizing leaders and managers in very different ways. Leaders are typically viewed as farsighted and even heroic visionaries who boldly blaze new trails. They can't be bothered with details. In contrast, a less-flattering portrayal of the manager is that of a facilitator who tends to the details of turning the leader's vision into reality. Accordingly, it has been said that leaders make chaos out of order and managers make order out of chaos. This dueling-stereotypes debate may be an amusing academic exercise, but it misses one important *practical* point: Today's leaner and continuously evolving organizations require people who can both lead *and* manage—in other words, the total package. The future belongs to those who can effectively blend the characteristics in Table 14.2.

In his own controversial way, Apple's CEO Steve Jobs is both a leader and a manager. He has

| Table 14.2 | Lead or Manage? Good Leaders Must Do Both |

BEING A LEADER MEANS	BEING A MANAGER MEANS
Motivating, influencing and changing behavior.	Practicing stewardship, directing and being held accountable for resources.
Inspiring, setting the tone, and articulating a vision.	Executing plans, implementing and delivering the goods and services.
Managing people.	Managing resources.
Being charismatic.	Being conscientious.
Being visionary.	Planning, organizing, directing and controlling.
Understanding and using power and influence.	Understanding and using authority and responsibility.
Acting decisively.	Acting responsibly.
Putting people first. The leader knows, responds to, and acts for his or her followers.	Putting customers first. The manager knows, responds to, and acts for his or her customers.
Leaders can make mistakes when: 1. they choose the wrong goal, direction or inspiration, due to incompetence or bad intentions; or 2. they over-lead; or 3. they are unable to deliver on [or] implement the vision due to incompetence or a lack of follow-through commitment.	Managers can make mistakes when: 1. they fail to grasp the importance of people as the key resource; or 2. they under-lead; they treat people like other resources [or like] numbers; or 3. they are eager to direct and to control but are unwilling to accept accountability.

Source: Reprinted from *Organizational Dynamics*, Vol. 33, Peter Lorenzi, "Managing for the Common Good: Prosocial Leadership," p. 286, Copyright 2004, with permission from Elsevier.

been described as a visionary, a micromanager, a showman, and a pop culture icon. His dictatorial management style has caused major problems for his business partners, yet no one can deny that his products routinely cause a sensation among consumers.[38] No one ever said leadership was easy.

The study of leadership has evolved as theories have been developed and refined by successive generations of researchers.[39] Something useful has been learned at each stage of development. We now turn to significant milestones in the evolution of leadership theory by examining the trait, behavioral styles, situational, and transformational approaches (see Figure 14.2).

| Figure 14.2 | The Evolution of Leadership Theory |

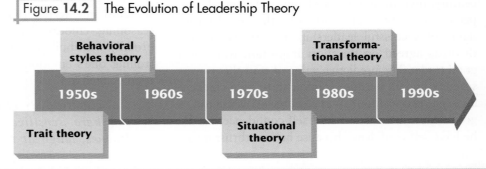

Leadership has many faces and directions today. For example, from left to right are Andrea Jung, CEO of Avon Products; actress and Avon Global Ambassador Reese Witherspoon; Joanne Sandler, executive director of UNIFEM (United Nations Development Fund for Women); and personal finance expert/television personality Suze Orman.

Larry Busacca/WireImage/Getty Images

Trait Theory

During most of recorded history, the prevailing assumption was that leaders are born and not made. Leaders such as Alexander the Great, Napoleon Bonaparte, and George Washington were said to have been blessed with an inborn ability to lead. This so-called great-man approach to leadership[40] eventually gave way to trait theory. According to one management scholar, people eventually accepted the idea that supposedly inborn leadership traits can be attained through education and experience, so researchers began to look for universal traits.[41]

As the popularity of the trait approach mushroomed during the second quarter of the twentieth century, literally hundreds of physical, mental, and personality traits were said to be the key determinants of successful leadership. Unfortunately, few theorists agreed on the most important traits of a good leader. The predictive value of trait theory was severely limited because traits tend to be a chicken-and-egg proposition: Was George Washington a good leader because he had self-confidence, or did he have self-confidence because he was thrust into a

leadership role at a young age? In spite of inherent problems, trait profiles provide a useful framework for examining what it takes to be a good leader.

AN EARLY TRAIT PROFILE. Not until 1948 was a comprehensive review of competing trait theories conducted. After comparing more than 100 studies of leader traits and characteristics, the reviewer uncovered moderate agreement on only five traits: intelligence, scholarship, reliability, social participation, and socioeconomic level.[42]

A MODERN TRAIT PROFILE: LEADERS WITH EMOTIONAL INTELLIGENCE. Daniel Goleman's 1995 book *Emotional Intelligence* popularized a concept that psychologists had talked about for years.[43] Whereas standard intelligence (IQ) deals with thinking and reasoning, emotional intelligence (EQ) deals more broadly with building social relationships and controlling one's emotions. Emotional intelligence has been defined as

> . . . good old street smarts—knowing when to share sensitive information with colleagues, laugh at the boss's jokes or speak

emotional intelligence the ability to monitor and control one's emotions and behavior in complex social settings

up in a meeting. In more scientific terms, . . . [emotional intelligence] can be defined as an array of noncognitive skills, capabilities and competencies that influence a person's ability to cope with environmental demands and pressures.[44]

Higher EQ scores indicate more polished social skills and greater emotional maturity (try the Action Learning Exercise at the end of this chapter). Interestingly, Goleman says that emotional intelligence should be evaluated by others because it is difficult to be objective about oneself in such an important domain.

Goleman and his colleagues recently cast emotional intelligence in terms of four leadership traits:

- *Self-awareness.* This essential component of emotional intelligence involves the ability to read one's own emotions and hence be better equipped to assess one's strengths and limitations.
- *Self-management.* Those who possess this trait do not let their moods and emotions disrupt honest and straightforward relationships.
- *Social awareness.* Those who possess this trait are able to read others' emotions and reactions and subsequently adapt in a constructive and caring fashion.
- *Relationship management.* Leaders who possess this trait are clear, enthusiastic, and convincing communicators who can defuse conflicts. They rely on kindness and humor to build strong relationships.[45]

Each of these traits can be learned, according to Goleman. A big step in the right direction is for managers to fully appreciate how their emotional outbursts and foul moods can poison the work environment. Leaders and followers alike need to exhibit greater emotional intelligence in order to build social capital in today's hectic and often stressful workplaces.[46]

THE CONTROVERSY OVER FEMALE AND MALE LEADERSHIP TRAITS. A second source of renewed interest in leadership traits is the ongoing debate about female versus male leadership traits. In an often-cited survey by Judy B. Rosener, female leaders were found to be better than their male counterparts at sharing power and information.[47] Critics have chided Rosener for reinforcing this traditional feminine stereotype.[48] Actually, a comprehensive review of 162 different studies found *no significant difference* in leadership styles exhibited by women and men. In real-life organizational settings, women did *not* fit the feminine stereotype of being more relationship-oriented, and men did *not* fit the masculine stereotype of being more task-oriented.[49] As always, it is bad practice to make prejudicial assumptions about individuals on the basis of their membership in a particular demographic category.

14c
Netflix Wants "Rare Responsible People"

The movie rental company hires experienced people who are mature, independent, possess the following traits, and [are] able to contribute right away:

- *Self-motivating.*
- *Self-aware.*
- *Self-disciplined.*
- *Self-improving.*
- *Acts like a leader.*
- *Doesn't wait to be told what to do.*
- *Never feels "that's not my job."*
- *Picks up trash lying on the floor.*
- *Behaves like an owner.*

QUESTIONS: What are the pros and cons of using a trait list such as this for hiring purposes? How do you measure up to this list of traits?

Source: Robert J. Grossman, "Tough Love at Netflix," *HR Magazine*, 55 (April 2010): 39.

Behavioral Styles Theory

During World War II, the study of leadership took on a significant new twist. Rather than concentrating on the personal traits of successful leaders, researchers working with the military began turning their attention to patterns of leader behavior (called leadership styles). In other words, attention turned from who the leader was to how the leader actually behaved. One early laboratory study of leader behavior demonstrated that followers overwhelmingly preferred managers who had a democratic style to those with an authoritarian style or a laissez-faire (hands-off) style.[50] An updated review of these three classic leadership styles can be found in Table 14.3.

For a number of years, theorists and managers hailed democratic leadership as the key to productive and happy employees. Eventually, however, their enthusiasm was dampened when critics noted how the original study relied on children as subjects and virtually ignored productivity. Although there is general agreement that these basic styles exist, debate has been vigorous over their relative value and appropriateness. Practical experience has shown, for example, that the democratic style does not always stimulate better performance. Some employees prefer to be told what to do rather than participating in decision making. This can be the result of cultural differences, as was the case when the world's largest television maker was created by the merger of China's TCL Corp. and France's Thomson. Soon after the merger, one TCL official commented on a cultural clash, noting that employees in China always agree with their leader, even when he is wrong, whereas employees from other cultures speak out and disagree.[51]

THE OHIO STATE MODEL. While the democratic style of leadership was receiving attention, a slightly different behavioral approach to leadership emerged. This second approach began in the late 1940s when a team of Ohio State University researchers defined two independent dimensions of leader behavior.[52] One dimension, called "initiating structure," was the leader's efforts to get things organized and get the job done. The second dimension, labeled "consideration," was the degree of trust, friendship, respect, and warmth that the leader extended to subordinates. By making a matrix out of these two independent dimensions of leader behavior, the Ohio State researchers identified four styles of leadership (see Figure 14.3).

This particular scheme proved to be fertile ground for leadership theorists, and variations of

Table 14.3   The Three Classic Styles of Leadership

	AUTHORITARIAN	DEMOCRATIC	LAISSEZ-FAIRE
Nature	Leader retains all authority and responsibility	Leader delegates a great deal of authority while retaining ultimate responsibility	Leader grants responsibility and authority to group
	Leader assigns people to clearly defined tasks	Work is divided and assigned on the basis of participatory decision making	Group members are told to work things out themselves and do the best they can
	Primarily a downward flow of communication	Active two-way flow of upward and downward communication	Primarily horizontal communication among peers
Primary strength	Stresses prompt, orderly, and predictable performance	Enhances personal commitment through participation	Permits self-starters to do things as they see fit without leader interference
Primary weakness	Approach tends to stifle individual initiative	Democratic process is time consuming	Group may drift aimlessly in the absence of direction from leader

Figure **14.3** Basic Leadership Styles from the Ohio State Study

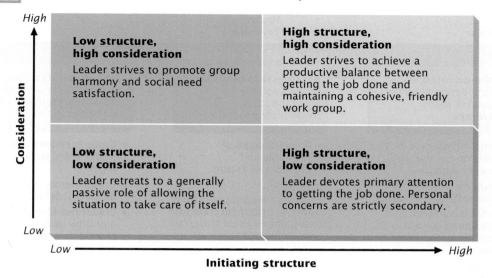

the original Ohio State approach soon appeared.[53] Leadership theorists began a search for the "one best style" of leadership. The high-structure, high-consideration style was generally hailed as the best all-around style. This "high-high" style has intuitive appeal because it embraces the best of both categories of leader behavior. But one researcher cautioned in 1966 that although there seemed to be a positive relationship between consideration and employee satisfaction, a positive link between the high-high style and work group performance had not been proved conclusively.[54]

Situational Theory

Convinced that no one best style of leadership exists, some management scholars have advocated situational or contingency thinking. Although numerous different situational-leadership theories have been developed, they all share one fundamental assumption: successful leadership occurs when the leader's style matches the situation. Situational-leadership theorists stress the need for flexibility. They reject the notion of a universally applicable style.[55] Research is under way to determine precisely when and where various styles of leadership are appropriate. Fiedler's contingency theory and the path-goal theory are introduced and discussed

here because they represent distinctly different approaches to situational leadership.

FIEDLER'S CONTINGENCY THEORY. Among the various leadership theories proposed so far, Fiedler's is the most thoroughly tested. It is the product of more than 30 years of research by Fred E. Fiedler and his associates. Fiedler's contingency theory gets its name from the the notion that a leader's performance depends on two things: (1) the degree to which the situation gives the leader enough control and influence to be successful, and (2) the degree to which the leader is motivated by being successful in completing the task *or* by developing healthy relationships with the members of his group.[56] These two motivational profiles are roughly equivalent to initiating structure (or concern for production) and consideration (or concern for people).

A consistent pattern has emerged from the many studies of effective leaders carried out by Fiedler and others.[57] As illustrated in Figure 14.4, task-motivated leaders seem to be effective in extreme situations when they have either very little control or a great deal of control over situational variables. In moderately favorable situations, however, relationship-motivated leaders tend to be more effective. Consequently, Fiedler and one of his colleagues summed up their findings by noting that "everything points to the conclusion that there is no such

Figure **14.4** | Fiedler's Contingency Theory of Leadership

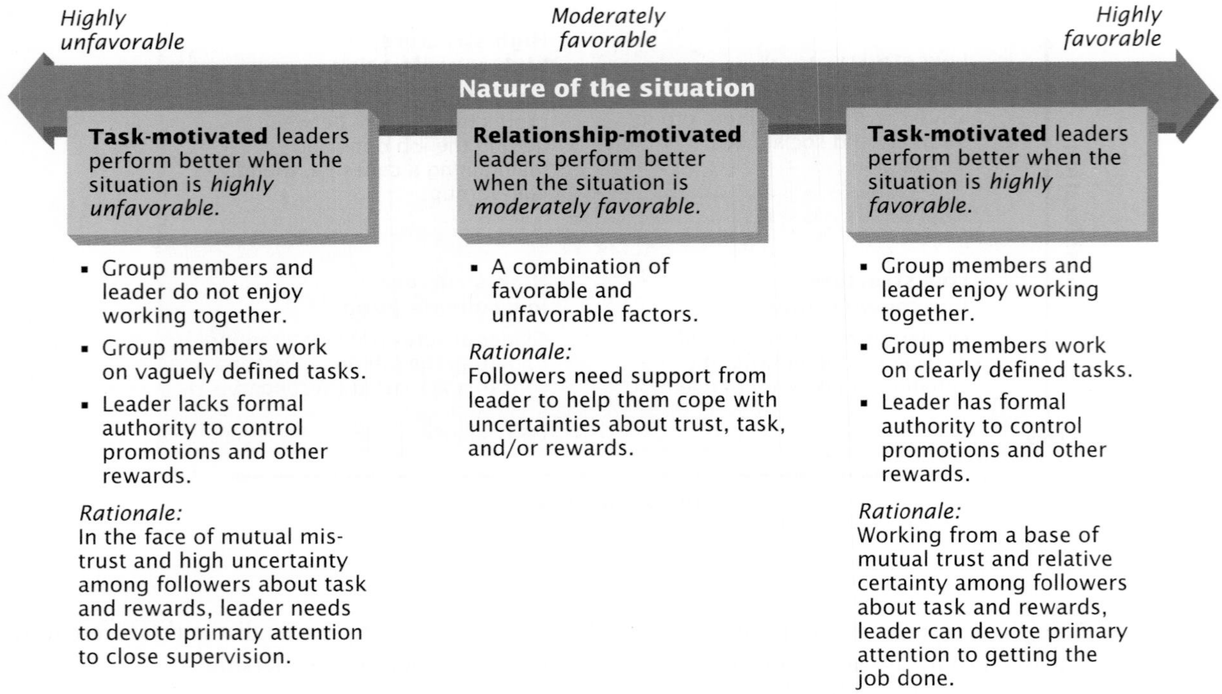

Highly unfavorable *Moderately favorable* *Highly favorable*

Nature of the situation

Task-motivated leaders perform better when the situation is *highly unfavorable.*

Relationship-motivated leaders perform better when the situation is *moderately favorable.*

Task-motivated leaders perform better when the situation is *highly favorable.*

- Group members and leader do not enjoy working together.
- Group members work on vaguely defined tasks.
- Leader lacks formal authority to control promotions and other rewards.

Rationale:
In the face of mutual mistrust and high uncertainty among followers about task and rewards, leader needs to devote primary attention to close supervision.

- A combination of favorable and unfavorable factors.

Rationale:
Followers need support from leader to help them cope with uncertainties about trust, task, and/or rewards.

- Group members and leader enjoy working together.
- Group members work on clearly defined tasks.
- Leader has formal authority to control promotions and other rewards.

Rationale:
Working from a base of mutual trust and relative certainty among followers about task and rewards, leader can devote primary attention to getting the job done.

thing as an ideal leader."[58] Instead, there are leaders, and there are situations. The challenge, according to Fiedler, is to analyze a leader's basic motivation and then match that leader with a suitable situation to form a productive combination. He believes it is more efficient to move leaders to a suitable situation than to tamper with their personalities by trying to get task-motivated leaders to become relationship-motivated leaders, or vice versa.

HOUSE'S UPDATED PATH-GOAL THEORY. Another situational-leadership theory is the path-goal theory, a derivative of expectancy motivation theory (see Chapter 12). Path-goal theory gets its name from the assumption that effective leaders can enhance employee motivation by (1) clarifying the individual's perception of work goals, (2) linking meaningful rewards to goal attainment, and (3) explaining how goals and desired rewards can be achieved. In short, leaders should motivate their followers by providing clear goals and meaningful incentives for reaching them. Path-goal theorists believe that motivation is essential to effective leadership.

According to path-goal theorists Robert J. House and Terence R. Mitchell, leaders can enhance motivation by adding to the number and types of payoffs that subordinates receive for work-goal attainment and clarifying the paths to these payoffs, both of which will also increase opportunities for personal fulfillment.[59] Best-selling author Marcus Buckingham, who has studied leaders for more than 20 years, adds that a leader's task is to make others feel more confident about the future. The more clearly a leader can articulate how the organization will overcome obstacles and beat its competitors, the more motivated, determined, and innovative the leader's followers will become.[60]

Personal characteristics of employees, environmental pressures, and demands on employees will all vary from situation to situation. Thus, House's updated path-goal model advises managers to rely contingently on eight categories of leader behavior:

- *Path-goal clarifying behaviors.* Make it clear how goal attainment is linked with meaningful rewards.

- *Achievement-oriented behaviors.* Set challenging goals, emphasize excellence, and seek continuous improvement while maintaining a high degree of confidence that employees will meet difficult challenges in a responsible manner.
- *Work facilitation behaviors.* Plan and coordinate work, make decisions, provide feedback and coaching, provide resources, remove roadblocks, and empower employees.
- *Supportive behaviors.* Be friendly and approachable, and show concern for employees' well-being.
- *Interaction facilitation behaviors.* Resolve disputes and encourage collaboration, diverse opinions, and teamwork.
- *Group decision behaviors.* Encourage group input, problem solving, and participation.
- *Networking behaviors.* Build bridges to influential people and represent the group's best interests to others.
- *Value-based behaviors.* Self-confidently formulate and passionately support a vision.[61]

The assumption that managers can and do shift situationally from one behavior pattern to another clearly sets path-goal theory apart from Fiedler's model. Recall that Fiedler claims managers cannot and do not change their basic leadership styles.

Limited research on the path-goal model has yielded mixed results.[62] One valuable contribution of path-goal theory is its identification of achievement-oriented leadership behavior. As managers deal with an increasing number of highly educated and self-motivated employees in advanced-technology industries, they will need to become skilled facilitators rather than just order givers or hand holders.

Transformational Leadership Theory

In his 1978 book *Leadership*, James McGregor Burns drew a distinction between transactional and transformational leadership. Burns characterized transformational leaders as visionaries who challenge people to achieve exceptionally high levels of morality, motivation, and performance.[63] Only transformational leaders, Burns argued, are capable of charting necessary new courses for modern organizations. Why? Because they are masters of change.[64] They can envision a better future, effectively communicate that vision, and get others to willingly make it a reality.

TRANSACTIONAL VERSUS TRANSFORMATIONAL LEADERS. Extending the work of Burns, Bernard Bass emphasized the importance of charisma in transformational leadership. Transformational leaders rely heavily on referent power. Wendy's Dave Thomas, Walmart's Sam Walton, and Southwest Airlines's Herb Kelleher exemplify charismatic leaders who engineered great success at their respective companies.[65] While acknowledging that transformational leaders exhibit widely different styles and tend to stir their fair share of controversy, Bass rounded out Burns's distinction between transactional and transformational leaders (see Table 14.4). Transactional leaders monitor people so that they do the expected, according to plan. In contrast, transformational leaders inspire people to do the unexpected, above and beyond the plan. This distinction can mean the difference between maintaining the status quo and fostering creative and productive growth.[66]

POSITIVE EVIDENCE. It is important to note that the distinction in Table 14.4 is not between bad and good leaders—both transactional and transformational leaders are needed today. This is where transformational leadership theory effectively combines the behavioral styles and situational approaches just discussed. To the traditional behavioral patterns of initiating structure and consideration have been

Vixit/Shutterstock.com

transformational leaders visionaries who challenge people to do exceptional things

Table 14.4 Transactional Versus Transformational Leaders

TRANSACTIONAL LEADER		TRANSFORMATIONAL LEADER	
Contingent reward	Contracts exchange of rewards for effort, promises rewards for good performance, recognizes accomplishments.	Charisma	Provides vision and sense of mission, instills pride, gains respect and trust.
Management by exception (active)	Watches and searches for deviations from rules and standards, takes corrective action.	Inspiration	Communicates high expectations, uses symbols to focus efforts, expresses important purposes in simple ways.
Management by exception (passive)	Intervenes only if standards are not met.	Intellectual stimulation	Promotes intelligence, rationality, and careful problem solving.
Laissez-faire	Abdicates responsibilities, avoids making decisions.	Individualized consideration	Gives personal attention, treats each employee individually, coaches, advises.

Source: Reprinted from *Organizational Dynamics* (Winter 1990). Bernard M. Bass et al., "From Transactional to Transformational Leadership: Learning to Share the Vision," Copyright 1990, with permission from Elsevier Science.

AP Photo/Michael A. Mariant

Alan Mulally had a stellar career at aircraft-maker Boeing before taking the CEO post at Ford Motor Company. Auto industry analysts bemoaned Mulally's total lack of experience in his new industry and predicted problems, yet his leadership skills later earned him CEO of the Year.

added charismatic and other behaviors.[67] Transformational leadership also needs to be situationally appropriate. Specifically, transformational leadership is needed in rapidly changing situations; transactional leaders can best handle stable situations.[68]

Available laboratory and field research evidence generally supports the transformational-leadership pattern. Followers of transformational leaders tend to perform better and to report greater satisfaction than followers of transactional leaders.[69]

Putting to Work What You've Learned by Using "Practical Intelligence" and Becoming a "Servant Leader"

Finding ways to practice leadership both on and off the job can help present and future managers develop their abilities. Serving in campus, community, or religious organizations, for example, will give you an opportunity to experiment with different leadership styles in a variety of situations. Leading effectively, like riding a bike, is learned only by doing.[70] This section offers some inspiration for polishing your leadership abilities.

PRACTICAL INTELLIGENCE. Yale University's Robert J. Sternberg believes that good leaders effectively blend three things: wisdom, intelligence, and creativity. What sort of intelligence? He explains: The ability to solve simple problems using past experience to shape and select environments is practical intelligence. These skills are used for managing oneself, others, and tasks.[71]

Because practical intelligence is a broad concept—involving both relationships and tasks—it includes and goes beyond emotional intelligence, discussed earlier. Significantly, Sternberg rejects the notion of "born leaders." Leadership is learned, he contends, because wisdom, practical intelligence, and creativity all can be learned.

Michael Dell, founder and CEO of Dell, Inc., is a true transformational leader, and he has the résumé to prove it. His vision, charisma, and communication skills earned him numerous accolades and have made him one of the richest men in the world.

Robert Galbraith/Reuters/Landov

SERVANT LEADERS. In addition to a working knowledge of the various leadership theories we have discussed in this chapter, aspiring leaders need a philosophical anchor point. This is where Robert K. Greenleaf's philosophy of the *servant leader* enters the picture as an instructive and inspiring springboard. The servant leader is an ethical person who puts *others*—not herself or himself—in the foreground. As a devout Quaker with years of real-world experience at AT&T, Greenleaf wove humility and a genuine concern for the whole person into his philosophy of leadership.[72] He portrayed the servant leader as one who, in addition to putting others first, has a clear sense of purpose in life, is a good listener, is trustworthy, and accepts others at face value. The servant leader tries to improve the world, first and foremost, through *self*-improvement. One person who embodied the servant leader philosophy was John Wooden, who coached the UCLA men's basketball team to an astounding ten national championships: "The great thing about Coach Wooden is that he is what he is," former player Bill Walton said prior to his coach's death at age 99 in 2010. He went on to describe Wooden as unpretentious, humble, and generous, with a desire to contribute to other people's success.[73] (See Ethics: Character, Courage, and Values.)

14d
Gender-Bender Mentoring

Procter & Gamble, Cincinnati, Ohio:

The consumer-products giant pairs junior female employees with a senior manager for reverse mentoring to help the mostly male higher-ups understand the issues women face.

QUESTION: What important lessons about today's work-life realities can young women teach older male bosses?

Source: Robert Levering and Milton Moskowitz, "The 100 Best Companies to Work For," *Fortune* (January 24, 2005): 74.

MENTORING

In spite of mountains of leadership research, much remains to be learned about why some people end up being good leaders whereas many others do not.[74] One thing is clear, though: mentors can make an important difference. Take, for example, the case

ETHICS: Character, Courage, and Values

Lola Gonzalez Laid Herself Off to Help Her Employees Keep Their Jobs

Like countless small-business owners, Lola Gonzalez agonizingly resolved to trim her firm's nine-person staff when the economic recovery began to sputter . . . [in early 2010].

Unlike other entrepreneurs, she picked an unlikely employee to lay off: herself.

The owner of Accurate Background Check in Ocala, Fla., says she couldn't bear to fire employees who have worked there for years. So she stopped paying herself a six-figure salary and got a job for less than half the pay as a social worker.

"How could you let somebody go that you trusted and that trusted you?" says Gonzalez, 51, who's still a social worker. . . .

Employees initially froze in fear [during her announcement], then erupted in laughter. Until they realized she was serious. . . .

Besides putting in a 40-hour week, . . . Gonzalez gets twice-weekly phone updates on goings-on at her business and still does certain background checks herself without getting paid.

For Discussion: Does Lola Gonzalez deserve to be called a servant leader? Explain.

Source: Excerpted from Paul Davidson, "How a Boss Saved Jobs: She Laid Herself Off," *USA Today* (November 26, 2010): 1B.

Anyone who has had a mentor knows how valuable the experience can be for all involved.

Alexander Raths/Shutterstock.Com

of Christine Day, CEO of the yoga apparel company Lululemon Athletica. Back when she worked in strategic planning at Starbucks, the senior VP of retail in North America, Bruce Craig, advised her to stop limiting herself to support roles, to become more visible, and to learn to accept critical feedback. After acting on his advice, Day went on to take the top position at Starbucks Asia Pacific,[75] which no doubt became a stepping stone to her current position. Let us explore this interesting process whereby leadership skills are acquired by exposure to role models and coaching.

Learning from a Mentor

The many obstacles and barriers blocking the way to successful leadership make it easy to understand why there is no simple formula for developing leaders. Abraham Zaleznik, the respected sociologist mentioned earlier, insisted that leaders must be nurtured under the wise tutelage of a mentor. A **mentor** is an individual who systematically develops another person's abilities through intensive tutoring, coaching, and guidance.[76] Some risks are involved for the mentor, however. As Zaleznik explained, mentors bet on the talent they perceive in people and can become emotionally invested in those people. Sometimes, the risks do not pay off, but the willingness to take risks is necessary for developing future leaders.[77]

A survey of 246 health care industry managers found higher satisfaction, greater recognition, and more promotion opportunities among managers with mentors than among those without.[78] Additionally, a study of turnover among more than 15,000 employees led the researchers to conclude, "People with mentors are twice as likely to stay as those without."[79] A recent survey of 3,417 managers and emerging leaders (57 percent women) by the Center for Creative Leadership revealed that 88 percent of those surveyed believe a mentor helps advance a person's career. They prefer a senior colleague (24 percent), an expert in the discipline (17 percent), or a chosen coach (16 percent).[80]

Dynamics of Mentoring

According to Kathy Kram, who conducted intensive biographical interviews with both members in 18 different senior manager–junior manager mentor relationships, mentoring fulfills two important functions: (1) a career enhancement function and (2) a psychological and social support function (see Table 14.5). Mentor relationships were found to average about five years in length.[81] Thus, a manager might have a series of mentors during the course of an organizational career. Also, as explained more recently by a team of researchers, there is a growing need for having more than one mentor at a time. Given the dynamic nature of global business, with its constantly changing technology and structures, it's nearly impossible to find a single mentor who possesses all of the knowledge required. But with multiple mentors working with multiple employees, an organization can turn these knowledgeable, well-developed people into a source of competitive advantage.[82]

Importantly, the junior member of a mentor relationship is not the only one to benefit. Mentors

Table **14.5**	Mentors Serve Two Important Functions	

CAREER FUNCTIONS*	PSYCHOSOCIAL FUNCTIONS**
Sponsorship	Role modeling
Exposure and visibility	Acceptance and confirmation
Coaching	Counseling
Protection	Friendship
Challenging assignments	

Source: Kathy E. Kram, "Phases of the Mentor Relationship," *Academy of Management Journal,* 26 (December 1983): 614 (Exhibit 1). Reprinted by permission.

*Career functions are those aspects of the relationship that primarily enhance career advancement.

**Psychosocial functions are those aspects of the relationship that primarily enhance a sense of competence, clarity of identity, and effectiveness in the managerial role.

often derive great intrinsic pleasure from seeing their protégés move up through the ranks and conquer difficult challenges. Mentors can freshen their technical knowledge and deepen their appreciation of diversity when coaching new talent. Moreover, by passing along their values and their technical and leadership skills to promising junior managers, mentors can wield considerable influence and power.[83]

New Approaches to Mentoring

Experts are divided on whether mentoring should be a formal or informal process. Major accounting firm KPMG prefers a carefully structured, two-pronged approach. The firm has developed a Web site to ensure that all junior staff members have mentors and all managers have protégés, and it uses social activities such as lunches and sporting events to encourage additional networking.[84]

Meanwhile, research suggests that informal relationships that arise naturally work better than formal structured pairings.[85] As the following list shows, the terms *informality* and *flexibility* best describe emerging trends in mentoring:

- *Speed mentoring.* In a timed event, college students rotate through brief meetings with experts to network and receive career coaching.
- *Informal mentoring:* New employees are encouraged to find a compatible mentor within the organization.
- *Reverse mentoring.* Senior executives gain technical and diversity exposure when paired formally or informally with younger employees.
- *Group mentoring.* Self-organizing social media and/or face-to-face groups of employees tackle topics and problems.
- *Anonymous mentoring.* Online exchanges take place between employees and outside consultants matched though background highlights and psychological testing.
- *Free-form mentoring.* For example, in 2009 IBM empowered employees to contact colleagues across the globe for advice on topics such as innovation and career paths.[86]

Traditional and modern approaches to mentoring can be blended to suit the situation.

BEHAVIOR MODIFICATION

This last approach to influencing behavior can be traced to two psychologists, John B. Watson and Edward L. Thorndike, who did their work in the early twentieth century. From Watson came the advice to concentrate on observable behavior. Accordingly, the philosophy of behaviorism maintains that observable behavior is more important than hypothetical inner states such as needs, motives, and expectations.[87] From Thorndike came an appreciation of the way in which consequences control behavior. According to Thorndike's classic law of effect, favorable consequences encourage behavior, whereas unfavorable consequences discourage behavior.[88] However, it remained for B. F. Skinner, the late Harvard psychologist, to integrate Watson's and Thorndike's contributions into a precise technology of behavior change.

behaviorism belief that observable behavior is more important than inner states

What Is Behavior Modification?

Skinner was the father of *operant conditioning*, the study of how behavior is controlled by the surrounding environment.[89] Although some find Skinner's substitution of environmental control for self-control repulsive and dehumanizing,[90] few deny that operant conditioning actually occurs. Indeed, much of our behavior is the product of environmental shaping. Rather, the debate centers on whether or not natural shaping processes should be systematically managed to alter the course of everyday behavior.[91] Advocates of behavior modification in the workplace believe they should be.[92]

Behavior modification is the practical application of Skinnerian operant-conditioning techniques to everyday behavior problems. Behavior modification (B. Mod.) involves systematically managing environmental factors to get people to do the right things more often and the wrong things less often. This is accomplished by managing the antecedents and/or consequences of observable behavior.

Managing Antecedents

An antecedent is an environmental cue that prompts an individual to behave in a given manner. Antecedents do not automatically *cause* the person to behave in a predictable manner, as a hot stove causes you to withdraw your hand reflexively when you touch it. Rather, we learn through experience to interpret antecedents as signals telling us it is time to behave in a certain way if we are to get what we want or to avoid what we do not want. This process is sometimes referred to as *cue control*. Domino's Pizza Inc., for example, exhibits posters showing helpful, work-related ideas and reminders, such as how to present the perfect pizza.[93]

Although it is often overlooked, the management of antecedents is a practical and simple way of encouraging good performance. As Table 14.6 indicates, there are two ways to manage antecedents. Barriers can be removed, and helpful aids can be offered. These steps ensure that the path to good performance is clearly marked and free of obstacles (which meshes with the path-goal theory of leadership).

Table 14.6 | Managing Antecedents

BARRIERS: REMOVE BARIERS THAT PREVENT OR HINDER THE COMPLETION OF A GOOD JOB. FOR EXAMPLE:	AIDS: PROVIDE HELPFUL AIDS THAT ENHANCE THE OPPORTUNITY TO DO A GOOD JOB. FOR EXAMPLE:
Unrealistic objectives, plans, schedules, or deadlines	Challenging yet attainable objectives
Uncooperative or distracting coworkers	Clear and realistic plans
Training deficiencies	Understandable instructions
Contradictory or confusing rules	Constructive suggestions, hints, or tips
Inadequate or inappropriate tools	Clear and generally acceptable work rules
Conflicting orders from two or more managers	Realistic schedules and deadlines
	Friendly reminders
	Posters or signs with helpful tips
	Easy-to-use forms
	Nonthreatening questions about progress
	User-friendly computer software and hardware

behavior modification systematic management of the antecedents and consequences of behavior | antecedent an environmental cue for a specific behavior

Managing Consequences

Managing the consequences of job performance is more complex than dealing strictly with antecedents, because there are four different classes of consequences. Each type of consequence involves a different process. Positive reinforcement and negative reinforcement both encourage behavior, but they do so in different ways. Extinction and punishment discourage behavior but, again, in different ways. These four terms have precise meanings that are often confused by casual observers.

POSITIVE REINFORCEMENT. Positive reinforcement encourages a specific behavior by immediately following it with a consequence the individual finds pleasing. For example, a machine operator who maintains a clean work area because he or she is praised for doing so has responded to positive reinforcement. As the term implies, positive reinforcement reinforces or builds behavior in a positive way.

NEGATIVE REINFORCEMENT. *Negative reinforcement* encourages a specific behavior by immediately withdrawing or terminating something a particular person finds displeasing. Children learn the power of negative reinforcement early in life when they discover that the quickest way to get something is to cry and scream until their parents give them what they want. In effect, the parents are negatively reinforced for complying with the child's demand by the termination of the crying and screaming. In other words, the termination or withdrawal of an undesirable state of affairs (for example, the threat of being fired) has an incentive effect. In a social context, negative reinforcement amounts to blackmail. "Do what I want, or I will continue to make your life miserable" are the bywords of the person who relies on negative reinforcement to influence behavior.

EXTINCTION. Through *extinction*, a specific behavior is discouraged by ignoring it. For example, managers sometimes find that the best way to keep employees from asking redundant questions is simply not to answer them. Just as a plant will wither and die without water, behavior will fade away without occasional reinforcement.

PUNISHMENT. *Punishment* discourages a specific behavior by the immediate presentation of an undesirable consequence or the immediate removal of something desirable. For example, a manager may punish a tardy employee by either assigning the individual to a dirty job or docking the individual's pay.

It is important to remember that positive and negative reinforcement, extinction, and punishment all entail the manipulation of the *immediate* or *direct* consequences of a desired or undesired behavior. If action is taken before the behavior, behavior control is unlikely. For instance, if a manager gives an employee a cash bonus *before* a difficult task is completed, the probability of the task being completed declines because the incentive effect has been removed. In regard to managing consequences, behavior modification works only when there is a contingent ("if…then") relationship between a specific behavior and a given consequence.

Positively Reinforce What Is Right About Job Performance (the Art of "Bucket Filling")

Proponents of behavior modification prefer to build up desirable behaviors rather than tearing down undesirable ones. Every undesirable behavior has a desirable counterpart that can be reinforced. For example, someone who comes in late once a week actually comes in on time four days a week. To encourage productive behaviors, managers are advised to focus on the positive aspects of job performance when managing consequences. Thus, positive reinforcement is the preferred consequence strategy.[94] This positive approach was effectively taken to heart by Preston Trucking, a Maryland shipping company, when managers decided to resolve a long-standing conflict with its truck drivers by instituting the Four-to-One Rule: For every criticism about a driver, a manager had to give four compliments. The drivers were skeptical at first, but eventually realized it signaled a shift to genuinely supportive supervision.[95]

This positive approach to modifying behavior is the central theme in the long-standing best-seller *The One Minute Manager,* which extols the virtues of "catching people doing something *right!*"[96] Positive reinforcement also is the core message in Tom Rath and Donald O. Clifton's best-selling book *How Full Is Your Bucket? Positive Strategies for Work and Life.* Rath and his now-deceased grandfather use the

positive reinforcement encouraging a behavior by providing a pleasing consequence

Jon Feingersh/Jupiter Images

Public positive reinforcement can have a powerful role modeling effect when skillfully managed. This employee is flattered by a handsome plaque and applause from her coworkers for a job well done

metaphor of a *bucket* to represent how a person feels and acts. One's bucket is filled by praise and other forms of positive reinforcement. Criticism and negativity empty one's bucket. On the basis of their Gallup surveys of a worldwide sampling of over 4 million employees, Rath and Clifton claim that "regular recognition and praise" boost productivity and satisfaction while reducing accidents and turnover. But they caution managers to use "positive interactions" to an appropriate extent—not too little, not too much. Citing recent research evidence, they recommend a ratio of positive to negative interactions (both at work and at home) of between 3 to 1 and 13 to 1. Less than a 3-to-1 ratio is flirting with corrosive negativity. A ratio greater than 13 to 1 communicates false optimism and lacks realism. Their conclusion: ". . . most of us don't have to worry about breaking the upper limit. The positive-to-negative ratios in most organizations are woefully inadequate and leave substantial room for improvement."[97]

14e
It's Nice to Be Appreciated

Last year Jennifer Lepird spent several weeks working long hours on a big deal. The 39-year-old Tucson-based human resources staffer at Intuit was part of a fast-moving acquisition team: Intuit was buying competitor Paycycle, and her job was to integrate its employees into Intuit's salary structure. She stayed up all night perfecting her spreadsheets as the deal was about to close.

Her immediate reward for that grueling overtime assignment? An e-mail from the acquisition team manager with a gift certificate worth a few hundred bucks. And she was thrilled. "The fact that somebody took the time to recognize the effort," she says, "made the long hours just melt away."

QUESTIONS: Given the proven motivational power of timely and well-deserved recognition, why do so many managers fall short in this regard? What can be done to create an organizational "culture of appreciation"?

Source: Telis Demos, "Motivate Without Spending Millions," *Fortune* (April 12, 2010): 37–38.

Schedule Positive Reinforcement Appropriately

Both the type and the timing of consequences are important in successful B. Mod. When a productive behavior is first tried out by an employee, a continuous schedule of reinforcement is appropriate. Under continuous reinforcement, every instance of the desired behavior is reinforced. For example, a bank manager who is training a new loan officer to handle a difficult type of account should praise the loan officer after every successful transaction until the behavior is firmly established. After the loan officer is able to handle the transaction, the bank manager can switch to a schedule of intermittent reinforcement.

As the term implies, intermittent reinforcement calls for reinforcing some, rather than all, of the desired responses.

The more unpredictable the payoff schedule is, the better the results will be. One way to appreciate the power of intermittent reinforcement is to think of the enthusiasm with which people play slot machines; these gambling devices pay off on an unpredictable intermittent schedule. In the same way, occasional reinforcement of established productive behaviors with meaningful positive consequences is an extremely effective management technique.[98]

(Now go do something nice for yourself as positive reinforcement for reading this chapter.)

---

continuous reinforcement rewarding every instance of a behavior | *intermittent reinforcement rewarding some, but not all, instances of a behavior*

SUMMARY

1. Influence is fundamental to management because individuals must be influenced to pursue collective objectives. Researchers have identified eight generic influence tactics used on the job: consultation (seeking participation of others), rational persuasion (reasoning with logic), inspirational appeals (appealing to someone's values or ideals), ingratiating tactics (using flattery or humility prior to a request), coalition tactics (seeking help in persuading others), pressure tactics (using intimidation, demands, or threats), upward appeals (seeking the support of higher management), and exchange tactics (trading favors).

2. The five basic types of power are reward, coercive, legitimate, referent, and expert power. Empowerment cannot work without a supporting situation, which may include a skilled individual, an organizational culture of empowerment, an emotionally mature individual with a well-developed character, and empowerment opportunities such as delegation, participation, and self-managed teams.

3. Formal leadership consists of influencing relevant others to voluntarily pursue organizational objectives. Informal leadership can work for or against the organization. Leadership theory has evolved through four major stages: trait theory, behavioral styles theory, situational theory, and transformational theory. A promising trait approach is based on Goleman's four dimensions of emotional intelligence: self-awareness, self-management, social awareness, and relationship management.

4. Researchers who differentiated among authoritarian, democratic, and laissez-faire leadership styles concentrated on leader behavior rather than personality traits. Leadership studies at Ohio State University isolated four styles of leadership based on two categories of leader behavior: initiating structure and consideration. A balanced high-structure, high-consideration style was recommended. According to Blake and his colleagues, a 9,9 style (high concern for both production and people) is the best overall style because it emphasizes teamwork.

5. Situational-leadership theorists believe there is no single best leadership style; rather, different situations require different styles. Many years of study led Fiedler to conclude that task-motivated leaders are more effective in either very favorable or very unfavorable situations, whereas relationship-motivated leaders are better suited to moderately favorable situations. The favorableness of a situation is dictated by the degree of the leader's control and influence in getting the job done. Path-goal leadership theory, an expectancy perspective, assumes that leaders are effective to the extent that they can motivate followers by clarifying goals and clearing the paths to achieving those goals and valued rewards. Unlike Fiedler, path-goal theorists believe that managers can and should adapt their leadership behavior to the situation.

6. In contrast to transactional leaders who maintain the status quo, transformational leaders are visionary, charismatic leaders dedicated to change. Greenleaf's philosophy of the servant leader helps aspiring leaders integrate what they have learned about leadership. The servant leader is motivated to serve rather than lead. Clear goals, trust, good listening skills, positive feedback, foresight, and self-development are the characteristics of a servant leader.

7. Mentors help develop less experienced people by fulfilling career and psychosocial functions. Mentors engage in intensive tutoring, coaching, and guiding. Mentors are role models for aspiring leaders. Six emerging trends in mentoring are speed mentoring, informal mentoring, reverse mentoring, group mentoring, anonymous mentoring, and free-form mentoring.

8. Behavior modification (B. Mod.) is the practical application of Skinner's operant conditioning principles. B. Mod. involves managing antecedents (removing barriers and providing helpful aids) and consequences to strengthen desirable behavior and weaken undesirable behavior. Proponents of B. Mod. prefer to shape behavior through positive reinforcement rather than negative reinforcement, extinction, and punishment. Continuous reinforcement is recommended for new behavior and intermittent reinforcement for established behavior.

TERMS TO UNDERSTAND

Influence, p. 388
Power, p. 391
Reward power, p. 392
Coercive power, p. 392
Legitimate power, p. 392
Referent power, p. 392
Expert power, p. 392

Empowerment, p. 393
Leadership, p. 394
Formal leadership, p. 394
Informal leadership, p. 394
Emotional intelligence, p. 396
Transformational leaders, p. 401
Mentor, p. 405

Behaviorism, p. 406
Behavior modification, p. 407
Antecedent, p. 407
Positive reinforcement, p. 408
Continuous reinforcement, p. 410
Intermittent reinforcement, p. 410

ACTION LEARNING EXERCISE

WHAT IS YOUR EMOTIONAL INTELLIGENCE (EQ)?[99]

Instructions: Evaluate each statement about your emotional intelligence on a scale of 1 = "not at all like me" to 10 = "very much like me." Try to be objective by viewing yourself through the eyes of key people in your life, such as family members, close friends, coworkers, and classmates. (*Note:* This instrument is for instructional purposes only because it was derived from a 25-item survey of unknown validity.)

_____   1. I usually stay composed, positive, and unflappable in trying situations.

_____   2. I am able to admit my own mistakes.

_____   3. I usually or always meet commitments and keep promises.

_____   4. I hold myself accountable for meeting my goals.

_____   5. I can smoothly handle multiple demands and changing priorities.

_____   6. Obstacles and setbacks may delay me a little, but they don't stop me.

_____   7. I seek fresh perspectives, even if that means trying something totally new.

_____   8. My impulses or distressing emotions don't often get the best of me at work.

_____   9. I usually don't attribute setbacks to a personal flaw (mine or somebody else's).

_____ 10. I operate from an expectation of success rather than from a fear of failure.

Total = _____

Interpretation: A score below 70 indicates a need for improvement. With sincere effort, one's emotional intelligence can be improved. It is part of a natural process of "growing up" and becoming mature in challenging social situations. People with low EQ scores are like porcupines—they're hard to hug.

FOR CONSIDERATION/DISCUSSION

1. What do you like or dislike about the concept of emotional intelligence?

2. Have you ever worked with or for someone who had high emotional intelligence? If so, describe that person and rate her or his effectiveness. Do the same for someone with low emotional intelligence.

3. What, if any, connection do you see between the concepts of emotional intelligence and servant leader? Explain.

4. How could you improve your emotional intelligence, in terms of the items on this test?

ETHICS EXERCISE

 DO THE RIGHT THING

SOME TRUTH ABOUT LYING

The study: [Columbia University Graduate School of Business professor] Dana Carney divided research subjects into two groups: bosses and employees. Bosses got larger offices and more power; they were asked, for instance, to assign employees' salaries. Half of all subjects were instructed by a computer to steal a $100 bill. If they could convince an interviewer they hadn't taken it, they could keep it. The other subjects were questioned as well. In the interviews, lying bosses displayed fewer involuntary signs of dishonesty and stress. On all measures, liars with power were hard to distinguish from subjects telling the truth.

The finding: A sense of power buffers individuals from the stress of lying and increases their ability to deceive others.

Source: Excerpted from Dana Carney, "Powerful People Are Better Liars," *Harvard Business Review*, 88 (May 2010): 32.

What are the ethical implications of the following interpretations?

1. It is always wrong to tell a lie, especially for managers and others in positions of authority. Lying is a bad habit and liars can't be trusted. If this is your belief, how faithfully do you adhere to it?

2. People in positions of power often have access to privileged information and cannot tell everyone everything they know. Lying either by commission (altering the facts) or omission (failing to reveal relevant facts) sometimes is a necessary evil when trying to get the job done in organizations.

3. Lying is a matter of degree, ranging from harmless little white lies ("Your new outfit makes you look thinner.") to deceitful bold-face lies ("My dog ate my research project."). Little white lies are okay as long as they don't hurt anyone, or maybe even help someone feel better. Do small lies generally lead to bigger lies? Explain.

4. Your own ethical interpretation?

MANAGERS-IN-ACTION VIDEO CASE STUDY

GREENSBURG, KANSAS

Leadership

Steve Hewitt, the Greensburg city manager, was faced with an immediate crisis following the tornado that destroyed his town. Beyond the first few days of managing urgent needs such as safety, power, and water, Hewitt faced the challenge of what to do next in the rebuilding effort. In this video, you will hear from several city officials, including the former mayor who resigned in the midst of the crisis. The impact of politics, power, and various leadership styles is revealed as Greensburg emerges from this natural disaster.

For more information about Greensburg, visit the Greensburg GreenTown Web site: http://www.greensburggreentown.org.

Before watching the video, answer the following questions:

1. What is the difference between a leader and a manager?

2. What is emotional intelligence and why is it important for leaders?

3. What are the essential qualities and characteristics of an effective leader?

After watching the video, answer the following questions:

4. Who revealed aspects of emotional intelligence in this video? What aspects were shown?

5. Why is Steve Hewitt's leadership style well suited to the rebuilding effort?

6. Describe Hewitt's approach to empowerment and explain why he was successful in empowering his employees.

CLOSING CASE

LEADERSHIP DEVELOPMENT GE-STYLE

As companies evolve, so do their leadership philosophies. And General Electric's John F. Welch Leadership Center at Crotonville has had more time to evolve than any other corporate university, as . . . [2006 marked] its 50th anniversary. In that half century, the center, in Ossining, N.Y., 30 miles outside of Manhattan, has turned out internal and external leaders ready to take on global-scale business challenges—and there's no sign of a slowdown.

"Crotonville is embedded in the GE culture and the GE values," GE Chief Learning Officer Bob Corcoran says. "All of our major change initiatives—cultural change and business change processes—have either originated at Crotonville as a result of best practice assessments and evaluations or executive leadership summits, or they have been broadcast, trained, amplified or rolled out with Crotonville as the change agent."

Corcoran himself is a 27-year GE veteran in human resources and executive leadership, and holds the distinction of being the first CLO and head of Crotonville who is a graduate of all of the executive development programs. . . .

Nominated executives stay in the Residence Building, a 190-bed facility where each room is a carbon copy of the next, reinforcing the level playing field Corcoran says he wants all attendees to be playing on. "Every person who comes here wears a little nametag; it doesn't say you're the [head] of health care, it doesn't say you're a junior finance accountant. It says your name and your business." He says employees are there to discuss values, processes and change initiatives, regardless of position. "It really is a place that fundamentally reinforces the concepts and principles of a meritocracy."

And while students are there, they'll be treated to lectures from not only leadership experts in the academic world (the late Peter Drucker taught there), but also GE leaders. In 25 years, [former CEO Jack] Welch and current Chairman and CEO Jeffrey Immelt have spoken at 329 of the last 330 executive-level courses at the facility, which is 60 miles from the GE headquarters in Fairfield, Conn. Welch, who missed one when he had heart bypass surgery, was known to speak up to six hours to students.

But lest one think taking leadership courses at Crotonville is a cushy reward for good behavior or a golf-centric retreat, Corcoran stresses that students, who represent each GE business, are there to work. "Our classes don't just go 8 to 5," he says, explaining [that] project work, evening lectures and roundtable discussions take up participants' time.

In the first of the three progressive courses, Manager Development Course (MDC), 75 to

80 students compete in an artificial intelligence marketplace via computer simulation following lectures that teach them business management basics. Instructors, who Corcoran says are two-thirds internal, one-third external, stress both theory and practical application. The format of the course, given eight times a year, Corcoran explains, is "concept, application, practice." And although it's the first of the top three courses, a GE executive won't be eligible for the program until 10 to 20 years into his or her career.

In the second and third courses, Business Manager Course (BMC) and Executive Development Course (EDC), respectively, not only do participants get assigned a real problem GE is facing, but also must present their findings to Immelt, who hand selects the problem. In BMC, given three times a year to 50 to 60 participants who are eligible about three to four years after MDC, the focus is on assessing and evaluating change with action-learning techniques, Corcoran says. The program typically involves a week of world travel, as many of the problems students are given hinge on staying competitive in a global market. The students conduct interviews and merge that into a recommendation for Immelt and his team.

EDC, meanwhile, focuses on changing GE's culture. The annual course is given to 35 individuals who are among the top 300 in the company and could potentially become one of the 170 GE corporate officers. "They get big issues to deal with," Corcoran says. There are guest lecturers, and students wrestle with broad-based solutions. Lectures are given in "The Pit" at Crotonville, which is a 100-seat amphitheater that Corcoran says truly puts the speaker in the spotlight. "When lecturers are there at the bottom, our classes don't sit quietly and say, 'Thank you very much,' and then talk badly about them when they leave. They smack them around live, and it doesn't matter if it's a vice president or not of GE." Participants also present their findings to Immelt and corporate officers.

While all this learning is happening under Immelt's scrutiny, Corcoran stresses that participants' experiences, successes and failures are not reported to supervisors. "We create a very, very safe learning environment. We fundamentally said Crotonville is a safe haven," Corcoran says. "You have to be free to make mistakes. The reality is that in the real world, in real life when you're not in the classroom, people learn most when they make mistakes. We encourage people to take risks; we encourage them to try."

There is no grading process during the courses, Corcoran says, stressing that it's more important that students take the lessons learned and apply [them] and create value in their jobs. "Potential's good, but results are better."

For Discussion

1. Referring to the section titled "Learning to Manage" in Chapter 1, do you think this is an effective way to teach leadership? Explain.

2. Is GE's Crotonville a better learning environment than the typical college classroom? Why or why not?

3. If you were a GE employee and were nominated to attend Crotonville, what would you look forward to the most (and what would you fear the most) about the experience? Explain.

4. How would you integrate a formal mentoring program with the Crotonville coursework?

5. All things considered, can leadership be taught or do some people just naturally have what it takes? Explain.

Source: Excerpted from Jacqueline Durett, "GE Hones Its Leaders at Crotonville," *Training*, 42 (May 2006): 25–27. Reprinted by permission of Billboard.

15

Change, Conflict, and Negotiation

Comstock Images/Jupiter Images

"Change begets conflict, conflict begets change."[1]

—DEAN TJOSVOLD

The Changing Workplace

IN SEARCH OF THE PAPERLESS OFFICE—PART 1

Although the promise of the paperless office has long eluded businesses, David Zugheri, co-founder of First Houston Mortgage, a mortgage bank based in Texas, really wanted to take a stab at it. Three years ago, his 125 employees were using about a million sheets of paper a year. The files for each of First Houston's 1,500 customers usually contained up to 250 pages, including applications, credit reports, tax returns, pay stubs, and other documents. And employees would often make two or three hard copies of each file to send to underwriters, title companies, and other parties involved in the mortgage approval process. Plus, because most of the documents contained sensitive customer information, First Houston was shelling out $550 a month to a shredding service.

Zugheri decided to buy a few multipage scanners, and one night, after all his workers had gone, he went around the office and unplugged every printer. The next morning, at 8 a.m., he announced a new rule: no paper. All documents would be scanned and stored digitally. An uproar ensued. Two employees threatened to quit. By noon, Zugheri had plugged the printers back in. "After playing a human punching bag for four hours, I realized that we couldn't just change our technology overnight," he says.

Source: Excerpted from Darren Dahl, "Trust Me: You're Gonna Love This—Getting Employees to Embrace New Technology," *Inc.*, 30 (November 2008): 41.

- **Identify** and **describe** four types of organizational change, according to the Nadler-Tushman model.
- **Explain** how people tend to respond differently to changes they like and those they dislike.
- **List** at least six reasons why employees resist change, and **discuss** what management can do about resistance to change.
- **Describe** how the unfreezing-change-refreezing metaphor applies to organization development (OD).
- **Describe** tempered radicals, and **identify** the 5Ps in the checklist for grassroots change agents.
- **Contrast** the competitive and cooperative conflict styles.
- **Identify** and **describe** five conflict resolution techniques.
- **Identify** and **describe** the elements of effective negotiation, and explain the advantage of added value negotiating (AVN).

OBJECTIVES

Being competitive in today's fast-paced global economy means managers must be able to understand and manage constant change. High among the top ten challenges for CEOs, according to a worldwide survey, was "speed, flexibility, and adaptability to change."[2] Case in point: Among the 200 product variations PepsiCo adds to its brands each year, it develops many products that appeal to ethnic tastes and health-conscious consumers.[3] In a recent *Fortune* magazine Q&A, PepsiCo's CEO Indra Nooyi commented that a strong manager must be willing to "lift and shift," meaning picking up ideas that are working in other places and adapting them to fit the manager's product, strategy, or region.[4]

As David Zugheri in the opening case now knows, rapid revolutionary changes and more deliberate evolutionary changes need to be balanced so that people both inside and outside the organization can handle them.[5] Also, as Xerox's recently retired CEO Anne Mulcahy learned from the school of hard knocks, it helps to be proactive rather than reactive. She told an interviewer, "It's hard to know exactly when change is needed, but better early than late."[6] The purpose of this chapter, then, is to explore the dynamics of organizational change and its natural by-product, conflict. We discuss change from organizational and individual perspectives, address resistance to change, and examine how to make change happen. We then consider the nature and management of conflict and conclude with a discussion of negotiation.

CHANGE: ORGANIZATIONAL AND INDIVIDUAL PERSPECTIVES

Researchers report a constant tension between opposing forces for stability and change in today's work organizations.[7] A productive balance is required. Too much stability and organizational decline begins. Too much change and the mission blurs and employees burn out. Today's managers need a robust set of concepts and skills to juggle stability and change. Let us tackle this major challenge for managers by looking at four types of organizational change and also at how individuals tend to respond to significant

changes. These twin perspectives are important because organizational changes unavoidably have personal impacts.

Types of Organizational Change

Consultant David A. Nadler and management professor Michael L. Tushman together developed an instructive typology of organizational change (see Figure 15.1). On the vertical axis of their model, change is characterized as either anticipatory or reactive. Anticipatory changes are any systematically planned changes intended to take advantage of expected situations. By contrast, reactive changes are those necessitated by unexpected environmental events or pressures. The horizontal axis deals with the scope of a particular change, either incremental or strategic. Incremental changes involve subsystem adjustments needed to keep the organization on its chosen path. Strategic changes alter the overall shape or direction of the organization. For instance, adding a night shift to meet unexpectedly high demand for the company's product is an incremental change. Switching from building houses to building high-rise apartment complexes would be a strategic change. Four resulting types of organizational change in the Nadler-Tushman model are tuning, adaptation, re-orientation, and re-creation.[8] These types of organizational changes—listed here and discussed in order of increasing complexity, intensity, and risk—require a closer look.

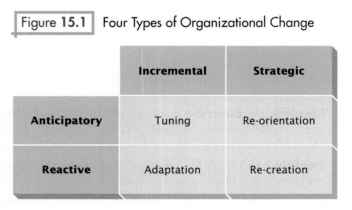

Figure 15.1 Four Types of Organizational Change

	Incremental	**Strategic**
Anticipatory	Tuning	Re-orientation
Reactive	Adaptation	Re-creation

Source: David A. Nadler and Michael L. Tushman, "Beyond the Charismatic Leader: Leadership and Organizational Change." Copyright ©1990 by the Regents of the University of California. Reprinted from the *California Management Review*, vol. 32, no. 2. By permission of the Regents. All rights reserved.

anticipatory changes planned changes based on expected situations | reactive changes changes made in response to unexpected situations | incremental changes subsystem adjustments required to keep the organization on course | strategic changes altering the overall shape or direction of the organization

TUNING. Tuning is the most common, least intense, and least risky type of change. Other names for it include preventive maintenance and the Japanese concept of *kaizen* (continuous improvement). The key to effective tuning is to actively anticipate and avoid problems rather than passively waiting for things to go wrong before taking action. For example, Du Pont tuned its marketing efforts by developing an Adopt-a-Customer program. The program lets blue-collar employees meet with customers to determine their needs and then represent the customers at the factory level.[9] This is a refreshing alternative to the traditional practice of waiting for customer complaints and only then trying to figure out how to fix them.

ADAPTATION. Like tuning, adaptation involves incremental changes. But this time, the changes are in reaction to external problems, events, or pressures. A common form of adaptation is updating product lines to keep up with changing consumer tastes and the competition. For example, consider how McDonald's is branching out into beverages, which is redefining consumers' habits of stopping in for something to drink. The fast food leader is now going head-to-head with convenience stores, supermarkets, and chains like Starbucks.[10] Care for a McDonald's smoothie or frappé?

RE-ORIENTATION. This type of change is anticipatory and strategic in scope. Nadler and Tushman call re-orientation "frame bending" because the organization is significantly redirected. Significantly, there is not a complete break with the organization's past. Consider this example of frame bending at Cisco Systems, the leading maker of Internet gear, after it had reported a 21 percent jump in sales. The increase came from Cisco's acquisition of Scientific Atlanta, a company that makes TV set-top boxes. The acquisition represents a major shift from Cisco's core business of networking equipment for big businesses to a broader vision featuring a complete range of networking products for business and consumers.[11]

Cisco's frame bending is motivated by a desire to broaden its customer base to avoid getting hurt, as it was when the Internet bubble burst in 2001.

RE-CREATION. Competitive pressures normally trigger this most intense and risky type of organizational change. Nadler and Tushman say it amounts to "frame breaking." A stunning example of frame breaking is the software giant Microsoft. In the mid-1990s, co-founder and then-CEO Bill Gates abruptly decided to tie his company's future to the Internet after initially dismissing it as a passing fad. Reinventing an already thriving company from the bottom

These ancient ruins from past civilizations in Rome, Italy, remind us that change is relentless. People, organizations, nations, and civilizations that attempt to stand still get left behind in a fast-changing world.

up—or frame breaking—was a risky move, but look how it has played out. As Jeffrey Katzenberg of DreamWorks noted at the time, "What they're doing is decisive, quick, breathtaking."[12]

Individual Reactions to Change

Ultimately, workplace changes of all types become a *personal* matter for employees. In fact, Stephen Haines, a management consultant, calls organizational change a myth because change happens on an individual level, even in the workplace.[13] A merger, for example, may mean a new job assignment for one person, a new boss for another, and a layoff for yet another. The first person may look forward to the challenge of a new assignment, whereas the second two may dread the prospect of adjusting to a new boss or finding a new job. Researchers tell us these people will tend to exhibit distinctly different response patterns.[14] Specifically, people tend to respond to changes they *like* differently than they do to changes they *dislike*. Let us explore these two response patterns with the goal of developing a contingency model for managers. It is important to note that both models are generic; that is, they apply equally to on-the-job and off-the-job changes.

HOW PEOPLE RESPOND TO CHANGES THEY LIKE. According to Figure 15.2, a three-stage adjustment is typical when people encounter a change they like. New college graduates, for instance, often see their unrealistic optimism (stage A) give way to

the reality shock (stage B) of earning a living before getting their life and career on track (stage C). Key personal factors—including attitude, morale, and desire to make the change work—dip during stage B. Sometimes the dip is so severe or prolonged that the person gives up, as, say, when newlyweds head for the divorce court. Stage B is thus a critical juncture where leadership can make a difference.[15]

HOW PEOPLE RESPOND TO CHANGES THEY FEAR AND DISLIKE. Although exact statistics are not available, the situation in Figure 15.3 is probably more common in the workplace than the one in Figure 15.2. In other words, on-the-job change generally is more feared than welcomed. Changes, particularly sudden ones, represent the unknown. Most of us fear the unknown. We can bring the model in Figure 15.3 to life by walking through it with Maria, a production supervisor at a dairy products cooperative. She and her coworkers face a major reorganization involving a switch to team-based production.

In stage 1, Maria feels a bit unsure and somewhat overwhelmed by the sudden switch to teams. She needs a lot more information to decide whether she really likes the idea. She feels twinges of fear. Stage 2 finds Maria joking with the other supervisors about how upper management's enthusiasm for teams will blow over in a few days, so there's no need to worry. Her attitude, mood, and desire for change improve a bit. After an initial training session on team-based management and participation, Maria begins to worry about her job security. Even

Figure 15.2 How People Tend to Respond to Changes They *Like*

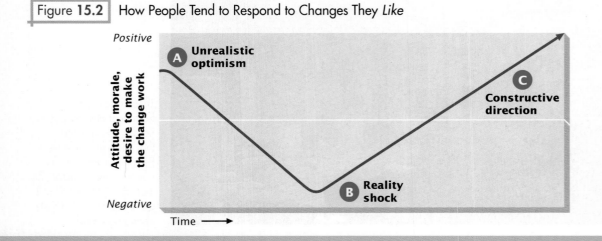

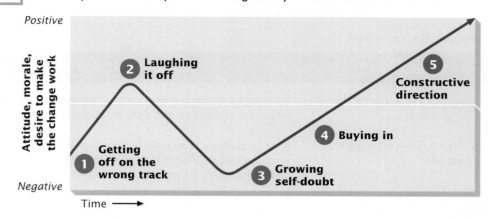

Figure 15.3 How People Tend to Respond to Changes They *Fear* and *Dislike*

if she keeps her job, she wonders whether she is up to the new way of doing things. Her morale drops sharply in stage 3. In stage 4, after a stern but supportive lecture from her boss about being a team player, Maria comes to grips with her resistance to the team approach. She resolves to stop criticizing management's "fad of the week" and to help make the switch to teams a success. Her attitude turns positive, and her morale takes an upswing in stage 5, as she tries participative management techniques and gets positive results. Additional training and some personal research and reading on team-based management convince Maria that this approach is the wave of the future.

Ten months after the switch to teams was announced, Maria has become an outspoken advocate for teams and participative management. Her job security is strengthened by a pending promotion to the training department, where she will coordinate all team training for supervisors. Unbeknownst to upper management, Maria has even toyed with the idea of starting her own consulting business, specializing in team management. Maria's transition from fear to full adaptation has taken months and has not been easy. But the experience has been normal and positive, including a timely boost from her manager between stages 3 and 4.

A CONTINGENCY MODEL FOR GETTING EMPLOYEES THROUGH CHANGES. Contingency managers, once again, adapt their techniques to the situation. The response patterns

in Figures 15.2 and 15.3 call for different managerial actions. Managerial action steps for both situations are listed in Table 15.1. When employees understand that stages B and 3 are normal and expected responses, they will be less apt to panic and more likely to respond favorably to managerial guidance through action steps C and 4 and 5.

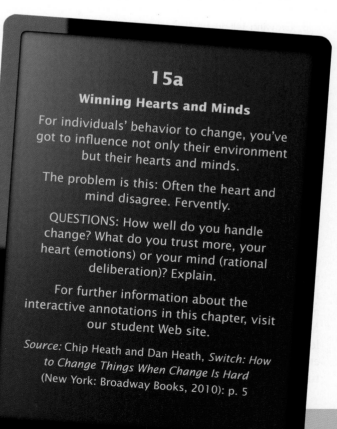

15a
Winning Hearts and Minds

For individuals' behavior to change, you've got to influence not only their environment but their hearts and minds.

The problem is this: Often the heart and mind disagree. Fervently.

QUESTIONS: How well do you handle change? What do you trust more, your heart (emotions) or your mind (rational deliberation)? Explain.

For further information about the interactive annotations in this chapter, visit our student Web site.

Source: Chip Heath and Dan Heath, *Switch: How to Change Things When Change Is Hard* (New York: Broadway Books, 2010): p. 5

Table 15.1	How to Help Individuals Deal with Change: A Contingency Approach

Situation: The person likes the change.

STAGE	MANAGERIAL ACTION STEPS
A. Unrealistic optimism: "What a great idea! It will solve all our problems."	Encourage enthusiasm while directing attention to potential problems and to the cooperation and work necessary to get the job done.
B. Reality shock: "This is going to be a lot harder than it seemed."	Listen supportively to negative feelings and neutralize unreasonable fears. Set realistic short-term goals. Build self-confidence. Recognize and reward positive comments and progress.
C. Constructive direction: "This won't be easy, but we can do it."	Set broader and longer-term goals. Encourage involvement. Emphasize group problem solving and learning. Celebrate individual and group achievements. Prepare for bigger and better things.

Situation: The person fears and dislikes the change.

STAGE	MANAGERIAL ACTION STEPS
1. Getting off on the wrong track: "What a dumb idea!"	Be a positive role model for the vision of a better way. Be a supportive listener and correct any misunderstanding.
2. Laughing it off: "Just another wild idea that won't go anywhere. Don't worry about it."	Same as action step A above.
3. Growing self-doubt: "I don't think I have what it takes."	Same as action step B above.
4. Buying in: "Okay, I'll give this thing a try."	Encourage the person to let go of the past and look forward to a better future. Build personal commitment. Recognize and reward positive words and actions.
5. Constructive direction: "This won't be easy, but we can do it."	Same as action step C above.

OVERCOMING RESISTANCE TO CHANGE

Dealing with change is an integral part of modern management. Change expert Ichak Adizes believes that the purpose of management, leadership, parenting, or governing is to solve the problems of today and prepare to solve the problems of tomorrow. Management is not needed when there are no problems, but there are always problems. And we should embrace those problems because they give us opportunities to manage, which makes us feel alive.[16]

Within the change typology just discussed, organizational change comes in all sizes and shapes. Often it's new and unfamiliar technology. It could be a reorganization, a merger, a new pay plan, or perhaps a new performance appraisal program. Whatever its form, change is like a stone tossed into a still pond. The initial impact causes ripples to radiate in all directions, often with unpredictable consequences. A common consequence of change in organizations is resistance from those whose jobs are directly affected. Both rational and irrational resistance can bring the wheels of progress to a halt. Management faces the challenge of foreseeing and neutralizing resistance to change. The question is, how? To answer that question, we need to examine why employees resist change.

Why Do Employees Resist Change?

Employees resist change for many reasons.[17] The following are the most common.

SURPRISE. Significant changes that are introduced on the spur of the moment or with no warning can create a threatening sense of imbalance in the workplace. Regarding this problem, an executive task force at J. C. Penney Co., the well-known retailer, determined that changes should be introduced incrementally, otherwise it can be counterproductive to change too much too quickly.[18]

INERTIA. Many members of the typical organization desire to maintain a safe, secure, and predictable status quo. The bywords of this group are "But we don't do things that way here." Technological inertia also is a common problem. Consider, for example, the history of the standard typewriter keyboard (referred to as the Qwerty keyboard because *Q, W, E, R, T,* and *Y* are the first six letters in the upper-left-hand corner). The layout dates from 1873, and was designed to slow down typists so they wouldn't jam the keys on the typewriter. But even as typewriters evolved and then gave way to modern keyboards, Qwerty has refused to replace the system with something faster. Thanks to resistance to change, today's high-tech marvels in personal computing come out of the box complete with an 1873-style keyboard! Supervisors and middle managers who fall victim to unthinking inertia can effectively kill change programs, and in the case of the Qwerty keyboard, experts estimate it has come at a cost of billions.[19]

MISUNDERSTANDING/IGNORANCE/ LACK OF SKILLS. Without adequate introductory or remedial training,

an otherwise positive change may be perceived in a negative light. This is precisely the situation Ann Fudge encountered in 2003 when she was hired as chair and CEO of Young & Rubicam, a troubled ad agency known for its turf battles. Borrowing concepts from Six Sigma, the rigid and almost religious quality-control program, Fudge tried to impose a more collaborative, efficient, and client-focused initiative that she dubbed FIT, for focus, innovation, and teamwork. Although some within the organization embraced the new outlook, most senior managers resisted her program, calling it "Sick Sigma."[20] Eventually, their resistance won out, and Fudge retired to focus on nonprofit work.[21]

EMOTIONAL SIDE EFFECTS. Those who are forced to accept on-the-job changes can experience a sense of powerlessness and even anger. The subsequent backlash can be passive (stalling, pretending not to understand) or active (vocal opposition, sabotage, or aggression).

15b
Let's go!

Carol Bartz, Yahoo CEO and breast cancer survivor:

I like change. Frankly, it's hard for me to understand why more people don't embrace it. I'm impatient with people and teams who don't move forward. "Fail fast-forward" is a favorite motto of mine. It's about not being afraid to fail; and if you do, identify it quickly and move ahead fast so no momentum is lost. I've never been interested in agonizing over what could have or should have happened. Just get going again.

QUESTIONS: How well would you do if you reported directly to Bartz? Do you think her battle with breast cancer back in 1992 affected her attitude about change and everyone having a sense of urgency? Explain.

Source: Carol Bartz, "Just Deal With It," *Fortune* (September 28, 2009): 115.

Employees resist change for many reasons, but after the economic crisis of 2008, unemployed Americans who were able to conquer their fears and proactively upgrade their skills were more likely to transition into new jobs sooner.

LACK OF TRUST. Promises of improvement are likely to fall on deaf ears when employees do not trust management. Conversely, managers are unlikely to permit necessary participation if they do not trust their people.

FEAR OF FAILURE. Just as many college freshmen have doubts about their chances of ever graduating, challenges presented by significant on-the-job changes can also be intimidating.

PERSONALITY CONFLICTS. Managers who are disliked by their people are poor conduits for change.

POOR TIMING. In every work setting, internal and/or external events can conspire to create resentment about a particular change. For example, an otherwise desirable out-of-state transfer would only make things worse for an employee with an ailing elderly parent.

LACK OF TACT. As we all know, it is not necessarily what is said that shapes our attitude toward people and events. *How* it is said is often more important. Tactful and sensitive handling of change is essential.

THREAT TO JOB STATUS/SECURITY. Because employment fulfills basic needs, employees can be expected to resist changes with real or imaginary impacts on job status or job security.

BREAKUP OF WORK GROUP. Significant changes can tear the fabric of on-the-job social relationships.[22] Accordingly, members of cohesive work groups often exert peer pressure on one another to resist changes that threaten to break up the group.[23]

PASSIVE-AGGRESSIVE ORGANIZATIONAL CULTURE. This subtle but potent form of resistance hides behind smiling faces. Passive-aggressive behavior becomes a major barrier to change when it becomes embedded in the organization's culture. For example, in a passive-aggressive organization, people typically attend meetings and appear to agree to a proposed change. Then they return to their desks, where they make snide comments about the change and refuse to act on it, hoping it will just drift away.[24]

COMPETING COMMITMENTS. Employees may not have a problem with the change itself, but rather with how it disrupts their pursuit of other goals. Such competing commitments are often unconscious and need to be skillfully brought to the surface to make progress. Consider this situation: Despite a commitment to teamwork, a person may refuse to collaborate in an attempt to avoid the conflict that naturally comes along with any team activity.[25]

These reasons for resisting change help demonstrate that participation is not a panacea. For example, imagine the futility of trying to gain the enthusiastic support of a team of assembly-line welders for a robot that will eventually take over their jobs. In extreme form, each reason for resisting change can become an insurmountable barrier to genuine participation. Therefore, managers need a broad array of methods for dealing with resistance to change. (See Green Management.)

Strategies for Overcoming Resistance to Change

Only in recent years have management theorists begun to give serious attention to alternative ways of overcoming resistance to change.[26] At least

Green Management: Toward Sustainability

AT&T's Alicia Abella Wants Better and Greener Communication Technologies

At AT&T, Alicia Abella is widely regarded for her efforts in developing long-distance collaboration tools. In her capacity as Executive Director of Innovative Services Research at AT&T Labs, she led a group of researchers dedicated to eliminating the need for plane travel and other commuting methods that potentially harm the environment or overuse energy resources. She has developed technologies that focus on teleconferencing, Web-based solutions, and iPhone App-based solutions that promote work and rapid-response collaboration across the globe. "We are really trying to enhance the way people are communicating with each other," [she said]. . . .

"Alicia is a change agent," said Chuck Kalmanek, vice president of Networking & Services Research. "She has a vision of innovative services that draws on her extensive experience in human-computer interaction and an intuitive understanding of how technologies like social networks change the way that users interact with each other and with our services."

For Discussion: What does Abella need to know about change and resistance to change to get people to adopt new communication technologies? How could AT&T's long-distance collaboration innovations affect how you live and work in the next few years?

Source: Excerpted from Joshua Molina, "Alicia Abella: A 'Change Agent' for AT&T, Also a Mentor to Young People," HispanicBusiness.com (April 7, 2010), **www.hispanicbusiness.com/news/2010/4/7/alicia_abella_a_change_agent_for.htm**, accessed June 28, 2010.

---

six options, including participation, are available in this area:

1. *Education and communication.* This strategy is appealing because it advocates prevention rather than cure. The idea here is to help employees understand the true need for a change as well as the logic behind it. Various media may be used, including face-to-face discussions, formal group presentations, or special reports or publications.

2. *Participation and involvement.* Once again, personal involvement through participation tends to defuse both rational and irrational fears about a workplace change. By participating in both the design

of a change and its implementation, one acquires a personal stake in its success.

3. *Facilitation and support.* When fear and anxiety are responsible for resistance to doing things in a new and different way, support from management in the form of special training, job stress counseling, and compensatory time off can be helpful. According to the CEO of Medtronic, the

The North American Free Trade Agreement (NAFTA) has caused political controversy in all three of the nations involved because citizens weren't prepared for change. These Mexican agricultural protestors worry that the removal of import tariffs on farm products under NAFTA will make them uncompetitive with U.S. farmers.

AP Photo/Eduardo Verdugo

heart pacemaker company facilitates employees' acceptance of a new product or innovation by first introducing it to a "venture team," consisting of people who are not emotionally attached to the old product. Once the team members have the new idea securely in place, they introduce it to the rest of the organization. At Medtronic, employees find it easier to accept gradual change coming from their peers, rather than having it imposed by top management.[27]

4. *Negotiation and agreement.* Sometimes management can neutralize potential or actual resistance by exchanging something of value for cooperation. An hourly clerical employee may, for instance, be put on a salary in return for learning how to operate a new Internet workstation.

5. *Manipulation and co-optation.* Manipulation occurs when managers selectively withhold or dispense information and consciously arrange events to increase the chance that a change will be successful. Co-optation normally involves token participation. Those who are co-opted with token participation cannot claim they have not been consulted, yet the ultimate impact of their input is negligible.

6. *Explicit and implicit coercion.* Managers who cannot or will not invest the time required for the other strategies can try to force employees to go along with a change by threatening them with termination, loss of pay raises or promotions, transfer, and the like.

As shown in Table 15.2, each of these strategies for overcoming resistance to change has advantages and drawbacks. Appropriateness to the situation is the key to success.

Now we turn our attention to implementing changes in organizations.

Table 15.2 Dealing with Resistance to Change

APPROACH	COMMONLY USED IN SITUATIONS	ADVANTAGES	DRAWBACKS
1. Education + communication	Where there is a lack of information or inaccurate information and analysis	Once persuaded, people will often help with the implementation of the change	Can be very time consuming if lots of people are involved
2. Participation + involvement	Where the initiators do not have all the information they need to design the change, and where others have considerable power to resist	People who participate will be committed to implementing change, and any relevant information they have will be integrated into the change plan	Can be very time consuming if participators design an inappropriate change
3. Facilitation + support	Where people are resisting because of adjustment problems	No other approach works as well with adjustment problems	Can be time consuming, expensive, and still fail
4. Negotiation + agreement	Where someone or some group will clearly lose out in a change, and where that group has considerable power to resist	Sometimes it is a relatively easy way to avoid major resistance	Can be too expensive in many cases if it alerts others to negotiate for compliance
5. Manipulation + co-optation	Where other tactics will not work or are too expensive	It can be a relatively quick and inexpensive solution to resistance problems	Can lead to future problems if people feel manipulated
6. Explicit + implicit coercion	Where speed is essential, and the change initiators possess considerable power	It is speedy and can overcome any kind of resistance	Can be risky if it leaves people mad at the initiators

Source: From "Choosing Strategies for Change," by John P. Kotter and Leonard A. Schlesinger, *Harvard Business Review* (July–August 2008), Exhibit 1, p. 136. Reprinted by permission of HBS Publishing.

MAKING CHANGE HAPPEN

In these fast-paced times, managers need to be active agents of change rather than passive observers or, worse, victims of circumstances beyond their control. This active role requires foresight, responsiveness, flexibility, and adaptability.[28] In this section, we focus on two approaches to making change happen: (1) organization development, a formal top-down approach, and (2) grassroots change, an unofficial and informal bottom-up approach.

Planned Change Through Organization Development (OD)

Organization development has become a convenient label for a host of techniques and processes aimed at making sick organizations healthy and healthy organizations healthier.[29] According to experts in the field, organization development (OD) refers to planned efforts to help individuals work together in their organizations more effectively by applying principles, methods, and concepts adapted from psychology, sociology, education, and management.[30]

Others simply call OD *planned change*. Regarding the degree of change involved, OD consultant and writer Warner Burke contends that organization development represents change in a broad, far-reaching aspect of the organization's culture, as opposed to change that solves a problem or improves a procedure.[31]

OD programs generally are facilitated by hired consultants, although inside OD specialists can also be found. Importantly, OD is a comprehensive, top-down approach to organizational change. It is not hit-or-miss training or piecemeal reorganizations. For instance, efforts to improve employee engagement led one team of frustrated consultants to this conclusion: We failed to realize that once the employees returned to work after the training, they faced organizational resistance to the very ideas we taught them. Organizational leaders must be involved and individuals must adjust their attitudes and behaviors if organizational change is to happen.[32] Thus, it is clear that OD is a concerted effort by *everyone* in the organization to change the culture.

THE OBJECTIVES OF OD. OD programs vary because they are tailored to unique situations. What is appropriate for one organization may be totally out of place in another. In spite of this variation, certain objectives are common to most OD programs. In general, OD programs develop social processes such as trust, problem solving, communication, and cooperation to facilitate organizational change and

Americans love their national parks. In fact, they're loving many of them to death. Here, Yosemite National Park ranger Jesse McGahey (right) educates a pair of rock climbers below Cathedral Peak about minimizing damage to the environment.

AP Photo/Al Golub

---

organization development (OD) planned change programs intended to help people and organizations function more effectively enhance personal and organizational effectiveness. More specifically, the typical OD program tries to achieve the following seven objectives:

1. Deepen the sense of organizational purpose (or vision) and align individuals with that purpose.
2. Strengthen interpersonal trust, communication, cooperation, and support.
3. Encourage a problem-solving rather than a problem-avoiding approach to organizational problems.
4. Develop a satisfying work experience capable of building enthusiasm.
5. Supplement formal authority with authority based on personal knowledge and skill.
6. Increase personal responsibility for planning and implementing.
7. Encourage personal willingness to change.[33]

Critics of OD point out that there is nothing really new in this list of objectives. Directly or indirectly, each of these objectives is addressed by one or another general management technique. OD advocates respond by saying general management lacks a systematic approach. They claim that the usual practice of teaching managers how to plan, solve problems, make decisions, organize, motivate, lead, and control contributes to a haphazard, bits-and-pieces management style. According to OD thinking, organization development gives managers a vehicle for systematically introducing change by applying a broad selection of management techniques as a unified and consistent package. This, they claim, leads to greater personal, group, and organizational effectiveness.

THE OD PROCESS. A simple metaphor helps introduce the three major components of OD.[34] Suppose someone hands you a coffee cup filled with clear, solid ice. You look down through the ice and see a penny lying tails up on the bottom of the cup. Now suppose that for some reason you want the penny to be frozen in place in a heads-up position. What can you do? There is really only one practical solution. You let the ice in the cup melt, reach in and flip the penny over, and then refreeze the cup of water. This is precisely how social psychologist Kurt Lewin recommended that change be handled in social systems. Specifically, Lewin told change agents to unfreeze, change, and then refreeze social systems.[35]

15c
Back to the Opening Case

From an OD perspective, what could David Zugheri have done to "unfreeze" the situation for successful change?

Unfreezing prepares the members of a social system for change, helps neutralize initial resistance, and gets them onboard. Sudden, unexpected change, according to Lewin, is threatening and socially disruptive.[36] But unfreezing can be used to ease the transition, as when deregulation forced Brooklyn Union Gas to reinvent itself and to compete in the marketplace as KeySpan. In this case, corporate ombudsman Kenny Moore came up with a clever idea to help managers adjust to this wrenching change. First he held a mock funeral, complete with tombstones and an urn, where managers mourned what they were losing. Other props, like a steamer trunk and a stork, represented the journey to a newly created organization. Then he asked the managers to write down what they would bring to their new organization, and had them create posters representing what the new KeySpan would look like. Allowing these key players to actively participate in a ceremony that represented the loss and re-birth of their organization helped them generate some excitement about the shift.[37]

Once the change has been introduced, **refreezing** is necessary to follow up on problems, complaints, unanticipated side effects, and any lingering resistance.[38] This seemingly simple approach to change spells the difference between systematic and haphazard change.

The OD model introduced here is based on Lewin's approach to handling change (see Figure 15.4). Diagnosis is carried out during the unfreezing phase. Change is then carefully introduced through tailor-made intervention. Finally, a systematic follow-up refreezes the situation. Each phase is critical to successful organizational change

unfreezing neutralizing resistance by preparing people for change | *refreezing* systematically following up a change program for lasting results

Figure 15.4 | A General Model of OD

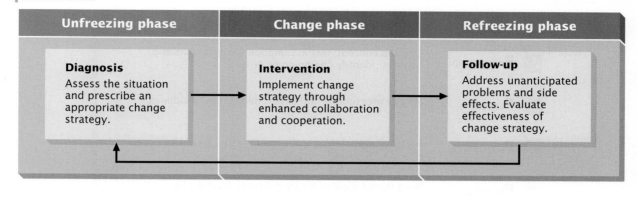

Unfreezing phase	Change phase	Refreezing phase
Diagnosis Assess the situation and prescribe an appropriate change strategy.	**Intervention** Implement change strategy through enhanced collaboration and cooperation.	**Follow-up** Address unanticipated problems and side effects. Evaluate effectiveness of change strategy.

and development. Still, it takes continual recycling through this three-phase sequence to make OD an ongoing system of planned change.

Unofficial and Informal Grassroots Change

OD is rationally planned, formal, systematic, and initiated by top management. As a sign of the times, many of today's organizations cannot be described in those terms. They tend to be spontaneous, informal, experimental, and driven from within. (Interestingly, employees in some of these modern organizations were empowered by earlier OD programs.) Unusual things can happen when empowered employees start to take the initiative, but they need to employ some critical skills along the way: getting buy in, answering opposition, building trust, and showing people how the change will help the organization reach its objectives. It helps to have a "fighter," someone who believes in the idea enough to sell it to top management.[39] This is not top-down change in the tradition

of OD. Rather, it involves change from inside the organization. Let us explore two perspectives on unofficial and informal grassroots change: tempered radicals and the 5P model.

TEMPERED RADICALS. This intriguing term and the concept it embraces come from Stanford professor Debra E. Meyerson. She defines tempered radicals as those who want to succed at work while retaining their personal values and identities, even if they clash with the corporate culture. They want to rock the boat but remain on board.[40] Meyerson's research has found many "square pegs in round holes" who identify powerfully with her concept of the tempered radical. They tend to work quietly yet relentlessly to advance their vision of a better organization.

If progressive managers are to do a good job of managing diversity, then they need to handle their tempered radicals in win-win fashion. Too often those with different ideas are marginalized and/or trivialized. When this happens, the organization's intellectual and social capital suffer greatly.

Mario Lopes/Shutterstock.com

tempered radicals people who quietly try to change the dominant organizational culture in line with their convictions

Figure **15.5** | The 5P Checklist for Change Agents

Key action steps	
✓ **P**reparation	Develop concept; test assumptions; weigh costs and benefits; identify champion or driver.
✓ **P**urpose	Specify measurable objectives, milestones, deadlines.
✓ **P**articipation	Refine concept while building broad and powerful support.
✓ **P**rogress	Keep things moving forward despite roadblocks.
✓ **P**ersistence	Foster realistic expectations and a sense of urgency while avoiding impatience.

Four practical guidelines for tempered radicals stem from Meyerson's research:

1. *Think small for big results.* Don't try to change the organization's culture all at once. Start small and build a string of steadily larger victories. Learn as you go. Encourage small, nonthreatening experiments. Trust and confidence in you and your ideas will grow with the victories.
2. *Be authentic.* Base your actions on your convictions and thoughtful preparation, not on rash emotionalism. Anger, aggression, and arrogance give people an easy excuse to dismiss you and your ideas.
3. *Translate.* Build managerial support by explaining the business case for your ideas.
4. *Don't go it alone.* Build a strong support network of family, friends, and coworkers to provide moral support and help advance your cause.[41]

THE 5P CHECKLIST FOR GRASSROOTS CHANGE AGENTS (TURNING IDEAS INTO ACTION). The 5P model consists of an easy-to-remember list for anyone interested in organizational change: *preparation, purpose, participation, progress,* and *persistence* (see Figure 15.5). The model is generic, which means that it applies to all levels in profit and nonprofit organizations of all sizes. Let us examine each item more closely.

- *Preparation.* Is the concept or problem clearly defined? Has adequate problem *finding* taken place? Are underlying assumptions sound? Will the end result be worth the collective time, effort, and expense? Can the change initiative be harnessed to another change effort with a high probability of success, or should it stand alone? Does the proposed change have a *champion* or a *driver* who has the passion and persistence to see the process through to completion?
- *Purpose.* Can the objective or goal of the change initiative be expressed in clear, measurable terms? Can it be described quickly to busy people? What are the specific progress milestones and critical deadlines?
- *Participation.* Have key people been involved in refining the change initiative to the extent of having personal "ownership" and willingness to fight for it? Have potential or actual opponents been offered a chance to participate? Have powerful people in the organization been recruited as advocates and defenders?
- *Progress.* Are performance milestones and intermediate deadlines being met? If not, why? Is support for the initiative weakening? Why? Have unexpected roadblocks been encountered? How can they be removed or avoided?
- *Persistence.* Has a reasonable sense of urgency been communicated to all involved? (*Note:* Extreme impatience can fray relationships and be stressful.) Has the change team drifted away from the original objective as time has passed? Does

everyone on the team have realistic expectations about how long the change process will take?

With situational adjustments for unique personalities and circumstances, the 5P approach can help ordinary employees create extraordinary change.[42] So sharpen your concept and take your best shot!

MANAGING CONFLICT

Conflict is intimately related to change and interpersonal dealings. Harvard's Abraham Zaleznik has written, "Because people come together to satisfy a wide array of psychological needs, social relations in general are awash with conflict." Given all of their differing opinions and dislikes, people should expect a few jabs and injuries in the course of working together toward a common objective.[43]

The term *conflict* has a strong negative connotation, evoking words such as *opposition, anger, aggression,* and *violence.*[44] But conflict does not have to be a negative experience. Based on research evidence that most organizational conflict occurs within a cooperative context, Dean Tjosvold offered this more positive definition: "**Conflict involves incompatible behaviors; one person interfering, disrupting, or in some other way making another's actions less effective.**"[45] This definition sets the scene for an important distinction between *competitive* (or destructive) conflict and *cooperative* (or constructive) conflict. Cooperative conflict is based on the win-win negotiating attitude discussed later in this chapter. Also, recall our discussion, in Chapter 13, of cooperative conflict as a tool for avoiding groupthink.

Dealing with the Two Faces of Conflict

Tjosvold contrasts competitive and cooperative conflict as follows: If people view conflict as opposing interests, they will see it as a fight for one party to subordinate the other. On the other hand, if people can keep their common goals in mind, they will view conflict as an opportunity to constructively solve a problem.[46]

Figure 15.6 graphically illustrates the difference between competitive and cooperative conflict. In the competitive mode, the parties pursue directly opposite goals. Each mistrusts the other's intentions and disbelieves what the other party says. Both parties actively avoid constructive dialogue and have a win-lose attitude. Unavoidably, the disagreement persists and they go their separate ways.[47] Does this self-defeating cycle sound familiar? Probably, because most of us at one time or another have suffered through a broken relationship or destructive conflict with someone else.

AP Photo/Christophe Ena

Bruce Patton teaches conflict management seminars in Harvard Law School's Program on Negotiation. For better or for worse, he calls conflict "a growth industry." He advises managers to not waste their time minimizing conflict, but rather to harness it in creative and constructive ways.

conflict incompatible behaviors that make another person less effective

In sharp contrast, the *cooperative* conflict cycle in Figure 15.6 is a mutually reinforcing experience serving the best interests of both parties. Cooperative conflict is standard practice at Anheuser-Busch, brewer of Budweiser beer. When faced with a major decision, the company assigns two or even three teams to argue the pros and cons of each alternative. Pat Stokes, one of the firm's top executives, notes, "We end up with decisions and alternatives we hadn't thought of previously."[48] Similarly, Intel's use of cooperative conflict has helped make the semiconductor maker a Silicon valley legend. The process, called "disagree and commit" makes engineers figure out new avenues for doing things quicker, more cost-effectively, and reliably.[49] Cooperative conflict thus can give creativity and innovation a boost."

As a skill-building exercise, you might want to use the cooperative conflict model in Figure 15.6 to salvage a personal relationship mired in competitive conflict. Show the cooperative model to the other party and suggest starting over with a new set of ground rules. Cooperative goals are the necessary starting point. This process can

15d
Let's Start a Good Clean Fight!

Jeff Weiss and Jonathan Hughes, management consultants:

Clashes between parties are the crucibles in which creative solutions are developed and wise trade-offs among competing objectives are made.

Larry Whitney, vice president, Federal Reserve Bank of New York:

You have to get people upset. When things get disruptive, people really get work done, and learning takes place.

QUESTIONS: Should managers try to stimulate conflict? How should they do it and how will they know if they've gone too far?

Sources: Jeff Weiss and Jonathan Hughes, "Want Collaboration? Accept—and Actively Manage—Conflict," *Harvard Business Review,* 83 (March 2005): 93; and as quoted in Fiona Haley, "Tough-Love Leadership," *Fast Company,* 86 (September 2004): 110.

Figure 15.6 | Competitive Versus Cooperative Conflict

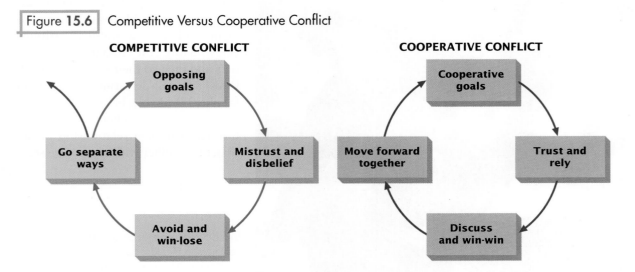

be difficult, yet very rewarding (see the Action Learning Exercise at the end of this chapter). Win-win conflict is not just a good idea; it is one of the keys to a better world. Some organizations facilitate win-win conflict with anger management training sessions.[50]

There are two sets of tools available for managing conflict.[51] The first we call conflict triggers, for stimulating conflict; the second involves conflict resolution techniques, used when conflict becomes destructive.

Conflict Triggers

A **conflict trigger** is a circumstance that increases the chances of intergroup or interpersonal conflict. As long as a conflict trigger appears to stimulate constructive conflict, it can be allowed to continue. But as soon as the symptoms of destructive conflict[52] become apparent, steps need to be taken to remove or correct the offending conflict trigger. Major conflict triggers include the following:

- *Ambiguous or overlapping jurisdictions.* Unclear job boundaries often create competition for resources and control. Reorganization can help to clarify job boundaries if destructive conflict becomes a problem (refer to the organization design alternatives discussed in Chapter 9).
- *Competition for scarce resources.* As the term is used here, *resources* include funds, personnel, authority, power, and valuable information. In other words, anything of value in an organizational setting can become a competitively sought-after scarce resource. Sometimes, as in the case of money and people, destructive competition for scarce resources can be avoided by enlarging the resource base (such as increasing competing managers' budgets or hiring additional personnel).[53]
- *Communication breakdowns.* Because communication is a complex process beset by many barriers, these barriers often provoke conflict. It is easy to misunderstand another person or group of people if two-way communication is hampered in some way. The battle for clear communication never ends.
- *Time pressure.* Deadlines and other forms of time pressure can stimulate prompt performance or trigger destructive emotional reactions. When imposing deadlines, managers should consider individuals' ability to cope.

- *Unreasonable standards, rules, policies, or procedures.* These triggers generally lead to dysfunctional conflict between managers and the people they manage. The best remedy is for the manager to tune into employees' perceptions of fair play and correct extremely unpopular situations before they mushroom.
- *Personality clashes.* It is very difficult to change one's personality on the job. Therefore, the practical remedy for serious personality clashes is to separate the antagonistic parties by reassigning one or both to a new job.[54]
- *Status differentials.* As long as productive organizations continue to be arranged hierarchically, this trigger is unavoidable. But managers can minimize dysfunctional conflict by showing a genuine concern for the ideas, feelings, and values of lower-level employees.[55]
- *Unrealized expectations.* Dissatisfaction grows when expectations are not met. Conflict is another by-product of unrealized expectations. Destructive conflict can be avoided in this area by taking time to discover, through frank discussion, what people expect from their employment. Unrealistic expectations can be countered before they become a trigger for dysfunctional conflict.

Managers who understand these conflict triggers will be in a much better position to manage conflict in a proactive and systematic fashion (see Valuing Diversity). Those who passively wait for things to explode before reacting will find conflict managing them. Worst-case scenarios involve workplace bullying,[56] aggression, and violence.

Resolving Conflict

Even the best managers sometimes find themselves in the middle of destructive conflict, whether it is due to inattention or to circumstances beyond their control. In such situations, they may choose to do nothing (some call this an *avoidance* strategy) or try one or more of the following conflict resolution techniques.[57]

PROBLEM SOLVING. When conflicting parties take the time to identify and correct the source of their conflict, they are engaging in problem solving. This

---

conflict trigger any factor that increases the chances of conflict

VALUING DIVERSITY

Needed: Innovators + Implementers

In our experience, innovation teams feel a hostility toward the people responsible for day-to-day operations. . . . The rich vocabulary of disdain includes *bureaucratic, robotic, rigid, ossified, staid, dull, decaying, controlling, patronizing* . . . and just plain old. Such animosity explains why most executives believe that any significant innovation initiative requires a team that is separate and isolated from the rest of the company. . . .

It is flat wrong. Isolation may neutralize infighting, but it also neuters innovation.

The reality is that an innovation initiative must be executed by a partnership that somehow bridges the hostilities—a partnership between a dedicated team and what we call the *performance engine*, the unit responsible for sustaining excellence in ongoing operations. Granted, such an arrangement seems, at first glance, improbable. But to give up on it is to give up on innovation itself.

For Discussion: Why does the diversity of employees' educational backgrounds, technical or professional fields, and job specializations inevitably lead to conflict in organizations? How can management get these diverse employees to team up, engage in cooperative conflict, and collaborate effectively?

Source: Excerpted from Vijay Govindarajan and Chris Trimble, "Stop the Innovation Wars," *Harvard Business Review*, 88 (July–August 2010): 77–78.

approach is based on the assumption that causes must be rooted out and attacked if anything is really to change. Problem solving (refer to our discussion of creative problem solving in Chapter 8) encourages managers to focus their attention on causes, factual information, and promising alternatives rather than on personalities or scapegoats. The major shortcoming of the problem-solving approach is that it takes time, but the investment of extra time can pay off handsomely when the problem is corrected instead of ignored and allowed to worsen.

SUPERORDINATE GOALS. Superordinate goals are typically big, valuable goals that are unattainable by any one individual or group working alone.[58] When a manager relies on superordinate goals to resolve destructive conflict, he or she brings the conflicting parties together and, in effect, says, "Look, we're all in this together. Let's forget our differences so we can get the job done." For example, a company president might remind the production and marketing department heads who have been arguing about product design that the competition is breathing down their necks. Although this technique often works in the short run, the underlying problem tends to crop up later to cause friction once again.

COMPROMISE. This technique generally appeals to those living in a democracy. Advocates of compromise say everyone wins because compromise is based on negotiation, on give-and-take.[59] However, as discussed in the next section, most people do not have good negotiating skills. They approach compromise situations with a win-lose attitude. Thus compromises tend to be disappointing, leaving one or both parties feeling cheated. Conflict is only temporarily suppressed when people feel cheated. Successful compromise requires skillful negotiation.

FORCING. Sometimes, especially when time is important or a safety issue is involved, management must simply step into a conflict and order the conflicting parties to handle the situation in a particular manner. Reliance on formal authority and the power of a superior position is at the heart of forcing. Consider this example involving Burger King's former CEO Gregory D. Brenneman: After he learned that feuding managers exchanged heated e-mails, he threatened to fire them if they persisted in this behavior.[60] As one might suspect, forcing does not resolve the conflict and, in fact, may serve to compound it by hurting feelings and/or fostering resentment and mistrust.

SMOOTHING. A manager who relies on smoothing says to the conflicting parties something like "Settle down. Don't rock the boat. Things will work out by themselves." This approach may tone down conflict in the short run, but it does not solve the underlying problem. Just like each of the other conflict resolution techniques, smoothing has its place. It can be useful when management is attempting to hold things together until a critical project is completed or when there is no time for problem solving or compromise and forcing is deemed inappropriate.

Problem solving and skillfully negotiated compromises are the only approaches that remove the actual sources of conflict. They are the only resolution techniques capable of improving things in the long run. The other approaches amount to short-run, stopgap measures. And managers who fall back on an avoidance strategy are simply running away from the problem. Nonetheless, as we have noted, problem solving and full negotiation sessions can take up valuable time—time that managers may not be willing or able to spend at the moment. When this is the case, management may choose to fall back on superordinate goals, forcing, or smoothing, whichever seems most suitable.[61]

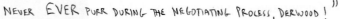

" NEVER EVER PURR DURING THE NEGOTIATING PROCESS, DERWOOD ! "

www.CartoonStock.com

NEGOTIATING

Negotiating is a fact of everyday life. Our negotiating skills are tested when we begin a new job, rent an apartment, live with a roommate, buy a house, buy or lease a car, ask for a raise or promotion, live with a spouse, divorce a spouse, or fight for custody of a child. Managers have even more opportunities to negotiate. Salespeople, employees, labor unions, other managers, and customers all have wishes that the organization may not be able to grant without some give-and-take. Sadly, most of us are rather poor negotiators.[62] Negotiating skills, like any other crucial communication skill, need to be developed through

Jim West/Alamy

With the rise of electronic communication, the volume of mail going through the U.S. Postal Service has been steadily decreasing since 2006. This change in the organization's need for personnel has prompted the USPS to engage in renegotiating its labor agreement with the employees' union.

negotiation decision-making process among interdependent parties with different preferences

diligent study and regular practice.[63] In fact, subjects in a study who had been trained in negotiating tactics negotiated more favorable outcomes than did those with no such training.[64] The quality of communication also matters, according to recent research. Higher-quality communication (e.g., greater clarity and responsiveness) led to better negotiation outcomes in both same-culture and cross-culture situations.[65]

Experts from Northwestern University define **negotiation** as "a decision-making process among interdependent parties who do not share identical preferences." They go on to say that in the negotiation process, each party gives up something and receives something in the relationship.[66] The scope of negotiations spans all levels of human interaction, from individuals to organizations to nations. Two common types of negotiation are *two-party* and *third-party negotiation*. This distinction is evident in common real estate transactions. If you sell your home directly to a buyer after settling on a mutually agreeable price, that is a two-party negotiation. It becomes a third-party negotiation when a real estate broker acts as a go-between for seller and buyer. Regardless of the type of negotiation, the same basic negotiating concepts apply. This final section examines three elements of effective negotiation and introduces a useful technique called *added value negotiating*.

15e
Negotiating a Pay Raise

Survey data:

In a survey of 3,600 professionals in 18 countries, 52% said "Yes" and 48% said "No" to the question: "Have you ever asked for or negotiated a pay raise?"

Advice from Dave Opton CEO of ExecuNet:

"Pull together the data you need to position yourself, including what your peers elsewhere are making and what you've contributed to the company. Think of yourself as a brand you have to sell. Explain the features." Many managers, he says, make the mistake of waiting to bring up money during a formal evaluation. "It's never a good idea, because those discussions tend to focus on how you can improve. Start a discussion about pay a few months beforehand."

QUESTIONS: Do you dislike asking for a pay raise? Why? How well would this advice work for you? Explain.

Sources: Jae Yang and Keith Carter, "Have You Ever Asked for or Negotiated a Pay Raise?" *USA Today* (March 9, 2009): 1B; and Anne Fisher, "How to Ask for—and Get—a Raise Now," *Fortune* (December 27, 2004): 47.

Elements of Effective Negotiation

A good way to learn about proper negotiation is to start from zero. This means confronting and neutralizing one's biases and faulty assumptions. Sports and military metaphors, for example, are usually inappropriate. Why? Because effective negotiators are not bent on beating the opposition or wiping out the enemy.[67] They have a much broader agenda. For instance, effective negotiators not only satisfy their own needs, they also enhance the other party's readiness to negotiate again. Trust is important in this regard.[68] Using this "clean slate" approach to learning, let us explore three common elements of effective negotiation.

ADOPTING A WIN-WIN ATTITUDE. Culture, as discussed in Chapter 4, has a powerful influence on individual behavior. In America, for example, the prevailing culture places a high value on winning and shames losing. You can be number one or be a loser, with little or nothing in between. America's cultural preoccupation with winning, while sometimes an admirable trait, can be a major barrier to effective negotiation.[69] A win-win attitude is preferable.

Stephen R. Covey, author of the best-selling books *The Seven Habits of Highly Effective People* and *The 8th Habit*, offered this instructive perspective: Win-win means seeking mutually beneficial solutions through an attitude of cooperation, not competition. It means finding the "Third Alternative," which is neither one party's answer nor the other's but a better combination of the two. The underpinning idea

Cupertino/Shutterstock.com

of win-win is that there is plenty for everybody. One doesn't have to win at someone else's expense.[70]

Replacing a culturally based win-lose attitude with a win-win attitude is quite difficult; deeply ingrained habits are hard to change. But change they must if American managers are to be more effective negotiators in today's global marketplace.[71] Tom's of Maine, famous for its toothpaste and other all-natural products, is a good role model. Founder and CEO Tom Chappell has built a values-driven company that pays its manufacturing employees in Maine 15 percent above the going rate and donates 10 percent of pretax profits to charity. He relies on a win-win attitude to grow his business, and begins his sales calls with top retailing executives by citing the values that the retailer and its customers have in common with Tom's. Focusing on shared values and goals helps Chappell convince retailers to carry his products, which are typically more expensive than average but are high quality and healthier for users.[72]

KNOWING YOUR BATNA. This odd-sounding label represents the anchor point of effective negotiations. It is an abbreviation for *best alternative to a negotiated agreement.* In other words, what will you settle for if negotiations do not produce your desired outcome(s)? Members of the Harvard Negotiation Project, which is responsible for the concept, call

BATNA "the standard against which any proposed agreement should be measured. That is the only standard which can protect you both from accepting terms that are too unfavorable and from rejecting terms it would be in your interest to accept."[73] In plain language, it adds up to "What is your bottom line?" or "What are you willing to settle for?" For example, a business seller's BATNA becomes the measuring stick for accepting or rejecting offers.

A realistic BATNA is good insurance against the three decision-making traps discussed in Chapter 8: framing error, escalation of commitment, and overconfidence. To negotiate without a BATNA is to stumble along aimlessly in the dark.

IDENTIFYING THE BARGAINING ZONE. Negotiation is useless if the parties involved have no common ground (see the top portion of Figure 15.7). At the other extreme, negotiation is unnecessary if both parties are satisfied with the same outcome. Midway, negotiation is necessary when there is a degree of overlap in the ranges of acceptable outcomes. Hence, the bargaining zone can be defined as the gap between the two BATNAs—the area of overlapping interests where agreement is possible[74] (see the middle portion of Figure 15.7). Because negotiators keep their BATNAs secret, each party needs to *estimate* the other's BATNA when identifying the likely bargaining zone.

bargaining zone the gap between two parties' BATNAs

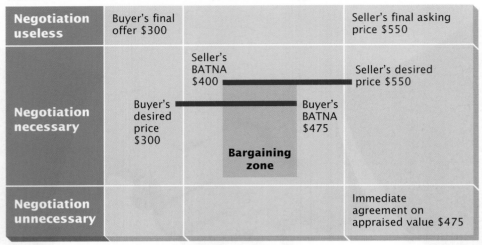

Figure 15.7 | The Bargaining Zone for Negotiators

Transaction: The sale of a used mountain bike with an appraised value of $475.

Added Value Negotiating

Win-win negotiation[75] is a great idea that can be difficult to implement on a daily basis. Managers and others tend to stumble when they discover that a win-win attitude, though necessary, is not all they need to get through a tough round of negotiations. A step-by-step process is also essential. Karl and Steve Albrecht's added value negotiating process bridges the gap between win-win theory and practice. Added value negotiating (AVN) is a five-step process involving the development of *multiple deals* that add value to the negotiating process.[76] This approach is quite different from traditional "single-outcome" negotiating that involves "taking something" from the other party. AVN comprises the following five steps:

1. *Clarify interests.* Both subjective (judgmental) and objective (observable and measurable) interests are jointly identified and clarified by the two parties. The goal is to find some *common ground* as a basis for negotiation.

2. *Identify options.* What sorts of value—in terms of money, property, actions, rights, and risk reduction—can each party offer the other? This step creates a *marketplace of value* for the negotiators.

3. *Design alternative deal packages.* Rather than tying the success of the negotiation to a single win-win offer, create a number of alternatives from various combinations of value items. This vital step, which distinguishes AVN from other negotiation strategies, fosters *creative agreement.*

4. *Select a deal.* Each party tests the various deal packages for value, balance, and fit. Feasible deals are then discussed jointly, and a *mutually acceptable deal* is selected.

5. *Perfect the deal.* Unresolved details are hammered out by the negotiators. Agreements are put in writing. *Relationships* are strengthened for future negotiations. Added value negotiating, according to the Albrechts, leads to healthy long-term relationships because it's based on openness and a commitment to value.[77]

SUMMARY

1. Managers need to do a much better job of managing the process of change. Nadler and Tushman's model identifies four types of organizational change by cross-referencing anticipatory and reactive change with incremental and strategic change. Four resulting types of change are tuning, adaptation, re-orientation (frame bending), and re-creation (frame breaking).

2. People who like a change tend to go through three stages: unrealistic optimism, reality shock, and constructive direction. When someone fears or dislikes a change, a more complex process involving five stages tends to occur: getting off on the wrong track, laughing it off, experiencing growing self-doubt, buying in, and moving in a constructive direction. Managers are challenged to help employees deal effectively with reality shock and self-doubt.

3. Inevitable resistance to change must be overcome if the organization is to succeed. Employees resist change for many different reasons, including (but not limited to) surprise, inertia, ignorance, lack of trust, fear of failure, passive-aggressive behavior, and competing commitments. Modern managers facing resistance to change can select from several strategies, including education and communication, participation and involvement, facilitation and support, negotiation and agreement, manipulation and co-optation, and explicit and implicit coercion.

4. Organization development (OD) is a systematic approach to planned organizational change. The principal objectives of OD are increased trust, better problem solving, more effective communication, improved cooperation, and greater willingness to change. The typical OD program is a three-phase process of unfreezing, change, and refreezing.

5. Unofficial and informal grassroots change can be initiated by tempered radicals, who quietly follow their convictions when trying to change the dominant organizational culture. Four guidelines for tempered radicals are (1) think small for big results, (2) be authentic, (3) translate, and (4) don't go it alone. The 5P checklist for grassroots change agents—*preparation, purpose, participation, progress,* and *persistence*—is a generic model for people at all levels in all organizations. Ordinary employees can achieve extraordinary changes by having a clear purpose, a cham.pion or driver for the change initiative, a measurable objective, broad and powerful support achieved through participation, an ability to overcome roadblocks, and a persistent sense of urgency.

6. Competitive conflict is characterized by a destructive cycle of opposing goals, mistrust and disbelief, and avoidance of discussion, coupled with a win-lose attitude. In contrast, cooperative conflict involves a constructive cycle of cooperative goals, trust and reliance, and discussion, coupled with a win-win attitude.

7. Conflict triggers can cause either constructive or destructive conflict. Destructive conflict can be resolved through problem solving, superordinate goals, compromise, forcing, or smoothing.

8. Three basic elements of effective negotiations are a win-win attitude, a BATNA (best alternative to a negotiated agreement) to serve as a negotiating standard, and the calculation of a bargaining zone to identify overlapping interests. Added value negotiating (AVN) improves on standard negotiation strategies by fostering a creative range of possible solutions.

TERMS TO UNDERSTAND

Anticipatory changes, p. 418
Reactive changes, p. 418
Incremental changes, p. 418
Strategic changes, p. 418
Organization development (OD), p. 427

Unfreezing, p. 428
Refreezing, p. 428
Tempered radicals, p. 429
Conflict, p. 431

Conflict trigger, p. 433
Negotiation, p. 435
Bargaining zone, p. 437
Added value negotiating, p. 438

ACTION LEARNING EXERCISE

PUTTING CONFLICT ON ICE

Instructions: Working alone or as a member of a team, read the following material on the iceberg of conflict. As instructed in the reading, focus on a specific conflict and then answer the seven sets of questions. Alternatively, both parties in a conflict can complete this exercise and then compare notes to establish interconnections and move toward resolution.

THE ICEBERG OF CONFLICT

One way of picturing the hidden layers and complexities of conflict is through the metaphor of the iceberg, as depicted in the following chart. You may want to identify additional layers besides the ones we cite, to reveal what is below the surface for you.

EXPLORING YOUR ICEBERG

Each level of the iceberg represents something that does not appear on the surface, yet adds weight and immobility to our arguments when we are in conflict. Beneath the iceberg, the chart identifies an "awareness of interconnection," meaning that we all have the capacity, when we go deep enough and are not stuck on the surface of our conflicts, to experience genuine empathy and awareness of our interconnection with each other—including the person who is upsetting us.

To understand the deeper layers of your iceberg and get to an awareness of interconnection, consider a conflict in which you are now engaged. Try to identify the specific issues, problems, and feelings that exist for you at each level of the iceberg. As you probe deeper, notice whether your definition of the conflict changes, and how it evolves. Become aware of any emotions that emerge as you look deeper. Fear or resistance to these feelings can keep the conflict locked in place and block you from reaching deeper levels. Allow

ICEBERG OF CONFLICT

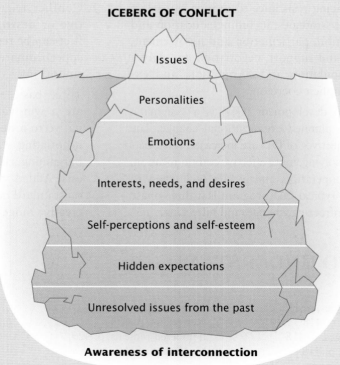

Issues

Personalities

Emotions

Interests, needs, and desires

Self-perceptions and self-esteem

Hidden expectations

Unresolved issues from the past

Awareness of interconnection

yourself to experience these feelings, whatever they are, and identify them to yourself or to someone you trust, so you can let them go. Try to answer the following questions for yourself and your opponent.

- Issues: What issues appear on the surface of your conflict?
- Personalities: Are differences between your personalities contributing to misunderstanding and tension? If so, what are they and how do they operate?
- Emotions: What emotions are having an impact on your reactions? How are they doing so? Are you communicating your emotions responsibly, or suppressing them?
- Interests, needs, desires: How are you proposing to solve the conflict? Why is that your proposal? What deeper concerns are driving the conflict? What do you really want? Why? What needs or desires, if satisfied, would enable you to feel good about the outcome? Why is that important? What does getting what you want have to do with the conflict?
- Self-perceptions and self-esteem: How do you feel about yourself and your behavior when you are engaged in the conflict? What do you see as your strengths and weaknesses?
- Hidden expectations: What are your primary expectations of your opponent? Of yourself? Have you clearly, openly, and honestly communicated your expectations to the other person? What would happen if you did? How might you release yourself from false expectations?
- Unresolved issues from the past: Does this conflict remind you of anything from your past relationships? Are there any unfinished issues remaining from the past that keep you locked in this conflict? Why?

Source: From Kenneth Cloke and Joan Goldsmith, *Resolving Conflicts at Work: A Complete Guide for Everyone on the Job*, pp. 114–116. Copyright © 2000 by Jossey-Bass. Reprinted with permission of John Wiley & Sons, Inc.

FOR CONSIDERATION/DISCUSSION

1. Did the issues and your perception of the conflict change as you worked through the iceberg? Explain.
2. Was there more (or less) to this conflict than you initially thought? Explain.
3. Which level of the iceberg was the most difficult to address? Why? Which was the easiest? Why?
4. What interconnections surfaced? How can they be used as a foundation for resolving the conflict?
5. How will this exercise affect the way you try to understand and resolve (or avoid) conflicts in the future?

ETHICS EXERCISE

 DO THE RIGHT THING

I'M WRONG!

Tyler Cowen, George Mason University economics professor: In your business dealings, the people with whom you butt heads are often those who have the most insight into you.

If someone thoroughly annoys you, chances are he has a good sense of your faults (maybe that's why you're annoyed!) or holds a point of view you don't often hear. Listen closely. Understanding the value of what your adversaries have to say will help you improve, giving you a big leg up. . . .

When you have an argument with your future spouse, about half the time you're in the wrong. Grasping that hard-to-accept fact is one of the best ways to save yourself from a costly divorce.

Source: Excerpted from Tyler Cowen, "Three Things to Tell a New Graduate," *Money,* 39 (May 2010): 35.

What are the ethical implications of the following interpretations?

1. Friends are friends and enemies are enemies. To say you're sorry is to show weakness, which encourages others to take advantage of you.

2. It is best to simply avoid those who annoy you to prevent conflict.

3. In appropriate situations, admitting you're wrong in an argument with a friend or loved one or in a disagreement with an adversary can actually boost your self-esteem and strengthen your public image.

4. Your own ethical interpretation?

MANAGERS-IN-ACTION VIDEO CASE STUDY

SCHOLFIELD HONDA

Change and Innovation

Roger Scholfield, owner of Scholfield Honda, shares his perspective on managing a constantly changing environment. He discusses Honda Corporation's 25-year business plan that incorporates everything from consumer safety to concerns for the environment. The car industry is a competitive market where businesses like Scholfield Honda must innovate to remain on top. In this video, you will learn about one employee, Lee Lindquist, who made a difference by initiating change. Discover Lindquist's secrets to getting his boss to agree to implement his idea, to sell natural-gas-powered vehicles. Lindquist avoids initial resistance to change but his dealership still has some challenges to overcome. What's next for this innovative business?

For more information about Scholfield Honda, visit its Web site: www.scholfieldhonda .com.

Before watching the video, answer the following questions:

1. Why is managing change an important topic to include in a management textbook?

2. Why do most people resist change?

3. How do you respond to change?

After watching the video, answer the following questions:

4. Who initiated change at Scholfield Honda?

5. How was Lindquist successful in getting the owner to agree to sell natural-gas-powered vehicles?

6. What can other business owners and managers learn from Roger Scholfield about embracing change for competitive advantage?

7. Scholfield Honda has a vision for ongoing change that includes increasing the sales of natural-gas-powered vehicles. The company faces a few challenges that are beyond its direct control. What do you suggest the company should do to develop a win-win approach and negotiate for the necessary infrastructure improvements?

CLOSING CASE

IN SEARCH OF THE PAPERLESS OFFICE—PART 2

After his first attempt at creating a paperless office tanked, Zugheri at First Houston Mortgage decided he needed to create an incentive: a more flexible work schedule. He paid a programmer about $30,000 to devise an electronic mortgage application, a tool for accepting electronic signatures, and a program to organize the company's electronic documents on its servers. Zugheri spent about three months designing a formal process for the saving, naming, and virtual handling of the files.

When he finally gathered his employees to demonstrate the new system, Zugheri emphasized the benefits for his workers, many of whom commuted an hour or more each day. Because the customer files would now be stored on an Internet-accessible server, employees would be able to work from home on Fridays, stay home with a sick child, or take a weeklong vacation without worrying about losing track of their accounts. "I could literally see their attitudes change through their body language," Zugheri says. "And I felt confident that when we left that room, we were all moving in the same direction."

Zugheri's company, which is in the process of changing its name to Envoy Mortgage after recent acquisitions, now employs about 475 people and has been praised by mortgage industry publications for its use of technology and for cutting back on paper waste. Though Zugheri concedes that his firm will never be completely free of paper, he is excited about the progress his employees have made—and that he is saving about $150,000 a year on paper and toner. But perhaps the greatest benefit of Zugheri's new system came in September, when Hurricane Ike devastated the Houston area. Even when 80 percent of his employees were unable to make it to the office because of flooded roads and debris, business continued to hum, as many of them were still able to log in via the Internet and do their work.

For Discussion

1. In terms of Figure 15.1, what type of change does this case involve? Explain your choice.

2. Why do you think David Zugheri's employees resisted the new digital scanning technology, discussed in Part 1 at the beginning of this chapter?

3. In the language of organization development (OD), why did the change in Part 1 fail and the change in Part 2 succeed?

4. In Part 2, can you detect an element of negotiation in Zugheri's approach? Explain.

5. Why do entrepreneurs such as Zugheri need to know about change, conflict, and negotiation if they want to achieve their strategic goals?

6. What is your personal experience with resistance to change in the workplace? Was the situation handled correctly or incorrectly? Explain. If incorrectly, how should the situation have been handled?

Source: Excerpted from Darren Dahl, "Trust Me: You're Gonna Love This—Getting Employees to Embrace New Technology," *Inc.*, 30 (November 2008): 41.

Organizational Control Processes

P5

CHAPTER 16 Organizational Control
and Quality Improvement

Organizational Control
and Quality Improvement

Bobby Bank/Getty Images News/Getty Images

*"We watch the numbers like a hawk every day. The biggest
measurement we have is how many customers love us."*[1]
—*WILLIAM WANG, FOUNDER AND CEO, VIZIO*

The Changing Workplace

APPLE TAKES A BITE OUT OF CUSTOMER SERVICE HASSLES

Among the many angry customers whom Jeremy Derr encountered during his time as an Apple Genius, the one he remembers best is the professional photographer with the bad FireWire port. "This guy had been dealing with the issue for weeks, so by the time he came in, he was pretty distraught," says Derr, who began working as a Genius at Apple's Houston Galleria store in 2002. Derr determined that the machine would need to go in for service and the repair would take a week. "That's when he absolutely lost it."

However great your product, something will invariably go wrong—and as the classic customer-service maxim goes, only then will the customer take the true measure of your firm. In recent years, companies of all kinds—but especially Apple's competitors in the computer and phone businesses—have adopted strategies that amount to customer avoidance rather than service. They shunt their customers off to outsourced call centers staffed with under-paid agents who read from scripts, or worse, send them to an online FAQ. When Google launched its Nexus One smartphone through its online store in January, it forgot to make any real people available to field support questions. It didn't take long for the company's online forums to be flooded with angry customers.

When Apple devised its retail strategy a decade ago, the company had a single overriding goal: to launch stores that were unlike anything that customers associated with the computer industry. Apple hired Ron Johnson from Target and George Blankenship from Gap. (Last year, Blankenship decamped to Microsoft's new retail-store effort.) Johnson began by asking shoppers to name their best customer-service experience, and he found that most of them agreed on a single setting, the hotel concierge desk. Their effort to re-create the same friendliness you'd find in a Four Seasons Hotel lobby led to the Genius Bar, which Johnson calls the "heart and soul" of every Apple Store.

OBJECTIVES

- **Identify** three types of control and the components common to all control systems.
- **Discuss** organizational control from a strategic perspective.
- **Identify** the four key elements of a crisis management program.
- **Identify** five types of product quality.
- **Explain** how providing a service differs from manufacturing a product, and identify the five service-quality dimensions.

- **Define** total quality management (TQM), and specify the four basic TQM principles.
- **Describe** at least three of the seven TQM process improvement tools.
- **Explain** how Deming's PDCA cycle can improve the overall management process.
- **Specify** and **discuss** at least four of Deming's famous 14 points.

Geniuses will look at any Apple product for free, regardless of where you bought your item. They'll take a stab at fixing non-Apple software, and they'll even help customers with non-tech-support tasks. "I once helped a woman learn iMovie so she could record her wedding reception," Derr says.

Apple doesn't charge for any of this. Customers pay only for repairs on out-of-warranty goods, and Derr notes that Geniuses have almost total leeway to waive these fees. How can Apple afford to be so generous? "It's a loss leader," says Derr, who left the Apple Store in 2006 to start a software company. "Sometimes someone comes in for help and decides to buy something on the way out."

That's exactly what happened with Derr's angry photographer. As the man ranted about being unable to do without his computer, Derr suggested that perhaps he should invest in another laptop as a backup. "It was like I'd said the magic words," Derr says. The photographer left the store with a brand-new machine.

Source: Excerpted from Farhad Manjoo, "Apple Nation," *Fast Company*, 147 (July–August 2010): 75–76.

Apple's never-ending quest for top-quality service teaches us an important management lesson. Strategies and plans, no matter how well conceived, are no guarantee of organizational success.[2] Those strategies and plans need to be updated and carried out by skilled and motivated employees amid changing circumstances and an occasional crisis. Adjustments and corrective action are inevitable. This final chapter helps present and future managers put this lesson to work by introducing fundamentals of organizational control, discussing crisis management, and exploring product and service quality.

FUNDAMENTALS OF ORGANIZATIONAL CONTROL

The word *control* suggests the operations of checking, testing, regulation, verification, and/or adjustment. As a management function, control is the process of taking the necessary preventive or corrective actions to ensure that the organization's mission and objectives are accomplished as effectively and efficiently as possible. Objectives are yardsticks against which actual performance can be measured. If actual performance is consistent with the appropriate objective, things will proceed as planned. If not, changes must be made. Successful managers detect (and even anticipate) deviations from desirable standards and make appropriate adjustments.[3] Those adjustments can range from ordering more raw materials to overhauling a production line; from discarding an unnecessary procedure to hiring additional personnel; from containing an unexpected crisis to firing a defrauder. Although the possible adjustments exercised as part of the control function are countless, the purpose of the control function is always the same: *Get the job done despite environmental, organizational, and behavioral obstacles and uncertainties.* Michael Dell, founder of the computer powerhouse bearing his name, admits that his company makes mistakes like any other, but that they focus on continuous improvement. In Dell's corporate culture, employees are trained to constantly ask how they can sell more, reduce costs, and enhance customer service.[4]

control taking preventive or corrective actions to keep things on track

Types of Control

Every open system processes inputs from the surrounding environment to produce a unique set of outputs. Natural open systems, such as the human body, are kept in life-sustaining balance through automatic feedback mechanisms. In contrast, artificial open systems, such as organizations, do not have automatic controls. Instead, they require constant monitoring and adjustment to control for deviations from standards. Figure 16.1 illustrates the control function. Note the three different types of control: feedforward, concurrent, and feedback.

FEEDFORWARD CONTROL (AND CHECKLISTS). According to two early proponents of feedforward control, "the only way [managers] can exercise control effectively is to see the problems coming in time to do something about them."[5] Feedforward control is the active anticipation of problems and their timely prevention, rather than after-the-fact reaction. Carpenters have their own instructive version of feedforward control: "Measure twice, cut once." It is important to note that planning and feedforward control are two related but different processes. Planning answers the question "Where are we going and how

Figure **16.1**   Three Types of Control

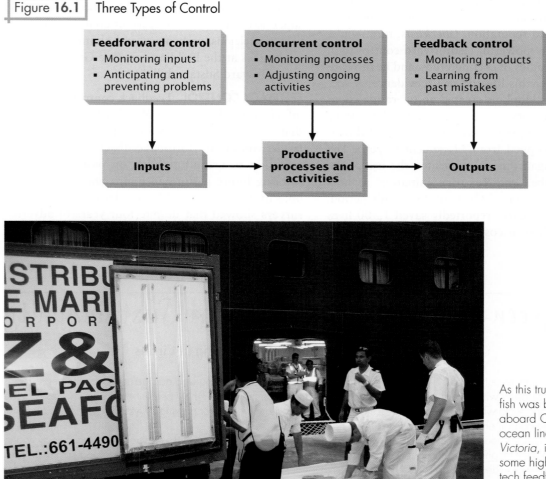

Feedforward control
- Monitoring inputs
- Anticipating and preventing problems

Concurrent control
- Monitoring processes
- Adjusting ongoing activities

Feedback control
- Monitoring products
- Learning from past mistakes

Inputs → **Productive processes and activities** → **Outputs**

As this truckload of fresh fish was being transferred aboard Cunard's new ocean liner, the *Queen Victoria*, in Costa Rica, some high-tech and low-tech feedforward control occurred. A ship's officer (right) scanned the fish with an electronic toxic chemical sniffer and a chef sniffed the fish with his nose.

Robert Kreitner

feedforward control active anticipation and prevention of problems, rather than passive reaction

will we get there?" Feedforward control addresses the issue "What can we do ahead of time to help our plan succeed?" For many industries—including agriculture, insurance, and transportation—feedforward control involves keeping a close eye on the weather and preparing for storms. For others, the focus is on food safety and avoiding food-borne illness. McDonald's hamburgers, for example, come from a packing plant that has been inspected by both McDonald's and a third party. The fast food giant is considered an industry leader in food safety.[6]

Product design, preventive maintenance on machinery and equipment, due diligence, and checklists also qualify as feedforward control. On a personal level, think of due diligence as refusing to go on a blind date without first researching the person's background and reputation. *Checklists*, meanwhile, are a simple yet powerful feedforward control tool, as proven in studies of cockpit crews and health care teams. Consider this life-and-death evidence: A specialist at Johns Hopkins created an operating room checklist for doctors and nurses, including basic steps like hand-washing with soap. Within a year, the infection rate dropped from 11 percent to zero. The state of Michigan then implemented the use of the checklist, dubbed the Keystone Initiative, at hospitals across the state.[7] Over an 18-month period, the Keystone Initiative reportedly saved 1,500 lives and $175 million in costs,[8] all because of a simple five-item checklist that helped busy health professionals remember the basics of good hygiene.

Of the three types of control, American managers tend to do the poorest job with feedforward control. Longer-term thinking, anticipating unintended consequences, better cross-functional communication, and checklists could help this situation.

CONCURRENT CONTROL. This second type of control might well be called real-time control because it deals with the present rather than with the future or past. Concurrent control involves monitoring and adjusting ongoing activities and processes to ensure compliance with standards.[9] When you adjust the water temperature while taking a shower, you are engaging in concurrent control. So, too, construction supervisors engage in concurrent control when they help electricians, carpenters, and plumbers with difficult tasks at the building site. (See Green Management: Toward Sustainability.)

FEEDBACK CONTROL. Feedback control is gathering information about a completed activity, evaluating that information, and taking steps to improve similar activities in the future. Feedback control permits managers to use information on past performance to bring future performance into line with planned objectives and acceptable standards. For example, surveys showed that despite four years of advertising using the quacking Aflac duck, 60 percent of

Green Management: Toward Sustainability

Tod Dykstra Wants Us to Stop Driving in Circles

[He glances out his] office window every day and sees waste. While a parking garage next door sits empty, roads are clogged with cars in search of cheaper metered spots on the street. "Thirty percent of driving in cities is made up of people who have gotten where they want to go and are looking for parking," Dykstra says. "Think about all those carbon emissions. It just doesn't seem right."

Dykstra, founder of Streetline Networks, a San Francisco company that makes traffic-control technology, wants to make it tougher to park cheaply or get away with not feeding the meter. Streetline's system lets parking authorities identify crowded streets and jack up parking-meter rates block by block. The idea is to encourage drivers to stop circling and get off the streets—either paying for a municipal garage or heading to a less crowded neighborhood. San Francisco and Los Angeles are now installing Streetline technology.

For Discussion: Why is this a good example of concurrent control in the quest for sustainability? Personally, do you think this is a good idea? Explain.

Source: Excerpted from Cliff Edwards, "Innovator: Tod Dykstra," *Bloomberg Businessweek* (June 14–20, 2010): 36.

concurrent control monitoring and adjusting ongoing activities and processes | *feedback control* checking a completed activity and learning from mistakes

respondents still did not know that the company sells insurance.[10] Critics of feedback control say it is like closing the gate after the horse (or duck?) is gone. Because corrective action is taken after the fact, costs tend to pile up quickly, and problems and deviations persist.

On the positive side, feedback control tests the quality and validity of objectives and standards. Objectives found to be impossible to attain should be made more reasonable. Those that prove too easy need to be toughened.

In summary, successful managers exercise all three types of control in today's complex organizations and fast-changing circumstances.[11] Feedforward control helps managers avoid mistakes in the first place; concurrent control enables them to catch mistakes as they are being made; feedback control keeps them from repeating past mistakes. Interaction and a workable balance among the three types of control are desirable.

Components of Organizational Control Systems

The owner-manager of a small business such as a dry-cleaning establishment can keep things under control by personally overseeing operations and making necessary adjustments. An electrician can be called in to fix a broken pressing machine, poor workmanship can be improved through coaching, a customer's complaint can be handled immediately, or a shortage of change in the cash register can be remedied. A small organization directed by a single, highly motivated individual with expert knowledge of all aspects of the operation represents the ideal control situation. Unfortunately, the size and complexity of most productive organizations have made firsthand control by a single person obsolete. Consequently, multilevel, multidimensional organizational control systems have evolved.

A study of nine large companies in different industries

sheds some light on the mechanics of complex organizational control systems.[12] After interviewing dozens of key managers, the researchers identified six distinct control subsystems (we have added a seventh):

1. *Strategic plans.* Qualitative analyses of the company's position within the industry
2. *Long-range plans.* Typically, five-year financial projections
3. *Annual operating budgets.* Annual estimates of profit, expenses, and financial indicators
4. *Statistical reports.* Quarterly, monthly, or weekly nonfinancial statistical summaries of key indicators such as orders received and personnel surpluses or shortages
5. *Performance appraisals.* Evaluation of employees through the use of management by objectives (MBO) or rating scales

16a
Quick Quiz

• North American companies, which spent an estimated $48.7 billion on airline tickets in 2009, could save almost $30 billion combined annually if they instituted and enforced stricter travel policies that required non-refundable tickets or the lowest logical fare.

• UPS now requires photo ID from customers shipping packages at retail sites globally, a month after explosives made it on to a UPS plane from a Yemen site.

QUESTION: What sort of control—feedforward, concurrent, or feedback—is involved in these two situations? Explain.

For further information about the interactive annotations in this chapter, visit our student Web site.

Sources: Dan Reed, "Companies Clamp Down on Travel Costs," *USA Today* (August 2, 2010): 4B; and "UPS to Demand Photo ID at Retail Sites," *USA Today* (December 8, 2010): 1B.

Managers at Chicago's busy O'Hare International Airport can't control the region's notoriously fickle weather. Yet they can use after-the-fact feedback controls such as snow removal to respond safely and efficiently to Mother Nature's wrath.

6. *Policies and procedures.* Organizational and departmental standard operating procedures referred to on an as-needed basis

7. *The organization's culture.* As discussed in Chapter 9, stories, rituals, and company legends have a profound impact on how things are done in specific organizations.[13] Employees who deviate from cultural norms are promptly straightened out with glances, remarks, or ridicule.

Complex organizational control systems such as these help keep things on the right track because they embrace three basic components that are common to all organizational control systems: objectives, standards, and an evaluation-reward system.[14]

OBJECTIVES. In Chapter 6, we defined an *objective* as a target signifying what should be accomplished and when. Objectives are an indispensable part of any control system because they provide measurable reference points for corrective action.[15] Yearly progress reports let managers know if they are on target or if corrective actions (such as creating a new advertising campaign) are necessary.

STANDARDS. Whereas objectives serve as measurable targets, standards serve as guideposts on the way to reaching those targets. Standards provide feedforward control by warning people when they are off track.[16] Golfers use par as a standard for gauging the

quality of their game. When the objective is to shoot par, a golfer who exceeds par on a hole is warned that he or she must improve on later holes to achieve the objective. Universities exercise a degree of feedforward control over student performance by establishing and following admission standards for grades and test scores. Businesses rely on many different kinds of standards, including those in purchasing, engineering, time, safety, accounting, and quality.

These standards are a vital first line of defense against increasingly sophisticated counterfeit products. Pharmaceutical companies, for instance, face an uphill battle: Fake drugs are so well produced that even experts can't tell the real from the copy. Counterfeiters even copy the security devices such as holograms on their packages.[17]

A proven technique for establishing challenging standards is benchmarking—that is, identifying, studying, and imitating the *best practices* of market leaders.[18] The central idea in benchmarking is to be competitive by striving to be as good as or better than the *best* in the business. The search for benchmarks is not necessarily restricted to one's own industry. Consider, for example, this recent talent swap between Procter & Gamble and Google. The two companies have been swapping employees to learn more about each other and about reaching customers.[19] The Walt Disney Company has even made a business out of benchmarking by conducting management training

benchmarking identifying, studying, and building upon the best practices of organizational role models

at its Disney Institute. One course is titled the Disney Approach to Quality Service.[20]

AN EVALUATION-REWARD SYSTEM. Because employees do not all achieve equal results, some sort of performance review is required to document individual and/or team contributions to organizational objectives. Extrinsic rewards need to be tied equitably to documented results and improvement. A carefully conceived and clearly communicated evaluation-reward arrangement can shape favorable effort→reward expectations, thus motivating better performance. CEO Paul R. Charron got Liz Claiborne Inc., the large apparel company, back on track by establishing a new metric for performance—direct operating profit—which he steadily reinforced until it became part of the corporate culture.[21] When integrated systematically, objectives, standards, and an equitable evaluation-reward system constitute an invaluable control mechanism.

Strategic Control

Managers who fail to complement their strategic planning with strategic control, as recommended in Chapter 7, will find themselves winning some battles but losing the war.[22] The performance pyramid in Figure 16.2 illustrates the necessarily tight linkage between planning and control. It is a strategic model because everything is oriented toward the strategic peak of the pyramid. Objectives based on the corporate vision (or mission) are translated downward during planning. As plans become reality, control measures of activities and results are translated up the pyramid. The flow of objectives and measures requires a good information system.

Criteria related to external effectiveness and those related to internal efficiency are distinguished in Figure 16.2 by color coding. Significantly, all of the external effectiveness areas are focused on the marketplace in general and on the *customer* in particular. According to the performance pyramid, control measures are needed for cycle time, waste, flexibility, productivity, and financial results. *Cycle time* is the time it takes for a product to be transformed from raw materials or parts into a finished good. Note that *flexibility* is related to both effectiveness and efficiency. A garden tractor manufacturer, for example, needs to be externally flexible in adapting to changing customer demands and internally flexible in training employees to handle new technology.

| Figure **16.2** | The Performance Pyramid for Strategic Control |

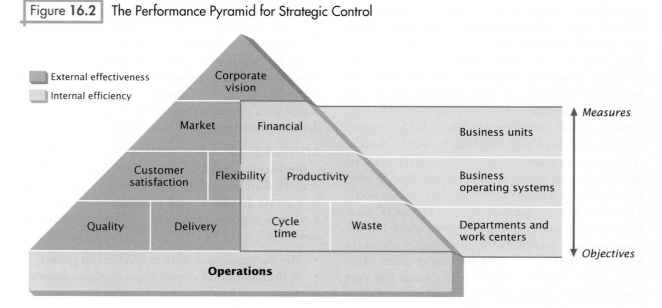

Source: C. J. McNair, Richard L. Lynch, and Kelvin F. Cross, "Do Financial and Nonfinancial Performance Measures Have to Agree?" *Management Accounting*, published by the Institute of Management Accountants, Montvale, N.J., 72 (November 1990): 30. Copyright by Institute of Management Accountants. Reprinted by permission.

Identifying Control Problems

Control problems have a way of quietly snowballing to overwhelming proportions. Progressive managers can take constructive steps to keep today's complex operations under control.[23] Two very different approaches are executive reality checks and internal auditing.

EXECUTIVE REALITY CHECK. In the executive reality check, top-level managers periodically work "in the trenches" to increase their awareness of operations. This was the premise behind the CBS television series *Undercover Boss*. One of the show's participants, Kimberly Schaefer, CEO of Great Wolf Resorts, pulled kitchen duty at one of her water parks and realized how much the corporation could improve by asking employees for their input. She commented, "It's amazing how much more you can learn when you don't think you're the smartest person in the room."[24] Executive reality checks not only alert top managers to control problems but also foster empathy for lower-level employees' problems and concerns. In addition to firsthand reality checks, an internal audit can identify weak spots and problems in the organizational control system.

INTERNAL AUDITS. There are two general types of auditing, external and internal. External auditing, generally performed by certified public accountants (CPAs), is the verification of an organization's financial records and reports. In the United States, the protection of stockholders' interests is the primary rationale for objective external audits. Of course, the Internal Revenue Service (IRS) and the Securities and Exchange Commission (SEC) also have a stake in external auditors' watchdog function. Ideally, external auditors help keep organizations honest by double-checking to see whether reported financial results are derived through generally accepted accounting principles and are based on material fact, not fiction.[25] Thanks to high-profile corporate and financial scandals, external auditing has been put under the microscope, and needed financial reforms such as the Sarbanes-Oxley Act of 2002 are now in place. Managers who "cook the books" run a greater risk than ever of paying stiff fines and doing jail time.[26] One of Sarbanes-Oxley's most notable requirements forces chief executive officers and chief financial officers to personally sign and certify their company's periodic financial statements and reports. Noncompliance carries heavy penalties, such as fines up to $1 million and/or a ten-year prison sentence, and willful violations result in fines up to $5 million and/or a 20-year sentence.[27] On the positive side, auditing is a hot job category these days.[28]

Internal auditing differs from external auditing in a number of ways. First, and most obviously, it is performed by an organization's staff rather than by outsiders. General Electric, for example, employs 500 internal auditors.[29] Second, internal auditing is intended to serve the interests of the organization as a whole. Also, as the following definition illustrates, internal auditing tends to be more encompassing than the external variety: "Internal auditing is the independent appraisal of the various operations and systems control within an organization to determine whether acceptable policies and procedures are followed, established standards are met, resources are used efficiently and economically, planned missions are accomplished effectively, and the organization's objectives are being achieved."[30]

The product of internal auditing is called a *process audit* by some and a *management audit* by others. Internal audits certainly are necessary, as discovered in a survey of 203 auditors: 92 percent found discrepancies in their companies' methods of accounting control.[31] To strengthen the objectivity of internal auditing, experts recommend that internal auditors report directly to the top person in the organization. In organization development terms, some "unfreezing" needs to be done to quiet the common complaint that internal auditing is a ploy used by top management for snooping and meddling. Timely and valid internal audits are a primary safeguard against organizational decline, as well as against theft and fraud.

SYMPTOMS OF INADEQUATE CONTROL. When a comprehensive internal audit is not available, a general checklist of symptoms of inadequate control can be a useful diagnostic tool. Although every situation has some unusual problems, certain symptoms are common:

- An unexplained decline in revenues or profits
- A degradation of service (customer complaints)
- Employee dissatisfaction (complaints, grievances, excessive absenteeism, turnover)
- Cash shortages caused by bloated inventories or delinquent accounts receivable

Sure, Brad Pitt can act. But can he keep the construction of eco-friendly homes in New Orleans' Lower 9th Ward under control? Brad reportedly does regular reality checks of progress on his pet project.

AP Photo/Bill Haber

- Idle facilities or personnel
- Disorganized operations (workflow bottlenecks, excessive paperwork)
- Excessive costs
- Evidence of waste and inefficiency (scrap, rework)[32]

Problems in one or more of these areas may be a signal that things are getting out of control.

CRISIS MANAGEMENT

The September 11, 2001, terrorist attacks on America were a symbolic wake-up call for any managers who had a lax attitude toward organizational crisis management programs. Companies that were already prepared stepped up their preparedness. FedEx, for example, now has 500 employees who serve as a committed security force[33] and spends nearly $600,000 a year for CEO Fred Smith's personal and family security.[34] Beyond terrorism, managers need to be vigilant for a vast array of trouble spots. They include everything from BP-size oil spills and Toyota-type product recalls to data theft, cyber attacks, and factory explosions.[35] In the age of social media, a crisis can arise in an instant and become a serious threat if uncontained. For example, two Domino's employees

posted a prank video on YouTube showing a person sneezing into a sandwich. Domino's immediately issued a video statement on YouTube and created a Twitter account to respond to questions. Even on a less dramatic scale, business-as-usual inevitably involves the occasional crisis that demands skillful crisis management and disaster recovery.[36,37]

Today, the diversity and scope of organizational crises strain the imagination. Experts on the subject define an *organizational crisis* as a low-probability yet high-impact occurrence that can seriously harm the company. While the cause, potential outcomes, and solution may not be clear, quick decisions must be made.[38] Obviously, managers need to "manage the unthinkable" in a foresighted, systematic, and timely manner. Enter the emerging discipline known as *crisis management*.

Crisis Management Defined

Traditionally, crisis management was viewed negatively, as "managerial firefighting"—waiting for things to go wrong and then scurrying to limit the damage. More recently, the term has taken on a more precise and proactive meaning. In fact, a body of theory and practice is evolving around the idea that managers should think about the unthinkable and expect the unexpected.[39] **Crisis management** is

crisis management anticipating and preparing for events that could damage the organization

Japan is prone to devastating earthquakes and tsunamis, which is why Tokyo firefighters are highly trained and well equipped by the Fire and Disaster Management Agency. Preparedness is what crisis management is all about.

Junko Kimura/Getty Images News/Getty Images

the systematic anticipation of and preparation for internal and external problems that could seriously threaten an organization's reputation, profitability, or survival.[40] Crisis management involves much more than an expedient public relations ploy or so-called spin control to make the organization look good amid bad circumstances. This new discipline is intertwined with strategic control.

Developing a Crisis Management Program

As illustrated in Figure 16.3, a crisis management program is made up of four elements. Disasters need to be anticipated, contingency plans need to be formulated, and crisis management teams need to be staffed and trained. Finally, the program needs to be perfected through realistic practice. Let us examine each of these elements.

CONDUCTING A CRISIS AUDIT. A crisis audit is a systematic way of seeking out trouble spots and vulnerabilities. Disaster scenarios become the topic of discussion as managers ask a series of "What if?" questions.[41] Lists such as the one in Table 16.1 can be useful during this stage. Some crises, such as the untimely death of a key executive, are universal and hence readily identified. Others are industry specific. For example, crashes are an all-too-real disaster scenario for passenger airline companies.

FORMULATING CONTINGENCY PLANS. A contingency plan is a backup plan that can be put into effect when things go wrong.[42] Whenever possible, each contingency plan should specify early warning signals, actions to be taken, and expected consequences of those actions. Detail is crucial, which is why Dow's contingency plan runs to 20 pages. It should include such decisions as who will act

---

Figure **16.3**   Key Elements in a Crisis Management Program

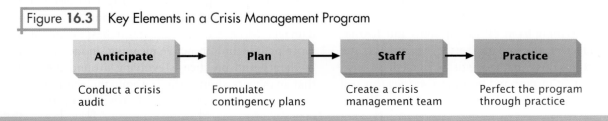

Anticipate	Plan	Staff	Practice
Conduct a crisis audit	Formulate contingency plans	Create a crisis management team	Perfect the program through practice

contingency plan a backup plan for emergencies

| Table **16.1** | An Organizational Crisis Can Come in Many Different Forms |

- Extortion
- Bribery
- Hostile takeover
- Information sabotage
- Product tampering
- Workplace bombing
- Vehicular fatality
- Terrorist attack
- Copyright infringement
- Plant explosion
- Environmental spill
- Sexual harassment
- Computer tampering
- Escape of hazardous materials
- Security breach
- Personnel assault
- Executive kidnapping
- Assault of customers
- Product/service boycott
- Product recall
- Work-related homicide
- Counterfeiting
- Malicious rumor
- Natural disaster that destroys corporate headquarters
- Natural disaster that disrupts a major product or service
- Natural disaster that eliminates key stakeholders
- Natural disaster that destroys organizational information base

Source: *Academy of Management Executive: The Thinking Manager's Source* by Christine Pearson & Judith Clair. Copyright 1998 by Academy of Management (NY). Reproduced with permission of Academy of Management (NY) in the format Textbook via Copyright Clearance Center.

CREATING A CRISIS MANAGEMENT TEAM. Organizational crisis management teams have been likened to the SWAT teams that police departments use for extraordinary situations such as hostage takings. Crisis management teams necessarily represent different specialties, depending on what kinds of crises are envisioned. For example, an electrical utility company might have a crisis management team made up of a media relations expert, an electrical engineer, a consumer affairs specialist, and a lawyer. In 1979, after a railroad car carrying its chemicals derailed near Toronto, Dow Chemical Canada developed a comprehensive crisis plan. Many years later when another accident occurred, Dow's plan kicked into action. Officials praised Dow for how quickly they addressed the situation and communicated information to the public.[44] As the case of Dow Chemical Canada illustrates, quick response and effective communication are the hallmarks of an effective crisis management team, which is why many companies now have such teams in place.

PERFECTING THE PROGRAM THROUGH PRACTICE. Like athletic teams, crisis management teams can achieve the necessary teamwork, effectiveness, and speed of response only through diligent practice. Simulations, drills, and mock disasters provide this

16b
The Truth About Crisis Management

Be honest, admit mistakes, and keep moving. That is perhaps the only way to cope with tragedy of any scale.

QUESTIONS: Why do executives in crisis situations such as the BP oil-spill disaster consistently ignore this simple advice? Is this equally good advice for dealing with a personal crisis? Explain.

Source: John Meacham, "What an Umpire Could Teach BP," *Newsweek* (June 14, 2010): 2.

as spokesperson for the company, which executives to notify in an emergency, and which media outlets to contact.[43] Both crisis audits and related contingency plans need to be updated at least annually and, if rapidly changing conditions dictate, more often.

invaluable practice.[45] Top-management support of such exercises is essential to provide good role models and underscore the importance of the activity. Reinforcing employee efforts in this area with an effective reward system can also encourage serious practice.

Experts say management's two biggest mistakes regarding organizational crises are (1) ignoring early warning signs and (2) denying the existence of a problem when disaster strikes. These mistakes cost Ford Motor Company roughly $3 billion when the company was forced to replace Firestone tires after more than 250 people died and many more were injured in car accidents.[46] A good crisis management program effectively eliminates these self-defeating mistakes. Nike, for example, is getting it right after initially responding with panic, anger, and denials to accusations of using sweatshops. Today, nearly 100 Nike employees oversee their outsourced operations to ensure fair labor practices.[47]

THE QUALITY CHALLENGE

Not too many years ago, North American industry was roundly criticized for paying inadequate attention to the quality of goods and services. Today, many organizations have achieved a dramatic turnaround. There is even a national trophy for quality in the United States that means prestige and lots of free media exposure for winners: the Malcolm Baldrige National Quality Award. Named for a former U.S. secretary of commerce, it was launched by Congress in 1987 to encourage and reward world-class quality.[48] Some observers claim the drive for quality was a passing fad. When asked whether the quality movement was a thing of the past, Tom Peters, the well-known management writer and consultant, answered that quality is no longer making headlines because it's become an accepted, ingrained part of every aspect of business.[49] Anyone tempted to dismiss quality as a once-hot topic past its prime should ponder the prospect of flying in a jet aircraft with substandard engine parts, for example. Quality is not always a life-or-death matter, but it certainly is a major *quality-of-life* factor for each of us.

The balance of this chapter builds a foundation of understanding about quality. The following questions will be answered: How are product and service quality defined? What does total quality management (TQM) involve? What is Deming management?

Defining Quality

According to quality expert Philip Crosby, the basic definition of quality is "conformance to requirements."[50] But whose requirements? The sound quality of an iPod may seem flawless to its new owner, adequate to the engineer who helped design it, and terrible to an accomplished musician. In regard to *service* quality, being put on hold for 30 seconds when calling a computer company's hot line may be acceptable for one person but very irritating for another. Because quality is much more than a simple either/or proposition, both product and service quality need to be analyzed. To do this, we will explore five types of product quality, the unique challenges faced by service organizations, and the ways in which consumers judge service quality.

Five Types of Product Quality

Other specialists in the field have refined Crosby's general perspective by identifying at least five different types of product quality: transcendent, product-based, user-based, manufacturing-based, and value-based.[51] Each represents a unique and useful perspective on product quality.

TRANSCENDENT QUALITY. Inherent value or innate excellence is apparent to the individual. Observing people's varied reactions to pieces of art in a museum is a good way to appreciate the subjectiveness of this type of quality. Beauty, as they say, is in the eye of the beholder.[52]

PRODUCT-BASED QUALITY. The presence or absence of a given product attribute is the primary determinant of this type of quality. Soft tissues, rough sandpaper, flawless glass, sweet candy, and crunchy granola exemplify product-based quality in very different ways. A cashmere sweater costing less than $100, for example, is unlikely to be pure cashmere, given the high cost of raw cashmere wool.[53]

USER-BASED QUALITY. Here, the quality of a product is determined by its ability to meet the user's expectations, preferences, and tastes. Does it get the job done? Is it reliable? Does it taste good? Customer

quality conformance to requirements

At the Bentley Motors Factory in Crewe, England, workers do a final quality inspection inside a glaring light tunnel, where imperfections can't hide. The quest for "transcendent quality," along with a world-class blend of the other four types of quality, helps explain a Bentley's six-figure price tag.

satisfaction surveys conducted by rating agencies such as *Consumer Reports*[54] give smart shoppers valuable input about user-based quality. Word-of-mouth advertising by happy customers has given Hyundai a big boost. In 2009, Hyundai surpassed Ford to take fourth place in sales worldwide. Toyota has long said that it feared the growth of Hyundai, and those fears just continue to grow stronger.[55]

MANUFACTURING-BASED QUALITY. How well does the product conform to its design specifications or blueprint? The closer the match between the intended product and the actual one, the higher the quality. Car doors designed to close easily, quietly, and snugly exhibit high quality if they do so. This category corresponds to Crosby's "conformance to requirements" definition of quality.

VALUE-BASED QUALITY. When you hear someone say, "I got a lot for my money," the speaker is describing value-based quality. Cost-benefit relationships are very subjective because they derive from human perception and personal preferences. About value, *Fortune* magazine observed that "[t]he concept can be nebulous because each buyer assesses value individually. In the end, value is simply giving customers what they want at a price they consider fair."[56] Discount retailers such as Big Lots and

Family Dollar successfully exploit this important type of product quality.

Unique Challenges for Service Providers

Services are a rapidly growing and increasingly important part of today's global economy.[57] Convincing evidence of this can be found in the annual *Fortune* 500 list of the largest U.S. companies by sales revenue. Among the top ten in 2010 were Walmart (retailing), Bank of America and J.P. Morgan Chase (banking), and AT&T (telecommunications). Walmart, a pure service business, topped the list, which has long been dominated by petroleum refiners and automobile companies. Walmart, with annual revenues exceeding $408 billion, has over 2.1 million employees.[58] (If Walmart were a city, it would be the fourth largest in the United States.) Indeed, the vast majority of the U.S. labor force now works in the service sector.

Because services are customer-driven, pleasing the customer is more important than ever. Experts say it costs five times more to win a new customer than it does to keep an existing one.[59] Still, U.S. companies lose an average of about 20 percent of their customers each year.[60] Service-quality strategists

Christopher Furlong/Getty Images News/Getty Images

emphasize that it is no longer enough simply to satisfy the customer. The strategic service challenge today is to *anticipate* and *exceed* the customer's expectations. Many managers of service operations, following the lead of Leon Leonwood Bean, the legendary founder of L.L. Bean Inc., regard customer satisfaction as an ethical responsibility. Bean's philosophy was that "no sale is really complete until the product is worn out and the customer is satisfied."[61] Bean surely would be proud that in a study of telephone service representatives nearly 100 years after he founded the company, L.L. Bean's reps rated tops in friendliness.[62]

To varying extents, virtually every organization is a service organization. Pure service organizations (such as daycare centers) and manufacturers that provide not only products but also delivery and installation services face similar challenges. Specifically, they need to understand and manage the following five distinctive service characteristics:[63]

1. *Customers participate directly in the production process.* Whereas people do not go to the factory to help build the cars and refrigerators that they eventually buy, they do need to be present when their hair is styled or a broken bone is set in a hospital emergency room.
2. *Services are consumed immediately and cannot be stored.* Hairstylists cannot store up a supply of haircuts in the same way that electronics manufacturer Intel can amass an inventory of computer chips.
3. *Services are provided where and when the customer desires.* McDonald's does more business by building thousands of restaurants in convenient locations around the world than it would if everyone had to travel to its Oakbrook, Illinois, headquarters to get a Big Mac and fries. Accommodating customers' sometimes odd schedules is a fact of life for service providers. Insurance salespersons generally work evenings and weekends during their clients' leisure periods.
4. *Services tend to be labor-intensive.* Although skilled labor has been replaced by machines such as automatic bank tellers in some service jobs, most services are provided by people to customers face to face. Consequently, the morale and

social skills of service employees are vitally important. In fact, customer service has been called a *performing art* requiring a good deal of "emotional labor."[64] It isn't easy to look happy and work hard for an angry customer when you're having a bad day, but good customer service demands it.

5. *Services are intangible.* Objectively measuring an intangible service is more difficult than measuring a tangible good, but it is both possible and necessary. For example, the Arizona State Retirement System recently documented improvement in key customer service indicators, such as reducing call wait times from 5 minutes to 15 seconds and refund processing from 25 days to 4 days or less.[65]

Because customers are more intimately involved in the service-delivery process than in the manufacturing process, we need to go directly to the customer for service-quality criteria. As service-quality experts tell us, the only valid standard of comparison

16c
Just One Question

Consumer behavior researchers studied the correlation between survey responses for 4,000 consumers and their loyalty to companies and products, as demonstrated by their actual purchases or recommendations to others. The best predictor across all industries was "How likely is it that you would recommend [company X] to a friend or colleague?"

QUESTIONS: As a customer, is the answer to this question a key indicator of your satisfaction? Explain why or why not. What other considerations affect whether you are a satisfied customer?

Source: Frederick F. Reichheld, "The One Number You Need to Grow," *Harvard Business Review*, 81 (December 2003): 50. For more, see Darren Dahl, "Would You Recommend Us? Perfect Your Service by Asking the Only Question That Matters," *Inc.*, 28 (September 2006): 40, 42.

is the level of customer satisfaction, which can be tricky to measure.[66] How, then, do consumers judge service quality?

Defining Service Quality

Researchers at Texas A&M University uncovered valuable insights about customer perceptions of service quality.[67] They surveyed hundreds of customers of various types of service organizations. The following five service-quality dimensions emerged: *reliability, assurance, tangibles, empathy,* and *responsiveness.* (You may find it helpful to remember these with the acronym RATER.)[68] Customers apparently judge the quality of each service transaction in terms of these five dimensions. (To better understand each dimension and to gauge your own service-quality satisfaction, take a moment now to complete the Action Learning Exercise at the end of this chapter.)

Which of the five RATER dimensions is most important to you? In the Texas A&M study, *reliability* was the most important dimension of service quality, regardless of the type of service involved. Anyone who has waited impatiently for an overdue airplane knows firsthand the central importance of service reliability.[69]

Specific ways to improve product and service quality are presented throughout the rest of this chapter.

AN INTRODUCTION TO TOTAL QUALITY MANAGEMENT (TQM)

Definitions of TQM are many and varied, which is not surprising for an area that has been subject to intense discussion and debate.[70] For our present purposes, total quality management (TQM) is defined as creating an organizational culture committed to the continuous improvement of skills, teamwork, processes, product and service quality, and customer satisfaction.[71] Consultant Richard Schonberger's shorthand definition calls TQM "continuous, customer-centered, employee-driven improvement."[72]

Our definition of TQM is anchored to *organizational culture* because successful TQM is deeply

embedded in virtually every aspect of organizational life. As discussed in detail in Chapter 9, an organization's culture encompasses all the assumptions its employees take for granted about how people should think and act. In other words, personal commitment to systematic continuous improvement needs to become an everyday matter of "that's just the way we do things here." For example, Dr. Frank P. Carrubba, chief technical officer at Philips, the huge Dutch electronics firm, believes it is never too early to get people thinking about quality. The quest for quality must begin in the earliest stages of research and permeate the entire company in order to create reliable products that customers value.[73]

As might be expected with a topic that received so much attention in a relatively short period of time, some unrealistic expectations were created. Unrealistic expectations inevitably led to disappointment and the need for a new quick fix.[74] However, managers with realistic expectations about the deep and long-term commitment necessary for successful TQM can make it work. TQM can have a positive impact if managers understand and enact these four principles of TQM:

1. Do it right the first time.
2. Be customer-centered.
3. Make continuous improvement a way of life.
4. Build teamwork and empowerment.[75]

Let us examine each of these TQM principles.

1. Do It Right the First Time

As noted in Chapter 1, the trend in recent practice has been toward designing and building quality into the product. This approach is much less costly than fixing or throwing away substandard parts and finished products, or experiencing a product recall crisis. Toy company Mattel learned the first lesson of TQM the hard way in 2007 when it had to recall millions of lead-tainted products that can cause serious injury or even death in children. The expense of lost revenues, damaged reputation, and potential government fines, in the long run, will no doubt outweigh the cost of ensuring the safety of materials used by Mattel's Chinese manufacturers and their subcontractors.[76] Schonberger, who studied many Japanese and U.S. factories firsthand, contends that "errors, if

total quality management (TQM) creating an organizational culture committed to continuous improvement in every regard any, should be caught and corrected at the source, i.e., where the work is performed."[77] Consider, for example, the work of a pastry chef. Kimberly Davis Cuthbert, owner of Sweet Jazmines, a Berwyn, Pennsylvania, made-to-order bakery, notes that baking is a science, and the steps and ingredients in each recipe must be replicated exactly each time.[78] A great many jobs in today's economy are like baking. Generally, comprehensive training in TQM tools and statistical process control is essential if employees are to accept personal responsibility for quality improvement.

2. Be Customer-Centered

Everyone has one or more customers in a TQM organization. They may be internal or external customers.[79] Internal customers are other members of the organization who rely on *your* work to get *their* job done. For example, a corporate lawyer employed by Marriott does not directly serve the hotel chain's customers by changing beds, serving meals, or carrying luggage. But that lawyer has an internal customer when a Marriott manager needs to be defended in court.

Regarding external customers, TQM requires all employees who deal directly with outsiders to be customer-centered. Being customer-centered means (1) anticipating the customer's needs, (2) listening to the customer, (3) learning how to satisfy the customer, and (4) responding appropriately to the customer.[80] Listening to the customer is a major stumbling block for many companies. But at Popchip, the natural snack company, listening to the customer is practically a religion. CEO Keith Belling

AP Photo/Jens Meyer

Total quality management (TQM) can be a life-and-death matter, as in the case of aircraft engine construction and field maintenance. So the next time you land safely on an airplane, whisper a "thank you" to skilled people such as these employees at N3 Engine Overhaul Services.

internal customers anyone in your organization who cannot do a good job unless you do a good job | *customer-centered* satisfying the customer's needs by anticipating, listening, and responding

answers every customer e-mail personally, and will often request further information and feedback. "It's such a learning experience," he adds.[81]

Appropriate responses to customers depend upon the specific nature of the business. For example, Table 16.2 lists good and bad customer service behaviors at a U.S. supermarket chain. Note that service-quality training led to very different patterns of behavior for the different jobs.

Vague requests to "be nice to the customer" are useless in TQM organizations. *Behavior*, not good intentions, is what really matters. As discussed in Chapter 14 in relation to behavior modification,

desirable behavior needs to be strengthened with *positive reinforcement*. A good role model in this regard is Ohio Health: "Ohio's largest health-care provider rewards everything: customer service, community service, stars of the month, and perfect attendance."[82]

3. Make Continuous Improvement a Way of Life

The Japanese word for "continuous improvement" is *kaizen*, which means improving the overall system by constantly improving the little details. TQM

| Table **16.2** | Turning a Supermarket into a Customer-Centered Organization |

EMPLOYEES	BEHAVIORS BEFORE THE CHANGE	BEHAVIORS AFTER THE CHANGE
Bag packers	Ignore customers Lack of packing standards	Greet customers Respond to customers Ask for customers' preference
Cashiers	Ignore customers Lack of eye contact	Greet customers Respond to customers Assist customers Speak clearly Call customers by name
Shelf stockers	Ignore customers Don't know store	Respond to customers Help customers with correct product location information Knowledgeable about product location
Department workers	Ignore customers Limited knowledge	Respond to customers Know products Know store
Department managers	Ignore customers Ignore workers	Respond to customers Reward employees for responding to customers
Store managers	Ignore customers Stay in booth	Respond to customers Reward employees for service Appraise employees on customer service

Source: Reprinted from *Organizational Dynamics*, Summer 1992, Randall S. Schuler, "Strategic Human Resource Management: Linking the People with the Strategic Needs of the Business," exhibit 4. Copyright 1992, with permission from Elsevier Science.

kaizen a Japanese word meaning "continuous improvement"

managers dedicated to *kaizen* are never totally happy with things. *Kaizen* practitioners view quality as an endless journey, not a final destination. They are always experimenting, measuring, adjusting, and improving. Rather than naïvely assuming that achieving zero defects necessarily means perfection has been attained, they search for potential and actual trouble spots. For instance, the quest for continuous improvement drives R. Todd Bradley, head of Hewlett-Packard's Personal Systems Group: Bradley explains, "You never let a win go to your head with competitors always on your heels." He is never satisfied that the company is as innovative, efficient, or customer-focused as it can be.[83]

There are four general avenues for continuous improvement:

- Improved and more consistent product and service *quality*
- Faster *cycle times* (in cycles ranging from product development to order processing to payroll processing)
- Greater *flexibility* (for example, faster response to changing customer demands and new technology)
- Lower *costs* and less *waste* (for example, eliminating needless steps, scrap, rework, and non-value-adding activities)[84]

Significantly, these are not trade-offs, as traditionally believed. In other words, TQM advocates reject the notion that a gain on one front must mean a loss on another. Greater quality, speed, and flexibility have to be achieved at lower cost and with less waste. This is an "all things are possible" approach to management. It requires diligent effort and creativity.

4. Build Teamwork and Empowerment

Earlier, we referred to TQM as employee-driven. In other words, it empowers employees at all levels in order to tap their full creativity, motivation, and commitment. *Empowerment*, as defined in Chapter 14, occurs when employees are adequately trained, provided with all relevant information and the best possible tools, fully involved in key decisions, and fairly rewarded for results.[85] TQM advocates prefer to reorganize the typical hierarchy into teams of people from different specialties.

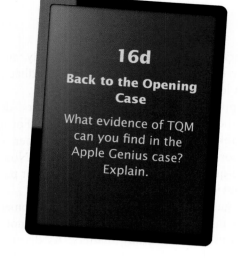

16d

Back to the Opening Case

What evidence of TQM can you find in the Apple Genius case? Explain.

In earlier chapters you encountered many ways to promote teamwork and employee involvement: suggestion systems (Chapter 11), employee engagement and self-managed teams (Chapter 12), teamwork and cross-functional teams (Chapter 13), and participative leadership (Chapter 14). Each can be a valuable component of TQM.

The Seven Basic TQM Process Improvement Tools

Continuous improvement of productive processes in factories, offices, stores, hospitals, hotels, and banks requires lots of measurement. Skilled TQM managers have a large repertoire of graphical and statistical tools at their disposal. The beginner's set consists of seven tools. A brief overview of each will help promote awareness and establish a foundation for further study.

FLOW CHART. A flow chart is a graphical representation of a sequence of activities and decisions. Standard flow-charting symbols include boxes for events or activities, diamonds for key decisions, and ovals for start and stop points. Flow charts show, for instance, how a property damage claim moves through an insurance company. Armed with knowledge of who does what to the claim, and in which sequence, management can streamline the process by eliminating unnecessary steps

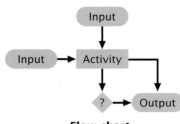

Flow chart

flow chart graphical display of a sequence of activities and decisions

or delays. Chapter 6 shows a sample flow chart as a planning and control tool. TQM teams have found flow charting to be a valuable tool for increasing efficiency, reducing costs, and eliminating waste.

CAUSE-AND-EFFECT ANALYSIS.

The fishbone diagram, named for its rough resemblance to a fish skeleton, helps TQM teams visualize important cause-and-effect relationships. (Some refer to fishbone diagrams as Ishikawa diagrams, in tribute to the Japanese quality pioneer mentioned in Chapter 2.) For example, did a computer crash because of an operator error, an equipment failure, a power surge, or a software problem? A TQM team can systematically track down a likely cause by constructing a fishbone diagram.

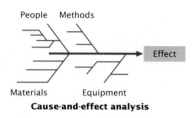
Cause-and-effect analysis

PARETO ANALYSIS.

This technique, popularized by quality expert Joseph M. Juran and discussed in Chapter 6, is named for the Italian economist Vilfredo Pareto (1848–1923). Pareto detected the so-called 80/20 pattern in many real-world situations: relatively few people or events (about 20 percent) account for most of the results or impacts (about 80 percent). It is thus most efficient to focus on the few things (or people) that make the biggest difference. The next time you are in class, for example, note how relatively few students offer the great majority of the comments in class. Likewise, a few students account for most of the absenteeism during the semester. In TQM, conducting a Pareto analysis involves constructing a bar chart by counting and tallying the number of times significant quality problems occur. The tallest bar on the chart, representing the most common problem, demands prompt attention. In a newspaper printing operation, for example, the most common cause of printing press stoppages for the week might turn out to be poor-quality paper. A quick glance at a Pareto chart would alert management of the need to demand better quality from the paper supplier.

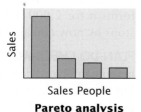
Pareto analysis

CONTROL CHART.

Statistical process control of repetitive operations helps employees keep key quality measurements within an acceptable range. A control chart is used to monitor actual versus desired quality measurements during repetitive operations. Consider the job of drilling a 2-centimeter hole in 1,000 pieces of metal. According to design specifications, the hole should have an inside diameter no larger than 2.1 centimeters and no smaller than 1.9 centimeters. These measurements are the upper control limit (UCL) and the lower control limit (LCL), respectively. Any hole diameters within these limits are of acceptable quality. Random measurements of the hole diameters need to be taken during the drilling operation to monitor quality. When these random measurements are plotted on a control chart, the operator has a handy visual aid that flags violations of the control limits and signals the need for corrective action. Perhaps the drill needs to be cleaned, sharpened, or replaced. This sort of statistical process control is considerably less expensive than having to redrill or scrap 1,000 pieces of metal with wrong-sized holes.

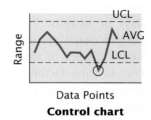
Control chart

HISTOGRAM.

A histogram is a bar chart showing whether repeated measurements of a given quality characteristic conform to a standard bell-shaped curve. Deviations from the standard signal the need for corrective action. The controversial practice of teachers "curving" grades when there is an abnormally high or low grade distribution can be implemented with a histogram.

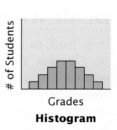
Histogram

SCATTER DIAGRAM.

A scatter diagram is used to plot the correlation between two variables. The figure to the right indicates a positive correlation. In other words, as the value of variable X increases, the value of variable Y tends to decrease. A design engineer for a sporting goods company would find this particular type

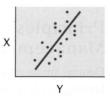

Scatter diagram

---

fishbone diagram a cause-and-effect diagram | Pareto analysis bar chart indicating which problem needs the most attention | control chart visual aid showing acceptable and unacceptable variations from the norm for repetitive operations | histogram bar chart indicating deviations from a standard bell-shaped curve | scatter diagram diagram that plots the relationship between two variables

of correlation while testing the relationship between various thicknesses of fishing rods and flexibility. The thicker the fishing rod, the lower the flexibility.

RUN CHART. Also called a time series or trend chart, a run chart tracks the frequency or amount of a given variable over time. Significant deviations from the norm signal the need for corrective action. Hospitals monitor vital body signs such as temperature and blood pressure with daily logs, which are actually run charts. TQM teams can use them to spot "bad days." For example, automobiles made in U.S. factories on a Friday or Monday historically have had more quality defects than those assembled on a Tuesday, Wednesday, or Thursday.

Before we move on to Deming management, an important point needs to be made. As experts on the subject remind us, "Tools are necessary but not sufficient for TQM."[86] Successful TQM requires a long-term, organizationwide drive for continuous improvement. The appropriate time frame is *years,* not days or months. Tools such as benchmarking and control charts are just one visible feature of that process. Invisible factors—such as values, learning, attitudes, motivation, and personal commitment—dictate the ultimate success of TQM.

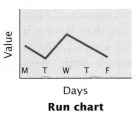

Run chart

DEMING MANAGEMENT

It is hard to overstate the worldwide impact of W. Edwards Deming's revolutionary ideas about management. His ideas have directly and indirectly created better and more productive work environments for countless millions of people. This section builds upon the historical sketch in Chapter 2 by examining basic principles of Deming management and Deming's famous 14 points.

Principles of Deming Management

Deming management is the application of W. Edwards Deming's ideas to revitalize productive systems by making them more responsive to the customer, more

democratic, and more efficient. This approach qualifies as a revolution because, when first proposed by Deming in the 1950s, it directly challenged the legacy of Taylor's scientific management.[87] Scientific management led to rigid and autocratic organizations unresponsive to customers and employees alike. Deming management proposed essentially the opposite approach. Some of the principles discussed next may not seem revolutionary today, precisely because Deming management has become ingrained in everyday *good* management.

QUALITY IMPROVEMENT DRIVES THE ENTIRE ECONOMY. Higher quality eventually means more jobs. Deming's simple yet convincing logic is presented in Figure 16.4. Quality improvement is a powerful engine driving out waste and inefficiency. Quality also generates higher productivity, greater market share, and new business and employment opportunities (see Window on the World). In short, everybody wins when quality improves.[88]

THE CUSTOMER ALWAYS COMES FIRST. In his influential 1986 text *Out of the Crisis,* Deming wrote, "The consumer is the most important part of the production line. Quality should be aimed at the needs of the consumer, present and future."[89] Of course, these are just inspirational words until they are enacted faithfully by individuals on the job.

DON'T BLAME THE PERSON, FIX THE SYSTEM. Deming management chides U.S. managers for being preoccupied with finding someone to blame rather than with fixing problems. His research convinced him that "the system"—meaning management, work rules, technology, and the organization's structure and culture—typically is responsible for upwards of 85 percent of substandard quality. People can and will turn out superior quality, *if* the system is redesigned to permit them to do so. Deming management urges managers to treat employees as internal customers, listening and responding to their ideas and suggestions for improvement. After all, who knows more about a particular job—the person who performs it for 2,000 hours a year or a manager who stops by now and again?

PLAN-DO-CHECK-ACT. Deming's approach calls for making informed decisions on the basis of hard data. His recommended tool for this process is what is popularly known as the PDCA cycle (plan-do-check-act

| Figure **16.4** | Everyone Benefits from Improved Quality |

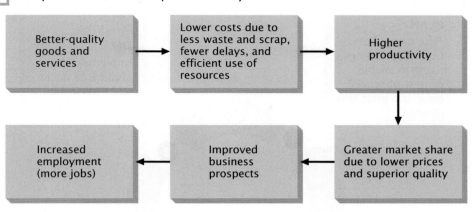

Source: Adapted from W. Edwards Deming, *Out of the Crisis* (Cambridge, Mass.: MIT Press, 1986), p. 3.

WINDOW ON THE WORLD

Chinese Appliance Maker Succeeds with a Lesson from Peter Drucker

Zhang Ruimin, CEO, Haier Group: When we founded Haier, in the 1980s, virtually all products were in short supply in China, and the key to reaping huge profits seemed to be maximizing sales. The vast majority of companies behaved accordingly and strove to get whatever products they could into the market. But at Haier we realized that a sole focus on generating huge profits today could not ensure our survival tomorrow. So we chose to focus on quality instead. Initially this approach made us appear to be falling behind competitors whose profits dwarfed ours. But when the supply-demand balance in China changed, lots of companies lost their customers and went bankrupt overnight. In contrast, we not only survived but strengthened our market position. We took to heart Peter Drucker's words "There is only one valid definition of business purpose: to create a customer."

For Discussion: How was Deming's emphasis on quality, as illustrated in Figure 16.5, brought to life at Haier? Tapping your entrepreneurial spirit, what business ideas do you have that could create customers?

Source: Zhang Ruimin, "Distance Has Been Eliminated," *Harvard Business Review*, 87 (November 2009): 81.

cycle). Deming preferred the term *Shewhart cycle*,[90] in recognition of the father of statistical quality control, Walter A. Shewhart, who is mentioned in Chapter 2. (Japanese managers call it the Deming cycle.) Whatever the label, the PDCA cycle reminds managers to focus on what is really important, use observed data, start small and build upon accumulated knowledge, and be research-oriented in observing changes and results (see Figure 16.5). The influence of Deming management was obvious at Intel when then-CEO Craig Barrett gave his employees a pep talk in a Webcast, reminding them there is nothing new about the principles of quality. He advised them to always plan, do, check, and act.[91]

Figure 16.5   Deming's PDCA Cycle

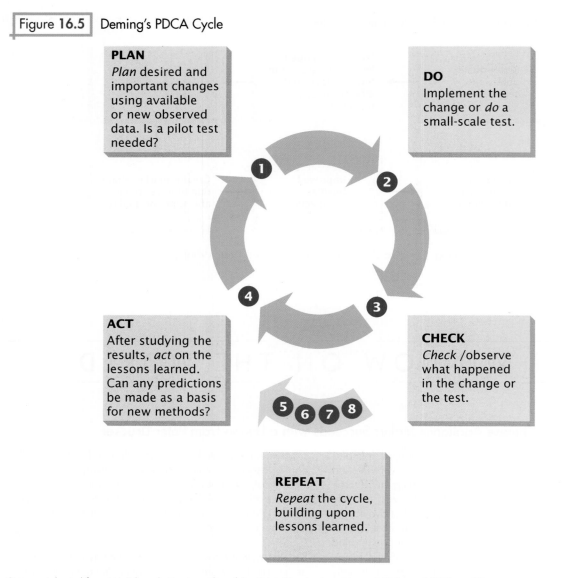

Source: Adapted from W. Edwards Deming, *Out of the Crisis* (Cambridge, Mass.: MIT Press, 1986), p. 88.

Deming's 14 Points

Deming formulated his 14 points to transform U.S. industry from what he considered to be its backward ways. Here is a summary of the 14 points that constitute the heart and soul of Deming management:[92]

1. *Constant purpose.* Strive for continuous improvement in products and services to remain competitive.

2. *New philosophy.* Western management needs to awaken to the realities of a new economic age by demanding wiser use of all resources.

3. *Give up on quality by inspection.* Inspecting for faulty products is unnecessary if quality is built in from the very beginning.

4. *Avoid the constant search for lowest-cost suppliers.* Build long-term, loyal, and trusting relationships with single suppliers.

5. *Seek continuous improvement.* Constantly improve production processes for greater productivity and lower costs.

6. *Train everyone.* Make sure people have a clear idea of how to do their job. Informally learning a new job from coworkers entrenches bad work habits.

7. *Provide real leadership.* Leading is more than telling. It involves providing individualized help.

8. *Drive fear out of the workplace.* Employees continue to do things the wrong way when they are afraid to ask questions about why and how. According to Deming, "No one can put in his best performance unless he feels secure. *Se* comes from the Latin, meaning without, *cure* means fear or care. *Secure* means without fear, not afraid to express ideas, not afraid to ask questions."[93] Lack of job security is a major stumbling block for quality improvement in America.

9. *Promote teamwork.* Bureaucratic barriers between departments and functional specialists need to be broken down. Customer satisfaction is the common goal.

10. *Avoid slogans and targets.* Because the *system* is largely responsible for product quality, putting pressure on individuals who feel they do not control the system breeds resentment. Posters with slogans such as "zero defects" and "take pride in quality" do nothing to help the individual measure and improve productive processes. Control charts and other process-control tools, in contrast, give employees direction and encouragement. Deming's approach tells managers that if they provide leadership and continually improve the system, the scoreboard will take care of itself.

11. *Get rid of numerical quotas.* When employees aggressively pursue numerical goals or quotas, they too often take their eyes off quality, continuous improvement, and costs. Hence, Deming management strongly rejects the practice of management by objectives (MBO),[94] discussed in Chapter 6.

12. *Remove barriers that stifle pride in workmanship.* Poor management, inadequate instruction, faulty equipment, and pressure to achieve a numerical goal get in the way of continuous improvement.

13. *Education and self-improvement are key.* Greater knowledge means greater opportunity. Continuous improvement should be the number one career objective for everyone in the organization.

14. *"The transformation is everyone's job."*[95] Virtually *everyone* in the organization plays a key role in implementing Deming management.

SUMMARY

1. Feedforward control is preventive in nature, whereas feedback control is based on the evaluation of past performance. Managers engage in concurrent control when they monitor and adjust ongoing operations to keep them performing up to standard. The three basic components of organizational control systems are objectives, standards, and an evaluation-reward system.

2. According to the performance pyramid, strategic control involves the downward translation of objectives and the upward translation of performance measures. Both external effectiveness and internal efficiency criteria need to be achieved.

3. The four elements of a crisis management program are (1) *anticipate* (conduct a crisis audit), (2) *plan* (formulate contingency plans), (3) *staff* (create a crisis management team), and (4) *practice* (perfect the program through practice).

4. Product quality involves much more than the basic idea of "conformance to requirements." Five types of product quality are transcendent, product-based, user-based, manufacturing-based, and value-based.

5. Service providers face a unique set of challenges that distinguish them from manufacturers. Because we live in a predominantly service economy, it is important to recognize these challenges: (1) direct customer participation, (2) immediate consumption of services, (3) provision of services at customers' convenience, (4) the tendency of services to be more labor intensive than manufacturing, and (5) the intangibility of services, making them harder to measure. Consumer research uncovered five service-quality dimensions: reliability, assurance, tangibles,

empathy, and responsiveness (RATER). Consumers consistently rank *reliability* number one.

6. Total quality management (TQM) involves creating a culture dedicated to customer-centered, employee-driven continuous improvement. The four TQM principles are

   • Do it right the first time.

   • Be customer-centered.

   • Make continuous improvement a way of life.

   • Build teamwork and empowerment.

7. Seven basic TQM process improvement tools are flow charts, fishbone diagrams, Pareto analysis, control charts, histograms, scatter diagrams, and run charts.

8. Deming's plan-do-check-act (PDCA) cycle forces managers to make decisions and take actions on the basis of observed and carefully measured data. This procedure removes quality-threatening guesswork. The PDCA cycle also helps managers focus on what is really important. PDCA work never ends, because lessons learned from one cycle are incorporated into the next.

9. Deming formulated his famous 14 points in an effort to revolutionize Western management practices. In summary, they urge managers to seek continuous improvement through extensive training, leadership, teamwork, and self-improvement. The points call for *doing away with* mass quality inspections, selecting suppliers only on the basis of low cost, fear, slogans, numerical quotas, and barriers to pride in workmanship. This transformation, according to Deming, is *everyone's* job.

TERMS TO UNDERSTAND

Control, p. 448
Feedforward control, p. 449
Concurrent control, p. 450
Feedback control, p. 450
Benchmarking, p. 452
Executive reality check, p. 454
Internal auditing, p. 454
Crisis management, p. 455

Contingency plan, p. 456
Quality, p. 458
Total quality management (TQM), p. 461
Internal customers, p. 462
Customer-centered, p. 462
Kaizen, p. 463
Flow chart, p. 464

Fishbone diagram, p. 465
Pareto analysis, p. 465
Control chart, p. 465
Histogram, p. 465
Scatter diagram, p. 465
Run chart, p. 466
Deming management, p. 466
PDCA cycle, p. 466

ACTION LEARNING EXERCISE

MEASURING SERVICE QUALITY

Think of the kind of treatment you have received in service establishments recently. Pick a specific restaurant, hair-styling salon, bank, airline, hospital, government agency, auto repair shop, department store, bookstore, or other service organization, and rate the kind of customer service you received, using the following five RATER factors. Circle one response for each factor and total them.

1. *Reliability:* ability to perform the desired service dependably, accurately, and consistently.

    Very poor   1   2   3   4   5   6   7   8   9   10   Very good

2. *Assurance:* employees' knowledge, courtesy, and ability to convey trust and confidence.

    Very poor   1   2   3   4   5   6   7   8   9   10   Very good

3. *Tangibles:* physical facilities, equipment, appearance of personnel.

    Very poor   1   2   3   4   5   6   7   8   9   10   Very good

4. *Empathy:* provision of caring, individualized attention to customers.

    Very poor   1   2   3   4   5   6   7   8   9   10   Very good

5. *Responsiveness:* willingness to provide prompt service and help customers.

    Very poor   1   2   3   4   5   6   7   8   9   10   Very good

    Total score = _____

SCORING KEY

1. 5–10: Cruel and unusual punishment.
2. 11–20: You call this service?
3. 21–30: Average, but who wants average service?
4. 31–40: Close only counts in horseshoes.
5. 41–50: Service hall-of-fame candidate.

FOR CONSIDERATION/DISCUSSION

1. If your service encounter was good (or bad), how many other people have you told about it? Why do people tend to pass along more stories about bad service than about good service?

2. Which of the five service-quality criteria was a major problem in the specific service situation you chose? What corrective actions should management take?

3. In the service situation you selected, which of the five criteria was most important to you? Why? Did you walk away satisfied? Why or why not?

4. If your present (or most recent) job involves rendering a service, how would you score yourself on the RATER factors? What needs to be done to improve your total score?

5. Does the most important RATER factor change for various types of service (for instance, a visit to the doctor versus flying on a commercial airliner)? Explain, with specific examples.

6. Generally speaking, which of the RATER factors is the weak link for today's service organizations? What remedies do you recommend?

ETHICS EXERCISE

 DO THE RIGHT THING

WHO'S REALLY NO. 1?

Matt Blumberg still laughs when he recalls the way his old presentation to investors used to raise eyebrows. It happened nearly every time he reached a certain slide. "It lets them know that our No. 1 stakeholder is our employee base, No. 2 is the customer, and No. 3 is the shareholder," says Blumberg, CEO and chairman of a New York City-based company called Return Path. "And that if they're not comfortable with that, they shouldn't invest in our company."

In the decade that has passed since Blumberg…[co-founded] Return Path, this dedication to employees has taken on varied forms: the flexible work policy that allows employees to conduct business from home. The monthly e-mail updates on the company's financial health [and training to understand the financial data in those e-mails].

Source: Excerpted from Jason Del Rey, "Testing a Company's Commitment to Transparency," *Inc.*, 32 (June 2010): 72.

What are the ethical implications of the following interpretations?

1. The customer was, is, and always should be number one at successful companies. Dissatisfied customers eventually guarantee the failure of any business. Any exceptions?

2. When employees truly believe they are management's number-one priority, they will be loyal and hard working and customer satisfaction and profits will be natural by-products.

3. In a corporation, shareholders are the owners and management's overriding job is to give them a good return on their investment. Any exceptions?

4. Your own ethical interpretation?

MANAGERS-IN-ACTION VIDEO CASE STUDY

PRESERVE® BY RECYCLINE

Quality Control

John Lively, director of operations for Preserve®, and Eric Hudson, founder and company president, share the challenges they face in controlling quality during a period of rapid growth. They discuss various performance measures, including meeting financial benchmarks, controlling manufacturing, and managing inventory. Learn how their commitment to measuring performance led to major operational decisions, including moving manufacturing to new partners who were more efficient and quality control conscious. Preserve's® focus on quality and meeting customer expectations combined with an ongoing concern for sustainability make this company one for other small business owners to emulate when preparing their total quality management plan.

For more information about Preserve®, visit its Web site: www.preserveproducts.com.

Before watching the video, answer the following questions:

1. Describe your impression of quality from a management perspective.

2. What does a product-focused company seek to control with its total quality management initiatives?

3. If there are inadequate controls in place, what are some of the possible symptoms that will become evident to managers over a period of time?

After watching the video, answer the following questions:

4. What are the major control issues facing the Preserve® brand today as it expands its product line?

5. Which of the three types of control discussed at the beginning of this chapter are evident with Preserve®?

6. Although the executives at Preserve® are doing many things right in controlling product development, there is room for improvement. How would you suggest the company should enhance its total quality management process to be prepared for future growth?

7. How has the company's commitment to quality and control given it a competitive edge in forming partnerships with customers and manufacturers?

CLOSING CASE

THE CURE

Here's a guarantee that will get your attention. Geisinger Health System, which runs three hospitals in central Pennsylvania, not only charges a flat fee on coronary-artery bypass surgery and all of the pre- and post-operative care that goes with it, but it also offers a warranty: If a preventable complication puts you back in the hospital within 90 days, Geisinger will eat the cost.

Geisinger's doctors and executives—who sound like management consultants with their talk of "unnecessary variation," "best practices," and "managing change in complex systems"—are trying to do more than reengineer heart surgery. They're turning this 92-year-old hospital network/insurance company in Danville, Pennsylvania, into an ambitious laboratory for organizational and financial experiments aimed at fixing American health care. And some of the ideas may actually work.

When CEO Glenn Steele, a surgeon and oncologist, was recruited from the University of Chicago medical school five years ago, Geisinger was recovering from a brief, unhappy merger with Penn State Hershey Medical Center that left it shaken but also open to change. This was ideal for Steele. Because Geisinger had its own hospitals and health-insurance plan, employed 600 doctors directly, and served a stable and therefore easily studied demographic, it was just the kind of place you'd pick if you wanted to test big hypotheses for reforming the health system.

On Steele's watch, Geisinger has expanded computerized patient records and established a venture unit to develop treatments for possible licensing. But the guarantee program, called Proven-Care, represents arguably the biggest challenge to the status quo.

To Steele, the underlying idea is simple enough: "We shouldn't get paid if we don't do the right thing." Most American health care is provided on a fee-for-service basis. If you have six operations and die, that's better financially for your hospital than if you have one procedure and go home. How to replace fee-for-service with pay-for-performance (P4P) has been the talk in medical policy circles for some time. P4P is often linked to "evidence-based medicine," which simply means doing what clinical data say works, rather than relying on habit, hopes, or tradition.

ProvenCare sets a fixed price—which includes a percentage of the historical costs of complications—for a given medical problem. That creates a powerful financial incentive to get things right the first time. Says Dr. Ronald Paulus, Geisinger's chief innovation and technology officer: "We had to put our money where our mouth was." Steele decided to start with coronary-artery bypass graft (CABG, pronounced *cabbage*) surgery because it's a high-volume, high-margin procedure that's well studied and has low mortality and complication rates.

"We did this to test whether we could take a very complex system across three hospitals with a huge number of people involved and reliably do something we promised we'd do," says Dr. Alfred Casale, formerly Geisinger's chief of cardiothoracic surgery and now chief medical officer of one of Geisinger's hospitals. Before, he explains, "if the physician's assistants got called to the bedside of somebody who had developed rapid atrial fibrillation [the irregular heart rhythm that happens about 20% of the time after a heart operation], the first thing they would ask wasn't, 'How is he?' It was, 'Whose is he?' Because what they would do next depended on the idiosyncrasies of the surgeon and the cardiologist."

ProvenCare eliminates that kind of variation. After studying guidelines adopted by the American Heart Association and the American College of Cardiology, as well as mountains of clinical research, Steele's seven cardiothoracic surgeons developed a list of 40 steps that should be taken—or at least considered—in the treatment of every CABG patient, from the first clinic visit to discharge. "None of the 40 things are new," Casale explains.

"Being certain that they are all being done all the time is the real innovation." It's not a question of inventing a secret sauce, he says, so much as guaranteeing "every hamburger that comes out of the place has the secret sauce in it."

For patients, of course, getting what's been proven to work is nothing more than we expect from a Jiffy Lube. But according to a 2003 *New England Journal of Medicine* paper, only 55% of American patients get all the treatment that is generally accepted as necessary for their problems. To make sure the number at Geisinger is near 100%, surgeons, pre- and post-operation, face a computer screen that asks a set of questions: Is the patient on a beta blocker? A statin? Were antibiotics given at least 60 minutes before surgery and discontinued after 48 hours? A staffer sends an email query if there's no response to any of the 40 steps.

There's a financial component to ProvenCare—doctors receive bonuses based in part on following the protocol—but Geisinger insists it's not trying to force its staff to practice what is pejoratively known in the industry as "cookbook medicine." A doctor who concludes there are good reasons not to do one of the 40 steps simply documents that decision in the patient's record. "What we're trying to do," Casale says, "is avoid the moment of smacking yourself on the head at the end of a procedure and saying, 'Jeez, I should have used antibiotics!'"

The results have been promising. A paper published in the fall of 2007 in the journal *Annals of Surgery* studied 181 CABG patients subject to the ProvenCare protocol between February 2006 and February 2007. Compared to nonchecklist patients, the ProvenCare group had 16% shorter hospital stays. Their bills were about 5% lower. While Casale admits that the study was small, he insists the results are still significant: "We've seen a 45% decrease in readmission rates, 60% decrease in neurologic complications—meaningful changes that you'd certainly be happy to get even if they don't meet a statistician's level for ringing a bell." He says surgeons opted to skip a step in only three cases.

The breakthrough so far hasn't revolutionized Geisinger's business; the company's sales force hasn't yet been able to attract new employers or insurance customers on the basis of ProvenCare, although it's in discussions with insurance giant Aetna. "The idea of mistake-proofing specific problems is at the center of the patient-safety movement and care improvement," says Dr. Troyen Brennan, Aetna's chief medical officer. "I give them great credit."

What Geisinger would really like, of course, is Brennan's business. Chief innovation officer Paulus is optimistic, predicting that new customers will come as the company expands the number of procedures and diseases covered, which now include total hip replacement, cataract surgery, and programs for managing diabetes.

In the meantime, Geisinger continues to compile success stories, including that of CEO Steele, who became patient No. 86 in the ProvenCare CABG program. "I was in and out of the hospital in two-and-a-half days," he says. Casale, who was Steele's surgeon, says the case opened his eyes to how complex a routine operation really is: "Two weeks after, the head of our IT group called me and said, 'Al, I just looked through [Steele's] chart, and I want to send you a list of everybody that accessed the medical record from the time he was seen in the clinic to two weeks post-op.' There were 113 people listed—and every one had an appropriate reason to be in that chart. It shocked all of us.

We all knew this was a team sport, but to recognize it was that big a team, every one of whom is empowered to screw it up—that makes me toss and turn in my sleep."

Which makes the value of that 40-step checklist very clear indeed.

For Discussion

1. How is feedforward control used in the CABG surgeries? What are the pros and cons of this approach?

2. How does Geisinger Health Systems effectively manage the three basic components of all organizational control systems—objectives, standards, and an evaluation-reward system?

3. Why was CEO Glenn Steele's unique "executive reality check" a great way to learn more about his organization and its "customers"?

4. Which of the four principles of TQM are evident in this case? Explain.

5. Which of Deming's 14 points are evident in this case? Explain.

Source: Peter Carbonara, "The Cure," *Fast Company*, 129 (October 2008): 82–86.

CHAPTER 1

1. Henry Mintzberg, "Third-Generation Management Development," *Training & Development* (March 2004): 30 (emphasis added).

2. Data from Milton Moskowitz, Robert Levering, and Christopher Tkaczyk, "100 Best Companies: The List," *Fortune* (February 8, 2010): 78. Also see Diane Brady, "Tony Hsieh," *Bloomberg Businessweek* (May 31–June 6, 2010): 88.

3. Joan Magretta, *What Management Is: How It Works and Why It's Everyone's Business* (New York: The Free Press, 2002), p. 7.

4. As quoted in Kathryn Tyler, "The Boss Makes the Weather," *HR Magazine*, 49 (May 2004): 93. Also see Ronald J. Rakowski, "Even 'Bad' Bosses Can Teach Something," *HR Magazine*, 54 (August 2009): 10.

5. Adapted from "Would You Lay Off Your Boss if You Could?" *USA Today* (November 10, 2009): 1B.

6. For more, see Steven M. Nakashima, "Executive Exemption Construed Narrowly," *HR Magazine*, 51 (November 2006): 118; and A. Kevin Troutman, "Deja Review," *HR Magazine*, 52 (February 2007): 58–62.

7. Ellen Van Velsor and Jean Brittain Leslie, "Why Executives Derail: Perspectives Across Time and Cultures," *Academy of Management Executive*, 9 (November 1995): 63. For related studies, see Frank Shipper and John E. Dillard Jr., "A Study of Impending Derailment and Recovery of Middle Managers Across Career Stages," *Human Resource Management*, 39 (Winter 2000): 331–345; and Clinton O. Longenecker, Mitchell J. Neubert, and Laurence S. Fink, "Causes and Consequences of Managerial Failure in Rapidly Changing Organizations," *Business Horizons*, 50 (March–April 2007): 145–155. Also see Teresa A. Daniel, "Tough Boss or Workplace Bully?" *HR Magazine*, 54 (June 2009): 82–86.

8. Jon Swartz, "Conway's Ethics Led to Firing," *USA Today* (October 5, 2004): 1B. For related research, see Bennett J. Tepper, "Consequences of Abusive Supervision," *Academy of Management Journal*, 43 (April 2000): 178–190.

9. Nanette Byrnes, "Pepsi Brings in the Health Police," *Bloomberg Businessweek* (January 25, 2010): 50.

10. Data from "The 500 Largest U.S. Companies," *Fortune* (May 3, 2010): F-3, F-45.

11. Brian Dumaine, "Myth: Driving Fewer Miles Is Good for the Environment," *Fortune* (April 12, 2010): 112.

12. See Kevin P. Coyne, Shawn T. Coyne, and Edward J. Coyne Sr., "When You've Got to Cut Costs Now," *Harvard Business Review*, 88 (May 2010): 74–82; and Donald S. Siegel, "Green Management Matters Only if It Yields More Green: An Economic/Strategic Perspective," *Academy of Management Perspectives*, 23 (August 2009): 5–16.

13. Frederik Balfour, "Singapore Leverages Its Liquid Smarts," *Bloomberg Businessweek* (May 3–9, 2010): 15.

14. Data from Victoria Markham, "America's Supersized Footprint," *Business Week* (October 30, 2006): 132; and "Yes, Drill Offshore for Oil, and Do Many Other Things, Too," *USA Today* (April 2, 2010): 12A.

15. Beth Kowatt, "The Future of Water," *Fortune* (October 12, 2009): 111.

16. See, for example, Brian Dumaine, "Nukes in My Backyard," *Fortune* (March 22, 2010): 36; Theunis Bates, "Supertiny Power Plants," *Fast Company*, 146 (June 2010): 38; and Anya Kamenetz, "From Big Oil to Big Algae," *Fast Company*, 147 (July–August 2010): 84–116.

17. Data from Anupreeta Das, Scott Kilman, and Liam Pleveen, "A $39 Billion Food Fight," *Wall Street Journal* (August 18, 2010): A1, A14; and www.census.gov/main/www/popclock.html.

18. See Sunanda Holmes, "Authors Explore Why So Many in World Are Starving," *USA Today* (November 30, 2009): 4B.

19. Diane Brady, "Wanted: Eclectic Visionary with a Sense of Humor," *Business Week* (August 28, 2000): 143.

20. See Jeanne C. Meister and Karie Willyerd, *The 2020 Workplace: How Innovative Companies Attract, Develop, and Keep Tomorrow's Employees Today* (New York: Harper Business, 2010).

21. Data from Michael Elliott, "The New Global Opportunity," *Fortune* (July 5, 2010): 96–102.

22. For a good historical perspective, see William J. Bernstein, *A Splendid*

Exchange: How Trade Shaped the World (New York: Grove Press, 2008).

23. Kathy Chu, "China Poised to Replace Japan as World's No. 2 Economy," *USA Today* (August 17, 2010): 3B.

24. Data from Mac Margolis, "Off the Deep End in Brazil," *Newsweek* (June 21, 2010): 4.

25. www.aboutmcdonalds.com/mcd/our_company.html, August 18, 2010.

26. Data from www.siemens.com/about/en/worldwide.htm, August 18, 2010.

27. Tara Kalwarski, "Global Winners," *Bloomberg Businessweek* (January 18, 2010): 60.

28. For good overviews of the offshoring controversy, see Diana Farrell, "Smarter Offshoring," *Harvard Business Review,* 84 (June 2006): 83–92; Ann E. Harrison and Margaret S. McMillan, "Dispelling Some Myths About Offshoring," *Academy of Management Perspectives,* 20 (November 2006): 6–22; and Michael Mandel, "The Real Cost of Offshoring," *Business Week* (June 18, 2007): 28–34.

29. See Fareed Zakaria, *The Post-American World* (New York: W.W. Norton, 2008).

30. Andy Grove, "How to Make an American Job," *Bloomberg Businessweek* (July 5–11, 2010): 50.

31. Employment data from Jia Lynn Yang, "Indian Call Center Lands in Ohio," *Fortune* (August 6, 2007): 23.

32. Paul Davidson, "Some Manufacturing Heads Back to USA," *USA Today* (August 6, 2010): 1B–2B. Also see Stefan Theil, "Europe's About-Face on Offshoring," *Newsweek* (January 11, 2010): 11; and Dexter Roberts, "The Right to Strike May Be Coming to China," *Bloomberg Businessweek* (August 9–15, 2010): 18–19.

33. A good historical overview of the quality movement can be found in R. Ray Gehani, "Quality Value-Chain: A Meta-Synthesis of

Frontiers of Quality Movement," *Academy of Management Executive,* 7 (May 1993): 29–42.

34. See Kenneth R. Thompson, "Confronting the Paradoxes in a Total Quality Environment," *Organizational Dynamics,* 26 (Winter 1998): 62–74; and Thomas J. Douglas and William Q. Judge Jr., "Total Quality Management Implementation and Competitive Advantage: The Role of Structural Control and Exploration," *Academy of Management Journal,* 44 (February 2001): 158–169.

35. See, for example, Sharon Begley, "The Evolution of an Eco-Prophet," *Newsweek* (November 9, 2009): 34–39; and "25 Green Myths Debunked," *Fortune* (April 12, 2010): 101–112.

36. For details on the U.S. Green Building Council's LEED (Leadership in Energy and Environmental Design) certification program, see www.usgbc.org.

37. See Betty Klinck, "Find a Green College: Check!" *USA Today* (April 20, 2010): 7D.

38. See Daniel McGinn, "The Greenest Big Companies in America," *Newsweek* (September 28, 2009): 34–54. Also see Alfred A. Marcus and Adam R. Fremeth, "Green Management Matters Regardless," *Academy of Management Perspectives,* 23 (August 2009): 17–26.

39. As quoted in Thomas L. Friedman, *Hot, Flat, and Crowded: Why We Need a Green Revolution—And How It Can Renew America,* release 2.0 (New York: Picador, 2009), p. 84.

40. As quoted in Geoff Colvin, "The Colvin Interview: Linda Fisher," *Fortune* (November 23, 2009): 46.

41. Paul Hawken, *The Ecology of Commerce: A Declaration of Sustainability* (New York: Collins Business, 1993), p. 139.

42. Gregory Unruh and Richard Ettenson, "Growing Green: Three Smart Paths to Developing Sustainable Products," *Harvard Busines Review,* 88 (June 2010): 94, 96. Also see David A. Lubin and

Daniel C. Esty, "The Sustainability Imperative," *Harvard Business Review,* 88 (May 2010): 42–50.

43. Based on Georg Kell and Peter Lacy, "Study: Sustainability a Priority for CEOs," *Bloomberg Businessweek* (June 25, 2010), www.businessweek.com/managing/content/jun2010/ca20100624_678038.htm. Also see Mark W. Johnson and Josh Suskewicz, "How to Jump-Start the Clean Tech Economy," *Harvard Business Review,* 87 (November 2009): 52–60; William Underhill, "The Next Industrial Revolution," *Newsweek* (December 14, 2009): 58–62; Matthew Philips, "Counting Carbon," *Newsweek* (January 11, 2010): 15; Daniel Gross, "Going for the Green," *Newsweek* (March 8, 2010): 20; and "Clearing the Air: Paytheon Is Passionate About Going Green," *Fortune* (May 3, 2010): 182.

44. See Allan Sloan, "If You Believe in Magic, Green Energy Will Be Our Salvation," *Fortune* (July 26, 2010): 59.

45. Data from Gene Koretz, "On Wall Street, Green Is Golden," *Business Week* (January 8, 2001): 30.

46. Drawn from David Lieberman and Matt Krantz, "Goldman Sachs Concedes Mistake, Settles SEC Suit," *USA Today* (July 16, 2010): 1B–2B; "GE Pays $23.4M to Settle Claims It Paid Kickbacks to Iraqi Officials," *USA Today* (July 28, 2010): 5B; and "Citigroup Pays $75M to Settle SEC Charges," *USA Today* (July 30, 2010): 2B.

47. Del Jones, "CEOs of the Future Get Formal Training to Take Giant Leap," *USA Today* (December 1, 2003): 2B. Also see Bill George and Peter Sims, *True North: Discover Your Authentic Leadership* (San Francisco: Jossey-Bass, 2007).

48. Julie Amparano, "As Ethics Crisis Grows, Businesses Take Action," *Arizona Republic* (November 24, 1996): D9.

49. See Janet Kornblum, "First U.S. Web Page Went Up 10 Years Ago," *USA Today* (December 11, 2001): 3D; Otis Port, "He Made the Net Work," *Business Week* (September 27,

2004): 20; and Otis Port, "Spinning the World's Web," *Business Week* (November 8, 2004): 16.

50. Data from "Internet Usage Statistics," June 30, 2010, www .internetworldstats.com/stats.htm.

51. Amy Campbell, "Social Media—A Definition," January 21, 2010, http://blogs.law.harvard.edu/ amy/2010/01/21/social-media-%E2%80%94-a-definition/.

52. Jon Swartz, "Time Spent on Facebook, Twitter, YouTube Grows," *USA Today* (August 2, 2010): 2B. Also see David Kirkpatrick, *The Facebook Effect: The Inside Story of the Company That Is Connecting the World* (New York: Simon & Schuster, 2010).

53. Don Tapscott, *Grown Up Digital: How the Net Generation Is Changing Your World* (New York: McGraw-Hill, 2009), p. 96.

54. See Nicholas Carr, *The Shallows: What the Internet Is Doing to Our Brains* (New York: W.W. Norton, 2010); "Internet Censorship: Showdown at the WTO," *Bloomberg Businessweek* (March 15, 2010): 12; Farhad Manjoo, "Multiple Choice," *Fast Company*, 145 (May 2010): 42–43; and Paul M. Barrett, "The Digital Future: You Know It When You See It," *Bloomberg Businessweek* (August 9–15, 2010): 86–87.

55. For related research, see Frank Shipper, "A Study of the Psychometric Properties of the Managerial Skill Scales of the Survey of Management Practices," *Educational and Psychological Measurement*, 55 (June 1995): 468–479; Frank Shipper and Charles S. White, "Mastery, Frequency, and Interaction of Managerial Behaviors Relative to Subunit Effectiveness," *Human Relations*, 52 (January 1999): 49–66; and Frank Shipper and Jeanette Davy, "A Model and Investigation of Managerial Skills, Employees' Attitudes, and Managerial Performance," *The Leadership Quarterly*, 13, no. 2 (2002): 95–120.

56. See Henri Fayol, *General and Industrial Management*, trans. Constance Storrs (London: Isaac Pitman & Sons, 1949).

57. Geoff Colvin, "Who's to Blame at BP?" *Fortune* (July 26, 2010): 60. Also see "After the Spill," *USA Today* (August 6, 2010): 9A.

58. Clark L. Wilson, *How and Why Effective Managers Balance Their Skills: Technical, Teambuilding, Drive* (Columbia, Md.: Rockatech Multimedia Publishing, 2003), pp. 13, 18–20.

59. See Scott Adams, *The Dilbert Principle* (New York: HarperBusiness, 1996).

60. "AMA Research," *Management Review*, 85 (July 1996): 10.

61. See Henry Mintzberg, "Managerial Work: Analysis from Observation," *Management Science*, 18 (October 1971): B97–B110.

62. Henry Mintzberg, "The Manager's Job: Folklore and Fact," *Harvard Business Review*, 53 (July–August 1975): 54. For Mintzberg's more recent thoughts about managing, see Jonathan Gosling and Henry Mintzberg, "The Five Minds of a Manager," *Harvard Business Review*, 81 (November 2003): 54–63.

63. As quoted in Alan Deutschman, "The CEO's Secret of Managing Time," *Fortune* (June 1, 1992): 136.

64. Jonathan Gosling and Henry Mintzberg, "Reflect Yourself," *HR Magazine*, 49 (September 2004): 151–152.

65. Adapted from Earnest R. Archer, "Things You Lose the Right to Do When You Become a Manager," *Supervisory Management*, 35 (July 1990): 8–9. Also see "Do I Have To?" *Business Week* (July 7, 2003): 14; and Nadine Heintz, "Why Can't We Be Friends?" *Inc.*, 26 (January 2004): 31–32.

66. See Eduardo Salas, Jessica L. Wildman, and Ronald F. Piccolo, "Using Simulation-Based Training to Enhance Management Education," *Academy of Management Learning and Education*, 8 (December 2009): 559–573; and Richard Barker, "No, Management Is *Not* a Profession," *Harvard Business Review*, 88 (July–August 2010): 52–60.

67. See Ron Zemke, "The Honeywell Studies: How Managers Learn to Manage," *Training* 22 (August 1985): 46–51.

68. Adapted from Robin Snell, "Graduating from the School of Hard Knocks?" *Journal of Management Development*, 8, no. 5 (1989): 23–30. Also see "Where CEOs Are Made," *Bloomberg Businessweek* (May 17–23, 2010): 20; and Katherine Bell, "Life's Work: Mario Batali," *Harvard Business Review*, 88 (May 2010): 132.

69. Brad Stone, "Nike's Short Game," *Newsweek* (January 26, 2004): 40–41.

70. See Linda A. Hill, "Becoming the Boss," *Harvard Business Review*, Special Issue: The Tests of a Leader, 85 (January 2007): 48–56; Caroline P. D'Abate, Mark A. Youndt, and Kathryn E. Wenzel, "Making the Most of an Internship: An Empirical Study of Internship Satisfaction," *Academy of Management Learning and Education*, 8 (December 2009): 527–539; and Douglas A. Ready, Jay A. Conger, and Linda A. Hill, "Are You High Potential?" *Harvard Business Review*, 88 (June 2010): 78–84.

71. Drawn from Jim Hopkins, "PCs, Immigrants Help Launch Millions of Little Firms," *USA Today* (October 30, 2002): 1B.

72. Data from "Global 500: The World's Largest Corporations," *Fortune* (July 26, 2010): F-1, F-6.

73. Data from Jennifer Schramm, "Benefits at Risk?" *HR Magazine*, 52 (February 2007): 74; and The Small Business Economy: A Report to the President—2008, www .docuticker.com/?p526754, accessed August 20, 2010.

75. Data from *ibid.*, p. 3.

76. Data from "Self-Employment Not Falling," July 1, 2009, www.smallbizlabs.com/2009/06/ selfemployment-not-falling .html.

77. See George Gendron, "The Failure Myth," *Inc.* (January 2001): 13; and Ben Levinson, "And Now for That Dream Job," *Business Week* (July 9–16, 2007): 60, 62.

78. See David R. Francis, "Spiking Stereotypes About Small Firms," *Christian Science Monitor* (May 7, 1993): 9; Gene Koretz, "A Surprising Finding on New-Business Mortality Rates," *Business Week* (June 14, 1993): 22; and James Aley, "Debunking the Failure Fallacy," *Fortune* (September 6, 1993): 21. For related reading, see Sydney Finkelstein, "The Myth of Managerial Superiority in Internet Startups: An Autopsy," *Organizational Dynamics,* 30 (Fall 2001): 172–185.

79. Data from Charles Burck, "Where Good Jobs Grow," *Fortune* (June 14, 1993): 22. Also see David Neumark, Junfu Zhang, and Brandon Wall, "Where the Jobs Are: Business Dynamics and Employment Growth," *Academy of Management Perspectives,* 20 (November 2006): 79–94.

80. For more on Birch's research, see Alan Webber, "Business Race Isn't Always to the Swift, But Bet That Way," *USA Today* (February 3, 1998): 15A. Also see "The Gazelle Theory," *Inc.,* 23 (May 29, 2001): 28–29.

81. See Howard Gleckman, "Whose Plan Is Healthier?" *Business Week* (May 24, 2004): 90, 92; and Jim Hopkins, "Rising Benefit Costs Hurt Small Businesses' Financial Health," *USA Today* (June 4, 2004): 1B–2B.

82. See Sandra Block, "She's Leader of the (Franchise) Pack," *USA Today* (October 12, 2009): 2B; and William E. Gillis and James G. Combs, "Franchisor Strategy and Firm Performance: Making the Most of Strategic Resource Investments," *Business Horizons,* 52 (November–December 2009): 553–561.

83. Adapted from Marc Ballon, "Hot Tips," *Inc.,* 21 (April 1999): 104.

84. Howard H. Stevenson and J. Carlos Jarillo, "A Paradigm of Entrepreneurship: Entrepreneurial Management," *Strategic Management Journal,* 11 (Summer 1990): 23 (emphasis added). Also see Donald F. Kuratko, "The Entrepreneurial Imperative of the 21st Century," *Business Horizons,* 52 (September–October 2009): 421–428; Robert Kiyosaki, "We Need Two School Systems," *USA Today* (February 10, 2010): 10A; David Whitford, "Can You Learn to Be an Entrepreneur?" *Fortune* (March 22, 2010): 63–66; and Daniel J. Isenberg, "How to Start an Entrepreneurial Revolution," *Harvard Business Review,* 88 (June 2010): 40–50.

85. Laura Petrecca, "On Their Way After a Steep Learning Curve," *USA Today* (July 6, 2010): 4B.

86. As quoted in Rob Walker, "Because Optimism Is Essential," Inc., 26 (April 2004): 150. Also see S. Trevis Certo and Samuel C. Certo, "Entrepreneurial Wisdom: Emerging Concept and Direction for Related Research," *Business Horizons,* 53 (July–August 2010): 413–417.

87. *Ibid.* Also see Robert D. Hof, "Jeff Bezos' Risky Bet," *Business Week* (November 13, 2006): 52–58.

88. As quoted in Bruce Rosenstein, "Inspiration for Entrepreneur Wannabes," USA Today (October 11, 2004): 9B. Also see Paul Keegan, "Working Without a Net," *Money,* 39 (March 2010): 96–101; and Joel Babbit, "Nature Called, He Listened," *Fortune* (April 12, 2010): 42.

89. Stephanie Armour, "UBUBU Boldly Launches Start-Up in Cyberspace," *USA Today* (June 19, 2000): 3B. Also see Marc Malone, "The Small Business Ego Trap," *Business Horizons,* 47 (July–August 2004): 17–22.

90. Steven Berglas, "GIs for Guts," *Inc.,* 22 (May 2000): 45.

91. Joshua Hyatt, "The Real Secrets of Entrepreneurs," *Fortune* (November 15, 2004): 186.

CHAPTER 2

1. John W. Gardner, *Self-Renewal: The Individual and the Innovative Society* (New York: Harper & Row, 1964), chap. 11.

2. For interesting historical perspectives, see Diane Coutu, "Leadership Lessons from Abraham Lincoln," *Harvard Business Review,* 87 (April 2009): 43–47; Alan Brinkley, "What Would Henry Do?" *Time* (April 19, 2010): 48–49; and Ian McGugan, "The Original Captain of Industry," *Bloomberg Businessweek* (August 2–8, 2010): 78–79.

3. Alonzo L. McDonald, as quoted in Alan M. Kantrow, ed., "Why History Matters to Managers," *Harvard Business Review,* 64 (January–February 1986): 82. Also see Arthur G. Bedeian, "The Gift of Professional Maturity," *Academy of Management Learning and Education,* 3 (March 2004): 92–98.

4. Barbara S. Lawrence, "Historical Perspective: Using the Past to Study the Present," *Academy of Management Review,* 9 (April 1984): 307. Also see George E. Smith, "Management History and Historical Context: Potential Benefits of Its Inclusion in the Management Curriculum," *Academy of Management Learning and Education,* 6 (December 2007): 522–533; and Albert Madansky, "Teaching History in Business Schools: An Outsider's View," *Academy of Management Learning and Education,* 7 (December 2008): 553–562.

5. See Morgan Witzel, *Fifty Key Figures in Management* (London: Routledge, 2003). A review of this book by W. Jack Duncan can be found in "Book Reviews," *Academy of Management Review,* 29 (October 2004): 687–689.

6. For a discussion in this area, see "How Business Schools Began," *Business Week* (October 19, 1963): 114–116. Also see John Trinkaus, "Urwick on the Business Academy," *Business Horizons,* 35 (September–October 1992): 25–29; and David D. Van Fleet and Daniel A. Wren, "Teaching History in Business Schools: 1982–2003," *Academy of Management Learning and Education,* 4 (March 2005): 44–56.

7. The top ten most influential management thinkers of the twentieth century, as selected by the readers of *Business Horizons* magazine, are discussed in Dennis

W. Organ, "And the Winners Are…," *Business Horizons,* 43 (March–April 2000): 1–3.

8. See Marian M. Extejt and Jonathan E. Smith, "The Behavioral Sciences and Management: An Evaluation of Relevant Journals," *Journal of Management,* 16 (September 1990): 539–551. For a list of 40 management-oriented periodicals, see Jonathan L. Johnson and Philip M. Podsakoff, "Journal Influence in the Field of Management: An Analysis Using Salancik's Index in a Dependency Network," *Academy of Management Journal,* 37 (October 1994): 1392–1407.

9. For advice on dealing with information overload, see Suzy Wetlaufer, "Thanks for Asking," *Harvard Business Review,* 80 (February 2002): 10.

10. See the instructive timeline in "Management Ideas Through Time," *Management Review,* 87 (January 1998): 16–19. Also see Daniel A. Wren and Ronald G. Greenwood, *Management Innovators: The People and Ideas That Shaped Modern Business* (New York: Oxford University Press, 1998).

11. For ideas about the related area of management as a profession, see Rakesh Khurana, "You Got a License to Run That Company?" *Harvard Business Review,* 82 (February 2004): 14; and Richard Barker, "No, Management Is *Not* a Profession," *Harvard Business Review,* 88 (July–August 2010): 52–60.

12. Craig C. Lundberg, "Is There Really Nothing So Practical as a Good Theory?" *Business Horizons,* 47 (September–October 2004): 10.

13. Kevin McCoy, "Domino's CEO Brandon Heads Back to College," *USA Today* (February 22, 2010): 1B. Also see Molly Peterson, "*Good to Great* Hits Grade School," *Bloomberg Businessweek* (February 15, 2010): 56–58.

14. See Henri Fayol, *General and Industrial Management,* trans. Constance Storrs (London: Isaac Pitman & Sons, 1949). An interesting review by Nancy M. Carter of Fayol's book can be found in Allen C. Bluedorn, ed., "Special Book Review Section on the Classics of Management," *Academy of Management Review,* 11 (April 1986): 454–456.

15. Stephen J. Carroll and Dennis J. Gillen, "Are the Classical Management Functions Useful in Describing Managerial Work?" *Academy of Management Review,* 12 (January 1987): 48.

16. Frank B. Copley, *Frederick W Taylor: Father of Scientific Management* (New York: Harper & Brothers, 1923), I: 3. Also see the brief profile of Taylor in "Taylorism," *Business Week: 100 Years of Innovation* (Summer 1999): 16.

17. For expanded treatment, see Frank B. Copley, *Frederick W Taylor: The Principles of Scientific Management* (New York: Harper & Brothers, 1911). A good retrospective review of Taylor's classic writings may be found in Bluedorn, ed., "Special Book Review Section on the Classics of Management," pp. 443–447. Robert Kanigel's *One Best Way,* a modern biography of Taylor, is reviewed in Alan Farnham, "The Man Who Changed Work Forever," *Fortune* (July 21, 1997): 114.

18. For an interesting update on Taylor, see Christopher Farrell, "Micromanaging from the Grave," *Business Week* (May 15, 1995): 34.

19. George D. Babcock, *The Taylor System in Franklin Management,* 2nd ed. (New York: Engineering Magazine Company, 1917), p. 31.

20. Taylor's seminal 1911 book *The Principles of Scientific Management* was recently selected by a panel of management experts as the most influential management book of the twentieth century: See Arthur G. Bedeian and Daniel A. Wren, "Most Influential Management Books of the 20th Century," *Organizational Dynamics,* 29 (Winter 2001): 221–225. Also see Oswald Jones, "Scientific Management, Culture and Control: A First-Hand Account of Taylorism in Practice," *Human Relations,* 53 (May 2000): 631–653.

21. For an alternative perspective and detailed critique of Taylor's experiments with pig iron handlers, see Charles D. Wrege and Richard M. Hodgetts, "Frederick W. Taylor's 1899 Pig Iron Observations: Examining Fact, Fiction, and Lessons for the New Millennium," *Academy of Management Journal,* 43 (December 2000): 1283–1291. Also see Sigmund Wagner-Tsukamoto, "An Institutional Economic Reconstruction of Scientific Management: On the Lost Theoretical Logic of Taylorism," *Academy of Management Review,* 32 (January 2007): 105–117.

22. Frederick W. Taylor, *Shop Management* (New York: Harper & Brothers, 1911), p. 22.

23. Frank B. Gilbreth and Lillian M. Gilbreth, *Applied Motion Study* (New York: Sturgis & Walton, 1917), p. 42. A retrospective review of the Gilbreths' writings, by Daniel J. Brass, can be found in Bluedorn, ed., "Special Book Review Section on the Classics of Management," pp. 448–451.

24. See Frank B. Gilbreth Jr. and Ernestine Gilbreth Carey, *Cheaper by the Dozen* (New York: Thomas Y Crowell, 1948).

25. For example, see the Gantt chart on p. 64 of Tom D. Conkright, "So You're Going to Manage a Project," *Training,* 35 (January 1998): 62–67.

26. For detailed coverage of Gantt's contributions, see H. L. Gantt, *Work, Wages, and Profits,* 2nd ed. (New York: Engineering Magazine Company, 1913). An interesting update on Gantt's contributions can be found in Peter B. Peterson, "Training and Development: The Views of Henry L. Gantt (1861–1919)," *SAM Advanced Management Journal,* 52 (Winter 1987): 20–23.

27. Good historical overviews of the quality movement include Ron Zemke, "A Bluffer's Guide to TQM," *Training,* 30 (April 1993): 48–55; R. Ray Gehani, "Quality Value-Chain: A Meta-Synthesis of Frontiers of Quality Movement," *Academy of Management Executive,* 7 (May 1993): 29–42; and Sangit Chatterjee and Mustafa Yilmaz, "Quality Confusion: Too Many Gurus, Not Enough

Disciples," *Business Horizons,* 36 (May–June 1993): 15–18. A look back at the roots of the quality movement can be found in Geoffrey Colvin, "A Concise History of Management Hooey," *Fortune* (June 28, 2004): 166–176.

28. Mary Walton, *Deming Management at Work* (New York: Putnam, 1990), p. 13. See John Hillkirk, "World-Famous Quality Expert Dead at 93," *USA Today* (December 21, 1993): 1B–2B; Peter Nulty, "The National Business Hall of Fame: W. Edwards Deming," *Fortune* (April 4, 1994): 124; Keki R. Bhote, "Dr. W. Edwards Deming—A Prophet with Belated Honor in His Own Country," *National Productivity Review,* 13 (Spring 1994): 153–159; Anne Willette, "Deming Legacy Gives Firms Quality Challenge," *USA Today* (October 19, 1994): 2B; and M. R. Yilmaz and Sangit Chatterjee, "Deming and the Quality of Software Development," *Business Horizons,* 40 (November–December 1997): 51–58.

29. See Jack Gordon, "An Interview with Joseph M. Juran," *Training,* 31 (May 1994): 35–41. Deming and Juran are saluted in Otis Port, "The Kings of Quality," *Business Week* (August 30, 2004): 20. See the obituary following Juran's death at age 103 in Stephen Miller, "Pioneer of Quality Control Kept Searching For 'A Better Way' to Make and Manage," *Wall Street Journal* (March 8–9, 2008): A7.

30. Zemke, "A Bluffer's Guide to TQM," p. 51. Also see Joseph M. Juran, "Made in U.S.A.: A Renaissance in Quality," *Harvard Business Review,* 71 (July–August 1993): 42–50.

31. See Armand V. Feigenbaum, "How Total Quality Counters Three Forces of International Competitiveness," *National Productivity Review,* 13 (Summer 1994): 327–330. More of Feigenbaum's ideas can be found in Del Jones, "Employers Going for Quality Hires, Not Quantity," *USA Today* (December 11, 1997): 1B; and Armand Feigenbaum and Donald S. Feigenbaum, "What Quality Means Today," *MIT Sloan Management Review,* 46 (Winter 2005): 96.

32. Crosby's more recent ideas may be found in Philip B. Crosby, *Completeness: Quality for the 21st Century* (New York: Dutton, 1992).

33. Edwin A. Locke, "The Ideas of Frederick W. Taylor: An Evaluation," *Academy of Management Review,* 7 (January 1982): 22–23. Also see David H. Freedman, "Is Management Still a Science?" *Harvard Business Review,* 70 (November–December 1992): 26–38.

34. See William Stevenson, *Operations Management* (New York: McGraw-Hill, 2008).

35. The Hawthorne studies are discussed in detail in F. J. Roethlisberger and William J. Dickson, *Management and the Worker* (Cambridge, Mass.: Harvard University Press, 1939). Dennis W. Organ's review of this classic book, in which he criticizes the usual textbook treatment of it, can be found in Bluedorn, ed., "Special Book Review Section on the Classics of Management," pp. 459–463. Also see Fred Kiel, "Flaws in the Selfish-Worker Theory," *Business Week* (October 6, 2008): 78.

36. See Ellen S. O'Connor, "The Politics of Management Thought: A Case Study of the Harvard Business School and the Human Relations School," *Academy of Management Review,* 24 (January 1999): 117–131.

37. See Henry C. Metcalf and L. Urwick, *Dynamic Administration: The Collected Papers of Mary Parker Follett* (New York: Harper & Brothers, 1942); Mary Parker Follett, *Freedom and Coordination* (London: Management Publications Trust, 1949). A review by Diane L. Ferry *of Dynamic Administration* can be found in Bluedorn, ed., "Special Book Review Section on the Classics of Management," pp. 451–454.

38. See L. D. Parker, "Control in Organizational Life: The Contribution of Mary Parker Follett," *Academy of Management Review,* 9 (October 1984): 736–745; Albie M. Davis, "An Interview with Mary Parker Follett," *Negotiation Journal,* 5 (July 1989): 223–225; and Dana Wechsler Linden, "The Mother of Them All," *Forbes* (January 16, 1995): 75–76.

39. See David Jacobs, "Book Review Essay: Douglas McGregor—The Human Side of Enterprise in Peril," *Academy of Management Review,* 29 (April 2004): 293–296.

40. For a case study of a military leader's transition from a Theory X style to a Theory Y style, see D. Michael Abrashoff, "Retention Through Redemption," *Harvard Business Review,* 79 (February 2001): 136–141.

41. John B. Miner, "The Rated Importance, Scientific Validity, and Usefulness of Organizational Behavior Theories: A Quantitative Review," *Academy of Management Learning and Education,* 2 (September 2003): 250–268.

42. For example, the new field of positive psychology has evolved into positive organizational behavior. See Martin E. P. Seligman and Mihaly Csikszentmihalyi, "Positive Psychology: An Introduction," *American Psychologist,* 55 (January 2000): 5–14; and Thomas A. Wright, "Positive Organizational Behavior: An Idea Whose Time Has Truly Come," *Journal of Organizational Behavior,* 24 (June 2003): 437–442.

43. See Jeffrey Pfeffer, "Building Sustainable Organizations: The Human Factor," *Academy of Management Perspectives*, 24 (February 2010): 34–45.

44. An interesting and instructive timeline of human resource milestones can be found in "Training and Development in the 20th Century," *Training,* 35 (September 1998): 49–56.

45. For a statistical interpretation of the Hawthorne studies, see Richard Herbert Franke and James D. Kaul, "The Hawthorne Experiments: First Statistical Interpretation," *American Sociological Review,* 43 (October 1978): 623–643. Also

see Stephen R. G. Jones, "Worker Interdependence and Output: The Hawthorne Studies Reevaluated," *American Sociological Review, 55* (April 1990): 176–190.

46. Russell L. Ackoff, "Science in the Systems Age: Beyond IE, OR, and MS," *Operations Research, 21* (May–June 1973): 664.

47. Charles J. Coleman and David D. Palmer, "Organizational Application of System Theory," *Business Horizons, 16* (December 1973): 77. Also see J. Brian Atwater, Vijay R. Kannan, and Alan A. Stephens, "Cultivating Systemic Thinking in the Next Generation of Business Leaders," *Academy of Management Learning and Education, 7* (March 2008): 9–25.

48. Chester I. Barnard, *The Functions of the Executive* (Cambridge, Mass.: Harvard University Press, 1938), p. 65.

49. *Ibid.,* p. 82. A retrospective review, by Thomas L. Keon, of Barnard's *The Functions of the Executive* can be found in Bluedorn, ed., "Special Book Review Section on the Classics of Management," pp. 456–459.

50. For details, see Lori Verstegen Ryan and William G. Scott, "Ethics and Organizational Reflection: The Rockefeller Foundation and Postwar 'Moral Deficits,' 1942–1954," *Academy of Management Review,* 20 (April 1995): 438–461.

51. Ludwig von Bertalanffy, "The History and Status of General Systems Theory," *Academy of Management Journal, 15* (December 1972): 411.

52. For an example of an economic/industrial hierarchy of organizations, see Figure 2 (p. 774) in Philip Rich, "The Organizational Taxonomy: Definition and Design," *Academy of Management Review,* 17 (October 1992): 758–781.

53. See Greg Lindsay, "The New New Urbanism," *Fast Company,* 142 (February 2010): 88–96.

54. Susan Albers Mohrman and Allan M. Mohrman Jr., "Organizational Change and Learning," in *Organizing for the Future: The New Logic for Managing Complex Organizations,* eds. Jay R. Galbraith, Edward E. Lawler III, and Associates (San Francisco: Jossey-Bass, 1993), p. 89. For an excellent overview of organizational learning, see David A. Garvin, "Building a Learning Organization," *Harvard Business Review, 71* (July–August 1993): 78–91. Also see Robert Aubrey and Paul M. Cohen, *Working Wisdom: Timeless Skills and Vanguard Strategies for Learning Organizations* (San Francisco: Jossey-Bass, 1995); and Timothy T. Baldwin and Camden C. Danielson, "Building a Learning Strategy at the Top: Interviews with Ten of America's CLOs," *Business Horizons, 43* (November–December 2000): 5–14.

55. For an excellent collection of readings, see *Harvard Business Review on Knowledge Management* (Boston: Harvard Business School Publishing, 1998). Also see Kenneth Husted and Snejina Michailova, "Dual Allegiance and Knowledge Sharing in Inter-Firm R&D Collaborations," *Organizational Dynamics, 39* (January–March 2010): 37–47; Deborah A. Peluso, "Preserving Employee Know-How," *HR Magazine, 55* (May 2010): 99; Jetta Frost, Margit Osterloh, and Antoinette Weibel, "Governing Knowledge Work: Transactional and Transformational Solutions," *Organizational Dynamics, 39* (April–June 2010): 126–136; and Martin W. Wallin and Georg von Krogh, "Organizing for Open Innovation: Focus on the Integration of Knowledge," *Organizational Dynamics, 39* (April–June 2010): 145–154.

56. For example, see Gary Weiss, "Chaos Hits Wall Street—The Theory, That Is," *Business Week* (November 2, 1992): 138–140.

57. See Benyamin Bergmann Lichtenstein, "Self-Organized Transitions: A Pattern amid the Chaos of Transformative Change," *Academy of Management Executive,* 14 (November 2000): 128–141; and Jay R. Galbraith, "The Multi-Dimensional and Reconfigurable Organization," *Organizational Dynamics, 39* (April–June 2010): 115–125.

58. Fred Luthans, *Introduction to Management: A Contingency Approach* (New York: McGraw-Hill, 1976), p. 28. Also see Henry L. Tosi Jr. and John W. Slocum Jr., "Contingency Theory: Some Suggested Directions," *Journal of Management,* 10 (Spring 1984): 9–26.

59. Y. K. Shetty, "Contingency Management: Current Perspective for Managing Organizations," *Management International Review,* 14, no. 6 (1974): 27.

60. For example, see Henry P. Sims Jr., Samar Faraj, and Seokhwa Yun, "When Should a Leader Be Directive or Empowering? How to Develop Your Own Situational Theory of Leadership," *Business Horizons, 52* (March–April 2009): 149–158.

61. See Joseph W. McGuire, "Management Theory: Retreat to the Academy," *Business Horizons,* 25 (July–August 1982): 37.

62. See Trish Reay, Whitney Berta, and Melanie Kazman Kohn, "What's the Evidence on Evidence-Based Management?" *Academy of Management Perspectives,* 23 (November 2009): 5–18; and Rob B. Briner, David Denyer, and Denise M. Rousseau, "Evidence-Based Management: Concept Cleanup Time?" *Academy of Management Perspectives,* 23 (November 2009): 19–32.

63. See Rosabeth Moss Kanter, "What Would Peter Say?" *Harvard Business Review,* 87 (November 2009): 64–70; and Alan M. Kantrow, "Why Read Peter Drucker?" *Harvard Business Review,* 87 (November 2009): 72–82.

64. Data from John A. Byrne, "How the Best Get Better," *Business Week* (September 14, 1987): 98–99.

65. Data from Ryan Underwood, "A *Field Guide* to the Gurus," *Fast Company,* 88 (November 2004): 104. Also see Jennifer Reingold and Christopher Tkaczyk, "Ten New Gurus Your Should Know," *Fortune* (November 24, 2008): 151–158.

66. See Del Jones, "It's Nothing Personal? On 'Apprentice,' It's All Personal," *USA Today* (March 26, 2004): 6B; and Del Jones and Bill Keveney, "10 Lessons of 'The Apprentice,'" *USA Today* (April 15, 2004): 1A, 5A.

67. See Elizabeth Spiers, "Library of the Living Dead," *Fast Company*, 124 (April 2008): 136; Marcus Alexander and Harry Korine, "The Susceptibility to Managerial Fads," *Harvard Business Review*, 86 (December 2008): 74; and "The Myth of Corporate Persistence," *Harvard Business Review*, 88 (May 2010): 18–19.

68. Craig M. McAllaster, "The 5 P's of Change: Leading Change by Effectively Utilizing Leverage Points Within an Organization," *Organizational Dynamics*, 33, no. 3 (2004): 321.

69. See Michael A. Hitt and R. Duane Ireland, "Peters and Waterman Revisited: The Unended Quest for Excellence," *Academy of Management Executive*, 1 (May 1987): 91–98.

70. Bruce G. Resnick and Timothy L. Smunt, "From Good to Great to…," *Academy of Management Perspectives*, 22 (November 2008): 6. Also see Bruce Niendorf and Kristine Beck, "*Good to Great*, or Just Good?" *Academy of Management Perspectives*, 22 (November 2008): 13–20.

71. Marc Gunther, "The End of Garbage," *Fortune* (March 19, 2007): 162.

72. Betty Klinck, "Litter, Litter Everywhere," *USA Today* (April 13, 2010): 10B.

73. Roben Farzad, "Cash for Trash," *Business Week* (August 4, 2008): 36.

CHAPTER 3

1. As quoted in R. Stanley Williams, "You Ain't Seen Nothin' Yet," *Business 2.0* (September 26, 2000): 168.

2. See "What You Need to Know Now," *Newsweek* (August 24–31, 2009): 50–70; Adrienne Fox, "At Work in 2020," *HR Magazine*, 55 (January 2010): 18–23; and Gregg Easterbrook, "The Boom Is Nigh: Why the Coming Recovery Will Hurt Like Hell," *Newsweek* (February 22, 2010): 48–49.

3. See Gary Hamel, *The Future of Management* (Boston: Harvard Business School Press, 2007); and Lynne C. Lancaster and David Stillman, *The M-Factor: How the Millennial Generation Is Rocking the Workplace* (New York: Harper Business: 2010).

4. Data from Rick Hampson, "In America's Next Decade, Change and Challenges," *USA Today* (January 5, 2010): 1A–2A; and Howard Fineman, "Showdown in America," *Newsweek* (June 14, 2010): 18.

5. Janet Kornblum, "'A Nation of Caregivers,'" *USA Today* (April 6, 2004): 6D. Also see Holly Dolezalek, "Boomer Reality," *Training*, 44 (May 2007): 16–21.

6. Data from Robert J. Samuelson, "Protecting the Welfare State," *Newsweek* (March 8, 2004): 37. Also see Tomoko Yamazaki and Komaki Ito, "Japan: Boosting Growth with Day Care," *Bloomberg Businessweek* (December 28, 2009–January 4, 2010): 96–97; and Aki Ito, "Bureaucrats Play Matchmaker in Japan," *Bloomberg Businessweek* (August 30–September 5, 2010): 12.

7. Laura Meckler, "Social Security Cuts Weighed by Panel," *Wall Street Journal* (August 20, 2010): A4. Also see the data in Robert Arnott, "Investing," *Fortune* (January 18, 2010): 28.

8. Jeanne C. Meister and Karie Willyerd, *The 2020 Workplace: How Innovative Companies Attract, Develop, and Keep Tomorrow's Employees Today* (New York: Harper Business, 2010), p. 44. Also see Sven C. Voelpel and Christoph K. Streb, "A Balanced Scorecard for Managing the Aging Workforce," *Organizational Dynamics*, 39 (January–March 2010): 84–90.

9. Pavel Alpeyev and Yoshinori Eki, "iPad Leads Apple to a New Market: The Elderly," *Bloomberg Businessweek* (August 16–29, 2010): 39.

10. Matthew Boyle, "Honey Nut Cheerios," *Bloomberg Businessweek* (August 16–29, 2010): 62.

11. Data from www.mediapost .com/publications/?fa=Articles. showArticle&art_aid=124694, accessed September 3, 2010.

12. PBS Nightly Business Report, September 3, 2010, www.pbs .org/nbr/site/onair/transcripts/ nbr_transcripts_100903/.

13. As quoted in *ibid*.

14. Geoff Colvin, "Failing the Test," *Fortune* (May 14, 2007): 39.

15. Greg Toppo, "Students' Reading Scores Show Little Progress," *USA Today* (March 25, 2010): 11B.

16. Data and quote from Stacy Teicher Khadaroo, "Graduation Rate for U.S. High-Schoolers Falls for Second Straight Year," *Christian Science Monitor* (June 10, 2010), www.csmonitor.com/USA/ Education/2010/0610/Graduation-rate-for-US-high-schoolers-falls-for-second-straight-year.

17. David A. Kaplan, "The STEM Challenge," *Fortune* (June 14, 2010): 25.

18. Stephanie Banchero, "Scores Stagnate at High Schools," *Wall Street Journal* (August 18, 2010): A1–A2.

19. Theresa Minton-Eversole, "Skills Deficiencies Threaten United States' Workforce Competence," *HR Magazine*, 54 (September 2009): 18.

20. Data from "To Create the Future," Special Advertising Section, *Harvard Business Review*, 88 (May 2010): 113–115. Also see Bill Gates, "A Quiet Revolution," *Newsweek* (February 1, 2010): 9.

21. Kathryn Tyler, "From Dependence to Self-Sufficiency," *HR Magazine*, 55 (September 2010): 36–37.

22. Excerpted from Christine Dugas, "For Boomers, Retirement Jobs Can Be a Tough Fit," *USA Today* (August 10, 2010): 2A. Also see Laura Lallos, "Retired—But in the Game," *Bloomberg Businessweek* (April 25, 2010): 62; and Ken Dychtwald, "I Retired. Now How

Do I Unretire?" *Fortune* (June 14, 2010): 50.

23. Excerpted from Paul Mayrand, "Older Workers: A Problem or the Solution?" *Proceedings: Textbook Authors Conference* (AARP: Washington, D.C., October 21, 1992), pp. 28–29; "Employer Attitudes towards Older Workers," Center for Retirement Research, http://crr.bc.edu; Gary M. Stern, "Hiring Older Workers," Small Business Review, 2011, http://smallbusinessreview.com; "Older Worker Injury and Illness Data from the CDC," www.stonehearthnewsletters.com, April 29, 2011; Terence M. McMenamin, "A Time to Work: Recent Trends in Shift Work and Flexible Schedules," Monthly Labor Review, Dec 2007; www.bls.gov.

24. Dan Kadlec, "How to Age-Proof Your Career," *Money*, 39 (May 2010): 120.

25. See Robert J. Samuelson, "The Quagmire of Inequality," *Newsweek* (June 11, 2007): 48. Also see Justin Fox, "Bridging America's Income Gap," *Harvard Business Review* 88 (September 2010): 122–123.

26. Jessica Bennett, Jesse Ellison, and Sarah Ball, "Are We There Yet?" *Newsweek* (March 29, 2010): 42–46. Also see Joanne Deschenaux, "Pay Gaps Persist Throughout Europe," *HR Magazine*, 54 (June 2009): 97–10.

27. See Nancy M. Carter and Christine Silva, "Women in Management: Delusions of Progress," *Harvard Business Review,* 88 (March 2010): 19–21; and Herminia Ibarra, Nancy M. Carter, and Christine Silva, "Why Men Still Get More Promotions Than Women," *Harvard Business Review,* 88 (September 2010): 80–85.

28. Ann M. Morrison and Mary Ann Von Glinow, "Women and Minorities in Management," *American Psychologist,* 45 (February 1990): 200 (emphasis added).

29. Ilene H. Lang, "Have Women Shattered Corporate Glass Ceiling?

No.," *USA Today* (April 15, 2010): 11A.

30. As quoted in Rhonda Richards, "More Women Poised for Role as CEO," *USA Today* (March 26, 1996): 2B. Also see "Top Barriers to Women in the Workplace," *USA Today* (March 1, 2010): 1B; Sylvia Ann Hewlett, Laura Sherbin, and Diana Forster, "Off-Ramps and On-Ramps Revisited," *Harvard Business Review*, 88 (June 2010): 30; and "Naïve Graduates," *Harvard Business Review*, 88 (September 2010): 27.

31. Based on Michelle K. Ryan and S. Alexander Haslam, "The Glass Cliff: Exploring the Dynamics Surrounding the Appointment of Women to Precarious Leadership Positions," *Academy of Management Review,* 32 (April 2007): 549–572.

32. www.sba.gov/faqs/, FAQ no. 26, accessed September 5, 2010.

33. See Robert J. Samuelson, "Insecurity Goes Upscale," *Newsweek* (July 19, 2010): 24.

34. Data from Adrienne Fox, "Part-Timers Make People Strategy Whole," *HR Magazine*, 55 (August 2010): 28–33.

35. Data from Todd J. Thorsteinson, "Job Attitudes of Part-Time vs. Full-Time Workers: A Meta-Analytic Review," *Journal of Occupational and Organizational Psychology,* 76 (June 2003): 151–177. Also see Nikos Bozionelos, "Does Treating the Permanent Workforce Well Matter to Temporary Employees?" *Academy of Management Perspectives,* 24 (February 2010): 84–86.

36. See Peter Coy, Michele Conlin, and Moira Herbst, "The Disposable Worker," *Bloomberg Businessweek* (January 18, 2010): 32–39.

37. Alan Gomez, "Rise Seen in Births to Illegal Dwellers," *USA Today* (August 12, 2010): 1A.

38. *Ibid.*

39. Haya El Nasser and Brad Heath, "Hispanic Growth Extends Eastward," *USA Today* (August 9, 2007): 1A. Also see Evan Thomas, "Twilight of the Wasps," *Newsweek*, May 24–31, 2010): 34.

40. Tamara Henry, "Societal Shifts Could Alter Education by Midcentury," *USA Today* (February 26, 2001): 6D.

41. Data from Kate Bonamici, "Going Long on Latinos," *Fortune* (February 23, 2004): 153; and Brian Grow, "Hispanic Nation," *Business Week* (March 15, 2004): 58–70.

42. Data from Eamon Javers, "The Divided States of America," *Business Week* (April 16, 2007): 67; and Chris Hawley, "For Many Mexicans, Migration Is a Two-Way Street," *USA Today* (July 26, 2007): 9A.

43. Data from Del Jones, "Setting Diversity's Foundation in the Bottom Line," *USA Today* (October 15, 1996): 4B.

44. For more, see David A. Thomas, "Diversity as Strategy," *Harvard Business Review,* 82 (September 2004): 98–108; Robert Rodriguez, "Diversity Finds Its Place," *HR Magazine,* 51 (August 2006): 56–61; Kathy Gurchiek, "Movies Are Vehicle for Diversity," *HR Magazine,* 54 (November 2009): 74; and Myrtle P. Bell, Mary L. Connerley, and Faye K. Cocchiara, "The Case for Mandatory Diversity Education," *Academy of Management Learning and Education,* 8 (December 2009): 597–609.

45. As quoted in Jack McDevitt, "Are We Becoming a Country of Haters?" *USA Today* (September 2, 1992): 9A. Also see Leslie C. Aguilar, *Ouch! That Stereotype Hurts: Communicating Respectfully in a Diverse World* (Dallas: The Walk the Talk Company, 2006); and Loriann Roberson and Carol T. Kulik, "Stereotype Threat at Work," *Academy of Management Perspectives,* 21 (May 2007): 24–40.

46. Adapted from Sheryl Hilliard Tucker and Kevin D. Thompson, "Will Diversity = Opportunity + Advancement for Blacks?" *Black Enterprise,* 21 (November 1990): 50–60; and Lee Gardenswartz and Anita Rowe, "Important Steps for Implementing Diversity Training," *Mosaics,* 8 (July–August 2002): 5.

47. Research support can be found in Joseph J. Martocchio, "Age-Related Differences in Employee Absenteeism: A Meta-Analysis," *Psychology and Aging*, 4 (December 1989): 409–414.

48. Data from Anne R. Carey and Sam Ward, "2 of 3 Americans Can't Name any U.S. Supreme Court Justices," *USA Today* (June 28, 2010): 1A. Also see Stephen Prothero, "Millennials Do Faith and Politics Their Way," *USA Today* (March 29, 2010): 9A.

49. Christopher Rugaber, "Google Uses Trade Tactic in Censorship Fight," *Arizona Republic* (June 24, 2007): D3.

50. Based in part on "Issues Management," http://pac.org/issues_management, accessed September 6, 2010.

51. Steven L. Wartick and Robert E. Rude, "Issues Management: Corporate Fad or Corporate Function?" *California Management Review*, 29 (Fall 1986): 124–140.

52. Michael Fitzgerald, "They Knew the Magic Word. Are Your Passwords Weak?" *Inc.*, 31 (November 2009): 114. Also see Tony Dokoupil, "A New Curb on Dirty Politicking in Maryland," *Newsweek* (June 7, 2010): 6.

53. Drawn from S. Prakash Sethi, "Serving the Public Interest: Corporate Political Action for the 1980s," *Management Review*, 70 (March 1981): 8–11. Also see Fredreka Schouten, "Health Groups Hiked Political Giving in '09," *USA Today* (February 17, 2010): 7A; and Paul M. Barrett and Jonathan D. Salant, "Why Companies Are Holding Fire," *Bloomberg Businessweek* (April 25–May 2, 2010): 36, 38.

54. Fredreka Schouten and Joan Biskupic, "It's a New Era for Campaign Spending," *USA Today* (January 22, 2010): 5A.

55. See Howard Fineman, "Free Speech By the Millions: Corporate Cash Plots a Comeback," *Newsweek* (September 21, 2009): 24; Ciara Torres-Spelliscy, "Spending on Politics? Tell Shareholders," *Business Week* (November 2,

2009): 80; and John C. Bogle, "It's Time to Stand Up to the Supreme Court," *Bloomberg Businessweek* (March 22–29, 2010): 100.

56. Based on James Mehring, "Soft Money's Flabby Return," *Business Week* (April 26, 2004): 30.

57. Michelle Kessler, "Techies Plug in to Capitol Hill Power," *USA Today* (June 23, 2004): 1B.

58. See Paul M. Barrett, Todd Shields, and Jonathan D. Salant, "An Internet Struggle with Bandwidth Aplenty," *Bloomberg Businessweek* (May 17–May 23, 2010): 28–29; and Robert Schmidt, "Big-Bank Nightmare on K Street," *Bloomberg Businessweek* (May 24–May 30, 2010): 30.

59. Data from Fredreka Schouten, "Health Care Groups Lobby at Record Pace," *USA Today* (October 22, 2009): 5A.

60. Conrad Wilson, "Shopper Without a Cause," *Business Week* (July 9–16, 2007): 14.

61. Sandra Sobiera, "Bush Signs Corporate Fraud Crackdown Bill," www.azcentral.com, July 31, 2002, p. 1. Also see David Henry, "Not Everyone Hates SarbOx," *Business Week* (January 29, 2007): 37; Theo Francis, "These Men Could Kill Sarbox," *Business Week* (November 30, 2009): 40–43; and Becky Quick, "No Perp Walks, No Jail Time. Why Prosecutors Are Going Easy on Wall Street," *Fortune* (July 5, 2010): 50.

62. Drawn from Nicholas Varchaver, "Long Island Confidential," *Fortune* (November 27, 2006): 172–186; Matthew Boyle and Chris Tkaczyk, "Corporate Convicts? Where Are They Now?" http://money.cnn.com/galleries/2008/fortune/0805/gallery.convicts.fortune/index.html, accessed September 6, 2010; and Diana B. Henriques, "Madoff Is Sentenced to 150 Years for Ponzi Scheme," *New York Times* (June 29, 2009), www.nytimes.com/2009/06/30/business/30madoff.html?_r=1. Also see John Waggoner, "Madoff's Gone But Ponzis Go On," *USA Today* (October 2, 2009): 1B–2B.

63. From Harry Maurer and Cristina Lindblad, "Trouble for China Mobile," *Bloomberg Businessweek* (January 11, 2010): 6–7.

64. Lawyer and survey data from Del Jones, "Lawyers, Wannabes on the Rise," *USA Today* (December 26, 2003): 5B.

65. "Briefly," *USA Today* (June 2, 2010): 1B.

66. See Michael Orey, "How Business Trounced the Trial Lawyers," *Business Week* (January 8, 2007): 44–50.

67. Marianne M. Jennings and Frank Shipper, *Avoiding and Surviving Lawsuits* (San Francisco: Jossey-Bass, 1989), p. 118 (emphasis added).

68. John R. Allison, "Easing the Pain of Legal Disputes: The Evolution and Future of Reform," *Business Horizons*, 33 (September–October 1990): 15. For more, see Michael Orey, "Arbitration Aggravation," *Business Week* (April 30, 2007): 38–39; and Jim Hanley, "Transformative Mediation," *HR Magazine*, 55 (April 2010): 64–65.

69. Jeannine Aversa, "Financing Isn't Their Strong Subject," *Arizona Republic* (April 4, 2004): D7.

70. U.S. Bureau of Labor Statistics, *Occupational Outlook Handbook*, 2010–11 edition, "Overview of the 2008–18 Projections," www.bls.gov/oco/oco2003.htm#employment, accessed September 7, 2010. Also see Rana Foroohar, "How to Build Again," *Newsweek* (July 19, 2010): 15.

71. *Ibid.* Also see Edward L. Glaeser and William R. Kerr, "The Secret to Job Growth: Think Small," *Harvard Business Review*, 88 (July–August 2010): 26.

72. Data from 1998–1999 *Occupational Outlook Handbook*, www.bls.gov.

73. David Lidsky, "Who's Next: Minnie Ingersoll," *Fast Company*, 145 (May 2010): 38.

74. See Paul Wiseman, "Outlook for Job Market Is Grim," *USA Today* (January 8, 2010): 1B–2B; Alison Young, "New RN Grads

Feel Squeeze for Jobs," *USA Today* (July 9, 2010): 1A; Michael Elliott, "The U.S. Isn't Alone: High Unemployment Rates Are the New Global Reality," *Fortune* (August 16, 2010): 36; and Peter Coy, "Job: Shop Clerk," *Bloomberg Businessweek* (August 16–29, 2010): 86.

75. Paul A. Samuelson, *Economics,* 10th ed. (New York: McGraw-Hill, 1976), p. 253.

76. Dan Kadlec, "What Your Kids Learned from the Crash," *Money,* 39 (September 2010): 100. Also see Peter Coy, "Smile, at Least It Isn't a Second Depression," *Bloomberg Businessweek* (December 28, 2009-January 4, 2010): 36, 38; and Rana Foroohar, "You Call This a Recovery?" *Newsweek* (August 16, 2010): 21.

77. Ranjay Gulati, Nitin Nohria, and Franz Wohlgezogen, "Roaring Out of Recession," *Harvard Business Review,* 88 (March 2010): 62–69.

78. Darrell Rigby, "Moving Upward in a Downturn," *Harvard Business Review,* 79 (June 2001): 100. Also see Geoff Colvin, "Time to Start Managing for the Next Recession," *Fortune* (October 12, 2009): 16; and Scott Cendrowski, "Singapore Airlines," *Fortune* (June 14, 2010): 22.

79. Daniel Gross, "The Revenge of the Business Cycle," *Fortune* (July 26, 2004): 58.

80. For an informative discussion of the value of economic forecasting, see Peter L. Bernstein and Theodore H. Silbert, "Are Economic Forecasters Worth Listening To?" *Harvard Business Review,* 62 (September–October 1984): 32–40.

81. Lawrence S. Davidson, "Knowing the Unknowable," *Business Horizons,* 32 (September–October 1989): 7.

82. Drawn from Jeffrey M. O'Brien, "Wii Will Rock You," *Fortune* (June 11, 2007): 82–92.

83. John Naisbitt and Patricia Aburdene, *Megatrends 2000* (New York: William Morrow, 1990), p. 21. Also see William J. Bernstein, *A Splendid Exchange: How Trade Shaped the World* (New York:

Grove Press, 2008); and Thomas L. Friedman, *Hot, Flat, and Crowded* (New York: Farrar, Straus and Giroux, 2009).

84. Thomas A. Stewart, "Welcome to the Revolution," *Fortune* (December 13, 1993): 67.

85. Data from www.chips.org, accessed September 7, 2010.

86. Data from "Global 500: The World's Largest Corporations," *Fortune* (July 26, 2010): F-1, F-6.

87. Data from www.toyota.com/about/our_business/our_numbers/images/2010USOperationsBrochure.pdf, accessed September 7, 2010.

88. Del Jones, "Foreign Firms Snap Up U.S. Rivals," *USA Today* (March 7, 2001): 6B.

89. Nicholas Bloom and John Van Reenen, "Why Do Management Practices Differ Across Firms and Countries?" *Journal of Economic Perspectives*, 24 (Winter 2010): 219.

90. Jerome B. Wiesner, "Technology and Innovation," in *Technological Innovation and Society,* ed. Dean Morse and Aaron W. Warner (New York: Columbia University Press, 1966), p. 11.

91. Walter Kiechel III, "How We Will Work in the Year 2000," *Fortune* (May 17, 1993): 39. Also see Jay Greene, "Where PCs Were Born," *Business Week* (February 26, 2007): 110.

92. For good reading on innovation, see Nathan Myhrvold, "Funding Eureka!" *Harvard Business Review,* 88 (March 2010): 40–50; Vijay Govindarajan and Chris Trimble, "Stop the Innovation Wars," *Harvard Business Review*, 88 (July–August 2010): 76–83; C. K. Prahalad and R. A. Mashelkar, "Innovation's Holy Grail," *Harvard Business Review*, 88 (July–August 2010): 132–141; and Lew McCreary, "Kaiser Permanente's Innovation on the Front Line," *Harvard Business Review,* 88 (September 2010): 92–97.

93. Data and excerpt from Michael Arndt and Bruce Einhorn, "The 50 Most Innovative Companies," *Bloomberg Businessweek* (April 25, 2010): 38. Also see

Arik Hesseldahl, "The iPad: More Than the Sum of Its Parts. $270 More, Actually," *Bloomberg Businessweek* (February 22, 2010): 24.

94. Brian Dumaine, "Closing the Innovation Gap," *Fortune* (December 2, 1991): 57.

95. Bill Breen, "The Thrill of Defeat," *Fast Company,* 83 (June 2004): 77. Also see Liz Szabo, "Vaccine Appears to Prevent Breast Cancer in Laboratory Mice," *USA Today* (June 2, 2010): 5D.

96. Based on Stratford Sherman, "When Laws of Physics Meet Laws of the Jungle," *Fortune* (May 15, 1995): 193–194.

97. As quoted in Jefferson Graham, "Apple, AT&T CEOs See iPhone as Industry Game-Changer," *USA Today* (June 29, 2007): 6B.

98. David Whitford, "A Human Place to Work," *Fortune* (January 8, 2001): 110. Also see Michael V. Copeland, "The Ultimate Personal Technology," *Fortune* (May 3, 2010): 55–56.

99. Robert J. Herbold, "Inside Microsoft: Balancing Creativity and Discipline," *Harvard Business Review,* 80 (January 2002): 73–74.

100. Gifford Pinchot III, *Intrapreneuring* (New York: Harper & Row, 1985), p. xvii. Also see Jeffrey H. Dyer, Hal B. Gregersen, and Clayton M. Christensen, "The Innovator's DNA," *Harvard Business Review*, 87 (December 2009): 60–67; and Feirong Yuan and Richard W. Woodman, "Innovative Behavior in the Workplace: The Role of Performance and Image Outcome Expectations," *Academy of Management Journal*, 53 (April 2010): 323–342.

101. Tim Smart, "Kathleen Synnott: Shaping the Mailrooms of Tomorrow," *Business Week* (November 16, 1992): 66.

102. Vince Luchsinger and D. Ray Bagby, "Entrepreneurship and Intra-preneurship: Behaviors, Comparisons, and Contrasts," *SAM Advanced Management Journal*, 52 (Summer 1987): 12.

103. Nokia (Finland), Lego (Denmark), Samsung (Korea), Ericsson (Sweden), and Adidas (Germany). In a survey of 1,000 American college students, only 4.4 percent had the correct answer for Nokia (53.6 percent said Japan). Correct answers for the other four brands, respectively, were 8.4 percent, 9.8 percent, 9.9 percent, and 12.2 percent.

CHAPTER 4

1. As quoted in Saren Starbridge, "Anita Roddick: Fair Trade," *Living Planet*, 3 (Spring 2001): 92.
2. Export data from "Trade to Expand by 9.5% in 2010 After a Dismal 2009, WTO Reports" (March 26, 2010), www.wto.org/english/news_e/pres10_e/pr598_e.htm. Also see Max Magni and Yuval Atsmon, "A Better Approach to China's Markets," *Harvard Business Review*, 88 (March 2010): 30–31; and Sheridan Prasso, "American Made… Chinese Owned," *Fortune* (May 24, 2010): 84–92.
3. Aaron Pressman, "Fished Out," *Business Week* (September 4, 2006): 60.
4. Data from "Trade to Expand by 9.5% in 2010 After a Dismal 2009, WTO Reports."
5. For specifics, see Anne D'Innocenzio, "Mattel to Recall Toy from China," *USA Today* (August 14, 2007): 1B; Brian Grow, Chi-Chu Tschang, Cliff Edwards, and Brian Burnsed, "Dangerous Fakes," *Business Week* (October 13, 2008): 34–44; Robert J. Samuelson, "China's $2.4 Trillion Stash," *Newsweek* (February 1, 2010): 17; Kate Linebaugh, Dionne Searcey, and Norihiko Shirouzu, "Secretive Culture Led Toyota Astray," *Wall Street Journal* (February 10, 2010): A1, A6; Stephen A. Stumpf and Peggy Chaudhry, "Country Matters: Executives Weigh In on the Causes and Counter Measures of Counterfeit Trade," *Business Horizons*, 53 (May–June, 2010): 305–314; and Frederik Balfour

and Tim Culpan, "Chairman Gou," *Bloomberg Businessweek* (September 13–19, 2010): 58–69.
6. "Going Global," *Inc.*, 29 (April 2007): 88. Also see John Lee, "Don't Underestimate India's Consumers," *Bloomberg Businessweek* (February 1–8, 2010): 84; and Bruce Einhorn, "Alan Mulally's Asian Sales Call," *Bloomberg Businessweek* (April 12, 2010): 40–43.
7. Nancy J. Adler with Allison Gundersen, *International Dimensions of Organizational Behavior*, 5th ed. (Mason, Ohio: Thomson SouthWestern, 2008), p. 5.
8. See Mauro F. Guillén and Estaban Garcia-Canal, "The American Model of the Multinational Firm and the 'New' Multinationals from Emerging Economies," *Academy of Management Perspectives*, 23 (May 2009): 23–35.
9. See Isin Guler and Mauro F. Guillén, "Home Country Networks and Foreign Expansion: Evidence from the Venture Capital Industry," *Academy of Management Journal*, 53 (April 2010): 390–410; Garry D. Bruton, "Business and the World's Poorest Billion—The Need for an Expanded Examination by Management Scholars," *Academy of Management Perspectives*, 24 (August 2010): 6–10; J Stewart Black and Allen J. Morrison, "A Cautionary Tale for Emerging Market Giants," *Harvard Business Review*, 88 (September 2010): 99–103; and Jo Jakobsen, "Old Problems Remain, New Ones Crop Up: Political Risk in the 21st Century," *Business Horizons*, 53 (September–October 2010): 481–490.
10. This six-step sequence is based on Alan M. Rugman, "A New Theory of the Multinational Enterprise: Internationalization Versus Internalization," *Columbia Journal of World Business*, 15 (Spring 1980): 23–29.
11. See Sandra Mottner and James P. Johnson, "Motivations and Risks in International Licensing: A Review and Implications for

Licensing to Transitional and Emerging Economies," *Journal of World Business*, 35 (Summer 2000): 171–188; and Thomas Y. Choi, Jaroslaw Budny, and Norbert Wank, "Intellectual Property Management: A Knowledge Supply Chain Perspective," *Business Horizons*, 47 (January–February 2004): 37–44.
12. Data from "Chip Licensing Deal," *USA Today* (November 27, 1996): 1B.
13. For related discussion, see Paul W. Beamish and Nathaniel C. Lupton, "Managing Joint Ventures," *Academy of Management Perspectives*, 23 (May 2009): 75–94; and "How To: Build Business Alliances," Guidebook, no. 3, *Inc.*, 32 (June 2010): 1–4.
14. Chris Woodyard, "A Special Delivery for FedEx," *USA Today* (April 7, 2010): 3B.
15. Robert S. Kaplan, David P. Norton, and Bjarne Rugelsjoen, "Managing Alliances with the Balanced Scorecard," *Harvard Business Review*, 88 (January–February 2010): 117. Also see Henrich R. Greve, Joel A. C. Baum, Hitoshi Mitsuhashi, and Timothy J. Rowley, "Built to Last But Falling Apart: Cohesion, Friction, and Withdrawal from Interfirm Alliances," *Academy of Management Journal*, 53 (April 2010): 302–322.
16. Adapted from Jeremy Main, "Making Global Alliances Work," *Fortune* (December 17, 1990): 121–126; and David Lei and John W. Slocum Jr., "Global Strategic Alliances: Payoffs and Pitfalls," *Organizational Dynamics*, 19 (Winter 1991): 44–62. Also see Srilata Zaheer and Akbar Zaheer, "Trust Across Borders," *Journal of International Business Studies*, 37 (January 2006): 21–29; Stewart Johnston and John W. Selsky, "Duality and Paradox: Trust and Duplicity in Japanese Business Practice," *Organization Studies*, 27 (February 2006): 183–205; and Yadong Luo, "The Independent and Interactive Roles of Procedural,

Distributive, and Interactional Justice in Strategic Alliances," *Academy of Management Journal,* 50 (June 2007): 644–664.

17. See Prashant Kale, Harbir Singh, and Anand P. Raman, "Don't Integrate Your Acquisitions, Partner with Them," *Harvard Budiness Review,* 87 (December 2009): 109–115.

18. John Yantis, "Future of Intel Lies in Easing Your Life," *Arizona Republic* (September 12, 2010): A20. Also see Serena Saitto, "Tech Companies Go Shopping Abroad," *Bloomberg Businessweek* (September 6–12, 2010): 31–32.

19. Joan Warner, "The World Is Not Always Your Oyster," *Business Week* (October 30, 1995): 132.

20. Data from Christopher Tkaczyk, "Colgate-Palmolive," *Fortune* (May 3, 2010): 39.

21. Based on Fons Trompenaars and Charles Hampden-Turner, *Riding the Waves of Culture: Understanding Cultural Diversity in Global Business,* 2nd ed. (New York: McGraw-Hill, 1998), pp. 191–192; Marie-Claude Boudreau, Karen D. Loch, Daniel Robey, and Detmar Straud, "Going Global: Using Information Technology to Advance the Competitiveness of the Virtual Transnational Organization," *Academy of Management Executive,* 12 (November 1998): 120–128; and Anil K. Gupta and Vijay Govindarajan, "Converting Global Presence into Global Competitive Advantage," *Academy of Management Executive,* 15 (May 2001): 45–56.

22. Stanley Reed, "Busting Up Sweden Inc.," *Business Week* (February 22, 1999): 52, 54. For other examples, see Bart Becht, "Building a Company Without Borders," *Harvard Business Review,* 88 (April 2010): 103–106; and Sophie Hares, "'Unmistakably Australian' News Corp. Moves to NYC," *USA Today* (April 7, 2004): 6B. Also see Daniel Gross, "Death on Our Shores," *Newsweek* (June 28–July 5, 2010): 36–39.

23. See David A. Lubin and Daniel C. Esty, "The Sustainability Imperative," *Harvard Business Review,* 88 (May 2010): 42–50.

24. Louis Lavelle and Geoff Gloeckler, "B-Schools: Help Wanted," *Bloomberg Businessweek* (April 12, 2010): 76. Also see Michelle Conlin, "Go East Young MBA," *Bloomberg Businessweek* (March 22–29, 2010): 86–87; and Jonathan P. Doh, "Why Aren't Business Schools More Global and What Can Management Educators Do About It?" *Academy of Management Learning and Education,* 9 (June 2010): 165–168.

25. See Kerri Anne Crowne, "What Leads to Cultural Intelligence?" *Business Horizons,* 51 (September–October 2008): 391–399; and Kok-Yee Ng, Linn Van Dyne, and Soon Ang, "From Experience to Experiential Learning: Cultural Intelligence as a Learning Capability for Global Leader Development," *Academy of Management Learning and Education,* 8 (December 2009): 511–526.

26. David C. Thomas and Kerr Inkson, *Cultural Intelligence: Living and Working Globally,* 2nd ed. (San Francisco: Berrett-Koehler, 2009), p. 16.

27. P. Christopher Earley and Elaine Mosakowski, "Toward Culture Intelligence: Turning Cultural Differences into a Workplace Advantage," *Academy of Management Executive,* 18 (August 2004): 155. Also see the cultural intelligence exercise on page 143 of P. Christopher Earley and Elaine Mosakowski, "Cultural Intelligence," *Harvard Business Review,* 82 (October 2004): 139–146.

28. Howard V. Perlmutter, "The Tortuous Evolution of the Multinational Corporation," *Columbia Journal of World Business,* 4 (January–February 1969): 11. Also see Malika Richards and Michael Y. Hu, "U.S. Subsidiary Control in Malaysia and Singapore," *Business*

Horizons, 46 (November–December 2003): 71–76.

29. Perlmutter and a colleague later added "regiocentric attitude" to their typology. Such an attitude centers on a regional identification (North America, Europe, and Asia, for example). See David A. Heenan and Howard V. Perlmutter, *Multinational Organization Development* (Reading, Mass.: Addison-Wesley, 1979).

30. Jessica Silver-Greenberg, "Land Rush in Africa," *Business Week* (December 7, 2009): 41.

31. Drawn from Brian Dumaine, "The New Turnaround Champs," *Fortune* (July 16, 1990): 36–44.

32. Based on Amy Borrus, "Can Japan's Giants Cut the Apron Strings?" *Business Week* (May 14, 1990): 105–106. For similar problems at Toyota, see Chris Woodyard, "Toyota's Reputation Needs Some TLC," *USA Today* (December 21, 2009): 1B–2B; Matthew Philips, "Toyota's 'Tylenol Moment,'" *Newsweek* (February 15, 2010): 12; and David Welch, "Oh, What a (Hideous) Feeling," *Bloomberg Businessweek* (February 15, 2010): 21–22.

33. Language data from U.S. Census Bureau, as cited in Allen Smith, "EEOC Settlement Reflects Challenges of English-Only Policies," *HR Magazine,* 54 (June 2009): 26.

34. Julia Lieblich, "If You Want a Big, New Market…," *Fortune* (November 21, 1988): 181.

35. Perlmutter, "The Tortuous Evolution of the Multinational Corporation," p. 16.

36. Andrew Johnson, "Forces of Globalization Intrigue Policy Scholar," *Arizona Republic* (December 10, 2006): D2.

37. Geoff Colvin, "How to Build Great Leaders," *Fortune* (December 7, 2009): 70.

38. Arvind V. Phatak and Mohammed M. Habib, "The Dynamics of International Business Negotiations," *Business Horizons,* 39 (May–June 1996): 34.

39. For more, see Adler with Gundersen, *International Dimensions of Organizational Behavior,* pp. 18–68;

and Georgia T. Chao and Henry Moon, "The Cultural Mosaic: A Metatheory for Understanding the Complexity of Culture," *Journal of Applied Psychology,* 90 (November 2005): 1128–1140.

40. As quoted in "How Cultures Collide," *Psychology Today,* 10 (July 1976): 69.

41. Trompenaars and Hampden-Turner, *Riding the Waves of Culture,* p. 3.

42. Data from www.aboutmcdonalds .com/mcd/our_company.html, accessed September 17, 2010.

43. Ronald Inglehart and Wayne E. Baker, "Modernization's Challenge to Traditional Values: Who's Afraid of Ronald McDonald?" *The Futurist,* 35 (March–April 2001): 18, 21. For similar conclusions, see Rana Foroohar and Mac Margolis, "The Other Middle Class," *Newsweek* (March 15, 2010): 42–43; and Rana Foroohar and Melinda Liu, "It's China's World: We're Just Living in It," *Newsweek* (March 22, 2010): 36–39.

44. Drawn from "Maine Hospital Open to Gown Redesign," *USA Today* (August 18, 2004): 12B.

45. See "How Cultures Collide," pp. 66–74, 97; Edward T. Hall, *The Hidden Dimension* (Garden City, N.Y.: Doubleday, 1996); and Mary Munter, "Cross-Cultural Communication for Managers," *Business Horizons,* 36 (May–June 1993): 69–78.

46. Ronald E. Dulek, John S. Fielden, and John S. Hill, "International Communication: An Executive Primer," *Business Horizons,* 34 (January–February 1991): 21.

47. For example, see Robert House, Mansour Javidan, Paul Hanges, and Peter Dorfman, "Understanding Cultures and Implicit Leadership Theories Across the Globe: An Introduction to Project GLOBE," *Journal of World Business,* 37 (Spring 2002): 3–10; Robert J. House, Paul J. Hanges, Mansour Javidan, Peter W. Dorfman, and Vipin Gupta, eds., *Culture, Leadership, and*

Organizations: The GLOBE Study of 62 Societies (Thousand Oaks, Calif.: Sage, 2004); Jiing-Lih Farh, Rick D. Hackett, and Jian Liang, "Individual-Level Cultural Values as Moderators of Perceived Organizational Support-Employee Outcome Relationships in China: Comparing the Effects of Power Distance and Traditionality," *Academy of Management Journal,* 50 (June 2007): 715–729; and Mansour Javidan, "Forward-Thinking Cultures," *Harvard Business Review,* 85 (July–August 2007): 20.

48. For more, see Mansour Javidan and Robert J. House, "Cultural Acumen for the Global Manager: Lessons from Project GLOBE," *Organizational Dynamics,* 29 (Spring 2001): 289–305.

49. This list is based on Edward T. Hall, "The Silent Language in Overseas Business," *Harvard Business Review,* 38 (May–June 1960): 87–96; Rose Knotts, "Cross-Cultural Management: Transformations and Adaptations," *Business Horizons,* 32 (January–February 1989): 29–33; and Adler with Gundersen, *International Dimensions of Organizational Behavior,* pp. 22–62.

50. For related research, see Juri Allik and Anu Realo, "Individualism-Collectivism and Social Capital," *Journal of Cross-Cultural Psychology,* 35 (January 2004): 29–49; and Alvin Hwang and Anne Marie Francesco, "The Influence of Individualism-Collectivism and Power Distance on Use of Feedback Channels and Consequences for Learning," *Academy of Management Learning and Education,* 9 (June 2010): 243–257.

51. For detailed discussion, see Allen C. Bluedorn, Carol Felker Kaufman, and Paul M. Lane, "How Many Things Do You Like to Do at Once? An Introduction to Monochronic and Polychronic Time," *Academy of Management Executive,* 6 (November 1992): 17–26.

52. Jefferson Graham, "Google Starts Searching Before You Finish Typing," *USA Today* (September 9,

2010): 1B. Multitasking is discussed in David H. Freedman, "Why Interruptions, Distraction, and Multitasking Are Not Such Awful Things After All," *Inc.,* 29 (February 2007): 67–68; Bruce Horovitz, "Alpha Moms Leap to Top of Trendsetters," *USA Today* (March 27, 2007): 1B–2B; and Ellen Nichols, "Hyper-Speed Managers," *HR Magazine,* 52 (April 2007): 107–110.

53. Stanley Reed and Robert Tuttle, "Qatar on the Cusp," *Bloomberg Businessweek* (March 20–29, 2010): 53.

54. See Carol Saunders, Craig Van Slyke, and Douglas R. Vogel, "My Time or Yours? Managing Time Visions in Global Virtual Teams," *Academy of Management Executive,* 18 (February 2004): 19–31.

55. Jerry Shine, "More US Students Tackle Japanese," *Christian Science Monitor* (November 25, 1991): 14.

56. Kathryn Tyler, "I Say Potato, You Say *Patata,*" *HR Magazine,* 49 (January 2004): 87.

57. Data from "Diverse Landscape of Newest Americans," *USA Today* (December 4, 2006): 8A; and "USA Today Snapshots: Learning the Lingo," *USA Today* (January 26, 2006): 1A.

58. See Nalini Tarakeshwar, Jeffrey Stanton, and Kenneth I. Pargament, "Religion: An Overlooked Dimension in Cross-Cultural Psychology," *Journal of Cross-Cultural Psychology,* 34 (July 2003): 377–394; Heather Johnson, "Taboo No More," *Training,* 41 (April 2004): 22–26; and Aijaz Ansari, "Buddhism Calls Many Low-Caste Indians," *Arizona Republic* (June 3, 2007): A25.

59. "Burger Boost," *USA Today* (October 11, 1995): 1B. Also see Michael Arndt, "A Misguided Beef with McDonald's," *Business Week* (May 21, 2001): 14.

60. See Peter B. Smith, "Nations, Cultures, and Individuals: New Perspectives and Old Dilemmas," *Journal of Cross-Cultural Psychology,* 35 (January 2004): 6–12.

61. Del Jones, "American CEO in Europe Blends Leadership Styles," *USA Today* (June 21, 2004): 4B.

62. See Geert Hofstede, *Culture's Consequences: Comparing Values, Behaviors, Institutions, and Organizations Across Nations,* 2nd ed. (Thousand Oaks, Calif.: Sage, 2001); Michael H. Hoppe, "An Interview with Geert Hofstede," *Academy of Management Executive,* 18 (February 2004): 75–79; John W. Bing, "Hofstede's Consequences: The Impact of His Work on Consulting and Business Practices," *Academy of Management Executive,* 18 (February 2004): 80–87; Harry C. Triandis, "The Many Dimensions of Culture," *Academy of Management Executive,* 18 (February 2004): 88–93; Bradley L. Kirkman, Kevin B. Lowe, and Cristina B. Gibson, "A Quarter Century of *Culture's Consequences:* A Review of Empirical Research Incorporating Hofstede's Cultural Values Framework," *Journal of International Business Studies,* 37 (May 2006): 285–320.

63. For related discussion, see Peter Cappelli, "The Future of the U.S. Business Model and the Rise of Competitors," *Academy of Management Perspectives,* 23 (May 2009): 5–10.

64. An extension of Hofstede's original work can be found in Geert Hofstede and Michael Harris Bond, "The Confucius Connection: From Cultural Roots to Economic Growth," *Organizational Dynamics,* 16 (Spring 1988): 4–21. Also see Sang M. Lee and Suzanne J. Peterson, "Culture, Entrepreneurial Orientation, and Global Competitiveness," *Journal of World Business,"* 35 (Winter 2000): 401–416; Ashleigh Merritt, "Culture in the Cockpit: Do Hofstede's Dimensions Replicate?" *Journal of Cross-Cultural Psychology,* 31 (May 2000): 283–301; and Galit Ailon, "Mirror, Mirror on the Wall: *Culture's Consequences* in a Value Test of Its Own Design," *Academy of Management Review,* 33 (October 2008): 885–904.

65. Nicholas Bloom and John Van Reenen, "Why Do Management Practices Differ Across Firms and Countries?" *Journal of Economic Perspectives,* 24 (Winter 2010): 207.

66. Based on discussion in Peter W. Dorfman, Paul J. Hanges, and Felix C. Brodbeck, "Leadership and Cultural Variation: The Identification of Culturally Endorsed Leadership Profiles," in Robert J. House, Paul J. Hanges, Mansour Javidan, Peter W. Dorfman, and Vipin Gupta, eds., *Culture, Leadership, and Organizations: The GLOBE Study of 62 Societies* (Thousand Oaks, Calif.: Sage, 2004), pp. 669–719. Also see Mansour Javidan, Peter W. Dorfman, Mary Sully de Luque, and Robert J. House, "In the Eye of the Beholder: Cross Cultural Lessons in Leadership from Project GLOBE," *Academy of Management Perspectives,* 20 (February 2006): 67–90; and David A. Waldman, Mary Sully de Luque, Nathan Washburn, Robert J. House, et al., "Cultural and Leadership Predictors of Corporate Social Responsibility Values of Top Management: A GLOBE Study of 15 Countries," *Journal of International Business Studies,* 37 (November 2006): 823–837.

67. Data from Dianne H. B. Welsh, Fred Luthans, and Steven M. Sommer, "Managing Russian Factory Workers: The Impact of U.S.-Based Behavioral and Participative Techniques," *Academy of Management Journal,* 36 (February 1993): 58–79. Also see Jack Welch and Suzy Welch, "The Riddle of Russia," *Business Week* (June 11, 2007): 88; Jason Bush, "Russia's Factories Shift Gears," *Business Week* (May 18, 2009): 50–51; and Tom Cahill, "Deadly Business in Moscow," *Bloomberg Businessweek* (March 1, 2010): 22–23.

68. Kristin Dunlap Godsey, "Thread by Thread," *Success,* 43 (April 1996): 8.

69. Developing Them," *Fortune* (May 28, 2007): 46.

70. Data from J. Stewart Black and Hal B. Gregersen, "The Right Way to Manage Expats," *Harvard Business Review,* 77 (March–April 1999): 52–63; and Gary S. Insch and John D. Daniels, "Causes and Consequences of Declining Early Departures from Foreign Assignments," *Business Horizons,* 45 (November–December 2002): 39–48.

71. Data from Robert O'Connor, "Plug the Expat Knowledge Drain," *HR Magazine,* 47 (October 2002): 101–107; and Carla Joinson, "No Returns," *HR Magazine,* 47 (November 2002): 70–77. Also see Lisbeth Claus, "International Assignees at Risk," *HR Magazine,* 55 (February 2010): 73–75; Mansour Javidan, Mary Teagarden, and David Bowen, "Making It Overseas," *Harvard Business Review,* 88 (April 2010): 109–113; and Lynn S. Paine, "The China Rules," *Harvard Business Review,* 88 (June 2010): 103–108.

72. Elisabeth Marx, *Breaking Through Culture Shock: What You Need to Succeed in International Business* (London: Nicholas Brealey Publishing, 2001), p. 7.

73. Based on Insch and Daniels, "Causes and Consequences of Declining Early Departures from Foreign Assignments."

74. List based on Rosalie L. Tung, "Selection and Training of Personnel for Overseas Assignments," *Columbia Journal of World Business,* 16 (Spring 1981): 68–78; and Mark E. Mendenhall, Gunter K. Stahl, Ina Ehnert, Gary Oddou, Joyce S. Osland, and Torsten M. Kuhlmann, "Evaluation Studies of Cross-Cultural Training Programs: A Review of the Literature from 1988 to 2000," in Dan Landis, Janet M. Bennett, and Milton J. Bennett, eds., *Handbook of Intercultural Training,* 3rd ed. (Thousand Oaks, Calif.: Sage, 2004), pp. 129–143. Also see Martha Frase, "Show All Employees a Wider World," *HR Magazine,* 52 (June 2007): 98–102.

75. Oliver Teves, "Filipinos Embrace the 'In' Job," *Arizona Republic* (December 6, 2003): D5.

76. See P. Christopher Earley and Randall Peterson, "The Elusive Cultural Chameleon: Cultural Intelligence as a New Approach to Intercultural Training for the Global Manager," *Academy of Management Learning and Education,* 3 (March 2004): 100–115.

77. Robert Moran, "Children of Bilingualism," *International Management,* 45 (November 1990): 93.

78. Based on Joann S. Lublin, "An Overseas Stint Can Be a Ticket to the Top," *Wall Street Journal* (January 29, 1996): B1, B5.

79. See Evan R. Goldstein, "What If 'English Only' Isn't Wrong?" *Wall Street Journal* (August 20, 2010): W9.

80. Based on Verne Harnish, "Step Up! Don't Miss the Biggest Opportunity in History!" *Fortune* (July 26, 2010): 54.

81. See Andrew Molinsky, "Cross-Cultural Code-Switching: The Psychological Challenges of Adapting Behavior in Foreign Cultural Interactions," *Academy of Management Review,* 32 (April 2007): 622–640.

82. See William W. Maddux, Adam D. Galinsky, and Carmit T. Tadmor, "Be a Better Manager: Live Abroad," *Harvard Business Review,* 88 (September 2010): 24.

83. Jessi Hempel, "It Takes a Village—And a Consultant," *Business Week* (September 6, 2004): 76.

84. See P. Christopher Earley, "Intercultural Training for Managers: A Comparison of Documentary and Interpersonal Methods," *Academy of Management Journal,* 30 (December 1987): 685–698. A comprehensive overview of 18 different cross-cultural training methods can be found in Table 3.3 on page 79 of Sandra M. Fowler and Judith M. Bloom, "An Analysis of Methods for Intercultural Training," in Dan Landis, Janet M. Bennett, and Milton J. Bennett, eds., *Handbook of Intercultural Training* (Thousand Oaks, Calif.: Sage, 2004), pp. 37–84.

85. An excellent resource book is J. Stewart Black, Hal B. Gregersen, and Mark E. Mendenhall, *Global Assignments: Successfully Expatriating and Repatriating International Managers* (San Francisco: Jossey-Bass, 1992). Also see Juan I. Sanchez, Paul E. Spector, and Cary L. Cooper, "Adapting to a Boundaryless World: A Developmental Expatriate Model," *Academy of Management Executive,* 14 (May 2000): 96–106; and Susan Meisinger, "Going Global: A Smart Move for HR Professionals," *HR Magazine,* 49 (March 2004): 6.

86. See Elisabeth Marx, *Breaking Through Culture Shock: What You Need to Succeed in International Business* (London: Nicholas Brealey Publishing, 2001); Annelies E. M. van Vianen, Irene E. De Pater, Amy L. Kristof-Brown, and Erin C. Johnson, "Fitting in: Surface- and Deep-Level Cultural Differences and Expatriates' Adjustment," *Academy of Management Journal,* 47 (October 2004): 697–709; and Crystal I. C. Farh, Kathryn M. Bartol, Debra L. Shapiro, and Jiseon Shin, "Networking Abroad: A Process Model of How Expatriates Form Support Ties to Facilitate Adjustment," *Academy of Management Review,* 35 (July 2010): 434–454.

87. See Stephenie Overman, "Mentors Without Borders," *HR Magazine,* 49 (March 2004): 83–85; Ann Pomeroy, "Protecting Expats Around the World," *HR Magazine,* 52 (April 2007): 16; and Mila Lazarova, Mina Westman, and Margaret A. Shaffer, "Elucidating the Positive Side of the Work-Family Interface on International Assignments: A Model of Expatriate Work and Family Performance," *Academy of Management Review,* 35 (January 2010): 93–117.

88. See Annette B. Bossard and Richard B. Peterson, "The Repatriate Experience as Seen by American Expatriates," *Journal of World Business,* 40 (February 2005): 9–28; Kathryn Tyler, "Retaining Repatriates," *HR Magazine,* 51

(March 2006): 97–102; and Alice Andors, "Happy Returns," *HR Magazine,* 55 (March 2010): 61–63.

89. Data from Rosalie L. Tung, "American Expatriates Abroad: From Neophytes to Cosmopolitans," *Journal of World Business,* 33 (Summer 1998): 125–144.

90. See Rosalie L. Tung, "Female Expatriates: The Model Global Manager?" *Organizational Dynamics,* 33, no. 3 (2004): 243–253.

91. David Stauffer, "No Need for Inter-American Culture Clash," *Management Review,* 87 (January 1998): 8. Also see Arup Varma, Linda K. Stroh, and Lisa B. Schmitt, "Women and International Assignments: The Impact of Supervisor-Subordinate Relationships," *Journal of World Business,* 36 (Winter 2001): 380–388.

92. See Louisa Wah, "Surfing the Rough Sea," *Management Review,* 87 (September 1998): 25–29; and Paula M. Caligiuri and Wayne F. Cascio, "Can We Send Her There? Maximizing the Success of Western Women on Global Assignments," *Journal of World Business,* 33 (Winter 1998): 394–416.

93. See Lynette Clemetson, "Soul and Sushi," *Newsweek* (May 4, 1998): 38–41.

94. For helpful tips, see Linda K. Stroh, Arup Varma, and Stacey J. Valy-Durbin, "Why Are Women Left Home: Are They Unwilling to Go on International Assignments?" *Journal of World Business,* 35 (Fall 2000): 241–255; and Brooke Kosofsky Glassberg, "10 Questions: Do Your Homework Before a Semester Abroad," *Budget Travel,* 9 (October 2006): 36, 38.

95. For more, see Timothy Dwyer, "Localization's Hidden Costs," *HR Magazine,* 49 (June 2004): 135–144; Michelle Tsai, "Shanghai Surprises: The Perils of Opening an Office in China," *Inc.,* 29 (March 2007): 47, 51; Calum MacLeod, "Whirlpool

Spins China Challenge into Turnaround," *USA Today* (April 5, 2007): 1B–2B; and Bob McDonald, "Unsolicited Advice," *Bloomberg Businessweek* (September 13–19, 2010): 52.

96. Excerpted from www.idg .com, accessed September 19, 2010. Also see www.idg.com/ www/HomeNew.nsf/docs/patrick_ mcgovern_bio.

97. Excerpted from Pat McGovern, "How to Be a Local, Anywhere," *Inc.*, 29 (April 2007): 112–114.

CHAPTER 5

1. Bruce Weinstein, "Take the YouTube Test," *Business Week* (June 29, 2009): 48.

2. See Fareed Zakaria, "Greed Is Good (To a Point)," *Newsweek* (June 22, 2009): 40–45; and Nathan T. Washburn, "Why Profit Shouldn't Be Your Top Goal," *Harvard Business Review*, 87 (December 2009): 23.

3. As quoted in Del Jones, "American CEO's Take on Europe," *USA Today* (August 20, 2007): 5B.

4. For an interesting look back at Rockefeller, see Jerry Useem, "Entrepreneur of the Century," *Inc.*, twentieth anniversary issue, 21 (May 18, 1999): 159–173.

5. Thomas M. Jones, "Corporate Social Responsibility Revisited, Redefined," *California Management Review*, 22 (Spring 1980): 59–60. Also see Dirk Matten and Jeremy Moon, "'Implicit' and 'Explicit' CSR: A Conceptual Framework for a Comparative Understanding of Corporate Social Responsibility," *Academy of Management Review*, 33 (April 2008): 404–424; C. K. Prahalad, "The Responsible Manager," *Harvard Business Review*, 88 (January–February 2010): 36; and Richard McGill Murphy, "Why Doing Good Is Good for Business," *Fortune* (February 8, 2010): 90–95.

6. For example, see Timothy M. Devinney, "Is the Socially Responsible Corporation a Myth? The Good, the Bad, and the Ugly of Corporate Social Responsibility," *Academy of Management Perspectives*, 23 (May 2009): 44–56; and "Where Does a Company's Responsibility End?" *Harvard Business Review*, 88 (July–August 2010): 18–19.

7. Nancy R. Lockwood, "Corporate Social Responsibility: HR's Leadership Role," 2004 Research Quarterly insert, *HR Magazine*, 49 (December 2004): 2. Also see Bill Drayton and Valeria Budinich, "A New Alliance for Global Change," *Harvard Business Review*, 88 (September 2010): 56–64.

8. See Louis W. Fry and John W. Slocum Jr., "Maximizing the Triple Bottom Line Through Spiritual Leadership," *Organizational Dynamics*, 37 (January–March 2008): 86–96.

9. Archie B. Carroll, "Managing Ethically with Global Stakeholders: A Present and Future Challenge," *Academy of Management Executive,* 18 (May 2004): 118. Also see Andrew Delios, "How Can Organizations Be Competitive But Dare to Care?" *Academy of Management Perspectives*, 24 (August 2010): 25–36.

10. *Ibid.*, pp. 117–118.

11. Tachi Kiuchi, "Fast Talk," *Fast Company*, 78 (January 2004): 64.

12. Alison Overholt, "The Good Earth," *Fast Company,* 77 (December 2003): 86. For an interesting update, see http:// planetgreen.discovery.com/ food-health/fetzer-vineyards- redesigned-bottles.html. Also see Alfred A. Marcus and Adam R. Fremeth, "Green Management Matters Regardless," *Academy of Management Perspectives*, 23 (August 2009): 17–26.

13. This distinction between the economic and the socioeconomic models is based partly on discussion in Courtney C. Brown, *Beyond the Bottom Line* (New York: Macmillan, 1979), pp. 82–83. Also see Richard Whitley, "U.S. Capitalism: A Tarnished Model?" *Academy of Management Perspectives*, 23 (May 2009): 11–22; and Luh Luh Lan and Loizos Heracleous, "Rethinking Agency Theory: The View from Law," *Academy of Management Review*, 35 (April 2010): 294–314.

14. See Robert J. Samuelson, "The Spirit of Adam Smith," *Newsweek* (December 2, 1996): 63; and David Ahlstrom, "Innovation and Growth: How Business Contributes to Society," *Academy of Management Perspectives*, 24 (August 2010): 11–24.

15. As quoted in Keith H. Hammonds, "Writing a New Social Contract," *Business Week* (March 11, 1996): 60.

16. Data from "Fortune 5 Hundred Largest U.S. Corporations," *Fortune* (April 16, 2001): F1.

17. Robert Kuttner, "Enron: A Powerful Blow to Market Fundamentals," *Business Week* (February 4, 2002): 20.

18. See Michael L. Barnett, "Stakeholder Influence Capacity and the Variability of Financial Returns to Corporate Social Responsibility," *Academy of Management Review,* 32 (July 2007): 794–816; and Anne-Claire Pache and Filipe Santos, "When Worlds Collide: The Internal Dynamics of Organizational Responses to Conflicting Institutional Demands," *Academy of Management Review*, 35 (July 2010): 455–476.

19. See Brian O'Keefe, "Meet the CEO of the Biggest Company on Earth," *Fortune* (September 27, 2010): 80–94.

20. See Jeffrey Pfeffer, "Shareholders First? *Not So Fast…*" *Harvard Business Review*, 87 (July 8, 2009): 90–91; and Gay Jervey, "Fast Talk: From Campus to Commerce," *Fast Company*, 144 (April 2010): 51–56.

21. Jayne O'Donnell, "UPS Workers Head to Haiti to Provide Help," *USA Today* (January 25, 2010): 4B.

22. These arguments have been adapted in part from Jones, "Corporate Social Responsibility Revisited," p. 61; and Keith Davis and William C. Frederick, *Business and Society: Management, Public Policy, and Ethics*, 5th ed. (New York: McGraw-Hill, 1984), pp. 28–41.

23. Davis and Frederick, *Business and Society*, p. 34. Also see John L. Campbell, "Why Would Corporations Behave in Socially Responsible Ways? An Institutional Theory of Corporate Social Responsibility," *Academy of Management Review*, 32 (July 2007): 946–967.

24. As quoted in "Trust in Business Rises Globally, Driven by Jumps in U.S. and Other Western Economies," www.edelman.com/trust/2010/, accessed January 26, 2010.

25. Drawn from Ian Wilson, "What One Company Is Doing About Today's Demands on Business," in *Changing Business-Society Interrelationships*, ed. George A. Steiner (Los Angeles: UCLA Graduate School of Management, 1975). Other models are presented in Homer H. Johnson, "Does It Pay to Be Good? Social Responsibility and Financial Performance," *Business Horizons*, 46 (November–December 2003): 34–40; Simon Zadek, "The Path to Corporate Responsibility," *Harvard Business Review*, 82 (December 2004): 125–132; and Michael E. Porter and Mark R. Kramer, "Strategy and Society," *Harvard Business Review*, 84 (December 2006): 78–92.

26. Mike France, "The World War on Tobacco," *Business Week* (November 11, 1996): 100. Also see Nanette Byrnes and Frederik Balfour, "Philip Morris Unbound," *Business Week* (May 4, 2009): 38–42.

27. "Review Questions Toyota's Legal Tactics in Product-Liability Lawsuits," *USA Today* (April 12, 2010): 5B. For more, see Jeff Green and Margaret Cronin Fisk, "Did Toyota's Traffic Cops Sway the Regulators?" *Bloomberg Businessweek* (March 1, 2010): 14, 16; and Sharon Silke Carty, "Toyota Recalls Lexus GX 460, Agrees to Fine," *USA Today* (April 20, 2010): 2B.

28. Peter Burrows, "Finally, a Big Green Apple," *Business Week* (October 5, 2009): 69.

29. As quoted in Abrahm Lustgarten, "Warm, Fuzzy, and Highly Profitable," *Fortune* (November 15, 2004): 194.

30. See Vincent Jeffries, "Virtue and the Altruistic Personality," *Sociological Perspectives*, 41, no. 1 (1998): 151–166. The case against altruism is presented in Edwin A. Locke and Terry W. Noel, "Right Problem, Wrong Solution: A Rejoinder to Mitroff's & Swanson's Call to Action," *The Academy of Management News*, 35 (October 2004): 4.

31. Based on Joseph Weber, "3M's Big Cleanup," *Business Week* (June 5, 2000): 96–98.

32. Data from Michael V. Russo and Paul A. Fouts, "A Resource-Based Perspective on Corporate Environmental Performance and Profitability," *Academy of Management Journal*, 40 (June 1997): 534–559. Also see Stefan Ambec and Paul Lanoie, "Does It Pay to Be Green? A Systematic Overview," *Academy of Management Perspectives*, 22 (November 2008): 45–62.

33. Based on Daniel B. Turban and Daniel W. Greening, "Corporate Social Performance and Organizational Attractiveness to Prospective Employees," *Academy of Management Journal*, 40 (June 1996): 658–672.

34. Joshua D. Margolis and Anger Elfenbein, "Do Well by Doing Good? Don't Count on It," *Harvard Business Review*, 86 (January 2008): 19.

35. Diane Brady and Duane Stanford, "Pepsi's Plan to Make Litter Green," *Bloomberg Businessweek* (April 28–May 2, 2010): 28–29.

36. Data from Christie Garton, "Companies Give in Kind, If Not in Cash," *USA Today* (August 9, 2010): 1B–2B. Also see Desda Moss, "The Value of Giving," *HR Magazine*, 54 (December 2009): 23–26; and Noelle Barton DeFazio and Caroline Preston, "Donations Might Not Increase for a While," *USA Today* (August 9, 2010): 3B.

37. Louis W. Fry, Gerald D. Keim, and Roger E. Meiners, "Corporate Contributions: Altruistic or For-Profit?" *Academy of Management Journal*, 25 (March 1982): 105.

38. For complete details, see Richard E. Wokutch and Barbara A. Spencer, "Corporate Saints and Sinners: The Effects of Philanthropic and Illegal Activity on Organizational Performance," *California Management Review*, 29 (Winter 1987): 62–77.

39. See Geoffrey B. Sprinkle and Laureen A. Maines, "The Benefits and Costs of Corporate Social Responsibility," *Business Horizons*, 53 (September–October 2010): 445–453.

40. As quoted in Heather Johnson, "The ROI of ROPI," *Training*, 41 (February 2004): 18.

41. Batia Wiesenfeld and Gino Cattani, "Business Through Hollywood's Lens," *Harvard Business Review*, 88 (October 2010): 146. Also see Steve Bates, "Survey: Business Ethics Improved During Recession," *HR Magazine*, 55 (January 2010): 13; and Ralph Nader, "Where Left and Right Converge," *Wall Street Journal* (August 18, 2010): A15.

42. See Kevin McCoy, "As Victims Cheer, 'Evil' Madoff Gets 150 Years," *USA Today* (June 30, 2009): 1A–2A; and James Bandler and Nicholas Varchaver, "How Bernie Did It," *Fortune* (May 11, 2009): 51–71.

43. Data from "Citigroup Pays $75M to Settle SEC Charges," *USA Today* (July 30, 2010): 2B; "GE Pays $23.4M to Settle Claims It Paid Kickbacks to Iraqi Officials," *USA Today* (July 28, 2010): 5B; David Lieberman and Matt Krantz, "Goldman Sachs Concedes Mistake, Settles SEC Suit," *USA Today* (July 16, 2010): 1B–2B; and "Hewlett-Packard Agrees to Fine," *USA Today* (August 31, 2010): 1B.

44. An excellent resource book is LaRue Tone Hosmer, *Moral Leadership in Business* (Burr Ridge, Ill.: Irwin, 1994). Also see the entire issue of *Organizational Dynamics*, 36, no. 2 (2007); and Arlen W. Langvardt,

"Building the Pipeline Through an 'Open Innovation' Strategy and a Focus on Ethics: An Interview with Young-Jin Kim, CEO and Chairman of Handok Pharmaceuticals Co.," *Business Horizons*, 53 (March–April 2010): 101–104.

45. See the five-article series on business ethics in the May 2004 issue *of Academy of Management Executive;* Terry Thomas, John R. Schermerhorn Jr., and John W. Dienhart, "Strategic Leadership of Ethical Behavior in Business," *Academy of Management Executive*, 18 (May 2004): 56–66; Dale Buss, "Corporate Com Passes," *HR Magazine*, 49 (June 2004): 127–134; and Jennifer Schramm, "Perceptions on Ethics," *HR Magazine*, 49 (November 2004): 176.

46. O. C. Ferrell and John Fraedrich, *Business Ethics: Ethical Decision Making and Cases* (Boston: Houghton Mifflin, 1991), pp. 10–11.

47. See, for example, Lawrence J. Walker and Karl H. Hennig, "Differing Conceptions of Moral Exemplarity: Just, Brave, and Caring," *Journal of Personality and Social Psychology*, 86 (April 2004): 629–647; John B. Cullen, K. Praveen Parboteeah, and Martin Hoegl, "Cross-National Differences in Managers' Willingness to Justify Ethically Suspect Behaviors: A Test of Institutional Anomie Theory," *Academy of Management Journal*, 47 (June 2004): 411–421; Scott J. Reynolds, "Moral Attentiveness: Who Pays Attention to the Moral Aspects of Life?" *Journal of Applied Psychology*, 93 (September 2008): 1027–1041; and Stephen A. Stumpf and Peggy Chaudhry, "Country Matters: Executives Weigh in on the Causes and Counter Measures of Counterfeit Trade," *Business Horizons*, 53 (May–June 2010): 305–314.

48. Del Jones, "48% of Workers Admit to Unethical or Illegal Acts," *USA Today* (April 4, 1997): 1A. Also see Ann Pomeroy, "Beware the 'Boiling Frog Syndrome,'" *HR Magazine*, 52 (May 2007): 12, 14; and Pamela Babcock, "Fraud by Employees Common, Hard to Detect," *HR Magazine*, 55 (February 2010): 14.

49. *Ibid.*, p. 2A.

50. Robert J. Grossman, "The Five-Finger Bonus: The Fraud Triangle at Work," *HR Magazine*, 48 (October 2003): 41. For a similar problem, see Dean Foust, "Why Did Indymac Implode?" *Business Week* (August 4, 2008): 24.

51. For related research and discussion, see Maurice E. Schweitzer, Lisa Ordonez, and Bambi Douma, "Goal Setting as a Motivator of Unethical Behavior," *Academy of Management Journal*, 47 (June 2004): 422–432; Marshall Schminke, Anke Arnaud, and Maribeth Kuenzi, "The Power of Ethical Work Climates," *Organizational Dynamics*, 36, no. 2 (2007): 171–186; and Lisa D. Ordonez, Maurice E. Schweitzer, Adam D. Galinsky, and Max H. Bazerman, "Goals Gone Wild: The Systematic Side Effects of Overprescribing Goal Setting," *Academy of Management Perspectives*, 23 (February 2009): 6–16.

52. Data from John F. Veiga, Timothy D. Golden, and Kathleen Dechant, "Why Managers Bend Company Rules," *Academy of Management Executive*, 18 (May 2004): 84–90.

53. William Rudelius and Rogene A. Buchholz, "Ethical Problems of Purchasing Managers," *Harvard Business Review*, 57 (March–April 1979): 12.

54. Vikas Anand, Blake E. Ashforth, and Mahendra Joshi, "Business as Usual: The Acceptance and Perpetuation of Corruption in Organizations," *Academy of Management Executive*, 18 (May 2004): 51. Also see Victoria L. Crittenden, Richard C. Hanna, and Robert A. Peterson, "The Cheating Culture: A Global Societal Phenomenon," *Business Horizons*, 52 (July–August 2009): 337–346; and Ellen Gibson, "When People Reckon It's O.K. to Cheat," *Business Week* (October 5, 2009): 25.

55. As quoted in Del Jones, "Military a Model for Execs," *USA Today* (June 9, 2004): 4B. Also see Bill George with Peter Sims, *True North: Discover Your Authentic Leadership* (San Francisco: Jossey-Bass, 2007).

56. See Ben Cohen and Mal Warwick, *Values-Driven Business: How to Change the World, and Have Fun* (San Francisco: Berrett-Koehler, 2006); and John A. Parnell and Eric B. Dent, "Philosophy, Ethics, and Capitalism: An Interview with BB&T Chairman John Allison," *Academy of Management Learning and Education*, 8 (December 2009): 587–596.

57. Del Jones, "CEO's Moral Compass Steers Siemens," *USA Today* (February 15, 2010): 3B.

58. As quoted in *ibid*.

59. Michael Schrage, "I Wasn't Fired," *Fortune* (January 21, 2002): 128.

60. For a landmark treatment of values, see Milton Rokeach, *Beliefs, Attitudes, and Values* (San Francisco: Jossey-Bass, 1968), p. 124; and Milton Rokeach and Sandra J. Ball-Rokeach, "Stability and Change in American Value Priorities, 1968–1981," *American Psychologist*, 44 (May 1989): 775–784. Also see Gregory R. Maio and James M. Olson, "Values as Truisms: Evidence and Implications," *Journal of Personality and Social Psychology*, 74 (February 1998): 294–311.

61. Rokeach, *Beliefs, Attitudes, and Values*, p. 124.

62. Based on Rick Wartzman, "Nature or Nurture? Study Blames Ethical Lapses on Corporate Goals," *Wall Street Journal* (October 9, 1987): 27. Also see Rana Foroohar, "The Recession Generation," *Newsweek* (January 18, 2010): 42–45; and Mary Beth Marklein, "Freshman Have Making Money on Their Minds," *USA Today* (January 21, 2010): 7D.

63. Data from "Jae Yang and Alejandro Gonzalez, "Would You Feel Comfortable Taking Items with You When Leaving a Job? *USA Today* (September 29, 2010): 1B.

64. See Gary R. Weaver and Bradley R. Agle, "Religiosity and Ethical

Behavior in Organizations: A Symbolic Interactionist Perspective," *Academy of Management Review,* 27 (January 2002): 77–97.

65. See Edward Soule, "Managerial Moral Strategies—In Search of a Few Good Principles," *Academy of Management Review,* 27 (January 2002): 114–124.

66. Excerpted from Hosmer, *Moral Leadership in Business,* pp. 39–41. © 1994, McGraw-Hill. Reproduced with permission of The McGraw-Hill Companies.

67. Harry Maurer and Cristina Lindblad, "Psst! Bank Info for Sale," *Bloomberg Businessweek* (February 15, 2010): 6.

68. See Archie B. Carroll, "In Search of the Moral Manager," *Business Horizons,* 30 (March–April 1987): 7–15. Also see Gary R. Weaver, "Ethics and Employees: Making the Connection," *Academy of Management Executive,* 18 (May 2004): 121–125.

69. Data from "The Stat," *Business Week* (December 29, 2003): 16.

70. Data from "Ethics Training a Low Priority," *USA Today* (January 29, 2004): 1B.

71. Peter Navarro, "Why Johnny Can't Lead," *Harvard Business Review,* 82 (December 2004): 17. Also see Donald O. Neubaum, Mark Pagell, John A. Drexler Jr., Frances M. McKee-Ryan, and Erik Larson, "Business Education and Its Relationship to Student Personal Moral Philosophies and Attitudes Toward Profits: An Empirical Response to Critics," *Academy of Management Learning and Education,* 8 (March 2009): 9–24; and David A. Kaplan, "MBAs Get Schooled in Ethics," *Fortune* (October 26, 2009): 27–28.

72. For details, see John A. Byrne, "The Best-Laid Ethics Programs...," *Business Week* (March 9, 1992): 67–69.

73. See Margery Weinstein, "Survey Says: Ethics Training Works," *Training,* 42 (November 2005): 15.

74. Based on discussion in "Top Execs Work with Corporate Boards on Ethics Programs," *HR Magazine,*

52 (January 2007): 16; Margery Weinstein, "Executing Ethics," *Training,* 44 (March 2007): 8; and Cynthia Kincaid, "The Right Stuff," *Training,* 46 (March–April 2009): 34–36.

75. For ground-breaking material on ethical advocates, see Theodore V. Purcell, "Electing an 'Angel's Advocate' to the Board," *Management Review,* 65 (May 1976): 4–11; Theodore V. Purcell, "Institutionalizing Ethics into Top Management Decisions," *Public Relations Quarterly,* 22 (Summer 1977): 15–20. Also see Dov Seidman, "The Case for Ethical Leadership," *Academy of Management Executive,* 18 (May 2004): 134–138; Robert M. Fulmer, "The Challenge of Ethical Leadership," *Organizational Dynamics,* 33, no. 3 (2004): 307–317; and Michael E. Brown, "Misconceptions of Ethical Leadership: How to Avoid Potential Pitfalls," *Organizational Dynamics,* 36, no. 2 (2007): 140–155.

76. See Mary C. Gentile, "Keeping Your Colleagues Honest," *Harvard Business Review,* 88 (March 2010): 114–117.

77. See Linda Klebe Trevino and Michael E. Brown, "Managing to Be Ethical: Debunking Five Business Ethics Myths," *Academy of Management Executive,* 18 (May 2004): 69–81.

78. Eleanor Bloxham, "What BP Was Missing on Deepwater Horizon: A Whistleblower," *Fortune* (June 22, 2010), http://money .cnn.com/2010/06/22/news/ companies/bp_horizon_macondo_ whistleblower.fortune/index.htm.

79. See Dan Vergano, "Is It Over? BP Caps Well, But More Hurdles Remain," *USA Today* (July 16, 2010): 1A–2A.

80. "Business's Big Morality Play," *Dun's Review* (August 1980): 56.

81. See K. Matthew Gilley, Christopher J. Robertson, and Tim C. Mazur, "The Bottom-Line Benefits of Ethics Code Commitment," *Business Horizons,* 53 (January– February 2010): 31–37; and

Eric Krell, "How to Conduct an Ethics Audit," *HR Magazine,* 55 (April 2010): 48–51.

82. See Gerard Beenen and Jonathan Pinto, "Resisting Organizational-Level Corruption: An Interview with Sherron Watkins," *Academy of Management Learning and Education,* 8 (June 2009): 275–289; Amanda Ripley and Maggie Sieger, "The Special Agent," *Time* (January 6, 2003): 34–40; Christine Dugas, "Spotlight Hits Whistle-Blower," *USA Today* (December 10, 2003): 3B; Alan Levin, "Pa. Hometown Proud of MP Who Blew Whistle on Scandal," *USA Today* (May 10, 2004): 4A; and "Soldier Accused of Leaking Iraq Video Faces Charges," *USA Today* (July 7, 2010): 4A.

83. Ralph Nader, "An Anatomy of Whistle Blowing," in *Whistle Blowing,* ed. Ralph Nader, Peter Petkas, and Kate Blackwell (New York: Bantam, 1972), p. 7. For a case study of whistle-blowing, see Ralph Hasson, "Why Didn't We Know?" *Harvard Business Review,* 85 (April 2007): 33–43.

84. See Peter Eisler, "Whistle-Blowers' Rights Get Second Look," *USA Today* (March 15, 2010): 6A; Joan Biskupic, "Supreme Court Restricts Whistle-Blower Lawsuits," *USA Today* (March 31, 2010): 7A; and Bill Leonard, "Whistle-Blower Protections Tucked into Health Care Reform Law," *HR Magazine,* 55 (June 2010): 16.

85. Data from Jayne O'Donnell, "$26.6M Won't Change Me, Whistle-Blower Says," *USA Today* (May 14, 2004): 2B. Also see Jesse Westbrook, "Whistleblowers Get a Raise," *Bloomberg Businessweek* (August 2–8, 2010): 31–32.

86. Jayne O'Donnell, "Complainants Take Risks Unfathomable to Most," *USA Today* (July 29, 2004): 1B. Also see Bill Leonard, "Blowing Whistle on Navy Recruitment Proves Costly," *HR Magazine,* 52 (March 2007): 25, 28.

87. Adapted from Kenneth D. Walters, "Your Employees' Right to Blow

the Whistle," *Harvard Business Review,* 53 (July–August 1975): 26–34, 161–162.

88. See D. Christopher Kayes, David Stirling, and Tjai M. Nielsen, "Building Organizational Integrity," *Business Horizons,* 50 (January–February 2007): 61–70; Steven P. Feldman, "Moral Business Cultures: The Keys to Creating and Maintaining Them," *Organizational Dynamics,* 36, no. 2 (2007): 156–170; and Carolyn Hirschman, "Giving Voice to Employee Concerns," *HR Magazine,* 53 (August 2008): 50–53.

CHAPTER 6

1. As quoted in Brent Schlender, "Peter Drucker Takes the Long View," *Fortune* (September 28, 1998): 170.

2. Data from Brad Stone, "Sell Your Friends," *Bloomberg Businessweek* (September 27–October 3, 2010): 64–72.

3. See Andreas M. Kaplan and Michael Haenlein, "Users of the World, Unite! The Challenges and Opportunities of Social Media," *Business Horizons,* 53 (January–February 2010): 59–68; Sharon Silke Carty, "New Ford Explorer to Make Debut on Facebook," *USA Today* (June 9, 2010): 3B; and Rick Hampson, Donna Leinwand, and Mary Brophy Marcus, "Has Social Networking Gone Too Far?" *USA Today* (October 1, 2010): 1A–2A.

4. Data from Michael Arndt, "Invasion of the Guatemalan Chicken," *Bloomberg Businessweek* (March 22–29, 2010): 72–73.

5. See Jim Collins, *How the Mighty Fall* (New York: HarperCollins, 2009); Laurence Capron and Will Mitchell, "Finding the Right Path," *Harvard Business Review,* 88 (July–August 2010): 102–107; and Michael A. Hitt, Katalin Takacs Haynes, and Roy Serpa, "Strategic Leadership for the 21st Century," *Business Horizons,* 53 (September–October 2010): 437–444.

6. See Kevin Buehler, Andrew Feeman, and Ron Hulme, "Owning the Right Risks," *Harvard Business Review,*

86 (September 2008): 102–110; René M. Stulz, "6 Ways Companies Mismanage Risk," *Harvard Business Review,* 87 (March 2009): 86–94; and Rich Miller and Simon Kennedy, "The Uncertainty Principle: Not Sure? Don't Spend," *Bloomberg Businessweek* (July 26–August 1, 2010): 11–12.

7. "Boeing Warns of 787 Delay," *USA Today* (July 16, 2010): 5B.

8. Based on discussion in Frances J. Milliken, "Three Types of Perceived Uncertainty About the Environment: State, Effect, and Response Uncertainty," *Academy of Management Review,* 12 (January 1987): 133–143. Also see Hugh Courtney, *20/20 Foresight: Crafting Strategy in an Uncertain World* (Boston: Harvard Business School Press, 2001): ch. 2. Uncertainty and fear are discussed in Jerry Useem, "A Brief History of Fear," *Fortune* (September 3, 2007): 84–86.

9. Kerry Sulkowicz, "Analyze This," *Business Week* (August 24–31, 2009): 25.

10. See Raymond E. Miles and Charles C. Snow, *Organizational Strategy, Structure, and Process* (New York: McGraw-Hill, 1978), p. 29. A validation of the Miles and Snow model can be found in Stephen M. Shortell and Edward J. Zajak, "Perceptual and Archival Measures of Miles and Snow's Strategic Types: A Comprehensive Assessment of Reliability and Validity," *Academy of Management Journal,* 33 (December 1990): 817–832. Also see the four articles accompanying David J. Ketchen Jr., "Introduction: Raymond E. Miles and Charles C. Snow's *Organizational Strategy, Structure, and Process,*" *Academy of Management Executive,* 17 (November 2003): 95–96.

11. Data from Joseph Weber, "Harley Investors May Get a Wobbly Ride," *Business Week* (February 11, 2002): 65.

12. Spencer E. Ante, "The Info Tech 100," *Business Week* (July 2, 2007): 64. For related reading about

prospectors, see Farhad Manjoo, "Box Tops," *Fast Company,* 137 (July–August 2009): 57; Alex Taylor III, "Here Comes the Electric Nissan," *Fortune* (March 1, 2010): 90–100; C. K. Prahalad, "Best Practices Get You Only So Far," *Harvard Business Review,* 88 (April 2010): 32.

13. William Boulding and Markus Christen, "First-Mover Disadvantage," *Harvard Business Review,* 79 (October 2001): 20–21 (emphasis added). Also see Jeremy C. Short and G. Tyge Payne, "First Movers and Performance: Timing Is Everything," *Academy of Management Review,* 33 (January 2008): 267–269.

14. Oded Shenkar, "Imitation Is More Valuable Than Innovation," *Harvard Business Review,* 88 (April 2010): 28–29. Also see Hongyan Yang, Corey Phelps, and H. Kevin Steensma, "Learning from What Others Have Learned from You: The Effects of Knowledge Spillovers on Originating Firms," *Academy of Management Journal,* 53 (April 2010): 371–389.

15. Mina Kimes, "The King of Low Cost Drugs," *Fortune* (August 17, 2009): 90.

16. Kevin Maney, "Kodak to Lay Off 15,000, Cut Manufacturing Capacity," *USA Today* (January 23, 2004): 4B.

17. Based on data in Ben Dobbin, "Kodak Cutting More Workers," *Arizona Republic* (January 23, 2004): D1–D2.

18. For details, see Jeffrey S. Conant, Michael P. Mokwa, and P. Rajan Varadarajan, "Strategic Types, Distinctive Marketing Competencies and Organizational Performance: A Multiple Measures Based Study," *Strategic Management Journal,* 11 (September 1990): 365–383.

19. See Matthew Sarkees and John Hulland, "Innovation and Efficiency: It *Is* Possible to Have It All," *Business Horizons,* 52 (January–February 2009): 45–55; and Donald Sull, "How To Thrive in Turbulent Markets,"

Harvard Business Review, 87 (February 2009): 78–88.

20. Based on Mary M. Crossan, Henry W Lane, Roderick E. White, and Leo Klus, "The Improvising Organization: Where Planning Meets Opportunity," *Organizational Dynamics*, 24 (Spring 1996): 20–35.

21. Based on Douglas MacMillan, "Twitter's Redesign Ruffles Feathers," *Bloomberg Businessweek* (September 27–October 3, 2010): 36–37.

22. "$1.4B Authorized to Restore Everglades," *USA Today* (December 12, 2000): 15A. For an update, see Brian Skoloff, "Water Again Flowing into Florida's Big Lake," *USA Today* (July 26, 2007): 4A.

23. Scott Adams, "Dilbert's Management Handbook," *Fortune* (May 13, 1996): 104. Also see Jack Welch and Suzy Welch, "State Your Business," *Business Week* (January 14, 2008): 80; and Nancy Lublin, "Wordplay," *Fast Company*, 140 (November 2009): 86.

24. Based on R. Duane Ireland and Michael A. Hitt, "Mission Statements: Importance, Challenge, and Recommendations for Development," *Business Horizons*, 35 (May–June 1992): 34–42. Also see Haley Rushing, "Managing with the Power of Purpose," *HR Magazine*, 55 (February 2010): 69.

25. Robert D. Hof, "Can Google Stay on Top of the Web?" *Business Week* (October 12, 2009): 48.

26. See Paul Leinwand and Cesare Mainardi, "The Coherence Premium," *Harvard Business Review*, 88 (June 2010): 86–92; and Roger L. Martin, "The Execution Trap," *Harvard Business Review*, 88 (July–August 2010): 64–71.

27. Dan Sullivan, "The Reality Gap," *Inc.*, 21 (March 1999): 119.

28. Anthony P. Raia, *Managing by Objectives* (Glenview, Ill.: Scott, Foresman, 1974), p. 24.

29. For an excellent and comprehensive treatment of goal setting, see Edwin A Locke and Gary P. Latham, *Goal Setting: A Motivational Technique That Works!* (Englewood Cliffs, N.J.: Prentice-Hall, 1984). Also

see Gary P. Latham and Edwin A. Locke, "Enhancing the Benefits and Overcoming the Pitfalls of Goal Setting," *Organizational Dynamics*, 35, no. 4 (2006): 332–340; and Erin Patton, "What Are the Characteristics of Good Strategic Objectives?" *HR Magazine*, 55 (April 2010): 23.

30. John A. Byrne and Heather Timmons, "Tough Times for a New CEO," *Business Week* (October 29, 2001): 66.

31. For example, see Margery Weinstein, "Time Is on Your Side," *Training*, 47 (February 2010): 114–117; and George Mannes, "What to Do When You Can't Do It All," *Money*, 39 (August 2010): 98–103.

32. Raia, *Managing by Objectives*, p. 54.

33. Brian Grow, "Thinking Outside the Big Box," *Business Week* (October 25, 2004): 70.

34. Richard Koch, *The 80/20 Principle: The Secret of Achieving More with Less* (New York: Currency Doubleday, 1998), p. 4.

35. Matthew Philips, "Dialing for Dollars," *Newsweek* (June 28–July 5, 2010): 19.

36. Elizabeth Esfahani, "How to Get Tough with Bad Customers," *Business 2.0*, 5 (October 2004): 52.

37. See Barbara Moses, "The Busyness Trap," *Training*, 35 (November 1998): 38–42; "The Time Trap," *Inc.*, 26 (June 2004): 42–43.

38. See Ellen Joan Pollock, "How I Got a Grip on My Workweek," *Business Week* (April 6, 2009): 84, 86; Leigh Buchanan, "Lighting a Fire Under Them," *Inc.*, 31 (September 2009): 86–90; and Caterina Fake, "If You Have to Have a Meeting, First, Drink Water," *Inc.*, 32 (March 2010): 73.

39. See Peter F. Drucker, *The Practice of Management* (New York: Harper & Row, 1954). For a short update on Drucker, see Thomas A. Stewart, "Effective Immediately," *Harvard Business Review*, 82 (June 2004): 10.

40. As an indication of the widespread interest in MBO, more than 700 books, articles, and technical

papers had been written on the subject by the late 1970s. For a brief history of MBO, see George S. Odiorne, "MBO: A Backward Glance," *Business Horizons*, 21 (October 1978): 14–24. An excellent collection of readings on MBO may be found in George Odiorne, Heinz Weihrich, and Jack Mendleson, *Executive Skills: A Management by Objectives Approach* (Dubuque, Iowa: Wm. C. Brown, 1980). Also see Henry H. Beam, "George Odiorne," *Business Horizons*, 39 (November–December 1996): 73–76.

41. T. J. Rodgers, "No Excuses Management," *Harvard Business Review*, 68 (July–August 1990): 87, 89.

42. For example, see Jan P. Muczyk and Bernard C. Reimann, "MBO as a Complement to Effective Leadership," *Academy of Management Executive*, 3 (May 1989): 131–139.

43. An interesting study of the positive and negative aspects of MBO may be found in Robert C. Ford and Frank S. McLaughlin, "Avoiding Disappointment in MBO Programs," *Human Resource Management*, 21 (Summer 1982): 44–49. Positive research evidence is summarized in Robert Rodgers and John E. Hunter, "Impact of Management by Objectives on Organizational Productivity," *Human Resource Management*, 76 (April 1991): 322–336.

44. For a critical appraisal of MBO core assumptions, see David Halpern and Stephen Osofsky, "A Dissenting View of MBO," *Public Personnel Management*, 19 (Fall 1990): 321–330. Deming's critical comments may be found in W. Edwards Deming, *Out of the Crisis* (Cambridge, Mass.: MIT Press, 1986), pp. 23–96; and Dennis W. Organ, "The Editor's Chair," *Business Horizons*, 39 (November–December 1996): 1.

45. See Richard Babcock and Peter F. Sorensen Jr., "An MBO Check-List: Are Conditions Right for Implementation?" *Management Review*, 68 (June 1979): 59–62.

46. Robert Rodgers and John E. Hunter, "Impact of Management by Objectives on Organizational Productivity," *Journal of Applied Psychology*, 76 (April 1991): 322.

47. See Robert Rodgers, John E. Hunter, and Deborah L. Rogers, "Influence of Top Management Commitment on Management Program Success," *Journal of Applied Psychology*, 78 (February 1993): 151–155.

48. For an excellent resource book, see James P. Lewis, *Fundamentals of Project Management*, 3rd ed. (New York: AMACOM, 2007).

49. Project Management Institute, "What Is Project Management?" www.pmi.org/en/About-Us/About-Us-What-is-Project-Management.aspx, accessed October 3, 2010.

50. Dean Foust, "Harry Potter and the Logistical Nightmare," *Business Week* (August 6, 2007): 9.

51. Data from David J. Lynch, "For Panama Canal, a New Era of Trade Is Coming," *USA Today* (August 6, 2009): 1A, 6A.

52. Louisa Wah, "Most IT Projects Prove Inefficient," *Management Review*, 88 (January 1999): 7. Also see Jennifer Gill, "Smart Questions for Your Tech Consultant," *Inc.*, 29 (January 2007): 45; Drew Robb, "Perfecting Project Management," *HR Magazine*, 54 (June 2009): 115–118; and Helen Walters, "Google Did," *Bloomberg Businessweek* (May 10–16, 2010): 56–62.

53. See Ryan Underwood, "OK, Everybody, Let's Do This! Managing Projects and Collaborating with Co-Workers," *Inc.*, 30 (July 2008): 40–42; Robert J. Grossman, "Managing the People Who Manage the Projects," *HR Magazine*, 54 (August 2009): 28–33; and Joel Spolsky, "When and How to Micromanage," *Inc.*, 31 (December 2009–January 2010): 33–34.

54. See Dean A. Shepherd and Donald F. Kuratko, "The Death of an Innovative Project: How Grief Recovery Enhances Learning," *Business Horizons*, 52 (September–October 2009): 451–458.

55. See recent issues of *Project Management Journal*, http://onlinelibrary.wiley.com/journal/10.1002/(ISSN)1938-9507.

56. Excerpted from a list of 26 attributes in "4.1 Software Attributes," www.project-manager.com.

57. Based on Sheila Simsarian Webber and Maria T. Torti, "Project Managers Doubling as Client Account Executives," *Academy of Management Executive*, 18 (February 2004): 60–71. Also see Sheila Simsarian Webber and Richard J. Klimoski, "Client-Project Manager Engagements, Trust, and Loyalty," *Journal of Organizational Behavior*, 25 (December 2004): 997–1013.

58. Jimmie West, "Show Me the Value," *Training*, 40 (September 2003): 62.

59. See the collection of book and resource reviews following J. Ben Arbaugh, "Introduction: Project Management Education: Emerging Tools, Techniques, and Topics," *Academy of Management Learning and Education*, 6 (December 2007): 568–569; and Kishore Sengupta, Tarek K. Abdel-Hamid, and Luk N. Van Wassenhove, "The Experience Trap," *Harvard Business Review*, 86 (February 2008): 94–101.

60. One example of the application of a flow chart is Sharon M. McKinnon, "How Important Are Those Foreign Operations? A Flow-Chart Approach to Loan Analysis," *Financial Analysts Journal*, 41 (January–February 1985): 75–78.

61. For examples of early Gantt charts, see H. L. Gantt, *Organizing for Work* (New York: Harcourt, Brace and Howe, 1919), ch. 8.

62. Gantt chart applications can be found in Tom D. Conkright, "So You're Going to Manage a Project," *Training*, 35 (January 1998): 64; and Andrew Raskin, "Task Masters," *Inc.* Tech 1999, no. 1 (1999): 62–72.

63. Ivars Avots, "The Management Side of PERT," *California Management Review*, 4 (Winter 1962): 16–27.

64. Additional information on PERT can be found in Nancy Madlin, "Streamlining the PERT Chart," *Management Review*, 75 (September 1986): 67–68; Eric C. Silverberg, "Predicting Project Completion," *Research Technology Review*, 34 (May–June 1991): 46–49; Robert L. Armacost and Rohne L. Jauernig, "Planning and Managing a Major Recruiting Project," *Public Personnel Management*, 20 (Summer 1991): 115–126; T. M. Williams, "Practical Use of Distributions in Network Analysis," *Journal of the Operational Research Society*, 43 (March 1992): 265–270; and Hooshang Kuklan, "Effective Project Management: An Expanded Network Approach," *Journal of Systems Management*, 44 (March 1993): 12–16.

65. Adapted in part from John Fertakis and John Moss, "An Introduction to PERT and PERT/Cost Systems," *Managerial Planning*, 19 (January–February 1971): 24–31.

66. See "Airbus Sees End to A380 Cancellations," *USA Today* (November 24, 2006): 5B.

CHAPTER 7

1. As quoted in Eugenia Levenson, Christopher Tkaczyk, and Jai Lynn Yang, "Indra Rising," *Fortune* (October 16, 2006): 145.

2. Data from C. Chet Miller and Laura B. Cardinal, "Strategic Planning and Firm Performance: A Synthesis of More Than Two Decades of Research," *Academy of Management Journal*, 37 (December 1994): 1649–1665.

3. Data from "U.S. Executives Cite Main Issues," *USA Today* (October 8, 2004): 1A.

4. As quoted in Daniel Lyons, "Jeff Bezos," *Newsweek* (January 4, 2010): 85. Also see Edward C. Baig, "Kindle Sales Stun Bezos: E-Books Fly Off Virtual Shelves at Amazon.com," *USA Today* (July 29, 2010): 3B; and Bryant Urstadt, "Diaper Vs. Goliath," *Bloomberg Businessweek* (October 11–17, 2010): 62–68.

5. See Gary Hamel, "Moon Shots for Management," *Harvard Business Review*, 87 (February 2009): 91–98.

6. See chapter 22 in Jeffrey Pfeffer, *What Were They Thinking? Unconventional Wisdom About Management* (Boston: Harvard Business School Press, 2007), pp. 147–153; and Jim Collins, *How the Mighty Fall: And Why Some Companies Never Give In* (New York: HarperCollins, 2009).

7. Data from "Most Employers Don't Share Company Strategy," *USA Today* (November 15, 2006): 1B.

8. Strategy making is discussed in Michael G. Jacobides, "Strategy Tools for a Shifting Landscape," *Harvard Business Review,* 88 (January–February 2010): 76–84; Henry Mintzberg, "We're Overled and Undermanaged," *Business Week* (August 17, 2009): 68; and Pankaj Ghemawat, "Finding Your Strategy in the New Landscape," *Harvard Business Review,* 88 (March 2010): 54–60.

9. John A. Byrne, "Strategic Planning," *Business Week* (August 26, 1996): 52.

10. Data from Joseph Weber, "Keeping Out of a Jam," *Business Week* (October 4, 2004): 104–106.

11. Based on a definitional framework found in David J. Teece, "Economic Analysis and Strategic Management," *California Management Review,* 26 (Spring 1984): 87. An alternative view calls for supplementing the notion of "fit" with the concept of "stretch," thus better accommodating situations in which a company's aspirations exceed its present resource capabilities. See Michael A. Hitt, Katalin Takacs Haynes, and Roy Serpa, "Strategic Leadership for the 21st Century," *Business Horizons,* 53 (September–October 2010): 437–444.

12. Based on discussion in Donald C. Hambrick and James W. Fredrickson, "Are You Sure You Have a Strategy?" *Academy of Management Executive,* 15 (November 2001): 48–59. Also see Christian Stadler, "The 4 Principles of Enduring Success," *Harvard Business Review,* 85 (July–August 2007): 62–72.

13. See John W. Upson and Annette L. Ranft, "When Strategies Collide: Divergent Multipoint Strategies Within Competitive Triads," *Business Horizons,* 53 (January–February 2010): 49–57.

14. Stephen Haines, "Become a Strategic Thinker," *Training,* 46 (October–November 2009): 64. For more on strategic thinking at work, see Jocelyn R. Davis and Tom Atkinson, "Need Speed? Slow Down," *Harvard Business Review,* 88 (May 2010): 30; and "Charlie Rose Talks to Eric Schmidt," *Bloomberg Businessweek* (September 27–October 3, 2010): 39.

15. Heather Johnson, "Learn or Burn," *Training* 41 (April 2004): 19. Also see Luc K. Audebrand, "Sustainability in Strategic Management Education: The Quest for New Root Metaphors," *Academy of Management Learning and Education,* 9 (September 2010): 413–428.

16. See Michael A. Hitt, et al., "Mergers and Acquisitions: Overcoming Pitfalls, Building Synergy, and Creating Value," *Business Horizons,* 52 (November–December 2009): 523–529.

17. Patricia Sellers, "P&G: Teaching an Old Dog New Tricks," *Fortune* (May 31, 2004): 168. Also see Max Jarman, "P&G Launches Chain of Tide Dry Cleaners," *Arizona Republic* (October 10, 2010): D2.

18. Amy Feldman, "The Tiger in Costco's Tank," *Fast Company,* 117 (July–August 2007): 38.

19. "Hotels Developing Multiple Personalities," *USA Today* (September 10, 1996): 4B.

20. See Brian Winter, "Could Chicken Manure Help Curb Climate Change?" *USA Today* (February 12, 2010): 1A–2A; and Rosalind Resnick, "Rewriting the Rules for E-cycling," *Fortune* (March 23, 2010): 138–139.

21. John Porretto, "Squeezing Diesel Out of Animal Fat," *USA Today* (April 17, 2007): 9B.

22. As quoted in Max Jarman, "Freeport CEO Stays Focused on Future," *Arizona Republic* (May 27, 2007): D2.

23. Jessie Scanlon, "The Shape of a New Coke," *Business Week* (September 8, 2008): 72.

24. See Michael E. Porter, *Competitive Strategy* (New York: Free Press, 1980), p. 35; and Michael E. Porter, *The Competitive Advantage of Nations* (New York: Free Press, 1990), p. 39. For updates see Carolin Decker and Thomas Mellewigt, "Thirty Years After Michael E. Porter: What Do We Know About Business Exit?" *Academy of Management Perspectives,* 21 (May 2007): 41–55; Michael E. Porter, "The Five Competitive Forces That Shape Strategy," *Harvard Business Review,* 86 (January 2008): 79–93; and Michael Porter and Nicolaj Siggelkow, "Contextuality Within Activity Systems and Sustainability of Competitive Advantage," *Academy of Management Perspectives,* 22 (May 2008): 34–56.

25. Porter, *The Competitive Advantage of Nations,* p. 37.

26. For more on brands, see Susan Fournier and Lara Lee, "Getting Brand Communities Right," *Harvard Business Review,* 87 (April 2009): 105–111; Mary Jo Hatch and Majken Schultz, "Of Bricks and Brands: From Corporate to Enterprise Branding," *Organizational Dynamics,* 38 (April–June 2009): 117–130; and Sunil Thomas and Chiranjeev Kohli, "A Brand Is Forever! A Framework for Revitalizing Declining and Dead Brands," *Business Horizons,* 52 (July–August 2009): 377–386.

27. Ron Zemke and Dick Schaaf, *The Service Edge* (New York: New American Library, 1989), p. 360. For more, see Doris Burke, "First: Planet Wal-Mart," *Fortune* (May 3, 2010): 27–28; Brian O'Keefe, "Meet the CEO of the Biggest Company on Earth," *Fortune* (September 27, 2010): 80–94; and Matthew Boyle and Carol Wolf, "To Boost Buying Power, Wal-Mart Woos Partners," *Bloomberg Businessweek* (October 11–17, 2010): 23–24.

28. Loizos Heracleous and Jochen Wirtz, "Singapore Airlines' Balancing Act," *Harvard Business*

Review, 88 (July–August 2010): 145.

29. See Leonard L. Berry and Kent D. Seltman, "Building a Strong Services Brand: Lessons from Mayo Clinic," *Business Horizons,* 50 (May–June 2007): 199–209.

30. For details, see Luis Ma. R. Calingo, "Environmental Determinants of Generic Competitive Strategies: Preliminary Evidence from Structured Content Analysis of *Fortune* and *Business Week* Articles (1983–1984)," *Human Relations,* 42 (April 1989): 353–369.

31. James F. Moore, *The Death of Competition: Leadership and Strategy in the Age of Business Ecosystems* (New York: HarperBusiness, 1996), p. 25. For relevant background material, see Warren Boeker, "Organizational Strategy: An Ecological Perspective," *Academy of Management Journal,* 34 (September 1991): 613–635; and James F. Moore, "Predators and Prey: A New Ecology of Competition," *Harvard Business Review,* 71 (May–June 1993): 75–86. Also see John Hagel III, John Seely Brown, and Lang Davison, "Shaping Strategy in a World of Constant Disruption," *Harvard Business Review,* 86 (October 2008): 80–89; and Marco Tortoriello and David Krackhardt, "Activating Cross-Boundary Knowledge: The Role of Simmelian Ties in the Generation of Innovations," *Academy of Management Journal,* 53 (February 2010): 167–181.

32. See Courtney Shelton Hunt and Howard E. Aldrich, "The Second Ecology: Creation and Evolution of Organizational Communities," in *Research in Organizational Behavior,* vol. 20, ed. Barry M. Staw and L. L. Cummings (Greenwich, Conn.: JAI Press, 1998), pp. 267–301; Peter Coy, "Sleeping with the Enemy," *Business Week* (August 21–28, 2006): 96–97; and DaeSoo Kim, "Process Chain: A New Paradigm of Collaborative Commerce and Synchronized Supply Chain," *Business Horizons,* 49 (September–October 2006): 359–367.

33. Jessi Hempel, "Clash of the Technology Titans," *Fortune* (January 18, 2010): 33–34.

34. See Jon Swartz, "Will Hurd's Sexual-Harassment Scandal Tarnish HP?" *USA Today* (August 9, 2010): 1B; Robert A. Guth and Joann S. Lublin, "Former H-P CEO Drafts Job Plan," *Wall Street Journal* (August 18, 2010): B3; www.bloomberg.com/news/2010–09–07/mark-hurd-joins-oracle-as-president-after-leaving-hp-as-phillips-resigns.html; and Brad Stone and Aaron Ricadela, "And Finally, My New No. 2 Is Way Better Than Yours," *Bloomberg Businessweek* (October 11–17, 2010): 35–36.

35. See Farhad Manjoo, "App Mania," *Fast Company,* 135 (May 2009): 72–79; and Peter Burrows, "Apple's Endlessly Expanding Universe," *Bloomberg Businessweek* (April 26–May 2, 2010): 92–99.

36. Moore, *The Death of Competition,* p. 61.

37. Jefferson Graham, "Apple Relaxes Restrictions for App Developers," *USA Today* (September 10, 2010): 1B.

38. See Ben Kunz, "Five Ways the 'iPad' May Change the World," *Bloomberg Businessweek* (January 18, 2010): 72; "It's Not Sci-Fi, It's (Augmented) Reality," *Fortune* (March 22, 2010): 27; Jessi Hempel, "Social Media Meets Retailing," *Fortune* (March 22, 2010): 30; and Marco R. della Cava, "It's an App World," *USA Today* (March 31, 2010): 1A–2A.

39. Michael Arndt, "L.L. Bean Follows Its Shoppers to the Web," *Bloomberg Businessweek* (March 1, 2010): 43.

40. Based on G. T. Lumpkin and Gregory G. Dess, "E-Business Strategies and Internet Business Models: How the Internet Adds Value," *Organizational Dynamics,* 33, no. 2 (2004): 161–173.

41. Michael E. Porter, "Strategy and the Internet," *Harvard Business Review,* 79 (March 2001): 76.

42. See "Serving Customers Online Gets Results—But It Costs More," *Harvard Business Review*, 88 (March 2010): 24; and "How to Optimize Your Site for Search," *Inc.* Guidebook, *Inc.*, 32 (July–August 2010): 1–4.

43. Data from Jon Swartz, "E-Tailers Ring Up a Record Holiday Week," *USA Today* (December 27, 2001): 3B.

44. For more on business and new media, see Andreas M. Kaplan and Michael Haenlein, "Users of the World, Unite! The Challenges and Opportunities of Social Media," *Business Horizons,* 53 (January–February 2010): 59–68; Felix Gillette, "Twitter, Twitter, Little Stars," *Bloomberg Businessweek* (July 19–25, 2010): 64–67; Biz Stone, "Social Media Grows Up," *Inc.*, 32 (September 2010): 162; and Douglas MacMillan, "Twitter's Redesign Ruffles Feathers," *Bloomberg Businessweek* (September 27–October 3, 2010): 36–37.

45. Su-Ting Yang, "Interaction," *Harvard Business Review*, 88 (May 2010): 20. Also see Max Chafkin, "Social Networking: Tell Your Friends About Us—How to Get Twitter Endorsements," *Inc.*, 32 (March 2010): 108, 110.

46. Sharon Silke Carty, "New Ford Explorer to Make Debut on Facebook," *USA Today* (June 9, 2010): 3B. Also see Joseph Galante, "Sometimes Groupon Coupons Work Too Well," *Bloomberg Businessweek* (June 14–20, 2010): 33–34; and John Waggoner, "Mutual Funds Invest in Twitter Accounts," *USA Today* (September 20, 2010): 2B.

47. April Joyner, "Social Networking: Who's Talking About You? Monitoring Your Online Reputation," *Inc.*, 32 (September 2010): 63–64. Also see Utpal M. Dholakia and Emily Durham, "One Café Chain's Facebook Experiment," *Harvard Business Review*, 88 (March 2010): 26; Ben Paynter, "Five Steps to Social Currency," *Fast Company*, 145 (May 2010): 44–47; Scott

Berinato, "Six Ways to Find Value in Twitter's Noise," *Harvard Business Review*, 88 (June 2010): 34–35; and Douglas MacMillan, "With Friends Like This, Who Needs Facebook?" *Bloomberg Businessweek* (September 13–19, 2010): 35–37.

48. For an alternative perspective, see Mahesh Gupta, Lynn Boyd, and Lyle Sussman, "To Better Maps: A TOC Primer for Strategic Planning," *Business Horizons*, 47 (March–April 2004): 15–26. Also see Kevin P. Coyne and John Horn, "Predicting Your Competitor's Reaction," *Harvard Business Review*, 87 (April 2009): 90–97.

49. Henry Mintzberg, "The Design School: Reconsidering the Basic Premises of Strategic Management," *Strategic Management Journal*, 11 (March–April 1990): 192. Also see Daniel P. Forbes, "Reconsidering the Strategic Implications of Decision Comprehensiveness," *Academy of Management Review*, 32 (April 2007): 361–376.

50. See Paul Leinwand and Cesare Mainardi, "The Coherence Premium," *Harvard Business Review*, 88 (June 2010): 86–92.

51. Drawn from David Welch, "Why VW Is the Car Giant to Watch," *Bloomberg Businessweek* (January 25, 2010): 44–48.

52. Richard F. Vancil, "Strategy Formulation in Complex Organizations," *Sloan Management Review*, 17 (Winter 1976): 18. Also see Brian J. Huffman, "Why Environmental Scanning Works Except When You Need It," *Business Horizons*, 47 (May–June 2004): 39–48.

53. As quoted in Fred Vogelstein, "It's Not Just Business, It's Personal," *Fortune* (November 15, 2004): 200.

54. "Is Your Company an Extrovert?" *Management Review*, 85 (March 1996): 7.

55. Rosabeth Moss Kanter, "Think Outside the Building," *Harvard Business Review*, 88 (March 2010): 34.

56. See Barbara B. Flynn, Sarah Jinhui Wu, and Steven Melnyk, "Operational Capabilities: Hidden in Plain View," *Business Horizons*, 53 (May–June 2010): 247–256.

57. Adapted from Andrew Bartmess and Keith Cerny, "Building Competitive Advantage Through a Global Network of Capabilities," *California Management Review*, 35 (Winter 1993): 78–103. Also see Robert L. Cardy and T. T. Selvarajan, "Competencies: Alternative Frameworks for Competitive Advantage," *Business Horizons*, 49 (May–June 2006): 235–245.

58. See David A. Thomas, "Diversity as Strategy," *Harvard Business Review*, 82 (September 2004): 98–108.

59. As quoted in Alan Webber, "The Old Economy Meets the New Economy," *Fast Company*, 51 (October 2001): 74. For more on strategic speed, see "Is Your Company Up to Speed?" *Fast Company*, 71 (June 2003): 81–86; and Hau L. Lee, "The Triple-A Supply Chain," *Harvard Business Review*, 82 (October 2004): 102–112.

60. For essential reading in this area, see Michael and James Champy, *Reengineering the Corporation: A Manifesto for Business Revolution* (New York: HarperBusiness, 1993); and James Champy, *Reengineering Management: The New Mandate for Leadership* (NewYork: HarperBusiness, 1995). Also see Gail L. Rein, "FEEL IT—A Method for Achieving Sustainable Process Changes," *Business Horizons*, 47 (May–June 2004): 75–81; and Daniel McGinn, "Re-engineering 2.0," *Newsweek* (November 22, 2004): 59.

61. According to Henry Mintzberg, there are four reasons why organizations need strategies: (1) to set direction, (2) to focus effort of contributors, (3) to define the organization, and (4) to provide consistency. For more, see Henry Mintzberg, "The Strategy Concept II: Another Look at Why Organizations Need Strategies," *California Management Review*, 30 (Fall 1987): 25–32.

62. Waldron Berry, "Beyond Strategic Planning," *Managerial Planning* 29 (March–April 1981): 14.

63. See Joseph L. Bower and Clark G. Gilbert, "How Managers' Everyday Decisions Create or Destroy Your Company's Strategy," *Harvard Business Review*, 85 (February 2007): 72–79; and Laurence Capron and Will Mitchell, "Finding the Right Path," *Harvard Business Review*, 88 (July–August 2010): 102–107.

64. Charles H. Roush Jr. and Ben C. Ball Jr., "Controlling the Implementation of Strategy," *Managerial Planning*, 29 (November–December 1980): 4. Also see Roger L. Martin, "The Execution Trap," *Harvard Business Review*, 88 (July–August 2010): 64–71; and Stanley F. Slater, Eric M. Olson, and G. Tomas M. Hult, "Worried About Strategy Implementation? Don't Overlook Marketing's Role," *Business Horizons*, 53 (September–October 2010): 469–479.

65. Donald C. Hambrick and Albert A. Cannella Jr., "Strategy Implementation as Substance and Selling," *Academy of Management Executive*, 3 (November 1989): 282–283.

66. As quoted in "How to Keep Your Company's Edge," *Business 2.0*, 4 (December 2003): 93.

67. William D. Guth and Ian C. Macmillian, "Strategy Implementation Versus Middle Management Self-Interest," *Strategic Management Journal*, 7 (July–August 1986): 321. Also see "How Hierarchy Can Hurt Strategy Execution," *Harvard Business Review*, 88 (July–August 2010): 74–75.

68. Alex Taylor III, "Fixing Up Ford," *Fortune* (May 25, 2009): 48–49.

69. See Robert S. Kaplan and David P. Norton, "Using the Balanced Scorecard as a Strategic Management System," *Harvard Business Review*, 85 (July–August 2007): 150–161.

70. See Homer H. Johnson and Sung Min Kim, "When Strategy Pales:

Lessons from the Department Store Industry," *Business Horizons*, 52 (November–December 2009): 583–593; and Stefan Cedergren, Anders Wall, and Christer Norström, "Evaluation of Performance in a Product Development Context," *Business Horizons*, 53 (July–August 2010): 359–369.

71. See Vasudevan Ramanujan and N. Venkatraman, "Planning and Performance: A New Look at an Old Question," *Business Horizons*, 30 (May–June 1987): 19–25.

72. See Ken McGee, "Give Me That Real-Time Information," *Harvard Business Review*, 82 (April 2004): 26; and Vaidyanathan Jayaraman and Yadong Luo, "Creating Competitive Advantages Through New Value Creation: A Reverse Logistics Perspective," *Academy of Management Perspectives*, 21 (May 2007): 56–73.

73. See Paul Saffo, "Six Rules for Effective Forecasting," *Harvard Business Review*, 85 (July–August 2007): 122–131.

74. See Kasey Wehrum, "Forecasting in a Crazy, Mixed-up World: Clues Are Hard to Find" *Inc.*, 31 (April 2009): 19–20; and Mina Kimes, "When He Talks, *the Street* Listens," *Fortune* (May 24, 2010): 29–30.

75. An excellent overview of forecasting techniques may be found in David M. Georgoff and Robert G. Murdick, "Manager's Guide to Forecasting," *Harvard Business Review*, 64 (January–February 1986): 110–120.

76. Jeff Green and Alan Ohnsman, "Toyota's Large-Pickup Identity Crisis," *Bloomberg Businessweek* (October 11–17, 2010): 24.

77. Based on C. W. J. Granger, *Forecasting in Business and Economics* (New York: Academic Press, 1980), pp. 6–10.

78. See Chris Woodyard, "Buyers Go After Big Cars Again," *USA Today* (January 26, 2009): 1B.

79. Duncan Martell, "Rumors Fly About iPod Upgrade," *USA Today* (October 12, 2004): 2B.

80. See Erick Schonfeld, "The Wisdom of the Corporate Crowd," *Business 2.0*, 7 (September 2006): 47–49.

81. See Steven Schnaars and Paschalina (Lilia) Ziamou, "The Essentials of Scenario Writing," *Business Horizons*, 44 (July–August 2001): 25–31; Hugh Courtney, "Scenario Planning," in *20–20 Foresight: Crafting Strategy in an Uncertain World* (Boston: Harvard Business School Press, 2001), pp. 160–165; William J. Worthington, Jamie D. Collins, and Michael A. Hitt, "Beyond Risk Mitigation: Enhancing Corporate Innovation with Scenario Planning," *Business Horizons*, 52 (September–October 2009): 441–450; and Frank Buytendijk, Toby Hatch, and Pietro Micheli, "Scenario-Based Strategy Maps," *Business Horizons*, 53 (July–August 2010): 335–347.

82. Steven P. Schnaars, "How to Develop and Use Scenarios," *Long Range Planning*, 20 (February 1987): 106.

83. See Darrell Rigby, "A Growing Focus on Preparedness," *Harvard Business Review*, 85 (July–August 2007): 21–22; Mike Eskew, "Stick with Your Vision," *Harvard Business Review*, 85 (July–August 2007): 56–57; and Suzanne Woolley, "Scouring the Globe for Emerging Risks," *Bloomberg Businessweek* (October 4–10, 2010): 55.

84. Leonard Fuld, "Be Prepared," *Harvard Business Review*, 81 (November 2003): 20.

85. *Ibid.*

86. Peter Coy and Neil Gross, "21 Ideas for the 21st Century," *Business Week* (August 30, 1999): 82.

87. See Burt Helm, "Online Polls: How Good Are They?" *Business Week* (June 16, 2008): 86–87; and Andrew O'Connell, "Reading the Public Mind," *Harvard Business Review*, 88 (October 2010): 27–29.

88. See Elie Ofek and Luc Wathieu, "Are You Ignoring Trends That Could Shake Up Your Business?" *Harvard Business Review*, 88 (July–August 2010): 124–131; and Barrett Sheridan, "Hit Detector," *Bloomberg Businessweek* (August 16–29, 2010): 83–84.

CHAPTER 8

1. Norm Brodsky, "The Thin Red Line," *Inc.*, 26 (January 2004): 49.

2. See S. Trevis Certo, Brian L. Connelly, and Laszlo Tihanyi, "Managers and Their Not-So-Rational Decisions," *Business Horizons*, 51 (March–April 2008): 113–119; Del Jones, "Being a Good Boss Is Like Being a Good Umpire," *USA Today* (October 20, 2008): 4B; and Dan Ariely, "The End of Rational Economics," *Harvard Business Review*, 87 (July–August 2009): 78–84.

3. Ellen McGirt, "Artist. Athlete. CEO." *Fast Company*, 148 (September 2010): 68.

4. Betty Beard, "Study: Complexity Dazes Executives," *Arizona Republic* (September 19, 2010): D2.

5. Morgan W. McCall Jr. and Robert E. Kaplan, *Whatever It Takes: The Realities of Managerial Decision Making*, 2nd ed. (Englewood Cliffs, N.J.: Prentice-Hall, 1990), p. 5.

6. Paul Hoversten, "Backers Hope Amenities Will Quiet Critics," *USA Today* (February 22, 1995): 2A.

7. Michael Parrish, "Former Arco Chief Still Gambling on Oil Strikes," *Los Angeles Times* (September 21, 1993): D1.

8. Andrew Campbell, Jo Whitehead, and Sydney Finkelstein, "Why Good Leaders Make Bad Decisions," *Harvard Business Review*, 87 (February 2009): 60, 62.

9. Eric W. K. Tsang, "Superstition and Decision-Making: Contradiction or Complement?" *Academy of Management Executive*, 18 (November 2004): 92. Also see "Hard Choices: Kai-Fu Lee," *Bloomberg Businessweek* (July 12–18, 2010): 80.

10. Justin Martin, "Tomorrow's CEOs," *Fortune* (June 24, 1996): 90.

11. See Dan Heath and Chip Heath, "In Defense of Feelings: Why Your Gut Is More Ethical Than Your

Brain," *Fast Company*, 137 (July–August 2009): 58–59.

12. Monica Hortobagyi, "Slain Students' Pages to Stay on Facebook," *USA Today* (May 9, 2007): 9D.

13. Steven M. Gillon, "Unintended Consequences: Why Our Plans Don't Go According to Plan," *The Futurist*, 35 (March–April 2001): 49.

14. See Edward Tenner, *Why Things Bite Back: Technology and the Revenge of Unintended Consequences* (New York: Vintage Books, 1996), ch. 1. Also see Stephen Haines, "The Rubik's Cube Effect," *Training*, 47 (March–April 2010): 48.

15. "Asian Carp Invasion," *Nature Conservancy* (Summer 2010): 12.

16. See, for example, Judy Keen, "Neighbors at Odds over Noise from Wind Turbines," *USA Today* (November 4, 2008): 3A; and Ania Wieckowski, "The Unintended Consequences of Cul-de-Sacs," *Harvard Business Review*, 88 (May 2010): 25.

17. Clark G. Gilbert and Matthew J. Eyring, "Beating the Odds When You Launch a New Venture," *Harvard Business Review*, 88 (May 2010): 95.

18. See Michael B. Metzger, "Problems with Probabilities," *Business Horizons*, 53 (January–February 2010): 15–19.

19. See David Champion, "Managing Risk in the New World," *Harvard Business Review*, 87 (October 2009): 69–75; and Nassim N. Taleb. Daniel G. Goldstein, and Mark W. Spitznagel, "The Six Mistakes Executives Make in Risk Management," *Harvard Business Review*, 87 (October 2009): 78–81.

20. Paul Raeburn, "A Biotech Boom with a Difference," *Business Week* (December 31, 2001): 52. Also see Faith Arner, "The High Cost of Drugs Hits a Drugmaker," *Business Week* (December 29, 2003): 14; and Julie Schmit, "Drugmakers Gamble Big on Generics," *USA Today* (August 24, 2004): 1B.

21. See John J. Medina, "The Science of Thinking Smarter," *Harvard Business Review*, 86 (May 2008): 51–54; Michelle Healy, "Mensa Gets on a Young Brain Wave," *USA Today* (October 11, 2010): 7D; and James G. March, *The Ambiguities of Experience* (Ithaca, N.Y.: Cornell University Press, 2010).

22. For related reading, see Alison Overholt, "Are You a Polyolefin Optimizer? Take This Quiz," *Fast Company*, 81 (April 2004): 37; and Michael J. Mauboussin, *Think Twice: Harnessing the Power of Counterintuition* (Boston: Harvard Business Press, 2009).

23. See Eugene Sadler-Smith and Erella Shefy, "The Intuitive Executive: Understanding and Applying 'Gut Feel' in Decision-Making," *Academy of Management Executive*, 18 (November 2004): 76–91; Erik Dane and Michael G. Pratt, "Exploring Intuition and Its Role in Managerial Decision Making," *Academy of Management Review*, 32 (January 2007): 33–54; and Eugene Sadler-Smith and Erella Shefy, "Developing Intuitive Awareness in Management Education," *Academy of Management Learning and Education*, 6 (June 2007): 186–205.

24. David Lieberman, "'Rolling Stone' Founder Keeps Things Fun," *USA Today* (June 11, 2007): 4B.

25. As quoted in Keith H. Hammonds, "Continental's Turnaround Pilot," *Fast Company*, 53 (December 2001): 100. Also see the first Q&A in Jack Welch and Suzy Welch, "When to Go with Your Gut," *Business Week* (September 4, 2006): 104; and Ap Dijksterhuis, "When to Sleep on It," *Harvard Business Review*, 85 (February 2007): 30–32.

26. For research on decision styles, see Susanne G. Scott and Reginald A. Bruce, "Decision-Making Style: The Development and Assessment of a New Measure," *Educational and Psychological Measurement*, 55 (October 1995): 818–831; and Stacey M. Whitecotton, D. Elaine Sanders, and Kathleen B. Norris, "Improving Predictive Accuracy

with a Combination of Human Intuition and Mechanical Decision Aids," *Organizational Behavior and Human Decision Processes*, 76 (December 1998): 325–348.

27. See Beverly Geber, "A Quick Course in Decision Science," *Training*, 25 (April 1988): 54–55; Alan E. Singer, Steven Lysonski, Ming Singer, and David Hayes, "Ethical Myopia: The Case of 'Framing' by Framing," *Journal of Business Ethics*, 10 (January 1991): 29–36; and Glen Whyte, "Decision Failures: Why They Occur and How to Prevent Them," *Academy of Management Executive*, 5 (August 1991): 23–31.

28. Irwin P. Levin, Sara K. Schnittjer, and Shannon L. Thee, "Information Framing Effects in Social and Personal Decisions," *Journal of Experimental Social Psychology*, 24 (November 1988): 527. For additional research evidence, see Myeong-Gu Seo, Brent Goldfarb, and Lisa Feldman Barrett, "Affect and the Framing Effect Within Individuals over Time: Risk Taking in a Dynamic Investment Simulation," *Academy of Management Journal*, 53 (April 2010): 411–431.

29. See Leslie C. Aguilar, *Ouch! That Stereotype Hurts: Communicating Respectfully in a Diverse World* (Dallas: The Walk the Walk Company, 2006).

30. For good background reading, see Barry M. Staw and Jerry Ross, "Knowing When to Pull the Plug," *Harvard Business Review*, 65 (March–April 1987): 68–74; and Barry M. Staw and Jerry Ross, "Understanding Behavior in Escalation Situations," *Science*, 246 (October 13, 1989): 216–220. Also see William S. Silver and Terence R. Mitchell, "The Status Quo Tendency in Decision Making," *Organizational Dynamics*, 18 (Spring 1990): 34–46.

31. See Joel Brockner, "The Escalation of Commitment to a Failing Course of Action: Toward Theoretical Progress," *Academy of Management Review*, 17 (January 1992): 39–61; Beth Dietz-Uhler, "The Escalation of Commitment in Political

Decision-Making Groups: A Social Identity Approach," *European Journal of Social Psychology,* 26 (July–August 1996): 611–629; Jennifer L. DeNicolis and Donald A. Hantula, "Sinking Shots and Sinking Costs? Or, How Long Can I Play in the NBA?" *Academy of Management Executive,* 10 (August 1996): 66–67; Marc D. Street and William P. Anthony, "A Conceptual Framework Establishing the Relationship Between Groupthink and Escalating Commitment Behavior," *Small Group Research,* 28 (May 1997): 267–293; Asghar Zardkoohi, "Do Real Options Lead to Escalation of Commitment?" *Academy of Management Review,* 29 (January 2004): 111–119; and Kin Fai Ellick Wong, Michelle Yik, and Jessica Y. Y. Kwong, "Understanding the Emotional Aspects of Escalation of Commitment: The Role of Negative Affect," *Journal of Applied Psychology,* 91 (March 2006): 282–297.

32. The second Q&A in Jack Welch and Suzy Welch, "Don't Count Brand America Out," *Business Week* (August 6, 2007): 96. A good case study of escalation can be found in John W. Mullins, "Good Money After Bad?" *Harvard Business Review,* 85 (March 2007): 37–48. Also see Tom Vanden Brook, "Gates Cuts Army Combat Vehicles," *USA Today* (May 1, 2009): 1A; and Ben Elgin and Keith Epstein, "It's a Bird, It's a Plane, It's Pork," *Business Week* (November 9, 2009): 46–48.

33. For related research evidence, see Itamar Simonson and Barry M. Staw, "Deescalation Strategies: A Comparison of Techniques for Reducing Commitment to Losing Courses of Action," *Journal of Applied Psychology,* 77 (August 1992): 419–426.

34. Sidney Finkelstein, *Why Smart Executives Fail—And What You Can Learn from Their Mistakes* (New York: Portfolio, 2003), pp. 223–224.

35. For an interesting exercise, see J. Edward Russo and Paul J. H. Schoemaker, "The Overconfidence Quiz," *Harvard Business Review,* 68 (September–October 1990): 236–237. Also see Burton G. Malkiel and Charles D. Ellis, "Dodge the 6 Biggest Investing Mistakes," *Money,* 39 (January–February 2010): 104–108.

36. Paul J. H. Schoemaker and Robert E. Gunther, "The Wisdom of Deliberate Mistakes," *Harvard Business Review,* 84 (June 2006): 111. Learning from mistakes and failure is discussed in Diane Brady, "Hard Choices: Carol Bartz," *Bloomberg Businessweek* (August 16–29, 2010): 100; and Seth Godin, "Redefining Failure," *Harvard Business Review,* 88 (September 2010): 34.

37. An excellent resource book is James G. March, *A Primer on Decision Making: How Decisions Happen* (New York: Free Press, 1994). Also see Thomas H. Davenport, "Make Better Decisions," *Harvard Business Review,* 87 (November 2009): 117–123.

38. Drawn from Gardiner Morse, "By Any Other Name," *Harvard Business Review,* 82 (November 2004): 30.

39. Gary Belsky and Thomas Gilovich, *Why Smart People Make Big Money Mistakes—And How to Correct Them: Lessons from the New Science of Behavioral Economics* (New York: Fireside, 1999), pp. 100–101.

40. For example, see Herbert A. Simon, *The New Science of Management Decision,* rev. ed. (Englewood Cliffs, N.J.: Prentice-Hall, 1977), p. 40.

41. See, for example, Herbert E. Kierulff, "The Replacement Decision: Getting It Right," *Business Horizons,* 50 (May–June 2007): 231–237.

42. See Dan Heath and Chip Heath, "The Heroic Checklist," *Fast Company,* 123 (March 2008): 66, 68.

43. Andrew S. Grove, *High Output Management* (New York: Random House, 1983), p. 98.

44. Simon, *The New Science of Management Decision,* p. 46.

45. See March, *A Primer on Decision Making,* pp. 8–9; and Rita Gunther McGrath and Ian C. MacMillan, "How to Get Unstuck," *Harvard Business Review,* 87 (May 2009): 20–21.

46. See Charles R. Schwenk, "The Use of Participant Recollection in the Modeling of Organizational Decision Processes," *Academy of Management Review,* 10 (July 1985): 496–503.

47. Chester I. Barnard, *The Functions of the Executive* (Cambridge, Mass.: Harvard University Press, 1938), p. 190.

48. For good background reading, see *Harvard Business Review on Knowledge Management* (Boston: Harvard Business School Publishing, 1998); and Nancy R. Lockwood, "Leveraging HR and Knowledge Management in a Challenging Economy," *SHRM Research Quarterly, HR Magazine,* 54 (June 2009): 1–10.

49. David W. De Long and Patricia Seemann, "Confronting Conceptual Confusion and Conflict in Knowledge Management," *Organizational Dynamics,* 29 (Summer 2000): 33.

50. See David A. Garvin, Amy C. Edmondson, and Francesca Gino, "Is Yours a Learning Organization?" *Harvard Business Review,* 86 (March 2008): 109–116.

51. Dorothy Leonard and Walter Swap, "Deep Smarts," *Harvard Business Review,* 82 (September 2004): 92. Also see Steven J. Armstrong and Anis Mahmud, "Experiential Learning and the Acquisition of Managerial Tacit Knowledge," *Academy of Management Learning and Education,* 7 (June 2008): 189–208; Deborah A. Peluso, "Preserving Employee Know-How," *HR Magazine,* 55 (May 2010): 99; and Margery Weinstein, "Netting Know-How," *Training,* 47 (September–October 2010): 26–29.

52. For more on tacit knowledge, see Roy Lubit, "Tacit Knowledge and Knowledge Management: The Keys to Sustainable Competitive Advantage," *Organizational Dynamics,* 29 (Winter 2001): 164–178; and Yoko Ishikura,

"Act Globally, Think Locally," *Harvard Business Review*, 85 (February 2007): 46.

53. See Katrina Pugh and Nancy M. Dixon, "Don't Just Capture Knowledge—Put It to Work," *Harvard Business Review*, 86 (May 2008): 21; Jean Thilmany, "Passing on Know-How," *HR Magazine*, 53 (June 2008): 100–104; "Knowledge Management Project of the Year," *Training*, 45 (November–December 2008): 40; and Shad Morris and James B. Oldroyd, "To Boost Knowledge Transfer, Tell Me a Story," *Harvard Business Review*, 87 (May 2009): 23.

54. See Kevin C. Desouza and Yukika Awazu, "Knowledge Management," *HR Magazine*, 48 (November 2003): 107–112.

55. Paul Kaihla, "The Matchmaker in the Machine," *Business 2.0*, 5 (January–February 2004): 52, 54.

56. See Margery Weinstein, "Are You LinkedIn?" *Training*, 47 (September–October 2010): 30–33.

57. Jeffrey Hsu and Tony Lockwood, "Collaborative Computing," *Byte*, 18 (March 1993): 113. For a contrary view, see David H. Freedman, "The Idiocy of Crowds: Collaboration Is the Hottest Buzzword in Business Today. Too Bad It Doesn't Work," *Inc.*, 28 (September 2006): 61–62.

58. Catherine Romano, "The Power of Collaboration: Untapped," *Management Review*, 86 (January 1997): 7.

59. George P. Huber, *Managerial Decision Making* (Glenview, Ill.: Scott, Foresman, 1980), pp. 141–142. Also see Cass R. Sunstein, "When Crowds Aren't Wise," *Harvard Business Review*, 84 (September 2006): 20–21; Erick Schonfeld, "The Wisdom of the Corporate Crowd," *Business 2.0*, 7 (September 2006): 47 49; Michael Useem, "How Well-Run Boards Make Decisions," *Harvard Business Review*, 84 (November 2006): 130–138; Joseph Weber, "Seeking Wisdom in a Crowd," *Business Week* (March 12, 2007): 14; and

Bob Frisch, "When Teams Can't Decide," *Harvard Business Review*, 86 (November 2008): 121–126.

60. As quoted in Ronald Henkoff, "A Whole New Set of Glitches for Digital's Robert Palmer," *Fortune* (August 19, 1996): 193. Also see Felix C. Brodbeck, Rudolf Kerschreiter, Andreas Mojzisch, and Stefan Schulz-Hardt, "Group Decision Making Under Conditions of Distributed Knowledge: The Information Asymmetries Model," *Academy of Management Review*, 32 (April 2007): 459–479.

61. See Eric Kearney, Diether Gebert, and Sven C. Voelpel, "When and How Diversity Benefits Teams: The Importance of Team Members' Need for Cognition," *Academy of Management Journal*, 52 (June 2009): 581–598; Aparna Joshi and Hyuntak Roh, "The Role of Context in Work Team Diversity Research: A Meta-Analytic Review," *Academy of Management Journal*, 52 (June 2009): 599–627; and George P. Huber and Kyle Lewis, "Cross-Understanding: Implications for Group Cognition and Performance," *Academy of Management Review*, 35 (January 2010): 6–26.

62. See Gayle W. Hill, "Group Versus Individual Performance: Are N + 1 Heads Better Than One?" *Psychological Bulletin*, 91 (May 1982): 517–539.

63. See, for example, David A. Kaplan, "Apps: Hot Course on Campus," *Fortune* (May 24, 2010): 22; Ellen McGirt, "Igor Pusenjak: iPhone App Developer, Lima Sky," *Fast Company*, 146 (June 2010): 79; David Welch, "GM Plots a New Road to New Technology," *Bloomberg Businessweek* (June 21–27, 2010): 39–40; and Geoff Colvin, "100,000 Transistors Now Cost Less Than a Grain of Rice. Here's Why That Matters," *Fortune* (September 6, 2010): 64.

64. Based on discussion in N. R. F. Maier, Mara Julius, and James Thurber, "Studies in Creativity: Individual Differences in the Storing and Utilization of

Information," *The American Journal of Psychology*, 80 (December 1967): 492–519.

65. Sidney J. Parnes, "Learning Creative Behavior," *The Futurist*, 18 (August 1984): 30–31. Also see Liz Welch, "Wolfgang Puck: From Potato Peeler to Gourmet-Pizza Tycoon," *Inc.*, 31 (October 2009): 86–88; Beth Kowitt, "Dunkin' Brands' Kitchen Crew," *Fortune* (May 24, 2010): 72–74; and Olga Kharif, "Innovator: Ronald Blum," *Bloomberg Businessweek* (October 11–17, 2010): 40.

66. As quoted in Ryan Underwood, "Fast Talk: Question Assumptions," *Fast Company*, 89 (December 2004): 44.

67. See Arthur Koestler, *The Act of Creation* (London: Hutchinson, 1969), p. 27.

68. See James L. Adams, *Conceptual Blockbusting* (San Francisco: Freeman, 1974), p. 35.

69. Michael Loeb, "Making a Case for Allergy Sufferers," *Business Week* (August 13, 2007): 66.

70. Minda Zetlin, "Nurturing Nonconformists," *Management Review*, 88 (October 1999): 30. Similar results were found in a parallel study reported in Bill Breen, "The 6 Myths of Creativity," *Fast Company*, 89 (December 2004): 75–78. Also see Robin Hanson, "The Myth of Creativity," *Business Week* (July 3, 2006): 134; and Seth Bornestein, "Refining Optical Microscopes? For Chu, That's 'Vegging Out,'" *USA Today* (July 8, 2010): 7D.

71. See Nadine Heintz, "Managing Employee Creativity Unleashed," *Inc.*, 31 (June 2009): 101–102; Mike Hawkins, "Create a Climate of Creativity," *Training*, 47 (January 2010): 12; "The Secret Reason Your Employees Won't Innovate," *Harvard Business Review*, 88 (April 2010): 26; Danielle Sacks, "Scott Belsky: Founder, CEO, Behance," *Fast Company*, 146 (June 2010): 106; "How to Hire for Creativity," *Inc.* Guidebook, *Inc.*, 32 (October 2010): 53–56.

72. As quoted in Abrahm Lustgarten, "A Hot, Steaming Cup of Customer Awareness," *Fortune* (November 15, 2004): 192. Also see Bruce Horovitz, "Starbucks Remakes Its Future," *USA Today* (October 18, 2010): 1B–2B.

73. See Charalampos Mainemelis, "Stealing Fire: Creative Deviance in the Evolution of New Ideas," *Academy of Management Review*, 35 (October 2010): 558–578.

74. List adapted from Roger von Oech, *A Whack on the Side of the Head* (New York: Warner Books, 1983). Reprinted by permission. Also see Christine Dugas, "Idea Guru Helps Work Kinks out of Others' Creations," *USA Today* (July 10, 2006): 5B.

75. Huber, *Managerial Decision Making*, p. 12. Also see Dan Roam, *The Back of the Napkin: Solving Problems and Selling Ideas with Pictures* (New York: Portfolio, 2008).

76. As quoted in Thomas Mucha, "How to Ask the Right Questions," *Business 2.0*, 5 (December 2004): 118.

77. See Michael Marquardt, *Leading with Questions: How Leaders Find the Right Solutions by Knowing What to Ask* (San Francisco: Jossey-Bass, 2005); Leigh Buchanan, "Armed with Data: How the Military Can Help You Learn from Your Mistakes," *Inc.*, 31 (March 2009): 98–100; Joel Spolsky, "When Good Problem Solving Goes Bad," *Inc.*, 31 (September 2009): 43–44; and "Two Leading Researchers Discuss the Value of Oddball Data," *Harvard Business Review*, 87 (November 2009): 26–27.

78. Louis S. Richman, "How to Get Ahead in America," *Fortune* (May 16, 1994): 48.

79. See Peter Burrows, "Virtual Meetings for Real-World Budgets," *Bloomberg Businessweek* (August 9–15, 2010): 36–37.

80. Adapted from Huber, *Managerial Decision Making*, pp. 13–15. Also see Norm Brodsky, "Problems, Problems: Are You Getting to the Root Causes?" *Inc.*, 26 (February 2004): 43–44; and John C. Camillus, "Strategy as a Wicked Problem," *Harvard Business Review*, 86 (May 2008): 98–106.

81. Marshall Sashkin and Kenneth J. Kiser, *Total Quality Management* (Seabrook, Md.: Ducochon Press, 1991), p. 153.

82. Adams, *Conceptual Blockbusting*, p. 7. Also see Jenny W. Randolph, J. Bradley Morrison, and John S. Carroll, "The Dynamics of Action-Oriented Problem Solving: Linking Interpretation and Choice," *Academy of Management Review*, 34 (October 2009): 733–756; and Dan Heath and Chip Heath, "Stop Solving Your Problems: Instead Look for the Folks Who Have Already Solved Them," *Fast Company*, 140 (November 2009): 82–83.

83. See Thomas H. Davenport, "How to Design Smart Business Experiments," *Harvard Business Review*, 87 (February 2009): 68–76; and Dan Ariely, "Why Businesses Don't Experiment," *Harvard Business Review*, 88 (April 2010): 34.

84. Drawn from Jonali Baruah and Paul B. Paulus, "Effects of Training on Idea Generation in Groups," *Small Group Research*, 39 (October 2008): 523–541.

85. For related research, see John J. Sosik, Bruce J. Avolio, and Surinder S. Kahai, "Inspiring Group Creativity: Comparing Anonymous and Identified Electronic Brainstorming," *Small Group Research*, 29 (February 1998): 3–31.

86. Jessi Hempel, "Big Blue Brainstorm," *Business Week* (August 7, 2006): 70. Also see Margery Weinstein, "The Building Blocks of Brainstorming," *Training*, 43 (May 2006): 44; Robert I. Sutton, "The Truth About Brainstorming," *Inside Business Week* (September 25, 2006): 17–24; Michael Myser, "When Brainstorming Goes Bad," *Business 2.0*, 7 (October 2006): 76; Burt Helm, "Wal-Mart, Please Don't Leave Me," *Business Week* (October 9, 2006): 84–89; and Chuck Salter, "Just Add Inspiration," *Fast Company*, 111 (January 2007): 100–101.

87. Jerry Useem, "Another Boss Another Revolution," *Fortune* (April 5, 2004): 112.

88. See Russell L. Ackoff, "The Art and Science of Mess Management," *Interfaces*, 11 (February 1981): 20–26. Also see Russell L. Ackoff, *Management in Small Doses* (New York: Wiley, 1986), pp. 102–103.

89. See March, *A Primer on Decision Making*, p. 18; Gina Imperato, "When Is 'Good Enough' Good Enough?" *Fast Company*, 26 (July–August 1999): 52; and Don Moyer, "Satisficing," *Harvard Business Review*, 85 (April 2007): 144.

90. Ackoff, "The Art and Science of Mess Management," p. 22.

91. As quoted in Kathy Chu, "Executive's Competitive Nature Fits at Walmart," *USA Today* (April 19, 2010): 4B.

92. "Empty the tacks from the box, tack the box to the wall, and stand the candle upright in the box."

CHAPTER 9

1. "Sam Walton in His Own Words," *Fortune* (June 29, 1992): 104.

2. For example, see Michael V. Copeland, "A Sick CEO's Full Disclosure," *Fortune* (October 18, 2010): 47–52.

3. As quoted in Keith H. Hammonds, "We, Incorporated," *Fast Company*, 84 (July 2004): 87.

4. See B. J. Hodge, William P. Anthony, and Lawrence M. Gales, *Organization Theory: A Strategic Approach*, 5th ed. (Upper Saddle River, N.J.: Prentice-Hall, 1996), p. 10. For a critical view of life in large organizations, see Harold J. Leavitt, "Big Organizations Are Unhealthy Environments for Human Beings," *Academy of Management Learning and Education*, 6 (June 2007): 253–263.

5. Adapted from Edgar H. Schein, *Organizational Psychology*, 3rd ed. (Englewood Cliffs, N.J.: Prentice-Hall, 1980), pp. 12–15.

6. Excerpted from "The 'Giving Life' Leader," Training, 47 (February 2010): 120. Also see Henry Mintzberg, "Rebuilding Companies as Communities," Harvard Business Review, 87 (July–August 2009): 140–143.

7. See Adam Smith, The Wealth of Nations (New York: Modern Library, 1937), p. 7.

8. For an interesting historical perspective, see Peter Coy, "Cog or Co-Worker?" Business Week (August 20–27, 2007): 58–60.

9. See the "Special Issue: Designing Organizations for the 21st-Century Global Economy," Organizational Dynamics, 39 (April–June 2010); and "How Hierarchy Can Hurt Strategy Execution," Harvard Business Review, 88 (July–August 2010): 74–75.

10. Elliot Jaques, "In Praise of Hierarchy," Harvard Business Review, 68 (January–February 1990): 127. Also see Harold J. Leavitt, "Why Hierarchies Thrive," Harvard Business Review, 81 (March 2003): 96–102.

11. For an interesting biography of Henry Ford, see Ann Jardim, The First Henry Ford: A Study in Personality and Business Leadership (Cambridge, Mass.: MIT Press, 1970), p. 40. Also see Sharon Silke Carty, "Model T Celebrates 100 Years," USA Today (September 29, 2008): 7B.

12. See Marc Cecere, "Drawing the Lines," Harvard Business Review, 79 (November 2001): 24.

13. For an interesting variation, see Beth Kowitt, "Latest CEO Accessory: A Chief of Staff," Fortune (January 18, 2010): 18.

14. See Steven Prokesch, "The Sustainable Supply Chain," Harvard Business Review, 88 (October 2010): 70–72.

15. See David A. Lubin and Daniel C. Esty, "The Sustainability Imperative," Harvard Business Review, 88 (May 2010): 42–50.

16. See Reuben E. Slone, John T. Mentzer, and J. Paul Dittmann, "Are You the Weakest Link in Your Company's Supply Chain?" Harvard Business Review, 85 (September 2007): 116–127; and "Is Your Supply Chain Sustainable?" Harvard Business Review, 88 (October 2010): 74.

17. For related research, see Andreas W. Richter, Michael A West, Rolf Van Dick, and Jeremy F. Dawson, "Boundary Spanners' Identification, Intergroup Contact, and Effective Intergroup Relations," Academy of Management Journal, 49 (December 2006): 1252–1269.

18. See Chris Argyris, "The Executive Mind and Double-Loop Learning," Organizational Dynamics, 11 (Autumn 1982): 4–22; and Chris Argyris, "Teaching Smart People How to Learn," Harvard Business Review, 69 (May–June 1991): 99–109.

19. See Peter M. Senge, The Fifth Discipline: The Art and Practice of the Learning Organization (New York: Doubleday, 1990).

20. David A. Garvin, "Building a Learning Organization," Harvard Business Review, 71 (July–August 1993): 78–91. Also see David A. Garvin, Amy C. Edmondson, and Francesca Gino, "Is Yours a Learning Organization?" Harvard Business Review, 86 (March 2008): 109–116.

21. David Lei, John Slocum, and Robert A. Pitts, "Designing Organizations for Competitive Advantage: The Power of Unlearning and Learning," Organizational Dynamics, 27 (Winter 1999): 30.

22. For more on learning organizations, see Ulrich Lichtenthaler, "Absorptive Capacity, Environmental Turbulence, and the Complementarity of Organizational Learning Processes," Academy of Management Journal, 52 (August 2009): 822–846; Jeffrey A. Martin and Kathleen M. Eisenhardt, "Rewiring: Cross-Business-Unit Collaborations in Multibusiness Organizations," Academy of Management Journal, 53 (April 2010): 265–301; and Peter M. Madsen and Vinit Desai, "Failing to Learn? The Effects of Failure and Success on Organizational Learning in the Global Orbital Launch Vehicle Industry," Academy of Management Journal, 53 (June 2010): 451–476.

23. Kim Cameron, "Critical Questions in Assessing Organizational Effectiveness," Organizational Dynamics, 9 (Autumn 1980): 70.

24. See Kenneth R. Thompson and Nicholas J. Mathys, "The Aligned Balanced Scorecard: An Improved Tool for Building High Performance Organizations," Organizational Dynamics, 37 (October–December 2008): 378–393; and Aapo Lansiluoto and Marko Jarvenpaa, "Greening the Balanced Scorecard," Business Horizons, 53 (July–August 2010): 385–395.

25. Winslow Buxton, "Growth from Top to Bottom," Management Review, 88 (July–August 1999): 11.

26. Alternative views of organizational effectiveness may be found in Gary L. Neilson, Karla L. Martin, and Elizabeth Powers, "The 17 Fundamental Traits of Organizational Effectiveness," Harvard Business Review, 86 (June 2008): 63; Saul Carliner, "Maybe ROI Really Is a Waste of Time," Training, 46 (June 2009): 14–15; and Geoff Colvin, "Many Performance Ratios Lie About a Company's Health," Fortune (January 18, 2010): 22.

27. See Michael Beer, "How to Develop an Organization Capable of Sustained High Performance: Embrace the Drive for Results-Capability Development Paradox," Organizational Dynamics, 29 (Spring 2001): 233–247; Edward E. Lawler III and Christopher G. Worley, Built to Change: How to Achieve Sustained Organizational Effectiveness (San Francisco: Jossey-Bass, 2006); and Jim Collins, How the Mighty Fall: And Why Some Companies Never Give In (New York: HarperCollins, 2009).

28. See Tom Burns and G. M. Stalker, The Management of Innovation (London: Tavistock, 1961), ch. 5.

29. See John A. Courtright, Gail T. Fairhurst, and L. Edna Rogers, "Interaction Patterns in Organic and Mechanistic Systems," *Academy of Management Journal,* 32 (December 1989): 773–802.

30. Ben Elgin, "Running the Tightest Ship on the Net," *Business Week* (January 29, 2001): 126. Also see Jon Swartz and Byron Acohido, "Who's Guarding Your Data in the Cybervault?" *USA Today* (April 2, 2007): 1B–2B.

31. As quoted in Leigh Buchanan, "The Art of Work," *Inc.,* 32 (June 2010): 78.

32. Jenny C. McCune, "The Change Makers," *Management Review,* 88 (May 1999): 17.

33. James D. Thompson, *Organizations in Action* (New York: McGraw-Hill, 1967), p. 59.

34. Based in part on Jay R. Galbraith, *Designing Organizations: An Executive Briefing on Strategy, Structure, and Process* (San Francisco: Jossey-Bass, 1995), pp. 24–37.

35. Catherine Arnst, "A Freewheeling Youngster Named IBM," *Business Week* (May 3, 1993): 136.

36. See Michelle Kessler, "It's Official: IBM Sells PC Unit to Chinese Company," *USA Today* (December 8, 2004): 1B; and Kevin Maney, "Pioneer IBM Finally Finds Its Way Out of the PC Wilderness," *USA Today* (December 8, 2004): 3B.

37. Based on "General Electric Reorganizes Some Businesses for Growth," *East Valley/Scottsdale Tribune* (December 5, 2003): B3. Also see Jeffrey R. Immelt, Vijay Govindarajan, and Chris Trimble, "How GE Is Disrupting Itself," *Harvard Business Review,* 87 (October 2009): 56–65; and Diane Brady, "Can GE Still Manage?" *Bloomberg Businessweek* (April 25, 2010): 26–32.

38. For related research, see Arturs Kalnins, "Divisional Multimarket Contact Within and Between Multiunit Organizations," *Academy of Management Journal,* 47 (February 2004): 117–128.

39. Adapted from "Dial 800, Talk to Omaha," *Fortune* (January 29, 1990): 16; Rhonda Richards, "Technology Makes Omaha Hotel-Booking Capital," *USA Today* (April 7, 1994): 4B; and Robert D. Kaplan, *An Empire Wilderness: Travels into America's Future* (New York: Random House, 1998), p. 59.

40. Cliff Edwards, "Shaking Up Intel's Insides," *Business Week* (January 31, 2005): 35.

41. For more, see Michael Hammer and James Champy, *Reengineering the Corporation: A Manifesto for Business Revolution* (New York: HarperCollins, 1993); James Champy, *Reengineering Management: The Mandate for New Leadership* (New York: HarperBusiness, 1995); Dutch Holland and Sanjiv Kumar, "Getting Past the Obstacles to Successful Reengineering," *Business Horizons,* 38 (May–June 1995): 79–85; and Michael Hammer, "The Process Audit," *Harvard Business Review,* 85 (April 2007): 111–123.

42. See Table 1 in N. Anand and Richard L. Daft, "What Is the Right Organization Design?" *Organizational Dynamics,* 36, no. 4 (2007): 329–344; and Ric Merrifield, Jack Calhoun, and Dennis Stevens, "The Next Revolution in Productivity," *Harvard Business Review,* 86 (June 2008): 72–80.

43. Rahul Jacob, "The Struggle to Create an Organization for the 21st Century," *Fortune* (April 3, 1995): 91.

44. David Kiley, "Coke Reorganizes; President Resigns," *USA Today* (March 5, 2001): 2B.

45. For an extensive bibliography on this subject, see David D. Van Fleet and Arthur G. Bedeian, "A History of the Span of Management," *Academy of Management Review,* 2 (July 1977): 356–372.

46. William H. Wagel, "Keeping the Organization Lean at Federal Express," *Personnel,* 64 (March 1987): 4–12.

47. Paul Kaestle, "A New Rationale for Organizational Structure," *Planning Review,* 18 (July–August 1990): 22.

48. Data from Gene Marcial, "On the Mend at J&J," *Business Week* (September 7, 2009): 67.

49. See Mina Kimes, "Why J&J's Headaches Won't Go Away," *Fortune* (September 6, 2010): 100–108.

50. Farhad Manjoo, "Apple Nation," *Fast Company,* 147 (July–August 2010): 75.

51. For example, see W. Chan Kim and Renée Mauborgne, "How Strategy Shapes Structure," *Harvard Business Review,* 87 (September 2009): 73–80; and Marcia W. Blenko, Michael C. Mankins, and Paul Rogers, "The Decision-Driven Organization," *Harvard Business Review,* 88 (June 2010): 54–62.

52. See Larry Bossidy, "The Job No CEO Should Delegate," *Harvard Business Review,* 79 (March 2001): 46–49; and Sharon Gazda, "The Art of Delegating," *HR Magazine,* 47 (January 2002): 75–78.

53. Adapted from Marion E. Haynes, "Delegation: There's More to It Than Letting Someone Else Do It!" *Supervisory Management,* 25 (January 1980): 9–15. Three types of delegation—incremental, sequential, and functional—are discussed in William R. Tracey, "Deft Delegation: Multiplying Your Effectiveness," *Personnel,* 65 (February 1988): 36–42.

54. Delegation styles of selected U.S. presidents are examined in Edward J. Mayo and Lance P. Jarvis, "Delegation 101: Lessons from the White House," *Business Horizons,* 31 (September–October 1988): 2–12.

55. Alex Taylor III, "Iacocca's Time of Trouble," *Fortune* (March 14, 1988): 79, 81.

56. Andrew S. Grove, *High Output Management* (New York: Random House, 1983), p. 60.

57. For practical advice on delegating, see Steve Sanghi, "Good Delegation Means Setting Objectives, Getting Results," *Arizona Republic* (August 1, 2010): D5.

58. "How Conservatism Wins in the Hottest Market," *Business Week* (January 17, 1977): 43.

59. As quoted in Jessi Hempel, "Putting Ads into Apps," *Fortune* (July 26, 2010): 16.

60. Adapted from William H. Newman, "Overcoming Obstacles to Effective Delegation," *Management Review,* 45 (January 1956): 36–41; and from Eugene Raudsepp, "Why Supervisors Don't Delegate," *Supervision,* 41 (May 1979): 12–15. Also see Francie Dalton, "Delegation Pitfalls," *Association Management,* 57 (February 2005): 65–72; and Tora Estep, "Devilish Delegation at the Department of Ominous Mechanical Mishaps," *Training and Development,* 59 (March 2005): 68–70.

61. For research on initiative, see Ronald Bledow and Michael Frese, "A Situational Judgment Test of Personal Initiative and Its Relationship to Performance," *Personnel Psychology,* 62 (Summer 2009): 229–258; and Gary J. Greguras and James M. Diefendorff, "Why Does Proactive Personality Predict Employee Life Satisfaction and Work Behaviors? A Field Investigation of the Mediating Role of the Self-Concordance Model," *Personnel Psychology,* 63 (Autumn 2010): 539–560.

62. Peter F. Drucker, *Managing the Non-Profit Organization* (New York: HarperCollins, 1990), p. 117. For related research, see Zhen Xiong Chen and Samuel Aryee, "Delegation and Employee Work Outcomes: An Examination of the Cultural Context of Mediating Processes in China," *Academy of Management Journal, 50* (February 2007): 226–238.

63. See, for example, Warren G. Bennis, *Changing Organizations* (New York: McGraw-Hill, 1966).

64. As quoted in Noel M. Tichy and Stratford Sherman, *Control Your Destiny or Someone Else Will: How Jack Welch Is Making General Electric the World's Most Competitive Corporation* (New York: Doubleday, 1993), p. 21.

65. See Raymond E. Miles, Charles C. Snow, Oystein D. Fjeldstad, Grant Miles, and Christopher Lettl, "Designing Organizations to Meet 21st-Century Opportunities and Challenges," *Organizational Dynamics,* 39 (April–June 2010): 93–103.

66. Excerpted from John Barry and Evan Thomas, "A War Within," *Newsweek* (September 20, 2010): 31–32.

67. Data from Patricia Sellers, "Now Is the Time to Invest," *Fortune* (October 16, 2006): 142. Also see the first Q&A in Jack Welch and Suzy Welch, "Lay Off the Layers," *Business Week* (June 25, 2007): 96.

68. As quoted in Adam Lashinsky, "Back2Back Champs," *Fortune* (February 4, 2008): 70.

69. See Jean Lipman-Blumen and Harold J. Leavitt, "Beyond Typical Teams: Hot Groups and Connective Leaders," *Organizational Dynamics,* 38 (July–September 2009): 225–233; Matthew J. Pearsall, Michael S. Christian, and Alexander P.J. Ellis, "Motivating Interdependent Teams: Individual Rewards, Shared Rewards, or Something in Between," *Journal of Applied Psychology,* 95 (January 2010): 183–191; Helen Walters, "Google Did," *Bloomberg Businessweek* (May 10–16, 2010): 56–62; and Liz Szabo, "Study: Teamwork Makes Surgery Safer," *USA Today* (October 20, 2010): 5D.

70. Toby Tetenbaum and Hilary Tetenbaum, "Office 2000: Tear Down the Walls," *Training,* 37 (February 2000): 60.

71. See Teddy Wayne, "Should Your Trainer Look Like This?" *Bloomberg Businessweek* (August 30–September 5, 2010): 81–83; and Bonnie Burn, "Teambuilding Dilemma," *Training,* 47 (September–October 2010): 42.

72. See Max Chafkin, "The Case, and the Plan, for the Virtual Company," *Inc.,* 32 (April 2010): 62–73; Nancy R. Lockwood, "Successfully Transitioning to a Virtual Organization: Challenges, Impact and Technology," *SHRM Research Quarterly, HR Magazine,* 55 (April 2010): 1–9; and Venkat

Ramaswamy and Francis Gouillart, "Building the Co-Creative Enterprise," *Harvard Business Review,* 88 (October 2010): 100–109.

73. Steve Hamm, "Linux Inc.," *Business Week* (January 31, 2005): 62.

74. Research on the behavioral implications of virtual organizations is reported in Deondra S. Conner, "Social Comparison in Virtual Work Environments: An Examination of Contemporary Referent Selection," *Journal of Occupational and Organizational Psychology,* 76 (March 2003): 133–147.

75. See David M. Slipy, "Anthropologist Uncovers Real Workplace Attitudes," *HR Magazine,* 35 (October 1990): 76–79; and David A Kaplan, "Studying the Gearheads," *Newsweek* (August 3, 1998): 62.

76. This definition is based in part on Linda Smircich, "Concepts of Culture and Organizational Analysis," *Administrative Science Quarterly,* 28 (September 1983): 339–358. Also see "What Is Culture?" *HR Magazine,* 54 (February 2009): 42–44; and Jason Daley, "Crating a Culture of Excellence," *Entrepreneur,* 38 (March 2010): 81–87.

77. Data from John E. Sheridan, "Organizational Culture and Employee Retention," *Academy of Management Journal,* 35 (December 1992): 1036–1056. For parallel findings, see Shelly Branch, "The 100 Best Companies to Work for in America," *Fortune* (January 11, 1999): 118–144. Also see Daniel R. Denison, Stephanie Haaland, and Paulo Goelzer, "Corporate Culture and Organizational Effectiveness: Is Asia Different from the Rest of the World?" *Organizational Dynamics,* 33, no. 1 (2004): 98–109.

78. For more, see Jerry Want, "When Worlds Collide: Culture Clash," *Journal of Business Strategy,* 24 (September 2003): 14–21; Pamela Babcock, "Is Your Company Two-Faced?" *HR Magazine,* 49 (January 2004): 42–47; and Richard O. Mason, "Lessons in

Organizational Ethics from the *Columbia* Disaster: Can a Culture Be Lethal?" *Organizational Dynamics,* 33, no. 2 (2004): 128–142. Also see Eric Krell, "How to Conduct an Ethics Audit," *HR Magazine,* 55 (April 2010): 48–51; and John L. Goolsby, David A. Mack, and James Campbell Quick, "Winning by Staying in Bounds: Good Outcomes from Positive Ethics," *Organizational Dynamics,* 39 (July–September 2010): 248–257.

79. David Kiley, "The New Heat on Ford," *Business Week* (June 4, 2007): 33.

80. Peter C. Reynolds, "Imposing a Corporate Culture," *Psychology Today,* 21 (March 1987): 38.

81. Based on Harrison M. Trice and Janice M. Beyer, *The Cultures of Work Organizations* (Englewood Cliffs, N.J.: Prentice-Hall, 1993), pp. 5–8.

82. As quoted in Stephen B. Shepard, "A Talk with Jeff Immelt," *Business Week* (January 28, 2002): 103.

83. See Jack Welch and Suzy Welch, "The Reverse Hostage Syndrome," *Business Week* (July 30, 2007): 92; and Michael Rosenthal, "From Putting Out Fires to Fueling Engagement," *Training,* 46 (March–April 2009): 56.

84. See Sally Maitlis and Thomas B. Lawrence, "Triggers and Enablers of Sensegiving in Organizations," *Academy of Management Journal,* 50 (February 2007): 57–84.

85. David A. Kaplan, "#1 SAS: The Best Company to Work For," *Fortune* (February 8, 2010): 64.

86. *Ibid.,* p. 57.

87. See Chip Jarnagin and John W Slocum Jr., "Creating Corporate Cultures Through Mythopoetic Leadership," *Organizational Dynamics,* 36, no. 3 (2007): 288–302.

88. "A. G. Lafley: Procter & Gamble," *Business Week* (January 13, 2003): 67.

89. For example, see Robert Berner, "My Year at Wal-Mart," *Business Week* (February 12, 2007): 70–74; "Many CFOs Don't 'Fit' Company Culture," *HR Magazine,* 52 (April 2007): 18; and Robert Riney,

"Heal Leadership Disorders," *HR Magazine,* 53 (May 2008): 62–66.

90. As quoted in Sandra Block, "Bridgeway Founder Wins with Integrity," *USA Today* (December 17, 2003): 5B.

91. For related research, see Elizabeth Wolfe Morrison, "Newcomers' Relationships: The Role of Social Network Ties During Socialization," *Academy of Management Journal,* 45 (December 2002): 1149–1160; Julia Balogun and Gerry Johnson, "Organizational Restructuring and Middle Manager Sensemaking," *Academy of Management Journal,* 47 (August 2004): 523–549; and Markku Jokisaari and Jari-Erik Nurmi, "Change in Newcomers' Supervisor Support and Socialization Outcomes After Organizational Entry," *Academy of Management Journal,* 52 (June 2009): 527–544.

92. Alan L. Wilkins, "The Culture Audit: A Tool for Understanding Organizations," *Organizational Dynamics,* 12 (Autumn 1983): 34–35.

93. See "How to Screen for Cultural Fit," *HR Magazine,* 54 (February 2009): 46–50; Leigh Buchanan, "Welcome Aboard. Now, Run! Rituals Bring New Hires into the Fold," *Inc.,* 32 (March 2010): 95–96; and Jennifer Taylor Arnold, "Ramping Up Onboarding," *HR Magazine,* 55 (May 2010): 75–78.

94. Rebecca Ganzel, "Putting Out the Welcome Mat," *Training,* 35 (March 1998): 54.

95. See Stephen Denning, "Stories in the Workplace," *HR Magazine,* 53 (September 2008): 129–132; and Shad Morris and James B. Oldroyd, "To Boost Knowledge Transfer, Tell Me a Story," *Harvard Business Review,* 87 (May 2009): 23.

96. Alan L. Wilkins, "The Creation of Company Cultures: The Role of Stories and Human Resource Systems," *Human Resource Management,* 23 (Spring 1984): 43.

97. Adapted from Terrence E. Deal and Allan A. Kennedy, *Corporate Cultures: The Rites and*

Rituals of Corporate Life (Reading, Mass.: Addison-Wesley, 1982), pp. 136–139.

98. Eight tips for maintaining the strength of an organization's culture are presented in Trice and Beyer, *Cultures of Work Organizations,* pp. 378–391. Also see: Calvin Leung, "Culture Club," *Canadian Business,* 79 (October 9–22, 2006): 115–120; Leigh Buchanan, "That's Chief *Entertainment* Officer," *Inc.,* 29 (August 2007): 86–94; and Robert M. Price, "Infusing Innovation into Corporate Culture," *Organizational Dynamics,* 36, no. 3 (2007): 320–328.

CHAPTER 10

1. Jack Welch and Suzy Welch, "So Many CEOs Get This Wrong," *Business Week* (July 17, 2006): 92.

2. See Ken Auletta, *Googled: The End of the World As We Know It* (New York: Penguin Press, 2009); and Dave Zielinski, "Building a Better HR Team," *HR Magazine,* 55 (August 2010): 65–68.

3. See Rita Zeidner, "Dave Ulrich: Getting HR Right," *HR Magazine,* 54 (August 2009): 21; Chih-Hsun Chuang and Hui Liao, "Strategic Human Resource Management in Service Context: Taking Care of Business by Taking Care of Employees and Customers," *Personnel Psychology,* 63 (Spring 2010): 153–196; and Suzanne Woolley, "Human Resources: New Priorities for Employers," *Bloomberg Businessweek* (September 13–19, 2010): 54.

4. Leon Rubis, "Analytical Graphics Works for Its Workers," *HR Magazine,* 49 (July 2004): 47.

5. Jeffrey B. Arthur, "Effects of Human Resource Systems on Manufacturing Performance and Turnover," *Academy of Management Journal,* 37 (June 1994): 670. Similar findings are reported in Heather Johnson, "Super HR," *Training,* 41 (August 2004): 18.

6. For example, see Laurie Bassi and Daniel McMurrer, "Maximizing Your Return on People,"

Harvard Business Review, 85 (March 2007): 115–123; Kathy Gurchiek, "Strategic Thinking, Communication Are Top HR Competencies," *HR Magazine,* 55 (May 2010): 18; and Linda Tepedino and Muriel Watkins, "Be a Master of Mergers and Acquisitions," *HR Magazine,* 55 (June 2010): 52–56.

7. See Bill Roberts, "Outsourcing in Turbulent Times," *HR Magazine,* 54 (November 2009): 42–47.

8. See Adrienne Fox, "China: Land of Opportunity and Challenge," *HR Magazine,* 52 (September 2007): 38–44; Bill Leonard, "The Doctor of HR," *HR Magazine,* 54 (December 2009): 34–35; and Peter Cappelli, Harbir Singh, Jitendra V. Singh, and Michael Useem, "Leadership Lessons from India," *Harvard Business Review,* 88 (March 2010): 90–97.

9. Bill Leonard, "Straight Talk," *HR Magazine,* 47 (January 2002): 46–51. Also see Veronica Flores Scarborough, "From Tech Side to People Side," *HR Magazine,* 55 (May 2010): 46–48.

10. Brian E. Becker, Mark A. Huselid, and Dave Ulrich, *The HR Scorecard: Linking People, Strategy, and Performance* (Boston: Harvard Business School Press, 2001), p. 4. Also see Bill Roberts, "Using a Road Map for HR Technology," *HR Magazine,* 55 (January 2010): 49–52; Margery Weinstein, "How's Your Human Capital ROI?" *Training,* 47 (February 2010): 12; and Brian C. Pinkham, Joseph C. Picken, and Gregory G. Dess, "Creating Value in the Modern Organization: The Role of Leveraging Technology," *Organizational Dynamics,* 39 (July–September 2010): 226–239.

11. "The 100 Best Companies to Work For," *Fortune* (February 4, 2002): 84. Also see Theresa Minton-Eversole, "Helping Students Stay in School," *HR Magazine,* 54 (December 2009): 28–32.

12. Scott Adams, "Dilbert's Management Handbook," *Fortune* (May 13, 1996): 99, 108.

13. As quoted in John Huey, "Outlaw Flyboy CEOs," *Fortune* (November 13, 2000): 246.

14. Data from Jeffrey Pfeffer, *The Human Equation: Building Profits by Putting People First* (Boston: Harvard Business School Press, 1998); and Jeffrey Pfeffer and John F. Veiga, "Putting People First for Organizational Success," *Academy of Management Executive,* 13 (May 1999): 37–48. Also see Bill Conaty, "Cutbacks: Don't Neglect the Survivors," *Bloomberg Businessweek* (January 11, 2010): 68; and Jeffrey Pfeffer, "Layoff the Layoffs," *Newsweek* (February 15, 2010): 32–37.

15. See Jim Collins, *Good to Great: Why Some Companies Make the Leap ... and Others Don't* (New York: HarperCollins, 2001); and Robert J. Grossman, "Close the Gap Between Research and Practice," *HR Magazine,* 54 (November 2009): 30–37.

16. Based on "What Are CEOs Thinking?" *USA Today* (May 3, 2001): 1B.

17. As quoted in Tim Talevich, "Carly Unplugged," *The Costco Connection,* 19 (June 2004): 19. Also see Myrtle P. Bell, Mary L. Connerley, and Faye K. Cocchiara, "The Case for Mandatory Diversity Education," *Academy of Management Learning and Education,* 8 (December 2009): 597–609.

18. Jessi Hempel, "How LinkedIn Will Fire Up Your Career," *Fortune* (April 12, 2010): 76. Also see Margery Weinstein, "Virtual Handshake," *Training,* 46 (September 2009): 18–22; Adrienne Fox, "Newest Social Medium Has Recruiters a-Twitter," 2010 HR Trendbook, *HR Magazine,* 54 (December 2009): 30; Geoff Gloeckler, "With Jobs Scarce, B-Schools Get Creative," *Bloomberg Businessweek* (March 15, 2010): 61–63; and Julia Schmalz, "Today's Job Seekers Add 'Social' to Networking," *USA Today* (May 10, 2010): 4B.

19. Sarah Kessler, "Go Ahead, Google Me," *Inc.,* 32 (October 2010): 30.

Also see Jessica Bennett, "Privacy Is Dead," *Newsweek* (November 1, 2010): 40–41.

20. William P. Smith and Deborah L. Kidder, "You've Been Tagged! (Then Again, Maybe Not): Employers and Facebook," *Business Horizons,* 53 (September–October 2010): 491. Also see Jena McGregor, "Beware of That Video Resume," *Business Week* (June 11, 2007): 12.

21. For more, see Richard A. Posthuma, Mark V. Roehling, and Michael A. Campion, "Applying U.S. Employment Discrimination Laws to International Employers: Advice for Scientists and Practitioners," *Personnel Psychology,* 59 (Autumn 2006): 705–739; and Michael Orey, "Fear of Firing," *Business Week* (April 23, 2007): 52–62.

22. Pamela Babcock, "Spotting Lies," *HR Magazine,* 48 (October 2003): 47. Also see Bill Leonard, "Fake Job Reference Services Add New Wrinkle to Screening," *HR Magazine,* 55 (January 2010): 9.

23. Merry Mayer, "Background Checks in Focus," *HR Magazine,* 47 (January 2002): 59. Also see Bill Leonard, "Researchers: Stolen Identities Often Slip Through E-Verify," *HR Magazine,* 55 (April 2010): 11; Betty Beard, "Immigration: Lawyers Flooded by Calls on Laws," *Arizona Republic* (June 6, 2010): D1–D2; and Miriam Jordan, "Policing Illegal Hires Puts Some Employers in a Bind," *Wall Street Journal* (July 15, 2010): A5.

24. Based on "Wal-Mart to Run Background Checks," *USA Today* (August 13, 2004): 1B.

25. Fred Vogelstein, "Google @$165: Are These Guys for Real?" *Fortune* (December 13, 2004): 106, 108. Also see Laura Petrecca, "With 3,000 Applications a Day, Google Can Be Picky," *USA Today* (May 19, 2010): 2B; and Rita Zeidner, "Recruiting? It's All About the Brand," *HR Magazine,* 55 (June 2010): 25.

26. See Sharon Fears, "The Demise of Job Descriptions," *HR Magazine,* 45 (August 2000): 184; Carla Joinson, "Refocusing Job Descriptions,"

HR Magazine, 46 (January 2001): 66–72; and Maria Greco Danaher, "Credentials Absent from Job Descriptions Considered," *HR Magazine,* 52 (April 2007): 113.

27. David A. Brookmire and Amy A. Burton, "A Format for Packaging Your Affirmative Action Program," *Personnel Journal,* 57 (June 1978): 294. Also see Robert J. Grossman, "Defusing Discrimination Claims," *HR Magazine,* 54 (May 2009): 46–51; and Bill Leonard, "Heed Financial Reform's Diversity Requirement," *HR Magazine,* 55 (September 2010): 13.

28. For details, see Gary L. Tidwell, Daniel A. Rice, and Gary Kropkowski, "Employer and Employee Obligations and Rights Under the Uniformed Services Employment and Reemployment Rights Act," *Business Horizons,* 52 (May–June 2009): 243–250. Also see Bill Leonard, "Help Soldiers Re-enter Civilian Workforce," *HR Magazine,* 55 (May 2010): 101; Lorri Freifeld, "Warriors to Workers," *Training,* 47 (September–October 2010): 14–18; and Kristena Hansen, "For Those Who Served," *Arizona Republic* (October 17, 2010): EC1.

29. See Rebecca R. Hastings, "States Ban Gender Identity Discrimination," *HR Magazine,* 52 (August 2007): 24, 26; Yoni Schoenfeld, "Asking and Telling in Israel," *Newsweek* (February 15, 2010): 13; Charles McLean and P. W. Singer, "Don't Ask. Tell," *Newsweek* (June 14, 2010): 32–33.

30. Data from Theresa Howard, "Coke Settles Bias Lawsuit for $192.5M," *USA Today* (November 17, 2000): 1B; and Stephanie Armour, "Bias Suits Put Spotlight on Workplace Diversity," *USA Today* (January 10, 2001): 1B–2B.

31. Data from "Boeing Settles Bias Case, Will Pay Up to $72.5 Mil.," *Arizona Republic* (July 17, 2004): D7.

32. See Charlene Marmer Solomon, "Frequently Asked Questions About Affirmative Action," *Personnel Journal,* 74 (August 1995): 61. For historical perspectives, see Janet Kornblum,

"Integration Makes Gains, But Perceptions Slower to Change," *USA Today* (April 6, 2004): 7D; and Roger O. Crockett, "Putting Words to the Dream," *Business Week* (July 12, 2004): 16.

33. See Jennifer Schramm, "Acting Affirmatively," *HR Magazine,* 48 (September 2003): 192; and Fred L. Fry and Jennifer R. D. Burgess, "The End of the Need for Affirmative Action: Are We There Yet?" *Business Horizons,* 46 (November–December 2003): 7–16.

34. For related discussion, see Robert J. Grossman, "Constant Inconsistency," *HR Magazine,* 48 (December 2003): 68–74; Margaret M. Clark, "While Some Employers See No Incentive for EEOC Mediation, Others Find Benefits," *HR Magazine,* 49 (January 2004): 36; Paul Oyer and Scott Schaefer, "The Bias Backfire," *Harvard Business Review,* 82 (November 2004): 26; Rita Zeidner, "Planning for EEO-1 Changes," *HR Magazine,* 51 (May 2006): 60–64; and Jathan Janove, "Retaliation Nation," *HR Magazine,* 51 (October 2006): 62–66.

35. Julia Lawlor, "Study: Affirmative-Action Hires' Abilities Doubted," *USA Today* (August 31, 1992): 3B. The complete study is reported in Madeline E. Heilman, Caryn J. Block, and Jonathan A. Lucas, "Presumed Incompetent? Stigmatization and Affirmative Action Efforts," *Journal of Applied Psychology,* 77 (August 1992): 536–554. Also see Beverly L. Little, William D. Murry, and James C. Wimbush, "Perceptions of Workplace Affirmative Action Plans," *Group & Organization Management,* 23 (March 1998): 27–47.

36. Yehouda Shenhav, "Entrance of Blacks and Women into Managerial Positions in Scientific and Engineering Occupations: A Longitudinal Analysis," *Academy of Management Journal,* 35 (October 1992): 897. Also see Mike McNamee, "The Proof Is in Performance," *Business Week* (July 15, 1996): 22. A female

executive's view can be found in "Helayne Spivak," *Fast Company,* 27 (September 1999): 113.

37. For example, see Jonathan Kaufman, "White Men Shake Off That Losing Feeling on Affirmative Action," *Wall Street Journal* (September 5, 1996): A1, A4. Also see William Atkinson, "Bringing Diversity to White Men," *HR Magazine,* 46 (September 2001): 76–83.

38. R. Roosevelt Thomas Jr., "From Affirmative Action to Affirming Diversity," *Harvard Business Review,* 68 (March–April 1990): 114. For an interview with R. Roosevelt Thomas, see Ellen Neuborne, "Diversity Challenges Many Companies," *USA Today* (November 18, 1996): 10B.

39. For more on diversity, see Alice H. Eagly and Linda L. Carli, "Women and the Labyrinth of Leadership," *Harvard Business Review,* 85 (September 2007): 62–71; Diane Cadrain, "Accommodating Sex Transformations," *HR Magazine,* 54 (October 2009): 59–62; Dahlia Lithwick, "Our Beauty Bias Is Unfair," *Newsweek* (June 14, 2010): 20; and Edna Gundersen, "Elton John: 'This Is Not the America I Love,'" *USA Today* (October 13, 2010): 3D.

40. As quoted in Ryan Underwood, "No Brakes," *Fast Company,* 86 (September 2004): 112.

41. Joel Schettler, "Equal Access to All," *Training,* 39 (January 2002): 44. Also see Sarah E. Needleman, "For Disabled, a Job Hunt Alternative," *Wall Street Journal* (July 15, 2010): B4; and Steve Taylor, "Surveys Highlight Gap in Disability Employment," *HR Magazine,* 55 (September 2010): 16.

42. See Jonathan A. Segal, "Presumed Disability," *HR Magazine,* 55 (May 2010): 95–98; Jonathan A. Segal, "ADA Game Changer," *HR Magazine,* 55 (June 2010): 121–126; and James B. Thelen, "The New Bermuda Triangle," *HR Magazine,* 55 (August 2010): 85–88.

43. Data from Anne R. Carey and Paul Trap, "Has Disability Law Opened

Doors?" *USA Today* (August 17, 2010): 1A.

44. Susan B. Garland, "Protecting the Disabled Won't Cripple Business," *Business Week* (April 26, 1999): 73. Also see J. Adam Shoemaker, "A 'Welcome Back' for Workers with Disabilities," *HR Magazine*, 54 (October 2009): 30–32; Donna M. Owens, "Hiring Employees with Autism," *HR Magazine*, 55 (June 2010): 84–90; and Jahna Berry, "A Helping Hand," *Arizona Republic* (July 9, 2010): D1–D2.

45. See Kathryn Tyler, "Ready to Be Heard," *HR Magazine*, 49 (September 2004): 70–76; Frank Jossi, "High-Tech Enables Employees," *HR Magazine*, 51 (February 2006): 109–115; and Stephen H. Wildstrom, "Tell Me a Story, Intel," *Bloomberg Businessweek* (December 14, 2009): 80.

46. See Dave Patel, "Testing, Testing, Testing," *HR Magazine*, 47 (February 2002): 112; Claire Bush, "Handwriting Could Tell Employer Lots About You," *Arizona Republic* (June 2, 2007): D5; Rita Zeidner, "The Other Face of Facebook," *HR Magazine*, 55 (February 2010): 22; and Jennifer Reingold, "Are You a Good Fit for Your Job?" *Fortune* (March 22, 2010): 48.

47. See Scott B. Parry, "How to Validate an Assessment Tool," *Training*, 30 (April 1993): 37–42.

48. See John Bacon, "Polygraphs Can Lie, Researchers Say," *USA Today* (October 9, 2002): 3A; James E. Wanek, Paul R. Sackett, and Deniz S. Ones, "Towards an Understanding of Integrity Test Similarities and Differences: An Item-Level Analysis of Seven Tests," *Personnel Psychology*, 56 (Winter 2003): 873–894; Holly Dolezalek, "Tests on Trial," *Training*, 42 (April 2005): 32–34; and David A. Kaplan, "Death to the SAT!!!" *Fortune* (November 1, 2010): 32.

49. Rod Kurtz, "Testing, Testing... ," *Inc.*, 26 (June 2004): 36.

50. See Kerry J. Sulkowicz, "The Corporate Shrink," *Fast Company*, 90 (January 2005): 38.

51. "Structured Interviewing: Avoiding Selection Problems," by Elliott D. Pursell, Michael A. Campion, and Sarah R. Gaylord, copyright November 1980. Reprinted with permission *of Personnel Journal*, Costa Mesa, Calif.; all rights reserved.

52. Barbara Whitaker Shimko, "New Breed Workers Need New Yardsticks," *Business Horizons*, 33 (November–December 1990): 35–36. For related research, see Allen I. Huffcutt and Philip L. Roth, "Racial Group Differences in Employment Interview Evaluations," *Journal of Applied Psychology*, 83 (April 1998): 179–189.

53. Practical tips on interviewing can be found in John Kador, *How to Ace the Brainteaser Interview* (New York: McGraw-Hill, 2005); Matt Bolch, "Lights. Camera ... Interview," *HR Magazine*, 52 (March 2007): 99–102; Amy Maingault, John Sweeney, and Naomi Cossack, "Interviewing, Management Training, Strikes," *HR Magazine*, 52 (June 2007): 43; Dan Heath and Chip Heath, "Hold the Interview," *Fast Company*, 136 (June 2009): 51–52; and Teddy Wayne, "Etiquette School for Dummies," *Bloomberg Businessweek* (October 18–24, 2010): 89–91.

54. Based on Pursell et al., "Structured Interviewing."

55. Based on Bruce Bloom, "Behavioral Interviewing: The Future Direction and Focus of the Employment Interview." Paper presented to the Midwest Business Administration Association, Chicago (March 27, 1998). Also see Andrea C. Poe, "Graduate Work," *HR Magazine*, 48 (October 2003): 95–100; and Joey George and Kent Marett, "The Truth About Lies," *HR Magazine*, 49 (May 2004): 87–91.

56. Del J. Still, *High Impact Hiring: How to Interview and Select Outstanding Employees*, 2nd ed., rev. (Dana Point, Calif.: Management Development Systems, 2001), pp. 53–54 (emphasis added).

57. Jeffrey Pfeffer, "Low Grades for Performance Reviews," *Business Week* (August 3, 2009): 68.

58. Kerry Sulkowicz, "Straight Talk at Review Time," *Business Week* (September 10, 2007): 16.

59. Samuel A. Culbert, "Get Rid of the Performance Review!" *Wall Street Journal* (October 20, 2008): R4. Also see Margery Weinstein, "Manager-Employee Gap Widens," *Training*, 46 (October–November 2009): 10; and "A Bad Review for Performance Reviews," *HR Magazine*, 55 (May 2010): 28.

60. Data from "What to Do with an Egg-Sucking Dog?" *Training*, 33 (October 1996): 17–21.

61. See Donald Kirkpatrick, *Improving Employee Performance Through Appraisal and Coaching* (New York: Amacom, 2005); Adrienne Fox, "Curing What Ails Performance Reviews," *HR Magazine*, 54 (January 2009): 52–56; Andrew Likierman, "The Five Traps of Performance Measurement," *Harvard Business Review*, 87 (October 2009): 96–101; and Karen S. Cravens, Elizabeth Goad Oliver, and Jeanine S. Stewart, "Can a Positive Approach to Performance Evaluation Help Accomplish Your Goals?" *Business Horizons*, 53 (May–June 2010): 269–279.

62. Adapted from Hubert S. Field and William H. Holley, "The Relationship of Performance Appraisal System Characteristics to Verdicts in Selected Employment Discrimination Cases," *Academy of Management Journal*, 25 (June 1982): 392–406. A more recent analysis of 51 cases that derived similar criteria can be found in Gerald V. Barrett and Mary C. Kernan, "Performance Appraisal and Terminations: A Review of Court Decisions Since *Brito* v. *Zia* with Implications for Personnel Practices," *Personnel Psychology*, 40 (Autumn 1987): 489–503.

63. See Paul Falcone, "Watch What You Write," *HR Magazine*, 49 (November 2004): 125–128.

64. For related research, see Todd J. Maurer, Jerry K. Palmer, and Donna K. Ashe, "Diaries, Checklists, Evaluations, and Contrast Effects in Measurement of Behavior,"

Journal of Applied Psychology, 78 (April 1993): 226–231.

65. Alan M. Webber, "How Business Is a Lot Like Life," *Fast Company,* 45 (April 2001): 135.

66. Matthew Boyle, "Performance Reviews: Perilous Curves Ahead," *Fortune* (May 28, 2001): 187. Also see Gail Johnson, "Forced Ranking: The Good, the Bad, and the Alternative," *Training,* 41 (May 2004): 24–34; and Sarah Boehle, "Keeping Forced Rankings," *Training,* 45 (June 2008): 40–46.

67. See David Kiley and Del Jones, "Ford Alters Worker Evaluation Process," *USA Today* (July 11, 2001): 1B; Earle Eldridge, "Ford Settles 2 Lawsuits by White Male Workers," *USA Today* (December 19, 2001): 3B; and Benjamin J. Romano, "Microsoft Alters Evaluations," *Arizona Republic* (December 18, 2006): D5.

68. See Jai Ghorpade, "Managing Five Paradoxes of 360-Degree Feedback," *Academy of Management Executive,* 14 (February 2000): 140–150; Angelo S. DeNisi and Avraham N. Kluger, "Feedback Effectiveness: Can 360-Degree Appraisals Be Improved?" *Academy of Management Executive,* 14 (February 2000): 129–139; William C. Byham, "Fixing the Instrument," *Training,* 41 (July 2004): 50; and the second Q&A in Jack Welch and Suzy Welch, "The Importance of Being Here," *Business Week* (April 16, 2007): 92.

69. See David A. Waldman, Leanne E. Atwater, and David Antonioni, "Has 360 Degree Feedback Gone Amok?" *Academy of Management Executive,* 12 (May 1998): 86–94; and Dennis E. Coates, "Don't Tie 360 Feedback to Pay," *Training,* 35 (September 1998): 68–78.

70. Frank Shipper, Richard C. Hoffman, and Denise M. Rotondo, "Does the 360 Feedback Process Create Actionable Knowledge Equally Across Cultures?" *Academy of Management Learning and Education,* 6 (March 2007): 33–50.

71. Based on Fred Luthans and Suzanne J. Peterson, "360-Degree Feedback with Systematic Coaching: Empirical Analysis Suggests a Winning Combination," *Human Resource Management,* 42 (Fall 2003): 243–256. Also see Angelo J. Kinicki, Gregory E. Prussia, Bin (Joshua) Wu, and Frances M. McKee-Ryan, "A Covariance Structure Analysis of Employees' Response to Performance Feedback," *Journal of Applied Psychology,* 89 (December 2004): 1057–1069.

72. Jennifer Reingold, "The $79 Billion Handoff," *Fortune* (December 7, 2009): 83–84.

73. Jeanne C. Meister and Karie Willyerd, *The 2020 Workplace: How Innovative Companies Attract, Develop, and Keep Tomorrow's Employees Today* (New York: HarperCollins, 2010), p. 155. Also see Adrienne Fox, "At Work in 2020," *HR Magazine,* 55 (January 2010): 18–23; and Bill Roberts, "Can They Keep Our Lights On?" *HR Magazine,* 55 (June 2010): 62–68.

74. Data from "2009 Training Industry Report: Executive Summary," *Training,* 46 (October–November 2009): 32–34.

75. Data from Ingy Bakir and Saul Carliner, "Training Spending Stuck in Neutral," *Training,* 47 (February 2010): 16–20.

76. Diane Brady, "Can GE Still Manage?" *Bloomberg Businessweek* (April 25, 2010): 28.

77. See, for example, "Best Practices and Outstanding Initiatives," *Training,* 47 (February 2010): 102–107; Bill Roberts, "Educate Yourself," *HR Magazine,* 55 (September 2010): 109–112; and Lorri Freifeld, "LMS Lessons," *Training,* 47 (September–October 2010): 20–23.

78. Margery Weinstein, "Mobile Learning News," *Training,* 44 (April 2007): 8. Also see Sarah Boehle, "Don't Leave Home Without It," *Training,* 46 (September 2009): 30–33.

79. As quoted in Meister and Willyerd, *The 2020 Workplace,* p. 41.

80. Kenneth N. Wexley and Gary P. Latham, *Developing and Training Human Resources in Organizations* (Glenview, Ill.: Scott, Foresman, 1981), pp. 75–77.

81. *Ibid.,* p. 77. Also see Dave Zielinski, "Training Games," *HR Magazine,* 55 (March 2010): 64–66; Marc Ratcliffe, "Spice Up Your Training," *Training,* 47 (March-April 2010): 18; and Holly Dolezalek, "Building Buzz," *Training,* 47 (March–April 2010): 36–38.

82. Based on Chapter 2 in Donald L. Kirkpatrick and James D. Kirkpatrick, *Evaluating Training Programs: The Four Levels,* vol. 1 of 2 (San Francisco: Berrett-Koehler, 2006), pp. 29–39. Also see Gail Dutton, "The $64,000 Question," *Training,* 46 (October–November 2009): 40–43; and Gail Dutton, "Are You Good, or Are You Grrrreat!" *Training,* 47 (March–April 2010): 34–35.

83. See Kimberly Eretzian Smirles, "Attributions of Responsibility in Cases of Sexual Harassment: The Person and the Situation," *Journal of Applied Social Psychology,* 34 (February 2004): 342–365; and Jennifer L. Berdahl, "Harassment Based on Sex: Protecting Social Status in the Context of Gender Hierarchy," *Academy of Management Review,* 32 (April 2007): 641–658.

84. Excerpted from Jahna Berry, "EEOC Files Lawsuits vs. 3 Ariz. Businesses," *Arizona Republic* (October 2, 2010): D1–D2.

85. Ruhal Dooley, "Parental Leave, Behavior at Work, Camera Use," *HR Magazine,* 49 (July 2004): 42.

86. Excerpted from Susan M. Schaecher, "Five-Week Employee Wins $1.2 Million in Harassment Claim," *HR Magazine,* 55 (July 2010): 66.

87. Data from Stephanie Armour, "More Men Say They Are Sexually Harassed at Work," *USA Today* (September 17, 2004): 1B. Also see Bill Leonard, "Survey: 10% of Employees Report Harassment at Work," *HR Magazine,* 55 (October 2010): 18.

88. Yvette Lee, "Electronic Harassment, Recruiters' Sources, Global Benefits," *HR Magazine*, 55 (September 2010): 24.

89. Sharon Jayson, "Teens Say Bullying Is Widespread," *USA Today* (October 26, 2010): 1A. Also see Nancy Gibbs, "Sticks and Stones. When Does Bullying Cross the Line from Cruel to Criminal?" *Time* (April 19, 2010): 64; Nanci Hellmich, "Chubby Kids Bullied More Often," *USA Today* (May 3, 2010): 7D; and Donna Leinwand, "Survey: 1 in 5 Teens 'Sext' Despite Risks," *USA Today* (June 24, 2009): 3A.

90. For a list of verbal and nonverbal forms of general harassment, see R. Bruce McAfee and Diana L. Deadrick, "Teach Employees to Just Say 'No!'" *HR Magazine*, 41 (February 1996): 86–89.

91. For details, see David E. Terpstra and Douglas D. Baker, "Outcomes of Federal Court Decisions on Sexual Harassment," *Academy of Management Journal*, 35 (March 1992): 181–190. Also see Jonathan A. Segal, "HR as Judge, Jury, Prosecutor and Defender," *HR Magazine*, 46 (October 2001): 141–154.

92. See Michael W. Johnson, "A 'Bifocal Approach' to Anti-Harassment Training," *HR Legal Report* (March–April 2007): 1, 5–8, www .shrm.org/law. Also see Spencer Morgan, "The End of the Office Affair?" *Bloomberg Businessweek* (September 20–26, 2010): 73–75.

93. "'Big Lag' in Treatment for Alcoholism Grows," *USA Today* (July 3, 2007): 9D. Also see Jon Saraceno, "Baseball Players, Alcohol Aren't Abnormal Mix," *USA Today* (May 9, 2007): 2C.

94. Data from "Almost 50% Have Used Illicit Drugs," *USA Today* (August 12, 2004): 1A. Also see Michael R. Frone, "Prevalence and Distribution of Illicit Drug Use in the Workforce and in the Workplace: Findings and Implications from a U.S. National Survey," *Journal of Applied Psychology*, 91 (July 2006): 856–869.

95. See "Teen Marijuana Use Rose Slightly in 2009," *USA Today* (December 15, 2009): 6D; Elizabeth Lopatto, "Vicodin," *Bloomberg Businessweek* (August 16–29, 2010): 69; and Eve Conant, "Pot and the GOP," *Newsweek* (November 1, 2010): 30–35.

96. Diane Cadrain, "Drug Testing Falls Out of Employers' Favor," *HR Magazine*, 51 (June 2006): 48.

97. Based on *Ibid.*

98. Data from Stephanie Armour and Del Jones, "Workers' Positive Drug Tests Decrease," *USA Today* (June 20, 2006): 3B; and Kathy Gurchiek, "Employer Testing Credited for Lower Drug-Use Rates," *HR Magazine*, 52 (June 2007): 36, 41. Also see Stephanie Armour, "Employers Grapple with Medical Marijuana Use," *USA Today* (April 17, 2007): 1B–2B.

99. Excerpted from Martha Mendoza, "U.S. War on Drugs Failing," *Arizona Republic* (May 14, 2010): A1, A4.

100. See Jonathan A. Segal, "Drugs, Alcohol and the ADA," *HR Magazine*, 37 (December 1992): 73–76; Jess McCuan, "When an Addict Seeks a Job," *Inc.*, 26 (March 2004): 30; and Margaret Fiester, "Drunk Driving," *HR Magazine*, 54 (November 2009): 20.

101. Janet Deming, "Drug-Free Workplace Is Good Business," *HR Magazine*, 35 (April 1990): 61. Also see Yvette Lee, "Drug Testing Time, Bankruptcy," *HR Magazine*, 54 (December 2009): 21. For extensive information, see www.dol.gov/asp/ programs/drugs/workingpartners/ faq.asp.

102. See Donna M. Owens, "EAPs for a Diverse World," *HR Magazine*, 51 (October 2006): 91–96; and Robert T. Whipple, "Stop the Enabling," *HR Magazine*, 55 (September 2010): 114–115.

103. Stuart Feldman, "Today's EAPs Make the Grade," *Personnel*, 68 (February 1991): 3. Also see Sharon Jayson, "More Workers Seek Housing Aid," *USA Today* (September 16, 2010): 1B.

CHAPTER 11

1. Laurence J. Peter, *Peter's Quotations* (New York: Bantam, 1977), p. 100.

2. Iris You, "Maureen Chiquet, Global CEO of Chanel, Speaks at Penn," *The Walk*, April 19, 2010, www.thewalkmagazine.com/ home/?p=2318.

3. Drew Robb, "From the Top: Technology Is Making It Easier for Executives to Communicate with Employees," *HR Magazine*, 54 (February 2009): 61.

4. "Wanted: Management Skills," *Training*, 41 (November 2004): 19.

5. Data from "3 Rs or 4 Cs?" *Training*, 47 (July–August 2010): 8.

6. Data from Jae Yang and Alejandro Gonzalez, "Can You Hear Me Now?" *USA Today* (November 23, 2009): 1B.

7. Keith Davis, *Human Behavior at Work: Organizational Behavior*, 6th ed. (New York: McGraw-Hill, 1981), p. 399.

8. For an instructive distinction between one-way (the arrow model) and two-way (the circuit model) communication, see Phillip G. Clampitt, *Communicating for Managerial Effectiveness* (Newbury Park, Calif.: Sage, 1991), pp. 1–24.

9. Rebecca R. Hastings, "Recession Stifling Managers' Communication?" *HR Magazine*, 55 (February 2010): 19.

10. See Chapter 3 in Nancy Adler with Allison Gundersen, *International Dimensions of Organizational Behavior*, 5th ed. (Mason, Ohio: Thomson SouthWestern, 2008), pp. 69–95; Bart Becht, "Building a Company Without Borders," *Harvard Business Review*, 88 (April 2010): 103–106; and Michael Harvey, Helene Mayerhofer, Linley Hartmann, and Miriam Moeller, "Corralling the 'Horses' to Staff the Global Organization of the 21st Century," *Organizational Dynamics*,

39 (July–September 2010): 258–268.

11. Ernest Gundling, "How to Communicate Globally," *Training & Development*, 53 (June 1999): 30. Also see David C. Thomas and Kerr Inkson, *Cultural Intelligence: Living and Working Globally*, 2nd ed. (San Francisco: Berrett-Koehler, 2009).

12. See Robert H. Lengel and Richard L. Daft, "The Selection of Communication Media as an Executive Skill," *Academy of Management Executive*, 2 (August 1988): 225–232. For a research update, see John R. Carlson and Robert W. Zmud, "Channel Expansion Theory and the Experiential Nature of Media Richness Perceptions," *Academy of Management Journal*, 42 (April 1999): 153–170. Also see Bruce Barry and Ingrid Smithey Fulmer, "The Medium and the Message: The Adaptive Use of Communication Media in Dyadic Influence," *Academy of Management Review*, 29 (April 2004): 272–292.

13. As quoted in Adam Lashinsky, "Lights! Camera! Cue the CEO!" *Fortune* (August 21, 2006): 27.

14. Erin Binney, "Is E-Mail the New Pink Slip?" *HR Magazine*, 51 (November 2006): 32.

15. Data from Rick Jervis, "Hispanic Worker Deaths Up 76%," *USA Today* (July 20, 2009): 1A.

16. Del Jones, "Do Foreign Executives Balk at Sports Jargon?" *USA Today* (March 30, 2007): 1B. Also see Stanley Bing, "Corporate Jargon," *Fortune* (March 19, 2007): 44.

17. Data from Louisa Wah, "An Ounce of Prevention," *Management Review*, 87 (October 1998): 9. Research on feedback recipients is reported in Angelo J. Kinicki, Gregory E. Prussia, Bin (Joshua) Wu, and Frances M. McKee-Ryan, "A Covariance Structure Analysis of Employees' Response to Performance Feedback," *Journal of Applied Psychology*, 89 (December 2004): 1057–1069.

18. Lindsey Gerdes, "The Best Places to Launch a Career," *Business Week* (September 24, 2007): 58. Also see Michael Rosenthal, "Performance Review 201," *Training*, 47 (July–August 2010): 44.

19. Frank Snowden Hopkins, "Communication: The Civilizing Force," *The Futurist*, 15 (April 1981): 39.

20. See Paul A. Argenti, Robert A. Howell, and Karen A. Beck, "The Strategic Communication Imperative," *MIT Sloan Management Review*, 46 (Spring 2005): 83–89; and John Hamm, "The Five Messages Leaders Must Manage," *Harvard Business Review*, 84 (May 2006): 114–123.

21. Phillip G. Clampitt, Robert J. DeKoch, and Thomas Cashman, "A Strategy for Communicating About Uncertainty," *Academy of Management Executive*, 14 (November 2000): 48.

22. *Ibid.*

23. *Ibid.*

24. "How to Communicate with Employees," *Inc.* Guidebook, no. 2, *Inc.*, 32 (May 2010): 4.

25. See Russ Juskalian, "How Lincoln Won the Civil War," *USA Today* (November 27, 2006): 10B.

26. "Reining in Office Rumors," *Inc.*, 26 (November 2004): 60.

27. Stephanie Armour, "Did You Hear the Story About Office Gossip?" *USA Today* (September 10, 2007): 2B.

28. Lisa A. Burke and Jessica Morris Wise, "The Effective Care, Handling, and Pruning of the Office Grapevine," *Business Horizons*, 46 (May–June 2003): 73–74.

29. Erin Ryan, "Why Your Firm May Need a Blog Policy," *Arizona Republic* (November 5, 2006): D5. Also see Janet Kornblum, "Rudeness, Threats Make the Web a Cruel World," *USA Today* (July 31, 2007): 1A–2A.

30. John W. Newstrom, Robert E. Monczka, and William E. Reif, "Perceptions of the Grapevine: Its Value and Influence," *Journal of Business Communication*, 11 (Spring 1974): 12–20.

31. See Roy Rowan, "Where Did *That* Rumor Come From?" *Fortune* (August 13, 1979): 130–137.

32. Giuseppe Labianca, "It's Not 'Unprofessional' to Gossip at Work," *Harvard Business Review*, 88 (September 2010): 28.

33. Daniel McGinn, "Managing Along the Cutting Edge," *Newsweek* (February 9, 2009): 46–47.

34. Tammy Galvin, "Nothing Ventured," *Training*, 41 (February 2004): 4.

35. Drawn from Albert Mehrabian, "Communication Without Words," *Psychology Today*, 2 (September 1968): 53–55. Also see Linda Talley, "Body Language: Read It or Weep," *HR Magazine*, 55 (July 2010): 64–65.

36. Pierre Mornell, "The Sounds of Silence," *Inc.*, 23 (February 2001): 117.

37. Excerpt from Brian Hickey, "People Packaging," *America West Airlines Magazine*, 5 (September 1990): 61. Reprinted by permission of the author.

38. Eric Spitznagel, "The Tragic Decline of Business Casual," *Bloomberg Businessweek* (October 11–17, 2010): 94. Also see Tim Murphy, "Coffee Kinesiology," *Bloomberg Businessweek* (October 25–31, 2010): 106–107.

39. See Jae Yang and Karl Gelles, "Biggest Grooming Red Flags for Job Interviews," *USA Today* (December 30, 2009): 1B.

40. This three-way breakdown comes from Dale G. Leathers, *Nonverbal Communication Systems* (Boston: Allyn & Bacon, 1976), ch. 2. Also see the second Q&A in Kerry Sulkowicz, "Nobody Loves a Tattletale," *Business Week* (August 6, 2007): 14.

41. Paul C. Judge, "High Tech Star," *Business Week* (March 15, 1999): 75.

42. Based on A. Keenan, "Effects of the Non-Verbal Behaviour of Interviewers on Candidates' Performance," *Journal of Occupational Psychology*, 49, no. 3 (1976): 171–175.

43. See Linda L. Carli, Suzanne J. LaFleur, and Christopher C. Loeber, "Nonverbal Behavior, Gender, and Influence," *Journal of Personality*

and *Social Psychology*, 68
(June 1995): 1030–1041.

44. For details, see Dore Butler and
Florence L. Geis, "Nonverbal
Affect Responses to Male and
Female Leaders: Implications for
Leadership Evaluations," *Journal of
Personality and Social Psychology*,
58 (January 1990): 48–59.

45. Based on Ben Brown, "Atlanta
Out to Mind Its Manners," *USA
Today* (March 14, 1996): 7C.
Also see Andrew L. Molinsky,
Mary Anne Krabbenhoft, Nalini
Ambady, and Y. Susan Choi,
"Cracking the Nonverbal Code:
Intercultural Competence and
Gesture Recognition Across
Cultures," *Journal of Cross-Cultural
Psychology*, 36 (May 2005):
380–395; Pamela Eyring,
"Broadening Global Awareness,"
Training and Development, 60
(July 2006): 69–71; and Gary
Stoller, "Doing Business Abroad?
Simple Faux Pas Can Sink You,"
USA Today (August 24, 2007):
1B–2B.

46. See Margery Weinstein, "Mind
Your Manners," *Training*, 46
(July–August 2009): 24–29; and
Teddy Wayne, "Etiquette School for
Dummies," *Bloomberg Businessweek*
(October 18–24, 2010): 89–91.

47. James R. Detert, Ethan
R. Burris, and David
A. Harrison, "Debunking Four
Myths About Employee Silence,"
Harvard Business Review, 88
(June 2010): 26. Also see Mina
Kimes, "How Can I Get Candid
Feedback from My Employees?"
Fortune (April 13, 2009): 24; and
Rita Zeidner, "Most Employees
Don't Speak Up," *HR Magazine*, 55
(September 2010): 22.

48. David Kirkpatrick, "Sam Palmisano:
IBM," *Fortune* (August 9, 2004):
96. IBM employee data from
"Global 500: The World's Largest
Corporations," *Fortune* (July 26,
2010): F-6.

49. For related research, see Wendy
R. Boswell and Julie B. Olson-
Buchanan, "Experiencing
Mistreatment at Work: The Role
of Grievance Filing, Nature of
Mistreatment, and Employee

Withdrawal," *Academy of
Management Journal*, 47
(February 2004): 129–139. Also
see Noelle C. Nelson, "Good
Grievances," *HR Magazine*, 51
(October 2006): 113–116; and
Carolyn Hirschman, "Giving
Voice to Employee Concerns,"
HR Magazine, 53 (August 2008):
50–53.

50. See Jack Welch, *Jack: Straight
from the Gut* (New York: Warner
Business Books, 2001), pp. 393–
394; and Palmer Morrel-Samuels,
"Getting the Truth into Workplace
Surveys," *Harvard Business Review*,
80 (February 2002): 11–118.

51. Charlotte Garvey, "Connecting
the Organizational Pulse to the
Bottom Line," *HR Magazine*,
49 (June 2004): 71. For another
example of survey feedback, see
Tom Vanden Brook, "Army Ditches
Velcro for Buttons," *USA Today*
(June 15, 2010): 1A.

52. Drawn from Robert J. Aiello,
"Employee Attitude Surveys: Impact
on Corporate Decisions," *Public
Relations Journal* (March 1983): 21.
Also see Lin Grensing-Pophal, "To
Ask or Not to Ask," *HR Magazine*,
54 (February 2009): 53–55.

53. Robert Levering and Milton
Moskowitz, "The 100 Best
Companies to Work For," *Fortune*
(January 12, 2004): 78. Also see
Barry Nalebuff and Ian Ayres,
"Encouraging Suggestive Behavior,"
Harvard Business Review, 82
(December 2004): 18.

54. Drawn from "First, People:
Dixon Schwabl," *Inc.*, 32
(June 2010): 64. Also see
Darren Dahl, "Pipe Up, People!
Rounding Up Staff Ideas," *Inc.*,
32 (February 2010): 80–81.

55. Paul Keegan, "Please, Just Don't
Call Us Cheap," *Business 2.0*, 3
(February 2002): 51.

56. Data from Robert Levering and
Milton Moskowitz, "The 100 Best
Companies to Work For," *Fortune*
(January 24, 2005): 84.

57. See James S. Larson, "Employee
Participation in Federal
Management," *Public Personnel
Management*, 18 (Winter 1989):
404 414.

58. Alison Stein Wellner, "Everyone's
a Critic," *Inc.*, 26 (July 2004):
38, 41.

59. Martha Frase-Blunt, "Meeting
with the Boss," *HR Magazine*, 48
(June 2003): 95.

60. Jack Ewing, "Nokia: Bring on the
Employee Rants," *Business Week*
(June 22, 2009): 50.

61. Anne Fisher, "Playing for Keeps,"
Fortune (January 22, 2007): 88.

62. "Exit Interviews Used Irregularly,"
Arizona Republic (February 25,
2001): D2. Also see Kathy
Gurchiek, "Execs Take Exit
Interviews Seriously," *HR Magazine*,
52 (January 2007): 34; and Terence
F. Shea, "Getting the Last Word,"
HR Magazine, 55 (January 2010):
24–25.

63. John Sweeney, "How Often Should
Exit Interview Results Be Presented
to Senior Managers? What Should
Be Reported?" *HR Magazine*, 55
(July 2010): 23.

64. Paul Kaihla, "Acing the Exit
Interview," *Business 2.0*, 5
(May 2004): 77. Also see
Margery Weinstein, "Netting
Know-How," *Training*, 47
(September–October 2010):
26–29.

65. Byron Acohido, "Work Anywhere
on Any Device," *USA Today*
(October 25, 2010): 3B.

66. David A. Kaplan, "The Best
Company to Work For," *Fortune*
(February 8, 2010): 62.

67. Linda Stone, "Living with
Continuous Partial Attention,"
Harvard Business Review, 85
(February 2007): 28.

68. Nicholas Carr, *The Shallows:
What the Internet Is Doing to
Our Brains* (New York: W.W.
Norton, 2010): pp. 129–130,
132. Also see Joel Spolsky, "A
Little Less Conversation," *Inc.*, 32
(February 2010): 28–29; Malcolm
Jones, "Slow Notion," *Newsweek*
(July 12, 2010): 58–59; and Marco
R. della Cava, "Attention Spans Get
Rewired," *USA Today* (August 4,
2010): 1D–2D.

69. Jena McGregor, "Putting Home
Depot's House in Order," *Business
Week* (May 18, 2009): 54. Also see
Vickie Elmer, "Why You Need a

Career Curator," *Fortune* (July 5, 2010): 33–34.

70. Data from Aliah D. Wright, "Employers, Employees Shun Policies on Social Networking," *HR Magazine*, 55 (February 2010): 18.

71. Data from Aliah D. Wright, "More Employees Visit Social Sites While Working," *HR Magazine*, 55 (September 2010): 21.

72. Excerpted from Wright, "Employers, Employees Shun Policies on Social Networking." p. 18.

73. Jae Yang and Sam Ward, "Does Your Company Audit and Monitor Postings to Social-Networking Sites?" *USA Today* (February 23, 2010): 1B.

74. For more, see Marco R. della Cava, "Twitter Power," *USA Today* (May 25, 2010): 1A–2A; Douglas MacMillan, "Washington's Web Cop Turns up the Heat," *Bloomberg Businessweek* (July 12–18, 2010): 39–40; Rick Hampson, Donna Leinwand, and Mary Brophy Marcus, "Has Social Networking Gone Too Far?" *USA Today* (October 1, 2010): 1A–2A; and Jon Swartz, "Privacy Breaches in Facebook Apps," *USA Today* (October 19, 2010): 2B.

75. See Margery Weinstein, "Employee E-mail Blunders," *Training* (September 2009): 8; and Rita Zeidner, "On the Menu: Abuse?" *HR Magazine*, 55 (January 2010): 15.

76. Charles E. Naquin, Terri R. Kurtzberg, and Liuba Y. Belkin, "The Finer Points of Lying Online: E-Mail Versus Pen and Paper," *Journal of Applied Psychology*, 95 (March 2010): 387.

77. Laura Petreccxa, "Feel Like Someone's Watching? You're Right," *USA Today* (March 17, 2010): 2B. Also see William P. Smith and Filiz Tabak, "Monitoring Employee E-Mails: Is There Any Room for Privacy?" *Academy of Management Perspectives*, 23 (November 2009): 33–48.

78. See Joanne Deschenaux, "New Jersey: Employee E-Mail with Attorney Is Private," *HR Magazine*, 55 (May 2010): 20.

79. Data from Jon Swartz, "Is the Future of E-Mail Under Cyberattack?" *USA Today* (June 15, 2004): 4B; and Jon Swartz, "Spammers Have Ignored Federal Law," *USA Today* (January 3, 2005): 1B.

80. See Paul Hemp, "10 Ways to Reduce E-mail Overload," *Harvard Business Review*, 87 (September 2009): 88; and Mark Cuban, "Don't Even Think About Calling," *Inc.*, 32 (March 2010): 71.

81. Alex Salkever, "What Is the Best Way to Manage a Torrential Amount of E-mail?" *Inc.*, 30 (January 2008): 60.

82. Data from "CTIA: The Wireless Association Releases Semi-Annual Survey on Wireless Trends," October 6, 2010, www.ctia.org/media/press/body.cfm/prid/2021. Also see Joel Stein, "America's Most Exclusive Club," *Bloomberg Businessweek* (August 9–15, 2010): 77–79; and Dan Reed, "Travelers Love Smartphones," *USA Today* (August 31, 2010): 4B.

83. Data from Chris Woodyard, "Some Offices Opt for Cellphones Only," *USA Today* (January 25, 2005): 1B.

84. See Michael Isikoff, "The Snitch in Your Pocket," *Newsweek* (March 1, 2010): 40–41; Allen Smith, "DOT Bans Texting For Commercial Drivers," *HR Magazine*, 55 (March 2010): 11; Robert Petrancosta, "There's a Reason We Can't Text and Drive: Science," *USA Today* (June 30, 2010): 11A; Rob Waters, "A Health Warning for a Wireless Age," *Bloomberg Businessweek* (July 12–18, 2010): 31–32; and Larry Copeland, "Most Teens Still Driving While Distracted," *USA Today* (August 2, 2010): 7A.

85. Roger Yu, "Videoconferencing Eyes Growth Spurt," *USA Today* (June 23, 2009): 3B. Also see Roger Yu, "More Hotels Invest in Videoconference Rooms," *USA Today* (July 1, 2009): 5B; "Online Videoconferencing Goes Hi-Def," *Inc.*, 32 (February 2010): 38; and Peter Burrows, "Virtual Meetings for Real-World Budgets," *Bloomberg Businessweek* (August 9–15, 2010): 36–37.

86. Data from Jae Yang and Adrienne Lewis, "Is Teleworking a Good Idea?" *USA Today* (October 28, 2008): 1B.

87. Data from Jennifer Schramm, "At Work in a Virtual World," *HR Magazine*, 55 (June 2010): 152.

88. Data from Rita Zeidner, "Home Is Where the Productivity Is," *HR Magazine*, 55 (July 2010): 20.

89. Max Chafkin, "Freelancer Tony Bacigalupo Longed for Co-Workers," *Inc.*, 32 (October 2010): 67. Also see Beth Kowitt, "Remote Working: Face Time Ain't Dead Yet," *Fortune* (June 14, 2010): 26; Peter Burrows, "Video Phones Are Coming. And This Time It's For Real," *Bloomberg Businessweek* (May 3–9, 2010): 33–34; and Ariel Schwartz, "Bring Your Robot to Work Day," *Fast Company*, 150 (November 2010): 72, 74.

90. Joelle Jay, "On Communicating Well," *HR Magazine*, 50 (January 2005): 87–90.

91. Patrick Barwise and Sean Meehan, "So You Think You're a Good Listener?" *Harvard Business Review*, 86 (August 2008): 22.

92. *Ibid.*

93. As quoted in Ann Pomeroy, "CEOs Emphasize Listening to Employees," *HR Magazine*, 52 (January 2007): 14.

94. Data from Cynthia Hamilton and Brian H. Kleiner, "Steps to Better Listening," *Personnel Journal,* 66 (February 1987): 20–21. Also see Ellen Gibson, "How a Doodle Serves Your Noodle," *Business Week* (April 6, 2009): 18.

95. This list has been adapted from John F. Kikoski, "Communication: Understanding It, Improving It," *Personnel Journal,* 59 (February 1980): 126–131; John L. DiGaetani, "The Business of Listening," *Business Horizons,* 23 (October 1980): 40–46; and P. Slizewski, "Tips for Active Listening," *HR Focus* (May 1995): 7.

96. "Listen Up, Leaders: Let Workers Do the Talking," *HR Magazine,* 48 (October 2003): 14.

97. Barbara Hagenbaugh, "Good Help Hard to Find for Manufacturers," *USA Today* (April 16, 2004):

1B. Also see Stanley Bing, "The Element's of Style," *Fortune* (August 20, 2007): 110; Craig Wilson, "It's Not Too Late to Mind Your Cursive P's & Q's," *USA Today* (January 14, 2009): 1D; and Jason Fried, "What's Your Point?" *Inc.*, 32 (May 2010): 41–42.

98. Patrick Welsh, "Txting Away ur Education," USA Today (June 23, 2009): 11A. Also see Don Campbell, "Plugging In, Tuning Out," *USA Today* (September 10, 2008): 11A; and Dennis Baron, *A Better Pencil: Readers, Writers, and the Digital Revolution* (New York: Oxford University Press, 2009).

99. Robert F. DeGise, "Writing: Don't Let the Mechanics Obscure the Message," *Supervisory Management*, 21 (April 1976): 26–28. Also see Peter Post, "The Note," *Training*, 47 (September–October 2010): 44.

100. Stuart R. Levine, "Make Meetings Less Dreaded," *HR Magazine*, 52 (January 2007): 107.

101. Anne R. Carey and Sam Ward, "Are Most Company Meetings a Waste of Time?" *USA Today* (September 20, 2010): 1A; Jason Fried, "We Rarely Have Meetings. I Hate Them. They're a Huge Waste of Time," *Inc.*, 31 (November 2009): 118–121; and Leigh Buchanan, "Networking: Sick of Canned Keynote Speeches? Try an Unconference," *Inc.* (December 2009–January 2010): 124–128.

102. As summarized in Michelle Archer, "Inject Some Drama, Structure in Office Meetings," *USA Today* (June 7, 2004): 11B. See Patrick M. Lencioni, *Death by Meeting: A Leadership Fable About Solving the Most Painful Problem in Business* (San Francisco: Jossey-Bass, 2004).

103. Data from Anne Fisher, "How Much PowerPoint Is Enough?" *Fortune* (May 31, 2004): 56. Also see Scott Kirsner, "Take Your PowerPoint and…," *Business Week* (May 14, 2007): 73–74; and John Brandon, "Yawn-Proof Presentations: Four Ways to Jazz Up Your PowerPoints," *Inc.*, 32 (March 2010): 47.

104. This list is based in part on discussions in Stephanie Armour, "Team Efforts, Technology Add New Reasons to Meet," *USA Today* (December 8, 1997): 2A; John E. Tropman, *Making Meetings Work: Achieving High Quality Group Decisions*, 2nd ed. (Thousand Oaks, Calif.: Sage, 2003); and Reldan S. Nadler, "Are You a Meeting Menace or Master?" *Training and Development*, 61 (January 2007): 10–11.

CHAPTER 12

1. As quoted in Nadira A. Hira, "You Raised Them, Now Manage Them," *Fortune* (May 28, 2007): 46.

2. Nitin Nohria, Boris Groysberg, and Linda-Eling Lee, "Employee Motivation: A Powerful New Model," *Harvard Business Review*, 86 (July–August 2008): 80.

3. For different perspectives on motivation, see Richard M. Steers, Richard T. Mowday, and Debra L. Shapiro, "The Future of Work Motivation Theory," *Academy of Management Review*, 29 (July 2004): 379–387; Edwin A. Locke and Gary P. Latham, "What Should We Do About Motivation Theory? Six Recommendations for the Twenty-First Century," *Academy of Management Review*, 29 (July 2004): 388–403; Margery Weinstein, "Frontline Motivation," *Training*, 44 (September 2007): 10; Russell E. Johnson, Chu-Hsiang (Daisy) Chang, and Liu-Qin Yang, "Commitment and Motivation at Work: The Relevance of Employee Identity and Regulatory Focus," *Academy of Management Review*, 35 (April 2010): 226–245; Leigh Buchanan, "The Secrets of Their Success," *Inc.*, 32 (April 2010): 92–93; and Nancy R. Lockwood, "Motivation in Today's Workplace: The Link to Performance," Research Quarterly, 2nd quarter, *HR Magazine*, 55 (July 2010): 1–10.

4. See A. H. Maslow, "A Theory of Human Motivation," *Psychological Review*, 50 (July 1943): 370–396; Bill Cooke, Albert J. Mills, and Elizabeth S. Kelley, "Situating Maslow in Cold War America: A Recontextualization of Management Theory," *Group and Organization Management*, 30 (April 2005): 129–152; and "Maslow's Pyramid Gets a Much Needed Renovation," *ASU News: Science & Tech*" (August 18, 2010), http://asunews.asu.edu/20100819_maslowspyramid.

5. Maslow, "A Theory of Human Motivation," p. 375.

6. See Jennifer Schramm, "Feeling Safe," *HR Magazine*, 49 (May 2004): 152.

7. Dean Foust, "Man on the Spot," *Business Week* (May 3, 1999): 142–143. Also see Duane D. Stanford, "Coke's Last Round," *Bloomberg Businessweek* (November 1–7, 2010): 54–61.

8. Patrick Lencioni, "The No-Cost Way to Motivate," *Business Week* (October 5, 2009): 84. Also see Jae Yang and Sam Ward, "Who Appreciates You the Most at Work?" *USA Today* (June 2, 2010): 1B.

9. For more, see William B. Swann Jr., Christine Chang-Schneider, and Katie Larsen McClarty, "Do People's Self-Views Matter? Self-Concept and Self-Esteem in Everyday Life," *American Psychologist*, 62 (February–March 2007): 84–94; Nanci Hellmich, "For Women, Bad Hair Days Are No Joke," *USA Today* (April 13, 2010): 10B; Diane Brady, "Out of Work, Not Out of Oomph," *Bloomberg Businessweek* (September 13–19, 2010): 51–52; and D. Lance Ferris, Huiwen Lian, Douglas J. Brown, Fiona X. J. Pang, and Lisa M. Keeping, "Self-Esteem and Job Performance: The Moderating Role of Self-Esteem Contingencies," *Personnel Psychology*, 63 (Autumn 2010): 561–593. (The first student to e-mail the author at r.kreitner@cox.net by December 31, 2012, about this endnote will receive a $100 grant for being a serious scholar.)

10. Maslow, "A Theory of Human Motivation," p. 382.

11. Brent Schlender, "Bill Gates: Life After Microsoft," *Fortune* (July 5, 2010): 94.

12. George W. Cherry, "The Serendipity of the Fully Functioning Manager," *Sloan Management Review,* 17 (Spring 1976): 73.

13. Vance F. Mitchell and Pravin Moudgill, "Measurement of Maslow's Need Hierarchy," *Organizational Behavior and Human Performance,* 16 (August 1976): 348. Also see Mike Hofman, "Embattled Hotelier Chip Conley Found Inspiration from an Unlikely Source: Psychologist Abraham Maslow," *Inc.,* 29 (October 2007): 42–45.

14. For example, see Ellen L. Betz, "Two Tests of Maslow's Theory of Need Fulfillment," *Journal of Vocational Behavior,* 24 (April 1984): 204–220.

15. Edward E. Lawler, *Motivation in Work Organizations* (Monterey, Calif.: Brooks/Cole, 1973), p. 34.

16. See Frederick Herzberg, Bernard Mausner, and Barbara Bloch Snyderman, *The Motivation to Work,* 2nd ed. (New York: Wiley, 1959).

17. "Office Bullying," *Bloomberg Businessweek* (November 1–7, 2010): 76. For more, see Kathy Gurchiek, "Job Satisfaction: Just How Bad?" *HR Magazine,* 55 (February 2010): 13.

18. Jennifer Schramm, "Post-Recession Job Dissatisfaction," *HR Magazine,* 55 (July 2010): 88.

19. Frederick Herzberg, "One More Time: How Do You Motivate Employees?" *Harvard Business Review,* 46 (January–February 1968): 56. For another view, see Dennis W. Organ, "The Happy Curve," *Business Horizons,* 38 (May–June 1995): 1–3. Herzberg's methodology is replicated in Susan G. Turner, Dawn R. Utley, and Jerry D. Westbrook, "Project Managers and Functional Managers: A Case Study of Job Satisfaction in a Matrix Organization," *Project Management Journal,* 29 (September 1998): 11–19.

20. James K. Harter, Frank L. Schmidt, and Theodore L. Hayes, "Business-Unit-Level Relationship Between Employee Satisfaction, Employee Engagement, and Business Outcomes: A Meta-Analysis," *Journal of Applied Psychology,* 87 (April 2002): 268. Also see Thomas A. Wright and Russell Cropanzano, "The Role of Psychological Well-Being in Job Performance: A Fresh Look at an Age-Old Quest," *Organizational Dynamics,* 33, no. 4 (2004): 338–351; and Stephen Miller, "HR, Employees Vary on Job Satisfaction," *HR Magazine,* 52 (August 2007): 32, 34.

21. See Robert J. House and Lawrence A. Wigdor, "Herzberg's Dual-Factor Theory of Job Satisfaction and Motivation: A Review of the Evidence and a Criticism," *Personnel Psychology,* 20 (1967): 369–389.

22. For example, see Peter W. Hom, "Expectancy Prediction of Reenlistment in the National Guard," *Journal of Vocational Behavior,* 16 (April 1980): 235–248; John P. Wanous, Thomas L. Keon, and Janina C. Latack, "Expectancy Theory and Occupational/Organizational Choices: A Review and Test," *Organizational Behavior and Human Performance,* 32 (August 1983): 66–86; Alan W. Stacy, Keith F. Widaman, and G. Alan Marlatt, "Expectancy Models of Alcohol Use," *Journal of Personality and Social Psychology,* 58 (May 1990): 918–928; and Anne S. Tsui, Susan J. Ashford, Lynda St. Clair, and Katherine R. Xin, "Dealing with Discrepant Expectations: Response Strategies and Managerial Effectiveness," *Academy of Management Journal,* 38 (December 1995): 1515–1543.

23. As quoted in "Leadership for the 21st Century: Lessons We Have Learned," *Newsweek* (September 25, 2006): 75.

24. See, for example, Edwin A. Locke and Gary P. Latham, *Goal Setting: A Motivational Technique That Works!* (Englewood Cliffs, N.J.: Prentice-Hall, 1984). Also see Edwin A. Locke, "Guest Editor's Introduction: Goal-Setting Theory and Its Applications to the World of Business," *Academy of Management Executive,* 18 (November 2004): 124–125; Gary P. Latham, "The Motivational Benefits of Goal-Setting," *Academy of Management Executive,* 18 (November 2004): 126–129; Gerard H. Seijts and Gary P. Latham, "Learning Versus Performance Goals: When Should Each Be Used?" *Academy of Management Executive,* 19 (February 2005): 124–131; Edwin A. Locke and Gary P. Latham, "Has Goal Setting Gone Wild, or Have Its Attackers Abandoned Good Scholarship?" *Academy of Management Perspectives,* 23 (February 2009): 17–23; and Gary P. Latham and Edwin A. Locke, "Science and Ethics: What Should Count as Evidence Against the Use of Goal Setting?" *Academy of Management Perspectives,* 23 (August 2009): 88–91.

25. See, for example, Edwin A. Locke, Keryll N. Shaw, Lise M. Saari, and Gary P. Latham, "Goal Setting and Task Performance: 1969–1980," *Psychological Bulletin,* 90 (July 1981): 125–152; Anthony J. Mento, Robert P. Steel, and Ronald J. Karren, "A Meta-Analytic Study of the Effects of Goal Setting on Task Performance: 1966–1984," *Organizational Behavior and Human Decision Processes,* 39 (February 1987): 52–83; Don VandeWalle, Steven P. Brown, William L. Cron, and John W. Slocum Jr., "The Influence of Goal Orientation and Self-Regulation Tactics on Sales Performance: A Longitudinal Field Test," *Journal of Applied Psychology,* 84 (April 1999): 249–259; and Gerard H. Seijts, Gary P. Latham, Kevin Tasa, and Brandon W. Latham, "Goal Setting and Goal Orientation: An Integration of Two Different Yet Related Literatures," *Academy of Management Journal,* 47 (April 2004): 227–239.

26. Gary P. Latham and Edwin A Locke, "Enhancing the Benefits and Overcoming the Pitfalls of Goal Setting," *Organizational Dynamics,* 35, no. 4 (2006): 332.

27. "ThermoSTAT," *Training,* 40 (July–August 2003): 16.

28. As quoted in Richard M. Smith, "Stay Hungry, Stay Humble," *Newsweek* (May 24–31, 2010): 56. Also see Jena McGregor, "Giving Back to Your Stars," *Fortune* (November 1, 2010): 53–54.

29. See Steven Kerr and Steffen Landauer, "Using Stretch Goals to Promote Organizational Effectiveness and Personal Growth: General Electric and Goldman Sachs," *Academy of Management Executive,* 18 (November 2004): 134–138; Karyll N. Shaw, "Changing the Goal-Setting Process at Microsoft," *Academy of Management Executive,* 18 (November 2004): 139–142; Jennifer Schramm, "Seeds of Discontent," *HR Magazine,* 52 (May 2007): 136; and Don Moyer, "Objective Selection," *Harvard Business Review,* 85 (June 2007): 144.

30. See Christopher Earley, Gregory B. Northcraft, Cynthia Lee, and Terri R. Lituchy, "Impact of Process and Outcome Feedback on the Relation of Goal Setting to Task Performance," *Academy of Management Journal,* 33 (March 1990): 87–105.

31. John Huey, "America's Most Successful Merchant," *Fortune* (September 23, 1991): 50. For an update, see Hank Gilman, "The Most Underrated CEO Ever," *Fortune* (April 5, 2004): 242–248.

32. Stephen Phillips and Amy Dunkin, "King Customer," *Business Week* (March 12, 1990): 91.

33. See Edwin A. Locke, "Linking Goals to Monetary Incentives," *Academy of Management Executive,* 18 (November 2004): 130–133; and Donald N. Sull and Charles Spinosa, "Promise-Based Management: The Essence of Execution," *Harvard Business Review,* 85 (April 2007): 78–86.

34. Lewis Carroll, *Alice's Adventures in Wonderland* (Philadelphia: The John C. Winston Company, 1923), p. 57.

35. Adapted from J. Richard Hackman, "The Design of Work in the 1980s," *Organizational Dynamics,* 7 (Summer 1978): 3–17. An instructive four-way analysis of job design may be found in Michael A. Campion and Paul W. Thayer, "Job Design: Approaches, Outcomes, and Trade-Offs," *Organizational Dynamics,* 15 (Winter 1987): 66–79. Also see Hayagreeva Rao, "What 17th-Century Pirates Can Teach Us About Job Design," *Harvard Business Review,* 88 (October 2010): 44.

36. Rick Wartzman, "Houston Turns Out to Be the Capital of the Egg Roll," *Wall Street Journal* (December 7, 1995): A1. Also see Gabriel Thompson, "A Gringo in the Lettuce Fields," *The Week* (February 5, 2010): 40–41. For interesting research about people who do society's "dirty work," see Blake E. Ashforth and Glen E. Kreiner, "'How Can You Do It?' Dirty Work and the Challenge of Constructing a Positive Identity," *Academy of Management Review,* 24 (July 1999): 413–434; Blake E. Ashforth, Glen E. Kreiner, Mark A. Clark, and Mel Fugate, "Normalizing Dirty Work: Managerial Tactics for Countering Occupational Taint," *Academy of Management Journal,* 50 (February 2007): 149–174; "How to Teach Pride in 'Dirty Work,'" *Harvard Business Review,* 85 (September 2007): 19–20.

37. Jean M. Phillips, "Effects of Realistic Job Previews on Multiple Organizational Outcomes: A Meta-Analysis," *Academy of Management Journal,* 41 (December 1998): 686. Also see Peter W. Hom, Roger W. Griffeth, Leslie E. Palich, and Jeffrey S. Bracker, "Revisiting Met Expectations as a Reason Why Realistic Job Previews Work," *Personnel Psychology,* 52 (Spring 1999): 97–112.

38. See Martha Frase-Blunt, "Ready, Set, Rotate!" *HR Magazine,* 46 (October 2001): 46–53; and Margaret Fiester, "Job Rotation, Total Rewards, Measuring Value," *HR Magazine,* 53 (August 2008): 33.

39. David Welch, "How Nissan Laps Detroit," *Business Week* (December 22, 2003): 60.

40. See Lee Smith, "The FBI Is a Tough Outfit to Run," *Fortune* (October 9, 1989): 133–140. Also see Michael A Campion, Lisa Cheraskin, and Michael J. Stevens, "Career-Related Antecedents and Outcomes of Job Rotation," *Academy of Management Journal,* 37 (December 1994): 1518–1542. For a condensed version of the foregoing study, see Susan Stites-Doe, "The New Story About Job Rotation," *Academy of Management Executive,* 10 (February 1996): 86–87.

41. See M. A. Howell, "Time Off as a Reward for Productivity," *Personnel Administration,* 34 (November–December 1971): 48–51.

42. Fred Luthans and Robert Kreitner, *Organizational Behavior Modification and Beyond: An Operant and Social Learning Approach* (Glenview, Ill.: Scott, Foresman, 1985), p. 192. Also see Diane L. Lockwood and Fred Luthans, "Contingent Time Off: A Nonfinancial Incentive for Improving Productivity," *Management Review,* 73 (July 1984): 48–52. The case for a six-hour work day is presented in "That's Why They Call It 'Work,'" *Fast Company,* 29 (November 1999): 194.

43. Data from Carla O'Dell and Jerry McAdams, "The Revolution in Employee Rewards," *Management Review,* 76 (March 1987): 30–33. For a recent example of CTO in action, see Thomas Petzinger Jr., "They Keep Workers Motivated to Make Annoying Phone Calls," *Wall Street Journal* (September 20, 1996): B1.

44. J. Richard Hackman and Greg R. Oldham, *Work Redesign* (Reading, Mass.: Addison-Wesley, 1980), p. 20. Also see Arne L. Kalleberg, "The Mismatched Worker: When People Don't Fit Their Jobs," *Academy of Management Perspectives,* 22 (February 2008): 24–40.

45. David Kirkpatrick, "How Safe Are Video Terminals?" *Fortune* (August 29, 1988): 71. For related research, see Michael A. Campion and Carol L. McClelland, "Interdisciplinary Examination of the Costs and Benefits of Enlarged Jobs: A Job Design Quasi-Experiment," *Journal of Applied Psychology,* 76 (April 1991): 186–198.

46. See J. Barton Cunningham and Ted Eberle, "A Guide to Job Enrichment and Redesign," *Personnel,* 67 (February 1990): 56–61; Roger E. Herman and Joyce L. Gioia, "Making Work Meaningful: Secrets of the Future-Focused Corporation," *The Futurist,* 32 (December 1998): 24–38; and Donna Fenn, "Redesign Work," *Inc.,* 21 (June 1999): 74–84.

47. As quoted in John Bowe, Marisa Bowe, and Sabin Streeter, eds., *Gig: Americans Talk About Their Jobs at the Turn of the Millennium* (New York: Crown Publishers, 2000), p. 30.

48. Hackman and Oldham, *Work Redesign,* pp. 78–80. Also see John W. Medcof, "The Job Characteristics of Computing and Non-Computing Work Activities," *Journal of Occupational and Organizational Psychology,* 69 (June 1996): 199–212; and Joan R. Rentsch and Robert P. Steel, "Testing the Durability of Job Characteristics as Predictors of Absenteeism over a Six-Year Period," *Personnel Psychology,* 51 (Spring 1998): 165–190.

49. See Deborah J. Dwyer and Marilyn L. Fox, "The Moderating Role of Hostility in the Relationship Between Enriched Jobs and Health," *Academy of Management Journal,* 43 (December 2000): 1086–1096; and Amy Wrzesniewski and Jane E. Dutton, "Crafting a Job: Revisioning Employees as Active Crafters of Their Work," *Academy of Management Review,* 26 (April 2001): 179–201.

50. See Bob Nelson and Dean R. Spitzer, *The 1001 Rewards & Recognition Fieldbook* (New York: Workman, 2002). Also see Drew Robb, "A Total View of Employee Rewards," *HR Magazine,* 52 (August 2007): 93–95.

51. As quoted in Yvette Armendariz and Kate Fitzgerald, "Gender-Specific Artificial Joints Reach Valley," *Arizona Republic* (October 21, 2006): D2.

52. Beth Kowitt, "Inside Trader Joe's," *Fortune* (September 6, 2010): 88, 96. For more, see www.traderjoes.com/.

53. James C. Cooper and Kathleen Madigan, "The Second Half Should Be Healthier," *Business Week* (August 13, 2001): 26. Also see Drew Robb, "Get the Benefits Message Out," *HR Magazine,* 54 (October 2009): 69–71; Joanne Sammer, "Big Picture on Drug Benefits," *HR Magazine,* 55 (March 2010): 32–38; and Gary B. Kushner, "Now It's Employers' Turn," *HR Magazine,* 55 (June 2010): 34–39.

54. See Darren Dahl, "The New Rules of Compensation," *Inc.,* 31 (July–August 2009): 91–97; Martha Frase, "Greener Pathways for Commuters," *HR Magazine,* 54 (September 2009): 59–62; Leslie A. Perlow and Jessica L. Porter, "Making Time Off Predictable and Required," *Harvard Business Review,* 87 (October 2009): 102–109; Joseph Galante, "Another Day, Another Virtual Dollar," *Bloomberg Businessweek* (June 21–27, 2010): 42, 44; and Stephen Miller, "Pay Incentives Planned to Limit Post-Recession Flight," *HR Magazine,* 55 (July 2010): 11.

55. See Karen M. Kroll, "Let's Get Flexible," *HR Magazine,* 52 (April 2007): 97–100; and Stephen Miller, "Voluntary Benefits' Widening Options," *HR Magazine,* 54 (December 2009): 17.

56. "Companies Offer Benefits Cafeteria-Style," *Business Week* (November 13, 1978): 116. Also see Anand Natarajan, "The Roll-Your-Own Health Plan," *Business Week* (January 26, 2004): 16.

57. For complete details, see Alison E. Barber, Randall B. Dunham, and Roger A. Formisano, "The Impact of Flexible Benefits on Employee Satisfaction: A Field Study," *Personnel Psychology,* 45 (Spring 1992): 55–75.

58. For more, see Joanne Sammer, "Weighing Pay Incentives," *HR Magazine,* 52 (June 2007): 64–68; Susan Lackey, "Fill Those Unpopular Shifts," *HR Magazine,* 54 (April 2009): 63–66; and Scott Ladd, "May the Sales Force Be with You," *HR Magazine,* 55 (September 2010): 105–107.

59. A good overview of equity theory can be found in Robert P. Vecchio, "Models of Psychological Inequity," *Organizational Behavior and Human Performance,* 34 (October 1984): 266–282.

60. See J. Stacy Adams and Patricia R. Jacobsen, "Effects of Wage Inequities on Work Quality," *Journal of Abnormal and Social Psychology,* 69 (1964): 19–25; Jerald Greenberg and Suzyn Ornstein, "High Status Job Title as Compensation for Underpayment: A Test of Equity Theory," *Journal of Applied Psychology,* 68 (May 1983): 285–297.

61. Data from Anne R. Carey and Suzy Parker, "'Underpaid' for the Work We Do," *USA Today* (September 15, 2008): 1A.

62. Data from Harry Maurer, "The Business Week: Hear This Mr. Semel," *Business Week* (June 25, 2007): 29. Also see John E. Core and Wayne R. Guay, "Is CEO Pay Too High and Are Incentives Too Low? A Wealth-Based Contracting Framework," *Academy of Management Perspectives,* 24 (February 2010): 5–19; A. G. Lafley, "Executive Pay: Time for CEOs to Take a Stand," *Harvard Business Review,* 88 (May 2010): 40; Geoff Colvin, "As Executive Compensation Becomes Topic A (Again), The Real Outrage Is *How* CEOs Are Paid, Not How Much," *Fortune* (May 3, 2010): 86; and Bill George, "Executive Pay: Rebuilding Trust in an Era of Rage," *Bloomberg Businessweek* (September 13–19, 2010): 56.

63. "What Has Undermined Your Trust in Companies?" *USA Today* (February 10, 2004): 1B.

64. "Continental CEO Declines Salary, Bonus," *USA Today* (January 5, 2010): 1B.

65. Chris Taylor, "On-the-Spot Incentives," *HR Magazine,* 49 (May 2004): 82. Also see Kathleen D. Vohs, "The Mere Thought of Money Makes You Feel Less Pain," *Harvard Business Review,* 88 (March 2010): 28–29.

66. See Matt Bolch, "Rewarding the Team," *HR Magazine,* 52 (February 2007): 91–93.

67. George Gendron, "Steel Man: Ken Iverson," *Inc.* (April 1986): 47–48.

68. The case *against* incentives is presented in Barry Schwartz, "The Dark Side of Incentives," *Business Week* (November 23, 2009): 84.

69. Employee involvement is thoughtfully discussed in Jay R. Galbraith, Edward E. Lawler III, et al., *Organizing for the Future: The New Logic for Managing Complex Organizations* (San Francisco: Jossey-Bass, 1993), chs. 6 and 7. Also see Richard L. Daft, "Theory Z: Opening the Corporate Door for Participative Management," *Academy of Management Executive,* 18 (November 2004): 117–121.

70. See W. Alan Randolph, "Navigating the Journey to Empowerment," *Organizational Dynamics,* 23 (Spring 1995): 19–32; Robert C. Ford and Myron D. Fottler, "Empowerment: A Matter of Degree," *Academy of Management Executive,* 9 (August 1995): 21–31; Jeffrey S. Harrison and R. Edward Freeman, "Special Topic: Democracy in and Around Organizations: Is Organizational Democracy Worth the Effort?" *Academy of Management Executive,* 18 (August 2004): 49–53; and Jeffrey L. Kerr, "The Limits of Organizational Democracy," *Academy of Management Executive,* 18 (August 2004): 81–97.

71. For details see James P. Guthrie, "High-Involvement Work Practices, Turnover, and Productivity: Evidence from New Zealand," *Academy of Management Journal,* 44 (February 2001): 180–190. Also see Abraham Sagie and Zeynep Aycan, "A Cross-Cultural Analysis of Participative Decision-Making in Organizations," *Human Relations,* 56 (April 2003): 453–473.

72. Adrienne Fox, "Raising Engagement," *HR Magazine,* 55 (May 2010): 35–36. Also see Bruce Louis Rich, Jeffrey A. LePine, and Eean R. Crawford, "Job Engagement: Antecedents and Effects on Job Performance," *Academy of Management Journal,* 53 (June 2010): 617–635; Rebecca R. Hastings, "Employee Engagement Gains Are Tenuous," *HR Magazine,* 55 (October 2010): 16; and Roland E. Kidwell, "Loafing in the 21st Century: Enhanced Opportunities—and Remedies—for Withholding Job Effort in the New Workplace," *Business Horizons,* 53 (November–December 2010): 543–552.

73. Data from Rita Zeidner, "Out of Sight but Not Off the Payroll," *HR Magazine,* 55 (September 2010): 22.

74. See Will Felps, Terence R. Mitchell, David R. Hekman, Thomas W. Lee, Brooks C. Holtom, and Wendy S. Harman, "Turnover Contagion: How Coworkers' Job Embeddedness and Job Search Behaviors Influence Quitting," *Academy of Management Journal,* 52 (June 2009): 545–561; and David G. Allen, Phillip C. Bryant, and James M. Vardaman, "Retaining Talent: Replacing Misconceptions With Evidence-Based Strategies," *Academy of Management Perspectives,* 24 (May 2010): 48–64.

75. Teresa M. Amabile and Steven J. Kramer, "What Really Motivates Workers," *Harvard Business Review,* 88 (January–February 2010): 44.

76. Drawn from Leigh Rivenbark, "Tools of Engagement," *HR Magazine,* 55 (February 2010): 48–52.

77. Gail Dutton, "YES! It's Monday," *Training,* 46 (July–August 2009): 32. Also see Katie Truss and Emma Soane, "Engaging the "Pole Vaulters" on Your Staff," *Harvard Business Review,* 88 (March 2010): 24; Martin Schmidt and Conrad Schmidt, "How to Keep Your Top Talent," *Harvard Business Review,* 88 (May 2010): 54–61; and Tony Schwartz, "The Productivity Paradox: How Sony Pictures Gets More Out of People by Demanding Less," *Harvard Business Review,* 88 (June 2010): 64–69.

78. Data from Fox, "Raising Engagement," p. 38.

79. Raj Aggarwal and Betty J. Simkins, "Open Book Management—Optimizing Human Capital," *Business Horizons,* 44 (September–October 2001): 5.

80. For more on OBM, see Tim R. V. Davis, "Open-Book Management: Its Promise and Pitfalls," *Organizational Dynamics,* 25 (Winter 1997): 7–20; Gretchen R. Vogelgesang and Paul B. Lester, "How Leaders Can Get Results by Laying It on the Line," *Organizational Dynamics,* 38 (October–December 2009): 252–260; and Leigh Buchanan, "Open-Book Management: *Mi* Number, *Su* Number," *Inc.,* 32 (June 2010): 85–86.

81. See W. Alan Randolph, "Rethinking Empowerment: Why Is It So Hard to Achieve?" *Organizational Dynamics,* 29 (Fall 2000): 94–107; Laurence Prusak and Don Cohen, "How to Invest in Social Capital," *Harvard Business Review,* 79 (June 2001): 86–93; Christopher A. Bartlett and Sumantra Ghoshal, "Building Competitive Advantage Through People," *MIT Sloan Management Review,* 43 (Winter 2002): 34 41; and Ginger L. Graham, "If You Want Honesty, Break Some Rules," *Harvard Business Review,* 80 (April 2002): 42–47.

82. As quoted in Hank Gilman, "The Most Underrated CEO Ever," *Fortune* (April 5, 2004): 244.

83. Heather Johnson, "Out with the Belly Flops," *Training,* 38 (December 2001): 22.

84. For more, see Ruth Wageman, "Critical Success Factors for Creating Superb Self-Managing Teams," *Organizational Dynamics,* 26 (Summer 1997): 49–61; Bradley L. Kirkman and Debra L. Shapiro, "The Impact of Cultural Values on Job Satisfaction and Organizational

Commitment in Self-Managing Work Teams: The Mediating Role of Employee Resistance," *Academy of Management Journal,* 44 (June 2001): 557–569; and Carol A. Beatty and Brenda A. Barker Scott, *Building Smart Teams: A Roadmap to High Performance* (Thousand Oaks, Calif.: Sage, 2004).

85. Data from "1996 Industry Report: What Self-Managing Teams Manage," *Training,* 33 (October 1996): 69.

86. Keith H. Hammonds, "Growth Search," *Fast Company,* 69 (April 2003): 79–80.

87. John Hoerr, "The Payoff from Teamwork," *Business Week* (July 10, 1989): 57. For related research evidence, see Rosemary Batt, "Who Benefits from Teams? Comparing Workers, Supervisors, and Managers," *Industrial Relations,* 43 (January 2004): 183–209; Simone Kauffeld, "Self-Directed Work Groups and Team Competence," *Journal of Occupational and Organizational Psychology,* 79 (March 2006): 1–21; and Abhishek Srivastava, Kathryn M. Bartol, and Edwin A. Locke, "Empowering Leadership in Management Teams: Effects on Knowledge Sharing, Efficacy, and Performance," *Academy of Management Journal,* 49 (December 2006): 1239–1251.

88. Adapted from David I. Levine, "Participation, Productivity, and the Firm's Environment," *California Management Review,* 32 (Summer 1990): 86–100. Christopher D. Zatzick and Roderick D. Iverson, "High-Involvement Management and Workforce Reduction: Competitive Advantage or Disadvantage?" *Academy of Management Journal,* 49 (October 2006): 999–1015.

89. Katherine I. Miller and Peter R. Monge, "Participation, Satisfaction, and Productivity: A Meta-Analytic Review," Academy of Management Journal, 29 (December 1986): 748.

90. As quoted in Paul B. Brown, "What I Know Now," *Fast Company,* 91 (February 2005): 96. Also see "Entrepreneurs Get Work/Life Lessons," *USA Today* (May 3, 2010): 5B.

91. Judith Warner, "Mommy Madness," *Newsweek* (February 21, 2005): 49. Also see Stephanie Armour, "Hi, I'm Joan, and I'm a Workaholic," *USA Today* (May 23, 2007): 1B–2B.

92. Sharon Jayson, "Working at Home: Family-Friendly?" *USA Today* (April 15, 2010): 1A. Also see Glen E. Kreiner, Elaine C. Hollensbe, and Mathew L. Sheep, "Balancing Borders and Bridges: Negotiating the Work-Home Interface Via Boundary Work Tactics," *Academy of Management Journal,* 52 (August 2009): 704–730.

93. As quoted in Sheila M. Puffer, "Changing Organizational Structures: An Interview with Rosabeth Moss Kanter," *Academy of Management Executive,* 18 (May 2004): 101. Also see Brad Harrington and Jamie J. Ladge, "Work-Life Integration: Present Dynamics and Future Directions for Organizations," *Organizational Dynamics,* 38 (April–June 2009): 148–157.

94. See Karen S. Kush and Linda K. Stroh, "Flextime: Myth or Reality?" *Business Horizons,* 37 (September–October 1994): 51–55; Susan Meisinger, "Flexible Schedules Make Powerful 'Perks,'" *HR Magazine,* 52 (April 2007): 12; and Ann Pomeroy, "Not Your Parents' Workplace," *HR Magazine,* 52 (August 2007): 12, 14.

95. Data from "More Women Value Flex Time," *USA Today* (August 1, 2000): 1B.

96. Mary Brophy Marcus, "Working Women Do the Most Caregiving," *USA Today* (December 10, 2009): 7D. Also see Kathy Gurchiek, "A Nationwide Focus on Workplace Flexibility," *HR Magazine,* 55 (May 2010): 104.

97. Robert Levering and Milton Moskowitz, "The 100 Best Companies to Work For," *Fortune* (January 12, 2004): 66.

98. Martha Frase, "Taking Time Off to the Bank," *HR Magazine,* 55 (March 2010): 42.

99. See Dominic Bencivenga, "Compressed Weeks Fill an HR Niche," *HR Magazine,* 40 (June 1995): 71–74; Cynthia R. Cunningham and Shelley S. Murray, "Two Executives, One Career," *Harvard Business Review,* 83 (February 2005): 125–131; and Susan Berfield, "Two for the Cubicle," *Business Week* (July 24, 2006): 88–91; and Jennifer Schramm, "Clockwork Productivity," *HR Magazine,* 55 (September 2010): 136.

100. Quoted material and data from Nancy R. Lockwood, "Work/Life Balance: Challenges and Solutions," 2003 Research Quarterly, *HR Magazine,* 48 (June 2003): 7.

101. For more, see Allen Smith, "FMLA Retaliation Claims Rise," *HR Magazine,* 55 (February 2010): 16; James B. Thelen, "The New Bermuda Triangle," *HR Magazine,* 55 (August 2010): 85–88; Allen Smith, "Leave to Care for Adult Children Expanded," *HR Magazine,* 55 (September 2010): 16; and Paul Falcone, "Curbing Intermittent FMLA Leave Abuse," *HR Magazine,* 55 (October 2010): 99–100.

102. Excerpts in this list from Milton Moskowitz, Robert Levering, and Christopher Tkaczyk, "100 Best Companies to Work For: The List," *Fortune* (February 8, 2010): 75–88.

103. See Elayne Robertson Demby, "Do Your Family-Friendly Programs Make Cents?" *HR Magazine,* 49 (January 2004): 74–78.

104. Stephen Miller, "Wellness Gets a Boost," *HR Magazine,* 55 (May 2010): 16; Margery Weinstein, "Fit to Lead," *Training,* 47 (July–August 2010): 40–42; Susan J. Wells, "Does Work Make You Fat?" *HR Magazine,* 55 (October 2010): 26–32; and Adrienne Fox, "How to Create a Skinny Operation," *HR Magazine,* 55 (October 2010): 34–39.

105. Daniel Yee, "Fit Workers Keep Insurance Costs Low," *Arizona Republic* (October 17, 2004): D3.

106. Moskowitz, Levering, and Tkaczyk, "100 Best Companies to Work For: The List," p. 88. For more, see Joel Schettler, "Successful Sabbaticals," *Training,* 39 (June 2002): 26; and Nadine Heintz, "Breaking Away," *Inc.,* 26 (October 2004): 44.

CHAPTER 13

1. As quoted in "From Wharton to War," *Fortune* (June 12, 2006): 108.

2. Data from Clinton O. Longenecker, Mitchell J. Neubert, and Laurence S. Fink, "Causes and Consequences of Managerial Failure in Rapidly Changing Organizations," *Business Horizons,* 50 (March–April 2007): 145–155. Also see Jae Yang and Adrienne Lewis, "People Skills Can Win Jobs," *USA Today* (December 1, 2009): 1B.

3. As quoted in "How Women Handle Success," *Business Week* (November 2, 2009): 70–71.

4. Robert Kreitner and Angelo Kinicki, *Organizational Behavior,* 9th ed. (New York: McGraw-Hill/Irwin, 2010), p. 14. For more, see David M. Sluss and Blake E. Ashforth, "Relational Identity and Identification: Defining Ourselves Through Work Relationships," *Academy of Management Review,* 32 (January 2007): 9–32; Michael J. Mauboussin, "When Individuals Don't Matter," *Harvard Business Review,* 87 (October 2009): 24–25; and Morten T. Hansen, "The Future Manager Is T-Shaped," *HR Magazine,* 55 (January 2010): 60.

5. See Marco R. della Cava, "Twitter Power: Learning From Ourselves, in Real Time," *USA Today* (May 25, 2010): 1A–2A; Rick Hampson, David Leinwand, and Mary Brophy Marcus, "Has Social Networking Gone Too Far?" *USA Today* (October 1, 2010): 1A–2A; and Andy Fixmer and Ronald Grover, "A Fresh Coat of Paint for MySpace," *Bloomberg Businessweek* (November 1–7, 2010): 42, 44.

6. Joseph A. Litterer, *The Analysis of Organizations,* 2nd ed. (New York: Wiley, 1973), p. 231.

7. For an excellent elaboration of this definition, see David Horton Smith, "A Parsimonious Definition of 'Group': Toward Conceptual Clarity and Scientific Utility," *Sociological Inquiry,* 37 (Spring 1967): 141–167. Also see Daniel J. Brass, Joseph Galaskiewicz, Henrich R. Greve, and Wenpin Tsai, "Taking Stock of Networks and Organizations: A Multilevel Perspective," *Academy of Management Journal,* 47 (December 2004): 795–817.

8. For related research, see Prithviraj Chattopadhyay, Malgorzata Tluchowska, and Elizabeth George, "Identifying the Ingroup: A Closer Look at the Influence of Demographic Dissimilarity on Employee Social Identity," *Academy of Management Review,* 29 (April 2004): 180–202; and Hongseok Oh, Myung-Ho Chung, and Giuseppe Labianca, "Group Social Capital and Group Effectiveness: The Role of Informal Socializing Ties," *Academy of Management Journal,* 47 (December 2004): 860–875.

9. For example, see Richard McDermott and Douglas Archibald, "Harnessing Your Staff's Informal Network," *Harvard Business Review,* 88 (March 2010): 82–89; and Joel Stein, "The Secret Cult of Office Smokers," *Bloomberg Businessweek* (May 10–16, 2010): 73–77.

10. David Krackhardt and Jeffrey R. Hanson, "Informal Networks: The Company Behind the Chart," *Harvard Business Review,* 71 (July–August 1993): 104. Also see Eugenia Levenson, "How the Office Really Works," *Fortune* (June 12, 2006): 118.

11. Jae Yang and Karl Gelles, "Is It Smart to Keep Personal and Professional Lives Separate?" *USA Today* (April 14, 2010): 1B.

12. Data from Jae Yang and Veronica Salazar, "Inviting Co-workers to Wedding," *USA Today* (September 22, 2010): 1B.

13. Data from Jae Yang and Karl Gelles, "Workplace Friendships," *USA Today* (April 13, 2010): 1B.

14. Excerpted from the second Q&A in Jack Welch and Suzy Welch, "From the Old, Something New," *Business Week* (November 20, 2006): 124.

15. See Laura Petrecca, "Hiring Family or Friends Can Be Boon or Bust," *USA Today* (October 11, 2010): 6B.

16. Excerpted from Chad Graham, "The Tangled Web of Social Media," *Arizona Republic* (May 17, 2009): D1–D2. Also see Jon Fortt and Michael V. Copeland, "Facebook for Business," *Fortune* (June 14, 2010): 38; and Margery Weinstein, "Are You LinkedIn?" *Training,* 47 (September–October 2010): 30–33.

17. See Cathy Olofson, "Let Outsiders In, Turn Your Insiders Out," *Fast Company,* 22 (February–March 1999): 46.

18. For related research, see Jennifer A. Chatman and Charles A. O'Reilly, "Asymmetric Reactions to Work Group Sex Diversity Among Men and Women," *Academy of Management Journal,* 47 (April 2004): 193–208; and Mark Van Vugt and Claire M. Hart, "Social Identity as Social Glue: The Origin of Group Loyalty," *Journal of Personality and Social Psychology,* 86 (April 2004): 585–598.

19. Peter Nulty, "Cool Heads Are Trying to Keep Commodore Hot," *Fortune* (July 23, 1984): 38, 40.

20. Albert A. Harrison, *Individuals and Groups: Understanding Social Behavior* (Monterey, Calif.: Brooks/Cole, 1976), p. 16. Also see Mark A. Griffin, Andrew Neal, and Sharon K. Parker, "A New Model of Work Role Performance: Positive Behavior in Uncertain and Interdependent Contexts," *Academy of Management Journal,* 50 (April 2007): 327–347; and Herminia Ibarra and Roxana Barbulescu, "Identity as Narrative: Prevalence, Effectiveness, and Consequences of Narrative Identity Work in Macro Work Role Transitions," *Academy of Management Review,* 35 (January 2010): 135–154.

21. See, for instance, Andrew Park, "Between a Rocker and a High Chair," *Business Week* (February 21, 2005): 86, 88; Hugh T. J. Bainbridge, Christina Cregan, and Carol T. Kulik, "The Effect of Multiple Roles on Caregiver Stress Outcomes," *Journal of Applied Psychology*, 91 (March 2006): 490–497; and Andrew Romano and Tony Dokoupil, "Men's Lib," *Newsweek* (September 27, 2010): 42–49.

22. Harrison, *Individuals and Groups*, p. 401.

23. For example, see Elisabeth K. Kelan and Rachel Dunkley Jones, "Gender and the MBA," *Academy of Management Learning and Education*, 9 (March 2010): 26–43.

24. Adapted from Daniel C. Feldman, "The Development and Enforcement of Group Norms," *Academy of Management Review*, 9 (January 1984): 47–53.

25. Gwendolyn Kelly, "Why This Med Student Is Sticking with Primary Care," *Business Week* (November 2, 1992): 125. Also see Catherine Arnst, "Are There Too Many Women Doctors?" *Business Week* (April 28, 2008): 104; and Rita Rubin, "Primary Care Doctors in Short Supply," *USA Today* (November 18, 2008): 7D.

26. For related research and reading, see Andrew Spicer, Thomas W. Dunfee, and Wendy J. Bailey, "Does National Context Matter in Ethical Decision Making? An Empirical Test of Integrative Social Contracts Theory," *Academy of Management Journal*, 47 (August 2004): 610–620; and Ben W. Heineman Jr., Avoiding Integrity Land Mines," *Harvard Business Review*, 85 (April 2007): 100–108.

27. From Group Effectiveness in Organizations by L. N. Jewell and H. J. Reitz (Scott, Foresman, 1981). Reprinted by permission of the authors. Also see Gerard Seijts and Jeffrey Gandz, "Gaining a Competitive Edge Through Rapid Team Formation and Development," *Organizational Dynamics*, 38 (October–December 2009): 261–269; and Matthew J. Pearsall,

Aleksander P. J. Ellis, and Bradford S. Bell, "Building the Infrastructure: The Effects of Role Identification Behaviors on Team Cognition Development and Performance," *Journal of Applied Psychology*, 95 (January 2010): 192–200.

28. Susan A. Wheelan and Felice Tilin, "The Relationship Between Faculty Group Development and School Productivity," *Small Group Research*, 30 (February 1999): 59.

29. For more, see Chao C. Chen, Xiao-Ping Chen, and James R. Meindl, "How Can Cooperation Be Fostered? The Cultural Effects of Individualism-Collectivism," *Academy of Management Review*, 23 (April 1998): 285–304. Also see Katherine J. Klein, Beng-Chong Lim, Jessica L. Saltz, and David M. Mayer, "How Do They Get There? An Examination of the Antecedents of Centrality in Team Networks," *Academy of Management Journal*, 47 (December 2004): 952–963.

30. See Vanessa Stéphane Côté and Christopher T. H. Miners, "Emotional Intelligence, Cognitive Intelligence, and Job Performance," *Administrative Science Quarterly*, 51 (March 2006): 1–28; Sharon Jayson, "Sociability: It's All in Your Mind," *USA Today* (September 25, 2006): 5D; and Daniel Goleman, *Social Intelligence: The New Science of Human Relationships* (New York: Bantam, 2007).

31. The following discussion of the six stages of group development is adapted from *Group Effectiveness in Organizations* by Linda N. Jewell and H. Joseph Reitz. Copyright 1981, Scott, Foresman and Company, pp. 15–20. Reprinted by permission. For ground-breaking research in this area, see Warren G. Bennis and Herbert A. Shepard, "A Theory of Group Development," *Human Relations*, 9 (1956): 415–437; Bruce W. Tuckman and Mary Ann C. Jensen, "Stages of Small-Group Development Revisited," *Group & Organization Studies*, 2 (December 1977): 419–427; and John F. McGrew, John G. Bilotta, and Janet M. Deeney, "Software Team Formation

and Decay: Extending the Standard Model for Small Groups," *Small Group Research*, 30 (April 1999): 209–234.

32. Jacqueline Durett, "There's No 'I' in 'Team,' But Maybe There Should Be," *Training*, 43 (September 2006): 12. Also see Ed Gash, "More Training Than Camp," *Training*, 43 (December 2006): 7.

33. For practical advice, see John E. Tropman, *Making Meetings Work: Achieving High Quality Decisions* (Thousand Oaks, Calif.: Sage, 2003); and Tim Ursiny, *The Coward's Guide to Conflict: Empowering Solutions for Those Who Would Rather Run Than Fight* (Naperville, Ill.: Sourcebooks, 2003).

34. See Brian R. Dineen, Raymond A. Noe, Jason D. Shaw, Michelle K. Duffy, and Carolyn Wiethoff, "Level and Dispersion of Satisfaction in Teams: Using Foci and Social Context to Explain the Satisfaction-Absenteeism Relationship," *Academy of Management Journal*, 50 (June 2007): 623–643.

35. See Jeanne M. Wilson, Paul S. Goodman, and Matthew A. Cronin, "Group Learning," *Academy of Management Review*, 32 (October 2007): 1041–1059.

36. For example, see Deondra S. Conner, "Human-Resource Professionals' Perceptions of Organizational Politics as a Function of Experience, Organizational Size, and Perceived Independence," *The Journal of Social Psychology*, 146 (December 2006): 717–732; Chu-Hsiang Chang, Christopher C. Rosen, and Paul E. Levy, "The Relationship Between Perceptions of Organizational Politics and Employee Attitudes, Strain, and Behavior: A Meta-Analytic Examination," *Academy of Management Journal*, 52 (August 2009): 779–801; and Smriti Anand, Prajya R. Vidyarthi, Robert C. Liden, and Denise M. Rousseau, "Good Citizens in Poor-Quality Relationships: Idiosyncratic Deals as a Substitute for Relationship Quality," *Academy of Management*

Journal, 53 (October 2010): 970–988.

37. See Del Jones and Bill Keveney, "10 Lessons of The Apprentice,'" *USA Today* (April 15, 2004): 1A, 5A; Del Jones, "America Loves to Hate Dastardly CEOs," *USA Today* (September 15, 2004): 1B–2B; and Ann Pomeroy, "Business Reality TV?" *HR Magazine,* 50 (January 2005): 14.

38. As quoted in Anne Fisher, "Putting Your Mouth Where the Money Is," *Fortune* (September 3, 2001): 238. Also see John Beeson, "Why You Didn't Get That Promotion," *Harvard Business Review*, 87 (June 2009): 101–105; Jeffrey Pfeffer, "Power Play," *Harvard Business Review*, 88 (July–August 2010): 84–92; and Jeff Kehoe, "How to Save Good Ideas," *Harvard Business Review*, 88 (October 2010): 129–132.

39. Marcia Stepanek, "How Fast Is Net Fast?" *Business Week* E.BIZ (November 1, 1999): EB 54.

40. Data from "9-to-5 Not for Everyone," *USA Today* (October 13, 1999): 1B.

41. Data from Jae Yang and Keith Simmons, "How Do You Deal with Office Politics?" *USA Today* (November 17, 2008): 1B.

42. See Casey Hawley, *100+ Tactics for Office Politics*, 2nd ed. (Hauppauge, N.Y.: Barron's, 2008); Rob Cross, Amanda Cowen, Lisa Vertucci, and Robert J. Thomas, "Leading in a Connected World: How Effective Leaders Drive Results Through Networks," *Organizational Dynamics*, 38 (April–June 2009): 93–105; and Michelle Conlin, "Make Yourself into a Rainmaker," *Money*, 39 (September 2010): 36.

43. Victor Murray and Jeffrey Gandz, "Games Executives Play: Politics at Work," *Business Horizons*, 23 (December 1980): 16.

44. Based on Andrew J. DuBrin, *Fundamentals of Organizational Behavior: An Applied Perspective,* 2nd ed. (Elmsford, N.Y.: Pergamon Press, 1978), p. 154.

45. Jared Sandberg, "Better Than Great—and Other Tall Tales of Self-Evaluations," *Wall Street Journal* (March 12, 2003): B1. Also see Del Jones, "To Brown-Nose or Not to Brown-Nose?" *USA Today* (November 18, 2009): 1B–2B; Margery Weinstein, "Tips to Neutralize Toxic Personalities," *Training*, 47 (March–April 2010): 13; Tanya Menon and Leigh Thompson, "Envy at Work," *Harvard Business Review*, 88 (April 2010): 74–79; and David J. Ketchen Jr. and M. Ronald Buckley, "Divas at Work: Dealing with Drama Kings and Queens in Organizations," *Business Horizons*, 53 (November–December 2010): 599–606.

46. Dan Farrell and James C. Petersen, "Patterns of Political Behavior in Organizations," *Academy of Management Review,* 7 (July 1982): 407. Also see Ori Brafman and Rom Brafman, "To the Vulnerable Go the Spoils," *Bloomberg Businessweek* (June 14–20, 2010): 71–73.

47. James R. Healey, "Covert Activity Saved Sports Car," *USA Today* (March 19, 1997): 1B.

48. Adapted from Dan L. Madison, Robert W. Allen, Lyman W. Porter, Patricia A. Renwick, and Bronston T. Mayes, "Organizational Politics: An Exploration of Managers' Perceptions," *Human Relations,* 33 (February 1980): 79–100.

49. Madison et al., "Organizational Politics," p. 97.

50. Based on DuBrin, *Fundamentals of Organizational Behavior,* pp. 158–170; David G. Baldwin, "How to Win the Blame Game," *Harvard Business Review,* 79 (July–August 2001): 55–62; and Marie G. McIntyre, *Secrets of Winning at Office Politics* (New York: St. Martin's Press, 2005).

51. Adapted from DuBrin, *Fundamentals of Organizational Behavior,* pp. 179–182.

52. See Gerard Beenen and Jonathan Pinto, "Resisting Organizational-Level Corruption: An Interview with Sherron Watkins," *Academy of Management Learning and Education,* 8 (June 2009): 275–289; and Jennifer J. Kish-Gephart, David A. Harrison, and Linda Trevino, "Bad Apples, Bad Cases, and Bad Barrels: Meta-Analytic Evidence About Sources of Unethical Decisions at Work," *Journal of Applied Psychology*, 95 (January 2010): 1–31.

53. See K. Matthew Gilley, Christopher J. Robertson, and Tim C. Mazur, "The Bottom-Line Benefits of Ethics Code Commitment," *Business Horizons*, 53 (January–February 2010): 31–37; Eric Krell, "How to Conduct an Ethics Audit," *HR Magazine*, 55 (April 2010): 48–51; and John L. Goolsby, David A. Mack, and James Campbell Quick, "Good Outcomes from Positive Ethics," *Organizational Dynamics*, 39 (July–September 2010): 248–257.

54. See Solomon E. Asch, *Social Psychology* (Englewood Cliffs, N.J.: Prentice-Hall, 1952), ch. 16.

55. For details, see Taha Amir, "The Asch Conformity Effect: A Study in Kuwait," *Social Behavior and Personality*, 12, no. 2 (1984): 187–190; Timothy P. Williams and Shunya Sogon, "Group Composition and Conforming Behavior in Japanese Students," *Japanese Psychological Research,* 26, no. 4 (1984): 231–234.

56. Data from Rod Bond and Peter B. Smith, "Culture and Conformity: A Meta-Analysis of Studies Using Asch's Line Judgment Task," *Psychological Bulletin,* 119 (January 1996): 111–137. Also see Francis J. Flynn and Scott S. Wiltermuth, "Who's with Me? False Consensus, Brokerage, and Ethical Decision Making in Organizations," *Academy of Management Journal*, 53 (October 2010): 1074–1089; and Bennett J. Tepper, "When Managers Pressure Employees to Behave Badly: Toward a Comprehensive Response," *Business Horizons,* 53 (November–December 2010): 591–598.

57. See Marilyn Elias, "Do We All Have a Dark Side? Psychologist Argues We Do in 'The Lucifer Effect,'" *USA Today* (March 14, 2007): 7D.

58. Irving L. Janis, *Groupthink*, 2nd ed. (Boston: Houghton Mifflin, 1982), p. 9. See also A. Amin Mohamed and Frank A Wiebe, "Toward a Process Theory of Groupthink," *Small Group Research*, 27 (August 1996): 416 430; Kjell Granstrom and Dan Stiwne, "A Bipolar Model of Groupthink: An Expansion of Janis's Concept," *Small Group Research*, 29 (February 1998): 32–56; the entire February–March 1998 issue of *Organizational Behavior and Human Decision Processes*; Annette R. Flippen, "Understanding Groupthink from a Self-Regulatory Perspective," *Small Group Research*, 30 (April 1999): 139–165; Jin Nam Choi and Myung Un Kim, "The Organizational Application of Groupthink and Its Limitations in Organizations," *Journal of Applied Psychology*, 84 (April 1999): 297–306; and Nandini Rajagopalan and Yan Zhang, "Recurring Failures in Corporate Governance: A Global Disease?" *Business Horizons*, 52 (November–December 2009): 545–552.

59. Adapted from a list in Janis, *Groupthink*, pp. 174–175.

60. *Ibid.*, p. 275.

61. For excellent discussions of the devil's advocate role, see Charles R. Schwenk, "Devil's Advocacy in Managerial Decision Making," *Journal of Management Studies*, 21 (April 1984): 153–168; and Richard A. Cosier and Charles R. Schwenk, "Agreement and Thinking Alike: Ingredients for Poor Decisions," *Academy of Management Executive*, 4 (February 1990): 69–74. For related reading, see Christopher Hitchens, "The Dogmatic Doubter," *Newsweek* (September 10, 2007): 40–42.

62. Adapted from a list in Janis, *Groupthink*, pp. 262–271.

63. See George S. Day and Paul J. H. Schoemaker, "Are You a 'Vigilant Leader'?" *MIT Sloan Management Review*, 49 (Spring 2008): 43–51; Jena McGregor, "Board Shakeups Made Easier," *Business Week* (August 10, 2009): 52; Mary C.

Gentile, "Keeping Your Colleagues Honest," *Harvard Business Review*, 88 (March 2010): 114–117; and Becky Quick, "Politics! Infighting! Gridlock! Welcome to the Newly Democratic Corporate Boardroom," *Fortune* (October 18, 2010): 80.

64. Barbara Kellerman, *Bad Leadership: What It Is, How It Happens, Why It Matters* (Boston: Harvard Business School Press, 2004), pp. 139–140. For a follow-up on Dunlap, see Ellen Florian, "Tough-Guy CEO Al Dunlap Is Getting in Touch with His Cuddly Side," *Fortune* (November 15, 2010): 142–143.

65. Other problems related in part to groupthink are discussed in Paul F. Levy, "The Nut Island Effect: When Good Teams Go Wrong," *Harvard Business Review*, 79 (March 2001): 51–59; and Michael Harvey, Milorad M. Novicevic, M. Ronald Buckley, and Jonathon R. B. Halbesleben, "The Abilene Paradox After Thirty Years: A Global Perspective," *Organizational Dynamics*, 33, no. 2 (2004): 215–226.

66. Ken Auletta, *Googled: The End of the World As We Know It* (New York: Penguin Press, 2009), p. 200.

67. Liz Szabo, "Study: Teamwork Makes Surgery Safer," *USA Today* (October 20, 2010): 5D. Also see Thomas H. Lee, "Turning Doctors into Leaders," *Harvard Business Review*, 88 (April 2010): 50–58.

68. An instructive distinction between work groups and teams is presented in Jon R. Katzenbach and Douglas K. Smith, "The Discipline of Teams," *Harvard Business Review*, 71 (March–April 1993): 111–120. Also see Jon R. Katzenbach and Douglas K. Smith, *The Wisdom of Teams: Creating the High-Performance Organization* (New York: HarperCollins, 1999); Carol A. Beatty and Brenda A. Barker Scott, *Building Smart Teams: A Roadmap to High Performance* (Thousand Oaks, Calif.: Sage, 2004); Gilad Chen, Lisa M. Donahue, and Richard J. Klimoski, "Training Undergraduates to Work in Organizational Teams," *Academy*

of Management Learning and Education, 3 (March 2004): 27 40; Caroline Verzat, Janice Byrne, and Alain Fayolle, "Tangling with Spaghetti: Pedagogical Lessons from Games," *Academy of Management Learning and Education*, 8 (September 2009): 356–369; and George P. Huber and Kyle Lewis, "Cross-Understanding: Implications for Group Cognition and Performance," *Academy of Management Review*, 35 (January 2010): 6–26.

69. See Alyssa Abkowitz, "They're on a Mission to Mars," *Fortune* (October 12, 2009): 39–41; and Adrienne Fox, "Don't Let Silos Stand in the Way," *HR Magazine*, 55 (May 2010): 50–51.

70. Excerpted from David Kiley, "Putting Ford on Fast-Forward," *Business Week* (October 26, 2009): 56–57.

71. Yuhyung Shin, "Conflict Resolution in Virtual Teams," *Organizational Dynamics*, 34, no. 4 (2005): 331. Also see Holly Dolezalek, "Virtual Leaders," *Training*, 46 (May 2009): 40–42.

72. For good overviews of available tools, see Bill Roberts, "Counting on Collaboration," *HR Magazine*, 52 (October 2007): 47–54; Darren Dahl, "Connecting the Dots: How to Choose the Right Collaboration Software for Your Company," *Inc.*, 31 (June 2009): 103–104; and Rachael King, "Mobile Apps Suit Up for the Office," *Bloomberg Businessweek* (November 8–14, 2010): 44–45.

73. See Jeanne Brett, Kristin Behfar, and Mary C. Kern, "Managing Multicultural Teams," *Harvard Business Review*, 84 (November 2006): 83–91.

74. "Fast Talk: The Recovery Business," *Fast Company*, 147 (July–August 2010): 54.

75. Michelle Conlin, "The Ideal Virtual Worker?" *Business Week* (July 27, 2009): 65.

76. See Arvind Malhotra, Ann Majchrzak, and Benson Rosen, "Leading Virtual Teams," *Academy of Management Perspectives*, 21

(February 2007): 60–70; Penelope Sue Greenberg, Ralph H. Greenberg, and Yvonne Lederer Antonucci, "Creating and Sustaining Trust in Virtual Teams," *Business Horizons,* 50 (July–August 2007): 325–333; Billie Williamson, "Managing at a Distance," *Business Week* (July 27, 2009): 64–65; Matthew J. Pearsall, Michael S. Christian, and Aleksander P. J. Ellis, "Motivating Interdependent Teams: Individual Rewards, Shared Rewards, or Something in Between?" *Journal of Applied Psychology*, 95 (January 2010): 183–191; and Yvette Lee, "Tele-terminating, Terminating Employees Abroad, Recruiting Diversity," *HR Magazine*, 55 (June 2010): 31.

77. See Joshua B. Wu, Anne S. Tsui, and Angelo J. Kinicki, "Consequences of Differentiated Leadership in Groups," *Academy of Management Journal*, 53 (February 2010): 90–106; Terri L. Griffith and John E. Sawyer, "Multilevel Knowledge and Team Performance," *Journal of Organizational Behavior*, 31 (October 2010): 1003–1031; and Jiing-Lih Farh, Cynthia Lee, and Crystal I. C. Fahr, "Task Conflict and Team Creativity: A Question of How Much and When," *Journal of Applied Psychology*, 95 (November 2010): 1173–1180.

78. See Hans J. Thamhain, "Managing Technologically Innovative Team Efforts Toward New Product Success," *Journal of Product Innovation Management*, 7 (March 1990): 5–18. Also see Paul F. Skilton and Kevin J. Dooley, "The Effects of Repeat Collaboration on Creative Abrasion," *Academy of Management Review*, 35 (January 2010): 118–134; and Martine R. Haas, "The Double-Edged Swords of Autonomy and External Knowledge: Analyzing Team Effectiveness in a Multinational Organization," *Academy of Management Journal*, 53 (October 2010): 989–1008.

79. See Stephen E. Kohn and Vincent D. O'Connell, *6 Habits of Highly Effective Teams* (Franklin Lakes, N.J.: Career Press, 2007).

80. See the entire July–September 2009 issue of *Organizational Dynamics*.

81. Three kinds of trust are discussed in Douglas A. Houston, "Trust in the Networked Economy: Doing Business on Web Time," *Business Horizons*, 44 (March–April 2001): 38–44. Also see F. David Schoorman, Roger C. Mayer, and James H. Davis, "An Integrative Model of Organizational Trust: Past, Present, and Future," *Academy of Management Review*, 32 (April 2007): 344–354; Sze-Sze Wong and Wai Fong Boh, "Leveraging the Ties of Others to Build a Reputation for Trustworthiness Among Peers," *Academy of Management Journal*, 53 (February 2010): 129–148; and Bart A. De Jong and Tom Elfring, "How Does Trust Affect the Performance of Ongoing Teams? The Mediating Role of Reflexivity, Monitoring, and Effort," *Academy of Management Journal*, 53 (June 2010): 535–549.

82. Jeffrey Pfeffer, "More Mr. Nice Guy," *Business 2.0*, 4 (December 2003): 78.

83. Del Jones, "CEO," *USA Today* (June 23, 2009): 1B–2B.

84. Haya El Nasser and Paul Overberg, "Census Response: 71% and Counting," *USA Today* (April 21, 2010): 1A.

85. Laurence Prusak and Don Cohen, "How to Invest in Social Capital," *Harvard Business Review*, 79 (June 2001): 90.

86. See Dale E. Zand, "Trust and Managerial Problem Solving," *Administrative Science Quarterly*, 17 (June 1972): 229–239.

87. See Lorri Freifeld, "Coveys Say Trust Is a Must," *Training*, 47 (January 2010): 16–18.

88. Adapted from Fernando Bartolomé, "Nobody Trusts the Boss Completely—Now What?" *Harvard Business Review*, 67 (March–April 1989): 137–139. Also see the excellent series of articles in the "Spotlight on Trust" section in the June 2009 issue of *Harvard Business Review*, pp. 53–77; and Patrick Lencioni, "The Power of Saying 'We Blew It,'" *Bloomberg Businessweek* (February 22, 2010): 84.

CHAPTER 14

1. Jack Welch and Suzy Welch, "Inventing the Future Now," *Business Week* (May 11, 2009): 76.

2. Ramin Setoodeh, "Calling Avon's Lady," *Newsweek* (January 3, 2005): 100–101. For a brief update on Jung, see Jessica Shambora and Beth Kowitt, "50 Most Powerful Women," *Fortune* (October 18, 2010): 131. Also see Adam Lashinsky, "The Enforcer," *Fortune* (September 28, 2009): 116–124.

3. See Gary Yukl and Cecilia M. Falbe, "Influence Tactics and Objectives in Upward, Downward, and Lateral Influence Attempts," *Journal of Applied Psychology*, 75 (April 1990): 132–140. For a comprehensive collection of readings on influence, see Lyman W. Porter, Harold L. Angle, and Robert W. Allen, *Organizational Influence Processes,* 2nd ed. (Armonk, N.Y: M.E. Sharpe, 2003). For related research, see Scott Sonenshein, "Crafting Social Issues at Work," *Academy of Management Journal*, 49 (December 2006): 1158–1172.

4. Adapted from Yukl and Falbe, "Influence Tactics and Objectives in Upward, Downward, and Lateral Influence Attempts." Also see Gary Yukl, Cecilia M. Falbe, and Joo Young Youn, "Patterns of Influence Behavior for Managers," *Group Organization Management,* 18 (March 1993): 5–28; Randall A. Gordon, "Impact of Ingratiation on Judgments and Evaluations: A Meta-Analytic Investigation," *Journal of Personality and Social Psychology,* 71 (July 1996): 54–70; Beth Azar, "More Powerful Persuasion," *Monitor on Psychology* (April 2010): 36–38; and Beth Kowitt, "I Deserve a Raise. Do I Dare Ask for One?" *Fortune* (July 5, 2010): 36.

5. See Robert B. Miller, Gary A. Williams, and Alden M. Hayashi,

The 5 Paths to Persuasion: The Art of Selling Your Message (New York: Warner Business, 2004); Del Jones, "Debating Skills Come in Handy in Business," *USA Today* (September 30, 2004): 3B; and Raymond T. Sparrowe, Budi W. Soetjipto, and Maria L. Kraimer, "Do Leaders' Influence Tactics Relate to Members' Helping Behavior? It Depends on the Quality of the Relationship," *Academy of Management Journal*, 49 (December 2006): 1194–1208.

6. See Jeffrey Pfeffer, "How to Turn on the Charm," *Business 2.0*, 5 (June 2004): 76; Jennifer Reingold, "Suck Up and Move Up," *Fast Company*, 90 (January 2005): 34; James D. Westphal and Ithai Stern, "Flattery Will Get You Everywhere (Especially If You Are a Male Caucasian): How Ingratiation, Boardroom Behavior, and Demographic Minority Status Affect Additional Board Appointments at U.S. Companies," *Academy of Management Journal*, 50 (April 2007): 267–288; and Nanette Byrnes, "Profiles in Sycophancy," *Business Week* (August 13, 2007): 12.

7. Linda Tischler, "IBM's Management Makeover," *Fast Company*, 88 (November 2004): 113.

8. See George F. Dreher, Thomas W. Dougherty, and William Whitely, "Influence Tactics and Salary Attainment: A Gender-Specific Analysis," *Sex Roles*, 20 (May 1989): 535–550; and Herman Aguinis and Susan K. R. Adams, "Social-Role Versus Structural Models of Gender and Influence Use in Organizations," *Group & Organization Studies*, 23 (December 1998): 414–446.

9. See Mahfooz A. Ansari and Alka Kapoor, "Organizational Context and Upward Influence Tactics," *Organizational Behavior and Human Decision Processes*, 40 (August 1987): 39–49.

10. Dean Tjosvold, "The Dynamics of Positive Power," *Training and Development Journal*, 38 (June 1984): 72.

11. See Janet O. Hagberg, *Real Power: Stages of Personal Power in Organizations*, 3rd ed. (Salem, Wis.: Sheffield Publishing, 2003); Jon Meacham, "The Story of Power," *Newsweek* (December 29, 2008–January 5, 2009): 32–35; Jeffrey Pfeffer, *Power: Why Some People Have It—and Others Don't* (New York: HarperCollins, 2010); and Michael Segalla, "Find the Real Power in Your Organization," *Harvard Business Review*, 88 (May 2010): 34–35. *(Note:* I would like to sincerely thank Carlton F. Harvey, Ph.D., for introducing me to Hagberg's fascinating book.)

12. Morgan McCall Jr., "Power, Influence, and Authority: The Hazards of Carrying a Sword," *Technical Report*, 10 (Greensboro, N.C.: Center for Creative Leadership, 1978), p. 5. For an interesting historical perspective of power, see Matt Miller, "What Makes History Happen?" *Fortune* (October 1, 2007): 78.

13. Based on Jeffrey Pfeffer, "Power Play," *Harvard Business Review*, 88 (July–August 2010): 84–92.

14. For more on these three effects of power, see Anthony T. Cobb, "An Episodic Model of Power: Toward an Integration of Theory and Research," *Academy of Management Review*, 9 (July 1984): 482–493. Also see C. Marlene Fiol, Edward J. O'Connor, and Herman Aguinis, "All for One and One for All? The Development and Transfer of Power Across Organizational Levels," *Academy of Management Review*, 26 (April 2001): 224–242.

15. Based on Edwin P. Hollander and Lynn R. Offermann, "Power and Leadership in Organizations: Relationships in Transition," *American Psychologist*, 45 (February 1990): 179–189.

16. See A. D. Amar, Carsten Hentrich, and Vlatka Hlupic, "To Be a Better Leader, Give Up Authority," *Harvard Business Review*, 87 (December 2009): 22–24.

17. "There Is No State Here Anymore," *Newsweek* (February 24, 1997): 42.

18. For related discussion, see Allan R. Cohen and David L. Bradford,

"Influence Without Authority: The Use of Alliances, Reciprocity, and Exchange to Accomplish Work," *Organizational Dynamics*, 17 (Winter 1989): 4–17; and Allan R. Cohen and David L. Bradford, *Influence Without Authority* (New York: Wiley, 1990).

19. See John R. P. French Jr. and Bertram Raven, "The Bases of Social Power," *Studies in Social Power*, ed. Dorwin Cartwright (Ann Arbor: University of Michigan Press, 1959), pp. 150–167. Eight different sources of power are discussed in Hugh R. Taylor, "Power at Work," *Personnel Journal*, 65 (April 1986): 42–49. Also see H. Eugene Baker III, "'Wax On—Wax Off: French and Raven at the Movies," *Journal of Management Education*, 17 (November 1993): 517–519.

20. Jeffrey M. O'Brien, "Amazon's Next Revolution," *Fortune* (June 8, 2009): 74.

21. John P. Kotter, "Power, Dependence, and Effective Management," *Harvard Business Review*, 55 (July–August 1977): 128. Also see Amanda J. Ferguson, Margaret E. Ormiston, and Henry Moon, "From Approach to Inhibition: The Influence of Power on Responses to Poor Performers," *Journal of Applied Psychology*, 95 (March 2010): 305–320.

22. For revealing case studies, see Barbara Kellerman, *Bad Leadership: What It Is, How It Happens, Why It Matters* (Boston: Harvard Business School Press, 2004). Also see Stanley Bing, "Crazy Bosses," *Fortune* (May 28, 2007): 49–54.

23. Ann Pomeroy, "Thanks, But No Thanks," *HR Magazine*, 49 (December 2004): 18.

24. Patricia Sellers, "What Exactly Is Charisma?" *Fortune* (January 15, 1996): 68. Also see Daniel Sankowsky, "The Charismatic Leader as Narcissist: Understanding the Abuse of Power," *Organizational Dynamics*, 23 (Spring 1995): 57–71.

25. See Scott E. Seibert, Seth R. Silver, and W. Alan Randolph, "Taking Empowerment to the Next Level: A Multiple-Level Model of Empowerment, Performance,

and Satisfaction," *Academy of Management Journal*, 47 (June 2004): 332–349; and Liz Wiseman and Greg McKeown, "Bringing Out the Best in Your People," *Harvard Business Review*, 88 (May 2010): 117–121.

26. As quoted in Laurel Shaper Walters, "A Leader Redefines Management," *Christian Science Monitor* (September 22, 1992): 14. For Frances Hesselbein's ideas about leadership, see Roundtable Discussion, "All in a Day's Work," *Harvard Business Review* (Special Issue: Breakthrough Leadership), 79 (December 2001): 54–66. Supportive research evidence for empowerment can be found in Abhishek Srivastava, Kathryn M. Bartol, and Edwin A. Locke, "Empowering Leadership in Management Teams: Effects on Knowledge Sharing, Efficacy, and Performance," *Academy of Management Journal*, 49 (December 2006): 1239–1251.

27. Adrienne Fox, "Raising Engagement," *HR Magazine*, 55 (May 2010): 39.

28. Based on discussion in Stephen R. Covey, *Principle-Centered Leadership* (New York: Simon & Schuster, 1991), pp. 214–216. Also see W. Alan Randolph, "Navigating the Journey to Empowerment," *Organizational Dynamics*, 23 (Spring 1995): 19–32; Xu Huang, Joyce Iun, Aili Liu, and Yaping Gong, "Does Participative Leadership Enhance Work Performance by Inducing Empowerment or Trust? The Differential Effects on Managerial and Non-Managerial Subordinates," *Journal of Organizational Behavior*, 31 (January 2010): 122–143; and Xiaomeng Zhang and Kathryn M. Bartol, "Linking Empowering Leadership and Employee Creativity: The Influence of Psychological Empowerment, Intrinsic Motivation, and Creative Process Engagement," *Academy of Management Journal*, 53 (February 2010): 107–128.

29. John A. Byrne, "The Environment Was Ripe for Abuse," *Business Week* (February 25, 2002): 119.

30. See Beth Kowitt and Kim Thai, "The Top Companies for Leaders," *Fortune* (December 7, 2009): 75–78; Christopher Meyer and Julia Kirby, "Leadership in the Age of Transparency," *Harvard Business Review*, 88 (April 2010): 38–46; and Tamara J. Erickson, "The Leaders We Need Now," *Harvard Business Review*, 88 (May 2010): 63–66.

31. See Mina Kimes, "P&G's Leadership Machine," *Fortune* (April 13, 2009): 22; Stephen Haines, "Bankrupt Leadership Development?" *Training*, 46 (June 2009): 64; and Margery Weinstein, "Missing Something?" *Training*, 47 (January 2010): 6.

32. Drawn from Joseph Kornik, "On the Minds of Managers... Skills Shortages and New Leadership," *Training*, 43 (June 2006): 16.

33. Peter F. Drucker, "What Makes an Effective Executive," *Harvard Business Review*, 82 (June 2004): 59.

34. Inspired by the definition in Andrew J. DuBrin, *Leadership: Research Findings, Practice and Skills*, 2nd ed. (Boston: Houghton Mifflin, 1998), p. 2. Also see Noel M. Tichy and Warren G. Bennis, "Making Judgment Calls: The Ultimate Act of Leadership," *Harvard Business Review*, 85 (October 2007): 94–102.

35. Catherine M. Dalton, "The Changing Identity of Corporate America: Opportunity, Duty, Leadership," *Business Horizons*, 48 (January–February 2005): 2–3. Also see Jack Zenger and Joseph Folkman, "Ten Fatal Flaws That Derail Leaders," *Harvard Business Review*, 87 (June 2009): 18; and Robert H. Schaffer, "Mistakes Leaders Keep Making," *Harvard Business Review*, 88 (September 2010): 86–91.

36. As quoted in Oren Harari, *The Leadership Secrets of Colin Powell* (New York: McGraw-Hill, 2002): p. 13.

37. See D. Scott DeRue and Susan J. Ashford, "Who Will Lead and Who Will Follow? A Social Process of Leadership Identity Construction in Organizations," *Academy of Management Review*, 35 (October 2010): 627–647.

38. Jessi Hempel, "Smartest CEO: Steve Jobs," *Fortune* (July 26, 2010): 83. Also see Brian O'Keefe, "Meet the CEO of the Biggest Company on Earth," *Fortune* (September 27, 2010): p. 88.

39. See Gary A. Yukl, *Leadership in Organizations*, 5th ed. (Upper Saddle River, N.J.: Prentice-Hall, 2001).

40. See David L. Cawthon, "Leadership: The Great Man Theory Revisited," *Business Horizons*, 39 (May–June 1996): 1–4; Dusya Vera and Antonio Rodriguez-Lopez, "Leading Improvisation: Lessons from the American Revolution," *Organizational Dynamics*, 36, no. 3 (2007): 303–319; and Gary H. Rawlins, "History's Leadership Qualities Still Valid," *USA Today* (August 24, 2009): 5B.

41. Fred Luthans, *Organizational Behavior*, 3rd ed. (New York: McGraw-Hill, 1981), p. 419. For interesting discussions about various leader traits, see David Rynecki, "An 18-Hole Character Test," *Business Week* (May 28, 2007): 92, 95; Del Jones, "First-Born Kids Grow Up to Be CEO Material," *USA Today* (September 4, 2007): 1B–2B; Don Schmincke, "Climb Higher," *HR Magazine*, 54 (June 2009): 121–124; Warren Bennis, "Acting the Part of a Leader," *Business Week* (September 14, 2009): 80; and "Best Leaders Bounce Back," *Training*, 47 (July–August 2010): 7.

42. Ralph M. Stogdill, "Personal Factors Associated with Leadership: A Survey of the Literature," *Journal of Psychology*, 25 (1948): 63.

43. See Daniel Goleman, *Emotional Intelligence* (New York: Bantam Books, 1995); Stéphane Côté and Christopher T. H. Miners, "Emotional Intelligence, Cognitive Intelligence, and Job Performance," *Administrative Science Quarterly*, 51 (March 2006): 1–28; John Antonakis, Neal M. Ashkanasy, and Marie T. Dasborough, "Does

Leadership Need Emotional Intelligence?" *The Leadership Quarterly*, 20 (April 2009): 247–261; and Dirk Lindebaum, "Rhetoric or Remedy? A Critique on Developing Emotional Intelligence," *Academy of Management Learning and Education*, 8 (June 2009): 225–237.

44. Michelle Neely Martinez, "The Smarts That Count," *HR Magazine*, 42 (November 1997): 72. Also see Roderick Gilkey, Ricardo Caceda, and Clinton Kilts, "When Emotional Reasoning Trumps IQ," *Harvard Business Review*, 88 (September 2010): 27; and "Interaction: When Emotional Reasoning Trumps IQ," *Harvard Business Review*, 88 (December 2010): 20–21.

45. Based on and adapted from Daniel Goleman, Richard Boyatzis, and Annie McKee, "Primal Leadership," *Harvard Business Review* (Special Issue: Breakthrough Leadership), 79 (December 2001): 49. Also see Daniel Goleman, Richard Boyatzis, and Annie McKee, *Primal Leadership: Realizing the Power of Emotional Intelligence* (Boston: Harvard Business School Press, 2002); and Daniel Goleman and Richard Boyatzis, "Social Intelligence and the Biology of Leadership," *Harvard Business Review*, 86 (September 2008): 74–81.

46. See Margery Weinstein, "Emotional Intelligence," *Training*, 46 (July–August 2009): 20–23; and Andrew O'Connell, "Emotional Intelligence: Smile, Don't Bark, in Tough Times," *Harvard Business Review*, 87 (November 2009): 27.

47. Data from Judy B. Rosener, "Ways Women Lead," *Harvard Business Review*, 68 (November–December 1990): 119–125. Also see "Interaction: Women CEOs: Why So Few?" *Harvard Business Review*, 88 (March 2010): 14–15; and Margery Weinstein, "Women Lead the Way," *Training*, 47 (July–August 2010): 16–20.

48. See "Ways Women and Men Lead," *Harvard Business Review*, 69

(January–February 1991): 150–160; and Herminia Ibarra and Otilia Obodaru, "Women and the Vision Thing," *Harvard Business Review*, 87 (January 2009): 62–70.

49. Data from Alice H. Eagly and Blair T. Johnson, "Gender and Leadership Style: A Meta-Analysis," *Psychological Bulletin*, 108 (September 1990): 233–256. A similar finding is reported in Robert P. Vecchio, "Leadership and Gender Advantage," *The Leadership Quarterly*, 13 (December 2002): 643–671.

50. Kurt Lewin, Ronald Lippitt, and Ralph K. White, "Patterns of Aggressive Behavior in Experimentally Created 'Social Climates,'" *Journal of Social Psychology*, 10 (May 1939): 271–299.

51. Dexter Roberts, "China Goes Shopping," *Business Week* (December 20, 2004): 34. Interpersonal differences in how leader behavior is interpreted are discussed in Jean-Francois Manzoni and Jean-Louis Barsoux, "The Interpersonal Side of Taking Charge," *Organizational Dynamics*, 38 (April–June 2009): 106–116.

52. For an informative summary of this research, see Edwin A. Fleishman, "Twenty Years of Consideration and Structure," in *Current Developments in the Study of Leadership*, ed. Edwin A. Fleishman and James G. Hunt (Carbondale: Southern Illinois University Press, 1973), pp. 1–40. Also see Vishwanath V. Baba and Merle E. Ace, "Serendipity in Leadership: Initiating Structure and Consideration in the Classroom," *Human Relations*, 42 (June 1989): 509–525.

53. Three popular extensions of the Ohio State leadership studies may be found in Robert R. Blake and Anne McCanse, *Leadership Dilemmas—Grid Solutions* (Houston, Tex.: Gulf Publishing, 1990); William J. Reddin, *Managerial Effectiveness* (New York: McGraw-Hill, 1970); and Paul Hersey and Kenneth

H. Blanchard, *Management of Organizational Behavior: Utilizing Human Resources*, 5th ed. (Englewood Cliffs, N.J.: Prentice-Hall, 1988), p. 171. Empirical lack of support for Hersey and Blanchard's situational leadership theory is reported in Jane R. Goodson, Gail W. McGee, and James F. Cashman, "Situational Leadership Theory: A Test of Leadership Prescriptions," *Group Organization Studies*, 14 (December 1989): 446–461.

54. See Abraham K. Korman, "Consideration, 'Initiating Structure,' and Organizational Criteria—A Review," *Personnel Psychology*, 19 (Winter 1966): 349–361.

55. For example, see Michael D. Watkins, "Picking the Right Transition Strategy," *Harvard Business Review*, 87 (January 2009): 47–53; Henry P. Sims Jr., Samer Faraj, and Seokhwa Yun, "When Should a Leader Be Directive or Empowering? How to Develop Your Own Situational Theory of Leadership," *Business Horizons*, 52 (March–April 2009): 149–158; and Adam M. Grant, Francesca Gino, and David A. Hofmann, "The Hidden Advantages of Quiet Bosses," *Harvard Business Review*, 88 (December 2010): 28.

56. Fred E. Fiedler, "Job Engineering for Effective Leadership: A New Approach," *Management Review*, 66 (September 1977): 29.

57. For an excellent comprehensive validation study, see Michael J. Strube and Joseph E. Garcia, "A Meta-Analytic Investigation of Fiedler's Contingency Model of Leadership Effectiveness," *Psychological Bulletin*, 90 (September 1981): 307–321.

58. Fred E. Fiedler and Martin M. Chemers, *Leadership and Effective Management* (Glenview, Ill.: Scott, Foresman, 1974), p. 91.

59. Robert J. House and Terence R. Mitchell, "Path-Goal Theory of Leadership," *Journal of Contemporary Business*, 3 (Autumn

1974): 85. The entire Autumn 1974 issue is devoted to an instructive review of contrasting theories of leadership.

60. As quoted in Michael Kelley, "The Clear Leader," *Fast Company*, 92 (March 2005): 66. Also see Marcus Buckingham, *The One Thing You Need to Know … About Great Managing Great Leading and Sustained Individual Success* (New York: Free Press, 2005).

61. Adapted from Robert J. House, "Path-Goal Theory of Leadership: Lessons, Legacy, and a Reformulated Theory," *The Leadership Quarterly*, 7 (Autumn 1996): 323–352.

62. For path-goal research, see Abduhl-Rahim A. Al-Gattan, "Test of the Path-Goal Theory of Leadership in the Multinational Domain," *Group & Organization Studies*, 10 (December 1985): 429–445; Robert T. Keller, "A Test of the Path-Goal Theory of Leadership with Need for Clarity as a Moderator in Research and Development Organizations," *Journal of Applied Psychology*, 74 (April 1989): 208–212; John E. Mathieu, "A Test of Subordinates' Achievement and Affiliation Needs as Moderators of Leader Path-Goal Relationships," *Basic and Applied Social Psychology*, 11 (June 1990): 179–189; and Retha A. Price, "An Investigation of Path-Goal Leadership Theory in Marketing Channels," *Journal of Retailing*, 67 (Fall 1991): 339–361.

63. See J. McGregor Burns, *Leadership* (New York: HarperCollins, 1978).

64. See Michael Maccoby, "Why People Follow the Leader: The Power of Transference," *Harvard Business Review*, 82 (September 2004): 76–85; Jane M. Howell and Boas Shamir, "The Role of Followers in the Charismatic Leadership Process: Relationships and Their Consequences," *Academy of Management Review*, 30 (January 2005): 96–112; and Bradley L. Kirkman, Gilad Chen, Jiing-Lih Farh, Zhen Xiong Chen, and Kevin B. Lowe, "Individual Power Distance Orientation

and Follower Reactions to Transformational Leaders: A Cross-Level, Cross-Cultural Examination," *Academy of Management Journal*, 52 (August 2009): 744–754.

65. A critique of charismatic leadership can be found in Joshua Macht, "Jim Collins to CEOs: Lose the Charisma," *Business 2.0*, 2 (October 2001): 121–122. Also see Alex Pentland, "We Can Measure the Power of Charisma," *Harvard Business Review*, 88 (January–February 2010): 34–35.

66. See Nathan P. Podsakoff, Philip M. Podsakoff, and Valentina V. Kuskova, "Dispelling Misconceptions and Providing Guidelines for Leader Reward and Punishment Behavior," *Business Horizons*, 53 (May–June 2010): 291–303.

67. See Joseph Seltzer and Bernard M. Bass, "Transformational Leadership: Beyond Initiation and Consideration," *Journal of Management*, 16 (December 1990): 693–703.

68. For research support, see David A. Waldman, Gabriel G. Ramírez, Robert J. House, and Phanish Puranam, "Does Leadership Matter? CEO Leadership Attributes and Profitability Under Conditions of Perceived Environmental Uncertainty," *Academy of Management Journal*, 44 (February 2001): 134–143.

69. For example, see Bernard M. Bass, "From Transactional to Transformational Leadership: Learning to Share the Vision," *Organizational Dynamics*, 18 (Winter 1990): 19–31; Warren Bennis, "The End of Leadership: Exemplary Leadership Is Impossible Without Full Inclusion, Initiatives, and Cooperation of Followers," *Organizational Dynamics*, 28 (Summer 1999): 71–80; James R. Detert and Ethan R. Burris, "Leadership Behavior and Employee Voice: Is the Door Really Open?" *Academy of Management Journal*, 50 (August 2007): 869–884; and Chip Jarnagin and John W. Slocum, Jr., "Creating Corporate Cultures Through Mythopoetic Leadership,"

Organizational Dynamics, 36, no. 3 (2007): 288–302.

70. See Mark E. Van Buren and Todd Safferstone, "The Quick Wins Paradox," *Harvard Business Review*, 87 (January 2009): 54–61; Haig R. Nalbantian and Richard A. Guzzo, "Making Mobility Matter," *Harvard Business Review*, 87 (March 2009): 76–84; and Jann E. Freed, "What Is Your Leadership Legacy?" *Training*, 47 (July–August 2010): 10–11.

71. Robert J. Sternberg, "WICS: A Model of Leadership in Organizations," *Academy of Management Learning and Education*, 2 (December 2003): 388. Also see Deborah Ancona, Thomas W. Malone, Wanda J. Orlikowski, and Peter M. Senge, "In Praise of the Incomplete Leader," *Harvard Business Review*, 85 (February 2007): 92–100; and Ronit Kark and Dina Van Dijk, "Motivation to Lead, Motivation to Follow: The Role of the Self-Regulatory Focus in Leadership Processes," *Academy of Management Review*, 32 (April 2007): 500–528.

72. For more on the servant leader philosophy, see Robert K. Greenleaf, *Servant Leadership: A Journey into the Nature of Legitimate Power and Greatness* (New York: Paulist Press, 1977); Walter Kiechel III, "The Leader as Servant," *Fortune* (May 4, 1992): 121–122; Larry C. Spears, *Reflections on Leadership: How Robert K. Greenleaf's Theory of Servant-Leadership Influenced Today's Top Management Thinkers* (New York: Wiley, 1995); Don M. Frick, *Robert K. Greenleaf: A Life of Servant Leadership* (San Francisco: Berrett-Koehler, 2004); and Joanne H. Gavin and Richard O. Mason, "The Virtuous Organization: The Value of Happiness in the Workplace," *Organizational Dynamics*, 33, no. 4 (2004): 379–392. Also see Peter Cairo, David L. Dotlich, and Stephen H. Rhinesmith, "The Unnatural Leader," *Training and Development*, 59 (March 2005): 26–31.

73. David Leon Moore, "Wooden's Wizardry Wears Well," *USA Today*

(March 29, 1995): 1C–2C. Also see Beth Harris, "Legendary UCLA Basketball Coach Wooden Dies," *Arizona Republic* (June 5, 2010): C1, C4. Other servant leaders are profiled in Jayne O'Donnell, "Ethan Allen's Kathwari Was Always a Leader," *USA Today* (June 25, 2007): 4B; Joel Spolsky, "My Style of Servant Leadership," *Inc.*, 30 (December 2008): 77–78; "CEO Dishes on Politics, Drug Prices," *USA Today* (March 2, 2010): 1B–2B; and Catherine M. Dalton, "Feeling Boxed in by the Big Boxes? Tools of the Trade for Successful Customer Relationship Management," *Business Horizons*, 53 (May–June 2010): 237–240.

74. See Barbara Kellerman, *Bad Leadership: What It Is, How It Happens, Why It Matters* (Boston: Harvard Business School Press, 2004); and Gabriella Salvatore, "Develop Tomorrow's Leaders," *Training*, 46 (May 2009): 14.

75. Christine Day, "Learn to Love the Spotlight," *Fortune* (November 10, 2008): 36. Also see Herminia Ibarra, Nancy M. Carter, and Christine Silva, "Why Men Still Get More Promotions Than Women," *Harvard Business Review*, 88 (September 2010): 80–88.

76. For more, see Kassandra Duane, "SpinVox CEO Christina Domecq on Making the Most of Mentors," *Harvard Business Review*, 86 (May 2008): 28; Susan J. Wells, "Tending Talent," *HR Magazine*, 54 (May 2009): 52–57; and David C. Pease, "Making Mentoring Memorable," *HR Magazine*, 54 (May 2009): 63–65.

77. Abraham Zaleznik, "Managers and Leaders: Are They Different?" *Harvard Business Review*, 55 (May–June 1977): 76.

78. For details, see Ellen A Fagenson, "The Mentor Advantage: Perceived Career/Job Experiences of Protégés Versus Non-Protégés," *Journal of Organizational Behavior*, 10 (October 1989): 309–320. More mentoring research findings are reported in Melenie J. Lankau and Terri A. Scandura, "An Investigation of Personal Learning in Mentoring Relationships: Content, Antecedents, and Consequences," *Academy of Management Journal*, 45 (August 2002): 779–790; Shana A. Simon and Lillian T. Eby, "A Typology of Negative Mentoring Experiences: A Multidimensional Scaling Study," *Human Relations*, 56, no. 9 (2003): 1083–1106; and Scott Tonidandel, Derek R. Avery, and McKensy G. Phillips, "Maximizing Returns on Mentoring: Factors Affecting Subsequent Protégé Performance," *Journal of Organizational Behavior*, 28 (January 2007): 89–110.

79. Margery Weinstein, "Stuck in the Middle," *Training*, 44 (July–August 2007): 8.

80. Lorri Freifeld, "Generation Management," *Training*, 47 (July–August 2010): 6.

81. For more, see Kathy E. Kram, "Phases of the Mentor Relationship," *Academy of Management Journal*, 26 (December 1983): 608–625.

82. Suzanne C. de Janasz, Sherry E. Sullivan, and Vicki Whiting, "Mentor Networks and Career Success: Lessons for Turbulent Times," *Academy of Management Executive*, 17 (November 2003): 79.

83. Based on J. Craig Anderson, "Mentors Lead Proteges to Success in Their Fields," *Arizona Republic* (June 5, 2010): D1–D2.

84. Nadira A. Hira, "You Raised Them, Now Manage Them," *Fortune* (May 28, 2007): 44.

85. See Erik Gunn, "Mentoring: The Democratic Version," *Training*, 32 (August 1995): 64–67.

86. Steve Hamm, "Match.com for Mentors," *Business Week* (March 23–30, 2009): 57. This list is based on discussions in Leon Rubis, "Engineering People as Well as Projects," *HR Magazine*, 53 (July 2008): 34–36; Sarah Boehle, "Millennial Mentors," *Training*, 46 (July-August 2009): 34–36; Greg Latshaw, "Students Make Career Matches," *USA Today* (April 7, 2010): 3A; and Jeanne C. Meister and Karie Willyerd, "Mentoring Millennials," *Harvard Business Review*, 88 (May 2010): 68–72.

87. For a contemporary perspective on behaviorism, see Richard J. DeGrandpre, "A Science of Meaning: Can Behaviorism Bring Meaning to Psychological Science?" *American Psychologist*, 55 (July 2000): 721–738.

88. See Edward L. Thorndike, *Educational Psychology: The Psychology of Learning* (New York: Columbia University Press, 1913), vol. II, p. 4.

89. For an instructive account of operant conditioning applied to human behavior, see B. F. Skinner, *Science and Human Behavior* (New York: Free Press, 1953), pp. 62–66. A good update is B. F. Skinner, "What Is Wrong with Daily Life in the Western World," *American Psychologist*, 41 (May 1986): 568–574. Also see Marilyn B. Gilbert and Thomas F. Gilbert, "What Skinner Gave Us," *Training*, 28 (September 1991): 42–48; and Janice Lloyd, "His Cats Know All the Tricks," *USA Today* (October 5, 2009): 7D.

90. For example, see Tom Kramlinger and Tom Huberty, "Behaviorism Versus Humanism," *Training & Development Journal*, 44 (December 1990): 41–45; and Alfie Kohn, "Challenging Behaviorist Dogma: Myths About Money and Motivation," *Compensation & Benefits Review*, 30 (March–April 1998): 27, 33–37.

91. For example, see Bob Filipczak, "Why No One Likes Your Incentive Program," *Training*, 30 (August 1993): 19–25; and Alfie Kohn, "Why Incentive Plans Cannot Work," *Harvard Business Review*, 71 (September–October 1993): 54–63.

92. For positive evidence and background, see Alexander D. Stajkovic and Fred Luthans, "A Meta-Analysis of the Effects of Organizational Behavior Modification on Task Performance, 1975–95," *Academy of Management Journal*, 40 (October 1997): 1122–1149; Fred Luthans and Alexander D. Stajkovic, "Reinforce for Performance: The Need to Go

Beyond Pay and Even Rewards," *Academy of Management Executive,* 13 (May 1999): 49–57; Cheryl Comeau-Kirschner, "Improving Productivity Doesn't Cost a Dime," *Management Review,* 88 (January 1999): 7; and Alexander D. Stajkovic and Fred Luthans, "Differential Effects of Incentive Motivators on Work Performance," *Academy of Management Journal,* 44 (June 2001): 580–590.

93. Dale Feuer, "Training for Fast Times," *Training,* 24 (July 1987): 28.

94. See Nadine Heintz, "Let's Give These Folks a Big Hand: Building a Culture of Appreciation," *Inc.,* (September 2009): 79–80; Scott Berinato, "Success Gets into Your Head—And Changes It," *Harvard Business Review,* 88 (January–February 2010): 28; Roy Saunderson, "Thank-You Training, CNN-Style," *Training,* 47 (September–October 2010): 40; and Nancy Lublin, "Two Little Words," *Fast Company,* 150 (November 2010): 56.

95. Alan Farnham, "The Trust Gap," *Fortune* (December 4, 1989): 74.

96. Kenneth Blanchard and Spencer Johnson, *The One Minute Manager* (New York: Berkley, 1982), p. 45 (emphasis added). Also see Kenneth Blanchard and Robert Lorber, *Putting the One Minute Manager to Work* (New York: Berkley, 1984).

97. Tom Rath and Donald O. Clifton, *How Full Is Your Bucket? Positive Strategies for Work and Life* (New York: Gallup Press, 2004), p. 57. Also see Kerry Hannon, "Praise Cranks Up Productivity," *USA Today* (August 30, 2004): 6B; and Richard F. Gerson and Robbie G. Gerson, "Effort Management," *Training and Development,* 60 (June 2006): 26–27.

98. For detailed treatment of B. Mod. in the workplace, see Fred Luthans and Robert Kreitner, *Organizational Behavior Modification and Beyond: An Operant and Social Learning Approach* (Glenview, Ill.: Scott,

Foresman, 1985). Also see Ahmad Diba, "If Pat Sajak Were Your CEO...," *Fortune* (December 18, 2000): 330; and Bobbie Gossage, "Lose Weight, Get a Toaster," *Inc.,* 27 (January 2005): 24.

99. Ten items excerpted from a 25-item survey in Anne Fisher, "Success Secret: A High Emotional IQ," *Fortune* (October 26, 1998): 293–298.

CHAPTER 15

1. Dean Tjosvold, *Learning to Manage Conflict: Getting People to Work Together Productively* (New York: Lexington, 1993), p. xi.

2. Ann Pomeroy, "CEO Challenges in 2004," *HR Magazine,* 49 (October 2004): 18. For instructive reading about change, see Jeffrey Hollender, "Giving Up the CEO Seat," *Harvard Business Review,* 88 (March 2010): 105–109; Vineet Nayar, "A Maverick CEO Explains How He Persuaded His Team to Leap into the Future," *Harvard Business Review,* 88 (June 2010): 110–113; and Steve Savage, "Why I Stepped Down," *Inc.,* 32 (September 2010): 186–187.

3. "The Best Managers: Steven Reinemund, PepsiCo," *Business Week* (January 10, 2005): 56.

4. As quoted in Patricia Sellers, "The Queen of Pop," *Fortune* (September 28, 2009): 108.

5. For good background reading on change, see Edward E. Lawler III and Christopher G. Worley, *Built to Change: How to Achieve Sustained Organizational Effectiveness* (San Francisco: Jossey-Bass, 2006); Gary Hamel with Bill Breen, *The Future of Management* (Boston: Harvard Business School Press, 2007); and Christopher G. Worley and Edward E. Lawler III, "Building a Change Capability at Capital One Financial," *Organizational Dynamics,* 38 (October–December 2009): 245–251.

6. As quoted in Del Jones, "Xerox CEO: Customers, Employees Come First," *USA Today* (December 15, 2003): 3B. Also see Rasika Welankiwar, "CARE CEO Helene

Gayle on Shaking Up a Venerable Organization," *Harvard Business Review,* 87 (April 2009): 22.

7. See Scott Sonenshein, "We're Changing—Or Are We? Untangling the Role of Progressive, Regressive, and Stability Narratives During Strategic Change Implementation," *Academy of Management Journal,* 53 (June 2010): 477–512.

8. Adapted from discussion in David A. Nadler and Michael L. Tushman, "Organizational Frame Bending: Principles for Managing Reorientation," *Academy of Management Executive,* 3 (August 1989): 194–204. Also see Robert H. Schaffer and Matthew K. McCreight, "Build Your Own Change Model," *Business Horizons,* 47 (May–June 2004): 33–38.

9. Drawn from Brian Dumaine, "Creating a New Company Culture," *Fortune* (January 15, 1990): 127–131.

10. Bruce Horovitz, "McDonald's Hopes New Cold Drinks Will Be Hot," *USA Today* (May 17, 2010): 1B. Also see Bruce Horovitz, "New Pizza Recipe Did Wonders for Domino's Sales," *USA Today* (May 5, 2010): 1B; and Diane Brady, "J. Patrick Doyle," *Bloomberg Businessweek* (May 3–May 9, 2010): 84.

11. Michelle Kessler, "Cisco's Risky Scientific-Atlanta Buy Pays Off as Quarterly Profit Surges," *USA Today* (August 9, 2006): 2B. For an update, see Jon Swartz, "Cisco Profit Up 8%, But It Misses Its Sales Forecast," *USA Today* (November 11, 2010): 4B. Other examples of frame bending can be found in Roger O. Crockett, "Will a Google Phone Change the Game?" *Business Week* (October 8, 2007): 38–39; Jon Fine, "The Wall Street Journalist," *Business Week* (July 14–21, 2008): 104; Roben Farzad and Christopher Palmeri, "Can Schwab Seize the Day?" *Business Week* (July 27, 2009): 36–39; and Christopher Palmeri, "Face-Lift for the One-Armed Bandit," *Bloomberg Businessweek* (December 21, 2009): 77.

12. Kathy Rebello, "Inside Mcrosoft," *Business Week* (July 15, 1996): 57.

Also see Mark W. Johnson, Clayton M. Christensen, and Henning Kagermann, "Reinventing Your Business Model," *Harvard Business Review*, 86 (December 2008): 51–59; and Jennifer Schramm, "The Pluses of 'Disruptive Change,'" *HR Magazine*, 54 (September 2009): 128.

13. Stephen Haines, "The Rollercoaster of Change," *Training*, 47 (November–December 2010): 56.

14. See Mitchell Lee Marks, "Workplace Recovery After Mergers, Acquisitions, and Downsizings: Facilitating Individual Adaptation to Major Organizational Transitions," *Organizational Dynamics*, 35, no. 4 (2006): 384–399; Boris Groysberg and Robin Abrahams, "Five Ways to Bungle a Job Change," *Harvard Business Review*, 88 (January–February 2010): 137–140; and Alison Beard, "Losing the Top Job—and Winning It Back," *Harvard Business Review*, 88 (October 2010): 136–138.

15. See Robert H. Miles, "Beyond the Age of Dilbert: Accelerating Corporate Transformations by Rapidly Engaging All Employees," *Organizational Dynamics*, 29 (Spring 2001): 313–321.

16. Ichak Adizes, *Mastering Change: The Power of Mutual Trust and Respect in Personal Life, Family Life, Business and Society* (Santa Monica, Calif.: Adizes Institute, 1991), p. 6.

17. See Jeffrey D. Ford, Laurie W. Ford, and Angelo D'Amelio, "Resistance to Change: The Rest of the Story," *Academy of Management Review*, 33 (April 2008): 362–377; Shaul Oreg, et al., "Dispositional Resistance to Change: Measurement Equivalence and the Link to Personal Values Across 17 Nations," *Journal of Applied Psychology*, 93 (July 2008): 935–944; Jeffrey D. Ford and Laurie W. Ford, "Decoding Resistance to Change," *Harvard Business Review*, 87 (April 2009): 99–103; Robert H. Schaffer, "Mistakes Leaders Keep Making," *Harvard Business Review*, 88 (September 2010): 86–91.

18. J. Alan Ofner, "Managing Change," *Personnel Administrator*, 29 (September 1984): 20.

19. Peter Coy, "The Perils of Picking the Wrong Standard," *Business Week* (October 8, 1990): 145. Also see Reena Jana, "Is Caps Lock the Next Dodo?" *Business Week* (July 27, 2009): 20.

20. Diane Brady, "Act II," *Business Week* (March 29, 2004): 76.

21. See Diane Brady, "Y&R's Fudge Heads for the Exit," *Business Week* (November 28, 2006), www .businessweek.com/bwdaily/dnflash/content/ nov2006/db20061128 277879. htm?chan=search.

22. See Leigh Buchanan, "The Office: The Departed," *Inc.*, 29 (August 2007): 128.

23. This list is based in part on John P. Kotter and Leonard A. Schlesinger, "Choosing Strategies for Change," *Harvard Business Review*, 86 (July–August 2008): 130–139; and Joseph Stanislao and Bettie C. Stanislao, "Dealing with Resistance to Change," *Business Horizons*, 26 (July–August 1983): 74–78.

24. Del Jones, "When You're Smiling, Are You Seething Inside?" *USA Today* (April 12, 2004): 2B.

25. Robert Kegan and Lisa Laskow Lahey, "The Real Reason People Won't Change," *Harvard Business Review*, 79 (November 2001): 86.

26. See Robert H. Miles, "Accelerating Corporate Transformations (Don't Lose Your Nerve!)," *Harvard Business Review*, 88 (January–February 2010): 68–75; and Jeffrey D. Ford and Laurie W. Ford, "Stop Blaming Resistance to Change and Start Using It," *Organizational Dynamics*, 39 (January–March 2010): 24–36.

27. As quoted in Del Jones, "Product Development Can Fill Prescription for Success," *USA Today* (May 30, 2000): 7B.

28. See Craig M. McAllaster, "The 5 P's of Change: Leading Change by Effectively Utilizing Leverage Points Within an Organization," *Organizational Dynamics*, 33, no. 3 (2004): 318–328; Nancy Hatch Woodward, "To Make Changes, Manage Them," *HR Magazine*, 52 (May 2007): 62–67; and Jack Welch and Suzy Welch, "What Change Agents Are Made Of," *Business Week* (October 20, 2008): 96.

29. See Robert N. Llewellyn, "When to Call the Organization Doctor," *HR Magazine*, 47 (March 2002): 79–83; Darin E. Hartley, "OD Wired," *Training and Development*, 58 (August 2004): 20–22; Stephen R. Covey, "Organizational Development," *Training*, 44 (April 2007): 40; and Nancy Lockwood, SHRM Research Quarterly, "Organization Development: A Strategic HR Tool," *HR Magazine*, 52 (September 2007): 1–9.

30. Philip G. Hanson and Bernard Lubin, "Answers to Questions Frequently Asked About Organization Development," in *The Emerging Practice of Organization Development*, ed. Walter Sikes, Allan Drexler, and Jack Grant (Alexandria, Va.: NTL Institute, 1989), p. 16 (emphasis added). For good background information on current OD practices, see W. Warner Burke, "The New Agenda for Organization Development," *Organizational Dynamics*, 26 (Summer 1997): 7–20; Chuck McVinney, "Dream Weaver," *Training & Development* 53 (April 1999): 39–42; and Ron Zemke, "Don't Fix That Company!" *Training*, 36 (June 1999): 26–33.

31. W. Warner Burke, *Organization Development: A Normative View* (Reading, Mass.: Addison-Wesley, 1987), p. 9. Also see John Austin, "Mapping Out a Game Plan for Change," *HR Magazine*, 54 (April 2009): 38–42; and John Stacey, "Culture Born of Collaboration," *HR Magazine*, 55 (July 2010): 30–32.

32. Tony Schwartz, "The Productivity Paradox: How Sony Pictures Gets More Out of People by Demanding Less," *Harvard Business Review*, 88 (June 2010): 65.

33. This list is based on Wendell French, "Organization Development Objectives, Assumptions, and Strategies," *California Management Review*, 12 (Winter 1969):

23–34; and Charles Kiefer and Peter Stroh, "A New Paradigm for Organization Development," *Training and Development Journal*, 37 (April 1983): 26–35.

34. See Robert J. Marshak, "Managing the Metaphors of Change," *Organizational Dynamics*, 22 (Summer 1993): 44–56; Craig L. Pearce and Charles P. Osmond, "Metaphors for Change: The ALPs Model of Change Management," *Organizational Dynamics*, 24 (Winter 1996): 23–35; and Ian Palmer and Richard Dunford, "Conflicting Uses of Metaphors: Reconceptualizing Their Use in the Field of Organizational Change," *Academy of Management Review*, 21 (July 1996): 691–717.

35. A successful application of Lewin's model at British Airways is discussed in Leonard D. Goodstein and W. Warner Burke, "Creating Successful Organization Change," *Organizational Dynamics*, 19 (Spring 1991): 4–17. Also see Gib Akin and Ian Palmer, "Putting Metaphors to Work for Change in Organizations," *Organizational Dynamics*, 28 (Winter 2000): 67–79; Richard S. Allen and Kendyl A. Montgomery, "Applying an Organizational Development Approach to Creating Diversity," *Organizational Dynamics*, 30 (Fall 2001): 149–161; and Mark Herron, "Training Alone Is Not Enough," *Training*, 39 (February 2002): 72.

36. For details on how poor "unfreezing" threatened the Hewlett-Packard/Compaq Computer merger plan, see Peter Burrows, "Carly's Last Stand?" *Business Week* (December 24, 2001): 62–70.

37. As quoted in Linda Tischler, "Kenny Moore Held a Funeral and Everyone Came," *Fast Company*, 79 (February 2004): 30.

38. For example, see Susan Berfield, "After the Layoff, The Redesign," *Business Week* (April 14, 2008): 54–56.

39. Bill Breen and Cheryl Dahl, "Field Guide for Change," *Fast Company*, 30 (December 1999): 384. Also see Keith H. Hammonds, "A Lever Long Enough to Move the World," *Fast Company*, 90 (January 2005): 60–63.

40. Debra E. Meyerson, *Tempered Radicals: How People Use Difference to Inspire Change at Work* (Boston: Harvard Business School Press, 2001), p. xi. Also see Debra E. Meyerson, "Radical Change, the Quiet Way," *Harvard Business Review*, 79 (October 2001): 92–100.

41. Adapted from "Tips for Tempered Radicals" in Keith H. Hammonds, "Practical Radicals," *Fast Company*, 38 (September 2000): 162–174.

42. For practical insights on organizational change, see Seth Godin, "Rules for Off-Roading at Work," *Fast Company*, 84 (July 2004): 95; Gary Hamel, "Break Free!" *Fortune* (October 1, 2007): 119–126; and Freek Vermeulen, Phanish Puranam, and Ranjay Gulati, "Change for Change's Sake," *Harvard Business Review*, 88 (June 2010): 70–76.

43. Abraham Zaleznik, "Real Work," *Harvard Business Review*, 67 (January–February 1989): 59–60.

44. For example, see Scott C. Douglas, Christian Kiewitz, Mark J. Martinko, Paul Harvey, Younhee Kim, and Jae Uk Chun, "Cognitions, Emotions, and Evaluations: An Elaboration Likelihood Model for Workplace Aggression," *Academy of Management Review*, 33 (April 2008): 425–451; James B. Thelan, "Is That a Threat?" *HR Magazine*, 54 (December 2009): 61–63; Diane Cadrain, "Campus Violence Reveals Background Screening Flaws," *HR Magazine*, 55 (May 2010): 13; and Signe Whitson, "Checking Passive Aggression," *HR Magazine*, 55 (June 2010): 115–116.

45. Dean Tjosvold, *Learning to Manage Conflict: Getting People to Work Together Productively* (New York: Lexington, 1993), p. 8.

46. *Ibid.* Also see Stuart D. Sidle, "Do Teams Who Agree to Disagree Make Better Decisions?" *Academy of Management Perspectives*, 21 (May 2007): 74–75; Saj-nicole A. Joni and Damon Beyer, "How to Pick a Good Fight," *Harvard Business Review*, 87 (December 2009): 48–57; and Jason Fried, "I Know You Are, But What Am I?" *Inc.*, 32 (July–August 2010): 39–40.

47. See "When Bosses Attack," *Training*, 42 (May 2005): 10; Amy Cortese, "Where Fight Club Meets the Office," *Business 2.0*, 6 (May 2005): 129; Johnnie L. Roberts, "Off with Their Heads!" *Newsweek* (July 30, 2007): 41–43; Maria Bartiromo, "Redstone: 'Legacies Are for Dead People,'" *Business Week* (August 6, 2007): 28–31; and Danielle Sacks, "Working with the Enemy," *Fast Company*, 118 (September 2007): 74–81.

48. Walter Kiechel III, "How to Escape the Echo Chamber," *Fortune* (June 18, 1990): 130. For other good material on constructive conflict, see Dean Tjosvold, Chun Hui, and Kenneth S. Law, "Constructive Conflict in China: Cooperative Conflict as a Bridge Between East and West," *Journal of World Business*, 36 (Summer 2001): 166–183.

49. Cliff Edwards, "Supercharging Silicon Valley," *Business Week* (October 4, 2004): 18. A different perspective of Intel's culture can be found in Dean Foust, "Where Headhunters Fear to Tread," *Business Week* (September 14, 2009): 42–44.

50. For more on anger and emotion in the workplace, see Deanna Geddes and Ronda Roberts Callister, "Crossing the Line(s): A Dual Threshold Model of Anger in Organizations," *Academy of Management Review*, 32 (July 2007): 721–746; Kathryn Tyler, "Helping Employees Cool It," *HR Magazine*, 55 (April 2010): 53–55; and Daniel L. Shapiro, "Relational Identity Theory: A Systematic Approach for Transforming the Emotional Dimension of Conflict," *American*

Psychologist, 65 (October 2010): 634–645.

51. For a good overview of managing conflict, see Kenneth Cloke and Joan Goldsmith, *Resolving Conflicts at Work: A Complete Guide for Everyone on the Job* (San Francisco: Jossey-Bass, 2000). Also see Jeff Weiss and Jonathan Hughes, "What Collaboration? Accept—and Actively Manage—Conflict," *Harvard Business Review,* 83 (March 2005): 92–101; Kelley Mollica, "Stay Above the Fray," *HR Magazine,* 50 (April 2005): 111–115; Stephen Covey, "7 Ways to Come Together," *USA Weekend* (January 15–17, 2010): 6–7; and Robin R. Vallacher, Peter T. Coleman, Andrzej Nowak, and Lan Bui-Wrzosinska, "Rethinking Intractable Conflict: The Perspective of Dynamical Systems," *American Psychologist,* 65 (May–June 2010): 262–278.

52. See Christine M. Pearson and Christine L. Porath, "On the Nature, Consequences and Remedies of Workplace Incivility: No Time for 'Nice'? Think Again," *Academy of Management Executive,* 19 (February 2005): 7–18; Weiss and Hughes, "Want Collaboration? Accept—And Actively Manage—Conflict," pp. 92–101; and Donny Ebenstein, "Removing 'Personal' from Interpersonal Tension," *Training,* 46 (September 2009): 48.

53. See Dean Tjosvold and Margaret Poon, "Dealing with Scarce Resources," *Group & Organization Management,* 23 (September 1998): 237–255.

54. See Hardy Green, "How to Get Rid of the, Uh, Jerks," *Business Week* (March 19, 2007): 14; the second *Q&A* in Kerry Sulkowicz, "(Not) the Life of the After-Work Party," *Business Week* (June 4, 2007): 18; David Silverman, "Surviving the Boss from Hell," *Harvard Business Review,* 87 (September 2009): 33–36; and Tom Krattenmaker, "In God-Fearing USA, Where Is the Decency?" *USA Today* (October 25, 2010): 11A.

55. See Bronwyn Fryer, "The Micromanager," *Harvard Business Review,* 82 (September 2004): 31–40.

56. See Bill Leonard, "Study: Bully Bosses Prevalent in U.S.," *HR Magazine,* 52 (May 2007): 22, 28; Michael Orey, "Try This Suit on for Size," *Business Week* (May 14, 2007): 14; the first Q&A in Kerry Sulkowicz, "One Snarls, the Other Doesn't," *Business Week* (June 18, 2007): 16; Wendy Koch, "Study: Bullies and Bullied More Likely Hit by Crime," *USA Today* (October 17, 2007): 2A; and Nancy Gibbs, "Sticks and Stones," *Time* (April 19, 2010): 64.

57. See Tim Ursiny, *The Coward's Guide to Conflict: Empowering Solutions for Those Who Would Rather Run Than Fight* (Naperville, Ill.: Sourcebooks, 2003), ch. 2; Paul Falcone, "Avoid Pre-Emptive Strikes," *HR Magazine,* 52 (May 2007): 101–104; Margery Weinstein, "Conquering Conflict," *Training,* 44 (June 2007): 56–58; and Kristin J. Behfar, Randall S. Peterson, Elizabeth A. Mannix, and William M. K. Trochim, "The Critical Role of Conflict Resolution in Teams: A Close Look at the Links Between Conflict Type, Conflict Management Strategies, and Team Outcomes," *Journal of Applied Psychology,* 93 (January 2008): 170–188.

58. Stephen P. Robbins, *Managing Organizational Conflict: A Nontraditional Approach* (Englewood Cliffs, N.J.: Prentice-Hall, 1974), p. 62.

59. See William H. Ross and Donald E. Conlon, "Hybrid Forms of Third-Party Dispute Resolution: Theoretical Implications of Combining Mediation and Arbitration," *Academy of Management Review,* 25 (April 2000): 416–427; Stephanie Armour, "Arbitration's Rise Raises Fairness Issue," *USA Today* (June 12, 2001): 1B–2B; and Jeanne M. Brett et al., "Sticks and Stones: Language, Face, and Online Dispute Resolution," *Academy*

of Management Journal, 50 (February 2007): 85–99.

60. Brian Grow, "Fat's in the Fire for This Burger King," *Business Week* (November 8, 2004): 70.

61. See M. Afzalur Rahim, "A Measure of Styles of Handling Conflict," *Academy of Management Journal,* 26 (June 1983): 368–376; and Meg Cadoux Hirshberg, "To Love, Honor, and Report To," *Inc.,* 32 (July–August 2010): 43–44.

62. See Olivia Barker, "Hagglers Thrive in New Economy," *USA Today* (March 16, 2009): 1D–2D; and Jillian Berman, "Negotiate Your Way to Savings," *USA Today* (July 30, 2010): 3B.

63. See Michael Kaplan, "How to Negotiate Anything: Seven Rules for Getting What You Want on Your Own Terms," *Money,* 34 (May 2005): 117–119; Reed Tucker, "Four Key Skills to Master Now," *Fortune* (October 30, 2006): 123–124; and "How to Negotiate Effectively," *Inc.* Guidebook, 2, no. 7, *Inc.,* 32 (November 2010): 65–68.

64. Data from Laurie R. Weingart, Elaine B. Hyder, and Michael J. Prietula, "Knowledge Matters: The Effects of Tactical Descriptions on Negotiation Behavior and Outcome," *Journal of Personality and Social Psychology,* 70 (June 1996): 1205–1217. Also see Gerben A. van Kleef, Carsten K. W. De Dreu, and Antony S. R. Manstead, "The Interpersonal Effects of Anger and Happiness in Negotiations," *Journal of Personality and Social Psychology,* 86 (January 2004): 57–76; and Leigh Thompson and Geoffrey J. Leonardelli, "The Big Bang: The Evolution of Negotiation Research," *Academy of Management Executive,* 18 (August 2004): 113–117.

65. Based on Leigh Anne Liu, Chei Hwee Chua, and Günter Stahl, "Quality of Communication Experience: Definition, Measurement, and Implications for Intercultural Negotiations," *Journal of Applied Psychology,* 95 (May 2010): 469–487.

66. Margaret A. Neale and Max H. Bazerman, "Negotiating Rationally: The Power and Impact of the Negotiator's Frame," Academy of Management Executive, 6 (August 1992): 42–51.

67. See Ian Mount, "How to Deliver an Ultimatum," Inc., 26 (October 2004): 101; and Deepak Malhotra and Max H. Bazerman, "Investigative Negotiation," Harvard Business Review, 85 (September 2007): 72–78; and Dan R. Dalton and Catherine M. Dalton, "On the Many Limitations of Threat in Negotiation, as Well as Other Contexts," Business Horizons, 52 (March–April 2009): 109–115.

68. See Danny Ertel, "Getting Past Yes: Negotiating as If Implementation Mattered," Harvard Business Review, 82 (November 2004): 60–68. Trust is explored in F. David Schoorman, Roger C. Mayer, and James H. Davis, "An Integrative Model of Organizational Trust: Past, Present, and Future," Academy of Management Review, 32 (April 2007): 344–354; Penelope Sue Greenberg, Ralph H. Greenberg, and Yvonne Lederer Antonucci, "Creating and Sustaining Trust in Virtual Teams," Business Horizons, 50 (July–August 2007): 325–333; and the series of articles in the "Spotlight on Rebuilding Trust" section in Harvard Business Review, 87 (June 2009): 53–77.

69. Cross-cultural negotiation is discussed in James K. Sebenius, "The Hidden Challenge of Cross-Border Negotiations," Harvard Business Review, 80 (March 2002): 76–85. Also see Deepak Malhotra, Gillian Ku, and J. Keith Murnighan, "When Winning Is Everything," Harvard Business Review, 86 (May 2008): 78–86.

70. Stephen R. Covey, The Seven Habits of Highly Effective People (New York: Simon & Schuster, 1989), p. 207. For more, see Stephen R. Covey, The 8th Habit: From Effectiveness to Greatness (New York: Free Press, 2004).

71. A good resource book is Roger Fisher and Danny Ertel, Getting Ready to Negotiate: The Getting to Yes Workbook (New York: Penguin, 1995). Also see Deborah M. Kolb and Judith Williams, "Breakthrough Bargaining," Harvard Business Review, 79 (February 2001): 88–97; and Ann Pomeroy, "Chameleons Win at Negotiation," HR Magazine, 52 (October 2007): 10, 12.

72. Sean Donahue, "Tom's of Mainstream," Business 2.0, 5 (December 2004): 73.

73. Roger Fisher and William Ury, Getting to Yes: Negotiating Agreement Without Giving In (Boston: Houghton Mifflin, 1981), p. 104. Also see Bert Spector, "An Interview with Roger Fisher and William Ury," Academy of Management Executive, 18 (August 2004): 101–108; Bridget Booth and Matt McCredie, "Taking Steps Toward 'Getting to Yes' at Blue Cross and Blue Shield of Florida," Academy of Management Executive, 18 (August 2004): 109–112; and Peter H. Kim and Alison R. Fragale, "Choosing the Path to Bargaining Power: An Empirical Comparison of BATNAs and Contributions in Negotiation," Journal of Applied Psychology, 90 (March 2005): 373–381.

74. See Chapter 9 in Max H. Bazerman and Margaret A. Neale, Negotiating Rationally (New York: Free Press, 1992), pp. 67–76. Also see Joan F. Brett, Gregory B. Northcraft, and Robin L. Pinkley, "Stairways to Heaven: An Interlocking Self-Regulation Model of Negotiation," Academy of Management Review, 24 (July 1999): 435–451; Geoffrey Cullinan, Jean-Marc Le Roux, and Rolf-Magnus Weddigen, "When to Walk Away from a Deal," Harvard Business Review, 82 (April 2004): 96–104; and Elliott Yama, "Purchasing Hardball, Playing Price," Business Horizons, 47 (September–October 2004): 62–66.

75. An informative and entertaining introduction to a four-step win-win model can be found in Ross R. Reck and Brian G. Long, The Win-Win Negotiator: How to Negotiate Favorable Agreements That Last (New York: Pocket Books, 1987).

76. Based on discussion in Karl Albrecht and Steve Albrecht, "Added Value Negotiating," Training, 30 (April 1993): 26–29.

77. Ibid., p. 29.

CHAPTER 16

1. As quoted in Tim Talevich, "CEO's Drive Helps Company Thrive," The Costco Connection," 23 (September 2008): 24–25.

2. See Michael G. Jacobides, "Strategy Tools for a Shifting Landscape," Harvard Business Review, 88 (January–February 2010): 76–84; and Pankaj Ghemawat, "Finding Your Strategy in the New Landscape," Harvard Business Review, 88 (March 2010): 54–60.

3. For example, see Ann Zimmerman, "'Controlled Chaos' Reigns for One Chain," Wall Street Journal (November 27–28, 2010): A4.

4. As quoted in Thomas A. Stewart and Louise O'Brien, "Execution Without Excuses," Harvard Business Review, 83 (March 2005): 106.

5. For example, see Harold Koontz and Robert W. Bradspies, "Managing Through Feedforward Control," Business Horizons, 15 (June 1972): 27.

6. Excerpted from Elizabeth Weise, "How McDonald's Makes Sure Its Burgers Are Safe," USA Today (December 30, 2009): 3B. Also see Julie Schmit, "Kellogg Scrutinizes Food Suppliers," USA Today (February 5, 2009): 1B; and Elizabeth Weise and Julie Schmit, "Nestlé Did Its Own Peanut Inspection," USA Today (March 20, 2009): 1B.

7. Catherine Arnst, "Make a List. Check It Twice," Bloomberg Businessweek (February 22, 2010): 79. For more, see Dan Heath and Chip Heath, "The Heroic Checklist," Fast Company, 123 (March 2008): 66, 68; and Liz

Szabo, "Checklist Reduces Surgery Deaths," *USA Today* (January 15, 2009): 8D.

8. Data from Atul Gawande, *The Checklist Manifesto: How to Get Things Right* (New York: Metropolitan Books, 2009), p. 44. Also see Gardiner Morse, "Health Care Needs a New Kind of Hero," *Harvard Business Review*, 88 (April 2010): 60–61.

9. See John R. Grout and John S. Toussaint, "Mistake-proofing Healthcare: Why Stopping Processes May Be a Good Start," *Business Horizons*, 53 (March–April 2010): 149–156.

10. Michael V. Copeland and Owen Thomas, "Hits & Misses," *Business 2.0*, 6 (January–February 2005): 130.

11. For a diverse selection of examples, see Barry Berman and Kunal Swani, "Managing Product Safety of Imported Chinese Goods," *Business Horizons*, 53 (January–February 2010): 39–48; Dan Reed, "Cracks in Wing Supports Found," *USA Today* (June 23, 2010): 3B; and Dan Heath and Chip Heath, "Blowing the Baton Pass," *Fast Company*, 147 (July–August 2010): 46, 48.

12. Based on Richard L. Daft and Norman B. Macintosh, "The Nature and Use of Formal Control Systems for Management Control and Strategy Implementation," *Journal of Management*, 10 (Spring 1984): 43–66.

13. See K. W. Platts and M. Sobótka, "When the Uncountable Counts: An Alternative to Monitoring Employee Performance," *Business Horizons*, 53 (July–August 2010): 349–357.

14. Based on Eric Flamholtz, "Organizational Control Systems as a Managerial Tool," *California Management Review*, 22 (Winter 1979): 50–59.

15. See Gary P. Latham and Edwin A. Locke, "Enhancing the Benefits and Overcoming the Pitfalls of Goal Setting," *Organizational Dynamics*, 35, no. 4 (2006): 332–340.

16. See Robert S. Huckman, "Are You Having Trouble Keeping Your Operations Focused?"

Harvard Business Review, 87 (September 2009): 91–95.

17. Kathy Chu, "Counterfeit Drugs Hurt Patients, Companies," *USA Today* (September 13, 2010): 2B. Also see Brian Grow, Chi-Chu Tschang, Cliff Edwards, and Brian Burnsed, "Dangerous Fakes," *Business Week* (October 13, 2008): 34–44.

18. For more, see Jeremy Shapiro, "Benchmarking the Benchmarks," *HR Magazine*, 55 (April 2010): 43–46.

19. "Google, Procter & Gamble Swap Jobs," *USA Today* (November 20, 2008): 1B.

20. See Margery Weinstein, "Part I: Keys to the Kingdom," *Training*, 45 (July–August 2008): 24–29.

21. Nanette Byrnes, "No Nonsense at Liz Claiborne," *Business Week* (July 5, 2004): 74.

22. For more on strategic control, see Michael Treacy and Jim Sims, "Take Command of Your Growth," *Harvard Business Review*, 82 (April 2004): 127–133; Holly Dolezalek, "What's in Your Budget?" *Training*, 44 (July–August 2007): 20–22; and Stefan Cedergren, Anders Wall, and Christer Norström, "Evaluation of Performance in a Product Development Context," *Business Horizons*, 53 (July–August 2010): 359–369.

23. See Jefferson Graham, "Apple Dramatically Chops iPhone Cost," *USA Today* (September 6, 2007): 1B; and "From Farm to Fork," *Fortune* (June 8, 2009): 28.

24. As quoted in "Secrets of an Undercover Boss," *Fortune* (September 27, 2010): 44.

25. See David Henry, "How Clean Are the Books?" *Business Week* (March 7, 2005): 108–110; Laureen A Maines, "Spotlight on Principles-Based Financial Reporting," *Business Horizons*, 50 (September–October 2007): 359–364; Ronald Jelinek and Kate Jelinek, "Auditors Gone Wild: The 'Other' Problem in Public Accounting," *Business Horizons*, 51 (May–June 2008): 223–233; and Kristian D. Allee, Laureen A. Maines, and David

A. Wood, "Unintended Economic Implications of Financial Reporting Standards," *Business Horizons*, 51 (September–October 2008): 371–377.

26. See Dan R. Dalton and Catherine M. Dalton, "Sarbanes-Oxley and the Guidelines of the Listing Exchanges: What Have We Wrought?" *Business Horizons*, 50 (March–April 2007): 93–100; Ann Pomeroy, "Sarbanes-Oxley Act 'Will Be Gone Soon,'" *HR Magazine*, 52 (August 2007): 12; Ann Pomeroy, "SOX Compliance Costs Still High," *HR Magazine*, 52 (September 2007): 12; and Dan R. Dalton and Catherine M. Dalton, "Corporate Governance in the Post Sarbanes-Oxley Period: Compensation Disclosure and Analysis (CD&A)," *Business Horizons*, 51 (March–April 2008): 85–92.

27. Jonathan A. Segal, "The Joy of Uncooking," *HR Magazine*, 47 (November 2002): 53. Also see Steve Rosenbush, "CFOs Are Feeling the Heat," *Business Week* (November 5, 2007): 15.

28. See Nanette Byrnes, "Green Eyeshades Never Looked So Sexy," *Business Week* (January 10, 2005): 44; and Nanette Byrnes, "The Comeback of Consulting," *Business Week* (September 3, 2007): 66–67.

29. Data from Justin Fox, "What's So Great About GE?" *Fortune* (March 4, 2002): 64–67.

30. Lawrence B. Sawyer, "Internal Auditing: Yesterday, Today, and Tomorrow," *The Internal Auditor*, 36 (December 1979): 26 (emphasis added). Also see H. David Sherman, Dennis Carey, and Robert Brust, "The Audit Committee's New Agenda," *Harvard Business Review*, 87 (June 2009): 92–99.

31. "The Stat," *Business Week* (July 19, 2004): 16.

32. This list is based in part on Donald W Murr, Harry B. Bracey Jr., and William K. Hill, "How to Improve Your Organization's Management Controls," *Management Review*, 69 (October 1980): 56–63.

33. CEO Fred Smith, as quoted in Matthew Boyle, "Fred Smith Delivers

the Goods," *Fortune* (August 23, 2004): 32.

34. Data from Del Jones, "Price of CEO Security Balloons," *USA Today* (September 8, 2009): 1B–2B.

35. See, for example, Dan Vergano, "Is It Over?" *USA Today* (July 16, 2010): 1A–2A; Chris Woodyard, "Toyota Sustains Another 'Black Eye,'" *USA Today* (July 2, 2010): 1B; Byron Acohido, "An Invitation to Crime: How a Friendly Click Can Compromise a Company," *USA Today* (March 4, 2010): 1A–2A; Gene Sloan, "On Disabled Cruise Ship, a 'Nightmare,'" *USA Today* (November 11, 2010): 1A–2A; Ben Paynter, "The Wire," *Bloomberg Businessweek* (November 29–December 5, 2010): 66–72, and Oren Dorell, "WikiLeaks Protests Use Botnets," *USA Today* (December 10, 2010): 1B.

36. Ben Levisohn and Ellen Gibson, "An Unwelcome Delivery," *Business Week* (May 4, 2009): 15. Also see Jeff Swartz, "Timberland's CEO on Standing Up to 65,000 Angry Activists," *Harvard Business Review*, 88 (September 2010): 39–43.

37. See Jia Lynn Yang, "Getting a Handle on a Scandal," *Fortune* (May 28, 2007): 26; and Ronald Heifetz, Alexander Grashow, and Marty Linsky, "Leadership in a (Permanent) Crisis," *Harvard Business Review*, 87 (July–August 2009): 62–69.

38. Christine M. Pearson and Judith A. Clair, "Reframing Crisis Management," *Academy of Management Review*, 23 (January 1998): 60. Also see Gilbert Probst and Sebastian Raisch, "Organizational Crisis: The Logic of Failure," *Academy of Management Executive*, 19 (February 2005): 90–105.

39. See Michael A. Roberto, Richard M. J. Bohmer, and Amy C. Edmondson, "Facing Ambiguous Threats," *Harvard Business Review*, 84 (November 2006): 106–113; Anisya Thomas and Lynn Fritz, "Disaster Relief, Inc.," *Harvard Business Review*, 84 (November 2006): 114–122; Judith A. Clair and Ronald L. Dufresne, "Changing

Poison into Medicine: How Companies Can Experience Positive Transformation from a Crisis," *Organizational Dynamics*, 36, no. 1 (2007): 63–77; and Ann Pomeroy "Protecting Employees in Harm's Way," *HR Magazine*, 52 (June 2007): 113–122.

40. See the definition in Elizabeth Woyke, "Getting on the Glitch List," *Business Week* (July 30, 2007): 10. See Alice M. Tybout and Michelle Roehm, "Let the Response Fit the Scandal," *Harvard Business Review*, 87 (December 2009): 82–88.

41. See Jennifer Reingold, "Mastering Disaster," *Fast Company*, 107 (July–August 2006): 38–39; Robert G. Eccles, Scott C. Newquist, and Roland Schatz, "Reputation and Its Risks," *Harvard Business Review*, 85 (February 2007): 104–114; Ariene Weintraub and Andrea Gerlin, "Lessons from the Pandemic That Wasn't," *Bloomberg Businessweek* (February 15, 2010): 24–25; and Betsy Feldman, "When the Storm Hits," *Fortune* (August 16, 2010): 12.

42. See Brahim Herbane, Dominic Elliot, and Ethne Swartz, "Contingency and Continua: Achieving Excellence Through Business Continuity Planning," *Business Horizons*, 40 (November–December 1997): 19–25; and Gardiner Morse, "What's the Plan?" *Harvard Business Review*, 82 (June 2004): 21–22.

43. Barbara Rudolph, "Coping with Catastrophe," *Time* (February 24, 1986): 53. Also see Eric Krell, "Be Ready to Meet the Press," *HR Magazine*, 54 (August 2009): 53–55.

44. William C. Symonds, "How Companies Are Learning to Prepare for the Worst," *Business Week* (December 23, 1985): 76. Also see Mark Lacter, "Face the Press. But Not Alone: How I Did It," *Inc.*, 29 (January 2007): 106–109; and Nitasha Tiku, "When Scandal Knocks," *Inc.*, 29 (August 2007): 26.

45. See Ann Zimmerman, "Wal-Mart's Emergency-Relief Team Girds for Hurricane Gustav," *Wall Street*

Journal (August 30, 2008): A3; and Beth Mirza, "Practice Violence Responses 'Just Like Fire Drills,'" *HR Magazine*, 55 (October 2010): 18.

46. "Ford Ends Tire-Replacement Program," *USA Today* (April 1, 2002): 2B. Also see David Kiley and James R. Healey, "Ford CEO Takes Recall Reins as More Questions Arise," *USA Today* (August 17, 2000): 1B–2B. Also see Rita Rubin, "FDA Says Recall of Adult Motrin 'Took Too Long,'" *USA Today* (October 1, 2010): 4A.

47. Stanley Holmes, "The New Nike," *Business Week* (September 20, 2004): 84.

48. For details about a recent winner, see Rita Zeidner, "Questing for Quality," *HR Magazine*, 55 (July 2010): 25–28.

49. Chris Woodyard, Bruce Horovitz, Gary Strauss, and Anne Willette, "Quality Guru Now Plugs Innovation," *USA Today* (February 27, 1998): 8B.

50. Philip B. Crosby, *Quality Without Tears: The Art of Hassle-Free Management* (New York: Plume, 1984), p. 64. For more, see Philip B. Crosby, *Completeness: Quality for the 21st Century* (New York: Dutton, 1992), p. 116. Also see Stephen Baker, "Why 'Good Enough' Is Good Enough," *Business Week* (September 3, 2007): 48.

51. Adapted in part from Ron Zemke, "A Bluffer's Guide to TQM," *Training*, 30 (April 1993): 48–55.

52. See Debanjan Mitra and Peter N. Golder, "Quality Is in the Eye of the Beholder," *Harvard Business Review*, 85 (April 2007): 26, 28.

53. See Lorrie Grant, "Don't Let Bargain 'Cashmere' Pull the Wool over Your Eyes," *USA Today* (December 10, 2004): 6B.

54. For more, see www .consumerreports.org.

55. Alex Taylor, "Hyundai Smokes the Competition," *Fortune* (January 18, 2010): 65.

56. Stratford Sherman, "How to Prosper in the Value Decade," *Fortune* (November 30, 1992): 91. Also see Gerald E. Smith and Thomas T. Nagle, "Frames of Reference and Buyers' Perception

of Price and Value," *California Management Review,* 38 (Fall 1995): 98–116.

57. See Robert C. Ford and David E. Bowen, "A Service-Dominant Logic for Management Education: It's Time," *Academy of Management Learning and Education,* 7 (June 2008): 224–243; and Andrew Von Nordenflycht, "What Is a Professional Service Firm? Toward a Theory and Taxonomy of Knowledge-Intensive Firms," *Academy of Management Review,* 35 (January 2010): 155–174.

58. Data from "Largest U.S. Corporations," *Fortune* (May 3, 2010): F1, F42.

59. Data from Patricia Sellers, "Getting Customers to Love You," *Fortune* (March 13, 1989): 38–49.

60. Data from Patricia Sellers, "What Customers Really Want," *Fortune* (June 4, 1990): 58–68.

61. Excerpted from Peter Nulty, "The National Business Hall of Fame," *Fortune* (April 5, 1993): 112, 114.

62. Data from Toddi Gutner, "Where Phone Service Is Warm and Fuzzy," *Business Week* (July 5, 2004): 103. For an interesting update, see Michael Arndt, "L.L. Bean Follows Its Shoppers to the Web," *Bloomberg Businessweek* (March 1, 2010): 43.

63. Based on discussions in M. Jill Austin, "Planning in Service Organizations," *SAM Advanced Management Journal,* 55 (Summer 1990): 7–12; Everett E. Adam Jr. and Paul M. Swamidass, "Assessing Operations Management from a Strategic Perspective," *Journal of Management,* 15 (June 1989): 181–203; Ron Zemke, "The Emerging Art of Service Management," *Training,* 29 (January 1992): 37–42; and Tim Breitbarth, Rob Mitchell, and Rob Lawson, "Service Performance Measurement in a New Zealand Local Government Organization," *Business Horizons,* 53 (July-August 2010): 397–403.

64. See, for example, Lorna Doucet, "Service Provider Hostility and Service Quality," *Academy of Management Journal,* 47 (October 2004): 761–771; Patricia B. Barger and Alicia A. Grandey,

"Service with a Smile and Encounter Satisfaction: Emotional Contagion and Appraisal Mechanisms," *Academy of Management Journal,* 49 (December 2006): 1229–1238; Markus Groth, Thorsten Hennig-Thurau, and Gianfranco Walsh, "Customer Reactions to Emotional Labor: The Roles of Employee Acting Strategies and Customer Detection Accuracy," *Academy of Management Journal,* 52 (October 2009): 958–974; and Devin Leonard, "Mad as Hell," *Bloomberg Businessweek* (August 16–29, 2010): 5–6.

65. Excerpted from "IT Plan Results in Significant Service Enhancements," *Financial Horizons* (Summer 2010): 2.

66. Ron Zemke and Dick Schaaf, *The Service Edge: 101 Companies That Profit from Customer Care* (New York: New American Library, 1989), p. 14. Also see Dave Dougherty and Ajay Murthy, "What Service Customers Really Want," *Harvard Business Review,* 87 (September 2009): 22; and Tony Hsieh, "Zappos's CEO on Going to Extremes for Customers," *Harvard Business Review,* 88 (July–August 2010): 41–45.

67. See Leonard L. Berry, A. Parasuraman, and Valarie A. Zeithaml, "The Service-Quality Puzzle," *Business Horizons,* 31 (September–October 1988): 35–43; Leonard L. Berry, A. Parasuraman, and Valarie A. Zeithaml, "Improving Service Quality in America: Lessons Learned," *Academy of Management Executive,* 8 (May 1994): 32–45; Leonard L. Berry, Kathleen Seiders, and Larry G. Gresham, "For Love and Money: The Common Traits of Successful Retailers," *Organizational Dynamics,* 26 (Autumn 1997): 7–23; Kathleen Seiders and Leonard L. Berry, "Service Fairness: What It Is and Why It Matters," *Academy of Management Executive,* 12 (May 1998): 8–20; Leonard L. Berry, Eileen A. Wall, and Lewis P. Carbone, "Service Clues and Customer Assessment of the Service Experience," *Academy*

of Management Perspectives, 20 (May 2006): 43–57; and Venkatesh Shankar, Leonard L. Berry, and Thomas Dotzel, "A Practical Guide to Combining Products and Services," *Harvard Business Review,* 87 (November 2009): 94–99.

68. Based on Paul Hellman, "Rating Your Dentist," *Management Review,* 87 (July–August 1998): 64.

69. See Leonard L. Berry and Ann M. Mirabito, "Innovative Healthcare Delivery," *Business Horizons,* 53 (March–April 2010): 157–169; and Matthew Dixon, Karen Freeman, and Nicholas Toman, "Stop Trying to Delight Your Customers," *Harvard Business Review,* 88 (July–August 2010): 116–122.

70. For example, see Thomas J. Douglas and William Q. Judge Jr., "Total Quality Management Implementation and Competitive Advantage: The Role of Structural Control and Exploration," *Academy of Management Journal,* 44 (February 2001): 158–169; William Roth and Terry Capuano, "Systemic Versus Nonsystemic Approaches to Quality Improvement," *Journal of Organizational Excellence,* 20 (Spring 2001): 57–64; Richard S. Allen and Ralph H. Kilmann, "Aligning Reward Practices in Support of Total Quality Management," *Business Horizons,* 44 (May–June 2001): 77–84; and Darius Mehri, "The Darker Side of Lean: An Insider's Perspective on the Realities of the Toyota Production System," *Academy of Management Perspectives,* 20 (May 2006): 21–42.

71. Inspired by a more lengthy definition in Marshall Sashkin and Kenneth J. Kiser, *Total Quality Management* (Seabrook, Md.: Ducochon Press, 1991), p. 25. Another good introduction to TQM is Arthur R. Tenner and Irving J. DeToro, *Total Quality Management: Three Steps to Continuous Improvement* (Reading, Mass.: Addison-Wesley, 1992). Also see the entire July 1994 issue of *Academy of Management Review.*

72. Richard J. Schonberger, "Total Quality Management Cuts a Broad

Swath—Through Manufacturing and Beyond," *Organizational Dynamics*, 20 (Spring 1992): 18.

73. "Aiming for the Stars at Philips," Special Advertising Section, Quality '92: Leading the World-Class Company, *Time* (September 21, 1992): 26.

74. See Brian Burnsed and Emily Thornton, "The Six Sigma Black Belts Are Back," *Business Week* (September 21, 2009): 64–65; and Theresa Minton-Eversole, "Lean Overtakes Six Sigma," *HR Magazine*, 55 (April 2010): 14.

75. Adapted and condensed from David E. Bowen and Edward E. Lawler III, "Total Quality-Oriented Human Resources Management," *Organizational Dynamics*, 20 (Spring 1992): Exhibit 1, 29–41.

76. See David J. Lynch, "Made in China," *USA Today* (July 3, 2007): 1B–2B; Bruce Horovitz, Greg Farrell, and Sharon Silke Carty, "Mattel's Stellar Reputation Tainted," *USA Today* (August 15, 2007): 1B–2B; and Jayne O'Donnell, "Mattel Recalls More Toys for Lead," *USA Today* (September 5, 2007): 1B.

77. Richard J. Schonberger, *Japanese Manufacturing Techniques: Nine Hidden Lessons in Simplicity* (New York: Free Press, 1982), p. 35.

78. Lorrie Grant, "Pastry Chef's Surprising Flavors Spell Sweet Success," *USA Today* (May 10, 2004): 3B.

79. See Roger Martin, "The Age of Customer Capitalism," *Harvard Business Review*, 88 (January–February 2010): 58–65.

80. See "How to: Know Your Customer Better," *Inc.* Guidebook, no. 16, in *Inc.*, 31 (September 2009): 1–4; Kasey Wehrum, "Sales Tips from the World's Toughest Customers," *Inc.*, 32 (April 2010): 94–97; and Brendan Gray, "Fine Tuning Market Oriented Practices," *Business Horizons*, 53 (July–August 2010): 371–383.

81. Laura Petrecca, "Popchips CEO Is an Eternal 'Poptimist,'" *USA Today* (April 12, 2010): 3B. Also see Rob Markey, Fred Reichheld, and Andreas Dullweber, "Closing the Customer Feedback Loop," *Harvard Business Review*, 87 (December 2009): 43–47.

82. Robert Levering and Milton Moskowitz, "100 Best Companies to Work For: The Rankings," *Fortune* (February 4, 2008): 77.

83. "R. Todd Bradley," *Business Week* (May 11, 2009): 35.

84. Based on discussion in Richard J. Schonberger, "Is Strategy Strategic? Impact of Total Quality Management on Strategy," *Academy of Management Executive*, 6 (August 1992): 80–87.

85. See Edward E. Lawler III, "Total Quality Management and Employee Involvement: Are They Compatible?" *Academy of Management Executive*, 8 (February 1994): 68–76.

86. Sashkin and Kiser, *Total Quality Management*, p. 42.

87. Based on discussion in Mary Walton, *Deming Management at Work* (New York: Perigee, 1990), p. 16.

88. See Brad Kenney, "Whatever Happened to Quality?" *Industry Week* (April 2008): 42–47.

89. W. Edwards Deming, *Out of the Crisis* (Cambridge, Mass.: MIT Press, 1986), p. 5.

90. See Figure 5 in Deming, *Out of the Crisis*, p. 88.

91. Gary D. Fackler, "Barrett Calls for Rededication to Intel Values," *Intel Circuit* (July 14, 2004): 3.

92. Adapted from discussion in Deming, *Out of the Crisis*, pp. 23–96; and Howard S. Gitlow and Shelly J. Gitlow, *The Deming Guide to Quality and Competitive Position* (Englewood Cliffs, N.J.: Prentice-Hall, 1987). Also see M. R. Yilmaz and Sangit Chatterjee, "Deming and the Quality of Software Development," *Business Horizons*, 40 (November–December 1997): 51–58.

93. Deming, *Out of the Crisis*, p. 59.

94. The debate is framed in Paula Phillips Carson and Kerry D. Carson, "Deming Versus Traditional Management Theorists on Goal Setting: Can Both Be Right?" *Business Horizons*, 36 (September–October 1993): 79–84.

95. Deming, *Out of the Crisis*, p. 24.

INDEXES

NAME INDEX

Abella, Alicia, 425
Ackoff, Russell, 230
Acohido, Byron, 119
Adams, James L., 232
Adams, Scott, 18, 157, 272
Adizes, Ichak, 37, 422
Adkerson, Richard C., 188
Adler, Nancy, 95
Affuso, Julian, 283
Aggarwal, Raj, 346
Albrecht, Karl, 438
Albrecht, Steve, 438
Alexander the Great, 396
Alice in Wonderland, 335
Alvarez, Carmen, 348
Amabile, Teresa M., 344
Amin, Idi, 121
Anand, Vikas, 136
Anderson, Ben, 205
Ariely, Dan, 220, 355
Arndt, Michael, 389
Asch, Solomon, 371–372
Ashforth, Blake, 136
Asinof, Lynn, 260
Auletta, Ken, 183
Ayub, Tahir, 114

Bacigalupo, Tony, 314
Bagley, Nate, 194
Bain, Alexander, 83
Baird, Julia, 14
Baker, Stephen, 46
Baldoni, John, 316
Baldwin, Bobby, 234–235
Ball, Lucille, 32
Ballmer, Steve, 25
Ballon, Marc, 22
Bander, Joseph, 259
Barley, Stephen, 82
Barnard, Chester I., 50–51, 59, 219
Barrett, Craig, 467
Bartolomé, Fernando, 379
Bartz, Carol, 423

Bass, Bernard M., 401, 402
Bean, Leon Leonwood, 460
Beckham, Victoria, 107
Bedbury, Scott, 20
Belling, Keith, 462–463
Bello, Marisol, 89
Bennett, Drake, 70
Benton, Emilia, 52
Berfield, Susan, 389
Bernasek, Anna, 160
Beyer, Janice M., 262
Bezos, Jeffrey P., 24, 155, 184, 392
Birch, David, 22
Blake, Robert R., 411
Blanchard, Kenneth, 56
Blankenship, George, 447
Blauwet, Cheri, 275
Bloom, Nicholas, 109
Blount, Sally, 98
Bluestein, Adam, 63
Blum, Justin, 114
Blumberg, Matt, 472
Bock, Laszlo, 269
Bonaparte, Napoleon, 396
Bonilla, Claire, 375
Bontempo, Robert, 121
Bossidy, Larry, 57
Boudway, Ira, 70
Boukadoum, Salah, 129
Bourzac, Katherine, 82
Bowlin, John, 389
Bradley, R. Todd, 464
Brady, Diane, 99, 194, 392
Bragg, Terry, 4
Brandon, David, 39
Bregman, Peter, 382
Brennan, Troyen, 475
Brenneman, Gregory D., 434
Bridges, Carolyn, 147
Brin, Sergey, 374
Briody, Dan, 313
Brodbeck, Felix C., 110
Brodsky, Norm, 208

Buchanan, Leigh, 61, 344
Buckingham, Marcus, 400
Buffett, Warren, 330
Burck, Charles, 57
Burgess, Calvin, 100
Burke, Warner, 427
Burns, James McGregor, 401
Burns, Tom, 37, 247, 248, 249, 263, 401
Burns, Ursula, 265
Busch, Kyle, 378
Bush, George W., 76
Bush, Jim, 48
Buxton, Winslow, 245
Byrne, John A., 57, 253

Cadrain, Diane, 289
Caldwell, Kelly, 375
Callagee, Cathy, 293
Campa, Gregg, 308
Campagnino, John, 273
Campbell, Amy, 13–14
Campion, Michael A., 279
Cappon, Daniel, 214
Carbonara, Peter, 475
Carey, Anne R., 128
Carney, Dana, 413
Carr, Nicholas, 311
Carroll, Archie B., 127, 139
Carrubba, Frank P., 461
Carter, Keith, 436
Carter, Majora, 229
Cartwright, Dorwin, 363
Casale, Alfred, 474
Chambers, John, 253, 298
Champy, James, 56
Chappell, Tom, 437
Charan, Ram, 57
Charron, Paul R., 453
Chenault, Kenneth, 48, 160
Cheops, 37
Cheshire Cat, 335
Chiquet, Maureen, 295–296
Cho, Emily, 305

Chouinard, Yvon, 132, 344
Christensen, John, 57
Chu, Kathy, 119
Claflin, Bruce L., 250
Clair, Judith, 457
Clampitt, Phillip G., 301–302, 318
Clemens, John, 317
Clifton, Donald O., 408–409
Cloke, Kenneth, 441
Coleman, Bill, 343
Collins, Bill, 12
Collins, James C., 56, 57, 273
Colvin, Geoffrey, 16, 68, 265, 367
Corcoran, Bob, 414–415
Coron, Edith, 94
Covey, Stephen R., 56, 436
Cowen, Tyler, 441–442
Coy, Peter, 282
Craig, Bruce, 405
Crosby, Philip B., 45, 59, 458, 459
Cross, Kelvin F., 453
Crystal, Graef, 354–355
Culbert, Samuel A., 280
Cuthbert, Kimberly Davis, 462

Dachis, Jeffrey, 174
Daft, Richard, 298
Dahl, Darren, 375, 385, 417, 443, 460
Dale, Richard, 363–364
Daley, Richard M., 90–91
Daniels, John D., 112
Dann, Jeremy B., 330
Darby, Joseph, 142
Davenport, Thomas H., 269
Davidson, Paul, 233, 404
Davis, Keith, 297
Day, Christine, 405
De la Cruz, Rosemary, 322
Dehne, Jason, 356
Del Rey, Jason, 472
Dell, Michael, 403, 448
Deming, W. Edwards, 11, 37, 44, 55, 59,
    163, 244, 466–468, 469
Demos, Telis, 409
Derr, Jeremy, 447–448
Dess, Gregory G., 193
Dewey, Joy, 287
Dolan, Paul, 127–128
Donnelly, James H., Jr., 246
Dorfman, Peter, 105, 110
Dowling, Daisy Wademan, 296
Dragone, Franco, 235, 236
Drake, Michael, 94
Drexler, Mickey, 295, 296
Drucker, Peter F., 37, 55, 150, 161, 162,
    226, 256, 394, 414, 467
Duarte, Deborah L., 376
Dugas, Christine, 134
Duncan, Gino, 147
Dunlap, Al, 374

Dunn, Brian, 194
Durkee, Brian, 120
Dykstra, Tod, 450

Eaton, Robert J., 129
Ebbers, Bernard, 76
Edelman, Richard, 131
Edison, Thomas, 224, 229
Edmondson, Amy C., 244
Edmunds, Mimi, 292
Edwards, Cliff, 450
Einhorn, Bruce, 30, 96, 119
Ellin, Abby, 129
Ellison, Marvin R., 311
Elmer, Vickie, 279
Emerson, Ralph Waldo, 294
Eno, Richard, 83
Esty, Daniel C., 200

Fakhraldeen, Sarah, 226
Falbe, Cecilia M., 390
Fayol, Henri, 15–16, 37, 39–41, 50, 59
Feigenbaum, Armand V., 45, 59
Fellini, Federico, 234
Fernando, Katherine Ann, 112
Ferraro, Gary P., 113
Fiedler, Fred, 37, 399–400, 401, 411
Finkelstein, Sydney, 217
Fisher, Anne, 370
Fisher, Linda, 12
Fleiss, Jenny, 191
Follett, Mary Parker, 37, 47, 48
Ford, Bill, Jr., 179, 180
Ford, Henry, 224, 241
Fortt, Jon, 292
Fox, Adrienne, 327
Foxton, Josh, 287
Franklin, Ben, 152
Friend, William, 306
Fudge, Ann, 423

Galbraith, Jay R., 258
Gantt, Henry L., 43, 44, 170, 176
Gardner, John W., 34
Garvin, David A., 244, 263
Gates, Bill, 25, 84, 330, 419
Gates, Robert, 257
Gautam, Vijay, 30
Gauthier, Daniel, 235
Gaylord, Sarah R., 279
Gee, Tom, 180, 181
George, Bill, 137
Gerzema, John, 61
Gibson, James L., 246
Gilbreth, Frank, 37, 43
Gilbreth, Lillian, 37, 43
Gino, Francesca, 244
Gladwell, Malcolm, 57
Glass, David, 345
Gokhale, Ketchki, 30
Gold, Mitchell, 62

Goldberg, Gary, 225
Goldberg, Lee, 23
Goldsmith, Joan, 441
Goleman, Daniel, 396–397, 411
Gonzales, Amy, 375
Gonzalez, Lola, 404
Gooden, Van, 91
Gordon, Jack, 376
Govindarajan, Vijay, 434
Graham, Katherine, 18
Graham, Stuart, 126
Greenberg, Elizabeth, 292
Greenblatt, Drew, 68
Greenleaf, Robert K., 404, 411
Griffin, Emily, 178, 355
Grossman, Robert J., 397
Grove, Andrew S., 10, 56, 255
Gunther, Marc, 8
Gupta, Vipin, 105, 110
Gurchiek, Kathy, 349

Hackman, J., 338
Hagwood, Neil, 30
Haines, Stephen, 186, 420
Haley, Fiona, 432
Hall, David E., 371
Hall, Edward T., 102, 104, 106
Hammer, Michael, 56
Hamoui, Omar, 256
Hampden-Turner, Charles, 103
Handy, Charles, 37
Hanges, Paul, 105, 110
Harrington, Noreen, 141
Harris, Jeanne, 269
Hart, Stuart L., 186
Hastings, Reed, 213
Hawley, Casey, 178
Hayward, Tony, 140
Headrick, Darin, 321
Heath, Chip, 199, 421
Heath, Dan, 199, 421
Hechinger, John, 308
Herzberg, Frederick, 328, 331–332,
    338, 352
Hesselbein, Frances, 393
Hewitt, Steve, 413–414
Hill, Gayle W., 224
Hilton, Paris, 107
Hinz, Werner, 221
Hitt, Michael A., 57, 58
Hofstede, Geert, 37, 108, 116
Hogan, Scott, 384
Holtom, Brooks C., 283
Holtsberg, Warren, 196
Horovitz, Bruce, 156
Horton, Robert, 226
Hosmer, 139
House, Robert J., 104, 105, 110,
    400–401
Hsieh, Tony, 3–4, 266–267
Hu Jintao, 372

Hudson, Eric, 30, 205, 472
Hufbauer, Gary, 81
Hughes, Jonathan, 432
Hurd, Mark, 191
Hurst, Mark, 312
Hussein, Saddam, 12
Hyatt, Joshua, 323
Hyman, Jenn, 191

Iacocca, Lee, 56, 255
Iem, Michael, 226–227
Iglesias, Brian, 20
Ignatius, Adi, 218
Immelt, Jeffrey R., 260, 414
Ingersoll, Minnie, 78
Inkson, Kerr, 99
Insch, Gary S., 112
Ireland, R. Duane, 57, 58
Ishikawa, Kaoru, 11, 37, 44, 59
Ivancevich, John M., 246

Jackson, Michael, 101
Janis, Irving, 372–373
Jarman, Max, 79
Jasinowski, Jerry, 68
Javidan, Mansour, 105, 110
Jayson, Sharon, 137, 313
Jewell, Linda N., 366
Jewell, Sally, 276
Jo, Mahendra, 136
Jobs, Steve, 38, 83, 132, 254, 394–395
John, Brad, 178
Johnson, Carla, 281
Johnson, Gail, 293
Johnson, Martha, 260
Johnson, Ron, 447
Johnson, Spencer, 56, 57
Jones, Carmen, 276
Jones, Del, 205
Jones, Hannah, 393
Jones, Papa Jo, 36
Jossi, Frank, 357
Jung, Andrea, 257, 388, 396
Juran, Joseph M., 37, 45, 55,
    59, 465
Juskalian, Russ, 38

Kacmar, Donna, 224
Kadlec, Dan, 78, 128
Kahn, Herman, 201
Kaiman, Lisa, 173
Kalmanek, Chuck, 425
Kamvar, Sep, 72
Kanter, Rosabeth Moss, 348
Kaplan, Amy, 123
Katzenberg, Jeffrey, 420
Kawasaki, Guy, 24
Kaye, Alan, 64
Kayes, D. Christopher, 100
Keighley, Geoff, 236
Kelleher, Herb, 25, 272–273, 401

Kelleher, Kevin, 184
Kellerman, Barbara, 374
Kelly, Clinton, 305
Kelly, Gwendolyn, 364
Kennedy, John, 392
Kensington, Larry, 316
Keys, Alicia, 329
Khan, Hani, 88–89
Kimani, Mungai, 122
Kindler, Jeffrey, 125
King, Martin Luther, Jr., 392
Kirchhoff, Bruce A., 21–22
Kirkpatrick, David, 151
Kirkpatrick, Donald L., 285, 290
Kistler, Matt, 165
Kiuchi, Tachi, 127
Klingelsmith, Bill, 310
Koehn, Nancy, 25
Kolditz, Tom, 199
Kopchinski, John, 125, 126
Kotter, John P., 426
Kowitt, Beth, 302
Kozlowski, Dennis, 76
Krafcik, John, 334
Kram, Kathy, 405
Kruguyrova, 333
Krupa, Gene, 36
Kumar, Sanjay, 76
Kuttner, Robert, 129

Lady Gaga, 305
Lafley, Alan G., 260–261
Laliberté, Guy, 235
Lamarre, Daniel, 235, 236
Latham, Gary P., 334, 335
Lauerman, John, 145
Lawler, Edward, 331
Lee, Mark, 119
Leiberman, David, 14
Leira, Kåre, 46
Lencioni, Patrick M., 317, 330
Lengel, Robert, 298
Leonard, Dorothy, 220
Leondis, Alexis, 355
Lepird, Jennifer, 409
Levering, Robert, 404
Levine, Stuart R., 317
Lewin, Kurt, 428
Lichtenstein, Benjamin
    Bregmann, 53
Lincoln, Abraham, 392
Lindquist, Lee, 442
Lively, John, 472
Lloyd, Glynn, 322–323
Locke, Edwin A., 334, 335
Lockwood, Nancy, 126
Longenecker, Clinton O., 382
Lorenz, Edward, 52
Lorenzi, Peter, 395
Löscher, Peter, 137
Lubin, David A., 200

Lubit, Roy, 220
Lublin, Joann S., 123
Lucas, George, 343
Lumpkin, G. T., 193
Lundberg, Craig C., 39
Lundin, Stephen C., 57
Luthans, Fred, 54
Lynch, Richard L., 453

Mackey, John, 156
MacLeod, Calum, 119
Madoff, Bernard, 76, 134
Magretta, Joan, 4
Maher, Grahame, 106
Maier, Matthew, 82
Majchrzak, Ann, 376
Malhotra, Arvind, 376
Malik, Om, 82
Manjoo, Farhad, 448
Mao Zedong, 107
March, James G., 285
Marchesini, Peter, 284
Markham, Julie, 13
Marklein, Mary Beth, 13
Martens, Phil, 179, 180, 181
Martin, C. F., 63
Martin, Chris, 62–63
Martin, Claire Frances, 63
Marx, Elisabeth, 111
Maslow, Abraham H., 328–331, 332,
    352, 361
Matlack, Carol, 10
Matsuda, Craig, 321
Mauboussin, Michael J., 209
Maury, Frédéric, 94
Mayer, Marissa, 106
Mayo, Elton, 37, 47
McAllaster, Craig M., 57
McCoy, Tony, 333
McCrum, Robert, 107
McDevitt, Jack, 73
McGahey, Jesse, 427
McGregor, Douglas, 47, 48–49
McKinstry, Nancy, 108
McMillon, Doug, 230
McNair, C. J., 453
Mehmood, Sajid, 226
Meinert, Dori, 142
Meister, Jeanne C., 65
Meussner, Mark, 326
Meyer, Erin, 94
Meyer, Ron, 387
Meyerson, Debra E., 429
Midamba, Noah, 121, 122
Miles, Raymond E., 154
Miles, Stephen A., 99
Miller, Eduardo, 187
Mintzberg, Henry, 2, 18, 195
Mironov, Vladimir, 88
Mitchell, Terence R., 400
Moen, Phyllis, 357

Moffett, James R., 188
Molina, Joshua, 425
Montgomery, John, 261
Monty, Scott, 194
Moore, James F., 56, 191–192
Moore, Joe, 91
Moore, Kenny, 428
Morgan, Pat, 375
Morse, Gardiner, 36
Morton, Rob, 261
Moskovitz, Dustin, 151
Moskowitz, Milton, 404
Muir, Cecelia, 349
Mulally, Alan R., 198, 259, 402
Mulcahy, Anne, 315, 392, 418
Myers, Kelly, 32–33

Nader, Ralph, 142
Nadler, David A., 418, 419, 439
Nam, Nguyen Than, 96
Nash, Laura L., 140
Navratilova, Martina, 334
Nelson, Willie, 101
Neubert, Mitchell, 382
Nichols, Scott, 337
Nohria, Nitin, 145
Nonaka, Kiujiro, 220
Nooyi, Indra, 6, 182, 418
Novak, William, 56
Nussenbaum, Evelyn, 304

Obama, Barack, 74, 257
Oldham, G., 338
Olson, Philip D., 24
Opton, Dave, 436
Orman, Suze, 396
Otellini, Paul, 252
Ouchi, William, 56

Pachter, Barbara, 362
Page, Larry, 257, 374
Page, Susan, 255
Palmer, Robert, 222
Palmisano, Samuel J., 228, 308
Pareto, Vilfredo, 465
Parker, Mark, 210
Paskin, Janet, 225
Patil, Prabhaker, 180, 181
Patton, Bruce, 431
Paul, Harry, 57
Paulus, Ronald, 474, 475
Pavlo, Walt, 135
Pearson, Christine, 457
Peña, Cotumanama "Toby", 322
Perlmutter, Howard, 99–100, 101
Pescovitz, David, 82
Peters, Sharon L., 350
Peters, Thomas J., 55–56, 57,
        58, 458
Petrecca, Laura, 20, 134

Pfeffer, Jeffrey, 58, 239, 272, 273, 280,
        290, 378, 388
Phillips, Bryce, 89, 266
Pilger, Christy, 122
Pilger, Dale, 121–122
Pilger, Eric, 122
Pilger, Nancy, 121–123
Pinchot, Gifford, 84–85
Pistorius, Brian, 384
Pitt, Brad, 455
Pittman, Robert, 183
Podolny, Joel, 359, 360
Polk, Rustin, 385
Porras, Jerry I., 56
Porter, Michael E., 189, 190, 192, 203, 360
Powell, Colin, 394
Pursell, Elliott D., 279

Rachner, Richard, 121
Raftery, Dan, 361
Raggio, Randle D., 148
Rahim, Ahmed, 120, 383
Rath, Tom, 408–409
Raynor, Michael, 156
Reed, Brian, 260
Reed, Dan, 451
Reichheld, Frederick F., 460
Reingold, Jennifer, 31–33
Reitz, Bonnie, 214
Reitz, H. Joseph, 366
Resnick, Bruce G., 57
Ressler, Cali, 356, 357
Richey, Samantha, 226
Rigby, Craig, 181
Roberts, Dexter, 114
Roberts, Wayne, 327
Robinson, Alan, 225
Rockefeller, John D., 126
Rockwood, Kate, 165
Roddick, Anita, 92
Rodgers, T. J., 162
Rokeach, Milton, 145
Romney, Mitt, 304
Rosen, Benson, 376
Rosener, Judy B., 397
Rosenfeld, Irene, 389
Rosensweig, Dan, 348
Rosing, Wayne, 346
Ross, Blake, 22
Ross, Gary, 289
Ross, Jerry, 216
Rothkopf, David, 102
Rowe, Mike, 336
Rowley, Coleen, 141
Rubin, Rita, 125, 289
Ruder, Brian, 211
Ruettgers, Michael C., 306
Ruimin, Zhang, 467
Russell, Steve, 211
Ruta, Gwen, 190

Sabin, Margaret, 350
Sachs, Vanda, 305
Sacks, Danielle, 393
Sadler-Smith, Eugene, 215
Saffo, Paul, 202
Salter, Chuck, 181, 229
Samuelson, Paul, 78
Sandler, Joanne, 396
Sandoval, Edgar, 368
Sankaran, Anand, 180, 181
Sauer, Patrick J., 317
Scanlan, Ed, 383–385
Schaefer, Kimberly, 454
Schein, Edgar, 240
Schiavoni, Angie, 72
Schlei, Andy, 292
Schlesinger, Leonard A., 426
Schmidt, Eric, 119, 196
Schmit, Julie, 190
Scholfield, Roger, 442
Schonberger, Richard, 461–462
Schrage, Michael, 137
Schuler, Randall S., 463
Schultz, Howard, 206–207, 218, 225, 330
Schwartz, Ariel, 246
Seidman, Dov, 377
Semel, Terry, 342
Sencion, John, 178
Seng, Chew Choon, 160
Senge, Peter, 244
Sexton, John, 308
Shabazz, Betty, 329
Shakespeare, 364
Shapiro, Jeremy, 269
Shefy, Erella, 215
Sherwin, Elton B., 22
Shewhart, Walter A., 44, 59, 467
Silver-Greenberg, Jessica, 355
Simkins, Betty J., 346
Skilling, Jeffrey, 76
Skinner, B. F., 406, 407, 411
Smircich, Linda, 262
Smisek, Jeff, 342
Smith, Adam, 128, 129, 241
Smith, Douglas, 240
Smith, Fred, 198, 455
Smolens, Michael, 110–111
Smucker, Richard K., 185
Smunt, Timothy L., 57
Snow, Charles C., 154
Snyder, Nancy Tennant, 376
Squillante, Frank, 390
Stafford, Ed, 134
Stahl, Moran, 121
Stalker, G. M., 37, 247, 248, 249, 263
Staw, Barry M., 216
Steele, Glenn, 473–475
Stegenga, Kurt, 322
Stemberg, Tom, 360
Stephens, Rex, 312

Sternberg, Robert J., 403
Still, Del J., 274
Stokes, Pat, 432
Stone, Linda, 311
Strauss, Frederick, 241
Sulkowicz, Kerry J., 154, 373
Sullivan, Dan, 159
Surowiecki, James, 222
Sutton, Robert I., 359
Sutton, Terry, 192
Swap, Walter, 220
Swartz, Jon, 153
Synnott, Kathleen, 85

Tapscott, Don, 14–15, 320
Tate, Patricia, 79
Tavares, Jose, 322
Taylor, Frederick W., 37, 41–43, 45, 54, 59, 170, 176
Thamhain, Hans. J., 377
Thiry, Kent, 239, 240
Thomas, Dave, 401
Thomas, David C., 99
Thomas, R. Roosevelt, Jr., 275
Thompson, James D., 249
Thompson, Jody, 356, 357
Thompson, John, 392
Thorndike, Edward L., 406
Thornton, B. Terry, 286
Tjosvold, Dean, 374, 416, 431, 432
Tkaczyk, Christopher, 48, 276
Tolva, John, 102
Torti, Maria, 168
Torvalds, Linus, 258
Tramiel, Jack, 364
Trap, Paul, 128
Trice, Harrison M., 262
Triebnig, Wolfgang, 309
Trimble, Chris, 434
Trimble, Kathy, 259
Trompenaars, Fons, 103
Trotman, Alex, 180
Truman, Harry, 255
Trump, Donald, 56, 368

Tsao, Audrey, 339
Tunstall, Joan, 312
Tushman, Michael L., 418, 419, 439

Valencia, Bert, 101
Van Reenen, John, 109
Vesterman, Jim, 358
Villalta, Paula, 335
von Bertalanffy, Ludwig, 51
von Oech, Roger, 225
Vroom, Victor H., 332

Walter, Elisse, 255
Walton, Bill, 404
Walton, Helen, 21
Walton, Sam, 21, 90, 238, 335, 345, 401
Wang, William, 446
Warren, James, 91
Washington, George, 396
Waterman, Robert H., Jr., 55–56, 57, 58
Watkins, Sherron Smith, 141
Watson, John B., 406
Webb, C. A., 205
Webb, Chick, 36
Webber, Sheila Simsarian, 168
Weber, Max, 37
Wederspahn, Gary, 121
Wei Chen, 93, 94
Weinstein, Bruce, 124
Weintraub, Arlene, 125
Weiss, Jeff, 432
Welch, Jack, 57, 216, 256, 268, 362, 376, 386, 414
Welch, Suzy, 216, 268, 362, 376, 386
Wellins, Richard, 31
Welsh, Patrick, 316
Wenner, Jann, 214
West, Amanda, 286
Westlund-Deenihan, Sandra, 233
Weston, Marti, 68
White, Christine, 309
Whitman, Meg, 75
Whitney, Larry, 432

Wieners, Brad, 222
Wigand, Jeffrey, 141
Williams, Archie, 360
Williams, Bob, 62
Willyerd, Karie, 65
Wilson, Clark L., 17, 26
Wilson, Craig, 343
Winston, Stephanie, 18
Winter, Caroline, 25, 72
Winterkorn, Martin, 195
Wiseman, Paul, 30
Witherspoon, Bill, 248–249
Witherspoon, Reese, 396
Wolfe, Jackson, 121
Womack, Brian, 119
Wong, Andrea, 360
Wooden, John, 404
Woodward, Joan, 37
Wozniak, Steve, 38
Wright, Aliah D., 321
Wright, Mary Ann, 179, 181
Wulfe, Mandy, 309

Yamazaki, Yoshitaka, 100
Yang, Jae, 436
Yeramyan, Pontish, 302
Yi Shen, Elisabeth, 94
Yorke, James, 52
Yukl, Gary, 390

Zachary, G. Pascal, 82
Zakaria, Fareed, 119
Zaleznik, Abraham, 394, 405, 431
Zand, Dale E., 378–379
Zander, Alvin, 363
Zemke, Ron, 19
Zey, Michael, 88
Zildjian, Avedis, 35, 36
Zildjian, Craigie, 35, 36
Zolli, Andrew, 205
Zuckerberg, Mark, 151, 152, 153
Zugheri, David, 417, 418, 443
Zuziak, Eric, 113

ORGANIZATIONAL INDEX

ABB Power Technologies, 187
Abercrombie & Fitch, 89
Accenture, 30
Accurate Background Check, 404
Acropolis, 241
Adelphia, 76
AdMob, 256
ADP Screening and Selection Services, 274
Aetna Life & Casualty, 337, 475

Aflac, 450–451
AK Environmental, 375
Amazon.com, 3, 24, 155, 184, 392
American Background Information Services Inc. (ABI), 274
American College of Cardiology, 474
American Express, 48, 160, 354
American Heart Association, 474
American Management Association (AMA), 18, 312

American Society for Testing and Materials, 106
Analytical Graphics Inc., 270
Anheuser-Busch, 432
Apple, 10, 68, 82, 83, 85, 111, 132, 189, 191, 192, 201, 254, 447, 448
Apple Genius, 447–448
Apple Store, 447, 448
The Apprentice, 368
Arrowhead Honda, 286

Arthur Andersen, 76, 259
Association of Test Publishers, 277
AT&T, 161, 404, 425, 459
Atlantic Richfield, 211
Avon, 257, 388
AXA, 97

Baidu, 119
Bank of America, 459
Basin Electric Power Cooperative, 389
Bentley Motors, 459
Best Buy, 194, 356–357
Bethlehem Steel, 41, 63
Bing, 14
Bit Literacy, 312
Bit Lots, 459
Bloomberg Businessweek, 10, 25, 38, 82
BMW, 10, 189
Boeing, 153, 209, 210, 259, 275
Boots, 211
BP Oil, 16–17, 97, 140, 141, 316
Bridgeway Funds, 261
Brigham Young University, 314
Brooklyn Union Gas, 428
Brown & Williamson, 141
Burger King, 107, 434
Business Research Lab, 308
Business Week, 129, 356
Buzz, 184

Canary Capital Partners, 141
Capgemini, 30
Capital One, 281–282
Cascade Engineering Inc., 69
Casino Arizona, 79
Caterpillar, 10, 189, 316
CB Richard Ellis (CBRE), 310–311
CBS, 354, 454
Center for Creative Leadership, 405
C.F. Martin & Company, 62–63
Chanel, 295–296
Chiapas International, 129
Chrysler, 199, 255
Chung's Gourmet Foods, 335
Cirque du Soleil, 234–236
Cirque Resort, 236
Cisco Systems, 253, 298, 313, 349, 350,
    375, 419
Citigroup, 12, 134
City Fresh Foods, 322–323
Club Cirque, 236
Coca-Cola, 97, 133, 183, 188, 252,
    275, 354
Coca-Cola Femsa, 329
Colgate-Palmolive, 97
Commodore International, 363
Compaq Computer, 222
Conoco, 282
ConocoPhillips, 188
Consumer Reports, 459
Continental Airlines, 214, 342

Corning Glass Works, 262
Corporate Executive Board, 142
Costco, 72, 187
Creative Artists Agency, 387
Creative Commons, 393
Crest, 189
CultureRx, 356, 357
Cypress Semiconductor Corporation,
    162, 163

Daimler, 96
Danube Knitware Ltd., 110
Darden Restaurants, 95
DaVita, 239, 240
Deepwater Horizon, 141
Dell, Inc., 10, 189, 403, 448
Denver International Airport, 210
Detroit Auto Show, 188
Detroit Medical Center, 259
Development Dimensions International
    (DDI), 31–32
Digital Equipment, 222
Discovery Channel, 336
Disney Institute, 261
Disney World, 235
Dixon Schwabl, 309
DM Bicycle Company, 147
Dominick's, 91
Dominion Farms, 100
Domino's Pizza Inc., 39, 407, 455
Dow Chemical Canada, 457
Dow Corning, 139–140
Dunkin' Donuts, 206
DuPont, 12, 419

eBay, 75, 192
Economist, 12
EMC Corp., 306
ENI, 97
Enron, 76, 129, 141, 259, 393
Envoy Mortgage, 443
Equal Employment Opportunity
    Commission (EEOC), 286
Ernst & Young, 308
European Commission, 351
evo, 89–90, 266
evogear, 89, 266

Facebook, 13, 14, 70, 128, 151, 152,
    153, 183, 184, 193, 194, 203,
    212, 273, 303, 310, 311, 320,
    321, 362
Family Dollar, 459
Fast Company, 38, 214
FBI, 336
Federal Express (FedEx), 198, 253, 455
Federal Reserve Bank of Philadelphia, 79
Fetzer Vineyards, 127–128
Fieldale Farms, 351
Financial Post, 71
Fire and Disaster Management Agency, 456

Firestone, 458
First Houston Mortgage, 417, 443
Flextronics, 291
Flickr, 14, 194
Ford Motor Company, 97, 179–181, 194,
    198, 199, 259, 282, 313, 375,
    458, 459
Fortune, 3, 7, 16, 38, 57, 71, 80, 81,
    129, 191, 257, 260, 273,
    370, 392, 459
Four Seasons hotel, 447
Fox News, 74
Foxconn, 10
Franklin Covey, 334
Freeport-McMoRan Copper
    & Gold, 188
The Futurist, 87–88

Gallup Poll, 184, 344, 409
Gap, 295
The Gap, 132
Geisinger Health System, 473–475
General Electric, 10, 12, 134, 246,
    250, 260, 283,
    414–415, 454
General Motors, 121, 199, 369
Genius Bar, 447
Gillette, 30
Girl Scouts of the USA, 393
Global Solutions, 32
Goldman Sachs, 9, 12, 134
Google, 14, 38, 74, 77, 82, 106, 119, 158,
    183, 184, 192, 196, 256, 257,
    269, 270, 272, 274, 320, 346,
    374, 447, 452
Great Wolf Resorts, 454
Guitar Hero, 183

Habitat for Humanity, 307
Hackett Group, 165
Haier Group, 467
Halliburton, 310
Harley-Davidson, 154–155
Harper University Hospital, 259
Harry Potter, 165
Harvard Business Review, 4, 55, 394
Harvard Business School, 145
Harvard Law School, 431
Heinz, 211
Hewlett-Packard (HP), 11, 12, 134, 191,
    222, 226, 464
Hillench & Bradsby, 133
Hitachi, 201
Holiday Inn, 23
Hollister Co., 88–89
Home Depot, 161, 311
Homewood Suites, 393
Honda Corporation, 180, 442
Honeywell, 19, 20, 26
Hyundai, 459
Hyundai USA, 334

IBM, 12, 30, 97, 102, 108, 228, 250, 308, 314, 390, 406
Inc. magazine, 24, 194, 303, 309
Infineon Technologies, 96
ING Bank, 161
ING Group, 97
Intel, 10, 69, 96, 189, 252, 255, 272
Interactive Annotation 1d, 23
Internal Revenue Service (IRS), 133, 454
International Red Cross, 243
Intuition, 283

J. C. Penney Co., 423
J. M. Smucker Co., 185
J. P. Morgan Chase, 459
Japanese Scientists and Engineers (JUSE), 44, 45
Jaypee Capital Services, 30
Jelly Belly Candy Co., 345
Jewel, 91
Jiffy Lube, 474
Johns Hopkins, 450
Johnson & Johnson (J&J), 254
Johnson Controls, 188
Johnson Financial Group, 350
Josephson Institute of Ethics, 137

KeySpan, 428
Kodak, 156
KPMG, 406
Kraft North America, 389

L. L. Bean Inc., 192, 460
Latinum Network, 68
Lawrence Berkeley National Laboratory, 12
Levi's, 132
Lexus, 189
Lifetime Networks, 360
Lingnan University, 374
LinkedIn, 14, 193, 273, 310, 311, 362
Linux, 258
Liz Claiborne Inc., 453
L. M. Ericsson, 97
Lodge at Vail, 309
Lululemon Athletica, 405

Maine Media Workshops, 292
Maine Medical Center, 103
Major League Baseball, 133
Management Review, 249
Marriott Hotels, 72, 187, 335, 462
Mattel, 461
Mayo Clinic, 190
McDonald's, 9, 23, 97, 103, 107, 183, 195, 206, 207, 419, 450, 460
MCI, 135
McKinsey & Company, 96
Medtronic, 84, 137, 425–426
Metabolix, 83
MGM Mirage, 236

Microsoft, 84, 119, 167, 183, 258, 273, 282, 375, 419, 447
Midvale Steel Works, 41, 170
Mirage Resorts, 234–235
Mitchell Gold + Bob Williams, 62
Mitre, 348–349
Moran, Stahl & Boyer International, 121, 122
Motorola, 196
MTV, 63, 183

N3 Engine Overhaul Services, 462
NASA, 259, 270, 393
National Assessment of Education Progress, 68
National Basketball Association, 23
National Institute on Alcohol Abuse and Alcoholism, 288
National Public Radio, 356
National Science Board, 68
NBC, 44
NBC-Universal, 250
NCR, 10
Nestlé, 97
Netflix, 213, 397
Networking & Services Research, 425
New Image, 305
New Leash on Life Animal Rescue, 363
New York Times, 356
Newsweek, 12, 71, 391
Nielsen, 14
Nike, 20, 132, 210, 367, 393, 458
Nintendo, 80
Nissan Motors, 10, 96, 336
Nokia, 97, 310
Norske Skog, 45, 46
Nucor Corporation, 343
Nugget Market, 350
Numi Organic Tea, 120, 383
Nustar Energy, 350
Nuts for Mutts, 363

Ocean Conservancy, 60
Office of National Drug Control Policy, 288
O'Hare International Airport, 452
Ohio Health, 463
Ohio State University, 398–399, 411
Omron, 196
Oracle, 191
Orkut, 184
Oticon Inc., 257

Patagonia, 132, 344
Pemex, 97
Penrose Hospital, 350
Pentair, Inc., 245
People and Innovation Lab (PiLab), 269
PeopleSoft, 6
PepsiCo, 6, 183, 418
Petrobrás, 97

Pew Research Center, 134, 378
Pfizer, 83, 125, 126
Phantasmagoria Factory, 234–236
Philip Morris, 131
Philips, 461
Pinnacol Assurance, 349
Pitney Bowes Inc., 85
Plan Fund, 129
Pollo Campero, 152
Popchip, 462
Poppa D's Nuts, 23
Preserve®, 30–31, 205, 472
Preston Trucking, 408
PricewaterhouseCoopers, 24, 111, 114, 300
Procter & Gamble, 30, 101, 185, 187, 217, 260–261, 282, 368, 404, 452
Project Management Institute, 164

Quad/Graphics, 310
Quality Float Works, 233
Queen Victoria, 449
Quest Diagnostics, 288

Rackspace, 327, 328
Radio Shack, 299
Rasmussen, 378
Razorfish, 174
Recreational Equipment Inc. (REI), 276
Recycline, 30–31, 205, 472
Red Lobster, 95
Reese, 187
Renault, 96
Return Path, 472
Ringling Bros. and Barnum & Bailey Circus, 235
Rock and Roll Hall of Fame, 214
Rolling Stone, 214
Roxbury Technology, 360

Salary.com, 343
Salt River Pima-Maricopa Indian Community, 79
Sam's Club, 90
Samsung Electronics, 95, 97
SAS, 260, 311
Scholastic, 164–165
Scholfield Honda, 442
Scientific Atlanta, 419
Seagate Technology, 10
7-Eleven, 23
Siemens, 97, 114, 137
Singapore Airlines, 160, 190
SiteROCK, 248, 249
60 Minutes, 356
Skanska, 126
The Sky Factory, 248–249
Skype, 313
Small Business Administration (SBA), 21, 71

Soap Hope, 129
Society for Human Resource
     Management, 314, 350
Solutions Marketing Group, 276
Sony Pictures, 291
Southern Company, 260
Southern Ohio Medical Center, 350
Southwest Airlines, 272–273, 401
Southwest Fire Use Training Academy
     (FUTA), 283
Standard Oil Company, 126
Staples, 360
Star Wars, 195
Starbucks, 72, 194, 206–207, 218, 225,
     330, 419
Starbucks Asia Pacific, 405
Stoneyfield Farm, 205
Streetline Networks, 450
Sun, 206
Sunbeam Corporation, 374
Sundance Channel, 229
Sunkist, 189
Susan G. Komen for the Cure, 133
Sweet Jazmines, 462

Talking Stick Resort, 79
Tandem Computers, 226–227
Tasty Catering, 303
TCL Corp., 398
Teva Pharmaceutical Industries, 155
Texaco, 275
Texas A&M University, 461
Texas Instruments, 95
Thomson, 398
3M Corporation, 132, 262
TNT, 313
Tom's of Maine, 437
Total Attorneys, 383–385

Toyota Motor, 10, 81, 97, 131–132, 180,
     195, 199, 247, 459
Trader Joe's, 339
Training magazine, 240, 283, 304,
     315, 346
The Travelers Companies, 69
Treasure Island casino, 235
Tupperware, 113
Twitter, 13, 14, 70, 74, 194, 203, 303,
     310, 311, 320, 455
Tyson Foods, Inc., 188, 286

UCLA, 13, 404
Undercover Boss, 454
Union Pacific, 8
United Health Group, 345
United Parcel Service (UPS), 6–7,
     129–130, 293
United Resource Recovery, 133
Universal Studios, 387
University of Buffalo School of
     Management, 77
U.S. Army Corps of Engineers, 157
U.S. Bureau of Labor Statistics, 77–78,
     299, 340
U.S. Census Bureau, 70
U.S. Department of Health and Human
     Services, 288
U.S. Department of Labor, 322
U.S. Naval Academy, 287
U.S. Navy Special Projects Office, 171
U.S. Postal Service (USPS), 435
U.S. Securities and Exchange Commission
     (SEC), 12, 454
USA Today, 112, 133, 142, 212

Ventiv Health, 284
VidyoOne, 313

Virginia Tech, 212
Volkswagen, 195

Wall Street Journal, 68, 369
Walmart, 10, 21, 90–91, 97, 130,
     165, 189, 190, 345,
     401, 459
Walmart International, 230
Walt Disney Company, 452
Walt Disney World, 261
Warner-Lambert, 142
Washington Post, 18
Waste Management, 133
Wave, 184
Wendy's, 401
Western Electric, 47
Whole Foods, 156
Winnebago Industries, 309
Wm. Wrigley Jr., 309
Wolters Kluwer, 108
Workday, 291–292
Working Woman, 71
World Trade Organization, 103
WorldCom, 76, 259

Xerox Corporation, 141, 265, 315,
     392, 418

Yahoo, 14, 119, 183, 342, 423
Yellowstone National Park, 198
Yosemite National Park, 427
Young & Rubicam, 423
YouTube, 13, 14, 183, 194, 203, 296, 311,
     320, 455

Zappos.com, 3–4, 266–267, 345
Zildjian Company, 35–36

SUBJECT INDEX

open-door policy, 309
overview, 296–297
planning for, 319–320
social media, 310
social networking, 311
strategies, 301–302
suggestion systems, 308–309
surveys, 308
in teams, 379
teleworking, 314
upward communication, 307–310
videoconference, 313–314
writing effectiveness, 316–317
Comparative management
     defined, 107–108
     GLOBE project and, 109–111

made-in-American management
     theories, 108
varying management styles,
     108–109
Compensation
     cafeteria, 340
     corporate CEO pay, 354–355
     employee, 340
Competence in teams, 379
Competition
     competing commitments as reason
          for employee resistance to
          change, 424
     competitive advantage, 189
     competitive scope, 189
     destructive, 370
Complex adaptive systems theory, 52–53

Compressed workweek, 349
Compromise, 434
The Concept of the Corporation
     (Drucker), 55
Concurrent control, 450
Concurrent engineering, 84
Condition of certainty, 213
Condition of risk, 213
Condition of uncertainty, 214
Conflict. *See also* Change
     competitive conflict, 431–433
     cooperative conflict, 431–433
     defined, 431
     in group development, 366
     iceberg of, 440–441
     resolving, 433–435
     triggers, 433

AAP. *See* Affirmative action program (AAP)
A-B-C priority system, 160–161
Acceptance, in groups, 368
Accommodative social responsibility
    strategy, 132
ADA. *See* Americans with Disabilities Act
    of 1990 (ADA)
Added value negotiating, 438
Administration Industrielle et Générale
    (Fayol), 39
Advertising
    advertising-based Internet business
        model, 193
    advocacy, 76
    profit-motivated, 133
Advocacy advertising, 76
Affirmative action program (AAP), 275.
        See also Equal employment
        opportunity (EEO)
Alcoholism, 288–289
Algebraic method for break-even analysis,
    173–174
Alternative dispute resolution (ADR), 77
Altruism, 132
Ambidextrous strategy, 156
Americans with Disabilities Act of 1990
    (ADA), 276
Analyzers, 155
Antecedent, 407
Anticipatory changes, 418
The Apprentice, 56
Assembly, local, 96
Attitudes toward international operations
    ethnocentric attitude,
        100–101
    geocentric attitude, 102
    polycentric attitude, 101–102
Attribute listing, 229
Audit
    crisis audit, 456
    internal audits, 454
    legal, 77
    management audit, 454
    process audit, 454
    stakeholder, 129
Authority
    chain of command, 241
    defined, 241
    hierarchy of, 241
Avoidance strategy, 433

B. Mod. *See* Behavior modification
    (B. Mod.)
Bad Leadership (Dunlap), 374
Bargaining zone, 437
BARS (behaviorally anchored rating
    scales), 281
BATNA, 437
Behavior modification (B. Mod.)
    antecedents, 407
    defined, 407

extinction, 408
    negative reinforcement, 408
    overview, 406
    positive reinforcement, 408, 410
    punishment, 408
Behavioral approach to management
    human relations movement, 46–49
    lessons from, 49–50
    organizational behavior, 49
Behavioral styles theory, 398–399
    Ohio State model, 398–399
Behaviorally anchored rating scales
    (BARS), 281
Behavior-based interview, 279, 291
Behaviorism, 406
Benchmarking, 452
Best alternative to a negotiated agreement
    (BATNA), 437
Bivariate analysis, 55
Body language, 305
Brainstorming, 228
Break-even analysis, 172–175
    algebraic method, 173–174
    fixed vs. variable costs, 173
    graphical method, 174
    limitations, 175
    strengths, 175
Break-even point, 173
Burns and Stalker model of contingency
    design, 247–249
Business cycles, 78–80
    cycle-sensitive decisions, 78–79
    defined, 78
    economic forecasts, 79–80
    timing, 78
Business ecosystem, 191
Business ethics, 134
Busyness trap, 161

Cafeteria compensation, 340
Campaign financing, 75
Capability profile, 196
Carpal tunnel syndrome, 336
Case studies
    change and innovation, 442–443
    changing environment, 89–90
    communications, 321–323
    corporate culture, 266–267
    ethics, 146–148
    group dynamics and teamwork,
        383–385
    human resource management,
        292–293
    international management, 120–123
    leadership development, 414–415
    management thought, 62–63
    motivating employees, 355–357
    planning and project management,
        178–181
    Preserve® by Recycline, 30–31
    problem solving, 233–236

quality control, 472–475
    sample of a day of managers, 31–33
    strategic management, 205–207
    team leading, 266
Cause-and-effect analysis, 465
Cell phones, 313
Centralization, 253–254
Chain of command, 241
Change. *See also* Organizational change
    grassroots change, 429–431
    individual reactions to, 420–422
    overcoming resistance to, 422–426
    planned change through organization
        development, 427–429
Chaos theory, 52–53
Charisma, 392
Charismatic/value-based leadership, 109
Cheaper by the Dozen (Gilbreth), 43
Checklists, 450
China
    Google censorship, 119
    myths and facts, 93–94
Civil Rights Act of 1964, 274, 286
Classical economic model, 128–129
Closed system
    contingency approach, 55
    general systems theory, 51
Cluster organization, 257–258
Coalition building, 75
Coalition tactics, 389
Codes of ethics, 140–141.
        See also Ethics
Coercive power, 392
Cohesiveness of groups, 363, 367
Collaborative computing, 221–222
Collectivist culture, 104–106
Commission-based Internet business
        model, 193
Commitment, 159
Communication
    body language, 305
    cell phones, 313
    contingency approach, 298–299
    decoding, 299–300
    defined, 297
    digital media, 310–314
    e-mail, 311–312
    encoding, 297
    exit interviews, 310
    feedback, 300
    grapevine, 302–304
    grievances, 308
    informal meetings, 309–310
    information overload, 311
    listening effectiveness, 315–316
    as managerial function, 16
    media richness, 298
    medium, 298
    meeting leadership, 317
    noise, 300
    nonverbal, 305–307

Conformity
  defined, 371
  the hot seat, 371–372
  immoral majority, 372
  research on, 371–372
Consensus approach to forecasting, 79–80
Consultation, 388
Contingency approach to management, 54–55
Contingency design
  Burns and Stalker model, 247–249
  centralization and decentralization, 253–254
  defined, 246–247
  departmentalization, 249–252
  explanation of, 246–247
  span of control, 252–253
Contingency management to decision making, 223–224
Contingency model
  individual reactions to change, 421
  for media selection, 298–299
Contingency plan, 456–457
Contingent time off, 337
Contingent workers, 71–72
Continuous reinforcement, 410
Contribution margin, 173
Contributive liberty, 139
Control
  components, 451–453
  concurrent, 450
  defined, 448
  executive reality check, 454
  feedback, 450–451
  feedforward, 449–450
  inadequate control, symptoms of, 454–455
  internal audits, 454
  as managerial function, 16–17
  strategic, 453
Control chart, 465
Corporate philanthropy, 133
Corporate social responsibility (CSR)
  altruism, 132
  arguments against, 130–131
  arguments for, 130
  benefits of, 132–134
  corporate philanthropy, 133
  defined, 126
  enlightened self-interest, 132–133
  global corporations, 127
  organizational benefits of, 133–134
  philanthropic responsibilities, 127
  transnational corporations, 127
  triple bottom line, 127
  voluntary action, 127–128
Cost focus strategy, 190
Cost leadership strategy, 189
CQ. See Cultural intelligence (CQ)
Creative leap, 230

Creativity
  defined, 224
  increasing, 225–226
  problem solving, 226–230
  testing, 232–233
  workplace, 225
Crisis audit, 456
Crisis management
  defined, 455–456
  overview, 455
  program development, 456–458
Critical path, 171
Cross-border mergers, 96
Cross-cultural effectiveness and global awareness, 98–103
  attitudes toward international operations, 99–102
  cultural imperative, 102–103
  manager competency, 99
Cross-cultural settings, media selection in, 298–300
  contingency approach, 298–299
  decoding, 299–300
  feedback, 300
  media richness, 298
  noise, 300
Cross-cultural training, 112–115
  combination of methods, 114
  culture assimilator, 112
  defined, 112
  documentary programs, 112
  field experience, 114
  integrated expatriate staffing system, 114–115
  language instruction, 112–113
  sensitivity training, 114
Cross-functional team, 374–375
Cross-sectional scenario, 201
Crystal ball gazing, 87–88
CSR. See Corporate social responsibility (CSR)
Cultural diversity. See Diversity
Cultural intelligence (CQ), 99
Cultural Intelligence: Living and Working Globally (Thomas & Inkson), 99
Culture. See also Diversity
  assimilator, 112
  defined, 102
  global awareness and, 102–103
  GLOBE project, 104
  high-context, 104
  interview bias and, 277
  looking into the cultural mirror, 117–118
  low-context, 104
  organizational. See Organizational culture
  passive-aggressive organizational culture, 424

single "Americanized" culture, 103–107
  societal culture, 103
  workforce communications, 322–323
Culture shock, 111
Customers
  customer classification department, 252
  customer service, 447
  customer-centered, defined, 462–463
  external, 44
  internal, 44, 462
  loyalty, 192–193
Cycles
  business cycles, 78–80
  cycle time, 453
  life-cycle benefits, 340
  MBO cycle, 162–163
  PDCA cycle, 466–467, 468
  project life cycle, 165–166

The Death of Competition: Leadership and Strategy in the Age of Business Ecosystems (Moore), 191
Decentralization, 253–254
Decision making. See also Groupthink; Problem solving
  complex streams of decisions, 210–212
  condition of certainty, 213
  defined, 210
  escalation of commitment, 216
  framing error, 215–216
  group-aided, 221–224
  information-processing styles, 214–215
  knowledge management, 219–221
  law of unintended consequences, 212
  as managerial function, 16
  model, 219
  nonprogrammed decisions, 218
  overconfidence, 216–217
  pooled, 211
  programmed decisions, 217–218
  risk, 213
  uncertainty and, 214
Decision rule, 218
Decoding, 299–300
Defenders, 154–155
Defensive social responsibility strategy, 131–132
Delegation
  advantages of, 255–256
  barriers to, 256
  defined, 254–255
  explanation of, 254–255
Delusion, in groups, 367
Deming management, 466–468
Demographics
  defined, 66
  education and workplace skills crisis, 68–69

of the new workforce, 66–68
older workers, 69–70
Departmentalization
  customer classification, 252
  defined, 249
  functional, 249–250
  geographic location, 250
  product-service, 250
  work flow process
    departments, 252
Differentiation strategy, 189
Direct foreign investments, 96
Disabled persons, 275–277
Discrimination, religious, 88–89. *See
    also* Equal employment
    opportunity (EEO)
Disillusion, in groups, 367–368
Dissatisfiers, 331–332
Distributive justice, 139
Diversity. *See also* Culture
  affirmative action and, 275
  collectivism, 104–106
  corporate culture, 260
  demographics of the new workforce, 66
  glass ceiling, 72
  individualism, 104–106
  innovators and implementers, 434
  interpersonal space, 106
  language, 106
  managing, 72–73
  quality-of-work-life programs, 348
  recruiting and, 273
  religion, 107
  sexual orientation, 276
  time, 106
  understanding of, 103–107
Division of labor, 240–241
Documentary programs, 112
Drug abuse, 288–289

*The Ecology of Commerce: A Declaration
    of Sustainability* (Fisher), 12
Ecomagination, 246
Eco-managers, 272
*Economic Control of Quality of
    Manufactured Product*
    (Shewhart), 44
Economic environment, 77–81
  business cycles, 78–80
  education and job outlook, 77–78
  global economy, 80–81
Economics
  classical economic model, 128–129
  efficiency and ethics, 139
  socioeconomic model, 129–130
Edisonian method of problem
    solving, 229
Education. *See also* Training
  job outlook and, 77–78
  learning organizations, 219, 244–245

remedial, 68–69
EEO. *See* Equal employment
    opportunity (EEO)
EEOC. *See* U.S. Equal Employment
    Opportunity Commission
    (EEOC)
Effect uncertainty, 153
The Effective Executive (Drucker), 55
Effectiveness
  balancing efficiency and, 6–7
  defined, 6
  of negotiation, 436–437
  organizational, 245
  of workplace teams, 376–377
Efficiency
  balancing effectiveness and, 6–7
  defined, 6
  ethics and, 139
Effort, coordination of, 240
The 8th Habit (Covey), 436
80/20 principle, 161. *See also* Pareto
    analysis
E-mail, 311–312. *See also* Internet
Emotional intelligence (EQ), 99,
    396–397, 412
Emotional side effects, 423
Empire building, 370
Employee
  change, resistance to, 423–424
  compensation, 340
  employee assistance program (EAP), 289
  participation and engagement,
    343–347
Employment. *See* Human resource
    management
Employment selection test, 277
Empowerment, 393, 464. *See also* Power
Encoding, 297
Enlightened self-interest, 132–133
Entrepreneurship. *See also* Small business
  defined, 23
  global entrepreneurs, 25
  limitations, 24–25
  temperament test, 27–29
  trait profile, 24
Environment
  crystal ball gazing, 87–88
  economic, 77–81
  globalization and, 8–10
  political-legal, 73–77
  social, 66–73
  sustainability and, 12, 26
  technological, 81–85
Environmental uncertainty, 153
EQ. *See* Emotional intelligence (EQ)
Equal employment opportunity (EEO)
  demographics of the new
    workforce, 71
  managing diversity, 73
  recruitment and selection, 273–274

Escalation of commitment, 216
Esteem needs, 330
Ethical advocate, 140
Ethics. *See also* Values
  admitting to being wrong, 441–442
  advocates, 140
  ambiguous situations, 135
  art of friendship, 382
  business ethics, 134
  call to action, 137
  codes of ethics, 140–141
  corporate CEO pay, 354–355
  corporate culture, 265–266
  cross-cultural training, 114
  death by project, 178
  defined, 134
  digital communications, 320–321
  employment discrimination, 88–89
  ethical hot spots, 135
  free Internet content vs.
    pirating, 205
  general principles, 138–139
  Google and Chinese
    censorship, 119
  laying off employees, 404
  making a difference, 13
  management, 29–30
  offshoring, 29–30
  organizational control, 472
  overtime, 233
  personal values as ethical anchors,
    137–138
  pressure from above, 135
  privacy issues, 291–292
  putting employees ahead of profits,
    218
  putting people first, 48
  rationalizing unethical conduct,
    136–137
  reawakening of, 12–13, 26
  recession in historical
    perspective, 61
  renewable energy, 190
  social responsibility, 129
  training, 139–140, 145
  truth and lying, 413
  whistle-blowing, 141–142
Ethnocentric attitude, 100–101
Evaluation-reward system, 453
Event outcome forecast, 200
Event timing forecast, 200
Exchange tactics, 389
Executive reality check, 454
Exit interviews, 310
Expatriate
  cross-cultural training, 112–115
  defined, 111
  failure of, 111–112
Expectancy, defined, 332
Expectancy theory, 332–333

Expert power, 392–393
Explicit knowledge, 220
Exporting, 96
Extinction, 408
Extrinsic rewards, 339, 340–343

Fairness in teams, 379
Family support services, 349–350
Family-friendly companies, 349
FCPA. *See* Foreign Corrupt Practices Act
    of 1977 (FCPA)
Federal Drug-Free Workplace Act of 1988,
    288–289
Feedback
    control, 450–451
    corrective action based on, 199
    media selection, 300
    nonverbal, 306–307
Feedforward control, 449–450
Fee-for-service-based Internet business
    model, 193
Fiedler's contingency theory, 399–400
Field experience, 114
The Fifth Discipline (Senge), 244
Fishbone diagrams, 228, 465
5P checklist for grassroots change agents,
    430–431
Fixed costs, 173
Flexible work schedules, 348–349
Flextime, 348–349
Flight 001 case study, 178, 355–356
Flow chart, 168–170, 464–465
FMLA. *See* U.S. Family and Medical Leave
    Act (FMLA)
Focused differentiation strategy, 190
Forcing as conflict resolution, 434
Forecasting
    benefiting from, 79–80
    consensus approach, 79–80
    defined, 199
    event outcome, 200
    event timing, 200
    informed judgment technique, 200–201
    scenario analysis, 201
    surveys, 201–202
    time series, 200
    trend analysis, 202
Foreign Corrupt Practices Act of 1977
    (FCPA), 114
Formal group, 362
Formal leadership, 394
Four-to-One Rule, 408
Framing error, 215–216
Frankenstein monster effect, 212
Free association, 228
Functional department, 249–250
The Functions of the Executive
    (Barnard), 50

Gantt charts, 170
Gender

glass ceiling and, 70–71, 72
    influence tactics and, 390
    leadership traits and, 396
General systems theory, 51
Generative strategy-making mode, 185
Geocentric attitude, 102
Geographic location department, 250
Glass ceiling, 70–71, 72
Global company
    defined, 97
    to transnational company, 97–98
Global economy, 80–81
Global Leadership and Organizational
    Behavior Effectiveness
    (GLOBE) project
    background, 104
    leadership lessons, 109–111
Globalization. *See also* Expatriate
    environment and, 8–10
    meeting world standards, 81
    as personal matter, 81
    working for foreign-owned
        companies, 81
GLOBE project. *See* Global Leadership
    and Organizational Behavior
    Effectiveness (GLOBE) project
Goal of organization, 240
Goals, superordinate, 434
Goal-setting theory, 333–335
    goal setting, defined, 334
    implications of, 335
    model, 334
    motivation by goals, 335
    personal ownership, 334–335
Golf for building relationships, 367
*Good to Great: Why Some Companies
    Make the Leap . . . and Others
    Don't* (Collins), 57, 273
Government requirements for ethical
    principles, 139
Grand strategy, 195
Grapevine, 302–304
Graphical method for break-even
    analysis, 174
Graphical planning
    PERT networks, 171–172
    scheduling with Gantt charts, 170
    sequencing with flow charts, 168–170
Grassroots change, 429–431
Great Recession, 78, 184
Green management
    biodegradable plastic, 83
    communication strategy, 303
    communication technologies, 425
    communications, 321–322
    community building through
        environmental problem
        solving, 229
    ecomagination, 246
    energy use for transport of goods, 8
    greenwashers, 134

human resources, 272
    organizational control, 450
    point person for sustainability, 393
    race for green technology, 98
    virtual environmental team, 375
    Walmart's sustainability project, 165
Greensburg, Kansas
    communications management,
        321–322
    decision making, 233–234
    leadership development, 413
    social responsibility, 146
Group. *See also* Teams
    attraction to, 363–364
    breakup of group as reason for
        employee resistance to
        change, 424
    cohesiveness, 363
    conformity, 371–372
    defined, 360–361
    development, 365–368
    formal, 362
    friendships in the workplace, 362
    groupthink, 372–374
    informal, 361–362
    norms, 364
    organizational politics, 368–370
    ostracism, 364
    roles, 364
Group development
    acceptance, 368
    characteristics of mature groups,
        365–366
    cohesion, 367
    conflict and challenge, 366
    delusion, 367
    disillusion, 367–368
    orientation, 366
    overview, 365
    stages of development, 366–368
Group-aided decision making
    advantages and disadvantages of, 223
    collaborative computing, 221–222
    contingency approach, 223–224
    dispersed accountability, 222–223
    group involvement in decisions, 222
Groupthink
    defined, 372–373
    preventing, 373–374
    symptoms of, 373
Groupware, 221–222
*Grown Up Digital: How the Net
    Generation is Changing Your
    World* (Tapscott), 320

Hawthorne studies, 47
Herzberg's Two-Factor Theory, 331–332
Hierarchy of authority, 241
High-context culture, 104
Histogram, 465
Horizontal organizations, 252

Horizontal specialization
    of organizations, 242
Horizontally loaded jobs, 337
Hourglass organization, 257
House's updated path-goal theory,
    400–401
*How Full Is Your Bucket? Positive
    Strategies for Work and Life*
    (Rath & Clifton), 408
*The HR Scorecard: Linking People,
    Strategy, and Performance*, 271
Human capital, 271–272
Human relations movement, 46–49
    Hawthorne studies, 47
    industrial humanism philosophy,
        47–49
    threat of unionization, 46–47
Human resource management
    affirmative action, 275
    age of human capital, 271–272
    alcohol and drug abuse, 288–289
    competitive advantage, 272–273
    defined, 270
    disabled persons, 275–277
    equal employment opportunity,
        274–277
    explanation of, 270–271
    interviewing, 277–279
    people-centered approach to,
        271–273
    performance appraisal, 280–282, 293
    recruitment and selection of,
        273–279
    sexual harassment, 286–288
    sustainable human resources, 272
    talent analytics, 269
    training, 283–286
*The Human Problems of an Industrial
    Civilization* (Mayo), 47
The Human Side of Enterprise
    (McGregor), 48
Humane-oriented leadership, 109

Idealize, 230
If Japan Can . . . Why Can't We?, 44
IM. *See* Issues management (IM)
Implementation gap, 12
Impression management, 99
In Search of Excellence (Peters &
    Waterman), 55, 57
Incremental changes, 418
Individual rights for ethical principles, 139
Individualistic culture, 104–106
Industrial humanism, 47–49
Industrial Revolution, 11
Inertia, 423
Influence tactics, 388–390
Informal group, 361–362
Informal leadership, 394
Information overload, 38, 311
Information processing, 214–215

Ingratiating tactics, 389
Innovation lag, 83–84
Innovation process, 82–84
    innovation lag, 83–84
    three-step process, 83
Inspirational appeals, 388
Instrumental value, 137–138
Intelligence quotient (IQ), 396–397
Interdisciplinary field of management
    theory, 38
Interdisciplinary input for
    decision-making, 211
Intermediate planning, 158
Intermittent reinforcement, 410
Internal audits, 454
Internal customers, 462
International management, defined, 95
Internationalization
    direct foreign investments, 96
    exporting, 96
    joint ventures, 96
    licensing, 95
    local assembly and packaging, 96
    local warehousing and selling, 96
Internet. *See also* Social networking
    business models, 192, 193
    customer loyalty, 192–193
    customized strategy, 192
    defined, 13
    description and applications, 14
    e-mail, 311–312
    free content vs. pirating, 205
    history of, 13
    recruiting for diversity, 273
    strategic management, 187–194
Interpersonal space, 106
Interviewing
    behavioral, 279
    behavior-based, 291
    criticism of, 277
    cultural bias, 277
    exit interviews, 310
    structured, 277–279
Intrapreneur, 84–85
Intrinsic rewards, 339
Iron law of responsibility, 131
Issues management (IM), 74

Job analysis, 274
Job description, 274
Job design
    defined, 335
    fitting jobs to people, 337–339
    fitting people to jobs, 335–337
    motivation through, 335–339
Job enlargement, 337
Job enrichment, 337–339
Job fairs, 271
Job rotation, 336–337
Job sharing, 349
Joint ventures, 96

Kaizen, 377, 419, 463–464
Kirkpatrick model of program evaluation,
    285–286
Knowledge management (KM)
    defined, 219
    exit interviews and, 310
    explicit knowledge, 220
    organizational learning and, 52
    software for, 221
    tacit knowledge, 220

Language
    cultural diversity, 106, 107
    instruction, 112–113
Law of unintended consequences, 212
Leadership
    behavioral styles theory, 398–399
    defined, 394
    female vs. male, 397
    formal, 394
    informal, 394
    leaders vs. managers, 394–395
    overview, 393–394
    practical intelligence, 403
    servant leaders, 404
    situational theory, 399–401
    trait theory, 396–397
    transformational leadership theory,
        401–403
Leadership (Burns), 401
Leadership styles
    charismatic/value-based, 109
    humane-oriented, 109
    participative, 109
    self-protective, 109
    team-oriented, 109
Leading, as managerial function, 16
Learning organizations, 219,
    244–245
Legal audit, 77
Legitimate power, 392
Lengel-Daft contingency model, 298
Licensing, 95
Life-cycle benefits, 340
Line and staff organization, 242
Listening guidelines, 315–316
Lobbying, 75–76
Longitudinal scenario, 201
Love needs, 330
Low-context culture, 104

Management
    audit, 454
    changing environment, coping with,
        8–15
    creativity, 224–226
    defined, 5
    of diversity, 72–73
    effectiveness and efficiency, 6–7
    entrepreneurship, 23–25
    ethics, 29–30. *See also* Ethics

Management (*continued*)
  green. *See* Green management
  limited resources and, 7–8
  open-book, 345
  organizational objectives,
      achieving, 6
  participative, 343
  practice and study of, 37–38
  small business, 21–25
  strategic. *See* Strategic management
  teamwork survey, 381–382
  TQM. *See* Total quality management
      (TQM)
  working with and through
      others, 5–6
Management by objectives (MBO)
  defined, 162
  goal setting, 334
  guidelines, 167
  limitations, 163–164
  manager roles, 167
  MBO cycle, 162–163
  project life cycle, 165–166
  project planning, 164–168
  software, 166–167
  strengths, 163–164
Management synergy, 188
Management thought
  behavioral approach, 46–50
  best sellers, 55–58
  case studies, 62–63
  contingency approach, 54–55
  information overload, 38
  interdisciplinary field, 38
  open-system thinking and recycling,
      60–61
  operational approach, 41–45
  systems approach, 50–53
  theory of, 38–39
  universal process approach, 39–41
Managers
  amoral, 139
  disadvantages of, 18–19
  eco-managers, 272
  expectancy theory relevance, 333
  functions, 15–17
  leaders vs., 394–395
  learning to manage, 19–25
  Maslow's theory relevance, 331
  middle-manager commitment, 198
  project manager roles, 167
  sample of a day, 31–33
  self-managed team resistance,
      346–347
  skills, 17
  video case study, 30–31
Manufacturing-based quality, 459
Market synergy, 187–188
Markup-based Internet business
      model, 193

Maslow's Hierarchy of Needs Theory,
      328–331
  esteem needs, 330
  love needs, 330
  physiological needs, 329
  relevance for managers, 331
  safety needs, 329
  self-actualization needs, 330–331
MBO. *See* Management by objectives
      (MBO)
Measuring sticks, 159
Mechanistic organizations, 247–249
Media richness, 298, 302
Medical marijuana, 289
Meetings
  informal, 309–310
  running, 317
Mentoring
  approaches to, 406
  dynamics of, 405–406
  gender-bender, 404
  learning from, 405
  mentor, defined, 404
  overview, 404–405
Mergers, cross-border, 96
Microbusiness, 21
Misunderstanding as reason for employee
      resistance to change, 423
Monochronic time, 106
Motivation
  defined, 328
  by goals, 335
  as managerial function, 16
  objectives, 159
  theories. *See* Motivation theories
  through employee participation and
      engagement, 343–347
  through job design, 335–339
  through quality-of-work-life programs,
      348–351
  through rewards, 339–343
Motivation theories
  expectancy theory, 332–333
  goal-setting theory, 333–335
  Herzberg's Two-Factor Theory,
      331–332
  Maslow's Hierarchy of Needs,
      328–331
Multitasking, 313
Multivariate analysis, 55

NAFTA. *See* North American Free Trade
      Agreement (NAFTA)
Negative reinforcement, 408
Negotiation
  added value, 438
  bargaining zone, 437
  BATNA, 437
  defined, 436
  effectiveness of, 436–437

  overview, 435–436
  win-win attitude, 436–437
Net Generation, 15
Noise, 300
Nonprogrammed decisions, 218
Nonverbal communication, 305–307. *See
      also* Communication
Norms of groups, 364
North American Free Trade Agreement
      (NAFTA)
  globalized economy and, 95
  political controversy of, 425
  single global marketplace, 80

Objectives
  defined, 158
  guidelines for writing, 159, 177–178
  importance of, 159
  management by, 162–168
  means-ends chain, 160
  objective probabilities, 213
  organizational control, 452
  planning and, 158–159
OD. *See* Organization development (OD)
Offshoring, 9–10, 29–30
Ohio State model, 398–399
The One Minute Manager (Hammer),
      56, 408
*The 1001 Rewards & Recognition
      Fieldbook*, 339
Open system
  contingency approach, 55
  general systems theory, 51
  of organizations, 242–244
  recycling and, 60–61
Open-book management, 345
Open-door communication policy, 309
Operational approach to management,
      41–45
  Gantt and, 44
  Gilbreths and, 43
  lessons from, 45
  pay incentives, 42–43
  quality advocates, 44–45
  standardization, 41–42
  systematic selection and training, 42
  Taylor and, 41–43
  time and task study, 42
Operational planning, 158
Operations management, 45
Optimize, 230
Organic organizations, 247–249
Organization
  changing shape of, 256–259
  cluster, 257–258
  defined, 240
  hourglass, 257
  learning, 244–245
  reconfigurable, 258
  virtual, 258–259

Organization chart
    defined, 241
    horizontal specialization, 242
    line and staff organization, 242
    purpose of, 241–242
    vertical hierarchy, 242
Organization development (OD), 427–429
Organizational behavior, 49
Organizational change. *See also* Change
    adaptation, 419
    anticipatory changes, 418
    incremental changes, 418
    reactive changes, 418
    re-creation, 419–420
    re-orientation, 419
    strategic changes, 418
    tuning, 419
Organizational control. *See* Control
Organizational culture
    characteristics, 260–261
    defined, 259
    explanation of, 259–260
    forms and consequences of, 261
    organizational X-ray, 264–265
    strengthening of, 262
Organizational effectiveness, 245
Organizational learning, 52
Organizational mission, 157–158
Organizational objectives of managers, 6
Organizational politics
    antidotes to political behavior, 370
    defined, 369
    destructive competition, 370
    empire building, 370
    making the supervisor look
        good, 370
    overview, 368–369
    posturing, 370
    power and loyalty cliques, 370
    research, 369–370
    social IOUs, 370
    tactics, 370
Organizational socialization,
        261–262
Organizational structure and effectiveness
    characteristics, 240–241
    cooperation, 241
    coordination of effort, 240
    division of labor, 240–241
    goals or purpose, 240
    hierarchy of authority, 241
    open systems, 242–244
    organization chart, 241–242
    organizational effectiveness, 245
    organizational learning, 239, 244–245
Organizational values, 261
Organizing, as managerial
        function, 16
Orientation programs, 261–262, 366
Ostracism, 364

Out of the Crisis (Deming), 44, 466
Outsourcing
    costly errors, 209
    offshoring, 9–10, 29–30
Overconfidence, 216–217

PAC. *See* Political action committee (PAC)
Packaging, local, 96
Paid-time-off (PTO) banks, 349
Paperless office, 417, 443
Pareto analysis
    defined, 45
    functions, 161
    total quality management, 465
    uses for, 45
Participative leadership, 109
Participative management, 343
Part-time workers, 71–72, 349
Passive-aggressive organizational culture,
        424
Pay. *See* Compensation
PDCA cycle, 466–467, 468
People-centered organizations, 271–273
Performance, improving with extrinsic
        rewards, 340–343
Performance appraisal
    alternate techniques, 281–282
    case study, 293
    defined, 280
    legally defensible, 280–281
Personal ownership of challenging goals,
        334–335
Personal virtues, 139
PERT networks
    in action, 171
    critical path, 171
    defined, 171
    negative aspects, 171–172
    PERT activity, 171
    PERT event, 171
    PERT times, 171
    positive aspects, 171–172
    terminology, 171
Philanthropy, 127, 133
Physiological needs, 329
Plan-do-check-act (PDCA) cycle, 466–467,
        468
Planning
    defined, 152, 157
    graphical, 168–172
    horizon, 158
    intermediate, 158
    as managerial function, 16
    objectives, 158–160
    operational, 158
    organizational mission, 157–158
    planning horizon, 158
    planning/control cycle, 161–162
    price planning, 173–174
    priorities, 160–161

    profit planning, 174
    project. *See* Project planning
    spontaneity and, 156
    strategic, 158
    uncertainty and, 152–156
Plastic, biodegradable, 83
Political action committee (PAC), 75
Political-legal environment, 73–77
    advocacy advertising, 76
    campaign financing, 75
    coalition building, 75
    general political responses, 74–75
    indirect lobbying, 75–76
    issues management, 74
    lobbying, 75
    management implications, 76–77
    personal legal accountability, 76
    politics, defined, 73
Polycentric attitude, 101–102
Polychronic time, 106
Positive evidence, 401–403
Positive reinforcement, 408, 410
Posturing, 370
Power
    coercive, 392
    defined, 391
    empowerment, 393, 464
    expert, 392–393
    legitimate, 392
    and loyalty cliques, 370
    overview, 390
    referent, 392
    reward, 391–392
Practical intelligence, 403
The Practice of Management (Drucker), 55
Predictability in teams, 379
Pressure tactics, 389
Price planning, 173–174
Priorities, 160–161
Proactive social responsibility strategy, 132
Problem solving. *See also* Decision making
    alternative solutions, 228–230
    conflict resolution, 433–434
    defined, 226
    evaluating the solution, 230
    fishbone diagrams, 228
    implementing the solution, 230
    organizational learning, 244
    problem, defined, 227
    problem identification, 226–228
    selecting a solution, 230
    stumbling blocks, 228
PROCEED model, 274
Process audit, 454
Product quality, evolution of, 11–12
Product technology, 83
Product-based quality, 458
Production technology, 83
Production-based Internet business
        model, 193

Product-service department, 250
Profit planning, 174
Program Evaluation and Review
    Technique. *See* PERT networks
Programmed decisions, 217
Project
    defined, 164
    life cycle, 165–166
    management software, 166–167
Project planning
    management and, 164–168
    management by objectives, 162–164
Prospectors, 155
PTO bank, 349
Punishment, 408
Purpose of organization, 240

Quality
    defined, 458
    manufacturing-based, 459
    product-based, 458
    service provider challenges, 459–461
    service quality, 461, 471
    transcendent, 458
    user-based, 458–459
    value-based, 459
Quality Is Free (Crosby), 45
Quality-of-work-life programs
    diversity and, 348
    family support services, 349–350
    flexible work schedules, 348–349
    sabbaticals, 351
    surveys, 353–354
    wellness programs, 351
Quick-fix mentality, 57, 58
Qwerty keyboard, 423

RATER acronym, 461
Rational persuasion, 388
Reactive changes, 418
Reactive social responsibility
    strategy, 131
Reactors, 156
Realistic job previews, 336
Reconfigurable organization, 258
Recruitment
    diversity in the Internet age, 273
    employment selection tests, 277
    equal employment opportunity,
        274–277
    interviewing, 277–279
    selection process, 273–274
Recycling, open-system thinking
    and, 60–61
Reengineering, 197, 252
Referent power, 392
Referral-based Internet business
    model, 193
Refreezing, 428
Relationship management, 397

Religion
    cultural diversity, 107
    employment discrimination, 88–89
    injunctions, 139
Resources, working with limited, 7–8
Respect in teams, 379
Response uncertainty, 153
Reward power, 391–392
Rewards
    belief that effort leads
        to reward, 340
    defined, 339
    employee compensation, 340
    equitable, 341–342
    evaluation-reward system, 453
    extrinsic, 339, 340–343
    intrinsic, 339
    linked to performance, 342–343
    satisfaction of individual needs, 340
Riding the Waves of Culture (Trompenaars
    & Hampden-Turner), 103
Risk
    condition of risk, 213
    decision making and, 213
Rokeach value survey, 138, 144–145
Roles of groups, 364
Run chart, 466

Sabbaticals, 351
Safety needs, 329
Sarbanes-Oxley Act, 76, 454
Satisfice, 230
Satisfiers, 331–332
Scatter diagram, 465–466
Scenario analysis, 201
Scheduling
    chronotype, 349
    flexible work schedules, 348–349
    flextime, 348–349
    with Gantt charts, 170
Scientific management, 41–43
    pay incentives, 42–43
    standardization, 41–42
    systematic selection and
        training, 42
    time and task study, 42
Scientific method of problem
    solving, 229
Self-actualization needs, 330–331
Self-awareness, 397
Self-interests, 139
Self-managed teams, 345–347
Self-management, 397
Self-protective leadership, 109
Selling, local, 96
Sensitivity training, 114
September 11, 2001 terrorist
    attacks, 202, 455
Servant leader, 404
Service provider challenges, 459–461

Service quality, 461, 471
*The Seven Habits of Highly Effective
    People* (Covey), 436
Sexual harassment, 286–288
*The Shallows: What the Internet
    Is Doing to Our Brains*
    (Carr), 311
Sherman Antitrust Act of 1890, 126
Situational analysis, 195–196
Situational theory
    explanation of, 399
    Fiedler's contingency theory, 399–400
    House's updated path-goal theory,
        400–401
Small business
    80-percent-failure-rate myth, 21–22
    career opportunities, 23
    entrepreneurship, 23–25
    gazelles, 22–23
    low-wage-jobs myth, 22–23
    microbusiness, 21
    myths, 21–23
    overview, 26
    small business, defined, 21
    statistics, 21
Smoothing as conflict resolution, 435
Social awareness, 397
Social capital, 360
Social environment, 66–73
    demographics of the new workforce,
        66–70
    diversity management, 72–73
    workplace inequalities, 70–72
Social IOUs, 370
Social media
    business models, 193–194
    defined, 13–14
    description and applications, 14
    strategic management, 187–194
    upward communications, 310
Social networking
    defined, 13
    workplace policy, 311
Social responsibility
    accommodation strategy, 132
    arguments against, 130–131
    arguments for, 130
    classical economic model, 128–129
    corporate. *See* Corporate social
        responsibility (CSR)
    corporate social responsibility,
        126–128
    defense strategy, 131–132
    history of, 126
    iron law of responsibility, 131
    personal, 128
    proaction strategy, 132
    reaction strategy, 131
    socioeconomic model, 129–130
Socialization, organizational, 261–262

Societal culture, 103
Socioeconomic model, 129–130
Software
    groupware, 221–222
    knowledge management, 221
    project management, 166–167
Span of control, 252–253
Staffing
    cross-cultural training, 112–115
    expatriate failure, 111–112
    foreign positions, 111–115
    integrated expatriate staffing system, 114–115
    local managerial talent, 115
    as managerial function, 16
    women on foreign assignments, 115
Stakeholder audit, 129
Standards, 452–453
State uncertainty, 153
Statistical process control, 465
S.T.E.P acronym, 345
Storytelling, 262
Strategic agility, 156
Strategic alliances, 96
Strategic changes, 418
Strategic control, 453
Strategic management
    business ecosystems, 191–192
    control, 198–199
    defined, 186
    forecasting, 199–202
    implementation, 197–198
    Internet and social media, 192–194
    Porter's competitive strategies, 189–190
    process, 194–197
    reasons for understanding of, 184–185
    synergy, 187–188
Strategic partnerships, 96
Strategic planning, 158
Strategy, defined, 186
Structured interview, 277–279
Subjective probabilities, 213
Subscription-based Internet business model, 193
Substance abuse, 288–289
Superordinate goals, 434
Supertasking, 313
Support in teams, 379
Surveys
    employee participation and engagement, 344–345
    management teamwork survey, 381–382
    quality-of-work-life programs, 353–354
    strategic management, 201–202
    upward communications, 308
Sustainability. See also Green management
    defined, 12
    environmentalism and, 12, 26

SWAT team, 457
SWOT analysis, 195–196, 204
Synergy, 187–188
Systematic management, 45
Systems approach to management, 50–53
    chaos theory, 52–53
    closed vs. open systems, 51
    complex adaptive systems, 52–53
    early systems perspective, 50–51
    general systems theory, 51
    knowledge management, 52
    lessons from, 53
    levels of systems, 51
    organizational learning, 52
    system, defined, 50

Tacit knowledge, 220
Targets, 159
Team-oriented leadership, 109
Teams. See also Group
    crisis management team, 457
    cross-functional, 374–375
    effectiveness of, 376–377
    management teamwork survey, 381–382
    overview, 374
    self-managed, 345–347
    SWAT team, 457
    trust and effectiveness, 378–379
    virtual, 375–376
Technological environment, 81–85
    innovation process, 82–84
    intrapreneurship, 84–85
    technology, defined, 81
Technological synergy, 188
Teleworking, 314
Tempered radicals, 429–430
Terminal value, 138
Terrorism, 202, 455
Theory X, 48
Theory Y, 48
360-degree review, 282
Time and culture, 106
Time series forecast, 200
Title VII, 274, 286
Total quality control, 45
Total Quality Control (Feigenbaum), 45
Total quality management (TQM)
    defined, 461
    evolution of product quality, 12
    flow charts, 168
    principles of, 461–464
    problem solving, 228
    process improvement tools, 464–466
TQM. See Total quality management (TQM)
Training. See also Education
    content and delivery, 283–285

cross-cultural. See Cross-cultural training
    defined, 283
    ethics, 139–140, 145
    Kirkpatrick model of program evaluation, 285–286
    program ingredients, 285
    purpose of, 283
    skill vs. factual learning, 285
Trait theory, 396–397
Transactional leadership, 401, 402
Transactive strategy-making mode, 185
Transcendent quality, 458
Transformational leadership theory, 401–403
Transnational company, 97–98
Trend analysis, 202
Triple bottom line, 127
Trust, lack of, as reason for employee resistance to change, 424
Trust and team effectiveness
    building, 379
    trust, defined, 378
    Zand's model of trust, 378–379

Uncertainty
    condition of uncertainty, 214
    coping with, 152–156
    decision making and, 211, 212–214
    effect, 153
    environmental, 153
    individual response, 153–154
    organizational response, 154–156
    planned action and spontaneity, 156
    response, 153
    state, 153
Unfreezing, 428
Uniformed Services Employment and Reemployment Rights Act, 275
Unintended consequences, 212
Universal process approach to management, 39–41
Universal rules for ethical principles, 139
Upward appeals, 389
Upward communication
    defined, 307
    exit interviews, 310
    grievance procedures, 308
    informal meetings, 309–310
    open-door policy, 309
    self-censorship, 307
    social media, 310
    suggestion systems, 308–309
    surveys, 308
U.S. Equal Employment Opportunity Commission (EEOC), 275
U.S. Family and Medical Leave Act (FMLA), 350

User-based quality, 458–459
Utilitarian benefits of ethical principles, 139

Values. *See also* Ethics
    decision making and, 211–212
    instrumental, 137–138
    organizational, 261
    Rokeach value survey, 138, 144–145
    terminal, 138
    value-based quality, 459
Variable costs, 173
Vertical hierarchy of organizations, 242
Vertically loaded jobs, 337, 346
Videoconference, 313–314
Vietnam War, 373
Virtual organization, 258–259

Virtual team, 375–376
Virtual working, 314
Vocational Rehabilitation Act of 1973, 288

Wagner Act of 1935, 46
Warehousing, local, 96
Web sites, sticky, 192–193
Wellness programs, 351
Whistle-blowing, 141–142
*Why Smart Executives Fail–and What You
        Can Learn from Their Mistakes*
        (Finkelstein), 217
Win-win attitude, 436–437
Women
    as expatriates, 115
    glass ceiling for, 70–71, 72

influence tactics and, 390
leadership traits and, 396
in the workforce, 66, 67
Work and Motivation (Vroom), 332
Work flow process department, 252
World Trade Organization
        (WTO), 80
World Wide Web. *See also* Internet
    description and applications, 14
    history of, 13
Writing guidelines, 316–317
WTO. *See* World Trade Organization
        (WTO)

Zand's model of trust, 378–379
Zero defects, 45